THE OXFORD 

INTERNATIONAL SECURITY

This *Oxford Handbook* is the definitive volume on the state of international security and the academic field of security studies. It provides a tour of the most innovative and exciting news areas of research as well as major developments in established lines of inquiry. It presents a comprehensive portrait of an exciting field, with a distinctively forward-looking theme, focusing on the question: what does it mean to think about the future of international security?

The key assumption underpinning this volume is that all scholarly claims about international security, both normative and positive, have implications for the future. By examining international security to extract implications for the future, the volume provides clarity about the real meaning and practical implications for those involved in this field. Yet, contributions to this volume are not exclusively forecasts or prognostications, and the volume reflects the fact that, within the field of security studies, there are diverse views on how to think about the future. Readers will find in this volume some of the most influential mainstream (positivist) voices in the field of international security as well as some of the best known scholars representing various branches of critical thinking about security. The topics covered in the *Handbook* range from conventional international security themes such as arms control, alliances and Great Power politics, to "new security" issues such as global health, the roles of non-state actors, cyber-security, and the power of visual representations in international security.

Alexandra Gheciu is a Professor at the Graduate School of Public and International Affairs, and Associate Director of the Centre for International Policy Studies, University of Ottawa. Her publications include, in addition to articles in leading academic journals, several books: *NATO in the 'New Europe': The Politics of International Socialization After the Cold War* (Stanford University Press, 2005); *Securing Civilization?* (Oxford University Press, 2008); *The Return of the Public in Global Governance* (co-edited with Jacqueline Best, Cambridge University Press, 2014, 2015); and *Security Entrepreneurs: Performing Protection in Post-Cold War Europe* (Oxford University Press, 2018). Prior to joining the University of Ottawa, she was a Research Fellow at the University of Oxford, and a Jean Monnet Fellow at the European University Institute, Florence. She has also been a visiting professor at Sciences Po, Paris and the Ca' Foscari University of Venice.

William C. Wohlforth is the Daniel Webster Professor of Government at Dartmouth. He is the author or editor of eight books and some 60 articles and book chapters on topics ranging from the Cold War and its end to unipolarity and contemporary U.S. grand strategy. He is a member of the Council of Foreign Relations and has served as a consultant for the National Intelligence Council and the National Bureau of Asian Research. His most recent book, with Stephen Brooks, is *America Abroad: The United States' Global Role in the 21st Century* (Oxford University Press, 2016).

THE OXFORD HANDBOOKS OF INTERNATIONAL RELATIONS

General Editors
Christian Reus-Smit of the University of Queensland and
Duncan Snidal of the University of Oxford

The *Oxford Handbooks of International Relations* is a twelve-volume set of reference books offering authoritative and innovative engagements with the principal sub-fields of International Relations.

The series as a whole is under the General Editorship of Christian Reus-Smit and Duncan Snidal, with each volume edited by a distinguished pair of specialists in their respective fields.

The series both surveys the broad terrain of International Relations scholarship and reshapes it, pushing each sub-field in challenging new directions. Following the example of the original Reus-Smit and Snidal *Oxford Handbook of International Relations*, each volume is organized around a strong central thematic by a pair of scholars drawn from alternative perspectives, reading its sub-field in an entirely new way, and pushing scholarship in challenging new directions.

THE OXFORD HANDBOOK OF

INTERNATIONAL SECURITY

Edited by

ALEXANDRA GHECIU

and

WILLIAM C. WOHLFORTH

Great Clarendon Street, Oxford, OX2 6DP,
United Kingdom

Oxford University Press is a department of the University of Oxford. It furthers the University's objective of excellence in research, scholarship, and education by publishing worldwide. Oxford is a registered trade mark of Oxford University Press in the UK and in certain other countries

First Edition published in 2018
First published in paperback 2020

Published in the United States of America by Oxford University Press
198 Madison Avenue, New York, NY 10016, United States of America

British Library Cataloguing in Publication Data
Data available

Library of Congress Cataloging in Publication Data
Data available

ISBN 978–0–19–877785–4 (Hbk.)
ISBN 978–0–19–885462–3 (Pbk.)

Acknowledgments

We are deeply grateful to many individuals for their invaluable help in producing this volume but our particular expression of gratitude goes to our contributors for their terrific work and for their patience during all the stages of this project. We would also like to thank Chris Reus-Smit and Duncan Snidal for the trust they placed in us when they invited us to edit this Handbook, and for their unwavering support and enthusiasm for our collection. Special thanks also go to Dominic Byatt, Sarah Parker, Olivia Wells, and all the other members of the OUP team, who provided extraordinary guidance as we navigated the long process of producing a volume of this magnitude. Last but not least, Randy Huang of Dartmouth College's class of 2019 provided crucial assistance in preparing our manuscript for submission. Each of us owes big intellectual debts to a list of colleagues too long to reproduce here—people who brainstormed with us about the state of the field and the real world of international security and its future. This volume would not have been possible without the amazing contributions of all these people—and many more colleagues, friends, and family members who were kind enough to share with us conversations about this volume, and who offered valuable suggestions, support, and friendship. They all have our heartfelt thanks. Needless to say, the responsibility for any remaining mistakes is entirely ours.

Contents

List of Figures

List of Tables

List of Abbreviations

ACD	Armed Conflict Data (Uppsala)
AFRICOM	US Africa Command
AIC	Akaike Information Criterion
AIDS	Acquired Immune Deficiency Syndrome
AIIB	Asian Infrastructure Investment Bank
ANSA	armed non-state actors
ANT	Actor-Network Theory
APL	anti-personnel landmines
APSA	American Political Science Association
APT	Advanced Persistent Threats
ASEAN	Association of Southeast Asian Nations
ATE	average treatment effect
ATT	Arms Trade Treaty
ATT	Average Treatment Effect on the Treated
AU	African Union
AUC	area under the curve
BLW	blinding laser weapons
BRICs	Brazil, Russia, India, and China
BRICS	Brazil, Russia, India, China, and South Africa
CA	comprehensive approach (to warfare)
CBPS	Covariate Balancing Propensity Score
CBRN	chemical, biological, radiological, and nuclear
CCP	Chinese Communist Party
CCW	Certain Conventional Weapons (1980 Convention)
CDC	Centers for Disease Control (US)
CIA	Central Intelligence Agency (US)
CM	cluster munitions
COW	Correlates of War

CR	classical realism
CSS	critical security studies
CSTO	Collective Security Treaty Organization
CVE	Countering Violent Extremism
DAC	Development Assistance Committee
DAG	Directed Acyclic Graph
DA-RT	data access and research transparency
DDR	Disarmament, Demobilization, and Reconstruction
DES	demographic and environmental stress
DFID	Department for International Development
DHS	Department of Homeland Security (US)
DRC	Democratic Republic of the Congo
ECOWAS	Economic Community of West African States
ECSP	Environmental Change and Security Program (Woodrow Wilson Center)
EEZ	exclusive economic zone
EITI	Extractive Industry Transparency Initiative
ELF	ethno-linguistic fractionalization
EU	European Union
EW	Expanded War
FATA	Federally Administered Tribal Areas (Pakistan)
FBI	Federal Bureau of Investigation (US)
FMLN	Farabundo Martí National Liberation Front (El Salvador)
GCC	Gulf Co-operation Council
GHSI	Global Health Security Initiative
GLMs	generalized linear models
GNI	Global Network Initiative
GOARN	Global Outbreak Alert and Response Network (WHO)
GPM	great power management
GWOT	Global War on Terror
HIPC	Heavily Indebted Poor Countries
HIV	human immunodeficiency virus
IAEA	International Atomic Energy Authority
ICC	International Criminal Court

ICISS	International Commission on Intervention and State Sovereignty
ICoC	International Code of Conduct
ICoCA	International Code of Conduct Association
ICRC	International Committee of the Red Cross
ICT	information and communications technology
IDs	infectious diseases
IEA	International Energy Agency
IGO	intergovernmental organization
IHL	international humanitarian law
IHR	International Health Regulations (WHO)
IMF	International Monetary Fund
INGO	international nongovernmental organization
IO	international organization
IO	*International Organization* (journal)
IPCC	Intergovernmental Panel on Climate Change
IPS	International Political Sociology
IR	International Relations
ISAF	International Security Assistance Force
ISR	intelligence, surveillance, and reconnaissance
ISSF	International Security Studies Forum
IUU	illegal, unauthorized and unreported
IV	instrumental variable
JETS	Journal Editors' Transparency Statement
JSF	Joint Strike Fighter
JSTARS	Joint Surveillance Target Attack Radar System
LASSO	Least Absolute Shrinkage and Selection Operator
LDP	Liberal Democratic Party
LNG	Liquefied Natural Gas
MID	Militarized Interstate Dispute
MMEs	multinational military exercises
MMI	multinational military intervention
MSE	mean square error
Mtoe	million tonnes of oil equivalent
NAM	Non-Aligned Movement

NATO	North Atlantic Treaty Organization
NCR	neoclassical realism
NGO	nongovernmental organization
NIC	National Intelligence Council (US)
NIMBY	"not in my backyard"
NNP	Non-Nuclear Principles (Japan)
NPR	nonproliferation regime
NPT	Nonproliferation Treaty
NSA	National Security Agency (US)
NSC	National Security Council (US)
ODA	official development assistance
ODNI	Office of the Director of National Intelligence
OECD	Organisation for Economic Co-operation and Development
OEF	Operation Enduring Freedom (GWOT)
OONI	Open Observatory of Network Interference
OPEC	Organization of the Petroleum Exporting Countries
OSCE	Organisation for Security and Cooperation in Europe
P-5	Permanent Five (of the UNSC)
PARIS	Political Anthropological Research for International Sociology
PLA	People's Liberation Army (China)
PMSCs	private military and security companies
PR	precision-recall (curve)
PRIO	Peace Research Institute Oslo (Norway)
R2P	Responsibility to Protect
RMA	revolution in military affairs
ROC	Receiver Operating Characteristic
RPAs	remotely piloted vehicles
RPD	Repeated Prisoner's Dilemma
RSC	regional security complex
SALW	small arms and light weapons
SCO	Shanghai Cooperation Organization
SDGs	Sustainable Development Goals (UN)
SIPRI	Stockholm International Peace Research Institute
SR	structural realism

SSR	security sector reform
SUTVA	stable unit treatment value assumption
TAN	transnational advocacy network
TWEED	Terrorism in Western Europe: Events Data
UAS	unmanned aerial systems
UDHR	Universal Declaration of Human Rights
UN	United Nations
UNCLOS	United Nations Convention on the Law of the Sea
UNDP	United Nations Development Program
UNESCO	United Nations Educational, Scientific and Cultural Organization
UNHCR	United Nations High Commissioner for Refugees
UNSC	United Nations Security Council
US	United States of America
USAID	United States Agency for International Development
USJFCOM	United States Joint Forces Command
USSR	Union of Soviet Socialist Republics
WBGU	German Advisory Council on Global Change
WHA	World Health Assembly (WHO)
WHO	World Health Organization
WMD	weapons of mass destruction
WTO	World Trade Organization

List of Contributors

Rita Abrahamsen is Professor in the Graduate School of Public and International Affairs at the University of Ottawa.

Fiona B. Adamson is Senior Lecturer in International Relations, Department of Politics and International Studies, SOAS, University of London.

Deborah Avant is Sié Chéou-Kang Chair for International Security and Diplomacy at the Josef Korbel School of International Studies at the University of Denver.

Michael Barnett is University Professor of International Affairs and Political Science at the George Washington University.

Didier Bigo is Professor of International Relations at King's College London and at Sciences Po, Paris.

Bear F. Braumoeller is Associate Professor of Political Science at The Ohio State University.

Thierry Bros is a visiting Professor at Sciences Po, Paris, and the author of the book *After the US Shale Gas Revolution*.

Joshua Busby is Associate Professor in the Lyndon B. Johnson School of Public Affairs at the University of Texas-Austin.

Barry Buzan is Emeritus Professor of International Relations at the LSE (formerly Montague Burton Professor), honorary professor at Copenhagen, Jilin, and China Foreign Affairs Universities, and a Senior Fellow at LSE Ideas.

Jonathan D. Caverley is Associate Professor of Strategy in the Strategic & Operational Research Department of the Naval War College's Center for Naval Warfare Studies and Research Scientist in Political Science and Security Studies at the Massachusetts Institute of Technology.

Jeffrey T. Checkel is Professor and Simons Chair in International Law and Human Security, School for International Studies, Simon Fraser University, Vancouver, BC, and Global Fellow, Peace Research Institute, Oslo.

Aaron Clauset is Assistant Professor in the Department of Computer Science and the BioFrontiers Institute at the University of Colorado, Boulder.

Lindsay Cohn is Senior Assistant Professor in the Department of National Security Affairs at the Naval War College.

Damon Coletta is Professor of Political Science at the United States Air Force Academy.

Dale C. Copeland is Professor in the Woodrow Wilson Department of Politics at the University of Virginia.

Audrey Kurth Cronin is Professor in the School of International Service at American University.

Ronald Deibert is Director of The Citizen Lab, Munk School of Global Affairs, University of Toronto.

Daniel Deudney is Associate Professor of Political Science at Johns Hopkins University.

Jennifer L. Erickson is Associate Professor in the Department of Political Science, Boston College.

Peter Feaver is Professor of Political Science and Public Policy at Duke University.

Matthew Fuhrmann is Professor of Political Science at Texas A&M University.

Alexandra Gheciu is an Associate Professor at the Graduate School of Public and International Affairs, and Associate Director of the Centre for International Policy Studies, University of Ottawa.

Kristian Skrede Gleditsch is Professor in the Department of Government at the University of Essex, director of the Michael Nicholson Centre for Conflict and Cooperation, and a research associate at the International Peace Research Institute, Oslo.

Lene Hansen is the Project Director of Images and International Security and a Professor of International Relations in the Department of Political Science at the University of Copenhagen.

Peter K. Hatemi is Distinguished Professor of Political Science, Co Fund in Microbiology and Biochemistry at Penn State University.

Virginia Haufler is Associate Professor in the Department of Government and Politics at the University of Maryland, College Park.

Chris Hendershot is a Research Associate for the Mobilizing Inuit Cultural Heritage project at York University.

Michael C. Horowitz is Associate Professor of Political Science at the University of Pennsylvania.

Ian Hurd is Associate Professor of Political Science, Northwestern University.

Anja P. Jakobi is Professor of International Relations and head of the Chair of International Relations at the Institute for Social Sciences, TU Braunschweig, Brunswick, Germany.

Robert Jervis is Adlai E. Stevenson Professor of International Affairs at Columbia University.

Audie Klotz is Professor of Political Science at Syracuse University.

Keith Krause is Professor at the Graduate Institute of International and Development Studies in Geneva.

Ronald R. Krebs is Beverly and Richard Fink Professor in the Liberal Arts, Professor of Political Science, University of Minnesota.

Sarah E. Kreps is Associate Professor in the Department of Government at Cornell University.

Andrew Kydd is Professor in the Department of Political Science, University of Wisconsin-Madison.

Adam M. Lauretig is a PhD candidate in Political Science at The Ohio State University.

Fred H. Lawson is James Irvine Professor of Government at Mills College.

Matteo Legrenzi is Associate Professor of International Relations at Ca' Foscari University of Venice.

Austin Long is Senior Political Scientist at the RAND Corporation.

Emma McCluskey is PhD candidate it War Studies at King's College, London.

Rose McDermott is David and Mariana Fisher University Professor of International Relations at Brown University.

David Mutimer is Professor of Political Science at York University.

Can E. Mutlu is Assistant Professor, Department of Politics, Acadia University.

Iver B. Neumann is based at the Norwegian Institute of International Affairs (NUPI).

Brendan O'Leary is Lauder Professor of Political Science at the University of Pennsylvania.

John M. Owen is Ambassador Henry J. and Mrs. Marion R. Taylor Professor of Politics, University of Virginia.

Sarah Percy is Associate Professor in the School of Political Science and International Studies at the University of Queensland.

Susan Peterson is Wendy & Emery Reves Professor of Government and International Relations Director, International Relations Program, College of William & Mary.

Daniel Philpott is Professor of Political Science, University of Notre Dame.

Adam Quinn is Senior Lecturer in International Politics, Department of Political Science and International Studies, University of Birmingham.

Sten Rynning is Professor of International Relations at the Department of Political Science, University of Southern Denmark.

Mark B. Salter is Professor at the School of Political Studies, University of Ottawa.

Nicholas Sambanis is Presidential Distinguished Professor, Department of Political Science, University of Pennsylvania.

Adam Sandor is a Post-Doctoral Researcher with the Centre Franco-Paix en Résolution des Conflits et Missions de Paix at the Université de Québec à Montréal.

Olivier Schmitt is Associate Professor of Political Science, Center for War Studies, University of Southern Denmark.

Hans Peter Schmitz is Associate Professor, Department of Leadership Studies at the University of San Diego.

Ole Jacob Sending is Research Director, Norwegian Institute of International Affairs (NUPI).

Laura Sjoberg is Associate Professor of Political Science, University of Florida.

Etel Solingen is Thomas T. and Elizabeth C. Tierney Chair in Peace Studies, Political Science School of Social Sciences, University of California, Irvine.

Necla Tschirgi is Professor of Practice, Human Security and Peacebuilding at the Joan B. Kroc School of Peace Studies, the University of San Diego.

Leslie Vinjamuri is Director of the Centre on Conflict, Rights and Justice, and Senior Lecturer (Associate Professor) in International Relations at SOAS University of London.

Jennifer M. Welsh is Professor and Chair in International Relations at the European University Institute, Florence.

Michael C. Williams is Professor in the Graduate School of Public and International Affairs at the University of Ottawa.

William C. Wohlforth is the Daniel Webster Professor of Government at Dartmouth College.

PART I

INTRODUCTION

CHAPTER 1

THE FUTURE OF SECURITY STUDIES

ALEXANDRA GHECIU AND
WILLIAM C. WOHLFORTH

THESE are fascinating times for practitioners and students of international security. More than a quarter-century following the end of the Cold War—and a century after the "war to end all wars"—questions about security remain among the most discussed and contested within the discipline of International Relations. Statements about international security can be found in abundance all around us: they suffuse the speeches of politicians of all political colors, dominate newspaper columns as well as the social media, flash across our television screens, and, simultaneously, are at the heart of a plethora of academic studies. Yet, among both academic circles and practitioners, there is little agreement over the nature and impact of key dynamics of international security, or even the very meaning of the term. As Krause and Williams (this volume) argue, "[t]his relativity of security—of who or what is being threatened, and from what or whom—has important consequences for understanding security relations between states, within states, and between non-state actors."

Following the collapse of communism and the end of the Cold War, Francis Fukuyama famously wrote about "the end of history" and many other prominent academics outlined a vision of a new era of peace and cooperation, based on liberal democracy, global capitalist forces, and/or a reinvigorated set of international organizations (van Evera 1990; Kaysen 1990; Russett 1994). This optimistic view was challenged, however, by those who warned that the post-Cold War era would be a time marked by renewed conflict, arms races, and even civilizational clashes (Mearsheimer 1990; Huntington 1993). Still other scholars regarded the collapse of Cold War political structures as a development that created the political and intellectual space needed to question old ways of thinking and advance a conception—and an agenda—of security focused on the well-being of individuals, environmental concerns, development, gender issues, or the status of underprivileged communities (Tuchman Matthews 1989; Roberts 1990; Peterson 1992; Homer-Dixon 1999). International security practices also seemed to undergo substantial change, leading to a proliferation of activities that would have been impossible during the Cold War. These included, for instance, a series of democracy-promotion activities as well as humanitarian interventions, conflict prevention initiatives and complex, UN-sponsored peacebuilding missions that were designed to address deep-rooted problems, promote stability in conflict-torn countries, and to avoid regional and international spillovers (Carothers 2006; Paris and Sisk 2009; Caplan 2012).

Just as (most) International Relations (IR) scholars were beginning to get used to the post-Cold War broadening of the security agenda, another set of events occurred that once again seemed to radically change the international landscape: the 9/11 terrorist attacks. Those events—and the US-led responses to them—generated unprecedented attention to the rise of non-state actors and their impact on the international security environment (Enders and Sandler 2006; Hoffman 2006; Pape 2006; Sageman 2008; Cronin 2009). At the same time, a series of scholars drew attention to what they perceived as the profoundly adverse effects of the new "War on Terror" on state–civil society relations around the world, including in liberal-democratic countries (Aradau and van Munster 2007; Bigo et al. 2015; Jarvis and Lister 2015). These critiques were accompanied by expressions of concern about the narrowing of the security agenda in the post-9/11 era—involving what could be seen as a reversal of post-Cold War intellectual and political developments. For instance, some prominent academics deplored the fact that the international community had missed a significant opportunity to break down the artificial boundary between security and development, and to formulate an agenda based on the recognition of the fundamental connection between these two fields (Baranyi, 2008; Newman 2010; Tschirgi et al. 2010). As Tschirgi (this volume) cogently argues, "the real consequence of 9/11 was not to deepen the links between security and development but to 'securitize' development by subordinating it to a militarized security agenda."

To further complicate matters, the great power agenda seemed to re-emerge. Russia annexed Crimea and stoked separatist conflict in Ukraine, intervened forcefully in support of the government in Syria's civil war, and stepped up more or less veiled threats concerning Central/East European countries. For its part, China continued active support of its claims in the South China Sea. These developments led many IR scholars to predict a return to Great Power rivalries (Mearsheimer 2014). Yet the new patterns of behavior also exhibited seemingly novel features falling under such rubrics as "hybrid" or "ambiguous" warfare. Whether these developments were truly novel or not, scholars were left to debate whether their traditional models were up the task of analyzing them.

While there is little agreement among IR scholars—or, indeed, practitioners—over the relative importance of various factors and actors, few would disagree with the view that today the international security landscape is far more complex than it has been in a long time. As Neumann and Sending (this volume) cogently argue, the contemporary period is characterized by "a proliferation in the types of actors that practice security, whether internally through the establishment of national security agencies alongside police and defence, or externally, through the role played by private security companies, NGOs offering risk assessments, or firms specializing in cybersecurity that the state is dependent upon."

In the first decades of the twenty-first century, conventional international security questions, including Great Power politics, arms control, economics of war and peace and nuclear proliferation (e.g. Buzan; Caverley; Copeland; Gleditsch and Clauset; Deudney; Erickson; Solingen, all in this volume) coexist and compete for attention with developments such as climate change, energy (in)security, cybersecurity threats, the power of visual representations, the role of non-state actors in the provision of (in)security, challenges posed by refugees and new patterns of migration, the rise of transnational crime or the growing role of the global South in international politics (Philpott; Avant and Haufler; Adamson, Abrahamsen, and Sandor; Busby; Bros; Cronin; Deibert; Hansen; Jakobi; Klotz; Kreps et al.; Percy; Peterson; Welsh). In a similar vein, as the chapters in Part V of this collection clearly demonstrate, twenty-first-century international security actors include entities that have long been at the heart of mainstream approaches (e.g. great powers and alliances), but also a broader set of regional and global institutions as well as more informal transnational networks, and powerful domestic groups and individual leaders (see the contributions by Buzan; Rynning and Schmitt; Hurd, Legrenzi, and Lawson; Schmitt; Sambanis and O'Leary; Horowitz; Feaver, Coletta, and Cohn). Together, these developments compel us to rethink some taken-for-granted categories and divides (e.g. between public and private spheres and between security and development), complicate the politics of national security (Krebs this volume), and raise new and interesting normative dilemmas and challenges (see Vinjamuri and Welsh, this volume).

In this multi-faceted environment, the relationship between the study and practice of security has also become more complex. In the words of Neumann and Sending (this volume), this relationship has become "more difficult to describe as a singular one: In some areas, the relationship between expertise and practice may be heavily institutionalized and dominated by a singular profession. This may be the case for certain areas of intelligence. In other areas, such as cybersecurity, the relationship between practice and expertise is different, being less firmly institutionalized and more open to competition from non-state actors." In essence, the evolving relationship between expertise and practice "can best be described as one of increased *differentiation*, where ever more actors perform ever more specialized tasks of both analyzing and of providing security" (Neumann and Sending, this volume).

This extraordinary complexity in practices and analyses of international security lies at the heart of our Handbook. The aim of this volume is to serve as the definitive statement of the state of international security and the academic field of security studies.

1.1 Why a New International Security Compendium?

The Handbook provides a tour of the most innovative and exciting new areas of research as well as major developments in established lines of inquiry. Even as it presents a comprehensive portrait of an exciting field, it has a distinctively forward-looking theme. All scholarly claims about international security, both normative and positive, have implications for the future. Asking thinkers about international security to extract implications for the future is a way to impose clarity about the real meaning and practical implications of their work. Inviting authors to be future-oriented is not synonymous with asking everyone to embrace the aim of making predictions. Indeed, this book reflects the fact that, within the field of security studies, there are diverse views on how to think about the future.

What does it mean to think about the future of international security? In practical terms, it means to ask questions such as: is fundamental change possible? Who are the agents and what are the processes or developments that can lead to change? How does one recognize fundamental change when one sees it? Conversely, what is the nature of structures or factors that prevent transformation in international security? What methods are suitable for analyzing those structures, processes, and agents? Are the ways scholars have studied international security up to now likely to be suitable in the years ahead? Contributors to this volume address these questions as they develop their arguments about the future of international security.

Future-oriented questions are woven through the study and practice of international security. Our purpose is to make them more explicit, as has been the case in some of the most influential scholarship ever produced in our field. Especially in the immediate aftermath of the Cold War's end, scholars generated a number of future-oriented works that would go on to shape inquiry and, in some cases, practice, for years. These include Barry Buzan's *People States and Fear*, Mearsheimer's "Back to the Future", Jervis's "The Future of World Politics: Will it Resemble the Past," and Acharia's "Will Asia's Past be its Future"—among others. While these works differ in how they see the connection between scholarship and thinking about the future, they have in common explicit efforts to address the questions we set forth above.

Building on such future-oriented works, this compendium makes a unique contribution to International Relations. By asking all contributors to think about the future, the *Handbook of International Security*—more than many existing collections of this kind— achieves a significant degree of unity. Encouraging both established leaders and rising stars of the field to push their arguments into the future yields a uniquely revealing picture of the state of international security studies at this critical juncture. It sheds unprecedented light on strengths and weaknesses in knowledge and provides a stocktaking of expert expectations—one we expect to be of intense interest not only to current scholars, practitioners, and journalists, but to future chroniclers of the evolution of knowledge in this critical area.

Before going any further it is important to clarify that contributions to this volume are not exclusively forecasts or prognostications. They engage history, the evolution of knowledge, theory, interpretation, debates, and empirical data. Indeed, thinking about the future implies a reflection of how we got "here"—however "here" might be conceptualized. While the past figures more prominently in some chapters (e.g. in Parts I and III) than in others, all the authors adopt some kind of historical perspective in developing their analyses and discussing key implications for the future. The purpose of this Handbook is to provide instructive conceptual clarity and to lead the field, rather than following it.

1.2 Reflecting the Diversity of the International Security Field

This Handbook includes a variety of approaches, reflecting the richness and diversity characteristic of the field of international security—and the fact that disagreements among scholars in this field revolve not only around the question of what is security, but also over how to study it. As the chapters in Part II amply demonstrate, thinking about international security continues to be organized around several highly influential schools of thought and methodological orientations (Sjoberg; Hendershot and Mutimer; Quinn; Barnett; Owen; Bigo and McCluskey; Lauretig and Braumoeller; Checkel; Mutlu, and Salter; Kydd; McDermott and Hatemi).

For a long time the study of security was powerfully influenced by (structural) realist thinking. Much scholarship on international security was thus "preoccupied with the four S's of states, strategy, science and the status quo" (Williams 2013: 3). The focus was on states as the key agents and referents of security in the international system, and on strategy "inasmuch as the core intellectual and practical concerns revolved around devising the best means of employing the threat and use of military force" (ibid.) Thinking about security sought to be scientific as it applied positivist methods in search of objective knowledge about the world. Finally, the conservative focus meant that little or no attention was paid to the possibility of radical transformation in the international realm. As Stephen Walt famously put it,

> Security studies seeks cumulative knowledge about the role of military force. To obtain it, the field must follow the standard canons of scientific research: careful and consistent use of terms, unbiased measurements of critical concepts, and public documentation of theoretical and empirical claims. (Walt 1991: 222)

From this perspective, the evolution of security studies is synonymous with the growth of scientific knowledge, involving a quest for timeless causal laws that govern patterns of human behavior. This approach to international security is grounded in an understanding of human subjects as instrumentally rational actors dealing with an external reality that is independent of their values and perceptions, and to which they can relate objectively. In a similar vein, the conception of state action as the instrumentally rational pursuit of self-interest lies at the heart of structural realist analyses of international security (Krause and Williams 1997: 40).

The chapters that follow reflect how far the field has come from the neorealism-dominated debates of the past. What constitutes broadly positivist research and the nature of criticism of the assumptions underlying such work have been transformed. It is worth recalling that a significant challenge to conventional thinking about international security came from approaches that are widely seen as falling under the broad umbrella of critical security studies, or CSS (Krause and Williams 1997; Hendershot and Mutimer this volume; Krause and Williams this volume). In their 1997 volume, Krause and Williams associate critical security studies with a particular orientation: the "appending of the term critical to security studies is meant to imply more an orientation toward the discipline than a precise theoretical label. . . . Practically, a broad definition allows many perspectives that have been considered outside of the mainstream of the discipline to be brought into the same forum" (Krause and Williams 1997: x–xi). As Hendershot and Mutimer (this volume) argue, "CSS does not denote a coherent set of views, an 'approach' to security; rather it indicates a desire. The initial desire was to study security/strategy differently than that which predominated during the Cold War" (see also Mutimer 2015). More recently, CSS has come to identify scholars who study securitizing processes, emancipatory potentials, discourses of threat and danger, gendered and sexed bodies, visual and emotional mediations, racialization and terror, logics, techniques, migration and borders, and material/non-human affects.

Arguably, the key challenge posed by CSS to dominant realist thinking involved primarily a process of framing security—and its study—as a political phenomenon (Nunes 2012). Security was conceptualized as more than a natural response to a self-evident truth, and security studies as more than the formulation of expert knowledge to address threats that exist "out there in the world." Critical security studies set out to go beyond previous moves to broaden and deepen the security agenda by re-examining concepts and methodologies hitherto taken for granted by security scholars. Importantly, critical scholars engaged in an analysis of the politics behind the construction of knowledge about security: ideas about security came to be seen as political insofar as they were the product of interpretation, contestation, and struggle among various actors. Furthermore, critical security scholarship also sought to shed light on the connection between security theory and the wider political order, examining the ways in which particular conceptions of security cannot be separated from broader ideas about how politics works or should work (Nunes 2012: 347). Scholars embracing this approach also sought to draw attention to the impact of ideas and practices of security upon the constitution of a particular political order, thereby conceptualizing security theorizing as a political activity in its own right.

Yet, Hendershot and Mutimer persuasively argue in this volume that the CSS orientation and critical stance has come with its own limitations. One of the key problems, their chapter suggests, is that despite its commitment to pay attention to the politics of security, critical security scholarship has not always engaged its own politics (see also Wibben 2016: 144, cited by Hendershot and Mutimer). In this context, "[d]espite avowed commitments to critique concepts and practices that sustain militarized, petro-chemical addicted, zero sum security relations, critical security scholars must also imagine the possibility that criticality can also affect domination and exploitation. That is to say, CSS needs to more thoughtfully consider its ongoing complicity amongst the settler colonial and imperial ordering of global relations. This analysis leads Hendershot and Mutimer to conclude: "there is no question that to have a future CSS must decolonize. CSS must accept its complicities, not to atone for a racist or imperial past, but to signal a willingness to work toward present possibilities of un-settling people, land and knowledge."

At the same time, what constitutes (for lack of better terms) mainstream or positivist international security research has undergone radical shifts since neorealism's heyday. For one thing, realism has morphed into a complex school of thought that is rediscovering its classical roots as it grapples with decades of cumulating critiques (Quinn, this volume). Advances in the social scientific implications of research in biology, evolution, and neuroscience are altering the foundations of core assumptions in the study of international security. Most notably, strict rationality assumptions no longer play the role in social science in general and international security studies in particular that they once did (Hatemi and McDermott). Increasingly sophisticated quantitative methods and more and better data expose some of the fallacies of earlier quantitative work and allow researchers to capture systemic and structural effects, historical contingency and individual agency in ways unforeseen two decades ago (Lauretig and Braumoeller; Horowitz). Some of these same advances have eroded the old qualitative–quantitative divide in international security research (Lauretig and Braumoeller). Even that epitome of scientism, mathematical game theory, has evolved in ways to better capture change and contingency (Kydd).

Not surprisingly, this diversity of views of what is security and how to study it is also reflected in thinking about the future. While our volume does not claim to be exhaustive, it does seek to capture some of the key differences in conceptions of the future of international security—ranging from mainstream positivist accounts to various branches of critical scholarship. Readers will find in this volume some of the most influential positivist voices in the field of international security. Yet, it should be noted that a positivist orientation does not dictate a uniform view about the role prediction plays in social science. Scholars committed to the principles of objective theory testing acknowledge classes of complex events that may defy forecasting and are sensitive to continuing limitations on the availability of good data regarding key predictors. But most nonetheless hold that thinking rigorously about the future and, indeed, more ambitious and precise forms of forecasting are valid and important goals of international security studies. For some, thinking about the future involves using massive empirical data informed by theory to predict developments in security affairs, ranging from overall trends to contingent forecasts of specific events, such as the probability of civil war or state breakdown (e.g. Lauretig and Braumoeller; Clauset and Gleditsch, this volume). Some see forecasting value in establishing the broad parameters of incentives for various kinds of international security behavior, stipulating that the balance of costs and benefits will in general affect the probability of certain classes of actions (Caverley). Others have an understanding of IR ontology that leads to a certain degree of skepticism about forecasting, holding that international security is perforce a historical science, but still contend that contingent predictions are a useful way to clarify theories and update them. For instance, Copeland (this volume) argues that theories of great power war will have little relevance to the modern nuclear age unless they incorporate within their deductive logics the importance of security-dilemma spiraling and the ongoing risk of inadvertent war. As he puts it, we need theories that show us "under what conditions states shift from peaceful cooperation to harder-line policies that consciously increase the risks of things getting out of hand."

Some scholars, while arguing that point prediction in International Relations is virtually impossible, seek to retain an ability to think analytically about the future by identifying and connecting chains of contingencies that could shape the future. From their perspective, a useful approach is the formulation of scenarios that map a set of causes and trends in future time. Scenarios are stories of how the future *might* unfold that are based on different combinations of causal variables, which may take on different values in different scenarios. By constructing scenarios, the aim is to identify various driving forces and then seek to combine these forces in logical chains that could generate a range of outcomes, rather than single futures. Scenarios are founded upon provisional assumptions and causal claims, which become the subject of revision and updating. For instance, in her chapter on transnational crime, Jakobi argues that despite the expansion of global crime governance in recent decades, presenting the future of crime, security, and its governance faces many unknowns. In her view, what type of crime will be most prominent in the future is dependent on technological progress, regulatory frameworks, and on political agendas. In addition to all these unknown background conditions—she goes on to argue—crimes differ in how they are governed today, and they are likely to differ in the future. Yet, three main points seem to be particularly important for future crime governance and security: the availability and use of data, the role of formal norms, and the different aspects of security—individual, national, and global. Different scenarios are plausible for each of these points, depending on whether to expect a linear development or major disruptions.

From the point of view of other scholars, even analyses based on a conception of contingent causal mechanisms do not go far enough. What is needed, from this perspective, is a stronger rejection of the positivist project, which starts from the recognition that the process of gaining knowledge about international security must involve a process of interpretation, including self-awareness of the researcher's own historical time and place. For scholars who are associated with the critical security camp, the aim of scholarship is not to identify objective laws and test hypotheses against a presumably independent reality of international security, but rather to understand the dynamics and implications of the construction of security practices in a particular historical and social context. This is to be done via a set of interpretive methods that can shed light on the ideational frameworks within which the relevant actors are acting, the rules they are following, as well as the social structures in which they are embedded, and that empower certain subjects at the expense of others, and enable a particular interpretation of threat to prevail at a given moment in time.

Consider, for instance, Didier Bigo and Emma McCluskey's chapter on the PARIS approach to studying processes of (in)security and (in)securitization. The PARIS approach (Political Anthropological Research for International Sociology) brings to the forefront the study of how different bodies of knowledge are labeling security, examining the tensions and controversies between and within practitioners and disciplinary fields in these labeling practices. Bigo and McCluskey place their emphasis on the different intellectual moves by which it is possible to study the relationship between the construction of the "security" label and the boundaries of the "security" practices that may be labeled by others' freedom, mobility, violence, or privacy. As opposed to viewing the two in opposition, the chapter conceptualizes the relation between security and insecurity as a mobius strip; a metaphor which demonstrates how one can never be certain of what constitutes the content of security and not insecurity. Consequently, a PARIS approach calls for the study of everyday (in)securitization processes and practices.

Far from regarding this diversity as a problem, our volume will use its core theme (the future) as an opportunity to clarify the differences among various approaches to international security.

1.3 Key Sub-themes in this Collection

In order to ensure clarity and unity, all contributors to this Handbook address a core theme: what does it mean to think about the future of international security? There are several sub-themes that structure the chapters as they address the core theme. While not all contributors pay equal attention to everything, all of them engage with several of these sub themes, which include: the relationship between continuity/change, the driving factors that are likely to affect the future; methods and approaches needed to study the factors that will shape the future; and also, in a broader perspective, normative questions about what the future should look like, and why.

Following an introductory part that frames the volume by providing a history of international security studies and an analysis of the evolving relationship between the study and practice of security (in Chapters 2 and 3), Part II clarifies the ways in which different approaches think about the future of international security, anticipate ways in which the boundary between security and insecurity will be drawn, address research trends, and envisage the future of the discipline—and the contributors' own approach within the discipline. Contributors also consider the different factors that are likely to shape the future of the field, and the evolution of the boundary between international security and other fields—including by reflecting on ways/areas in which IR scholars might need to borrow from other fields.

The key aim of Part III is to analyse what could be called the "big swings" in the field: these are broad patterns or sets of developments that transcend specific issues and are likely to affect a variety of challenges/actors in international security—including the challenges and opportunities addressed in Part IV and the actors examined in Part V. Building on this analysis of big swings, Part IV provides concrete illustrations of the ways in which different IR scholars think about the future. The main goal of this Part is to address some key security challenges, problems, and questions that are likely to be prominent in the future. It is important to keep in mind that our Handbook does not claim to offer an exhaustive account of all relevant international security issues. Finally, Part V focuses on actors that can be expected to play important roles in the twenty-first-century security environment. Contributors to this Part examine the degree to which they expect change/continuity in the constitution and behavior of these actors. Relevant questions include: how do those actors respond to ideational and/or material forces? How are they likely to evolve, and how much freedom to maneuver will various actors have in addressing the dominant security challenges? What types of power will they be able to exercise and what (if any) forms of pathological behavior might they engage in? Last but not least, how should these actors behave in the future?

In the chapters that follow, some of the sharpest minds in the field of International Relations grapple with these questions. Along the way, they provide a comprehensive (if not exhaustive) stocktaking of what scholars think they know about war and peace, how they think they know it, and where they think their field of inquiry and international security more broadly are headed.

References

Acharia, Amitav. 2003/2004. Will Asia's Past be its Future? *International Security*, 28(3): 149–64.

Aradau, Claudia and Rens van Munster. 2007. Governing Terrorism through Risk: Taking Precautions, (Un)knowing the Future. *European Journal of International Relations*, 13 (1): 89–115.

Baranyi, Stephen. 2008. *The Paradoxes of Peacebuilding Post-9/11*. Vancouver: UBC Press.

Bigo, Didier, Evelien Brouwer, Sergio Carrera, Elspeth Guild, Emmanuel-Pierre Guittet, Julien Jeandesboz, Francesco Ragazzi, and Amandine Scherrer. 2015. The EU Counter-Terrorism Policy Responses to the Attacks in Paris: Towards an EU Security and Liberty Agenda. *CEPS Liberty and Security in Europe (81). Available at:* http://www.ceps.eu/system/files/LSE81Counterterrorism.pdf

Buzan, Barry. 1991. *People, States and Fear*. London: Harvester Wheatsheaf.

Caplan, Richard. 2012. *Exit Strategies and State Building*. New York: Oxford University Press.

Carothers, Thomas (ed.). 2006. *Promoting the Rule of Law Abroad: In Search of Knowledge*. New York: Carnegie Endowment for International Peace.

Cronin, Audrey Kurth. 2002/3. Behind the Curve: Globalization and International Terrorism. *International Security*, 27(3): 30–58.

Cronin, Audrey Kurth. 2009. *How Terrorism Ends: Understanding the Decline and Demise of Terrorist Campaigns*. Princeton, NJ: Princeton University Press.

Enders, Walter and Todd Sandler. 2006. *The Political Economy of Terrorism*. New York: Cambridge University Press.

Fukuyama, Francis. 1992. *The End of History and the Last Man*. London: Penguin Books.

Hoffman, Bruce. 2006. *Inside Terrorism*. New York: Columbia University Press.

Homer-Dixon, Thomas. 1999. *Environment, Scarcity, and Violence*. Princeton, NJ: Princeton University Press.

Huntington, Samuel. 1993. The Clash of Civilizations. *Foreign Affairs*, 72(3): 22–49.

Jarvis, Lee and Michael Lister (eds.) 2015. *Critical Perspectives on Counter-Terrorism*. London: Routledge.

Jervis, Robert. 1991–92. The Future of World Politics: Will it Resemble the Past? *International Security*, 16(3): 39–73.

Kaysen, Carl. 1990. Is War Obsolete? *International Security*, 14(4): 42–64.

Krause, Keith and Michael C. Williams. 1997. *Critical Security Studies: Concepts and Cases*. London: UCL Press.

Mearsheimer, John. 1990. Back to the Future: Instability in Europe after the Cold War. *International Security*, 15(1): 5–57.

Mearsheimer, John. 2014. *The Tragedy of Great Power Politics* (updated edition). London and New York: W.W. Norton & Co.

Mutimer, David. 2015. Critical Security Studies: A Schismatic History, In A. Collins, (ed.), *Contemporary Security Studies*, 4th edn, pp. 87–107. Oxford: Oxford University Press.

Newman, Edward. 2010. Peacebuilding as Security in "Failing" and Conflict-Prone States. *Journal of Intervention and Statebuilding*, 4: 305–22.

Nunes, Joao. 2012. Reclaiming the Political: Emancipation and critique in security studies. *Security Dialogue*, 43(4): 345–61.

Pape, Robert. 2006. *Dying to Win: The Strategic Logic of Suicide Terrorism*. New York: Random House.

Paris, Roland and Timothy Sisk. (2009). *The Dilemmas of Statebuilding: Confronting the Contradictions of Postwar Peace Operations* (Security and Governance Series). London; New York: Routledge.

Peterson, Spike V. 1992. *Gendered States*. Boulder, CO: Lynne Rienner.

Roberts, Brad. 1990. Human Rights and International Security. *Washington Quarterly*: 65–75.

Russett, Bruce. 1994. *Grasping the Democratic Peace*. Princeton, NJ: Princeton University Press.

Sageman, Marc. 2008. *Leaderless Jihad: Terror Networks in the Twenty-First Century*. Philadelphia, PA: University of Pennsylvania Press.

Tschirgi, Necla, M. Lund, and F. Mancini (eds.) 2010. *Security and Development: Searching for Critical Connections*. Boulder, CO: Lynne Rienner.

Tuchman Matthews, Jessica. 1989. Redefining Security. *Foreign Affairs*, 68 (2): 162–77.

Van Evera, Stephen. 1990–91. Primed for Peace: Europe after the Cold War. *International Security*, 15(3): 7–57.

Walt, Stephen. 1991. The Renaissance of Security Studies. *International Studies Quarterly*, 35: 211–39.

Williams, Paul D. 2013. *Security Studies: An Introduction*, 2nd edn. London: Routledge.

CHAPTER 2

SECURITY AND "SECURITY STUDIES"

Conceptual Evolution and Historical Transformation

KEITH KRAUSE AND MICHAEL C. WILLIAMS

2.1 Introduction

The quest for security is one of the most powerful dynamics of modern politics. Few claims are as politically potent as those cast within the imperative of "security," and few can mobilize such enormous political, social, and economic resources. In the pursuit of "national" security, more than one trillion US dollars are spent worldwide each year on military institutions and instruments, with many billions more on police and paramilitary institutions. In the name of national security covert and often extra-legal operations of intelligence services are undertaken and justified, immune from public scrutiny. And in the most extreme case, governments can demand that individuals kill and die in the name of security. Yet the term "security" is not restricted to the realm of military affairs and national security. One of the confounding aspects of the concept is the way in which it has been attached to an array of domestic, international, and transnational issues. Programs of social security are associated with the welfare state, while calls to promote environmental or economic security, or individual concerns with food security or health security all foster the impression that the search for security is omnipresent, and that the concept can be applied to areas far removed from the realms of war, conflict, and violence.

To ask "what is security and security studies?" is thus to grapple with an ambiguous, contested, and controversial concept and discipline. What one person, group, society, or state perceives as a threatening source of insecurity, another may not. To some, widespread individual ownership of firearms furthers their security, while to others it is a source of insecurity. To one state, the possession of a specific weapons system is essential to its defense, to another it appears deeply threatening. For one social group, the right to educate their children in a particular faith or language is vital to their cultural survival as a group; to their neighbors it may appear as a threat needing to be suppressed. Even if one restricts analysis to the realm of *national* security, the complexities do not disappear. The question of the security of the *nation*—of who belongs and who does not—has been at the heart of many recent conflicts and wars. This relativity of security—of who or what is being threatened, and from what or whom—has important consequences for understanding security relations between states, within states, and between non-state actors.

The indeterminacy and ambiguity of security has led some to view any attempt to discuss so broad and multi-dimensional a concept as futile (Wolfers 1952; Buzan 1991; Baldwin 1997). Yet the ambiguities of security are no different than those of other contested political concepts, such as freedom, democracy, or power. Contrasting visions of what it is and how it ought to be achieved are essential elements of political debates and decisions, and the central place of security in political life makes it too important to ignore. Rather than despairing at conflicting or imprecise definitions, or seeing these as a result of fuzzy thinking, our aim in this chapter is to trace some of the shifting meanings, practices, and institutions of security to show how and why these have changed as part of a complex historical process of dealing with the place of violence and order in modern political and social life. Our goal is to avoid imposing an anachronistic contemporary vision of what security is or ought to be, and instead to uncover and explain some of the different understandings that individuals, societies, and ruling elites have had of security at different times and places.

To capture these different understandings while avoiding presenting an account of the progressive development of the discipline, the chapter is organized around three themes: movement, rupture, and dissent. The first captures the mainstream account (and history) of the progressive development of the discipline of security studies; the second captures the breaks with previous scholarship that are reflected in the literature; the third captures the always-present dissenting voices that resisted the disciplining dimension of the mainstream account. In parallel, we briefly trace the symbiotic but not always tight relationship between the *conceptual* ("security studies") and the *socio-political* (institutions and practices) realms of security, best pictured as a loose strand of DNA, with different "bonds" of connection, some distant, some close. The chapter thus traces some of the main moments in the history of security practices and security studies, attempting to highlight moments of greatest convergence and divergence in the two evolving strands. It briefly reviews pre-twentieth-century contributions to highlight some of the antecedents to contemporary debates, and concentrates on the twentieth century in greatest detail. Given the future-oriented nature of this volume, the past (distant and recent) is presented with an eye to the near-future, both in terms of expected continuities and transformations.

2.2 Antecedents

The language of security has deep Roman and Greek roots (Rothschild 1995; Arends and Frederik 2008) connected with images of freedom from care or concern, but the crystallization of a distinctly modern preoccupation with security coincides with the rise of the modern state. Security, for Thomas Hobbes, is a precondition for civil and law-governed life, and requires political institutions to provide that which individuals in the state of nature cannot obtain, since "we cannot expect security from others, or assure it to ourselves" (Hobbes 1998 (1651): 26).

This conceptualization of security did not produce a discipline of security studies; rather, it provided an explanation and justification for the increased centralization of state power and its growing monopoly over the legitimate use of force. What did emerge, however, was systematic thought on strategy and warfare at the service of this new form of state power. "Strategic studies" can thus credibly claim to be a precursor of mainstream security studies, defined by one of its foremost proponents as "*the study of the threat, use and control of military force* ... [that is] the conditions that make the use of force more likely, the ways that the use of force affects individuals, states and societies, and the specific policies that states adopt in order to prepare for, prevent or engage in war" (Walt 1991: 212, emphasis in original). The tight bond between the development of state power, the increasing scope and scale of warfare, and strategic thought was reflected in the close relationship of strategic thinkers and the "science" of war to actual state policies and practices. This covered such diverse domains as the seventeenth-century development of fortifications to secure borders (Vauban) and systematic forms of training and drill for soldiers (Maurice of Nassau), battlefield deployment and tactics in the Napoleonic era (Jomini), or the importance of twentieth-century military innovations such as air power (Douhet) (Mead Earle 1944; Paret 1986; Parker 1996).

By the late nineteenth century strategic thought began to take on a more *conceptual* or theoretical cast, as well as a simply practical one, with the development of geopolitical doctrines that attempted to explain the underlying forces shaping nation states, conflict between states, and the evolution of world politics. These ranged from the more purely geographic ideas of continental versus naval powers (Halford Mackinder and Alfred Thayer Mahan), to the racially-tinged, Social Darwinist and Hegelian ideas of German geopolitical thought that fused state power to the destiny of peoples (Friedrich Ratzel, Karl Haushofer). Dissent from this vision of strategy at the service of the state was not absent, however, and the increasing scope and scale of modern warfare spurred humanist thinkers to posit "peace projects" on a grand scale. These ranged from the early fourteenth-century projects of Dante and Dubois, nostalgic for the hegemonic unity of Latin Christendom, to those of scholars such as William Penn, the Abbé de St Pierre and Immanuel Kant who attempted to reconcile the anarchic nature of the state system with an end to war (Arcidiacono 2011). While these projects did not form a *discipline* of "peace research," they served in important ways as the backdrop to twentieth-century efforts at security governance and institution-building that explicitly claimed this heritage, in particular under the umbrella of *collective security* within the League of Nations (Kennedy 1987).

This *external* vision of securing the state against external military threats, linked tightly to strategy and policy, was facilitated by increasing levels of *domestic* safety and public order, generated by the growing administrative power of the state (Eisner 2003).

From the French Revolution forward, as the state mobilized and subjected greater numbers of its citizens to the risks of violence from warfare in the name of the national and territorial state, it also assumed greater responsibility for their well-being and protection and a larger role in the management of society and the population. This increasing concern with "policing" society in its narrow sense implicated institutional development and differentiation in three ways: the expansion of the police as an institution (Bayley 1975), the slow elimination of the armed forces' role in providing domestic order, and the "pacification" of the state's relations with its subjects (rule of law, elimination of arbitrary exercises of state power such as punishment, detention, torture, and deprivation of rights). More broadly, it involved the development of what Michel Foucault termed the "conduct of conduct": the shaping of forms of subjectivity and social action, and the development of new forms of governing the self and society ("governmentality") that had the security of populations as their heart (Foucault 2003). Policing in this broader sense is not only about "negative security" (preventing people from acting in certain ways and punishing them if they do so), but also about fostering the creation of particular kinds of individuals and social orders.

All of these (external, internal, state-society) dimensions of security practices can be presented both as *trade-offs* between liberty and security, but also as *productive*; as part of complex processes of structuring conceptions of freedom and agency in ways that support specific visions of security. Consider, for instance, the elimination of duelling in the eighteenth and nineteenth centuries. This prohibition involved much more than the development of state capacities to prevent or punish duelling. It also involved a marginalization of heroic conceptions of aristocratic honor, a shift which made duelling seem uncivilized, illegitimate, and even absurd, in addition to being illegal. "Policing" society here combined with the evolution of the police to bring about a shift in security practices that was itself symptomatic of much broader processes of state consolidation and social and political transformation. Such a process was fundamental in the consolidation of the capacity for violence in the hands of the state during the process of state formation in Europe. While institutional developments in security provision were complex and diverse, they all involved a centralization of security structures (policing) within the state, an extension of state power and surveillance throughout a given territory, and a growing distinction between the institutions of internal security and those responsible for external security.

2.3 Movement: Consolidating Cold War Security Studies

The early twentieth-century study of security is most easily identified as a rupture with nineteenth-century strategic thought, and the ascendance of two strands of work that presaged (and influenced) subsequent scholarship. The first strand is best described as analyses into the conditions of peace, much of which—associated with the League of Nations experiment in collective security and various forms of disarmament—was normatively oriented and tightly linked to the concerns of particularly internationalist policy elites (Webster 2006). Although it broke definitely with nineteenth-century strategic thought and great power diplomacy, regarded as in part responsible for the tragedies of the Great War, the foundations of such conceptual and institutional innovations as collective security were in fact extensions of earlier thought about the balance of power (Niemeyer 1952; Ashworth 2006). Later work on security regimes (Jervis 1982) and security communities (Adler and Barnett 1998) can be seen as following in these footsteps, albeit with a much more scholarly focus. The second strand focused on the problem of war, and its major contribution, Quincy Wright's collaborative *A Study of War* (Wright 1942), was "notable for its inattention to problems of national strategy and national security" (Fox, quoted in Baldwin 1995: 120). It arguably stands along with Lewis Richardson's *Statistics of Deadly Quarrels* (Wilkinson 1980) at the origins of what its proponents now call the "scientific study of war" (see Section 1.6). The only major strategic studies contribution (Mead Earle 1944) was predominantly historical (except for the epilog on the Nazi concept of war).

The mainstream of security studies that emerged in the early Cold War period was not, however, an extension of these two strands. It emerged out of the matrix of the Second World War and geopolitical confrontation between East and West, was in part a reaction to the failures of multilateral security institutions of the interwar period, and narrowed its focus of security primarily to the security of the state (and its citizens) from external military threats (Baldwin 1995). In one sense, this was coherent with the nineteenth-century vision of state–society relations and of domestic order/international anarchy. More importantly though, early scholarship was predominantly America-centric and policy driven, and cohered will the geopolitical rise of the United States and the crystallization of the concept of "national security," which made its first appearance in the late 1940s (Bock and Berkowitz 1966). By 1947 national security had been institutionalized in the American National Security Act, the National Security Council (NSC), and the "national security state," in which domestic "security" concerns were occluded by the predominance of an externally-oriented focus for the word. As Daniel Yergin noted, "at certain moments, unfamiliar phrases suddenly become common articles of political discourse, and the concepts they represent become so embedded in the national consciousness that they seem always to have been with us" (Yergin 1978: 195)—so it was with the phrase "national security."

The subsequent evolution of mainstream security studies in the four decades until the mid-1980s has been sketched by Steven Walt, David Baldwin, and others (Walt 1991; Kolodziej 1992; Baldwin 1995). Security studies scholarship focused on such topics as weapons proliferation, nuclear deterrence theory, military strategy in counter-insurgency wars, arms control, the security dilemma, alliance formation and dynamics, the offence–defense balance, and other such topics (for examples, see Snyder 2007; Shiping 2010; Williams and Viotti 2012). Research by communities of scholars in each of these areas ebbed and flowed according to broader developments in International

Relations theory and methods. Deterrence theory occupied center stage in the 1950s and 1960s (Schelling 1980; Kaplan 1991; Morgan 2003); arms control was a focus in the 1970s; alliance theory re-emerged at the end of the Cold War, and so forth. Although scholars such as Walt celebrated this as a "renaissance," associated with increasing rigor, methodological sophistication, and theoretical inclination in research (Walt 1991: 211), others took a more skeptical view of these claims, highlighting the narrowness of the conception of security that underpinned this work, and its implicit claim for the primacy of security (as a precondition for political and economic life, and not subject to diminishing margin returns). As Baldwin put it, security studies "has tended to focus on *one* set of means by which security may be pursued ... military statecraft," and has "tended to assert the primacy of military security over other goals" (Baldwin 1995: 129, 127, emphasis in original).

While the broad outlines of mainstream security studies scholarship are captured by this account, the narrative obscures at least three issues. First, to scholars working outside the United States, the curious conflation of American national security concerns with the scholarly discipline of "international security studies" (treated synonymously, as in the title of a major journal in the field) smacked of academic imperialism, and obscured the way in which mainstream security studies was deeply enmeshed with current American policy concerns: deterrence, counter insurgency, arms control, terrorism. Second, the subjects covered by security studies tended to occlude much scholarship that directly concerned "issues of war and peace" or the use of force, but was not directly oriented toward immediate political concerns. This was especially the case for the large literature on the "causes of war" (Levy 1998; Levy and Thompson 2011), and the scholarship associated from the early 1960s with the Correlates of War project (COW) (Suzuki et al. 2002). Mainstream security studies resembled much more a revival of nineteenth and early twentieth century geopolitics (with an admixture of strategic thought), stripped of its tainted legacy and presented as a form of "grand strategy" to analyze the competition between the rival superpowers and their blocs. Finally, "dissent" was confined to the margins, with peace research and disarmament advocates in particular effectively cut off from the mainstream of the discipline (Rogers and Ramsbotham 1999), and pursuing their own intellectual agendas through such bodies as the International Peace Research Association, the *Journal of Peace Research* (both launched in 1964), or the publications of the Stockholm International Peace Research Institute (founded in 1966).

2.4 Dissent: Broadening and Deepening Security Studies

The past three decades have seen wide-ranging debates over how security should be studied, understood, and practically provided (Kolodziej 2005; Williams 2008; Buzan and Hansen 2009; Collins 2010; Bourbeau 2015). At the core of these debates has been *dissent*: questioning whether the mainstream way of studying security (of the state, from primarily external military threats) in International Relations is adequate. While the mainstream view of security studies was always contested, two aspects of the post-Cold War critique were most telling. The first pointed out that in the name of "state security" the security of individual citizens is most often threatened. This is clearest when the individual is compelled to go to war, and the security of the state requires the sacrifice of the security of the individual. This paradox is even starker in situations where the state—in the name of "national security"—declares certain individuals or citizens as threats. In many places, the major threats to individuals come from the security institutions of their own states (from the intelligence and "security" services, or from militaries aligned with one social group, political faction, or regime) rather than from any external sources (Davenport 2007).

The second challenge argued that the focus of traditional security studies on states and interstate war fails to capture many of the most intense dynamics of contemporary security relations: in the areas of national identity and culture; with the security of groups, individuals, or the biosphere; with questions of state stability or fragility; with economic dislocation, and global flows of people and information; and with structures and institutions of security cooperation. Environmental, economic, demographic, and other transformations posed significant threats to the well-being of states and peoples for which military force was largely irrelevant, and that traditional conceptions of security were ill-equipped to recognize. In his classic work, *People, States and Fear*, Barry Buzan argued that "a notion of security bound to the level of individual states and military issues is inherently inadequate" (Buzan 1991: 29). He, and a legion of subsequent scholars, went on to develop an expanded agenda for security studies that included different sources of insecurity, including economic and environmental dynamics, as well as political and military factors (Buzan 1991, and for an overview of one issue Brauch et al. 2008; Floyd and Matthew 2013). *Broadening* security studies thus refers to the need to address threats and sources of insecurity beyond the military security of the territorial state, the most prominent of which have been environmental or economic challenges, but which have also included issues such as transnational migration, global health, food, energy, or human rights.

As the criticisms of "narrow," traditional views of security gathered force, proponents of these views argued that the concept of security needed also to be *deepened* to include different referent objects including individuals, sub-state groups, states, regions, the global system, and the biosphere, to capture the complexity of contemporary security dynamics and the political and ethical issues involved in studying and practicing security. *Deepening* the security agenda involves moving away from an exclusive focus on the state, toward individuals or social groups below the level of the state (societal or human security) (Buzan et al. 1998; Hanlon and Christie 2016), or to institutions and structures above it (regional security arrangements, or wider cooperative security mechanisms) (Buzan and Waever 2003; Neack 2017). In each case, shifting the referent object for security (what is being secured; from what threats) reveals new and important elements and dynamics of contemporary security, yet also reveals the difficulty in analyzing these dynamics: "if everything that causes a decline in human well-being is labelled a 'security' threat, the term loses any analytical usefulness and becomes a loose synonym of 'bad'" (Deudney 1990: 463–4).

A further extension of the broadening/deepening argument holds that the negative view of security as threat is too conservative. Precisely because security is so evocative, and because it captures vital vulnerabilities of the human condition as no other term does, it is crucial that it be understood positively, defined broadly, and mobilized politically. Conditions of insecurity defined as threats to life or well-being are everywhere: poverty, disease, environmental degradation (Booth 2007). On this account, the promotion of security has an emancipatory dimension, liberating people from various forms of physical and structural violence, empowering them to control their own futures (Nunes 2012).

The challenge presented by broadening and deepening the concept of security has generated significant debate. The most straightforward reaction from mainstream security studies has been to argue that "in considering the problem of security in international politics, the place to start is with war" (Morgan 2006: 1). This reaction may reflect the power of entrenched scholarly (and policy) paradigms, or an ahistorical and unquestioning acceptance of the fusion of security and war. It is also, however, underpinned by a dual theoretical and practical claim: while new issues might represent important problems, they do not represent threats that warranted being labeled as security issues; and that if security is broadened to refer to issues beyond the security of the state from military threats, it could be expanded to mean anything. This would not only lead to analytic anarchy, it would also mean that security studies would be unable to contribute to understanding the most important issues on its agenda, those of war and peace (Mearsheimer 1994). Both of these concerns represent important challenges that have not always been taken seriously by advocates of a broadened or deepened agenda.

2.5 Rupture: Securitization Theory

A second, radically different, reaction both to "broadening and deepening" and to mainstream security studies came in the development of securitization theory (Buzan et al. 1998; Balzacq 2011). Unlike those who rejected the ambiguities of security by retreating to the supposedly secure foundations of prevailing orthodoxies, securitization theory embraced the apparent indeterminacy of the concept and sought to transform it into a basis for theoretical clarity. To do this it is necessary to relinquish the idea that security has an essential meaning or fixed condition: what are considered security issues in different times by different people is variable. But this does not imply that security is a meaningless term or that security studies is condemned to conceptual chaos. On the contrary, in securitization theory, security represents a "speech act," involving the naming of particular phenomena as "existential threats," and having that declaration accepted by a relevant audience. The concept of security is not important for what it *means*; it is important for what it *does*: for the way it marks an issue as one of survival, requiring the adoption of emergency measures and the suspension of normal rules of social and political life.

While securitization theory retains elements of the traditional view of security, particularly its association with existential fear, extreme situations, and the potential for violence, it delinks the concept from any specific object to be secured (such as the state), or a specific type of threats (originating solely from external, military forces, for example). Anything can in principle be an object to be secured: for instance, the government, the territorial state, and the nation are analytically separable referent objects that connect and conflict in practice and that often need to be distinguished in order to understand how they are combined in specific situations. In the same way, the economy, social identity, and the environment can be threatened referent objects and international corporations, migrants, HIV/AIDS, or global warming can represent threats. The analytic question thus becomes what security claims (speech acts) are made, by whom, and with what success in a given context. Security analysts recognize that these processes are underway when an actor invokes "existential threats"—processes in which mainstream conceptions and traditional institutions of state security have considerable power in setting the security agenda—but they are not exclusive, unchallengeable, or unchallenged.

Unlike much of mainstream security studies *and* many of its critics, securitization theory does not necessarily regard security as a positive thing in which "more is better." Since defining a security issue casts it within logics of fear, extremity, and emergency, securitizing an issue carries significant risks to groups such as refugees or migrants, for example. Accordingly, issues should only be securitized with a full appreciation of the potentially negative implications of doing so, and great caution should be exercised. More positive action involves *removing* an issue from the security agenda: "desecuritizing" it, and placing it within the sphere of "normal" politics where debate, negotiation, and compromise, rather than the politics of fear and emergency rule the day (Aradau 2004).

This vision of security, and particularly its division between "security" and "normal" politics provides another opening onto contemporary debates about security governance and the management of risk by networks of security professionals distinct from political elites and policy-makers. The divide between normal and securitized politics has become increasingly blurred by the rise of mentalities, technologies, and practices to manage risk and forecast security threats. Risk management practices are partly a response to the changing landscape of global security, with analysis including non-traditional as well as traditional sources of threat: to airline passengers on commercial flights as well as modern air forces; to computer hackers as well as columns of tanks; to self-radicalized violent extremists and organized terrorist groups; and to transnational non-state actors as well as state militaries. As a consequence, massive intellectual and material resources are now directed toward data collection and analysis, toward developing profiles and algorithms that can render this expansive and complex new security terrain visible and manageable.

In this way, the focus on concepts of risk in security studies opens up another of the fundamental conceptual and practical distinctions that has traditionally underpinned security studies, the divide between security inside and outside the state. As security issues and threats have become globalized, so too has the practice of policing stretched beyond borders, and as domestic threats are linked to transnational networks, domestic policing has become increasingly militarized. The two faces are often entwined, as for instance when drug trafficking, illicit arms supplies or transnational terrorism are involved; or when foreign fighters return to their "home" states and "home-grown" extremists act with global connections. Contemporary security challenges often thus cut across and partially erase the conceptual and institutional divides between internal and external security concerns. One could even argue that the post-9/11 security condition is one in which the external has become the internal: the War on Terror, and the very name and function of the Department of Homeland Security is *about* external threats having intruded into the sphere of domestic political, social, and economic life.

2.6 Retrenchment: "What Has War Got to do with this?"

Both the "dissent" and "rupture" outlined above occlude or even exclude questions of war and violence. Yet even mainstream security studies, despite a commitment to studying the *use of force* is increasingly isolated in scholarly terms from research and analysis on actual wars and armed conflicts (with the exception of terrorism)—representing a decisive rupture with the heritage of strategic studies. Current mainstream research concentrates more on what could be called geopolitics or grand strategy, focusing (from the webpage of *International Security*) on topics such as: the causes and prevention of war, ethnic conflict and peacekeeping, terrorism and homeland security, European, Asian, and regional security, US foreign policy, arms control and weapons proliferation, International Relations theory, and diplomatic and military history. One reason for this can be found in the changing nature of warfare itself: the decline of great power and interstate wars has meant that actual war-fighting takes place predominantly in the global South, involves a range of state and non-state actors, and/or is asymmetric in nature (Münkler 2005; Kaldor 2013). Even within the dissenting strands of security studies, only recently has attention been paid to the study of war as a phenomenon and "in a world made in no small measure by ongoing histories of organised violence, we lack a social science of war."

One result is that the study of the organization for and the conduct of wars and armed conflict is increasingly the preserve of scholars working within the tradition of the "scientific study of international conflict." Work regarding the recruitment and dynamics of armed groups, the logic of civil wars, mass killing and genocide, civilian victimization and the analysis of factors leading to violence is published, for example, in outlets such as *Civil Wars, or Terrorism and Political Violence*; the *Journal of Peace Research*; or the *Journal of Conflict Resolution*. These examples cover the ends of the spectrum ranging from contemporary strategic issues to research on peace and post-conflict peacebuilding; and much of this scholarship is driven by a concern with data-driven or model-based methods of social science, directly drawing upon the groundwork laid by the Correlates of War and the work of Nordic peace researchers in the 1980s and beyond (Urdal et al. 2014). For a discipline whose mainstream is oriented around "the study of the threat, use and control of military force" (Walt 1991: 212), this result is at best paradoxical, and has seen the rise of calls from more critical sociological approaches to return war to a more central place in security studies (Barkawi and Brighton 2011).

2.7 On (Future) Securities

As even this brief survey shows, the field of security studies is now rich in both its theoretical perspectives and empirical concerns. This diversity is both a strength—in that research covers a wide array of topics from diverse approaches—and a weakness—in that there is no agreed core to the discipline, and perhaps even "two solitudes" of security studies as the wide gulf between mainstream and other approaches testifies (see Hayes 2015). Any attempt to map its present and future contours would thus likely result in failure. In this final section we can only offer clues for thinking about the future of security studies, based on the diverse understandings of security and security studies outlined in this chapter.

To begin, our account highlights that security is a historically shifting set of social and political practices, not an objective condition or fixed set of perceptions. Who is being secured, from what, and by what means, has evolved throughout history. Security studies has ebbed and flowed along with these shifting practices, and the orientation it takes cannot be separated from them. Security studies is not "basic research." Embedding an analysis of security within the broader evolution of the relationships between states, societies, and institutions of organized violence leads us to scrutinize the foundations of any particular conception of security, rather than to declare one of them correct for all times and places. Nor can security be reduced solely to the existential threats to an individual, a state, or a society. While these are important, it is crucial to examine the ways in which risks are transformed into threats, and how particular issues become accepted as security issues. And it is equally important to examine the conditions under which security issues become de-intensified to the point where they are considered only to be challenges to be met through normal politics; in short, how relations of insecurity can be transformed into stable and pacific relations and systems.

The study of security will also not be reduced to violence and warfare, but war, as the ultimate expression of the potential for organized violence, is central to how security has been understood and practiced. But this needs to be set in a wider context of the processes by which individuals and communities determine what—or who—constitutes threats to their safety and well-being, since these processes tell us much about an individual's (or a community's) vision of themselves, their identity and their values—and of what they are willing to fight, kill, and die for. Traditional issues of interstate war and peace continue to present challenges that will be central to security studies. However it does not follow that this requires scholars and analysts to restrict the analysis of security only to these issues. It recognizes the many different *forms* of contemporary organized violence (large and small; highly or loosely organized; materially or politically motivated), shares mainstream security studies' concern with the institutions and instruments of coercion, but looks beyond the military, beyond war, and beyond the external exercise of force by states (Barkawi 2011).

In an increasingly globalized world, the question is also not whether the state should or should not be the focus of security studies, but rather how security provision came to be synonymous with the state, and how contemporary social and political challenges and transformations have an impact on that specific historical resolution. This is important in those parts of the globe where fragile states never provided security to their citizens, and where predatory rule represented the greatest source of insecurity. It also applies within states where the historically formed practices and processes through which internal and external forms of security provision became institutionally and politically distinct are eroding or being challenged. Too narrow or timeless a vision of security restricts our understanding of the role of the state as a political institution with a certain relationship to a community that may be emancipatory, protective, or repressive. It also hinders us from analysing many of the most important aspects of contemporary insecurities, and potentially developing creative or effective responses to them that are not bounded by the state.

Finally, treating security as a concept that has a history and that exists within a wider social and political field means that the evolution of the concept and practice of security, and the relationship between the two, is an important subject of inquiry in itself. Stressing the connections between theory and practice does not mean either that theories drive reality, or that they are simply a reflection of it. Bringing the two into a clearer relation and showing how different understandings of the concept of security are historically contingent can illuminate both changes in the concept and in the practices of security. Ultimately, the powerful "sign of security" serves to structure the mentalities, values, conceptions of the self, of social order, and of the condition of security that are embedded in institutions that we encounter on a nearly everyday basis. In this way, debates over security and the scope and ambit of security studies are connected to broader values and political judgments about desirable forms of domestic and global order.

References

Adler, E. and M. Barnett (eds.) 1998. *Security Communities*. Cambridge: Cambridge University Press.

Aradau, C. 2004. Security and the Democratic Scene: Desecuritization and Emancipation. *Journal of International Relations and Development*, 7(4): 388–413.

Arcidiacono, B. 2011. *Cinq types de paix: une histoire des plans de pacification perpétuelle (XVIIe–XXe siècles)*. Paris: PUF.

Arends, J. and M. Frederik 2008. From Homer to Hobbes and Beyond—Aspects of "Security" in the European Tradition. *Globalization and Environmental Challenges*, 3: 263–77.

Ashworth, L. M. 2006. Where are the Idealists in Interwar International Relations? *Review of International Studies*, 32(2): 291–308.

Baldwin, D. 1995. Security Studies and the End of the Cold War. *World Politics*, 48(1): 117–41.

Baldwin, D. 1997. The Concept of Security. *Review of International Studies*, 23(01): 5–26.

Balzacq, T. (ed.) 2011. *Securitization Theory*. London: Routledge.

Barkawi, T. 2011. From War to Security: Security Studies, the wider Agenda and the Fate of the Study of War. *Millennium*, 39(3): 701–16.

Barkawi, T. and S. Brighton. 2011. Powers of War: Fighting, Knowledge, Critique. *International Political Sociology*, 5: 126–43.

Bayley, D. H. 1975. The Police and Political Development in Europe. In C. Tilly and G. Ardant (eds.), *The Formation of National States in Western Europe*, pp. 328–39. Princeton, NJ: Princeton University Press.

Bock, P. G. and M. Berkowitz. 1966. The Emerging Field of National Security. *World Politics*, 19(1): 122–36.

Booth, K. 2007. *Theory of World Security*. Cambridge: Cambridge University Press.

Bourbeau, P. 2015. *Security: Dialogue across Disciplines*. Cambridge: Cambridge University Press.

Brauch, H. G., O. Ú. Spring, C. Mesjasz, J. Grin, P. Dunay, N. C. Behera, B. Chourou, P. Kameri-Mbote, and P. H. Liotta (eds.). 2008. *Globalization and Environmental Challenges: Rreconceptualizing Security in the 21st Century*, vol. 3. Berlin: Springer Science & Business Media.

Buzan, B. 1991. *People, States and Fear*. London: Macmillan.

Buzan, B. and L. Hansen. 2009. *The Evolution of International Security Studies*, Cambridge: Cambridge University Press.

Buzan, B. and O. Waever. 2003. *Regions and Powers: The Structure of International Security*. Cambridge: Cambridge University Press.

Buzan, B., O. Waever, and J. de Wilde. 1998. *Security: A New Framework for Analysis*. Boulder, CO: Lynne Reinner.

Collins, A. (ed.). 2010. *Contemporary Security Studies*, 2nd edn. Oxford: Oxford University Press.

Davenport, C. 2007. *State Repression and the Domestic Democratic Peace*. Cambridge: Cambridge University Press.

Deudney, D. 1990. The Case against Linking Environmental Degradation and National Security. *Millennium*, 19(3): 461–76.

Eisner, M. 2003. Long-term Historical Trends in Violent Crime. *Crime and Justice*, 30: 83–142.

Floyd, R. and R. Matthew. 2013. *Environmental Security: Approaches and Issues*. London: Routledge.

Foucault, M. 2003. *Society Must Be Defended: Lectures at the Collège de France, 1975–1976*. New York: Picator.

Hanlon, R. J. and K. Christie. 2016. *Freedom from Fear, Freedom from Want: An Introduction to Human Security*. Toronto: University of Toronto Press.

Hayes, J. 2015. Securitization Forum: End, or Beginning? *Available at:* http://duckofminerva.com/tag/securitization

Hobbes, T. 1998 (1651). *De Cive (On the Citizen).* Edited and translated by Richard Tuck and Michael Silverthorne. Cambridge: Cambridge University Press.
Jervis, R. 1982. Security Regimes. *International Organization*, 36(2): 357–78.
Kaldor, M. 2013. *New and Old Wars: Organised Violence in a Global Era.* Chichester: John Wiley & Sons.
Kaplan, F. 1991. *The Wizards of Armageddon.* Stanford, CA: Stanford University Press.
Kennedy, D. 1987. The Move to Institutions. *Cardoso Law Review*, 8(5): 841–988.
Kolodziej, E. A. 1992. Renaissance in Security Studies? Caveat lector! *International Studies Quarterly*, 36(4): 421–38.
Kolodziej, E. 2005. *Security and International Relations.* Cambridge: Cambridge University Press,.
Levy, J. 1998. The Causes of War and the Conditions of Peace. *Annual Review of Political Science.* 1(1): 139–68.
Levy, J. S. and W. R. Thompson. 2011. *Causes of War.* Chichester: John Wiley & Sons.
Mead Earle, E. (ed.). 1944. *Makers of Modern Strategy: Military Thought from Machiavelli to Hitler.* Princeton, NJ: Princeton University Press.
Mearsheimer, J. J. 1994. The False Promise of International Institutions. *International Security*, 19(3): 5–49.
Morgan, P. M. 2003. *Deterrence Now.* Cambridge: Cambridge University Press.
Morgan, P. M. 2006. *International Security: Problems and Solutions.* Washington, DC: CQ Press.
Münkler, H. 2005. *The New Wars.* Cambridge: Polity.
Neack, L. 2017. *National, International, and Human Security: A Comparative Introduction.* Lanham, MD: Rowman & Littlefield.
Niemeyer, G. 1952. The Balance-Sheet of the League Experiment. *International Organization*, 6(4): 537–58.
Nunes, J. 2012. Reclaiming the Political: Emancipation and Critique in Security Studies. *Security Dialogue*, 43(4): 345–61.
Paret, P. (ed.). 1986. *Makers of Modern Strategy from Machiavelli to the Nuclear Age.* Princeton, NJ: Princeton University Press.
Parker, G. 1996. *The Military Revolution: Military Innovation and the Rise of the West, 1500–1800*, 2nd edn. Cambridge: Cambridge University Press.
Rogers, P. and O. Ramsbotham. 1999. Then and Now: Peace Research—Past and Future. *Political Studies*, 47(4): 740–54.
Rothschild, E. 1995. What is Security? *Daedalus*, Summer: 53–97.
Schelling, T. C. 1980. *The Strategy of Conflict.* Cambridge, MA: Harvard University Press.
Shiping, T. 2010. Offence-defence Theory: Towards a Definitive Understanding. *The Chinese Journal of International Politics*, 3: 213–60.
Snyder, G. H. 2007. *Alliance Politics.* Ithaca, NY: Cornell University Press.
Suzuki, S., V. Krause, and J. D. Singer. 2002. The Correlates of War Project: A Bibliographic History of the Scientific Study of War and Peace, 1964–2000. *Conflict Management and Peace Science*, 19(2): 69–107.
Urdal, H., G. Østby, and N. P. Gleditsch. 2014. Journal of Peace Research. *Peace Review: A Journal of Social Justice*, 26(4): 500–4.
Walt, S. M. 1991. The Renaissance of Security Studies. *International Studies Quarterly*, 35(2): 211–39.
Webster, A. 2006. From Versailles to Geneva: The Many Forms of Interwar Disarmament. *Journal of Strategic Studies*, 29(2): 225–46.

Wilkinson, D. O. 1980. *Deadly Quarrels: Lewis F. Richardson and the Statistical Study of War*. Oakland: University of California Press.
Williams, P. 2008. *Security Studies: An Introduction*. London: Routledge.
Williams, R. E., Jr., and P. R. Viotti. 2012. *Arms Control: History, Theory, and Policy: History, Theory, and Policy*, 2 vols, Santa Barbara, CA: ABC-CLIO.
Wolfers, A. 1952. "National Security" as an Ambiguous Symbol. *Political Science Quarterly*, 67(4): 481–502.
Wright, Q. 1942. *A Study of War*. Chicago: University of Chicago Press.
Yergin, D. H. 1978. *Shattered Peace: The Origins of the Cold War and the National Security State*. Boston, MA: Houghton Mifflin.

CHAPTER 3

EXPERTISE AND PRACTICE

The Evolving Relationship between the Study and Practice of Security

IVER B. NEUMANN AND OLE JACOB SENDING*

3.1 Introduction

Twenty years ago, in the introduction to the landmark volume on *The Culture of National Security* (1996), Peter Katzenstein noted that students of world politics had all but slept through the end of the Cold War as they had been preoccupied with debating the relative merits of neorealism and neoliberalism. Having ignored domestic political factors, including nationalism, and also important economic factors, the then-dominant theories of world politics had quite simply failed to make sense of what was going on. Our era is similarly marked by significant transformations: there are power-political changes in East Asia, with territorial disputes and struggles for regional political dominance; uncertainty about the future role of the United States with the election of Donald Trump, and of the European Union with the United Kingdom having voted to leave. There is state failure and insurgency in parts of Africa and the Middle East. Russian and Turkish regimes exhibit clear fascist tendencies and face economic problems at home.

One may therefore ask whether we once again face a similar problem of being preoccupied with theories that can only offer what Jon Elster (1985: 20) once called "precision in the second decimal" in terms of explaining contemporary and future changes in international security. This volume notes that security as a field of study is significantly more diverse and open to outside influences than ever before and so, we must think, will be better able to offer at least *partial* answers. We should stress partiality, for the study of security has proliferated and broken off into distinct sub-fields and with a wide array of theoretical tools and methods. There simply is no one theory or paradigm that can claim comprehensive authority on international security *tout court*. This is not first and foremost a reflection of an "end of theory" or disciplinary uncertainty. Rather, it reflects a

* Support from the Research Council of Norway through the project "Evaluating Power Political Repertoires" (project number 250419) is gratefully acknowledged.

proliferation in the types of actors that practice security, whether internally through the establishment of national security agencies alongside police and defence, or externally, through the role played by private security companies, NGOs offering risk assessments, or firms specializing in cybersecurity that the state is dependent upon (Abrahamsen and Williams 2010). This proliferation of types of security and the actors involved in performing them is reflected in the topics studied and analytical tools used by students of international security (Leander 2005).

In short, the relationship between the study and practice of security has not only changed considerably over the last twenty years, but has also become more difficult to describe as a singular one: in some areas, the relationship between expertise and practice may be heavily institutionalized and dominated by a singular profession. This may be the case for certain areas of intelligence. In other areas, such as cybersecurity, the relationship between practice and expertise is different, being less firmly institutionalized and more open to competition from non-state actors. We think that the evolving relationship between expertise and practice, which is the topic under discussion here, can best be described as one of increased *differentiation*, where ever more actors perform ever more specialized tasks of both analyzing and of providing security. More technically, security used to be dominated by a principle of segmentary (territorially delimited) differentiation but has increasingly been dominated by functional differentiation, where specialization and division of labour are less framed and conditioned by a national frame of reference (Buzan and Alberts 2010). Our contention is that the relative strength of the national framing has declined and that the functional differentiation has increased over the last three decades, resulting in a transnationalization in what is increasingly a market for security expertise.

While our purpose here is not a historical one, the historical backdrop matters for our appreciation of the present: the signaling of state interests to its own subjects and to the outside world is, among other things, a way of gaining one single voice and so appear to the world as an integrated unit. In this sense, the professional study of security has historically been intimately tied to the state's attempts at formulating specific, and unifying, interests, as expressed, for example, in institutionalized systems for intelligence gathering at the hands of the state. The evolving relationship between the study and practice of security can therefore tell us something about changes in how the state rules over time. We explore this dimension through an analysis of the proliferation of the types of actors that are engaged both in the study, and in the practice, of security for or on behalf of the state. Our present—and we think our future—will be marked by the proliferation not only of types of actors engaged in the production of knowledge about security (such as the International Crisis Group) but also in the practice of security, since different kinds of actors tend to do things differently. As a consequence of this proliferation, it will also be marked by category-defying practices of security, as seen by the move in the direction of so-called "hybrid warfare" and in the realm of cybersecurity.

3.2 From Brother via King's Hand to War Cabinet

European states made war, and war made states (Tilly 1992). The process of state formation was historically organized around kin and clan, then tribes, some of which became polities, that consolidated around the state. This process was in large measure one of differentiation of advisors, from the King and his brothers (biological or otherwise), then to non-kin advisors, followed by schools being set up to train students on matters important for how the King could rule most effectively. In this sense, the evolution of the study of how to rule and secure the regime was integral to the evolution of the state. We see this in how generals, advisors to the King, and intelligence officers have historically occupied positions where the study and practice of security have gone hand in hand.

Max Weber (1978: 973) famously stressed how bureaucracies ideally try to order and standardize their work by imposing routines. As a direct result of the differentiation of state organs, Army and Navy Ministries, or, to use a more up-to-date terminology, Defense Ministries, emerged in Europe in the eighteenth century. They were supposed to secure a measure of kingly, and later civilian, control over matters military. By imposing overarching political goals on a military organization they were also supposed to inscribe matters military within an overall political logic.[1] Today, as a result of emulation, almost all states have Defense Ministries (with the exception being states that lease their defense functions to allies, such as Costa Rica and Nauru). Defense Ministries are similar regarding form (isomorphic), not only because they were copied at their inception, but also because states follow one another's institutional set-ups in search of what is sometimes called institutional form or best practices (Meyer and Rowan 1977).

If wars make states, and states make wars, it is hardly coincidental that knowledge about warfare takes precedence. In a self-help system like the states system, where poor knowledge about the military strengths and intentions of other states may lead to annihilation, this kind of knowledge comes at a premium. It sharpens a state's will to use resources and produce state-of-the-art knowledge production to know that one's state may be soundly beaten if knowledge production is not up to snuff. It is hardly surprising, then, that the first area in which non-European states began to copy European ones, was military matters. For example, the first translations from European languages into Russian (from the early seventeenth century) concern military manuals.

As a result of such structural factors, we may observe how states' ways of establishing knowledge-producing institutions are converging as they come into closer contact. From the late nineteenth century onwards, models that emerged in the West have been emulated not only where military manuals are concerned, but also where other security practices are concerned. This does not mean that the world has become or is becoming homogenous in this regard. When a specific phenomenon is emulated in a different setting, it will not be realized in its emulated form, but will rather be hybridized as it is being emulated. The result is something new.

The bureaucratization of security policy, then, is not simply a question of institutional form. It has immediate consequences for the substance of security policy. For example, bureaucratic organizations do not like crises, for they interrupt the flow of work. Crises are events—unique happenings—and, so, unpredictable and unwieldy, where bureaucracies will try to make their environments as stable and predictable as possible (Scott 1999). One upshot of this is that Defense Ministries are organized around analyzing and planning for a range of different contingencies, which helps explain why Defense Ministries spend so much of their resources on analyses and education. Similar trends may be traced where the question of military institutions themselves are concerned.[2]

Since the Second World War, as internationalization and then globalization have brought states and societies closer, the sheer number of people involved in producing knowledge about security matters has increased. Defense Ministries have expanded, and further state differentiation has spawned ever new institutions concerned with security. One place where this may be seen is in the development of units with responsibility for managing piracy or terrorism. Interestingly, the wars in Iraq and Afghanistan precipitated the development of new security tactics such as counter insurgency, which emulated past colonial experience as well as ushering in a new way of operating for the military (Friis 2012). A similar trend of a differentiation of security into a range of special skills can be observed at the international level as well: The first United Nations (UN) peace operations, starting with troops deployed as a UN Emergency Force during the Suez crisis in the early 1950s, were positioned between the warring parties with a mandate to observe the truce. Over time, the UN has built up ever more specialized expertise within the UN Secretariat. This mix of expertise is deployed as part of the UN's efforts to actively hunt insurgents, to protect civilians, and to engage in peacebuilding (Thakur 2006).

One added value of looking at differentiation is that we can capture the evolving relationship between the study and practice of security as a product of specialization and competition (differentiation). This has significant consequences, for it means that we attribute less autonomy to the study of security than is often assumed in the study of expert groups. While we concur with Stampnitzky (2013) that terrorism was "invented" as a distinct category to analyze and act on, we do not see this process as one that is unrelated to how states govern more generally—it is conditioned by structural features in how states are expected to operate, in keeping with what world polity scholars have long argued (Meyer and Rowan 1977; Neumann and Sending 2010). Similarly, the role of maritime security specialists has been central in defining the practices through which to engage pirates off the coast of Somalia and elsewhere (Cullen and Berube 2012). But this process—and the causal power of expert groups to shape policy—is here seen as structured by dynamics beyond the agency of such expert groups (Sending 2015). Take the number of think tanks, pundits, and consultants that have exploded over the last two decades. At one level, this is a professionalization of the study of security. At another level, it is an emerging "market" for specialized skills that seek to create and respond to a demand from states for analyses and tools with which to engage their environment (Henriksen and Seabrooke 2016). The specialization is not unique to actors outside the state, however. The number of military universities has increased, as has the number of military officers with master and doctoral degrees from non-military universities. This trend is most pronounced in North America and Europe, although many states are now establishing institutions that look similar in form. There are exceptions, of course. In India, security expertise is hard to find outside of the ministries and a handful of select elite institutions. Possible explanations for this include a lack of funds, a Gandhian heritage, and a factor of special interest to us here, namely the first Foreign Minister Nehru's dogged determination to keep knowledge production about foreign affairs at large in-house (Behera 2007).[3]

Expertise is a highly specialized skill. We would, therefore, expect it to reside with specialists. And so it does. And yet, knowledge is inextricably mixed up with how statehood is re-presented and "enacted" and so the holder of the office of defense or foreign minister is generally recognized as that country's foremost "expert" on security matters simply by virtue of how he or she re-presents statehood in times of crises. If we consider expertise as a social category to be explained—and we should—then we see that being able to speak as a representative of the state confers significant authority not only to act in the name of the state, but also to interpret the world for the state. State actors are not only "in" authority, where authority resides in the office, but are in fact also recognized as "an" authority, where the authority is seen to reside in the special capacity and knowledge of the person, independently of the office held (Friedman 1990; Sending 2015).

This particular combination of types of authority in persons holding office, which is often without any foundation regarding the special knowledge one might have thought to be required, touches on a defining question for the social sciences, namely that of anchoring the epistemic order in the state (Weber 1958; Bourdieu 2014). Hegel wrote about the Prussian state at the start of the nineteenth century, but his idealization of the state and the statesman may still be recognized in how states organize knowledge production. Processes such as entering into the career tracks of diplomats, or being admitted into a country's intelligence community, are generally competitive, elitist, and defined by the search for "knowledge and proof of ability" among a large pool of applicants. By the same token, the history of the social sciences in general, and of the study of security in particular, are intimately linked to the history of the evolution of the state.

3.3 The Academic Study of Security

Our analysis of differentiation in how states organize and are involved in knowledge production about security is also reflected, we think, in the evolution of academic analyses of security. In the interwar period, with the establishment of the League of Nations and the emphasis on legal mechanisms for conflict prevention, security was analyzed as an end to be achieved through a wide range of strategies. As one commentator notes, "During this period international relations scholars believed that democracy, international understanding, arbitration, national self-determination, disarmament, and collective security were the most important ways to promote international peace and security" (Baldwin 1995: 119). A representative work like Quincy and Louise Wright's *The Study of War* (1942) treated war as something to be avoided, as opposed to treating it as an instrument of statecraft. The first decade after the Second World War was a significant one for the institutionalization of International Relations as a discipline, with security at its very core. At this time, security was seen as one of several objectives, on a par with economic welfare, and it was not solely linked to the systemic features of the international system but also to domestic politics, even concerns with individual freedom (cf. Baldwin 1995: 121–3; van Münster and Sylfest 2016).

During the Cold War, the institutionalization of security studies took off in Europe and North America, with graduate programs being developed and research institutions emerging to offer analyses as well as an arena for so-called "informed debate"—often under Chatham House rules (opinions may be repeated, but not ascribed to a named speaker) to facilitate engagement between academics and practitioners—about security policy. The institutionalization of this highly selective and exclusionary "public" meant that there was a very close relationship between analysts and practitioners of security, and where the broader public had little access to debates about a country's security policy. Indeed, it is no exaggeration to say that—then as now—proximity and access to government circles is the single most important resource in establishing a position of recognized expertise on matters of national or international security. One of the more celebrated texts describing the dynamics of United States–Soviet relations during the Cold War was not the product of an outside academic, but was written by George Kennan, a diplomat at the US Embassy to Moscow. Inversely, in the US as elsewhere, there is a long tradition of recruiting security advisors and planners of foreign policy from top ranked universities. Examples include Henry Kissinger and Condoleeza Rice as National Security Advisors and later Secretaries of State, and Stephen Krasner and Anne Marie Slaughter as Directors of Policy Planning at the State Department.

One implication of differentiation concerns the institutional flexibility that comes from cross-fertilization and hybridization. A social order that includes not only variously organized clusters of security experts, but also a network formal and informal relations between these experts, allows the state apparatus to appropriate and make use of different registers of expertise depending on the situation. Above, we gave the historical example of the Ottoman Empire. Consider today's Turkey, where new clusters of security experts that have emerged since the 1970s or so are now under direct attack from the regime. If the regime's slogan of neo-Ottomanism means de-differentiation, then we are likely to see that the decimation of semi-independent security knowledge producers in Turkey may have a detrimental effect on Turkish external security policy, as policy-makers will have access to a decreasing pool of security expertise on different topics.

Early explanations of why knowledge production tends to continue on the basic of already established representations drawn up from within rather than on gathering new knowledge about what was happening outside tended to focus on psychological factors. In 1962, Festinger formulated his influential theory about cognitive dissonance. The basic idea was that humans tend to think in terms of wholes. Phenomena that do not conform to the already established mental image of a certain phenomenon, will tend to be read out or seen in a way that conforms to already established mental images. A well-known overall psychological reading of how such knowledge production proceeds, was Robert Jervis's (1976) book *Perception and Misperception in International Relations*. One weakness of such studies had to do with the area of generalization, which concerned individuals. In order for a number of people, for example the majority of a decision-making elite or the entire elite of a particular state, to perceive things in a similar manner, one will also have to factor in social factors. An early attempt to do this was made by Irving Janis (1972; also Park 1990), who launched the concept of group-think in order to capture how one way of representing a phenomenon such as a security threat would come to prevail. Such analyses of knowledge production are still useful.

The United States has the largest and most differentiated pool of security knowledge producers. Being a political and intellectual leader spells having an element of hegemony on thinking, which means that structural forces are afoot that will lead other security experts elsewhere to emulate American perspectives. This is, of course, a well-known dynamic. In the mainstream debates about international security after the end of the Cold War, scholars elsewhere tended to adopt the perspectives, if not always the interests, of the position of the United States. Hegemonic stability theory, for example, subsumed the question of security under the question of the conditions under which a hegemon could conceivably maintain and expand its position. Perhaps most well-known is the exchange between John Mearsheimer (1994) and Robert Keohane and Lisa Martin (1995) on the relative merits of realism and institutionalism. For all the theoretical importance of that debate for IR scholarship on the generic features of interstate politics, it was nonetheless a debate that replaced a focus on security as such with one on the calculations of statesmen. In so doing, security was an epiphenomenon of/derivate of changes in the international order, not a specific object of analysis in its own right. We see the same dynamic in theories of "order" or "balancing," the focus on systemic features and strategic balancing tends to overshadow how security threats emerge from non-predictable events whose sources are beyond such a concept.

In our perspective, then, these analyses, important as they are on substance, are first and foremost contemporary examples of the kind of expert knowledge that characterizes how governance is now organized. This process calls for self-reflection. The role of expert knowledge in security policy has been a central concern for those who are interested in the so-called knowledge-policy nexus in world politics. While Ernst Haas did not write about security policy per se, the leitmotif for his explorations in *When Knowledge is Power* (1990) was how different types of learning generates distinct modes of international cooperation and "political integration", thereby overcoming the security dilemma. Perhaps the most significant development over the last three decades was the publication of the special issue of *International Organization* on so-called "epistemic communities" (Haas 1992). For Peter M. Haas and his collaborators, such communities, formed by like-minded experts, are important because they may, under certain conditions, shape international policy, including international security policy. Adler

(1992) analyzed how, for example, a US-based epistemic community advocating nuclear arms control, prevailed to shape the 1972 Antiballistic Missile Arms Control Treaty. This study and the ones it inspired were primarily interested in countering theories that did not leave much explanatory room for expert knowledge, or for non-state actors (Cross 2007). Haas and his followers organized their analytical tools around the actors in question, defined as an epistemic community, and explored the causal pathways through which they could shape policy. In so doing, they necessarily had to insulate "knowledge" from political conditioning, for if it could be shown that the knowledge claims of an epistemic community were significantly shaped by pre-existing political interests, their role would ultimately be epiphenomenal.

This was important, for it further strengthened the image of knowledge production as autonomous from policy making, and it did not ask what type of knowledge could ever become authoritative in the eyes of policy-makers. From a very different vantage point, the early post-structural work in IR theory in the late 1980s and early 1990s took issue with dominant representations of statehood and security (Campbell 1992). Ashley and Walker highlighted the importance of questioning sovereignty and of unmasking the so-called "great debates" to identify what functions these served in terms of securing for IR a level of authority in speaking on behalf of the scholarly community vis-à-vis state actors. Shapiro (1990) and Klein (1990) both followed this script in their exploration of security-related themes in the special issue of *International Studies Quarterly* edited by Ashley and Walker. Perhaps most importantly, Ashley's sustained critique of neorealism in his 1984 article in *International Organization*, pointed to the importance of distinguishing between categories of analysis and categories of practice. For Ashley, realism is a generic practice category, not an analytical one. Here we have the reason why Ashley pointed to the need for critically informed analyses of the categories used by "statesmen" in their conduct of security policy—categories that should not be taken at face value as had been the tradition in security studies and foreign policy.

One interpretation of this development is that the academic discipline of IR, and of security studies, had by the 1980s achieved a level of specialization and differentiation from direct policy issues that allowed a more critical reflection to emerge on how the object of analysis—the state, the international system, security—was defined in the first place. The scholarship originating in Aberystwyth and Copenhagen around the same time—as discussed elsewhere in this volume—is an expression of a similar development (see Krause and Williams, this volume).

This is not all new: historically, mercenaries, privateers, missionaries, and other "private" actors have been important components of how states, and certainly empires, have ruled both as providers of knowledge, and as implementers of policy (cf. Steinmetz 2007). What is distinct about the present is that these non-state actors are not appropriated by or under the control of any one state. They operate with significant resources, independent mandates, and specialized expertise that is mobilized vis-à-vis both states and international organizations to shape specific policy decisions. This development relates directly to our overarching point about how the state governs: the state plays a new or different role, harnessing tools from a variety of actors. This is very much on display in the emerging area of cybersecurity, where most states are completely dependent on private firms, which have the know-how to provide such services (Kello 2013).

More actors are involved in claiming to speak on, or for, others and more actors are used by states to "do" security, as in the case of so-called hybrid warfare. One implication for the study of security is to go back to Mitchell's (1991) insight about the state—that it is a product of boundaries being drawn and re-drawn, and our task as analysts is to capture the practices through which the state emerges as somehow standing above society. In the field of security, there is ample room for fine-grained analyses of how different images and forms of statehood emerge from ever more specialized practices of security. For example, the state that emerges from practices of cyber security appears distinct from that which emerges from, say, protecting civilians against terrorist threats.

3.4 Conclusion

As the European state emerged as an ever stronger force, the differentiation of functions led to ever more fine-grained institutionalization. Contact between European states and other polities led to copying and hybridization, so that, by the twentieth century, what was once a characteristically European knowledge order of security had gone global. The previous century was also the time when Western polities saw this differentiation spill across formal state boundaries, so that loci of security knowledge popped up outside of the formal state apparatus as well. The degree to which this differentiation process has been copied and hybridized explains most of the variation between different state knowledge orders in the contemporary world.

The key loci of security knowledge to emerge outside of immediate state control were academic disciplines. During the Cold War, such knowledge tended to be directly tied to the formulation of state interest. After the Cold War, knowledge production with direct ties to state interests was complemented by knowledge production with more indirect ties to state knowledge production. It is significant that security studies initially emerged as a sub-discipline of International Relations and Political Science, for it meant that this kind of knowledge production was part and parcel of the general emergence of knowledge within those disciplines. Here we have one reason why the new psychologically-oriented studies of security, which emerged in the 1970s and built on research findings from outside International Relations and Political Science, were marginalized by more socially-oriented studies after the end of the Cold War.

At the present juncture, as was the case after the end of the Cold War, new developments in world politics invite changes in knowledge production. A major challenge for scholars is to acknowledge these challenges on their own terms, rather than to resort to path dependency and group-think in producing even more studies of already well-known phenomena within an already well-known knowledge order. This brings us to our final point: security can be studied in different ways, and one should be cognizant of the character of the institutional framework within which "security" is studied. Our interpretation of the nexus between expertise and practice as one of differentiation is in part aimed at capturing how the study of security has historically had a tendency to follow not so much the specific interests of any given state ("politics"), but the broader institutional parameters within which such interests have been articulated ("the political"). "Politics" refers to manifest behavior within established institutional settings, and it is the hallmark of most social scientific analyses. The "political" refers to the very register within which some phenomena emerge as amenable to empirical analyses and others do not. Reflecting on the latter aspect is important, for focusing solely on manifest behavior "neglects ... the constituted character of data: their insertion into frames of reference, and particularly into the generative framework of 'the political' or the polity." (Dallmayr 1993: 110). It is our hope that the study of security also looks at the "constituted character of data" and thereby makes the distinction between the practice and study of security part and parcel of the analysis of security. Luckily, such epistemologically sensitive analyses are now beginning to emerge (Stampnitzky 2013), and they seem to us to heed Richard Ashley's observation thirty years ago that the study of politics is an integral part of politics inasmuch as the former continually reproduces some categories and not others. When we are now facing the potential for a major shake-up of established strategies for security with the election of Donald Trump as US President, it seems all the more important for security scholars to not budge but to stick to their commitment to uncovering different dimensions of security, both national and international.

Notes

1. Here we have one social backdrop to the famous strategic debate between Jomini, who advocated building to a decisive battle, and Clausewitz, who did not favour the putting of so much stock in any one single battle (Paret 1986).
2. After the Napoleonic Wars, Prussia saw a further differentiation of state organs when the invention of the Military High Command emerged (Holborn 1986). This model has also been copied by other states as a mark of statehood. It is no coincidence, for example, that during the period of decolonization, the first order of business in planning for independence was the establishment of a military force, with a high command with direct links to the office of the head of state (cf. Eyre and Suchman 1996; Mitchell 1991).
3. As seen from an academic standpoint, this means that Indian security policy is rarely studied by anybody other than a select and isolated few, who tend to focus on a narrow band of issues. In the 1980s and 1990s, it was adherence to the nuclear Nonproliferation Treaty. In this millennium, it has been India's campaign to be recognized as a fully-fledged great power. There is a seeming inconsistency here, for other aspiring great powers, first and foremost China and Brazil, have spent the same period building up an internationally active corps of security policy researchers, and a state like Russia has tried to internationalize their relevant academic milieus (albeit with limited success).

References

Abrahamsen, Rita and Michael C. Williams. 2010. *Privatising Africa's Everyday Security*. Cambridge: Cambridge University Press.

Adler, Emmanuel. 1992. The Emergence of Cooperation: National Epistemic Communities and the International Evolution of the Idea of Nuclear Arms Control, *International Organization*, 46(1): 101–45.

Baldwin, David. 1995. Security Studies and the End of the Cold War, *World Politics*, 48: 117–41.

Behera, Navnita Chadha. 2007. Re-Imagining IR in India, *International Relations of the Asia-Pacific*, 7(3): 341–68.

Bourdieu, Pierre. 2014. *On the State*. London: Polity.

Buzan, Barry and Mathias Albert. 2010. Differentiation: A Sociological Approach to International Relations Theory. *European Journal of International Relations*, 16(3): 315–37.

Campbell, David. 1992. *Writing Security*. Minneapolis, MN: University of Minnesota Press.

Cross, Ma'ia K. Davis. 2007. *The European Diplomatic Corps*. Basingstoke: Palgrave Macmillan.

Cullen, Patrick and Claude Berube (eds.). 2012. *Maritime Private Security: Market Responses to Piracy, Terrorism and Waterborne Security Risks in the 21st Century*. Abingdon: Routledge.

Dallmayr, Fred. 1993. Postmetaphysics and Democracy. *Political Theory*, 21(1), 101–27.

Elster, Jon. 1985. *Sour Grapes. Studies in the Subversion of Rationality*. Cambridge: Cambridge Univerity Press.

Eyre, Dana P. and Mark C. Suchman. 1996. Status, Norms and the Proliferation of Conventional Weapons: An Institutional Theory Approach, In Peter Katzenstein (ed.), *Cultures of National Security*, pp. 79–113. New York: Columbia University Press.

Festinger, Leon. 1962. Cognitive Dissonance. *Scientific American*, 207(4): 93–107.

Friedman, R. B. 1990. On the Concept of Authority in Political Philosophy. In Joseph Raz (ed.), *Authority*. New York: New York University Press.

Friis, Karsten. 2012. Which Afghanistan? Military, Humanitarian, and State-building Identities in the Afghan Theater. *Security Studies*, 21(2).

Haas, Ernst. 1990. *When Knowledge is Power*. Stanford, CA: University of California Press.

Haas, Peter M. 1992. Introduction: Epistemic Communities and International Policy Coordination. *International Organization*, 46(1): 1–35.

Henriksen, Lasse Folke and Leonard Seabrooke. 2016. Transnational Organizing: Issue Professionals in Environmental Sustainability Networks, *Organization* 23(5): 722–41.

Holborn, Hajo. 1986. The Prussian-German School: Moltke and the Rise of the General Staff. In Peter Paret (ed.), *Makers of Modern Strategy from Machiavelli to the Modern Age* pp. 281–95. Oxford: Clarendon.

Janis, Irving L. 1972. *Victims of Groupthink: A Psychological Study of Foreign-Policy Decisions and Fiascoes*. Boston: Houghton Mifflin.

Jervis, Robert. 1976. *Perception and Misperception in International Politics*. Princeton, NJ: Princeton University Press.

Katzenstein, Peter. (ed.) 1998. *The Culture of National Security*. New York: Columbia University Press.

Kello, Lucas. 2013. The Meaning of the Cyber Revolution: Perils to Theory and Statecraft. *International Security*, 38(2): 7–40.

Keohane, Robert O. and Lisa L. Martin. 1995. The Promise of Institutionalist Theory. *International Security*, 20(1): 39–51.

Klein, Bradley S. 1990. How the West Was One: Representational Politics of NATO. *International Studies Quarterly*, 34(3): 311–25.

Leander, Anna. 2005. The Power to Construct International Security: On the Significance of Private Military Companies. *Millennium: Journal of International Studies*, 33(3): 803–25.

Mearsheimer, John. J. 1994. The False Promise of International Institutions. *International Security*, 19(3): 5–49.

Meyer, John. W and Brian Rowan. 1977. Institutionalized Organizations: Formal Structure as Myth and Ceremony. *American Journal of Sociology*, 83(2): 340–63.

Mitchell, Timothy. 1991. The Limits of the State: Beyond Statist Approaches and Their Critics. *The American Political Science Review*, 85(1): 77–96.

Neumann, Iver B. and Ole Jacob Sending. 2010. *Governing the Global Polity: Practice, Rationality, Mentality.* Ann Arbor, MI: Michigan University Press.

Paret, Peter. 1986. Clausewitz. In Peter Paret (ed.), *Makers of Modern Strategy from Machiavelli to the Modern Age*, pp. 186–213.Oxford: Clarendon.

Park, W. W. 1990. A Review of Research on Groupthink. *Journal of Behavioral Decision Making*, 3(4): 229–45.

Scott, James C. 1999. *Seeing Like a State.* Princeton, NJ: Princeton University Press.

Sending, Ole Jacob. 2015. *The Politics of Expertise: Competing for Authority in Global Governance.* Ann Arbor: University of Michigan Press.

Shapiro, Michael J. 1990. Strategic Discourse/Discursive Strategy: The Representation of "Security Policy" in the Video Age. *International Studies Quarterly*, 34(3): 327–40.

Stampnitzky, Lise. 2013. *Disciplining Terror: How Experts Invented "Terrorism."* Cambridge: Cambridge University Press.

Steinmetz, George. 2007. *The Devil's Handwriting: Precoloniality and the German Colonial State in Qingdao, Samoa, and Southwest Africa.* Chicago: University of Chicago Press.

Thakur, Ramesh. 2006. *The United Nations, Peace and Security: From Collective Security to the Responsibility to Protect.* Cambridge: Cambridge University Press.

Tilly, Charles. 1992. *Coercion, Capital and European States, A.D. 990–1992.* Oxford: Blackwell.

Van Münster, Rens and Casper Sylvest. 2016. *Nuclear Realism: Global Political Thought During the Thermonuclear Revolution.* London: Routledge.

Weber, Max. 1958. Science as a Vocation. *Daedalus*, 87(1): 111–34.

Weber, Max. 1978. *Economy and Society.* Berkeley, CA: University of California Press.

Wright, Quincy and Louise Wright. 1942. *A Study of War.* Chigaco: University of Chicago Press.

PART II

APPROACHES TO INTERNATIONAL SECURITY

A

Schools of Thought

CHAPTER 4

FEMINIST SECURITY AND SECURITY STUDIES

LAURA SJOBERG

In 1988, J. Ann Tickner (1988) pointed out that "international relations is a man's world, a world of power and conflict in which warfare is a privileged activity."[1] Thirty years into feminist contributions to International Relations (IR), there is an extent to which that statement remains true, and is likely to be true well into the future. While even initial embraces predicted that feminist insights would "fundamentally change IR's greatest debates" (Keohane 1989), the trajectory of feminist inquiry in IR generally and security studies specifically has been rocky.[2] The achievements of feminist research for advancing knowledge about security have been, in my view, nothing short of amazing, but "feminist theorists have rarely achieved the serious engagement with other IR scholars for which they have frequently called" (Tickner 1997), and many have stopped calling for engagement at all (e.g. Wibben 2011; Sylvester 2013). This chapter looks at the foundations and trajectory of Feminist Security Studies, engaging both its debates and its difficulties. It then considers security studies *as if* feminisms had transformed it, and uses that theorizing to consider futures for Feminist Security Studies.

The importance of feminist approaches is, as V. Spike Peterson (1992: 197) explains, that "'real world' events are not adequately addressed by androcentric accounts that render women and gender issues invisible." Feminist approaches use *gender lenses* (Peterson and Runyan 1993: 21) to look for gender in international security, and observe what is then made visible.[3] When feminists in security studies use the word "gender," they are referring to more than what sex someone appears to be when you look at them. They are referring to the divisions that we see and the divisions that we make between those we understand to be men and those we understand to be women—but they are also referring to the ways that traits associated with those people *and* their perceived sex (which we call masculinities and femininities) operate in social and political life—at the individual level, in social interaction, in workplaces, in organizations, in politics, and everywhere else across the global that tropes, perceptions, and labels that we might identify as "gendered" exist. As Marysia Zalewski (1995) notes, "the driving force of feminism is its attention to gender and not simply women. . . . The concept, nature, and practice of gender are key."

But what does that mean? It means rather than focusing on what women do in the security realm and what men do, Feminist Security Studies is interested in "thinking about gendered social structures that select for and value gendered characteristics" (Sjoberg 2013: 47). Gendered social structures are applied to, and have effect on, people, but they are also applied to governments, organizations, corporations, behaviors, and other elements of global politics which people who associate the terms "gender" and "sex" (male and female) might not immediately think to analyze as gendered. Instead, Feminist Security Studies looks to consider where gendered assumptions, gendered labels, and gendered hierarchies impact how a wide variety of actors act, and are responded to, in global politics. Masculinization can be seen as a move of claiming or acknowledging power, while feminization can be used to devalue or devalorize, for example (Peterson 2010). Feminist Security work, then, asks "what assumptions about gender (and race, class, nationality, and sexuality) are necessary to make particular actions meaningful" (Wilcox 2009) in international security, and, indeed, to make international security itself meaningful (Shepherd 2008).

These sorts of questions are not commonly asked in traditional security studies. In 2009, I pointed out that there had been very little cross-pollination between feminist work addressing security issues and "mainstream" publications in security studies (Sjoberg 2009: 187). While, in the intervening years, some engagement has happened, that engagement remains both very new and very thin.[4] When I say that it remains very new, I mean both that the *term* Feminist Security Studies and the idea that security studies (proper) should engage with feminism is a product of this millennium, even though feminist scholars both inside and outside of disciplinary IR have been studying security for significantly longer.

This chapter proceeds in three sections., First, it looks to situate Feminist Security Studies within and around security studies, substantively, intellectually, and categorically. Second, it discusses some of the major contributions of Feminist Security Studies, in general terms and with examples. Finally, it looks for the potential futures of Feminist Security Studies itself and security studies more broadly with the integration of feminist theorizing.

4.1 Situating Feminist Security Studies

Feminist Security Studies is both unique to IR and not unique to IR. The sense in which it is not unique to IR is that feminist researchers have been interested in security both broadly defined (personal safety, economic security, physical security) and in traditional terms (war, terrorism, conflict) since the inception of feminist theorizing. Early work such as Betty Reardon's (1985) *Sexism and the War System* and Birgit Brock-Utne's (1985) *Educating for Peace* linked sexism and conflict, feminism and the seeking of peace. Later analysis has been more complicated—asking how assumptions about sex, gender, and sexuality are embedded in both the phenomenon of international security and the study thereof (e.g. Wilcox 2009; Shepherd 2008).

Yet Feminist Security Studies *in* IR also directly and explicitly addresses the concerns and issues that IR scholars have engaged with over the years. For example, some have mapped Feminist Security Studies onto IR's grand theoretic, or paradigmatic, approaches. In this exercise, one might map feminist approaches onto different paradigmatic approaches to IR. Feminist realism is interested in gender, structure, and power.[5] Feminist liberalism is interested in including women in the legal and social structures of the international arena (e.g. Caprioli and Boyer 2001). Feminist constructivism focuses on the role of ideas about gender in global politics (e.g. Prugl 1999). Feminist critical theory explores gender significations in global politics (e.g. Chin 1998). Feminist poststructuralism explores how gendered meanings constitute global politics (e.g. Shepherd 2008). Feminist postcolonialism focuses on the intersection of colonial relations of domination and gender relations (e.g. Chowdhury and Nair 2002). These categories, though, are both oversimple (much work crosses their boundaries) and somewhat dated (for example, postcolonialism has given way to decolonialism, and not a lot of work self-identifies in these categories anymore). They also pin IR feminism to IR rather than feminist theorizing, which is a permissive condition of some shallow thinking about sex, gender, and sexuality.[6] Alternatively, one might map contributions to Feminist Security Studies in terms of typologies of feminisms, where liberal feminisms focus on women's inclusion,[7] radical feminisms focus on the fundamental nature of women's oppression (e.g. MacKinnon 1982), socialist feminisms link sex and class oppression (e.g. Haraway 1987), eco-feminisms focus on the links between gender oppression and environments, queer feminisms focus on the intersections of gender and sexuality (e.g. Detraz 2009), and cultural feminisms highlight the deleterious effects of masculinized behaviors and stereotypes (e.g. Alcoff 1988). This typology also has a number of weaknesses, given that much feminist work in IR combines approaches in feminist theorizing, and that one of the key strengths of Feminist Security Studies is the ability to converse both with feminist IR (which has starting points in disciplinary IR) and disciplinary IR more generally.

As such, I argue that the exercise of categorizing different *types* of work in Feminist Security Studies is useful only as a heuristic exercise to detail and think about various potential contributions to the enterprise of studying security from a feminist perspective. That heuristic exercise demonstrates that there are a wide variety of directions, both commensurable and incommensurable, in which feminist sensibilities might lead security studies. Rather than rehearsing categorizations or segmenting incommensurabilities, this section will highlight commonalities that feminist approaches to security studies might hold, and some ways that different feminisms might follow that common ground to different theoretical contributions.

One thing that feminist work in security studies shares is "a normative and empirical concern that the international system is gender-hierarchical," where the normative concern is that gender hierarchy is wrong, and the empirical concern is that ignoring it gives inaccurate and incomplete explanations. The normative concern that gender hierarchy is wrong is just that—an understanding that gender (whether conceptualized as biological sex, social conditioning, or discursive signification) influences people's positions in the world such that people, things, and institutions associated with femininities are seen, and treated, differently than people, things, and institutions associated with masculinities. This difference is not equally distributed or randomly assigned—instead, associations with femininity *devalue* while associations with masculinity *add value* (Peterson 2010). This normative concern manifests in many forms of scholarly analysis, from advocacy for women's legal inclusion to advocacy to throw off the gender-subordinating chains of capitalist social and political order. In this way, "knowledge is contextual, contingent, and interested" (Maynard and Purvis 1994)—both in the context of the feminist normative commitment to rejecting gender hierarchy (however defined) and in feminist analysis of research which either refuses or neglects to reject gender hierarchy (which can be characterized as having a knowledge-interest in the status quo) (Tickner 1997; Sjoberg 2012).

The empirical concern that ignoring gender hierarchy gives inaccurate and incomplete explanations of how global politics works follows from the understanding that gender hierarchy is prevalent in global politics, but often ignored by scholars looking to account for the constitution of or explain causal processes in global politics. Most scholars whose work can be understood as being within Feminist Security Studies argue that gender is both constitutive and causal in global politics, where gender is a constitutive feature of the identity and interactions of actors as well as a proximate cause of political behavior (Sjoberg 2009: 196). Different scholars focus on different parts of that chain, but to all of them, gender is key to the analysis of global politics generally and international security specifically (Sjoberg 2013). This understanding of the centrality of gender to the processes of international security inspires feminist scholars to "ask what assumptions about gender (and race, class, nationalist, and sexuality) are necessary to make particular statements, policies, and actions meaningful" in global politics, at various levels of analysis (Wilcox 2009).

Going from the abstract to the specific requires asking how the orientation of looking for what gender means and how it functions in global politics shapes definitions of and understandings of security. In 2009, as a number of feminist scholars were looking to understand the contours of Feminist Security Studies, I argued that four manifestations of their common foundations could be found (Sjoberg 2009). First, I argued that different areas of Feminist Security Studies work shares a "broad understanding of what counts as a security issue and to whom security should be applied" (Sjoberg 2009: 199). In this argument, I was referencing the debate in security studies between those who would "broaden" the definition of security beyond interstate war (e.g. Krause and Williams 1996) and those who would limit the study of security to the study of the actions of state militaries (e.g. Walt 1991). In that debate, feminist work has largely been in the camp of the wideners. Feminists have argued that threats to women's security can and often do come from members of their own households or representatives of their own states (e.g. Nussbaum 2005). Feminist have pointed out that threats to women's security come not only from guns, bombs, and fists but also from inadequate access to nutrition, health care, and birth control (e.g. Cohn 2013). They have shown that statist views of global politics marginalize women (e.g. Hudson 2005). Feminist have demonstrated that broader definitions of what constitutes threats to security can provide broader paths to tempering security threats, especially by recognizing the importance of foregrounding values associated with femininities.

Second, I argued that Feminist Security Studies researchers share an interest in understanding the gendered nature of the values prized in the realm of international security (Sjoberg 2009: 200). This also manifests in different ways in different Feminist Security Studies research, but can be found across wide varieties of the work. For example, liberal feminists often see the gendered nature of values prized in the international arena in sex-based or even primordial terms. This can be seen in the recent increase of work using an FEA (feminist evolutionary analytic) to think about security, where scholars argue that the evolutionary drive to heterosexual sex positions men and women in a way that both subordinates women ("naturally") and causes war and conflict ("instinctually") (e.g. Hudson et al. 2011). By contrast, recent work looking at masculinities in war and conflict has suggested that expectations about the sex, gender, and sexuality of members of militaries are necessary features both of the constitution of military organizations and the ability to convince soldiers and citizens of hierarchies among both states and militaries (e.g. Belkin 2012). In this analysis, association with values understood to be masculine and association with values understood to be feminine are *constitutive of rank* and *determinative of result* in security situations in important, if complicated, ways.[8]

The third commonality I suggested was that scholars in Feminist Security Studies recognize "the broad and diverse role that feminists see gender playing in the theory and practice of international security" where "it is necessary, conceptually, for understanding international security, it is important in analyzing causes and predicting outcomes, and it is essential to thinking about solutions to promoting positive change in the security realm" (Sjoberg 2009: 200–1, 201). Early feminist work in peace studies as well as IR tended to suggest the availability of *degendering* global politics, suggesting that it is possible to recognize the ways in which gender subordination structures political interactions and then correct for them in a straightforward way. Feminist Security Studies work of all paradigmatic or epistemological stripes has tended to characterize this relationship as more complicated, arguing that gender is interwoven in international processes at almost every step of political interaction, and should be treated as both multi-faceted and embedded (e.g. Wibben 2011; Sjoberg 2013). As Laura Shepherd (2016) notes, this shared tenet also looks different in practice when it is carried out by different researchers. She explains that "some FSS scholars take the lives and experiences of women in the context of security politics and practices as their central concern, while others engage with FSS as a series of critical investigations of how the category of gender itself and the corollary identities we associate with subjects come to have meaning in the world through security politics and practices" (Shepherd 2016). *Both* of these disparate approaches argue that the influence of gender in security is widespread and embedded, but they treat its widespread nature substantively differently and see a different source of its embeddedness.

The fourth commonality that I noted in 2009 was that Feminist Security Studies work shares the view that "the omission of gender from work on international security does not make that work gender-neutral or unproblematic" (Sjoberg 2009: 202). This might be the most radical tenet Feminist Security Studies shares. In this view, Feminist Security Studies is not another paradigm like realist work or constructivist work—where it offers a different perspective than other paradigmatic alternatives based on a different worldview. Instead, it argues that security studies *across paradigmatic approaches* is incomplete and exclusive inasmuch as it is blind to the gendered nature of the analysis it undertakes and the gendered nature of the global political phenomena that it observes. In this view, Feminist Security Studies is not seeking the *inclusion* of gender, either as a variable of analysis or as a perspectival approach, but instead the *transformation* of security studies.

While I think that these categories that I developed in 2009 still have utility in accounting for some of the dimensions of Feminist Security Studies, my views have expanded and the field has both changed and diversified in the intervening time. First, I started to see the substance of Feminist Security Studies as residing more in the argument than in the resolution of the argument between different feminisms (Sjoberg 2011). Second, Carol Cohn's question about whether Feminist Security Studies is "feminist security" studies (with an emphasis on the security concerns inspired by feminist theorizing) or feminist "security studies" (with an emphasis on feminist interpretations of the traditional concerns of security studies) led to a discussion of the pros and cons of engaging with disciplinary IR.

Some feminist scholars have cautioned against engaging with, or intellectually "facing" toward, disciplinary IR generally and security studies specifically. Early in the development of feminist theorizing in IR, Sarah Brown (1988) warned that "the danger in attempts to reconcile international relations and feminism ... lies in the uncritical acceptance by feminists of objects, methods, and concepts which presuppose the subordination of women." In response to this danger, as Judith Squires and Jutta Weldes (2007: 185) note, feminist "scholars are now actively reconstructing IR without reference to what the mainstream asserts rightly belongs inside the discipline ... it is more effective to refuse to engage in disciplinary navel-gazing." This leads to Feminist Security Studies focused on "feminist security" that looks different to Feminist Security Studies focused on "security studies" (Cohn 2011).

Others have argued for the full integration of sex and gender into the traditional concerns of security studies, treating gender as a variable to analyze security situations and strategic decision-making (Hudson et al. 2009). The position that I have taken is a middle ground between the two—looking for a Feminist Security Studies that both cannot be ignored by security studies and does not fundamentally alter its intellectual orientations to fit with traditional assumptions either about the form of security inquiry or about the appropriate subject matter of security analysis. I label this approach "constructive engagement" with disciplinary IR and security studies—looking for conversation and perhaps even compromise while insisting on the importance of studying the gendered dynamics of security politics on the global level, rather than conflating sex and gender or ignoring either or both (Sjoberg 2013).

If how to situate Feminist Security Studies within or around the constructs of "mainstream" IR or security studies is the subject of some controversy, so is the relationship between Feminist Security Studies and other critical approaches to the study of security in global politics. While there are some who assume that feminist theorizing is akin to or subsumed within "broader" (read: malestream) critical approaches to security (e.g. Booth 2007), others worry that critical approaches to security often replicate the gender-blindnesses of "mainstream" security studies. For example, Christine Sylvester (2007) points out that the widely-lauded CASE Collective (2006) manifesto of the theoretical and political tenets of Critical Security Studies (CSS) does not include feminist or gender-based concerns in the article-length text at all, and mentions them only as an aside in a footnote. Sylvester (2007) argues that this is a visible instantiation of a deeper problem in critical security, where male scholars who self-identify as critical engage in a self-congratulatory refusal to acknowledge remaining gender concerns in their otherwise-emancipatory intellectual frameworks.

Even were other critical approaches to security to engage feminism more directly, it is not immediately clear that Feminist Security Studies has an easy intellectual affinity with other approaches generally understood to be critical. Feminist Security Studies has been distinguished, for example, from human security theorizing, by the recognition that the "human" is a gendered concept and that human bodies have gender-distributed needs and significations.[9] Feminist Security Studies has been distinguished from the Copenhagen school by the recognition that there are gendered power dynamics in securitization (Sjoberg 2009: 208–11). Feminist Security Studies has been distinguished from practice theory by the gendered implications of embodiment for notions of practice (e.g. Wilcox 2013). Still, for as many times as Feminist Security Studies has been distinguished from or critical of other critical approaches to the study of security, it has been likened to or paired with them as frequently.

All of this is to say that there is no *one* Feminist Security Studies, no *one* position of Feminist Security Studies in the field, and no *one* on-balance normatively correct way to handle feminist security theorizing around global politics. Instead, the contributions of Feminist Security Studies revolve around some common assumptions, handled differently, and explored differently, to produce a wide variety of insights for security studies.

4.2 Feminist Insights for Security Studies

With these various ontological, epistemological, and methodological approaches, feminists have shown gender bias in security's core concepts—the state, violence, war, peace, and even security itself, and have urged redefinition and reinterpretation (Sjoberg 2009: 197). They have shown that seeing women and gender in war and conflict is crucial to understanding both how those conflicts came to be and what happens in them

(Sjoberg 2009: 198). This has been as true for "traditional" security issues like nuclear strategy and the non-combatant immunity principle as it has been for traditionally hidden security issues like marriage and household finance.[10] The breadth and depth of feminist work in international security has touched almost all (imaginable) parts of the field of security studies—from arguing that gender hierarchy is a system-level influence in global politics (Sjoberg 2012) to seeing that global security politics takes place in the everyday living of women's lives (Enloe 2010; Parashar 2013). There is not sufficient space in this chapter to explore each contribution, or to find representative categories, for the diversity of this work. Instead, I will briefly discuss four diverse examples, and their contribution to the study of security.

First, I discuss a book that pre-dates the use of the term "Feminist Security Studies," Ann Tickner's (1992) *Gender in International Relations*. Tickner (1992) draws a picture of "global security" (which is the subtitle of the book) that includes not only military issues and what is traditionally thought of as state security, but also (and with equal weight), human rights issues, political economy issues, and environmental issues. Tickner's (1992) claim is that those issues affect the viability and security of people's lives (especially women's) as much, if not more than, traditional military security issues, both on a macro-level and everyday. It is Tickner's contention that it is important to pay attention to *insecurity* as the flip side of "security," and that *insecurity* is gendered. When she characterizes insecurity as gendered, Tickner is making parallel claims that *women* are more likely to be in insecure positions in global politics, and that women's insecurity is often shaped by negative treatment *because of* their gender. Tickner provides evidence for this claim both by showing how women are similarly situated across a wide variety of security issues, and by showing how associations with femininity signify devalorization in many security discourses. Both of these insights have been used, built on, and complicated in the more than two-decade development of Feminist Security Studies since the writing of this crucial book.

The second piece of work that I will highlight is a very different one—Aaron Belkin's (2012) *Bring Me Men*. Like Tickner, Belkin (2012) suggests that gender stereotypes are key to understanding how people's roles are cast in security politics. Unlike Tickner, however, Belkin is interested in how gender stereotypes frame *men's* roles in security politics. While Tickner allows for the possibility, it is not her focus. Belkin observes a particular militarized masculinity that he demonstrates governs perceptions of individual fitness for participation in, and success in, the United States military—something that work before this book had looked into in some depth (e.g. Enloe 2000; Hooper 2001). Belkin (2012) explains, however, that this militarized masculinity is not simple and unidirectional, but instead *built on* its opposite—a culture of sexualization and homoeroticism. Contending that understanding *both* the image of the straight, brave, masculine soldier *and* the homoerotic undertones that render that image possible is key to understanding not only how the US military functions, but also the United States' self-perception of its place in the world, Belkin (2012) argues for careful tracing of the relationships between gender tropes and security structures.

The third piece of work that I would like to highlight—Megan MacKenzie's (2012) *Female Soldiers in Sierra Leone*, also argues that careful tracing of the relationships between gender tropes and security structures is key, though in a very different environment. While Belkin (2012) explores the complexity of stereotypical *and lived* masculinities; MacKenzie (2012) explores the differences between stereotypical and lived femininities. By paying attention to female soldiers who both defied and lived with/through stereotypical expectations of what women can and/or should be, MacKenzie (2012) demonstrates that the category of "woman" is broader than is often perceived. *Female Soldiers in Sierra Leone* also shows that policies that underestimate and/or pigeonhole women are not only inaccurate but can have deleterious effects—where Disarmament, Demobilization, and Reconstruction (DDR) programs that failed to take account either of the existence of female soldiers or of the complexity of their lived gender roles were ineffective in demobilizing combatants. MacKenzie (2012) argues that a sex-aware approach will not suffice in such situations, nor will an approach that makes traditional assumptions about what women are and what they need. Instead, looking at the multi-faceted and multidirectional influences of gender socialization and gendered expectations is key to understanding not only what is going on in any given security environment, but also how to improve security (MacKenzie 2012).

The fourth book that I will highlight situates the study of gender in global security with the study of race and colonialism. In *Gender and Global Politics in the Asia-Pacific*, editors Bina D'Costa and Katrina Lee-Koo (2009), along with the chapter authors, make the argument that many of these nuances about the ways that gender works in global security can be found in people's everyday lives, or the "low politics" of the global arena. The book uses localized and contextualized knowledge to argue both for the importance of context itself and for the intersection of race, gender, geography, and political economy in shaping security/insecurity in both personal life and global politics (D'Costa and Lee Koo 2009). The authors suggest that feminist approaches to security include feminist politics of region (Pettman 2009), feminist and decolonial politics of resistance (George 2009; Huynh 2009), and political economies of gendered and raced security *as constitutive of security* (Peterson 2009). This work (D'Costa and Lee Koo 2009), and work like it, shows that the feminist interest in contextualization can reach both thinking about gender and thinking about the many other factors that surround gender in global security.

These four examples are not meant to be either comprehensive or representative—instead, they are meant to show some of the many approaches to feminist theorizing about security generally, and Feminist Security Studies specifically, that can contribute to security theorizing generally and security studies specifically an understanding of both the centrality and contextuality of gender analysis. This shared contribution across diverse (and even divergent) feminist work on security can, I argue, provide insights into future paths for Feminist Security Studies.

4.3 Looking Forward for Feminist Security Studies

One of the questions that inspired Feminist Security Studies specifically and Feminist International Relations generally was articulated by Cynthia Enloe when she looked at the cannon of IR scholarship at the time. She asked—"where are the women?"—a question that at once suggests that the study of global politics paid attention to *the men* and *where the men are*, rather than to *the women* and where they are. When Enloe asked that question 30 years ago, IR and security studies could be characterized as neglecting the existence and roles of women in global politics.

Now, if we looked for women in global politics, they would be both much more visible and much more frequently analyzed than when Cynthia Enloe first inquired about where women were, and J. Ann Tickner characterized International Relations as a man's world. There are those who would say that the increased visibility of women in global politics has changed the mission of, or even the need for, feminist work in security studies. I would argue that this is an overstatement. While women have become increasingly visible in global politics, it is all the more important now to ask which women remain invisible, where the women who remain invisible are, and how they are made invisible by perceptions of what women are and perceptions of what security is. Women who engage in political and even sexual violence in global politics, for example, often remain invisible because of an attachment to the idea that there is a relationship between women and peace (e.g. Sjoberg and Gentry 2007; Sjoberg 2016). Minority women are often either invisible or sensationalized in security situations (where states either ignore them or claim to be fighting *for* them) (e.g. Spivak 1988). Asking "where are the women?" might be a more nuanced question now for security studies than it was when there were *no* women identifiable in security scholarship, but it is still an important question in a variety of ways.

Even to the extent that security studies has "discovered" some of the women in international security, I argue that feminism in security studies is increasingly relevant. Even when women are visible in security, as I mentioned in the previous paragraph, questions addressing which assumptions about gender (and race and class) make particular understandings about how the world works possible remain (and even become more) important. Instead of looking *just* for where women are and where men are, Feminist Security Studies moving forward looks for where *gender* is—gendered tropes, gendered perceptions, the assignment of gendered traits, and gendered significations. While the answer to the question "where are the women?" is *everywhere*, and never more visible, J. Ann Tickner's (1988) characterization of global security as a man's world also, importantly, remains true. If Feminist Security Studies has succeeded in calling attention to the existence and importance of women in international security, as well as questioning the boundaries of what counts as security, it has not yet succeeded in *transforming* security studies.

By *transforming* security studies, I mean that Feminist Security Studies (and feminist IR more generally) have suggested that no part of security studies should remain undisturbed and unchanged by the understanding that not only sex but also gender matters. Realists should have different understandings of power; liberals should have different understandings of cooperation and regimes; constructivists should have different understandings of the social; critical theorists should have different understandings of the emancipatory—all informed by the notion that the phenomena they study are heavily influenced by ideas and practices of and about gender. In Caron Cohn's (2011) words, this Feminist Security Studies is both "Feminist Security" Studies (that is, with a feminist perspective about what constitutes security being the main object of study) and Feminist "Security Studies" (looking to transform disciplinary and/or mainstream security studies. Looking forward, pursuing both of these paths for Feminist Security Studies is key to making the most use of the insights that the diverse field has already brought to the study of global politics.

Pursuing the first path might mean a transformation of Feminist Security Studies that puts its emphases and its attention more squarely outside the purview of traditional security studies—demonstrating the importance of *feminist* security concerns such as women's lives, household security, economic stability, and freedom from sexual assault while refusing to link them to interstate or civil war or terrorism. The idea behind this path would be to draw security studies outside of its own thinking with compelling arguments about the major sources of *insecurity* in global politics. It would rely on the changed subject matter of security studies to change the conceptual and epistemological contours of current thinking. Pursuing the second path, on the other hand, requires more hybrid work—work that does not forget what is *feminist* about Feminist Security Studies, but uses those tools to engage with and perhaps even individually transform work in security studies. The idea behind this path would be to (continue to) produce work that looked to contribute to different areas of security studies *by* questioning the epistemological and empirical assumptions in the current work in those areas. It would rely on convincing current security scholars that their work (on its own terms) is incomplete. Both paths are currently being pursued to one degree or another; in my view, they should both continue to be pursued. Both face Herculean odds if they are looking to change the face of security studies. Barriers include narrow definitions of policy relevance (e.g. Desch 2015); narrow understandings of the appropriate subject matter of security studies (e.g. Walt 1991); a drive to quantify gender and fit it into positivist epistemological assumptions (e.g. Reiter 2015); path-dependence in a field that has been resistant to change (e.g. Waltz 2000); and just plain sex-essentialist assumptions about how the world works (e.g. Thayer 2000). I do not see these barriers as insurmountable, though I cannot deny frustration at confronting them constantly. But I see the work produced by those confrontations as both valuable in itself regardless of its transformative success *and* important because of the importance of pursuing transformation even against potentially insurmountable odds. If thinking about gender really is key to thinking about security, as I believe it is, I think it is neither possible nor ethical to stop trying to convince others to understand.

Notes

1. This piece was in the special issue on "Women and IR," often seen as the launch of feminist IR.
2. See extensive discussion in Sjoberg (2009)
3. For a discussion of visibility, see Sjoberg (2016).

4. see, e.g., recent discussion in Sjoberg et al. (2016)
5. In very different ways, Elshtain (1985), Tickner (1988), True (2010), and Sjoberg (2012) have done feminist realist analysis, though this is a less-used category than the others that follow here.
6. See, e.g., discussion in Brown (1988).
7. See discussion in Prugl (2015).
8. See further discussion in Sjoberg (2014).
9. E.g., discussion in Sjoberg (2009).
10. For traditional security issues, see, e.g., Cohn (1987); Sjoberg (2006). For traditionally hidden security issues, see, e.g., True (2012); Enloe (2016).

References

Alcoff, Linda. 1988. Cultural Feminism Versus Post-Structuralism: The Identity Crisis in Feminist Theory. *Signs*, 13(3): 405–36.

Belkin, Aaron. 2012. *Bring Me Men: Military Masculinity and the Benign Façade of American Empire, 1898-2001*. New York: Columbia University Press.

Booth, Ken. 2007. *Theory of World Security*. Cambridge: Cambridge University Press.

Brock-Utne, Birgit. 1985. *Educating For Peace*. Oxford: Pergamon.

Brown, Sarah. 1988. Feminism, International Theory, and International Relations of Gender Inequality. *Millennium*, 17(3): 461–75.

Caprioli, Mary and Mark Boyer. 2001. Gender, Violence, and International Crisis. *Journal of Conflict Resolution*, 45(4): 503–18.

CASE Collective. 2006. Critical Approaches to Security in Europe: A Networked Manifesto. *Security Dialogue*, 37(4): 443–87.

Chin, Christine. 1998. *In Service and Servitude*. New York: Columbia University Press.

Chowdhury, Geeta and Sheila Nair (eds.). 2002. *Power, Postcolonialism, and International Relations*. New York: Routledge.

Cohn, Carol. 1987. Sex and Death in the World of Rational Defense Intellectuals. *Signs*, 12(4): 687–718.

Cohn, Carol. 2011. "Feminist Security Studies": Toward a Reflexive Practice. *Politics & Gender*. 7(4): 581–6.

Cohn, Carol (ed.). 2013. *Women and Wars*. London: Polity.

D'Costa, Bina and Katrina Lee-Koo (eds.). 2009. *Gender and Global Politics in the Asia-Pacific*. London: Palgrave Macmillan.

Desch, Michael. 2015. Technique Trumps Relevance: The Professionalization of Political Science and the Marginalization of Security Studies. *Perspectives on Politics*, 13(2): 377–93.

Detraz, Nicole. 2009. Environmental Security and Gender: Necessary Shifts in an Evolving Debate. *Security Studies*, 18(2): 345–69.

Elshtain, Jean Bethke. 1985. Reflections on War and Political Discourse: Realism, Just War, and Feminism in a Nuclear Age. *Political Theory*, 13(1): 39–57.

Enloe, Cynthia. 2000. *Maneuvers*. Berkeley: University of California Press.

Enloe, Cynthia. 2010. *Nimo's War, Emma's War: Making Feminist Sense of the Iraq War* Berkeley: University of California Press.

Enloe, Cynthia. 2016. A Flick of the Skirt: A Feminist Challenge to IR's Coherent Narrative. *International Political Sociology*, 10(4): 320–31.

George, Nicole. 2009. Shifting Terrains of Transnational Engagement. In Bina D'Costa and Katrina Lee-Koo (eds.), *Gender and Global Politics in the Asia-Pacific*, pp. 175–94. London: Palgrave Macmillan.
Haraway, Donna. 1987. A Manifesto for Cyborgs: Science, Technology, and Socialist Feminism in the 1980s. *Australian Feminist Studies*, 2(3): 1–42.
Hooper, Charlotte. 2001. *Manly States*. New York: Columbia University Press.
Hudson, Heidi. 2005. "Doing" Security as though Humans Matter: A Feminist Perspective on Gender and the Politics of Human Security. *Security*, 36(2): 155–74.
Hudson, Valerie, Mary Caprioli, Bonnie Ballif-Spanvill, Rose McDermottl, and Chad F. Emmett. 2009. The Heart of the Matter: The Security of Women and the Security of States. *International Security*, 33(3): 7–45.
Hudson, Valerie, Donna Lee Bowen, and Perpetua Lynne Nielsen. 2011. What is the Relationship between Inequity and Violence against Women? Approaching the Issue of Legal Enclaves. *Politics & Gender*, 7(4): 453–92.
Huynh, Kim. 2009. One Woman's Everyday Resistance. In Bina D'Costa and Katrina Lee-Koo (eds.), *Gender and Global Politics in the Asia-Pacific*, pp. 129–42. London: Palgrave Macmillan.
Keohane, Robert. 1989. International Relations Theory: Contributions of a Feminist Standpoint. *Millennium*, 18(2): 245–53.
Krause, Keith and Michael C. Williams. 1996. Broadening the Agenda of Security Studies: Politics and Methods. *Mershon International Studies Review*, 40(Supplement 2): 229–54.
MacKenzie, Megan. 2012. *Female Soldiers in Sierra Leone: Sex, Security, and Post-Conflict Development*. New York: New York University Press.
MacKinnon, Catharine A. 1982. Feminism, Marxism, Method, and the State: An Agenda for Theory. *Signs*, 7(3): 515–44.
Maynard, Mary and June Purvis (eds.). 1994. *Researching Women's Lives from a Feminist Perspective*. London: Taylor and Francis.
Nussbaum, Martha. 2005. Women's Bodies: Violence, Security, and Capabilities. *Journal of Human Development*, 6(2): 167–83.
Parashar, Swati. 2013. What Wars and "War Bodies" Know about International Relations. *Cambridge Review of International Affairs*, 26(4): 615–30.
Peterson, V. Spike. 1992. 'Transgressing Boundaries: Theories of Knowledge, Gender, and International Relations. *Millennium*, 21(2): 183–206.
Peterson, V. Spike. 2009. Gendered Economies in the Asia-Pacific. In Bina D'Costa and Katrina Lee-Koo (eds.), *Gender and Global Politics in the Asia-Pacific*, pp. 39–56. London: Palgrave Macmillan.
Peterson, V. Spike. 2010. Gendered Identities, Ideologies, and Practices in the Context of War and Militarism. In Laura Sjoberg and Sandra Via (eds.), *Gender, War, and Militarism*. Santa Barbara, CA: Praeger Security International.
Peterson, V. Spike and Anne Sisson Runyan. 1993. *Global Gender Issues*. Boulder, CO: Westview Press.
Pettman, Jan Jindy. 1996. A Feminist Politics of Region? In Bina D'Costa and Katrina Lee-Koo (eds.), *Gender and Global Politics in the Asia-Pacific*, pp. 211–32. London: Palgrave Macmillan.
Prugl, Elisabeth. 1999. *The Global Construction of Gender*. New York: Columbia University Press.

Prugl, Elisabeth. 2015. Neoliberalising Feminism. *New Political Economy*, 20(3): 614–31.
Reardon, Betty. 1985. *Sex and the War System*. New York: Teachers' College Press.
Reiter, Dan. 2015. The Positivist Study of Gender and International Relations. *Journal of Conflict Resolution*, 59(7): 1301–26.
Shepherd, Laura J. 2008. *Gender, Violence, and Security*. London: Zed Books.
Shepherd, Laura J. 2016. Feminist Security Studies. In Jill Steans and Daniela Tepe-Belfrage (eds.), *Handbook on Gender and World Politics*. Cheltenham: Edward Elgar.
Sjoberg, Laura. 2006. Gendered Realities of the Immunity Principle: Why Gender Analysis Needs Feminism. *International Studies Quarterly*, 50(4): 889–910.
Sjoberg, Laura. 2009. Introduction to *Security Studies:* Feminist Contributions. *Security Studies*, 18(2): 184–214.
Sjoberg, Laura. 2011. Looking Forward, Conceptualizing Feminist Security Studies. *Politics & Gender*, 7(4): 600–4.
Sjoberg, Laura. 2012. Gender, Structure, and War: What Waltz Couldn't See. *International Theory*, 4(1): 1–38.
Sjoberg, Laura. 2013. *Gendering Global Conflict: Towards a Feminist Theory of War*. New York: Columbia University Press.
Sjoberg, Laura. 2014. *Gender, War, and Conflict*. London: Polity.
Sjoberg, Laura. 2016. *Women as Wartime Rapists* New York: New York University Press.
Sjoberg, Laura and Caron Gentry. 2007. *Mothers, Monsters, Whores*. London: Zed Books.
Sjoberg, Laura, Kelly Kadera, and Cameron G. Thies. 2016. Reevaluating Gender and IR Scholarship: Moving Beyond Reiter's Dichotomies toward Effective Synergies. *Journal of Conflict Resolution*, 59(7): 1301–26.
Spivak, Gayatri. 1988. Can the Subaltern Speak? In Cary Nelson and Lawrence Grossberg (eds), *Marxism and the Interpretation of Culture*, pp. 271–313. London: Palgrave.
Squires, Judith and Jutta Weldes. 2007. Beyond Being Marginal: Gender and International Relations in Britain. *British Journal of Politics and International Relations*, 9(2): 185–203.
Sylvester, Christine. 2007. Anatomy of a Footnote. *Security Dialogue*, 38(4): 547–58.
Sylvester, Christine. 2013. Passing American Security. *International Studies Perspectives*, 14(4): 444–6.
Thayer, Bradley. 2000. Bringing in Darwin: Evolutionary Theory, Realism, and International Politics. *International Security*, 25(2): 124–51.
Tickner, J. Ann. 1988. Hans Morgenthau's Principles of Political Realism: A Feminist Reformulations. *Millennium*, 17(3): 429–40.
Tickner, J. Ann. 1992. *Gender in International Relations: Feminist Perspectives on Global Security*. New York: Columbia University Press.
Tickner, J. Ann. 1997. You Just Don't Understand: Troubled Engagements Between Feminists and IR Theorists. *International Studies Quarterly*, 41(4): 611–32.
True, Jacqui. 2010. Feminism and Realism in International Relations, Paper presented at OCIS IV, Auckland, New Zealand.
True, Jacqui. 2012. *The Political Economy of Violence against Women*. Oxford: Oxford University Press.
Walt, Stephen. 1991. The Renaissance of Security Studies. *International Studies Quarterly*, 35(2): 211–39.
Waltz, Kenneth. 2000. Structural Realism after the Cold War. *International Security*, 25(1): 5–41.
Wibben, Annick. 2011. *Feminist Security Studies: A Narrative Approach*. London: Routledge.

Wilcox, Lauren. 2009. Gendering the Cult of the Offensive. *Security Studies*, 18(2): 214–40.

Wilcox, Lauren. 2013. Impossible Queer Practices, presented at the 2013 International Feminist Journal of Politics at the University of Sussex, May 17–20, 2013.

Zalweski, Marysia. 1995. Well, What is the Feminist Perspective on Bosnia? *International Affairs*, 71(2): 339–56.

CHAPTER 5

CRITICAL SECURITY STUDIES

CHRIS HENDERSHOT AND DAVID MUTIMER

To consider a future for Critical Security Studies (CSS) it bears reiterating that CSS should not be considered a subdiscipline of Security Studies or International Relations. Born of the "failure of political realism" to predict and account for the end of the Cold War (Mutimer 2016: 83) and growing and diversifying in response to the global War on Terror (see Mutimer 2014), CSS is not so much a unified academic project as it is a heuristic amalgam of modes of studying security that are not "conventional." In other words, CSS "does not denote a coherent set of views, an 'approach' to security; rather it indicates a desire" (Mutimer 2015: 88). The initial desire was to study security differently to the studies of state-centric strategies of militarized defense that predominated during the Cold War (Mutimer 2015: 88). Some of the most influential works produced in the early years include: *Security and Emancipation* (Booth 1991), *Writing Security: United States Foreign Policy and the Politics of Identity* (Campbell 1992), *Critical Security Studies: Concepts and Cases* (Krause and Williams 1997), and *Security: A New Framework for Analysis* (Buzan et al. 1998). These works re-conceptualized what security meant and how it mattered through constructivist, post-structural, post-Marxian, and post-positivist metatheories.

The racialized and sexualized discourses of threat, the emphasis on military and intelligence solutions, and the anti-terror legislation of the global War on Terror colluded to greatly expand the socio-political remit of who or what could be(come) a security concern. Simultaneously, digitization and the global proliferation of information and communications technology produced new, inventive, and invasive ways of monitoring, predicting, and/or neutralizing potential security threats. These "new" practices and processes of security opened up theoretical and empirical possibilities, while also issuing an array of different ethical challenges than those faced in the 1990s. Analysis of biopower and violence (see Dauphinee and Masters 2007), biometrics (see Muller 2008), surveillance (see Bell 2006), privatization (see Leander 2005), critical infrastructure (see Aradua 2010), sexualized torture (see Richter-Montpetit 2007), improvised explosive devices (see Grove 2016), drones and targeted killing (see Grayson 2016), and algorithmic security (see Amoore and Raley 2017) represent only a cross-section of the various ways that critical security research has been conducted since the turn of the twenty-first century.

The diversity of research conducted across the 30 years of CSS is both demonstrative of the "open" (Wibben 2016) possibilities of studying security critically and a consequence of dissatisfaction with the theoretical, referential, or ethical exclusions (see Mutimer 2009) among various modes of study. These exclusions also mean that CSS does not capture and cannot claim provenance of all "critical" understandings of security. Accordingly, what CSS is and means, who a CSS scholar is, and how security is critically studied is fraught with "controversy, contestation and even conflict" (Mutimer et al. 2013: 3). So much so that some critically committed scholars "consciously" eschew the CSS "label" altogether (Mutimer et al. 2013: 3). As this section of the Handbook attests, Feminist Security Studies, Constructivisms, and International Political Sociology need to be recognized as distinct non-conventional studies in and of security.

Our problematizing of the nomenclature is not intended to be a simple criticism. A future for CSS is not imperiled because of a lack of coherence within critical study. Rather the troublesome existence of CSS is foregrounded in order to circumscribe the predictive possibilities of this chapter. Loose affiliations and amorphous meaning do not easily lend themselves to prediction. Thus, what follows is an effort to provoke the present with the intention of keeping open the possibility of an unsettling and unsettled future. To be unsettling, CSS must (continue to) commit to unconventional inquisitiveness through refusing the disciplining of knowledge and embracing a reflexive accounting of the pernicious political practices and processes that have made the Anglo-European study of security possible. By refusing to be disciplined, the future of CSS is opened up to methods of knowledge production that can push the meaningfulness of critical studies of security beyond the Anglo-European academy. Research that is not over-determined by institutionalized academic imperatives can in turn invigorate "criticality" as researchers must consider how their relationship with the academy affects what knowledge is produced. Embracing a reflexive accounting is thus a method of foregrounding both personal and institutional complicities with the very politics that CSS has sought to contest. Critical security scholarship must be an exercise of critique through self-implication so as to expose the limits of a study and thereby keep open the possibility for further reflection and other ways of knowing. A most pressing political complicity, that will require un-settling work, is our ongoing implication in the violence of colonialism.

For non-Indigenous critical security scholars living and working in North America, the violent securing of the settler-colonies of Canada, the United States, and Mexico cannot be ignored. To work with and for a future that supports Indigenous sovereignty over land, language, and creative practice, CSS must become un-settled. An un-settled CSS works for decolonization. To be un-settled is to seriously consider if and how CSS can support ongoing struggles against colonial domination and disposition. Unsettling exercises can and should support un-settling efforts, but to become un-settled is not synonymous with being unsettled. Being unsettled can allow CSS to foster scholarship that understands that "the desired outcomes of decolonization are diverse and located at multiple sites in multiple forms, represented by and reflected in Indigenous sovereignty over land and sea, as well as over ideas and epistemologies" (Sium et al. 2012: II). Creating an academic space in which decolonization and Indigenous sovereignty can be understood through security should unsettle critical security research that has long ignored or excluded Indigenous Peoples. Nonetheless, security conventions can be and are routinely unsettled without any consideration of the settler-colonial and imperial conventions that continue to determine what security means and how it matters. To become un-settled is to first take account of complicities in (the ongoing) colonial exploitations of people, land, and knowledge. CSS must accept its complicities, not to atone for a racist or imperial past, but to signal a willingness to work toward present possibilities of un-settling people, land, and knowledge. Accounting for complicities is only a first and arguably the least demanding of un-settling exercises required of CSS. The more meaningful efforts must be the enactment of myriad methods of support for people whose very existence is a resistance and repudiation of the violence of colonization/imperialism. Such support must extend beyond the disciplinary or career expectations of being an academic, for example research, teaching, and administration, to include financial, emotional, and socio-political support for the everyday efforts of people to ensure Indigenous futures. Ironically, this means considering the unsettling possibility that CSS should have no future.

5.1 Unsettling Study?

At its simplest, the unsettling of CSS means the sustenance and invigoration of an investigative ethic that is dissatisfied with the security questions being asked, who is doing the asking and answering, and how different questions can be posed and thought through. This is not a demanding ask of CSS. Divergence from the conventional and contesting the status quo has been the lynchpin of CSS for the past 30 years. As previously mentioned, a "schismatic history" (Mutimer 2015) also demonstrates that critical conventions are and need to be open to being challenged. The various modes of critically studying security that have constituted CSS are both instructive and insightful. For instance, post-positivist, post-Marxian, and post-structural analyses have been pivotal in pushing the social and geopolitical curiosity of CSS (see Mutimer 2014). Feminist (see Wibben 2010; Cohn 2011; Shepherd 2013), postcolonial/non-Western (see Bilgin 2010; Dixit 2014), and post-human/new material (see Herschinger 2015; Mitchell 2016) theories alongside a thorough consideration of methodologies (see Salter and Mutlu 2013; Aradau et al. 2014; Wilcox 2016) have deepened the analytical and political possibilities of CSS in the second decade of the twenty-first century. What needs to be cast aside from the past and present of CSS is the (rhetorical) institutionalization of contentions and divergences. Differences among schools of thought can invigorate questioning (see CASE Collective 2006; Sylvester 2007; de Larrinaga and Salter 2014), but it can also settle knowledge into camps that become more concerned with "self-protective exclusivity"

(Sylvester 2010: 608). Decamping is imperative to unsettling. To be unsettled is to work with a reality that is open to engagement with difference, if not detraction, and humbly to accept that the politics of the Anglo-European academy place unnecessary limits on the possibilities of knowledge production.

For instance, pressures to only produce "useful" knowledge, a lack of funding, and uncertain employment opportunities work against unsettling academic exercises. Critical scholars must be particularly wary of making peer-review, promotion, and funding decisions that discipline possibilities for study. In other words, innovation and impact should not be the primary drivers of determining which projects are funded, what research is published where, and who is recruited for prestigious titles and regular compensation. The disciplinary work that established CSS as a legitimate academic exercise need not be forgotten among unsettling moves. Such work, and its narrative, is instructive of how criticality functions within the Anglo-European academy. Nevertheless, CSS needs to foster earnestly the development and dissemination of modes of study that will affect extra-disciplinary meanings and matters. Supporting creative projects that pull in non-academic collaborators can push critical security knowledge into unfamiliar conversations and expose it to unfamiliar audiences. Playing with forms of dissemination that are not strictly textual elucidations of a research project will unsettle a political-economics of academic publishing that paywalls access and impels "careerist" imperatives into the production of academic knowledge. Disciplinary pressure is certainly not unique to CSS, which is why refusing to become settled can ensure that CSS is open to the inquisitiveness of scholars across the global academy, as well permitting collaboration with knowledge producers that work in and through non-academic practices.

Another key aspect of an unsettled future is a commitment to a reflexive accounting of the politics of being a critical security scholar. Academics strive to stay abreast of and are willing to produce literature that reflects upon the limitations of contemporary scholarship—including their own work. Critical security scholars have been particularly dutiful with reflexive critiques (see Bourne and Bulley 2011; Browning and McDonald 2013; Nyman 2016). Significantly provocative reflections include: "CSS still focuses too much on what policymakers themselves regard as 'security' practices" (Montesinos Coleman and Rosenow 2016: 213); "Critical scholarship in security, with few exceptions, has been reluctant to engage its own politics" (Wibben 2016: 144); "the accomplishments of [CSS] are arguably modest in what pertains to engaging with practical transformative politics" (Nunes 2012: 346). Criticisms such as these need to be taken seriously otherwise CSS risks settling for referents, methods, and ethics that are merely rearranging deck chairs on the *Titanic*. To focus on security already carries the risk of reiteratively centralizing security. Or as Montesinos Coleman and Rosenow (2016) warn, "The perpetual recentering of Security reflects a fetishism [that diverts] attention from unspeakable violences that sustain the problematization of Security" (2016: 213). Therefore, critical security scholars must always be open to questioning the conceptual value of security. By questioning security as an academic concept, critical security scholars can more thoroughly consider how to produce knowledge that affects possibilities for more equitable and sustainable global political–economic relations.

Reflecting upon conceptual limits can be unsettling, but it is not sufficiently accountable. Critical scholars must take a thorough accounting of the allocations (or appropriations) of time, space, energy, and finances that sustain, or in another word, secure the continued possibilities of academic work. Put bluntly, the academic work of CSS cannot be enacted on a basis of innocence. CSS cannot be reflexively accountable if colonial/imperial, militarized, petro-chemical dependent, or zero-sum security relations are only analyzed antagonistically. As cited above, critical security scholars have tackled the varying manifestations of pernicious security relations. These studies are crucial to a thorough understanding of how threats become threats and who and what suffers, and benefits, from the practices that are enacted to neutralize that which is (made) threatening. To do unsettling work, to be reflexively accountable, requires CSS to be more open about its complicities with the hierarchies, inequities, and dispositions that security work produces and exploits. As Wibben (2016) contends, Security Studies is "implicated in creating and maintaining the insecurities and injustices that critical scholarship should aim to transform" (2016: 147). While we agree, CSS is also a constituent and is constitutive of how security matters and what it means. We contend that CSS must also be open to accounting for its complicities. For example, at present, the Anglo-European academy is beholden to inequitable systems of energy production, finance, land ownership, and prestige. To work toward an unsettling future means accounting for how these political-economic circumstances determine where and why critical security knowledge is produced in order to "transform and reimagine" (Moran et al. 2016: 134) how that knowledge should be produced.

The past 30 years of critical security research matters as much for the theories, methods, and ethics of critique that have been produced as it does for the political-economics that have permitted a privileged few people and institutions to do and receive (compensatory) recognition for producing such knowledge. Taking account of complicities should be an exercise of invigorating research that more thoroughly acknowledges, understands, and supports the security knowledge produced by and through the people, places, and things that are denied the privileges associated with being an academic. In doing so, the future of CSS can become increasingly open to supporting and producing research that is more meaningful and transformative to the people, places, and things that have been and continue to be burdened with enduring pernicious enactments of security.

5.2 Un-settling Security

Despite avowed commitments to critique concepts and practices that sustain militarized, carbon dependent, or zero-sum security relations, critical security scholars must also imagine the possibility that criticality can still affect domination and exploitation. That is to say, CSS needs to more thoughtfully consider its ongoing complicity with the settler-colonial and imperial ordering of global relations. As two scholars who live and work on the traditional territory of the Haudenosaunee, the Métis, and most recently, the territory of the Mississauga of the Credit River (CAUT 2016) and are thus sustained through the occupation of this territory, we must immediately confront our complicity in settler-colonialism. Or to paraphrase Sundberg (2014: 35), as citizens of a settler-colonial state, we "have a profound obligation and responsibility to confront the widespread implications of colonialism in [our] scholarship and to ask what [security] thought has to become to face the political, philosophical, and ethical challenges of decolonizing." Without a vigorous un-settling, CSS will be incapable of working for and with "Indigenous sovereignty in its material, psychological, epistemological, and spiritual forms" (Sium et al. 2012: v).

What must be more readily confronted is that criticality does not obviate complicity with colonialism, imperialism, and racialized domination. Expansive referents, non-positivistic metatheories, and openness to difference can certainly create the intellectual space to read and cite the work of Patrick Wolfe (2006) or Glen Coulthard (2014) or Sarah Hunt (2014). Or to consider how the Asubpeeschoseewagong First Nation, the Standing Rock Sioux Tribe, and/or Native Hawaiians are affected by and affect security politics. Critical scholars who focus on the security politics of the Arctic are already including Indigenous concerns and knowledge in their analysis. Using securitization theory, Greaves (2016) engages with Inuit and Sámi discourses "in order to explain variation in different understandings of (in)security" among Indigenous Peoples as well as recognizing how colonial agendas constrain the capacities of Indigenous Peoples "to advance a conception of (in)security that is distinct from those of settler governments" (2016: 462–3). Harrington and Lecavalier (2014) work through an emancipatory approach in order to understand how Inuit discourse, particularly that which is articulated by and through the Inuit Circumpolar Council, and traditional knowledge "offers an important emancipatory alternative to traditional practices of environmental security" (2014: 114).

Yet, inclusion and recognition of Indigenous Peoples and knowledge does not necessarily un-settle the academy (Ahenakew 2016). Greater inclusion need not contest the fact that the academic study of security, whether it be traditional or critical, is not possible without (settler) colonialism/imperialism. Ontologically, the world of nation states, citizens, consumers, the environment, water, and food cannot exist as referents of security because they do not exist as such without colonial rearrangements of economics, geographies, and politics (see Byrd 2011; Samson and Gigoux 2017). Epistemologically, notions of threat and danger are entwined with colonial determinations of the civilized, productive, and/or human (see Tuck and Gaztambide-Fernández 2013). Methodologically, the Anglo-European "modernization" of academic knowledge production does not occur without the discovery, classification, and collection of "native" people, flora, and fauna (Tuhiwai Smith 2012). Politically, the educational authority of Anglo-European universities rests, in many instances literally, on the coercive disposition of land, suppression of language, and spiritual and creative practice, as well as the ignorance of traditional knowledge (see Todd 2016). Only through honestly confronting this (ongoing) complicity with colonialism can critical security scholarship sincerely consider, support, and enact decolonial possibilities.

As decolonization is not a metaphor "for other things we want to do to improve our societies and schools" (Tuck and Yang 2012: 3) we, the settler/imperial scholars, cannot assume that openness to differing modes of thought, extra-disciplinary meaning, and reflexive accountability (that is, holding ourselves accountable for our complicities with structures and practices of domination) can assure decolonial possibilities. They may be necessary, but cannot be considered sufficient. Nor are indigenizing curricula, acknowledging occupied land, and/or calling for/echoing calls for the decolonization of CSS enough. As settler scholars, we must support the work of Indigenous scholars to conduct and present their research "on its own terms" (Ahenakew 2016: 327)—that is, not filtered "through the frames of Western Epistemology" (Ahenakew 2016: 327). One method for supporting Indigenous knowledge sovereignty is the transformation of peer adjudication processes, particularly those which determine which research projects are funded. Settler scholars cannot assume to be the only or even appropriate peers. Colonial disposition, not comprehension of a universal or modern understanding of the world, is what secured and secures the knowledge authority of settlers over and above Indigenous Peoples. Un-settling CSS will require exercises that work to support the knowledge authority of Indigenous thinkers—thinkers who may or may not work in or for the Anglo-European academy. Un-settling CSS will also require performing non-academic work. Settler scholars must provide material support to protest and advocacy movements. Universities located on occupied land must make longer-term financial investments in Indigenous-led economic, social, cultural, and educational efforts.

To do this decolonial work will require settler scholars to consult and collaborate with Indigenous thinkers, activists, and elders. Un-settling CSS will require both the making and giving back of time, space, and sustenance to permit Indigenous thinkers and activists to sustain and safeguard their pasts, presents, and futures. Non-Indigenous CSS scholars must understand that "decolonization is a messy, dynamic, and a contradictory process" (Sium et al. 2012: ii) in order never to suggest that we know a better way. We as settler scholars working through unsettling security must also seriously entertain the possibility that decolonization means no future for CSS.

5.3 What Future?

Questioning whether security can actually be done critically is a vitally important reflexive exercise (see Neocleous 2008; Hynek and Chandler 2013). To be unsettling and un-settled means imagining the possibility that criticality can expose colonial/imperial, militarized, petro-chemical dependent, or zero-sum security relations, but not resist or transform these pernicious relations. If CSS is to have a future it cannot rest on an ideological commitment to progressive improvement of scholarship that can in turn inform emancipatory and/or anti-capitalist efforts to reconcile pernicious security practices.

The people, places, and things that are bearing (or being forced to bear) the burden of pernicious security practices should not have to wait for a future in which CSS figures out how to transform or decolonize security. To orient transformative thinking toward a "better" future is tantamount to passing the buck and refusing to be held accountable for the problematic security practices of the present. Furthermore, to become un-settled, CSS cannot be reliant on promises of greater openness to and dialogue with Indigenous thinkers, activists, and elders. Presuming potentials for progressive change installs a future that continues to privilege settler possibilities (see Baldwin 2012). That is to say, resolving the depravations and exploitations of colonialism as a future possibility, rather than a present actuality, erases current struggles by Indigenous Peoples to refuse colonial domination while re-establishing settler timelines for resolution, reconciliation, or restitution.

Perhaps presuming that CSS can have a future is an unreflexive reiteration of the value of survival that still sits at the core of conventional security studies (see Auchter 2016). Desires for survival can be unsettling and un-settling when they are enacted by and through the people whom security and colonial practices have targeted and continue to target for disposition and harm. For CSS to become unsettled and un-settling, however, it is crucial that scholars and their collaborators consider how settler or Anglo-European desires for survival can be transformed and reimagined as not coming at the expense of the survival of "others." One method is to imagine that CSS does not have a future. By thinking through what the dissolution of CSS would, could, or should entail can allow scholars and collaborators to comprehend how present knowledge practice works to (re-)settle the critical study of security.

Working as though CSS does not or should not have a future can open such collaborations to the possibilities of repatriating the time, space, energy, and finances that currently constitute and sustain CSS to Indigenously-led efforts to decolonize. Tuck and Gaztambide-Fernández (2013: 80) are clear that an "Indigenous futurity does not require the erasure of now-settlers" and thus to suggest a possible end for CSS is an unnecessary provocation. As such, an unsettling and un-settled future for CSS need not result in dissolution, but a rearranging is necessary. Just as the upheaval with the end of the Cold War permitted CSS to find and seize conceptual and political-economic space within the Anglo-European academy, to have a future CSS must recognize and enact the current moment as one that is open to decolonial, extra-disciplinary, and reflexively accountable possibilities.

References

Ahenakew, C. 2016. Grafting Indigenous Ways of Knowing Onto Non-Indigenous Ways of Being. *International Review of Qualitative Research*, 9(3): 323–40.

Amoore, L. and R. Raley. 2017. Securing with Algorithms: Knowledge, Decision, Sovereignty. *Security Dialogue*, 48(1): 3–10.

Aradau, C. 2010, Security that Matters: Critical Infrastructure and Objects of Protection. *Security Dialogue*, 41(5): 491–514.

Aradau, C., J. Huysmans, A. Neal, and N. Voelkner (eds.). 2014. *Critical Security Methods: New Frameworks for Analysis*. Abingdon: Routledge.

Auchter, J. 2016. Paying Attention to Dead Bodies: The Future of Security Studies? *Journal of Global Security Studies*, 1(1): 36–50.

Baldwin, A. 2012. Whiteness and Futurity Towards a Research Agenda. *Progress in Human Geography*, 36(2): 172–87.

Bell, C. 2006. Surveillance Strategies and Populations at Risk: Biopolitical Governance in Canada's National Security Policy. *Security Dialogue*, 37(2): 147–65.

Biligin, P. 2010. The "Western-Centrism" of Security Studies: "Blind Spot" or Constitutive Practice?, *Security Dialogue*, 41(6): 615–22.

Booth, K. 1991. Security and Emancipation. *Review of International Studies*, 17(4): 313–26.

Bourne, M. and D. Bulley. 2011. Securing the Human in Critical Security Studies: The Insecurity of a Secure Ethics. *European Security*, 20(3): 453–71.

Browning, C. S. and M. McDonald. 2013. The Future of Critical Security Studies: Ethics and the Politics of Security. *European Journal of International Relations*, 19(2): 235–55.

Buzan, B., O. Wæver, and J. de Wilde. 1998. *Security: A New Framework for Analysis*. Boulder, CO: Lynne Rienner.

Byrd, J. A. 2011. *The Transit of Empire: Indigenous Critiques of Colonialism*. Minneapolis, MN: University of Minnesota Press.

Campbell, D. 1992. *Writing Security: United States Foreign Policy and the Politics of Identity*. Minneapolis, MN: University of Minnesota Press.

CASE Collective. 2006. Critical Approaches to Security in Europe: A Networked Manifesto. *Security Dialogue*, 37(4): 443–87.

CAUT. 2016. CAUT Acknowledging Traditional Territory, Canadian Association of University Teachers *Available at*: https://www.caut.ca/docs/default-source/professional-advice/list---territorial-acknowledgement-by-province.pdf?sfvrsn=12, accessed 12 September 2017.

Cohn, C. 2011. "Feminist Security Studies": Toward a Reflexive Practice. *Politics & Gender*, 7(4): 581–6.

Coulthard, G. S. 2014. *Red Skin, White Masks*. Minneapolis, MN: University of Minnesota Press.

Dauphinee, E. and C. Masters. (eds.). 2007. *The Logics of Biopower and the War on Terror: Living, Dying, Surviving*. New York: Palgrave Macmillan.

de Larrinaga, M. and M. B. Salter. 2014. Cold CASE: A Manifesto for Canadian Critical Security Studies. *Critical Studies on Security*, 2(1): 1–19.

Dixit, P. 2014. Decolonizing Visuality in Security Studies: Reflections on the Death of Osama bin Laden. *Critical Studies on Security*, 2(3): 337–51.

Grayson, K. 2016. *Cultural Politics of Targeted Killing: On Drones, Counter-Insurgency, and Violence*. New York: Routledge.

Greaves, W. 2016. Arctic (in) security and Indigenous peoples: Comparing Inuit in Canada and Sámi in Norway, *Security Dialogue*, 47(6): 461–80.

Grove, J. 2016. An Insurgency of Things: Foray into the World of Improvised Explosive Devices. *International Political Sociology*, 10(4): 332–51.

Harrington, C. and E. Lecavalier. 2014. The Environment and Emancipation in Critical Security Studies: The Case of the Canadian Arctic, *Critical Studies on Security*, 2(1): 105–19.

Herschinger, E. 2015. The Drug Dispositif: Ambivalent Materiality and the Addiction of the Global Drug Prohibition Regime. *Security Dialogue*, 46(2): 183–201.

Hunt, S. 2014. Ontologies of Indigeneity: The Politics of Embodying a Concept. *Cultural Geographies*, 21(1): 27–32.

Hynek, N. and D. Chandler. 2013. No Emancipatory Alternative, No Critical Security Studies. *Critical Studies on Security*, 1(1): 46–53.

Krause, K. and M. C. Williams. 1997. *Critical Security Studies: Concepts and Cases*. Minneapolis, MN: University of Minnesota Press.

Leander, A. 2005. The Power to Construct International Security: On the Significance of Private Military Companies. *Millennium*, 33(3): 803–26.

Mitchell, A. 2016. Posthuman Security: Reflections from an Open-ended Conversation *E-International Relations*, 25 January 2016, viewed 1 January 2017. *Available at:* http://www.e-ir.info/2016/01/25/posthuman-security-reflections-from-an-open-ended-conversation/

Montesinos Coleman, L. and D. Rosenow. 2016. Security (Studies) and the Limits of Critique: Why We Should Think through Struggle. *Critical Studies on Security*, 4(2): 202–20.

Moran, M., A. M. Friis Kristensen, and C. Athanassiou. 2016. Introduction De/Re-constructing the Political: How Do Critical Approaches to 'Security' Frame our Understanding of the Political?, *Critical Studies on Security*, 4(2): 133–6.

Muller, B. 2008. Securing the Political Imagination: Popular Culture, the Security Dispositif and the Biometric State. *Security Dialogue*, 39(2–3): 199–220.

Mutimer, D. 2009. My Critique is Bigger than Yours: Constituting Exclusions in Critical Security Studies, Special Issue on "Security and Exclusion". *Studies in Social Justice*, 3(1): 9–22.

Mutimer, D. 2014. Security and Social Critique. In M. Kaldor and I. Rangelov (eds.), *The Handbook of Global Security Policy*, pp. 31–50. London: Blackwell.

Mutimer, D. 2015. Critical Security Studies: A Schismatic History in A. Collins (ed.), *Contemporary Security Studies*, 4th edn, pp. 87–107. Oxford: Oxford University Press.

Mutimer, D. 2016. Critical Security Studies in M. Dunn Cavelty and T. Balzacq (eds.), *Routledge Handbook of Security Studies*, 2nd edn, pp. 80–92. Abingdon: Routledge, available from ProQuest ebrary. [1 January 2017].

Mutimer, D., K. Grayson, and J. M. Beier. 2013. Critical Studies on Security an Introduction. *Critical Studies on Security*, 1(1): 1–12.

Neocleous, M. 2008. *Critique of Security*. Montreal/Kingston: McGill-Queens University Press.

Nunes, J. 2012. Reclaiming the Political: Emancipation and Critique in Security Studies. *Security Dialogue*, 43(4): 345–61.

Nyman, J. 2016. What is the Value of Security? Contextualising the Negative/Positive Debate. *Review of International Studies*, 42(5): 821–39.

Richter-Montpetit, M. 2007. Empire, Desire and Violence: A Queer Transnational Feminist Reading of the Prisoner "Abuse" in Abu Ghraib and the Question of "Gender Equality". *International Feminist Journal of Politics*, 9(1): 38–59.

Salter, M. B. and C. E. Mutlu (eds.). 2013. *Research Methods in Critical Security Studies: An Introduction*. New York: Routledge .

Samson, C and C. Gigoux. 2017, *Indigenous Peoples and Colonialism Global Perspectives*. Malden, MA: Polity Press,.

Shepherd, L. J. 2013. The State of Feminist Security Studies: Continuing the Conversation. *International Studies Perspectives*, 14(4): 436–9.

Sium, A., C. Desai, and E. Ritskes. 2012. Towards the 'Tangible Unknown': Decolonization and the Indigenous Future. *Decolonization: Indigeneity, Education & Society*, 1(1): I–XIII.

Smith, L. T. 2012. *Decolonizing Methodologies: Research and Indigenous Peoples*, 2nd edn. New York: Zed Books .

Sundberg, J. 2014. Decolonizing Posthumanist Geographies. *Cultural Geographies*, 21(1): 33–47.
Sylvester, C. 2007. Anatomy of a Footnote. *Security Dialogue*, 38(4): 547–58.
Sylvester, C. 2010. Tensions in Feminist Security Studies, *Security Dialogue*, 41(6): 607–14.
Todd, Z. 2016. An Indigenous Feminist's Take on the Ontological Turn: "Ontology" is Just Another Word for Colonialism. *Journal of Historical Sociology*, 29(1): 4–22.
Tuck, E. and R. A. Gaztambide-Fernández. 2013. Curriculum, Replacement, and Settler Futurity. *Journal of Curriculum Theorizing*, 29(1): 72–89.
Tuck, E. and K. W. Yang. 2012. Decolonization is not a Metaphor. *Decolonization: Indigeneity, Education & Society*, 1(1): 1–40.
Wibben, A. T. 2010. *Feminist Security Studies: A Narrative Approach*. New York: Routledge.
Wibben, A. T. 2016. Opening Security: Recovering Critical Scholarship as Political. *Critical Studies on Security*, 4(2): 137–53.
Wilcox, L. 2016. Securing Methods, Practicing Critique: A Review of Methods and Critical Security Studies. *International Studies Review*, 18(4): 702–13.
Wolfe, P. 2006. Settler Colonialism and the Elimination of the Native. *Journal of Genocide Research*, 8(4): 387–409.

CHAPTER 6

REALISMS

ADAM QUINN

6.1 Introduction

Realism is one of the longest-established approaches to the study of security, and a cornerstone in the construction of International Relations as a distinct discipline in the twentieth century. But the longevity of the label—and its ubiquity in disciplinary surveys over decades—gives a misleading impression of the constancy and uniformity of the intellectual framework to which it refers. This will be old news to veterans of realism's internal debates, which have been extensive. Those uninitiated in realism's rolling conversation within and about itself, however, might be surprised by the range of difference encompassed by the alternative versions of realism established in the literature.

Rival conceptions of realism have diverged on fundamental issues: whether rigorous theory can work at all below the system level; the extent to which prediction of state behaviour is possible; the meaning of "rationality" and its applicability to states' actions; whether realism's function is merely explanatory or also prescriptive/normative; and the role if any of ideas in driving behavior. This chapter will not resolve what qualifies as the "realest" realism. That would be hard to do other than by fiat, given the length of time over which different strands have made accepted use of the label. It will, however, elucidate in more detail some of these important points of divergence, and draw out the implications for realism's efforts to look to the future in the study and practice of international security.

6.2 Mapping the Schools of Realism

Most accounts of realism make central—rightly—the distinction between two variants that emerged sequentially during the twentieth century: classical and structural. The first, original, realism manifested in the scholarship of Hans J. Morgenthau and E. H.

Carr, published in the aftermath of the outbreak of the Second World War. Its *raison d'être* was to serve as critique and counterpoint to liberal ideas of the period, which realists thought overestimated the viability of suppressing international aggression and war through law, institutions, and appeals to a common interest in peace. Liberal "idealists," this realism contended, failed to appreciate the primacy of power and the irreconcilability of states' interests in accumulating it for their rival purposes.

The second realism arrived with Kenneth Waltz's *Theory of International Politics* (2010/1979). Waltz explicitly criticized, disavowed, and disengaged from significant parts of previously existing realism. His starting proposition was that Morgenthau (1966) and those who followed him were fundamentally misguided in seeking to identify universal behavioral laws applicable to states or individuals by building bottom-up from the cataloguing of recorded events. The goal, he proposed, should not be to try and discern through aggregated observations which attributes of states and statesmen generate the outcomes of war and peace. Rather it should be to explain the consistency with which the *same* outcome—conflict—manifests in international life despite the striking diversity of individuals' and states' characteristics. To account for this, he proposed, only a theory of *system* would do. In pursuit of such a theory, he found his organizing principle in anarchy; that is, in the absence of any sovereign authority above states analogous to that existing in domestic politics. Operating in such an environment, he argued, states wanting to preserve their continued autonomous existence had an incentive to achieve a balance against concentrations of power that might otherwise ultimately dominate them. States that failed to heed this incentive entirely would be selected out of the system, losing their sovereignty. Those which made sub-optimal but less catastrophic choices would, in general, be socialized over time into more appropriate behavior.

With the advent of this distinction came the new terminological regime: a previously existing realism baptized retrospectively as "classical," while Waltz's theory and subsequent work in the furrow he ploughed becoming "neo-" or "structural" realism. Realist scholarship in the years since can be classified into three major categories, to which this chapter will refer as we proceed:

- *Structural Realism (SR)* accepts Waltz's premises regarding the purpose and parameters of theorizing and seeks to develop and refine an account of international politics on that basis.
- *Neoclassical Realism (NCR)* accepts the fundamentals of a Waltzian structural model, or refined variant thereof. But it proposes that it is (a) desirable to provide a supplementary account of how, when, and why some state behavior diverges from optimal responses to systemic incentives, and (b) possible to identify stable, consistent rules governing such divergence.
- *Classical Realism (CR) Redux* is, like neoclassical realism, interested in the role of factors below the international-systemic level. But rather than grafting "unit-level" attributes onto a structural model as "intervening variables" as NCR does, CR advocates reprising the original methodological and normative facets of

classical realism. This contrasts with the positivistic scientific aspirations of both SR and NCR.

Inevitably, presentation of the taxonomy in this stark form makes the frontiers between categories seem more rigid and impermeable than tends to be the case in the work of actually existing scholars. Nevertheless, these categories do provide a useful framework for exploring the key points of principled intellectual divergence within contemporary realism. Let us now examine how this plays out in regard to some particular issues.

6.3 Is Realism a Predictive Theory?

A key point of divergence between realists is whether the approach can generate robust predictions—and to what degree success in that regard determines worth. None of the three strands claims to be capable of generating comprehensively accurate predictions down to the level of every state's behavior in every case. But each questions the plausibility of attaining such total predictive power for different reasons, and those differences are instructive.

6.3.1 Structural Realism and Prediction

In Waltz's SR theory, the possibility of knowing what every state will do on any given occasion is ruled out from first principles as unrealizable. What it offers instead is an account of how systemic incentives generate a pattern of behavior toward which states—on aggregate, not individually—will gravitate consistently over the long term. In combining incentives, selection, and socialization in a system-level account, SR borrows substantially and explicitly from a simple outline of the economic theory of the market (Waltz 2008). States may vary in their internal structures, values, desires, and types of leader. But for each, continued survival as an autonomous entity is always a precondition for achieving other goals. From this Waltz deduces there will be a tendency for states to balance against rival concentrations of power, since this is necessary to secure that fundamental interest.

Crucially, this does not require the claim that all states respond optimally to systemic incentives. It does not even require the claim that as a matter of descriptive empirical fact—as distinct from operationally useful theoretical assumption—*every* state is primarily motivated by survival. States that persistently show reckless disregard for their own survival will be destroyed, that is, selected out. States that do seek survival but make poor choices in pursuit of it will, presuming they avoid the relatively rare fate that is total destruction, be subject to painful costs. Over time this will lead them either to correct their course, or else be overtaken in power by states whose behavior better matches the reward structure of the system.

SR in Waltz's formulation therefore *is* predictive. But—importantly—not at the level of the individual state. It posits two things. First, a predictable pattern of balancing behavior on the part of states on aggregate over the long term. Second, that states will, in general, experience punishment and reward in proportion to how appropriately they respond to the system's incentives.

In the years since, many have followed in Waltz's footsteps. This has meant a sizable tranche of literature (for an excellent survey, the steps of which we need not retread here, see Taliaferro 2000/01) in which contributors generally (a) accept the centrality of the SR framework, while (b) proposing some refinement of their own regarding the specifics of how incentives and capabilities interact to produce a certain pattern of behavior. The content of each offshoot on the family tree of SR varies, but all generate hypotheses that are—in principle at least—amenable to testing against historical cases or future events. At the least, empirical case evidence is relevant to confirming—or disproving—the existence of whatever pattern of behavior they expect. In addition, to the extent it is claimed states self-consciously adapt to systemic incentives—that is, are socialized—empirical evidence might also be used in tracing the process by which this occurs.

While pursuing this agenda, some structural realists (e.g. Mearsheimer 2001a, 2001b) have concluded that the pattern of international behavior tends toward expansionist pursuit of ever-greater power. Others have stayed closer to Waltz in discerning a more defensively oriented pattern (e.g. Walt 1987, 1995). "Balancing behavior" is the aspect of SR that has received most attention. This is both because it is the clearest empirically testable prediction derivable from the theory, and also one that appears to have direct relevance to the order arising after the end of the Cold War. Faced with the puzzle of the United States maintaining, since 1991, a sizable relative power advantage over all other major powers, some, such as Layne (2012), Mearsheimer (2001a, 2001b), and Waltz himself (2000), have predicted the emergence of balancing against the United States—albeit while acknowledging the likelihood of a time lag while systemic incentive translates into actual behavior. Others have argued, contrarily, that a unipolar distribution so heavily stacked in favor of one power deters others from challenging the status quo, whether alone or through alliances (Brooks and Wohlforth, 2008).

This latter, balancing sceptical realism can interweave comfortably with the account previously provided by hegemonic stability theory (Gilpin 1981). Both agree that hegemonic power, once established, is unlikely to be challenged by coordinated resistance. If and when it is destabilized, it is more likely to be because of an increase in the capabilities of lesser powers brought about by differential rates of economic growth and technological capacity. Such focus on states' internal development of capabilities has been amplified in the most recent SR scholarship: Rosato and Parent (2015) argue that although the evidence for *external* balancing may be rickety, SR's predictive power is vindicated if we focus on the regularity with which *internal* balancing has occurred. That is to say: great powers are—justifiably—wary of the reliability of alliances when contending with a stronger power, but have with much more consistency tended to arm themselves against rivals, and emulate their organizational and doctrinal innovations.

6.3.2 Neoclassical Realism and Prediction

NCR (Rose 1998) softens yet simultaneously expands realism's claim to predictive power. It softens it by acknowledging that the patterns of system-incentivized behavior it imports from SR are in practice routinely disrupted by other variables. It expands it by suggesting we can derive, from case research, law-like rules about which variables have what consequences, allowing us to anticipate deviation from structure-driven patterns with some precision (Lobell et al. 2009; Ripsman et al. 2016). As this author (Quinn 2013) has noted previously, particular NCR scholars have varied widely in the variable that they propose "intervenes" between systemic incentive and state action:

> According to assorted neoclassical realists, these mediating variables include, *inter alia*: divisions between and within elites in the foreign policy executive (Lobell 2003; Lobell et al. 2009); entrenched strategies formed at the national level during previous historical periods (Brawley 2009); the need or desire of parts of the governing class to appeal to nationalist sentiment, even in contexts of economic interdependence (Sterling-Folker 2009); embedded ideological constructions in the domestic political culture within which national foreign policy must be justified (Dueck, 2004, 2006, 2009); the ability of powerful domestic forces to shape the pursuit of the national interest by threatening the security in office of the government (Ripsman 2009); the capacity of some states relative to others to "extract" resources for the purposes of foreign policy (Taliaferro 2009); and the role of a strong, coherent state, with a complementary ideology, in making expansionary policy on the part of a state possible (Schweller 2008, 2009)

Each of these accounts certainly does propose something predictable about the world that should be amenable to testing against events, for example Schweller's would lead us to expect certain types of state response to an external threat based on the structure of domestic institutions. Each is based on a qualitative analysis of case study evidence. However, it should be noted that if we were to credit them *all* with being accurate, it becomes most challenging to preserve the ultimate compatibility with Waltz's account of structure that NCR claims. This is for two reasons. First, because theoretically it opens the door to an uncontrollable proliferation of variables of precisely the kind Waltz condemned in principle as a dysfunctional feature of IR scholarship prior to imposing the brutalist parsimony of his *Theory*. A structural purist would therefore complain that NCR presents the illusion of greater predictive and descriptive accuracy by reaching down to the level of state behavior, but at the price of giving over realism's research agenda to the endless accumulation of ad hoc variables that supposedly account for every difference in case outcome. The second reason is because the scope and duration of the divergences from structural imperative posited by NCR is unclear. Does NCR want to claim only that these intervening variables produce occasional anomalies that—while interesting—are insufficiently frequent or lasting to ultimately disrupt the predictions of long-term aggregate state behavior on which SR rests (Rathbun 2008)? Or is its goal "bolder: to build a causal model... whereby state-level attributes drive states to act contrary to supposed systemic imperatives in ways that are not merely anomalous, but are predictable, recurrent and lasting" (Quinn 2013).

6.3.3 Classical Realism Redux and Prediction

Scholars who advocate rediscovering the neglected virtues of classical realism, and their reapplication in the contemporary practice of IR scholarship, have made the predictive pretensions of SR and NCR a major point of departure. Barkin (2009) emphasizes in his interrogation of prediction's place in classical realism that it is at heart "a theory of foreign policy, not a theory of system constraints," thus underlining its distinction from a structural approach. Unlike NCR, however, CR does not understand "theory of foreign policy" to mean a deterministic account of rules governing state action. Rather, in focusing on the situation facing national decision-makers, it seeks to emphasize their agency and the non-determined nature of their choices. In doing so it also engages in a kind of exhortation, to the effect that political actors should embrace prudence and circumspection given the inescapable uncertainty of the future and of the outcomes of their actions.

Kirshner (2015: 156), who has called for a "renaissance" of CR, criticizes "purportedly scientific and, in particular, economistic approaches to IR theory," which in his view have displaced "an older, classical realist tradition with its emphasis on choice, contingency, history, ideology, uncertainty, and unpredictability." He portrays CR as committed to a *kind* of objectivity, but at the same time skeptical about IR's ability to successfully imitate the natural sciences in making prediction central to its utility. One can "describe, explain, understand and anticipate," he proposes, but not predict with the same kind of credibility. When it comes to international politics there are simply too many explanatory variables, and too many behavioral relationships in play, for circumstances to ever precisely replicate in the way required to allow construction of a rigorous predictive theory. In addition, Kirshner emphasizes—as does Barkin—the disruptive effect of the reflexivity of actors on models that try to extrapolate from the historical record into the future, neglecting the feedback effect of learning to which IR scholarship itself contributes: "Structural realists model their states as amnesiacs innocent of historical legacies, and their statesmen as caretakers arranging the deckchairs on ships guided by inexorable currents beyond their control." (2015: 168).

6.4 Is Realism a Theory of Rational Action?

Advocates for reprising the classical realist approach often foreground its reservations about attributing too much rationality to states or leaders. Kirshner sets up CR as a counterpoint not just to structuralism but also to what he calls "hyperrationalism," an approach he characterizes as involving "misapplication of economic theories and analogies to the study of IR" (Kirshner 2015: 156). He criticizes the "rational expectations" model of state behavior for its reliance on positing an implausibly high level of information and capacity for calculation on the part of actors:

> This scepticism ... is not a rejection of the scientific study of politics but a conservative regard for what social science can hope to achieve. Classical realists model their actors as rational, but not hyperrational, essentially as Keynes described them: doing the best they can to advance their interests in an uncertain world. (Kirshner 2015: 178)
>
> ... In the context of uncertainty, classical realists tend to model states in the abstract as rational muddlers—essentially rational, purposeful and motivated—but not as hyperrationalist automatons, Presented with a range of plausible policy options in an uncertain, contingent world, the choices states make will reflect the distinct historical experience, ideological context, and political contestations of the moment. (Kirshner 2015: 179)

Barkin (2003) similarly argues that although classical realism wants the *study* of politics to have a rational cast, this should not be conflated with supposing political actors *themselves* are strictly rational. He also notes, citing Guzzini, that as a matter of disciplinary history, "the argument that human nature is power-seeking [was] replaced by the assumption that the state is rational" during the shift toward a more aspirationally "scientific" study of International Relations. (Barkin 2003: 236). By implication, the assumption of rationality was not a mainstay of prior classical models. Rathbun (2016), in his version of revived classical realism, suggests setting aside entirely the question of whether actions can be judged rational by reference to their aims, or the efficacy of their end–means calculation. He defines rationality instead as a thought process certain individual decision-makers may, or may not, have the temperamental disposition to follow.

It is also a premise of neoclassical realism's project that rational action is not to be expected uniformly across states. NCR provides an account of variation from optimal behavior by states, with the explanatory weight falling on intervening variables of myriad kinds—cultural, organizational, institutional, or political. We might note, however, that logically such a theory only functions if it can posit a stable account of what optimal behavior would look like, against which actual behavior may then be evaluated. Simply put, one can only have a theory of divergence if there is something to diverge from. NCR finds this in its acceptance of structural realism (Rathbun 2008). But as noted in Section 6.3.2, there is some unresolved tension within the approach as to whether it merely seeks to account for anomalies, or, more boldly, to propose wider new behavioral rules of greater lasting consequence. Does the force of structure always win out in the end or can divergent behavior be sustained indefinitely (Quinn 2013)? If the former, simply importing a structural realist model does resolve the "divergence from what" question. If the latter, things get trickier, since—as we are about to note later in this section—in structural realism it is by observing socialization and selection in action that we actually define what optimality and rationality *are*. Without socialization and selection, the "sub-optimal" and "irrational" becomes simply the different.

Since other strands of realism rely on some standard outside actually-existing state behavior against which any particular action might be evaluated, the following question therefore takes on no small importance: Does structural realism's account of the system and its incentives entail a theory of rationality? Certainly some who have built on Walz's foundation have explicitly framed their account as one involving rationality. Most prominently, Glaser (2003, 2010) provides an account of when conflict or cooperation occur based on the interaction of state capabilities, information, and motive (the latter meaning whether a state is satisfied with basic security or is "greedy"). Still, Glaser is clear that his theory is more focused on providing an account of *what rational states would do* than on making the empirical claim that states do in fact behave rationally. And since his theory takes differences in state motive as given at its starting line, it allows for different courses of action in otherwise identical circumstances to be considered equally rational.

For a more parsimonious structural realism such as Waltz's—which ascribes to all states a single fundamental motive—the question is more stark: Does obeying the imperatives of the system equate to rationality? Or to put a sharper point on it: Does divergence constitute *irrational* behavior? As it happens, Waltz (2010/1979) himself speaks to this point, making it apparent in the process that he sets a rather low bar for what it means for rationality to pertain. In the *Theory of International Politics* he explains this by reference to his favored analogy of the market:

> Firms are assumed to be maximizing units. In practice, some of them may not even be trying to maximize anything. Others may be trying, but their ineptitude may make this hard to discern. Competitive systems are regulated, so to speak, by the "rationality" of the more successful competitors. What does rationality mean? It means only that some do better than others, whether through intelligence, skill, hard work, or dumb luck. They succeed in providing a wanted good or service more attractively or cheaply than others do. Either their competitors emulate them or they fall by the wayside. (Waltz 2010/1979: 77)

Rationality for Waltz, therefore, reduces to something very basic indeed; perhaps to no more than that the systemic outcome simply "is what it is." Referring to the imputed centrality of rationality to his theory in later years, he was even more blunt:

> I do not even know what 'rational actor' means empirically. ... Some [people] are going to do better than others; some are going to be a lot smarter; some are going to be a little bit luckier than others; some are going to be better at cheating than others. All those things affect outcomes, but rationality—in its empirical form—has really little to do with it. The notion of rationality is a big help in constructing a theory. ... But in the real world, does anybody think "I'm rational, or you're rational"? Let alone, that states could be rational? It has no empirical meaning. (interview, cited in Bessner and Guilhot 2015: 111)

Taking all this into account, it might seem odd, therefore, that some prominent skeptics of realism, when seeking to boil it down to its irreducible core alone, should have alighted on a "commitment to the assumption of rational state behaviour" (Legro and Moravcsik 1999: 54). As respondents to Legro and Moravcsik noted at the time, an emphasis on "rationalism" seems to contradict Waltz's own extremely limited claims for the power and relevance of rationality (Feaver et al. 2000). Feaver puts his finger on the essential point: realism is entirely comfortable with the occurrence in practice of a great deal of state behavior running counter to what realists think systemic pressures incentivize. Structural realism's expectation, however, is that such behavior will be "punished" by the system and thus state behavior on the whole "constrained." This, in fact, is the true core of structural realism. Feaver noted in 2000 that the question of whether and how such punishment actually unfolds in practice had been "undertheorized": "how systematic are system constraints, really?" (Feaver et al. 2000: 167).

6.5 Is Realism Prescriptive/Normative?

At first glance, structural realism might seem to facilitate disengaging from prescription when it comes to the actions of states or their leaders. In practice, however, even realists who emphasize structure have not tended to steer clear: Mearsheimer (2014), Walt (2016) and others frequently offer evaluations of the wisdom of national policies and dispense judgment and advice. Does this make sense?

As established in Section 6.3.1, even the most emphatically structural realist allows that there is scope for variation between states in their choices, albeit within constraints imposed by the system. To the extent that we allow for some agency in selecting the substance of that variation, this opens up the space for prescription to be meaningful. It is within the capacity of individual states to decide to at least *try* and buck the system. At the same time, Waltz's model, in which the accumulated outcomes of selection and socialization generate a distinction between what is rational and what is not, seems to provide a strong normative standard against which to measure state policy. Unless, that is, we are to regard the theory as implying no favor for the policies it characterizes as optimal and rational, which seems implausible.

Mearsheimer places himself in a somewhat tighter bind than Waltz. His theory's central proposition (2001b) is that states are power-maximizers, but at the same time he talks of "reckless" states (2009) and his policy recommendations tend toward commending the wisdom of restraint (2014). Does this not amount to criticizing states for doing no more than acting in line with what his own framework tells us is to be expected? Whereas the defensive realist sets up a norm of rational self-interested action while suggesting real-world state action does in fact generally abide by it, the offensive realist seems at once to identify a prevailing pattern of behavior *and* the undesirability of that behavior with regard to states' true interests. One might conclude that continuing to dispense policy advice when one conceives of the international system in such tragic terms—as an account of predestined self-harm—implies the greatest commitment of all to the inherent worthiness of normative prescription. After all, it suggests a willingness to persevere despite being convinced that more often than not good advice will fail to be heeded, and entails advocating not for adherence to a prevailing behavioral norm, but for valiant efforts at resistance in spite of the powerful pull of self-destructiveness.

Neoclassical realism walks a similar line in expecting one kind of behavior and recommending another. In adopting a structural realism as a foundation, NCR imposes a framework of expectation—whether tacitly or explicitly—regarding what rational self-interest demands of states. Since its *raison d'être* is to then provide accounts of divergence from this standard, we might therefore reasonably conclude that some measure of criticism, aimed at the level of the decision-making unit, is implied. Schweller (2008), for one example, is not merely observing a correlation between the arrangement of domestic politics and institutions and a certain pattern of state behavior, but also linking this to a judgment as to whether and when states act *adequately* to address external threats. For another example, authors who focus on the role of ideology and culture in limiting policy choice (Dueck 2006, 2009; Quinn 2010) often pair that with concern that this serves to close off some strategically sensible options from consideration.

Classical realism meanwhile is the most overtly normative of the realist approaches. Its lesser attachment to prediction and its emphasis on contingency and agency foreground the idea that prescription is purposeful. As Barkin (2009) puts it:

> [T]he need for prescription underlines the possibility that prediction might fail. This is the case inasmuch as it involves having to tell decision makers to do what they have been predicted to do, or having to warn them not to do what it has been predicted they will not do anyway. To the extent therefore that we expect that prescription might work, we must accept that prediction might fail. (Barkin 2009: 245)

For Barkin, classical realism is at heart a "theory of foreign policy, not a theory of system constraints" (Barkin 2009: 241). By this he means not—as a structural or neoclassical realist would—an explanatory account of how foreign policy *will* unfold, but rather an injunction as to the disposition leaders should bring to the task of making decisions. Similarly, Williams (2004) in advocating renewed attention to Morgenthau's CR, emphasizes the demand it places on leaders to make "critical normative and political judgements" (2004: 635). For Morgenthau, he says, approvingly:

> While it was essential to recognise objectively the dynamics and power relations involved in collective identity formation, and the intrinsic relationship between politics and power, it was equally essential to develop an ethical and evaluative stance towards these dynamics. If realism was not to descend into a crude realpolitik, and if a recognition of the centrality of power in politics was not to result in the reduction of politics to nothing more than power and violence, critical judgement was essential. (Williams 2004: 657)

That classical realism would seek to open up the space first for agency and then for critical thinking by actors should not surprise us when we recall that its foundational puzzle was that states frequently do "the wrong thing," and that it is therefore worthwhile to exhort them to do otherwise (Quinn 2010, 2014).

6.6 Do "ideas matter" in Realism?

Ideas do not play the primary role in structural and neoclassical realist accounts. But they certainly do feature within the universe posited by those frameworks. This is true in three regards. First, because state leaders—and national cultures for that matter—have ideas about the ideal world they wish to see realized. Survival as an autonomous entity is the fundamental drive of states according to realism, but that is because it is the *sine qua non* of their pursuit of myriad other things they value. Most such "next-step" goals involve ideals of political or economic order toward which actors wish to see progress. We should not confuse realism's claim that states will, anomalies excepted, prioritize survival over abstract ideological purism with a denial that states invest importance in their "idea of the good" once they have a baseline of security from which to proceed.

Second, structural realism is in large part an account of how the pressures of anarchy *moderate and modify* other drivers, some of which are ideational. As a matter of intellectual history, Waltz's structural realist theory came into being in order to make the case that democratic domestic politics could, despite its vicissitudes, be reconciled with the need to provide competently for national security, because of the socializing effect of the international system (Bessner and Guilhot 2015). Similar arguments are made today by realists regarding highly ideological states such as Iran and North Korea.

Third, for some variants of NCR, ideas account for sub-optimal behaviour, whether directly in the form of ideology and culture (Dueck 2006, 2009) or indirectly in the form of institutional structure (Schweller 2008) or domestic political coalitions (Lobell 2002).

When we consider classical realism, ideas are not merely present but absolutely central. We have noted in Section 6.5—and therefore need not labor here—Williams' point that Morgenthau's realism demanded actors reflect critically on their own political and ethical position. In reprising prominently this dimension of classical realism, the movement for CR Redux seeks not only to remind realists that, however tacitly, they inevitably assume a normative position, but also that it is a vital imperative to keep one's own values in perspective. It is here that Barkin finds the space and grounds for his thesis that there is an underappreciated overlap between realism's fundamentally relativistic take on political values, and critical-constructivist frameworks of analysis.

People, especially groups and nations, are prone to identifying their own ideological convictions with universal values, and to rationalizing the pursuit of their own interests as somehow demanded by the universal good. Pointing this out and criticizing this human tendency was central to the *oeuvre* not just of Morgenthau but also Carr (1995) and Niebuhr (2005, 2008). Barkin emphasizes this strand of "moral scepticism" which represents "a key difference between idealism and realism":

> Idealism recognises a single ideal, a universal political morality towards which we should strive. Realism argues that no universal political morality exists. ... [W]hen we justify a use of power to ourselves as being for moral purposes, we may simply be fooling ourselves and rationalizing an action as moral that we want to take for other reasons. As such, even though power is hollow without political morality, the classical realist argument is that we must, nonetheless, apply to that morality, ours as well as others, a certain scepticism when it is used to justify power. (Barkin 2003: 337–8).

CR thus not only opens up the space for agency and prescription—it also makes the meta-ethical move of insisting that, at the most fundamental level, the values and preferences guiding our own actions exist in a relationship of equivalence with those of others. And it wishes actors to become and remain conscious of this equivalence. In this regard, CR, it might be argued, is a more dispassionately relativistic theory than many "critical" approaches.

If realism can be skeptical about rationality and encompass a major role for ideas, the question may then arise: Is it any longer a distinct theoretical paradigm? This has certainly been a matter of animated debate (Legro and Moravcsik 1999; Feaver et al. 2000). One plausible possibility lies its conviction about the limits constraining change. Realism *does* have a place for change. Even Gilpin's (1981) account of hegemonic stability, for example, is concerned with how it ultimately is destabilized. And almost every realist account treats the distribution of power as something dynamic not static. Nevertheless, realism offers accounts of only limited change *within* a system centered on an indissoluble core of antagonism between interests.

This is not simply a failure of imagination. Realists, even when prompted to reflect on the possibilities, are actively skeptical of the viability of certain kinds of radical transformation in human political relations. Specifically, realism believes it is a core truth about humans that they form groups. States happen to be the dominant organizational form this has taken in the modern era, but the universal tendency pre-dates the state, and by implication realists are confident it would outlive it. This observation has been a mainstay of classical realists through the years, brought into focus especially by Niebuhr (2005, 2008), alongside his emphasis on human collectives' consistent failure to recognize the moral equivalence of their own interests relative to those of others. More recently, Sterling-Folker (2002) has even speculated on a biological root to the grouping impulse. Whether or not we go that far, it is quite right, as she argues, that future dialogue between realism and liberal constructivism should most usefully focus on the proposition that "there may be limitations on how human beings construct their social realities" (Sterling-Folker 2002: 76).

6.7 Conclusion

There is little risk that realism's centrality to international security scholarship will go unrecognized in any survey. The risk is greater that its diversity might go underappreciated. Some realisms attribute significant weight to their ability to make predictions at the system level. Others claim to be able to divine law-like relationships between state attributes and future behavior. And yet others still actively emphasize the importance of contingency and agency. Some realists have a strong conception of rational action—or at least proceed as though they do—against which state actions can be judged anomalous, even deviant. Others are skeptical of "rationality," doubting not just whether states or people behave rationally, but also whether it is possible to give the very concept itself thick and stable meaning.

Some realisms are normative only tacitly: they have a standard for optimal system-incentivized behavior against which to judge the actual, and we might reasonably infer that they approve of what is optimal. Others, in particular classical realism as revived in a twenty-first-century incarnation, are invested in restoring ethical and meta-ethical considerations to the foreground. For some realism, ideas matter in the sense that states and leaders have them and their efforts in pursuit will be moderated by the pressures of the international system. Others see realism itself as an intellectual project that challenges political actors to put their own beliefs and values in perspective alongside those of others, avoiding the lure of chauvinism and universalism. One thing that binds realists together is skepticism toward claims by radicals that some new order may be realized, through "resistance," which overcomes altogether the human tendency toward grouping and the exercise of power within structures that follow from it. Realism allows for change: material, ideational, and institutional. But perhaps more than anything, realism believes in limits.

References

Barkin, J. S. 2003. Realist Constructivism. *International Studies Review*, 5: 325–42.

Barkin, J. S. 2009. Realism, Prediction and Foreign Policy. *Foreign Policy Analysis*, 5: 233–246.

Bessner, D. and Guilhot, N. 2015. How Realism Waltzed Off: Liberalism and Decisionmaking in Kenneth Waltz's Neorealism. *International Security*, 40(2): 87–118.

Brawley, M. R. 2009. Neoclassical Realism and Strategic Calculations: Explaining Divergent British, French and Soviet Strategies towards Germany between the World Wars. In S. E. Lobell, N. M. Ripsman, and J. W. Talliafero (eds.), *Neoclassical Realism, the State and Foreign Policy*, pp. 75–98. Cambridge: Cambridge University Press.

Brooks, S. G. and W. C. Wohlforth 2008. *World Out of Balance: International Relations and the Challenge of American Primacy*. Princeton, NJ: Princeton University Press.

Carr, E. H. 1995. *The Twenty Years Crisis 1919–1939*. London: Macmillan (first published 1939).

Dueck, C. 2004. Ideas and Alternatives in American Grand Strategy, 2000–2004. *Review of International Studies*, 30(4): 511–35.

Dueck, C. 2006. *Reluctant Crusaders: Power, Culture and Change in American Grand Strategy*. Princeton, NJ: Princeton University Press

Dueck, C. 2009. Neoclassical Realism and the National Interest: Presidents, Domestic Politics, and Major Military Interventions. In S. E. Lobell, N. M. Ripsman, and J. W. Talliafero (eds.), *Neoclassical Realism, the State and Foreign Policy*, pp. 139–69. Cambridge: Cambridge University Press.

Feaver, Peter D., G. Hllmann, R. L. Schweller, J. W. Taliaferro, W. C. Wohlforth 2000. Correspondence: Brother Can You Spare a Paradigm (Or Was Anybody Ever a Realist?). *International Security*, 25(1): 165–9.

Gilpin, R. 1981. *War and Change in World Politics*. Cambridge: Cambridge University Press.

Glaser, C. L. 2003. Structural Realism in a More Complex World. *Review of International Studies*, 29: 403–14.

Glaser, C. L. 2010. *Rational Theory of International Politics*, Princeton, NJ: Princeton University Press.

Kirshner, K. 2015. The Economic Sins of Modern IR Theory and the Classical Realist Alternative. *World Politics*, 67(1): 155–83.

Layne, C. 2012. "This Time it's Real: The End of Unipolarity and the Pax Americana. *International Studies Quarterly*, 56: 1-11.

Legro, J. W. and J. Moravcsik. 1999. Is Anybody Still a Realist? *International Security*, 24(2): 5–55.

Lobell, S. E. 2002. War is Politics: Offensive Realism, Domestic Politics, and Security Strategies. *Security Studies*, 12(2): 165–95.

Lobell, S. E. 2003. *The Challenge of Hegemony: Grand Strategy, Trade and Domestic Politics*, Ann Arbor: University of Michigan Press.

Lobell, S. E., N. M. Ripsman, and J. W. Talliafero (eds). 2009. *Neoclassical Realism, the State and Foreign Policy*. Cambridge: Cambridge University Press.

Mearsheimer, J. J. 2001a. "The Future of the American Pacifier. *Foreign Affairs*, 80(5): 46–61.

Mearsheimer, J. J. 2001b. *The Tragedy of Great Power Politics*. New York: W.W. Norton & Co. (updated 2014).

Mearsheimer, J. J. 2009. Reckless States and Realism. *International Relations*, 23(2): 241–26.

Mearsheimer, J. J. 2014. Why the Ukraine Crisis Is the West's Fault, *Foreign Affairs*, Sep/Oct. *Available at:* https://www.foreignaffairs.com/articles/russia-fsu/2014-08-18/why-ukraine-crisis-west-s-fault

Morgenthau, H. J. 1966. *Politics among Nations: The Struggle for Power and Peace*, 3rd edn. New York: Knopf.

Niebuhr, R. 2005. *Moral Man and Immoral Society: A Study in Ethics and Politics*. London and New York: Continuum (first published 1932).

Niebuhr, R. 2008. *The Irony of American History*. Chicago and London: University of Chicago Press (first published 1952).

Quinn, A. 2010. *US Foreign Policy in Context: National Ideology from the Founders to the Bush Doctrine*. London and New York: Routledge.

Quinn, A. 2013. Kenneth Waltz, Adam Smith and the Limits of Science: Hard choices for Neoclassical Realism. *International Politics*, 50(2): 159–82.

Quinn, A. 2014. Does the Flaw Lie Within US? Classical Realism and Unrealistic Policy. *Global Society*, 28(2): 241–65.

Rathbun, B. 2008. A Rose by Any Other Name: Neoclassical Realism as a Logical and Necessary Extension of Structural Realism. *Security Studies*, 17(2): 294–321.

Rathbun, B. 2016. "The Prince" Among Men: Bismarck, the Psychology of Realism, and International Relations', unpublished paper, presented at University of Birmingham June 1, 2016. *Available at:* http://www.birmingham.ac.uk/schools/government-society/centres/iccs/news/2016/05/p-psychology-realism-international-relations.aspx

Ripsman, N. M. 2009. Neoclassical Realism and Domestic Interest Groups. In S. E. Lobell, N. M. Ripsman, and J. W. Talliafero (eds.), *Neoclassical Realism, the State and Foreign Policy*, pp. 170–93. Cambridge: Cambridge University Press.

Ripsman, N. M., J. W. Taliaferro, S. E. Lobell 2016. *Neoclassical Realist Theory of International Politics*, Oxford: Oxford University Press.

Rosato, S. and Parent, J. 2015. Balancing in Neorealism. *International Security*, 40(2): 51–86.

Rose, G. 1998. Neoclassical Realism and Theories of Foreign Policy. *World Politics*, 51(1): 144–72.

Schweller, R. L. 2008. *Unanswered Threats: Political Constraints on the Balance of Power*. Princeton, NJ: Princeton University Press.

Schweller, R. L. 2009. Neoclassical Realism and State Mobilization: Expansionist Ideology in the Age of Mass Politics. In S. E. Lobell, N. M. Ripsman, and J. W. Talliafero (eds.), *Neoclassical Realism, the State and Foreign Policy*, pp. 227–30. Cambridge: Cambridge University Press.

Sterling-Folker, J. 2002. Realism and the Constructivist Challenge: Rejecting, Reconstructing, or Rereading. *International Studies Review*, 4(1): 73–97.

Sterling-Folker, J. 2009. Neoclassical Realism and Identity: Peril Despite Profit across the Taiwan Strait. In S. E. Lobell, N. M. Ripsman, and J. W. Talliafero (eds.), *Neoclassical Realism, the State and Foreign Policy*, pp. 99–138. Cambridge: Cambridge University Press.

Taliaferro, J. 2000/01. Security Seeking under Anarchy: Defensive Realism Revisited. *International Security*, 25(3): 128–61.

Taliaferro, J. W. 2009. Neoclassical Realism and Resource Extraction: State Building for Future War. In S. E. Lobell, N. M. Ripsman, and J. W. Talliafero (eds), *Neoclassical Realism, the State and Foreign Policy*, pp. 194–226. Cambridge: Cambridge University Press.

Walt, S. 1987. *The Origin of Alliances*. Ithaca, NY: Cornell University Press.

Walt, S. 1995. Alliance Formation and the Balance of World Power. *International Security*, 19: 9.

Walt, S. 2016. What Would a Realist World have Looked like? *Foreign Policy*, 8 January.

Waltz, K. N. 2000. Structural Realism after the Cold War. *International Security*, 25(1): 5–41.

Waltz, K. N. 2008. Realist Thought and Neorealist Theory. In K. N. Waltz, *Realism and International Politics*, pp. 67–82. New York: Routledge.

Waltz, K. N. 2010. *Theory of International Politics*. Long Grove, IL: Waveland Press (first published 1979).

Williams, M. C. 2004. Why Ideas Matter in International Relations: Hans Morgenthau, Classical Realism, and the Moral Construction of Power Politics. *International Organization*, 58: 633–65.

Williams, M. C. 2009. Waltz, Realism and Democracy. *International Relations*, 23(3): 328–40.

CHAPTER 7

CONSTRUCTIVISM

MICHAEL BARNETT

7.1 Introduction

Constructivism's social theoretic foundations formed in the 1980s as a result of a set of critiques of mainstream International Relations (IR) theory. Drawing from established figures like Max Weber and Emile Durkheim, seminal contributions by rising stars such as Anthony Giddens, and critical and postmodern theories from the social sciences and the humanities, a handful of scholars of IR began to identify a littany of social theoretic limitations of mainstream IR theories. The critiques were wide-ranging, but the most compelling were those that claimed that the discipline's twin towers of realism and institutionalism were founded on a "thin" view of social life. In contrast, the critiques offfered the promise of a richer alternative that treated actors as the sociological creatures they are.

However impressive the social theoretic critique, before the mainstream would consider constructivism a viable alternative it had to demonstrate an empirical pay-off, and not just in any sub-field but in the discipline's core research agenda, namely security. And at this moment an event caught the mainstream completely off guard: the end of the Cold War. Realist theories, whose credentials were burnished in security politics, were unprepared for this radical turn of events, and their theoretical toolkit was ill-equipped to provide much more than ad hoc insight. Much like the Soviet Union at the time, realist and institutionalist theories found themselves downsized, humbled, and demoralized. Although constructivist and other alternative theories of international relations did not possess a ready-made explanation, at least they were now starting at the same place and, argued constructivists, they had the social theoretic tools to explain the unpredictable.

Constructivist scholars pounced on this opportunity by assailing mainstream theories with four broad lines of inquiry: (1) an attack on the mainstream's social theoretic foundations and an insistence on a fuller conception of global and social life; (2) an interrogation of some of the fundamental concepts of the discipline, including anarchy, sovereignty, and state interests, demonstrating that these are not natural kinds but rather are social constructs that need to be explained and whose effects can be polymorphous; (3) offering their alternative explanations to the end of the Cold War, with a focus on a thick conception of ideas; and, (4) demonstrating how a constructivist sensibility could offer an alternative account of existing security patterns and point to security developments that were outside the mainstream's sight line (Katzenstein 1996; Wendt 1999). In short, constructivist IR was demonstrating how the social, and not only the material, matters for the conduct of security relations. The realist response to the constructivist challenge was what one might expect from a hegemon under attack from a lesser power—anything from annoyance to abject hostility. For instance, my recollection is that Peter Katzenstein's first choice of publisher for his *The Cultures of National Security*, was Cornell University Press, which arguably had (and still has) the premier series in security studies. The series editors, though, rejected the manuscript, with extreme prejudice.

Constructivism, along with many other schools of thought, incuding critical theory, historical sociology, and feminism, produced a different way of understanding how the world "hangs together" (Ruggie 1988), alongside a fundamental re-assessment of theory, practice, and meaning of international/global/transnational security. Section 7.2 provides a tailored overview of the basic conceptual vocabulary of constructivism, with particular attention to how it potentially re-orients our understanding of theory and practice of security. Section 7.3 picks up the Handbook's charge to consider how constructivism might consider a major trend in international security: the institutionalization and internationalization of the belief that the "international community" has a responsibility to reduce unnecessary harm to humans. In other words, it addresses how the principle of humanity has emerged to compete with the principle of state security, and the effects this development has had on patterns of global security. In the conclusion, I shift from explanatory to emancipatory theory, and consider whether the internationalization and institutionalization of the reduction of human suffering is necessarily part of human progress, and whether humanity can hope to compete with the state.

7.2 Constructivism

Constructivism is a social theory and not a substantive theory of international politics. Social theory is broadly concerned with how to conceptualize the relationship between agents and structures; for instance, what is the relationship between states and the structure of international politics? Substantive theory offers specific claims and hypotheses about patterns in world politics; for instance, why do democratic states tend not to wage war on one another? In this way, constructivism is best compared with rational choice (Fearon and Wendt 2002). Rational choice is a social theory that offers a framework for understanding how actors operate with fixed preferences that they attempt to maximize under a set of constraints. It makes no claims about the content of those preferences; they could be world domination or religious salvation. Nor does it assume anything about the content of the constraints; they could be guns or ideas. Rational choice offers no claims about the actual patterns of world politics. Like rational choice, constructivism is a social theory that is broadly concerned with the relationship between agents and structures, but it is not a substantive theory. Constructivists, for instance, have different arguments regarding the rise of sovereignty; the impact of human rights norms on states; and the reasons for the rise of human security and the evolution of the international commuity's "responsibility to protect." To begin the process of generating substantive claims, scholars must delineate who are the principal actors, what are their identities, interests, and capacities, and what is the content of the normative structures that constitutes and constrains them.

So, what does it mean to say that the world is "socially-constructed"? Like most social theories, social constructivism has lots of moving parts and analytical layers, which can be sources of disagreement and generate rival camps. That said, they all begin with the fundamental insight that social reality is a product of human consciousness; consciousness is created and constituted through knowledge that shapes meaning and categories of understanding and action; such knowledge and meanings can be institutionalized in social life; and this institutionalization, in turn, shapes the construction of social reality. What follows are some of the key terms that provide the social theoretic underpinnings for constructivism, and that are most useful for explaining key issues regarding the transformation of international security.

To begin, "constructivism is about human consciousness and its role in international life" (Ruggie 1998: 856). This focus on human consciousness suggests a commitment to idealism and holism, which, according to Wendt (1999), represent the core of constructivism. Idealism demands that we take seriously the role of ideas in world politics. The world is defined by material and ideational forces. But these ideas are not akin to beliefs or psychological states that reside inside our heads. Instead, these ideas are social. Our mental maps are shaped by collectively held ideas such as knowledge, symbols, language, and rules. Idealism does not reject material reality but instead observes that the meaning and construction of that material reality is dependent on ideas and interpretation. The balance of power does not objectively exist out there, waiting to be discovered; instead, states debate what is the balance of power, what is its meaning, and how they should respond. Constructivism also accepts some form of holism or structuralism. The world is irreducibly social and cannot be decomposed into the properties of already existing actors. The emphasis on holism can make it seem like actors are automatons. But holism allows for agency, recognizing that agents have some autonomy and their interactions help to construct, reproduce, and transform those structures. The commitment to idealism and holism explains why much of constructivist international relations has been more interested in demonstrating the existence and effects of these socially-constructed worlds than on the ability and capacity for actors to transform them.

This constructed reality can appear as an objective reality, which relates to the concept of social facts. There are those things whose existence is dependent on human agreement, and those things whose existence is not. Brute facts such as rocks, flowers, gravity, and oceans exist independently of human agreement, and will continue to exist even if humans disappear or deny their existence. Social facts, on the other hand, are often treated as part of the "natural order of things" when, in fact, their existence is dependent on human agreement. Money, refugees, terrorism, human rights, and sovereignty are social facts. Their existence depends on human agreement, they will only exist so long as that agreement exists, and their existence shapes how we categorize the world and what we do. Human agreement does not depend on the existence of a contract made between two voluntary actors, but rather comes from underlying structures that give us the language, categories, and meanings to make sense of the world. Accordingly, constructivists often refer to background knowledge, scripts, and the taken-for-granted nature of the many organizing concepts of our world.

The social construction of reality depends on knowledge—that is, discourse, symbols, rules, concepts, and categories that individuals use to map, construct, interpret, and make meaningful the world. Reality does not exist out there waiting to be discovered; instead, historically produced and culturally bound knowledge enables individuals to construct and give meaning to reality. In other words, existing categories help us to understand, define, and make sense of the world. Symbols never exist in isolation but rather are interpreted in relationship to other symbols. Moreover, symbolic systems invariably entail processes of categorization and classification, which underlie distinction and difference, and these symbolically-defined differences often become the source of hierarchy and differential social capacities. In short, symbols are important to boundary construction, providing a source of identity, meaning, and protection to its members, and help to generate distintions between "us" and "them." In this regard, these classification systems, to the extent that they organize reality and practices, are central to human action. As Berger and Luckmann (1966) famously observed, systems of meaning and categorization generate the "everyday reality" that is connected to the practical aspect of getting things done. There are lots of ways to understand collective violence, and one of the unfortunate features of a bloody twentieth century is that we have more categories to discriminate between forms of violence, from civil war to ethnic cleansing, to crimes against humanity, to genocide. None of these categories existed out there, waiting to be discovered. Instead, these were socially constructed, becoming part of the mapped experience that actors used to make sense of the world beginning in the twentieth century.

These categories and classification systems not only help to map social reality, for they also provide categories of meaning. Following Max Weber's (1949: 81) insight that "we are cultural beings with the capacity and the will to take a deliberate attitude toward the world and to lend it significance," constructivists attempt to recover the meanings that actors give to their practices and the objects that they construct. These derive not from private beliefs but rather from culture. In contrast to the rationalist presumption that culture, at most, constrains action, constructivists argue that culture informs the meanings that people give to their action. Sometimes constructivists have presumed that such meanings derive from a hardened culture. But because culture is fractured and society comprises different interpretations of what is meaningful activity, scholars need to consider these cultural fault lines and treat the fixing of meanings as an accomplishment that is the essence of politics. Some of the most important debates in world are about how to define particular activities such as human rights, security, humanitarian intervention, and sovereignty. These orienting concepts can have various meanings, and, importantly, states and non-state actors will fight to have their preferred meaning collectively accepted and hegemonic.

It is not only the "external reality" that is socially constructed, for so, too, are the very actors. Different structures are productive of different categories of actors. States and non-state actors are defined by the underlying structure of sovereignty. The modern category of the state distinguishes those who are citizens from those who are not. These different categories come with different kinds of social capacities—that is, they are responsible for processes of enabling and empowerment and disabling and disempowerment. Structures not only produce the very categories of actorhood; they also shape identities and interests. Actors are not born outside of and prior to society, as individualism claims. Instead, actors are produced and created by their cultural environment: nurture, not nature. This points to the importance of identity and the social construction of interests. The American identity shapes national interests. All states might have an interest in security, but their understandings of what security means and how it can best be achieved can be linked to identity. For instance, the US' post-Second World War preference for multilateralism is often seen as an externalization of its commitment at home to institutions designed to respect autonomy, check against arbitrary power, distribute authority to create proper checks and balances, and maintain stability. Not all is fair in love, war, or any other social endeavor, and adhering to the contemporary laws of war is often interpreted not only as a statement about rational calculations but also about one's "civilizational" identity.

This process of sorting, categorization, and classification can be value-neutral and free of judgment, yet, as I have already noted, quite often it stratifies and ranks (Bially Mattern and Zakarol 2016). As Durkeim and Mauss (1963: 8) wrote: "to classify is not only to form groups; it means arranging these groups according to particular relations. … There are some which are dominant, others which are dominated, and still others which are independent of each other." This process of sorting and the effects of classification, in short, are bound up with power. A security problem is not just another kind of social problem, but rather one that demands greater attention and gravity than others. This is why groups that want to convince others of the seriousness of their issue often use the discourse of "security." And not all problems that are seen as implicating "security" are treated as equally important—national security, environmental security, food security are typically ranked in terms of their import. Male and female are not just categories based on biology, but, historically and culturally speaking, generate radically uneven social capacities and relations of superordination and subordination. And such classifications, which become part of society and its institutions, can have differential effects on the security of men and women.

These claims about the effects of knowledge provide a very different approach to understanding power. Most International Relations theorists treat power as the ability of one state to compel another state to do what it otherwise would not, and tend to focus on the material technologies, such as military firepower and economic statecraft, which have this persuasive effect. Constructivists have offered two important additions to this view of power. The forces of power go beyond the material; they also can be social (Barnett and Duvall 2005). And, power is not only constraining but also constituing. Simply put, the effects of power go beyond the ability to change behavior to include how knowledge, the fixing of meanings, and the construction of identities allocate differential rewards and capacities. If development is defined as per capita income, then some actors, namely states, and some activities, namely industrialization, are privileged; however, if development is defined as basic needs met, then other actors, namely peasants and women, gain voice, and other activities, namely small-scale agricultural initiatives, microfinance and cottage industries, are both visible and desirable. International humanitarian law tends to assume that "combatants" are men and "civilians" are women, children, and the elderly. This gendered nature of the "civilian," can have perverse effects, including generating a system of "women and children first" even when men between the ages of 15 and 50 are at greater risk (Carpenter 2003).

The idealism and holism that undergirds constructivism also shapes its treatment of norms and rules. Rules come in two basic varieties. Regulative rules regulate already existing activities—rules for the road determine how to drive; the rules of the laws of war regulate who and when someone can be legally killed during war. Constitutive rules create the very possibility for these activities. Sovereignty produces states with certain kinds of privileges, including the monopoly of the means of force, and responsibilities, including an acceptance of the principle of non-interference, and the meaning of the purpose of force (Finnemore 2004). In other words, the rules of sovereignty not only regulate state practices but also make possible the very idea of a sovereign state. Constitutive rules also help to define what is considered to be an act of war and whether parties are involved in an international or internal armed conflict. The norms also vary in terms of their institutionalization, that is, how much they are taken for granted (Finnemore and Sikkink 1999). Relatedly, rules are not static, but rather are revised through practice, reflection, and arguments by actors regarding how they should be applied to new situations (Crawford 2002). Indeed, actors often attempt to alter the norms and their meanings that subsequently guide and constitute state identities and interests. For instance, the International Committee of the Red Cross not only attempts to "teach" states what are the laws of war, but also encourages changes in domestic institutions and law in order to increase the likelihood that states see compliance not just as consistent with "best practices" but also as symbolic of their civilized nature.

Constructivist IR has been used to explain both permanency and transformation. Drawing from sociological theories, constructivist approaches tend to focus on how underlying structures create order in global life. To understand why actors act the way they do, constructivists have tended to examine not choices made under constraint but rather how the underlying structures compel actors to adopt actions that reproduce the status quo. It is not to say that constructivist theories treat actors as cultural dupes, with no mind of their own, no room to reflect on their choices, and no agency whatsoever;

however, the sociological tradition from which it draws privileges the underlying structures in which actors are embedded. For these reasons, constructivism tends to emphasize path dependence and cite favorably historical institutionalist methods when explaining change (Fioretos 2011).

Yet constructivists also want to examine processes of transformation. After all, if the world is socially-constructed, then a series of questions become part of the research agenda. When are agents, sometimes called normative entrepreneurs, able to produce a change in the structure? Why and how does something become "taken for granted"? What are the processes by which one social reality becomes hegemonic, and, likewise, under what conditions does a once-hegemonic social reality become destabilized and uprooted? What are the alternative social realities that might have existed, but do not? Sovereignty did not always exist. What were the exogenous shocks, contingencies, historical accidents, the conjunction of material and ideational forces, and strategic actions that led the organization of world politics into a secularized, modernist state system with rules such as the principle of non-interference and no authority superior to the state?

7.3 Securing Humanity

As this Handbook illustrates, the study and practice of international security is no longer under the grip of the state. This is particularly pronounced in two global trends. The first is the movement away from the security of states to the security of humanity. The security of states still matters considerably, and, indeed, continues to dominate most other concerns. Yet there is greater attention to the security of humans, with the expectation that the state's role is to serve the security and welfare of its people. The other trend is how the security of humanity is to be accomplished, with the state now being accompanied by an array of international organizations and non-state actors. In short, security has been humanized and internationalized. I am not claiming that these trends have eroded or supplanted the patterns and practices associated with a system produced by and for the state and its security. Instead, I am pointing to how these trends have become embedded in the definition and practices of international security. Although constructivist theories have drawn from both micro and macro theories to explain international change, transformation of this type generally requires historical-sociological approaches that can address foundational changes in the meaning, provision, and beneficiaries of security (also see Linklater 2011, 2014).

7.3.1 Humanity

The human is not a biological fact but rather is a social construct. The creation and rise of "humanity" as a concept of analysis and practice owes to processes of the Enlightenment and religious change in the late eighteenth and nineteenth centuries (Haskell 1985;

Wilson and Brown 2009; Linklater 2011). Among the many transformative effects of the Enlightenment, two are most important for understanding the emergence of humanity. One was the revolutionary claim that all individuals are humans, all humans are equal and capable of reason, and because humans form a common species, they are obligated to "treat fellow humans as family" (Wilson and Brown 2009: 43). The other was the introduction of a new regime of sympathy, a concern for the suffering of others (Festa 2010). It was not enough to feel human; humans also needed to act humanely. Conversely, the neglect, indifference, or cause of unnecessary suffering became a mark of one's inhumanity. Many of the same underlying processes associated with the Enlightenment also left their mark on Christianity, including the emergence of new forms of evangelicalism. Evangelicalism is a broad-brush term that can refer to any of the many Christian denominations that emerged with the Reformation, but in the late eighteenth century the evangelical movement contained several defining features that oriented it toward saving humanity: a belief that all humans are children of Christ and form a single humanity.

A consequence of this new regime of sympathy was the emergence of reform movements, most targeted at home, but also the transnational mobilization in defense of humanity. The inaugural, and perhaps the most famous, episode was the formation of the transnational movement to abolish the slave trade and slavery. Although the discourses of humanity presumed that all humans were equal, it did not mean that all humans had successfully developed their humanity. Emancipation from slavery brought new responsibilities. Many of the leading abolitionists at the time did not believe that slaves had developed the right qualities to govern themselves, and so they recommended new forms of paternalism. Such beliefs became a staple of many colonial projects, including the belief that the civilized West had a responsibility to bring Christianity, education, literacy, and other attributes of civilization to these backward populations (McCarthy 2009: 169). These civilizing missions were not only good for the uncivilized—they also helped the civilized reaffirm their own sense of humanity.

Histories of the International Relations of the nineteenth century typically focus on the revolutionary effects of ideologies of nationalism and the emerging system organized around nation states, but under the radar (and largely associated with the domestic sphere) were additional processes that reshaped both the character of modern authority, namely, secularization, and the object of the sacred. Secularization has many definitions, and has gone through ups and downs, both in history and scholarly fashion, but the fundamental observation is a shift in authority from the religious to the secular. But, as Durkheim (2008 (1949)) famously observed, the "sacred" can be part of the "secular." In contrast to the profane, which is part of the "everyday," the sacred is invested with transcendental reverence and is regarded as "superior in dignity and power to profane things." Humans can associate the sacred with natural or artificial objects, and to animals, men, or to objectifications of human culture.

The sacred serves the critical function of helping produce and sustain the broader community. Writing against the emerging (and still quite dominant) view in the West that society is formed and maintained on the basis of self-interest, Durkheim argued that shared social ideas, beliefs, and practices form the basis of society. Humans can and do exist in two realms: one that is moral and collective, and the other that is self-regarding, utilitarian, and private. Yet even liberal, atomized, and market-driven societies that celebrate individualism are bound by common values and a shared culture. According to Durkheim, the sacred induces individuals to become more morally- and community-minded than they otherwise might be, including those in seemingly secular societies. Simply put, seemingly secular beliefs, practices, and institutions can have a sacred quality and function to produce and bind a moral community, including elements of the nation and the state (Cavanaugh, 2011). Nationalism has strong elements of the sacred, amounting to a "civil religion." The highest expression of nationalism is "sacrificing" oneself for one's country, and those sacrifices are often memorialized and commemorated in sacred spaces. The possibility of the sacred in secularism is also evident, according to Durkheim, in the sacralization of the human. Simply put, the human can become sacred, "the object of a sort of religion ... a common faith" (Cladis 2008: xxviii; Durkheim (2008 (1949): 61). This process of sacralization is bound up with the growing belief in human rights and universal human dignity; "every single human being has increasingly, and with ever-increasing motivational and sensitizing effects, been viewed as sacred" (Joas 2013: 5). Every soul is sacred.

The gift of life is not only a blessing but also generates obligations to sacralized others (Joas 2013: 7). We must treat others with dignity. We have negative duties, as we must avoid action that produces unnecessary and foreseeable harm. We also have positive duties and an obligation to "prevent and alleviate human suffering wherever it may be found," "to protect life and health and to ensure respect for the human being," and to "promote mutual understanding, friendship, co-operation and lasting peace among all peoples" (Pictet 1979). It is through our actions that we not only demonstrate the humanity of others—we also enact and perform our own humanity. Respecting others' dignity, reducing unnecessary suffering, and creating the conditions for a full and vibrant life, are sacred tasks. And, as part of the sacred, it serves to create a moral community, limiting the otherwise corrosive effects of a society built on self-interest.

The state was part of this equation, viewed as having a responsibility for protecting and advancing the welfare of its population, not unlike the role of the shepherd to its flock. Foucault argued that this was part of the broader shift from a theological to a rational order. For Foucault, this concern with the security and the welfare of the population is bound with modern governance, which is the project to "secure the welfare of the population, the improvement of its condition, the increase of its wealth, longevity, health," and the betterment of its general well-being (Foucault 1991: 100). But this feature of governance has expanded beyond the state and its citizens to include the international community and humanity; there now exists a humanitarian governance, "the administration of human collectivities in the name of a higher moral principle that sees the preservation of life and the alleviation of suffering as the highest value of action" (Fassin 2007: 151).

The sacralization of humanity, the sense of obligation to distant others, and humanitarian governance became increasingly internationalized beginning in the twentieth century. The argument is not that somehow the logic of the states system became subsumed to the logic of humanity, that the pursuit of state security became subordinated to the defense of human security, or even that states were truly prepared to define their interests in ways that incorporated broader humanity concerns. Rather, the argument is that increasingly states and non-state actors were expected to take into account the effects of their policies on humanity and consider how they might reduce unnecessary suffering; that is, humanity became increasingly entangled with state sovereignty.

There has been a progression, or at least an extension, of areas of concern over the last century. The League of Nations established the first-ever international mechanisms to protect minorities and refugees. The Second World War made self-evident that states were not the only actors at risk of destruction. Accordingly, the United Nations' Charter pledged to represent the security of both states and peoples, even if the deck was stacked against the latter; the Geneva Conventions codified new protections for civilians during war; the Universal Declaration of Human Rights established a set of universal rights that transcended the state and that all states were supposed to respect; and the Genocide Convention declared that something must be done when designated groups of peoples are threatened with their annihilation.

The end of the Cold War raised the principle of humanity to a new level, not only because traditional power politics no longer occupied the center ring but also because of the growing understanding that more people were threatened, rather than protected, by their state. Although the international human rights movement had been picking up momentum since the 1970s (Moyn 2010), with the end of the Cold War the movement crossed into the express lane. The "new wars" of the 1990s made clear that civilian casualties were no longer an unfortunate incident of war but rather an intended effect. Consequently, humanitarian relief became increasingly in demand, and the aid system expanded dramatically (Barnett 2011). There was a growing recognition of the "two sovereignties": an external sovereignty that depended on the state's legitimacy in the community of states, and an internal sovereignty that depended on the state's legitimacy in its domestic community (Annan 1999). The addition of internal sovereignty was understood as also incorporating "human security," which had the effect of expanding what counted as a threat (Kaldor 2007). And there were sub-categories of humanity that deserved special attention because they had specialized needs or because their needs tended to be obscured when placed in the mass of humanity. Refugees had been a protected class since the First World War, but other displaced peoples, including internally-displaced peoples, became subjects of concern. Women's rights expanded into security and a broader women's peace and security agenda (Willett 2010). Children and the disabled also became the object of greater protection. Individuals were threatened not only by the gun but also by the environment and by public health pandemics such as HIV/AIDS and Ebola (Rushton and Youde 2014).

All this concern for humanity would have come to naught without the expansion of new forms of assistance by a metropolis of actors. International humanitarian law, criminal law, and human rights law coalesced into a "humanity's law" that was supposed to provide more protections for populations and punish the violators and perpetrators (Teital 2011). The International Criminal Court's universal jurisdiction included crimes of aggression, war crimes, and crimes against humanity. A growing coterie of international and non-state actors became armed with resources for the purposes of protecting humanity and improving the welfare of the world's most vulnerable populations. The UN system expanded dramatically and in new directions. Operating in the name of humanity, the population of nongovernmental organizations (NGOs) exploded. A stunning complex of actors became involved in "saving failed states" and post-conflict reconstruction, aiming to transform civil wars into civil societies. Peacekeeping and peacebuilding, despite their checkered track record, continued to be deployed in large numbers and maintain their ambitious agenda. Many of these initiatives had the backing of states, but not always. The laws of war expanded in ways that were not always to the liking of states; the Ottawa Treaty banned landmines, and other movements have set their sights on other kinds of weapons systems that fail to adequately discriminate between civilians and combatants. States, because of their sovereignty, are still expected to be the first line of defense, but when they either fail in their responsibilities, or are a source of threat, then their sovereignty can become suspended by the international community. However limited the possibility that states will follow through on these sanctions, it remains something that hangs over the heads of states.

If there is a greater concern with humanity than ever before, it owes not only, or even mainly, to a moral revolution. As in all transformations, a combustible mixture of material and ideational forces have created new structures of possibility. There is certainly some degree of sincerity on the part of some states and many organizations, as they genuinely want to reduce unnecessary suffering. Yet we should also maintain a healthy dose of cynicism, for many states and organizations have attempted to appropriate the misfortunes of others to advance their existing interests. There is growing fear that many of these distant threats might descend on the state's doorstep—the displaced person in Syria might become the refugee in Germany; the SARS virus in China might ignite a pandemic throughout the rest of the region; the collapse of the state might become the source material for extremist groups and terrorism. Most "humanitarian" interventions are hardly humanitarian but, rather, are motivated by more base interests. As in previous bursts of humanitarian concern, other material factors have also become important, such as growing economic interdependence, new transportation, and communication technologies that make it possible to know and do something more quickly than ever before, and growing wealth that provides new resources.

7.4 Conclusion: Explanatory and Emancipatory Theory

The body of this chapter has provided a taste of how constructivist International Relations theory might be employed to explain central features of the transformation of international security. Yet constructivist theory is more than explanatory and descriptive; its relationship to critical theory also injects it with a heavy dose of normative theory. Specifically, critical theory is one part explanatory and one part emancipatory theory. To unmask the hidden structures of power and oppression is not enough—it is equally important to ask what can be done to give individuals greater control over their lives. Such normative objectives also inform metrics of human progress. Progress in IR might be assessed in any number of ways—wealth, mastery over nature, democracy, freedom, and number of wars and deaths due to war—but a critical theory sensibility insists that we make human emancipation the touchpoint.

Constructivists have not established what kind of normative benchmark might be used to judge whether one outcome is superior to another, in terms of its emancipatory element or some other measure, but they are constantly implicitly and explicitly arguing that one outcome is superior to another on normative grounds (Price 2008). Although I do not know of a balance sheet by a constructivist that attempts to calculate whether international security has experienced progress (although on human rights see Sikkink 2017), there is a sense in which the internationalization and institutionalization of the human represents several giant steps in the right direction. The rising category of the "human," and its displacement or sharing of the stage with the state, is generally viewed as evidence of civilizing processes. Human rights, human security, human capabilities, humanitarianism, and virtually anything with the modifier "human," is almost always interpreted as a sign of progress. The same can be said about many of the institutional innovations that assert our global duty to alleviate suffering whenever possible and act in ways that do not do harm to others. The growth of NGOs, global civil society, and other kinds of non-state actors are almost always treated as a victory of sorts—in part because they are seen as representatives of the people and acting in the name of "humanity." Responsibility to protect is hailed as a moral breakthrough. And part of this global duty of care is that states and others in positions of power should be held accountable for actions that are intentionally or recklessly injurious to others. The categories of war crimes and crimes against humanity, now institutionalized in the International Criminal Court, are widely viewed as evidence that individuals should be held accountable for harms caused to peoples. The world now has in place a myriad of global institutions whose mandate is to enhance the security and welfare of individuals and vulnerable populations—indeed, there seems to be a different UN agency for every conceivable category of people and for every possible threat to their security. This might be evidence of progress. But it also could be evidence of a humanitarian "fig leaf." Do the very existence of the laws of war suggest moral progress—or do they represent new mechanisms that help to legitimate a system of war?

Humanity is constantly under threat. There is much talk about humanity, but does humanity really portend emancipation? Without endorsing Carl Schmitt's infamous saying that whoever evokes the name of humanity cheats, some of these developments that are taken as a mark of human progress, because they are assumed to be emancipatory, might represent new forms of domination. The thrust of an emancipatory ethos is that individuals have the ability to have some say over their lives, which includes the capabilities to enable them to make choices that affect their ability to live their lives as they define it. But to what extent can global institutions be trusted to reflect the wishes, desires, welfare, and security needs of local populations from which they are spatially (and often culturally) distant (Barnett 2017)?

These critiques of the potential excesses of global security have led to an interesting reconsideration of the state as a unit of protection. One of the pragmatic reasons for the development of global institutions was the belief that the state was unable to properly represent and protect the interests of its population. Given this shortcoming, other global actors were assigned (or, more accurately, assumed) a "responsibility to protect." And they frequently justified their new roles in the name of "humanity." Yet can and should they play that role? There are, in fact, various movements that see a properly constructed state as a better promoter of security, at least in the long run. These movements need not necessarily treat "humanity" as a threat, but the recent resurgence of nationalism and populism has certainly crowded out humanity. At the very least, the discourse of humanity only suggests that individuals and organizations will consider the welfare of non-members, not that they will necessarily do so.

References

Annan, Kofi. 1999. *Two Concepts of Sovereignty*. New York: United Nations.

Barnett, Michael. 2011. *Empire of Humanity: A History of Humanitarianism*. Ithaca, NY: Cornell University Press.

Barnett, Michael (ed.). 2017. *Paternalism Beyond Borders*. New York: Cambridge University Press.

Barnett, Michael and Raymond Duvall. 2005. Power in International Politics. *International Organization*, 59(1): 39–75.

Berger, Peter and Thomas Luckmann. 1966. *The Social Construction of Reality*. New York: Anchor Books.

Bially Mattern, Janice and Ayse Zarakol. 2016. Hierarchies in World Politics. *International Organization*, 70(3): 623–54.

Carpenter, R. Charli. 2003. "Women and Children First": Gender, Norms, and Humanitarian Evacuation in the Balkans 1991–95. *International Organization* 57(4): 661–94.

Cavanaugh, William. 2011. *Migrations of the Holy*. Grand Rapids, MI: Wm. B. Erdmanns.

Cladis, Mark. 2008. Introduction. In Emile Durkheim, *Elementary Forms of Religious Life*. New York: Oxford University Press.

Crawford, Neta. 2002. *Argument and Change in World Politics: Ethics, Decolonization, and Humanitarian Intervention*. Cambridge: Cambridge University Press.

Durkheim, Emile. 2008. *The Elementary Forms of Religious Life*. New York: Oxford.

Durkheim, Emile and Marcel Mauss. 1963. *Primitive Classification*. Chicago: University of Chicago Press.

Fassin, D. 2007. Humanitarianism: A Nongovernmental Government." In Michael Feher (ed.), *Nongovernmental Politics*, pp. 149–60. New York: Zone Books.

Fearon, J. and Wendt, A. 2002. Rationalism vs. Constructivism. In W. Carlneas, B. Simmons, and T. Risse (eds.), *Handbook of International Relations*. Thousand Oaks, CA: Sage.

Festa, Lynn. 2010. Humanity Without Feathers. *Humanity*, 1(1): 3–27.

Finnemore, M. 2004. *The Purpose of Intervention*. Ithaca, NY: Cornell University Press.
Finnemore, M. and Sikkink, K. 1999. International Norms and Political Change. In P. Katzenstein et al. (eds.), *Explorations and Controversies in World Politics*. Cambridge, MA: MIT Press.
Fioretos, Orfeo. 2011. Historical Institutionalism in International Relations. *International Organization*, 65(2): 367–99.
Foucault, M. 1991. Governmentality. In G. Burchell, C. Gordon, and P. Miller (eds.), *The Foucault Effect: Studies in Governmentality*, pp. 87–104. Chicago: University of Chicago Press.
Haskell, Thomas. 1985. Capitalism and the Origins of the Humanitarian Sensibility, Part 1. *Americal Historical Review*, 90: 339–61.
Joas, Hans. 2013. *The Sacredness of the Person: A New Genealogy of Human Rights*. Washington, DC: Georgetown University Press.
Kaldor, Mary. 2007. *Human Security*. Boston, MA: Polity Press.
Katzenstein, Peter (ed.), 1996. *The Culture of National Security*. New York: Columbia University Press.
Linklater, Andrew. 2011. *The Problem of Harm in World Politics: Theoretical Investigations*. New York: Cambridge University Press.
Linklater, Andrew. 2017. *Violence and Civilization in the Western States-System*. New York: Cambridge University Press.
McCarthy, Thomas. 2009. *Race, Empire, and the Idea of Human Development*. New York: Cambridge University Press.
Moyn, Samuel. 2010. *The Last Utopia*. Cambridge, MA: Harvard University Press.
Pictet, Jean. 1979. *The Fundamental Principles of the Red Cross*. Geneva: ICRC.
Price, Richard (ed.). 2008. *Moral Limit and Possibility in World Politics*. New York; Cambridge: Cambridge University Press.
Ruggie, John. 1988. What Makes the World Hang Together? Neo-utilitarianism and the Social Constructivist Challenge. *International Organization*, 52(4): 855–85.
Rushton, Simon and Jeremy Youde. 2014. *Routledge Handbook of Global Health Security*. Abingdon: Routledge.
Sikkink, Kathryn. 2017. *Evidence for Hope: Making Human Rights Work in the 21st Century*. Princeton, NJ: Princeton University Press.
Teitel, Ruti G. 2011. *Humanity's Law*. New York: Oxford University Press.
Weber, Max. 1949. *The Methodology of the Social Sciences*. New York: Free Press.
Wendt, Alexander. 1999. *A Social Theory of International Politics*. Cambridge: Cambridge University Press.
Willett, Susan. 2010. Introduction: Security Council Resolution 1325: Assessing the Impact on Women, Peace and Security. *International Peacekeeping*, 17(2): 142–58.
Wilson, Richard and Richard Brown. 2009. *Humanitarianism and Suffering*. New York: Cambridge University Press.

CHAPTER 8

LIBERAL APPROACHES

JOHN M. OWEN

A century ago, liberals wanted to overturn the existing global order. Today, they want to retain and extend it. Liberalism's conservatism is a tribute to its hard-won success over the past century. Visions once chimerical—of stable peace in Europe, a world free of formal empires, high economic interdependence among most states, low global military spending—were realized over the course of the twentieth century and have come to seem normal.

The global liberal order is built upon ideas that have come to be put into practice as *institutions*, or established, broadly recognized rules or ways of conducting social interaction. These ideas derived from liberal theory and scholarship over the centuries, and indeed an emphasis on institutions is what diverse liberal social-scientific approaches to international security have in common. Some liberal scholars stress domestic institutions, such as constitutionalism, democracy, and capitalism.[1] Others stress international institutions that regulate economic transactions, human rights, weapons proliferation, and other activities. The broad liberal tradition in International Relations recognizes both levels of analysis, and indeed is open to endogeneity between the two—for example that democracies trade more with one another and that the resulting higher national income reinforces democracy (Russett and Oneal 2001).

Liberals generally see institutions as causes. They are not the only causes of security outcomes, or even always the chief ones. Institutions do not erase material power or its effects. But they do mediate between power and outcomes. Liberal approaches to international security imply the counterfactual: add, remove, or alter institutions, and states will be more or less secure, have more or fewer wars, fight more or less destructively. Thus, when liberals think about the future of international security, they think not only of shifts in material power but also of change and continuity in domestic and international institutions. The remarkable material gains of China since the 1980s are bound to be consequential, but for liberals China's domestic institutions are likewise crucial. What China does with its increasing power, including how far it abides by or tries to change international institutions, turns in part on whether it remains a Market-Leninist state or becomes a multi-party democracy.

8.1 Liberalism and Security

In (IR) scholarship, liberalism often is thought to be uneasy with security or high politics, more at home with political economy or low politics. In fact, security always has been a central concern of liberal political theory. The security that concerns liberalism, however, is first that of the *individual*, particularly his or her person and property. National and international security are instrumental to individual security (Owen 2010b). Of course, liberalism is also concerned with the individual's liberty, but liberals argue that, under the right institutions, liberty and security complement rather than compete with one another. Liberals differ as to what those institutions are, but one prominent account, seen in the late eighteenth-century thinkers James Madison (2003: 319) and Immanuel Kant (1983: 126), argues for institutions that balance self-interested actors.

8.1.1 Institutions

Social scientists tell a number of stories about institutions. Sociologists take a top-down or structural approach, in which institutions open certain options for agents and close others (Powell and DiMaggio 2012). Economists take a bottom-up approach, in which agents construct and use institutions to lower transaction costs and make interaction more efficient (Coase 1960). Liberalism's approach is closer to that of the economists. Individuals build institutions to serve their preferences. Without institutions, IR would be disordered and rife with inefficiencies contradicting the interests of powerful and weak alike. In some times and places institutions are imposed by the powerful upon the weak, and produce fear and conflict; thus the Athenians' aphorism in Thucydides' famous Melian Dialogue: "the strong do what they can and the weak suffer what they must" (Thucydides 1998: 352). In other times and places institutions are freely agreed upon by all and produce trust and cooperation. States themselves are complexes of institutions, some nested in others, some informal and evolving. Not the unitary rational actors envisaged by realism, states are instead arenas of competition among societal actors, each with different utility functions. Who wins the competition affects the state's foreign policy, and so domestic institutions matter a great deal.[2] States come in two ideal types. Constitutional or liberal regimes are mutually agreed upon by freely-choosing individuals and allowing those individuals' preferences to influence foreign policy; they provide individual security, liberty, prosperity. Despotic or authoritarian regimes are imposed from above, block citizen influence on foreign policy, and produce insecurity, servitude, and poverty.

An early division among liberal thinkers concerned whether liberal institutions scale up to the international level—whether sovereign liberal states can build rules and practices that safeguard the security and liberty of each. Hobbes and Rousseau say no, and are categorized as realists. Locke leaves room for more international cooperation in the state of nature. Kant goes further and argues that liberal international institutional architecture is actually inevitable, but only among republics, that is, states that separate the legislative from the executive power. Kant's influence endures, both for the comprehensiveness of his vision and his prediction of the democratic peace, or the absence of war among liberal democracies (Doyle 1983; Russett 1994; Owen 1997; Cederman and Gleditsch 2004). Recently, Deudney (2008) has pushed the logic further and argued that today's destructive technologies will drive humanity toward a global federation.

Institutional complexes, then, span the international and domestic realms. Here is where we see most starkly that institutions are inescapable but that not all institutions are the same. Not every state is Bismarck's Germany, nor are all international systems like that of Europe in the late nineteenth century. Some states are more like the Third Reich, some systems more like the nightmare of Europe 1939–45. Some states are more like today's Federal Republic of Germany, some systems like today's European Union. The quality of interaction among liberal states will be different from that among nonliberal states, or that between liberal and nonliberal states. Liberal states build among themselves what each has within its borders: institutions that share information, reduce transaction costs, build trust, and encourage agents to invest in relationships for mutual gain. Nonliberal states have less inclination or ability to build and remain in such relationships, because they are constitutionally prone to arbitrariness (Gaubatz 1996; Martin 2000; Lipson 2013). Liberal states show little sign of trying to counter-balance America's unprecedented global military dominance; nonliberal states such as Russia and China have taken such steps, albeit gingerly (Owen 2000/2001).

Skeptics argue that institutions are consequences, not causes: states that want to cooperate for reasons of interest do so, and institutions are simply the result of their cooperation (Mearsheimer 1994). Liberalism can grant a selection effect: it is liberal democracies that tend to form, remain in, and comply with liberal international institutions. But those same international institutions feed back into their member states and strengthen their domestic institutions and preferences. Were the particular rules of international institutions inconsequential, non-democracies would not be so wary of liberal institutions, nor would democracies spend so many resources trying to influence them (Koremenos et al. 2001).

8.1.2 Liberalism and Its Alternatives

Liberalism's differences with realism are straightforward. Realism insists that the human race is trapped in a world where might makes right and insecurity is pervasive and perpetual. The best that can be achieved is a stable distribution of power (be it bipolar, multipolar, or unipolar), and attempts to break out of this system will only make matters worse. Liberalism finds those claims excessively pessimistic, and insists that some types of institutions can and do mitigate the problems described by realism. Some versions of liberalism contain an implicit teleology, in which the human race is destined to pull itself out of the dangerous state of nature, if only gradually. Other versions simply maintain that it is possible for people to make the world more or less peaceful, depending on who has power, what their preferences are, and how capable they are of learning. What liberals agree on is that institutions make the difference.

Liberalism and realism also differ as to the efficacy of liberal democracy in international politics. When it comes to navigating the perils of diplomacy, traditional realism regards liberal democracies as deficient because they constrain executive action by popular will and law (Kennan 1951; Lippmann 1997; Tocqueville 2002: 217–18). Structural realists, by contrast, abstract from domestic regime type, implying that liberal-democratic institutions are inconsequential. Recent liberal scholarship argues that liberal states enjoy security advantages in the international system. They do not fight one another (see the earlier reference to Kant), and tend to win the wars they do fight—either because they fight better or because they are wiser about which wars to fight (Lake 1992; Reiter and Stam 2002). Their superior ability to reveal information about their capabilities and preferences (Fearon 1994; Schultz 2001) allows them to focus on fewer potential enemies. Public choice literature adds that the right institutions give individuals incentives to innovate, invent new technologies, increase productivity, and create opportunities for others in their societies; those institutions are generally liberal-democratic ones (Rosenberg and Birdzell 2008; Acemoglu and Robinson 2012).

Liberalism stands in a different relation to constructivism. The two paradigms have in common an emphasis on norms and ideas and greater hope in long-term peace and cooperation than does realism. But liberalism, like modern realism, is a rationalist theory. The agents for liberalism are individuals rather than states, but liberalism is methodologically individualist and takes actors' preferences as exogenous. Social interaction reduces to bargaining over goods. Institutions themselves are a product of bargaining. Constructivism, by contrast, is holistic, taking preferences to be endogenous to or derived from social interaction; institutions, for constructivists, structure preferences and bargaining (Wendt 1992; Fearon and Wendt 2002). Although liberal scholarship allows for states' preferences to change through interaction—how else to think about the change from the Third Reich to the Federal Republic of Germany?—in its treatment of individuals, liberalism is necessarily rationalist.

Furthermore, whereas constructivism sees norms as socially constructed, liberalism sees at least norms concerning the good life as given or natural. For liberals, human beings value individual security and liberty more highly than other goods, such as fame, religious devotion, art, or even power. When states do not achieve international cooperation, liberalism regards it as a puzzle (and looks to institutions for the solution). Constructivism, at least not its radical form, denies human nature as such, positing instead that identities and desires are plastic and contingent.

8.2 Liberalism, Institutions, and the Future of International Security

What do liberal approaches imply about the future of international security? Liberalism directs our attention to change and continuity in institutions both domestic and international. Change the institutions, and the world may come to resemble the war of all against all depicted by realism. Maintain, broaden, and deepen extant liberal-democratic institutions, and the current order should persist. Change and continuity matter at both the domestic and international levels, because the two levels influence each other.

What changes institutions, then? Institutions are path-dependent, inasmuch as they tend to pay increasing returns to their members and the opportunity costs of defecting from them tend to rise over time (Ikenberry 2001). So stability is built into any institutional complex. Yet, institutions change. Some scholars argue for gradual evolution: a set of interacting agents find that some new problem is not adequately addressed by existing institutions; agents formulate various ideas for addressing the problem; they try out some of these ideas; the winning ideas—those that appear to powerful actors best at addressing the problem, or most consistent with the existing matrix of institutions and habits—become institutionalized (Hodgson 2002). Others argue for abrupt change: a crisis emerges, disrupts normal patterns of interaction, and presses or enables agents to build new institutions (Legro 2005). For the sake of simplicity, I only consider the latter source of change. International history suggests two general types of crisis that can alter institutions:

1. Power shifts, e.g., triggered by major-power wars such as the Napoleonic Wars or the World Wars of the twentieth century (Ikenberry 2001; Gunitsky 2014).
2. Sustained economic crises, such as in the 1870s (which wrecked the emergent norm of free trade in Europe) and the 1930s (which did the same and also helped fascism supplant liberal democracy) (Findlay and O'Rourke 2007).

One type of power shift I consider is "traditional," a textbook case of power transition: the rise of China and concomitant relative decline of the United States. The second type is non-traditional: transnational terrorism, or the continuing ability of non-state actors to threaten the security of dozens of states. I also consider a type of economic distress, one less dramatic than that of the 1930s but possibly as consequential: the continuing stagnation of the native working classes in most Western countries.

8.2.1 Global Power Shifts

Liberalism recognizes that in an anarchical international system, differences in states' power to hurt and conquer other states is crucial. But the purposes to which states put their power matter as well, and domestic and international institutions directly affect those purposes. Hence the spectacular economic growth of China since the 1980s is bound to be consequential for international security not simply because Beijing can convert its new wealth to military power, but because the country's persistent Leninist political system increases the probability that it will put its power to purposes contrary to those of the United States. America remains the world's only military superpower and doubtless will do for some time to come (Brooks and Wohlforth 2008), but by definition it is declining in material terms relative to China.

Global power shifts advanced the liberal world order in the twentieth century. The Second World War devolved power from Western Europe to the United States and the Soviet Union; each superpower built an international order that competed against that of the other (Lake 1996). In Western Europe and Japan, the United States simultaneously promoted liberal democracy within states (Owen 2010a) and spun a cobweb of international rules regulating relations among states (Ikenberry 2012). US allies relinquished their empires in exchange for American guarantees of security and stable economic growth. The United States protected not only the territorial integrity of these states but also their liberal-democratic regimes. The US-sponsored order was far more coercive in poor countries and regions; there, where the Soviets were actively competing for elite and mass loyalty, Washington did not trust democrats to be liberal and anti-Soviet, and supported authoritarians who stayed out of the Soviet camp and opened themselves to trade and investment (Poznansky 2015). As the USSR began to liberalize itself in the late 1980s, more and more Third World elites began to sour on socialism and anti-Americanism and to embrace the liberal international order (Owen and Poznansky 2014). Thus the globalization of the 1990s.

China accepted many of the economic aspects of the liberal institutional order, and grew at a spectacular rate after the 1970s. Measured in constant US dollars, the Chinese economy is on track to surpass the American economy sometime in the next two decades (World Bank 2016). In both international trade and finance, China already is a global player: it is the world's biggest exporter (World Trade Organization 2016), and in 2015 launched the Asian Infrastructure Investment Bank (AIIB) as an alternative to older US- and Europe-dominated international financial institutions. China's military spending in 2014 was 1.9 percent of its GDP, compared to 3.5 percent of GDP for the United States. China's ruling Communist Party (CCP) does not seem interested in building the country into a global military superpower. Instead, it appears most concerned to secure the country's access to raw materials, assert what it sees as China's rights in the East and South China seas, and challenge long-standing US military and political predominance there.

China is no liberal democracy. The CCP clearly is determined to maintain its monopoly on political power, and under Chairman (and Chinese President) Xi Jinping has identified liberal democracy as a serious ideological threat emanating from the West.

The rise of Market-Leninist China is important for several reasons. First, the CCP could try to alter, directly or indirectly, some of the liberal characteristics of the global complex of institutions that the West has underwritten for decades. China has prospered under the current complex, and one could ask why the CCP would seek to change a system under which it is winning. But it is clear that the Chinese leadership believe international institutions to be biased in a liberal direction and suspect that the West uses them to contain China. Human rights institutions are the most obvious case. China's representatives on the UN Human Rights Council have promoted "universality," or the avoidance of singling out individual countries, and also rules giving heavy agenda influence to the state under review (Nathan 2015: 164–7). The China-sponsored AIIB attaches fewer conditions to loans than the Western-dominated International Monetary Fund (IMF) and World Bank.

Second, China's ongoing success as an authoritarian capitalist state could lead elites in other states in Asia and beyond to conclude that the "China Model" is viable or even superior to liberal democracy (Halper 2010). A number of studies find that the intermittent but significant growth in the number of democracies over the past centuries is partly a result of international diffusion (Brinks and Coppedge 2006). Authoritarianism spreads as well (Ambrosio 2010; Gunitsky 2017). The rise of China could roll back liberal democracy in East Asia and elsewhere. State elites could conclude that the China Model offers the quickest and best route to economic growth. They also could be attracted to the China Model simply because of China's prestige.

Thus two vital questions liberalism will ask about international security in the coming years are: Will China continue to rise? And, will it liberalize by allowing opposition parties and meaningful political competition on the state and national level?

8.2.2 Terrorism

The rise of transnational terrorism since 2001 constitutes a different kind of global power shift. The so-called Islamic State, al-Qaeda, and other jihadist entities are not states, and certainly have far less power than the United States, France, India, and others. But they do have what Thomas Schelling called the "power to hurt," that is, to damage countries' populations and property without defeating them on the battlefield (Schelling 1966). Hence these networks have the power to terrorize populations and topple governments. An al-Qaeda attack in Madrid in 2004 almost certainly helped doom the Spanish government of José María Aznar. Each government understands that if it is judged by its constituents to have failed to stop a terrorist attack, it may be voted out of office. Hence the expensive security measures in so many countries today, from heightened airport security to greater monitoring of private communication to violations of civil liberties; and thus two long wars led by the United States (Afghanistan and Iraq). Transnational terrorists can and do impose enormous costs on rich, powerful states.[3]

Discontent with Western domination has existed as long as Western countries have had empires. Only recently has that discontent been mobilized and channeled into terrorist networks that penetrate the Western countries themselves. This power shift is heavily driven by technological change: cheap communication and international travel make it possible for militant leaders to disseminate their messages widely, recruit and train, and plant cells virtually anywhere. Jihadist terrorism is also not likely to disappear any time soon, because its causes are robust. The deep cause is a prolonged legitimacy crisis in many Muslim-majority countries, particularly in North Africa, the Middle East, and Central and South Asia over the right way to order society. On one level, there are two sides, Islamists and secularists. Within the Islamist camp are a number of competitors—Sunni *versus* Shia, pro- *versus* anti-Western—who show no sign of giving up (Owen 2015).

Sharia is not going to become the law of the land in Western countries. Rather, the threat to liberal institutions from ongoing jihadist terrorism comes from efforts by threatened liberal democracies to defend themselves. Terrorists' use of cyberspace to communicate, recruit, spy, and move money has provoked already capable Western intelligence agencies to develop new capabilities and norms. In the United States since September 2001 the federal government has assumed new powers, including to gather meta-data on all telephone calls; to torture terrorism suspects; to kill US citizens suspected of terrorism without due process; and to compile, by opaque procedures and without appeal, lists of Americans who are prohibited from flying. Some of these powers have been rescinded or modified. But a trade-off familiar to liberal democracies remains real: in times of threat, a liberal-democratic government is under great pressure to shed the institutional constraints that make it what it is—transparent, predictable, accountable, and legitimate. Some officials or departments in the government will be tempted to exploit the insecurity to grab more power than is warranted (Eddington 2015). Indeed, for liberal IR theory, long-term national and international security depend on liberal-democratic institutions within states. An additional trade-off appears, then, between short-term security (served by increasing monitoring and intrusiveness by police and intelligence) and long-term security (served by decentralizing power). If the jihadist threat is not ended or contained, the international liberal order could weaken.

8.2.3 Sustained Economic Stagnation in the West

The third potential threat to liberal institutions, not entirely separable from the first two, emanates from within liberal democracies themselves. It is a loss of confidence among large segments of their publics in the liberal international order. Majorities continue to support liberal democracy *within* their countries, although populist-nationalist political parties and candidates have been rising and attracting anti-democratic extremists. The chief threat is to the *international* side of liberalism: the long-standing aspiration to free movement of goods, capital, and labor.

As discussed in Section 8.2.1, globalization is a liberal project. It accelerates technological and managerial innovation and raises aggregate wealth. It may undermine itself, however, inasmuch as economic openness always creates losers as well as winners. Workers in economic sectors in which their country is at a comparative disadvantage lose their jobs and find their lives disrupted. Losers from globalization will naturally try to reverse it; thus economists' theory of endogenous protectionism, in which international trade is self-undermining (Treffler 1993). Insofar as their governments do not adequately address their grievances, globalization's losers will provide opportunities for new political movements and parties. In the second decade of the twenty-first century, to the surprise of many political analysts, the international liberal order appears weak in its heartlands of Europe and North America. In the United States in 2016, one of the two major parties nominated a populist who seemed determined to end America's role as underwriter of the global liberal order. In Europe, a majority of voters in the United Kingdom voted to withdraw their country from the EU, while populist parties showed greater strength in Continental Europe than at any time since the 1930s.

Some analysts attribute the rise of populist nationalism to the distribution of gains and losses from globalization. The losers are working-class natives with falling prospects for higher paying jobs and stable careers for themselves and their offspring. In the United States, supporters of Donald Trump in the Republican state primary elections tended to be white and to lack a university education. Between 1990 and 2013 the employment rate of this population group fell from 76 percent to 68 percent. These also are the people who believe that neither political party pays them any attention (Thompson 2016).[4] Economist Branko Milanovic finds that the global "upper middle class"—corresponding to the working and middle classes in rich countries—is the only segment of society that has lost from the freer movement of goods, labor, and capital since the 1980s. Globalization has lifted millions of people out of poverty, but those between the 70th and 95th percentiles of wealth in Figure 8.1 (reproduced from Milanovic n.d.) might be less inclined than those above the 95th percentile to celebrate.

Automation, resulting from liberalism's attachment to technological innovation, also bears some blame for the shape of this curve (Brynjolfsson and McAfee 2011). Yet it is a mistake to reduce the political turmoil of the 2010s to economics. Liberal internationalism is also a cultural phenomenon (Hunter and Yates 2002): it presses a kind of

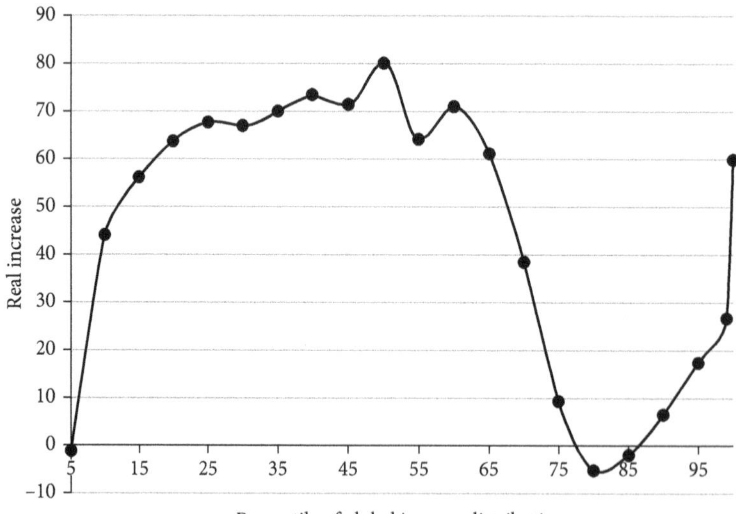

FIGURE 8.1 Change in real income between 1988 and 2008 at various percentiles of global income distribution (calculated in 2005 international dollars)

Note: The vertical axis shows the percentage change in real income, measured in constant international dollars. The horizontal axis shows the percentile position in the global income distribution. The percentile positions run from 5 to 95, in increments of five, while the top 5% are divide into two groups: the top 1% and those between the 95th and 99th percentiles.

rootlessness upon people and societies; it either erases or denigrates and trivializes local differences and traditions, reducing them to tastes in food, music, and art that are then mashed together and recombined. The culture of globalization is well-suited to cosmopolitan elites—professionals in banking, business, law, academia, foundations, and so on—but not to those who, by necessity or choice, stay in one place. The latter know well enough that globalizers tend to assume a moral authority and to look down on their more rooted counterparts as quaint at best and barriers to progress at worst.

International liberalism always has brought these stresses, but some analysts believe the wealthy liberal countries are near a collective tipping point. Perhaps one immediate cause is the waves of immigration that hit the United States (from Latin America) and Western Europe (from the Southwest Asia, North Africa, and Eastern Europe) in recent years. The populist-nationalists are in full-throated opposition to this immigration and appeal to a more ethnically homogeneous past. Another immediate cause, perhaps, was the renewal of jihadist terrorism in 2015–16, with murderous attacks in Paris, Brussels, California, and Florida. Those attacks, coupled with accelerated immigration from the Middle East, aggravated the sense many had of feckless and unaccountable governing elites

In any case, rising political opposition to globalization in its countries of origin bears watching. No doubt remedies are available, and the rejiggering of political coalitions may yield creativity. Still, liberal theory itself says that democracy is a social contract; if enough individuals believe the contract has been violated, they may revoke it and seek a new one. If a return to Hitler's Europe is highly unlikely, a return to Bismarck's—with more nationalism and attention to relative gains—is more imaginable than it was in the 1990s.

8.3 The Future of Liberal Approaches

What of the future of liberal scholarship about security? Liberalism has made enormous contributions to the study of security by treating institutions not as a mere consequence of cooperation, but as causes of it. The literatures on democratic peace, economic interdependence, and international institutions and cooperation fall squarely in the liberal tradition: all argue that institutions are consequential and imply that people and governments have real choices.

The liberal paradigm has weaknesses. Like any rationalist tradition, it has difficulty dealing with downward causation from institutions; it cannot adopt constructivism's holism. This means that liberalism's version of hegemony must be limited to such phenomena as direct coercion and paying for international public goods (such as keeping open global commons such as sea and air routes and the Internet); liberalism shies away from what Steven Lukes calls the second and third faces of power (the power to set agendas and to mold others' preferences) (Lukes 1974). It is prone to dismiss critiques of liberal hegemony from the left and the right (Schmitt 2008).

Within its limits, however, liberal IR scholarship has much to contribute over the coming years to the academic study of security. An ongoing trend to complicate Kant's simple dichotomy by explicating distinctions among both liberal and nonliberal institutions should continue. A descent from high theory reveals a staggering variety of institutional complexes around the world. Some countries that formally qualify as liberal-democratic could come up short in various ways, and others that might not qualify as liberal-democratic could nonetheless exhibit some of the properties associated with liberalism. Elman (2000) argues that presidential and parliamentary democracies are different. Potter and Baum (2015) argue that democracies with more opposition parties tend to be more restrained from using force. Dafoe and Weiss (2015) argue that nondemocratic governments also incur audience costs when they make threats; if so, then one putative advantage of liberal democracies partly disappears. Narang and Talmadge (2017) argue that civil–military relations differ across both democracies and nondemocracies, with consequences for international security.

More important still, liberal approaches to security also ought to focus more on explaining changes in institutions—domestic, international, or both. First, liberal scholars should try to endogenize the various types of event that can trigger institutional change. Liberal internationalism is bound to create losers, and those losers are bound to try to repay internationalism by ending it. We can extend the endogeneity question to the tectonic global power shift to China. After all, the CCP implemented its semi-liberalizing reforms to make China a wealthy and secure country, and succeeded beyond anyone's expectations. Had China remained mired in Maoism, it would be difficult to see the power shift we are seeing and the resulting challenge to liberal internationalism. Harrison and Mitchell (2013) argue that the predominance of the West is under threat, but not liberal internationalism itself; rather, rising powers will carry on the system under which they rose.

Second, although most liberal scholars would recognize a partial congruence between domestic and international institutions—liberal democracies participate in more liberal international institutions—we know too little about this congruence. What is it about liberal states that render them a better fit for liberal internationalism? By what mechanisms do liberal international institutions strengthen democracy within countries? How do these mechanisms break down? Although some institutional complexes, such as the EU (European Union) and NATO (the North Atlantic Treaty Organization), require that new members be liberal democracies, the same clearly is not true of many other liberal international institutions. Most countries, including some prominent nondemocratic ones such as China, Russia, and Saudi Arabia, are members of the WTO (World Trade Organization). Greece and Turkey were members of NATO while going through authoritarian periods during the Cold War (and in the 2010s Turkey descended again into authoritarianism). Will the liberal international complex of institutions pull China into political reform? That has been the long-term hope of liberals, and South Korea, Taiwan, and Chile were all authoritarian countries that liberalized as they participated in the global economy. On the other hand, will the CCP hang on to power and pull international institutions in its direction?

Third, and related, liberal scholarship should explore more fully and rigorously evolutionary logic to explain change and continuity. Evolution lurks in the shadows of much work on institutions. Although some liberal scholarship may tell a stylized story of rational agents designing institutions to solve collective problems, most scholarship in fact points to such mechanisms as competition, learning, and copying. In other words, institutions emerge and spread by an evolutionary process, in which the fittest institutions survive and unfit ones die away. Agents scour the world for information about which policies and institutions work best and either copy those that do or, if they find "best practices" threatening, build defenses against them. Some studies of institutional and normative change are explicitly evolutionary (Kahler 1995; Florini 1996). Tang (2013) argues that the world has evolved from an offensive-realist to a defensive-realist one.

Evolutionary logic is more realistic than standard rationalism, inasmuch as it assumes that agents' rationality is bounded (Simon 1982). Agents have limited resources, including information, cognitive ability, and time. Bounded rationality means that institutions may be imperfectly copied, sub-optimal, and produce unintended consequences. Thus evolution need not imply any teleology or progress. Evolution also presumes political competition within and among states, and hence eludes a perennial realist charge of utopianism. It is the elites' need for security that drives them to look for information about which institutions work best and to imitate success. Nor need evolutionary logic imply that states are selected out of the international system. States do die (Fazal 2011), but much more typically they adapt; it is policies and institutions that die.

Finally, evolution does not necessarily exclude differences in power and interest. In biology, evolutionary theory has come to recognize the ability of agents to shape their environments and thereby alter which phenotypes (traits) are selected for. Beavers build dams to solve local problems (to increase food supply and protect themselves from predators), but dams in turn select for beavers who know how to build them. Organisms and environment co-evolve (Lewontin 2001; Odling-Smee et al. 2003). Just so, leaders of powerful states may shape their social and material environments in ways that select for and against particular institutions. The United States has co-evolved with the international system by building liberal internationalism; China and other rising powers may attempt to do the same.

An explicit and rigorous evolutionary approach would focus scholars' attention on mechanisms of change and help advance our ability to address questions such as the effects of the rise of China on liberal internationalism and vice versa; the sources and regional consequences of Russia's descent back into authoritarianism; the effects of US relative decline on democracy and liberal internationalism; and the persistence of authoritarianism in the Middle East and its consequences for security in the region. For liberals, these questions about the links between domestic and international institutions are questions about security—the security of the international community, nations, and the individuals that compose them. Domestic and international institutions clearly have evolved and will continue to do so. So should liberal approaches to international security.

Notes

1. One highly prominent account reduces liberal IR theory to the analytical priority of domestically generated preferences over international structures and interaction (Moravcsik 1997). Clearly such preferences are important to liberalism, but the broad liberal tradition, traceable at least to Kant, stresses the centrality of institutions within and among states.
2. The interwar debate between the realist Carl Schmitt and the liberal Harold Laski continues to reward today's reader. See Schmitt (2008).
3. Neta Crawford (2014) estimates that, as of 2014, the War on Terror cost the United States $4.4 trillion (including wars and homeland security). Notwithstanding that Iraq had nothing to do with the 9/11 attacks, those attacks clearly made the war more likely; see e.g. Woodward (2004); Packer (2005).
4. For deeper treatments of this group see Murray (2012); Putnam (2015).

References

Acemoglu, D. and J. Robinson. 2012. *Why Nations Fail: The Origins of Power, Prosperity, and Poverty*. London: Profile Books.

Ambrosio, T., 2010. Constructing a Framework of Authoritarian Diffusion: Concepts, Dynamics, and Future Research. *International Studies Perspectives*, 11(4): 375–92.

Brinks, D. and M. Coppedge. 2006. Diffusion is No Illusion: Neighbor Emulation in the Third Wave of Democracy. *Comparative Political Studies*, 39(4): 463–89.

Brooks, S. G. and W. C. Wohlforth. 2008. *World Out of Balance: International Relations and the Challenge of American Primacy*. Princeton, NJ: Princeton University Press.

Brynjolfsson, E. and A. McAfee. 2011. *Race against the Machine*. Digital Frontier Publishing.

Cederman, L. E. and K. S. Gleditsch. 2004. Conquest and Regime Change: An Evolutionary Model of the Spread of Democracy and Peace. *International Studies Quarterly*, 48(3): 603–29.

Chow, D. C. K. 2016. Why China Established the Asia Infrastructure Investment Bank. *Ohio State Public Law Working Paper* 333. *Available at:* http://papers.ssrn.com/sol3/papers.cfm?abstract_id=2737888, accessed April 15. 2016.

Coase, R. H. 1960. The Problem of Social Cost. In *Classic Papers in Natural Resource Economics*, pp. 87–137. Basingstoke: Palgrave Macmillan.

Crawford, N. 2014. U.S. Costs of Wars through 2014: $4.4 Trillion and Counting. Typescript, Boston University. *Available at:* http://watson.brown.edu/costsofwar/files/cow/imce/figures/2014/Costs%20of%20War%20Summary%20Crawford%20June%202014.pdf, accessed June 24, 2016.

Dafoe, A. and J. C. Weiss. 2015. Authoritarian Audiences in International Crises: A Real-History Survey-Experiment of Diversionary Incentives and Audience Costs in China. Typescript, Yale University.

Deudney, D. 2008. *Bounding Power: Republican Security Theory from the Polis to the Global Village*. Princeton, NJ: Princeton University Press.

Doyle, M. W. 1983. Kant, Liberal Legacies, and Foreign Affairs, Part I. *Philosophy & Public Affairs*, 12(3): 205–35.

Eddington, P. 2015. The Patriot Act Is Not Fit for Purpose. Nor Is Its Replacement. *Newsweek* (June 1, 2015). *Available at:* http://www.newsweek.com/patriot-act-not-fit-purpose-nor-its-replacement-337970, accessed July 5, 2016.

Elman, M. F. 2000. Unpacking Democracy: Presidentialism, Parliamentarism, and Theories of Democratic Peace. *Security Studies*, 9(4): 91–126.

Fazal, T. M. 2011. *State Death: The Politics and Geography of Conquest, Occupation, and Annexation*. Princeton, NJ: Princeton University Press.

Fearon, J. D. 1994. Domestic Political Audiences and the Escalation of International Disputes. *American Political Science Review*, 88(3): 577–92.

Fearon, J. and A. Wendt. 2002. Rationalism v. Constructivism: A Skeptical View. In W. Carlneas, B. Simmons, and T. Risse (eds.), *Handbook of International Relations*, pp. 52–72. Thousand Oaks, CA: Sage

Findlay, R. and K. H. O'Rourke. 2007. *Power and Plenty: Trade, War, and the World Economy in the Second Millennium* (Vol. 51). Princeton, NJ: Princeton University Press.

Florini, A. 1996. The Evolution of International Norms. *International Studies Quarterly*, 40(3): 363–89.

Gaubatz, K. T. 1996. Democratic States and Commitment in International Relations. *International Organization*, 50(1): 109–39.

General Office, Central Committee of the Communist Party of China, 2013. Document No. 9. Beijing. *Available at:* https://www.chinafile.com/document-9-chinafile-translation, accessed June 22, 2016.

Gunitsky, S. 2014. From Shocks to Waves: Hegemonic Transitions and Democratization in the Twentieth Century. *International Organization*, 68(3): 561–97.

Gunitsky, S. 2017. *Aftershocks: Great Powers and Domestic Reforms in the Twentieth Century*. Princeton, NJ: Princeton University Press.

Halper, S. 2010. *The Beijing Consensus: How China's Authoritarian Model Will Dominate the Twenty-First Century*. New York: Basic Books.

Harrison, E. and S. M. Mitchell. 2013. *The Triumph of Democracy and the Eclipse of the West*. Basingstoke: Palgrave Macmillan.

Hodgson, G. M. 2002. The Evolution of Institutions: An Agenda for Future Theoretical Research. *Constitutional Political Economy*, 13(2): 111–27.

Hunter, J. D. and J. Yates. 2002. In the Vanguard of Globalization: The World of American Globalizers. In P. L. Berger and S. P. Huntington (eds.), *Many Globalizations: Cultural Diversity in the Contemporary World*, pp. 323–57. Oxford: Oxford University Press.

Ikenberry, G. J. 2001. *After victory: Institutions, Strategic Restraint, and the Rebuilding of Order after Major Wars*. Princeton, NJ: Princeton University Press.

Ikenberry, G. J. 2012. *Liberal Leviathan: The Origins, Crisis, and Transformation of the American World Order*. Princeton, NJ: Princeton University Press.

Kahler, M. 1995. *International Institutions and the Political Economy of Integration*. Washington, CD: Brookings Institution Press.

Kant, I. 1983. To Perpetual Peace, a Philosophical Sketch. In I. Kant, *Perpetual Peace and Other Essays*, ed. Ted Humphrey. Indianapolis: Hackett (first published 1795).

Kennan, G. F. 1951. *American Diplomacy*. Chicago: University of Chicago Press.

Koremenos, B., Lipson, C. and Snidal, D. 2001. The Rational Design of International Institutions. *International Organization*, 55(4): 761–99.

Lake, D. A. 1992. Powerful Pacifists: Democratic States and War. *American Political Science Review*, 86(1): 24–37.

Lake, D. A. 1996. Anarchy, Hierarchy, and the Variety of International Relations. *International Organization*, 50(1): 1–33.

Legro, J. W. 2005. *Rethinking the World: Great Power Strategies and International Order*. Ithaca, NY: Cornell University Press.

Lewontin, R. C. 2001. *The Triple Helix: Gene, Organism, and Environment*. Cambridge, MA: Harvard University Press.

Lippmann, W. 1997 (1922). *Public Opinion*. New York: Free Press.

Lipson, C. 2013. *Reliable Partners: How Democracies Have Made a Separate Peace*. Princeton, NJ: Princeton University Press.

Lukes, S. 1974. *Power: A Radical View*. London: Macmillan.

Madison, J. 2003. Federalist No. 51. In Alexander Hamilton, John Jay, and James Madison, *The Federalist*. Signet (first published 1788).

Martin, L. 2000. *Democratic Commitments: Legislatures and International Cooperation*. Princeton, NJ: Princeton University Press.

Mearsheimer, J. J. 1994. The False Promise of International Institutions. *International Security*, 19(3): 5–49.

Milanovic, B. n.d. Global Income Inequality by the Numbers: In History and Now. Typescript. Washington, DC: World Bank.

Moravcsik, A. 1997. Taking Preferences Seriously: A Liberal Theory of International Politics. *International Organization*, 51(4): 513–53.

Murray, C. 2012. *Coming Apart: The State of White America, 1960–2010*. Crown Forum.

Narang, V. and C. Talmadge. 2017. Civil–Military Pathologies and Defeat in War: Tests Using New Data. *Journal of Conflict Resolution*, forthcoming.

Nathan, A. J. 2015. China's Challenge. *Journal of Democracy*, 26(1): 164–7.

Odling-Smee, F. J., K. N. Laland, and M. W. Feldman 2003. *Niche Construction: The Neglected Process in Evolution* (No. 37). Princeton, NJ: Princeton University Press.

Owen, J. M. 1997. *Liberal Peace, Liberal War: American Politics and International Security*. Ithaca, NY: Cornell University Press.

Owen, J. M. 2000/01. Transnational Liberalism and U.S. Primacy. *International Security*, 26(3): 117–52.

Owen, J. M. 2010a. *The Clash of Ideas in World Politics: Transnational Networks, States, and Regime Change, 1510–2010*. Princeton, NJ: Princeton University Press.

Owen, J. M. 2010b. Liberalism and Security. In Robert A. Denemark (ed.), *The International Studies Encyclopedia*. John Wiley.

Owen, J. M. 2015. *Confronting Political Islam: Six Lessons from the West's Past*. Princeton, NJ: Princeton University Press.

Owen, J. M. and M. Poznansky 2014. When Does America Drop Dictators? *European Journal of International Relations*, 20(4): 1072–99.

Packer, G. 2005. *The Assassins' Gate: America in Iraq*. New York: Farrar, Straus and Giroux.

Potter, P. and M. Baum. 2015. Information, Popular Restraint, and the Democratic Peace. Typescript, University of Virginia.

Powell, W. W. and P. J. DiMaggio (eds.), 2012. *The New Institutionalism in Organizational Analysis*. Chiacgo: University of Chicago Press.

Poznansky, M. 2015. Stasis or Decay? Reconciling Covert War and the Democratic Peace. *International Studies Quarterly*, 59(4): 815–26.

Putnam, R. D. 2015. *Our Kids: The American Dream in Crisis*. New York: Simon & Schuster.

Reiter, D. and A. C. Stam. 2002. *Democracies at War*. Princeton, NJ: Princeton University Press.

Rosenberg, N. and l. E. Birdzell. 2008. *How the West grew Rich: The Economic Transformation of the Industrial World*. New York: Basic Books.

Rousseau, J.-J. 1997. *The Social Contract and Other Later Political Writings*, ed. Victor Gourevitch. Cambridge: Cambridge University Press (first published 1762).

Russett, B. 1994. *Grasping the Democratic Peace: Principles for a Post-Cold War World*. Princeton, NJ: Princeton University Press.

Russett, B. M. and J. Oneal. 2001. *Triangulating Peace: Democracy, Interdependence, and International Organizations*. London: W.W. Norton.

Schelling, T. C. 1966. *Arms and Influence*. New Haven, CT: Yale University Press.

Schmitt, C. 2008. *The Concept of the Political: Expanded Edition*. Chicago: University of Chicago Press (first published 1932).

Schultz, K. A. 2001. *Democracy and Coercive Diplomacy* (Vol. 76). Cambridge: Cambridge University Press.

Simon, H. A. 1982. *Models of Bounded Rationality: Empirically Grounded Economic Reason* (Vol. 3). Cambridge, MA: MIT Press.

Tang, S. 2013. *The Social Evolution of International Politics*. Oxford: Oxford University Press.

Thompson, D. 2016. Who Are Donald Trump's Supporters, Really? *The Atlantic* (March 1). *Available at:* http://www.theatlantic.com/politics/archive/2016/03/who-are-donald-trumps-supporters-really/471714/, accessed June 23, 2016.

Thucydides, 1998. *The Landmark Thucydides*, ed. Robert B. Strassler, trans. C. W. Crawley. New York: Free Press (composed 411 BC).

Tocqueville, A. de 2002. *Democracy in America*, trans. Harvey C. Mansfield and Delba Winthrop. Chicago: University of Chicago Press (first published 1835).

Treffler, D. 1993. Trade Liberalization and the Theory of Endogenous Protection: An Econometric Study of U.S. Import Policy. *Journal of Political Economy*, 101(1): 138–60.

United Nations Development Program. 2002. *Arab Human Development Report*. New York: United Nations Publications.

Wendt, A. L. 1992. Anarchy is What States Make of it: The Social Construction of Power Politics. *International Organization*, 46(2): 391–425.

Wildau, G. and T. Mitchell. 2016. China GDP growth slips to 6.7% as stimulus eases slowdown. *Financial Times* (April 15). *Available at:* https://next.ft.com/content/faa4576c-0203-11e6-9cc4-27926f2b110c, accessed June 23, 2016.

Woodward, B. 2004. *Plan of Attack*. New York: Simon & Schuster.

World Bank. 2016. http://data.worldbank.org/data-catalog/GDP-PPP-based-table, and http://data.worldbank.org/indicator/NY.GDP.MKTP.CD, both accessed June 22, 2016.

World Trade Organization. *Available at:* http://stat.wto.org/CountryProfile/WSDBCountryPFView.aspx?Country=CN&, accessed June 22, 2016.

The Worries about China's Slowing Growth. *Economist* (January 19, 2016). *Available at:* http://www.economist.com/blogs/economist-explains/2016/01/economist-explains-11, accessed June 22, 2016.

CHAPTER 9

WHAT IS A PARIS APPROACH TO (IN)SECURITIZATION? POLITICAL ANTHROPOLOGICAL RESEARCH FOR INTERNATIONAL SOCIOLOGY

DIDIER BIGO AND EMMA MCCLUSKEY

9.1 From Paris to PARIS, Deconstructing the Territorial and Nationalist Oppositions, Building New Relations

NUMEROUS publications or "manuals" regarding security studies oppose three different schools of Critical Security Studies (CSS) by naming them after "cities": Aberystwyth, Copenhagen, and Paris. These so-called schools are more often than not portrayed as isolated rivals, pursuing different research agendas and arguing over what it means to be "critical" with regards to security. This naming can be a useful trick for students to remember who is who, but it bears a form of essentialism and culturalism, blocking the understanding of the difference between more linguistic and communicational approaches on one side and more political anthropology and sociological approaches on the other (Wæver 2004; Booth 2005; Peoples and VaughanWilliams 2010; Salter and Mutlu 2012; Shepherd 2013). Even worse, this is a mistake as it is precisely the dialogue between the authors from these so-called schools which has permitted each position to evolve and to take into consideration the arguments as they developed. Though sometimes using different terminologies, the scholars of all three schools nonetheless expressed more or less the same kind of reasoning.

This is why the relation between the so-called Copenhagen and Paris schools is more adequately approached if one sees the process of convergence and the critical dialogue between them, rather than by trying to create two essentialist narratives whereby no influence occurred and only distinctions persist. The first discussions along these lines, which occurred in 1994, were about the terminology of "securitization," which at the time had not been published by Ronnie Lipschutz and was merely a working paper of The Copenhagen Centre (Wæver 1993). Two years later, there was another meeting in Paris for a colloquium organized by Anne Marie Le Gloannec where Ole Wæver presented a piece on insecurity and identity; an endless dialectic that Pierre Hassner and Didier Bigo discussed (Wæver 1997). We will not develop here the 20 years of dialogue that ensued, apart from saying that what was established was a strong sense that common to all parties was a critique of the way in which security was analyzed in the leading US journals and the way a sub-discipline of security studies narrowly focused on mostly military and strategic dimensions. The critique of this approach had already led to the creation of the journal *Cultures et Conflits* in 1989 in Paris where sociologists, historians, anthropologists, and political scientists combined their efforts to propose an alternative vision of the post-bipolar world (Bigo and Hermant 1990). In Copenhagen it led to the book *The European Security Order Recast: Scenarios for the Post-Cold War Era*, which was among the first books born out of the collaboration between Barry Buzan and the Copenhagen group; Ole Wæver, Morten Kelstrup, Pierre Lemaitre, and Elzbetia Tromer (Buzan et al. 1990).

In both publications, the accent was put on the critique of viewing security solely as an answer to threats and insecurity, as if the world of security agencies was just reacting to external events and was not constructing the boundaries between security and insecurity. Against this functionalist approach—that paradoxically deprives the agents of a field of action of their agency and considers them as just reactionary—it was necessary to explain the conditions under which the social and political construction that enacts a process of securitization occurs. Emerging mainly from the security agencies and the professionals of politics, this is a process which in fact organizes the very differentiation between practices of security and practices of violence, fear, and insecurity.

9.2 Avoiding Essentialist Readings

As has been explained in detail in the CASE collective (CASE Collective 2006), what was at stake was creating a "collective intellectual" in the way Pierre Bourdieu has suggested (Lenoir 2005).[1] This notion points to a group that can offer different competences and which dares to enter into a serious discussion of the presupposition on which other disciplines are built, in order to deconstruct the common sense and to rebuild from the ruins of the Kings way, different transversal paths, different lines of flights.[2] The CASE collective was to be a way of opposing the mainstream doxa of International Relations (IR) by building a counter-hegemony regrouping diverse strands of CSS camps living on the margins of IR, especially in International Relations departments and in Europe which despaired of ever having a voice in journals or at conferences. The deconstruction of the assumptions of IR, which were so deeply rooted in English-speaking countries, was far more difficult to operate in the US than anywhere else. By connecting the sociological dimension of the European research, the translation of French theorists, and the strength of political theorists in some IR departments in North America, however, the symbolic power of the "dissidents" was sufficient to create "alternatives" to mainstream IR built on the US political science of the 1970s (Ashley and Walker 1991). In that sense, the CASE collective has been a success in that it has tied a generation of scholars and the students of that time to the core of a series of contemporary problems of utmost importance: critical infrastructure, risk and surveillance, digital activities, environmental changes, and ambiguities of humanitarianism, for example. However, the CASE Collective was also in part a failure in that it was often misread and contributed to diffusing the narrative of three opposing schools of CSS—Aberystwyth, Copenhagen, and Paris—naming them in a very culturalist manner after cities, and reducing the very strong debates in each place as if they were three different schools of thought (CASE Collective 2006). A serious reading of the CASE collective text shows that its purpose was, on the contrary, not to oppose the so-called schools but to build an International Political Sociology (IPS) that could instead emancipate. Its aim was, first, to free IR scholars from the premises of a US political science and, second, to liberate the sociologists from their methodological nationalism and their tendencies to avoid the idea of "international" in favor of jumping immediately to the concept of "global society." Additionally, this approach tried to bring the political theorists back to contemporary problems instead of a focusing on a history of ideas of great dead white men (Bigo and Walker 2007a, 2007b).

Nevertheless the imperative of the "publish or perish" culture and the need to have "manuals" for first-year students, or even Masters students, considering them not bright enough to understand complex ideas and supposing that they require simplification, has led to a series of false oppositions. Repeated again and again, this factionalization plays on the standardization of narratives concerning each "place" without analyzing, for each of them, the internal debates and the trajectories of the different individuals, as well as the ways in which the debates have been institutionalized through centers inside universities or within journals.

9.3 Beyond Political Science Assumptions, a Political and Anthropological Approach

Concerning Paris, the idea of a Paris school of thought opposed to Copenhagen or Aberystwyth has therefore been popularized, but makes no sense at all, and induces a culturalism that should be strongly rejected. The journal *Cultures et Conflits* located in Paris has certainly been and still is one of the major spaces for debates around the sociology of conflicts and security and has gathered people around the Francophone world, living in Paris, but also London, Amsterdam, Brussels, or Canada and the US because they were sharing a political and anthropological approach. We therefore need to move from the label of Paris as a city center to the travels and the travelers that gathered there, and if Paris has to be evoked, it should not be as a "place" but as an acronym of a Political Anthropological Research for International Sociology or a PARIS problematization. This conceptualization permits an understanding of what is at stake in the process of (in)securitization as well as in other processes of (un)freedomization or of (in)equalization of conditions that are occurring in our contemporary present.

And this problematization (*problematique*) or line of thought, which is built on an anthropological, sociological, and political base, mobilizes in many places: in London, in Rio, in Ottawa, in Johannesburg, and in Singapore as much as in Paris, and also includes some authors located in Copenhagen or Aberystwyth.[3]

What is specific to a Political Anthropological Research for International Sociology is de facto the combination of knowledge organized in a transdisciplinary way. This contrasts with other combinations more tempted by linguistics and semiotics for the study of conflicts and peace processes, or by a defense of IR as a sub-discipline of political science that has to be built on the legacy of the Anglo-US founding (and funding) fathers, while nevertheless being emancipatory.

Clearly, the three lines of thought have their legitimate place in a broader IPS approach, but we will here concentrate, for obvious reasons, on how IPS is practiced by the Paris problematization, exemplified in this instance around the dimension of (in)security. Once again, however, it is important to repeat that methodologically the PARIS–IPS approach strongly rejects the traditional dividing lines derived from political sciences, such as the opposition between, on one side, a theoretical and norm-oriented constructivism lacking empirical observations, and, on the other side, an empirical often cynical positivist research lacking a situated theoretical approach reflexive on its conditions of production (Bigo et al. 2010; Bigo and Walker 2007a).

9.4 For a PARIS–IPS of (In) Securitization Processes

What we have just explained means that the approach concerning the practices encapsulated in the language as security or insecurity and their various delineations of danger, risk, fear, response to violence, or relation to liberty, will not be discussed in the same way that an IR approach discusses them, even critical strands. Authors of PARIS will look at the discursive activities concerning security enacted by practitioners following pragmatic justifications of their work activities, and by the practitioners who theorize the practices of other actors, that is, theories coming from think-tanks or, in a more distant way, from academic disciplines. They will also strongly reject a specialization/hierarchization of knowledge and will not consider that the scholarship coming from historians, sociologists, and criminologists is less important than IR scholarship, under the pretext that they deal with less serious questions about security. Speaking about human beings' sense of protection will not be subordinated to IR specialists' preoccupations with the "survival" of a referent object, be it the nation state or democratic aspirations for emancipation (Booth 1992; Buzan et al. 1998; Walt 1991). The process by which a specific label of security or/and insecurity is connected with other terminologies, in terms of proximity or opposition, will be more important than the isolation of a true meaning of security through space and time in order to build a concept and a theory of security or securitization.

For a PARIS approach, "security" therefore, first and foremost, will not be divided into different disciplinary "objects" under which security is restricted to one qualification by discipline. It will instead recognize how the term has been used to describe very different practices inside the disciplines which cannot be subsumed under one main category (e.g. survival, but also human needs for IR; personal safety, fear of crime, but also urban policing and computer hacking for criminology; self-identity and group thinking for psychology; social security and flexisecurity[4] in the welfare state for economics; risk management and catastrophic risk for sociology; privacy, personal guarantee, and human rights for all individuals for law). This delimitation of disciplinary boundaries by experts is not a knowledge construction, but an expertise mimicking it, with the effect of hiding the struggles and hierarchies inside these discursive activities and their competition for a certain truth. Analyzing the modalities of veridiction of truth claims and their competition will therefore be the first reflexive move to construct a research question around a topic labeled "security."

Second, a PARIS approach will concern itself with the lived experiences of people affected by the practices of those who claim they can decide what is security, insecurity, and fate. Be they direct or indirect victims, be they amateurs of security, or just indifferent to the debates but affected by them, these people are all central to the analysis of the field of practices of (in)security. In taking seriously the political-anthropological element of a PARIS problematization, the significance of livable lives and experiences, which may be considered marginal or unimportant to IR or political science, will be central and form the core of the field. These experiences will not be determined by the elite discourses but by the practices revealing resistances to or escape from their power, and the building of centrifugal and disperse dynamics, which prevent the concentration of power and symbolic power in the hands of the bureaucratic elites. Resonating with recent scholarship that focuses its attention on people's experiences of (in)security in various spheres such as the "Critical Anthropology of Security" (Maguire et al. 2014), a PARIS approach refuses to reduce robust political-anthropological analysis to an add-on for IR theorists to undertake small ethnographic fieldwork projects in the name of methodological pluralism (Salter and Multu 2012). Instead, political anthropology will be chosen as the core investigation to analyze symbolic power and field dynamics and trajectories in order to explore the very continuities and contradictions of everyday experiences of unease and (in)security, so pertinent now in an era where (in)security discourses and practices are making ever deeper inroads into more mundane aspects of day-to-day life (Basaran et al. 2017).[5]

The third move of a PARIS approach will combine the first two in order to develop a socio-historical approach analyzing the social forces that have the capacity to impose a meaning at a certain period, and the dynamics that construct change in the long run. For example, security as a "term of art" is historically determined with very different meanings over time, running from equivalent to wisdom, to an act of contrition and self-sacrifice, to a juridical guarantee, to a sin, to a fear of collective death, of crime, of having a mobile phone stolen (Gros 2006; Foucault et al. 2007; Wæver 2010; Burgess 2011). The socio-historical or socio-genesis of power practices will try to uncover the tensions and aporia that are revealed when putting these connotations and their related bodies of knowledge together with the positions of power of the different actors. To initiate this research, the study of the primary metaphors delineating these forms of knowledge can be useful as metaphors often build the boundaries of what each discipline labels "security" and "insecurity" and calls the "object" of security (Kubálková et al. 1998). How each discipline masks the physical and symbolic violence of this very gesture is also revealed. Research into the trajectories of these metaphors, or of the "hotbeds of meanings" they produce, explains why it makes no sense to try to analyze security as "something," as a permanent concept, as an object belonging to a specific discipline studying an "external reality" (e.g. military or strategic studies, or even International Relations) as any labeling is both (i.e. the something and its external reality). It has its own "social" life and is the product of a world of our making. To put it differently, the world, in order to maintain its realness, has to be constructed with meanings that are constantly reproduced and translated to cope with change. These meanings, however, do not converge into one natural social world called society bounded by a state but are in fact always objects of transactions; conversions between multiple professional and cultural worlds (Rancière 1987; Ashley and Walker 1991; Bigo 2011).

Consequently, a very diverse array of practices of justifying ambiguous ways of governing others (often involving violence) coming from diverse professional worlds and heterogeneous bodies of knowledge are both enabled and hidden by the terminology of security and its overflows (risk, vulnerability, resilience).

9.5 A Paris Approach for the Art of Writing the (In)Securitization Processes across Fields of Power

So, when all the actors of so many different social universes jump on the terminology and impose their own significations, PARIS–IPS research will take very seriously what all the actors say about the different meanings of security, how they relate to technologies and objects to stabilize their meanings, even if the boundaries they trace do not fit with an academic discipline.

The fourth move is to look at the disputes and controversies the actors create, and to reconstruct their trajectories and bifurcations or settlements. This also implies going beyond the sole controversies to analyze the power struggles the actors engage with and the ones that blind them because they share the same doxa. Typically, this implies looking at the transformative discursive practices of the actors, when a terminology is translated from one universe to another one to understand how it reflects, or not, a change of mode of veridiction and a change in the relations between fields of power (for example security in computer hacking and security in biology in terms of struggles around the notions of anti-virus; this is the same for the prevention of catastrophe between seismology and its translation in management studies and IR counter-terrorism approaches regarding so-called predictive policing). It also implies, of course, rejecting the idea that academic writing can decide, instead of the actors, what constitutes a true definition of security (Bonditti and Olsson 2017).

Therefore, this approach insists on symbolic power as a main category of analysis and refuses to have a "regressive" academic habitus in order to maintain a tradition in the name of "clarity" of knowledge, of the purity and simplicity of a concept, or in the name of the authority of the discipline (Swartz 2013). Political science and IR have been very resilient on this subject and they often survive by the way they directly use the argument of the necessity of their own survival as a discipline to maintain the local dominant epistemological positions abandoned by other disciplines for a while, and often with no shame, but with a cynical pride (Guilhot 2008). IPS, on the contrary, insists on the multiplicity of possibilities of investigations in the social sciences and humanities, and has doubts about explanations and predictions of human practices, for reasons which have to do also with a reflexivity concerning policing, surveillance, and security (Jeandesboz 2016).

It creates a huge difference about the art of writing CSS, and it is perhaps on this point that we strongly disagree with Ole Wæver when he presents securitization theory as a theory in the Waltzian sense in his response in the journal *Security Dialogue* to various criticisms (Wæver 2011). Far from trying to mathematize by a formalist approach the real in order to predict it, by mimicking the physics of the last century and by applying a neo-platonic view of the world, an IPS approach will try to respect the diversity of human practices of traversal fields of actors and the heterogeneity of the plural worlds of these plural (in)dividuals (Bigo 2017).

To recap what we have said so far, security cannot be divided into different disciplinary "objects" and cannot become the object of one theory of securitization. The list of contradictions, heterogeneities, or different attributions of ethical values regarding security that reveal a panorama of different forms of disciplinary knowledge shows that the search for a unifying principle is always a search for a dominant position that has no chance of encapsulating the different practices. Consequently, the academic struggles to impose one theory led by a concept of security can continue forever (Gallie 1956). Security, as a notion, is permanently contested, whatever the social universe in which the terminology is deployed.

Furthermore, these definitions of security can often be seen as being in complete opposition to each other. For example, privacy as personal safety may be described as a danger, an insecurity in IR digital security discourses, which consider privacy to be an obstacle, a shadow that obscures and anonymizes potential criminals. More importantly, security, as a notion, and whatever the social universe, is always the object of competition between actors seeking to control its content, so paradoxically the only communality is that security is always the object of struggles (Bigo 1994; Huysmans 1995, 2002, 2014; Bigo and Tsoukala 2008). This is why "security claims" belong to the realm of politics and politicization, they are not a different domain, beyond normal politics.

On the contrary, this is a key lesson for studying political life today, especially when the political players do not debate freedom and democracy anymore, and instead construct a consensus in which terrorism seemingly justifies any form of coercive action called security, counter-terrorism, or counter radicalization. The consensus around security by politicians is diminishing reasoning, and democratic debates. It creates a doxa of a world dominated by fear and unease that help right-wing movements to impose their view of security and to silence their views on freedom, equality, and solidarity.

Furthermore all security claims, even the most benign, imply a struggle around the legitimacy of some ambiguous practices involving violence or control of an actor's behavior, beyond the political scene. Certainly, many practices, which we call security or protection in everyday life are not, as such, an object of direct contestation. Often these practices are seen as forms of freedom. For instance, in our home countries of France and the UK, it seems that we can choose what to eat, drink, or wear, as well as where we want to go, or what we publish on the Internet about ourselves. But these practices can become a security issue when they reach the boundaries of somebody else's freedom, for example because of scarcity, lack of equality and redistribution, forms of property, beliefs in primordial identities. Why? Because the temptation of the various practitioners is to refuse to change the previous practices when they are contested, and to continue by claiming that they are vital to assure security, that they are a legitimate reaction to a danger, a risk, a threat, and are de facto justified. The claim may also be used to mobilize support in favor of previous actions, which themselves were considered illegitimate. This logic operates at the personal level, but also with regard to collectivities and their identities. Politicization and creation of social movements which contend power often come from the initial disputes about the boundaries of security that diminish forms of freedom, and do not diminish insecurities whatsoever. On the contrary, these disputes develop them by escalating the violence or by creating the image of a perpetual emergency. This (in)securitization process and its possible escalation is in that case the sixth move to develop in terms of investigation.

9.6 The Necessity of a "Seppuku" of Security and CSS

As we have contended, security is a label whose limits are constructed by the relationship with other labels like freedom, mobility, and privacy.[6] The label masks the symbolic violence and arbitrariness which present security as a norm for good or necessity in the making of the boundary with insecurity and the acts classified as "violent," "criminal," or even "terrorist."[7] Security, therefore, is not a concept and has no autonomy. Security studies are a form of imposture (deception). They cannot exist as a sub-discipline having its own set of rules, because security does not describe a class of specific objects or facts.[8] Security is then never absolute, integral, total, or global, except for a "securititarian ideology," that some "securocrats" promote, and which is often hidden by the idea of a legitimate field of security studies. The academic field of security studies is mainly an illusio imposed by academic actors who maintain their positions as an elite by providing a securitarian ideology to the professionals of politics when they need one, and by giving them the argument for a series of techniques and procedures that "maximize" and "globalize" security as if it were something good or at least necessary. The recent politics, too quickly called populism, are of that sort. But, in practice, a process of (in)securitization always reaches a limit, and security appears as a reversal, a tipping point, invoking and materializing other qualifications that imply a limitation while trying to eradicate them. It is central to an understanding that security presupposes political judgments about freedom, property, mobility, privacy, and democracy and often tends to refuse to recognize the practices associated with these other concepts, by trying to colonize them under positive labels like protection and humanity. Some researchers like Neocleus have considered that only an "anti-security" stance can solve this "no limit" of security and they have a strong point, with which we agree. But by the same token, they seem to reproduce the move they contest with anti-security as a label (Neocleous 2011). PARIS researchers consider they have to take distance with both positions and to show that each disciplinary knowledge organizes the network of relations to security very differently, and that the struggles inside and between fields cannot be subsumed under the argument of a general complicity of all the actors revealed by a researcher.

The web of significations coming from these contradictory bodies of knowledge shows quite immediately that in a certain body of knowledge security is the name given to certain practices that might otherwise be called by other disciplines insecurity, violence, coercion, fear, freedom, mobility, or opportunity. The boundaries of these practices, which are subsumed into the catch-all term "security," vary according to the trajectory of disciplinary bodies of knowledge, as well as historical and political reasons. One of the main sites of disagreement with traditional approaches is about this "isolation" of security and its closure as an objective category, an eternal value, a central concept organizing life, a right more fundamental than freedom, or even a justification to save a collectivity. To subsume, security, as a concept, has no "essence." Therefore, like Lewis Caroll's hunting of the snark, the quintessential meaning of security has no end(s). To try to reverse it, is also hopeless. The right question is not what security means, but what security does (CASE Collective 2006; Balzacq et al. 2010).

9.7 A Transdisciplinary Approach: Transversal Fields of Power, (In)Securitization and Effects on Lived Experiences in Everyday Practices

What does security do today? The answer may look simple. For many readers and researchers it is not even a question, it is common sense: what security does is to diminish insecurity. But what is the relation of security to insecurity? Do we have a simple relation under which security is the solution to insecurity? Is it possible to achieve "security" as it is so often claimed? Indirectly, could we have a management, a governance of security, which is based on the eradication or at least a limitation of insecurity? The paradox of a large part of the literature on security is that the answer is assumed to be positive: the more security, the less insecurity.

The IR discipline (including some authors of CSS) has surprisingly not engaged to a great extent with this question of insecurity and the social construction of threat and violence. Security has been analyzed as a form of social construction, but simultaneously as an "answer" to insecurity and violence coming from the real world or the "environment." The debate between the IR specialists has therefore been more around the notion of security as a contested concept, than about insecurity. Insecurity has been seen as unproblematic, as the reverse of security. It comes as no surprise that so many works dealing with different definitions of security nevertheless converge de facto towards an essentialist definition of insecurity as threat. To favor the achievement of a real/true security supposes that security is regarded as a positive value and insecurity as a negative value (Williams 2011).

In most of the literature the two terminologies of security and insecurity are not only opposed, but simultaneously essentialized and considered as coming "from the real world." Or, even when security is de-essentialized, contested and re-constructed, it is often to maintain an essentialist view of insecurity as the reference to the real world and the threats coming out of it. Consequently the role of institutions and of performative effects are recognized in the framing of the security "solution," but the violence is a given and insecurity is "bad." A "soft" constructivism can emerge as a middle ground position about the social construction of norms and the "real world" of the "realists": Stuart Croft, Terry Terriff, Stuart James, Patrick Morgan (Terriff et al. 1999), or Philippe David (David and Roche 2002) or even at some point Thierry Balzacq when he speaks of security policies and instruments (Balzacq 2008). But is it possible just to assume that "we" know what insecurity is or that our normative choices are the right ones as it is assumed in many resolutions concerning the responsibility to protect or deradicalization? Could we assume that if the objective is to promote peace we are justified in using military means?

Could we describe a situation objectively as insecurity if we do not anticipate what the situation will be after the (non)intervention? Insecurity is a political judgment about a situation regarding its past and its future. Jef Huysmans has insisted on this point in his first book: "This interpretation broadens the notion of insecurity from threat definition to the political and institutional framing of policy issues in what can be referred to as 'domains of insecurity'" (Huysmans 2006). So we strongly agree: what is at stake is a politics of insecurity, but we add something to that claim: to emphasize insecurity while maintaining the two opposite sides of security and insecurity may be misleading, and this is why we prefer to speak of (in)security practices and an (in)securitization process in order to insist on the consubstantiality of security and insecurity, especially in a state of violence reformulating previous states of war.

The naming of security is a political act as is the naming and framing of insecurity. Both are the emerging part of a larger political process of (in)securitization, which implies sacrifice, decisions, and symbolic domination concerning the legitimacy of the measures taken. Depending on power relations, the measures and routinized practices will be called violence, insecurity, or security and safety, or even lack of chance and fate. These power relations certainly affect the field of the politics professional, but they do not affect them alone. These power relations come into play in each bureaucratic or technical field as soon as the actors try to manage (in)security by using either coercion, surveillance, or the pastoral techniques of integration, prevention, and prediction. The process of politicization in each professional universe is driven by the permanent struggles among the actors concerning claims to define the domains of insecurity and of security, the refusal to accept them, and the competitions they engage in to determine in their own universes what is security, what is insecurity, and what is fate.

The relation of (in)security can thus be described as a Mobius strip. To specify exactly what is meant by that, one has to think that in the wording itself we do not have two terminologies that are in opposition. We do not even have two sides generating a dynamics of co-constitution of the opposite, nor do we have a chiasm inside the word security. We have only one side in a non-orientable surface (as in a Mobius strip) that we have to call (in)security, or an (in)securitization process. We have a unique phenomenon of (in)security even if it appears, depending on the point of view that actors have, as security for some and for others as its opposite, insecurity. The Mobius strip is constituted of one band, and looks like it has opposite sides, but when someone is asked to point out exactly where the opposite side begins, he realizes that if he can see a border and name the two sides, other actors, placed in front of him will not contest that a border exists, but will contest his choice of naming the inside and the outside. In our case, what is contested is what is security and what is insecurity (Bigo 2001, 2016). It is this intersubjectivity and the impossibility of common agreement about where is the inside and where is the outside which blocks the phenomenon of closure and exclusion that a circle performs. It is not possible to assert for sure the territory of the security enclosure (circle or domain) and to exclude, to purify it from insecurity, because in a Mobius strip someone will just affirm the exact contrary concerning the postition of the inside and the outside, the content of what is security and what is insecurity. And it seems central in understanding the logic at work. Actors disagree about what is security and what is insecurity. They may have inverse positions, but at the same time they agree about the places of the boundaries and they are surprised if they are obliged to trace them to realize that where they have seen an opposition, they can only find a continuity. They look for the distinction between security and insecurity and they find only (in)security as a practice, as the practical sense of their everyday life. And this is the last move and the key of the research to be developed under a PARIS approach. What is essential is understanding the moments in which the individuals in their practices feel they are (in)secure because of the relations and processes they are immersed in. This is what a political anthropology has to observe and investigate. It has little to do with a feeling, a psychological move, a psyche of anxiety, or with discourse and communication. It has to do with their places in different fields of power and where they are positioned. It has to do with their "practical sense."

Notes

1. The article was published in *Security Dialogue* as the result of a meeting in Paris of the Challenge programme led by Didier Bigo and the cost action led by Jef Huysmans. The idea to create a collective intellectual came from a late-night discussion between all the members of the group who co-signed a paper concerning the responsibility of intellectuals, be they organic or specific, to work individually and often to act to reproduce the myth of a clear difference between legitimate and illegitimate violence, of a clear border between security and insecurity, that their own concept will cut through forever.
2. The Bourdieusian terminologies employed by PARIS; field, doxa, illusio, and practical sense, refer to Bourdieu's theory that agents and their social positions are located within specific settings (fields) and operate according to the particular logic of the game at play within these settings (practical sense). The belief by all involved that this "game" is worth playing (illusio) leads to a sort of taken-for-grantedness of the arbitrariness of the values and assumptions which inform an agent's actions within the field (doxa). For a more detailed, highly accessible introduction to these concepts, see Bourdieu and Wacquant (1992) and for a more developed analysis, see Swartz (2013).
3. But we have to say that we leave to the groups in Copenhagen or to Aberystwyth the task of transforming their approach into an acronym respecting the place (good luck to Aberystwyth).
4. This model was introduced in Scandinavia and adopted by the European Commission with the aim of combining flexibility in the labor market within a globalized economy with a degree of social protections for employees.
5. The book *International Political Sociology: Transversal Lines*, which is the first of the IPS Routledge collection, gives a long series of topics that can be studied through this anthropological approach, and the next volume will further develop the links between a Paris IPS approach and the anthropology of globalization.
6. "Seppuku" in the heading, of course, literally refers to the form of Japanese ritual suicide by disembowelment, also known as harikiri.
7. Nelson Mandela's labeling as a terrorist being the most striking example of this point.

8. It is in this respect that we are calling for a "seppuku" of the label. Contrary to conceiving of CSS as a sub-discipline of IR and accepting a political science understanding of Security, we are, for a multiplication of topics and problematizations, engaging with security as limiting freedom, equality, and solidarity.

References

Ashley, Richard K. and R. B. J. Walker. 1991. Reading Dissidence/ Writing the Discipline: Crisis and the Question of Sovereignty in International Studies. *International Studies Quarterly*, 34(3): 367–416.

Balzacq, Thierry. 2008. The Policy Tools of Securitization: Information Exchange, EU Foreign and Interior Policies. *Journal of Common Market Studies*, 46(1): 75–100.

Balzacq, Thierry, Tugba Basaran, Didier Bigo, Emmanuel-Pierre Guittet, and Christian Olsson. 2010. Security Practices. International Studies Encyclopedia Online. ed, Robert A. Denemark, Blackwell Publishing. Blackwell Reference Online, accessed March 18, 2010.

Basaran, Tugba, Didier Bigo, Emmanuel-Pierre Guittet, and R. B. J. Walker. 2017. *International Political Sociology: Transversal Lines* Abingdon: Routledge.

Bigo, Didier. 1994. The European Internal Security Field: Stakes and Rivalries in a Newly Developing Area of Police Intervention. In Malcolm Anderson and Monica Den Boer (eds.), *Policing across National Boundaries*, pp. 161–173. London: Pinter Publications.

Bigo, Didier. 2001. The Moebius Ribbon of Internal and External Security(ies). In Mathias Albert, David Jacobson, and Yosef Lapid (eds.), *Identities, Borders, Orders: Rethinking International Relations Theory*. Minneapolis, MN; London: University of Minnesota Press.

Bigo, Didier. 2011. Pierre Bourdieu and International Relations: Power of Practices, Practices of Power. *International Political Sociology*, 5(3): 225–58.

Bigo, Didier. 2016. The Moebius strip of national and world security. *Available at:* http://explosivepolitics.com/blog/the-mobius-strip-of-national-and-world-security/, accessed August 20, 2016.

Bigo, Didier. 2017. International Political Sociology: Rethninking the International Through Dynamics of Power. In Tugba Basaran, Didier Bigo, Emannuel-Pierre Guittet, and R. B. J Walker (eds.), *International Political Sociology: Transversal Lines*. Abingdon: Routledge.

Bigo, Didier and Daniel Hermant. 1990. La prolongation des conflits: introduction. *Cultures et Conflits*, 1(1): 2–15.

Bigo, Didier and Anastasia Tsoukala. 2008. *Terror, Insecurity and Liberty: Illiberal Practices of Liberal Regimes After 9/11*. London. New York: Routledge.

Bigo, Didier and R. B. J. Walker. 2007a. Political Sociology and the Problem of the International. *Millenium. Journal of International Studies*, 35(3): 725–39.

Bigo, Didier and R. B. J. Walker. 2007b. International, Political, Sociology. *Editorial: International Political Sociology*, 1: 1–5.

Bigo, Didier, Sergio Carrera, Elspeth Guild, and Rob Walker. 2010. *Europe's 21st Century Challenge: Delivering Liberty and Security*. Aldershot: Ashgate.

Bonditti, Philippe and Olsson, Christian. 2017. Violence, War and Security Knowledge: Between Practical Theories and Theoretical Practices. In Tugba Basaran, Didier Bigo, Emannuel-Pierre Guittet, and R. B. J Walker (eds.), *International Political Sociology: Transversal Lines*. Abingdon: Routledge.

Booth, Ken. 1992. Security and emancipation. *Review of International Studies*, 17(4): 313–26.

Booth, Ken. 2005. *Critical Security Studies and World Politics*. Boulder, CO: Lynne Rienner.

Bourdieu, Pierre and Wacquant, Loic. 1992. *An Invitation to Reflexive Sociology*. Cambridge: Polity.

Burgess, J. Peter. 2011. *The Ethical Subject of Security: Geopolitical Reason and the Threat Against Europe*. Abingdon: Routledge.

Buzan, Barry, Morten Kelstrup, Pierre Lemaitre, Elzbetia Tromer, and Ole Wæver. 1990. *The European Security Order Recast. Scenarios for the post-Cold War Era*. London: Pinter Publishers & Center for Peace and Conflict Research, University of Copenhagen.

Buzan, Barry, Ole Wæver, and Jaap de Wilde. 1998. *Security: A New Framework for Analysis*. Boulder, CO: Lynne Rienner).

CASE Collective. 2006. Critical Approaches to Security in Europe: A Networked Manifesto. *Security Dialogue*, 37(4): 443–87.

David, Charles-Philippe and Jean-Jacques Roche 2002. Théories de la Sécurité. *Politique étrangère*, 68(2): 435–6.

Foucault, Michel, Michel Senellart, and Arnold I. Davidson. 2007. *Security, Territory, Population: Lectures at the Collège de France, 1977–1978* Basingstoke; New York: Palgrave Macmillan.

Gallie, Walter B. 1956. Essentially Contested Concepts. *Proceedings of the Aristotelian Society*, 56: 167–98.

Gros, Frederic. 2006. *Etats de violence, essai sur la fin de la guerre*, edn NRF Paris: Gallimard.

Guilhot, Nicolas. 2008. The Realist Gambit: Postwar American Political Science and the Birth of IR Theory. *International Political Sociology*, 2(3): 281–304.

Huysmans, Jef. 1995. "Migrants as a Security Problem: Dangers from Securitizing Societal Issues. in R. Miles and D. Thränhardt (eds.), *Migration and European Integration. The Dynamics of Inclusion and Exclusion*, pp. 53–72. London: Pinter).

Huysmans, Jef. 2002. "Defining Social Constructivism in Security Studies: The Normative Dilemma of Writing Security. *Alternatives*, 27: 41–62.

Huysmans, Jef. 2006. The Politics of Insecurity. Fear, Migration and Asylum in the EU. London: Routledge.

Huysmans, Jef. 2014. *Security Unbound: Enacting Democratic Limits*. London: Routledge.

Jeandesboz, Julien 2016. "Interroger la 'vie sociale des méthodes' dans les approches critiques de la sécurité: expertise et enquête sur les questions de sécurité européenne. in Emmanuel-Pierre Guittet (ed.), *Questions de méthodes: Savoir-faire des études critiques de sécurité*, pp. 33–57. Paris: Cultures et Conflits-L'Harmattan.

Kubálková, V., Onuf, Nicholas Greenwood, and Kowert, Paul. 1998. *International Relations in a Constructed World*. Armonk, NY: M. E. Sharpe.

Lenoir, Remi 2005. "L'habitus scientifique: Pierre Bourdieu et l'intellectuel collectif. *Regards sociologiques*, 30: 119–30.

Maguire, Mark, Catarina Frois, and Nils Zurawski. 2014. *The Anthropology of Security: Perspectives from the Frontline of Policing, Counter-Terrorism and Border Control*. London: Pluto Press.

Neocleous, Mark. 2011. *Anti-security* Ottawa; Red Quill Books.

Peoples, Columba and Nick VaughanWilliams. 2010. *Critical Security Studies: An Introduction*. Abingdon: Routledge.

Rancière, J. 1987. *Le maître ignorant: cinq leçons sur l'émancipation intellectuelle*. Paris: Fayard.

Salter, Mark B. and Can E. Multu. 2012. The Discursive Turn. Introduction. in Mark B. Salter and Can E. Mutlu (eds.), *Research Methods in Critical Security Studies: An Introduction*, pp. 113–20. New York: Routledge.

Shepherd, Laura J. 2013. *Critical Approaches to Security: An Introduction to Theories and Methods*. Abingdon: Routledge.

Swartz, David L. 2013. *Symbolic Power, Politics, and intellectuals: The Political Sociology of Pierre Bourdieu*. Chicago; University of Chicago Press.

Terriff, Terry, Stuart Croft, Lucy James, and Patrick M. Morgan. 1999. *Security Studies Today*. Cambridge: Polity Press.

Wæver, Ole. 1993. Securitization and Desecuritization. *Working Paper*, 5: 31.

Wæver, Ole. 1997. European security identities. *Journal of Common Market Studies*, 34(1): 103–32.

Wæver, Ole. 2004. Aberystwyth, Paris, Copenhagen, New "Schools" in Security Theory and their Origins between Core and Periphery. Paper presented at the annual meeting of the International Studies Association, Montreal, Canada, March 17–20, 2004.

Wæver, Ole. 2010. Towards a Political Sociology of Security Studies. *Security Dialogue*, 41(6): 649–58.

Wæver, Ole. 2011. Politics, Security, Theory. *Security Dialogue*, 42(4–5): 465–80.

Walt, Stephen M. 1991. The Renaissance of Security Studies. *International Studies Quarterly*, 35(2): 211–39.

Williams, P. 2011. *Security Studies: An Introduction*, 2nd edn. Abingdon: Routledge.

B

Methods: Methodological Implications of Thinking about the Future of International Security from Different Perspectives

CHAPTER 10

STATISTICS AND INTERNATIONAL SECURITY

ADAM M. LAURETIG AND BEAR F. BRAUMOELLER

10.1 Introduction

Students of international security have been gathering data about conflict for a very long time (see, e.g., Wright 1942). Over time, the sophistication of quantitative analysis has grown as new generations of scholars seek out newer and better methods to capture important features of international relations data (Beck and Zeng 1999; Braumoeller 2003; Cranmer and Menninga 2012). There have been useful correctives along the way—see especially Achen (2002), Clarke and Primo (2007), and Schrodt (2014)—and in all candor, those correctives have largely fallen on willfully deaf ears. Nevertheless, the overall trend in the statistical study of international security has been in the direction of progress.

There's only one problem: In a very fundamental sense, we don't know what we're doing.[1] Quantitative International Relations (IR) scholars overwhelmingly tend to use statistical models for purposes for which they were not intended and should not be utilized, treating description, causal inference, and prediction as interchangeable. This is a very real problem, and it is time that we face up to it.

The origins of the problem are not too difficult to describe. Most quantitative IR scholars can remember having received the warning that statistical models like regression do nothing more than describe correlations among variables, and that correlation does not mean causation. We all nodded and made a note of that point. Nevertheless, when we read quantitative work in our IR seminars, we looked for stars on the variables of interest and assumed that the statistically significant variable "caused" the effect of interest.

When it came time to do our own research, most of us simply threw our list of variables into a generalized linear model, turned the crank,[2] looked for $p < .05$, and then wrote up the results. We did not actually use the word "cause" in our write-ups, but overwhelmingly the analyses were presented as causal—increasing the variable of interest by 1 would cause a β increase in y. Sometimes, we would even say our variables "predict" a β-unit change in y, further muddying the conceptual waters.

IR scholars are far from unique in this regard. Morgan and Winship (2014) note that, starting in the 1960s and 1970s, methodologists in the social sciences were eager to claim that the methods they described were amenable to a causal interpretation. In the "age of regression" that followed, practitioners proved all too eager to throw caution to the wind when it came to interpreting the partial correlations represented by regression coefficients.

Our point in this chapter is simple: it is time to come back down to earth and actually do the sort of work that we have been claiming to do for decades. In this chapter, we demonstrate that doing so is far from impossible, though it does demand that observational data be treated with the respect and caution that they deserve.

Regression models, logits, probits, and other generalized linear models (GLMs) are fundamentally *descriptive* models: they describe the correlation between a dependent variable and some vector of independent variables. If correlation is all that is needed—if, for example, we just want to know whether democratic dyads are less likely to go to war than other pairs of states—description suffices. If we want to know *why* democratic dyads are less likely to go to war, however, we are attempting to make a causal claim. If we seek to assess the future conflict propensities of pairs of states based on their level of democracy, we are attempting to *predict* their future behavior.

Causal models are carefully designed to achieve *identification*: due to the design of the study or the statistics used to carry it out, we believe that we are identifying a causal effect, where manipulating X *changes* Y, if units under study are otherwise identical, rather than simply a correlation. Identification cannot simply be assumed. If the research design warrants a causal interpretation (say, the data come from an experiment), GLMs, crosstabs, and simple difference-of-means tests can bear a causal interpretation. If the design does not warrant a causal interpretation, as it typically does not in observational settings, some other research design or modeling procedure must typically be brought to bear before results can credibly be said to have a causal interpretation.

While causal modeling is built around the idea of approximating a laboratory experiment using statistical methods, the goal in *prediction* is to maximize one's ability to predict an outcome Y given a set of variables X, with the model evaluated according to some measure of how well it can predict observations that were not used to generate its parameters (Ward et al. 2010) rather than by the statistical significance of individual coefficients.

In the remainder of this chapter, we will explore methods such as matching and instrumental variables for causal inference, and the elastic net and random forests for prediction, all of which are available in the free statistical software R. We encourage the interested reader to explore these packages and their worked examples for themselves in order to get a feel for how these procedures work.

10.2 Causal Inference

Experiments are held as the gold standard for causal evidence: the analyst can manipulate everything of interest and randomization ensures that the subjects vary systematically only in terms of the treatment (Hyde 2015). However, experimental results in International Relations often encounter problems of external validity. For example, people experiencing war may respond differently than undergraduates competing for money in a laboratory (Driscoll and Maliniak 2016). Simply put, there is no substitute for real-world observational data for conflict scholars. Unfortunately, this is where causal inference becomes difficult.

In order to gain some traction on the problem, we must first specify what we mean by "causation."

10.2.1 Manipulation and Potential Outcomes

The manipulation account of causation, originally developed in the philosophy of science literature (Sekhon 2004 provides an accessible review), is based on the idea that, if a proposed cause actually does produce a given effect, the manipulation of the cause will result in the manipulation of the effect (but not vice versa) (Holland 1986).

The manipulation account of causation was introduced to the statistics literature as the *potential outcomes framework* by Rubin (1974) and has become the most popular framework for causal inference in current political science research methodology (Keele 2015). The potential outcomes framework was designed to approximate an experiment when the analyst only has observational data to estimate causal effects. Mathematically, the potential outcomes framework states that in a population with an outcome Y and a treatment D (using notation from Morgan and Winship 2014), assuming binary treatments and outcomes, every individual has a potential treatment $d_i = 1$ or $d_i = 0$, and a potential outcome y_i^1 when $d_i = 1$ or y_i^0 when $d_i = 0$. However, the scholar runs into what Holland (1986: 947) named the "fundamental problem of causal inference": we only observe one treatment and outcome for each individual.

$$Y = Y^1 \text{ if } D = 1$$

$$Y = Y^0 \text{ if } D = 0$$

or, more simply:

$$Y = DY^1 + (1 - D)Y^0$$

If we *could* re-run history and observe treated and untreated outcomes for the same individuals, causal inference would be simple: we could just compare the two and see how big a difference the treatment makes.

In practice, we have to condition for the effects of confounders. Randomizing the treatment is the simplest way to do so. The effects of the cause can then be observed in the difference in means of the treated and control group. The "broadest possible average effect" (Morgan and Winship 2014: 46), which can be calculated using this set-up is the average treatment effect, which, using the expectation operator $E[.]$ from probability theory is:

$$E[Y^1] - E[Y^0]$$

By subtracting the average of the treated outcomes from the control outcomes, we can observe the effect of treatment in the population. If we satisfy two simple (but strong) assumptions, we can claim that this subtraction represents a *causal* effect, and that this effect is identified. In Figure 10.1, this can be seen by subtracting the means of the two distributions, which results in the average treatment effect.

Two assumptions need to be satisfied to make a causal claim: the stable unit treatment value assumption (SUTVA) and the independence assumption. SUTVA "is simply the a priori assumption that the value of Y for unit u when exposed to treatment t will be the

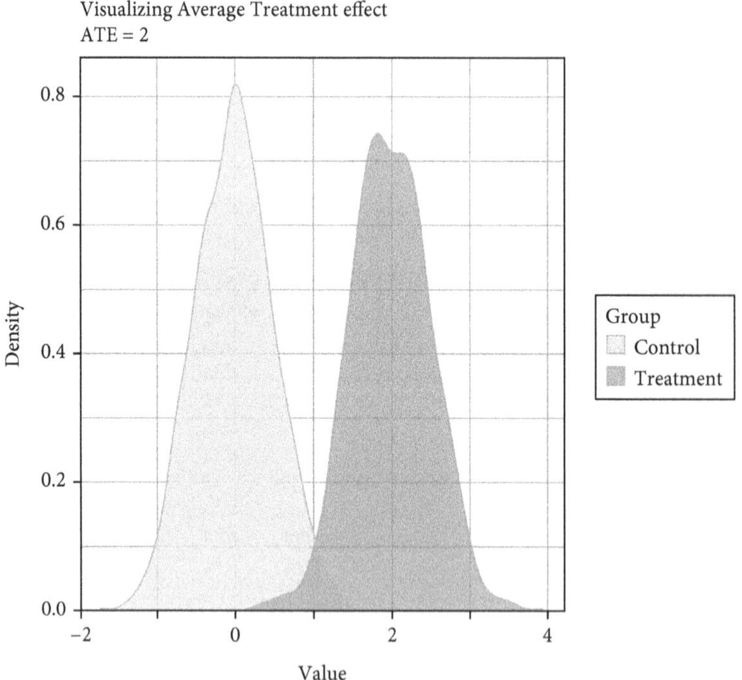

FIGURE 10.1 Visualizing average treatment effect

Note: ATE = 2.

same no matter what mechanism is used to assign treatment t to unit u and no matter what treatments the other units receive" (Morgan and Winship 2014: 48). SUTVA thus means that any individual is not affected by the treatment assigned to other individuals.

The independence assumption states that knowing that a unit was assigned to the treatment group tells you nothing about the counterfactual outcome for the control group, and equivalently, assigning a unit to the control group tells you nothing about its counterfactual treatment. Formally:

$$(Y^0, Y^1) \perp\!\!\!\perp D$$

where $\perp\!\!\!\perp$ denotes independence, and D denotes treatment, the counterfactual is independent of the treatment (Morgan and Winship 2014). The key is that the treatment only "flows" forward to the outcome, that the outcome does not tell you anything about the treatment, and that all variation in D is completely random. This is referred to by Rubin (1978: 42) as "ignorability."

10.2.2 Accounting for Nonrandom Treatment

Using only these assumptions, we can engage in causal inference, though as Manski (1990) demonstrated, our inferences will typically be very imprecise. To make progress, we must account for whether observations select into treatment—are the characteristics of observations *endogenous to*, or caused in part by, their propensity for receiving the treatment D? If these characteristics exist and are not accounted for, they can bias our estimate of the average treatment effect. Fortunately, as Rubin (1978) noted, if we can *condition* on those characteristics S that affect treatment, we can refer to the remaining variation as "ignorable."

To understand what is meant by "conditioning," we return briefly to the example of regression. In its simplest form, regression takes the form

$$Y = \beta_0 + \beta_1 D + \beta_2 \mathbf{X} + \epsilon$$

Y represents an outcome, D represents the proposed cause of that outcome, $\mathbf{X}$ represents a set of confounders, $\beta_0 - \beta_2$ are coefficients to be estimated, and ϵ represents the error term. In order to believe that β_1 accurately captures the causal effect of D on Y in the context of the potential outcomes framework—that is, that increasing D by 1 will cause a β_1-unit change in Y—we must also believe the following:[3]

1. D causes Y
2. ϵ causes Y
3. ϵ does not cause D
4. Y does not cause D
5. Nothing that causes ϵ also causes D.

Assumptions 1 and 2 are typically unproblematic and 4 is typically justified by theory. To believe assumptions 3 and 5, however, we have to believe that the proposed cause D is not caused either by an omitted variable in the error term or by a cause of an omitted variable in the error term. In other words, D must either be truly exogenous or its causes must be both distinct from and uncorrelated with ϵ.

In the densely interconnected and interactive world of human behavior, these are heroic assumptions. In the case of democratic peace, for example, it is entirely possible that unmodeled variation in peaceful and conflictual behavior influences the probability that a state will become or remain democratic (see, e.g., Reuveny and Li 2003), violating assumption 3. Similarly, an unmodeled confounder, like liberal political norms, could influence both conflict behavior and democracy (Weart 2000), violating assumption 5. In either case the treatment, democracy, is nonrandom with respect to the characteristics of the units.

Conditioning on the variables that influence treatment, broadly speaking, involves introducing information about those variables into the analysis. Done sensibly, conditioning makes identification plausible in observational data. Conditioning cannot typically be done without making *some* assumptions about the process of treatment, however, and the plausibility of identification hinges critically on the plausibility of the assumptions necessary to produce it.

10.2.2.1 *Matching*

Perhaps the most well-known technique for causal inference in political science is matching, originally developed by Rubin (1973). The goal of matching is to approximate the randomization in an experiment, to obtain the best possible estimate of the effect of the treatment on the outcome (Rubin 2008). Treatment is viewed as a probabilistic (usually binary) outcome, for which one estimates the *propensity score*, the probability of receiving treatment. After the propensity score is estimated, treated observations are "matched" to untreated ones, optimizing balance to find those control observations which are most similar to the treated observations.

The key identifying assumption for causal inference is *selection on observables*: all variables that influence nonrandom selection must be observed and incorporated into the analysis. Once they have been, it becomes possible to compare treated and untreated groups without leveraging many additional assumptions—a substantial advantage. However, selection on observables can be a challenging assumption to meet even under ideal circumstances (Sekhon 2009; Keele 2015).

The main advantage to matching is that it enables the analyst to take into account stratification in their data. Using the example above, if X perfectly predicts the probability of receiving treatment D so that there is a "selection effect," by matching on X the analyst can compare treated and control groups, recovering the Average Treatment Effect on the Treated (the ATT). In this case, given a binary treatment and outcome, we are interested in $E[Y_i^1 \mid D_i = 1] - E[Y^0 \mid D_i = 1]$, since we believe the treated and untreated groups are drawn from different populations (Sekhon 2009). While we cannot observe this, by conditioning on the variables $\mathbf{X}$ in the population which lead to selection into treatment, $E[Y_i^1 \mid D_i = 1, \mathbf{X}] - E[Y^0 \mid D_i = 0, \mathbf{X}]$, we can estimate the "observational equivalent" of the ATE (Sekhon 2009). Modeling this using regression returns a biased estimate of β_1, however, since this selection effect violates assumption 3 something in ϵ is causing D. Matching helps to account for this.

There are a variety of ways to estimate the propensity score. Traditionally, the simplest way was to use predicted probabilities from a logistic regression (Rosenbaum and Rubin 1983). Once the propensity score is estimated and a balanced set of cases is selected, the analyst subtracts the control outcomes from the treated outcomes to find the ATE and conducts a simple t-test to see if the difference in means is significant. If the difference in means is significant, we assume that the treatment had an effect on the outcome.

However, the traditional propensity-score approach is sensitive to misspecification (Imai and Ratkovic 2014), scholars should use other techniques for calculating propensity scores, such as optimization using genetic algorithms, known as "genetic matching" (Diamond and Sekhon 2013) or a method of moments estimator which also optimizes balance, the Covariate Balancing Propensity Score (CBPS) (Imai and Ratkovic 2014).

10.2.2.2 *Instrumental Variables*

Instrumental variables (IVs) have a long lineage in econometrics and in the 1990s were adopted for explicitly identifying causal effects (Angrist et al. 1996). Instruments were originally developed to address issues of endogenous predictors, where in

$$Y = \beta_0 + \beta_1 D + \beta_2 X + \epsilon$$

D and Y are correlated through ϵ, violating either assumption 3 or assumption 5 at the start of Section 10.2.1 or both, depending on the source of the correlation. The goal of instrumental variables modeling is to find a source of exogenous variation (Z) that causes variation in Y *only* through D, so that if we look at the relationship between Y and the variation in D we can attribute to Z to infer causality. The key identifying assumption, therefore, is that Z does not cause Y except via D.

IV modeling requires estimating a multiple-equation model, either a two-stage least squares or a simultaneous likelihood model. In the first equation, an instrument Z is estimated for X, where Z only affects Y through D, so that $D = Z\pi + on$, where π is the effect of Z on X. The predicted values (X^*) are then used in place of D in the second equation for Y. $Y = \alpha + D^*\beta + \epsilon$ then returns an unbiased estimate of β, as long as the covariance between Z and ϵ is asymptotically 0, that the instrument Z only effects the outcome Y through the mediating variable D, known as the "exclusion restriction" (Sovey and Green 2011: 190). This relationship can never truly be tested; the analyst must provide a plausible theoretical reason for their instrument choice, such that asymptotically, the exclusion restriction might be met. The analyst must also avoid the "weak instrument problem": asymptotically, the covariance between Z and D asymptotically must not equal zero, otherwise, substantial bias will result (Sovey and Green 2011).

10.2.2.3 *Binary Outcomes and Simultaneous Equations*

Another complication with instrumental variables crops up in the case of the nonlinear models, like logit and probit, that are the bread and butter of quantitative international security studies. Because the theory behind instrumental variables was developed in the context of the linear model, the IV method does not translate especially well to the nonlinear case (Greene 2009).

The solution to nonrandom treatment in nonlinear models involves modeling the sources of both treatment and outcome in simultaneous equations. The model that captures the logic of endogenous binary treatment most intuitively is the *recursive bivariate probit* model, which has seen surprisingly little use in political science:

$$Y^* = \beta_0 + \beta_1 D + \beta_2 \mathbf{X} + \epsilon$$

$$D^* = \gamma_0 + \gamma_1 \mathbf{W} + \upsilon$$

$$-1 \leq \rho(\epsilon, \upsilon) \leq 1$$

Simply put, treatment is a function of **W** and the outcome is a function of treatment and **X**. The impact of residual unobserved confounders is captured in the correlation (ρ) between ϵ and υ.

In this model, identification can take place even if all variables that influence selection are not observed and measured, so one need not assume selection on observables as in matching. Instead, identification is obtained both via the exclusion restriction (at least one variable in **W** must be legitimately excluded from **X**) and via functional-form assumptions (e.g. that the link functions for the two equations are probits and the distribution of the error terms follows a cumulative normal distribution). To reduce reliance on strong functional-form assumptions, Braumoeller et al. (2017) have introduced a flexible recursive bivariate model to political science that allows the user to relax many of the parametric assumptions of the standard model.

10.2.2.4 *Other Tools for Causal Inference*

We have only scratched the surface of a vast literature on tools for causal inference. Among those techniques we did not address were regression discontinuities, difference-in-differences (Angrist and Pischke 2008), inverse propensity score weighting and doubly robust estimation (Morgan and Winship 2014), and the role of time in causal inference (Blackwell 2013). Mediation analysis is a rapidly growing sub-field of the causal inference literature, with a focus on the mechanisms by which the treatment affects the outcome (Imai et al. 2011). The development of sensitivity analyses has provided another flourishing literature in causal inference: building on the work of Manski (1990), scholars build tests to examine how strong assumptions have to be to make a particular design work (Mebane and Poast 2013).

Finally, there is the graphical approach to causality, developed by Pearl (2009) and Spirtes et al. (1993), which expresses causality in the form of Directed Acyclic Graphs (DAGs) and conditional probabilities. Though the graphical and potential outcomes frameworks are mathematically equivalent (Morgan and Winship 2014), the clean representation of the graphical model can clarify the math and intuitions of the equivalent potential outcomes model. Despite their origins in computer science rather than the social sciences and the relative recency of their development, DAGs have begun to make some inroads into political science (see, e.g., Blackwell 2013; Imai et al. 2014).

10.2.2.5 *The Next Frontier: Interference*

As discussed at the start of Section 10.2.1, one of the key assumptions in causal inference is SUTVA, the stable unit treatment value assumption, in particular, a lack of interference, where subject *i*'s treatment does not affect subject *j*'s outcome, and vice versa. Network effects, which are often present in International Relations data, raise challenging issues for causal inference: how does one (for example) match on dyads? Not accounting for network structures can bias our inferences: we are no longer measuring $Y = DY^1 + (1-D)Y^0$, but rather $Y = (DY^1 + \text{other stuff}) + ((1-D)Y^0 + \text{other stuff})$; not accounting for this "other stuff" biases our estimate of the average treatment effect.

Some solutions are available, but no consensus exists regarding a "best" or "default" solution. If observations are grouped and interference occurs within but not between groups, a multilevel model is appropriate. By fitting a model with slopes and intercepts which vary across groups, one can isolate the effect of treatment (Gelman and Hill 2006). However, if the analyst suspects that there is a complex network structure driving the observed outcomes (Cranmer et al. 2012), the modeling strategy will need to involve these network structures. The analyst could make use of a variety of approaches to network causal inference developed in epidemiology and biostatistics (Ogburn and VanderWeele 2014), statistics (Athey 2016), or political science (Bowers et al. 2013). The downside to these methods is that they often require a far larger N (more observations) than International Relations data can provide and also usually fail to take time (T) into account.

An open challenge for the field is developing a method to take advantage of the data structures common in international security data: a small N ($\approx$ 150 countries or 22,350 dyads per year), but a large T, with the Correlates of War extending from 1816 to 2010 (Palmer et al. 2015). Future work could attempt to leverage this longitudinal structure to estimate causal effects over time in the presence of interference.

10.2.3 What Can Causal Inference Offer IR?

At first, the promise of causal inference for students of IR seems great: simply switching from ordinary probit to recursive bivariate probit would not be much of a challenge for most practitioners, and the results would more plausibly capture causal effects.

However, since we assume causation requires manipulation, simply changing the model does not mean we are suddenly "doing causal inference." We must think about the design underlying our models.

The key insight from the study design literature is that the design of a causal study should be robust, relying on several tests of the underlying theoretical cause, rather than just a single test (Keele and Minozzi 2013). Rosenbaum (2010) refers to this as testing for the "reasons for effects," while causal inference is usually interested in the "direct causes." We might also ask what else a theory implies, to assess the strength of our theorized cause.

For example, hypothesis testing in the Democratic Peace literature is often reduced to one or two dependent variables (MIDs or wars from Palmer et al. 2015), and an independent variable (regime, usually coded by Polity score; see Marshall and Jaggers 2002). Scholars run a handful of regressions, tweaking "control variables," but rarely looking at alternative measures of the outcomes or treatments upon which their theory depends.

What might they do instead? In asking what their particular theory of the Democratic Peace implies, they might ask if they would expect to see similar patterns if they operationalize regime differently (as Weeks 2014 did), or if they operationalize conflict differently. For example, rather than examining wars, if a scholar expects that democratic dyads are more pacific, they might use event data (Schrodt et al. 2008)[4] and investigate whether there are fewer "conflictual" events and more "cooperative" events between democracies, as compared to autocracies. They could also, following Keele and Minozzi (2013), utilize an array of different research designs and statistical models designed for causal inference (matching, instrumental variables, natural experiments, and the like) in an attempt to triangulate an answer.

Regardless, the challenges of causal inference do not justify inaction. If the goal is to move beyond simplistic regression models and make causal claims, scholars, even in the presence of data which make standard causal inference techniques difficult, can use the principles of causal inference to better test the causal claims in many IR theories.

10.3 Prediction

Prediction gets a bad rap in International Relations. Kenneth Waltz (1979) dismissed it and later argued that "tests [of theory] are always problematic" and that prediction should not be the goal of theory (Waltz 1997, 2016). This approach has been contested by Ward et al. (2010) and Schrodt (2014) among others, who argue that predictive modeling is the ultimate test for the validity of theory. We argue, following Shmueli (2010), that explanation (causal inference) is fundamentally different than prediction. Both have utility, but scholars should not confuse causal models for predictive ones or vice versa.

What is prediction? Following Shmueli (2010), we define prediction as using models or algorithms to predict unobserved values of Y, given some set of predictors X. Models "trained" on some existing data where both X and Y are known are then "tested" on some new data, where one might only have X. The scholar then "predicts" the new Y values. In the remainder of this section, we will review the process of prediction, how to assess predictive models, and conclude with a sample of various techniques that IR scholars can use for prediction.

10.3.1 The Process of Prediction

Unlike causal inference, prediction is usually not interested in coefficient values, statistical significance, or "the exact role of each variable in terms of an underlying causal structure," (Shmueli 2010: 300) but, rather, in modeling the data-generating process to best approximate Y given X. Many of the approaches used for prediction are "algorithmic:" The model is a "black box" for approximating the best model of Y, given X (Breiman 2001b). The goal of these models is to choose some combination of variables which optimizes some function (mean-squared error, Akaike Information Criterion (AIC), etc.) to find the best fit. Unlike GLMs, where the data-generating process is (more or less) linear and additive, many algorithmic predictive models can capture nonlinear, non-additive aspects of a data-generating process.

How does the analyst determine if a model is predicting well? The common technique for testing predictive models in the absence of new data is cross-validation. The data are partitioned into "training" and "test" sets, with models fitted on the training data and not allowed to "see" the test data, and then x-values from the test data are used to predict new y-values, which are then compared to the observed y-values in the test data. This *out-of-sample* prediction, has become more common in political science, especially since the publication of King and Zeng (2010).

10.3.2 Assessing Predictive Models

Once the analyst has fit a variety of models and wants to find the model that best captures their data-generating process, they need to decide on a criterion to assess their predictive model. If the analyst fits a model by maximum likelihood, they can use the AIC, which takes the model deviance and adds a penalty for number of predictors, penalizing predictors which only add noise (McElreath 2016 provides an easy-to-understand derivation of the AIC). The result is a model fit criterion which asymptotically measures out-of-sample prediction (Gelman and Hill 2006). However, there is no guarantee the assessment holds in finite samples, especially if the coefficient distributions are not Gaussian (McElreath 2016). Instead, while scholars can (and should!) use AIC in their models, they should also choose among metrics that are designed to work with observed out-of-sample predictions.

The simplest of these is mean-squared error (MSE):

$$MSE = \frac{1}{n}\sum_{i=1}^{n}(y_i - \hat{f}(x_i))^2$$

MSE squares the difference between actual (y_i) and predicted ($\hat{f}(x_i)$) outcomes and then takes the average (James et al. 2013). A smaller MSE means better out-of-sample fit, the squared term penalizes outliers more severely. The MSE is most useful for assessing non-binary outcomes; the squared term simply provides the absolute value in the binary case: $(0-1)^2 = (1-0)^2$.

For binary outcomes, like MID/war onset, a broad literature on assessment has developed in the machine learning community. One tool in particular, the Receiver Operating Characteristic (ROC) curve, has become a standard tool for assessing out-of-sample fit. Originally developed in signal processing during the Second World War, ROC curves were imported to political science by King and Zeng (2001). Generating the ROC curve requires taking the predicted probabilities generated by a binary outcome model, using these probabilities to predict a binary outcome, and then comparing the correctly predicted outcomes to the incorrectly predicted outcomes (James et al. 2013), for the entire probability range $[0,1]$ generated by the model. This creates a curve, and "area under the curve" (AUC) can be used to assess binary predictive model fit; a higher AUC indicates a larger proportion of true positives compared to false positives, the model is predicting more "correct" than "incorrect" outcomes. If a model has an AUC below .5, the number of true positives is less than the number of false positives, and the model is doing worse than flipping a coin to predict the outcome (Davis and Goadrich 2006). The ROC curve can be used both in- and out-of-sample; in our examples, we calculate it for out-of-sample prediction.

It is worth noting that if we have far more 0s than 1s, an ROC curve will not always find the best model for predicting 1s, since it will treat predicting true positives for both 0 and 1 as equally important. If we care more about 1 than 0, this is not helpful. The precision-recall (PR) curve, built for data with highly-imbalanced dependent variables will be far more useful. Using the same probabilities generated by a binary model that ROC curves use, PR curves divide the number of correctly predicted ones (precision) by the total number of ones predicted at each point on the predicted probability (recall). The PR curve, like the ROC curve, provides a useful metric to evaluate models and penalizes models that do well on AUC by generating mostly zeroes. Indeed, models that perform the best on precision-recall perform the best on AUC, but the converse does not hold (Davis and Goadrich 2006); security scholars interested in predicting conflict would be wellserved by validating their models using precision-recall curves.

10.3.3 Varieties of Predictive Models

A broad variety of models for prediction exist in the statistics and machine learning literature, and entire books have been written on them (see Hastie et al. 2009; James et al. 2013)[5]

In this section we will focus on three common models—the generalized linear model, the elastic net, and the random forest—and illustrate these models on a simulated dataset with a rare outcome.[6] The GLM in this case is a logistic regression. The elastic net, implemented in the "glmnet" package in R, comes from Zou and Hastie (2005) by way of Hastie et al. (2009), and grows out of Tibshirani's (1996) work on the LASSO (an acronym for "Least Absolute Shrinkage and Selection Operator"). The elastic net penalizes overly complex models, regularizing coefficients by forcing them toward zero to prevent overfitting, unless they add predictive power. A key advantage to the elastic net for security scholars is that, unlike traditional regression, it works when there are more variables than observations, even when these variables are highly correlated. Since the elastic net is built around a GLM, it runs relatively quickly, even with large datasets.

Random forests, originally developed by Breiman (2001a), are a black box tool for regression and prediction which improve upon regression trees by creating an ensemble of trees that split outcomes based on predictors and, by iterating this process many times (1000 in our simulation), reduce overfitting, bias, and variance. The key advantage to random forests is that they make no functional form assumptions about the data-generating process and so are more flexible than a GLM-based approach.

In the following simulation, we generated 1000 observations with 100 possible variables. The outcome is highly skewed, with $\approx 10\%$ 1s. The outcome data are generated from the first 35 of these variables; models are trained on 80 percent of the data and tested on the remaining 20 percent. ROC and precision-recall curves are used to measure model fit in out-of-sample prediction (Figures 10.2 and 10.3).

Examining this outcome, the elastic net outperforms both logistic regression and the random forest. In the ROC curve, the best-predicting model should hug the upper-left corner: the elastic net makes a sizable predictive improvement on both the random forest and the logistic regression. In the precision-recall curve, the best-predicting model should hug the top right corner, again the elastic net does best. While the logistic regression appears to perform better than the random forest, its recall is zero below this $\approx .55$ cutoff, so, while it may predict these zeroes (peace) correctly, as scholars, we are not interested in this, since it cannot tell us when there is a one (war). When the analyst uses these plots to check their analyses, they should keep in mind potential differences in the two, and check both, to make sure their results are not the results of particular model specifications and/or quirks in the data.

10.4 Combining Prediction and Causal Inference?

As we hope to have demonstrated, prediction and causal inference are different tasks, and those tasks are typically best accomplished with different modeling approaches. However, several machine learning techniques for prediction are also contributing to causal inference, as datasets become so large that traditional methods no longer work.

A new and exciting set of developments for security scholars is the use of machine learning approaches for causal inference in high-dimensional data (see Athey 2015 for a general overview) which use predictive methods in the service of causal inference.

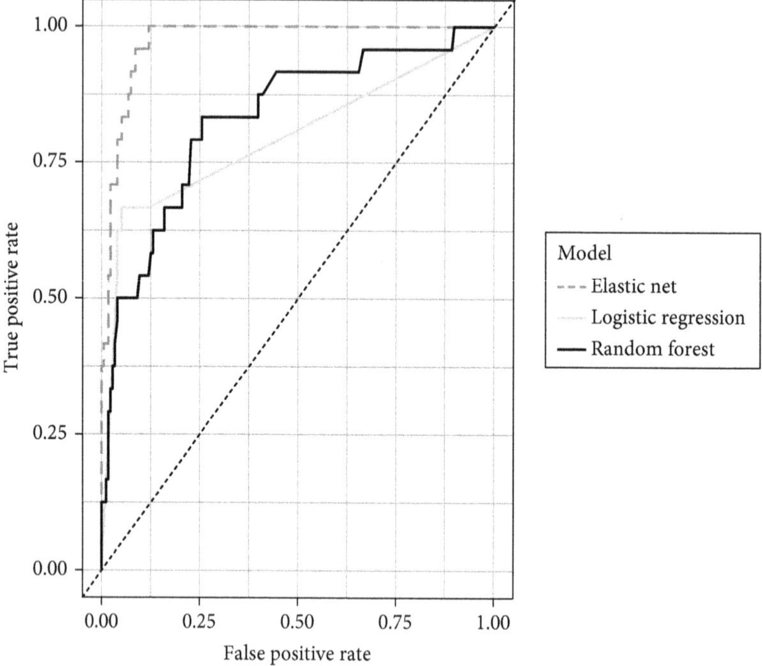

FIGURE 10.2 ROC plot for three models

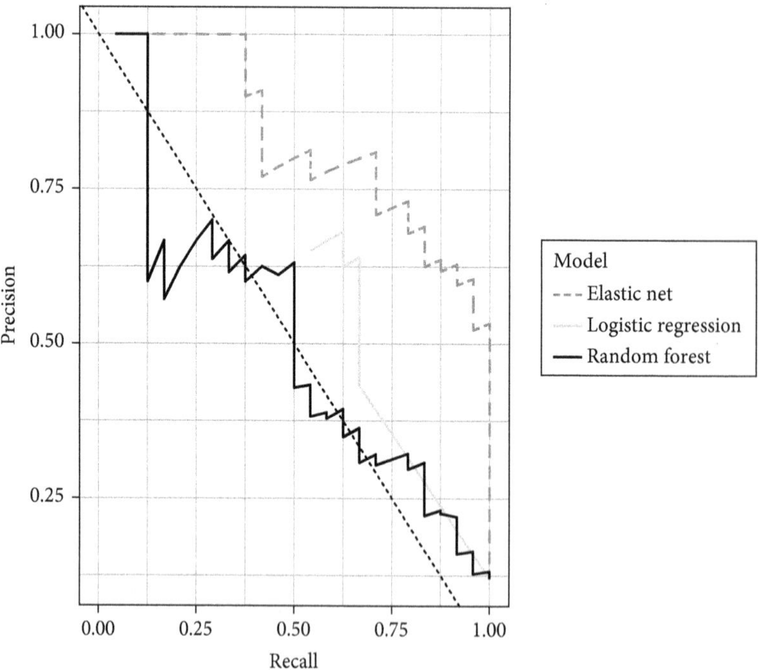

FIGURE 10.3 Precision-recall curve plot for three models

Propensity scores are essentially a prediction task, and when dozens (or hundreds) of variables can potentially play a role in the propensity score, traditional methods like logistic regression are overwhelmed. Machine learning methods can be used to build propensity scores from large collections of variables using ensembles of models, and then standard causal inference techniques are used to estimate effects. Van der Laan and Rose (2011) provide a suite of methods for this approach, and Samii et al. (2016) provide a political science example. Similarly, Hill (2012) suggests using Bayesian Additive Regression Trees, a Bayesian variation on random forests, to flexibly model response to treatment, without making parametric assumptions about the distribution of the outcome.

Recent work by economists using machine learning techniques for causal inference holds promise for security scholars as well. As Belloni et al. (2014) and Athey and Imbens (2016) discuss, an analyst facing hundreds of possible variables to include in a causal analysis can either select a handful in an ad hoc manner, or use machine learning tools like the LASSO or random forests to select the subset of variables which matter for analysis, and are the asymptotically best choice. Particularly in an era of "big data," where scholars will have access to hundreds of variables and hundreds of thousands of observations, tools like these are a promising path for dealing with large datasets.

10.5 Conclusion

In this chapter, we have discussed the difference between prediction and causal inference in statistics, and what this means for scholars of international security. Following Shmueli (2010), we sought to highlight that these are two different activities, with different goals, modeling strategies, and methods to analyze data. We do not set the two up as competing approaches in a zero-sum empirical game, but rather as different ways to evaluate the empirics underlying theories, each of which is well-suited to a different set of statistical tools.

We leave with the hope that our discussion of the distinction between prediction and causation and our call for better quantitative research will lead to improvements in the field of international security and bring our everyday methods more in line with our traditions of strong theorizing and effective data-gathering.

Notes

1. The junior author of this piece should be held blameless for the blunt tone of this and the remaining paragraphs in this section.
2. God only knows how many times (Gelman and Loken 2014).
3. Although we have read many definitions of endogeneity, user Bill's is the clearest and most succint: http://stats.stackexchange.com/questions/59588/what-do-endogeneity-and-

exogeneity-mean-substantively. Because we cannot improve on Bill's list of five assumptions, we have reproduced them here almost verbatim, with notation slightly tweaked to be in line with Morgan and Winship (2014).

4. These are daily-level events data that record a variety of concrete actions, from "made a speech" to "employ aerial weapons."
5. Availableonlinefromtheauthors:http://www-bcf.usc.edu/gareth/ISL/ISLRSixthPrinting.pdf, http://statweb.stanford.edu/tibs/ElemStatLearn/printings/ESLIIprint10.pdf, http://www.inference.phy.cam.ac.uk/itprnn/book.pdf,http://web4.cs.ucl.ac.uk/staff/D.Barber/pmwiki.php?n=Brml.online Barber (2012) and MacKay (2003).
6. All code is available for replication at https://github.com/adamlauretig/Statisticsandinternationalsecurity.

References

Achen, Christopher H. 2002. Toward a New Political Methodology: Microfoundations and ART. *Annual Review of Political Science*, 5(1): 423–50.

Angrist, Joshua D. and Jörn-Steffen Pischke. 2008. *Mostly Harmless Econometrics: An Empiricist's Companion*. Princeton, NJ: Princeton University Press.

Angrist, Joshua D., Guido W. Imbens, and Donald B. Rubin. 1996. Identification of Causal Effects Using Instrumental Variables. *Journal of the American Statistical Association*, 91(434): 444–55.

Athey, Susan. 2015. Machine Learning and Causal Inference for Policy Evaluation. In *Proceedings of the 21th ACM SIGKDD International Conference on Knowledge Discovery and Data Mining*, pp. 5–6. Syndey: ACM.

Athey, Susan and Guido Imbens. 2016. The State of Applied Econometrics—Causality and Policy Evaluation. *arXiv preprint arXiv:1607.00699*.

Athey, Susan, Dean Eckles, and Guido W. Imbens. 2016. Exact P-values for Network Interference. *Journal of the American Statistical Association*. Doi/10.1080/01621459.2016.1241178.

Barber, David. 2012. *Bayesian Reasoning and Machine Learning*. Cambridge: Cambridge University Press.

Beck, Nathaniel, Gary King, and Langche Zeng. 1999. Improving Quantitative Studies of International Conflict: A Conjecture. *American Political Science Review*, 94(1): 21–36.

Belloni, Alexandre, Victor Chernozhukov, and Christian Hansen. 2014. High-Dimensional Methods and Inference on Structural and Treatment Effects. *The Journal of Economic Perspectives*, 28(2): 29–50.

Blackwell, Matthew. 2013. A Framework for Dynamic Causal Inference in Political Science. *American Journal of Political Science*, 57(2): 504–20.

Bowers, Jake, Mark M. Fredrickson, and Costas Panagopoulos. 2013. Reasoning about Interference between Units: A General Framework. *Political Analysis*, 21(1): 97–124.

Braumoeller, Bear F. 2003. Causal Complexity and the Study of Politics. *Political Analysis*, 11(3): 209–233.

Braumoeller, Bear F., Giampiero Marra, Rosalba Radice, and Aisha Bradshaw. 2017. Flexible Causal Inference for Political Science. *Political Analysis*, forthcoming.

Breiman, Leo. 2001a. Random Forests. *Machine Learning*, 45(1): 5–32.

Breiman, Leo. 2001b. Statistical Modeling: The Two Cultures (with comments and a rejoinder by the author). *Statistical Science*, 16(3): 199–231.

Clarke, Kevin A. and David M. Primo. 2007. Modernizing Political Science: A Model-Based Approach. *Perspectives on Politics*, 5(4): 741–53.

Cranmer, Skyler J., Bruce A. Desmarais, and Elizabeth J. Menninga. 2012. Complex Dependencies in the Alliance Network. *Conflict Management and Peace Science*, 29(3): 279–313.

Davis, Jesse and Mark Goadrich. 2006. The Relationship between Precision-Recall and ROC Curves. In *Proceedings of the 23rd International Conference on Machine Learning*, pp. 233–40. Pittsburgh, PA: ACM.

Diamond, Alexis and Jasjeet S Sekhon. 2013. Genetic Matching for Estimating Causal Effects: A General Multivariate Matching Method for Achieving Balance in Observational Studies. *Review of Economics and Statistics*, 95(3): 932–45.

Driscoll, Jesse and Daniel Maliniak. 2016. Did Georgian Voters Desire Military Escalation in 2008? Experiments and Observations. *The Journal of Politics*, 78(1): 265–80.

Gelman, Andrew and Jennifer Hill. 2006. *Data Analysis Using Regression and Multilevel/Hierarchical Models*. Cambridge: Cambridge University Press.

Gelman, Andrew and Eric Loken. 2014. The Statistical Crisis in Science: Data-Dependent Analysis—A "Garden of Forking Paths"—Explains Why Many Statistically Significant Comparisons Don't Hold Up. *American Scientist* 102(6): 460.

Greene, William H. 2009. Discrete Choice Modeling. In Terence C. Mills and Kerry Patterson (eds), *Palgrave Handbook of Econometrics*, Vol. 2 (Applied Econometrics), pp. 473–556. Basingstoke: Palgrave Macmillan.

Hastie, Trevor, Robert Tibshirani, and Jerome Friedman. 2009. *The Elements of Statistical Learning*. Vol. 1 Springer series in statistics. Berlin: Springer.

Hill, Jennifer L. 2012. Bayesian Nonparametric Modeling for Causal Inference. *Journal of Computational and Graphical Statistics*. Doi/10.1198/jcgs.2010.08162

Holland, Paul W. 1986. Statistics and Causal Inference. *Journal of the American Statistical Association*, 81(396): 945–60.

Hyde, Susan D. 2015. Experiments in International Relations: Lab, Survey, and Field. *Annual Review of Political Science*, 18: 403–24.

Imai, Kosuke and Marc Ratkovic. 2014. Covariate Balancing Propensity Score. *Journal of the Royal Statistical Society: Series B (Statistical Methodology)*, 76(1): 243–63.

Imai, Kosuke, Luke Keele, Dustin Tingley, and Teppei Yamamoto. 2011. Unpacking the Black Box of Causality: Learning about Causal Mechanisms from Experimental and Observational Studies. *American Political Science Review*, 105(4): 765–89.

James, Gareth, Daniela Witten, Trevor Hastie, and Robert Tibshirani. 2013. *An Introduction to Statistical Learning*. Vol. 6. Berlin: Springer.

Keele, Luke. 2015. The Statistics of Causal Inference: A View from Political Methodology. *Political Analysis*, 23(3): 313–35.

Keele, Luke and William Minozzi. 2013. How Much is Minnesota Like Wisconsin? Assumptions and Counterfactuals in Causal Inference with Observational Data. *Political Analysis*, 21(2): 193–216.

King, Gary and Langche Zeng. 2001. Improving Forecasts of State Failure. *World Politics*, 53(4): 623–58.

McElreath, Richard. 2016. *Statistical Rethinking: A Bayesian Course with Examples in R and Stan*. Vol. 122 Boca Raton, FL: CRC Press.

MacKay, David J. C. 2003. *Information Theory, Inference and Learning Algorithms*. Cambridge: Cambridge University Press.

Manski, Charles F. 1990. Nonparametric Bounds on Treatment Effects. *The American Economic Review*, 80(2): 319–23.

Marshall, Monty G. and Keith Jaggers. 2002. Polity IV project: Political regime characteristics and transitions, 1800–2002. *Available at:* http://www.systemicpeace.org/polityproject.html, accessed August 30, 2107.

Mebane, Walter, R Jr. and Paul Poast. 2013. Causal Inference without Ignorability: Identification with Nonrandom Assignment and Missing Treatment Data. *Political Analysis*, 21(2): 233–51.

Morgan, Stephen L. and Christopher Winship. 2014. *Counterfactuals and Causal Inference*. Cambridge: Cambridge University Press.

Ogburn, Elizabeth L., and Tyler J. VanderWeele. 2014. Vaccines, Contagion, and Social Networks. *arXiv preprint arXiv:1403.1241*.

Palmer, Glenn, Vito d'Orazio, Michael Kenwick, and Matthew Lane. 2015. The MID4 Dataset, 2002–2010: Procedures, Coding Rules and Description. *Conflict Management and Peace Science*, 32(2): 222–42.

Pearl, Judea. 2009. *Causality*. Cambridge: Cambridge University Press.

Reuveny, Rafael and Quan Li. 2003. The Joint Democracy–Dyadic Conflict Nexus: A Simultaneous Equations Mode." *International Studies Quarterly*, 47: 325–46.

Rosenbaum, Paul R. 2010. *Design of Observational Studies*. Vol. 10. Berlin: Springer.

Rosenbaum, Paul R. and Donald B. Rubin. 1983. The Central Role of the Propensity Score in Observational Studies for Causal Effects. *Biometrika* 70(1): 41–55.

Rubin, Donald B. 1973. Matching to Remove Bias in Observational Studies. *Biometrics*, 159–83.

Rubin, Donald B. 1974. Estimating Causal Effects of Treatments in Randomized and Nonrandomized Studies. *Journal of Educational Psychology*, 66(5): 688.

Rubin, Donald B. 1978. Bayesian Inference for Causal Effects: The Role of Randomization." *The Annals of Statistics*, 6(1): 34–58.

Rubin, Donald B. 2008. For Objective Causal Inference, Design Trumps Analysis. *The Annals of Applied Statistics*, 2(3): 808–40.

Samii, Cyrus, Laura Paler, and Sarah Zukerman Daly. 2016. Retrospective Causal Inference with Machine Learning Ensembles: An Application to Anti-recidivism Policies in Colombia. *Political Analysis*, 24(4): 434–56.

Schrodt, Philip A. 2014. Seven Deadly Sins of Contemporary Quantitative Political Analysis. *Journal of Peace Research*, 51(2): 287–300.

Schrodt, Philip A., Omür Yilmaz, Deborah J. Gerner, and Dennis Hermreck. 2008. The CAMEO (Conflict And Mediation Event Observations) Actor Coding Framework. In *Annual Meeting of the International Studies Association*.

Sekhon, Jasjeet S. 2004. Quality Meets Quantity: Case Studies, Conditional Probability, and Counterfactuals. *Perspectives on Politics*, 2(2): 281–93.

Sekhon, Jasjeet S. 2009. Opiates for the Matches: Matching Methods for Causal Inference. *Annual Review of Political Science*, 12: 487–508.

Shmueli, Galit. 2010. To Explain or to Predict? *Statistical Science*, 25(3): 289–310.

Sovey, Allison J. and Donald P Green. 2011. Instrumental Variables Estimation in Political Science: A Readers' Guide. *American Journal of Political Science*, 55(1): 188–200.

Spirtes, Peter, Clark N. Glymour, and Richard Scheines. 1993. *Causation, Prediction, and Search*. Cambridge, MA: MIT Press.

Tibshirani, Robert. 1996. Regression Shrinkage and Selection via the LASSO. *Journal of the Royal Statistical Society. Series B (Methodological)*, 267–88.

Van der Laan, Mark J. and Sherri Rose. 2011. *Targeted Learning: Causal Inference for Observational and Experimental Data*. Berlin: Springer Science & Business Media.

Waltz, Kenneth N. 1979. *Theory of International Politics*. Long Grove, IL: Waveland Press.

Waltz, Kenneth N. 1997. Evaluating Theories. *American Political Science Review*, 91(4): 913–17.

Ward, Michael D. 2016. Can We Predict Politics? Toward What End? *Journal of Global Security Studies*, 1(1): 80–91.

Ward, Michael D., Brian D. Greenhill, and Kristin M. Bakke. 2010. The Perils of Policy by p-value: Predicting Civil Conflicts. *Journal of Peace Research*, 47(4): 363–75.

Weart, Spencer R. 2000. *Never At War: Why Democracies Will Not Fight One Another*. New Haven, CT: Yale University Press.

Weeks, Jessica L. P. 2014. *Dictators at War and Peace*. Ithaca, NY: Cornell University Press.

Wright, Quincy and Louise Leonard Wright. 1942. *A Study of War*. Chicago: University of Chicago Press.

Zou, Hui and Trevor Hastie. 2005. Regularization and Variable Selection via the Elastic Net. *Journal of the Royal Statistical Society: Series B (Statistical Methodology)*, 67(2): 301–20.

CHAPTER 11

METHODS IN CONSTRUCTIVIST APPROACHES

JEFFREY T. CHECKEL

11.1 Introduction

METHODS follow from theory and theoretical choice. Constructivists have made a number of theoretical bets—on the constitutive power of language and practice, and on thinking of cause in terms of causal and social mechanisms—that then require the use of particular methods. Reading across constructivist scholarship, the methods most commonly referenced are process tracing and case studies (conventional constructivists) or discourse, ethnography and textual analysis (interpretive constructivists). Notably—given the significant epistemological and ontological differences among these scholars—they increasingly converge on a concern with process, in both theory and method.

This chapter is not about the choices constructivists make about methods. Rather, I take their methods at face value and instead explore how well they are used. Are the methods specified and operationalized? Are clear standards articulated? That is, are we given some metric for determining that an application of, say, discourse analysis, is *good* discourse analysis? Are the methods and their execution explicit and transparent, or implicit and vague?

This chapter's core argument is that constructivists can and need to do better in their use of methods. Partly, such weaknesses are a function of constructivism's relative youth, with empirical explorations—which, of necessity, require methods—only really appearing since the mid-1990s. In addition, early empirical work was more concerned with showing that constructivism added value—norms matter, say. Over the past decade, though, researchers have sought to develop more fine-grained arguments—when, under what conditions, and through what mechanisms norms matter, say. And the latter requires a more systematic application of methods.

However, constructivists also need to do better with methods because the social science world around them is changing. Our training in and expectations for the use of qualitative techniques—the ones typically employed by these scholars—are increasingly ambitious. This means future constructivist work on security will need to be much more explicit and transparent in its use of methods.

The chapter proceeds as follows. I begin with some clarifications and delimitations, in particular, justifying my relatively broad-tent understanding of constructivism as well as international security. I then document my claim that constructivists have come to adopt—theoretically—a processual view of the social world. Section 11.4—the chapter's core—assesses how well constructivists apply methods. In the conclusion, I look to the future, arguing that these scholars must double down on method while never losing sight of the precept that method always follows from and is secondary to theory.

11.2 Constructivism and International Security

A fundamental criterion for the constructivism considered in this chapter is that it be empirical; otherwise, it would have no need for method(s). I consider constructivist scholarship on security that is both positivist (so-called conventional constructivism) and interpretive. The latter includes scholars whose work bridges these supposed epistemological divides within constructivism, but it excludes critical security studies as this research is covered elsewhere in the Handbook (Salter and Mutlu, this volume).

Regarding international security, it has become a broad field, as reflected in the diverse themes in this volume—from arms control, to diasporas, to cybersecurity, to nuclear proliferation, to global health. My only addition will be to consider constructivist work on civil war. At first glance, internal conflict might seem to have little connection to *international* security. However, both scholarship (Checkel 2013b) and real-world events (the Syrian civil war that continues as I write in late 2016) demonstrate that civil wars have international and transnational dimensions that inevitably link them to regional and international security.

11.3 The Turn to Process

In an important sense, process has always been central to constructivism. At a foundational level, the ontological stance of mutual constitution favored by many constructivists—which highlights the interaction of agency and structure—is a processual view of the social world. In Wendt's (1999) path-breaking book, causal mechanisms—the process stuff connecting things—play a key role. Despite this, early empirical work exhibited a clear bias toward structure—be it discourses shaping policy (Doty 1993), or norms clashing with other norms (Checkel 1999).

Over the past 10 years, however, a broad cross-section of constructivists has shown growing interest in theorizing process—which mirrors similar moves in political science generally (Hall 2003; Bennett 2013) and in sociology (Hedstrom and Ylikoski 2010). The majority of conventional constructivists now theorize in terms of causal mechanisms (Kelley 2004a, 2004b; Checkel 2007; Risse et al. 2013). Building upon the processual view inherent in mechanisms (Gerring 2007), Kathryn Sikkink—a leading conventional constructivist—advocates a theoretical agenda of agentic constructivism, which is "concerned with the micro-foundations of creating and constituting new actors and new conditions of possibility. It looks at those parts of social processes where new actors take on and challenge (and sometimes change) existing logics of appropriateness" (Sikkink 2011: 9). Here, too, one sees process coming to the fore. Still other conventional constructivists have turned to agent-based modeling as a way to analyze the social processes through which norms emerge or identities change (Hoffmann 2005; Nome and Weidmann 2013).

Theorizing in this process-based way is not the exclusive preserve of constructivists with a positivist orientation. Prominent interpretive constructivists now theorize in terms of what they call social mechanisms, which—again—are all about process (Guzzini 2011; Pouliot 2015). Other interpretive constructivists devote considerable time to theorizing practices, which produce social effects and generate macro phenomena of interest. If this hints at a role for process, then Adler and Pouliot make the link crystal clear—highlighting "the processual nature of practice ontology" (Adler and Pouliot 2015; see also Neumann 2002; Pouliot 2010).

If my analysis here is correct, one should expect to see several broad methodological trends in constructivist work on international security. For one, over time, this scholarship should become more methodologically self-conscious. However, equally important, it should increasingly turn to those methods best suited for measuring process. Whether or not the empirical record supports such claims is the subject of Section 11.4.

11.4 Constructivist Methods in Action

With constructivism and international security defined as in Section 11.2, the data for my analysis come from a review of relevant work in the following journals, for the time period 1996–2016: *American Political Science Review, Civil Wars, Cooperation and Conflict, European Journal of International Relations, International Organization, International Security, International Studies Quarterly, Journal of Conflict Resolution, Journal of Peace Research, Security Dialogue, Security Studies*, and *World Politics*. In addition, research monographs by constructivists from the major university and academic presses were consulted.

The picture that emerges from this survey is of a constructivist literature on security that is not terribly concerned with methods. Of course, methods do get mentioned and sometimes are done well. In fact, though, the best methods applications are by interpretive scholars and researchers working on the edges of constructivism. On the former, my claim may be somewhat surprising given the received wisdom—at least in North America—that conventional constructivists are more likely to get methods right because of their positivist orientation. By the latter, I refer to the work of several students of civil war who study key constructivist dynamics (emotions, norms, frames), but who would not self-identify as constructivists.

To document these findings, I begin by assessing five security monographs where the methods are done well. I then turn to articles, surveying nearly 100 published over a 20-year period and exploring what methods with what degree of rigour are employed.

11.4.1 Research Monographs

With more space than a journal article, one would expect a book to elaborate its methods more clearly. The manuscripts discussed here—in chronological order—were not chosen at random. Among the constructivist books on security I reviewed, they stand out for the clear and operational way methods are employed—clear because readers understand what methods will be utilized and operational because one actually sees the methods at work in the empirics. Three of the five monographs are authored by interpretive constructivists; the other two were written by students of civil war.[1]

In this sense, the chosen books are the exception that proves the rule, with most other constructivist works leaving their methods to operate only implicitly in the empirics and case studies. This makes it more difficult for readers to judge how well they are used—for example, in Finnemore's (2003) and Gheciu's (2005) otherwise excellent studies. In making such a critique, however, it is important to remember that both books were written over a decade ago, when training in and expectations/standards for methods were different from today—a point to which I return in the concluding section.

11.4.1.1 *Soviet and Russian Foreign Policy*

Drawing upon a broad array of sources from sociology, social psychology, and social theory, Ted Hopf (2002a)—in his study of Soviet and Russian foreign policy—seeks to recover the social origins of identity in constructivist theory. More important for my purposes, he tells us how—via what sources and methods—he will use this theory to recover inductively Russian understandings of their own identities. Hopf's (2002a, 23–38) careful discussion and justification of his sources and textual methods, of the dangers of pre-theorization, of reliability, and the like are a must-read. His operational discussion and transparency regarding methods are on a par with contemporary expectations and standards, althrough the work dates from 2002.

All is not perfect here, however, as the methods for the second part of his argument, where Hopf explores the influence of identity discourses on specific Soviet/Russian foreign policy choices, are implicit. In particular, the process tracing in his case studies remains hidden in the narrative. However, with this latter weakness, the author is in very good company, as many contemporary constructivist studies of security continue to invoke process tracing more as a metaphor than as an analytic tool (Hopf 2012; Grynaviski 2014).

11.4.1.2 *Civil War and Rebel Mobilization*

In her book on the civil war in El Salvador, Elisabeth Wood (2003) argues that norms and emotions played a key role in the rebellion. She documents this through a rigorous combination of interviews (panel design), political ethnography, and inductive process tracing. She explicitly addresses the potential sources of bias in interview data (and how one deals with it) and devotes an entire chapter to operationalizing her interviews and ethnography (Wood 2003: ch.2). By operationalize, I mean that readers have a clear understanding of how the methods are used to gather data and draw inferences. And, as others have noted (Lyall 2015), her process tracing is systematic and clear. Writing in 2003, Wood was already adhering to many of the best practices for the method that were first fully articulated only a decade later (Bennett and Checkel 2015).

11.4.1.3 *China and the World*

In his study of China's relations with Asian regional and international organizations, Johnston (2008) sets a method-data standard for conventional constructivist studies of identity. In terms of data, he makes extensive use of interviews (over 120), while explicitly addressing the weaknesses (misremembering, strategic dissimulation) inherent in this particular data source (Johnston 2008: 4143). He also does not stop with interviews, instead triangulating across multiple data streams, including public documents, Chinese academic literature, and private communications among Chinese bureaucrats.

Regarding methods, he takes seriously the challenge of measuring a process such as identity change, rigorously employing a form of process tracing. This means he first operationalizes his three causal mechanisms of identity change, asking (in the jargon) what would be the observable implications if they were at work in the Chinese case. He then presents carefully structured narratives, where readers get a real sense of what mechanisms were at work with what effects (Johnston 2008: ch.1 and *passim*).

11.4.1.4 *Russia–NATO Relations*

Applying practice theory to a study of post-Cold War security relations between Russia and NATO, Vincent Pouliot (2010) adds a missing processual dimension to work on security communities (Adler and Barnett 1998). He does so in a way that is both theoretically innovative and methodologically rigorous. On the former, interpretive constructivists have for many years claimed that the best way to study language is through the examination of texts and discourse. In contrast, Pouliot argues that we must move beyond the mere study of texts to consider also what actors *do*, their practice.

Regarding methodology, Pouliot devotes an entire chapter to it (2010: ch.3; see also Pouliot 2007). And it is a must-read for interpretive constructivist students of security, setting a high (but entirely reachable) standard for an "interpretive methodology" (2010: 61) that will uncover the process through which practices form. Pouliot thinks hard about how to measure practices, ideally through ethnography and participant observation. Since these were not feasible given his sensitive subject matter, Pouliot instead lays out and justifies a combination of interviewing, triangulation, and an interpretive form of process tracing (see also Pouliot 2015) to recover practices in his case.

11.4.1.5 *International Organizations and Post-Conflict Interventions*

Severine Autesserre (2010) uses a focus on mechanism and process to explore post-conflict interventions by international organizations (IOs). Building upon earlier constructivist work on IOs as social entities (Barnett and Finnemore 2004), but in a much more methodologically self-conscious manner, Autesserre documents how a powerful framing mechanism shapes the understanding and actions of these intervening organizations. This is an argument about how process—framing dynamics first theorized by sociologists—shapes what IOs do and the effects they have. To make the argument, Autesserre conducts multi-sited ethnography, semi-structured interviews (over 330) and document analysis, spending a total of 18 months in the field (Autesserre 2010: 31–7).

While she never explicitly cites process tracing, this is in fact a central technique she employs, and it is carefully executed. For example, while she does not use the language of observable implications, Autesserre does just this throughout the study's empirical chapters, exploring what she ought to see if the dominant frame and peacebuilding culture is at work (Autesserre 2010: chs. 2–5). She measures these frame effects by carefully triangulating across multiple data streams. Thus, she examines UN documents, reports findings from field observations and—more ethnographically—engages in participant observation, all with the purpose of documenting both the frame's existence and its effects (Autesserre 2009: 261–3). This triangulation increases confidence in the validity of Autesserre's inferences.

A final point worth emphasizing is that both Autesserre (2010) and Wood (2003) carried out their process tracing in unstable, post-conflict situations, which raises additional challenges, including enhanced incentives for interviewees to lie, personal safety concerns, and ethical issues. It thus all the more remarkable that their methods are so clear and transparent.

11.4.2 Articles

Before turning to constructivist journal articles on international security, several preliminary comments are in order. Naturally, the length limitations of articles compared to books leave authors less space for discussion or operationalization of methods. Some publications—the *Journal of Peace Research*, for example—have addressed this technical obstacle by allowing qualitative methods and data discussions to be placed in online appendices that do not count against word limits.

In addition, journals clearly differ in the extent to which they expect empirical studies to engage with methods. A constructivist study in *International Organization* (*IO*) is more likely to have a detailed methods discussion than one published in *Cooperation and Conflict*. Finally, these differences in editorial profile and readership mean certain journals are over-represented in my sample. Many more constructivist security articles are published in the *European Journal of International Relations* than, say, in *World Politics*.

With these comments in mind, there is a striking fact about the majority of the articles I surveyed. While they usually mention methods at some point, little effort is made to operationalize them. This finding holds independent of journal or time period, and prompts five observations.

First, and to start on a positive note, overall, constructivists working on security have come to devote more attention to methods in their articles. In some cases, this may be general discussions—how to operationalize particular methods, or the techniques required by constructivism (Hopf 2007; Pouliot 2007, 2008, 2015). However, in many instances, empirical studies are now clear about the methods that stand behind their findings (Krebs 2015b; Vaughan-Williams and Stevens 2016). This is a notable change from 10–15 years ago, when it was common to mention methods only in passing (Checkel 2001; Berg and Ehin 2006).

Second and more critically, readers are often told that the research uses a particular method, but the article's empirical material does not show how. The author may know the work the methods are doing and whether or not they are doing it well; for the reader, it is much more difficult to tell. Process tracing, for example, is typically invoked in this manner (Hegghammer 2010; Bettiza and Dionigi 2015; Mitzen 2015; Lantis 2016).

Put differently, the method is not operationalized; it is not clear how an author will employ it to gather data and draw explanatory inferences. Operationalization would also make clear that the author is aware of a given method's limitations—and how he/she might compensate or control for them. Absent this, one has the "method as metaphor" problem, where a method is invoked with no elaboration. This particular weakness remains—unfortunately—widespread in the constructivist literature on security (Mattern 2001; Widmaier 2007; Agius 2013; Dolan 2013; Ben-Josef Hirsch 2014; Fiaz 2014, among many others).

Third, there are of course exceptions to my assessment here, and these are often articles by interpretive constructivists. One example is Hopf's (2002b) study of legitimization dynamics in the post-Soviet space, where he employs a combination of discourse analysis and focus-group methods to reconstruct how people understand the transition from communism. However, he does much more than state his methods. Instead, Hopf justifies their choice, explicitly considers their limitations, and thinks operationally, asking what are the testable implications that his methods seek to uncover.[2]

Fourth, articles by students of civil war that invoke–theorize–document constructivist dynamics are typically very well executed, providing a clear and operational use of their methods. Thus, in her study of peacebuilding failures after civil wars, Autesserre (2009) utilizes a carefully specified ethnography as well as interviewing to document convincingly the role played by frames. In her research on socialization in post-civil war

Guatemala, Bateson (2017) employs process tracing in such a way that readers see how it allows her to gather data and advance specific causal claims. Fujii (2017b) explores how broader social processes shape socialization dynamics in the Bosnian civil war, with her methods being a combination of textual analysis and an interpretive form of interviewing where readers understand what she is able to infer from the interviews and why (Fujii 2010, 2017a). For all three authors, methodologically speaking, it is anything but "method as metaphor."

Fifth and as a direct consequence of the growing theoretical interest in process among constructivist students of security (Section 11.3), one sees increased attention to methods that seek to measure it. Thus, one sees process tracing employed by conventional constructivists (Kelley 2004b; Hegghammer 2010; Bettiza and Dionigi 2015; Lantis 2016). Interpretive constructivists also increasingly turn to process tracing in their empirical studies—albeit in a slightly modified form given their epistemological differences (Guzzini 2012: ch.11; Pouliot 2015; see also Norman 2016).

Scholars who highlight practices have also devoted considerable attention to developing methodological tools appropriate for capturing their processual nature (Pouliot 2007). More recently, Krebs (2015b, 2015c) has sought to develop an account of legitimation dynamics in the national security arena where process-based methods play a key role. These include process tracing, narrative analysis, and the use of rhetorical modes. And the latter are operationalized as either arguing or storytelling, both of which add a process dimension to the study of language.

11.5 Taking Constructivist Methods Seriously: Opportunities and Dangers

In this final section, I begin by contextualizing my critique of constructivists and their use of methods. I then point to two trends—the revolution in qualitative methods and the new emphasis on research transparency—to argue that these scholars must do better methodologically. The section concludes with a warning—to keep methods in their (proper, secondary) place.

11.5.1 Guess What? Constructivists Have Good Company

My review of constructivists working on international security agrees wholeheartedly with Pouliot's (2010: 52) comment that constructivism "would certainly benefit from engaging more systematically and coherently with pressing methodological issues ... making its standards of validity more explicit and amenable to non-constructivist ways of doing research." And the rub for constructivists is in the last part of Pouliot's critique—making their methodological standards more explicit.

Throughout this chapter, I have used the term operationalization, but my concern is the same. It is simply not good enough to state "In this article, I use a combination of ethnography, interviews and process tracing to ..." Readers also need some sense—to continue the example—for how the three methods were used to gather the data and advance explanatory-causal-narrative inferences. In turn, the latter requires an author to address explicitly the biases and weaknesses in their methods. Put differently, operationalization forces one to the applied level, and application can only be based on some sense of "this is how we do it well"—standards, in other words.

Invoking standards, however, pushes me to nuance and contextualize my critique of constructivist security work in two ways. First, while I have not systematically surveyed empirical work on international security by other schools and groups of scholars—realists or students of critical security studies, say—my very strong sense is that the identical critique regarding poorly operationalized methods would be applicable to their work. Constructivists, in other words, are in good company.

Consider one example. For the better part of 20 years, empirically oriented international security scholars have been debating how one explains the peaceful end to the Cold War. Was it ideas? Material power? A combination of the two? The disagreement is, of course, to some extent rooted in a particular scholar's theoretical priors. However, in a review of the relevant literature, Evangelista (2015) persuasively argues that the indeterminacy of the debate is also explained by method—more precisely, by poorly operationalized process methods. This has made it more difficult for others to evaluate the rigor and quality of the evidence advanced by researchers with competing theoretical explanations.

Second, when I critique constructivists for coming up short on methods, I am implicitly applying some standard. But whose standard and based on what? If constructivists used primarily quantitative methods, these questions would be easier to answer. Quantitative researchers do have certain community expectations of how to present and operationalize their methods—from reporting confidence intervals, to making their data available for replication. Qualitative researchers currently have no similar community standards—although this is changing (see Section 11.5.2).

Thus, the methodological standard I impose here—to be both explicit and operational—is my own. However, it is not pulled out of thin air, but emerges from my own work on methodology (Checkel 2008a, 2008b; Bennett and Checkel 2015; Checkel 2015), professional engagement with methodological issues (through the Organized Section on Qualitative and Multi-Method Research of the American Political Science Association [APSA]), service on journal editorial boards (*International Organization, European Journal of Political Research*), and lecturing and graduate workshops on methods throughout Europe and the Americas.

11.5.2 Social Science Is Changing

Methodologically, the biggest challenge for constructivists studying international security arises not internally, from the choice of particular methods or data problems;

instead, it comes from the outside—by which I mean the rapidly evolving expectations for the use of qualitative methods in political science.

Two trends are driving these expectations. Most important, the period since the turn of the millennium has witnessed nothing short of a revolution in qualitative methods. It is seen in the publication of numerous books and edited volumes devoted not just to method A, but—crucially—also how to do method A well. This includes work on case studies (George and Bennett 2005; Gerring 2006), discourse analysis (Hansen 2006; Neumann 2008), interpretive interviewing (Fujii 2017a), and process tracing (Beach and Pedersen 2013; Bennett and Checkel 2015)—to name just a few.

This revolution is also seen in the significant improvement in graduate training, mainly through the availability of qualitative methods courses outside university departments. This includes the "short courses" held in conjunction with APSA's annual convention; the winter and summer methods schools offered by the European Consortium for Political Research; and the two-week long Institute for Qualitative and Multi-Method Research at Syracuse University.

The second trend that is raising expectations for users of qualitative methods is the DA-RT initiative, or data access and research transparency (Symposium 2014, 2015, 2016). In 2011–12, this started as an initiative of APSA, with a focus on incorporating DA-RT principles into the Association's ethics guidelines. However, beginning in late 2014, a number of political science journal editors sought to bring these principles more broadly into professional publishing norms. This led to the promulgation of a Journal Editors' Transparency Statement (JETS), which—as of early 2017—has been adopted by over 27 leading American and European political science journals.[3]

JETS and DA-RT have clear implications for constructivist work on international security. Specifically, there is now a requirement (for publication in the 27 journals) and expectation (in the discipline) that authors demonstrate both production transparency and analytic transparency with regards to their methods and data. The former requires digital archiving—that is, making publicly available your qualitative data (field notes, interview protocols, etc.). The latter requires authors to specify clearly the analytic procedures upon which their published claims rely.

Both requirements may sound innocuous, but they are not. They contain significant—and unresolved—tensions along ethical, epistemological and practical dimensions (see, especially, Symposium 2016). Consider one example. Implementing analytic transparency may involve authors creating a so-called transparency index, where the reader of a journal article can follow links to the actual source material (say, full interview protocol or full archival document) used to make specific inferential claims. What, though, if that source material—as will often be the case—is in a foreign language? Is the author required to translate it? If so, how do we know she will not cheat—only translating in a way that confirms her argument? Amazingly, JETS/DA-RT do not even address this issue.

While there is significant debate and pushback against both DA-RT and JETS,[4] my own sense is these innovations are here to stay—eventually perhaps in some modified form. This means constructivist students of international security will need to work even harder at their methods. Indeed, *not a single book or article reviewed in this chapter* meets the methods/data expectations of DA-RT/JETS.

11.5.3 Keeping Methods Where They Belong

My final set of comments may come as a surprise, especially given the message of this chapter so far, which might be summarized as "more methods, yes, and better too." Simply put, one can have too much focus on methods.

I opened the chapter with a truism: "Methods follow from theory and theoretical choice." One of the great things about constructivism—including its work on international security—is the theoretical fresh air it has brought to the field. Arguments about practices (Pouliot 2010), socialization (Johnston 2008), and the role of language in structuring politics—discourse, yes, but also theory on arguing and persuasion (Deitelhoff 2009)—have helped us create a set of social theories of international security. It would thus be a pity if such bold theorizing were now overshadowed by method.

And there are legitimate grounds to worry. Among quantitative IR scholars, it has been noted (Mearsheimer and Walt 2013), that the heavy focus on methods has reduced theory to "simplistic hypothesis testing." From this perspective, there is a clear villain to the story: "The quants made us do it!" While there is an element of truth to such a claim, it is only one small part of the story. Indeed, for many qualitative IR scholars—including some constructvists surveyed here—theory is now little more than a list of mechanisms that do not travel or generalize in any meaningful way (Checkel 2013a, 2015, 2016).

At a deeper level, we socialize graduate students to get their work published fast and in the best IR journals. Of course, writing articles is important, but their length limitations, the nature of the review process and the need to write oneself into the current debates and literature encourage a pull-theory-off-the-shelf approach. The debates over DA-RT and the JETS policy will further incentivize younger scholars to think in such theoretically small ways.

To paraphrase that renowned IR scholar, Austen Powers, we would appear to have lost our theoretical mojo. So, yes, constructivist students of international security do need to work harder at their methods, especially at the operational level. At the same time, they should not relegate theory to the back seat, but instead be ambitious about their theoretical aims and terms. Here, we would all benefit from Rosenau's ideas about creative theorizing. Written over 35 years ago, his words still ring true today: "To think theoretically one must be playful about international phenomena ... to allow one's mind to run freely ... to toy around" (Rosenau 1980: 35). The implication is to think outside the box, to get outside your comfort zone—and to keep methods in their proper, secondary place.[5]

Notes

1. If I had instead chosen six books to review, the sixth would have been Krebs (2015a), another study by an interpretive constructivist that stands out for its systematic and operational use of methods.

2. Other interpretive constructivist work on security where the methods are both explicit and operationalized includes Price 1995 (genealogy); Deitelhoff (2009) (discourse; content analysis); Krebs 2015b (narrative methods); and Shepherd 2015 (discourse methods).
3. Specifically on JETS, see http://www.dartstatement.org/2014-journal-editors-statement-jets (accessed January 14, 2017).
4. Two websites are especially helpful for tracking the debate: Dialogue on DA-RT (http://dialogueondart.org/); and Qualitative Transparency Deliberations (https://www.qualtd.net/). Accessed January 14, 2017.
5. I thank Martha Snodgrass for research assistance.

References

Adler, Emanuel and Michael Barnett (eds.). 1998. *Security Communities*. Cambridge: Cambridge University Press.

Adler, Emanuel and Vincent Pouliot. 2015. Fulfilling the Promises of Practice Theory in IR. *ISQ Online* [14 December] . *Available at:* http://www.isanet.org/Publications/ISQ/Posts/ID/4956/Fulfilling-The-Promises-of-Practice-Theory-in-IR, accessed January 14, 2017.

Agius, Christine. 2013. Performing Identity: The Danish Cartoon Crisis and Discourses of Identity and Security. *Security Dialogue*, 44(3): 241–58.

Autesserre, Severine. 2009. Hobbes and the Congo: Frames, Local Violence and International Intervention. *International Organization*, 63(2): 249–80.

Autesserre, Severine. 2010. *The Trouble with the Congo: Local Violence and the Failure of International Peacebuilding*. Cambridge: Cambridge University Press.

Barnett, Michael and Martha Finnemore. 2004. *Rules for the World: International Organizations in Global Politics*. Ithaca, NY: Cornell University Press.

Bateson, Regina. 2017. Rethinking Socialization: The Case of Guatemala's Civil Patrols. *Journal of Peace Research*, 54(5).

Beach, Derek and Rasmus Brun Pedersen. 2013. *Process-Tracing Methods: Foundations and Guidelines*. Ann Arbor, MI: University of Michigan Press.

Ben-Josef Hirsch, Michal. 2014. Ideational Change and the Emergence of the International Norm of Truth and Reconciliation Commissions. *European Journal of International Relations*, 20(3): 810–33.

Bennett, Andrew. 2013. The Mother of all Isms: Causal Mechanisms and Structured Pluralism in International Relations Theory. *European Journal of International Relations*, 19(3): 459–81.

Bennett, Andrew and Jeffrey T. Checkel, (eds.). 2015. *Process Tracing: From Metaphor to Analytic Tool*. Cambridge: Cambridge University Press.

Berg, Eiki and Piret Ehin. 2006. What Kind of Border Regime is in the Making? Towards a Differentiated and Uneven Border Strategy. *Cooperation and Conflict*, 41(1): 53–71.

Bettiza, Gregorio and Filippo Dionigi. 2015. How Do Religious Norms Diffuse? Institutional Translation and International Change in a Post-Secular World Society. *European Journal of International Relations*, 21(3): 621–46.

Checkel, Jeffrey T. 1999. Norms, Institutions, and National Identity in Contemporary Europe. *International Studies Quarterly*, 43(1): 84–114.

Checkel, Jeffrey T. 2001. Why Comply? Social Learning and European Identity Change. *International Organization*, 55(3): 553–88.

Checkel, Jeffrey T. (ed.). 2007. *International Institutions and Socialization in Europe*. Cambridge: Cambridge University Press.

Checkel, Jeffrey T. 2008a. Process Tracing. In Audie Klotz (ed.), *Qualitative Methods in International Relations: A Pluralist Guide*, ch. 8. New York: Palgrave Macmillan.

Checkel, Jeffrey T. 2008b. Bridging the Gap? Connecting Qualitative and Quantitative Methods in the Study of Civil War (Symposium). *Qualitative Methods: Newsletter of the American Political Science Association Organized Section for Qualitative and Multi-Method Research*, 6(1): 13–29.

Checkel, Jeffrey T. 2013a. Theoretical Pluralism in IR: Possibilities and Limits. In Walter Carlsnaes, Thomas Risse, and Beth Simmons (eds.), *Handbook of International Relations*, ch. 9. end edn. London: Sage.

Checkel, Jeffrey T. (ed.). 2013b. *Transnational Dynamics of Civil War*. Cambridge: Cambridge University Press.

Checkel, Jeffrey T. 2015. Mechanisms, Process, and the Study of International Institutions. In Andrew Bennett and Jeffrey T. Checkel (eds.), *Process Tracing: From Metaphor to Analytic Tool*, ch. 3. Cambridge: Cambridge University Press.

Checkel, Jeffrey T. 2016. Mechanisms, Method and the Near-Death of IR Theory in the Post-Paradigm Era. Paper Presented at the IR 2030 Workshop, August 27, University of Wyoming.

Deitelhoff, Nicole. 2009. The Discursive Process of Legalization: Charting Islands of Persuasion in the ICC Case. *International Organization*, 63(1): 33–65.

Dolan, Thomas M. 2013. Unthinkable and Tragic: The Psychology of Weapons Taboos in War. *International Organization*, 67(1): 37–63.

Doty, Roxanne Lynn. 1993. Foreign Policy as Social Construction: A Post-Positivist Analysis of U.S. Counterinsurgency Policy in the Philippines. *International Studies Quarterly*, 37: 297–320.

Evangelista, Matthew. 2015. Explaining the Cold War's End: Process Tracing all the Way Down? In Andrew Bennett and Jeffrey T. Checkel (eds.), *Process Tracing: From Metaphor to Analytic Tool*, ch. 6. Cambridge: Cambridge University Press.

Fiaz, Nazya. 2014. Constructivism Meets Critical Realism: Explaining Pakistan's State Practice in the Aftermath of 9/11. *European Journal of International Relations*, 20(2): 491–515.

Finnemore, Martha. 2003. *The Purpose of Intervention: Changing Beliefs about the Use of Force*. Ithaca, NY: Cornell University Press.

Fujii, Lee Ann. 2010. Shades of Truth and Lies: Interpreting Testimonies of War and Violence. *Journal of Peace Research*, 47(2): 231–41.

Fujii, Lee Ann. 2017a. Relational Interviewing for Social Science Research: An Interpretive Approach. London: Routledge.

Fujii, Lee Ann. 2017b. 'Talk of the Town': Explaining Pathways to Participation in Violent Displays. *Journal of Peace Research*, 54(5). Doi: 10.1177/0022343317714300.

George, Alexander and Andrew Bennett. 2005. *Case Studies and Theory Development in the Social Sciences*. Cambridge, MA: MIT Press.

Gerring, John. 2006. *Case Study Research: Principles and Practices*. Cambridge: Cambridge University Press.

Gerring, John. 2007. Review Article: The Mechanismic Worldview—Thinking Inside the Box. *British Journal of Political Science*, 38(1): 161–79.

Gheciu, Alexandra. 2005. *NATO in the 'New Europe': The Politics of International Socialization after the Cold War*. Stanford, CA: Stanford University Press.

Grynaviski, Eric. 2014. *Constructive Illusions: Misperceiving the Origins of International Cooperation*. Ithaca, NY: Cornell University Press.

Guzzini, Stefano. 2011. Securitization as a Causal Mechanism. *Security Dialogue*, 42(4-5): 329–41.

Guzzini, Stefano. 2012. Social Mechanisms as Micro-Dynamics in Constructivist Analysis. In Stefano Guzzini (ed.), *The Return of Geopolitics in Europe? Social Mechanisms and Foreign Policy Identity Crises*, ch. 11. Cambridge: Cambridge University Press.

Hall, Peter. 2003. Aligning Ontology and Methodology in Comparative Politics. In James Mahoney and Dietrich Rueschemeyer (eds.),*Comparative Historical Analysis in the Social Sciences*, ch. 11. Cambridge: Cambridge University Press.

Hansen, Lene. 2006. *Security as Practice: Discourse Analysis and the Bosnian War*. London: Routledge.

Hedstrom, Peter and Petri Ylikoski. 2010. Causal Mechanisms in the Social Sciences. *Annual Review of Sociology*, 36: 49–67.

Hegghammer, Thomas. 2010. The Rise of Muslim Foreign Fighters: Islam and the Globalization of Jihad. *International Security*, 35(3): 53–94.

Hoffmann, Matthew. 2005. *Ozone Depletion and Climate Change: Constructing a Global Response*. Albany, NY: State University of New York Press.

Hopf, Ted. 2002a. *Social Construction of International Politics: Identities and Foreign Policies, Moscow, 1955 and 1999*. Ithaca, NY: Cornell University Press.

Hopf, Ted. 2002b. Making the Future Inevitable: Legitimizing, Naturalizing and Stabilizing. the Transition in Estonia, Ukraine and Uzbekistan. *European Journal of International Relations*, 8(3): 403–36.

Hopf, Ted. 2007. The Limits of Interpreting Evidence. In Richard Lebow and Mark Lichbach (eds.), *Theory and Evidence in Comparative Politics and International Relations*, ch. 3 New York: Palgrave Macmillan.

Hopf, Ted. 2012. *Reconstructing the Cold War: The Early Years, 1945–58*. New York: Oxford University Press.

Johnston, Alastair Ian. 2008. *Social States: China in International Institutions, 1980–2000*. Princeton, NJ: Princeton University Press.

Kelley, Judith. 2004a. *Ethnic Politics in Europe: The Power of Norms and Incentives*. Princeton, NJ: Princeton University Press.

Kelley, Judith. 2004b. International Actors on the Domestic Scene: Membership Conditionality and Socialization by International Institutions. *International Organization*, 58(3): 425–57.

Krebs, Ronald. 2015a. *Narrative and the Making of US National Security*. Cambridge: Cambridge University Press.

Krebs, Ronald. 2015b. Tell Me a Story: FDR, Narrative, and the Making of the Second World War. *Security Studies*, 24(1): 131–70.

Krebs, Ronald. 2015c. How Dominant Narratives Rise and Fall: Military Conflict, Politics, and the Cold War Consensus. *International Organization*, 69(4): 809–45.

Lantis, Jeffrey. 2016. Agentic Constructivism and the Proliferation Security Initiative: Modeling Norm Change. *Cooperation and Conflict* 51(3): 384–400.

Lyall, Jason. 2015. Process Tracing, Causal Inference, and Civil War. In Andrew Bennett and Jeffrey T. Checkel (eds.), *Process Tracing: From Metaphor to Analytic Tool*, ch. 7. Cambridge: Cambridge University Press.

Mattern, Janice Bially. 2001. The Power Politics of Identity. *European Journal of International Relations*, 7(3): 349–97.

Mearsheimer, John and Stephen Walt. 2013. Leaving Theory Behind: Why Simplistic Hypothesis Testing Is Bad for International Relations. *European Journal of International Relations*, 19(3): 427–57.

Mitzen, Jennifer. 2015. Illusion or Intention? Talking Grand Strategy into Existence. *Security Studies*, 24(1): 61–94.

Neumann, Iver. 2002. Returning Practice to the Linguistic Turn: The Case of Diplomacy. *Millennium—Journal of International Studies*, 31(3): 627–51.

Neumann, Iver. 2008. Discourse Analysis. In Audie Klotz (ed.), *Qualitative Methods in International Relations: A Pluralist Guide*, ch. 5. New York: Palgrave Macmillan.

Nome, Martin and Nils Weidmann. 2013. Conflict Diffusion via Social Identities: Entrepreneurship and Adaptation. In Jeffrey T. Checkel (ed.), *Transnational Dynamics of Civil War*, ch. 7. Cambridge: Cambridge University Press.

Norman, Ludvig. 2016. *The Mechanisms of Institutional Conflict in the European Union*. London: Routledge.

Pouliot, Vincent. 2007. 'Sobjectivism': Toward a Constructivist Methodology. *International Studies Quarterly*, 51(2): 359–84.

Pouliot, Vincent. 2008. The Logic of Practicality: A Theory of Practice of Security Communities. *International Organization*, 62(2): 257–88.

Pouliot, Vincent. 2010. *International Security in Practice: The Politics of NATO-Russia Diplomacy*. New York: Cambridge University Press.

Pouliot, Vincent. 2015. Practice Tracing. In Andrew Bennett and Jeffrey T. Checkel (eds.), *Process Tracing: From Metaphor to Analytic Tool*, ch. 9. Cambridge: Cambridge University Press.

Price, Richard. 1995. A Genealogy of the Chemical Weapons Taboo. *International Organization*, 49(1): 73–103.

Risse, Thomas, Stephen Ropp, and Kathryn Sikkink. (eds.). 2013. *The Persistent Power of Human Rights: From Commitment to Compliance*. New York: Cambridge University Press.

Rosenau, James. 1980. *The Scientific Study of Foreign Policy, Revised Edition*. London: Frances Pinter.

Shepherd, Laura. 2015. Constructing Civil Society: Gender, Power and Legitimacy in United Nations Peacebuilding Discourse. *European Journal of International Relations*, 21(4): 887–910.

Sikkink, Kathryn. 2011. Beyond the Justice Cascade: How Agentic Constructivism Could Help Explain Change in International Politics. Paper presented at the Princeton IR Colloquium, 21 November, Princeton University.

Symposium. 2014. Openness in Political Science. *PS: Political Science & Politics*, 47(1): 19–83.

Symposium. 2015. Transparency in Qualitative and Multi-Method Research. *Qualitative & Multi-Method Research: Newsletter of the American Political Science Association Organized Section for Qualitative and Multi-Method Research*, 13(1): 2–64.

Symposium. 2016. Data Access and Research Transparency (DA-RT). *Comparative Politics Newsletter: The Organized Section in Comparative Politics of the American Political Science Association*, 26(1) (Spring): 10–64.

Vaughan-Williams, Nick and Daniel Stevens. 2016. Vernacular Theories of Everyday (in) Security: The Disruptive Potential of Non-Elite Knowledge. *Security Dialogue*,47(1): 40–58.

Wendt, Alexander. 1999. *Social Theory of International Politics*. Cambridge: Cambridge University Press.

Widmaier, Wesley W. 2007. Constructing Foreign Policy Crises: Interpretive Leadership in the Cold War and War on Terrorism. *International Studies Quarterly*, 51(4): 779–94.

Wood, Elisabeth Jean. 2003. *Insurgent Collective Action and Civil War in El Salvador*. New York: Cambridge University Press.

CHAPTER 12

METHODS IN CRITICAL SECURITY STUDIES

MARK B. SALTER AND CAN E. MUTLU

12.1 Introduction

In the last three decades, the sub-field of critical security studies (CSS) has flourished and diversified. Ranging from securitization theory that focuses on the discursive construction of security, to the International Political Sociology approach that looks at everyday implications of security practices, to new materialist perspectives that marshal object-oriented philosophy, such a plurality of perspectives comes with agreements, disagreements, and silences. Whereas differences over various interpretations of the meaning of criticality sustain disagreements, agreements are structured around an appreciation of the political significance, and everyday implications, of security as a signifier of values. With those debates about the meaning of criticality, however, comes a lack of consensus about method.

A number of important collections have surveyed the ontology of security methods, but our goal in this chapter is to prose a different approach: methods, rather than methodology (Salter and Mutlu 2013; Shepherd 2013; Aradau et al. 2014; Peoples and Vaughan-Williams 2014). In this chapter, we argue for a more pragmatic focus on the "how" of CSS. We will ask a basic empirical question about CSS: how do we do what we do? This question leads us to identify research methods, and especially principles of research design that are used by multiple schools. We focused on methods as tools of clarity and mutual-intelligibility, instead of disciplining techniques for making different approaches commensurable (Mutlu and Salter 2014). In other words, the language of methods is common within our critical community, even when the theoretical frameworks diverge substantially, and we wager that this common methods language is an essential marker of the limits of the critical community. Rather than taking an authoritative, singular, disciplining approach to taking sides and setting out the orthodox or correct use of a given method, we illustrate here a more pluralist framework structured around different turns as either established or future directions of the field: corporeal, discursive, ethnographic, field analysis, and object-oriented methods. This does not mean that the turns are discrete. Discourse is material, objects are interrogated discursively, ethnographers might study professional fields, etc. The first subsection presents our best pitch for being explicit about clean research design. We start with research design, because the standards of clarity, fit, and reflexivity are crucial for the integrity of all critical methods in security studies. We focus here on methods, and provide a short introduction to the method and the key works within that turn. We then survey each of the five turns and provide some essentials for researchers conducting their work on issues related to these approaches.

12.2 Research Design

Research design is a crucial stage of the overall scientific project, which can be overlooked in advanced, theory-heavy handbooks. To illustrate the methodological coherence of diverse theoretical traditions in CSS, we asked: What counts as clear, coherent, and reflexive research design in CSS? How do we design clarity, coherence, and reflexivity into our projects? We started with some common assumptions about the critical community broadly, informed by multiple strands of social theory, and identified four shared postures: social and political is messy; agency is everywhere; causality is emergent rather than efficient; and scholarship is inherently political (Salter and Mutlu 2013: 2). We take the recognition of the messiness of the social and political world as a condition that is not solved by parsimonious theory, as with traditional theories based on more scientific theories of social science. Rather, following Law (2004) and Squire (2013), we feel our studies should mirror the messiness of the world, and so while we take rigor extremely seriously, we do not aim to ape the scientific method of the natural sciences. Similarly, we posit that agency does not simply reside in rational actors and their institutions, but allows for a more plural and varied understanding of agency that grants the capacity to have consequences to ideas, norms, language structures, national and organizational cultures, identities, and even material forces and objects. Borrowing again from social theory, we do not want to reproduce positivist or reductionist models of social or political causation. Instead, we agree that casual models cannot predict particular constellations of effect, but rather the "present" is always assembled by different forces, ideas, institutions, values, and discourses. Finally, there is a collective sense that studying or writing about politics and security in particular is not an objective, scientific, or neutral act. If we accept that the expression of knowledge represents a particular power politics, a regime of truth, then we must take responsibility for the knowledge we produce and the power politics that we resist or reproduce with our studies.

Security practices play an important role in shaping everyday life; critical security scholars actively engage with the everyday and the connection between security and politics in traditional and unexpected places. In particular, there is not the presumption that states are unitary, rational, or even calculating actors, but rather that we can trace the relations of security actors across a number of different scales and levels of analysis. However, this leads to vulnerability to the charge that security is so deep and wide that everything is security. The second issue is related to this first point: some critical security scholars can have their theoretical approaches determine their methodological choices, instead of having the empirical world drive the process. The organizing logic of "schools" in CSS is sometimes counter-productive, leading to jargon-heavy footnote battles about which Foucault or the correct reading of Bourdieu that presume particular methods that might be ill-suited to a research site. Putting the sociology of the discipline first can restrict the methodological rigor and diversity of approaches by encouraging researchers to ask certain questions that work well with certain methods, instead of asking questions that correspond with the empirical realities that they are trying to address. It reduces the richness of the empirical field to a plug-and-play research design. As a result, the broader field could be left with the impression that securitization theorists focus on linguistic, discursive methods, while international political sociologists focus on Bourdieusian practice approaches; feminists focus on corporeal methods, while rehabilitated Marxists engage with the material. In fact, we observe and celebrate the fact that scholars from all sides of the critical community use these methodological tools as they find them useful. Finally, critical security studies scholars are often extremely concerned with foregrounding their criticality and the wagers of their political position, due to a shared epistemology that is invested heavily in post-positivism and interpretivism and a keen sensitivity to the politics of their knowledge production—sometimes at the cost of clarity.

However, whatever theoretical frame one is using, broad standards of proof in social science can address these three issues and help research projects to become clearer, which leads to better debate (Jackson 2017). To address these concerns, we encourage researchers to think carefully about three propositions:

1. In relation to the question of *coherency*, we asked: "What counts as a compelling argument in the tracing of competing logics, cultures, and meanings?"
2. In relation to the question of *criticality*, we asked: "What is a reasonable articulation of a critical position, if we are seeking engagement and not objectivity?"
3. In relation to the question of *sufficiency*, we asked: "When can we stop our actual data retrieval in interpretivist methods, such as genealogy, ethnography, field, somatic, object or, discourse analysis?" (Salter and Mutlu 2013: 15).

In encouraging researchers to tackle these questions, we intend to push our colleagues to think about research design more seriously and systematically. This is not a call for the replicability or reproducibility of the natural science model (which itself is suspect). Instead it is a call motivated purely by a concern with legibility. Interpretivism does not lend itself to reproducibility. There is neither a way nor a reason to make ethnographic research meet the standards of quantitative datasets: they have different purposes, they explain different phenomena, and focus on different scales of social relations. That is not to say that there are no standards whatsoever for determining the quality of an ethnographic research. Instead, scholars who work on interpretivist approaches must be held to their own proper standards. In addressing questions about methods, we must be transparent about preferences along the way and acknowledge their limitations. We must be clear and transparent about our object of analysis, our research question, the method we have chosen, and our rationale behind that selection, as well as an a priori understanding of the kinds of data that will count as true, or sufficient for the purposes of that project. In addressing the challenges we have identified above, we ask researchers to answer three simple questions to reflect on their interpretivist research design:

1. *Clarity*: how much can we remove and still remain the essential research question?
2. *Fit*: what method is appropriate for the object of study?
3. *Reflexivity*: what is the role of the researcher in interpretivist methodology?(Salter and Mutlu 2013: 15).

Whereas a clear research question is important for identifying core social relations that are under investigation, it does not necessarily result in a clean or simple answer. In other words, the demand for a clear research question is not a call for the simplification of social complexity. Clear research questions can, and do, lead to messy explanations. An emphasis on clarity, in this regard, forces the researcher to think carefully about the relationship between the questions they ask and the social reality they engage with. Moving beyond the question of clarity, we encourage researchers to think carefully about the relationship between methods and objects of study. In stark contrast to our positivist friends, we assert that different methods are appropriate for different objects of study; methodological fluidity is central to CSS scholars.

To demonstrate our approach, we survey the multiple methods used in the different turns. Again, in contrast to the notion of schools that might focus on a sociological genealogy of debates and personnel, we start with some core premises of each mode of study and where they start, agnostic to the goal at which they are directed.

12.3 Corporeal Methods

From trying to understand the political effects of a Syrian boy's lifeless body on a beach in Turkey (Parashar 2015; Wibben 2016), to studying affective metrics used by airport security personnel (Adey 2009; Frowd and Leite 2013), to understanding personal and international effects of rape as a weapon of war (Kirby 2013), affects, emotions, and other somatic markers are researched through the use of corporeal methods. Taking their lead from feminist and postcolonial theories, corporeal methods are suitable for projects that start with the body, bodily reactions, and study the socio-political structures of meaning and values in which the body is situated and through which the body is constructed. "Corporeal" represents a meta-concept that covers concepts and theories related to the (human) body. They fit well with projects that focus on affects, bodies, and emotions. Recent focus on corporeal methods in CSS has taken the form of tracing and rendering explicit the differential valuation of gender, race, (dis)ability, queerness, or biology within the everyday, the state, the interstate system, or the global. A clear research design in corporeal method-driven research projects takes discourses and practices of security as "as institutions, cultural norms that shape knowledge, perceptions, and representations of the body" (Salter and Mutlu 2013: 140).

Some researchers use corporeal methods because they start with theories borrowed from neuroscience, psychology, biology, or other branches of natural sciences that focus on the psycho-somatic. Yet, the tendency among critical security studies scholars is to either focus on (auto/ethnographic) narratives of experience as data (Wibben 2011), particularly as a supplement or corrective to purely policy or discursive analyses of bodies and/or emotions, or focus on technology, new materialism and affect theory to explain transformations of social phenomena (Grove 2015). This is especially important as short of doing medical experiments, it is difficult to measure affective and emotional responses to security politics. In general, scholars that use corporeal methods rely on auto-ethnography, interviews, participant observation to gather data on affective and emotional reactions to security-related issues. These methods allow researchers to build bridges between the somatic and the social through the corporeal. Auto-ethnography and narrative methods, in particular, are suitable for reflexive research designs that place an emphasis on the intersubjective relationship between the researcher and the research subject.

Some of the more influential examples of contemporary uses of corporeal methods in critical studies include books on the gendered nature of nationalism, militarism, or the international (Enloe 2000, 2001; Weber 1995, 2016); the racial dynamics of international law and institutions (Vucetic 2011), the privileging of particular norms about intellectual capacity in studies of genocide, trauma, and sexual violence in conflict (Howell 2011; Kirby 2011); the regulation of particular microbes and bodies (Elbe 2005, 2006).These germinal works bring together different aspects of corporeal analysis by discussing affects, emotions, and the somatic in order to understand the relationship between the social and the corporeal as a significant site of security politics.

Corporeal approaches allow us to study the significance of the human body, and the social relations that surround its subjugation to (in)security practices. Whether we are looking at it from a feminist, new materialist, or humanist point of view, corporeal approaches present an opening to understand and theorize the impact of security practices on the human body.

12.4 Discursive Methods

Another well-established path for critical work is the analysis of language and its constructions, ranging from the quantitative critical discourse analysis to the very linguistic

Austinian speech act theory from which securitization theory is derived, to the much more abstract Foucauldian genealogy that traces particular regimes of truth. In its early phase, we can identify a discursive turn in the Third Debate, in which scholars informed by post-structuralism and postmodernism decentred the state as the key locus of action, and instead focused on the way that the discourse of anarchy, states, and the international system created the conditions for certain arguments to be made, about the possibility of the good life (Ashley and Walker 1990; Walker 1993), the construction of security (Campbell 1998), or the effect of media on the description of the real (Der Derian 2009). Scholars influenced by this strand then focused on the way that meaning was constructed and knowledge produced about the international system, through culture, identity, and orders (Lapid and Kratochwil 1996). Discourses, of course, are not simply linguistic, but also refer to systems of images, ideas, and narrative structures that triangulate the meaning of security to wider identity politics. Meaning is taken to be constructed contextually, and so the valuation of different political arrangements, policies, or identities can be traced through the deconstruction of terms, arguments, rhetoric from policy documents, speeches, popular or high culture, and ephemera.

Broadly, there are two logics to understand the role of discourse. A constructivist or interpretivist approach argues that language games structure the meaning of real events and represent the conditions of possibility for certain politics or policies. It is not possible to create an argument for the invasion of Iraq, for example, without establishing the facts and the case for war that operate within the generally accepted logics of intervention and international relations (Der Derian 2009a, 2009b). These kinds of studies, then, look at the rationalizations, justifications, and world-building structures of particular discourses, such as cultural artifacts like movies, state foreign policies, or international norms for intervention (Debrix and Weber 2003; Weber 2016). Foucauldian genealogies of truth regimes have been particularly useful in tracing the evolution of particular institutions and dispositions that are structured by the production of knowledge and the politics of truth (Dillon 1996; Hamilton 2013). A correspondence theory of language argues that discourses represent ideas, values, and practices, and that speech can be connected to unobservable phenomena or beliefs. In this kind of approach, utterances are understood as strategic resources in contests for meaning between actors: language serves particular interests, and is used intentionally. In this model, politicians and professionals use particular exceptional language in order to gain the authority to assert competence over a particular domain and the capital it provides (Bigo 2002; Adler-Nissen 2013). One of the primary modes of interrogating discourse has been through securitization theory (Buzan et al. 1998). Building on an Austinian notion that language is performative, simply calling an issue or object a matter of security that has an effect in the world, these studies often focus on speeches (Balzacq 2011), media reports, or images (Williams 2003; Bourbeau 2011), or expert discourses (Balzacq 2008). To varying degrees, each of these approaches looks at the grammatical, discursive, or conceptual links between issues and the values of security. Discursive approaches are some of the most flexible tools used across the sub-field, and, as with any analytic framework, it becomes crucial for scholars to identify how they choose what data to study, how that language or sign is to be interpreted, and the messy causal mechanisms that connect language to politics.

12.5 Ethnographic Methods

A more experiential method for understanding the construction of meaning in context comes from ethnography, and critical security scholars have been tentatively engaging with this kind of reflexive method. Inspired by anthropology, Geertz described ethnography as "thick description" (Geertz 1973), Vrasti (2008) argues that contemporary anthropology puts the question of reflexivity at its core. Rather than simply reporting on the culture of an "other," ethnographers examine how the self and other are mutually constituted through interactions, paying close attention to the impact on the researcher themselves. Distinct from practice-inspired approaches that assume there is a external social reality that can be observed by the researcher, ethnographers assume that social reality is created, co-constituted by the researcher (Kurowska and Tallis 2013). Johnson (2014), for example, follows the path of irregular migrants, accounting for both the conditions of her subjects and her own position and perspectives. Consequently, researchers like Lisle, Johnson, and Bourne (Bourne et al. 2015) approach these security issues tangentially through the laboratory. Because security cultures are extremely difficult to penetrate or to participate in, this is a challenging and difficult research design, which a few scholars have documented (Cohn 1987; Der Derian 2009b; Gusterson 1996; Salter 2008).

12.6 Field Methods

The insight that meaning was constructed contextually also led to the inference that not all meanings would be verbalized or discoverable in language, and yet still existed and had an effect. Bourdieu's insights on the development of site-specific common sense and the unconsciousness but consistency of everyday practice has been useful for scholars investigating particular fields. Bigo's (2002) early work was revolutionary in this community as he described the cadre of "professionals of unease" who shared meanings, practices, a similar common sense of the "rules of the game" across institutions, borders, and jurisdictions. The "thinking tools" of habitus, doxa, and capital illuminate the social dynamics of security fields: the day-to-day practice that sets out the conditions of possibility, the unsaid common sense of the actors, and the production of material and discursive resources (Leander 2008). This kind of sociological work requires more than documentary analysis, but active involvement in the professional sphere to understand what counts as common sense, how capital is generated and circulated, and what the boundaries of that field might be. After the end of the Cold War, and particularly with the strengthening of European transnational institutions, it was particularly useful to suspend the assumed categories of national, subnational, and supranational authorities in order to see what connections really existed. This kind of practice approach has been used to study the EU, certain diplomatic dynamics and institutions like NATO (Pouliot 2010), security (Williams 2007; Abrahamsen and Williams 2010), and international mobility.

12.7 Material Methods

Objects play an active role in social relations. They mediate, regulate, and at times they even act at a capacity that could be interpreted as agency. Bennett (2010) refers to this as the "thing-power" of actants. This understanding of objects stems from Object-Oriented Ontology (Harman 2002), that rejects anthropocentrism, or the privileging of human agency over other forms of agency, in the social sciences. Material methods, thus, have a wider definition of agency that comes to recognize the capacity of objects, ideas, humans, and institutions to have political and social effects on their surroundings. This strong position on the multiplicity of agency starts with the capacity of materials, objects, and things—as well as human actors—to have effects in the world. In CSS, this results in a focus on the social and political life of security objects and technologies. Whether it is the role of algorithms (Amoore 2013), drones (Pugliese 2013), or improvised-explosive devices (Grove 2016), there is a vibrant research agenda within CSS that looks at both the role and agency of objects and technology in security practices. "Given the a priori emphasis on (in)security practices within critical security studies, analysis of insecurity objects presents an opportunity for a methodological study of insecurity practices" (Salter and Mutlu 2013: 179).

This opportunity allows us to ask some provocative questions on the role of objects in security studies: How do we theorize the increasing reliance on technology in security practices? What is the relationship between security and architecture (Muller et al. 2016)? How does the materiality of security practices, such as the physicality of tear gas (de Larrinaga 2016) shape crowd control practices? Or how do we come to conceptualize the culture impact of the continuous presence of drones in places like the Gaza Strip, the Federally Administered Tribal Areas (FATA) in Pakistan, or Yemen? These questions highlight some of the puzzles researchers are trying to tackle in relation to the role of objects in CSS. Object-oriented research provides a way to follow, or trace, the *social life of things*, as they interact with the international.

Although there are historical materialists within the critical community, the most prevalent model for material methodology derives from the broader Science and Technology Studies community, and Actor-Network Theory (ANT) developed by Callon (1986), Law (1991), Mol (1999), Latour (2002, 2005, 2013), among others. Starting from a sociological perspective, ANT theorists found that the construction of scientific knowledge was not simply linguistic, abstract, or non-material, but relied on a broader set of material actors including: machines, recording devices, notepads, microscopes, and then their translations into notes, papers, and articles, that mediate, regulate, and act within a broader ecology of social relations. Rather than relying on "pre-existing scales of analysis," this method attempts to flatten the focus of the study, and to reflexively and meticulously trace: how (social) relations are formed and what actors have an effect, or agency.

In many ways, the material methods build on the existing contributions of the "field methods" in CSS and their practice-oriented research framework. The object-oriented approach of material methods present an avenue for understanding how objects mediate the relationship between discursive and practical constructs by tracing the agency of objects.

12.8 The Future of Methods

Our intellectual project starts with an insistence that there need not be an orthodox consensus about each of the methods of CSS to have a coherent conversation about the object of security studies. We feel it is more important to be politically engaged than scholastically fighting each other over which Foucault lecture to cite. Our intention is not to assert a doctrinaire version of any particular turn, but rather to illustrate the rich panoply of methods that scholars use to tackle the question of security and indicate the leverage and the weakness of each approach. This is not to say that there are not substantial differences between the theoretical stakes at play in these methods, but rather that high theoretical battles distract time and attention from the engaged character of critical work. As such, we advocate strongly that CSS scholars focus on our core design principles (clarity, fit, reflexivity) and then render the methods of that research project as plainly and clearly as possible, so that the relationship between the object and the critique of security are open. A Zen koan instructs: "Hold tightly with an open hand."

It is imperative for the community of critical security scholars to clearly articulate the stakes of its research designs in a manner that allows for mutual intelligibility, and intelligibility outside of our citation collective. We have set out some basic methods that are used in this field to positively assert a set of tools that critical scholars share and that are used in different theoretical traditions. Deriving the standards of clarity, fit, and reflexivity from wider social theory and interpretivist methodological work, we aim to set out standards by which critical scholarship can be judged, not on its ethical claims or on its particular take on criticality, but rather on the grounds of rigor.

References

Abrahamsen, Rita, and Michael C. Williams. 2010. *Security Beyond the State: Private Security in International Politics*. Cambridge ; New York: Cambridge University Press.

Adey, Peter. 2009. Facing Airport Security: Affect, Biopolitics, and the Preemptive Securitisation of the Mobile Body. *Environment and Planning D: Society and Space*, 27(2): 274–95.

Adler-Nissen, Rebecca (ed.). 2013. *Bourdieu in International Relations*. London: Routledge.

Amoore, Louise. 2013. *The Politics of Possibility: Risk and Security beyond Probability*. Durham: Duke University Press.

Aradau, Claudia, Jef Huysmans, Andrew Neal, and Nadine Voelkner. 2014. *Critical Security Methods: New Frameworks for Analysis*. Abingdon: Routledge.

Ashley, Richard K. and R. B. J. Walker. 1990. Conclusion: Reading Dissidence/Writing the Discipline: Crisis and the Question of Sovereignty in International Studies. *International Studies Quarterly*, 34(3): 367–416.

Balzacq, Thierry. 2008. The policy tools of securitization: Information Exchange, EU Foreign and Interior Policies. *Journal of Common Market Studies*, 46(1): 75–100.

Balzacq, Thierry (ed.). 2011. *Securitization Theory: How Security Problems Emerge and Dissolve*. London: Routledge.

Bennett, Jane. 2010. *Vibrant Matter: A Political Ecology of Things*. Durham: Duke University Press.

Bigo, Didier. 2002. Security and Immigration: Toward a Critique of the Governmentality of Unease. *Alternatives: Global, Local, Political*, 27(1): 63–92.

Bourbeau, Philippe. 2011. *The Securitization of Migration*, London: Routledge.

Bourne, M., H. Johnson, and D. Lisle. 2015. Laboratizing the Border: The Production, Translation and Anticipation of Security Technologies. *Security Dialogue*, 46(4): 307–25.

Buzan, Barry, Ole Wæver, and Jaap de Wilde. 1998. *Security: A New Framework for Analysis*. Lynne Rienner Publishers.

Callon, Michel. 1986. Some Elements of a Sociology of Translation: Domestication of the scallops and fishermen of St. Briefcase Bay. In John Law (ed) *Power, Action, Belief?: A New Sociology of Knowledge?* pp. 196–223. Abingdon: Routledge.

Campbell, David. 1998. *Writing Security: United States Foreign Policy and the Politics of Identity*. Revised edn. Minneapolis: University of Minnesota Press.

Cohn, Carol. 1987. Sex and Death in the Rational World of Defense Intellectuals. *Signs* 12(4): 687–718.

Debrix, Francois, and Cynthia Weber (eds.). 2003. *Rituals of Mediation: International Politics and Social Meaning*. Minneapolis: University of Minnesota Press.

Der Derian, James. 2009a. *Critical Practices in International Theory*. New York: Routledge.

Der Derian, James. 2009b. *Virtuous War: Mapping the Military-Industrial-Media-Entertainment-Network*. 2nd edn. New York: Routledge.

Dillon, Michael. 1996. *Politics of Security: Towards a Political Philosophy of Continental Thought*. London: Routledge.

Elbe, Stephan. 2005. AIDS, security, biopolitics. *International Relations*, 19 (4): 403–19.

Elbe, Stephan. 2006. Should HIV/AIDS be securitized? The Ethical Dilemmas of Linking HIV/AIDS and Security. *International Studies Quarterly*, 50 (1): 119-144.

Enloe, Cynthia. 2000. *Maneuvers: The International Politics of Militarizing Women's Lives*. Berkeley: University of California Press.

Enloe, Cynthia. 2001. *Bananas, Beaches and Bases: Making Feminist Sense of International Politics*. Updated edition with a New Preface. Berkeley: University of California Press.

Frowde, Philippe M. and Christopher C. Leite. 2013. In Mark B. salter and Can E. Mutlu (eds) *Research Methods in Critical Security Studies: An Introduction*. pp.149–53. Abingdon: Routledge.

Geertz, Clifford. 1973. *The Interpretation of Cultures: Selected Essays*. New York: Basic Books.

Grove, Jairus. 2016. An Insurgency of Things: Foray into the World of Improvised Explosive Devices. *International Political Sociology*, October 31.

Grove, Nicole Sunday. 2015. The Cartographic Ambiguities of HarassMap: Crowdmapping Security and Sexual Violence in Egypt. *Security Dialogue*, 46(4): 345–64.

Gusterson, Hugh. 1996. *Nuclear Rites: A Weapons Laboratory at the End of the Cold War*. Berkeley: University of California Press.

Hamilton, John T. 2013. *Security: Politics, Humanity, and the Philology of Care*. Princeton, NJ: Princeton University Press.

Harman, Graham. 2002. *Tool-Being: Heidegger and the Metaphysics of Objects*. Chicago: Open Court.

Howell, Alison. 2011. *Madness in International Relations: Psychology, Security, and the Global Governance of Mental Health*. Abingdon: Routledge.

Jackson, Patrick T. 2017. *The Conduct of Inquiry in International Relations*. 2nd edn. New York: Routledge, 2017.

Johnson, Heather L. 2014. Ethnographic Translations: Bringing Together Multi-Sited Studies. *Critical Studies on Security*, 2(3): 362–5.

Kirby, P. 2013. How Is Rape a Weapon of War? Feminist International Relations, Modes of Critical Explanation and the Study of Wartime Sexual Violence. *European Journal of International Relations*, 19(4): 797–821.

Kurowska, X. and B. C. Tallis. 2013. Chiasmatic Crossings: A Reflexive Revisit of a Research Encounter in European Security. *Security Dialogue*, 44(1): 73–89.

Lapid, Yosef and Friedich V. Kratochwil. 1996. *The Return of Culture and Identity in IR Theory*. Boulder: Lynne Rienner.

Larrinaga, Miguel de. 2016. (Non)-Lethality and War: Tear Gas as a Weapon of Governmental Intervention. *Critical Studies on Terrorism*, 9(3): 522–40.

Latour, Bruno. 2002. *Aramis, or the Love of Technology*. Cambridge, MA: Harvard University Press.

Latour, Bruno. 2005. *Reassembling the Social: An Introduction to Actor-Network Theory*. Oxford: Oxford University Press.

Latour, Bruno. 2013. *An Inquiry into Modes of Existence: An anthropology of the moderns*. Cambridge: Harvard University Press.

Law, John (ed.). 1991. *A Sociology of Monsters: Essays on Power, Technology and Domination*. Sociological Review Monograph 38. London: Routledge.

Law, John. 2004. *After Method: Mess in Social Science Research*. International Library of Sociology. London; New York: Routledge.

Leander, Anna. 2008. Thinking Tools. In Audie Klotz and Deepa Prakash (eds.), *Qualitative Methods in International Relations*, pp. 11–27. Research Methods Series. Basingstoke: Palgrave Macmillan.

Mol, Annemarie. 1999. Ontological Politics. A Word and Some Questions. *The Sociological Review*, 47(S1): 74–89.

Muller, Benjamin, Thomas N. Cooke, Miguel de Larrinaga, Philippe M. Frowd, Deljana Iossifova, Daniela Johannes, Can E. Mutlu, and Adam Nowek. 2016. Collective Discussion: Ferocious Architecture: Sovereign Spaces/Places by Design. *International Political Sociology*, 10(1): 75–96.

Mutlu, Can E. 2015. How (Not) to Disappear Completely: Pedagogical Potential of Research Methods in International Relations. *Millennium-Journal of International Studies*, 43(3): 931–41.

Mutlu, Can E. and Mark B. Salter. 2014. Commensurability of Research Methods in Critical Security Studies. *Critical Studies on Security*, 2(3): 353–5.

Parashar, Swati. 2016. On Images, Stories, and the Need to Hear More. *E-International Relations. Available at:* http://www.e-ir.info/2015/10/08/on-images-stories-and-the-need-to-hear-more/, accessed December 8, 2016.

Peoples, Columba and Nick Vaughan-Williams. 2014. *Critical Security Studies: An Introduction*. Abingdon: Routledge.

Pouliot, Vincent. 2010. *International Security in Practice: The Politics of NATO-Russia Diplomacy*. Cambridge: Cambridge University Press.

Pugliese, Joseph. 2013. *State Violence and the Execution of Law: Biopolitcal Caesurae of Torture, Black Sites, Drones*. Abingdon; New York: Routledge.

Salter, Mark B. 2008. Securitization and Desecuritization: A dramaturgical analysis of the Canadian Air Transport Security Authority. *Journal of International Relations and Development*. 11(4): 321–349.

Salter, Mark B. 2013. Expertise in the Aviation Security Field. In Mark B. Salter and Can E. Mutlu (eds.), *Research Methods in Critical Security Studies: An Introduction*, pp. 105–8. Abingdon: Routledge.

Salter, Mark B. and Can E. Mutlu. 2013. *Research Methods in Critical Security Studies: An Introduction*. Abingdon: Routledge.

Shepherd, Laura J. (ed.) 2013. *Critical Approaches to Security: An Introduction to Theories and Methods*. Abingdon: Routledge.

Squire, Vicki. 2013. Attending to mess. In Mark B. Salter and Can E. Mutlu (eds.) *Research Methods in Critical Security Studies: An Introduction*, pp. 1–11. Abington: Routledge.

Vucetic, Srdjan. 2011. *The Anglosphere: A Genealogy of a Racialized Identity in International Relations*. Stanford, CA: Stanford University Press.

Walker, R. B. J. 1993. *Inside/Outside: International Relations as Political Theory*. Cambridge; New York: Cambridge University Press.

Walters, William. 2015. Secrecy, Publicity and the Milieu of Security. *Dialogues in Human Geography*, 5(3): 287–90.

Weber, Cynthia. 1995. *Simulating Sovereignty: Intervention, the State and Symbolic Exchange*. Cambridge: Cambridge University Press.

Weber, Cynthia. 2016. *Queer International Relations: Sovereignty, Sexuality and the Will to Knowledge*. Oxford: Oxford University Press.

Wibben, Annick T. R. 2011. *Feminist Security Studies: A Narrative Approach*. London; New York: Routledge.

Wibben, Annick T. R. 2016. On Doing 'something' … as Academics | Duck of Minerva. *Available at:* http://duckofminerva.com/2015/09/on-doing-something-as-academics.html, accessed December 8, 2016.

Williams, Michael. 2003. Words, Images, enemies: securitization and International Politics. *International Studies Quarterly*, 47(4): 511–31.

Williams, Michael. 2007. *Culture and Security: Symbolic Power and the Politics of International Security*. New York: Routledge.

CHAPTER 13

GAME THEORY AND THE FUTURE OF INTERNATIONAL SECURITY

ANDREW KYDD

13.1 INTRODUCTION

GAME theoretic analyses of international security are now commonplace. They have touched on many important questions in the discipline, such as war and peace, alliances and burden-sharing, arms racing and arms control, and international cooperation. Because the mathematical structure of the models lends itself to verification and elaboration, the game theoretic literature has been unusually cohesive and cumulative. Families of closely related models have developed, analyzing common mechanisms in varying settings and in combination with each other (Kydd 2015).

But does game theory have anything to say about the *future* of international security, the subject of this volume? At first blush, the answer might seem to be no. Especially if what we are really interested in is how the future will differ from the present, or how things will change. Game theory seems inherently biased toward explaining continuity. The foundational concept in game theory, the Nash equilibrium, is a pattern of behavior from which no one has an incentive to deviate, if they believe that others will fulfill their part of the equilibrium. Actors playing Nash equilibrium strategies should therefore be expected to *keep on* playing them, potentially ad infinitum. As a result, game theory is very good at explaining continuity, but the subject of change has been somewhat neglected.

However, game theory does have a lot to offer for those who want to understand change. Game theoretic models can be used to analyze change in three ways. The first approach is to take our essentially static models and ask how the equilibrium behavior would shift in response to an *exogenous* change in a parameter that we think is changing over time. For instance, we may be interested in whether the development of a particular technology, like drone warfare, will make war more or less likely. To analyze this question, we can take an off-the-shelf model of war initiation and identify some parameters in it that are affected by the technological innovation. With drone warfare, we could surmise that the more drones the states field, the lower the cost of war, since drones will take the place of manned platforms that put pilots at risk. Lowering the cost of war in standard crisis bargaining models usually makes war more likely, so we could then infer that adding drones to the arsenals of the states will make war more likely.

The second approach is to construct dynamic models that describe endogenous processes of change. Here, change is built into the equilibrium. Three aspects of the game are often analyzed in this fashion. First, in signaling and learning models, beliefs can alter over time, so states learn about each other and the state of the world, and then act based on their new beliefs. Second, the relative power of the states may change. If states choose to develop a technology, such as nuclear weapons, in the first round, they then have the option to use it in the second. Finally, even the number of players in the game can change. In balance of power models, states can gang up on other states, and if they defeat and absorb them, the next round takes place with one fewer state.

The third approach is to use evolutionary game theory to look at how behavior changes over time if the population of actors playing the game evolves. In evolutionary game theoretic models, the players play simple games, but face some kind of selection pressure, so that players that do well increase their representation in the system while those doing badly dwindle in number. The actors may be distinguished by what strategy they pursue, or by their preferences. Evolutionary game theory has been used since the 1980s to analyze the emergence and breakdown of cooperation, the number and nature of states, and the prevalence of war in the system. It is this third approach which holds out the greatest promise for analyzing large-scale historical change, including speculation about the future.

But why use game theory to think about the future and how it will be different from the present? First of all, because we don't have any data on the future, we need theory to guide our speculation. What characteristics should that theory have, beyond the usual desiderata? Ideally, we should want a coherent body of theory that helps us understand the past and present, and that is based on lower-level assumptions that we think will continue to hold true into the future. If the basic assumptions remain reasonably accurate, the overall theory should continue to be useful as well. The game theoretic approach fits this description. The fundamental axioms of human behavior that the theory is founded on may be disputable, but it is not obvious why they should be less accurate as time goes by. So long as states pursue their interests as best they can given their beliefs in a condition of anarchy, the game theoretic approach will have much to say about international security affairs.

In what follows, I will illustrate with examples from the literature how static, dynamic, and evolutionary game theoretic models can be used to analyze the future of international security.

13.2 Static Models and Exogenous Sources of Change

Even static, normal form games can be useful in thinking about change if we consider the payoffs in the matrices as variables that can change over time. Consider the Cooperation Dilemma illustrated in Table 13.1. Each side may cooperate or defect. Mutual cooperation yields payoff *R*, (reward) while mutual defection leads to *P* (punishment). Defecting while the other side cooperates gives one the payoff *T* (temptation) while cooperating while the other side defects leads to *S* (sucker's payoff). What is the equilibrium of the game? It depends on the order of the payoffs. In the Prisoner's Dilemma, the payoffs are ranked $T > R > P > S$. In this case both players have a "dominant strategy" to defect, in that they prefer to defect no matter what the other side is expected to do. Mutual defection is therefore the only equilibrium in the game.

What if there is an exogenous change in the payoffs, such that the reward for mutual cooperation, *R*, becomes better than the temptation to exploit the other side, *T*? Then the preference order is $R > T > P > S$, which corresponds to the Stag Hunt or Assurance game. In the new game, there are two Nash equilibria: mutual defection and mutual cooperation. A change in the preference ranking of two outcomes has opened up new behavioral possibilities. For example, when Argentina and Brazil transitioned from authoritarian rule to democracy in the 1980s they also abandoned their nuclear competition. If democratic states view the advantages of nuclear weapons as lower and the costs as higher than authoritarian states, it could explain why mutual cooperation became possible as a result of the regime transition.

Repeated normal form games might seem better than one shot games for thinking about change, since they take place over time (Oye 1986). Unfortunately, the standard repeated normal form game actually has no greater purchase on when cooperation starts or stops than the static games on which they are based. If the actors care enough about the future, cooperation is possible, if they do not, it isn't. Some analysts, however, have tried to tweak the repeated game framework to address change. For instance, Laitin and Greif (2004) use a repeated game to study endogenous institutional change. They introduce the concept of "quasi-parameters," which are parameters of the game that vary over the long term. In the Cooperation Dilemma of Table 13.1, for instance, cooperation over

Table 13.1 Cooperation dilemma

		Player 2	
		Cooperate	Defect
Player 1	Cooperate	*R, R*	*S, T*
	Defect	*T, S*	*P, P*

time could reinforce the value for R, making cooperation more valuable in the future. Conversely, it could weaken R, leading to an eventual collapse in cooperation.[1]

Another approach is to construct a dynamic model with a built-in, but still exogenous, source of change. The classic example is the preventive war literature. These models take place over time with at least two periods, representing the present and the future. The usual assumption is that relative power is shifting, for exogenous, usually economic, reasons. The fact that one state is growing faster than the other means that deals which are satisfactory in the present may not be in the future. In response, states may engage in redistributive bargaining in the future, and possibly in the present as well. However, if the shift in power is too great and the conflicts of interest between the states too important, the declining power may attack preventively in the present because it fears that in the future it will be exploited or attacked (Fearon 1995; Powell 2006; Bas and Coe 2012). These models are dynamic, but they do not explain how behavior will be different in the future. Rather, they explain how fear of future changes can affect present behavior.

Timing games, such as the war of attrition, are an interesting case of an essentially static game that nonetheless is concerned with predicting when an event will take place (Fearon 1994). In these games, the players fight over a prize, and pay a cost as they fight over it. The first player to quit loses and the player holding out longer wins the prize. The player's strategies can be thought of as a length of time they are willing to fight before quitting. With incomplete information about the player's costs for fighting or valuation of the prize, equilibria can be found in which "tougher" types, those with lower costs or higher valuations for the prize, fight longer, and so are more likely to win in the end. The outcome of the war is decided by relative toughness or the balance of interest between the two sides. Such games have been applied to the duration and level of escalation of international crises, and to the length of wars of attrition. Fearon argues that this logic also explains long-term international conflicts, such as the Cold War, better than competing repeated Prisoner's Dilemma models (Fearon 1998).

Even static game theoretic models can therefore be used to analyze the effects of changes in exogenous parameters, like the cost of war, the value for cooperation, the relative strength of the parties, etc. If we have strong reasons to believe that exogenous changes in important variables are occurring, we can often turn to existing models to analyze their effects.

13.3 Dynamic Models featuring Endogenous Change

While static games can be useful, we might wish to endogenize the sources of change, and study why the change happens, along with what effect it will have. This section discusses models that can help with this task. Games that embody endogenous sources of change in international relations often focus on three factors, the beliefs, capabilities, and the number of actors.

13.3.1 Endogenous Beliefs

Beliefs are important in several strands of international relations theory. First, as structural realists point out, international anarchy makes security an important value for states, and the search for security can lead to conflict via the "security dilemma" (Jervis 1978; Waltz 1979). However, since security is actually a positive sum good, for the search for security to cause problems there must be some chance that some states have more aggressive motivations than just security (Schweller 1996). If motivations are fundamentally opaque, therefore, states are doomed to conflict (Mearsheimer 2001; Rosato 2014/15), whereas if they can be communicated then cooperation becomes easier (Kydd 1997a). In other words, the level of international trust is a critical variable. States that distrust each other will behave very competitively, whereas states that trust each other can transcend the pernicious effects of anarchy.

Game theory has contributed to this debate from the beginning. Jervis's original analysis of the security dilemma made use of the Stag Hunt and Prisoner's Dilemma models to examine how factors like the offense/defense balance and the advent of nuclear weapons affected the likelihood of cooperation (Jervis 1978). In my own work on the related spiral model (Jervis 1976), I developed a game in which initial arms decisions could exacerbate mutual fears, which then cause further competition or even preemptive attacks (Kydd 1997b). The model can be used to shed light on competitive spirals that worsen mutual fears, such as that before the First World War. I examine the flip side, reassurance, using a related game in which states have the opportunity to cooperate on smaller initial issues to send reassuring signals, build mutual trust, and so foster subsequent cooperation (Kydd 2000a, 2005). I apply these models to one of the greatest transformations in the international system: the end of the Cold War, focusing on the reassuring aspects of Gorbachev's initiatives toward the West, such as the 1987 Intermediate Range Nuclear Forces Treaty.

Beliefs and belief change are also very important in bargaining. Bargaining theory suggests that if states have complete information, or shared beliefs, about each other and the state of the world, they are more likely to reach negotiated settlements that avoid conflict or war (Fearon 1995). This insight has led to an extensive literature on uncertainty and signaling in the context of crisis bargaining. Two different types of signals are distinguished in the literature: "costly signals" which have some inherent cost and derive their credibility from that cost, and "cheap talk," or ordinary verbal communication, which is typically only credible when the interests of the communicating states are aligned. Fearon (1994) argued that some leaders pay "audience costs" when they go back on their word in international bargaining. In particular, democracies, because they have mechanisms for holding their leaders accountable, are better at generating audience costs, and so are better at communicating their resolve in international bargaining.

This logic helps explain the democratic peace, and has become a staple of game theoretic (Schultz 2001), and experimental work (Tomz 2007).

Other scholars have used models of cheap talk to study diplomatic communication (Kurizaki 2007). The most extensive work on this topic is by Trager (2010, 2016), who argues for the importance of diplomacy in shaping international perceptions. In one of his models, the credibility of the communication stems from the negative consequences that arise if one's threats are believed. If the worst a state can do in response to a threat is to ignore it, then threats are not costly, and so not credible. However, states can do more than just ignore a threat, they can actively work against the interests of the threatener, which makes even verbal threats potentially costly. An example Trager discusses is Bismarck's decision in 1876 to inform Russia very delicately that Germany would not want to see Austria weakened. Even such a mild threat was enough to convey to Russia that in the event of a Russian confrontation with Austria, Germany would side with Austria. This led to a lasting deterioration in Russo–German relations that culminated in the war of 1914.

Belief change is also at the heart of tipping models and informational cascades. Sometimes international change can be surprising, sweeping, and dramatic. Examples include the Eastern European revolutions in 1989, the "color revolutions" of the early 2000s, the Arab Spring of 2011, and the Ottawa treaty banning landmines in 1996. Timur Kuran argued that the revolutions of 1989 were so unexpected because everyone falsified their preferences to avoid punishment (Kuran 1990). When the regimes began to falter, however, more protesters were willing to go out, which in turn persuaded more to come out, in a self-reinforcing cascade. (See also Karklins and Peterson 1993; Lohmann 1994.) While the instability of the Eastern European regimes helps explain why they were so suddenly swept away, the landmines treaty provides an example where there is no obvious instability to start with. Prior to the early 1990s, landmines were a normal part of military arsenals. However, the after-effects of indiscriminate landmine dispersal in several countries plagued by civil war led to an international campaign against them, which quickly gained support and led to a treaty in which many states agreed to ban the weapons (Price 1998). Similar analyses have been applied to the issue of the nuclear non-proliferation treaty (Coe and Vaynman 2015).

Belief change can be a powerful force in international relations. When states become more trusting, they can relax tensions and cooperate. If they come to view their interests in conflict, they can prepare for war or even make it more likely. States in bargaining situations that can signal their preferences may be able to reach agreement where others cannot. The transparency of democratic states is often held to be one of the reasons for the democratic peace. Finally, rapid cascades of belief change can sweep regions or even the globe, leading to dramatic changes over a large area.

13.3.2 Endogenous Capabilities

A second class of models focusing on endogenous change are the arms race models, particularly those that connect arms decisions with bargaining or war initiation.

When states build weapons or otherwise augment their capabilities, it alters the balance of power with other states and may give them options they did not have before. The superpowers called the shots in the Cold War because their capabilities dwarfed those of other states. Within certain bounds, states choose how powerful they will be, and those choices have consequences. Those choices also affect states' beliefs about each other's motivations, so these models overlap to some extent with those of the previous section.

Jervis's "deterrence model" distills the hawk perspective that building armaments both creates strength and communicates resolve, thereby deterring challengers (Jervis 1976; Kydd 2000b). Powell (1993, 1999: ch. 2) formalized the "guns vs. butter" trade-off, in which states choose a level of power and then have the option to attack or not. A counterintuitive result, since replicated in other models, is that the cost of arming for deterrence in a peaceful equilibrium could be too great, leading the states to choose war instead. Slantchev (2005, 2011) analyzes a game in which two states choose their level of military power and then bargain over an indivisible good that is valued by both of them. The challenger's valuation is unknown to the state that currently holds the good. The more power the challenger creates, the better they will do if it comes to war. This enables the challenger to commit itself to fighting, by altering its payoff for war. It also signals resolve to the defender, and so encourages them to surrender the good peacefully.[2]

Another approach to endogenous power is taken by Hirshleifer (1995, 2001).[3] He models a competitive environment in which the states allocate their efforts between developing their own current resources (peaceful investment) and building military power to defend one's resources and if possible take those of the other states. He derives optimal military spending equilibria which in turn determine the share of territory held by each state. The more decisive military contests are, the more the states will have to invest in defense and predation.

Models of endogenous power and bargaining have found an important application to the question of nuclear proliferation. For decades, analysts have overestimated the number of states that would choose to build nuclear weapons (Hymans 2006: ch. 1). Game theorists have begun to analyze the question of under what conditions states will pursue the bomb. Alexandre Debs and Nuno Monteiro (2014) examine a model in which a great power opposed to proliferation confronts a smaller power that is considering developing nuclear weapons. If the smaller power developed nuclear weapons, it would shift the balance of power in their favor, leading to better outcomes in subsequent bargaining. They show that if the arms decision were easily detectable, the great power would deter the smaller state from proliferating by threatening to attack if they do so. If the decision to pursue the program is unobservable, however, then the small state may choose to go for nuclear weapons, and the great power may choose to attack, not knowing for sure whether the small power is actually pursuing nuclear weapons. In fact, as preventive war gets cheaper or more effective, the likelihood of "mistaken" preventive wars, launched when the small power is not actually trying to proliferate, goes up. They apply the model to the US invasion of Iraq in 2003, and a wide range of other historical cases (Debs and Monteiro 2017).

Bas and Coe (2016a, 2016b) have a different take on the proliferation question. In their model, the decision to try to get nuclear weapons is observable, the question is how successful the program is. Getting nuclear weapons takes time and some states are better at it than others. Observing states that might want to intervene to stop proliferation tend to wait until they see evidence of real progress before attacking, so preventive wars, and deals to buy off proliferators, are often found at the end of a process rather than early on. The Iranian nuclear deal of 2015 fits this logic.

Models of endogenous capabilities can contribute to important debates on arms racing and arms control, the future of relations between great powers, the likelihood of preventive war and the spread of nuclear weapons. Such issues are of obvious importance in connection with the rise of China, the future of the Middle East, and United States relations with Russia, among other topics.

13.3.3 Endogenous Players

In addition to the beliefs and capabilities of the players, some models make the size and even number of the players endogenous. These models can address truly fundamental questions about the nature of the international system.

Some models in this vein are inspired by the classical literature on the balance of power in European politics. Harrison Wagner (1986) first attempted to model an *n* person system in which states have the option to attack each other and eliminate competitors. He used a non-cooperative game framework (in which agreements are unenforceable) and showed among other results, that three power systems would be stable in the sense that no power would be eliminated, but they would fight until one power had half the world's resources, and so the other two would have to unite against it to preserve themselves. In an alternative approach, using cooperative game theory (with enforceable agreements), Niou et al. (1989) also find that systems in which one state has half the world's resources are stable, but that some weaker states may be "inessential," in that eliminating them does not diminish any other state's ability to survive in subsequent rounds. Interestingly, these models only predict conquest and elimination, never secession. The number of states in these models can only go down, never up.[4]

Alesina and Spolaore (1997, 2003) focus on the "optimal size" of nations. In their framework, states benefit from being larger because it increases the gains from trade within the state, whereas heterogeneity, for instance among different ethnic groups, imposes a cost on greater size. The optimal size is found by equating the benefits of trade and costs of heterogeneity. They find, among other results, that democratization promotes secession, and that international economic integration also supports smaller countries, by reducing the economic penalties of small size.

Thus, even fundamental aspects of the international system, like the number and size of states, can be made endogenous in rationalist models. There are, therefore, a wide variety of tools available for analyzing change in international security relations, even at the macro-historical scale.

13.4 Evolutionary Game Theory and the Arrow of History

While the models discussed above provide insights into important aspects of international change, perhaps the best set of tools in the rationalist tradition for the study of long-term historical change are those of evolutionary game theory. In evolutionary game theory, we typically make somewhat weaker assumptions about the rationality of the actors, and study the evolution of different "types" of actor over time. What the type of actor means is context dependent. Evolutionary game theoretic models have been applied to the largest questions about the past and the future. They have been used to support arguments that humanity, and indeed life in general, is progressing toward higher and more complex forms of organization that will be more and more peaceful. However, other evolutionary arguments have been made to support the idea that war will always be with us.

The belief in progress, the perfectability of humanity, the eventual elimination of war, etc. originated in the Enlightenment and is widespread today. Francis Fukuyama (1992) famously argued that with the end of the Cold War we had reached the "end of history." Widely read books by Steven Pinker (2011) and Joshua Goldstein (2011) claim to show an overall decline in human conflict, including war. Pinker takes a macro-historical perspective and traces the decline in overall violence to the progress of civilization, while Goldstein focuses more specifically on the development of UN peacekeeping since the end of the Cold War. In the realm of International Relations theory, these ideas have been prominent in constructivism. Alexander Wendt (1999) argued that history is progressing from a Hobbesian state of nature full of violence and destruction, through a Lockean international society where there is still competition but of a more limited nature, to an eventual Kantian society based on international friendship and shared identities. He took it further to argue that a "world state" is not only desirable but inevitable (Wendt 2003). While such claims might seem speculative, and far from the restrictive, hidebound rationalist approach, in a sense evolutionary game theory got there first, and with more compelling arguments.

The key rationalist insight is that conflict is inefficient because it destroys resources or diverts effort from peaceful production to struggling over the ownership of what has been produced. Therefore, actors who can figure out a way to avoid conflict will do "better" in some sense than those that engage in it. This fundamental idea shows up in the analysis of the Prisoner's Dilemma, in which the mutual defect equilibrium is worse for both players than mutual cooperation (Oye 1986). It also appears in the analysis of bargaining, in which, as Fearon (1995) stressed, because war is inefficient, there will usually be deals available that both sides prefer to fighting. Both of these models emphasize, of course, that conflict is possible, and in some cases advantageous to individual actors. However, the broader point remains that conflict is inefficient, and if actors can figure out a way to avoid it, they will be jointly better off.

Robert Axelrod (1984) stressed these ideas in his pioneering application of evolutionary game theory to International Relations. He based his analysis on the Repeated Prisoner's Dilemma (RPD). In the RPD, there are many different equilibria, assuming that the states value the future sufficiently. Axelrod set out to find out which strategies would do well in the RPD environment against a diverse array of competitors. He staged a series of computer tournaments in which a variety of possible strategies were initially equally represented and then subject to an evolutionary process in which strategies that did well reproduced at higher rates than strategies that did poorly. He found that the simple strategy called Tit for Tat—cooperating on the first move and then doing whatever the other side just did—was quite successful and could sustain cooperation against itself and a wide variety of other strategies. Subsequent analyses have focused on the role of noise, and identified modified versions of Tit for Tat that are more robust under perturbations (Signorino 1996; Bendor and Swistak 1997). Cederman (1997, 2001) further developed the evolutionary approach using "agent based models" in which the agents follow specified rules of behavior in competitive environments. He used it to endogenize the number and characteristics of states, and study the spread of democracy and the democratic peace.[5] The upshot of this tradition of modeling is that the inefficiency of conflict generates a powerful evolutionary incentive in favor of strategies and actors who can figure out ways to cooperate, often through contingent strategies that reward cooperation from others and punish defection. Popular discussions of these models have argued that they help account for the evolution of social behavior in animals and development in human cultures from simple and warlike to more complex and peaceful (Wright 2000, Nowak 2012).

While these evolutionary game theoretic models support the progress narrative, alternative evolutionary models have darker implications. Predator–prey models in biology focus on the relationship between predators, like wolves, and prey, such as deer (Berryman 1992). The more wolves there are, the fewer deer there will be, so the wolves will have less to eat and diminish in population. If the wolves become scarce, the deer will multiply, making more food available for the wolves, and leading to an increase in the wolf population. These simple dynamics can lead either to a steady state ratio between wolves and deer, or a boom and bust cycle in which the populations of wolves and deer rise and fall in sinusoidal patterns. What (usually) does not happen is a millenarian golden age for deer in which there are no more wolves to worry about.

In a similar vein, Little and Zeitzoff (2017) present an evolutionary version of the canonical Fearon (1995) take-it-or-leave-it bargaining model with grim predictions for the future of war. They start from the premise that states with a taste for conflict can extract more in bargaining from other states, because they have a higher reservation value or bottom line in the bargaining. Hawks will therefore be able to extract more from doves when they are engaged in bargaining. Such a taste for conflict could thus be selected for by evolutionary mechanisms, leading to more and more belligerent leaders or states. The downside, of course, is that when hawks meet hawks, the result tends to be war, rather than easy predation. As a result, if the proportion of hawks increases, the advantage of belligerence diminishes because it is better to do somewhat worse in the bargaining as a dove, rather than fight a war as a hawk. The result is an equilibrium proportion of more and less belligerent types, hawks and doves, in the population. The hawks never go away, and neither do the doves. Interestingly, and contrary to the more optimistic evolutionary game theoretic analyses, the likelihood of war can never go to zero in the model, because it is the chance of war that imposes an evolutionary penalty on hawkishness. If war were eliminated, then everyone would want to be hawkish because they could then extract more from the remaining doves, without worrying about war with other hawks.

Evolutionary game theory, therefore, has much to contribute to macro-historical debates about progress and human destiny. Some models support the idea that there is a powerful incentive to cooperate broadly and deeply, so that individuals, cultures, and countries that manage to do so will outcompete those who do not. Alternative models have more pessimistic implications, supporting the idea that humanity may never escape war and violence.

13.5 Conclusion

Game theory, the formal theory of strategic interaction, is admittedly most naturally suited to the study of short-term interactions between rational, self-interested agents. However, even static models can provide insight into international change through the consideration of the impact of exogenous parameters on models of war, bargaining, collective action, etc. A variety of models also focus on endogenous changes in beliefs (learning), capabilities (especially military power), and the number and characteristics of states (the balance of power and the size of states literature). For the study of long-term historical trends and their projections into the future, however, evolutionary game theory is perhaps the most appropriate. It has been used to back up arguments that the world is on course to greater complexity, larger-scale organization, and more pacific behavior overall. However, some models suggest that conflict will always be with us, because the more peaceful we become, the greater the gains from predation. How these conflicting ideas can be reconciled will have to wait for future study.

Notes

1. See also Milgrom et al. (1990) and Bueno de Mesquita (2000).
2. See also Meirowitz and Sartori (2008); Jackson and Morelli (2009); Baliga and Sjostrom (2008); Fearon (2016).
3. See also Skaperdas (1992).
4. See also Acemoglu et al. (2008).
5. See also de Marchi and Page (2014).

References

Acemoglu, Daron, Georgy Egorov, and Konstantine Sonin. 2008. Coalition Formation in Non-Democracies. *Review of Economic Studies*, 75(4): 987–1009.

Alesina, Alberto and Enrico Spolaore. 1997. On the Number and Size of Nations. *Quarterly Journal of Economics*, 112(4): 1027–56.

Alesina, Alberto and Enrico Spolaore. 2003. *The Size of Nations*. Cambridge, MA: MIT Press.

Axelrod, Robert. 1984. *The Evolution of Cooperation*. New York: Basic Books.

Baliga, Sandeep and Thomas Sjostrom. 2008. Strategic Ambiguity and Arms Proliferation. *Journal of Political Economy*, 116(6): 1023–58.

Bas, Muhammet A. and Andrew J. Coe. 2012. Arms Diffusion and War. *Journal of Conflict Resolutionu*, 56(4): 651–74.

Bas, Muhammet A. and Andrew J. Coe. 2016a. A Dynamic Theory of Nuclear Proliferation and Preventive War. *International Organization*, 70(4): 655–85.

Bas, Muhammet A. and Andrew J. Coe. 2016b. Give Peace a (Second) Chance: A Theory of Nonproliferation Deals. Manuscript.

Bendor, Jonathan and Piotr Swistak. 1997. The Evolutionary Stability of Cooperation. *American Political Science Review*, 91(2): 290–307.

Berryman, Alan A. 1992. The Origins and Evolution of Predator-Prey Theory. *Ecology*, 73(5): 1530–5.

Bueno de Mesquita, Bruce. 2000. Popes, Kings and Endogenous Institutions: The Concordat of Worms and the Origins of Sovereignty. *International Studies Review*, 2(2): 93–118.

Cederman, Lars-Erik. 1997. *Emergent Actors in World Politics*. Princeton, NJ: Princeton University Press.

Cederman, Lars-Erik. 2001. Modeling the Democratic Peace as a Kantian Selection Process. *Journal of Conflict Resolution*, 45(4): 470–502.

Coe, Andrew J. and Jane Vaynman. 2015. Collusion and the Nuclear Nonproliferation Regime. *Journal of Politics*, 77(4): 983–97.

Debs, Alexandre and Nuno P. Monteiro. 2014. Known Unknowns: Power Shifts, Uncertainty and War. *International Organization*, 68(1): 1–31.

Debs, Alexandre and Nuno P. Monteiro. 2017. *Nuclear Politics: The Strategic Causes of Proliferation*. Cambridge: Cambridge University Press.

De Marchi, Scott and Scott E. Page. 2014. Agent-Based Models. *Annual Review of Political Science*, 17: 1–20.

Fearon, James D. 1994. Domestic Political Audiences and the Escalation of International Disputes. *American Political Science Review*, 88(3): 577–92.

Fearon, James D. 1995. Rationalist Explanations for War. *International Organization*, 49(3): 379–414.

Fearon, James D. 1998. Bargaining, Enforcement and International Cooperation. *International Organization*, 52(2): 269–305.

Fearon, James D. 2016. Cooperation, Conflict and the Cost of Anarchy. Manuscript.

Fukuyama, Francis. 1992. *The End of History and the Last Man*. New York: Avon.

Goldstein, Joshua. 2011. *Winning the War on War: The Decline of Armed Conflict Worldwide*. New York: Plume.

Hirshleifer, Jack. 1995. Anarchy and Its Breakdown. *Journal of Political Economy*, 103(1): 26–52.

Hirshleifer, Jack. 2001. *The Dark Side of the Force*. Cambridge: Cambridge University Press.

Hymans, Jacques. 2006. *The Psychology of Nuclear Proliferation: Identity, Emotions and Foreign Policy*. Cambridge: Cambridge University Press.

Jackson, Matthew O. and Massimo Morelli. 2009. Strategic Militarization, Deterrence and Wars. *Quarterly Journal of Political Science*, 4(4): 279–313.

Jervis, Robert 1976. *Perception and Misperception in International Politics*. Princceton, NJ: Princeton University Press.

Jervis, Robert. 1978. Cooperation Under the Security Dilemma. *World Politics*, 30(2): 167–214.

Karklins, Rasma and Roger Peterson. 1993. Decision Calculus of Protesters and Regimes: Eastern Europe 1989. *Journal of Politics*, 55(3): 588–614.

Kuran, Timur. 1990. Now out of Never: The Element of Surprise in the Eastern European Revolutions of 1989. *World Politics*, 44(1): 7–48.

Kurizaki, Shuhei. 2007. Efficient Secrecy: Public vs. Private Threats in Crisis Diplomacy. *American Political Science Review*, 101(3): 543558.

Kydd, Andrew. 1997a. Sheep in Sheep's Clothing: Why Security Seekers Do Not Fight Each Other. *Security Studies*, 7(1): 114–55.

Kydd, Andrew. 1997b. Game Theory and the Spiral Model. *World Politics*, 49(3): 371–400.

Kydd, Andrew. 2000a. Trust, Reassurance and Cooperation. *International Organization*, 54(2): 325–57.

Kydd, Andrew. 2000b. Arms Races and Arms Control: Modeling the Hawk Perspective. *American Journal of Political Science*, 44(2): 222–38.

Kydd, Andrew. 2005. *Trust and Mistrust in International Relations*. Princeton, NJ: Princeton University Press.

Kydd, Andrew. 2015. *International Relations Theory: The Game Theoretical Approach*. Cambridge: Cambridge University Press.

Laitin, David and Avner Greif. 2004. A Theory of Endogenous Institutional Change. *American Political Science Review*, 98(4): 633–52.

Little, Andrew T. and Thomas Zeitzoff. 2017. A Bargaining Theory of Conflict with Evolutionary Preferences. *International Organization*, 71(3): 523–57.

Lohmann, Suzanne. 1994. The Dynamics of Informational Cascades: The Monday Demonstrations in Leipzig, East Germany, 1989–1991. *World Politics*, 47(1): 42–101.

Mearsheimer, John. 2001. *The Tragedy of Great Power Politics*. London: W.W. Norton.

Meirowitz, Adam and Anne Sartori. 2008. Strategic Uncertainty as a Cause of War. *The Quarterly Journal of Political Science*, 3(4): 327–52.

Milgrom, Paul R., Douglass C. North, and Barry R. Weingast. 1990. The Role of Institutions in the Revival of Trade: The Law Merchant, Private Judges, and the Champagne Fairs. *Economics and Politics*, 2(1): 1–23.

Niou, Emerson M. S., Peter C. Ordeshook, and Gregory F. Rose. 1989. *The Balance of Power: Stability in International Systems*. Cambridge: Cambridge University Press.

Nowak, Martin A. with Roger Highfield. 2012. *Supercooperators: Altruism, Evolution and Why We Need Each Other to Succeed*. New York: Free Press.

Oye, Kenneth (ed.). 1986. *Cooperation Under Anarchy*. Princeton, NJ: Princeton University Press.

Pinker, Steven. 2011. *The Better Angels of Our Nature: Why Violence has Declined*. New York: Viking.

Powell, Robert. 1993. Guns, Butter, Anarchy. *American Political Science Review*, 87(1): 115–32.

Powell, Robert. 1999. *In the Shadow of Power*. Princeton, NJ: Princeton University Press.

Powell, Robert. 2006. War as a Commitment Problem. *International Organization*, 60(1): 169–203.

Price, Richard. 1998. Reversing the Gun Sights: Transnational Civil Society Targets Land Mines. *International Organization*, 52(3): 613–44.

Rosato, Sebastian. 2014/15. The Inscrutable Intentions of Great Powers. *International Security*, 39(3): 48–88.

Schultz, Kenneth. 2001. *Democracy and Coercive Diplomacy*. Cambridge: Cambridge University Press.

Schweller, Randall. 1996. Neorealism's Status Quo Bias: What Security Dilemma? *Security Studies*, 5(3): 90–121.

Signorino, Curtis S. 1996. Simulating International Cooperation Under Uncertainty. *Journal of Conflict Resolution*, 40(1): 152–205.

Skaperdas, Stergios. 1992. Cooperation, Conflict and Power in the Absence of Property Rights. *American Economic Review*, 82(4): 720–39.

Slantchev, Branislav. 2005. Military Coercion in Interstate Crises. *American Political Science Review*, 99(4): 533–47.

Slantchev, Branislav. 2011. *Military Threats: The Costs of Coercion and the Price of Peace*. Cambridge: Cambridge University Press.

Tomz, Michael. 2007. Domestic Audience Costs in International Relations. *International Organization*, 61(3): 821–40.

Trager, Robert. 2010. Diplomatic Calculus in Anarchy: How Communication Matters. *American Political Science Review*, 104(2): 347–68.

Trager, Robert. 2016. *Diplomacy: Communication and the Origins of International Order*. Cambridge: Cambridge University Press.

Wagner, R. Harrison. 1986. The Theory of Games and the Balance of Power. *World Politics*, 38(4): 546–76.

Waltz, Kenneth. 1979. *Theory of International Politics*. London: Random House.

Wendt, Alexander. 1999. *Social Theory of International Relations*. Cambridge: Cambridge University Press.

Wendt, Alexander. 2003. Why a World State is Inevitable. *European Journal of International Relations*, 9(4): 491–542.

Wright, Robert. 2000. *Nonzero: The Logic of Human Destiny*. New York: Vintage.

CHAPTER 14

BIOLOGY, EVOLUTION, AND INTERNATIONAL SECURITY

ROSE MCDERMOTT AND PETER K. HATEMI

14.1 Introduction

The dominant theories in International Relations (IR) over the last century have provided important insight into some of the motives for institutional human behavior, from power to economic incentives to social forces. Yet, one of the most puzzling aspects of security studies is that the majority of past and current research is based on assumptions about human nature that we know are not true, yet we treat them as though they accurately represent human values and incentives. Rather, many of the central paradigms in IR rest on notions of human nature that failed to garner widespread empirical support. For example, realism derives from notions of classical rationality originating from micro-economic theory. While such incentives can shape human behavior in some domains, such a model does not, and cannot, explain powerful human drives that easily and often overwhelm financial motives or self-interest, such as hunger, thirst, sleep, sex, or altruism. Similarly, constructivism rests on sociological notions of intersubjectivity that again provide some explanations in some domains of social behavior, such as the influences exerted by social networks, but it fails to explain, address, or even allow for, the kind of individual-level decision-making and information processing essential for understanding critical issues, such as leader choice. The problem is not that these models are always wrong, but rather the cases where they are right are used by advocates who then overgeneralize and assume they apply to domains of behavior well beyond their demonstrated areas of application.

As a field, we are not alone in our myopia; recent work in law points to the way that the criminal justice system fails to deliver justice as a result of the exact same kind of neglect (Benforado 2015). In most respects, this is understandable and results from the nature of scientific research. The field began during a time when knowledge was absent or in nascent form. However, continuing such traditions today becomes increasingly problematic as incorrect assumptions continue to dominate the theories and associated research that permeate the field.

Political scientists often note that the discipline is a borrowing field, extracting notions from fields such as micro-economics or psychology, to develop theories about structural realism or social learning, for example (Waltz 1979; Krosnick and McGraw 2002). What is less often recognized is that such borrowing incorporates a temporal lag, so that the ideas that are borrowed are most often decades out of date, and the fields that introduced them have moved forward while political science has not kept up. It should be noted, for example, drawing on the discipline that has generated much of the research in political science, that many of the most high status economists today work in the area of behavioral economics, and have long ago discarded reliance on the classical assumptions of rationality which gave birth to the field (Camerer et al. 2005).

Kahneman and Tversky's (1979; Tversky and Kahneman 1974) revelations documenting the descriptive processes underlying human choice and decision-making lay to rest any notion of humans as rational, even in the most strict monetary domains. Yet political science in general, and IR in particular, continues to cling to rational choice as a viable model for understanding human behavior writ large, despite the overwhelming amount of empirical evidence that refutes its ontological assumptions (Weingast 1995; Ostrom 1998). This does not mean that rational choice cannot garner useful predictions in a more constrained manner, as indeed was the case with original micro-economic theory and the IR work conducted around its assumptions by such progenitors as Bruce Bueno de Mesquita and colleagues (Bueno de Mesquita et al. 2005). However, as has been the case with micro-economics, in order to move toward a more comprehensive model of human behavior, it becomes important to recognize some inherent limitations in the models which animate our current understandings.

The last half century of research has shown that biological and evolutionary theories prove essential for studying all facets of human behavior, and its methods have provided critically important insights and empirical observations about how we think, feel, and behave (Barkow et al. 1992). There is no aspect of human behavior, including those involving international security, that do not exist as some function of evolution and biological factors (Hatemi and McDermott 2011a; Lopez et al. 2011; Klofstad et al. 2012; Petersen and Aaroe 2012; McDermott and Hatemi 2013; Lockyer and Hatemi 2014; Petersen 2015). Indeed, evolutionary approaches are the only means to explain why the human architectures for decision-making are universal, while at the same time there is great variation within such architectures depending on local ecology. The fundamental biological aspects of human nature deeply and profoundly inform our understanding of the decisions people make when confronting war and or trying to promote peace (Johnson et al. 2006; Rosen 2007; McDermott et al. 2009).

Yet, as noted, current dominant understandings in international security, especially those drawn from notions of classical economic rationality, do not accurately map onto identified human cognitive architecture and processes. Indeed, many notions in international security simply do not reflect empirical reality and therefore are limited in their ability to accurately predict human behavior; this is certainly true for the violent actions we care about the most (Siever 2008). Therefore, in a spirit combining hope and humility, this chapter aims to help guide the course of our field's future trajectory and argue for a greater inclusion of biological factors into the study of IR. In so doing, we provide an overview of potential fertile ground for further investigation for improving real-world policy and decision making in the realms of aggression, violence, and war, topics which perpetually and enduringly preoccupy scholars of International Relations.

14.2 Bringing Biology to the Study of Conflict

Since the dominant paradigms of IR were developed, the theories, methods, and approaches in the behavioral sciences have changed precipitously. Our goal here is not to provide a complete review of such progress; we guide interested readers to relevant and significant prior work which provides the foundation for this development (Schultz et al. 1997; Filley et al. 2001; Sanfey et al. 2003; McDermott 2004; Camerer et al. 2005; Fries et al. 2005; de Aguirre 2006; Hariri and Holmes 2006; Hibbing and Smith 2007; Kaplan et al. 2007; Miczek et al. 2007; Smith et al. 2007; Siever 2008; Hatemi and McDermott 2011b, 2014; Lopez et al. 2011; Victoroff et al. 2011; Waldman et al. 2011; Hibbing et al. 2013; Buckholtz and Meyer-Lindenberg 2014; Jost et al. 2014). Instead, here we provide the big picture findings and examine how these insights can and should influence our work going forward. So, what have we learned about human biological and psychological processes that can inform our understanding of International Relations?

14.2.1 Core Findings

Subsuming individualist theories under evolutionary theory has resulted in a more accurate and comprehensive approach to understanding the human psychological architecture. Evolution is the only current theory that provides a means to explain and predict the entire sequence and panoply of human activity, from genes through brain processes, environment, and social development to inform all aspects of decision-making involving complex social and political behavior. Evolution provides a descriptively accurate and predictively powerful model for understanding and explaining human motives, mechanisms, and outcomes.

One of the most important insights evolutionary models provide is that behavior results not only from current circumstances, but also from selection pressures that may go back millennia. Importantly, this does not diminish the importance of environmental triggers and cues. Rather, just the opposite is true: evolutionary forces have resulted in humans privileging certain environmental stimuli over others, such as those related to reproduction and survival, and developed and instantiated highly complex processes that offer flexible and adaptive repertoires of responses to various environmental contingencies. This means that many processes and outcomes we care about, from risk propensity and threat perception to in-group defense and cooperation and conflict are deeply informed by evolutionary selection pressures adapted to current environmental conditions. So conflicts over oil in the Middle East represent not only the immediate conflicts of interest, but also reflect more ancient tendencies around perception and responses to threat, as well as desires for in-group defense and out-group annihilation. Such insights can help explain in part how seemingly minor conflicts can quickly grow into major conflagrations, among other things.

Moreover, evolution provides leverage for explicating why people differ even within the categories of social similarities defined by the demographics favored by survey methodologists. Standard scales of ethnicity, age, sex, and political leanings only explain so much of the variance in any outcome of interest. That is simply because most people vary in an infinity of ways according to the millions of polymorphisms that vary across individuals; genetic forces are multifactorial, polygenic, and indirect, but that does not mean they do not exert an enormous amount of influence, in total, over a wide array of outcomes, including perception, emotion, cognition, and behavior. But, in even more subtle and powerful ways, such forces, however unconscious, also inform more complex and enduring life choices, such as the occupations and friendship networks a person selects into, choice of mate, and interpersonal interaction styles. This is because from an evolutionary standpoint, biological influences never operate in isolation, but rather interact in reciprocally intertwined ways with environmental forces. And, from a neurobiological standpoint, environment is not merely restricted to external forces, as many social scientists assume, but rather includes internal and distinct physiological processes as well, such as the in utero environment a child experiences prior to being born (Van den Bergh et al. 2005).

From the standpoint of IR, such issues may seem peripheral, but think about how individuals who are conceived in environments of war, famine, and deprivation might be affected for their entire lives by the consequences of those developmental influences. Think of a simple example. If a baby is born into an environment of deprivation, environmental features such as famine, or even anxiety on the part of a mother who has been raped, inevitably send neurochemical signals to the child in utero through the mother's physiology; long before the child is born, certain genes become more likely to be expressed while others are less so. For example, consider the biology of expecting mothers who gave birth to children during the famine in Holland toward the end of the Second World War; the famine resulting in changes in the genetic expression of the mothers, which resulted in a cohort of children with heightened insulin sensitivity giving them a lifesaving advantage through their differential ability to extract calories. But these children are now at a much greater risk for diabetes and other health problems, and they have continued to pass these famine-related epigenetic processes to the next generation (Painter et al. 2005; Heijmans et al. 2008; Tremblay 2008; Tremblay and Szyf 2010). Similarly, one could easily imagine that a child born into an environment of conflict might show greater genetic expression on pathways related to the proclivity to fight for survival, generating more conflict across generations, particularly if such a child grew up in an environment where loss spurred a desire for further revenge and violence. Examining this possibility in greater detail provides only one of many research possibilities for scholars of IR who may be interested in regional differences in the likelihood of war, for example.

It is now established that individual differences in our DNA and neurological functions are reflected in all those cognitive and emotional traits that guide complex decisions including those in International Relations involving decisions to go war, who to fight against, when to aggress and when to withdraw, how to lead, and when not to intervene. Aggression, anxiety, assertiveness, bonding, cognition, communication, compulsivity, cooperation, executive control, group affiliation, impulsivity, intellect, learning, memory, mood regulation, morality, perceived fairness, pro-sociality, pursuit of power, reward dependence, reactions to fear, stress and threat, resilience, risk-taking, self-interest, social attachment, and trust, to name only a few of these traits, differ greatly by one's disposition, and are regulated by genetic and neurological processes that differ across humans (Madsen 1985; Rushton et al. 1986a, 1986b; Wise 2004; Kosfeld et al. 2005; Hariri and Holmes 2006; Crockett et al. 2008; Israel et al. 2009; McDermott et al. 2009; Ebstein et al. 2010; Loewen et al. 2013).

In particular, evolution has resulted in emotional processes that quickly and automatically, but indirectly, guided us toward what worked best for our ancestors who confronted similar problems over time; and often emotion is the mechanism that informs us about what we should do. Emotion works like an operating system in a computer whereby it signals which program to bring up based on the perceived needs of the user at the time (Tooby and Cosmides 1988). When confronting a predator, fear works to protect a person by making them run or hide or freeze or fight without second thought; the desire to get away for example, is simply experienced as overwhelming. Similarly, anger functions to defend against violations of all sorts, including threats presented from in- or out-group members. Sadness compels a person to slow down so that vital processes can be preserved in a time of grief and so on. These emotions did not come out of nowhere and there are universal physiological markers and facial expressions for at least the seven most basic emotions, suggesting evolutionary selection and genetic instantiation of major pathways that privilege their operation (Ekman and Oster 1979). These are not irrational forces unnecessarily inciting violence, for example, regardless of what economists or political theorists have implied; rather, these emotions have been preserved precisely because, from an evolutionary standpoint, they proved exquisitely rational by encouraging their possessors to defend against others who posed realistic threats to survival by siphoning resources, stealing mates or livestock, or engaging in direct attack. Thus, at a neurocomputational level, emotions worked to increase the probability that our ancestors were more likely to achieve reproductive success, and so such tendencies are preserved in a modern environment that may nonetheless be less suited to their activation and operation.

Emotions may or may not exert an enormous impact at the level of the individual actor. Indeed, leaders can both direct and manipulate emotions for their own purposes, including their own personal political ambition. Although leaders who fail to represent their constituency consistently have lost their lies or their positions across evolutionary time (Boehm 1999), it can prove more difficult to track such cheaters in the very large modern political context. Successful and effective leaders rely on emotional entrepreneurship to define the boundaries of identity, which serves to categorize and distinguish members of the in-group and out-group, and encourage fence sitters to join in a fight lest their position be exploited by the other side (McDermott 2010).

The involvement of all these central psychological processes makes sense because decisions in the realm of International Relations fundamentally encompass the same issues of survival, cooperation, and reproduction that confronted our ancestors; the general decision-making processes are the same because they involve the same interpersonal motives, constraints, and incentives (Lumsden and Wilson 1981; Axelrod 1984; Eaves et al. 1989; Ridley 1993; Cosmides and Tooby 1997; Boehm 1999; Hibbing and Smith 2007; Hatemi et al. 2011; Hatemi and McDermott 2011a; Petersen and Aaroe 2012; Hibbing et al. 2013). Modern-day issues involving security and foreign policy are reflections of the prehistoric need to protect one's in-group, defend against potential out-groups and ensure the survival of offspring; views on immigration, for example, mirror the primal need to recognize and protect against unknown and potentially "dangerous" others. What may appear irrational in a modern context emerges, in part, from the benefits that derived to communities who reduced pathogen contagion by limiting exposure to new diseases for which they had not yet had the time to develop immunity. The manifestation of these concerns are of course more complicated because human populations have grown from small tribes to massive societies, with borders, institutions, and governments, and modern technology has changed the speed and scale of transportation, communication, and lethality of warfare. However, while the processes through which individual preferences are made have changed from personal and direct to indirect and institutional, the underlying psychological connection between the core issues that are important to humans, focusing on safety, access to resources, and reproduction, remain the same. That is, the same emotional and cognitive processes are instigated and engaged when individuals are faced with small group decisions as when mobilizing a whole country for war (Hatemi and McDermott 2011a, 2012a; Lopez et al. 2011; Lopez and McDermott 2012; Hibbing et al. 2013; Lockyer and Hatemi, 2014).

14.2.2 Implications

This line of research holds profound implications for a field that has developed on the assumption that not only will all people faced with similar incentives behave identically, but at least one which also posits that states will do the same (Waltz 1979) and others which assume that all states are the same with the exception of the regime type. Institutionalists, for example, may counter that it does not matter if people vary as long as institutional structures remain sufficiently strong to constrain, incentivize, and thereby guide and control human behavior (Weingast 1995). This may be true as far as it goes but fails to recognize two important, albeit implicit, aspects of such an approach.

First, institutions are not *sui generis*; rather, they are built by people seeking to pursue certain goals using certain incentives. This means that certain goals, regardless of how normatively desirable these might be, such as peace, are privileged over other goals by those building the institutions. Such institutions may then take on a life of their own, as we know (Martin and Simmons 1998), but that does not mean they do not continue to serve the needs of their progenitors. And indeed, this has been the accusation leveled recently by those who oppose the capitalist, democratic superstructure imposed by the World Bank, the World Trade Organization, the Import–Export Bank and other financial institutions set up at the end of the Second World War, which were explicitly designed to serve the interests of the United States. Goals of peace and stability, however laudatory, nonetheless place asymmetric burdens on different kinds of economies and political structures in ways designed to incentivize the creation of democratic and capitalist systems. Only willful ignorance can assume such institutions were established by nature itself and not driven by human goals and desires which varied based on the values of who won and who lost the war, among many other factors.

Second, as work in behavioral economics so aptly demonstrates, incentives can only move human behavior at the margins (Camerer et al. 2005). More money can drive most people to do many things they might not do otherwise. But even a lot of money will not drive the majority of people to do things they really do not want to do, such as kill a member of their family. In other words, there are limits to what incentives can do to change human nature, and those limits inform us about the underlying drives that guide human behavior. Most people want to take care of their family members and protect them from harm, even at great personal cost. Many people prefer sex to many other pursuits, sometimes at great risk to their health or even life, even when other activities might offer a lot of money, or they engage in sexual behaviors that risk their health and even their life. The vast majority of people fear illness and death, and motivating people to overcome these fears often requires very strong social, and not financial, incentives as we know from studies showing that men in combat fight not so much for ideology as for their comrades in arms.

Regardless of the normative instructions of classical economists, any normal person who honestly faces the mirror of introspection knows that not all decisions, especially important ones that involve emotional investment, occur in seemingly rational ways. Indeed, this is one of the core problems in raising health care costs; we invest disproportionate amounts of money on the last six months of life not because it is rational to do so (i.e. people will not get better and rarely even improve their quality of life), but rather because it is emotionally hard to let loved ones go, or to justify not doing everything possible to improve their prospects for survival. Of course, this is partly because our notion of what rationality is has been hijacked by those who construct the term almost exclusively in financial cost–benefit terms (for a critique, see McDermott 2004). But rationality from a biological perspective is not about individuals' access to money, but rather about species survival and reproductive success; that means that much of what otherwise may appear to be irrational from an economic standpoint makes perfect sense from a biological one. This does not mean that risking death in combat is illogical; if men who might otherwise not be able to find mates can do so through bride capture or other resources gained by fighting, then the behavior is completely rational from an ecological standpoint. Similarly, people who risk themselves, or kill themselves in suicide missions, in ways that may or do benefit their relatives are similarly behaving in an utterly rational way from a biological perspective, even as those actions may confound standard economic analysis. In addition, much that appears rational from an economic perspective requires enormous incentives in order to get people to comply. Saving for retirement may be rational from an economic perspective in the modern world, but natural selection is very unlikely to have designed a psychological mechanism that privileges money over social capital, since money is a latter-day invention, while friends and family were necessary to survive over millennial time. This is not to say we cannot or do not privilege money over social capital; humans are also adaptive, and have the ability to transcend or transform their evolutional incentives in numerous ways, particularly as people have learned to use money to circumvent the need for social capital by outsourcing caring to paid labor.

IR scholars benefit by recognizing that emotions are both hard-wired as well as socialized and that most people do not act like the automaton rational actors that economic analysis and dominant theories would like us to. Human behavior does not result from the normatively bound rules that rational actor models would have us believe but rather revolve around the theory of mind and emotional motivations that have been genetically instantiated across evolutionary time to aid survival in complex political and social environments not so unlike modern psychological challenges in many underlying ways.

Several other substantive areas in the domain of International Relations, or in areas relevant to it, have already been examined from this perspective. These include examinations of foreign policy, and how neurobiological approaches can improve our understanding of how best to identify those at greatest risk for engaging in political violence (Hatemi and McDermott 2012b), and also how individual differences in tendencies toward physical aggression affect attitudes toward interventionist foreign policy and complex moral dilemmas (McDermott and Hatemi 2016). Such areas of importance in International Relations need not, and increasingly should not, be limited to the domain of military action. Work on religious attitudes and practices from a genetic perspective (Eaves et al. 2008), as well as work on the interaction between genes and culture (McDermott and Hatemi 2013) has begun as well and holds promise for a greater understanding of the ways in which institutions can intervene or help shape transformations in these areas for good or ill.

14.2.3 Questions to Address Going Forward

If we take evolutionary and biological models seriously going forward, then what questions do we want to ask and answer using the novel analytic lens afforded by these insights? What are the big questions of interest to International Relations that should be tackled from this perspective?

Certainly understanding the nature of group strength and identity will prove critical to better understanding the causes of conflict and any potential avenues for achieving peace without war. How quickly do powerful groups form? How important does a particular identity, whether ethnic or sectarian or otherwise, need to be in order to instigate a physiological response to increase the desire to defend it against others who differ to the point of violence? What features of human psychological architecture can help promote tolerance for diversity, and under what conditions are these operative? Further empirical examination of the relationship between emotions, especially shame and humiliation, and subsequent behaviors undertaken in defense of the ego, could do a lot to enlighten our theories of International Relations. This is particularly important because many of the most influential paradigms in International Relations, such as realism and rational choice, are based on concepts drawn from micro-economic theory that rest on assumptions of rationality that do not comport with overriding human psychological mechanisms. Such an insight goes far in explaining why many of our well-worn theories have not been able to make much progress in ensuring peace.

Furthermore, the nature and function of leadership remains key to any study of violence and war. We still know little about how democratic leaders garner support from their nations for wars or other campaigns, since without such support, wars could never be fought, much less won. But even more critically, how does a leader motivate people to risk their lives in combat or through other ideological motives and incentives? What defines such a leader? Highly effective political leaders differ in some important regards from charismatic military leaders, and yet neither type is common. What explains those who emerge as leaders from the background of other potential candidates? There is a great deal of potential for additional exploration of aspects of these phenomena, particularly in distinguishing the difference between types of leadership; for example, how the nature, function, and manifestation of effective political versus military leadership may vary (McDermott et al. 2017). At the very least, the emotional expressions, motivations, and encouragements of leaders must be rigorously studied, and explicitly incorporated, into our models of state interactions going forward if we are to achieve any realistic understanding of how leaders and followers interact and affect one another in decisions around war.

There are many areas of great and enduring interest and importance in IR that could be greatly enlightened by approaches rooted in the examination of both universal human nature as well as explorations of individual differences within that universality. Indeed, many of these big unanswered questions in IR can be directly addressed by a more explicit consideration of the evolutionary motives that drive complex social and political behavior, and can be more directly studied using biological tools and techniques.

Obviously a lot of the big questions that remain unanswered, perhaps even unaddressed, revolve around terrorism. How can the human mind be extrinsically motivated or hijacked into blowing itself up? And how can we examine individual variance in the midst of powerful socialization? If socialization were as supreme as many wish it to be, then how come with the millions of children being raised and trained in jihadist madrassas, only a minority become terrorists? The majority, subjected to the exact same external environmental pressures, deprivations, and losses, do not. No one doubts that social forces are very powerful, but in these questions, social forces have nothing to say about why people differ when faced with the same social pressures, making it impossible to predict who among the indoctrinated poses a real threat. But here is where biology may help provide some answers, since this varies across individuals regardless of the similarity in the social forces to which they are exposed and subjected.

Perhaps the domain in which such work may show most immediate effect lies in just this kind of examination of individual combatants from a neurobiological perspective. In many areas where war is endemic and catastrophic losses common, many people nonetheless do not take up arms and instead strive toward the peaceful resolution of contentious issues. What makes the difference between those who fight and those who do not? Is there a way to screen for individuals who are most susceptible to becoming suicide bombers or terrorists for example? How about screening for Special Forces? And among those who serve in a regular army, how does the stress of combat and the individual propensity for impulsivity play out on the battlefield and affect risk for injury or retention? Who is at greatest risk of traumatic brain injury in the face of blast and who is at greatest risk of post-traumatic stress in the wake of combat? Answers to such questions will only come at the level of individual examination and inquiry.

14.3 Conclusion

It is important to acknowledge that it is still early days in the basic scientific exploration of many of these foundational neurobiological processes. Some of these notions may get overturned as we learn more; certainly all will become more sophisticated and nuanced as we come to understand more about these mechanisms and how they interact. But that does not mean that we cannot, and should not, begin to incorporate more empirically valid conceptions of human psychological behavior and processes into our models of IR, not only to make them more descriptively accurate, but also to render them more predictively useful.

As models and methods from neurobiology become more incorporated into wider swaths of scientific enterprise and more disciplines, IR, as with political science more broadly, needs to begin to adapt and incorporate these central notions if it hopes to stay relevant to larger public intellectual and policy debates. The reasons for this are not limited to the selfish desire for funding which of course often dominates academic motives, however subterranean, but more meaningfully directly impacts the extent to which the wider public as well as leaders consider our work relevant and accessible. Discussions of DNA are endemic in popular culture, permeating everything from leader's speeches to television, music, and literature. Any discipline that ignores the importance of these influences is destined to be cast aside as irrelevant at best, and antediluvian at worst. If we hope to join with other scientists across disciplinary divides to solve pressing social problems, including those posed by violence spurred by ethnic and sectarian divisions both at home and abroad, an increasingly necessary enterprise if we are to make progress in addressing such concerns, then International Relations would benefit by moving beyond the notion that only institutions and organizations and larger political structures determine international outcomes. Anyone who has watched the recent ISIS-inspired truck attacks in Nice, Berlin, and Israel must realize intuitively that the days of states maintaining anything close to exclusive control over the instruments of coercion are long gone. And if scholars of International Relations are going to begin to address those issues seriously, investigating the motivations for individual behavior, including those at the biological level, is a necessary start. As with evolution itself, those models which do not adapt to these increasingly important aspects of individual behavior, including terrorist action, in IR, will not survive as meaningful and influential models for understanding the world or influencing public policy, even if they remain dominant in obscure enclaves of solely academic endeavor, resigned to irrelevance in the larger world.

It can be tempting to ask how this research will affect the practice of IR. But as Morganthau (1948) noted long ago, theory does not influence practice so much as practice influences theory. And as the prominence of individual and non-state actors continues to grow beyond the ability of state actors to adequately contain them, we will see how the real world of IR will increasingly force the proper recognition of the force of individual actors, and thus on the very biological, social, and environmental structures which comprise them.

References

Axelrod, R. 1984. *The Evolution of Cooperation*. New York: Basic Books.

Barkow, J. H., L. E. Cosmides, and J. E. Tooby. 1992. *The Adapted Mind: Evolutionary Psychology and the Generation of Culture*. New York: Oxford University Press.

Benforado, A. 2015. *Unfair: The New Science of Criminal Injustice*. New York: Crown.

Boehm, C. 1999. *Hierarchy in the Forest: The Evolution of Egalitarian Behavior*. Cambridge, MA, Harvard University Press.

Buckholtz, J. W. and A. Meyer-Lindenberg. 2014. 7 Genetic Perspectives on the Neurochemistry of Human Aggression and Violence. In Turan Cani (ed.), *The Oxford Handbook of Molecular Psychology*, p. 121. Oxford: Oxford University Press.

Bueno de Mesquita, B., A. Smith, R. M. Siverson, and J. D. Morrow. 2005. *The Logic of Political Survival*. Cambridge, MA: MIT Press.

Camerer, C., G. Loewenstein, and D. Prelec. 2005. Neuroeconomics: How Neuroscience Can Inform Economics. *Journal of Economic Literature*, 43(1): 9–64.

Cosmides, L. and J. Tooby. 1997. Evolutionary Psychology: A Primer. *Evolutionary Psychology: a primer*. Blogpost.

Crockett, M. J., L. Clark, G. Tabibnia, M. D. Lieberman, and T. W. Robbins. 2008. Serotonin Modulates Behavioral Reactions to Unfairness. *Science*, 320: 1739.

De Aguirre, M. I. 2006. Neurobiological Bases of Aggression, Violence, and Cruelty. *Behavioral and Brain Sciences*, 29: 228–9.

Eaves, L. J., H. J. Eysenck, and N. G. Martin. 1989. *Genes, Culture, and Personality: An Empirical Approach*. London; San Diego: Academic Press.

Eaves, L. J., P. K. Hatemi, E. C. Prom-Wormley, and L Murrelle. 2008. Social and Genetic Influences on Adolescent Religious Attitudes and Practices. *Social Forces*, 86: 1621–46.

Ebstein, R. P., S. Israel, S. H. Chew, S. Zhong, and A. Knafo. 2010. Genetics of Human Social Behavior. *Neuron*, 65: 831–44.

Ekman, P. and H. Oster. 1979. Facial Expressions of Emotion. *Annual Review of Psychology*, 30: 527–54.

Filley, C. M., B. H. Price, V. Nell, T. Antoinette, et al. 2001. Toward an Understanding of Violence: Neurobehavioral Aspects of Unwarranted Physical Aggression: Aspen Neurobehavioral Conference Consensus Statement. *Cognitive and Behavioral Neurology*, 14: 1–14.

Fries, A. B. W., T. E. Ziegler, J. R. Kurian, S. Jacoris, and S. D. Pollak. 2005. Early Experience in Humans Is Associated with Changes in Neuropeptides Critical for Regulating Social Behavior. *Proceedings of the National Academy of Science U S A*, 102: 17237–40.

Hariri, A. R. and A. Holmes. 2006. Genetics of Emotional Regulation: The Role of the Serotonin Transporter in Neural Function. *Trends in Cognitive Sciences*, 10: 182–91.

Hatemi, P. K., N. A. Gillespie, L. J. Eaves, B. S. Maher, et al. 2011. A Genome-Wide Analysis of Liberal and Conservative Political Attitudes. *Journal of Politics*, 73: 271–285.

Hatemi, P. K. and R. McDermott. 2011a. Evolution as a Theory for Political Behavior. In: P. K. Hatemi and R. McDermott, (eds.), *Man is by Nature and Nurture a Political Animal*. Chicago: University of Chicago Press.

Hatemi, P. K. and R. McDermott. 2011b. *Man is by Nature a Political Animal: Evolution, Biology, and Politics*. Chicago, IL: University of Chicago Press.

Hatemi, P. K. and R. McDermott. 2012a. The Genetics of Politics: Discovery, Challenges, and Progress. *Trends in Genetics*, 28: 525–33.

Hatemi, P. K. and R. McDermott. 2012b. A Neurobiological Approach to Foreign Policy Analysis: Identifying Individual Differences in Political Violence. *Foreign Policy Analysis*, 8: 111–29.

Hatemi, P. K. and R. McDermott. 2014. The Study of International Politics in the Neurobiological Revolution: A Review of Leadership and Political Violence. *Millenium*, 43: 92–123.

Heijmans, B. T., E. W. Tobi, A. D. Stein, H. Putter, et al. 2008. Persistent Epigenetic Differences Associated with Prenatal Exposure to Famine in Humans. *Proceedings of the National Academy of Sciences*, 105: 17046–9.

Hibbing, J. R. and K. B. Smith. 2007. The Biology of Political Behavior: An Introduction. *The ANNALS of the American Academy of Political and Social Science*, 614: 6–14.

Hibbing, J. R., K. B. Smith, and J. R. Alford. 2013. *Predisposed: Liberals, Conservatives, and the Biology of Political Differences*. Abingdon: Routledge.

Israel, S., E. Lerer, I. Shalev, F. Uzefovsky, et al. 2009. The oxytocin receptor (OXTR) Contributes to Prosocial Fund Allocations in the Dictator Game and the Social Value Orientations Task. *PLoS One*, 4: e5535.

Johnson, D. D., R. McDermott, E. S. Barrett, J. Cowden, et al. 2006. Overconfidence in Wargames: Experimental Evidence on Expectations, Aggression, Gender and Testosterone. *Proceedings of the Royal Society B: Biological Sciences*, 273: 2513–20.

Jost, J. T., H. H. Nam, D. M. Amodio, and J. J. Van Bavel. 2014. Political Neuroscience: the Beginning of a Beautiful Friendship. *Political Psychology*, 35: 3–42.

Kahneman, D. and A. Tversky. 1979. Prospect Theory: An Analysis of Decision under Risk. *Econometrica*, 47: 263–92.

Kaplan, J. T., J. Freedman, and M. Iacoboni, 2007. Us versus Them: Political Attitudes and Party Affiliation Influence Neural Response to Faces of Presidential Candidates. *Neuropsychologia*, 45: 55–64.

Klofstad, C. A., R. McDermott, and P. K. Hatemi. 2012. Do Bedroom Eyes Wear Political Glasses? The Role of Politics in Human Mate Attraction. *Evolution and Human Behavior*, 33: 100–8.

Kosfeld, M., M. Heinrichs, P. J. Zak, U. Fischbacher, and E. Fehr. 2005. Oxytocin Increases Trust in Humans. *Nature*, 435: 673–6.

Krosnick, J. A. and K. M. McGraw. 2002. Psychological Political Science Versus Political Psychology True to its Name: A Plea for balance. In: K. Monroe (ed.), *Political Psychology*. Mahwah, NJ: Erlbaum.

Lockyer, A. and P. K. Hatemi. 2014. Resolving the Difference between Evolutionary Antecedents of Political Attitudes and Sources of Human Variation. *Canadian Journal of Political Science / Revue canadienne de science politique*, 47(3): 549–68.

Loewen, P. J., C. T. Dawes, N. Mazar, M. Johannesson, et al. 2013. The Heritability of Moral Standards for Everyday Dishonesty. *Journal of Economic Behavior & Organization*, 93: 363–6.

Lopez, A. C. and R. McDermott. 2012. Adaptation, Heritability, and the Emergence of Evolutionary Political Science. *Political Psychology*, 33(3): 343–62.

Lopez, A. C., R. McDermott, and M. B. Petersen. 2011. States in Mind: Evolution, Coalitional Psychology, and International Politics. *International Security*, 36: 48–83.

Lumsden, C. J. and E. O. Wilson. 1981. *Genes, Mind, and Culture: The Coevolutionary Process*, Cambridge, MA: Harvard University Press.

Madsen, D. 1985. A Biochemical Property Relating to Power Seeking in Humans. *The American Political Science Review*, 79: 448–57.

Martin, L. L. and B. A. Simmons. 1998. Theories and Empirical Studies of International Institutions. *International Organization*, 52; 729–57.

McDermott, R. 2004. The Feeling of Rationality: The Meaning of Neuroscientific Advances for Political Science. *Perspectives on Politics*, 2: 691–706.

McDermott, R. 2010. *Emotional Manipulation of Political Identity. Manipulating Democracy: Democratic Theory, Political Psychology, and Mass Media*. London: Routledge.

McDermott, R. and P. K. Hatemi. 2013. Political Ecology: On the Mutual Formation of Biology and Culture. *Political Psychology*, 35: 111–27.

McDermott, R. and P. K. Hatemi. 2016. The Relationship between Physical Aggression, Foreign Policy and Moral Choices: Phenotypic and Genetic Findings. *Aggressive Behavior*, 43(1): 37–46.

McDermott, R., D. Tingley, J. Cowden, G. Frazzetto, and D. D. Johnson. 2009. Monoamine oxidase A gene (MAOA) Predicts Behavioral Aggression Following Provocation. *Proceedings of the National Academy of Sciences*, 106: 2118–23.

McDermott, R., A. C. Lopez, and P. K. Hatemi. 2017. An Evolutionary Approach to Political Leadership. *Security Studies*, 25(4): 677–98.

Miczek, K. A., R. M. De Almeida, E. A. Kravitz, E. F. Rissman, et al. 2007. Neurobiology of Escalated Aggression and violence. *The Journal of Neuroscience*, 27: 11803–6.

Morganthau. H. 1948. *Politics Among Nations*. New York: A. A. Knopf.

Ostrom, E. 1998. A Behavioral Approach to the Rational Choice Theory of Collective Action: Presidential Address, American Political Science Association, 1997. *American Political Science Review*, 92: 1–22.

Painter, R. C., T. J. Roseboom, and O. P. Bleker. 2005. Prenatal Exposure to the Dutch Famine and Disease in Later Life: An Overview. *Reproductive Toxicology*, 20: 345–52.

Petersen, M. B. 2015. Evolutionary Political Psychology: On the Origin and Structure of Heuristics and Biases in Politic. *Political Psychology*, 36(S1): 45–78.

Petersen, M. B. and L. Aaroe. 2012. Is the Political Animal Politically Ignorant? Applying Evolutionary Psychology to the Study of Political Attitudes. *Evolutionary Psychology*, 10: 802–17.

Ridley, M. 1993. *The Red Queen: Sex and the Evolution of Human Nature*, Harmondsworth: Penguin Books Ltd.

Rosen, S. P. 2007. *War and Human Nature*. Princeton, NJ: Princeton University Press.

Rushton, J. P., D. W. Fulker, M. C. Neale, D. K. B. Nias, and H. J. Eysenck. 1986a. Altruism and Aggression: The Heritability of Individual Differences. *Journal of Personal and Social Psychology*, 50: 1192–8.

Rushton, J. P., C. H. Littlefield, and C. J. Lumsden. 1986b. Gene-culture Coevolution of Complex Social Behavior: Human Altruism and Mate Choice. *Proceedings of the National Academy of Sciences U S A*, 83: 7340–3.

Sanfey, A. G., J. K. Rilling, J. A. Aronson, L. E. Nystrom, and J. D. Cohen. 2003. The Neural Basis of Economic Decision-making in the Ultimatum Game. *Science*, 300: 1755–8.

Schultz, W., P. Dayan, and P. R. Montague. 1997. A Neural Substrate of Prediction and Reward. *Science*, 275: 1593–9.

Siever, L. 2008. Neurobiology of Aggression and Violence. *American Journal of Psychiatry*, 165: 429–42.

Smith, K. B., C. W. Larimer, L. Littvay, and J. R. Hibbing. 2007. Evolutionary Theory and Political Leadership: Why Certain People Do Not Trust Decision Makers. *The Journal of Politics*, 69: 285–99.

Tooby, J. and L. Cosmides. 1988. *The Evolution of War and its Cognitive Foundations. Evolution and Human Behavior Annual Meeting*. Ann Arbor, MI: Michigan.

Tremblay, R. E. 2008. Understanding Development and Prevention of Chronic Physical Aggression: Towards Experimental Epigenetic Studies. *Philosophical Transactions of the Royal Society of London B: Biological Sciences*, 363: 2613–22.

Tremblay, R. E. and M. Szyf. 2010. Developmental Origins of Chronic Physical Aggression and Epigenetics. *Epigenomics*, 2: 495–9.

Tversky, A. and D. Kahneman. 1974. Judgment under Uncertainty: Heuristics and Biases. *Science*, 185: 1124–31.

Van Den Bergh, B. R., E. J. Mulder, M. Mennes, and V. Glover. 2005. Antenatal Maternal Anxiety and Stress and the Neurobehavioural Development of the Fetus and Child: Links and Possible Mechanisms. A Review. *Neuroscience & Biobehavioral Reviews*, 29: 237–58.

Victoroff, J., S. Quota, J. R. Adelman, B. Celinska, et al. 2011. Support for Religio-political Aggression among Teenaged Boys in Gaza: Part II: Neuroendocrinological Findings. *Aggressive Behavior*, 37: 121–32.

Waldman, D. A., P. A. Balthazard, and S. J. Peterson. 2011. Leadership and Neuroscience: Can we Revolutionize the Way that Inspirational Leaders are Identified and Developed? *The Academy of Management Perspectives*, 25: 60–74.

Waltz, K. 1979. *Theory of International Politics*. Boston, MA: MacGraw-Hill.

Weingast, B. R. 1995. A Rational Choice Perspective on the Role of Ideas: Shared Belief Systems and State Sovereignty in International Cooperation. *Politics & Society*, 23: 449–64.

Wise, R. A. 2004. Dopamine, Learning and Motivation. *Nature Reviews Neuroscience*, 5: 483–94.

PART III

MAJOR ISSUES FOR TWENTY-FIRST-CENTURY SECURITY

CHAPTER 15

SYSTEMIC THEORY AND THE FUTURE OF GREAT POWER WAR AND PEACE

DALE C. COPELAND

THIS chapter is animated by a simple question: Are the core systemic theories of great power war and peace still relevant in the modern age of intercontinental missiles and the threat of thermonuclear war? Put somewhat differently, could one seriously imagine either China or the United States choosing to launch a major war against the other, as great powers did as recently as 1914, 1939, and 1941? If our initial reaction is to answer "no" to both versions of the question, it might seem clear that causes-of-war scholarship needs a fundamental refocus of its efforts—away from its traditional emphasis on great power war toward issues of regional conflicts, civil strife, or perhaps great power coercion short of war (e.g. economic sanctions). It does seem self-evident that neither Beijing nor Washington would see any "value" in deliberately initiating a full-scale conflict against the other.[1] But if the experience of the Cold War has taught us anything, it is that great powers in the nuclear age can still get frightenly close to total war through escalating suspicions, military mobilizations, and events such as the 1962 Cuban Missile Crisis. Indeed, a fundamental goal of US policy-makers for the past three decades, both Democratic and Republican, has been the avoidance of a new cold war with China, precisely because of the risks of an unintended escalation to great power war that accompany such intense rivalries.

To show that our theories of war are still relevant to the modern era, therefore, it is imperative that we demonstrate that they can explain why states shift from cooperation toward hard-line policies that increase the likelihood of either a cold war competition or an actual crisis that could spiral to nuclear war. Unfortunately, few of our most well-known systemic theories of war, including classical realism, power transition theory, neorealism, and the bargaining model of war, are presently set up to do this.[2] Almost invariably, these theories are built around the logical premise that actors either initiate war or they do not, depending on certain specified conditions. Such a premise may help to create a foundation for explaining why states might "choose" war over peace—usually within the larger paradigm of "rational choice" theory. But they typically are not equipped to explain why leaders might engage in actions that knowingly increase the risk of a slide into an inadvertent war, that is, a war that, prior to the action taken (e.g. crisis initiation), no actor would ever want to see come about.[3]

The purpose of this chapter is to help correct this oversight, both by discussing theories that are already set up to explain behavior that increases the likelihood of spiraling into war, and also to suggest ways that other theories might be adjusted to achieve this necessary goal. In this sense, the chapter's objective is not to argue that some theories are better than others simply because they capture the problem of inadvertent spiraling. Rather, it is to show that all theories of great power war, are relevant in the modern age, must be attuned to this problem, and adjusted accordingly, even if deductive or formal theorizing is made much more complicated in the process.

15.1 Theories of Great Power War and the Nuclear Question

The problem of building useful theories of great power war in the nuclear age was identified more than half a century ago by Thomas Schelling. Schelling's argument was straightforward: given that states cannot actually use nuclear weapons in the traditional Clausewitzian sense—to grab and hold territory to advance national political objectives—they are at best only devices to coerce others into offering concessions they would not otherwise make (Schelling 1966).[4] Yet how they do this is unique. Great powers with nuclear weapons are in the ultimate Chicken game. They both might like to get the other to "swerve" by conceding on a particular foreign policy issue or territorial interest. Yet if they had to choose, both sides greatly prefer continued peace or even a humiliating swerve to actual thermonuclear war.[5] For Schelling, this means that states, to get what they want, can only "manipulate the risk" of an slide into nuclear war by pulling the other onto the slippery slope to war and hoping it swerves first. In a world where no state is rational to initiate nuclear war, it might still be rational for each side to use the risk of an inadvertent nuclear war to achieve its foreign policy ends. The Berlin and Cuban crises of 1961–62, as Schelling suggests, can be seen in this light. Needless to say, there are few leaders that would want to use this tool of statecraft on an ongoing basis (sometimes when one rocks the boat, it does go over).[6] And because cold wars increase the chance of crises breaking out, leaders are also disinclined to fall into such intense rivalries if they can avoid them.

Any theory of great power war worth its salt, therefore, must be able to explain why great powers that have been peacefully cooperating for some time—the United States and China since 1985, for example—would ever take actions that might lead to a cold war or to crises that raise the prospect of an undesired slide into nuclear conflict.

Surprisingly, however, there are very few such theories in the field of International Relations. Consider some of the most prominent theories of great power politics and war, and how they fare in a world of nuclear weapons.

15.1.1 Classical Realism

Classical realists argue that systems where states exist in a "balance of power," with all great powers essentially equal in relative power, are likely to be peaceful.[7] Great power wars occur only when one state becomes significantly superior in military power and can thus contemplate a bid to take over the system. Multipolar systems make this more difficult, since smaller great powers can use alliances to deter superior actors by raising the costs of war and the risks of defeat. But such actors, as Germany showed twice in the twentieth century, may still decide to take on the system because of their superiority in military power (Morgenthau 1978; Gulick 1962). Yet such a theory, as it stands, has little predictive power in a world of nuclear second strike capability. Even a state with overwhelming "nuclear superiority" in the number of weapons and launch vehicles—such as the United States in the 1950s and today—would be extremely unlikely to launch a war against another nuclear power. It would take only a few retaliatory strikes by the other to make "victory" meaningless and war thus irrational.[8]

15.1.2 Power Transition Theory

The same problem hangs over classical realism's main challenger, power transition theory (or hegemonic stability theory). It argues that the presence of one hegemonically dominant state keeps the peace, while the rise of the second-ranked great power to essential equality with the former hegemon leads to war. The rising actor initiates war at this point of "power transition" because it now has incentives to alter the system through war to get the goodies (status, territory, economic concessions) that it has been historically denied.[9]

Power transition theory has a fundamental logical flaw at its heart: actors still rising in power always have an incentive to avoid war so they can fight later if necessary at less cost and risk. This means that any "power transition" point of military equality has no magical causal power to drive rising states into an initiation of war (Copeland 2000: 13–14).[10] The theory, however, makes even less sense when the equality of power is measured in terms of nuclear weapons. A China that grew to equality with the United States in nuclear throw-weight might believe the Chicken game was now between equal Mac trucks, rather than (as previously) a Mac truck and a VW bug. But thermonuclear war is still thermonuclear war, and no great power would willingly choose it just to gain goodies it believes it deserves. To be sure, such a state might be more willing to engage in Schellingesque "rocking the boat" to play upon the other's unwillingness to risk drowning in a nuclear sea. Yet as with classical realism, we cannot understand the triggers for such risk-taking behavior without theorizing the causal mechanisms linking changes in the distribution of power with the willingness of actors to assume increased risks of inadvertent war through hard-line policies.[11] Otherwise, power transition theory has little practical value in today's world, even if the logical flaw that argues that rising powers initiate conflicts is corrected.

15.1.3 Neorealism

Neorealist theories of great power war are similarly limited by their failure to deal with inadvertent war. Kenneth Waltz (1979, 1989) and John Mearsheimer (2001) have argued that bipolar systems are more stable than multipolar systems, mainly because the level of uncertainty is greater in the latter than the former, leading some actors to initiate wars that they think they can win quickly and easily. Yet surprisingly, both theorists are also famous for arguing that nuclear weapons provide the ultimate deterrent, making wars between nuclear great powers very unlikely, essentially regardless of the polarity of the system. Aside from the fact that the Cold War is their only example of bipolar stability—meaning any "peace" from 1945 to 1990 was clearly overdetermined by the presence of nuclear weapons[12]—the Waltz–Mearsheimer neorealist logic cannot explain variations in the probability of great power war across time by invoking a constant such as polarity. Why did dangerous nuclear crises that risked nuclear war occur in the early 1960s, but were few and far between after 1965 and especially after 1985?

One might argue that Mearsheimer's theory does have an extra variable drawn from classical realism and deterrence theory—the relative equality or inequality of the military power balance—to explain changes in the propensity of war within multipolarity or bipolarity. Yet because he seeks to explain only why states might choose to initiate war, not why they might decide to engage in hard-line policies that increase the risk of inadvertent war, he has no theoretical explanation for why great powers might consciously accept the risks that cold wars and nuclear crises entail in the modern world—or why they might indeed moderate their policies to avoid these risks. Mearsheimer's "offensive" version of neorealism might seem to suggest that because states are forced to assume the worst about the other's intentions, they will be continually engaging in assertive behavior to expand their spheres, even at the risk of actual great power war. But this constant—the worst-case assumption—cannot explain why for decades states such as the United States and China after 1985 would be so prudently cautious in their diplomatic relations.[13]

More to the point, a theory based on a worst-case assumption cannot explain the conditions under which either side might decide to initiate behaviors that would indeed get them into a cold war or worse. Mearsheimer might invoke the costs of nuclear war as a cost parameter keeping the two moderate in behavior.[14] But costs and risks are two separate variables—one involves "given" expenses after war occurs, the other the probability that war occurs at all. Without a theory to explain the willingness to get out on the slippery slope to a nuclear war, therefore, offensive neorealism is only a theory of sphere consolidation and low-level incremental expansion, not a theory that helps us explain the conditions for great power war and peace.

15.1.4 Bargaining Model of War

We will see in a moment that the defensive realist strand of neorealism, when combined with a dynamic view of relative power, does help us overcome the limitations of the offensive realist position. But for now it is worth investigating the value of perhaps the most influential theory of international conflict for the last two decades, namely, the bargaining model of war. The original formulation of the model (Fearon 1995) identified two main ways that a "rationalist" war between powerful actors could come about: information asymmetries and commitment problems.[15] In the first mechanism, if two great powers have private information about their own willingness to pay the costs of war, they might initiate a crisis or small-scale war against a third party, thinking the other great power lacks the resolve to fight to defend its interests. If costly signals through mobilization and public statements of resolve fail to overcome the information asymmetry, both sides may fail to make sufficient concessions for a deal that both sides prefer to war, leading one of the states to initiate actual great power war. In the second mechanism, one state fears the other's future intentions, either in the short term or long term. The other may be unable to credibly promise not to attack later because it has an incentive to hide its true desires. This may lead the first state to attack now because it believes the other is preparing for immediate attack (preemptive war) or because it believes the other is growing in military power and will attack later once it has reached a point of military advantage (preventive war). Either way, the inability of states to commit to being nice later can lead actors fearing a diminution of their military position to attack now for fear of the future.

Fearon's bargaining model of war has had an enormous impact on the studies of both coercion through crisis and war itself.[16] The model helps us establish the conditions under which states will or will not reach a bargain that both might otherwise prefer to have to fight a war. Yet when it comes to the study of great power war in the nuclear era, it suffers from the same problem previously discussed. In pretty well every formalization of the bargaining model logic, states are assumed to simply choose war as better than the next best alternative, namely, either the status quo (if the actor forgoes a "crisis stage" and simply attacks) or "backing down" (within any crisis that might arise).[17] Such a theoretical move is driven by the focus of uncertainty about the other's current intentions or resolve, with the presumption that if a state believes the other is Chicken, it will push forward, but if it believes the other has Prisoners' Dilemma or Stag Hunt payoffs and thus will indeed choose war over backing down, then making a deal is preferred.[18] But in the nuclear age, direct great power conflict is and always remains a Chicken game, since no state would rationally choose to initiate a war that would lead to thermonuclear destruction. As Schelling stresses, no state can credibly claim to prefer war to giving up a small part of its sphere or to the loss of a neutral third party. But it can still credibly communicate its willingness to risk an uncontrollable slide into general war that it knows it neither prefers to the status quo nor to making concessions.[19]

This means that bargaining approaches to war, if they are going to be relevant to modern great power politics, must build in to their logics the exogenous risks of inadvertent spiraling to war that rise as both a function of overall hostility levels (as when states shift from relative peace to cold war) and the intensity of any crises that arise within an ongoing rivalry. More specifically, they must work from the assumption that states make their calculations based on their probabilistic assessments of the risks of action versus the risks of non-action, that is, of becoming more hard-line versus staying more soft-line.

15.1.5 Defensive Realism

This is where the insights of defensive realism have proved particularly helpful. Defensive realists stress the tragic reality of security dilemmas: the inability of one state to increase its security through things such as arms buildups and alliances without simultaneously diminishing the security of other states, either because such actions can suggest that the first state may be preparing for war or because they improve its relative ability to fight and win in a war. Other states can be expected to respond with similar measures, measures that end up reducing the security of the state that starts the ball rolling. Actors can thus find themselves in a spiral of increasing hostility and mistrust that puts both sides on a "hair-trigger" and increases the chances that dangerous crises may occur that lead to actual war (Jervis 1976, 1978; Glaser 1997, 2010; Booth and Wheeler 2008; Kydd 2005; Van Evera 1999). For this reason, defensive realists reject the worst-case assumption of offensive realists, arguing that such an assumption will lead to overly hard-line policies by both parties and a reduction, not a "maximization," of the security of the players (Glaser 2010).

Defensive realism has proved particularly useful in explaining why states that have been relatively peaceful with each other—or even allies, as the United States and Russia had been during the Second World War—might fall into a spiral of arms racing and hostile posturing that greatly increases the risks of great power war. The main problem with defensive realism is a simple one: it assumes that the leaders are not aware of the risks of spiraling prior to the spiral, and that "if only" they had been aware, or had understood that the other was also seeking security, they would not have upped the ante through hard-line policies that trigger the spiral. Yet a properly defined rationalist logic must assume that leaders do indeed understand the problem of security dilemmas, and that they know they can trigger undesired escalation by their own policies. If we start with this assumption, the puzzle of great power politics becomes this: Why do actors ever switch from moderate policies that keep the risks of spiraling low to hard-line actions that knowingly increase those risks? If the "crash" in nuclear Chicken is so unacceptable, why do actors ever engage in actions that increase the risk of one?[20]

There is a deeper issue lurking behind this question. Scholars and policy officials have understood for decades that any great power stand-off in the nuclear era is similar to the 1950s game of teenagers driving toward each other at breakneck speeds, hoping to get the other to swerve first. Yet International Relations (IR) theorists rarely ask the prior question: Why do actors decide to "get on the road" in the first place? Why not use moderation and quiet bargaining to avoid putting one's reputation on the line, and thus being forced into playing such a dangerous game?[21] If great power leaders are aware of the perils of security-dilemma spiraling, as they clearly are,[22] we must turn to an investigation of exogenous factors that change leaders' calculation, leading them to accept the increased risks of spiraling and inadvertent war. If the life of great powers is about trade-offs, then their willingness to "up the ante" in the nuclear age will be a function of the kinds of things that force leaders to make choices they would otherwise not want to make.

15.1.6 Dynamic Neorealism

My own scholarly efforts to grapple with the above problems have led me to seek to integrate the insights of offensive realism and defensive realism into a more dynamic neorealist view of international politics. This dynamic neorealist position stresses the factors external to a state that can change its assessment of its long-term power position and security, and thus its willingness to accept the risks of spiraling. Declining power has been a major reason for large-scale wars between great powers in the pre-nuclear era.[23] Yet leaders of nuclear great powers also worry about relative decline. They know that they face difficult least-of-many-evils decisions to deal with it. If they continue with moderate policies in an effort to avoid spiraling, they know that the state may become more vulnerable to attack later on or be subject to efforts by growing adversaries to whittle down the state's sphere of influence. Yet if they switch to more hard-line policies in order to avert decline, they might increase the probability of an inadvertent slide into war through a spiral of hostility and mistrust (Copeland 2000: ch. 2 and 2015: 8–12, 42–4, 430–1). What factors will drive an actor's decision to shift to increasingly hard-line behavior, despite knowledge of the risks of triggering a security-dilemma spiral? By focusing our attention on these factors, within a logic that accepts that great power decision-making is all about trade-offs, we can begin to build a theoretical foundation that can predict when great powers, even in the nuclear age, will adopt policies that lead to cold wars and dangerous crises such as occurred in 1961 and 1962.

The first most obvious factor is a leader's assessment of the depth and inevitability of any decline currently taking place. If decline is seen as a short-term downward "blip" on an otherwise optimistic growth trajectory, then it is highly unlikely that a state would risk setting off a cold war spiral, let alone initiate a full-blown nuclear crisis. China since 1990 has occasionally experienced temporary economic problems. But because its overall trends have been so positive, it has been very reluctant to do anything that might spark a return to cold war politics. A state anticipating steep decline if it remains cooperative, on the other hand, is much more likely to turn to containment to prevent this decline, notwithstanding the greater probability of great power war. This was the

US situation in 1945 coming out of the Second World War. Harry Truman understood that continuing the wartime cooperation with the Soviet Union would only allow it to develop its now larger territorial base of power in Eurasia. He thus decided to end economic lend-lease aid, restrict reparation payments from western Germany, and expand on Roosevelt's policy of projecting US air power from bases surrounding the Soviet Union. He was well-aware by mid-1945 that such policies would spark a cold war, but he adopted them as better than allowing the Soviets to grow unimpeded.[24]

Fortunately the United States has been in a more favorable situation over the last three decades than it faced in 1945. China may be closing the GNP gap, but there is no reason to think it will inevitably overtake America in total economic or technological power. And when one considers per capita GNP, it is clear that the United States will remain supreme for a long time to come (Brooks and Wohlforth 2015–16). This means that while Washington might "pivot" to Asia to signal its commitment to Asian allies, it has no need to embark on a Trumanesque containment of China, especially given the downside risks that a new cold war would entail (Copeland 2000: 24045, 2015: 436–44).

A key related factor is a state's expectations of the future commercial environment, and how any actions it undertakes to shore up its position might shape the other's expectations of future trade. Trade between great powers and their spheres is a major source of economic growth for the actors. If they expect other great powers will continue this trade into the future, they will have reason to maintain relatively moderate policies. This will avoid pushing the other into restrictive commercial policies that destroy current trade benefits. It will also reduce the chance that the states might invoke a "trade-security spiral," whereby actions by one great power to contain the other's economic growth lead the second actor to build up its military strength and control over its commercial sphere, which only leads the first actor to increase its economic restrictions out of fear of the other's long-term intentions (Copeland 2015: 10–12, 39–49, 429–39).

The dramatic changes in the US–Japanese relationship from 1920 to 1941 illustrate the importance of the trade dimension in great power politics. In the 1920s, when trade relations were positive, Tokyo and Washington enjoyed a period of cooperation and peace. After 1929 and especially after 1940, trade fell dramatically, pushing the Japanese government into territorial policies that only heightened Washington's desire to tighten the economic screws. The result of course was the Pacific War. Severe economic restrictions during the Cold War also greatly exacerbated the level of hostility between the United States and Russia. Fortunately, the American and Chinese governments seemed to have learned from these dangerous periods of history, and have acted to avoid any trade–security spiraling sparked by such things as third-party instability in the Middle East or territorial questions in Central Asia or the South China Seas (Copeland 2015: chs. 4–6, 442–4).

A third important parameter is a declining state's estimate of the likelihood of a rising state doing damage to its sphere later on, or actually launching a major war against it (Copeland 2000: 38–9). As the bargaining model correctly points out, rising states have great difficulty in credibly signaling their commitment to be peaceful in the future, once they have more power. In the pre-1945 era, this problem of uncertainty was particularly severe, since declining actors could indeed imagine that the rising state might think it was worth its while to launch an all-out war after it had gained pre-eminence. German civilian and military leaders in 1914 and 1939, for example, unanimously agreed that the rising Russian state might very well expand westward if it grew to a dominant position. The presence of nuclear weapons and secure second strike capability greatly reduces this concern. But the fear that the rising state, if its base is allowed to grow, will increase its efforts to whittle down the dominant state's sphere to further its economic or power projection capability is still a real one. This of course has been a primary issue shaping talk of a "rising China threat" for the last two decades of US foreign policy.

The question of whether or not a rising state will embark on aggressive policies later reveals the value of including domestic- and individual-level variables as a complement to the systemic forces discussed so far. In a pure systemic set-up, we might assume that the declining actor is so uncertain about what type of actor it will face later, once the rising state has peaked in power, that its estimate of its likelihood of being aggressive is only a function of how big it will likely become. In the real world, of course, states in decline will not rely solely on any estimate of the depth of decline, but will also ask the question: What kind of state is the riser likely to be in 15 or 20 years, after it has become much more powerful?[25] In particular, any argument that incorporates security-dilemma insights must ask whether the other's expected future type will make it more or less likely to engage in the kinds of risky behaviors that can cause an action–reaction spiral to inadvertent war. Ideologically extreme states such as Stalinist Russia in the early 1950s or revolutionary Iran in the 1980s will clearly make declining states much more worried about the future. China's move away from Maoist extremism toward capitalist-based integration has predictably reduced fears that a growing China will shift to territorial expansionism down the road. Set against the clear risks of war associated with hard-line containment, both Republican and Democratic administrations have understandably maintained cooperative policies that serve to further bind China to the globalized world system.

15.2 Reformulating Systemic Theory

We have seen so far that systemic theory can still be relevant in the nuclear age, as long as it incorporates within its deductive logic actor awareness of military and trade-based security dilemmas and the concomitant risks of spirals to inadvertent war. If we start from the assumption that leaders are conscious of the difficult trade-offs in international politics, we can see why they usually prefer to maintain moderate politics (to avoid spiraling) but occasionally feel obliged to switch to hard-line policies to maintain their power positions in the face of what would otherwise be significant decline. Yet we have seen that most of the key systemic theories of great power war have not yet incorporated the risks of inadvertent war into their core causal logics. This section of the chapter will suggest a few ways to help these theories make this move, and thus re-establish their relevance in the contemporary age.

Classical realist theories of war can be improved by assuming that when nuclear states are significantly dominant in relative military power, they will be more likely to accept the risks of inadvertent spiraling to great power war.[26] The prediction here is that nuclear great powers will still be wary of setting off an uncontrollable escalation to war, but that when they are significantly superior, they will think it easier to "rock the boat" to get the other side to swerve. The Mac truck and the VW Bug in nuclear Chicken both fear the DD outcome, but the driver of the Mac truck might reasonably think the other will chicken out first as a crisis escalates.[27] Classical realists have implicitly done this when explaining such things as the US willingness to escalate the Cuban crisis of 1962; American naval and nuclear superiority put the balance of power in Washington's favor, explaining why the Americans would pull both sides out further on the slippery slope to nuclear war.[28] By more explicitly theorizing the role of security-dilemma spiraling, such realists would make their own theory more applicable to contemporary relations with China. Still, because of its static nature, the classical realist argument has trouble explaining why nuclear states would ever get on the road to play Chicken in the first place, either by initiating a cold war or a nuclear crisis. Bringing in power trends and the problem of decline would help correct this problem.

Power transition theory, as we have seen, suffers from the logical flaw of assuming that rising states seek war at points of power equality, even though they are still on an upward power trajectory. But we can correct this concern by bringing in the classical realist point that in any snapshot of time, the more relative power a state has, the more it is willing to take risks of escalation to war. When a rising power is weak, it will be cautious. If over many years it has built up its power so that it is closer to equality, it will be more willing to defend its interests when they are threatened. In the nuclear age, this means that power transition theory could argue that a now equal great power might see itself no longer as a VW Bug but as a near-equal Mac truck, and that it "won't be pushed around anymore." Note, however, that its greater willingness to accept the risks of inadvertent war is not a function of its rising power trend—that trend will make it want to buy time for further growth, all things being equal—but rather the result of the new snapshot of relative power (see note 10 above). Power transition theory can thus be seen as ultimately grounded in classical realist thinking: taking snapshots of the distribution of power over time, it predicts that the more relative military power a state has, the more it will be willing to risk war. Yet when we bring trend lines back in, we see that a formerly inferior state will still be cautious if equal but still rising in power, because it knows that war later is better than war now. The true initiator of great power conflict will thus logically be states anticipating decline, either because of long-term internal problems or expectations that trade will increasingly be restricted and will not be restored.[29]

The neorealist theories of war must also explicitly incorporate defensive realist insights on spiraling if they are to remain relevant. In the end, as we saw earlier, Mearsheimer's offensive realism uses a classical realist logic about power differentials to argue that in either bipolar or multipolar systems, it is superior states that are the ones mostly likely to initiate war, with near-equal states being deterred by the balance of power. Once the risk of inadvertent war is built into the logic, a reformulated neorealism would mirror the predictions of the adjusted classical realist argument: dominant great powers will risk inadvertent nuclear war more readily than states that are only equal or in fact inferior in military power. Yet even with this reformulation, neorealism could not explain why actors, even dominant ones, would be moderate in behavior for long periods of time, and then suddenly shift to hard-line policies that increase the chances of nuclear war. Neorealism is still too static, focusing as it does on snapshots of relative power. Declining power trends must be incorporated to explain the conditions under which strong powers might decide to accept the risks associated with cold war and nuclear crisis.[30]

The future task for the bargaining model of war is to set its insights within a framework that recognizes the ever-present problem of security-dilemma spiraling. The easiest way to do this is to formalize the idea that initiating a crisis, as opposed to simply starting a war, entails a series of "stages" or "moments" on a slippery slope, each one of which is associated with a higher exogenous probability that both actors will fall into the abyss of nuclear war. The probability of inadvertent war can be expected to increase for a variety of reasons: trigger-happy commanders, accidents that lead to incentives to preempt, or the over-commitment of reputations as regional nuclear skirmishes break out. Assuming that leaders understand the Schelling logic, and will manipulate the growing exogenous risk of war to get the other to back down, bargaining theory can then show under what conditions states might decide to keep playing nuclear Chicken in order to force a "negotiated deal" that both prefer to continued crisis (as opposed to "war" itself, as is assumed in almost every recent version of the bargaining model).

Work by Branislav Slantchev (2013) sets a standard for other bargaining theorists when it comes to understanding "crisis bargaining" through manipulation of risk. But even once the general bargaining model of war has been corrected to account for the risk of nuclear war in a crisis, it must still deal with the question of why great powers would ever get out on the road to nuclear Chicken in the first place. Can bargaining theory predict when and under what conditions China and the United States might leave behind the economic and political cooperation of the past 30 years and embark on a new round of cold war politics? Here bargaining theory is limited by its focus on the mechanisms of bargaining itself, and its bracketing of the underlying propelling forces might push states to use coercion during periods of peaceful cooperation. Dynamic theories focusing on the security concerns of declining actors can supplement bargaining models by revealing the different parameters that can make a moderate state start to lean to more hard-line actions, including cold war containment, military arms racing, and the occasional initiation of nuclear crises.

15.3 Conclusion

This chapter has shown that theories of great power war will have little relevance to the modern nuclear age unless they incorporate within their deductive logics the importance of security-dilemma spiraling and the ongoing risk of inadvertent war. Given the existential concerns associated with cold wars and crises, it seems clear that most nuclear great powers will want to avoid heated confrontations by maintaining moderate policies, most of the time. The puzzle of conflict for the present day can thus be boiled down to this: Why would a United States or a China ever embark on policies that knowingly could lead to a new cold war, let alone initiate a nuclear crisis of the kind we saw in 1961–62? The defensive realist insight into the tragic reality of spiraling and inadvertent war brings us part of the way to an answer. But to go further, we need theories that show us under what conditions states shift from peaceful cooperation to harder-line policies that consciously increase the risks of things "getting out of hand." Parameters that capture the intensity of a state's decline, its expectations of future trade, and the likelihood of a rising state doing damage later are all useful starting points for future research. Clearly much more theoretical work must be done before we can offer great power leaders the kind of advice that will help states maintain their security while keeping the risk of nuclear war to a bare minimum. But in an age when any future "world war" would likely be our last, there can be no denying of the importance of such scholarly efforts.

Notes

1. Even pessimists about the world's ability to avoid nuclear war—such as Dan Deudney in this volume—assume that the main danger lies not in the choices of great powers vis-à-vis each other, but rather in their interactions with smaller state and non-state actors in the system.
2. Due to space, I focus only on theories emphasizing systemic factors as causes of war. Unit-level arguments stressing the role of domestic politics and leader psychology have an advantage over systemic theories in explaining how nuclear war might occur, given their emphasis on the potentially self-defeating or irrational side of human decision-making. At the end of the chapter, I will briefly mention how unit-level and systemic theories can be integrated into a fuller explanation of war and conflict.
3. On this definition, see (George 1991: xi, 545). On the risks of inadvertent nuclear war during a crisis, see (Schelling 1966; Frei 1983; Betts 1987; Jervis 1989; Blair 1993).
4. Nuclear weapons also serve important deterrence functions, of course.
5. In the traditional set-up of the Chicken game, cooperation or "CC" gives both players a utility payoff of 3, getting the other to swerve is worth 4, swerving yourself is 2, and the "crash" of "DD" has a payoff of 1 (such that each player's preferences are DC > CC > CD > DD). A nuclear Chicken game has the same ordering of preferences, but might be better represented by a mutual DD payoff of –100 or –200 each, to remind us of the truly horrific nature of the crash.

6. And Sechser and Fuhrmannn 2017 show just how rarely this tool is employed historically.
7. For more on the various forms of realism discussed in this chapter, see Adam Quinn, this volume.
8. So-called neoclassical realists might be able to solve the problem by incorporating unit-level pathologies that lead to errors in crisis decision-making. Unfortunately, such realists have not yet built a theory of great power war that incorporates the risk of inadvertent nuclear war through irrational missteps and domestic pressures. See the edited volume by Lobell et al. (2009), as well as Ripsman et al. (2016).
9. See in particular Organski and Kugler (1980); Gilpin (1981); Kugler and Organski (1989); Tammen et al. (2000).
10. There is a common conceptual confusion that seems to provide power transition theory with some empirical support. When previously weak states have narrowed the gap in relative conventional power, they sometimes start to act more assertively (Germany after 1895, for example). Yet this is only because the differential of relative power is now more equal, which allows the formerly weaker state to advance its interests—not because the state with a rising power trajectory is destined to become more aggressive. In short, power transition theory fails to separate the causal effects of *snapshots* in the distribution of power from the effects of *dynamic trends* in any distribution. As I discuss later, power transition theorists are closer to classical realists than they think. Classical realists, using a series of snapshots of the power balance, can explain why states that were significantly inferior become increasingly assertive as they become more equal—they are relatively less deterred over time. The dynamics of the power balance, however, must still be taken into account: if these states are still on an upward power trajectory, they have strong incentives not to push too hard, and especially to avoid war until their power has peaked (Germany after 1913, given the newly rising Russian state).
11. Compare this to Kugler and Organski (1989: 185–90), who adamantly deny that the theory needs to be adjusted in any way to accommodate the reality of nuclear weapons.
12. See Copeland (1996) for an examination of three other (clearly unstable) cases of bipolarity: Sparta–Athens and Rome–Carthage in the ancient world and the French–Hapsburgs of the early sixteenth century.
13. Offensive realism, when it comes to the US–Chinese relationship, thus turns into a normative theory: Washington and China *should* be more hard-line and expansionist than they have been, if they want to respond rationally to the pressures of the anarchic system. The main problem, of course, is that holding to a worst-case assumption in a nuclear realm is a highly *irrational* way to behave (and US and Chinese leaders fortunately know this).
14. This would be consistent with Mearsheimer's claim that high conventional costs of war can deter expansionism (2001: 37).
15. A third possibility, wars due to the indivisibility of a particular good, are unlikely, precisely because states can use side-payments to overcome the problem.
16. A small representative sample would include Goemans (2000); Powell (2002, 2006); Wagner (2007); Ramsay (2004); Slantchev (2013); Schultz (2001); Kydd (2005); Reiter (2003, 2009). My own thinking about war has been strongly influenced by Fearon's work, notwithstanding my concerns for its limitations (Copeland 2000: 45–9, 2015: 12–13, 39–41).
17. The two are often combined by bringing in a small third party that one state attacks out of the blue, which leads to a crisis when the other major state counter-mobilizes, leading to a crisis that may or may not be resolved without war.

18. See references in note 16. Two notable exceptions of bargaining scholars that do incorporate into their logics the autonomous or exogenous risks of spiraling as a crisis proceeds are Powell 1990 and Slantchev (2013). As I note in Section 15.2, however, they do not examine why rational actors would ever get themselves into a crisis in the first place, knowing that it might force them to take risky escalatory steps.
19. Schelling (1966). In other words, the question of "resolve" in nuclear scenarios is not about "willingness to pay the costs of war"—the traditional bargaining model assumption—but rather the willingness to risk a war no state could possibly prefer to a negotiated peace.
20. See Copeland (2015: 12–13, 42–6, 430–31; and 2000: ch. 2).
21. Bargaining-model theorists that do incorporate the importance of exogenous increases in the risk of inadvertent war into their analyses, such as Powell (1990) and Slantchev (2013), invariably start with the fact of a crisis itself. They do not consider why the actors put themselves on the road to Chicken by choosing the hard-line actions that force a competition of prestige and reputation.
22. Snyder and Diesing (1977), for example, found that in 13 of 16 major crisis cases, leaders were highly conscious that their own actions might cause events to get out of hand.
23. Copeland (2000, 2015); Weisiger (2013). For further discussion and references regarding the preventive motive for war, see Levy (1989, 2008).
24. Copeland (2000, ch. 6); Copeland (2015, ch. 6).
25. See Copeland (2000: 38–9, 238–40 and 2015: 46–7, 435–6, 445–6), which builds on some of the insights of Stephen Walt's (1996) balance-of-threat theory.
26. In my own work, I build this point in as an additional parameter that shapes the willingness of a declining state to shift to more hard-line policies (see Copeland, 2000, 38–9).
27. China has felt the sense of its inferiority since it backed away from its hard-line stance over Taiwan in the 1995–96 stand-off in the East China Sea. Its subsequent efforts to build its military power in the region can be seen as a way to create a more "equal" Chicken scenario in any future Taiwan crisis, increasing the chance that Washington will be the one to swerve.
28. See Betts (1987).
29. We can thus predict that China, as long as it is still on an upward trajectory, will be relatively cautious about pushing too hard for territorial changes in Asia, whether over its border with India or in the East and South China Seas. China's "new and improved" snapshot level of relative power does give it more incentive to defend its interests in the region, but its upward trend line gives it an incentive not to provoke a superior but relatively declining United States. It is a shift to preventive containment by a declining America that is more likely to set off a spiral to cold war or a nuclear crisis in Sino–American relations. See Copeland (2015: 436–44; and 2000: 240–5).
30. Fortunately, because of China's huge population, it will always have a much smaller per capita income than the United States, even if it overtakes America in total GNP (Brooks and Wohlforth, 2015–16; Copeland 2000: 242). This means that leaders in Washington can rationally continue to allow China to "catch up" in relative power rather than having to switch to the kind of hard-line preventive containment employed against the Soviet Union after 1945. The benefits of such a switch (maintaining US dominance) would not be worth the considerable risks (a new cold war and the attending chance of another 1962-type nuclear crisis).

References

Betts, Richard K. 1987. *Nuclear Blackmail and Nuclear Balance*. Washington, DC: Brookings.

Blair, Bruce G. 1993. *The Logic of Accidental Nuclear War*. Washington, DC: Brookings.

Booth, Ken and Nicholas J. Wheeler. 2008. *The Security Dilemma: Fear, Cooperation, and Trust in World Politics*. New York: Palgrave.

Brooks, Stephen G. and William C. Wohlforth. 2015–16. The Rise and Fall of the Great Powers of the Twenty-First Century: China's Rise and the Fate of America's Global Position. *International Security*, 40(3): 7–53.

Copeland, Dale. 1996. Neorealism and the Myth of Bipolar Stability: Toward a Dynamic Realist Theory of Major War. *Security Studies*, 5(3): 29–89.

Copeland, Dale. 2000. *The Origins of Major War*. Ithaca, NY: Cornell University Press.

Copeland, Dale. 2015. *Economic Interdependence and War*. Princeton, NJ: Princeton University Press.

Fearon, James D. 1992. Threats to Use Force. PhD dissertation, Department of Political Science, University of California, Berkeley.

Fearon, James D. 1995. Rationalist Explanations for War. *International Organization*, 49(3): 577–92.

Frei, Daniel. 1983. *Risks of Unintentional Nuclear War*. New York: UN Institute for Disarmament Research.

George, Alexander L. (ed.). 1991. *Avoiding War: Problems of Crisis Management*. Boulder, CO: Westview.

Gilpin, Robert. 1981. *War and Change in World Politics*. Cambridge: Cambridge University Press.

Glaser, Charles. 1997. The Security Dilemma Revisited. *World Politics*, 50(1): 171–201.

Glaser, Charles. 2010. *Rationalist Theory of International Politics*. Princeton, NJ: Princeton University Press.

Goemans, H. E. 2000. *War and Punishment: The Causes of War Termination and the First World War*. Princeton, NJ: Princeton University Press.

Gulick, Edward V. 1962. *Europe's Classical Balance of Power*. New York: Norton.

Jervis, Robert. 1976. *Perception and Misperception in International Politics*. Princeton, NJ: Princeton University Press.

Jervis, Robert. 1978. Cooperation under the Security Dilemma. *World Politics*, 30(2): 167–214.

Jervis, Robert. 1989. *The Meaning of the Nuclear Revolution*. Ithaca, NJ: Cornell University Press.

Kugler, Jacek and A. F. K. Organski. 1989. The Power Transition: A Retrospective and Prospective Evaluation. In Manus I. Midlarksy (ed.), *Handbook of War Studies*. Boston, MA: Unwin Hyman.

Kydd, Andrew. 2005. *Trust and Mistrust in International Politics*. Princeton, NJ: Princeton University Press.

Levy, Jack S. 1987. Declining Power and the Preventive Motivation for War. *World Politics*, 40(1): 82–107.

Levy, Jack S. 2008. Preventive War and Democratic Politics. *International Studies Quarterly*, 52(1): 1–24.

Lobell, Steven E., Norrin M. Ripsman, and Jeffrey W. Taliaferro (eds.). 2009. *Neoclassical Realism, the State, and Foreign Policy*. Cambridge: Cambridge University Press.

Mearsheimer, John. J. 2001. *The Tragedy of Great Power Politics*. New York: Norton.

Morgenthau, Hans J. 1978. *Politics Among Nations*, 5th rev. edn. New York: Alfred A. Knopf.

Organski, A. F. K. and Jacek Kugler. 1980. *The War Ledger*. Chicago: University of Chicago Press.

Powell, Robert. 1990. *Nuclear Deterrence Theory*. Cambridge: Cambridge University Press.

Powell, Robert. 2002. Bargaining Theory and International Conflict. *Annual Review of Political Science*, 5(1): 1–30.

Powell, Robert. 2006. War as a Commitment Problem. *International Organization*, 60(1): 169–203.

Ramsay, Kristopher W. 2004. Politics at the Water's Edge: Crisis Bargaining and Electoral Competition. *Journal of Conflict Resolution*, 48(3): 459–86.

Reiter, Dan. 2003. Exploring the Bargaining Model of War. *Perspectives on Politics*, 1(1): 27–43.

Reiter, Dan. 2009. *How Wars End*. Princeton, NJ: Princeton University Press.

Ripsman, Norrin M., Jeffrey W. Taliaferro, and Steven E. Lobell. 2016. *Neoclassical Realist Theory of International Politics*. Oxford: Oxford University Press.

Schelling, Thomas C. 1966. *Arms and Influence*. New Haven, CT: Yale University Press.

Schultz, Kenneth. 2001. *Democracy and Coercive Diplomacy*. Cambridge: Cambridge University Press.

Sechser, Todd S. and Matthew Fuhrmann. 2017. *Nuclear Weapons and Coercion*. Cambridge: Cambridge University Press.

Slantchev, Branislav. 2013. *Military Threats: The Cost of Coercion and the Price of Peace*. Cambridge: Cambridge University Press.

Snyder, Glenn and Paul Diesing. 1977. *Conflict Among Nations*. Princeton, NJ: Princeton University Press.

Tammen, Ronald et al. 2000. *Power Transitions: Strategies for the 21st Century*. New York: Chatham House.

Van Evera, Stephen. 1999. *Causes of War: Power and the Roots of Conflict*. Ithaca, NY: Cornell University Press.

Wagner, R. Harrison. 2007. *War and the State*. Ann Arbor, MI: University of Michigan Press.

Walt, Stephen M. 1996. *Revolution and War*. Ithaca, NY: Cornell University Press.

Waltz, Kenneth. 1979. *Theory of International Politics*. New York: Random House.

Waltz, Kenneth. 1989. The Origins of War in Neorealist Theory. In Robert I. Rotberg and Theodore K. Rabb (eds.), *The Origins and Prevention of Major War*. Cambridge: Cambridge University Press.

Weisiger, Alex. 2013. *Logics of War: Explanations for Limited and Unlimited Conflicts*. Ithaca, NY: Cornell University Press.

CHAPTER 16

TRENDS IN CONFLICT
What Do We Know and What Can We Know?

KRISTIAN SKREDE GLEDITSCH AND
AARON CLAUSET

16.1 Introduction

Trends has been a central topic since the inception of research on conflict and violence. Many early debates revolved around contending claims about the causes of war, with different implications for the frequency of war and the possibility for change. While some insist that the risk of war is essentially constant and inescapable, others see warfare as a more dynamic phenomenon that can increase or decrease in frequency and severity with other features such as social organization and development (see, e.g., Gat 2005; Fry 2006; Pinker 2015). Recent debates over whether war is in decline have reignited interest in trends in conflict. Some argue that we see clear evidence of a decline in conflict, especially after the Cold War, following a broader decline in many types of violence with deeper historical roots (see, e.g., Gurr 2000; Payne 2004; Goldstein 2011; Pinker 2011). This is a remarkable contrast to the extreme pessimism that prevailed at the end of the Cold War, where many argued that conflict was becoming more common and predicted an increasingly violent world (Mearsheimer 1990; Kaplan 1994). The decline of war thesis is not without its critics, who express a host of reservations ranging from challenges to the underlying data, claims that certain types of conflict do not decline, as well as more fundamental concerns over limits to our ability to make inferences about trends from existing data.

Much of the debate on trends in conflict involves technical issues about data and modeling, but at the core of the debate lie fundamental questions about what we can learn from the past about the present and the future. Is the long peace between the major powers since 1945 a remarkable fact, indicating a decline in war, or fully compatible with random fluctuation? If war has declined, can we say something about the possible role of specific factors such as democratic institutions, economic interdependence, and nuclear weapons, or the implications for future conflict (e.g. Mearsheimer 1990; Russett 1990; Gaddis 1992/93; Schelling 2005)? Does the decline of conventional conflict mask an increase in unconventional violence (see, e.g., Kaldor 2013; Gray 2015)? What can we say about the future and what constitutes informative evidence?

In this chapter we provide a non-technical overview of the contending positions and the concepts necessary to understand the current debate on the decline of conflict. We first consider trends in the raw number of armed conflicts or states involved in conflicts, followed by trends in the severity of interstate and civil wars, and trends in alternative measures of conflict. We then consider the role of distributions, and the timing of conflicts. Throughout, we consider whether trends may have emerged or changed at particular points in history, such as the end of the Second World War or the end of the Cold War. We conclude with some thoughts on how to advance research on trends in conflict.

16.2 Measures of Conflict Trends

Many questions about trends in conflict are inherently descriptive. The many contemporary data sources on conflict following pioneering efforts of scholars such as Richardson (1960) should in principle allow for assessing such questions, but the availability of data alone has not led to a consensus. Indeed, data rarely speak directly for themselves, and conclusions can often depend on the specific measures used.

16.2.1 Number of Armed Conflicts

Discussions of trends in conflict often count absolute incidence or events. Although theoretical definitions of conflict tend to stress incompatibilities rather than specific means (Most and Starr 1989), most data tend to focus on violent events. One common data source is the Uppsala Armed Conflict Data (ACD, see Gleditsch et al. 2002), which focus on episodes of armed interactions, with at least one state actor, over a governmental or a territorial incompatibility, causing at least 25+ deaths in a calendar year. Based on the identity of the actors, the ACD distinguish among (i) *interstate conflicts*, (ii) *intrastate* or *civil conflicts* between a state and a non-state actor, (iii) *internationalized civil conflicts* where other states participate on the side of the government, and (iv) *extrasystemic conflicts* where states fight non-state actors in overseas colonies.

Panel (a) in Figure 16.1 plots the number of ongoing armed conflicts from 1945 through 2015. Interstate conflicts have been relatively rare since 1945, and extrasystemic conflicts disappeared after the independence of the last major overseas colonies

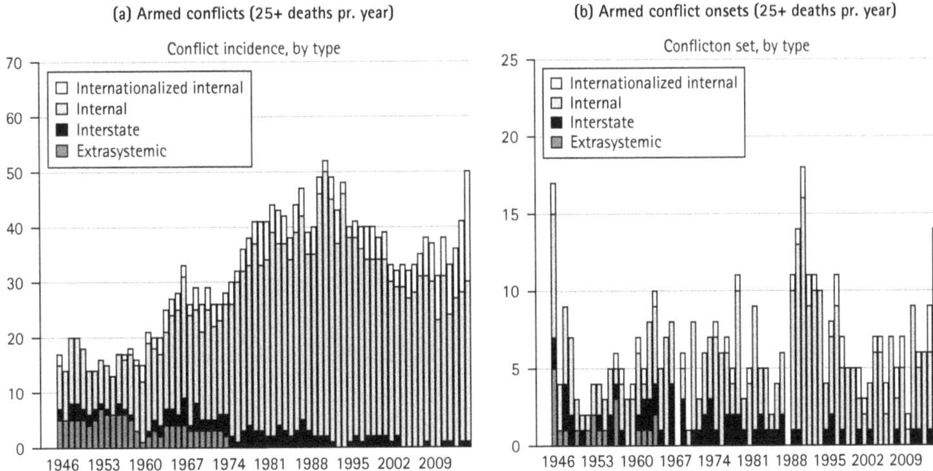

FIGURE 16.1 Uppsala armed conflict data

controlled by Portugal in the early 1970s. At the same time, civil wars appear to have become more common as decolonialization accelerated in the 1960s. The number of civil wars peaked shortly after the end of the Cold War, but subsequently declined. This is the best known and least controversial claim of a decline of war. Although the number of ongoing civil conflicts has gone up in the most recent years, the number that reaches the more severe threshold of 1000+ deaths remains below the post-Cold War peak.

Overall incidence does not distinguish between new and ongoing conflicts. Moreover, duration or the length of conflict episodes tends to differ by conflict type, as civil wars on average last much longer than interstate conflicts. Panel (b) in Figure 16.1 indicates new conflict outbreaks, counting only the first year in a new conflict. Save for the artificial spike in 1946 (where all ongoing conflicts "start" at the beginning of the dataset), the early 1990s sees the largest spike in new conflicts, reflecting the dissolution of Yugoslavia and the USSR.

16.2.2 States in Conflict

Many other factors that could affect the absolute number of conflicts also change over time. In particular, since definitions tend to stress state involvement, the number of conflicts identified may depend on the number of states. If there is a fixed probability of conflict between a pair of states, for example, the total expected number of conflicts must increase as the number of states N grows.[1] The idea of a fixed probability of war may be unrealistic, but many suggest that the risk of interstate conflict increases with the number of states (e.g. Harrison and Wolf 2012). Moreover, decolonialization introduced weak states plausibly at higher risk of challenges from non-state actors (e.g. Fearon and

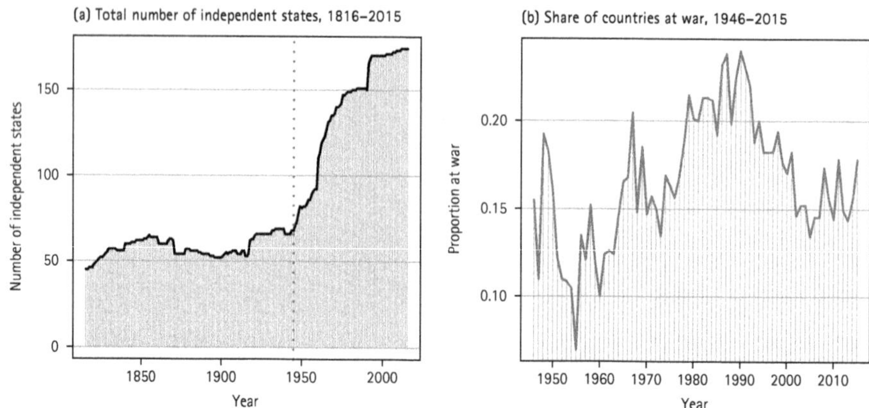

FIGURE 16.2 Number of states and states at war

Laitin 2003). Finally, one weak state can have multiple civil wars that cannot be considered independent.

In light of this it may be useful to normalize measures of conflict by the number of states. Panel (a) in Figure 16.2 shows the growth in the number of independent states, based on the Gleditsch and Ward (1999) list. The number of independent states increased rapidly after 1945, and more than doubled by 2015. In Panel (b) in Figure 16.2 we plot the share of states involved in armed conflict (irrespective of type) since 1945. We see an increasing share of countries with conflict following decolonialization, and an even more notable downward trend after the Cold War.

16.2.3 Conflict Severity

The measures used in Figures 16.1 and 16.2 count armed conflicts equally, but they differ dramatically in severity or the number killed. Some such as the Iran–Iraq war in the 1980s generate millions of battle deaths, while others such as the 1998 Omagh bombing in Northern Ireland (29 fatalities) just exceed the annual threshold. This speaks in favor of scaled measures of the extent of war or weighting by the severity of wars.

One simple measure of conflict severity is the number of battle deaths. Panel (a) in Figure 16.3 displays the summed battle deaths in armed conflitcs, drawing on Lacina and Gleditsch (2005) as well as more recent updates by the Uppsala Conflict Data Program. Although interstate wars are relatively rare compared to civil wars, the former tend to kill more than the latter. We also see a clear decline in total battle deaths over the period, starting before the end of the Cold War, and particularly notable after the end of the very severe Iran–Iraq conflict in the late 1980s.

Absolute deaths may be a problematic severity measure since population increases over time. If the risk of war is proportional to the number of people of fighting age, for example, we should expect more wars and deaths with a larger population. To use an

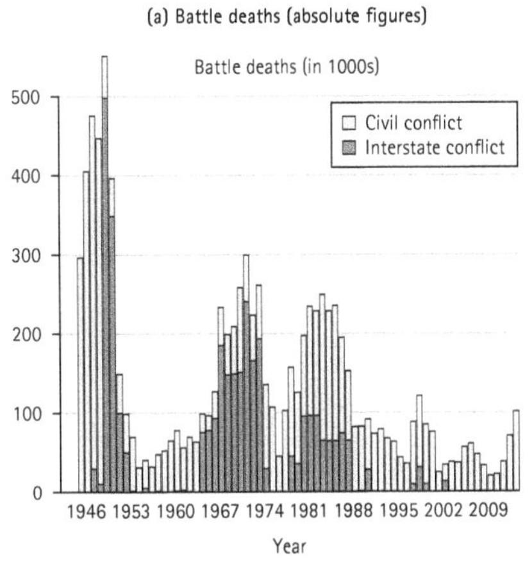

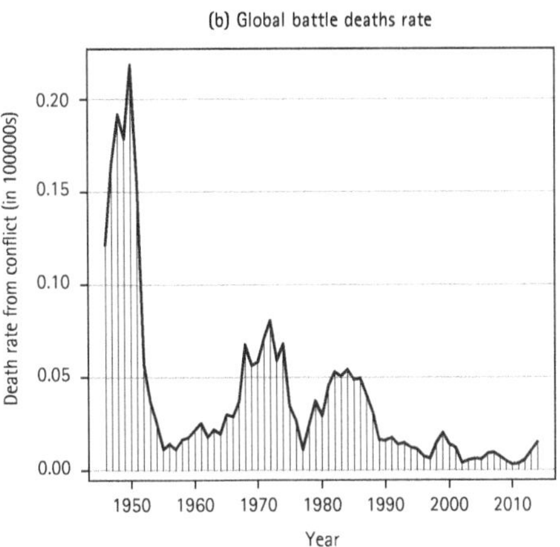

FIGURE 16.3 Battle deaths from conflict

analogy, the total incidence of cancer may increase with a growing population, even if the relative or per capita rate of cancer declines. As such, it may be appropriate to standardize conflict deaths by world population. Panel (b) in Figure 16.3 displays global battle deaths as a rate over global population in 100,000s, using data from the United Nation's population division. This indicates a strong decline in the battle death per capita rate over time.

16.3 Longer Time Series

Limiting analyses of trends in conflict to the post-Second World War period leaves a relatively short series, without the preceding major wars. Panel (a) in Figure 16.4 plots the absolute incidence of wars—defined as armed conflicts claiming at least 1000+ casualties over a conflict—going back to 1816, based on the most recent Expanded War (EW) data (Gleditsch 2004).[2] In Panel (b) we scale wars by the number of participating states, since some wars counted as a single event—such as the First and Second World Wars—have many participants. These figures indicate an even more dramatic decline in recorded wars after the end of the Cold War. This reflects how many ongoing armed conflicts with 25+ deaths per year after the post-Cold War conflict peak do not reach the cumulative 1000+ war threshold.

Figure 16.5 displays battle deaths for the longer time series on wars. Panel (a) shows absolute deaths while panel (b) shows deaths as a rate compared to global population. The picture is consistent with many points made already for the shorter time series, including less severe conflict. Interstate conflicts tend to be more severe but less frequent, and the decline in conflict after the end of the Cold War is still prominent. Although the World Wars stand out as extremely severe events, the average death rates for the nineteenth-century seem similar to the post-1945 period.

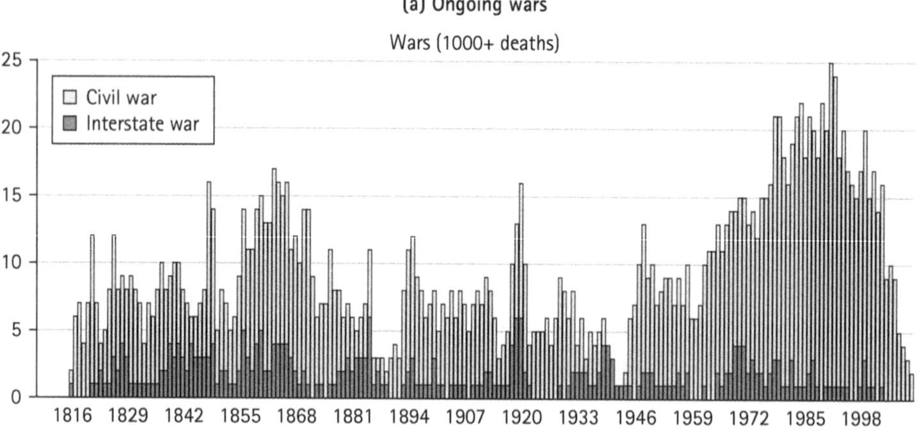

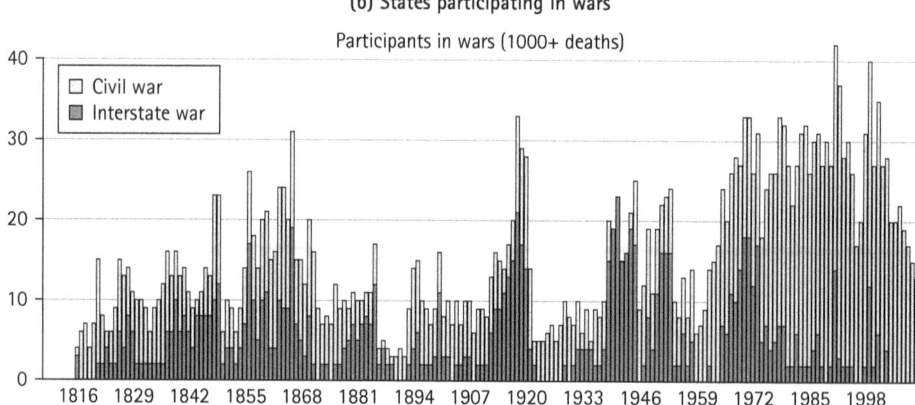

FIGURE 16.4 Expanded conflict data, frequency

16.4 Alternative Conflict Measures

The measures considered so far require organized violence, specific incompatibilities, and some minimum casualties. Alternative conflict measures generally dispense with one or more of these criteria, and some researchers have claimed to find divergent patterns contradicting the decline in violence using these. We focus on two important alternative measures, namely interstate crises and terrorism.

Measures of interstate crises dispense with the casualties requirement. Many key events during the Cold War such as the Cuban Missile Crisis did not involve direct casualties, but could be seen as periods of tension where war potentially could have broken out. The Military Interstate Dispute (MID) data focus on "the threat, display or use of military force short of war by one member state ... explicitly directed toward the

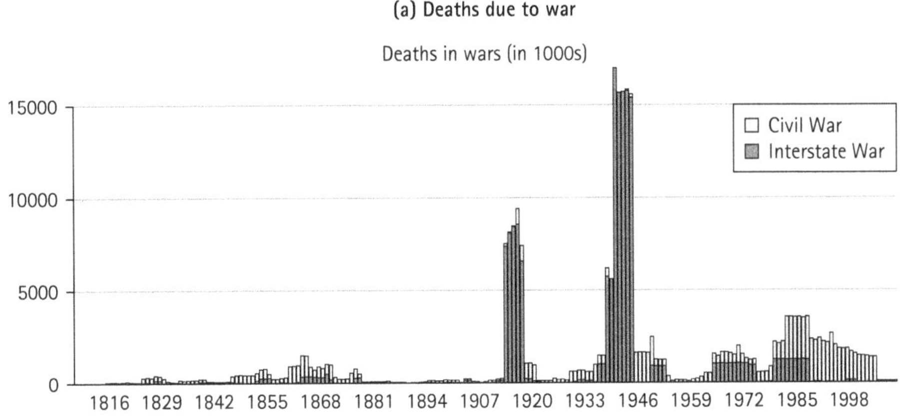

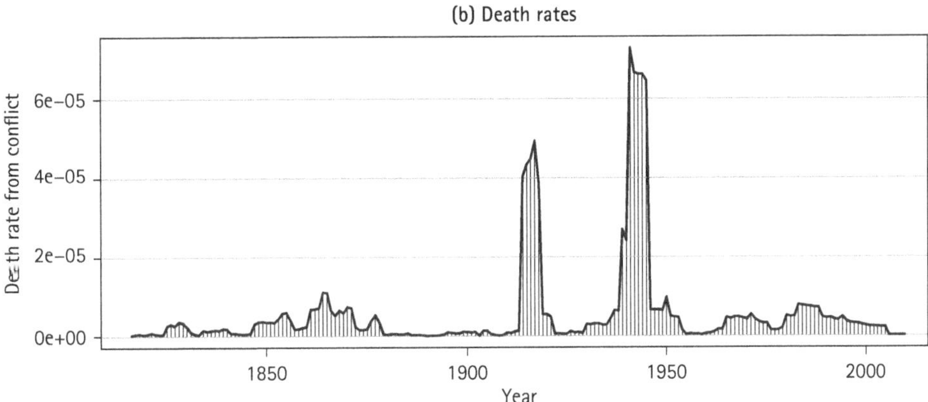

FIGURE 16.5 Expanded conflict data, severity

government, official representatives, official forces, property, or territory of another state" (Jones et al. 1996: 163). Panel (a) in Figure 16.6 shows how the number of ongoing MIDs increases steadily with time, unlike the number of wars. Based on an analysis of these data, Harrison and Wolf (2012: 1055), claim that "[w]ars are increasingly frequent, and the trend has been steadily upward since 1870."

Although MIDs do not decline to the same extent as armed conflicts after the Cold War, extending the concept of war to events without casualties is controversial. Figure 16.6 shows that most MIDs are non-lethal and do not involve any casualties. As such, perhaps the most remarkable trend in these data is that interstate disputes seem to escalate to violence at a lower rate over time (Gleditsch and Pickering 2014). Our ability to identify disputes and lower intensity conflicts may decline the further we go back in time, especially outside the developed world. Non-fatal events are likely to be recorded at a much higher rate in more recent years with increasing media coverage, and this may explain the apparent growth in non-fatal MIDs over the period.

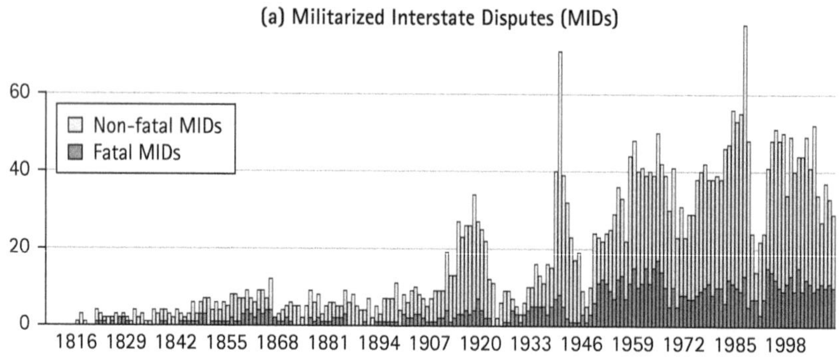

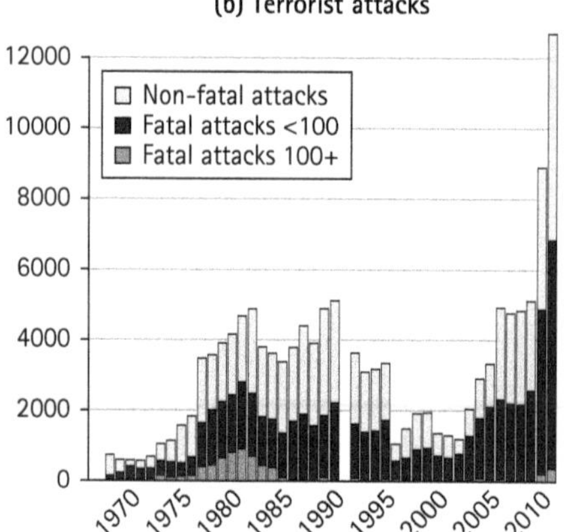

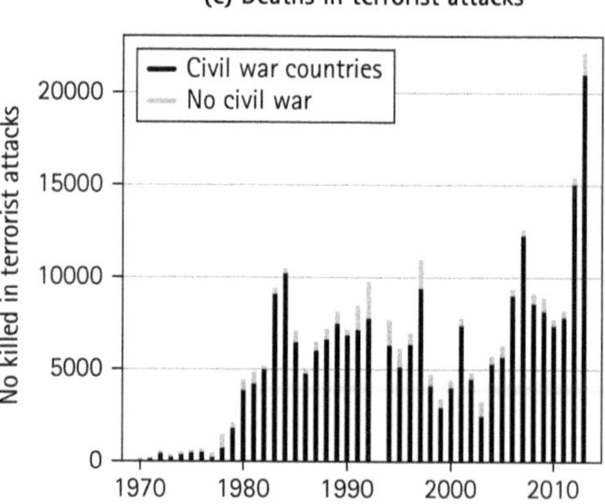

FIGURE 16.6 Alternative conflict data

Many argue that there has been a dramatic increase in the number of terrorist attacks after 9/11 (see, e.g., http://bit.ly/28MRq5k), and that we are witnessing a transformation of political violence, where any apparent decrease in conventional violence simply masks an increase in irregular violence (see, e.g., Kaldor 2013; Gray 2015). Terrorism is a contested concept, but can plausibly be distinguished from conventional armed conflicts by the emphasis on indirect attacks, intended to coerce or send a message to a different audience, rather than direct attacks between the antagonists. Thus, terrorist attacks need not entail organized violence (i.e. attacks may be carried out by lone wolves), the incompatibility or perpetrator can be unclear, the specific victims may be irrelevant, and events are identified based on intent to harm rather than casualties.

The Global Terrorism Data documents individual attacks since 1970 (see LaFree and Dugan 2007). The count of terrorist attacks in panel (b) in Figure 16.6 suggests a different pattern than civil wars, with a similar decrease in the immediate aftermath of the Cold War, but then followed by an increase after the mid-2000s, and especially after 2010.

However, a number of issues call for caution in interpreting this as support for increasing terrorist violence replacing conventional civil war. Binning by lethality reveals that most attacks are not lethal. The number of severe lethal events remains low and was higher during the 1980s, partly due to plane bombings. We are likely to have better reporting of less severe events over time, and some argue that changing data collection practices undermine comparisons (Pape et al. 2014). Finally, others argue that the concept of terrorism has become extended to all attacks against civilians, especially in Afghanistan and Iraq (Human Security Report 2007).[3]

Panel (c) shows that most deaths due to terrorism take place in countries already at civil war. This is not consistent with strong claims of a transformation of violence, where terrorism is said to occur instead of conventional violence, but rather suggests that terrorism is increasingly used in ongoing civil wars (Polo and Gleditsch 2016).

16.5 Conflict Distributions and Comparisons

Looking at conflict trends in the observed data can be criticized for not comparing against a null model, or interrogating the likely amount of variation that one should expect given a plausible underlying distribution. For example, our confidence in a sample estimate, such as a poll estimate of the share intending to vote for a candidate in an election, should be considered proportional to the likely variability. In a poll, the margin of error depends on the variation among the respondents and sample size. All else being equal, an estimate from a small poll has more uncertainty than an estimate from a larger poll, and averaging the results from many polls entails less uncertainty than the estimate of a single poll.

The sample analogy here may strike some readers as odd, since the historical record or the observed data are normally thought of as the population. However, comparisons to a null model or distributional comparisons may be useful or quantify uncertainty through measures of expected variation (see Berk et al. 1995). If we think of the observed data on conflict as one iteration of history, we may ask how much variation we could expect to see from one iteration to another, given the observed data and specific assumptions. Beyond the idea of alternative or counterfactual histories, we may also be interested in uncertainty over predictions about future events, based on what we know from the observed data.

16.5.1 The Timing of Wars

Richardson (1944) developed an influential model of the timing of wars in terms of the number of outbreaks by year. His analysis suggested that the distribution of annual war outbreaks over the period 1820–1929 was consistent with a Poisson process, a common distribution for the number of independent random events over a time interval, where there is a constant "very small probability of an outbreak of war somewhere on the globe on every day" (Richardson 1944: 243) and "an absence of any drift toward more or fewer wars" (1944: 246). We can think of this random distribution as a null model for assessing claims about trends in observed conflict data. Many studies find that a Poisson distribution provides a plausible fit to other conflict datasets (see, e.g., Houweling and Kuné 1984; Mansfield 1988).

The idea that the distribution of conflict is random does not sit easily with much research on the causes of war.[4] Failing to reject a Poisson distribution for the overall timing of wars does not mean that individual outbreaks must be entirely random. Richardson himself found some evidence that wars were contagious, in the sense that an ongoing war increased the likelihood of outbreaks among neighbors and that countries with more borders were more likely to see wars. Research has uncovered many state/relational characteristics associated with differences in the risk of interstate conflict, including power-preponderance, geographic distance, and a tendency for conflict to recur (see Bremer 1992; Goertz and Diehl 1993), or country profiles at greater risk of civil war (see Sambanis 2002).

At the same time, dyadic or monadic research rarely considers implications for global conflict distributions. If specific features believed to be relevant to conflict change over time, then we should see shifts in either the probability or timing of conflict. We return to this point later.

16.5.2 The Frequency–Severity Distribution of Conflict and Power Laws

Another important conflict distribution model considers the frequency of wars of a particular magnitude or severity. Richardson (1948) found that the frequency and severity of conflicts appeared to follow a so-called power law, where the frequency of an event is an inverse power of severity, or the number of casualties. More formally, the frequency of wars of a given severity x scale as $P(x) \propto x^{-\alpha}$, where $\alpha \approx 2$ is the scaling exponent. In a power law, multiplying the severity level by a given factor yields a proportional division of the frequency. The ratio of these values is given by the "scaling parameter" α, and distribution is said to be "scale free", since this relationship holds for all values of the power law.

Plotting the complementary cumulative distribution function $P(X \geq x)$ of a power law on doubly-logarithmic axes will appear as a straight line with a slope $\alpha - 1$, at least in the tail of the distribution above some minimum value x_{min}. Panel (a) in Figure 16.7 displays Richardson's original plot of the frequency and severity of deadly quarrels. Due to binning, the individual data points show up as horizontal lines. Panel (b) provides a more recent example from Cederman (2003), using the Correlates of War interstate war data (Small and Singer 1982), suggesting an approximately linear relationship between log cumulative frequency and severity.

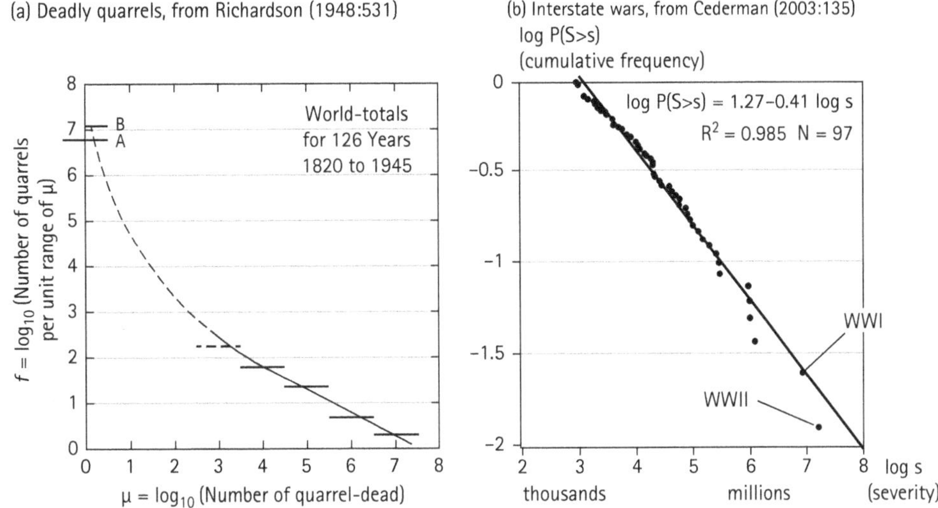

FIGURE 16.7 Power laws in conflict frequency and severity data

Power laws differ from normal distributions as their heavy tail implies a substantial fraction of observations far away from the center. For a phenomenon that plausibly follows a normal distribution, such as height of individuals (upper panel in Figure 16.8), the mean (168cm) has a clear interpretation as a "typical" value. Values around the mean are common; one would expect about 95 percent of all observations to fall within two standard deviations (*ca* 20cm) of the mean, and values of multiple standard deviations above the mean are essentially impossible. However, in a power law distribution, large events substantially above the mean are relatively common.

Many phenomena display a power law distribution, at least in the upper tail (Clauset et al. 2009). The distribution of cities with more than 50,000 inhabitants in the United States in the lower panel in Figure 16.8 does not resemble a normal distribution. The average is 155,400, while the standard deviation is 379,499. Large cities the size of New York City—population over 8 million, more than 20 standard deviations above the average—would be extremely unlikely under a normal distribution.

By contrast, if individual heights in the US population followed a power law, then we should expect many individuals to be multiple standard deviations above average height. More precisely, we would expect nearly 60,000 individuals to be as tall as the tallest adult male on record (2.72m), 10,000 as tall as an adult male giraffe, and 180 million individuals no more than 17cm tall.

If war severity and frequency follows a power law, then we should expect most wars to have limited severity, but the risk of severe wars can be high, even if such events have not been observed over a long period. The severity distribution of terrorist events also appears to follow a power law distribution, and Clauset and Woodard (2013) use this fact to estimate the likelihood of a terrorist event with the same or larger magnitude as the 9/11 attacks over the decade 2012–21. The precise estimate depends on the specific assumptions used, but their forecasts indicate a likelihood ranging from 19 percent

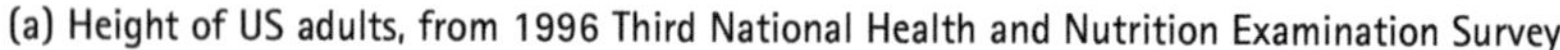

(a) Height of US adults, from 1996 Third National Health and Nutrition Examination Survey

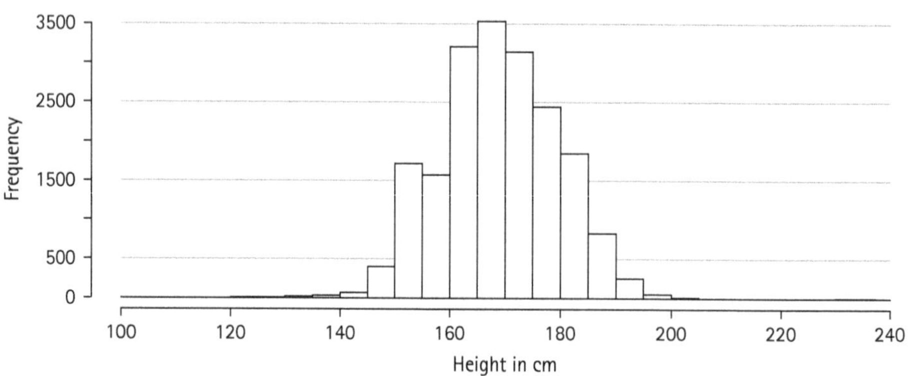

(b) 2010 population estimate of US incorporated cities of 50,000+, US Census Bureau

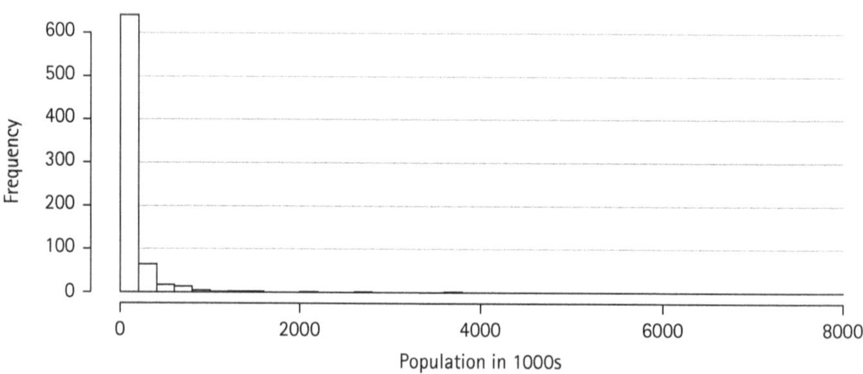

FIGURE 16.8 Real-world distributions

to 46 percent. Thus, although the 9/11 attacks were more severe than previous terrorist attacks, it is not an "outlier" based on a plausible distributional model. More generally, the large variability in heavy-tailed distributions makes it difficult to tell whether a trend exists in observed data, since even draws from an unchanged distribution with no trend can exhibit periods of peace and more conflict just by chance.

16.6 The Decline of War and the New Conflict Trends Debate

The relative lack of severe interstate conflict in the post-Second World War era—which Gaddis (1986) has called "the long peace"—inspired speculation on whether there has been some structural shift in the risk of conflict. Some attribute international stability to the stabilizing effects of bipolarity or deterrence through nuclear weapons (Waltz 1979; Schelling 2005), while others have argued that changes in norms and values have prevented major interstate wars, or highlight changes in characteristics believed to influence interstate conflict such as democracy or economic interdependence (see, e.g., Mueller 1989; Russett 1990).

However, others have worried that wars are becoming more common. Many argued that the Cold War rivalry between the superpowers exerted a stabilizing influence, and that its end would usher in renewed interstate conflict (Mearsheimer 1990; Huntington 1993). The increase in civil wars following the breakup of the former Yugoslavia and the perceived instability in the former Soviet Union fueled perceptions of an explosion of ethnic civil war and a "coming anarchy" (Kaplan 1994). These claims were widely shared among scholars and policy-makers of all kinds of backgrounds and persuasions (for an interesting review of pessimism after the end of the Cold War, see Mueller 1994).

This received wisdom that war was becoming more common was regarded as so self-evident, few bothered to consult the data. One of the first empirical studies, Wallensteen and Sollenberg (1995), however, actually found a declining number of conflicts over the period 1989–94 but received only limited attention. An op-ed piece in the *Los Angeles Times* on the decline in warfare by Wilson and Gurr (1999) generated more attention, and discussed possible explanations based on greater ethnic accommodation and conflict management efforts Goldstein (2011).

The current decline of war thesis is to a large extent associated with Pinker's (2011) *The Better Angels of Our Nature: Why Warfare has Declined*. Pinker notes the post-Cold War decline in civil wars and the decline of interstate conflict after 1945 discussed in this chapter, and makes a more ambitious claim about a long-term decline in violence, noting extreme levels of deaths due to violence in pre-historic states, and a remarkable decline in homicide.

Although some have disputed the data themselves (Harrison and Wolf 2012; Gray 2015), few see this as a fundamental challenge to evidence for the decline of war, and there is in our view at best modest evidence for a transformation to unconventional conflict.

A more challenging criticism questions the relative lack of emphasis on mechanisms and the broad nature of the decline of war thesis. Some of the proposed explanations are rather nebulous, especially the notion of a civilizing process (see Elias 2000/1939), where it is unclear if the decline of violence is a clearly separate outcome, caused by the former. It is also not obvious whether any single mechanism can be expected to account for such a diverse range of violence, and some argue that looking at specific types of conflict and scope conditions can allow us to learn more about the relevant mechanisms (Cederman et al. 2017). However, this is primarily a call for theoretical elaboration and differentiation between conflict types rather than a challenge to the decline of war thesis per se.

Cirillo and Taleb (2016) present a more fundamental challenge, emphasizing the problems in drawing conclusions about trends and the likelihood of future severe wars, given the statistical properties of conflict data noted by Richardson. They stress that measures of central tendency such as the mean from the observed data are not informative. Rather than the small wars and events emphasized by those who see a decline of violence, we should focus on what statistics allow us to say about the expected likelihood of the very big wars.

The absence of severe wars over a long period alone does not constitute evidence about fundamental changes in the pattern of war.

Using a new dataset on deaths in wars with at least 3000 casualties over the two most recent millennia (1–2015), normalized by global population, Cirillo and Taleb (2016) argue that their analysis provides no basis for rejecting the null hypothesis that wars follow an independent Poisson process, without any change in the frequency and severity of conflict. To reject this null we would need much more data, i.e., "the absence of a conflict generating more than, say, 5 million casualties in the last sixty years [is] highly insufficient to state that their probability has decreased over time, given that the average inter-arrival time is 93.03 years, with a mean absolute deviation of 113.57 years!" (Cirillo and Taleb 2016: 7).

Some see this critique as a devastating blow to the decline of war thesis, but Pinker and many others dispute this. The emerging debate has generated some light on important issues, but also a great deal of heat and inflammatory language, and has so far primarily taken place in comments and blogposts rather than journal articles (see Beauchamp 2015; Roodman 2015; Spagat 2015; Pinker n.d.; Taleb n.d.; Ulfelder n.d.). We try to outline here what we see as the main issues.

16.6.1 What Can We Know About Conflict Trends?

At one level, one may question what there is to debate, as there is, in principle, no inconsistency between claiming that the world currently sees less violence than prior periods and simultaneously acknowledging that history involves elements of chance, where some events could have played out differently, and that it is difficult to make predictions about the future (see, e.g., Clauset 2017; Tetlock and Belkin 1996; Tetlock and Gardner 2015). Pinker and others argue that Cirillo and Taleb attack a straw man, and a position on trends and prediction that they do not take.

Looking beyond the surface, however, there are some clearer disagreements and divergent views on what constitutes evidence. Pinker and others see the decline of many forms of violence outside large-scale warfare such as homicide and interpersonal violence as relevant information that strengthens our confidence in a decline of warfare. Cirillo and Taleb dismiss anything beyond their preferred null of no change in the frequency of major warfare, making it harder to shift prior beliefs.

There is also an underlying disagreement on what we can learn from history and the nature of prediction. Pinker and others would argue that changes in prevalent views on war and the use of violence have important real-world implications. War was once considered heroic and glorious, and conquest for long a conventional motive, while the use of force is now normally only justified on defensive grounds. Some see this as indicative of a shift to politics by agreements and stronger governing institutions, beyond simply an accidental avoidance of conflict (see also Mueller 1989; Goertz et al. 2016). Delineating alternative testable propositions is a common method to try to "maximize leverage" when dealing with limited data (King et al. 1994).

Detailing mechanisms can also help provide more specific tests of implications for conflict trends. Cederman et al. (2017), for example, examine if a decline in ethnic civil conflict after the end of the Cold War could plausibly be attributed to changes in ethnic accommodation, democratization, and peacekeeping. Their results suggest a clear structural break, and some evidence that the risk of conflict decreases and prospects for conflict termination increase after following changes in individual countries.

There has also been renewed interest in out-of-sample prediction of conflict and instability and some evidence of progress in predictive ability (see, e.g., Ward et al. 2013; Tetlock and Gardner 2015). In general, claims about the future can and should be evaluated based on our understanding of the mechanisms believed to have produced changes and our confidence that these will endure (see, e.g., Hughes et al. 2014; Spagat n.d.; Ulfelder n.d.).

Re-examining the debate in this way helps suggests possible ways to advance research on conflict trends. Instead of limiting ourselves to a single null hypothesis of unchanging warfare that can only be rejected after very long periods with the absence of extreme events, can we come up with more informative alternative tests? For example, if there has been a shift in the underlying distribution of war, what would be the plausible changes to the distribution, and would we be able to detect it? Can we gain more information by examining distributions of different types of warfare? Roodman (2015) notes that Cirillo and Taleb's analysis suggest that wars of at least 1 million should happen every 26.71 years, yet we have seen no such conflicts between the major powers since 1945. How unlikely is such an outcome, based on models of past conflict between major powers? Is the relative absence of severe interstate conflicts consistent with specific limiting factors? Do existing studies on territorial conflict management offer hope that disputes in East Asia will not escalate to severe wars (Goertz et al. 2016)? Should we use different models of expected war frequencies and duration for the civil wars that are most prominent in current global warfare? How can we rigorously integrate data on the frequency and severity of different types of conflicts? How fragile are the mechanisms believed to have reduced the risk of war since the Second World War?

These are complex questions that are far from trivial to answer, and raise important theoretical and methodological issues. However, they are in our view answerable and worthy of attention. Conflict trends and modeling distributions deserve a prominent place in conflict research.[5]

Notes

1. More formally, the number of possible pairwise interactions between states increases by $[N \times (N-1)]/2$.
2. Unlike the Correlates of War data (Small and Singer 1982), the EW data do not impose a European-centric definition of states, which can undercount global warfare.

3. By contrast, previous violence against civilians such as the Rwandan genocide was not generally considered terrorism at the time.
4. Some have suggested that war outbreaks should be random in a bargaining framework, as any observable factors that influence the outcome of armed contests should be factored into demands and concessions (Gartzke 1999). However, this presumes prior incompatibilities, and the empirical research can be seen as identifying dyads that are more or less likely to have incompatibilities rather than the use of force.
5. We are grateful for helpful discussions and comments from the volume editors, Baris Ari, Rebecca Cordell, Nils Petter Gleditsch, Philip Nelson, Steve Pickering, and Steven Pinker.

References

Beauchamp, Zack. 2015. This fascinating academic debate has huge implications for the future of world peace. *Available at:* http://www.vox.com/2015/5/21/8635369/pinker-taleb, accessed August 19, 2017.

Berk, Richard A., Bruce Western, and Robert E. Weiss. 1995. Statistical Inference for Apparent Populations (with discussion). *Sociological Methodology*, 25: 421–85.

Bremer, Stuart A. 1992. Dangerous Dyads: Conditions Affecting the Likelihood of Interstate War, 1816–1965. *Journal of Conflict Resolution*, 36(2): 309–41.

Cederman, Lars Erik. 2003. Modeling the Size of Wars: From Billiard Balls to Sandpiles. *American Political Science Review*, 97(1): 135–50.

Cederman, Lars-Erik, Kristian Skrede Gleditsch, and Julian Wucherpfennig. 2017. Predicting the Decline of Ethnic War: Was Gurr Right, and For the Right Reasons? *Journal of Peace Research*, 54: (2):298–312.

Cirillo, Pasquale and Nassim Nicholas Taleb. 2016. On the statistical properties and tail risk of violent conflicts. *Physica A: Statistical Mechanics and its Applications*, 452(15): 29–45.

Clauset, Aaron. 2017. Trends and Fluctuations in the Severity of Interstate Wars. Typescript, University of Colorado, Boulder.

Clauset, Aaron and Ryan Woodard. 2013. Estimating the Historical and Future Probabilities of Large Terrorist Events. *Annals of Applied Statistics*, 7(4): 1838–65.

Clauset, Aaron, Maxwell Young, and KristianSkrede Gleditsch. 2007. On the Frequency of Severe Terrorist Events. *Journal of Conflict Resolution*, 51(1): 1–31.

Clauset, Aaron, Cosma R. Shalizi, and Mark E. J. Newman. 2009. Power-law Distributions in Empirical Data. *SIAM Review*, 51(4): 661–703.

Elias, Norbert. 2000/1939. *The Civilizing Process: Sociogenetic and Psychogenetic Investigations*. Oxford: Blackwell.

Fearon, James D. and David D. Laitin. 2003. Ethnicity, Insurgency, and Civil War. *American Political Science Review*, 91(1): 75–90.

Fry, Douglas P. 2006. *Beyond War: The Human Potential for Peace*. Oxford: Oxford University Press.

Gaddis, John Lewis. 1986. The Long Peace: Elements of Stability in the Postwar International System. *International Security*, 10(4): 99–142.

Gaddis, John Lewis. 1992/93. International Relations Theory and the End of the Cold War. *International Security*, 17: 5–58.

Gartzke, Erik. 1999. War Is in the Error Term. *International Organization*, 53(3): 567–587.

Gat, Azar. 2005. *War in Human Civilization*. Oxford and New York: Oxford University Press.

Gleditsch, Kristian Skrede. 2004. A Revised List of Wars Between and Within Independent States, 1816–2002. *International Interactions*, 30(4): 231–62.
Gleditsch, Kristian Skrede and Steve Pickering. 2014. Wars are Becoming Less Frequent: A Reply to Harrison and Wolf. *Economic History Review*, 67(1): 214–30.
Gleditsch, Kristian Skrede and Michael D. Ward. 1999. Interstate System Membership: A Revised List of Independent States since 1816. *International Interactions*, 25: 393–41.
Gleditsch, Nils Petter, Peter Wallensteen, Mikael Erikson, Margareta Sollenberg, and Håvard Strand. 2002. Armed Conflict, 1945–99: A New Dataset. *Journal of Peace Research*, 39(5): 615–37.
Goertz, Gary and Paul F. Diehl. 1993. Enduring Rivalries: Theoretical Constructs and Empirical Patterns. *International Studies Quarterly*, 37(1): 147–71.
Goertz, Gary, Paul F. Diehl, and Alexandru Balas. 2016. *The Puzzle of Peace: The Evolution of Peace in the International System*. Oxford: Oxford University Press.
Goldstein, Joshua S. 2011. *Winning the War on War*. Hialeah, FL: Dutton.
Gray, John. 2015. Steven Pinker is wrong about violence and war. *Available at:* https://www.theguardian.com/books/2015/mar/13/john-gray-steven-pinker-wrong-violence-war-declining, accessed August 19, 2017.
Gurr, Ted Robert. 2000. Ethnic Warfare on the Wane. *Foreign Affairs*, 79: 52–64.
Harrison, Mark and Nikolaus Wolf. 2012. The Frequency of Wars. *Economic History Review*, 54(3): 1055–76.
Houweling, H. W. and J. B. Kuné. 1984. Do Outbreaks of War Follow a Poisson-Process? *Journal of Conflict Resolution*, 28(1): 51–61.
Hughes, Barry B., Devin K. Joshi, Jonathan D. Moyer, Timothy D. Sisk, and Jos'e R. Solórzano. 2014. *Strengthening Governance Globally (Patterns of Potential Human Progress, Volume 5)*. Boulder, CO: Paradigm Publishers.
Human Security Report. 2007. *Human Security Report*. Vancouver: Human Security Report Project.
Huntington, Samuel P. 1993. The Clash of Civilizations? *Foreign Affairs*, 72(3): 22–49.
Jones, Daniel M., Stuart A. Bremer, and J. David Singer. 1996. Militarized Interstate Disputes, 1816–1992: Rationale, Coding Rules, and Empirical Applications. *Conflict Management and Peace Science*, 15(2): 163–213.
Kaldor, Mary. 2013. In Defence of New Wars. *Stability: International Journal of Security and Development*, 2(1). Doi: http://doi.org/10.5334/sta.at.
Kaplan, Robert D. 1994. The Coming Anarchy: How Scarcity, Crime, Overpopulation, Tribalism, and Disease are Rapidly Destroying the Social Fabric of our Planet. *Atlantic Monthly*.
King, Gary, Robert O. Keohane, and Sidney Verba. 1994. *Designing Social Inquiry: Scientific Inference in Qualitative Research*. Princeton, NJ: Princeton University Press.
Lacina, Bethany and Nils Petter Gleditsch. 2005. Monitoring Trends in Global Combat: A New Dataset of Battle Deaths. *European Journal of Population Studies*, 21(2–3): 145–66.
LaFree, Gary and Laura Dugan. 2007. Introducing the Global Terrorism Database. *Terrorism and Political Violence*, 19(2): 181–204.
Mansfield, Edward D. 1988. The Distribution of Wars Over Time. *World Politics*, 44(1): 21–51.
Mearsheimer, John J. 1990. Back to the Future: Instability in Europe after the Cold War. *International Security*, 15(4): 5–56.
Most, Benjamin A. and Harvey Starr. 1989. *Inquiry, Logic, and International Politics*. Columbia, SC: University of South Carolina Press.

Mueller, John. 1989. *Retreat from Doomsday: The Obsolescence of Major War*. New York: Basic Books.

Mueller, John. 1994. The Catastrophe Quota: Trouble After the Cold War. *Journal of Conflict Resolution*, 38(3): 355–75.

Pape, Robert, Keven Ruby, Vincent Bauer, and Gentry Jenkins. 2014. How to fix the flaws in the Global Terrorism Database and why it matters. *Available at:* https://www.washingtonpost.com/news/monkey-cage/wp/2014/08/11/how-to-fix-the-flaws-in-the-global-terrorism-database-and-why-it-matters/, last accessed August 19, 2017.

Payne, James L. 2004. *A History of Force: Exploring the Worldwide Movement against Habits of Coercion, Bloodshed, and Mayhem*. Sandpoint, ID: Lytton.

Pinker, Steven. 2011. *The Better Angels of Our Nature: Why Violence Has Declined*. New York: Viking.

Pinker, Steven. 2015. The Decline of War and Conceptions of Human Nature. *International Studies Review*, 15(3): 400–5.

Pinker, Steven. n.d. Fooled by Belligerence: Comments on Nassim Taleb's "The Long Peace is a Statistical Illusion". *Available at:* https://stevenpinker.com/files/pinker/files/comments_on_taleb_by_s_pinker_1.pdf, accessed August 19, 2017.

Polo, Sara M. T. and Kristian Skrede Gleditsch. 2016. Twisting Arms and Sending Messages: Terrorist Tactics in Civil War. *Journal of Peace Research*, 53(6): 815–29.

Richardson, Lewis F. 1944. The distribution of wars in time. *Journal of the Royal Statistical Society*, 57(3–4): 242–50.

Richardson, Lewis F. 1948. Variation of the Frequency of Fatal Quarrels With Magnitude. *Journal of the American Statistical Association*, 43(244): 523–46.

Richardson, Lewis F. 1960. *Statistics of Deadly Quarrels*. Chicago and Pittsburgh, PA: Quadrangle/Boxwood.

Roodman, David. 2015. Little Greek letters become weapons in war of words over trend in violence. *Available at:* http://davidroodman.com/blog/2015/05/19/little-greek-letters-become-weapons-in-war-of-words-over-trend-in-violence/, accessed August 19, 2017.

Russett, Bruce M. 1990. A more democratic and therefore more peaceful world. *World Futures*, 29(4): 243–63.

Sambanis, Nicholas. 2002. A Review of Recent Advances and Future Directions in the Quantitative Literature on Civil War. *Defense Economics*, 13(1): 215–43.

Schelling, Thomas C. 2005. An Astonishing Sixty Years: The Legacy of Hiroshima. *American Economic Review*, 96(4): 929–93.

Small, Melvin and J. David Singer. 1982. *Resort to Arms: International and Civil Wars, 1816–1980*. Beverly Hills, CA: Sage.

Spagat, Michael. 2015. Is the Risk of War Declining? Stats.org. *Available at:* http://www.stats.org/is-the-risk-of-war-declining/, accessed August 19, 2017.

Spagat, Michael. n.d. What is the Risk of World War III. Significance Magazine. *Available at:* https://mikespagat.wordpress.com/2016/01/17/forecasting-world-war-iii, last accessed 19 August 2017/.

Taleb, Nassim Nicholas. n.d. The "Long Peace" is a Statistical Illusion. http://www.fooledbyrandomness.com/pinker.pdf, accessed April 19, 2017.

Tetlock, Philip E. and Aaron Belkin (eds.). 1996. *Counterfactual Thought Experiments in World Politics: Logical, Methodological, and Psychological Perspectives*. Princeton, NJ: Princeton University Press.

Tetlock, Philip E. and Dan Gardner. 2015. *Superforecasting: The Art and Science of Prediction*. Random House.

Ulfelder, Jay. n.d. About That Apparent Decline in Violent Conflict. . . . *Available at:* https://dartthrowingchimp.wordpress.com/2015/05/22/about-that-apparent-decline-in-violent-conflict/

Wallensteen, Peter and Margareta Sollenberg. 1995. After the Cold War: Emerging Patterns of Armed Conflict 1989–94. *Journal of Peace Research*, 32(3): 345–60.

Waltz, Kenneth N. 1979. *Theory of International Politics*. Reading, MA: Addison-Wesley.

Ward, Michael D., Nils W. Metternich, Cassy L. Dorff, Max Gallop, Florian M. Hollenbach, Anna Schultz, and Simon Weschle. 2013. Learning from the Past and Stepping into the Future: Toward a New Generation of Conflict Prediction. *International Studies Review*, 15: 473–90.

Wilson, Ernest J., III and Ted Robert Gurr. 1999. Fewer Nations Are Making War. LA Times, August 22.

CHAPTER 17

LEADERS, LEADERSHIP, AND INTERNATIONAL SECURITY

MICHAEL C. HOROWITZ

17.1 INTRODUCTION

IN 2017, the President of the United States is Donald Trump, a political outsider, with no prior governing experience, the relevance of leaders for international politics seems more obvious and important than ever. It would be difficult to find a serious student of global affairs that thinks US foreign policy would look exactly the same under Donald Trump as it would have under Hillary Clinton, his Democrat opponent in the 2016 Presidential election in the United States. On Syria policy, while Clinton advocated a no-fly zone, Trump promoted closer ties with Russia and Bashir al-Assad to crack down on ISIS (Holland 2016). In the Asia-Pacific, during the Presidential campaign, Trump questioned the value of US alliances with Japan and South Korea and implied that they might need to seek their own nuclear weapons instead of relying on the US extended nuclear umbrella, while Clinton spoke of improving relations with US allies and partners in the region (Condon 2016). These different approaches mean the Trump administration will likely yield an outcome for the United States and the world at least somewhat different than if Clinton had been elected.

Yet, from the perspective of nearly all of the dominant approaches to the study of international politics over the last two generations, who won 2016 the election in the United States was irrelevant from the perspective of American foreign policy. Pressure from the international system, interest groups in the United States, and norms shared by the United States and other nations, should play the key roles driving US foreign policy according to most theories of international politics (realism, liberalism, and constructivism).

The results of the 2016 Presidential election in the United States may represent a critical case for testing the importance of leaders in international politics. In the first year of his presidency, initial actions from the Trump administration suggest deviations from a relatively consistent US strategy of deep engagement with the world are possible. There is significant uncertainty, however, about whether the Trump Administration's foreign policy will be more of a minor repair or a large change in US strategy.

If, after the Trump administration concludes, nothing much has changed about American foreign policy, from US strategy in Syria to the US approach to the Asia-Pacific, to America's relationships with its allies and partners in Europe, it would probably represent powerful evidence of the constraints that leaders around the world, even in the United States, face.

On the other hand, the early 2010s have already seen close elections whose outcomes have promoted leaders promising, and beginning to implement, very different policies, than those that came before. Just in 2016, in the United Kingdom, the close vote in favor of Brexit led to the resignation of Prime Minister David Cameron, an advocate of UK integration in Europe, and the elevation of Prime Minister Teresa May, whose primary job will be to navigate UK withdrawal from the European Union (Dewan and Isaac 2016). In the Philippines, a narrow win for Duterte created potential changes in the national security strategy of the Philippines—a cancelation of military exercises with the United States, a discussion of ejecting US forces from the Philippines, and a move toward closer ties with China (Blanchard 2016; Denyer 2016). In both cases, it is hard to argue that these outcomes were inevitable due to structural or other forces. These elections turned on several small, contingent, political factors. And both demonstrate the importance of leaders in international politics. Put another way, Waltz's (1959) first image is back with a vengeance.

This chapter will explore the role of leaders in international politics, and especially in the international security realm. It begins by reviewing the literature on leaders and, specifically, how and why the academic study of international politics came to minimize the role of leaders. It then describes three different ways that leaders have relevance for international politics, building on a recent renaissance in political science research on leaders. The chapter concludes by discussing the future of international security and the role that the study of leaders should play.

17.2 Where Did the Leaders Go? International Relations Scholarship and the First Image

In the nineteenth century, historian Thomas Carlyle (1935) wrote that "the history of the world is but the biography of great men." He expressed a feeling, common, at the time, that heads of state played an outsized role in determining the trajectories of their countries. After all, the nineteenth century was still an age full of kings and other hereditary rulers, even if change around the world due to the Industrial Revolution and other factors was already in progress. The average person in a country was significantly disconnected from how that country operated. Alliances between countries seemed to change on a dime, due to the whims of leaders. How could Napoleon III decide to declare war on Prussia because he felt insulted by a letter Bismarck leaked to the press? What was the rapid shift in the relationship between Prussia and the Austro-Hungarian empire from allies in the Schleswig-Holstein war of 1860 to enemies in the Seven Weeks War of 1866 A head cold could fundamentally change how a country operated in the world, as when Czarina Elizabeth of Russia died in 1762 and her replacement, Czar Peter, broke an alliance with France and Austria to settle with Prussia (Byman and Pollack 2001: 107).

Yet, someone regarded as one of the most important leaders of that century, Prussian (then German) Chancellor Otto von Bismarck, was already in the process of articulating a vision of politics that came to dominate the study of International Relations (IR) in the United States for the last two generations. He said "Man cannot create the current *of events.* He can only float with it and steer" (Lee 1988: 89). Similarly, US President Abraham Lincoln said "I claim not to have controlled events, but confess plainly that events have controlled me" (Donald 1995: 514; Jervis 2013: 154).

Since the early Cold War, IR scholarship, especially in the US, has sided with Bismarck and Lincoln over Carlyle. Why is that? Multiple reasons may explain why interest in studying leaders declined during the Cold War, and then continued long after the Cold War ended (until the renaissance described in Section 17.3). First, with the advent of the Cold War and nuclear weapons, more powerful forces, such as the struggle between democracy/capitalism and communism, animated those interested in global politics. The ability of countries to destroy themselves and the world with nuclear weapons also shifted scholars to asking questions about the world, as opposed to about countries.

Second, the development of the modern social sciences occurred in part due to advances in the mid-twentieth century in computing, econometrics, and game theory (Horowitz et al. 2015). These advances led scholars to begin putting a premium on the rigor of their insights and their ability to test those insights using the scientific method. Studying the personality of leaders and how leaders made a difference in national policy appeared archaic in the face of the desire for falsifiable hypothesis testing, even among scholars using qualitative methods, and innovations such as the Correlates of War dataset, which let International Relations scholars try to understand the macro conditions that made war and peace more likely (Singer and Small 1972). Similarly, the focus of game theorists on formal logics of behavior led to an emphasis on strategic interaction and the need to assume the similarity of motivations and beliefs across individuals, even heads of state (Schelling 1960). This assumption meant, however, ruling out the importance of leaders from the beginning. A focus on "clock-like" models of international politics, to quote Karl Popper (1966), necessitated the choice.

The implication was a decline in research on leaders. As Elizabeth Saunders writes, "In the last few decades, however, international relations theorists—with the notable exception of those who take a psychological approach—have rarely focused on leaders" (Saunders 2009: 120).[1] These trends combined in the rise of realism as a theory of international politics (Byman and Pollack 2001; Horowitz et al. 2015). Kenneth Waltz (Waltz 1959: 1979) articulated his famous three images of international politics. He argued that the first level, the individual level, was the least powerful because it was not possible to systematically understand the role of human nature in politics, and national and international factors played a more powerful role in constraining and shaping the behavior of nations. The desire to more effectively model the behavior of states, and the belief that understanding leaders was not possible due to the lack of good theory and data, led more scholars over time to reject studying leaders. James Rosenau famously described states as "billiard balls" (Rosenau 1971) and attempts to study leaders as too "idiosyncratic" (Rosenau 1966) for the serious study of politics. Essentially, even if leaders did matter at times, it was too hard to generalize the ways they made decisions (Byman and Pollack 2001: 108), relegating leaders to the "error term," so to speak, of models of international politics.

Critiques of the importance of leaders in international politics are not simply a relic of age-old decisions made by the IR field. The belief that leaders do not play a critical role in shaping global politics was articulated by Robert Jervis, who argued that three factors limit the influence of leaders. First, most leaders who rise to power in a given country tend to share similar beliefs, due to macro-influences at the national or even international level. Second, leaders are socialized in office, by everything from the intelligence reports they receive, which are often delivered by the same people who informed their predecessor, to the diplomats who advise them and execute their foreign policy. Third, leaders are constrained because countries are constrained, both by their level of power, the actions that are seen as appropriate in the international system, and interest groups whose support is necessary for the leader to stay in office (Jervis 2013: 155–6).

For leaders to matter in the most important sense, there have to be reasons to think that having a particular leader in power at a particular period of time mattered—otherwise, while a given leader may have made a decision, almost any elite from that country might have made a similar decision, meaning the identity of the leader was not crucial (Greenstein 1969).

A textbook case of this is arguably the invasion of Iraq by the United States and several of its allies and partners in 2003. In 2000, a closely contested election in the United States between George W. Bush and Al Gore ended with the United States Supreme Court making a decision about rules surrounding the counting of ballots that gave the White House to Bush. This made the election of Bush, as opposed to Gore, as close to a "random" event as is possible from the perspective of IR research. Gore could have easily been President—and nearly was.

As President, Bush then engaged in a series of actions, from withdrawing from the anti-ballistic missile treaty with Russia to invading Iraq (Kagan and Kristol 2004), that many believe Al Gore would not have done. This clearly illustrated the relevance of leaders in international politics—or did it? Frank Harvey (2011) argues that, faced with the September 11, 2001 attacks and the need to prevent Saddam Hussein from building new military capabilities, a President Gore very well may have invaded Iraq. Moreover, Robert Jervis argues that even Bush may not have mattered for US foreign policy, stating that "there may be nothing particularly Bush-like, neoconservative, or American about the invasion of Iraq" (Jervis 2013: 175). These kinds of counterfactuals are extremely difficult, however. Counterfactual history is fraught with risks in general (Tetlock and Belkin 1996; Ferguson 2000), given the inability to actually re-run history in a controlled laboratory, meaning all we really have is the evidence in front of us.

There are also reasons to think that leaders should matter a great deal in driving some of the most important decisions for the study of international security. First, it is leaders who ultimately make decisions about whether countries should go to war. While their electorates, bureaucratic politics, and advisors matter (Allison 1971; Bueno de Mesquita et al. 2003; Saunders 2017), the buck stops with leaders when it comes to making choices about how to respond in a crisis, or whether to escalate a dispute to war (Horowitz et al. 2015). Second, the areas where leaders focus highlight, both domestically and internationally, the priorities of a leader and involve choices about where to spend political capital. For example, US President George H. W. Bush's personal involvement with attempts to regulate the proliferation of chemical weapons, both as Vice President and then as President, likely played a key role in driving the conclusion of the Chemical Weapons Convention.

Leaders also make decisions about the pursuit of key weapons technologies that shape national behavior. Fuhrmann and Horowitz (2015) show that leaders with prior experience as a rebel are significantly more likely to pursue nuclear weapons than other types of leaders due to their understanding of the instability of national sovereignty and predisposition, due to efficacy beliefs drawn from their success as a rebel, toward risk taking (on efficacy beliefs, also see Kennedy 2011). The appointment of lower-level national security officials also influences foreign policy, even though the leader does not necessarily have direct control over those policies. In more autocratic countries, and especially personalist regimes, where the checks on the leader are reduced, individual-level variation in leaders could play an even larger role on a variety of foreign policy issues (Weeks 2014; Horowitz et al. 2015).

What, then, is to be done? This chapter argues that recent research shows scholars can build more powerful models of international politics by incorporating leaders into how scholars think about the world. The study of leaders therefore has profound implications for the study of international security as a whole.

17.3 Leaders and International Security: A New Beginning

One of the biggest macro trends in academia over the last 30 years has been the behavioral revolution. From Kahnamen and Tversky (1979; Tversky and Kahnamen 1973) in psychology to behavioral economics (Camerer et al. 2011), scholars have taken a greater interest in unpacking the black box of individual rationality and showing the cognitive and other biases that influence how people, groups, bureaucracies, and countries make decisions.

Interestingly, the sub-field of political psychology stood out as an exception, throughout the Cold War and the 1990s, to overall trends away from studying leaders within the sub-field of international security. For example, studies of personality (Etheridge 1978; Hermann 1980, 1984; Kowert and Hermann 1997), judgment in foreign policy (George 1980; Goldgeier 1994; Renshon and Larson 2002; McDermott 2008), beliefs about the use of force (Herrmann and Keller 2004), and prospect theory (McDermott 2001; McDermott et al. 2008) represent key areas of research that continued even as overall research on leaders declined within the sub-field of international security, as well as International Relations as a whole.

It is natural, in some ways, that as other fields, as well as political science, turn back to studying the features that make us human, the study of leaders would rise in prominence again. Additionally, the creation of new datasets on heads of state around the world (Goemans et al. 2009) as well as the educational, family, and military background experiences of those leaders (Ellis et al. 2015), makes broader investigation of leader-driven phenomena vastly more plausible than a generation ago. There are several mechanisms through which variation in the attributes of leaders can shape policies relevant for international security—and this new generation of research is exploring those mechanisms and pointing the way toward future research as well.

First, the personalities of leaders have been a fascination for students of politics since Thucydides (1972) wrote about Pericles' bearing and rhetorical ability to shape Athenian public opinion. George and George's (1964) study of Woodrow Wilson's personality demonstrated how his stubbornness and idealism, as well as his relationship with his wife and Colonel House, shaped the character of the Treaty of Versailles, as well as the negotiations during the ratification process that led to its rejection by the United States Senate. This is an area of research that continued even as overall research on leaders declined (for example, see work by Margaret Hermann (1980, 1984; Hermann and Keller 2004), as well as Rose McDermott (2001, 2008; McDermott et al. 2008)).

Advances in theory and method mean international security studies can now more systematically understand the personalities of those leaders and how they shape their behavior. To give two recent examples, Saunders (2009) shows that Kennedy and Eisenhower's beliefs about the utility of intervention drove the different ways they approached international politics, and especially decision-making concerning Vietnam. Andrew Kennedy (2011), alternatively, shows how the different beliefs of Mao and Nehru concerning their personal efficacy in diplomacy and foreign policy profoundly influenced Chinese and Indian foreign policy in the early Cold War.

Second, investigating the background experiences of leaders may shed critical information on how leaders evaluate the costs and benefits of war and peace, as well as shaping how others evaluate them. Horowitz and colleagues (2015) demonstrate that the background experiences of leaders systematically shapes their conflict propensity by influencing their risk attitudes. They show that the strength of these effects on the probability of militarized disputes and war is similar to most realist and domestic political variables, and that the effects of leaders are stronger in more autocratic regimes with smaller selectorates—precisely those regimes where leaders are less constrained. Research on leader backgrounds also highlights the way specific background experiences, from a leader's age (Horowitz et al. 2005), to other factors, shape risk attitudes. Southern US Presidents, for example, with stronger views of honor and defending honor, have different conflict behavior than non-southern Presidents (Dafoe and Caughey 2016). Leaders with military service but no conflict experience, such as Kaiser Wilhelm II, have positive associations about the use of force and feelings of expertise from their military service, but none of the corresponding understanding of the costs that come from facing death in combat (Horowitz and Stam 2014). This makes them more likely to start conflicts.

Former rebels, in particular, also seem particularly prone to dangerous behavior. Revolutionary leaders, a subset of former rebels, often transfer their radical stance to domestic politics abroad, leading to more conflictual behavior (Colgan 2013). Former rebels, as referenced in Section 17.2, are also more likely to seek nuclear weapons, and potentially may be more likely to seek other kinds of advanced weapons as well (Fuhrmann and Horowitz 2015).

Third, the study of leaders and international security outcomes naturally leads to questions about the role of reputation in international politics. Both realist (Press 2005) and constructivist (Mercer 1996) approaches to the study of reputation assume that reputations adhere (or do not) to countries, but recent research suggests that countries and leaders evaluate the specific leader they are interacting with, as well as the history of the country involved (Renshon et al. forthcoming). This influences issues ranging from intelligence assessments (Yarhi-Milo 2014) to overall militarized interactions (Weisiger and Yarhi-Milo 2015) and can be driven by leader backgrounds as well as other factors (Dafoe and Caughey 2016; Kertzer 2016).

Fourth, some of the most significant work on leaders in international security involves studies concerning how the turnover of leaders influences the international security environment. Uncertainty is generally thought to make military conflicts more likely, because if leaders were certain how a conflict would work out prior to its beginning, they would find another way to resolve the dispute and "pay" the costs without sacrificing human life (Fearon 1994). Leadership turnover often leads to periods of heightened uncertainty, as both allies and adversaries wonder what policies the new administration of a country will pursue. This uncertainty is further heightened when the leadership turnover involves an irregular leadership transition, such as the rise to power of a new regime through a coup, revolution, or other illicit activity, or a wholesale regime change, such as the shift of a regime from an autocracy to a democracy (Chiozza and Goemans 2004, 2011; Colaresi 2004).[2]

Concern about losing power further influences leader decision-making concerning conflicts. Alexander Debs and Hein Goemans (2010) show that the less a leader worries about losing office if they make concessions, the more willing they are to bargain with potential adversaries. Since autocratic leaders are significantly more likely to lose their lives when leaving office than leaders of democracies, issues surrounding leaders could therefore play an important role in explaining the democratic peace. Sarah Croco (2011) demonstrates that the responsibility leaders feel for conflicts varies depending on whether they were in office when a conflict started. This influences their willingness to settle a conflict versus double down and continue fighting, because leaders who feel more responsible for a conflict, and that their selectorate will hold them accountable, are more likely to continue fighting.

17.4 Leaders and International Security: Future Avenues

Academic research on leaders in the international security realm is poised to grow in several areas, in addition to those noted in this chapter, over the next decade. Waltz's three images have given way to a more integrated notion of international politics where scholars can explore questions such as what explains when leaders have a more or less significant impact in international politics, or how domestic politics and leaders interact to produce national security policy.

One potential area for research involves the intersection of leaders and bureaucratic politics. A natural extension of the work on the background experiences of leaders is to explore how the backgrounds of key advisors to Presidents and Prime Ministers, such as Foreign Affairs Ministers/Secretaries of States and Defense Ministers/Secretaries of Defense, shape national policy choices. Such work could explicate the relationship between the leader and advisors, as well as the role that bureaucratic leaders at the sub-national level play in driving national policies. Saunders' (2017) work represents and broad and important start. Like the study of leaders, research on bureaucratic politics, once a large area of research in international politics, has declined in recent decades. There is no reason why this must be the case, however. Research by scholars in comparative politics on the "deep state," for example, or the way that bureaucratic institutions can impede change even when the overall government shifts, has continued. Advances in survey research could also give scholars the opportunity to better understand the preferences of policy leaders, further bringing together research on leaders and that on bureaucratic politics (Renshon 2015).

Another area of investigation with great relevance for the international security environment could be how leader attributes shape reputations, bringing together two of the research areas outlined above with broader scholarship on reputation and international security. For example, it is possible that leaders with prior military experience are viewed as more knowledgeable about military affairs than leaders without those experiences, meaning potential adversaries treat them with more deference in crisis situations. Alternatively, leaders may be most comfortable when interacting with leaders most like them. Leaders facing off against potential adversaries whose leaders have similar background experiences might view those actors as easier to understand, reducing uncertainty and making conflict less likely.

Perceptions of similarity that make conflict less likely might also be based in personality, rather than particular experiences. Some pundits noting US President Donald Trump's affinity for more autocratic personalities and leaders, such as Vladimir Putin, initially speculated that this could influence the probability of US–Russian cooperation, as well as US cooperation with other leaders perceived to be "strong," such as Orbán in Hungary. It will take careful empirical research to unpack the interaction between leaders, reputations, and international conflict further.

How leaders evaluate their own national power and that of potential adversaries could signify an interesting intersection between more realist understandings of the role of material power, constructivist notions of culture, and the study of leaders. For example, culturally-driven views of societies can influence threat perceptions (Fischerkeller 1997). Leaders who represent particular selectorates in society may be more likely to feature the biases of that selectorate. Scholars have traditionally thought about this in terms of the ideology of political parties (e.g. left-wing versus right-wing), but this is another way that the identity of a leader matters. Moreover, shifts in leader perspectives could influence national threat perceptions, and thus issues such as military deployments or investments. For example, in the United States, the type of defense posture necessary to ensure military superiority over China in the Asia-Pacific is likely to differ from the posture that would maximize America's ability to defeat the Islamic State. To be fair, this type of leader-based investigation fails one of the tests Jervis outlined for the causal power of leaders—the idea that, for leaders to matter, the "replacement leader" would have to have different preferences from the leader on the quantity of interest. Yet, such a situation could potentially emerge in the United States. For example, Donald Trump elucidated a different view of the world in the 2016 Republican Primary and general election than other Republican candidates such as Marco Rubio.

17.5 Conclusion

Once cast aside in the interest of macro debates about realism versus liberalism versus constructivism, the study of leaders has returned over the last several years for several reasons. The creation of new datasets on leaders and leader attributes has made the systematic study of leaders easier than it was before. Moreover, building on the behavioralist revolution in other fields, coming out of psychology, there is more acknowledgment by international security scholars of the way individual-level biases and perceptions shape political sciences. The advent of survey experiments, in particular, also provides a mechanism for scholars to explore the micro-foundations of beliefs to see how leader attributes influence how the public reacts, allowing them to ask questions about reputation, credibility, war, and peace.

The election of Donald Trump in the United States provides an opportune moment to consider the role of leaders in the study of international security. For example, questions about Trump's temperament and Clinton's health in the 2016 campaign recall research on leader illness and how that can lead to more volatile decision-making (McDermott 2008). Whether Trump's temperament is actually more volatile than past American leaders is not the point. Instead, that there is vibrant public debate about the personality of the President and how it is influencing US foreign policy suggests the relevance of research on leaders. Donald Trump's presidency may represent a natural experiment of sorts, as well as a hard case for leader-driven theories. Constitutional republics such as the United States place some of the largest constraints on leaders in the world. Prime Ministers in parliamentary systems often have greater freedom of action if their party is behind them, as do some types of autocratic leaders—especially more personalist leaders. Thus, President Trump is more constrained than many leaders around the world.

Finally, the Trump administration also highlights beliefs in the national security community about the importance of bureaucratic leadership at the subnational level. The belief that US foreign policy might vary in meaningful ways when Michael Flynn was replacted with H. R. McMaster as national security advisor suggests that it is not just the head of state that matters, but their advisors as well (Saunders 2017). Thus, the Trump administration case is poised to provide unique insights into the role of leaders in international politics across multiple dimensions. Policy debates aside, this means the study of leaders in international security could represent one of the most important areas of research for understanding the foreign policy of the most powerful country in the world in the years ahead.

Notes

1. Also see Saunders (2011).
2. Though beyond the scope of this chapter since it falls less into the domain of international security, research also suggests that leadership turnover influences trade relationships (McGillivray and Smith 2004) and international cooperation (McGillivray and Smith 2005).

References

Allison, Graham T. 1971. *Essence of Decision: Explaining the Cuban Missile Crisis.* New York: Little, Brown.

Blanchard, Ben. 2016. Duterte aligns Philippines with China, says U.S. has lost. *Reuters*, October 20. *Available at:* http://www.reuters.com/article/us-china-philippines-idUSKCN12KoAS

Bueno de Mesquita, Bruce, James D. Morrow, Randolph M. Siverson, and Alastair Smith. 2003. *The Logic of Political Survival.* Cambridge, MA: MIT Press.

Byman, Daniel L. and Kenneth M. Pollack. 2001. Let us now Praise Great Men: Bringing the Statesman back in. *International Security*, 25(4): 107–46.

Camerer, Colin F., George Loewenstein, and Matthew Rabin. 2011. *Advances in Behavioral Economics.* Princeton, NJ: Princeton University Press.

Carlyle, Thomas. 1935. *On Heroes, Hero-Worship, and the Heroic in History*. London: Oxford University Press.

Chiozza, Giacomo and Hein E. Goemans. 2004. International Conflict and the Tenure of Leaders: Is War still ex post Inefficient? *American Journal of Political Science*, 48(3): 604–19.

Chiozza, Giacomo and Hein E. Goemans. 2011. *Leaders and International Conflict*. New York: Cambridge University Press.

Colaresi, Michael. 2004. When Doves Cry: International Rivalry, Unreciprocated Cooperation, and Leadership Turnover. *American Journal of Political Science*, 48(3): 555–70.

Colgan, Jeff D. 2013. Domestic Revolutionary Leaders and International Conflict. *World Politics*, 65(4): 656–90.

Condon, Stephanie. 2016. Donald Trump: Japan, South Korea Might Need Nuclear Weapons. *CBS News*, March 29. *Available at:* http://www.cbsnews.com/news/donald-trump-japan-south-korea-might-need-nuclear-weapons/

Croco, Sarah E. 2011. The Decider's Dilemma: Leader Culpability, War Outcomes, and Domestic Punishment. *American Political Science Review*, 105(3): 457–77.

Dafoe, Allan and Devin Caughey. 2016. Honor and War. *World Politics*, 68(2): 341–31.

Debs, Alexandre and Hein E. Goemans. 2010. Regime Type, the Fate of Leaders, and War. *American Political Science Review*, 104(3): 430–45.

Denyer, Simon. 2016. Philippine leader Duterte Now Wants U.S. Troops Out "In the Next Two Years". *The Washington Post*, October 26. *Available at:* https://www.washingtonpost.com/world/philippines-duterte-now-wants-us-troops-out-in-two-years/2016/10/26/32bec8a5-8584-4d95-8e9d-4d7762865055_story.html

Dewan, Angela and Lindsay Isaac. 2016. David Cameron to Resign Wednesday as Theresa May to become British PM. *CNN*, July 11. *Available at:* http://www.cnn.com/2016/07/11/europe/britain-politics-may-leadsom/

Donald, David. 1995. *Lincoln*. New York: Simon & Schuster.

Ellis, Cali M., Allan C. Stam, and Michael C. Horowitz. 2015. Introducing the LEAD Dataset. *International Interactions*, 41(4): 718–41.

Etheridge, Lloyd S. 1978. Personality Effects on American Foreign Policy, 1898–1968: A Test of Interpersonal Generalization Theory. *American Political Science Review*, 72(2): 434–51.

Fearon, James D. 1994. Signaling versus the Balance of Power and Interests: An Empirical Test of a Crisis Bargaining Model. *Journal of Conflict Resolution*, 38(2): 236–69.

Ferguson, Niall. 2000. *Virtual History: Alternatives and Counterfactuals*. New York: Basic Books.

Fischerkeller, Michael P. 1997. David versus Goliath: The Influence of Cultural Judgements on Strategic Preference. PhD, Political Science, The Ohio State University, Columbus, OH.

Fuhrmann, Matthew and Michael C. Horowitz. 2015. When Leaders Matter: Rebel Experience and Nuclear Proliferation. *Journal of Politics*, 77(1): 72–87.

George, Alexander L. 1980. *Presidential Decisionmaking in Foreign Policy: The Effective Use of Information and Advice*. Boulder, CO: Westview Press.

George, Alexander L. and Juliette L. George. 1964. *Woodrow Wilson and Colonel House: A Personality Study*. Mineola, NY: Dover Publications.

Goemans, Henk E., Kristian S. Gleditsch, and Giacomo Chiozza. 2009. Introducing Archigos: A Dataset of Political Leaders. *Journal of Peace Research*, 46(2): 269–83.

Goldgeier, James M. 1994. *Leadership Style and Soviet Foreign Policy: Stalin, Khrushchev, Brezhnev, Gorbachev*. Baltimore, MD: The Johns Hopkins University Press.

Greenstein, Fred I. 1969. *Personality and Politics, Problems of Evidence, Inference, and Conceptualization*. Chicago, IL: Markham Publishing Co.

Harvey, Frank P. 2011. *Explaining The Iraq War: Counterfactual Theory, Logic, and Evidence*. New York: Cambridge University Press.

Hermann, Margaret G. 1980. Explaining Foreign Policy Behavior Using the Personal Characteristics of Political Leaders. *International Studies Quarterly*, 24(1): 7–46.

Hermann, Margaret G. 1984. Personality and Foreign Policy Decision Making: A Study of 53 Heads of Government. In D. A. Sylvan and S. Chan (eds.), *Foreign Policy Decision-Making: Perceptions, Cognition, and Artificial Intelligence*. New York: Praeger.

Herrmann, Richard K. and Jonathan W. Keller. 2004. Beliefs, Values, and Strategic Choice: U.S. Leaders' Decisions to Engage, Contain, and Use Force in an Era of Globalization. *Journal of Politics*, 66(2): 557–80.

Holland, Steve. 2016. Trump says he would consider alliance with Russia over Islamic State. *Reuters*, July 25. *Available at:* http://www.reuters.com/article/us-usa-election-trump-idUSKCN1052CJ

Horowitz, Michael C. and Allan C. Stam. 2014. How Prior Military Experience Influences the Future Militarized Behavior of Leaders. *International Organization*, 68(3): 527–59.

Horowitz, Michael, Rose McDermott, and Allan C. Stam. 2005. Leader Age, Regime Type, and Violence International Conflict. *Journal of Conflict Resolution*, 49(5): 661–85.

Horowitz, Michael C., Allan C. Stam, and Cali M. Ellis. 2015. *Why Leaders Fight*. New York: Cambridge University Press.

Jervis, Robert. 2013. Do Leaders Matter and How Would We Know? *Security Studies*, 22(2): 153–79.

Kagan, Robert and William Kristol. 2004. The Right War for the Right Reasons. *The Weekly Standard* 9 (23). *Available at:* http://www.weeklystandard.com/Content/Public/Articles/000//3/735tahyk.asp

Kahneman, Daniel and Amos Tversky. 1979. Prospect Theory: An Analysis of Decision under Risk. *Econometrica: Journal of the Econometric Society*, 47:263–91.

Kennedy, Andrew. 2011. *The International Ambitions of Mao and Nehru: National Efficacy Beliefs and the Making of Foreign Policy*. New York: Cambridge University Press.

Kertzer, Joshua D. 2016. *Resolve in International Politics*. Princeton, NJ: Princeton University Press.

Kowert, Paul A. and Margaret G Hermann. 1997. Who Takes Risks? Daring and Caution in Foreign Policy Making. *The Journal of Conflict Resolution*, 41(5): 611–37.

Lee, Stephen J. 1988. *Aspects of European History 1789–1980*. Reprint, illustrated edn. London: Routledge.

McDermott, Rose. 2001. *Risk-taking in International Politics: Prospect Theory in American Foreign Policy*. Ann Arbor, MI: University of Michigan Press.

McDermott, Rose. 2008. *Presidential Leadership, Illness, and Decision Making*. Cambridge: Cambridge University Press.

McDermott, Rose, James H. Fowler, and Oleg Smirnov. 2008. On the Evolutionary Origin of Prospect Theory Preferences. *The Journal of Politics*, 70(2): 335–50.

McGillivray, Fiona and Alastair Smith. 2004. The Impact of Leadership Turnover on Trading Relations Between States. *International Organization*, 58: 567–600.

McGillivray, Fiona and Alastair Smith. 2005. The Impact of Leadership Turnover and Domestic Institutions on International Cooperation. *Journal of Conflict Resolution*, 49(5): 639–60.

Mercer, Jonathan. 1996. *Reputation and International Politics*. Ithaca, NY: Cornell University Press.

Popper, Karl R. 1966. Of Clouds and Clocks: An Approach to the Problem of Rationality and the Freedom of Man. St. Louis: Washington University Press.

Press, Daryl G. 2005. *Calculating Credibility: How Leaders Assess Military Threats*. Ithaca, NY: Cornell University Press.

Renshon, Jonathan. 2015. Losing Face and Sinking Costs: Experimental Evidence on the Judgment of Political and Military Leaders. *International Organization*, 69(3): 659–95.

Renshon, Jonathan, Allan Dafoe, and Paul Huth. Forthcoming. Leader Influence and Reputation Formation in World Politics. *American Journal of Political Science*, forthcoming.

Renshon, Stanley A. and Deborah W. Larson (eds.). 2002. *Good Judgment in Foreign Policy: Theory and Application*. New York: Rowman and Littlefield.

Rosenau, James N. 1966. Pre-Theories and Theories of Foreign Policy. In B. R. Farrell (ed.), *Approaches to Comparative and International Politics*, pp. 27–92. Evanston, IL: Northwestern University Press.

Rosenau, James N. 1971. *The Scientific Study of Foreign Policy*. New York: Free Press.

Saunders, Elizabeth N. 2009. Transformative Choices: Leaders and the Origin of Intervention Strategy. *International Security*, 34(2): 119–61.

Saunders, Elizabeth N. 2011. *Leaders at War: How Presidents Shape Military Interventions*. Ithaca, NY: Cornell University Press.

Saunders, Elizabeth N. 2017. No Substitute for Experience: Presidents, Advisers, and Information in Group Decision-Making. *International Organization*, 71(S1): S219–47.

Schelling, Thomas C. 1960. *The Strategy of Conflict*. Cambridge, MA: Harvard University Press.

Singer, J. David and Melvin Small. 1972. *The Wages of War, 1816-1965: A Statistical Handbook*. New York: John Wiley.

Tetlock, Philip and Aaron Belkin (eds.). 1996. *Counterfactual Thought Experiments in World Politics: Logical, Methodological, and Psychological Perspectives*. Princeton, NJ: Princeton University Press.

Thucydides. 1972. *History of the Peloponnesian War*. Translated by R. Warner and M. Finley. London: Penguin UK.

Tversky, Amos and Daniel Kahneman. 1973. Availability: A Heuristic for Judging Frequency and Probability. *Cognitive Psychology*, 5(2): 207–32.

Waltz, Kenneth N. 1959. *Man, the State, and War*. New York: Columbia University Press.

Waltz, Kenneth N. 1979. *Theory of International Politics*. New York: McGraw-Hill.

Weeks, Jessica L. P. 2014. *Dictators at War and Peace*. Ithaca, NY: Cornell University Press.

Weisiger, Alex and Keren Yarhi-Milo. 2015. Revisiting Reputation: How Past Actions Matter in International Politics. *International Organization*, 69(2): 473–95.

Yarhi-Milo, Keren. 2014. *Knowing the Adversary: Leaders, Intelligence, and Assessments of Intentions in International Relations*. Princeton, NJ: Princeton University Press.

CHAPTER 18

THE POLITICS OF NATIONAL SECURITY

RONALD R. KREBS

In his seminal *Theory of International Politics*, Kenneth Waltz famously threw up his hands at "the infinite proliferation of variables" confronting the analyst of "the aims, policies, and actions of states." He was deeply skeptical of the prospects for developing any "valid generalizations" regarding the domestic drivers of foreign policy (Waltz 1979: 65). Thankfully, in the nearly 40 years since, scholars have paid little attention to Waltz's warning. As a result, there is now a robust and theoretically diverse literature on how domestic political actors, institutions, and ideas shape foreign policy, including national security policy.

However, existing approaches have succeeded largely by ignoring domestic *politics*—by turning an analytical blind eye to the contingent strategems political agents devise and pursue as they struggle for power and over policy. Recent scholarship has begun to give the politics of national security its due, exploring the techniques and tools that politicians employ to fix the contours of debate and to forge supportive elite coalitions. In combination, these research programs with distinct rationalist and constructivist roots shed light on key aspects of the making of national security: how the policy menu is constructed, what policy is pursued, how it is legitimated, and how it is sustained. Together they point toward a research agenda centered around the often-ignored, yet crucial, process of mobilization.[1]

This chapter proceeds in four sections. First, I review the existing literature at the intersection of domestic affairs and national security. Second, I argue for bringing politics back into the study of national security via mobilization and its constituent processes, including legitimation and coalition management. Third, in keeping with this handbook's focus on the future, I reflect on three contemporary developments—the rise of the transnational, the information and communication technologies revolution, and the fragmentation of authority and political community—that complicate the politics of mobilization. Finally, from this vantage point, I consider the future of grand strategy and briefly advance the case for an alternative: pragmatism.

18.1 Domestic Affairs and National Security: Existing Approaches

The now-rich scholarly literature on the domestic bases of national security has sought to account for three important phenomena: the sources of actors' interests, the production of the national collective's goals, and the state's capacity for action. It typically highlights causes drawn, alone or in combination, from actor (interest group) preferences, institutional design, and national culture and identity. With the caveat that this brief review cannot do justice to the existing literature, and must necessarily proceed highly selectively, the following discussion is organized around those three key phenomena.

A structural realist stance remains a useful conceptual baseline. Imagine a state concerned with little but its survival and security and thus deeply, even exclusively, attentive to its strategic circumstances. Imagine an international system that issued clear dictates regarding how states should position themselves for success. National security policy would then derive from these systemic imperatives. In the real world, however, states do not always, or perhaps even regularly, hew to the system's decrees. Realists have thus long invoked domestic factors to explain why states do not conform to the system's demands, even in the realm of high politics (Rathbun 2008; Ripsman et al. 2016). The domestic sources of policy pathology are varied—powerful lobbies (Mearsheimer and Walt 2007), liberal political culture (Layne 2006), underdeveloped state institutions (Zakaria 1998), and divided elites (Schweller 2006). But they serve a common analytical purpose: they are constraints on the state's capacity to act in accordance with systemic pressures.

This structural realist baseline, however, presumes that similarly situated observers would draw similar conclusions about what those systemic pressures are and what those pressures demand. But they would not, which is why Arnold Wolfers characterizes national security as "an ambiguous symbol" (Wolfers 1962: 151). Nations do not experience threats the same way, he notes: "some may find the danger to which they are exposed entirely normal and in line with their modest security expectations while others consider it unbearable to live with these same dangers." The international system is inarticulate: reasonable people can, and do, disagree about the lessons of recent and historical events. Even if there is consensus on the identity and magnitude of the threats facing the nation, the system normally does not prescribe how security-conscious states should respond—arms or alliances, military confrontation or diplomacy. In short, there is no systemic baseline from which to measure irrational deviations for which one can reflexively blame domestic politics.

Consequently, important streams of literature focus on how interests, institutions, and ideas rooted in domestic politics define what states seek to achieve in the international arena—that is, their national interest. It stands to reason that domestic interest groups seek a foreign policy that furthers their goals (Moravcsik 2008: esp. 236–7). This is most obvious in democracies, but all but the most totalitarian regimes provide points of entry for actors beyond the state to shape the policy-making process. Perhaps because many scholars think economic interests are the most powerful, or perhaps because these interests lend themselves to parsimonious theorizing, we know the most about their effects on security policy. It appears that those who profit materially from international engagement tend to favor a more expansive conception of the national interest and a more interventionist foreign policy (Trubowitz 1998, 2011; Fordham 2008) and to be more responsive to international norms (Solingen 2007). Those whose prosperity rests on open trade tend to back a liberal world order, sustained by international law and collective security (Narizny 2007). However, economic gain is just one motive around which groups can coalesce, along with identity (e.g. national or ethnoreligious) and principle (e.g. human rights).

Not all security preferences factor equally into the definition of "the national interest," for political institutions differentially empower actors and channel preference aggregation. Many scholars, for instance, presume that democratic institutions largely, if imperfectly, reflect the popular will. They therefore argue that democracies should, compared to less representative regimes, either be slow to use military force because it would lead to soldiers' deaths or conversely be reckless because their militaries replace men with machines (Caverley 2014); choose their wars more wisely (Reiter and Stam 2002); and puncture "myths of empire," which serve a narrow segment of elites, before those myths become too costly (Snyder 1991). However, these arguments do not persuade because they rest on a naïve model of democratic representation and accountability. Democracies' foreign policies reflect the views of business leaders and experts more than the will of the people (Jacobs and Page 2005) and, more generally, (Achen and Bartels 2016). Democratic publics rarely punish leaders who back down in a crisis or reward those who stand firm (Snyder and Borghard 2011; Trachtenberg 2012), and democracies are not particularly savvy when it comes to picking fights or dropping damaging imperial ventures (Downes 2009).

However, the larger institutional insight has merit. Some institutions make it easier for "selectorates" to hold leaders accountable, and the government's aims reflect that group's worldview and interests (Weeks 2014). Institutions with many "veto points" in foreign affairs provide more opportunities for outsiders to shape the national interest. Democracies with more intense partisan competition foster a more politically knowledgeable and active citizenry, increasing democratic responsiveness (Baum and Potter 2015). National leaders in presidential and semi-presidential systems have more authority over foreign and national security policy than do their counterparts in parliamentary regimes (Canes-Wrone et al. 2008).[2] As a result, individual leaders' backgrounds and beliefs weigh especially heavily in these systems (Saunders 2011; Horowitz et al. 2015). While legislatures are not entirely sidelined, it is the executive that sets the security agenda and produces the initiatives to which legislators react and which they sometimes seek to restrain.[3]

Finally, existing literature suggests that collective identity and culture also define the national interest. Relatively stable conceptions of the national self shape what state representatives imagine to be possible and desirable in global affairs and what threats and opportunities they perceive. Thus the arguably unique American sense of national mission has underpinned its impulse to spread liberal democracy and has impeded advocates of a realist foreign policy (Dueck 2006). Thanks to earlier quests for world power that ended in disaster, Germany and Japan embraced a pacifist identity and eschewed global ambitions (Berger 1998). Liberal powers, accustomed to non-violent conflict resolution at home, expect the same from fellow liberals in foreign policy, no matter their conflicts of interest (Owen IV 1998).

However the national interest is defined, states can pursue those aims in very different ways. Interests, institutions, and ideas again feature centrally in the existing literature. The distribution of interests affects what tools of statecraft policy-makers employ (Milner and Tingley 2015). If impacted industries are powerful, they may prevent the state from levying economic sanctions. If a military has invested heavily in air- and sea-based technology-intensive weapons platforms, it may oppose pivoting to manpower-intensive, ground-based counter insurgency. If governing elites are highly divided, the state will have difficulty mobilizing resources and balancing against rising challengers (Schweller 2006).

Political institutions also affect what resources decision-makers have available and what policy instruments they find attractive. Ambitious leaders cannot follow through on their dreams if primitive institutions of extraction cannot generate sufficient funds (Zakaria 1998). They gravitate toward those policy tools over which they have greater control, which may explain why US presidents incline toward the use of force (Milner and Tingley 2015: 23–6). Features of political institutions can also facilitate (or impede) states' ability to negotiate effectively in international politics. Institutions that increase accountability, promote political competition, or boost transparency bolster the capacity for credible commitment and information transmission, thereby imparting an advantage in bargaining (Schultz 2001).[4] Political systems that require the ratification of international agreements by another branch of government give negotiators a lever for wringing concessions (Putnam 1988).

Finally, normative commitments shape what means decision-makers view as legitimate or at least as politically sustainable. Moral revulsion against nuclear weapons has underpinned nuclear non-use (Tannenwald 2007), and ideological comity has shaped alliance patterns (Haas 2005). The mass public's moral commitments have supposedly prevented democratic decision-makers from embracing brutal counter insurgency or entertaining war against fellow democracies (Hayes 2013; Merom 2003). However, it is not clear that democratic publics have punished leaders severely for transgressions, nor is it even clear that they view these behaviors as transgressive—as their normative commitments may not run deep or extend beyond national borders (Valentino et al. 2006; Sagan and Valentino 2016).

In short, over the last three decades, scholars have shed substantial light on how economic interest groups acquire preferences with respect to security, how political institutions shape how states define and pursue the national interest, how identity and culture affect both preferences and behavior, and how that same triumvirate of forces both makes available and limits the resources and tools on which states draw. However, they have paid too little attention to countries and regions beyond the United States and Europe (I confess a personal mea culpa) and have too swiftly presumed that the American experience is generalizable.

Equally troubling, existing scholarship—whether realist, liberal, or constructivist in flavor—is overwhelmingly structuralist and static. Preferences are treated as the product of fixed economic interests. Institutions are theorized as aggregating individual preferences, favoring particular actors, and channeling behavior. Elite and ethnic divides are cast as stable impediments to collective action. National identity and culture are treated either as permanent collective characteristics or as effectively fixed, despite their contingent origins. Structuralism's appeal is understandable: it facilitates parsimonious, predictive theory, highlights the constraints on even inventive political actors, and draws attention to enduring features of the political scene.

But structuralism comes at a cost: it is blind to, and even shunts aside, politics. When political actors confront constraints, they do not treat them as permanent features of the political landscape that so radically shrink the menu that choice is eliminated or meaningless. They are agents. They make choices that are both fundamentally unpredictable and very much consequential (Kirshner 2015). They labor creatively, and presumably not futilely, to attract allies and marginalize rivals, to persuade others of their rectitude or to coerce others rhetorically into endorsing their stance, to leverage institutional rules and roles, to overcome societal divides by reframing issues, and to legitimate their political agendas. This everyday politics of national security, this lived reality, makes hardly a dent in the vast scholarship on the domestic sources of foreign policy. However, this omission overlooks important dynamics and mechanisms and impoverishes our explanations of how nations make security policy.

18.2 Bringing Politics Back in to Security: A Research Agenda

By security policy, I mean those measures ostensibly designed to limit the state's vulnerability to attack and coercion and thereby to promote the corresponding public feeling of safety. Because security policy sometimes seeks to advance these ends indirectly, its scope can be large.[5] However, security policies informed by good intentions may not actually bolster national security or cultivate public confidence; via unintended and unforeseen dynamics, they may in practice lead to insecurity. Policies that pretend to security can also have covert agendas, including fostering public fear. I identify security policy here by its explicit, overt purposes.

Security policy is inherently political in two senses. First, the problem it purports to rectify—insecurity—is necessarily the product of political action (Weldes et al. 1999). Critics from the left treat security as the default position and assume that threats are inflated to serve ulterior motives, and critics from the right treat insecurity as the default and assume that threats are downplayed, out of *naïveté* or misplaced loyalties. But neither security nor insecurity are the "natural" state of affairs. Political actors promote discourses of security or insecurity, and nurture the corresponding public emotions, via rhetorical "speech acts"—by asserting vulnerability, by promising security—and thereby shape the political terrain (Wirls 1992, 2010). Second, although actors invoke security to silence opposition, it is not a rhetorical trump card that sweeps away all debate in the name of urgency. Invoking "security" does not shift an issue into the apolitical realm that Carl Schmitt termed "the exception" (contra Buzan et al. 1998). Security politics is distinctive and confined, but debates over national security are nevertheless often passionate.

Security policy is a two-step process, and both steps are shot through with high-stakes politics. The first is the fixing of the foundations of debate and thus the menu of legitimate policy options. This step is easily overlooked because the menu is typically presented as common sense, rather than as the product of contingent political action. Even scholars sensitive to how ideas drive strategic choice in foreign and security affairs rarely explore the processes by which that menu is composed (notably, Legro 2005). The second step entails devising and sustaining policy. This does not involve merely selecting a policy dish from the menu, but making sure it is fully cooked and properly garnished—not just once, but for repeat orders. This step rests on the creation and continual management of a supportive coalition. Even scholars sensitive to the challenge of mobilization tend to focus on structural impediments and neglect the mechanisms through which policies are rendered legitimate and elite coalitions are forged and maintained (notably, Schweller 2006).

18.2.1 Fixing the Narrative, Constituting the Policy Menu

In national security, as in other domains, contestation is the lifeblood of politics.[6] But it is never unstructured. Some premises go unquestioned and even unspoken, striking participants and observers as common sense, but they are always the product of human agency. Debates over national security are often underpinned by dominant narratives—such as the Cold War consensus or the post-9/11 Terror narrative—that weave present challenges, past failures and triumphs, and potential futures into a coherent tale, and thereby impart meaning and order to global affairs. These narratives constitute the terrain on which politicians, pundits, and activists battle. They set the boundaries of the legitimate, limiting what political actors can publicly justify and therefore what policies they may pursue, thereby privileging particular courses of action and impeding others. No wonder that political actors seek not only to purchase or compel others' assent to particular policies, but devote resources and energy to the quest for narrative dominance.

However, if actors commonly strive to lay this narrative foundation, why do some aspiring narratives triumph over competitors, while others fall by the wayside? And when do dominant narratives come undone? These questions on the bases of legitimation and the construction of choice have received little attention compared to the instrumental and normative considerations that enter into security policy—yet are arguably more important. Moreover, they suggest a conceptual and theoretical turn away from an allegedly stable national identity toward the contingent politics of meaning and the processes by which it becomes temporarily stabilized.

One intuitive answer is that charismatic, well-funded, or institutionally empowered individuals manipulate debate, including by inserting wedge issues and deceiving the public (Kaufmann 2004; Schuessler 2015). There is some truth to this, but politicians know that their efforts often fall short. Moreover, even brilliant orators do not stand outside or transcend social structures that they sway at will. Critical constructivist and post-structuralist scholarship has revealed dominant articulations for what they are, has explored how they are configured and how they silence alternatives, and has identified common processes through which they are assembled (Campbell 1998; Weldes 1999; Fierke 2007; Williams 2007). But these approaches have not explained why some narratives acquire the status of common sense, while others remain contested, while still others are ignored or treated as beyond the pale. This requires exploring contending speakers' concrete articulations, those speakers' social and political positionality, and the constitution of key audiences (Bially Mattern 2005: 12, 93).

In a study of US national security debates and policy, employing multiple methods to analyze cases and data ranging from the 1930s to the 2000s, I suggest an account that knits together three elements: the rhetorical demands of the environment, the authority speakers bring to bear, and the rhetorical modes they adopt. I argue that in unsettled times—when multiple narratives legitimately swirl about the public sphere—presidents can advance their narrative ambitions by adopting the rhetoric of storytelling (Krebs 2015: chs. 2–4). This same basket of factors explains when dominant narratives endure and when they collapse. Rather than shocking failure impelling narrative breakdown, I maintain that even substantial battlefield setbacks encourage the political opposition to offer only narrow policy criticism that ironically reproduces the dominant narrative, in whose terms the mission had been legitimated. However, by bolstering the authority of its "owners," victory in war and coercive diplomacy make narrative change possible (Krebs 2015: chs. 5–8).

Others will hopefully build upon this initial foray. How have dominant narratives of national security coalesced and collapsed outside the United States—in countries that have felt the pressures of global politics more intensely and have waged costly wars on their own territory? How have other configurations of narrative authority shaped these dynamics—in parliamentary or semi-presidential regimes, or where militarism rules? What is the scope for civil society groups to move national security debate? Do more fine-grained rhetorical choices affect the fate of narrative projects? These questions await answers.

18.2.2 Mobilizing and Managing Coalitions

National security experts typically prefer to focus on the substance of policy and strategy and seem to hold domestic politics in contempt. But, regardless of policy's virtues, its ultimate success rests on the mobilization and maintenance of a supportive coalition and thus on domestic political acumen. Building and sustaining that coalition requires the effective legitimation of policy and the management of elites.

Legitimation—the articulation before key audiences of publicly acceptable reasons for action and policy—is an essential first step toward an enduring coalition. In both domestic and foreign affairs, it is necessary whenever publics of whatever scope must be mobilized and wherever there is a reasonable chance that the glare of public attention will turn (Goddard and Krebs 2015). Those who do not bother to legitimate their claims or whose claims to legitimacy fail to pass over the bar have few public advocates, and their few advocates are ignored or disdained. As the tendon binding concrete policies to underlying narratives, legitimation reflects that narrative structure enables but also constrains: not all policies can be legitimated, which is why decision-makers sometimes opt for covert action and why political actors, subject to the pressures of "rhetorical coercion," sometimes give way (Krebs and Jackson 2007). But legitimation also entails strategy—carefully constructing arguments to persuade or compel, framing preferred policies in the most attractive light, leveraging credibility, delivering an authentic performance.

Effective legitimation draws from the universe of "rhetorical commonplaces" that prevailing narratives provide (Jackson 2006). It guarantees that critics cannot dismiss one's stance as beyond the boundaries of the acceptable, as worthy of nothing but derision. But legitimation can sometimes achieve much more, silencing opponents by depriving them of the materials out of which to construct a sustainable counterargument. Adolf Hitler's rhetoric of "national self-determination" had this coercive effect on British advocates of rapid rearmament (Goddard 2015). Similarly, the post-9/11 War on Terror made it very difficult for leading Democrats to oppose the Iraq War (Krebs and Lobasz 2007). Much of politics revolves around this battle of contending legitimations, and successful legitimation tilts the tables. Existing scholarship has identified some key mechanisms and scope and facilitating conditions, but we still have much to learn about how and when legitimation strategies reconfigure politics.

Although effective legitimation promises a seat at the table and narrows the rhetorical field of play, it does not alone ensure a stable, supportive elite coalition. Such a coalition is essential for mobilizing societal resources and for managing public opinion, even in many autocracies. Outside purely totalitarian regimes, contending elites can shape policy and impede its implementation in many ways—from rallying allies in the bureaucracy to withholding funding to going public. These elites do not merely reflect pre-existing mass preferences, and the divides among them are not fixed. There is then substantial room for leadership in mobilizing elite support and limiting opposition. Leaders employ various techniques to that end, ranging from coercion (threatening punishment to compel adherence) to bargaining (offering side-payments or limited policy concessions to procure compliance) to manipulation (managing information flows to co-opt and declaw elites) (Bueno de Mesquita et al. 2004; Saunders 2015). Leaders' choices are not unconstrained: regime structures affect how broad a coalition they need, what costs opposed elites might impose, what techniques of coalition management are available and which are most appealing. But their choices are important too. Existing scholarship has only begun to catalog these techniques. Future research might explore how different kinds of regimes prompt different forms of elite coalition formation and management, how leaders choose among the varied strategies and tactics available to them, under what conditions particular strategies and tactics are most likely and most successful, and what unintended consequences they spawn (for initial efforts, see Saunders and Wolford 2016).

This research agenda goes a long way toward bringing politics back into the making of national security. Deliberations behind closed doors, the substance of strategy, and the moment of decision remain important. But so too are the deeply political processes that precede and follow—from the fixing of premises to the legitimation of policy to the management of elites.

18.3 The Future of Politics and National Security

Backward-looking research on politics and national security may mislead, however, if the future will look little like the past. Three big changes are now under way with potentially transformative implications: the rise of the transnational, the information and communications technology revolution, and the decline of authority. All three are vexing the politics of national security and making the already challenging task of mobilization yet more daunting.

Recent decades have witnessed the rise of the transnational as a sphere of political organization and mobilization (Adamson 2005; Barnett and Sikkink 2008). Some argue that we can no longer speak of "domestic politics," even in the security arena: "all politics is local" has given way to "all politics is transnational." It follows that the politics of mobilization need to be reconceptualized in a world of transnational challenges, activism, and coordination. It is true that attentive audiences are now more numerous and diverse and located beyond national borders. Transnational action rests on legitimation in a transnational space—not just in multiple distinct domestic arenas—and it is more challenging: there are fewer shared rhetorical resources and even fewer settled bases for legitimation, and speakers addressing varied audiences are more vulnerable to charges of hypocrisy. Still, the transnational imperative bites less deeply in the security domain, where relationships are often *inter*national and thus where national leaders typically take charge of mobilizing local coalitions. Moreover, with respect to resource extraction, mobilization remains almost exclusively a domestic affair. Nevertheless, the rise of the transnational has complicated legitimation.

So too has the revolution in information and communications technologies (ICT). Thanks to ICTs, government has become more transparent, albeit unevenly and episodically. Officials know that, well before formal declassification, every email or text message they send could become public. Arguably, the prospect of Wikileaks-style revelations should make policy more reflective of mass preferences, since a better informed public should be better able to hold officials accountable if they deviate from its wishes. However, it does not seem likely that ICTs are helping promote democratic responsiveness. Accountability is elusive not just because officials keep secrets. It is also elusive because publics and their representatives have limited capacity for oversight. And it is elusive because, although elections are a chief mechanism of accountability, they are only occasional and therefore encapsulate diverse policy dimensions: even well-informed voters might re-elect politicians despite their dissatisfaction with foreign policy. Moreover, excessive transparency has a dark side: it hinders mobilization if leaders fear they will be punished for compromising principles and making backroom deals and if they are therefore reluctant to offer side-payments to stabilize elite coalitions. ICT-promoted transparency is likely polarizing politics and destabilizing policy coalitions, in national security and other domains, without any countervailing gain in responsiveness.

Finally, mobilization is still more imposing in a political and cultural milieu in which traditional claims to authority hold less sway and in which the bonds of community are eroding—what the historian Daniel Rodgers has aptly called our "age of fracture" (Rodgers 2011). As social networks become increasingly homogeneous with respect to class and political ideology, there are fewer shared bases for legitimation, and the flexibility needed to build and maintain coalitions is more scarce. The new media environment has further fueled this trend: its ever-expanding array of both entertainment and news allows the disinterested to revel in their ignorance and news junkies to feed their passion more richly than ever in partisan and ideological echo chambers. It is not that publics no longer yearn for community and narrative order. They do—and they continue to look to the nation's leaders to explain a world changing so rapidly, and seemingly inexplicably, around them. But satisfying that demand is difficult when audiences for "hard news" are shrinking, when numerous voices are clamoring for attention in the media marketplace, when swiftly moving events continually dislocate efforts to make public sense of them, and when the zones of shared rhetorical commonplaces are contracting.

A composite picture emerges from these three vectors of change. They are making the core tasks of mobilization—setting the terms of debate, legitimating policy, forging and sustaining a supportive elite coalition—increasingly difficult. And they are making national security leadership, at least as we have traditionally conceived of it, nearly impossible.

18.4 The End of Grand Strategy?

These growing mobilization challenges may also mark the death knell of grand strategy. Grand strategy is "a state's theory about how it can best 'cause' security for itself" (Posen 1984: 13). Strategists define a national interest, identify threats, and prioritize among them; allocate scarce resources and energy; and fashion appropriate policy responses, bringing the nation's assets into alignment with its ends abroad. Strategy informs the present, but it is perhaps even more valuable as a guide to the future: it issues broad instructions to policy-makers regarding how they should address challenges as yet unforeseen. In implementing strategy, policy-makers must be somewhat flexible and must adapt to changing circumstances, but a strategy that changes too much, too rapidly, and too often is not worth the name: strategy's value supposedly lies in allowing policy-makers to steer a steady ship amidst the storms that regularly roil the seas of global politics. Yet coherent and consistent strategy has often fallen victim to bureaucratic pulling and hauling, pressure from other branches of government, the limits of human cognition, and the inherent complexity of global politics (Betts 2000). But grand strategy is also politically demanding, requiring leaders to rally broad and enduring coalitions. As mobilization proves increasingly elusive, strategy is increasingly an illusion—and a costly one, if leaders pursue unwise policies to maintain the charade.

But what alternative is there to keeping up the appearance of strategy? Allow me, in closing, to offer a modest plea for pragmatism (Edelstein and Krebs 2015: 115–16). Like its strategic counterpart, a pragmatic approach to foreign-policy making begins with a specification of national goals and values. But, recognizing that strategy merely pretends to stability and consistency, a pragmatic approach seeks to make a virtue out of the necessity of constant adaptation. Whereas strategy embeds a dominant narrative of national security and thus confines debate to that terrain, a pragmatic foreign policy sustains narrative pluralism and facilitates less constrained debates over policy's virtues and vices. In place of the spectacle of strategizing, it has the potential to promote deliberation and creative innovation. Whereas strategy prizes consistency, pragmatism liberates policy-makers from the pressure of foolish consistency and thus avoids costly errors for the sake of that hobgoblin. A pragmatic culture of national security policy making would free officials to embrace experimentation, acknowledge failure, jettison losing propositions, and try again. Whereas grand strategy rests on broad and enduring coalitions, a pragmatic approach is better suited to our fractured age. It would facilitate mobilization, since the coalition needed to sustain individual policy initiatives, as opposed to a totalizing grand strategy, could be assembled on narrower grounds. It would make managing the politics of national security easier, as leaders could then assemble a revolving cast of otherwise strange bedfellows and shell out more limited side-payments.

Pragmatism is not without intellectual and policy obstacles, notably on what grounds officials and leaders selectively engage the world, allocate attention and resources, and avoid lurching from crisis to crisis. But strategy's grip has been so tight, even on pragmatism's home turf of the United States, that pragmatism has received scant consideration as an alternative approach to foreign and national security policy. That seems terribly unpragmatic.

Notes

1. For a similar call, to focus on mobilization processes at the global level, see Goddard and Nexon (2016).
2. Though presidential authority is dependent on which policy instruments he or she employs: see Milner and Tingley (2015: chs. 5–6).

3. Conditional on partisan interests, the extent and diffuseness of policy's distributive consequences, and the intensity of ideological divides: see Howell and Pevehouse (2007: esp. 19–21, 34–40); Milner and Tingley (2015).
4. Whether democracies enjoy a credibility advantage is much debated: for a skeptical view, see Downes and Sechser (2012).
5. Virtually all public policies have ramifications for national security. However, not all initiatives are explicitly justified on security grounds. A policy falls into the "security" domain when its advocates make the security ramifications central to their brief.
6. This paragraph and the next draw freely on Krebs (2015: ch. 1).

References

Achen, Christopher H. and Larry M. Bartels. 2016. *Democracy for Realists: Why Elections Do Not Produce Responsive Government*. Princeton, NJ: Princeton University Press.

Adamson, Fiona. 2005. Globalisation, Transnational Political Mobilisation, and Networks of Violence. *Cambridge Review of International Affairs*, 18(1): 31–49.

Barnett, Michael and Kathryn Sikkink. 2008. From International Relations to Global Society. In Christian Reus-Smit and Duncan Snidal (eds.), *The Oxford Handbook of International Relations*, ch. 3. Oxford: Oxford University Press.

Baum, Matthew A. and Philip B. K. Potter. 2015. *War and Democratic Constraint: How the Public Influences Foreign Policy*. Princeton, NJ: Princeton University Press.

Berger, Thomas U. 1998. *Cultures of Antimilitarism: National Security in Germany and Japan*. Baltimore, MD: The Johns Hopkins University Press.

Betts, Richard K. 2000. Is Strategy an Illusion? *International Security*, 25(2): 5–50.

Bially Mattern, Janice. 2005. *Ordering International Politics: Identity, Crisis, and Representational Force*. New York: Routledge.

Bueno de Mesquita, Bruce, James D. Morrow, Randolph M. Siverson, and Alastair Smith. 2004. *The Logic of Political Survival*. Cambridge, MA: MIT Press.

Buzan, Barry, Ole Wæver, and Jaap de Wilde. 1998. *Security: A New Framework for Analysis*. Boulder, CO: Lynne Rienner.

Campbell, David. 1998. *Writing Security: United States Foreign Policy and the Politics of Identity*. Revised edn. Minneapolis: University of Minnesota Press.

Canes-Wrone, Brandice, William G. Howell, and David E. Lewis. 2008. Toward a Broader Understanding of Presidential Power: A Reevaluation of the Two Presidencies Thesis. *Journal of Politics*, 70(1): 1–16.

Caverley, Jonathan D. 2014. *Democratic Militarism: Voting, Wealth, and War*. Cambridge: Cambridge University Press.

Downes, Alexander B. 2009. How Smart and Tough Are Democracies? Reassessing Theories of Democratic Victory in War. *International Security*, 33(4): 9–51.

Downes, Alexander B. and Todd S. Sechser. 2012. The Illusion of Democratic Credibility. *International Organization*, 66(3): 457–89.

Dueck, Colin. 2006. *Reluctant Crusaders: Power, Culture, and Change in American Grand Strategy*. Princeton, NJ: Princeton University Press.

Edelstein, David M. and Ronald R. Krebs. 2015. Delusions of Grand Strategy. *Foreign Affairs*, 94(6): 109–16.

Fierke, K. M. 2007. *Critical Approaches to International Security*. Cambridge: Polity Press.

Fordham, Benjamin O. 2008. Economic Interests and Public Support for American Global Activism. *International Organization*, 62(1): 163–82.

Goddard, Stacie E. 2015. The Rhetoric of Appeasement: Hitler's Legitimation and British Foreign Policy, 1938–1939. *Security Studies*, 24(1): 95–130.

Goddard, Stacie E. and Ronald R. Krebs. 2015. Rhetoric, Legitimation, and Grand Strategy. *Security Studies*, 24(1): 5–36.

Goddard, Stacie E. and Daniel H. Nexon. 2016. The Dynamics of Global Power Politics: A Framework for Analysis. *Journal of Global Security Studies*, 1(1): 4–18.

Haas, Mark L. 2005. *The Ideological Origins of Great Power Politics, 1789–1989*. Ithaca, NY: Cornell University Press.

Hayes, Jarrod. 2013. *Constructing National Security: US Relations with India and China*. Cambridge: Cambridge University Press.

Horowitz, Michael C., Allan C. Stam, and Cali M. Ellis. 2015. *Why Leaders Fight*. Cambridge: Cambridge University Press.

Howell, William G. and Jon C. Pevehouse. 2007. *While Dangers Gather: Congressional Checks on Presidential War Powers*. Princeton, NJ: Princeton University Press.

Jackson, Patrick Thaddeus. 2006. *Civilizing the Enemy: German Reconstruction and the Invention of the West*. Ann Arbor, MI: University of Michigan Press.

Jacobs, Lawrence R. and Benjamin I. Page. 2005. Who Influences U.S. Foreign Policy? *American Political Science Review*, 99(1): 107–23.

Kaufmann, Chaim. 2004. Threat Inflation and the Failure of the Marketplace of Ideas: The Selling of the Iraq War. *International Security*, 29(1): 5–48.

Kirshner, Jonathan. 2015. The Economic Sins of Modern IR Theory and the Classical Realist Alternative. *World Politics*, 67(1): 155–83.

Krebs, Ronald R. 2015. *Narrative and the Making of U.S. National Security*. Cambridge: Cambridge University Press.

Krebs, Ronald R. and Patrick T. Jackson. 2007. Twisting Tongues and Twisting Arms: The Power of Political Rhetoric. *European Journal of International Relations*, 13(1): 35–66.

Krebs, Ronald R. and Jennifer K. Lobasz. 2007. Fixing the Meaning of 9/11: Hegemony, Coercion, and the Road to War in Iraq. *Security Studies*, 16(3): 409–51.

Layne, Christopher. 2006. *The Peace of Illusions: American Grand Strategy from 1940 to the Present*. Ithaca, NY: Cornell University Press.

Legro, Jeffrey W. 2005. *Rethinking the World: Great Power Strategies and International Order*. Ithaca, NY: Cornell University Press.

Mearsheimer, John J. and Stephen M. Walt. 2007. *The Israel Lobby and U.S. Foreign Policy*. New York: Farrar, Straus, & Giroux.

Merom, Gil. 2003. *How Democracies Lose Small Wars: State, Society, and the Failures of France in Algeria, Israel in Lebanon, and the United States in Vietnam*. Cambridge: Cambridge University Press.

Milner, Helen V. and Dustin Tingley. 2015. *Sailing the Water's Edge: The Domestic Politics of American Foreign Policy*. Princeton, NJ: Princeton University Press.

Moravcsik, Andrew. 2008. The New Liberalism. In Christian Reus-Smit and Duncan Snidal (eds.), *The Oxford Handbook of International Relations*, pp. 234–54. Oxford: Oxford University Press.

Narizny, Kevin. 2007. *The Political Economy of Grand Strategy*. Ithaca, NY: Cornell University Press.

Owen IV, John M. 1998. *Liberal Peace, Liberal War: American Politics and International Security*. Ithaca, NY: Cornell University Press.
Posen, Barry R. 1984. *The Sources of Military Doctrine: France, Britain, and Germany Between the World Wars*. Ithaca, NY: Cornell University Press.
Putnam, Robert D. 1988. Diplomacy and Domestic Politics: The Logic of Two-Level Games. *International Organization*, 42(3): 427–60.
Rathbun, Brian C. 2008. A Rose by Any Other Name: Neoclassical Realism as the Logical and Necessary Extension of Structural Realism. *Security Studies*, 17(2): 294–321.
Reiter, Dan and Allan C. Stam. 2002. *Democracies at War*. Princeton, NJ: Princeton University Press.
Ripsman, Norrin M., Jeffrey W. Taliaferro, and Steven E. Lobell. 2016. *Neoclassical Realist Theory of International Politics*. New York: Oxford University Press.
Rodgers, Daniel T. 2011. *Age of Fracture*. Cambridge, MA: Harvard University Press.
Sagan, Scott D. and Benjamin A. Valentino. 2016. Just a War Theory? American Public Opinion on Ethics in Military Combat. Unpublished manuscript, Stanford University and Dartmouth College.
Saunders, Elizabeth N. 2011. *Leaders at War: How Presidents Shape Military Interventions*. Ithaca, NY: Cornell University Press.
Saunders, Elizabeth N. 2015. War and the Inner Circle: Democratic Elites and the Politics of Using Force. *Security Studies*, 24(3): 466–501.
Saunders, Elizabeth N. and Scott Wolford. 2016. Two Logics of Democracies at War: How Elites Shape Public Accountability and Foreign Policy in Democracies. Unpublished manuscript, George Washington University and University of Texas at Austin.
Schuessler, John M. 2015. *Deceit on the Road to War: Presidents, Politics, and American Democracy*. Ithaca, NY: Cornell University Press.
Schultz, Kenneth A. 2001. *Democracy and Coercive Diplomacy*. Cambridge: Cambridge University Press.
Schweller, Randall L. 2006. *Unanswered Threats: Political Constraints on the Balance of Power*. Princeton, NJ: Princeton University Press.
Snyder, Jack L. 1991. *Myths of Empire: Domestic Politics and International Ambition*. Ithaca, NY: Cornell University Press.
Snyder, Jack and Erica D. Borghard. 2011. The Cost of Empty Threats: A Penny, Not a Pound. *American Political Science Review*, 105(3): 437–56.
Solingen, Etel. 2007. *Nuclear Logics: Contrasting Paths in East Asia and the Middle East*. Princeton, NJ: Princeton University Press.
Tannenwald, Nina. 2007. *The Nuclear Taboo: The United States and the Non-Use of Nuclear Weapons Since 1945*. Cambridge: Cambridge University Press.
Trachtenberg, Marc. 2012. Audience Costs: An Historical Analysis. *Security Studies*, 21(1): 3–42.
Trubowitz, Peter. 1998. *Defining the National Interest: Conflict and Change in American Foreign Policy*. Chicago, IL: University of Chicago Press.
Trubowitz, Peter. 2011. *Politics and Strategy: Partisan Ambition and American Statecraft*. Princeton, NJ: Princeton University Press.
Valentino, Benjamin, Paul Huth, and Sarah Croco. 2006. Covenants Without the Sword: International Law and the Protection of Civilians in Times of War. *World Politics*, 58(3): 339–77.
Waltz, Kenneth N. 1979. *Theory of International Politics*. Reading, MA: Addison-Wesley.
Weeks, Jessica L. P. 2014. *Dictators at War and Peace*. Ithaca, NY: Cornell University Press.

Weldes, Jutta. 1999. *Constructing National Interests: The United States and the Cuban Missile Crisis*. Minneapolis, MN: University of Minnesota Press.

Weldes, Jutta, Mark Laffey, Hugh Gusterson, and Raymond Duvall (eds.). 1999. *Cultures of Insecurity: States, Communities, and the Production of Danger*. Minneapolis, MN: University of Minnesota Press.

Williams, Michael C. 2007. *Culture and Security: Symbolic Power and the Politics of International Security*. Abingdon: Routledge.

Wirls, Daniel. 1992. *Buildup: The Politics of Defense in the Reagan Era*. Ithaca, NY: Cornell University Press.

Wirls, Daniel. 2010. *Irrational Security: The Politics of Defense from Reagan to Obama*. Baltimore, MD: The Johns Hopkins University Press.

Wolfers, Arnold. 1962. *Discord and Collaboration*. Baltimore, MD: Johns Hopkins University Press.

Zakaria, Fareed. 1998. *From Wealth to Power: The Unusual Origins of America's World Role*. Princeton, NJ: Princeton University Press.

CHAPTER 19

RELIGION AND INTERNATIONAL SECURITY

DANIEL PHILPOTT

Some time prior to the Iranian Revolution of 1979, CIA analyst Earnest Oney broached to his bosses a study of religious leaders in Iran. Scholar of Iran, James A. Bill, describes the response:

> His bureaucratic superiors vetoed the idea, dismissing it as "sociology." The work climate was such that he was sometimes condescendingly referred to by others in the government as "Mullah Ernie." It was not until the revolution and after his retirement that he was able to do his study on the force of religion in Iran. He did it for the agency on contract—*after* the force of religion had been felt not only in Iran but by America as well (Bill 1988: 417).

The Iranian Revolution, wrought by Shia Islam, created a crisis in US foreign policy, brought down a US president, realigned Middle Eastern politics, and led to a war between Iran and its neighbor, Iraq—a majority Shia state then controlled by a secularist Sunni regime—that lasted eight years and took an estimated one million lives.

During the 1990s, religiously-inspired terrorism expanded rapidly and displayed itself most spectacularly in the attacks of September 11, 2001. Combatting this terrorism then preoccupied the foreign policies of the United States, European states, and other countries like India, Indonesia, Russia, and Nigeria and shaped their alignments and relations with countries like Pakistan and Saudi Arabia.

Civil war in Iraq and Afghanistan became the besetting dilemmas of the United States and its allies in the past decade-and-a-half and have been propelled by religion, as have conflicts in Iraq and Syria, where the Islamic State and other Islamist militant groups battle government authorities.

Since the Iranian Revolution, religion has also contributed critically to conflicts in Tajikistan, Kashmir, Yugoslavia, Algeria, Sri Lanka, the Philippines, Chechnya, Sudan, India, Burma, Israel–Palestine, and other locales. Earnest Oney was right and sociology—as well as political science, religious studies, and related fields—has been struggling to catch up ever since. Until about 2000, religion had little place in the international relations sub-field of political science. In the period 1980–99, only six or so articles in four leading International Relations journals—*International Organization, International Studies Quarterly, World Politics,* and *International Security*—featured religion as an important influence in International Relations (Philpott 2001: 9). Since that time, corresponding to global events, a body of scholarship on religion and international relations has arisen in which war, violence, and security are central topics. This strand of study remains small in proportion to newspaper headlines.

Why did not International Relations (IR) scholars study religion prior to this period? How does the absence and then the appearance of scholarship on religion in international politics correspond to historical reality? What themes, theses, and prescriptions for policy have emerged?

19.1 The Rise and Fall of Secularism in International Relations

Why has religion arisen recently in IR thought? The better question may be: Why was it absent in the first place? Religion scholar Martin Riesebrodt has written in his recent book, *The Promise of Salvation* (2011: xiii, 19), that "[r]eligion's promise ... remains astonishingly constant in different historical periods and cultures." He elaborates, "[a] ll humans belong to the same species" and manifest "universal characteristics ... and thus are not arbitrarily or infinitely variable or unbridgeably different." Arguably, then, what needs to be explained is the rise of a historically anomalous outlook that denies the reality and relevance of religion.

That outlook is the secularization thesis, one of the central themes in modern Western thought and politics. Secular—or secularism or secularization—has many meanings (Philpott 2009: 185). The one that confronts religion most sharply—history's most influential antithesis to religion—holds that religion is an irrational atavism receding in its influence on human affairs and destined to disappear in the face of modernity's inexorable forces: science, economic progress, free inquiry, technological advancement, political liberalization, and democratization. Originating in the Enlightenment, the theory seemed to have triumphed in the late 1960s when the cover of *Time* magazine read "Is God Dead?" and when Peter Berger, one of the great sociologists of the past generation, told the *New York Times* that by "the 21st century, religious believers are likely to be found only in small sects, huddled together to resist a worldwide secular culture" (Berger 1968).

IR theory has been secular from its origins. The founders of both the realist and liberal traditions (see Doyle 1997) built their theories around their view that religion's influence on politics was in decline. Niccolo Machiavelli, Hobbes, Jean-Jacques Rousseau, John

Locke, Adam Smith, and Immanuel Kant all viewed the state as a distinct body politic—a Leviathan, Hobbes called it—that was constituted apart from religion and was free from ecclesiastical authority from without and superior to such authority within. They viewed the purpose of the state not in the way that medieval thinkers like Thomas Aquinas had viewed it—inculcating virtue or preserving the Church—but rather in terms of what Cardinal Richelieu called *Raison d'Etat*. For realists, this included security and power, defined in terms of military capacity, wealth, land, population, and other hard resources. Liberals, too, counseled these ends, but thought them achievable through international norms and institutions, free commerce, and liberal democratic governance. Early International Relations theorists did not merely depict a world of politics without religion but also prescribed and celebrated it. Machiavelli saw religion as enfeebling while the later thinkers saw it as the cause of wars across Europe and thus something to be tamed. They placed morality on a foundation of reason, not revelation. Rousseau went so far as to recommend the invention of a civic religion that would buttress the state and to advocate the death penalty for violating its precepts (Rousseau 1994: 223).

All of these secular commitments persist in modern IR theory, both liberal and realist. Hans Morgenthau, perhaps the leading realist of the twentieth century, held that politics is not and could not be pursued in religious terms. In 1962, he wrote that:

> The moral problem of politics is posed by the inescapable discrepancy between the commands of Christian teaching, of Christian ethics, and the requirements of political success. It is impossible, if I may put it in somewhat extreme and striking terms, to be a successful politician and a good Christian. (Morgenthau 1962: 102)

Steeped in the thought of Friedrich Nietzsche, Morgenthau posited power as the central category in international politics and prescribed that statecraft be pursued through a form of consequentialism, "the morality of the national interest." Religious actors and ideas were either irrelevant or inimical to this pursuit.

The secularism of IR thought corresponded to the onset and expansion of secularism in global politics. The Peace of Westphalia of 1648 is iconic. Although scholars disagree about whether Westphalia was the origin of the modern international system (see Krasner 1993; Philpott 2001; Osiander 2001; Nexon 2009; de Carvalho et al. 2011), the surrounding century was one in which the states system was consolidated as secular. By Westphalia, the sovereign state had become the predominant form of political authority in Europe while the transnational temporal authority of the Catholic Church was sharply curtailed. Following Westphalia, religiously motivated interventions saw a sharp diminuendo. Within states, both Catholic and Protestant, there arose Erastianism, the subordinating of churches to state authority. The rise of nationalism directed popular loyalties away from religion and toward "faith in the nation," as the title of Anthony Marx's book put it (Marx, 2003). Secularism deepened with the French Revolution, which, following Rousseau's script, created for the first time a regime that rejected Christianity and sought to strip the Church even of its own ecclesial authority. Parties and regimes inspired by the revolution carried this secularism into the nineteenth and twentieth centuries and triumphed in France, Italy, several Latin American countries, Mexico in the 1920s, and certain European colonies, among other places. In the twentieth century, Communist regimes and Nazi Germany advanced hostility to religion to levels as yet unseen. After the Second World War, a transnational network of secular leaders in postcolonial regimes in the Arab world as well as Kenya, Indonesia, Iran, and Sri Lanka, sought to place their countries' politics on a secular footing (Shah and Philpott 2011: 37–46).

It was right around the time that Berger and *Time* magazine proclaimed the death of religion that, in retrospect, secularism had reached its peak and the resurgence of religion's influence in global politics began. Beginning in the late 1960s, a sharp growth in political activity took place in every major religion in every area of the world. A global Islamic resurgence, the rise of Jewish nationalism after the Six Day War, the political engagement of the Catholic Church following the Second Vatican Council, the rise of Hindu and Buddhist nationalism, the rise of the Religious Right in the United States, the growth of Christianity in China, religious terrorism, religious civil war, and religion's important role in the "third wave" of democratization all exemplified the trend. Through these events, religious engagement in politics rose, or, to turn the matter on its head again, secularism fell.

In 1998, Peter Berger humbly retracted his prediction of 30 years earlier, declaring that "the world today … is as furiously religious as it ever was" (Berger 1999: 2). By then, a small body of scholarship on religion in global politics—little of it by political scientists—had appeared, covering topics like fundamentalism, religious nationalism, desecularization, and Islam (Rapaport 1984; Marty and Appleby 1991, 1993, 1994, 1995; Little 1991; Juergensmeyer 1993; Casanova 1994; Esposito 1999). What brought religion into political science—explosively at that—was Samuel Huntington's *Foreign Affairs* article (1993) and then trade press book (1996) holding that a "clash of civilizations" based on religious identities would define major conflicts in global politics in the coming historical era. Huntington's thesis was debated furiously around the world in embassies, universities, and the media. Whatever the merits or shortcomings of his argument, Huntington had perceived religion's resurgence in global politics at a time when few other political scientists had. Over the next decade, a group of other political science IR scholars challenged the secularization thesis and sought to adumbrate frameworks for studying religion (Fox 2001; Philpott 2001; Fox 2002; Petitio and Hatzopoulos 2003; Fox and Sandler 2004; Thomas 2004; Philpott 2007; Hurd 2008). During that same decade, the attacks of September 11 took place, seemingly vindicating Huntington and establishing beyond doubt the relevance of religion to IR and to international security in particular.

19.2 Recent Scholarship on Religion and Security

What are some of the themes in this emergent area of inquiry? Most of the scholarship grapples in one way or another with religion's relationship to armed conflict: war, especially civil war, and terrorist violence. A few scholars pose the question in the widest way, asking whether religion is inherently violent. Proponents of a strong form of the secularization theory persist, holding that religion is violent by nature. A group of writers who attained popularity as the "new atheists" hold this view (Harris 2005; Dawkins 2006; Dennett 2006; Hitchens 2007). Theologian William Cavanaugh (2009) identifies a group of other scholars who hold the view and summarizes their explanation for religion's violence: religion is irrational, inherently divisive, and absolute.

Cavanaugh takes issue, though, arguing against what he calls the "myth of religious violence." The myth, he explains, is the idea that "religion is a transhistorical and transcultural feature of human life, essentially distinct from 'secular' features such as politics and economics, which has a peculiarly dangerous inclination to promote violence" (Cavanaugh 2009: 3). The lesson of the myth is that religion must be marginalized in order to keep safe the secular nation state, which is natural and stable.

Demurring, Cavanaugh challenges the notion that religion is a general phenomenon of which there are separate types as well as the distinction between religious and secular violence, which he finds incoherent. What is considered religion and what is considered secular differs from setting to setting and results from different configurations of power. The configuration behind the myth of religious violence is the rise of the Western state, which supplanted religious authority in early modern Europe and propounded the myth of religious violence to legitimate its authority. The secular state and its attendant ideologies, though, have proven just as absolute, divisive, and irrational as religion has been alleged to be. Cavanaugh conducts a close historical analysis of the "religious wars" of early modern Europe, by which secular liberals—and, recall, the early theorists of International Relations—justified the state and concludes that they were as much about political power, economics, and related causes as they were about religion (Cavanaugh 2009: 3–14).

Strong echoes of Cavanaugh can be found in the arguments of political analysts Jeroen Gunning and Richard Jackson, who question the concept of "religious terrorism," that has been so prominent in Western analysis since September 11. To Gunning and Jackson, the distinction between religion and secular terrorism is indefensible conceptually and empirically and serves to delegitimize "religious" actors while legitimizing questionable counter-terrorist policies (Gunning and Jackson 2011).

A broader range of scholars does not argue that religion is (or is not) inherently violent but rather views religion as a force with potential for both violence and peace and offers explanations for why it takes either form. Historian R. Scott Appleby (2000), for instance, argues for the "ambivalence of the sacred" and explores both religious violence and religious peacebuilding. Political scientist Jonathan Fox, one of the pioneering voices in the current wave of scholarship, identified in the Minorities at Risk dataset a subset of ethnic conflicts where the warring groups are of different religions and called them "ethnoreligious conflicts." In 2002, he identified 105 out of 268 disputes in the world, or 39 percent, as ethnoreligious (Fox 2002: 70–1). Political scientist Monica Duffy Toft (2007: 103), in her work on religious civil wars, shows that from 1940 to 2000, 42 out of 133 civil wars, or 32 percent, have involved religion. She divides these conflicts into two kinds: those in which religion shapes the identity of warring factions and those in which religion shapes the identity as well as the ends of these factions. Several scholars, contra Gunning and Jackson, have argued that religion fashions a unique form of terrorism, one that is performative and expressive rather than merely strategic, and is conducted as a divine duty, a cosmic war, or an apocalyptic struggle (Rapaport 1984; Ranstorp 1996; Hoffman 1998: 94–9; Juergensmeyer 2003; Stern 2003: 6–8; Moghadam 2008a, 2008b). For these scholars, religion is one form of violence and violence is one form of religion.

Some scholars in this category have offered innovative accounts of how religion shapes violence. One of the most creative of these is political scientist Ron Hassner, who, in his book, *War on Sacred Grounds* (2009), shows how religion, understood not just as theology but also as ritual, symbol, and community, renders sacred sites objects of armed conflict. In a successor book, *Religion on the Battlefield* (2016), Hassner depicts how religion shapes, enables, and constrains the very conduct of war. Into this category also falls religious studies scholar Michael Sells (1996), who shows how Yugoslavia's wars of the 1990s were sparked by "folk religion" that is theologically impoverished but rich in ritual, lore, and ethnicity and thus ripe for exploitation by bellicose demagogues. Of this type, too, is the work of Shane Barter and Ian Zatkin-Osburn, who study religious conflict in Southeast Asia through the religious credentials of rebel leaders, recruitment networks, public discourse, and, most innovatively, burial practices (Barter and Zatkin-Osburn 2014).

A common theme among this set of scholars is that religious violence has increased in recent decades. Bruce Hoffmann, arguably the leading scholar of religious terrorism, shows that while in 1968, all of the world's 11 terrorist groups were secular, religious terrorist groups appeared in the early 1980s and grew to 46 percent of the world's 56 terrorist groups by the mid-1990s (Hoffman 1998: 90–4). Political scientist Assaf Moghadam (2008a, 2008b) focuses on suicide terrorists and shows their religious motivation and their sharp expansion since their debut in 1981. Toft reports that religious civil wars have increased sharply in proportion to all civil wars from 19 percent of civil wars in the 1940s to 50 percent of civil wars in the 2000s (Toft 2006: 9). Peace scholar Isak Svensson likewise shows that religious civil wars have become increasingly common in the Middle East and North Africa (Svensson 2013).

Another common, yet also debated, thesis is that religious forms of violence are more severe than other forms. Toft, for instance, finds that religious civil wars result in more casualties and non-combatant deaths and last longer than non-religious civil wars (Toft 2007). Both Fox and political scientist Philip Roeder adduce quantitative evidence that religious conflicts are more intense (last longer, have more deaths) than non-religious conflicts (Roeder 2003; Fox 2004). Susanna Pearce's (2005), nuanced study of 278 territorial conflict phases shows that religious conflicts are more intense than other ones but also that the relationship disappears when religious goals are taken into account and that no religion manifests a higher or lower intensity than others. In like spirit, Svensson finds that religious wars are more difficult to resolve than civil wars, explains that the reason lies not in religious identities but rather in explicitly religious demands, and argues that religion nonetheless carries resources for conflict resolution (Svensson 2012,

2013). Political scientists Andreas Hasenclever and Volker Rittberger argue that religion carries a propensity to escalate conflicts by rendering them conflicts of values rather than interests, increasing the willingness of parties to make sacrifices, decreasing trust, and lowering the possibility of conflict resolution (Hasenclever and Rittberger 2000). Focusing on suicide terrorism, political scientist Peter Henne finds that religious ideology sharply increases the death toll of attacks even when terrorist groups' goals and organizational nature are controlled for (Henne 2012). Quite a different view than these, though, is that of political scientist Matthew Isaacs (2016), who confronted the question of why religious conflicts are comparatively more violent by studying the religious rhetoric of 495 political organizations from 1970 to 2012 and found that, in fact, previous engagement in violence makes religious rhetoric more likely and not the reverse. For Isaacs, religion is more an instrument than an initiator.

A version of this debate—one that is more hotly contested in the public sphere—is whether Islam in particular is prone to violence. Toft (2006: 15, 2007: 113–14), for instance, reports that one or both parties were Muslim in 34 of 42, or 81 percent, of religious civil wars; that 58 percent of all states that have fought civil wars have majority Muslim populations; and that 9 out of 10 religious civil wars fought between groups of the same faith have involved Muslims. Fox (2004: 68) also reports that conflict rose among Muslims during the 1990s. Toft (2007) attributes the disproportionate presence of Islam to the absence of internal war on the scale of the early modern religious wars, which brought tolerance to Christianity; the nearness of Islam's holiest sites to both Israel and to vast oil reserves; and the presence of jihadist ideology. In a separate piece, Toft and Yuri Zhukov (2015) showed that in the North Caucasus, Salafi-Jihadi militant groups were more difficult to defeat than nationalist rebel groups in good part because the ideology of the Islamists linked them to transnational sources of support. My own research (Philpott 2007: 520) found in that in 2007, 91 percent of all religious terrorist groups were radical Islamist ones.

Other scholars, though, argue that Islam itself is not the source of greater violence. In a study of casualties resulting from terrorist attacks, political scientist James Piazza (2009) discovers that death rates are more attributable to groups' organizational structures and goals than to their ideology or religion. Namely, groups with universal and abstract goals inflict more casualties than ones with concrete, strategic goals. On the same side of the debate, Indra de Soysa and Ragnhild Nordås (2007) show that Muslim societies actually experience lower levels of terrorism than others, that location in the Arab region explains what appears to be due to Islam, and that Catholic societies experience the worst levels of terrorism among populations defined by religiosity.

Finally, among the scholarship that views religion as diverse in its behaviors is an effort to explain the "political ambivalence" of religion by identifying two influences on the behavior of religious actors (Philpott 2007; Toft et al. 2011). First is the institutional independence of political and religious authority, which is roughly a combination of religious freedom and separation of religion and state (see Fox 2008). The second is political theology, or the doctrines about political authority and justice that religious actors derive from their more foundational theology. Religious actors who enjoy institutional independence and who hold a political theology that favors liberalism, democracy, reconciliation, or a restrictive doctrine of war are more likely to take action in favor of democracy, peacemaking, or reconciliation. By contrast, religious actors who practice little institutional independence from their state—either through being marginalized from or acting in close collaboration with the state—and who espouse a political theology that favors violence or religious authoritarianism are more prone to undertake violence or to support dictatorship.

Supportive of this theory is the work of social scientists who demonstrate a relationship between the denial of religious freedom and religious violence (Grim and Finke, 2011; Saiya 2015, 2015). Brian J. Grim and Roger Finke (2011: 70–87), for instance, show that "government restriction of religion" as well as the restriction of religion on the part of non-state actors beget violent persecution. Nilay Saiya shows how states which hinder religious freedom contribute to four kinds of violence—domestic religious terrorism, international religious terrorism, religious civil wars, and interstate conflicts—while states that favor religious freedom are far less prone to such violence. Thus, Saiya argues, we can speak of a "religious freedom peace" (2015: title).

19.3 Religious Freedom: A Normative Lesson?

The religious freedom peace: might this be a normative lesson, a policy prescription to emerge from the recent wave of scholarship on religion and security? It is surely not the only such lesson but it is one that is linked closely with the analyses in this scholarship (for a thoughtful piece on the ethics of religion and violence, see Lynch 2014). A human right that protects the religious belief and practice of persons and communities, religious freedom entails an enduring, principled commitment to respect and share citizenship with people of different religions and of different views toward the same religion. Were religious freedom ensconced in law, institutions, culture, and the teachings of religious traditions themselves, might it serve as an antidote to religious violence and intolerance?

Religious freedom is ensconced in international norms and law, including the Universal Declaration of Human Rights, the International Covenant on Civil and Political Rights, and other conventions. In 1998, the United States Congress overwhelmingly passed the International Religious Freedom Act, which created a standing foreign policy apparatus, including an ambassador-at-large, to promote religious freedom around the world. In more recent years, the European Union, the United Kingdom, Austria, Germany, Italy, the Netherlands, Norway, and Canada have adopted religious freedom into their foreign policies in one way or another (though Canada has just reversed course). All of these laws and policies are vehicles through which religious freedom has been and might be further widened. But they are not without controversy.

ve of critics of religious freedom have arisen from the academy, promi- m political scientist Elizabeth Shakman Hurd, whose 2008 book, *The rism in International Relations*, stands as one of the central contribu- nt revival of religion in IR scholarship. There, she criticized the field secularism and marginalization of religion. In her more recent work (2015), she criticizes religious freedom proponents for committing the opposite error: privileging religion analytically and promoting religious freedom politically to the exclusion of all else. Hurd has also co-edited a volume containing 27 statements from a variety of scholars in this same school (Sullivan et al. 2015). Let us call these scholars the "new critics of religious freedom" (see also Mahmood 2016).

Though the arguments of the new critics are wide-ranging, their views can be summarized in four propositions. First, religious freedom differs so strongly in its meanings across time and place that there simply is no single thing to which everyone has a right. A strong implication is that Westerners ought not to render universal what is in fact their own parochial principle. Second, what accounts for how religious freedom is defined in this or that place is rather the power and the interests of those doing the defining. Running through the new critics' writings is the imprint of philosopher Michel Foucault and his view that principles and knowledge are forms of power. Several of the new critics hold that religious freedom is a tool of American as well as Christian power. Third, modern religious freedom is a product of particular developments in Western history, especially the Protestant Reformation and the secularization that followed in its wake. This view, many of the critics derive from anthropologist Talal Asad (see 1993, 2003). Like Asad and echoing Cavanaugh, they believe that the concept of religion and the principle of religious freedom are products of modernity. Fourth is a prescription: Westerners ought not to export religious freedom.

These propositions, though, admit of criticism. With respect to the first proposition, numerous thinkers, both past and contemporary, have defended the universality of religion as a human phenomenon and the validity of religious freedom as a basic human right. Though the new critics point to diverse expressions of religion and views of religious freedom, it does not follow from this diversity that defensible versions of these principles do not exist.

The second proposition, that religious freedom is a product and tool of power, is difficult to square with the reality of global power. The United States, than whom no state is more powerful or more committed to religious freedom, thus far has marginalized religious freedom in its foreign policy, regularly subordinating it to security and economic interests. To the degree that the US and other Western powers do promote religious freedom, they do so on behalf of powerless religious minorities, on whose behalf there is little incentive for anyone to advocate.

The third claim, that religious freedom is a product of modern Western history, is subject to scrutiny as well. Religious freedom long pre-dates the Protestant Reformation and Enlightenment and was espoused by early Christian thinkers like Lactantius and Tertullian (Shah 2015). Its history is fraught, too, in the modern West, where the French Revolution and its successor movements sharply curtailed the freedom of the Catholic

Church and the Soviet Union and Nazi Germany violated religious freedom more tha. any other regime in all of history. Religious freedom can be found in non-Christian religions as well, as in the Quran's injunction, "Let there be no compulsion in religion."

From this analysis follows a conclusion that takes issue with the fourth proposition: there is no reason why states should refrain from promoting religious freedom beyond their borders. Arguably there are advantages to promoting it multilaterally and integrating with other foreign policy and security goals. If the analysis of Saiya (2015), Toft et al. (2011), and others (Farr 2008) is correct, there is a complementarity to be realized between religious freedom and the reduction of terrorism and armed conflict, the settlement of civil wars, and the promotion of democracy.

19.4 Into the Future?

Is the study of religion and international security here to stay? Yes, as long as religion's engagement with politics is here to stay. There are reasons to believe that this is the case. Recall that I turned the puzzle of religious resurgence on its head. People have always been religious and are still so. A 2012 study by the Pew Research Center showed that in 2010, 84 percent of the world's population was affiliated with a religion. What needs to be accounted for is why an ideology that forcibly supplanted religion's role in politics encountered decline.

Ironically, the forces that have laid low secularist regimes are some of the very ones that secularization theorists predicted would bring down religion: political openness, the free exchange of ideas, and the advance of technology. The regimes that have suppressed religion have typically been brutal dictatorships—necessarily so, for they have ruled over populations that are usually far more religious. The Republic of Turkey, for instance, was founded in 1923 as a strongly secularist regime based on nationalism and modernization, and for decades repeatedly overturned elections that returned majorities for Muslim parties. Finally, in 2002, Turkey took a stride toward democracy by allowing the Justice and Development Party, an Islamic party, to govern after it won a national election. More generally, the secular ideologies of the "Bandung Generation" of the 1950s and 1960s and of Communist regimes around the world in the twentieth century have been drained of prestige by economic stagnation, corruption, and popular weariness with the denial of freedom. A global wave of democratization beginning around 1974 has created space for religious movements to ply their political wares.

Religiously-based politics has also thrived on modern travel, communication technology, and the global increase in flows of people and ideas across borders. Pope John Paul II's global travels, for instance, often placed him in a position to challenge dictatorships. Al Qaeda has made strong use of cell phones and computers. Jewish and Hindu diaspora populations in the United States use media and the Internet to support religious nationalism in Israel and India. Empowered by globalization and modernization, politically engaged religious actors have become transnational ones.

modernization, and democratization are here to stay, whatever their als. Under these conditions, religious people will not remain confined and worship but will strive to influence their societies and their gov- and for ill, and will insist on the freedom to do so. There will remain ...n, for scholars of religion and global politics.

References

Appleby, R. S. 2000. *The Ambivalence of the Sacred: Religion, Violence, and Reconciliation*. Lanham, MD: Rowman & Littlefield.

Asad, T. 1993. *Genealogies of Religion: Discipline and Reasons of Power in Christianity and Islam*. Baltimore, MD: The Johns Hopkins University Press.

Asad, T. 2003. *Formations of the Secular: Christianity, Islam, Modernity*. Stanford, CA: Stanford University Press.

Barter, S. and I. Zatkin-Osburn. 2014. Shrouded: Islam, War, and Holy War in Southeast Asia. *Journal for the Scientific Study of Religion*, 53(1): 187–201.

Berger, P. L. 1968. A Bleak Outlook is Seen For Religion. *New York Times*, Sunday February 25, p. 3.

Berger, P. L. 1999. The Desecularization of the World: An Overview. In P. L. Berger, *The Desecularization of the World: Resurgent Religion and World Politics*. Washington, DC: Eerdmans/Ethics and Public Policy Center.

Bill, J. A. 1988. *The Eagle and the Lion: The Tragedy of American–Iranian Relations*. New Haven, CT: Yale University Press.

Bosco, R. M. 2014. *Securing the Sacred: Religion, National Security, and the Western State*. Ann Arbor, MI: University of Michigan Press.

de Carvalho, Benjamin, Halvard Leira, and John Hobson 2011. The Myths that Your Teachers Still Tell You about 1648 and 1919. *Millennium*, 39(3): 735–58.

Casanova, J. 1994. *Public Religions in the Modern World*. Chicago, IL: University of Chicago Press.

Cavanaugh, W. C. 2009. *The Myth of Religious Violence: Secular Ideology and the Roots of Conflict*. Oxford: Oxford University Press.

Dawkins, R. 2006. *The God Delusion*. Boston, MA: Houghton Mifflin Co.

Dennett, D. C. 2006. *Breaking the Spell: Religion as a Natural Phenomenon*. New York: Viking.

Doyle, M. 1997. *Ways of War and Peace: Realism, Liberalism, and Socialism*. New York: W.W. Norton.

Esposito, J. 1999. *The Islamic Threat: Myth or Reality?* Oxford: Oxford University Press.

Farr, T. 2008. *World of Faith and Freedom: Why International Religious Liberty is Vital to American Security*. Oxford: Oxford University Press.

Fox, J. 2001. Religion: An Oft Overlooked Element of International Studies. *International Studies Review*, 3(3): 53–73.

Fox, J. 2002. *Ethnoreligious Conflict in the Late 20th Century: A General Theory*. Lanham, MD: Lexington Books.

Fox, J. 2004. Religion and State Failure: An Examination of the Extent and Magnitude of Religious Conflict from 1950 to 1996. *International Political Science Review*, 25(1): 55–76.

Fox, J. 2008. *A World Survey of Religion and the State*. Cambridge: Cambridge University Press.

Fox, J. and S. Sandler. 2004. *Bringing Religion into International Relations*. New York: Palgrave-Macmillan.

Grim, Brian J. and R. Finke. 2011. *The Price of Freedom Denied: Religious Persecution and Conflict in the Twenty-First Century.* Cambridge: Cambridge University Press.

Gunning, J. and R. Jackson. 2011. What's So "Religious" About "Religious" Terrorism? *Critical Studies on Terrorism*, 4(3): 369–88.

Harris, S. 2005. *The End of Faith: Religion, Terror, and the Future of Reason.* New York: W.W. Norton.

Hasenclever, A. and V. Rittberger. 2000. Does Religion Make a Difference? Theoretical Approaches to the Impact of Faith on Political Conflict. *Millenium: Journal of International Studies*, 29(3): 654–9.

Hassner, R. E. 2009. *War on Sacred Grounds.* Ithaca, NY: Cornell University Press.

Hassner, R. E. 2016. *Religion on the Battlefield.* Ithaca, NY: Cornell University Press.

Henne, P. S. 2012. The Ancient Fire: Religion and Suicide Terrorism. *Terrorism and Political Violence*, 24(1): 38–60.

Hitchens, C. 2007. *God is Not Great: How Religion Poisons Everything.* New York: Twelve.

Hoffman, B. 1998. *Inside Terrorism.* New York: Columbia University Press.

Huntington, S. P. 1993. The Clash of Civilizations? *Foreign Affairs*, 72(3): 22–49.

Huntington, S. P. 1996. *The Clash of Civilizations and the Remaking of World Order.* New York: Simon and Schuster.

Hurd, E. S. 2008. *The Politics of Secularism in International Relations.* Princeton, NJ: Princeton University Press.

Hurd, E. S. 2015. *Beyond Religious Freedom: The New Global Politics of Religion.* Princeton, NJ: Princeton University Press.

Isaacs, M. 2016. Sacred Violence or Strategic Faith? Disentangling the Relationship between Religion and Violence in Armed Conflict. *Journal of Peace Research*, 53(2): 211–25.

Juergensmeyer, M. 1993. *The New Cold War? Religious Nationalism Confronts the Secular State.* Berkeley, CA: University of California Press.

Juergensmeyer, M. 2003. *Terror in the Mind of God: The Global Rise of Religious Violence.* Berkeley, CA: University of California Press.

Kimball, C. 2002. *When Religion Becomes Evil.* San Francisco, CA: Harper.

Krasner, S. D. 1993. Westphalia and All That. In J. Goldstein and R. O. Keohane (eds.), *Ideas and Foreign Policy: Beliefs, Institutions, and Political Change*, pp. 253–64. Ithaca, NY: Cornell University Press.

Little, D. 1991. *Ukraine: The Legacy of Intolerance.* Washington, DC: United States Institute of Peace.

Lynch, C. 2014. A Neo-Weberian Approach to Studying Religion and Violence. *Millennium: Journal of International Studies*, 43(1): 273–90.

Mahmood, S. 2016. *Religious Difference in a Secular Age: A Minority Report.* Princeton, NJ: Princeton University Press.

Marty, M. E. and R. S. Appleby. 1991. *Fundamentalisms Observed.* Chicago, IL: University of Chicago Press.

Marty, M. E. and R. S. Appleby. 1993. *Fundamentalisms and the State: Remaking Polities, Economies, and Militance.* Chicago, IL: University of Chicago Press.

Marty, M. E. and R. S. Appleby. 1994. *Accounting for Fundamentalisms: The Dynamic Character of Movements.* Chicago, IL: University of Chicago Press.

Marty, M. E. and R. S. Appleby. 1995. *Fundamentalisms Comprehended.* Chicago, IL: University of Chicago Press.

Marx, A.W. 2003. *Faith in Nation: The Exclusionary Origins of Nationalism.* New York: Oxford University Press.

008a. Motives for Martyrdom: Al-Qaida, Salafi Jihad, and the Spread of *International Security*, 33(3): 46–78.

008b. *The Globalization of Martyrdom: Al Qaeda, Salafi Jihad, and the de Attacks*. Baltimore, MD: The Johns Hopkins University Press.

962. The Influence of Reinhold Niebuhr in American Political Life and ght. In H. R. Landon (ed.), *Reinhold Niebuhr: A Prophetic Voice of Our Time*, pp. 97–110. Greenwich, CT: Seabury Press.

Nexon, D. 2009. *The Struggle for Power in Early Modern Europe: Religious Conflict, Dynastic Empires, and International Change*. Princeton, NJ: Princeton University Press.

Osiander, A. 2001. Sovereignty, International Relations, and the Westphalian Myth. *International Organization*, 55(2): 251–87.

Pearce, S. 2005. Religious Rage: A Quantitative Analysis of the Intensity of Religious Conflicts. *Terrorism and Political Violence*, 17(3): 333–52.

Petitio, F. and P. Hatzopoulos (eds.). 2003. *Religion in International Relations: The Return from Exile*. New York: Palgrave.

Pew Research Center 2012. *The Global Religious Landscape: A Report on the Size and Distribution of the World's Major Religious Groups as of 2010*. Washington, DC: Pew Research Center.

Philpott, D. 2001. *Revolutions in Sovereignty: How Ideas Shaped Modern International Relations*. Princeton, NJ: Princeton University Press.

Philpott, D. 2007. Explaining the Political Ambivalence of Religion. *American Political Science Review*, 101(3): 505–25.

Philpott, D. 2009. Has the Study of Global Politics Found Religion? In M. Levi, S. Jackman, R. and Rosenblum (eds.), *Annual Review of Political Science*, Volume 12. Palo Alto CA: Annual Reviews.

Piazza J. A. 2009. Is Islamist Terrorism more Dangerous?: An Empirical Study of Group Ideology, Organization and Goal Structure. *Terrorism and Political Violence*, 21(1): 62–88.

Ranstorp, M. 1996. Terrorism in the Name of Religion. *Journal of International Affairs*, 50(1): 41–60.

Rapaport, D. 1984. Fear and Trembling: Terrorism in Three Religious Traditions. *American Political Science Review*, 78(3): 658–77.

Riesebrodt, M. 2011. *The Promise of Salvation: A Theory of Religion*. Trans. S. Rendall. Chicago, IL: University of Chicago Press.

Roeder, Philip G. 2003. Clash of Civilizations and Escalation of Domestic Ethnopolitical Conflicts. *Comparative Political Studies* , 36(5): 509–40.

Rousseau, J. J. 1994. The Social Contract. In R. D. Masters and C. Kelly (eds.), *The Collected Writings of Rousseau*, Volume 4. Trans. J. R. Bush, R. D. Masters, and Kelly C. Hanover. NH: Dartmouth College and the University Press of New England.

Saiya, N. 2015. The Religious Freedom Peace. *The International Journal of Human Rights*, (19)3: 369–82.

Saiya, N. and Scime, A. 2015. Explaining Religious Terrorism: A Data-mined Analysis. *Conflict Management and Peace Science*, (32)5: 487–512.

Sells, M. A. 1996. *The Bridge Betrayed: Religions and Genocide in Bosnia*. Berkeley, CA: University of California Press.

Shah, T. S. 2015. The First Enlightenment: The Patristic Roots of Religious Freedom. In D. A. Yerxa (ed.), *Religion and Innovation: Antagonists or Partners?*, pp. 59–73. London and New York: Bloomsbury Academic.

Shah, T. and D. Philpott. 2011. The Fall and Rise of Religion in International Relations: Histor and Theory. In J. Snyder (ed.), *Religion and International Relations Theory*, pp. 24–59. New York: Columbia University Press.

Snyder, J. (ed.) 2011. *Religion and International Relations Theory*. New York: Columbia University Press.

de Soysa, I. and R. Nordås. 2007. Islam's Bloody Innards? Religion and Political Terror, 1980–2000. *International Studies Quarterly*, (51)4: 927–43.

Stern, Jessica 2003. *Terror in the Name of God: Why Religious Militants Kill*. New York: Harper Collins.

Su, A. 2016. *Exporting Freedom: Religious Liberty and American Power*. Cambridge, MA: Harvard University Press.

Sullivan, W. F., E. S. Hurd, S. Mahmood, and P. G. Danchin. 2015. *Politics of Religious Freedom*. Chicago, IL: University of Chicago Press.

Svensson, I. 2012. *Ending Holy Wars: Religion and Conflict Resolution in Civil Wars*. St Lucia, Qld: University of Queensland Press.

Svensson, I. 2013. One God, Many Wars: Religious Dimensions of Armed Conflict in the Middle East and North Africa. *Civil Wars*, 15(4): 411–30.

Thomas, S. 2004. *The Global Resurgence of Religion and the Transformation of International Relations: The Struggle for the Soul of the Twenty-First Century*. New York: Palgrave Macmillan.

Toft, M. D. 2006. Religion, Civil War, and International Order. Belfer Center for Science and International Affairs Discussion Paper 2006-03, July.

Toft, M. D. 2007. Getting Religion? The Puzzling Case of Islam and Civil War. *International Security*, 31(4): 97–131.

Toft. M. D. and Y. M. Zhukov. 2015. Islamists and Nationalists: Rebel Motivation and Counterinsurgency in Russia's North Caucasus. *American Political Science Review*, 109(2): 222–38.

Toft, M. D., D. Philpott, and T. Samuel Shah. 2011. *God's Century: Resurgent Religion in Global Politics*. New York: W.W. Norton.

CHAPTER 20

THE FUTURE OF INTERNATIONAL SECURITY NORMS

LESLIE VINJAMURI

Perhaps never more than before, the time is ripe for debating the future of international norms. Contemporary politics have proved to be a trigger for renewed public debate on a topic that has garnered significant scholarly attention for a long time. Many people are asking whether the foundations of the international liberal order—both institutional and normative—are at risk of disintegrating. Norms that govern international security are at the heart of this order. In the past three decades, especially, moral, legal, and ethical considerations have been taken seriously, from the expectation that decisions about the use of force should be taken collectively, to the assumption that war should be designed to minimize civilian casualties, that states have a responsibility to stop perpetrators of mass atrocities, and that those who try to kill in this way should be prosecuted for their crimes. States are often strategic in their embrace of norms, but few states and even fewer democracies, have openly contested the sanctity of this normative context.

Today, many fear that the greatest threat to liberalism rests not in the erosion of formal institutions, but in the risk that contemporary politics in the West poses for norms that are integral to the liberal international order. Contemporary expressions of alarm may merely be hyperbolic. US Presidents have more autonomy in the foreign policy arena than at home, but sceptics may be right: a single individual seems unlikely to create a major shift in international norms, even when that individual is the leader of a major power like the United States.

Indeed, how one understands norm creation and normative change will shape expectations about the future. Theories of norms may offer some insights into the future of international security norms. International Relations (IR) scholars commonly define norms as collectively shared expectations of appropriate behavior in a particular area of international politics held by actors who share a common identity (e.g. Katzenstein 1996). Norms governing the use of economic sanctions, military force, and specific categories of weapons, and those for rebuilding post-conflict states and dealing with questions of responsibility and accountability for mass atrocities have taken on a more central role in the international liberal order. The demand for civilian protection and for discrimination between combatants and non-combatants has permeated many dimensions of international security. The norm that states should be responsible for preventing atrocities and also protecting their people from atrocities has grown in prominence alongside the demand that individuals (and not states) should be held accountable for crimes against humanity, genocide and war crimes.

This chapter considers the future of some of the dominant international security norms that underpin contemporary international politics. First it surveys the dominant international security norms that have defined the post-Cold War era. Many if not most of these have roots in the interwar period or in the years following the Second World War if not earlier. Next it considers theoretical arguments about the sources of norms and normative change. Finally, it considers prospects for the future in light of theoretical arguments about normative change. A key question for the future is whether the backlash against efforts to infuse security policies with humanitarian and human rights norms, the reluctance by states to enforce these norms, and the rise of new powers that do not embrace these norms will lead to a substantial erosion of existing norms.

20.1 Normative Contestation after the Cold War

Normative contestation in the security arena has been a constant feature of the post-Cold War era. Some depict a different story, arguing that backlash is a natural concomitant of progress and has no meaningful or lasting impact (Dancy and Sikkink 2017). Others argue that efforts to introduce moral and ethical concerns into the security arena have subsequently constrained state power even when such measures were initially adopted for strategic purposes (Sagan 2016). Those more skeptical have argued that authoritarian states have pursued a variety of strategies to circumvent liberal norms (Cooley and Schaaf 2017).

In the 1990s, security norms were infused with human rights and humanitarian standards in response to internal wars that broke out in Somalia, Yugoslavia, Rwanda, East Timor, Kosovo, and beyond. This was not without a rigorous debate about the legitimacy and legality of humanitarian intervention (Moore 1998; Buchanan 1999; Henkin, 1999; Wheeler 2000; Holzgrefe and Keohane 2003; Bellamy 2007). The notion that security stopped where sovereignty began was openly contested and l for a recasting of the sovereignty norm (Duke 1994; ICISS 2001; ren and Sylvan 2002; Macklem 2008). The decade following the ıcks was marked by intense normative contestation between offi- d scholars who adopted different positions about the optimal bal- ..onal security on the one hand, and civil liberties and human rights on the other (Rejali 2003, 2009; Ackerman 2004, 2006; Joyner 2004; Gearty 2005, 2010; Cole and Dempsey 2006; Sanders 2011; Sikkink 2012; David 2016). A long-simmering debate about the BRICS (Brazil, Russia, India, China, and South Africa), especially China, the decline of American power, and Russia's new place in the international order was the structural backdrop for the immediate events that provoked intense debate about specific norms and policies (Jervis 1982; Wohlforth 1999; Buzan 2010; Ikenberry 2011; Kurowska 2014; Stephen 2014).

A third period, one that began with the financial crisis in 2008, has inspired a different kind of debate about international norms. The source of normative contestation had its origins more firmly in the domestic and regional politics of European liberal democracies and also the United States. The United Kingdom's vote to exit the European Union, followed a few months later by the election of Donald Trump has generated significant debate about the future of multilateralism and of the liberal international order (Walt 2016; Mead 2017). Trump campaigned on a platform that rejected America's long-standing commitment to providing security for Japan and South Korea; threatened to abandon NATO, the centerpiece of Western security since 1949; put human rights and democracy promotion at arms length; embraced the use of torture, including waterboarding, for terrorists; and refused to hold a firm line against Russia for its violation of the territorial integrity of Ukraine in its illegal annexation of Crimea. Within weeks of his inauguration, many analysts questioned whether the new administration had loosened the rules of engagement to make protecting civilians less of a priority (Kahl 2017). If the new US leadership showed a very certain disregard for specific commitments, it also seemed to reject the fundamental procedural norms that guided US policy since the end of the Second World War—most importantly a commitment to multilateralism in international security affairs, especially with respect to Europe, but also increasingly in Asia and beyond.

Some scholars and pundits have argued that a Trump presidency will bring a delayed adjustment to the new realities of American power which has not only declined in relative terms, but is also no longer defined by the imperative of balancing Soviet power (Posen 2014; Walt 2017). Adjustment is long overdue and reflects underlying structural changes brought about by the end of the Cold War. Institutions, and also norms, are sticky and change is often delayed. Others suggest that the liberal international order has taken on a life of its own, providing collective benefits and securing liberal norms and values by providing a framework for that enables states to work together on global problems. The advantages of liberal internationalism have and should endure long into the future (Keohane et al. 2009; Lindberg 2015; Patrick 2016; Risse 2016).

20.2 Security Norms: Multilateralism, Democracy Promotion, Civilian Protection, and Human Rights Trials

Norms governing international security can be grouped into different categories. I focus on four in particular that have been central to the post-Cold War era, but that may now be under severe threat: first, the norm that legitimacy is defined by multilateralism and, more specifically, some notion of collective consent especially but exclusively when it comes to using military force; second, the norm that democracy is critical for peace and stability, and that international organizations are a mechanism for consolidating democracy and, by extension, building a more stable world order; third, the norm that wars must be fought in ways that discriminate between civilians and combatants and that weapons must be regulated to reflect this imperative; and finally, a fourth basket of norms that has gained increasing prominence deals with the problem of enforcement against those who violate norms that protect civilians. The Responsibility to Protect talks about prevention and protection and the accountability norm underscores the need for trials of those who perpetrate mass atrocities (Bellamy 2009; Hurd 2011; Welsh 2016).

First among these is the norm that collective decision-making is key to the legitimacy of foreign policy decisions and that this is especially the case for decisions about the use of military force. Martha Finnemore (1996) argues that multilateralism has been especially important in giving legitimacy to humanitarian interventions. Even when formal institutional structures are circumvented, states have looked for alternative venues that allow them to secure collective legitimacy. In many cases, deadlock on the United Nations Security Council has prevented this body from achieving its mandate of sanctioning or denying the use of military force for international peace and security. Most famously, the Security Council authorized the use of a multinational force in 1990 when Iraq invaded Kuwait. In 2003, though, the United States, knowing it would not be able to secure a Security Council authorization, sought to build a coalition of the willing to give legitimacy to its invasion of Iraq (Franck 1990; Keohane 2006; Tago, 2007; Kreps 2008).

The multilateral norm has been especially strong when it comes to authorizing the use of force for humanitarian operations where there is no overwhelming or obvious national security interest and a general consensus exists that war is a matter of choice rather than necessity. Ethical and moral considerations have continued to shape expectations for best practices about how to fight wars and rebuild post-war states. Collective decision-making in the form of multilateralism, regionalism, or even coalitions of the willing has been taken as inherently more moral than unilateral resort to the use of force. And, despite the fact that the ability of the Security Council to act has often been impeded by China and Russia for reasons that have little to do with moral, ethical, or legal considerations, there continues to be a premium placed on securing the approval of the Security Council to authorize the decision to use military force.

A second basket of international security norms that has underpinned international and regional organizations links democracy and democracy promotion to peace and stability (Brzezinski 1995; Pevehouse 2002; Epstein 2005). In the post-Cold War era, the expectation among liberal states has been that existing organizations would be extended both in terms of their membership and their practices to help secure democracy not simply for its inherent value, but also for its role in building a more stable order. Once designed solely to protect the sovereignty and territoriality of member states by deterring external aggressors or building markets, the new post-Cold War expectation has been that existing international and regional organizations would now seek to assist new members in consolidating democracy at home (Gheciu 2005). Organizations like the OSCE (Organisation for Security and Cooperation in Europe) turned to election monitoring as one instrument for securing this new normative commitment.[1] NATO was extended to include multiple new members (Koremenos et al. 2001), and the UN authorized multiple new peacekeeping operations designed to reconfigure domestic institutions (Barnett and Finnemore 2004; Howard 2007; Sambanis 2008).

A third important set of norms is grounded in the principle of distinction (between civilians and combatants) in fighting wars and regulating weapons. This principle has guided campaigns to regulate different categories of weapons (Price 1998; Jefferson 2014). Some campaigns have met with more success than others. The Nonproliferation Treaty requires nuclear weapons states to work toward reducing and eliminating their nuclear arsenals, but few world leaders take seriously the idea that nuclear weapons should be destroyed in full. Nonetheless, Nina Tannenwald (1999) argues that there is a nuclear weapons taboo that explains the non-use of nuclear weapons by the United States since it dropped atomic bombs on Hiroshima and Nagasaki. (Others are more skeptical and argue that deterrence is a more apt explanation for the non-use of nuclear weapons in the post-war period.)

In many cases, weapons that are inherently indiscriminate have been subject to campaigns designed to galvanize support for a ban on their use. In 1997, the Convention prohibiting the use of chemical weapons came into force. That same year, the Ottawa Treaty, prohibiting the use of anti-personnel mines, was adopted (Price 1998). The turn to drone warfare has been justified in part on the assumption that drones have the ability to minimize not only risk to drone operators, but also to drastically curtail civilian deaths (ODNI 2016). Although this finding has been heavily contested by scholars such as Sarah Kreps and Geoffrey Wallace (2016), it continues to shape perceptions about drone usage and to guide decision-making.

The principle of distinction has also guided strategic decisions about fighting wars. Some scholars argue that support for the norm that civilian casualties must be limited and proportionate to the benefits of using military force has gained increasing force over the past four decades, especially in the United States. While norms of civilian distinction have a long history in just war theory, mechanisms for enforcing these norms have been adopted across many liberal democracies. One scholar argues that in the years following the Vietnam War, the US military placed a greater emphasis on training its forces in the laws of war, paying greater attention to civilian casualties (Kahl 2007). This corresponded with a decrease in the number of civilian deaths since Vietnam. Other scholars have also argued that the US military exercised "courageous restraint" in both Afghanistan and Iraq, attempting to reduce non-combatant deaths, when fighting wars of counterinsurgency. Although this was driven by legal and moral considerations, it also had the unintended and positive consequence of local populations sharing more information with US forces about insurgents (Rosen 2009; Rubinstein and Roznai 2011; Felter and Shapiro 2017).

A fourth basket of international "atrocities prevention and prosecution" norms designed to enforce and punish violators who intentionally kill civilians has developed rapidly during the post-Cold War period. Although these norms evolved over many years, they gained institutional backing in the 2000s. In 2002, prosecutorial norms became firmly embedded by the creation of the International Criminal Court (Bosco 2014; Hurd 2010; Schiff 2008). The expectation that individuals who committed the most heinous international crimes should be put on trial has been remarkably uncontested in principle. In practice, the pursuit of sitting heads of state alleged to be responsible for war crimes has generated an intense and sustained backlash, and has also been the subject of an intense scholarly debate about the effects of these measures on human rights, democracy, and peace (Snyder and Vinjamuri 2004; Kim and Sikkink 2010; Sikkink 2011; Jo and Simmons 2016; Snyder 2017; Vinjamuri 2017).

The adoption of the Responsibility to Protect (R2P) in 2005 was the culmination of a protracted period of debate about the standards and procedures that should govern humanitarian intervention, a debate that intensified after NATO's air campaign in Kosovo. R2P established guidelines for preventing crimes against humanity, genocide and other war crimes but also, importantly, for using military force to protect civilians who were subject to these crimes (Welsh 2016).

Each of these two norms has attempted to develop independent standards for evaluating the morality and legality of crimes and the necessity of action and also to anchor these in the decision-making authority of the Security Council (Bosco 2009). The prosecution norm has moved the idea of accountability away from the state and to the individual (Sikkink 2011). R2P instead recognizes the responsibility of the state to protect its people.

20.3 Normative Change: Drivers and Disruptors

What does IR scholarship tell us about the source of international norms? Two explanations stand out. The first looks to powerful states and their internal normative structures as key determinants of international security norms. Others emphasize the role of change-agents that actively seek to construct, diffuse, and consolidate new norms. Unlike explanations that stress state power and norms, change-agents do not merely seek to reflect existing norms. Instead, they seek to create new ones and may actively engage in trying to constrain the behavior of hegemonic powers as well as smaller states.

20.4 Rising Powers as Norm Disruptors

Scholars who place great emphasis on the role of hegemonic powers in constructing international norms have been especially attentive to the challenge posed by rising powers. Since Goldman Sachs released its study on the rise of Brazil, Russia, India, and China (the original BRICs as defined by Jim O'Neil of Goldman Sachs 2001) the threat posed by emerging powers has dominated public debate about the future of international politics. Hegemonic powers have the greatest ability to shape international norms, but emerging powers, even democratic ones, pose a threat to the stability of these norms. For example, India actively shuns the idea of intervening in the internal affairs of other states for human rights or humanitarian purposes.

Rising authoritarianism and the concomitant decline of democracy in Turkey and Russia also threaten to undermine existing normative frameworks. Turkey's crackdown on human rights may not have a significant impact on existing international norms, but it creates a significant barrier to any attempt to extend their geographical influence. Russia has actively engaged in a regional strategy of "counter norming," designed to circumvent and also undermine Western norms (Cooley and Schaaf 2017) and offering another example of how regional powers can block the geographical extension of important international norms. South Africa, also an important and influential regional power, has engaged in "strategic backlash," seeking to undermine existing norms of accountability embedded in the International Criminal Court (ICC) (Vinjamuri 2017). When Sudan's President Bashir, under arrest warrant by the ICC, visited South Africa, its government came under pressure to arrest him but refused to do so. South Africa later issued a statement indicating that pressure to arrest a sitting head of state undermined its own approach to the peaceful resolution of conflicts and attempted to withdraw from the ICC, but was later challenged by its own courts.

It is the rise of China, though, which has triggered an unparalleled fear and concern among many who note that China rejects liberal norms that are embraced by democracies across Europe and in the United States (Johnston 2003; Ikenberry 2008). Some scholars suggest that the implications for regional and global governance would be considerable if China were to replace the United States as the dominant power (Foot and Walter 2011; Clark 2014; Drezner 2014; Stephen 2014). China disregards human rights at home, and denies the legitimacy of humanitarian interventions abroad. Its seeming disregard for collective decision-making on matters concerning international peace and security presents a challenge to existing norms. Despite recent efforts to promote a regional bank for infrastructure projects (the Asian Infrastructure Investment Bank) and the Regional Comprehensive Economic Partnership, it has until very recently given scant attention to the idea of security cooperation in Asia. Despite issuing a recent white paper on the subject (Ministry of Foreign Affairs of the People's Republic of China 2017),

China's genuine commitment to collective security seems to be limited. On the global stage, China has been a reluctant partner, paying little regard for the United Nations Security Council as a forum for advancing significant initiatives.

20.5 Major Powers and Domestic Normative Shifts

Hegemons play a central role in determining which norms will shape international politics. Historically, liberal states were the most prominent supporters of international war crimes tribunals. This reflected their own domestic commitment to legalism (Bass 2002). Hegemonic powers have actively sought to socialize new states and elites in smaller powers have sometimes accepted these norms. Ikenberry and Kupchan (1990) have argued that projecting a set of norms is a key part of the hegemonic exercise of power.

One implication of this is that internal normative change in hegemonic powers can have dramatic reverberations abroad. Even in the context of a period of relative stability in the overall distribution of power, the potential for disruption and change is considerable. Domestic change can also alter the future course of international security norms.

John Ruggie (1983) wrote about the shift away from embedded liberalism, which triumphed in the post-war era. Embedded liberalism was marked by a shared commitment to the welfare state and to accommodations for labor. After the economic crisis of the 1970s, neoliberalism came to dominate. International institutions remained stable in a formal sense, but the dominant norms in the major powers were soon reflected in international institutions such as the World Bank and the International Monetary Fund (IMF).

Western liberal democracies have also been a locus of normative contestation on issues of war and peace, first during the global War on Terror, and more recently with the chain of events that began with the 2008 financial crisis and extended through a refugee crisis, the United Kingdom's vote to exit the European Union, and the election of Donald Trump. In each of these periods, leaders have adopted rhetoric and policies that have challenged dominant international security norms. This was most evident in the debate that emerged over the use of torture following the US invasion of Iraq (Gilligan and Nesbitt 2009; Gross 2010; Barnes 2016).

20.6 Transnational Networks and Normative Socialization

Transnational networks of civil society activists seek to disrupt the status quo by creating and consolidating new norms. Activist networks draw on symbolic politics and other forms of leverage to harness state power on behalf of a norm. International networks link up with local civil society actors, enabling these groups to circumvent the repressive politics of national governments and placing external power on these states to reform. This is the "boomerang effect" (Keck and Sikkink 1998). Risse, Ropp, and Sikkink in two volumes (published more than a decade apart) have developed a theory of how norms develop. Under pressure to conform, states pay lip service to norms, that allows other actors to draw on this language and pressure them to take norms more seriously. Eventually norms take on a life of their own and achieve a status where they are "taken for granted" (Risse et al. 1999 and 2013).

In their second volume, Risse and colleagues (2013) acknowledge that in many cases, norms do not progress beyond the initial phases of norms development. The lack of state capacity is one reason for this; norms that require states to have the ability to implement and enforce them lose traction where institutions are weak. A second impediment to the consolidation of new norms comes when states adopt national security narratives as a justification for undercutting human rights norms, for example, that threaten to impinge on state interests and autonomy. Both the United States and China have used national security as a mechanism for short changing human rights (Burke-White 2004; Schofer 2015; Human Rights Watch 2017).

Despite these qualifications, norm theories in IR have tended to underestimate the significance of backlash and counter-norming strategies. The future of norms depends crucially on whether norms adopted for strategic purposes have the unintended effect of constraining the future actions of those who designed them, or whether the backlash that norms inspire leads to their demise.

20.7 Technological Change

Technological change will continue to be one of the most potent disruptors of international security norms. In some cases, technology may increase expectations to comply with new security norms. By enhancing knowledge of atrocities, new technologies create political pressure to engage in humanitarian operations designed to protect those at risk (Axworthy and Dorn 2016). The rush to develop norms for regulating new technologies has often been driven by the desire to restrict access. This drive is more intense when technology is cheaper and easier to develop and therefore more likely to diffuse rapidly. The development of drone technology and the anticipated spread of this technology has galvanized efforts to develop the appropriate standards for drone use (Walzer 2016). This is complicated by the reality that many technologies can be deployed for multiple purposes (Kreps et al. 2017). Drones hold the potential not only to destroy, but also to support humanitarian operations.

Critics argue that drones have enabled the United States to move into a state of perpetual war and that drone technology makes it easier for states to violate the sovereignty norm by conducting sustained but low intensity warfare (Enemark 2014). But, drone usage is often justified on the basis that drones are highly discriminate and minimize civilian casualties, thereby bolstering existing normative frameworks. Other technologies, like autonomous weapons, create new challenges and opportunities (Horowitz 2016). Simply evaluating autonomous weapons systems on the basis of whether they have a greater ability to discriminate, as compared with the incidence of human error, is unlikely to be sufficient.

20.8 Are International Security Norms Durable?

Few people observing international politics in the months on either side of 2017 are likely to make the case for the durability of international security norms. Multilateralism appears to have been setback. The 45th President of the United States of America has made clear that he supports torture, articulated his ambivalence toward the most substantial multilateral and regional frameworks in the international system, namely the United Nations, the European Union, NATO, the World Bank and the IMF, and, apparently, loosened the rules of engagement to permit more civilian killing. The process of infusing security with human rights and humanitarian norms has been setback. NATO's intervention in Libya generated reluctance to embrace the Responsibility to Protect. African states mobilized against the ICC when it pressed too far to arrest Kenya's leaders. And across Europe, there has been a backlash against open borders as one by one European states have attempted to restrict access to refugees and migrants.

Still, there is a strong case to be made that the future of norms that regulate how wars are fought, the weapons that are legitimately and legally used, and the frameworks in which decisions are made will be similar to the past in at least one sense: norms of multilateralism, discrimination, humanitarianism, and human rights have been constantly violated at the same time that they continue to be regarded. Donald Trump's attack on multilateralism has been unique in its vitriol, but it is not the first time that the principle that the use of force should necessarily be multilateral has come under scrutiny.

Several points are key here. First, the stability of the civilian immunity norm has always been tenuous. Some IR scholars suggest that even democracies do not wholeheartedly embrace the norm, and will disregard the norm at times. Democratic leaders suffer when wars continue indefinitely. Their incentives to accelerate and intensify attacks on civilians increase as wars go on. Alexander Downes (2008) has argued that democracies that find themselves in wars of attrition will adopt strategies that inflict high levels of civilian deaths if they believe this will bring wars to a close more quickly. But recent scholarship suggests that rebel actors also take international humanitarian law into account. Those whose ambition is to form their own state and seek international recognition are more likely to comply than rebels who do not share these goals (Stanton 2016; Fazal 2017).

Second, the evidence on public attitudes is also mixed. One study finds that a strategy aimed at ending wars quickly despite high levels of civilian deaths is likely to backfire (Valentino 2016). But when faced with the potential of a grave security threat, public attitudes on the use of indiscriminate force against an enemy are less concerned with civilian killing. One recent experimental survey of public attitudes toward the use of nuclear weapons found that faced with a grave threat from Iran, Americans would support dropping a nuclear bomb (Sagan and Valentino 2015). The public's role in serving as a moderating influence on executive action when it comes to using force in ways that recognize important norms may be far less than has been previously assumed.

Third, despite recent politics, the more serious challenges to international security norms are likely to come not from the democracies of the West, but from rising powers, authoritarianism (this is not new), and transitional states (where debate is robust, and some very important scholarship sees human rights treaties as having some of their most important and positive effects) (Simmons 2009).

Norms calling for the protection and prosecution of civilians have generated a fierce backlash from multiple corridors. Libya has proved to be a serious setback for the "hard edge" of R2P. In the aftermath of NATO's air campaign in Libya, critics argued that R2P had once again become a veneer for regime change (Brockmeier et al. 2016). The prosecution norm has gained more secure institutional backing in the past two decades, but the ICC's efforts to prosecute sitting heads of state and other elite party officials in Kenya and Sudan has generated an intense backlash across Africa.

The future of international norms will depend in part on the strategies that are deployed to push back and unravel existing norms. Those that seek to create new norms or adapt existing norms in ways that create an alternative type of path-dependence, especially one that alters the balance between state sovereignty and individual rights, will have a more lasting impact on future norms than backlash that is merely tactical and limited to immediate outbursts (Vinjamuri 2017).[2]

Notes

1. The OSCE has a long history of election observation around the world, recently including the April 2017 constitutional referendum in Turkey, the presidential election in France, and the November 2016 US presidential election (OSCE 2017).
2. I would like to thank Lauren Dickey for her excellent research assistance.

References

Ackerman, B. 2004. The Emergency Constitution. *Yale Law Journal*, 113(5): 1029–91.

Ackerman, B. 2006. *Before the Next Attack: Preserving Civil Liberties in the Age of Terrorism*. New Haven, CT: Yale University Press.

Axworthy, L. and A. Dorn. 2016. New Technology for Peace & Protection: Expanding the R2P Toolbox. *Daedalus*, 145(4): 88–100.

Ayoob, M. 2002. Humanitarian Intervention and State Sovereignty. *International Journal of Human Rights*, 6(1): 81–102.

Barnes, J. 2016. The "War on Terror" and the Battle for the Definition of Torture. *International Relations*, 30(1): 102–24.

Barnett, M. and M. Finnemore. 2004. The Power of Liberal International Organizations. In Michael Barnett and Raymond Duvall (eds.), Power in Global Governance, pp. 161–84. Cambridge: Cambridge University Press.

Bass, G. 2002. *Stay the Hand of Vengeance: The Politics of War Crimes Tribunals*. Princeton, NJ: Princeton University Press.

Bellamy, A. 2007. Motives, Outcomes, Intent and the Legitimacy of Humanitarian Intervention. *Journal of Military Ethics*, 3(3): 216–32.

Bellamy, A. 2009. *Responsibility to Protect*, Cambridge: Polity.

Bosco, D. 2009. *Five to Rule Them All: The UN Security Council and the Making of the Modern World*. Oxford: Oxford University Press.

Bosco, D. 2014. *Rough Justice: The International Criminal Court in a World of Power Politics*. Oxford: Oxford University Press.

Brockmeier, S., O. Stuenkel, and M. Tourinho. 2016. The Impact of the Libya Intervention Debates on Norms of Protection. *Global Society*, 30(1): 113–33.

Brzezinski, Z. 1995. A Plan for Europe. *Foreign Affairs*, 74(1): 26–42.

Buchanan, A. 1999. The Internal Legitimacy of Humanitarian Intervention. *Journal of Political Philosophy*, 7(1): 71–87.

Burke-White, W. 2004. Human Rights and National Security: The Strategic Correlation. *Harvard Human Rights Journal*, 17(249): 249–80.

Buzan, B. 2010. China in International Society: Is "Peaceful Rise" Possible? *Chinese Journal of International Politics*, 3(1): 5–36.

Clark, I. 2014. International Society and China: The Power of Norms and the Norms of Power. *Chinese Journal of International Politics*, 7(3): 315–40.

Cole, D. and J Dempsey. 2006. *Terrorism and the Constitution: Sacrificing Civil Liberties in the Name of National Security*. New York: New Press.

Cooley, A. and M. Schaaf. 2017. Grounding the Backlash: Regional Security Treaties, Counternorms, and Human Rights in Eurasia in Stephen Hopgood, Jack Snyder, and Leslie Vinjamuri (eds.), *Human Rights Futures*, pp. 159–88. New York: Cambridge University Press.

Dancy, G. and K. Sikkink. 2017. Human Rights Data, Processes, and Outcomes: How Recent Research Points to a Better Future. In Stephen Hopgood, Jack Snyder, and Leslie Vinjamuri (eds.), *Human Rights Futures*, pp. 24–59. New York: Cambridge University Press.

David, J. 2016. Uncloaking Secrecy: International Human Rights Law in Terrorism Cases. *Human Rights Quarterly*, 38(1): 58–84.

Downes, A. 2008. *Targeting Civilians in War*. Ithaca, NY: Cornell University Press.

Drezner, D. 2014. *The System Worked: How the World Stopped Another Great Depression*. Oxford: Oxford University Press.

Duke, S. 1994. The State and Human Rights: Sovereignty versus Humanitarian Intervention. *International Relations*, 12(2): 25–48.

Enemark, C, 2014. Drones, Risk, and Perpetual Force. *Ethics & International Affairs*, 28(3): 365–81.

Epstein, R. 2005. NATO Enlargement and the Spread of Democracy: Evidence and Expectations. *Security Studies*, 14(1): 63–105.

Fazal, T. M. 2017. Rebellion, War Aims & the Laws of War. *Daedalus*, 146(1): 71–82.

Felter, J. and J. Shapiro. 2017. Limiting Civilian Casualties as Part of a Winning Strategy: The Case of Courageous Restraint. *Daedalus*, 146(1): 44–58.

Finnemore, M. 1996. Constructing Norms of Humanitarian Intervention. In Peter J. Katzenstein (ed.), *The Culture of National Security: Norms and Identities in World Politics*. New York: Columbia University Press.

Foot, R. and A. Walter. 2011. *China, the United States, and Global Order*. Cambridge: Cambridge University Press.

Franck, T. 1990. *The Power of Legitimacy Among Nations*. Oxford: Oxford University Press.

Gearty, C. 2005. 11 September 2001, Counter-terrorism, and the Human Rights Act. *Journal of Law and Society*, 32(1): 18–33.

Gearty C. 2010. *Escaping Hobbes: Liberty and Security for Our Democratic (Not Anti-Terrorist Age*. London: London School of Economics and Political Science.

Gheciu, A. 2005. *NATO in the "New Europe": The Politics of International Socialization after the Cold War*. Stanford, CA: Stanford University Press.

Gilligan, M. and N. Nesbitt. 2009. Do Norms Reduce Torture? *Journal of Legal Studies*, 38(2): 445–470.

Gross, M. L. 2010. *Moral Dilemmas of Modern War: Torture, Assassination, and Blackmail in an Age of Asymmetric Conflict*. Cambridge: Cambridge University Press.

Henkin, L. 1999. Kosovo and the Law of "Humanitarian Intervention". *American Journal of International Law*, 93(4): 824–8.

Holzgrefe, J. L. and R. Keohane. (eds.), 2003. *Humanitarian Intervention: Ethical, Legal, and Political Dilemmas*. Cambridge: Cambridge University Press.

Horowitz, M. 2016. The Ethics & Morality of Robotic Warfare: Assessing the Debate over Autonomous Weapons. *Daedalus*, 145(4): 25–36.

Howard, L. M. 2007. *UN Peacekeeping in Civil Wars*. Cambridge: Cambridge University Press.

Human Rights Watch. 2017. World Report 2017: China. *Available at:* https://www.hrw.org/world-report/2017/country-chapters/china-and-tibet, accessed April 20, 2017.

Hurd, I. 2010. *International Organizations: Politics, Law, Practice*. Cambridge: Cambridge University Press.

Hurd, I. 2011. Is Humanitarian Intervention Legal? The Rule of Law in an Incoherent World. *Ethics & International Affairs*, 25(3): 293–313.

Ikenberry, G. J. 2008. The Rise of China and the Future of the West: Can the Liberal System Survive?. *Foreign Affairs*, 87(1): 23–37.

Ikenberry, G. J. 2011. The Future of the Liberal World Order: Internationalism After America. *Foreign Affairs*, 90(3): 56–68.

Ikenberry, G. J. and C. Kupchan. 1990. Socialization and Hegemonic Power. *International Organization*, 44(3): 283–315.

International Commission on Intervention and State Sovereignty (ICISS). 2001. *The Responsibility to Protect*. Ottawa: International Development Research Centre.

Jefferson, C. 2014. Origins of the Norm against Chemical Weapons. *International Affairs*, 90(3): 647–61.

Jervis, R. 1982. Security Regimes. *International Organization*, 36(2): 357–78.

Jo, H. and B. Simmons. 2016. Can the International Criminal Court Deter Atrocity? *International Organization*, 70(3): 443–75.

Johnston, A. I. 2003. Is China a Status Quo Power? *International Security*, 27(4): 5–56.

Joyner, C. 2004. The United Nations and Terrorism: Rethinking Legal Tensions Between National Security, Human Rights, and Civil Liberties. *International Studies Perspectives*, 5(3): 240–57.

Kahl, C. 2007. In the Crossfire or the Crosshairs? Norms, Civilian Casualties, and U.S. Conduct in Iraq. *International Security*, 32(1): 7–46.

Kahl, C. 2017. Like Middle East Wars? You're Gonna Love President Trump. *Politico*. *Available at:* http://www.politico.com/magazine/story/2017/04/like-middle-east-wars-youre-gonna-love-president-trump-214985, accessed April 19, 2017.

Katzenstein, P. (ed.). 1996. *The Culture of National Security: Norms and Identity in World Politics*. New York: Columbia University Press.

Keck, M. and K. Sikkink. 1998. *Activists Beyond Borders: Advocacy Networks in International Politics*. Ithaca, NY: Cornell University Press.

Keohane, R. 2006. The Contingent Legitimacy of Multilateralism. GARNET Working Paper No. 09/06.

Keohane, R., S. Macedo, and A. Moravcsik. 2009. Democracy-Enhancing Multilateralism. *International Organization*, 63(1): 1–31.

Keren, M. and D. Sylvan (eds.). 2002. *International Intervention: Sovereignty Versus Responsibility*. London: Taylor & Francis.

Kim, H. and K. Sikkink. 2010. Explaining the Deterrence Effect of Human Rights Prosecutions for Transitional Countries. *International Studies Quarterly*, 54(4): 939–63.

Koremenos, B., C. Lipson, and D. Sindal. 2001. The Rational Design of International Institutions. *International Organization*, 55(4): 761–99.

Kreps, S. 2008. Multilateral Military Interventions: Theory and Practice. *Political Science Quarterly*, 123(4): 573–603.

Kreps, S. and G. P. R. Wallace. 2016. International law, Military Effectiveness, and Public Support for Drone Strikes. *Journal of Peace Research*, 53(6): 830–44.

Kurowska, X. 2014. Multipolarity as Resistance to Liberal Norms: Russia's Position on Responsibility to Protect. *Conflict, Security & Development*, 14(4): 489–508.

Lindberg, T. 2015. What is the International Community? in Chester Crocker, Fen Osler Hampson, and Pamela Aal (eds.), *Managing Conflict in a World Adrift*. Washington, DC: U.S. Institute of Peace.

Macklem, P. 2008. Humanitarian Intervention and the Distribution of Sovereignty in International Law. *Ethics and International Affairs* 22(4): 369–93.

Mead, W. R. 2017, The Jacksonian Revolt: American Populism and the Liberal Order. *Foreign Affairs*, 96(2): 2–6.

Ministry of Foreign Affairs of the People's Republic of China. 2017. China's Policies on Asia-Pacific Security Cooperation. *Available at:* http://www.fmprc.gov.cn/mfa_eng/zxxx_662805/t1429771.shtml, accessed on April 20, 2017.

Moore, J. (ed.). 1998. *Hard Choices: Moral Dilemmas in Humanitarian Intervention*. Lanham, MD: Rowman & Littlefield.

Office of the Director of National Intelligence (ODNI). 2016. *Summary of Information Regarding U.S. Counterterrorism Strikes Outside Areas of Active Hostilities*. *Available at:* https://www.dni.gov/index.php/newsroom/reports-and-publications/214-reports-publications-2016/1392-summary-of-information-regarding-u-s-counterterrorism-strikes-outside-areas-of-active-hostilities, accessed April 20, 2017.

O'Neil, J. 2001. Building Better Global Economic BRICs. Goldman Sachs Global Economics Paper No. 66.

Organisation for Security and Cooperation in Europe (OSCE). 2017. *Elections*. *Available at:* http://www.osce.org/odihr/elections, accessed April 18, 2017.

Patrick, S. 2016. World Order: What, Exactly, are the Rules? *Washington Quarterly*, 39(1): 7–27.

Pevehouse, J. 2002. Democracy from the Outside-In? International Organization and Democratization. *International Organization*, 56(3): 515–49.

Posen, B. 2014. *Restraint: A New Foundation for U.S. Grand Strategy*. Ithaca, NY: Cornell University Press.

Price, R. 1998. Reversing the Gun Sights: Transnational Civil Society Targets Land Mines. *International Organizations*, 52(3 (1998): 613–44, 628.

Rejali, D. 2003. Modern Torture as a Civic Marker: Solving a Global Anxiety with a New Political Technology. *Journal of Human Rights*, 2(2): 153–71.

Rejali, D. 2009. *Torture and Democracy*. Princeton, NJ: Princeton University Press.

Risse, T. 2016. *Domestic Politics and Norm Diffusion in International Relations: Ideas do not Float Freely*. Abingdon: Routledge.

Risse, T., S. Ropp, and K. Sikkink. 1999. *The Power of Human Rights: International Norms and Domestic Change*. Cambridge; Cambridge University Press.

Risse, T., S. Ropp, and K. Sikkink. 2013. *The Persistent Power of Human Rights: From Commitment to Compliance*. Cambridge: Cambridge University Press.

Rosen, R. 2009. Targeting Enemy Forces in the War on Terror: Preserving Civilian Immunity. *Vanderbilt Journal of Transnational Law*, 42(3): 683–95.

Rubinstein, A. and Y. Roznai. 2011. Human Shields in Modern Armed Conflicts: The Need for a Proportionate Proportionality. *Stanford Law & Policy Review*, 22(1): 93–135.

Ruggie, J. G. 1983. International Regimes, Transactions, and Change: Embedded Liberalism in the Postwar Economic Order. in Stephen Krasner ed., *International Regimes*, Cornell University Press, pp. 195–232.

Sagan, S. 2016. Ethics, Technology & War. *Daedalus*, 145(4): 6–11.

Sagan, S. and B. Valentino. 2015. Public Opinion, Commitment Traps, and Nuclear Weapons Policy. Centre for International Security and Cooperation, Stanford University.

Sambanis, N. 2008. Short- and Long-Term Effects of United Nations Peace Operations. *World Bank Economic Review*, 22(1): 9–32.

Sanders, R. 2011. (Im)plausible Legality: The Rationalisation of Human Rights Abuses in the American "Global War on Terror". *International Journal of Human Rights*, 15(4): 605–26.

Schiff, B. 2008. *Building the International Criminal Court*. Cambridge: Cambridge University Press.

Schofer, M. 2015. Human Rights and National Security Post 9/11. *Security and Human Rights*, 26(2-4): 294–307.

Sikkink, K. 2011. *The Justice Cascade: How Human Rights Prosecutions are Changing World Politics*. New York: W.W. Norton & Company.

Sikkink, K. 2012. Tortured. *Utne*(169): 40–4.

Simmons, B. A. 2009. *Mobilizing for Human Rights: International Law in Domestic Politics*. Cambridge: Cambridge University Press.

Snyder, J. 2017. Empowering Rights through Mass Movements, Religion, and Reform Parties. in Stephen Hopgood, Jack Snyder, and Leslie Vinjamuri (eds.), *Human Rights Futures*, pp. 88–113. New York: Cambridge University Press.

Snyder, J. and L. Vinjamuri. 2004. Trials and Errors: Principle and Pragmatism in Strategies of International Justice. *International Security*, 28(3): 5–44.

Stanton, J. A. 2016. *Violence and Restraint in Civil War: Civilian Targeting in the Shadow of International Law*. Cambridge: Cambridge University Press.

Stephen, M. 2014. States, Norms and Power: Emerging Powers and Global Order. *Millennium*, 42(3): 888–96.

Tago, A. 2007. Why do States Join US-led Military Coalitions?: The compulsion of the Coalition's Missions and Legitimacy. *International Relations of the Asia-Pacific*, 7(2): 179–202.

Tannenwald, N. 1999. The Nuclear Taboo: The United States and the Normative Basis of Nuclear Non-Use. *International Organization*, 53(3): 433–68.

Valentino, B. 2016. Moral Character or Character of War? American Public Opinion on the Targeting of Civilians in Times of War. *Daedalus*, 145(4): 127–38.

Vinjamuri, L. 2017. Human Rights Backlash. in Stephen Hopgood, Jack Snyder, and Leslie Vinjamuri (eds.), *Human Rights Futures*, pp. 114–34. New York: Cambridge University Press.

Walt, S. 2016. The Collapse of the Liberal World Order. *Foreign Policy. Available at:* http://foreignpolicy.com/2016/06/26/the-collapse-of-the-liberal-world-order-european-union-brexit-donald-trump/,accessed April 19, 2017.

Walt, S. 2017. America's New President is Not a Rational Actor. *Foreign Policy. Available at:* http://foreignpolicy.com/2017/01/25/americas-new-president-is-not-a-rational-actor/, accessed April 20, 2017.

Walzer, M. 2016. Just & Unjust Targeted Killing & Drone Warfare. *Daedalus*, 145(4): 6–11.

Welsh, J. 2016. The Responsibility to Protect after Libya & Syria. *Daedalus*, 145(4): 75–87.

Wheeler, N. 2000. *Saving Strangers: Humanitarian Intervention in International Society*. Oxford: Oxford University Press.

Wohlforth, W. 1999. The Stability of a Unipolar World. *International Security*, 24(1): 5–41.

CHAPTER 21

THE ECONOMICS OF WAR AND PEACE

JONATHAN D. CAVERLEY

WITH apologies to Charles Tilly, war made the economy, and the economy made war. While neoclassical economics tends to start with a benign world full of property rights and free of predation, many prerequisites for such a world—sovereign credit markets, central banks, freedom of navigation—originate in warmaking and violence. This relationship continued to shape the international politics of the twentieth century. The punitive economic punishments in the First World War's Treaty of Versailles helped produce Weimar Germany's economic collapse and the Second World War's advent. The Cold War's Marshall Plan permanently shaped the economic nature of Western (and Eastern) Europe. The Vietnam War led Nixon to close the gold window. And the collapse of the Soviet Union, largely due to the pressures of competing militarily with the United States, led to both American unipolarity and the extreme economic interdependence we call "globalization."

Lest we think that such links are passé, the potential unraveling of both globalization and unipolarity (addressed below in Section 21.2) cannot be separated from the increasing security competition between the United States and aspiring great powers. In a rare statement of unvarnished truth by the American political class, the Obama administration sold the Trans-Pacific Partnership free trade pact as a means of competing against China, rather than of increasing gains from trade (Obama 2016). The continued relevance of the subject, given trends in contemporary international politics, drives this chapter.

This Handbook asks "what [about international security] is likely to change and what is likely to stay the same?" It is generally accepted that much about the politics of war is immutable, but have the *economics* of war evolved?

Those occupying the commanding heights of the global economy seem to think so. In 2015 the World Economic Forum (2015: 7) labeled "interstate conflict" the number one "global risk," because "2015 differs markedly from the past, with rising technological risks, notably cyber-attacks, and new economic realities, which remind us that geopolitical tensions present themselves in a very different world from before. Information flows instantly around the globe and emerging technologies have boosted the influence of new players and new types of warfare." Given this newly-found anxiety among Davos Men (and the occasional Woman), this chapter examines potential changes in the relationship between war and both national and global economies.[1]

The chapter makes three major points. First, it highlights one major change in the economics of war and peace. The economic futility of conquest is both a rare spot of agreement in our field and an insufficiently appreciated development in international politics. Second, it skeptically reviews predictions of major change in two economic forces thought to make war less likely: unipolarity and globalization. Finally, the chapter explores other possible economic underpinnings to the perceived increase in conflict risk identified above, drawing upon recent research on the economics of *going to war*. Dramatic changes do appear to be taking place here, but they largely reinforce the current state of international affairs.

21.1 Conquest Does Not Pay

The field largely agrees on what *has* changed in the relationship between economics and war. The most direct link between these two practices—going to war in the pursuit of wealth—is largely irrelevant to contemporary international politics. The opportunity cost of war in terms of prosperity (for most states) seems profoundly high, and the gains from conquest seem equally low (Brooks 1999, 2005; Crescenzi 2003; Kim 2014).[2] While few debates in IR ever die, current scholarship is surprisingly reticent to argue that "conquest still pays," the last major attempt being two decades old (Liberman 1998). Oil, so often blamed for conflict (Klare 2001), is rarely its direct cause (Schultz 2015; Meierding 2016; Colgan 2014). Some predict water wars in the future (Starr 2016), but evidence remains scarce to date (Wolf 1999).

None of the world's ongoing large-scale conflicts and plausible future ones—Indian–Pakistani tensions in Kashmir, Russian aggression in its Near Abroad, Saudi flailing in Yemen, the multinational cockpit of Syria and Iraq—can plausibly be described primarily as economic disputes. Even China's maritime "land reclamation" seems largely an attempt to protect itself from economic coercion and to expand its influence and prestige rather than a quest for rapidly depleting fisheries or unproven undersea resources.

But while its direct economic gains may have dissipated, war—as Richard Betts (1999) glumly observes—still seems to find a way, and thus the economics of *producing* war continue to matter greatly. Richer states have bigger ambitions. The scale economies of war shape international politics in profound ways. Even if many rich countries seem to lack the willingness to fight, wealth remains an essential prerequisite for war (and perhaps more broadly for "power"); arming and fighting are not free.

21.2 The Robustness of Unipolarity and Globalization

Any investigation of the contemporary economics of war must reckon with the twin facts underpinning post-Cold War politics: the awesome relative economic and military power of the United States, and the current high degree of mutual economic interdependence among states, firms, and people. Whereas one senior IPE scholar as late as 2008 described hegemonic stability theory as "passé" (Cohen 2008: 9), a new generation of scholarship has explored the mutual influence of unipolarity and globalization (Kirshner 2006a; Mastanduno 2009).

There is a general assumption that, combined, these forces reduce the probability of war.[3] While vague in many respects, hegemonic stability theory and its cousin "power transition theory" nonetheless make it clear that rapid and large power shifts make war more likely and that globalization in general makes war less likely. Realists and liberals can agree that the *decline* of American unipolarity, economic interdependence, or both bode poorly for peace.

And prospects appear grim. Trade makes up a smaller percentage of global GDP than before the 2007 economic crisis. The Doha round of global trade talks continues to flounder. Two United States-led trade agreements also appear stalled, supported by neither major 2016 presidential candidate. The Great Firewall of China restricts the exchange of information between the world's largest economy by purchasing power and the rest of the world (and protects indigenous competitors like Alibaba and Weibo). The one-two punch of Europe's internal fiscal imbalances and Brexit threaten the continued operation, much less the deepening, of the world's most successful project of international economic integration. The United States recently elected a president vocally antagonistic toward free trade, international institutions, and liberal norms.

Even scholars once at the forefront of linking globalization to American power see both as declining. Mastanduno (2009: 123) finds that "U.S. dominance in the international security arena no longer translates into effective leverage in the international economic arena." It appears to be of the United States' own doing. Many point to a self-defeating imbalance between US military spending and economic power (Layne 1993, 2012).[4] Others underscore American sins such as excessive debt, failed wars, sclerotic government, profligate energy use, and the friability of the ideas underpinning the "Washington Consensus" (Freidman and Mandelbaum 2011). Kirshner (2006b: 5), who has done so much to analyze globalization's empowerment of the United States, now argues that the United States, "saddled by national debt, fiscal deficits, and record trade imbalances," is losing ground.[5]

But like Hymen Roth in *Godfather II*, the United States has been dying of the same heart attack for decades. American relative supremacy and increasing global interdependence both pre-date the Cold War's end, as do predictions of their demise. Responding to a previous wave of declinism, Susan Strange cannily identified the robustness of this relationship (Strange 1987, 1998). Strange's case still stands. To make this case I turn to several political economic truisms.

First, one cannot explain change with a constant; the continued structural advantages of the United States, especially relative to China, are hard to deny (Beckley 2011; Brooks and Wohlforth 2015). Although US actions may deserve some credit, much of it is dumb luck, such as the recent finding that 60 percent of economically viable oil production at $60 a barrel is in American shale (Crooks 2016). As Bismarck noted, God watches over fools, drunkards, and the United States. Nor are many of America's sins all that new. Indeed its sclerotic domestic government has at times been considered the source of American power, constraining it from its worst excesses (Friedberg 2000; Colaresi 2014).

Second, voice does not imply exit (Hirschman 1970); indeed, squeals are often the only tool available when an actor cannot exit an asymmetric relationship. What Kirshner (2016) labels as "chronic squabbling" is not evidence of decline. If weaker partners do not complain during a round of economic bargaining, the stronger side is not squeezing hard enough.

Third, and relatedly, new ideas do not necessarily presage decline. Kirshner (2014) identifies a "New Heterogeneity" and Grabel (2011) a new "productive incoherence" over international economic management. Kirshner (2016) argues that the Global Financial Crisis will present a "learning moment" in world politics, and that "much of that learning will take place outside of the United States." I suspect that the United States will learn what it wants, and then other states will learn what they can. Periods of idea-shopping can certainly lead to change, but there must be no mistake about which state will get to decide among those alternatives. For example, TPP, ostensibly written in a time of relative US decline, seems to be largely a United States-generated document and is designed to exclude its primary potential international challenger (Allee and Lugg 2016). And yet Donal Trump, the newly elected US President, rejected the pact as not being a sufficiently "good deal" for the United States.

Fourth, the perception of declining American agency is endogenous to structure. Many identify periodic US congressional squabbling over the debt ceiling and government shutdowns as evidence of: (1) financial overstretch and (2) a deadlocked government inacpable of competently managing its own economy, much less the world's. But the United States can indulge in these high jinks precisely because the international market is unable to discipline it. As embarrassing as they are, ill-advised invasions of Asian countries and brinksmanship with sovereign debt are symptoms of power, not signs of its decline.

The final, related social science truism that applies is that inefficiency and other forms of "bad behavior" tend to suggest the presence of rent rather than competition. The United States has tremendous slack in the system which allows it to provide side-payments to states for putting up with its hegemony. Scale and winner-take-all economies are readily apparent not only in the defense industry, but also in information technology and finance, where the United States continues to dominate. If anything this is getting stronger; what separates this century from the last, according to Anne-Marie Slaughter

(2009), is that "the state with the most connections will be the central player." The United States remains at the center of this network (Oatley et al. 2013; Starrs 2013).

21.3 Stretching the Sinews of Power

So far this chapter has argued that, while conquest does not seem to pay economically, there remain many reasons for states to use their military and thus leverage their economy accordingly. It then argued that transitions in the large, international political-economic forces of unipolarity and globalization range from slow to non-existent. This section narrows the chapter's scope further by addressing potential changes in the production of one specific good or service: war.

The economics of warmaking matter greatly for the likelihood and conduct of both war and peace. The number of substantive issues on this front has steadily grown: the advent of military drones and robotics, renewed attention to nuclear proliferation, the strange rearmament of an economically reeling Russia, the development of "anti-access" weaponry to resist US power projection, and the estimated short-term cost of the Iraq and Afghanistan campaigns to the United States alone at $1.6 trillion (Belasco 2014).[6] Research has accumulated accordingly.

Like the larger field of IR, much recent study of the production of military power and war has been shaped by unipolarity and globalization. From the 1991 Gulf War to the apparently triumphant United States invasions of Iraq and Afghanistan, security studies largely focused on the implications of the so-called "RMA," the revolution in military affairs (Adamsky 2010; Dombrowski and Ross 2008), both a product of globalization and a hallmark of American power. Perhaps most importantly, the capabilities it made possible were relatively inexpensive for the United States, making the venerable idea of "imperial overstretch" appear less relevant.

More recently, alongside the larger fears of deteriorating unipolarity, some predict a fading of the stunning imbalance in global military capability. American struggles in Iraq and Afghanistan, the financial crisis, and newly aggressive, rapidly arming China and Russia have led many, not least in the Pentagon, to reconsider the robustness of this advantage. From a broad historical perspective, this makes sense. Traditionally, military power stems from economic growth (Gilpin 1981; Kennedy 1988). And there is no denying the shrinking wealth gap between the United States and the rest of the world. Globalization, and the apparently easy availability of sophisticated technology, reinforces this capability diffusion.

Yet Brooks and Wohlforth (2015: 9) argue that the "greatly enhanced difficulty of converting economic capacity into military capacity makes the transition from a great power to a superpower much harder now than it was in the past." Even developed countries with a track record of large militaries and defense industries may struggle; Rachel Epstein (2006: 231) argues that "globalization may well undermine the state's ability to provide certain public goods, including defense, at a level of expenditure acceptable to

European politics" (see also Schilde 2016). Will these trends continue? Are more states or fewer likely to be able afford arming and fighting in the future?

21.3.1 Finding Bucks for the Bang

The cost of, and the ability to pay for, arming and war have always driven the approach states take to advance their interests. Major British defense reform efforts for example tend to follow economic crises rather than any objective change in that country's strategic environment (Smith 2009: 47). Change in GDP is the single best predictor of the change in military spending. A state can of course buck the tyranny of economic growth in its strategic behavior. The Russian military, which only started issuing socks to its recruits a decade ago (Kramer 2013), has bounced back in quite remarkable fashion. But there are limits; the Kremlin's defense budget is currently being cut in recognition of its economic troubles (due, in part, to the economic sanctions following its invasion of Crimea).

We do not appear to be in an era of massive rearming or of large swings in the balance of military investment (and thus of capability). Figure 21.1 shows that global defense spending as a percentage of world GDP has hardly budged since the Cold War's end. Even an "aggressive," rising power such as China is spending a mere 2 percent of its economy on defense.[7] Among "Heavily Indebted Poor Countries" (HIPC) spending as a percentage of the economy has never been lower (World Bank 2015).

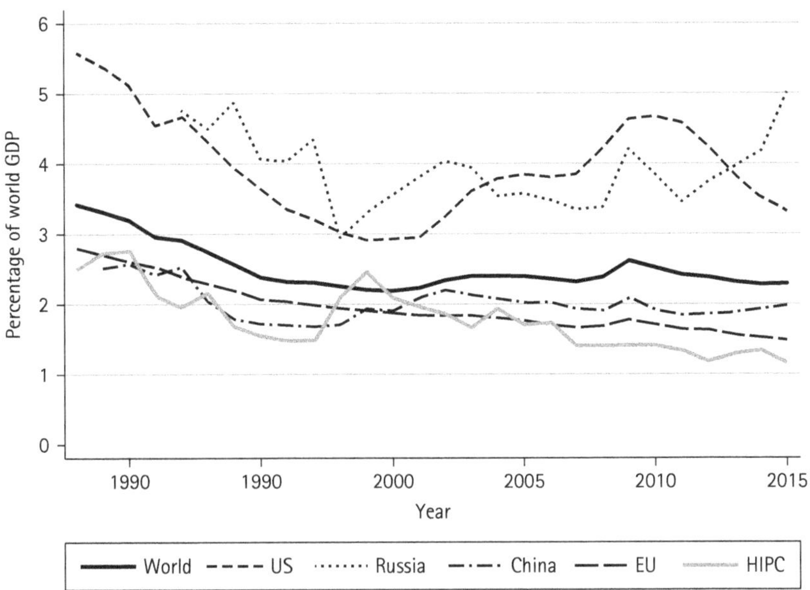

FIGURE 21.1 Military spending as percent of GDP, 1989–2015

Source: SIPRI.

Perhaps lower spending is due to war becoming more affordable. The evolution of the US defense budget suggests this. Its Second World War effort peaked at 37.5 percent of GDP. At the Cold War's height, US defense spending hovered around 10 percent. The Korean War cost a modest 13.2 percent and Vietnam 9.5 percent. The US military then internalized the previously hidden labor costs of conscription by shifting to a volunteer force, and war got cheaper anyway. Despite ongoing conflicts in Iraq, Afghanistan, and elsewhere, US spending peaked at 4.9 percent of GDP in 2010, and even that is partly a function of a contracting economy. The United States managed to invade and occupy (albeit with poor results) two massive countries for a mere 1.2 percent of GDP (Daggett 2010).

But it is not clear that war is so affordable for any other country. In Syria, Russia displayed considerable logistic capability in deploying forces, generated a high sortie rate from its small air wing, and pulled off sophisticated operations such as launching a cruise missile from a submarine. But the United States has performed these operations routinely for a quarter century. At the peak of the Syrian operation, Russia deployed 4000 personnel and 28 aircraft. The US war in Afghanistan is officially over, but the United States still has 10,000 personnel there (not counting contractors). Russia claims to have flown 5000–9000 air sorties from October 2015 to July 2016 (McDermott 2016). In the first seven months of 2016 alone, the United States pursued over 30,000 sorties in Operation Inherent Resolve, and another 23,000 in Afghanistan and other parts of Central Command (US Air Forces Central Command 2016). Judging by spending in Figure 21.1, the United States displays enormous economies of scale relative to its only serious rival in power projection capability.

Modern war is pricy. While inflation in the price of acquiring weapons routinely outstrips that for other products (Hartley and Solomon 2016), much of the economic effort required is not reflected in the costs of hardware. Indeed, the production of military capability resembles the rest of the modern economy in that services are where the money is. Saudi Arabia bought 72 Typhoon aircraft from the UK in 2008 for 4.3 billion pounds sterling; arming them cost 5 billion, and supporting them added another 10 (Smith 2009: 141).

And like the other aspects of the modern economy, the United States dominates this "service sector." Karl Mueller (2006: 148) describes the "deceptively inconspicuous" aspects of modern war—intelligence collection, military command and control, training simulators—all American specialties. To paraphrase Eisenhower, aspiring powers talk strategy, but a superpower talks logistics. Military transportation, refueling, and command and control are almost exclusively the province of the United States, even when "leading from behind." France, for example, had to rely on American military transport to fight its relatively miniscule Operation Serval in Mali.

Given these rather low levels of global military effort, as well as developments in capital-intensive technology (in both the traditional notion of capital and the human version), producing military capability has become an exercise in fiscal rather than social mobilization (Caverley 2014). Research has shifted accordingly, and the literature on war finance has grown considerably over the past decade.

The ability to extract resources from society, particularly tax revenue, drives the projection of military power. Capella Zielinski's (2016: 5) ambitious book revisits an age-old dilemma for governments seeking to pay for war: you can depend on your public or you can depend on other states. Capella Zelinski finds that leaders are more likely to engage in direct resource extraction to finance a war when they fear inflation, when public support for the war is high, and when the state has the capacity to extract revenue.

How states manage this dilemma shapes conflict behavior. As with so much of the field, the first cut in war financing focuses on regime type. Democracies seem to have more difficulty in mobilizing resources for large wars (Carter 2015), and shifting away from non-military spending (Carter and Palmer 2016). Democratic leaders are punished more often than non-democratic ones for large mobilization costs, and thus differences in the conflict behavior of democracies and dictatorships should be largest when waging war requires a significant mobilization effort (Carter and Palmer 2015).

Good international credit allows for more military spending and responsiveness to international threats (DiGiuseppe 2015b). In general, contemporary states have largely avoided financing their wars through tax increases and inflation, regardless of regime type (Carter and Palmer 2016). In the United Kingdom and the United States, survey experiments show that borrowing shields the public from the direct costs of war, giving leaders greater latitude in how they carry out war (Flores-Macias and Kreps 2015). Again, regime type appears to play a role. Schultz and Weingast (2003) argue that states with better access to credit, specifically democracies, enjoy a significant military advantage in long-standing rivalries (see also DiGiuseppe 2015a). On the other hand, Shea (2014) finds that not only do borrowing costs have a substantial effect on war outcomes, but democracies are more sensitive to these costs than are non-democracies.

So while current research suggests a democratic disadvantage in raising wartime funds, it is hard to say whether this outweighs the fact that arming and war are growing more expensive in capital and less dependent on labor, an advantage for democracies which are generally wealthier than other regime types. Democracies are also flush with human capital, an essential component of modern military power (Biddle and Long 2004). Finally the costs of arming and war may vary within democracies, and are manipulable through tax policy (Caverley 2014; Kriner et al. 2015).

Once again it is hard not to recognize the unique American advantages in the context of this stream of research. The United States has succeeded in making copious use of military force less salient to its public (if not the rest of the world). The United States has one of the world's most progressive *federal* tax systems making the cost of conflict small for the average voter-taxpayer (Caverley 2014: 29), unrivaled abilities to borrow on the international credit market, and the most capitalized military on the planet. These are not coincidences. United States' military adventures are funded by a few rich Americans and a lot of poor Chinese.

21.3.2. What Can You Buy?

Once money is found, what can it buy? Given secular trends in rising labor costs and accelerating information technology, advanced weapons appear to be the place to invest, potentially making the RMA no longer the exclusive province of the United States. While the concern that, "Over time, all states—not just the U.S. and its allies—will share access to much of the technology underpinning the modern military" (Defense Science Board 1999), is as old as the RMA itself (Bitzinger 1994), many regard this process to be finally accelerating, with renewed focus on the ability of non-top tier countries (particularly China) to design (often from stolen blueprints), build, and operate advanced conventional weapons rivaling the United States' (Work 2015).

Regardless of whether they are bullish and bearish students on the prospects of military technology diffusion, scholars agree that the "information age" differs from the "industrial age." Much of the bulls' case rests on the potential military application of readily available civilian technologies. In a poll of defense experts, nearly three-quarters think that commercial companies' influence on the defense sector will grow significantly by 2030 (Horowitz 2014). Coupled with a "second mover advantage" (Singer 2009: 239) this could lead to widespread proliferation of advanced weapons. Horowitz (2012: 223), speculates that "military technology . . . could become increasingly 'lootable.'" Bears point out that this diffusion has yet to happen on any appreciable scale, identifying a host of factors that make "copying" high end military technology all but impossible (Neuman 2006; Caverley 2007; Gholz 2007). Gilli and Gilli (2016) usefully divide the process of diffusion into two daunting components. First, a country faces a "platform challenge" in designing, developing, and manufacturing a combat-effective weapon system. Second, that country then must deal with the "adoption challenge," ensuring access to the required infrastructural and organizational support (see also Horowitz 2010: 27–34). Moreover, like much of the modern economy, software is harder to copy, and thus more valuable, than hardware (Goldman and Andres 1999: 123).

Much of the substantive focus has revolved around the proliferation of remotely piloted vehicles, also known as "drones," whose military potential has captured the imagination of both the world and academia. Well-established national security thinkers (Singer 2009; Zegart 2015) have predicted that "drones are going to revolutionize how state and non-state actors threatened the use of violence."[8] It is true that many countries are developing such weapons (Fuhrmann and Horowitz 2017). Lower-end drones are certainly cheap and provide a measure of tactical awareness, and perhaps very limited strike capability, that have previously only been the province of the United States. But in general, drones' ability to alter the international status quo remains limited (Horowitz et al. 2017: 14–15). Larger, more sophisticated ones, capable of carrying out large attacks from a distance, surveilling across a massive spectrum and area, appear just as out of reach as ever for almost all states (Gilli and Gilli 2016). Drones, like much military capability, will probably bifurcate in terms of sophistication (Caverley and Kapstein 2016).

It is far too early to tell which side will prove correct, but I do caution against scholars making worst case assumptions about the United States and best case ones about rivals. Joint Strike Fighter (JSF) plans obtained through cyber-espionage may have saved China some development costs for its J-31 knockoff. But the ongoing, 1.5-trillion-dollar struggle by Lockheed Martin—which presumably also has the blueprints—to produce a viable production-ready fighter suggests that plans are far from enough. The JSF program costs the United States about $12.4 billion, annually; a third to a quarter of China's entire procurement budget. Second-mover advantages will have to be massive to overcome this disparity in scale.

Perhaps civilian technology will close the capability gap, but a statement like "access to cutting-edge technology from Silicon Valley could very well give large countries with large ambitions, like China, the boost they need to surpass the United States" gives much of the game away (Horowitz 2014). Civilian tech firms cluster because that makes it easier to incorporate each other's innovations. Unless it is actually *simpler* to incorporate civilian technology into military platforms than into other civilian products, until China has its own Silicon Valley it is unlikely to have a cutting-edge military. The direction in which the gap between civilian and military applications is changing has yet to be answered conclusively. At the same time, it may be immaterial from a perspective of power. More than any other country, the United States excels at both.

Former Lockheed Martin CEO Norm Augustine (1997) famously and facetiously predicated that, based on cost trends, by 2054 the entire US defense budget would purchase just one tactical aircraft to be shared by the Navy and Air Force (the Marines would get Leap Day). Perhaps he is not far off, but that one American aircraft is going to be a heck of a plane, and will probably be the only one left in the world.

21.4 Conclusion

It is in the nature of most social scientists to focus on change, or variables. This is understandable and correct, given that we live in a time of great economic transformations. But by focusing on how these transformations might affect the international system, in particular with respect to globalization and unipolarity, scholars have forgotten the importance of identifying continuity in many crucial forces. Moreover, some changing factors are only doing so slowly. Finally several of the most important changes make the United States relatively stronger, not weaker.

In reviewing the capacity for change in the economics of war and peace, this chapter has taken several strong stances. First, the economics of conquest appear to have made war for financial gain a bad investment. Second, both globalization and US military and even economic preponderance will decline slowly, if at all. Finally, the financing of modern military power, and thus of warfare, continues to become prohibitive for all but the most wealthy and/or most aggressive states.

Writing in early 2017, one cannot conclude a chapter such as this without acknowledging that a new potential source of change in the economics of war and peace has emerged. The new positions apparently avowed by the Trump administration (with a Republican Congress and Supreme Court)—protectionism, nativism, rejection of international institutions and alliances, suspicion of liberal norms—look nothing like the policies usually blamed on United States decline reviewed in this chapter. Ironically, but not surprisingly, the largest prospect for undermining the American-advantaged status quo described in this chapter is a brand of illiberalism that comes from within the United States itself.[9]

Notes

1. This chapter does not address the economic *approach* to war and peace: statistical analysis (and the desperate search for exogenous instruments) and formal models. Instead it focuses on the broader idea of "economics" as the "production, consumption, and transfer of goods and services." On the other hand, this chapter shares the economic approach's materialist ontology, trusting that other chapters will cover alternatives. I also take to heart this Handbook's focus on "International Security." The amount of interstate war is at an almost historical low, yet the wide-scale death and destruction in the ostensibly "civil" conflicts of Syria, Iraq, Afghanistan, South Sudan, Yemen, and Libya would be inconceivable without neighboring (and not so neighboring) states employing their own military forces directly or indirectly. Much of the work reviewed here is from political science; see the excellent Ron Smith (2009) overview from the field of economics.
2. This is subtly different than the large literature on economic interdependence and peace. Interdependence can influence *any* reason to go to war. This section focuses on the argument that the economic value of conquest is pretty minimal, but there are plenty of other reasons to fight remaining.
3. Although see Monteiro (2014).
4. There are more structural approaches as well (Kupchan 2002; Zakaria 2009). Other analysis suggests unipolar durability (Norrlof 2014).
5. It is difficult to assess how unusual an individual as Donald Trump (or the domestic coalition that made him possible) fits into my argument, but he does not appear to result from any of the declinists' mechanisms either.
6. $4–8 trillion once interest payments and veterans' health care are considered (Crawford 2016).
7. Note that China is not very transparent about spending, but one would have to be off by a lot to suggest that China is shifting its economy to rapidly arm itself into superpower status.
8. More modest estimates of their impact exist (Davis et al. 2014).
9. The author would like to thank Peter Dombrowksi and Mauro Gilli for very helpful comments.

References

Adamsky, D. 2010. *The Culture of Military Innovation: The Impact of Cultural Factors on the Revolution in Military Affairs in Russia, the US, and Israel.* Ithaca, NY: Cornell University Press.

Allee, T. and A. Lugg. 2016. Who Wrote the Rules for the Trans-Pacific Partnership? *Research & Politics*, 3(3).

Augustine, N. R. 1997. *Augustine's Laws* 6th edn. Reston, VA: American Institute of Aeronautics and Astronautics.

Beckley, M. 2011. China's Century? *International Security*, 36(3): 41–78.

Belasco, A. 2014. *The Cost of Iraq, Afghanistan, and Other Global War on Terror Operations Since 9/11.* Washington, DC: CreateSpace Independent Publishing Platform.

Betts, R. K. 1999. Must War Find a Way?: A Review Essay. *International Security*, 24(2): 166–98.

Biddle, S. and S. Long. 2004. Democracy and Military Effectiveness: A Deeper Look. *Journal of Conflict Resolution*, 48(4): 525–46. *Available at:* papers2://publication/uuid/F1B76636-D3F8-412B-A152-5F7A02B86E04.

Bitzinger, R. A. 1994. The Globalization of the Arms Industry. *International Security*, 19(2): 170–98.

Brooks, S. G. 1999. The Globalization of Production and the Changing Benefits of Conquest. *Journal of Conflict Resolution*, 43(5): 646–70.

Brooks, S. G. 2005. *Producing Security: Multinational Corporations, Globalization, and the Changing Calculus of Conflict.* Princeton, NJ: Princeton University Press.

Brooks, S. G. and W.C. Wohlforth. 2015. The Rise and Fall of the Great Powers in the 21st Century: China's Rise and the Fate of America's Global Position. *International Security*, 40(3): 7–53.

Cappella Zielinski, R. 2016. *How States Pay for Wars.* Ithaca, NY: Cornell University Press.

Carter, J. 2015. The Political Cost of War Mobilization in Democracies and Dictatorships. *Journal of Conflict Resolution*, 61(8): 1758–94.

Carter, J. and G. Palmer. 2015. Keeping the Schools Open While the Troops are Away: Regime Type, Interstate War, and Government Spending. *International Studies Quarterly*, 59(1): 145–57.

Carter, J. and G. Palmer. 2016. Regime Type and Interstate War Finance. *Foreign Policy Analysis*, 12(4): 695–719.

Caverley, J. D. 2007. United States Hegemony and the New Economics of Defense. *Security Studies*, 16(4): 598–614.

Caverley, J. D. 2014. *Democratic Militarism: Voting, Wealth, and War.* Cambridge: Cambridge University Press.

Caverley, J. D. and E. B. Kapstein. 2016. Who's Arming Asia? *Survival*, 58(2): 167–84.

Cohen, B. J. 2008. *International Political Economy: An Intellectual History.* Princeton, NJ: Princeton University Press.

Colaresi, M. P. 2014. *Democracy Declassified: The Secrecy Dilemma in National Security.* Oxford: Oxford University Press.

Colgan, J. D. 2014. *Petro-Aggression: When Oil Causes War.* Cambridge: Cambirdge University Press.

Crawford, N. C. 2016. *US Budgetary Costs of Wars through 2016: $4.79 Trillion and Counting.* Providence.

Crescenzi, M. J. C., 2003. Economic Exit, Interdependence, and Conflict. *Journal of Politics*, 65(3): 809–32.

Crooks, E. 2016. US shale is lowest-cost oil prospect. *Financial Times*, pp. 9–12.

Daggett, S. 2010. Costs of Major U.S. Wars. *Congressional Research Service Report*.

Davis, L. E., M. J. McNerney, and J. S. Chow. 2014. *Armed and Dangerous? UAVs and U.S Security*, Washington, DC: RAND.

Defense Science Board. 1999. *Final Report: Globalization and Security*. Washington, DC.

DiGiuseppe, M. 2015a. The Fiscal Autonomy of Deciders: Creditworthiness and Conflict Initiation. *Foreign Policy Analysis*, 11(3): 317–38.

DiGiuseppe, M. 2015b. Guns, Butter, and Debt: Sovereign Creditworthiness and Military Expenditure. *Journal of Peace Research*, 52(5): 680–93.

Dombrowski, P. and A. L. Ross. 2008. The Revolution in Military Affairs, Transformation, and the Defense Industry. *Security Challenges*, 4(4): 57–80.

Epstein, R. 2006. Divided Continent: Globalization and Europe's Fragmented Security Response. In J. Kirshner (ed.), *Globalization and National Security*, pp. 231–57. New York London: Routledge.

Flores-Macias, G. A. and S. E. Kreps. 2015. Borrowing Support for War: The Effect of War Finance on Public Attitudes toward Conflict. *Journal of Conflict Resolution*: 1–30.

Freidman, T. L. and M. Mandelbaum. 2011. *That Used to Be Us: How America Fell Behind in the World It Invented and How We Can Come Back*. New York: Farrar Straus and Giroux.

Friedberg, A. L. 2000. *In the Shadow of the Garrison State*. Princeton, NJ: Princeton University Press.

Fuhrmann, M. and M. C. Horowitz. 2017. Droning On: Explaining the Proliferation of Unmanned Aerial Vehicles. *International Organization*, 71(2); 397–418.

Gholz, E. 2007. Globalization, Systems Integration, and the Future of Great Power War. *Security Studies*, 16(4): 615–36.

Gilli, A. and M. Gilli. 2016. The Diffusion of Drone Warfare? Industrial, Organizational and Infrastructural Constraints. *Security Studies*, 25(June): 50–84.

Gilpin, R. G. 1981. *War and Change in World Politics*. Cambridge: Cambridge University Press.

Goldman, E. O. and R. B. Andres. 1999. Systemic Effects of Military Innovation and Diffusion. *Security Studies*, 8(4): 79–125.

Grabel, I. 2011. Not your Grandfather's IMF: Global Crisis, "Productive Incoherence" and Developmental Policy Space. *Cambridge Journal of Economics*, 35(5): 805–30.

Hartley, K. and B. Solomon. 2016. Special Issue: Defence Inflation. *Defence and Peace Economics*, 27(2): 172–5.

Hirschman, A. O. 1970. *Exit, Voice, and Loyalty: Responses to Decline in Firms, Organizations, and States*. Cambridge, MA: Harvard University Press.

Horowitz, M. C. 2010. *The Diffusion of Military Power*. Princeton, NJ: Princeton University Press.

Horowitz, M. C. 2012. Information-Age Economics and the Future of East Asian Security Environment. In A. Goldstein and E. D. Mansfield (eds.), *The Nexus of Economics, Security, and International Relations in East Asia*. Stanford, CA: Stanford University Press.

Horowitz, M. C. 2014. The Looming Robotics Gap: Why America's global dominance in military technology is starting to crumble. *Foreign Policy* 206. *Available at:* http://foreignpolicy.com/2014/05/05/the-looming-robotics-gap/

Horowitz, M. C., S. E. Kreps, and M. Fuhrmann. 2017. The Consequences of Drone Proliferation: Separating Fact From Fiction. *International Security*, 41(2): 7–24.

Kennedy, P. 1988. *The Rise and Fall of the Great Powers: Economic Change and Military Conflict from 1500 to 2000*. New York: Random House.

Kim, N. K. 2014. Testing Two Explanations of the Liberal Peace: The Opportunity Cost and Signaling Arguments. *Journal of Conflict Resolution*, 58(5): 894–919.

Kirshner, J. (ed.). 2006a. *The Globalization of National Security*. London: Routledge.

Kirshner, J. 2006b. Globalization and National Security. In J. Kirschner (ed.), *The Globalization of National Security*. London: Routledge.

Kirshner, J. 2014. *American Power after the Financial Crisis*. Ithaca, NY: Cambridge University Press.

Kirshner, J. 2016. Dollar Diminution and New Macroeconomic Constraints on American Power. In J. Suri and B. Valentino (eds.), *Sustainable Security: Rethinking American National Security Strategy*. Oxford; New York: Oxford University Press.

Klare, M. 2001. *Resource Wars: The New Landscape of Global Conflict*. New York: Henry Holt.

Kramer, A. 2013. Russian Military Ordered to Switch to Socks. *New York Times*.

Kriner, D., B. Lechase, and R. Cappella Zielinski. 2015. Self-interest, Partisanship, and the Conditional Influence of Taxation on Support for War in the USA. *Conflict Management and Peace Science*: 1–22.

Kupchan, C. 2002. *The End of the American Era: U.S. Foreign Policy and the Geopolitics of the Twenty-first Century*. New York: Knopf.

Layne, C. 1993. The Unipolar Illusion: Why New Great Powers Will Rise. *International Security*, 17(4): 5–51.

Layne, C. 2012. This Time It's Real: The End of Unipolarity and the Pax Americana. *International Studies Quarterly*, 56(1): 203–13.

Liberman, P. 1996. *Does Conquest Pay? The Exploitation of Occupied Industrial Societies*. Princeton, NJ: Princeton University Press.

McDermott, R. 2016. Putin the "Peacemaker" Ends Operations in Syria. *Eurasia Daily Monitor*. 13(51). *Available at:* https://jamestown.org/program/putin-the-peacemaker-ends-operations-in-syria/

Mastanduno, M. 2009. System Maker and Privilege Taker: The United States and the International Political Economy. *World Politics*, 61(1): 121–54.

Meierding, E. 2016. Dismantling the Oil Wars Myth. *Security Studies*, 25(2): 258–88.

Monteiro, N. 2014. *Theory of Unipolar Politics*. Cambridge: Cambridge University Press.

Mueller, K. P. 2006. The Paradox of Liberal Hegemony. In J. Kirshner (ed.), *Globalization and National Security*, pp. 143–70. New York London: Routledge.

Neuman, S. G. 2006. Defense Industries and Global Dependency. *Orbis*, 50(3): 429–51.

Norrlof, C. 2014. Dollar Hegemony: A Power Analysis. *Review of International Political Economy*, 21(5): 1042–70.

Oatley, T., W. K. Winecoff, A. Pennock, and S. B. Danzman. 2013. The Political Economy of Global Finance: A Network Model. *Perspectives on Politics*, 11(1): 133–53.

Obama, B. 2016. President Obama: The TPP would let America, not China, lead the way on global trade. *The Washington Post*.

Schilde, K. 2016. European Military Capabilities: Enablers and Constraints on EU Power? *Journal of Common Market Studies*, 55(1): 37–53.

Schultz, K. A. 2015. Mapping Interstate Territorial Conflict A New Data Set and Applications. *Journal of Conflict Resolution*, 61(7): 1565–90.

Schultz, K. A. and B. Weingast. 2003. The Democratic Advantage: Institutional Foundations of Financial Power in International Competition. *International Organization*, 57(1): 3–42.

Shea, P. E. 2014. Financing Victory: Sovereign Credit, Democracy, and War. *Journal of Conflict Resolution*, 58(5): 771–95.

Singer, P. W. 2009. *Wired for War: The Robotics Revolution and Conflict in the 21st Century*. New York: Penguin.

Slaughter, A. 2009. America's Edge: Power in the Networked Century. *Foreign Affairs*, 88(February): 94–53.

Smith, R. 2009. *Military Economics: The Interaction of Power and Money*. Basingstoke: Palgrave Macmillan.

Starr, J. R. 1991. Water Wars. *Foreign Policy*, 82: 17–36.

Starrs, S. 2013. American Economic Power Hasn't Declined—It Globalized! Summoning the Data and Taking Globalization Seriously. *International Studies Quarterly*, 57(4): 817–30.

Strange, S. 1987. The Persistent Myth of Lost Hegemony. *International Organization*, 41(4): 551–74.

Strange, S. 1998. *States and Markets*. London: Bloomsbury.

US Air Forces Central Command, 2016. *Combined Forces Air Component Commander 2010–2015 Airpower Statistics*, Tampa Bay, FL. *Available at:* http://www.afcent.af.mil/AboutUs/AirpowerSummaries.aspx

Wolf, A. T. 1999. "Water Wars" and Water Reality: Conflict and Cooperation Along International Waterways. In S. Longeran (ed.), *Environmental Change, Adaptation, and Security*, pp. 251–65. Berlin: Springer.

Work, B. 2015. Deputy Secretary of Defense Speech: The Third U.S. Offset Strategy and its Implications for Partners and Allies. *Available at:* http://www.defense.gov/News/Speeches/Speech-View/Article/606641/the-third-us-offset-strategy-and-its-implications-for-partners-and-allies

World Bank, 2015. *World Development Indicators*. Washington, DC: World Bank.

World Economic Forum, 2015. *Global Risks 2015: Insight Report*. Geneva. *Available at:* www.weforum.org/risks

Zakaria, F. 2009. *Post-American World and the Rise of the Rest*. New York: Penguin.

Zegart, A. B. 2015. The Coming Revolution of Drone Warfare. *Wall Street Journal*: 18–21.

CHAPTER 22

THE CHANGING GEOGRAPHY OF GLOBAL SECURITY

FIONA B. ADAMSON

22.1 Introduction

The global rise in populist nationalism has led many commentators to argue that the world is set to enter a "post-globalization" period. Political developments such as "Brexit" and "global Trumpism" point to the ongoing relevance of the state as a key actor in international security. Yet, many of the most pressing and complicated contemporary security challenges—such as terrorism; climate change; complex humanitarian emergencies; mass migration and refugee flows; cyber-warfare; and transnational political violence—transcend the territorial confines of the state and do not fit easily within traditional models of national security. Indeed, the rise of populist nationalism can, in many respects, be understood as a reaction to changes in the underlying "landscape" of global security. Due to a combination of technological, economic, and political developments, the idea of the container state (Agnew 1994)—in which the territorial boundaries of the state are assumed to provide protection against external security threats—has become increasingly anachronistic and obsolete.

This chapter surveys the changing geography of international security and examines its implications for the future. Its starting premise is that security practices—like all human behavior—are embedded in and enabled by particular types of spatial configurations (Gregory and Urry 1985). The spatial configuration that has dominated most analyses of the security environment has been the nation state, which operates according to a particular territorial and bounded logic (Mann 1984). New information and communication technologies (ICTs), however, have transformed the human relationship with space and distance, while global markets have created forces that challenge territorial forms of sovereignty and democracy (Rosenau 2003; Stein 2016). As a result, numerous "non-national" spaces are becoming increasingly important for understanding global security dynamics. These include cities, cyberspace, the high seas, border regions, diasporas, refugee camps, prisons, and detention centers. At the same time, state security practices themselves are transforming in ways that blur distinctions between internal and "external" security. All these developments suggest the need to examine security discourse, policies, and practice beyond the spatial confines of the state.

The rest of this chapter proceeds in the following manner. First, it discusses the role that territoriality has played in the conceptualization of security, including the ways in which a "methodological nationalist" bias has helped to shape the field's historical focus on nation states and national interests. Second, it describes the blurring between "zones of war" and "zones of peace" that is challenging models of national security and leading to a rise in security practices such as surveillance, policing, and incarceration. The chapter then goes on to analyze how technology has led to new configurations of power such as diasporic networks and global cities. Finally, the chapter suggests the utility of borrowing conceptual tools and methodologies from geography, sociology, and anthropology as a means of re-spatializing the study of global security.

22.2 Territorial States, Methodological Nationalism, and Security Studies

Shaped by the historical experiences of the First World War, Second World War and the Cold War, mainstream approaches to international security have traditionally focused on issues of "national security" and the sources of conflict and cooperation among states. Dominant theories and approaches in the field reflect this state-centric focus. The ability to treat the territorial state as a "unit" or "actor" has allowed for the emergence of a body of state-centric work in security studies based on strategic interaction, rational choice assumptions, bargaining, and game theory (Schelling 1980; Axelrod and Keohane 1985). Entire sub-fields of security studies, such as the study of nuclear strategy, coercive diplomacy, and deterrence all rely heavily on these statist assumptions, which inform a wide-ranging literature on alliances, arms races, conflict spirals, and security dilemmas (Jervis 1978; Walt 1990; Snyder 2007).

These assumptions, however, also mean that the field has been marked by a "methodological nationalism" that has obscured the importance of spaces beyond the state (Adamson 2016). Methodological nationalism refers to the naturalization of the nation state by the social sciences, and arguably produces at least three underlying biases: it ignores the fundamental role that the ideology of nationalism has played in structuring the modern world; it assumes that the territorial borders of the state are the relevant boundaries for studying social phenomena; and it leads researchers to identify with the interests of their own national unit (Wimmer and Schiller 2003). As a result, the state has in many respects come to be seen as a natural social and political unit in security studies—despite the fact that it is just one of many possible spatial regimes of control and governance (Ruggie 1993; Elden 2013). Nomadic societies, empires, and city states (Doyle 1986; MacKay et al. 2014; Spruyt 1996) are all examples of alternative forms of rule and governance that do not conform to the territorial logic of nation states.

The methodological nationalism of security studies has never been an accurate reflection of empirical reality. The history of nation states has been closely connected with warmaking and has been marked by large-scale forms of violence against civilians such as ethnic cleansing, population exchanges, and programs of assimilation and homogenization (Tilly 1990; Rae 2002; Mann 2005). Moreover, security studies as a whole has not done an adequate job of examining the history of violence and destruction that accompanied European imperialism, or movements toward decolonization. It also has a poor record of documenting and analyzing the use of state violence internally—such as human rights violations or mass killings and genocide that take place within states (Valentino 2013). These blind spots reflect the fact that the modern field of security studies has often been based on the view from state capitals in North America and Europe rather than the global South.

Nevertheless, the centrality of territory and states to the modern understanding of security is clear. Warfare has historically been linked to territory—defending and protecting it, or attacking, annexing, and occupying it (Lasswell 1941). Military battleground strategies have traditionally focused on how to engage with a particular terrain or geography (von Clausewitz 2008; Elden 2010). Internal conflicts and civil wars are considered more or less resolvable based on whether territory is viewed as divisible or indivisible (Toft 2005; Goddard 2006). In effect, the territorial organization of nation states has structured modern conceptions of the relationship between territory, war, and security—including how we define wars and political violence and which bodies count as being lost in battle (Krause 2017).

The physical borders of the state have often been idealized as offering a "protective shell" against external threats (Andreas 2003; Maier 2016). Even for advanced industrialized states, however, this image did not reflect reality in the twentieth century. The role of territory in warfare changed significantly with the age of nuclear weapons. Suddenly there was the possibility that warfare could result in the annihilation of the planet rather than just the annexation or occupation of territory. Although the "hard shell" of the territorial state had been eroding previously with the advent of aerial warfare, the nuclear revolution fundamentally changed the nature of warfare, creating an impetus for a system of collective security for territorial states (Herz 1957).

22.3 The Blurring of Zones of War and Peace

The Global War on Terror (GWOT) that ensued following the terrorist attacks of September 11, 2001 led to further shifts in the relationship between territory and international security, including the blurring of what constitutes "zones of war" and "zones of peace" (Elden 2009; Gros 2010). Transnational networks of non-state actors who use political violence and terror are not new, but the scale of the 9/11 attacks shifted perceptions and challenged perceived distinctions between "inside" and "outside," or domestic and external approaches to state security (Walker 1992; Adamson 2005). This was reflected in the declaration by the 9/11 Commission Report (2004) that the "US Homeland is the Planet." It was also reflected in the practices and tools that defined the GWOT, which included surveillance technology, drone warfare, covert activities and a global network of extra-juridical spaces or "black sites." In the post-9/11 context a central strategic problem was the lack of clear geographic boundaries with which to define "the enemy." Terms such as "sanctuaries," "safe havens," operating environments," "enabling environments," and "terrain complexity" were employed as a way of delineating relevant geographical spaces in armed conflict (Innes 2008).

The use of drone warfare has further challenged traditional spatial imaginaries of conflict by physically separating combatants from the battlefield. Spaces of warfare become blurred with spaces of ordinary civilian life when drone operators can return to their homes and families at the end of a day of remote-control combat (Wilcox 2015). Furthermore, there is an increasing realization that counter insurgency strategies and equipment used in distant locales can be re-imported to domestic contexts and applied to populations at "home" via the militarization of policing, when social protest is likened to a nascent insurgency. More generally, war has shifted from territories to individual human bodies—whether through the precision targeting and killing of individuals in drone strikes by the United States, or the use of suicide terrorism by non-state actors—a strategy which employs the human body as a weapon (Bargu 2014).

The system of black sites and spatial confinement such as the Guantanamo Bay Detention Camp that emerged during the War on Terror constituted a "war in the shadows" that was rendered largely invisible in state-centric approaches to security (Khalili 2012). These same techniques of spatial confinement and control can be seen as disrupting the territorial landscape of states—and as constituting a competing "carceral geography" that incarcerates some populations within states while facilitating the movement of others (De Genova and Peutz 2010; Silverman 2015; Moran 2016). Prisons and detention centers—often privately run and managed—have emerged as illiberal spaces of exception used to marginalize and confine populations viewed as threatening—whether potential terrorists, criminals or—increasingly—migrants, refugees, and failed asylum seekers. The latter have been portrayed by some actors as "others" or enemies that challenge both the territorial order of states, and the national identities and interests of particular states. Indeed, the figure of the refugee or stateless person increasingly points to the limits of liberal state-based notions of citizenship, belonging, and human rights (Haddad 2008). Similarly, the existence of quasi-permanent refugee camps in states such as Lebanon, Algeria, Pakistan, and Kenya that disrupts and challenges the ontology of the international states system and blurs the boundaries between spaces of global humanitarianism, spaces of state sovereignty, and spaces of conflict and confinement.

The blurring of zones of war and peace means that shared spaces take on different meanings to different populations. For example, the Mediterranean Sea has become an extension of war zones in many respects: refugees attempt to escape violent conflict, organized crime networks engage in human smuggling, state actors send military patrols, and nongovernmental organizations (NGOs) and private actors send ships to rescue refugees and migrants. At the same time, the Mediterranean also continues to function as a space of tourism, commerce, trade, and transport—despite the fact that the perilous journey of crossing the Mediterranean results in many more deaths annually than would be required to code conflicts as "wars" in major datasets on international and internal conflict.[1]

The erasure of clear lines between spaces of war and peace can also be seen in the growing importance of cities in the new global security environment. Cities and their transport systems, infrastructure, and public spaces have become focal points for larger global political struggles. Terrorist attacks in cities as diverse as Paris, London, Brussels, Baghdad, Manchester, Kabul, New York, Madrid, Moscow, Barcelona, St Petersburg, Berlin, Istanbul, Ankara, Beirut, Tunis, Nairobi, Bangkok, Jakarta, Mumbai, Lahore, and Abuja make headlines around the world and play into larger global narratives about terrorism. Indeed, in the past several decades 75 percent of the incidents of political violence labeled as "terrorism" have occurred in cities (Ljungkvist 2015; Savitch 2014). Cities are increasingly characterized by surveillance and policing activities focused on containing urban unrest Counter insurgency specialists now identify cities as new battlegrounds in asymmetric conflicts, thus suggesting a future blurring of military, counter insurgency and policing activities (Kilcullen 2015). Moreover, securing and policing cities has become a lucrative business for private and for-profit security companies (Abrahamsen and Williams 2007).

Like cities, virtual space is also increasingly being securitized. Cyberspace activity is subject to extensive surveillance and monitoring by state agencies such as the US National Security Agency (NSA) or multinational corporations, but has also become an arena itself of conflict between various mixes of state and non-state actors, through cyber-warfare, cyber-attacks and so-called "cyber exploitation." Security mechanisms such as deterrence, compellence, and collective defense depend on clearly delineated and identifiable rational unitary actors, yet cyberspace is an arena that blurs lines between peaceful and hostile activities and that facilitates diffuse identities and networked structures to the extent that it is often unclear which actors represent which constituencies (Kello 2013).

The networked structure of the Internet challenges national boundaries and territorially-defined divisions between "insider" and "outsider," facilitating the emergence of new sub- and transnational identities. In the context of advanced globalization, imagined communities can stretch far beyond the state and into wholly new spaces (Deibert 2000). This both increases global connectivity and leads to the emergence of global publics and a global public sphere, but may simultaneously lead to new forms of fractionalization, rivalry, and identity-based political contestation that do not correspond to specific territorial locations.

22.4 New Geographies of Power Beyond the State

The emergence of new spaces of global security that blur the line between war and peace is indicative of a shift in geographies of power. A traditional way of measuring shifts in power has been to examine the balance of power across territorial states. In this context, the question of the rise of "emerging powers" and the decline of the United States and other Western powers has taken on significance for understanding the future of international security. Yet, a focus on changes in the balance of power across states ignores deeper changes to the overall distribution of power that transcend any particular state.

Spatial relations often reflect broader power relations. For example, spatial relations in humanitarian crisis situations are often a microcosm of larger global North–South inequalities. Examining how humanitarian aid is physically and spatially organized helps to illuminate aspects of identity and power relations that impact on human security, and that are not reducible to states and their interests. International humanitarian aid workers congregate in the lobbies of international hotels and drive around in white SUVs while the victims of conflict are confined to refugee camps (Smirl 2015). Globalized humanitarian crises involve the engagement of multiple types of actors—such as aid workers, representatives of international organizations, or foreign fighters—who share the same physical space, but are connected to very different types of networks and power. International and local actors will often have competing frames and understandings of the same conflict (Autesserre 2014; Bakke 2014). They exist side-by-side but may inhabit different life worlds and participate in different global imaginaries.

Similarly, the Internet can have the effect of replicating or perpetuating existing global inequalities and importing them into new contexts. For example, global online identity politics are largely conducted in English, with key nodes and websites located in the global North, and are dominated by discourses of human rights (Kumar 2016). The world wide web has become a non-territorial space for the enactment of identity politics, accompanied by new forms of symbolic politics. Yet, while such activities transcend the territorial boundaries of states, they may nevertheless be affected by and reflect the geopolitics of the interstate system. In many cases, territoriality continues to play an important symbolic role in online politics, via the use of alternative maps and cartographic images (Kashmir, Khalistan, Kurdistan, Palestine, Tamil Eelam, the Islamic Caliphate) to contest dominant geopolitical narratives and provide a counter-hegemonic virtual alternative to existing territorial-juridical realities.

At the same time new technologies also have disruptive effects that produce alternative non-state geographies of power. For example, in comparing the effect of cyberspace on structures of global finance and structures of global activism, Sassen (2012: 459) notes that in the case of finance cyberspace has simultaneously elevated the power of "subnational scales such as the global city, and supranational scales, such as global markets, where previously the national scale was dominant." The opposite is the case in the political realm, where weak and previously isolated locally embedded actors can "go global," forming coalitions and alliances with other actors online, thus engaging in transnational action without physically moving.

These changes empower new actors and create new concentrations of power that become sites of political resistance and contestation. The emergence of global networks, for example, empowers smaller, weaker non-state actors by allowing them to coordinate with like-minded constituencies around the globe. This increases the salience of asymmetric forms of warfare and conflict, which renders traditional "national" security policies ineffective. Diverse local actors become enmeshed in larger global networks as local settings become "microenvironments on global circuits" (Sassen 2012: 466, 468). Thus, a single actor or small network operating in Manchester or Paris can be linked to similarly small networks in Libya, Syria, or elsewhere, meaning that very different types of political spaces become part of connected global circuits of extremist violence. Such tactical innovations challenge the nature of conventional warfare and "postmodern" conflicts therefore become wars of hearts and minds that are conducted in part via multimedia communications networks (Sassen 2012; Betz 2015).

Networks facilitate connections across different sites and spaces in the global economy—such as cities, cyberspace, and border regions. They operate on a different logic from hierarchical institutions and political orders. Within networks, power exists in particular nodes and positions and with brokers who can act as a bridge across different networks (Jackson and Nexon 1999; Goddard 2009; Hafner-Burton et al. 2009). Network structures have thus come to dominate both the forms that security threats take—such as de-territorialized terrorist networks—as well as institutionalized forms of security responses and governance (Krahmann 2005; Sageman 2011).

Technology has created incentives for the rise of networked structures and has also empowered actors such as diaspora groups that transcend the territorial borders of states, while still remaining tied to their politics. The existence of such transnational diasporas has a broader structural impact as it challenges the fit between the "state" as a territory or bureaucratic structure and the "nation" or identity of a state (Adamson and Demetriou 2007). Diasporic political entrepreneurs can take advantage of political opportunity structures that emerge in an integrated global economy to mobilize transnationally to engage in politics beyond the state. The emergence of transnational diaspora politics does not always correlate with increased cosmopolitanism, but often instead involves the globalization of localized conflicts and identities (Lyons and Mandaville 2010).

Diaspora politics has an impact on the global security environment in several different ways. First, violent conflict can generate diasporas when populations are forced to leave to escape persecution or violence, as in the case of the Tamil, Kurdish, Eritrean, and Syrian diasporas (Lyons 2007). Second, diasporas can play a role in the dynamics of internal conflicts and civil wars by shifting the local balance of power via the transfer of resources or by engaging in protest, lobbying, or other political activities (Collier et al. 1999; Adamson 2013; Koinova 2013). Third, diasporas can globalize and transnationalize of civil wars via activities that create spillover effects in their countries of residence. Finally, diaspora politics can also be a force for conflict resolution, development and transitional justice (Shain 2002; Smith and Stares 2007; Brinkerhoff 2011; Koinova and Karabegović 2017).

The role of transnational diasporas in the global security environment also points to the ways in which transnational forces and external factors shape power relations in intra-state conflicts (Gleditsch 2007; Salehyan et al. 2011; Checkel 2013). Transnational ethnic groups, diasporas, refugees, foreign fighters, international organizations, multinational corporations, and other actors can all have impacts on the dynamics of "internal" conflicts, meaning that what appear to be "local" conflicts are often more accurately analyzed as manifestations of larger structural and systemic factors (Hironaka 2005).

The shift in global power relations brought about by ICTs also helps to explain the importance that global cities play in the new security environment. Cities may be desirable targets due to the density of their infrastructure and population, but also due to the symbolic role they play as repositories of global power, finance, and culture. Cities are at once embedded in particular national spaces and contexts, subject to the jurisdiction of national governments. But they also transcend these national spaces, acting as nodes in global networks and circuits of finance, knowledge, and exchange. Indeed, cities can be thought of as quasi-autonomous centers of global power that transcend and coexist with nation states: they develop independent relations with other cities, compete with one another for resources and status, form alliances, and join their own global institutions. They also develop their own urban identities, and autonomous security policies. The paradoxical and multi-faceted dimensions of global cities—as spaces of cosmopolitanism and capitalism, as well as spaces marked by intense inequalities, increasing surveillance, policing, and securitization—make them key spaces for theorizing contemporary security.

22.5 Analyzing the New Security Landscape: Methods and Approaches

Understanding the future landscape of international security requires methods and tools that move beyond the "territorial trap" of methodological nationalism, and that allow us to examine the relations that emerge across very different types of spaces and actors. Disciplines such as geography, sociology, anthropology, and critical geopolitics all provide a number of useful resources for engaging with the changing geography of international security. These include concepts such as scale; approaches that focus on networks, fields, and assemblages; and methods that range from the use of big data and quantitative analysis to ethnographic and practice-based approaches. Utilizing such approaches does not mean throwing out traditional conceptions of power, identity, and interest, but rather thinking about how they operate in contexts beyond the state.

Notions of scale and scalar processes can be helpful in understanding some of the dynamics and configurations that define the new security landscape. Whereas levels-of-analysis approaches to international security sought to distinguish between the national (or domestic) and the international, scalar approaches help to show how different levels are connected with one another or are intertwined (Sjoberg 2008). For example, global cities are not just physical spaces but they are also sites of multiple and interlinking power relations that operate at many levels, from the micro-level of the physical body, to the local, national, and global (Massey 2005). The idea of the "local" has traditionally been associated with physical or geographic proximity, embedded in a nested hierarchy that includes the national and the global, but new technologies disrupt these hierarchies by enabling "multiscalar transactions and simultaneous interconnectivity" meaning that issues and conflicts in one locale can easily diffuse to other sites and spaces, in the process becoming transnationalized and globalized (Sassen 2012).

The notion of scale shift in particular helps to shed light on how some forms of political violence "go global" and become inserted into new contexts. "Scale shift" has been applied to social movements to understand how and when actors move issues to different geographic levels (Tarrow and McAdam 2005) such as when a "national" issue becomes a global concern or a global discourse becomes transferred into a local arena. A similar dynamic exists in the use of political violence by non-state actors. Terrorist attacks in global cities are an example of the use of scalar strategies and processes by relatively weak, violent non-state actors: the use of violence creates an "upward" scale shift by provoking global media coverage of a "local" event in a way that helps to shape and construct global security narratives. If the media plays along, it is an effective way of globalizing fear. On the other hand, a "downward" scale shift can be seen when transnational or long-distance conflicts become embedded in new local contexts. An example would be the emergence of rival local neighborhood street gangs based on identity cleavages in homeland civil wars, as has happened in Toronto and London around the Tamil conflict in Sri Lanka (Orjuela 2011) and in cities in Sweden and Germany around the Kurdish conflict in Turkey (Baser 2016).

The existence of such transnational connections and circuits has led to an increased interest in the use of network analysis in security studies. Network approaches fit well with both qualitative methods and ethnography but also with formal methods that use big data to visualize complex relations that transcend any particular territory. For example, geospatial analysis can be used to map the distribution and concentration of various factors across space, such as natural resources or populations, and may also be combined with agent-based modeling approaches and complexity theory to examine the dynamics of complex humanitarian crises; the diffusion of violent conflicts; or the spread of health emergencies and epidemics (Ward and Gleditsch 2002; Vogt et al. 2015; Pickering 2017: 139–82).

Other forms of ontological theorizing provide useful templates for conducting empirical research on different spatial configurations beyond the state. For example, the notion of the assemblage has been helpful for conceptualizing the complex and variegated relations and interests that converge around issues such as private security, military intervention, and policing (Abrahamsen and Williams 2009; Bachmann et al. 2014). An assemblage approach suggests an object of research composed of a set of relations and connections that transcend particular places or levels of analysis. It is concerned with aggregating relationships rather than delineating particular territorial units. Assemblage and field theory approaches thus both fit well with a move toward practice-based and ethnographic methods in International Relations (Adler and Pouliot 2011; Berling 2012; Bueger and Gadinger 2014). A commonality of these approaches is that they have been agnostic about the particular units or spaces to be investigated, and they allow for a focus on process and meaning in ways that get beyond traditional debates about ideational and material factors.

For example, examining piracy as a "community of practice" provides a helpful means of conceptualizing and analyzing a non-territorial feature of the security environment without reducing it to a "unit" or "actor" (Bueger 2013). Similarly, Bourdeausian field theory provides a useful way of understanding how domestic police forces are increasingly linked to each other beyond state borders, sharing common identifications and sets of relations via narratives and discourses around global crime that produce a transnational field of security professionals (Bigo 2011). Such approaches point to the fruitfulness of taking an inductive and ethnographic approach to the new security environment—one in which assumptions about the relevant spaces for understanding international security dynamics are not assumed a priori but rather become objects of investigation.

22.6 Conclusions

Whereas security studies has focused disproportionately on issues of interstate conflict, understanding the future of international security requires moving past the national frame and paying greater attention to spaces and sites beyond the state. Such spaces include refugee camps, global cities, cyberspace, diasporas, and other locales and spatial configurations that transcend or coexist with territorial states. The emergence of such spaces as important sites of global security discourses and practices also leads us to examine the reconfiguration of global power relations in ways that cut across territorial states. This challenges classical notions about the balance of power by directing our attention to non-territorial configurations of power such as asymmetric forms of warfare and conflict with non-state actors and networks.

Concepts and approaches drawn from disciplines such as geography, sociology, anthropology, and critical geopolitics provide a useful starting point for analyzing and understanding the social and power relations that characterize non-territorial security challenges and responses. Assemblage, field theory, and network analysis approaches provide templates that focus on social relations rather than territorial units, while incorporating notions of scale and methods such as geospatial analysis provides additional avenues for treating space as "a constituent aspect that must be conceptualized explicitly and probed systematically" rather than an assumed and unproblematized background (Sewell 2001: 51–2).

Despite recent trends indicating the re-assertion of nationalism, larger structural changes in world politics still point to the necessity of understanding security dynamics beyond the spatial confines of the state. The increased connectivity brought about by information and communication technologies (ICTs) and other features of advanced globalization will require state policy-makers and other actors to continue to grapple with security issues in "non-national" spaces that traverse territorial boundaries. The blurring of the lines between zones of war and zones of peace will mean a decrease in the effectiveness of policies—such as deterrence or strategic bargaining—that rely on the assumption of states as unitary actors. Instead, the changing geography of international security leads to a greater emphasis on non-territorial security policies such as policing, surveillance, and the use of information warfare. A major challenge for the future will be to find ways to work together to foster global security and stability in this changed environment without sacrificing other important collective goods such as civil liberties, privacy, and freedom of movement.

Note

1. A figure of 4812 migrants died crossing the Mediterranean in 2016. Data from the Missing Migrants Project, International Organization for Migration (IOM): https://missingmigrants.iom.int/migrant-deaths-worldwide-top-7100-over-half-mediterranean

References

Abrahamsen, R. and M. C. Williams. 2007. Securing the City: Private Security Companies and Non-State Authority in Global Governance. *International Relations*, 21(2): 237–53.

Abrahamsen, R. and M. C. Williams. 2009. Security Beyond the State: Global Security Assemblages in International Politics. *International Political Sociology*, 3(1): 1–17.

Adamson, F. B. 2005. Globalisation, Transnational Political Mobilisation, and Networks of Violence. *Cambridge Review of International Affairs*, 18(1): 31–49.

Adamson, F. B. 2013. Mechanisms of Diaspora Mobilization and the Transnationalization of Civil War. J. T. Checkel (ed.), *Transnational Dynamics of Civil War*, pp. 63–88. Cambridge: Cambridge University Press.

Adamson, F. B. 2016. Spaces of Global Security: Beyond Methodological Nationalism. *Journal of Global Security Studies*, 1(1): 19–35.

Adamson, F. B. and M. Demetriou. 2007. Remapping the Boundaries of "State" and "National Identity": Incorporating Diasporas into IR Theorizing. *European Journal of International Relations*, 13(4): 489–526.

Adler, E. and V. Pouliot. 2011. *International Practices: Introduction and Framework*. Cambridge Studies in International Relations. Cambridge: Cambridge University Press.

Agnew, J. 1994. The Territorial Trap: The Geographical Assumptions of International Relations Theory. *Review of International Political Economy*, 1(1): 53–80.
Andreas, P. 2003. Redrawing the Line: Borders and Security in the Twenty-first Century. *International Security*, 28(2): 78–111.
Autesserre, S. 2014. *Peaceland: Conflict Resolution and the Everyday Politics of International Intervention*. Cambridge: Cambridge University Press.
Axelrod, R. and R. O. Keohane. 1985. Achieving Cooperation under Anarchy: Strategies and Institutions. *World Politics*, 38(1): 226–54.
Bachmann, J. C. Bell, and C. Holmqvist. 2014. *War, Police and Assemblages of Intervention*. Abingdon: Routledge.
Bakke, K. M. 2014. Help wanted? The Mixed Record of Foreign Fighters in Domestic Insurgencies. *International Security*, 38(4): 150–87.
Bargu, B. 2014. *Starve and Immolate: The Politics of Human Weapons*. New York: Columbia University Press.
Baser, B. 2016. *Diasporas and Homeland Conflicts: A Comparative Perspective*. Abingdon: Routledge.
Berling, T. V. 2012. Bourdieu, International Relations, and European Security. *Theory and Society*, 41(5): 451–78.
Betz, D. 2015. *Carnage and Connectivity: Landmarks in the Decline of Conventional Military Power*. Oxford: Oxford University Press.
Bigo, D. 2011. Pierre Bourdieu and International Relations: Power of Practices, Practices of Power. *International Political Sociology*, 5(3): 225–58.
Brinkerhoff, J. M. 2011. Diasporas and Conflict Societies: Conflict Entrepreneurs, Competing Interests or Contributors to Stability and Development?, *Conflict, Security & Development*, 11(2): 115–43.
Bueger, C. 2013. Practice, Pirates and Coast Guards: The Grand Narrative of Somali Piracy. *Third World Quarterly*, 34(10): 1811–27.
Bueger, C. and F. Gadinger. 2014. *International Practice Theory: New Perspectives*. Berlin: Springer.
Checkel, J. T. 2013. *Transnational Dynamics of Civil War*. Cambridge: Cambridge University Press.
Collier, P. and A. Hoeffler. 1999. *Greed and Grievance in Civil War*. Policy Research Working Papers. The World Bank.
De Genova, N. and N. Peutz 2010. *The Deportation Regime: Sovereignty, Space, and the Freedom of Movement*. Durham, NC: Duke University Press.
Deibert, R. 2000. *Parchment, Printing, and Hypermedia: Communication and World Order Transformation*. New York: Columbia University Press.
Doyle, M. W. 1986. *Empires*. Ithaca, NY: Cornell University Press.
Elden, S. 2009. *Terror and Territory: The Spatial Extent of Sovereignty*. Minneapolis: University of Minnesota Press.
Elden, S. 2010. Land, Terrain, Territory. *Progress in Human Geography*, 34(6): 799–817.
Elden, S. 2013. *The Birth of Territory*. Chicago: University of Chicago Press.
Gleditsch, K. S. 2007. Transnational Dimensions of Civil War. *Journal of Peace Research*, 44(3): 293–309.
Goddard, S. E. 2006. Uncommon Ground: Indivisible Territory and the Politics of Legitimacy. *International Organization*, 60(1): 35–68.

Goddard, S. E. 2009. Brokering Change: Networks and Entrepreneurs in International Politics. *International Theory*, 1(2): 249–81.
Gregory, D. and J. Urry. (eds.). 1985. *Social Relations and Spatial Structures:* Critical Human Geography. Basingstoke: Macmillan Education.
Gros, F. 2010. *States of Violence: An Essay on the End of War*. Chicago: University of Chicago Press.
Haddad, E. 2008. *The Refugee in International Society: Between Sovereigns*. Cambridge: Cambridge University Press.
Hafner-Burton, E. M., M. Kahler, and A. H. Montgomery. 2009. Network Analysis for International Relations. *International Organization*, 63(3): 559–92.
Herz, J. H. 1957. Rise and Demise of the Territorial State. *World Politics*, 9(4): 473–93.
Hironaka, A. 2005. *Neverending Wars: Weak States, the International Community, and the Perpetuation of Civil War*. Cambridge, MA: Harvard University Press.
Innes, M. A. 2008. Protected Status, Sacred Sites, Black Holes and Human Agents: System, Sanctuary and Terrain Complexity. *Civil Wars*, 10(1): 1–5.
Jackson, P. T. and D. H. Nexon. 1999. Relations before States: Substance, Process and the Study of World Politics. *European Journal of International Relations*, 5(3): 291–332.
Jervis, R. 1978. Cooperation under the Security Dilemma. *World Politics* , 30(2): 167–214.
Kello, L. 2013. The Meaning of the Cyber Revolution: Perils to Theory and Statecraft. *International Security*, 38(2): 7–40.
Khalili, L. 2012. *Time in the Shadows: Confinement in Counterinsurgencies*. Stanford, CA: Stanford University Press.
Kilcullen, D. 2015. *Out of the Mountains: The Coming Age of the Urban Guerrilla*. Oxford: Oxford University Press.
Koinova, M. 2013. Four Types of Diaspora Mobilization: Albanian Diaspora Activism For Kosovo Independence in the US and the UK. *Foreign Policy Analysis*, 9(4): 433–53.
Koinova, M. and D. Karabegović. 2017. Diasporas and Transitional Justice: Transnational Activism from Local to Global Levels of Engagement. *Global Networks—A Journal of Transnational Affairs*, 17(2): 212–33.
Krahmann, E. 2005. Security Governance and Networks: New Theoretical Perspectives in Transatlantic Security. *Cambridge Review of International Affairs*, 18(1): 15–30.
Krause, K. 2017. Bodies Count: The Politics and Practices of War and Violent Death Data. *Human Remains and Violence: An Interdisciplinary Journal*, 3(1): 90–115.
Kumar, P. 2016. *Diaspora 2.0: Mapping Sikh, Tamil and Palestinian Online Identity Politics*. PhD Thesis. SOAS, University of London.
Lasswell, H. D. 1941. The Garrison State. *The American Journal of Sociology*, 46(4): 455–68.
Ljungkvist, K. 2015. *The Global City 2.0: From Strategic Site to Global Actor*. Abingdon: Routledge.
Lyons, T. 2007. Conflict-generated Diasporas and Transnational Politics in Ethiopia. *Conflict, Security and Development*, 7(4): 529–49.
Lyons, T. and P. Mandaville. 2010. Think Locally, Act Globally: Toward a Transnational Comparative Politics. *International Political Sociology*, 4(2): 124–41.
MacKay, J., J. Levin, G. de Carvalho, K. Cavoukian, and R. Cuthbert. 2014. Before and After Borders: The Nomadic Challenge to Sovereign Territoriality. *International Political Science Review*, 51(1): 101–23.
Maier, C. S. 2016. *Once Within Borders*. Cambridge, MA: Harvard University Press.

Mann, M. 1984. The Autonomous Power of the State: Its Origins, Mechanisms and Results. *Archives europeennes de sociologie. European Journal of Sociology. Europaisches Archiv fur Soziologie*, 25(2): 185–213.

Mann, M. 2005. *The Dark Side of Democracy: Explaining Ethnic Cleansing*. Cambridge: Cambridge University Press.

Massey, D. 2005. *For Space*. London: Sage.

Moran, D. 2016. *Carceral Geography: Spaces and Practices of Incarceration*. Abingdon: Routledge.

Orjuela, C. 2011. Violence at the Margins: Street Gangs, Globalized Conflict and Sri Lankan Tamil Battlefields in London, Toronto and Paris. *International Studies*, 48(2): 113–37.

Pickering, S. 2017. *Understanding Geography and War*. New York: Palgrave Macmillan.

Rae, H. 2002. *State Identities and the Homogenisation of Peoples*. Cambridge: Cambridge University Press.

Rosenau, J. N. 2003. *Distant Proximities: Dynamics Beyond Globalization*. Princeton, NJ: Princeton University Press.

Ruggie, J. G. 1993. Territoriality and Beyond: Problematizing Modernity in International Relations. *International Organization*, 47(1): 139–74.

Sageman, M. 2011. *Leaderless Jihad: Terror Networks in the Twenty-First Century*. Philadelphia: University of Pennsylvania Press.

Salehyan, I., K. S. Gleditsch, and D. E. Cunningham. 2011. Explaining External Support for Insurgent Groups. *International Organization*, 65(4): 709–44.

Sassen, S. 2012. Interactions of the Technical and the Social: Digital Formations of the Powerful and the Powerless. *Information, Communication and Society*, 15(4): 455–78.

Savitch, H. V. 2014. *Cities in a Time of Terror: Space, Territory, and Local Resilience*. Abingdon: Routledge.

Schelling, T. C. 1980. *The Strategy of Conflict*. Cambridge, MA: Harvard University Press.

Sewell, W. H., Jr. 2001. Space in Contentious Politics. In R. R. Aminzade (ed.), *Silence and Voice in the Study of Contentious Politics*, pp. 51–88. New York: Cambridge University Press Cambridge.

Shain, Y. 2002. The Role of Diasporas in Conflict Perpetuation or Resolution. *SAIS Review*, 22(2): 115–44.

Silverman, S. J. 2015. Carceral Spaces: Mobility and Agency in Imprisonment and Migrant Detention. *Social & Cultural Geography*, 16(7): 863–4.

Sjoberg, L. 2008. Scaling IR Theory: Geography's Contribution to Where IR Takes Place. *International Studies Review*, 10(3): 472–500.

Smirl, L. 2015. *Spaces of Aid: How Cars, Compounds and Hotels Shape Humanitarianism*. London: Zed Books Ltd.

Smith, H. A. and P. Stares. 2007. *Diasporas in Conflict: Peace-makers or Peace-wreckers?* Tokyo: United Nations University Press.

Snyder, G. H. 2007. *Alliance Politics*. New York: Cornell University Press.

Spruyt, H. 1996. *The Sovereign State and Its Competitors: An Analysis of Systems Change*. Princeton, NJ: Princeton University Press.

Stein, A. A. 2016. The Great Trilemma: Are Globalization, Democracy, and Sovereignty Compatible? *International Theory*, 8(2): 297–340.

Tarrow, S. and D. McAdam. 2005. Scale Shift in Transnational Contention. In D. della Porta (ed.), *Transnational Protest and Global Activism*, pp. 121–150. Lanham, MD: Rowman and Littlefield.

The 9/11 Commission Report: Final Report of the National Commission on Terrorist Attacks Upon the United States, official government edition. Washington, DC: US Government Printing Office, 2004.

Tilly, C. 1990. *Coercion, Capital and European States, AD 990–1992*. Cambridge, MA: Basil Blackwell.

Toft, M. D. 2005. *The Geography of Ethnic Violence: Identity, Interests, and the Indivisibility of Territory*. Princeton, NJ: Princeton University Press.

Valentino, B. A. 2013. *Final Solutions: Mass Killing and Genocide in the 20th Century*. Ithaca, NY: Cornell University Press.

von Clausewitz, C. 2008. *On War*. Princeton, NJ: Princeton University Press.

Vogt, M., N.-C. Bormann, S. Rüegger, L.-E. Cederman, P. Hunziker, and L. Girardin, L. 2015. Integrating Data on Ethnicity, Geography, and Conflict: The Ethnic Power Relations Data Set Family. *The Journal of Conflict Resolution*, 59(7): 1327–42.

Walker, R. B. J. 1992. *Inside/Outside*. Cambridge: Cambridge University Press.

Walt, S. M. 1990. *The Origins of Alliances*. Ithaca, NY: Cornell University Press.

Ward, M. D. and K. S. Gleditsch. 2002. Location, Location, Location: An MCMC Approach to Modeling the Spatial Context of War and Peace. *Political Analysis: An Annual Publication of the Methodology Section of the American Political Science Association*, 10(3): 244–60.

Wilcox, L. B. 2015. *Bodies of Violence: Theorizing Embodied Subjects in International Relations*. Oxford: Oxford University Press.

Wimmer, A., and N. G. Schiller. 2003. Methodological Nationalism, the Social Sciences, and the Study of Migration: An Essay in Historical Epistemology. *International Migration Review*, 37(3): 576–610.

CHAPTER 23

THE GREAT DEBATE

The Nuclear-Political Question and World Order

DANIEL DEUDNEY

23.1 Contested Legacies

Hiroshima was "the day humanity began taking its final exam" as futurist Buckminster Fuller has observed (Fuller 1969: 56). While outright failure has not happened yet, the prospects for passing and moving on to the next grade do not look very promising. Experts disagree strongly on basic questions, unexpected surprises abound, and the contours of the debates over fundamentals periodically shift in major ways. The future, unfortunately, is likely to continue these patterns: avoiding the ultimate civilizational failure of nuclear war is unlikely to persist indefinitely.

The bombing of Hiroshima in 1945 marks the beginning of a new era in human history in which human capacities of destruction began to pose an existential threat to civilization and humanity. This ominous new reality has triggered a great debate about how to achieve security in a nuclear world. Even before nuclear weapons were brought into existence during the Manhattan Project or used on Japan during the waning days of the Second World War, contentious debate over their implications for humanity and international politics was underway among nuclear scientists (Boyer 1985). Across the seven decades of the nuclear era, controversy over these great engines of destruction has been a prominent, and immensely complex, facet of contemporary global civilization. These disputes have spilled into virtually every domain of human thought, particularly in the United States and Europe. Despite their high stakes, debates over nuclear weapons among theorists of international politics are marked by little consensus. At the core of these arguments is a very simple question, the nuclear-political question: What political arrangements are necessary for security from nuclear weapons? This question poses a dark puzzle upon whose successful resolution rests the fate of civilization, and perhaps human survival.

Unfortunately, there is little prospect for inductively answering this question in any fully convincing manner by recourse to empirical facts. While a great many answers have been offered to this question, and many experts are confident they have the answer to it, their answers and confidence are not soundly based on empirical vindication, but rather on a combination of deductive theory and problematic interpretations of a limited number of highly ambiguous historical episodes.[1] Any satisfactory answer to the nuclear-political question would require convincing responses to two key questions: How probable is nuclear use? And what happens after nuclear weapons are used? Because nuclear weapons have not been used since 1945, it is impossible to say with any confidence *why* they have not been used.

Attempts to answer these questions tend to hinge on conflicting interpretations of two defining events of the nuclear age, the Cuban Missile Crisis and the end of the Cold War. For some, these events demonstrate that the basic lessons of pre-nuclear security strategy—have more power and resolve—still hold true. But for others these events demonstrate more or less the opposite lesson, that only by recognizing a common peril, and accepting mutual restraints, can security be realized in the nuclear age. Despite the difficulty in definitively answering the nuclear-political question, practical nuclear choices rest inescapably on how these questions are answered.

The debate over the nuclear-political question has passed through three rounds, each quite different in character, which this chapter surveys. This evolution has been propelled in part by actual real-world developments, in both technology and politics, as well as by conceptual impasses and innovations. In the first round, running from about 1945 to 1960, "nuclear one world" ideas about the need for revolutionary transformations in world political order were prevalent and widely debated. In the second and longest-running phase of the debate, the concept of deterrence was central, with vigorous disputes about its stability and prerequisites. In the wake of the unexpected end of the Cold War, and in response to renewed concerns over proliferation, and nuclear terrorism, a third round in the great debate has taken shape. The contemporary nuclear landscape of nuclear controversy is in many ways a break from the main lines of thought during the second Cold War round of the debate, while at the same time returning in some important ways to concerns that were paramount in the first round, but which were marginalized during the second. Most importantly, the confidence in the stabilizing role of deterrence marking the second round of the debate has been significantly weakened. As this has happened, more radical ideas about both using and eliminating nuclear weapons have become increasingly prominent.

23.2 Nuclear One Worldism and Its Conceptual Impasses

The first round of the great debate over the nuclear-political question was dominated by a distinctive set of assumptions, expectations, and aspirations. Overall, the first round was dominated by "nuclear one worldism," the view that nuclear weapons pose a fundamental challenge to the core security-providing function of the state and state-system, and that only the creation of a world government configured as a state with a centralized monopoly of violence could prevent a civilizational catastrophe. In part, such nuclear one world arguments derived from the widespread assumption and expectation that nuclear world war would occur in the absence of such a reconfigured world political order, and that the time for averting such a disastrous war was very short. It is notable that such apocalyptic thinking predominated in a period before large numbers of nuclear weapons were built and deployed, before thermonuclear weapons were invented, and before the full planetary ecological consequences of a general nuclear war were understood. The basic of the nuclear one world view is nicely encapsulated by Secretary of War Henry Stimson's September 1945 memorandum to President Truman, where he observed that nuclear explosives constitute "a new control by man over the forces of nature too revolutionary and dangerous to fit into the old concepts." The development of these new destructive capabilities "caps the climax of the race between man's growing technical power for destructiveness and his psychological power of self-control and group control—his moral power." Given this, "our method of approach to the Russians is a question of the most vital importance in the evolution of human progress" and requires an abandonment of "the old custom of secrecy and nationalistic military superiority relying on international caution to proscribe the future use of the weapon" (Stimson and Bundy 1947: 644). In short, nuclear weapons mark a revolutionary change in violence capacity, which in turn necessitates a revolutionary change in world politics.

The most theoretically sophisticated nuclear one world statement on the crisis of the state-system produced by nuclear weapons is found in John Herz's 1959 book, *International Politics in the Atomic Age* (Herz 1959).[2] His account provides the most extensive attention to the specifics of the material transformation brought about by the introduction of nuclear explosives. He argues that the most basic function of states is providing security through military control of territory, which requires territorial "impermeability." It is not enough for a state apparatus to aspire to, claim, or even be recognized as having, statehood. The state apparatus must be capable of making good its claim in war with other states. States are driven to consolidate as the technological foundations of military viability show increasing scale effects, a process which has been underway since the dawn of history. With the advent of nuclear weapons, no state can maintain a protective "shell." Every state has become "permeable," and therefore another consolidation can be expected. When "not even half the globe remains defensible against the all-out onslaught of the new weapons," the "power of protection, on which political authority was based in the past, seems to be in jeopardy for any imaginable entity." Humans inhabit a "planet of limited size," but "the effect of the means of destruction has become absolute" (Herz 1959: 13). Destructive power has expanded, but the human habitat has not expanded, so the human species now relates to destructive force in an historically unprecedented manner. Nuclear explosives have produced "the most radical change in the nature of power and the characteristics of power units since the beginning of the modern state system," or perhaps "since the beginnings of mankind."

This development "presages the end of the territorial protective function of state power and territorial sovereignty" and the "chief external function of the modern state therefore seems to have vanished" (Herz 1959: 13).

The arguments of the classical nuclear one worlders are easily and often confused with types of "idealism," due to their optimism that needed changes in world politics could be readily achieved, and because the world state solution had long been advocated by self-consciously idealist writers. However, the nuclear one world argument is fundamentally "realist" because it holds that power, and particularly material capacities of violence, determine political outcomes, and set the parameters for viable security-providing units. To the degree that early nuclear one worldism and statism was utopian, it was fundamentally a "realist" utopia, yet another state to mediate between survival goals and violence capabilities. Unfortunately, the thinking of the nuclear one worlders, despite all their rhetoric about "fundamentally new ways of thinking," is at its core very traditional and unimaginative, because they essentially envision the adjustment of world politics to nuclear weapons taking a time-worn pattern of extending the *scale* of the security-providing unit to match the spatial scale at which technology permits security to be provided. In essence the nuclear one worlders proclaimed: "The states are dead, long live the state!"

The nuclear one worlders conceptualized a world government as a world state with a monopoly of violence capacity and authority with universal, planet-wide scope. Although they disagreed about other attributes of a world state, they agreed that a world state required at least the deep disarmament of the existing states, and the establishment of a worldwide centralized military apparatus capable of coercing all other actors. In sum, nuclear one world theorists thought the state had been fatally compromised in its ability to provide security by the emergence of nuclear weapons, and that a worldwide state was necessary.

With these two basic ideas framing their thinking, nuclear one world theorists engaged in a far-reaching debate about how such an entity might be created, as well as how it could be prevented from becoming a comprehensively oppressive world tyranny. The basic puzzle is laid out by Hans Morgenthau, who, despite his widespread reputation as a "founder of realism" (at least in the United States), held strong nuclear one world views: "How can the atomic power be transferred to the control of supranational institutions that will prevent its use on behalf of a particular national interest without submerging the autonomous life of individual nations in a universal tyranny?" (Morgenthau 1960: 171).[3]

There are four main variants of nuclear one worldism, each offering a different answer to this puzzle: (1) the *imperial world statism* of James Burnham; (2) the *maximal world federalism* of the Chicago Committee to Frame a World Constitution; (3) the *tragic nuclear one worldism* of Hans Morgenthau; and (4) *minimal world federalism* (Deudney 2007). Could a non-repressive world state be created? Burnham argued that nuclear weapons made a world state inevitable in the near future, and therefore the United States should take the lead in establishing it by whatever means necessary (Burnham 1947).[4] The Maximalists argued that the preconditions of world community to support a non-repressive world state were present or imminent. Morgenthau responded that a crucial precondition for the creation of a non-repressive world state was a strong sense of world community, and that national communities would remain strong for the foreseeable future. The Minimalists replied that a world security state, or what they referred to as a "minimalist state," could and should be established immediately, without the existence of a world community. This debate, which has largely disappeared from the attention of international theorists, is of continuing interest because it clearly put the topic of political tyranny at the center of the debate over the nuclear-political question. This debate casts the peril facing humanity in the nuclear world as having two faces, the *crash* of a general nuclear war, and the *crush* of comprehensive despotism.

Overall, these classical nuclear one worldist images of a world government as a world state as the remedy to the nuclear security problem reached something of a conceptual impasse. Recognizing that the move from world anarchy to world hierarchy entails grave security risks, they attempted to envision a variety of internal restraints on hierarchy, from concessions stimulated by fear of revolt to world community, but none of their remedies seem particularly feasible within the time frame they anticipated was necessary. Despite the widespread recognition that nuclear weapons pose a fundamental threat, there has been no discernable trend toward the creation and empowerment of a world government with state-like capabilities and authorities. No state or popular antinuclear movement, has been willing to trade the perils of nuclear anarchy for the perils of nuclear hierarchy, to "leap from the (nuclear) frying pan, into the (world state) fire." This conceptual impasse is rooted in the "over-stated" character of the nuclear one worlders' conceptualization of a worldwide security arrangement appropriate to the nuclear problem. Solutions to this impasse are most likely to be found in a more careful analysis of the material dimensions of the nuclear revolution, and in architectures of mutual restraint that are alien to the statist and realist conceptualization of political order.

23.3 The Cold War Trinity: Deterrence, Strategy, and Arms Control

The great debate over the nuclear-political question entered its second round during the middle and late Cold War. The landscape of thinking in this round came to be centered around the concept of nuclear deterrence, the notion that nuclear forces, if properly configured, would render the initiation of a nuclear war suicidal, and thus very unlikely. If adversaries had the capability to retaliate after a first strike, nuclear war would not be a "rational" act of statecraft, and therefore no state would start one. Although this vision of a solution to the problem of nuclear security had been clearly articulated by Bernard Brodie and others during the late 1940s, it came to occupy the center of thinking about the nuclear problem only during the late 1950s and 1960s (Brodie 1946). Within a deterrence-centered framework for thinking about nuclear security, there remained a set of basic disagreements centered around the question of how many nuclear weapons, prepared for which missions, were needed to achieve deterrence.

On this question, there were sharp divides that coalesced into three fairly distinct schools of theory and practice, *simple deterrence, war strategism*, and *arms control.* Together these three schools of thought about the nuclear revolution made up a sort of theoretical trinity, sharing a very broad set of common assumptions within which this round of the great debate was conducted. The simple deterrence school viewed nuclear deterrence as extremely robust, almost an automatic consequence of the presence of a minimum number of nuclear weapons, but both the war strategists and arms controllers saw it as potentially fragile and in need of augmentation—but in opposite ways.

At the center of the trinity was the simple or minimum deterrence school, perhaps best represented by the theorists Robert Jervis and Kenneth Waltz, which held that simply achieving a capacity for mounting a secure second strike was sufficient, because the level of destruction that even a small handful of nuclear weapons could produce was so great.[5] On both flanks of this simple deterrence view were variants of deterrence thinking that were sharply at odds with each other. Disagreements between these two wings of the nuclear theoretical trinity played out in theory and practice at virtually every turn during the Cold War.

On one side there were the war strategists, such as Herman Kahn and Colin Gray, who held that achieving deterrence required the deployment of large numbers of nuclear weapons prepared for prompt use for a wide range of missions and scenarios. Although holding that nuclear war could and should be avoided through deterrence, the war strategists held that the demands of achieving deterrence were dauntingly high, and that only by preparing for an extremely wide range of nuclear use contingencies could use actually be avoided. War strategists were largely suspicious of arms control, seeing it as "impossible when necessary, and unnecessary when possible," and as a flimsy "house of cards" lacking resilience (Gray 1992).

On the other side, there were the arms controllers, such as Thomas Schelling, Hedley Bull, and the members of the Harvard Arms Control School and the Princeton Deep Arms Control School. They held that mutual restraints on nuclear forces were desirable to avoid situations in which states would find themselves in predicaments where it was circumstantially rational to do things that were irrational in relation to their more basic security interests.[6] Arms controllers also emphasized that it was desirable to "lengthen the fuse" by slowing down the tempo of likely nuclear use scenarios, in order to reduce the dangers stemming from the dauntingly complex and tightly coupled force structures that had emerged in the rapid arms build-ups of the 1950s and 1960s.[7] Arms controllers viewed their project as making for a less "fail deadly" form of deterrence, rather than as leading to a significant alteration of the international anarchical system, and they emphasized that they were aiming to reform and moderate, not substantially replace the interstate system. A telling indicator of the grip that deterrence had on this wide spectrum of thinking about the nuclear-political question during the Cold War, was that even Jonathan Schell, whose work raised such radical questions about prevalent nuclear policies and thinking, cast his nuclear alternative, laid out in his book *The*

Abolition (1984), as a way to have the maximally safe version of deterrence possible, in effect allowing the world to "have its cake and eat it too."[8]

Despite their great differences, members of the war strategist and arms control schools were united in the centrality they attached to deterrence. All three schools also converged in being largely indifferent to the internal regime attributes of nuclear states, and the problem of despotism and freedom is never in play. The Soviet Union was viewed with deep suspicion and hostility by most Western nuclear analysts, but its despotic government was never viewed as an obstacle to "rational" deterrence. Although a world security order based on nuclear deterrence has come to be normalized, particularly by realist international theorists, it entails a radical departure in the relationships among military power, interstate anarchy, and security prevalent before the nuclear era. In the deterrence world, interstate anarchy has been pacified, and the dynamics of anarchy that, at least according to realists, contributed to the chronic condition of interstate war have been largely neutered. This view of deterrence as the source of a secure world order, while largely conservative in practical terms, is quite radical conceptually. While the nuclear one worlders advanced a conceptually conservative way of thinking about world nuclear politics with revolutionary practical implications, the deterrence schools advance a conceptually revolutionary approach that is deeply conservative in its practical implications.

Throughout the long decades of the Cold War, it was widely assumed that this great conflict was an effectively permanent feature of world politics that might be managed, but never eliminated. The unexpected, and unexpectedly peaceful, end of this conflict in the late 1980s, followed shortly by the collapse of Communist Party rule and the Soviet Union itself, was, like the end of other major wars among great powers, marked by an elaborate negotiated settlement. The Cold War settlement was largely centered on a set of far-reaching reductions in nuclear forces. Although no one had anticipated this outcome, each of the three schools rushed to claim at least partial credit, each claiming that the implementation of its favored policies had steered the world to this positive outcome. Another completely unexpected development of considerable importance was the convergence of the leaders of the United States and the Soviet Union on a general understanding of the grave threat posed by nuclear war that in its sweeping nature and urgency harkened back to "nuclear one world" view which had otherwise so completely disappeared from elite nuclear policy debates. Despite his vigorous anti-Communism, and long support of increased military spending, US President Ronald Reagan also strongly believed in completely eliminating nuclear weapons, as did Soviet President Mikhail Gorbachev.[9]

The unexpected end of the Cold War is not the only major development over the nuclear era that was unanticipated. Most surprising are the underlying physical bases for nuclear weapons: a rare element—uranium—can be coaxed into releasing, pound per pound, a millions times more energy than chemical high explosives, and then the thermonuclear processes fueling the sun and stars could also be harnessed to produce explosions thousands of times larger than the one that obliterated Hiroshima. Also unexpected were the discoveries that a full-scale nuclear war would possibly render extinct all the higher life forms on the planet—including humans—by destroying the thin layer of ozone in the stratosphere blocking potent solar radiations, and that the soot from many burning cities could plunge the planet into a "nuclear winter" in which agricultural production would be severely curtailed for years (Schell 1981; Ehrlich et al. 1984). Although now taken for granted, it is surely surprising that the Soviet Union and the United States could deploy tens of thousands of nuclear weapons in a vast global-spanning network of bases and mobile platforms over several decades without a single weapon ever being detonated.

Despite the great reduction in nuclear arsenals at the end of the Cold War, these changes did not move the anarchical interstate system any closer to a world government as a world state along the lines envisioned by the nuclear one world theorists. To grasp the actual trajectory of institutional change produced by arms control and potentially resulting from the realization of deep arms control, a "modified nuclear one worldism" is necessary. Instead of seeing the development of nuclear weapons (and space weapons, most notably ballistic missiles) as requiring an expansion in the *scale* of the state to universal dimensions, it is more accurate to see them as rendering obsolete the dominant security practices of the pre-nuclear era, which together compose the "real-state mode of protection." Security practices produce, and are supported by, the emergence of security structures (understood as configurations of legitimate authority), and real-state practices generate hierarchical structures at the unit-level and anarchic structures at the system level. The body of theory and practice known as "realism" is essentially the "operating manual" for the key actors of the real-state mode of protection and its attendant hierarchical and anarchical structures. Such a mode of protection is viable in a material context marked by limited violence volume and limited violence velocity because the core real-state practices of mobilization, concentration, and employment are suited to solving security problems in such contexts. But their pursuit in material situations of violence abundance and high violence velocity, such as characterize the nuclear era, produce dysfunctional over-mobilization and hyper-concentration.

In contrast, the practices (and attendant political structures) of a "republican-federal mode of protection" are suited to provide security in situations of high violence volume and velocity, because they slow, de-mobilize, and de-couple. Such approaches were historically marginal in pre-nuclear times because they did what was not needed and could not do what was needed. The practices of this alternative mode of protection are present in the emergent arms control efforts of the nuclear era. Over time, their pursuit produces political structures that are not anarchical or hierarchical. Instead, the resulting political structures are "negarchical," in the sense that they are a set of mutual restraints, and amount to a type of world confederate republic, not a world hierarchical state. This way of viewing the revolutionary security challenge posed by the development of nuclear weapons provides an image of the world political order that would be produced by the realization of the full arms control project.[10]

23.4 The Third Round: Bombs Away?

Beginning around 1990 with the end of the Cold War and extending to the present, a third round of the great debate over the nuclear-political question has emerged. Like the previous two rounds, the third is marked by sharp disagreements, and is driven by real-world developments. And like the first two rounds, the third has been defined by a set of assumptions and parameters that give it an overall unity. This round of the debate has been centered on the problems of proliferation of nuclear weapons and nuclear "terrorism" by non-state actors (Paul 1999; Ikle 2006; Bracken 2012). The new debate has several important similarities with the first: the assumption that the probability of nuclear use is fairly high, a limited faith in deterrence, and the recognition that the internal features of polities, as well as the prospects for political freedom, are at stake in choices about nuclear weapons.

Historical eras rarely have sharp beginnings and ends, but for the third round of the great debate on the nuclear-political question, the terrorist attacks of September 11, 2001, now known forever simply as "9/11," come close to playing such a role. These attacks are a marker not so much for what they were, but for what they implied lay ahead. Like a bolt of lightning in a dark night, these attacks illuminated an ominous new landscape of security threat. The attacks and the "anthrax letters" that followed in their wake seemed to many observers to indicate that non-state actors, perhaps backed by revisionist or "rogue" states, had both the capability and the intent to inflict major damage on the civil populations of even the most powerful states.[11] A perilous new landscape has been glimpsed, but what are the contours of the new terrain, and what must be done to be secure in it? It is these questions that the third round of the great debate seeks to answer.

The single most important feature of arguments in the third round of the nuclear-political debate is a widespread sense that deterrence, the central anchor of nuclear thinking in the second round, has been significantly compromised as the foundation of nuclear non-use. This diminished confidence in deterrence has several sources. As nuclear capability spreads, or "proliferates" into the possession of more states, and as it "leaks" into the hands of non-state actors, the assumptions of classical nuclear deterrence are seen as no longer operating as robustly as they did during the Soviet-American Cold War. New nuclear states are not as likely to possess the many ancillary technical and institutional features that marked the nuclear force structures of the United States and USSR. A truly nuclear multipolar system would potentially be subject to the dynamics of complexity and unintended consequences that have historically marked multipolar systems.[12] Anti-missile defenses, slowly but surely maturing technologically, raise anxieties about the ability of "second strike" forces to retaliate effectively.[13] Incremental improvements in the accuracy of ballistic missiles, combined with the waning of "oceanic opacity" (which has allowed submarine-based nuclear weapons to be a secure second strike basing mode), have created new fears about the possibilities for successful preemptive first strikes (Kristensen et al. 2017). At the same time, technological developments in missile accuracy are leading some strategists to believe that advanced "conventional" (i.e. non-nuclear) munitions can achieve disarming first strikes with minimal "collateral damage," thus making a range of counterforce options not only again "thinkable," but even attractive (Lieber and Press 2006). Confidence in nuclear deterrence is also being undermined by a growing realization that cyber-attacks may undermine the capacity of states to reliably direct their nuclear forces (Gatzke and Lindsay 2017).

Perhaps most importantly, non-state actors, such as cults and religious extremist groups, are widely seen as much less subject to deterrence than states, because they do not have territory against which to retaliate, and because they may be able to keep their role as an attacker hidden, thus creating a problem of "attribution" never present during the Soviet-American rivalry (Weitz 2011). The attempt by the Japanese cult Aum Shrinikyo to acquire nuclear weapons, and the marketing of nuclear "starter kits" by the Pakistani nuclear official A. Q. Khan also provided ominous indications that both proliferation and leakage were growing features of the world security landscape.[14] For all these reasons, the third round of the great debate is, if not post-deterrence, then certainly "deterrence-challenged."

As the stabilizing weight of the deterrence anchor of the Cold War trinity has weakened in its restraining and unifying role, there has been a partial liberation, and a partial radicalizing, of both the two subordinate wings of the Cold War deterrence trinity, war strategism and arms control. Each of these schools of nuclear thinking has taken on new practical relevance and has been rapidly innovating in their policy agendas, but in radically opposite directions.

The war strategism of the Cold War round of the great debate has evolved into an agenda of coercive counter-proliferation. No longer confident that new actors with nuclear weapons will be subject to the restraining logic of nuclear deterrence, nuclear-possessing states have increasingly turned to military pre-emption and preventive war to forestall the diffusion of nuclear capabilities into the hands of others (Lavoy et al. 2000). This turn to coercive counter-proliferation has been most visible in the actions of Israel, in its attack on Iraqi and then Syrian nuclear reactors, and in the advocacy by its prime minister of an American attack on the nuclear facilities of Iran. This way of dealing with the problem of proliferation and leakage was also evident in the approach of the United States to Iraq in the wake of the terrorist attacks of late 2001.

Arms control has also been extended and radicalized as deterrence has come to be seen as less robustly reliable. This can be seen in the "Zero Nuclear" movement which has been endorsed by several retired leading public officials in the United States from the late Cold War era and the recent UN treaty banning all nuclear weapons.[15] It is also visible in the revived interest in the comprehensive control of all fissionable material and the Fissile Material Cut-off Treaty (FMCT) (Feiveson et al 2014). Because all nuclear weapons depend on fissionable uranium or plutonium, a worldwide regime to halt the production of such specialized and readily identifiable material would simultaneously advance the goals of interstate disarmament, nonproliferation, and anti-terrorism.

American policy has lurched between these two new approaches, but with little success in either direction. The Bush–Cheney administration embraced the radicalized war strategist agenda of counter-proliferation in Iraq, only to discover that Iraq did not have a significant nuclear weapons program.[16] In contrast, the Obama administration sought with only modest success to advance the deeper arms control agenda, by reviving American–Russian arms control and moving toward deep reductions, by rounding up the fissionable material that is dispersed around the world in research reactors, and by its declaratory embrace of a nuclear-free world.

Despite their obvious differences, both these schools of thought have an important point of convergence, a focus on the materials to make nuclear weapons as well as the systems to "deliver" them. Both also see the current international nuclear order as unstable, and they advance measures and policies which, if implemented, would result in significant changes in the international system.

Both the radicalized war strategists and the deep arms controllers also attach great importance to the internal political features of states, in contrast to the general indifference of the Cold War schools on this topic, thus returning to a concern that played a pivotal role in the first round of the debate. More specifically, political freedom and despotism have returned as outcomes at stake in the third round of the nuclear-political debate. For strategists, many committed to "neo-conservative" ideas about the deep superiority of liberal democracy and the need to expand it by force of arms, the fact that many emerging nuclear states are authoritarian means they cannot be reliably deterred, making more "forward leaning" measures necessary. At the same time, the absence of state capacity and authority, present in many "failed states" and "smashed states" (such as Afghanistan, Iraq, and Libya) is seen as a threat to powerful, orderly, and prosperous states, because such areas provide opportunities for transnational terrorist networks to operate.

For the deepened and radicalized versions of the arms control arguments that have emerged over the course of the third round of the nuclear debate, political freedom and despotism are also at stake. The key point is that counter-terrorism strengthens state security apparatuses at the expense of individual liberty and political democracy. The long record of modern counter-terrorism, which emerged in the later nineteenth century in response to the new threat of "dynamite terrorism," demonstrates that when states are compelled to fight terrorists, liberty and democracy are diminished proportionately. For the United States, 9/11 produced the "Patriot Act."[17] A "nuclear 9/11," the detonation of a nuclear weapon in a major city, would produce pressures for an even more intrusive and powerful state, and a "super Patriot Act." This means that the survival of liberal constitutional democracy now increasingly hinges on the successful completion of the nuclear arms control project (Deudney 2010). To the extent that this is the case, the problem of freedom and despotism, exiled from the debates on the nuclear political–political question since the intellectual collapse of nuclear one worldism and its world state agenda, is now back in play at the center of the debate.

23.5 Avoiding the Ultimate Failure

Humanity's final exam is not easy. Expert answers to the nuclear-political question remain in sharp disagreement; events are ambiguous; and the unanticipated repeatedly happens. Given the stakes in getting the right answers and pursuing the right course, this conceptual uncertainty should be deeply unsettling, and should evoke special caution and deep humility. As the horizon of the future fills with other catastrophic and existential threats such as climate change, designer plagues, and runaway artificial intelligence, it is becoming increasingly evident that the overall modern project of advancing the human estate by harnessing science and technology is producing a cornucopia of increasingly potent "double-edged swords" and that nuclear war is not alone in posing a "final exam" for humanity. Despite all the dispute and complexity of these increasingly numerous and ominous technological possibilities, it seems safe to assume that the deeply ingrained pattern of rapidly weaponizing new technologies, usually in secret, is, sooner or later, a sure path to unprecedented catastrophe for modern civilization and humanity.

Although nuclear war is the oldest of these technogenic threats to civilization and human survival, and although important steps to restraint, particularly at the end of the Cold War, have been achieved, the nuclear world is increasingly changing in major ways, and in almost entirely dangerous directions. The third "bombs away" phase of the great debate on the nuclear-political question is more consequentially divided than in the first two phases. Even more ominously, most of the momentum lies with the forces that are pulling states toward nuclear-use, and with the radical actors bent on inflicting catastrophic damage on the leading states in the international system, particularly the United States. In contrast, the arms control project, although intellectually vibrant, is largely in retreat on the world political stage. The arms control settlement of the Cold War is unraveling, and the world public is more divided and distracted than ever. With the recent election of President Donald Trump, the United States, which has played such a dominant role in nuclear politics since its scientists invented these fiendish engines, now has an impulsive and uninformed leader, boding ill for nuclear restraint and effective crisis management.

Given current trends, it is prudent to assume that sooner or later, and probably sooner, nuclear weapons will again be the used in war. But this bad news may contain a "silver lining" of good news. Unlike a general nuclear war that might have occurred during the Cold War, such a nuclear event now would probably not mark the end of civilization (or of humanity), due to the great reductions in nuclear forces achieved at the end of the Cold War. Furthermore, politics on "the day after" could have immense potential for positive change. The survivors would not be likely to envy the dead, but would surely have a greatly renewed resolution for "never again." Such an event, completely unpredictable in its particulars, would unambiguously put the nuclear-political question back at the top of the world political agenda. It would unmistakeably remind leading states of their vulnerability It might also trigger more robust efforts to achieve the global regulation of nuclear capability. Like the bombings of Hiroshima and Nagasaki that did so much to catalyze the elevated concern for nuclear security in the early Cold War, and like the experience "at the brink" in the Cuban Missile Crisis of 1962, the now bubbling nuclear caldron holds the possibility of inaugurating a major period of institutional innovation and adjustment toward a fully "bombs away" future.

Notes

1. For the theory-based origins of different understandings of the nuclear revolution, see Connelly (2012).
2. For Herz and other public intellectuals from the 1950s, see van Munster and Sylvest (2016).
3. Morgenthau, 1960, 171. For Morgenthau's tortured thinking on nuclear weapons, see Craig (2004).
4. For scenarios of US nuclear use, see Quester (2000).
5. This view seems to be approximately realized in the force structures of the secondary nuclear states. See Goldstein (2000).
6. The logic of arms control is laid out in Schelling and Halperin (1961) and Bull (1961).
7. For "lengthening the fuse" see, Feiveson et al. (1999). For complexity and tight coupling, see Perrow (1984). For nuclear applications, see Sagan (1993).
8. One peculiarity of Schell's work was his attack on "arms control," when his preferred agenda of "abolition" was really just the furthest stage of arms control. Like other arms controllers, the appeal of the abolitionist program is held by Schell to rest upon "lengthening the fuse." See Schell (1998 and 2000).
9. For Reagan's abolitionism and its origins, see Lettow (2005) and Mann (2009). For Gorbachev, see Shenfeld (1987) and Zubok (2007).
10. For further discussion, see Deudney (2000a, 2000b, and 2007).
11. For synoptic evaluations, see Allison (2004), Ferguson and Potter (2006), and Flannery (2016).
12. The stability of a genuinely multipolar nuclear great power system is remarkably underexplored. For some recent pessimistic observations, see Sokolski (2015).
13. The system destabilizing potentials of the deployment of anti-missile capabilities are explored in Wirtz and Larssen (2001).
14. For the Aum cult, see Kaplan and Marshall (1996) and Lifton (1999). For the Khan network, see Correra (2006), Langewiesche (2007), and Montgomery (2005).
15. For Zero Nuclear, see Schultz and Goodby (2015) and Perkovitch and Acton (2008). For the UN Treaty, see Fihn (2017).
16. For the many puzzles of the Iraq case, see Jervis (2005).
17. For the ways in which the "Global War on Terrorism" triggered by 9/11 has produced a global cascade of anti-constitutional measures, see Scheppele (2004 and 2006). For US impacts, see Crotty (2004).

References

Allison, Graham. 2004. *Nuclear Terrorism: the Ultimate Preventable Catastrophe*. New York: Henry Holt.

Boyer, Paul. 1985. *By the Bombs Early Light: American Thought and Culture at the Dawn of the Atomic Age*. New York: Pantheon.

Bracken, Paul. 2012. *The Second Nuclear Age: Strategy, Danger, and the New Power Politics*. New York: St. Martin's Press.

Brodie, Bernard. 1946. War in the Atomic Age, and Implications for Military Strategy. Both in B. Brodie (ed.), *The Absolute Weapon: Atomic Power and World Order*. New York: Harcourt, Brace & Co.

Burnham, James. 1947. *The Struggle for the World.* New York: John Day.
Connelly, Matthew. 2102. "General, I Have Fought Just as Many Nuclear Wars as You Have:" Forecasts, Future Scenarios, and the Politics of Armageddon, *American Historical Review*, 117(5); 1431–60.
Correra, Gordon. 2006. *Shopping for Bombs: Nuclear Proliferation, Global Insecurity, and the Rise and Fall of the A.Q. Khan Network.* Oxford: Oxford University Press.
Craig, Campbell. 2004. *Glimmer of a New Leviathan: Total War in the Realism of Niebuhr, Morgenthau, and Waltz.* New York: Columbia University Press.
Crotty, William (ed.), 2004. *The Politics of Terror: The U.S. Response to 9/11.* Boston: Northeastern University Press.
Deudney, Daniel. 2000a. Regrounding Realism: Anarchy, Security, and Changing Material Contexts. *Security Studies*, 10(1): 1–45.
Deudney, Daniel. 2000b. Geopolitics as Theory: Historical Security Materialism. *European Journal of International Relations*, 6(1): 77–108.
Deudney, Daniel. 2007. Anticipations of World Nuclear Government. In D. Deudney, *Bounding Power: Republican Security Theory from the Polis to the Global Village*, ch. 9. Princeton, NJ: Princeton University Press.
Deudney, Daniel. 2010. Omniviolence, Arms Control, and Limited Government. In Jeffrey Tulis and Stephen Macedo (eds.), *The Limits of Constitutionalism*, pp. 297–316. Princeton, NJ: Princeton University Press.
Ehrlich, Paul R., Carl Sagan, David Kennedy, and Walter Orr Roberts. 1984. *The Cold and the Dark: The World After Nuclear War.* New York: Norton.
Feiveson, Harold A. (ed.). 1999. *The Nuclear Turning Point: A Blueprint for Deep Cuts and De-altering of Nuclear Weapons.* Washington: Brookings.
Feiveson, Harold A., Alexander Glaser, Zia Mian, and Frank von Hippel. 2014. *Unmaking the Bomb: A Fissile Material Approach to Nuclear Disarmament and Nonproliferation.* Cambridge, MA: MIT Press.
Ferguson, Charles D. and William C. Potter. 2006. *The Four Faces of Nuclear Terrorism.* New York: Routledge.
Fihn, Beatrice. 2017. The Logic of Banning Nuclear Weapons, *Survival*, 59(1): 43–50.
Flannery, Francis, 2016. *Understanding Apocalyptic Terrorism: Countering the Radical Mindset.* Abingdon: Routledge.
Fuller, R. Buckminster. 1969. *Operating Manual for Spaceship Earth.* Carbondale: Southern Illinois University Press.
Gatzke, Erik and Jon R. Lindsay. 2017. Thermonuclear Cyberwar. *Journal of Cybersecurity*, February: 1–12.
Goldstein, Avery. 2000. *Deterrence and Security in the 21st Century: China, Britain, and Enduring Legacy of the Nuclear Revolution.* Stanford, CA: Stanford University Press.
Gray, Colin S. 1992. *House of Cards: Why Arms Control Must Fail.* Ithaca, NY: Cornell University Press.
Herz, John. 1959. *International Politics in the Atomic Era.* New York: Columbia University Press.
Ikle, Fred Charles. 2006. *Annihilation from Within: the Ultimate Threat to Nations.* New York: Columbia University Press.
Jervis, Robert. 2005. *American Foreign Policy in a New Era.* New York: Routledge
Kaplan, David E. and Andrew Marshall. 1996. *The Cult at the End of the World: The Terrifying Story of the Aum Doomsday Cult, from the Subways of Tokyo to the Nuclear Arsenals of Russia.* New York; Crown Publishing.

Kristensen, Hans M., Matthew McKinzie, and Theodore A. Postol. 2017. How US Nuclear Force Modernization is Undermining Strategic Stability: The Burst-Height Compensating Super-fuze. *Bulletin of the Atomic Scientists*, March.

Langewiesche, William. 2007. *The Atomic Bazaar: The Rise of the Nuclear Poor*. New York: Farrar, Strauss & Giroux.

Lavoy, Peter R., Scott D. Sagan, and James J. Wirtz (eds.). 2000. *Planning the Unthinkable: How New Powers Will Use Nuclear, Biological, and Chemical Weapons*. Ithaca, NY: Cornell University Press.

Lettow, Paul. 2005. *Ronald Reagan and His Quest to Abolish Nuclear Weapons*. New York: Random House.

Lieber, Kier A. and Daryl G. Press. 2006. The End of MAD? The Nuclear Dimension of U.S. Primacy. *International Security*, 30(4): 7–44.

Lifton, Robert Jay. 1999. *Destroying the World to Save It: Aum Shrinikyo, Apocalyptic Violence, and the New Global Terrorism*. New York: Henry Holt.

Mann, James. 2009. *The Rebellion of Ronald Reagan: A History of the End of the Cold War*. New York: Viking.

Montgomery, Alexander H. 2005. Ringing in Proliferation: How to Dismantle an Atomic Bomb Network. *International Security*, 20(2): 153–87.

Morgenthau, Hans J. 1960. *On the Purpose of American Politics*. Chicago: University of Chicago Press.

Mueller, John. 2009. *Atomic Obsession: Nuclear Alarmism from Hiroshima to Al-Qaeda*. Oxford: Oxford University Press.

van Munster, Rens and Casper Sylvest. 2016. *Nuclear Realism: Global Political Thought during the Thermonuclear Revolution*. Abingdon: Routledge.

Paul, T. V. 1999. Great Equalizers or Agents of Chaos? Weapons of Mass Destruction and the Emerging International Order. In T. V. Paul and John A. Hall (eds.), *International Order and the Future of World Politics*. Cambridge: Cambridge University Press.

Perkovitch, George and James M. Acton. 2008. *Abolishing Nuclear Weapons*, International Institute for Strategic Studies, Adelphi Paper No. 396. Abingdon: Routledge.

Perrow, Charles. 1984. *Normal Accidents: Living with High-Risk Technologies*. New York: Basic Books.

Quester, George. 2000. *Nuclear Monopoly*. New Brunswick: Transaction.

Sagan, Scott D. 1993. *The Limits of Safety: Organizations, Accidents and Nuclear Weapons*. Princeton, NJ: Princeton University Press.

Schell, Jonathan. 1981. *The Fate of the Earth*. New York: Knopf.

Schell, Jonathan. 1984. *The Abolition*. New York: Knopf.

Schell, Jonathan. 1998. *The Gift of Time: The Case for Abolishing Nuclear Weapons Now*. New York: Henry Holt.

Schell, Jonathan. 2000. The Folly of Arms Control. *Foreign Affairs*, 79(5): 22–46.

Schelling, Thomas and Morton Halperin. 1961. *Strategy and Arms Control*. New York: The Twentieth Century Fund, (re-issued 1985, with new introduction).

Scheppele, Kim Lane. 2004. Law in a Time of Emergency: States of Exception and the Temptations of 9/11. *University of Pennsylvania Journal of Constitutional Law*, 6(5).

Scheppele, Kim Lane. 2006. The Migration of Anti-Constitutional Ideas: The Post-9/11 Globalization of Public Law and the International State of Emergency. In Sujit Choudhry (ed.), *The Migration of Constitutional Ideas*. New York: Cambridge University Press.

Schultz, George and James Goodby. (eds.). 2015. *The War That Must Never Be Fought*. Stanford, CA: Hoover Institution Press.

Shenfield, Stephen. 1987. *The Nuclear Predicament: Explorations in Soviet Ideology*. London: Routledge & Kegan Paul.

Sokolski, Henry D. 2015. *Underestimated: Our Not So Peaceful Nuclear Future*. Washington: Non Proliferation Policy Education Center.

Stimson, Henry L. and McGeorge Bundy. 1947. *On Active Service in Peace and War*. New York: Harper & Brothers.

Weitz, Richard. 2011. Nuclear Forensics: False Hopes and Practical Realities. *Political Science Quarterly*, 126(1): 53–75.

Wirtz, James J. and Jeffrey A. Larsen (ed.). 2001. *Rocket's Red Glare: Missile Defense and the Future of World Politics*. Boulder, CO: Westview,.

Yoshihara, Toshi and James R. Holmes (eds.). 2012. *Strategy in the Second Nuclear Age: Power, Ambition, and the Ultimate Weapon*. Washington, DC: Georgetown University Press.

Zubok, Vladislav M. 2007. *A Failed Empire: The Soviet Union in the Cold War from Stalin to Gorbachev*. Chapel Hill: University Press of North Carolina.

CHAPTER 24

PUBLIC–PRIVATE INTERACTIONS AND PRACTICES OF SECURITY

DEBORAH AVANT AND VIRGINIA HAUFLER

Most people connect security issues with what we think of as "public" and attach them to a particular collective endeavor such as a community or a nation.[1] Imagining public authorities as those charged with ensuring the security of their followers is a key part of contractarian narratives of governance. What we see as "public" is often tied to governance and settles whose safety is deemed important and who is threatening or expendable. In the modern era the state has embodied this collective endeavor, and the control and management of violence have been seen as core elements of state practice. We argue here that in recent years, interactions among intellectuals, governments, transnational activists, and companies have broadened the idea of security, changing who or what should be secured, and shifting our understanding of what is public. A focus on these interactions should inform our thinking about the future of global security.

History shows that the degree to which different forms of violence are collective endeavors handled by states has varied. Organizations outside of government have been integral participants in defining public, private, and the line separating the two. Nongovernmental organizations have nearly always participated in the practice of security, though in different ways across time and space. Historical examples include the British East India Company or the London Missionary Society in the nineteenth century, both of which undertook "private" pursuits that were pivotal in shifting governmental roles in controlling violence and providing security (Avant and Haufler 2014).

In the current era, these practices have been affected by globalization, understood here as social, economic, and technological processes that increase connections among people and organizations (Held et al. 1999). With these increased connections have come claims to broader views of both security and the public, opening the way for the participation of various "private" actors including multinational corporations, advocacy NGOs, implementing NGOs, and private military and security companies (PMSCs) in the practice of security. These new actors have not only broadened participation in security, but have also changed its practice.

We illustrate our argument in three parts. In Section 24.1, we examine how global changes inspired debate among public intellectuals and academics over how to define security in the post-Cold War moment. This debate and its new language opened avenues for different arguments about public and private, as well as about security itself. In the second section, we explore how the use of this language fostered interactions that changed perspectives about who authorizes security, with particular implications for company behavior, practices, and interactions in the security realm. In Section 24.3, we turn to changes in who provides security and how this has influenced ideas about what distinguishes legitimate from illegitimate force. We conclude with a brief discussion of current developments that might reinforce—or disrupt—contemporary practices.

24.1 Public–Private Interactions and the Redefinition of Security

In 1989 Jessica Tuchman Matthews wrote a *Foreign Affairs* article calling for a redefinition of security. Mathews particularly sought to include environmental and demographic concerns: "Environmental strains that transcend national borders are already beginning to break down the sacred boundaries of national sovereignty, previously rendered porous by the information and communication revolutions and the instantaneous global movement of financial capital." (Mathews 1989). In the debate that ensued, Daniel Deudney (1991) called her logic "muddled thinking," and Stephen Walt (1991) held that including topics such as environmental hazards in security would destroy the intellectual coherence of the field. Soon after, the United Nations introduced the concept of "human security" (UNDP 1994), which uses the individual as the referent for security and linked the security of individuals to economic and social conditions in ways that traditional security advocates saw as misguided (Paris 2001). European scholars then began analyzing the process by which something became a security issue, or was "securitized" (van Munster 2012). The securitization literature implied that what security means shifts over time, depending on claims about an issue's relevance to security and the acceptance of those claims. At the same time, this literature still accepted the traditional assertion that evoking security implied a special role for the state (Williams 2003).

This debate over what we should "secure" was opened by a prominent public intellectual, carried on by academics in academic journals, and further broadened by representatives at the UN. As Matthews made explicit, the debate was partly a response to processes of globalization, but it was also made opportune by the Cold War's end, which opened possibilities for re-shaping the security priorities of prominent states like the United States. And while Matthews sought to direct attention to environmental challenges, others fought to bring security's urgency to additional issues in order to frame them in a way that would garner attention and action.

This debate has not been resolved. Its various protagonists continue to call for and analyze "security"—but with different meanings and in different ways. The word "security" appears in studies of many different issues: environmental security, economic security, food security, human security, national security, international security, collective security. These point to sources of risk well beyond traditional military threats, including everything from pandemics and women's oppression, to financial contagion, and more. These have been taken up by governments as guides to policy, as when Japan, Canada, and South Africa each committed themselves to principles of human security and shifted their agendas accordingly (Brysk 2009). Even when not taken up explicitly in government policy, different parts of government including military organizations adopted the language of security for a wider array of risks. So have companies, NGOs, international organizations (IOs), and policy analysts. The privileged role for the state and the enmity over issues attached to security that securitization theorists expected to see was visible in some of these new issue areas. In others, the process demonstrated malleability in the degree to which security invokes enmity or is tied to the state (Avant 2007). These dynamics affected both who authorizes security and how we have come to understand the laws of war.

24.2 Broadened Security and Shifts in who Authorizes Security

Governments often seek to monopolize violence by claiming not just the sole right to exercise it, but the right to define which violence is threatening and how its populations should understand violent experiences. But this ability to shape security practices by defining violence and threat is not confined to governments. Other organizations also make claims about which threats we should be concerned about; which ones justify a response and by whom; and what or who we should protect. Sometimes they are successful in gaining acceptance and legitimacy for their claims from other groups and even from governments. In other cases, organizations make no claims themselves, but become the target of claims made by others—either as a source of threat or as a source of protection.

In the current era, transnational activists and social movements often adopt the language of security when making appeals about the issues they organize to address. They link problems such as threats to human rights, democracy, or the environment to security in order to gain attention and pressure others to action. Although some activists operate across borders, most of their efforts focus on local conflicts (Della Porta and Tarrow 2005). Local activists appeal to transnational groups by framing conflicts in the global language of human rights and environmental protection in order to gain support for their cause (Keck and Sikkink 1998). As a result, the international community becomes more likely to view environmental degradation in localities such as the Niger River delta as a source of insecurity, and local activists more concerned about unemployment and inequality nevertheless frame their cause in the language of environment and human rights for an international audience (Bob 2002; Oduah 2016). In either case, organizations identify themselves as principled actors working for the common good and speaking for communities who have too little voice, which gives them authority to determine the content of security concerns locally and internationally. As such, they take on a public role—identifying threats to the common good or to particular communities.

Through their claims in recent years, these organizations have pushed commercial actors to take on more public roles (Brysk 2009; Della Porta and Tarrow 2005; Risse et al. 2013). Consider the direct naming and shaming of companies by activist campaigns seeking to mobilize citizens, consumers, and policy-makers on issues of common concern (Soule 2009; Friman 2015). They target prominent companies, such as Nike or Shell Oil, or criticize the global supply chains that obscure the role of specific firms (MacDonald 2014). These campaigns occur within the context of larger movements that seek to re-shape global norms, such as the corporate social responsibility movement (Tsutsui and Lim 2015) or the broader global justice movement (Della Porta and Tarrow 2005).

In enlisting transnational corporations to address local violence in the areas where companies operate, these activists also authorize a broader public role for commercial actors (Haufler 2001, 2010b; Fort 2008; Dietelhoff and Wolf 2013). Transnational companies are identified as a source of grievance, complicit in government violence against communities, and engaging in what has been labeled "militarized commerce" (Forcese 2001). But they are also viewed as having more resources and capacity to resolve these conflicts and end the violence—and are thus given authority to act (Haufler 2010b). These campaigns typically enroll other NGOs concerned about related issues within the broader definition of security—human rights, environment, corruption—thus further securitizing these issues. For instance, the transnational campaign against the trade in "conflict" diamonds that financed war in Angola, Sierra Leone, and the DRC (Democratic Republic of the Congo) garnered support from literally hundreds of NGOs which tied their own issues to this one (Tamm 2004; Haufler 2010a). These campaigns build on and reinforce broad definitions of security and work to pull private actors into public roles.

The effort to enlist companies into conflict prevention has found significant support among international institutions and governments. The UN Global Compact facilitated the growing acceptance of business as a security actor through regular dialogues beginning in 2001, and eventually launched the Business4Peace platform to support corporate conflict prevention activities in 2015. The UN Security Council in 2014 discussed the role of business in conflict prevention, peacekeeping, and post-conflict peacebuilding for the first time. Individual governments have adopted policies that identify commercial actors as part of security processes, reflected in recent legislation in the United States and the EU that requires companies to report their trade in conflict minerals.

Conflict-affected governments and communities often expect corporations to take on security responsibilities, even when those companies are reluctant to do so.

In response, some corporations have adopted new practices. Urged by activists to adopt "conflict sensitive business practices" (International Alert 2005), they have begun analyzing the impact of their own investments and operations on local stability and human rights practices. Many are adopting transparency policies, reporting on their operations, plans for the future, and payments to government. They engage more directly with the local communities in which they operate, and participate in multi-stakeholder processes and institutions at both the local and international levels (Ruggie 2013). Examples include the participation of the diamond industry in the Kimberley Process Certification Scheme, the oil and gas industry in the Extractive Industries Transparency Initiative (EITI), and due diligence initiatives regarding global supply chains in general.[2] In some cases, business has been a key supporter in peace negotiations, as in Mozambique at the end of its civil war and currently in South Sudan. These interactions link local conflicts to broader global norms at the same time as they connect a broader set of issues to security. They expand the range of actors involved in both defining and providing security and give companies authority in security affairs.

Some observers argue that transnational corporations need to develop their own corporate foreign policy and engage in corporate diplomacy (Chipman 2016). As Ciepley argues, corporations have never been truly "private" actors but are government-like, and as such, need to abide by principles of geopolitical due diligence regarding transnational risk in both home and host countries (Ciepley 2013). Their contemporary role requires them to engage more fully with local and international stakeholders, building a positive reputation as a legitimate participant with a "social license to operate" (Zandvliet and Anderson 2009; Ruggie 2013; Henisz 2014). Fort goes so far as to argue that companies should explicitly pursue peace as a corporate policy (Fort 2015). These arguments blur lines between public and private actors and recognize that company practices endow firms with the authority to determine the contours of security.

A striking example of the implications of this change is the evolving behavior of Chinese companies in Africa. The rise of Chinese economic and political power is typically framed as an evolving geostrategic competition with the United States. But this misses the ways in which Chinese engagement abroad is having an impact on China itself. Chinese companies have become the most significant investors in Africa in recent years, especially in resource-rich areas. These companies are generally thought to be more willing to invest in weakly governed regions than their Western counterparts[3] (Chen et al. 2015; Matfess 2015), and Chinese investors are assumed to be preferable to governments concerned about conditionality. The Chinese government has a long-standing policy of not intervening in local affairs which reinforces assumptions that neither the government nor firms pay attention to environmental or social issues (Saferworld 2011).

However, Chinese investments are prone to the same risks from local conflict dynamics that have been problematic for Western investors, and face some of the same pressures (Patey 2014; Patey and Chun 2015). A number of critical observers argue that Chinese companies should take into account the impact their operations have on the potential for violence. As one remarks, “Whether China likes it or not, it plays a significant role in peace and security in Africa; negatively, through its absence, and positively, through an increased partnership with African states and institutions working for peace and security” (Iyasu 2013). A number of recent analyses go further to argue that China is incrementally and unofficially moving away from its policy of non-interference, in response to its experience in specific and varying African contexts (Verhoeven 2014; Aidoo and Hess 2015).

Indeed, Chinese company practices on the ground are becoming more similar to those of Western firms. Even state-owned oil companies participate in multi-stakeholder engagement processes such as the EITI, and Chinese companies are about as transparent concerning their payments to governments as Western ones (Matfess 2015; Schjolberg Marques 2015). An increasing number now issue corporate social responsibility reports detailing their efforts to promote sustainability and engage with local communities (Liu 2015). The main Chinese association for mining recently published social responsibility guidelines for mining investments abroad, including due diligence standards on conflict similar to those developed by the OECD.[4] In South Sudan, Chinese investors are undertaking social engagement on the ground and participating in international peace talks[5] (Johnson 2014; Alessi and Xu 2015). These corporate actions suggest a shift away from policies of non-interference in response to both particular crises in different African countries and more general expectations about the role that companies play in global affairs (Alessi and Xu 2015). Observers see Chinese firms as having responsibility and authority in security affairs and expect that they will take on a more public role.

The debate over whether we need to redefine security gave a wider range of actors opportunities to determine what security is about—who or what needs to be protected, and what risks should be evaluated. They provided space for activists to promote new expectations for corporations in contributing to peace and stability in the areas where they invest. Those expectations entailed a larger role for companies in assessing their own impact on conflicts. They led firms to change their practices to reduce risk and instability, and to influence who or what gets secured in specific contexts. These expectations were reinforced by international organizations and some governments, which have essentially authorized public practices for firms in security affairs—even when contrary to some government policy.

24.3 Claims about who Can Deliver Security and Shifting Meanings in the Laws of War

In Section 24.2, we looked at how interactions between activists and companies—reinforced by other authorities—gave companies more authority to influence the definition of security and adopt policies to mitigate risk. In this section, we look at how public–private interactions—and claims about them—have also shaped who delivers security and, in turn, the global norms that govern legitimate violence. Domestic political movements in the United States and the UK combined with larger structural changes such as the end of the Cold War increased transnational connections to generate a significant role for "private" commercial security providers. Often organized transnationally, private military and security companies (PMSCs) deliver security services all over the globe (Singer 2003a; Avant 2005; Abrahamsen and Williams 2010). PMSCs provide a wide variety of services, overlapping with both military and policing functions, to both governmental and nongovernmental clients. Claims about the inability or unwillingness of government forces to serve "public" or collective concerns have also animated the rise in sub-state or transnational armed groups—called "militia," "rebel," or "terrorist." These groups also claim to deliver security to some communities, and to use legitimate violence against others. Traditionally, both commercial and sub-state or transnational armed groups have been viewed as "private," illegitimate managers of violence precisely because they are not state actors.

As commercial and non-commercial non-state armed groups have increasingly managed violence, they have run up against arguments that challenge their legitimacy. In this section we examine how their claims to legitimacy, alongside problem-solving efforts to affect their behavior, have led to changes in the norms governing war—particularly the way we think about just war and international humanitarian law (IHL). Both rebel groups and PMSCs challenge the categories on which just war and IHL rest. Because militias, rebels, and terrorists are not states (which are assumed to be public authorities), they do not have the proper standing to enter a war justly. Furthermore, their strategies often blur the lines between combatant and civilian, something that violates a fundamental tenet of IHL. Similarly, PMSCs can operate on the battlefield but are often not covered by military justice systems and occupy a middle area between combatant and civilian. This led some to claim there was a "vacuum of [international] law" surrounding their actions (Singer 2003). Both rebel movements and PMSCs, however, have made some strides toward greater legitimacy by claiming their behavior is in pursuit of, or consistent with, common concerns.

Historically, rebel forces often claim to better represent public ends than the governments they oppose. Some rebel groups also take it upon themselves to exercise restraint with regard to non-combatants—observing some principles of *jus in bello*.[6] One of the fundamental tenets of Mao's doctrine was a focus on winning the hearts and minds of the population among which the guerrilla forces swam. While these forces committed what could be regarded as "murder" by their surreptitious assassinations of military forces or political leaders, they often took pains to distinguish between members of the regime against which they fought and members of the civilian population to whom they turned for support. In practice rebel armies vary in the degree to which they protect or brutalize the population. Jeremy Weinstein's study of rebel forces begins with a contrast between the 1981 rebel force behavior in Lukumbi Village, Uganda (largely respectful and protecting of civilians) and rebel behavior in Maringue Village, Mozambique in 1979 (largely un-respectful of civilians) (Weinstein 2006).

Beyond particular behavior toward civilians, some rebel groups have actually pledged support for IHL as the FMLN (Farabundo Martí National Liberation Front) did in El Salvador. In other cases, as with the Lord's Resistance Army in Uganda, the rebels have espoused doctrine that is fundamentally at odds with IHL. Hyeran Jo examined the data to explain why some rebels (51 percent of the groups she examines) comply with IHL and others (22 percent) do not. She looked at rebel commitment to international law and rebel compliance in three areas: civilian killing, the use of child soldiers, and the treatment of detainees (Jo 2015).[7] Her analytical categories demonstrate the concerns many international experts pay attention to in assessing legitimate management of force: the treatment of vulnerable groups and a commitment to established international norms and practices. By associating themselves with accepted public authorities—governments and international law—otherwise suspect rebel groups believe they can generate greater acceptance, and even legitimacy. Groups with a persistent political wing, governance aims, and openness to transnational actors were those most likely to pledge respect for IHL.

The ICRC (International Committee of the Red Cross) has consistently encouraged respect for IHL regardless of the status of militant groups (whether labeled rebels or terrorists). While careful not to endorse these groups as legitimate, the ICRC has focused its efforts on engendering respect for *jus in bello* principles. In pursuit of this respect, the ICRC is prepared to engage with any actor willing to work toward those principles. Another Swiss-based NGO, Geneva Call, specifically aims to work with armed non-state actors (ANSA) to encourage their respect for international humanitarian norms.[8] Concerned that the IHL focus on states leaves non-state armed actors without a clear logic for abiding by IHL, Geneva Call educates and trains these ANSA about *jus in bello* principles and offers them a chance to issue a "Deed of Commitment" to refrain from sexual violence, to ban landmines, and/or to protect children. Though both the ICRC and Geneva Call avoid discussing the legitimacy of these actors per se, the implicit presumption is that groups who make this commitment are more legitimate than those who do not.

Academics have not been so shy. Michael Gross proposes an ethics even for those seeking violent political change, considering both the relative justice of their resistance as well as the justice of their tactics (Gross 2015). In keeping with the logic here, just resistance requires it to generate self-determination, a dignified life, and an acceptable level of public consent. Just tactics must reduce potential harm to non-combatants, and "permissible targeting turns on liability" (Gross 2015: 9).[9] Thus different "private" actors such as the ICRC, Geneva Call, and academic analysts have made claims about what "private" (rebel) forces should do in order to act "public."

The logic surrounding PMSCs is a little different from the logic regarding non-state armed groups. As more military and security services began to be delivered and financed by the private sector in the 1990s a debate broke out over the conditions, if any, under which they were legitimate. Representatives of some governments and international lawyers claimed that PMSCs could gain legitimacy through right *authorization*. If these companies were authorized by states, they could be considered legitimate as an extension of right authority. Though states would delegate authority to PMSCs they would remain responsible for their actions. But because authorizing private forces changes the way states operate, this can lead a government to avoid constitutional or public checks—thus leading the state itself to behave less in keeping with public or common concerns (Avant and Sigelman 2010). This logical move, then, was not satisfying to many observers of the rise in PMSCs.

What has gained more traction is an approach that looks at the range of relationships between states and private forces, and to think concretely about how states should relate to PMSCs in order to be congruent with their general international legal obligations. This approach was initiated by the ICRC (along with the Swiss government) in 2007 and involved governments as well as representatives from PMSCs and civil society in a multi-stakeholder process to develop the relevant guidelines. The resulting Montreux Document outlines legal obligations and best practices for contracting states (those who contract with PMSCs), home states (those states where PMSCs are incorporated), and territorial states (those states on whose territory PMSCs operate).[10] The logical follow-on step was to extend the principles of IHL to PMSCs. In the wake of the Montreux Document process, the ICRC and Swiss again initiated a multi-stakeholder process to come up with an international code of conduct (ICoC) for security services.[11] The ICoC was signed in 2010 and an organization to implement it, the International Code of Conduct Association (ICoCA), was launched in 2013. As of June 2016 the ICoCA has 6 government members, 16 civil society members, and 101 company members. Private national and international standards have been built on the Montreux/ICoC principles and at the five-year anniversary of the Montreux Document the government signatories formed a Montreux Document Forum (Avant 2016).

Together the Montreux Document and ICoC provide an integrated framework for best practices among governments and PMSCs. The standards based on this framework can be written into contracts and then enforced through contract law. The multi-stakeholder ICoCA promises oversight and monitoring of the ICoC, along with coordination with both standards bodies and the Montreux Document Forum. Though many of these instruments are non-binding, they have driven changes in government regulation, with governments including the United States making them a part of legal requirements in ways that promise enforcement.

More importantly, the interactions among various academic and civil society claims, companies, and governments have also contributed to a shift in the focus of international humanitarian law. As with the rebel example, these claims have concentrated on the *behavior* of actors rather than being concerned about the category into which they fall. The Montreux Document claimed to introduce nothing new, but simply to interpret what government obligations under existing IHL meant for private security providers. However, stretching these principles to an additional set of actors has furthered the idea that public behavior is more about what an actor *does* than who it *is*.

These two instance show how "private" actors can gain acceptance and legitimacy for their actions by claiming to behave in keeping with public concerns. Though the particular claims of non-state armed groups and commercial security providers are quite different, they have both pledged to constrain their behavior in accord with IHL principles. These pledges and their acceptance by others have been stabilizing in that they prescribe and reinforce behavior for nongovernmental security providers consistent with IHL. It has also, though, altered the meaning of "public" in IHL, giving more emphasis to behavior that respects public norms than it does to incorporation by a state (Avant and Haufler 2014: 51). Claims in the Responsibility to Protect (R2P) doctrine support a similar change from a different angle by arguing that states only access their "public" status if they uphold their responsibilities by acting in keeping with common concerns. This refocus, in turn, may allow even more space for other types of nongovernmental security providers in IHL.

24.4 Public–Private Interactions and the Future of Security

Debate around the definition of security provided space for public–private interactions that fostered security roles for different actors and envisioned the public in new ways. Pulling these various actors into global norms has led to adjustments that reinforce a broader view of both security and the public. But in what we have sketched in this chapter, these dynamics have drawn various new threads spun by globalization into familiar patterns. Similar trends in the past, however, tell us that these patterns can be erased or redrawn as well as extended (Ciepley 2013; Avant and Haufler 2014). As we look to the future, two particular developments could disrupt the trends we have discussed in Section 24.3: security in the cyber world and nationalist reactions to globalization itself.

In the cyber world, technology has generated new political spaces that bear little connection to territory (Adamson 2016: 25). Cyberspace is arguably a public arena involving issues of common concern to be secured. However, what is to be secured, who defines it, and who provides security are all contested. Rather than seeing governments as protectors of this public space, they are often viewed as part of the threat. The Global Network Initiative (GNI), for instance, seeks to insulate cyberspace from government pressures that may, as their homepage puts it, "conflict with the internationally recognized human rights of freedom of expression and privacy."[12] Much of the infrastructure of the Internet is owned and organized by private companies, such as Google or Facebook. But the services they provide lead many people to see them as public actors. Our discussions in this chapter might suggest that they, too, will be drawn into public norms. The norms defining common concerns in cyberspace, though, are murky and contested (Finnemore and Hollis 2016). The Internet provides tools that can put power in the hands of individuals but also reinforce the capacities of governments. The threats posed in cyberspace appear quite distant from the violence concerns in traditional security but cyber tools can both affect violent capacities and have dire consequences for stability and legitimacy.

Cyberspace is thus not easily situated in the normative space that has grown around the incorporation of commercial and activist organizations thus far.

The new online media have been credited with reducing the cost of mobilization for social change. Ironically, some of this mobilization has allowed attacks on the very globalization responsible for the growth of the cyber world (Cronin 2002–03). These movements, cutting across left–right divisions, seek to reassert nationalism or localism. The Brexit vote is a dramatic example of this, but populist sparks can be seen all over Europe, in the United States, and in Russia and China (Weiss 2014). More extreme versions like ISIS have taken the use of globalization's tools to new levels, using new media to mobilize support (Cronin, Chapter 34 this volume). The "common" concerns espoused by these groups or movements are narrow and inward-looking, contrasting markedly with the expansive view of the public we discuss in this chapter. They harken back to a simpler time and promote practices that would erase broader concerns and reinforce more traditional, national, views of security—protecting "us" against "them" with violence.

Though pointing to different logics of disruption, the cyber world and nationalist mobilization work in tandem. Because the cyber world touches nearly every dimension of the physical world, how cybersecurity is imagined, what norms it builds on, and how its practices unfold will have dramatic consequences for how we think of security, who provides it, and what governs their behavior. Whether these trends portend further broadening, a dramatic break with existing practices, or a return to traditional security depends on unfolding interactions between technology companies, advocacy organizations, governments, movements, and others. These interactions will decide how we see the public and its security in the future.

Notes

1. Public defined here as issues of common concern (Best and Gheciu 2014).
2. Corporate participation in the security arena is uneven and it is not clear whether it has significantly reduced violence. Nevertheless, these practices influence who and what gets secured, and who provides security.
3. Data on Chinese investment abroad is difficult to obtain and interpret, and there are ongoing debates over the amount and significance of it (Brautigam 2011; Shinn 2012).
4. The OECD Due Diligence Guidance for Responsible Supply Chains of Minerals from Conflict-Affected and High-Risk Areas.
5. At the same time, the Chinese government has sold arms and ammunition to the government of South Sudan, which may have undermined the peace, so Chinese engagement is not always peace promoting (Matfess 2015).
6. The just war tradition consists of both claims about the justness of the decision to enter a war (*jus ad bellum*) and claims about the justness of behavior undertaken in prosecuting a war (*jus in bello*). *Jus in bello*'s cardinal principles are discrimination between civilians and combatants (targeting only combatants) and proportionality of means (violence should be used proportionately to the injustice suffered).
7. Her dataset covers 1990–2010 and includes rebel groups in violent engagement with government forces that have produced at least 25 battle deaths.

8. http://www.genevacall.org/.
9. Neither mercenaries nor PMSCs are included in Gross's analysis.
10. See https://www.eda.admin.ch/eda/en/fdfa/foreign-policy/international-law/international-humanitarian-law/private-military-security-companies/montreux-document.html.
11. Defined as: guarding and protection of persons and objects, such as convoys, facilities, designated sites, property or other places (whether armed or unarmed), or any other activity for which the Personnel of Companies are required to carry or operate a weapon in the performance of their duties. See the ICoC, available at: http://icoca.ch/en/the_icoc.
12. See https://www.globalnetworkinitiative.org/.

References

Abrahamsen, Rita and Michael Williams. 2010. *Security Beyond the State: Private Security in International Politics.* Cambridge: Cambridge University Press.

Adamson, F. B. 2016. Spaces of Global Security: Beyond Methodological Nationalism, *Journal of Global Security Studies*, 1(1): 19–35.

Aidoo, Richard and Steve Hess. 2015. Non-Interference 2.0: China's Evolving Foreign Policy towards a Changing Africa. *Journal of Current Chinese Affairs*, 44(1): 107–39.

Alessi, Christopher and Beina Xu. 2015. *China in Africa.* CFR Backgrounder. Updated: April 27, 2015.

Avant, Deborah. 2005. *The Market for Force: The Implications of Privatizing Security.* Cambridge: Cambridge University Press.

Avant, Deborah. 2007. NGOs, Corporations, and Security Transformation in Africa. *International Relations*, 21(2): 143–61.

Avant, Deborah. 2016. Pragmatic Networks and Transnational Governance of Private Military and Security Services. *International Studies Quarterly*, 60(2): 330–42.

Avant, Deborah and Virginia Haufler. 2014. The Dynamics of "Private" Security Practices and their Public Consequences: Transnational Organizations in Historical Perspective. In Jacqueline Best and Alexandra Gheciu (eds.), *The Return of the Public in Global Governance.* Cambridge: Cambridge University Press.

Avant, Deborah and Lee Sigelman. 2010. Private Security and Democracy: Lessons from the United States in Iraq. *Security Studies*, 19(2): 230–65.

Best, Jacqueline and Alexandra Gheciu (eds.). 2014. *The Return of the Public in Global Governance.* Cambridge: Cambridge University Press.

Bob, Clifford. 2002. Political Process Theory and Transnational Movements: Dialectics of Protest among Nigeria's Ogoni Minority. *Social Problems*, 49(3): 395–415.

Brautigam, Deborah. 2011. *The Dragon's Gift: The Real Story of China in Africa.* Oxford: Oxford University Press.

Brysk, Allison. 2009. *Global Good Samaritans: Human Rights as Foreign Policy.* Oxford: Oxford University Press.

Chen, Wenjie, David Dollar, and Heiwai Tan. 2015. *Why is China Investing in Africa? Evidence from the Firm Level.* Washington, DC: The Brookings Institution.

Chipman, John. 2016. Why Your Company Needs a Foreign Policy. *Harvard Business Review.* September: 37–43.

Ciepley, David. 2013. Beyond Public and Private: Toward a Political Theory of the Corporation. *American Political Science Review*, 107(1): 139–58.

Cronin, Audrey. 2002–03. Behind the Curve: Globalization and International Terrorism. *International Security*, 27(3): 30–58.

Della Porta, Donatella and Sidney Tarrow. 2005. *Transnational Protest and Global Activism*. Lanham, MD: Rowman & Littlefield.

Deudney, Daniel. 1991. Muddled Thinking. *Bulletin of the Atomic Scientists*, 47(3): 22.

Dietelhoff, Nicole, and Klaus Dieter Wolf. 2013. Business and Human Rights: How Corporate Norm Violators become Norm Entrepreneurs. In Thomas Risse, Stephen C. Ropp and Katherine Sikkink (eds.), *The Persistent Power of Human Rights: From Commitment to Compliance*, pp. 222–38. New York: Cambridge University Press.

Finnemore, Martha and Duncan Hollis. 2016. Constructing Norms for Global Cybersecurity. *American Journal of International Law*. 110(3): 425–79.

Forcese, Craig. 2001. Militarized Commerce in Sudan's Oil Fields: Lessons for Canadian Foreign Policy. *Canadian Foreign Policy*, 8(3): 37–56.

Fort, Timothy L. 2008. *Prophets, Profits, & Peace: How Businesses Can Become Instruments of Peace and Foster Religious Harmony*. New Haven, CT: Yale University Press.

Fort, Timothy. 2015. *The Diplomat in the Corner Office: Corporate Foreign Policy*. Stanford, CA: Stanford University Press.

Friman, H. Richard. 2015. *The Politics of Leverage in International Relations: Name, Shame, and Sanction*. Basingstoke: Palgrave Macmillan.

Gross, Michael. 2015. *The Ethics of Insurgency: A Critical Guide to Just Guerilla War*. Cambridge: Cambridge University Press.

Haufler, Virginia. 2001. Is There a Role for Business in Conflict Management? In Chester Crocker, Fen Hampson, and Pamela Aall (eds.), *Turbulent Peace*. Washington, DC: United States Institute of Peace.

Haufler, Virginia. 2010a. The Kimberley Process Certification Scheme: An Innovation in Governance and Conflict Prevention. *Journal of Business Ethics* Special Issue 89(4): 409–16.

Haufler, Virginia. 2010b. Corporations in Zones of Conflict: Issues, Actors, and Institutions. In Deborah Avant, Martha Finnemore, and Susan Sell (eds.), *Who Governs the Globe?*, pp. 102–30. Cambridge: Cambridge University Press.

Held, David, Anthony McGrew, David Goldblatt, and Jonathan Perraton. 1999. *Global Transformations: Politics, Economics, and Culture*. Stanford, CA: Stanford University Press.

Henisz, Witold. 2014. *Corporate Diplomacy: Building Reputations and Relationships with External Stakeholders*. Sheffield: Greenleaf Publishing.

ICoC. 2010. International Code of Conduct for Private Security Providers. *Available at:* http://psm.du.edu/media/documents/regulations/global_instruments/multi_stakeholder/icoc/icoc_eng.pdf

International Alert. 2005. *Conflict-Sensitive Business Practice: Guidance for Extractive Industries*. London: International Alert.

Iyasu, Alula. 2013. China's Non-Interference Policy and Growing African Concerns. *African Arguments. Available at:* http://africanarguments.org/2013/07/18/china%E2%80%99s-non-interference-policy-and-growing-african-concerns/ July 18

Jo, Hyeron. 2015. *Compliant Rebels: Rebel Groups and International Law in World Politics*. Cambridge: Cambridge University Press.

Johnson, Keith. 2014. China's African Adventure. *Foreign Policy*. April 24, 2014.

Keck, Margaret E. and Kathryn Sikkink. 1998. *Activists Beyond Borders: Advocacy Networks in International Politics*. Ithaca, NY: Cornell University Press.

Liu, Meng. 2016. *Is Corporate Social Responsibility China's Secret Weapon?* World Economic Forum]. March 17, 2017. *Available at:* https://www.weforum.org/agenda/2015/03/is-corporate-social-responsibility-chinas-secret-weapon/.

MacDonald, Kate. 2014. *The Politics of Global Supply Chains*. Cambridge: Polity Press.

Matfess, Hilary. 2015. Should you worry about China's investments in Africa? *The Monkey Cage*. September 9, 2015. *Available at:* https://www.washingtonpost.com/blogs/monkey-cage/wp/2015/09/09/should-you-worry-about-chinas-investments-in-africa/

Matthews, Jessica. 1989. Redefining Security. *Foreign Affairs*, Spring.

Oduah, Chika. 2016. Trouble is Brewing in Nigeria's Oil Country. *Foreign Policy*. June 15.

Paris, Roland. 2001. Human Security: Paradigm Shift or Hot Air? *International Security* 26(2): 87–102.

Patey, Luke. 2014. *The New Kings of Crude: China, India, and the Global Struggle for Oil in Sudan and South Sudan*. London: Hurst.

Patey, Luke and Zhang Chun. 2015. Improving the Sino-African Relationship: What Beijing Can Do. *Foreign Affairs* December 7.

Risse, Thomas, Stephen C. Ropp, and Katherine Sikkink. 2013. *The Persistent Power of Human Rights: From Commitment to Compliance*. New York: Cambridge University Press.

Ruggie, John Gerard. 2013. *Just Business: Multinational Companies and Human Rights*. New York: W.W. Norton & Co.

Saferworld. 2011. *China's growing role in African peace and security*.

Schjolberg Marques, Ines. 2015. Chinese Companies as Transparent as Others. *EITI News*, May 22.

Shinn, David. 2012. China's Investments in Africa. *China–United States Focus*. November 1, 2012.

Singer, Peter W. 2003a. *Corporate Warriors: the Rise of the Privatized Military Industry*. Ithaca, NY: Cornell University Press.

Singer, Peter W. 2003b. War, Profits and the Vacuum of Law: Privatized Military Firms and International Law. *Columbia Journal of International Law*, 42: 521.

Soule, Sarah A. 2009. *Contention and Corporate Social Responsibility*. Cambridge: Cambridge University Press.

Tamm, Ingrid J. 2004. Dangerous Appetites: Human Rights Activism and Conflict Commodities. *Human Rights Quarterly*, 26(3): 687–704.

Tsutsui, Kiyoteru and Alwyn Lim. 2015. *Corporate Social Responsibility in a Globalizing World*. New York and Cambridge: Cambridge University Press.

United Nations Development Program (UNDP). 1994. *Human Development Report 1994: New Dimensions of Human Security*. *Available at:* http://hdrnet.org/426/

van Munster, Rens. 2012. *Securitization*. Oxford Bibliographies. *Available at:* http://www.oxfordbibliographies.com/view/document/obo-9780199743292/obo-9780199743292-0091.xml

Verhoeven, Harry. 2014. Is Beijing's NonInterference Policy History? How Africa is Changing China. *The Washington Quarterly*, 37(2): 55–70.

Walt, Stephen. 1991. The Renaissance of Security Studies. *International Studies Quarterly*, 35(2): 211–39.

Weinstein, Jeremy. 2006. *Inside Rebellion: The Politics of Insurgent Violence*. Cambridge: Cambridge University Press.

Weiss, Jessica Chen. 2014. *Powerful Patriots: Nationalist Protest in China*. Oxford: Oxford University Press.

Williams, Michael C. 2003. Words, Images, Enemies: Securitization and International Politics. *International Studies Quarterly*, 47(4): 511–31.

Zandvliet, Luc, and Mary Anderson. 2009. *Getitng it Right*. Sheffield: Greenleaf Publishing.

CHAPTER 25

NUCLEAR PROLIFERATION

The Risks of Prediction

ETEL SOLINGEN

25.1 Introduction

This Handbook's editors invited contributors to think about the future of international security while identifying key agents, processes, and structural drivers of transformation. This is a tall order. This chapter organizes the existing literature on nuclear proliferation accordingly. Section 25.2 briefly reviews existing theoretical tools for predicting proliferation or nonproliferation, spanning a range of agents (states, regimes, dominant coalitions, and individuals), structures, and processes. Section 25.3 distills relevant considerations for exploring future scenarios in East Asia, a good laboratory for understanding failed past predictions and conditions for potential transformations of its nuclear order. Section 25.4 concludes with an assessment of where the field stands in its potential for estimating proliferation trends.

25.2 Theoretical Tools for Predicting Nonproliferation

25.2.1 Neorealism

Neorealism was once the orthodoxy for explaining why some states seek nuclear weapons and others renounce them. Its foremost exponent, Kenneth Waltz, considered it unwise to lump his theory, offering specific predictions on the topic, with other versions of neorealism. Waltz identified an anarchic international structure as the dominant driver of nuclear behavior, and states as the key agents responding to those constraints.

While anarchy arguably renders all states insecure—compelling self-help—nuclear weapons provide security, stability, and diminished chances of war. Alluring for its simplicity, this theory provides valuable insights, explains some cases reasonably well, and retains some *prima facie* appeal (Solingen 2007: 26–9). Yet its dominance has been challenged. As the "most likely" explanation, neorealism should effortlessly crowd out other theories yet it competes with them heavily in what should be its best arena for empirical validation. Three major problems stand out.

First is the massive and growing set of empirical anomalies:

- Anarchy, uncertainty, and self-help apply to most if not all states, yet most have not developed nuclear weapons; indeed, an overwhelming majority has renounced them.
- Even more modest predictions by Waltz—18 to 30 nuclear weapons states—have not materialized
- Several acutely vulnerable states have *not* gone nuclear, even when rivals did (e.g. Egypt, Vietnam, but also Japan, South Korea, and others)
- States without *existential* threats *contemplated* nuclear weapons (e.g. Argentina, Brazil)

When scholars attempt to deal with these anomalies, a second problem emerges, explanatory inconsistency:

- Hegemonic protection had disparate effects, with some renouncing nuclear weapons but not others.
- Alliances are insufficient for explaining nuclear abstention, with some allies abstaining but not others (e.g. Britain, France) (Waltz 1979, 1981)
- Many states restrained nuclear ambitions without superpower guarantees (e.g. Egypt, Brazil).
- Comparable structural conditions can (and have) lead to very different choices; multipolarity, for example, predicts increased nuclearization yet has led to different outcomes across time and space (e.g. East Asia, the Middle East).
- States have shifted toward or away from nuclear weapons over time even absent major structural changes (e.g. Taiwan, South Korea).

These problems of explanation reveal deeper conceptual limitations:

- Unfalsifiability (many options can be made to fit vague notions of security maximization a posteriori).
- Under-determination (inconclusive corollaries lead to multiple possible outcomes); it fails to explain many cases easily, at high levels of confidence and parsimony, and is incomplete in explaining most others.

Other branches of neorealism more amenable to domestic considerations discussed in the next sections may partially alleviate some of these problems but only at the cost of parsimony, a feature that neorealism prizes highly. Over the last two decades some studies began challenging previously unquestioned confidence in this theory as the driving force of all nuclear decisions (Solingen 1994a, 1994b; Ogilvie-White 1996; Sagan 1996). This has led to new efforts to rectify some of the noted deficiencies (Debs and Monteiro 2016).

25.2.2 Neoliberal Institutionalism

Neoliberal institutionalist scholarship is far more sensitive than neorealism to states' ability to "mitigate the effects of anarchy, produce mutual gains, and avoid shared harm" (Jervis 1999: 45), and to their rational incentives to join international institutions that enhance information, enforce compliance, and serve their interests at lower costs than self-help. These institutional agents can arguably moderate brute power, and states' expectations of repeated institutional interactions can alter their strategic calculus (Axelrod and Keohane 1985). The nonproliferation regime (NPR) that emerged around its core Nonproliferation Treaty (NPT) has undoubtedly performed some of the functions attributed to such institutions.[1] As a presumed driver of non/proliferation, however, this institutional approach has important limitations, including:

- The NPR *may* mitigate but not eliminate security dilemmas.
- Several NPT signatories developed clandestine weapons programs (e.g. Iraq, North Korea).
- There are inconsistencies in non-compliance rulings (e.g. South Korea, Egypt).
- Regime imperfections and other considerations have kept states from joining the NPR (e.g. India, Pakistan, Israel).
- We lack systematic evidence that the NPR accounts for *all or most* cases of nuclear abstention, although we also lack systematic evidence to the contrary (Solingen 2007).[2]
- Potential selection bias warns against imputing excessive causal weight to the NPR; states may have joined for a wide range of reasons that were causally prior to joining the treaty (e.g. South Africa, Japan).
- Causally prior drivers (in the direction of nuclear abstention) can also explain subsequent compliance better than fears of detection and punishment.
- The NPR is less than a stable bargain but rather one subject to challenges from various quarters (e.g. potential new proliferators, New Agenda Coalition on upholding the NPT's Article VI, the 2017 Treaty on the Prohibition of Nuclear Weapons, and others).

Because nuclear choices are highly sensitive to Prisoner's Dilemma situations and problems of collective action, a neoliberal institutionalist perspective does not constitute a "most likely" theory in this arena. And yet, the fact that the NPT is among the most highly subscribed international treaties compels its serious consideration as a source of nuclear restraint.

25.2.3 Norms

Constructivist approaches draw attention to how international norms emerge and converge, emphasizing socialization and normative pressure (Finnemore and Sikkink 1998; Barnett and Finnemore 1999; Johnston 2001; Klotz and Lynch 2007). States arguably join institutions not simply as a function of a material cost–benefit analysis but also because they share common purposes and beliefs. The horrors of Hiroshima and Nagasaki led to important work by Schelling (1976, 2000) and Tannenwald (2007) on the emergence of a taboo explaining nuclear non-*use*. Efforts by others (Rublee 2009) to apply normative insights to explain non-*acquisition* are less persuasive for several reasons.[3]

- A large segment of the expert community has been socialized into the framework of canonical deterrence theory, which assumes that nuclear acquisition obviates use. If nuclear weapons are designed to prevent war, according to this worldview (Jervis 1989), then such weapons may conform to a consequentialist "conditional morality" (Nye 1988)
- Many states considered or pursued nuclear options even after Hiroshima and Nagasaki (not just Iran, Iraq, North Korea, Libya, and Syria but also Sweden, Switzerland, and many others).[4]
- Insufficient systematic evidence is available to ascertain that strong norms against acquisition have indeed taken root for all or most states.
- Proposals for universal nuclear disarmament, including some backed by prominent experts (e.g. Global Zero) have failed to yield fruit. The conclusion of the Nuclear Weapon Ban Treaty in 2017 is an important milestone but one facing innumerable challenges.
- There is overwhelming domestic support for nuclear weapons among nuclear weapons' states, and rising levels of support among some presumed to have been restrained by anti-nuclear norms (e.g. South Korea).
- All nuclear arsenals are undergoing modernization.
- Coercion, material dis/incentives and other rational factors are at play in many cases of abstention.
- Failure to specify the domestic politics explaining normative receptivity (Checkel 1997).

25.2.4 Domestic Models of Political Survival

All approaches discussed thus far suffer from a common omission: a proper theory stipulating why and how domestic politics underlie nuclear choices, modifying the impact of international power, institutional, or normative considerations. Internal disagreements over nuclear choices are empirical facts, suggesting that conceptions of threats are not simple derivatives of abstract balances of power. Particular leaders and regimes interpret and define "structural insecurity" differently. Furthermore, the latter should not be conflated with *regime* survival or insecurity. Nor can rational-institutional and normative dis/incentives regarding nuclear weapons be understood without reference to the relative domestic receptivity to either. What might explain such receptivity?

Models of regime survival stemming from competing orientations to the global political economy offer important clues for estimating nuclear choices since the NPT's inception (Solingen 1994a, 1994b, 2007). Leaders and supportive coalitions rely on two Weberian ideal-typical models to gain and retain power: internationalizing and inward-looking, respectively. Findings suggest that nuclear aspirants were more likely to emerge in domestic and regional contexts dominated by inward-looking models than in internationalizing ones. The two models entail different grand strategies, each with domestic, regional, and global referents. Inward-looking models stake their political survival on rejecting integration in the global economy and associated institutions inimical to their strategy. Hostile to international markets, foreign investment, and technology, these models favor economic protectionism, self-sufficiency, sprawling state enterprises, ancillary military-industrial complexes, and nationalism, policies that shield their constituencies. Inward-looking models are less keen on cooperative regions that both undermine allocations to those constituencies and deprive them from opportunities to promote hyper-nationalist myths.[5] Such models thus incur fewer costs from exploiting nuclear weapons as tools in nationalist-protectionist platforms. There are strong synergies across the domestic, regional, and international pillars of their favored strategy. North Korea's *juche* (autarkic) approach is archetypical but several Middle Eastern states have exhibited similar profiles.

Internationalizing models lowered the likelihood of nuclear weapons' acquisition through several causal mechanisms. First, their emphasis on economic growth through global integration entailed strong incentives to avoid political, economic, reputational, and opportunity costs of nuclearization that could harm internationalizing objectives. Second, those objectives also required: resources for compensating constituencies adversely affected by economic openness; restrained military expenditures, lest they crowd out the resources needed for internationalizing the economy; expanded private economic activities; and lower barriers to trade and foreign investment. Third, these models also required a cooperative region not prone to nuclearization that would free up resources for domestic reform; reduce uncertainty; encourage foreign investment; and signal a commitment to stability and growth. Nuclear weapons programs, by contrast, strengthen bureaucracies and industrial complexes opposed to such reforms; rattle neighbors and endanger their own reforms; and encumber efforts to promote exports, competitiveness, macroeconomic and political stability, and global access. Finally, internationalizing models endorse global rules and institutions that encourage their favored strategies. Nuclear abstention enhances synergies across those strategies' domestic, regional, and global pillars. East Asian states embraced variants of this model since the 1960s. Notably, after China's 1964 nuclear test under Mao's inward-looking model only North Korea acquired nuclear weapons.

Domestic models of political survival were omitted from the theoretical menu until recently despite their utility for weighing and re-ordering the relative importance of other drivers, including structural power, norms, and institutions. Those models explain synchronic variation in nuclear preferences across states and overtime variation within the same state; varying compliance with NPR commitments; varying readings of security dilemmas as more (or less) intractable; variance in ranking alliances higher than self-reliance or vice versa; variance in relative receptivity to external sanctions and inducements;[6] why and when external coercion and inducements may be effective; and why nuclear designs were renounced where one might have expected them. Since 1968 every decision to renounce nuclear weapons by states that had entertained them was nested in broader shifts toward internationalizing models (e.g. post-Franco Spain, Sadat's Egypt, post-apartheid South Africa, Brazil, Argentina, South Korea, Japan, Taiwan, Libya in 2003, and several European powers). Most defiant nuclear courses unfolded under inward-looking models (Saddam Hussein, Muammar Qaddafi, the Kim dynasty, Ahmadinejad, Assad's Syria, and others). The two patterns find support across different regional security contexts and diverse associations with hegemons, yet important caveats and scope conditions should be noted:

- The association between respective models and nuclear choices is neither deterministic nor inevitable.
- Inward-looking models arguably provide necessary but insufficient conditions for seeking nuclear weapons.
- A region's center of gravity (internationalizing or inward-looking) can modify domestic preferences toward or away from nuclear weapons.
- Temporal sequences in nuclear weapons' acquisition matter: when nuclearization precedes the inception of internationalizing models (e.g. China, Israel), subsequent denuclearization may be harder. It is far more costly politically to abandon nuclear weapons than to cancel a program prior to fruition, as one might expect from prospect theory (McDermott 1998). Dis/incentives emanating from a global political economy arguably operate more forcefully at earlier stages both in the inception of internationalizing models and in the consideration of nuclear weapons.

The expansion of quantitative studies has not ended contestation over the relative weight of the theoretical drivers reviewed thus far (Solingen and Wan 2017). Supply-side studies building on Meyer's (1986) landmark proposition that technological momentum inevitably leads to proliferation have yielded competing findings (Fuhrmann 2009; Kroenig 2009; Kemp 2014). Technological determinism exhibits significant anomalies including a substantial number of "most likely cases" that renounced nuclear weapons and "least likely cases" that pursued them (Solingen 2007). As Lewis (2016) argued, whether or not states decide not to acquire nuclear weapons has often far more to do with restraint than with technological barriers, given a 65-year-old technology. Studies considering neorealist variables differed in their conceptualization of security, the weight of enduring rivalries, the likelihood of "reactive proliferation," and the effect of security guarantees, among others (Singh and Way 2004; Jo and Gartzke 2007). Some studies argued that personalist regimes are more likely to pursue nuclear weapons (Ways and Weeks 2014); others that nonproliferation norms act most strongly on democratic or democratizing states (Mueller and Schmidt 2010). Yet most autocratic leaders have renounced nuclear weapons and abided by their NPT commitments; both democracies and autocracies have acquired nuclear weapons; and the outstanding non-NPT members are either stable democracies (India and Israel) or intermittently democratic (Pakistan).

Bell's (2015) sophisticated statistical study concluded that quantitative studies failed to offer strong explanations or predictions for proliferation patterns because they neglect indirect causal pathways that are difficult to capture; have little to say about those drivers' causal strength; include too many variables relative to the number of cases; rely on proxy variables that gauge underlying concepts poorly; and focus on different dependent variables (nuclear exploration, pursuit, acquisition). Hence, findings regarding weak correlations between many variables and proliferation offer no proof whatsoever that those variables indeed lack causal effects on proliferation and nonproliferation. Furthermore, wide discrepancies regarding the appropriate "universe of cases" exist, along with serious concerns that the typical "universe"—that is, nearly all states in the system—exacerbates heterogeneity and decreases validity (Debs and Monteiro 2016; Solingen and Malnight 2016). Statistical studies also ignore temporal effects, treating states as monolithic entities following continuous, coherent pathways. They often exclude contextual factors that are hard to capture, measure, or operationalize such as the role of the NPR (beyond membership), political-economy models (beyond trade ratios), or perceptions of status (beyond capacity). Endogeneity is rampant and the dominant direction of causality often unclear. Some of these shortcomings can afflict qualitative studies as well. The lack of consensus across theoretical and methodological studies suggests that the task of predicting nuclear futures—as nuclear weapons themselves—is pregnant with risk.

25.3 Japan's Enigma and Proliferation Scenarios in East Asia

East Asia is an especially appropriate focus for this chapter's assignment: the region's trajectory has failed to conform to various theories; offers "crucial cases" for testing them; and has been a focal point as a proliferation-prone region. Suggesting that Japan and South Korea might be better off with their own nuclear weapons, President Donald Trump exacerbated such concerns, but they are not new. Waltz and others predicted decades ago that Japan was highly likely to acquire nuclear weapons,[7] and that such development does not break alliances apart: "Great powers ... must expect to take care of themselves" and "How long can Japan ... live alongside other nuclear states while denying [itself] similar capabilities?" (Waltz 1993: 66, 2000: 34). Even strong supporters of the alliance in Japan sustained concerns with US commitments. Makoto Momoi, former head of Japan's Defense Research Institute, referred to the alliance as "a Bible. You may know every word in it, and believe it to be true, but can you really be sure of salvation?"[8] After Nixon's trip to China (without consulting Japan) Momoi added: "you can say that we've put the Bible away. It's something around the home, but the children don't read it any longer." In an anarchic neorealist world, concerns with alliance commitments could never be fully put to rest. As a Japanese vice-admiral once put it, "the nuclear umbrella held by the U.S. must surely be useful, but for complete faith there is the nuclear umbrella opened by oneself."

Such predictions notwithstanding, Japan has not acquired nuclear weapons as of mid-2017, an outcome especially incompatible with the premise that states do best by relying on their own deterrent. What makes this abstention an even more difficult anomaly for neorealism is that Japan has witnessed—over six decades—the nuclearization of no less than three of its neighbors (the Soviet Union, China, and a rabid North Korean regime that conducted six nuclear tests). With so many thresholds crossed, imminent predictions that Japan would go nuclear should have come to pass. Nor was Japan's abstention the product of US coercion; there was no strong Japanese demand for nuclear weapons that required US pressure to halt it. Nixon's 1969 "Guam doctrine" called for greater self-reliance by Asian allies and unleashed a renewed sense of abandonment by the United States. Nixon even suggested to Premier Sato in 1972 that Japan faced an unacceptable choice to either develop "its own deterrent power however unpalatable vis-à-vis its neighbors, who are armed with nuclear weapons, or... come to an accommodation with them" (Solingen 2007: 61) and the United States exerted no pressure on Japan to ratify the NPT.

Japan's nuclear abstention does not provide strong support for neoliberal institutionalism either. There is little evidence that the nascent NPT played any role in its critical 1970s decisions. Nor did the NPR's institutional failures—notably regarding North Korea—alter those decisions. A norms-based approach tracing abstention to Hiroshima and Nagasaki may explain the rise of some pacifist constituencies. Yet the "nuclear allergy" was far from strong when Japan delayed signing the NPT by 18 months; attached an unusual addendum to its signature, taking note of Article X allowing legal withdrawal three months after notification; delayed ratification by nearly *seven* years; and conducted various studies on nuclear options. All these, as well as surveys and archives, provide enough evidence that Japan did not consider nuclear weapons' acquisition an "unthinkable" taboo at the time of its crucial decisions (Samuels 1996; Solingen 2007). Premier Sato was awarded the Nobel Peace Prize for Japan's 1967 Three Non-Nuclear Principles (NNP, not to possess, manufacture, or introduce nuclear weapons into Japan's sea or air). Yet Sato also conveyed to Ambassador Reischauer explicitly—and to Keidanren leaders—his personal preference for a nuclear Japan. Indeed the NNP never became law and contestation regarding Article 9 of the Constitution (renouncing the right of belligerency but not explicitly "defensive" nuclear weapons) persists. Embracing the US nuclear umbrella did not precisely signal nuclear abstinence either. Japan informed the International Court of Justice in 1994 that it did not necessarily view nuclear weapons' use as illegal. Nor did Japan sign the 2014 "Humanitarian Pledge" calling for a new legal framework prohibiting nuclear weapons or the 2017 Nuclear Weapon Ban Treaty. If neither great power status nor the NPT or norms were crucial drivers, what explains nuclear abstention in this case? And what might reverse this trajectory?

The Yoshida doctrine, at the heart of the dominant Liberal Democratic Party's (LDP) model of political survival, was a decisive component of nuclear restraint. This "economy first" strategy hinging on economic growth deflated Communist subversion and rallied LDP factions, bureaucracies, big business and finance, energy and farming interests, smaller and medium-sized business, and even most opposition parties. The model overwhelmed more inward-looking right and left extremes, including those favoring rearmament or nuclear weapons. It also quadrupled Japan's share of global trade and exports; turned it into the third largest economy in the 1960s; and yielded stability and continued LDP dominance. The model thus provided the glue for a nuclear abstention package that logrolled essential constituencies. Nuclear weapons would have heightened uncertainty, threatened the economic miracle, and unraveled Japan's regional "peace diplomacy" and global access. Peak industrial associations strongly endorsed NPT ratification. Japan's nuclear energy program was doomed without international support; its economic miracle was doomed without nuclear energy; and the LDP was doomed without the economic miracle. A secret study ordered by Sato on the desirability of nuclear weapons (1968–70) concluded that the domestic political and international diplomatic costs would be too high and that Japan's security would be far better advanced through the Yoshida model.

The behavior of Sato—and of his post-war precursors and successors—also challenges a view that psychological profiles of leaders predict nuclear choices (Hymans 2006), an approach that neglects the political context. Premiers Kishi, Yoshida, Sato, Nakasone, Koizumi, Fukuda, Abe, and others may have arguably favored a nuclear armed Japan privately but did not (could not) act on those proclivities (Solingen 2010b). Indeed, the confluence of major external threats (North Korea's repeated nuclear and missile tests) and leaders with arguably strong private penchants for nuclear weapons failed to yield different outcomes than abstention. That still remains the case for Abe Shinzo, who imbibed a hardline approach from his grandfather Kishi.

What does all this suggest for future scenarios regarding not just Japan but also South Korea and Taiwan? After all, neorealism's most authoritative proponent (Waltz 1979) argued that a strong theory must be able to predict accurately a priori and that its usefulness is judged not only by its explanatory but also its predictive powers. Given elastic and subjective definitions of balance of power, self-help, insecurity, and power itself, predictions based on such assumptions remain questionable. The nuclearization of three neighbors and China's dramatic rise have not yet altered Japan's nuclear abstention. We must nonetheless consider a scenario where East Asia exhibits more nuclear weapons' states, but how do we get there? Debs and Monteiro (2016) argue that states will proliferate when (a) they enjoy high relative power; (b) can deter a preventive strike; (c) they have a great power ally that can deter a preventive strike but falls short in reliability; (d) the great power ally has expansive foreign policy interests not covered under the alliance; and (e) the ally allows them to proliferate as long as the risk of entrapment is low. Assessing all these conditions is rather difficult, particularly because concepts such as "relative power," "level of security threat," and "great power reliability" among others remain open to subjective estimates and hence, to elusive predictions. The consequential changes in balance of power—beyond the ones we already observed—that should trigger discontinuities in nuclear policy remain unclear. Furthermore, each one of conditions (a) to (e) may lead to different—often contradictory—scenarios.

Indeed, regarding US extended deterrence alone, widespread disagreement remains on whether security guarantees alone account for nuclear abstention, whether US coercion or persuasion were more important, and other enigmas related to alliances (Solingen 1994b, 2007; Knopf, 2012; Debs and Monteiro 2016). Waltz's (1981) precept that "internal balancing is more reliable and precise than external balancing" cannot be discounted. Nor can his prediction that "nuclear weapons make alliances obsolete." Even alliances that qualify as "best practices" do not preclude dilemmas of abandonment and entrapment, and sometimes outright nuclearization (e.g. Britain and France). The fundamental logic of survival trumps the idea that states can substitute self-help for external protection. Anarchic international structures preclude a division of labor, especially since hegemonic commitments falter recurrently as in East Asia over the decades, particularly under presidents Jimmy Carter, Nixon, and, more recently, President Donald Trump.[9]

Competing neorealist perspectives thus leave us with abundant open-endedness. Scenarios hinging on external threats could do better by considering the domestic political landscapes that heighten or dampen the pressure to respond to such threats with nuclear weapons. Neoclassical realism (Wohlforth 1993), for instance, is more amenable to including such drivers for explaining non-balancing, under-balancing, or nuclear abstention even when some "objective" reality out there—a nuclear North Korea or a more menacing China—would have arguably compelled otherwise.

The typical neoliberal institutionalist scenario often invokes the NPR's collapse as the prelude to nuclear cascades. This external shock of major proportions, however, could lead to different scenarios, only some featuring more nuclear weapons states. Others find the potential for such cascades to be overstated (Potter and Mukhatzhanova 2010). From Japan's and South Korea's standpoints, the NPR has already failed to guarantee their security. Furthermore, China's permanent seat in the UNSC enables it to dilute sanctions on the Kim dynasty, which continues to boost its nuclear capabilities dramatically (Solingen 2013, 2016). Nor does the NPR provide more protection to Taiwan than it would have in its absence. Failures of collective action and rising Prisoner's Dilemma situations should make some East Asian states "most-likely-cases" for going nuclear, per this theory's logic.

Some constructivist and critical theory tools leave us with even more open-ended scenarios, a feature entirely compatible with these approaches' epistemology and reservations regarding prediction (Abraham 2010). One might nonetheless distill a scenario that upholds norms against nuclear acquisition, perhaps in tandem with progress toward Global Zero, hard as it may seem under current circumstances. By contrast, the emergence of a rival norm could lead to a scenario of more nuclear weapons' states driven by issues of memory, nationalism, and history that fuel Hobbesian mistrust, turning East Asia into a "most likely case" for nuclearization. As norms and ideas "don't float freely," evaluating these different scenarios might be more fruitful if they incorporated particular domestic conditions that help consolidate one norm or the other in each case (Risse Kappen 1994; Checkel 1997), which leads us back to domestic models of political survival.

As argued, expectations from these models are not deterministic; they only suggest that internationalizing models make the development of nuclear weapons less likely than inward-looking ones. They are indeed falsifiable: internationalizing models may embrace nuclear weapons and inward-oriented ones may abandon them. Specific scope conditions may alter expected outcomes. First, the extent to which the regional context shares a congruent orientation toward the global political economy (either positive or negative) can modify nuclear preferences within individual states. A region's center of gravity is consequential for nuclear outcomes, making acquisition more likely, even for isolated internationalizers facing an inward-looking strategic cluster. Second, temporality matters; abandoning nuclear weapons once they exist is different—more costly politically—from abandoning a program prior to fruition, as prospect theory suggests it is far more costly politically to eliminate actual weapons than reverse steps before acquisition. Leaders and publics value more—and are averse to losing—what they have ("endowment effect") than what they might get in an uncertain future. Hence, eliminating existing nuclear weapons is expected to be harder than reversing programs before nuclear weapons are acquired. Reversals are much harder when nuclear weapons acquisition precedes the inception of internationalizing models (e.g. China, India, Israel). Third, political survival models are a dynamic category and hence entail no linear or irreversible trajectory in either direction.

Four possible scenarios emerge from this framework: two would validate the argument, the other two would falsify it. The vertical axis in Table 25.1 reflects the respective models, internationalizing and inward-looking. The horizontal axis maps two outcomes: more nuclear weapons states or no new nuclear weapons states (status quo). Scenario 1 points to the continuity of internationalizing models in "usual suspect" East Asian states and continued nuclear abstention—despite inward-looking North Korea—an outcome compatible with the framework's expectations.[10] Scenario 2 entertains a widespread East Asian turn to inward-looking models while retaining NPT-compliant nuclear abstention, an anomaly for the framework. Scenario 3 entails continued dominance of internationalizing models that proceed to acquire nuclear weapons, another anomaly. Scenario 4 features a massive regional shift toward inward-looking models that abandon nuclear abstention, confirming the framework's expectations. A Chinese leadership that overturns internationalization, for instance, might heighten the odds that neighbors follow suit and reverse prior nuclear restraint. Global and regional downward economic spirals can be a major source of domestic turns and shifts toward hyper-nationalism. Although this trend seems evident in different parts of the world, it has yet to reach the shores of East Asia.

Table 25.1 Models of survival and nuclear outcomes: East Asia

		Models of political survival	
		Internationalizing	Inward-looking
Nuclear outcomes	No new nuclear weapons states	1 Compatible	2 Anomaly
	New nuclear weapons states	3 Anomaly	4 Compatible

Similar scenarios can be constructed for the Middle East. The region's past inward-looking trajectory already conforms to the attempted acquisition of nuclear weapons in Iraq (prior to 2003), Egypt (prior to 1974), Iran, Libya, and Syria. Israel is reported to possess a sophisticated nuclear arsenal and others surface in studies of potential candidates for future proliferation, including Saudi Arabia and Turkey (Cambpell et al. 2004). Waltz (2012) envisaged a nuclear-armed Iran and Syria but later predicted that "once Iran crosses the nuclear threshold . . . . No other country in the region will have an incentive to acquire its own nuclear capability," an odd prediction given a multipolar context that should, per Waltz's theory, lead to further nuclearization. The jury is out on the JCPOA but few observers pin its fate on anything other than domestic competition between Iran's internationalizing and inward-looking camps. Statements by President Trump during the election campaign and barriers to Iran's reintegration in the global economy strengthen the latter camp. The Middle East continues to defy the existence of a nuclear taboo curtailing acquisition.

25.4. Conclusions

As the editors suggest, thinking about our theories' implications for the future enhances clarity about our claims. This chapter has reviewed proliferation patterns in recent decades; assessed the record and shortcomings of past predictions; explored conceptual debates underlying predictions; and highlighted the risks of prediction, particularly in this domain. The good news for the discipline is that a promising research agenda attentive to complex systemic effects, reputation, domestic veto-points, dynamics of the global economy, and regime survival seems to be replacing analytically impoverished, policy-deficient, grossly inaccurate forecasts, and stale accounts of states' nuclear choices. All theoretical formulations can benefit from improvements. First, they must be cast in falsifiable terms, with greater precision, and aim at better specification of threshold conditions.[11] Second, they must provide clearly defined, a priori testable propositions, avoiding circularity and ex-post-facto rationalizations. Third, they must stipulate the kind of evidence that would challenge or corroborate their expectations. Fourth, they must tighten up rules and procedures for (quantitative or qualitative) data gathering and analysis. Fifth, they must assess findings against competing theoretical claims. Seventh, they must develop ways to discover, dissect, and assess indirect causal pathways, even if they are more difficult to work with. Eight, they must be attentive to temporality and context; choices for or against nuclear weapons are fluid and change over time (Levite 2002). Above all, attention to complexity, contingency, and historical context can enhance predictive accuracy. Tetlock (2005) branded parsimony "snake oil," the enemy of accuracy. Good forecasting must tolerate ambiguity and dissonance, embrace self-criticism, and integrate relevant drivers previously omitted, at great analytical cost, or substituted by invalid proxies.

A unified field theory capable of predicting proliferation may not be in our grasp. Furthermore, much to our dismay, our theories may not work for eternity. Even those that may have done well explaining the past may be less useful for predicting the future. Even if they were to work forever, our ability to manipulate and control drivers is limited. It is emblematic of the challenges inherent in the study of international diffusion that no consensus exists on whether the present outcome—nine nuclear weapons' states—is a success story of non-diffusion (no runaway dominos) or a slow-moving increase in nuclear weapon states that could dangerously approach rapid diffusion along an S-shaped curve (Solingen 2012). Nor is there consensus on whether a presumed success might be a triumph of restraint—many states permanently opting not to convert technical capabilities into weapons—or of hedging. Substantive disagreement remains over whether the NPT is an impressive, most highly subscribed international security treaty gathering 190 states, or a frail firewall unable to prevent determined violations. Further contention exists on whether the IAEA is an effective mechanism for diffusing nuclear energy or one unintendedly spreading nuclear weapons' know-how, and whether learning and socialization within the broader nonproliferation regime buttresses its survival or fails to stem its deterioration. Deep discrepancy also remains among those for whom the diffusion of nuclear weapons is a great equalizer—"more is better" in Waltz's unforgettable rendition—and those for whom such diffusion is a recipe for wholesale destruction of the world as we know it.

Our overview raises many additional questions that the discipline will continue to address, particularly regarding change. Will changes in the NPR be evolutionary or revolutionary? Will they occur through implosion or explosion? Will they be re-ordering or counter-ordering? Will rising powers such as China alter the NPR as we know it today? Will what comes next be more coherent or less coherent? Will this evolution be linear or ridden with discontinuities? Will learning about the horrors of nuclear war become, once and for all, sedimented into an enduring normative firewall? Or will nuclear weapons "long be with us," in another Waltz's (1995) formulation. Will the domestic, regional or the global levels be more promising arenas of change? These and other uncertainties militate against our ability to discern all likely paths to continuity and change in the world of nuclear proliferation.

Notes

1. The regime also includes the Nuclear Suppliers Group, the Zangger Committee, the Comprehensive Test Ban Treaty, the Additional Protocol, and nuclear-weapon-free zones, among others. The IAEA Board of Governors and the UN Security Council act as enforcement mechanisms on safeguard agreements. For a comprehensive analysis of this regime, see Wan (2013) and Wan and Solingen (2017).
2. Betts (2000: 69) argued that one should be able to name at least one specific country that would have sought nuclear weapons or tested them, but refrained from doing so because of the NPT. He found none that come to mind. Egypt's former Minister of Foreign Affairs Nabil Fahmy argued that very few non-nuclear weapons states joined the treaty because it responded to their immediate security concerns and that most did so for political or economic reasons and had otherwise no reason to pursue nuclear weapons (Carnegie Endowment Conference 2006).
3. Schelling (1976: 80) himself made clear that "the most severe inhibitions are undoubtedly those on the actual use of nuclear weapons, not on the possession of them."
4. According to Mueller and Schmidt (2010) 36 states are known to have once started nuclear weapons activities.
5. On "myth-making" and nuclear weapons, see Lavoy (1993).
6. The more inward-looking the target, the less effective are coercion and positive inducements (Solingen 2012). See also Miller (2014).
7. Pierre Gallois, Herman Khan, and Nixon himself were among them. A 1957 National Intelligence Estimate advanced that Japan was highly likely to go nuclear within a decade <http://nsarchive.gwu.edu/NSAEBB/NSAEBB155/>. Kissinger argued that "We must have no illusion: Failure to resolve the North Korean nuclear threat in a clear-cut way will sooner or later lead to the nuclear armament of Japan—regardless of assurances each side offers the other" (Kissinger 2003).
8. All references to Makoto in Endicott (1975: 63).
9. http://www.nytimes.com/2016/11/16/opinion/the-trump-effect-on-tokyo.html?ref=world.
10. Following North Korea's launching of nuclear-capable missiles unto Japan's exclusive economic zone in 2016, defense minister Inada Tomomi discounted Japan's consideration of nuclear weapons "at the moment" while declaring that Japan's constitution has "no restrictions on the types of weapons that Japan can possess as the minimum necessary." Premier Abe immediately added that "there is no way that Japan will either possess nuclear weapons or consider possessing such arms" <https://nuclear-news.net/2016/08/07/abe-rules-out-possibility-that-japan-will-possess-nuclear-weapons/>. Nearly 60 percent of polled South Koreans arguably supported an indigenous nuclear deterrent in 2016 but the government restated its non-nuclear course <http://www.koreatimes.co.kr/www/news/nation/2016/09/205_214598.html.
11. On how non-falsifiable predictions undermine the quality of professional discourse and our ability to improve policy, see Tetlock and Scoblic (2015).

References

Abraham, Itty. 2010.Who's Next?' Nuclear Ambivalence and the Contradictions of Non-proliferation Policy. *Economic & Political Weekly*, October 23, xlv(43): 48–56.

Axelrod, R. and R. O. Keohane. 1985. Achieving Cooperation under Anarchy: Strategies and Institutions. *World Politics*, 38(1): 226–54.

Barnett, Michael, and Martha Finnemore. 1999. The Politics, Power, and Pathologies of International Organizations. *International Organization*, 53 (4): 699–732.

Bell, M. S. 2015. Examining Explanations for Nuclear Proliferation. *International Studies Quarterly*. *Available at:* http://papers.ssrn.com/abstract=2630614

Betts, Richard K. 2000. Universal Deterrence or Conceptual Collapse? Liberal Pessimism and Utopian Realism. In Victor A. Utgoff (ed.), *The Coming Crisis: Nuclear Proliferation, U.S. Interests, and World Order*, pp. 51–86. Cambridge, MA: MIT Press.

Campbell, Kurt M., Robert J. Einhorn, and Mitchell B. Reiss (eds.). 2004. *The Nuclear Tipping Point: Why States Reconsider Their Nuclear Choices*. Washington, DC: Brookings Institution Press.

Carnegie Endowment. 2006. Nonproliferation Conference. *Available at:* http://carnegieendowment.org/

Checkel, Jeffrey T. 1997. *Ideas and International Political Change: Soviet/Russian Behavior and the End of the Cold War*. New Haven, CT: Yale University Press.

Debs, Alexander and Nuno Monteiro. 2016. *The Strategic Causes of Proliferation*. Cambridge: Cambridge University Press.

Endicott, John E. 1975. *Japan's Nuclear Option: Political, Technical, and Strategic Factors*. New York: Praeger.

Finnemore, Martha and Kathryn Sikkink. 1998. International Norm Dynamics and Political Change. *International Organization*, 52(4): 887–917.

Fuhrmann, M. (2009). Spreading Temptation: Proliferation and Peaceful Nuclear Cooperation Agreements. *International Security*, 34(1): 7–41.

Hymans, J. E. 2006. *The Psychology of Nuclear Proliferation: Identity, Emotions, and Foreign Policy*. Cambridge: Cambridge University Press.

Jervis, R. 1989. *The Meaning of the Nuclear Revolution*. Ithaca, NY: Cornell University Press.

Jervis, R. 1999. Realism, Neoliberalism, and Cooperation: Understanding the Debate. *International Security*, 24(1): 42–63.

Jo, D.-J. and E. Gartzke. (2007). Determinants of Nuclear Weapons Proliferation. *The Journal of Conflict Resolution*, 51(1): 167–94.

Johnston, Alastair I. 2001. Treating International Institutions as Social Environments. *International Studies Quarterly*, 45(4): 487–515.

Kemp, R. S. (2014). The Nonproliferation Emperor Has No Clothes. *International Security*, 38(4): 39–78.

Kissinger, Henry. 2003. Why We Can't Withdraw from Asia. *Washington Post*, June 15.

Klotz, Audie and Cecelia Lynch. 2007. *Strategies for Research in Constructivist International Relations*. Abingdon: Routledge.

Knopf, J. (ed.). 2012. *Security Assurances and Nuclear Nonproliferation*. Stanford, CA: Stanford University Press.

Kroenig, M. 2009. Importing the Bomb: Sensitive Nuclear Assistance and Nuclear Proliferation. *Journal of Conflict Resolution*, 53(2): 161–80.

Lavoy, P. R. (1993). Nuclear Myths and the Causes of Nuclear Proliferation. *Security Studies*, 2(3-4): 192–212.

Levite, A. (2002). Never Say Never Again: Nuclear Reversal Revisited. *International Security*, 27(3): 59–88.

Lewis, Jeffrey. 2016. "Sorry, Fareed: Saudi Arabia Can Build a Bomb Any Damn Time It Wants To." *Foreign Policy*, June 12.

McDermott, Rose. 1998. *Risk-taking in International Politics: Prospect Theory in American Foreign Policy*. Ann Arbor: University of Michigan Press.

Meyer, S. M. 1986. *The Dynamics of Nuclear Proliferation*. Chicago: University of Chicago Press.

Miller, Nicholas L. 2014. The Secret Success of Nonproliferation Sanctions. *International Organization*, 68 (4): 913–44.

Mueller, H. and Schmidt, A. 2010. The Little-Known Story of Deproliferation: Why States Give Up Nuclear Weapons Activities. In W. C. Potter and G. Mukhatzhanova (eds.), *Forecasting Nuclear Proliferation in the 21st Century: The Role of Theory* (Vol. 1, pp. 124–158). Stanford, CA: Stanford University Press.

Nye, J. S., Jr. 1988. U.S.–Soviet Cooperation in a Nonproliferation Regime. In A. L. George, P. J. Farley, and A. Dallin (eds.), *U.S. Soviet Security Cooperation*, pp. 336–52. New York: Oxford University Press.

Ogilvie-White, T. (1996). Is There a Theory of Nuclear Proliferation? An Analysis of the Contemporary Debate. *The Nonproliferation Review*, 4(1): 43–60.

Potter, W. C. and G. Mukhatzhanova (eds.). 2010. *Forecasting Nuclear Proliferation in the 21st Century: The Role of Theory* (Vol. 1) and *Forecasting Nuclear Proliferation in the 21st Century: A Comparative Perspective* (Vol. 2). Stanford Security Studies. Stanford, CA: Stanford University Press.

Risse-Kappen, Thomas. 1994. Ideas Don't Float Freely. *International Organization*, 48(2): 185–214.

Rublee, M. R. 2009. *Nonproliferation Norms: Why States Choose Nuclear Restraint*. Athens, GA: University of Georgia Press.

Sagan, S. D. 1996. Why Do States Build Nuclear Weapons? Three Models in Search of a Bomb. *International Security*, 21(3): 54–86.

Samuels, R. J. 1996. *Rich Nation, Strong Army: National Security and the Technological Transformation of Japan*. Ithaca, NY: Cornell University Press.

Schelling, T. C. 1976. Who Will Have the Bomb? *International Security*, 1(1): 77–91.

Schelling, T. 2000. A Half-Century without Nuclear War. *The Key Reporter*, 65(3): 3–5.

Singh, S. and C. R. Way. 2004. The Correlates of Nuclear Proliferation: A Quantitative Test. *Journal of Conflict Resolution*, 48(6): 859–85.

Solingen, Etel. 1994a. The Domestic Sources of Regional Regimes: The Evolution of Nuclear Ambiguity in the Middle East. *International Studies Quarterly*, 38(2): 305–37.

Solingen, Etel. 1994b. The Political Economy of Nuclear Restraint. *International Security*, 19(2): 126–69.

Solingen, Etel. 2007. *Nuclear Logics: Contrasting Paths in East Asia and the Middle East*. Princeton, NJ: Princeton University Press.

Solingen, Etel. 2010a. Domestic Models of Political Survival: Why Some Do and Others Don't (Proliferate). In W. C. Potter and G. Mukhatzhanova (eds.), *Forecasting Nuclear Proliferation in the 21st Century: The Role of Theory*, Vol. 1, pp. 38–57. Stanford, CA: Stanford University Press.

Solingen, Etel. 2010b. The Perils of Prediction: Japan's Once and Future Nuclear Status. In William C. Potter and Gaukhar Mukhatzhanova (eds.), *Forecasting Nuclear Proliferation in the 21st Century: A Comparative Perspective*. Stanford, CA: Stanford University Press.

Solingen, Etel. 2012. Of Dominoes and Firewalls: The Domestic, Regional, and Global Politics of International Diffusion. *International Studies Quarterly*, 56(4): 631–44.

Solingen, Etel. 2013. Three Scenes of Sovereignty and Power. In Martha Finnemore and Judith Goldstein (eds.), *Back to Basics: Rethinking Power in the Contemporary World*. Oxford: Oxford University Press.

Solingen, Etel. 2016. Rashomon in North Korea: Comparing Northeast Asian approaches. *Asian Journal of Comparative Politics*, 1(2): 108–21.

Solingen, Etel. and Joshua Malnight. 2016. More Noise than Signal in Proliferation Studies? *International Studies Quarterly*, Blog posted February 10.

Solingen, Etel. and Wilfred Wan. (2017) International Security: Critical Junctures, Developmental Pathways, and Institutional Change. In Orfeo Fioretos (ed.), *International Politics and Institutions in Time*. Oxford and New York: Oxford University Press.

Tannenwald, N. 2007. *The Nuclear Taboo: The United States and the Non-Use of Nuclear Weapons since 1945*. New York: Cambridge University Press.

Tetlock, P. 2005. *Expert Political Judgment: How Good is It? How Can We Know?* Princeton, NJ: Princeton University Press.

Tetlock, P. and J. Peter Scoblic. 2015. The Power of Precise Predictions. *New York Times*, October 2.

Waltz, Kenneth N. 1979. *Theory of International Politics*. Boston, MA: Addison-Wesley.

Waltz, Kenneth N. 1981. The Spread of Nuclear Weapons: More May Better. *Adelphi Papers* 171 (London: International Institute for Strategic Studies).

Waltz, Kenneth N. 1993. The Emerging Structure of International Politics. *International Security*, 18 (2): 44–79.

Waltz, Kenneth. 1995. Peace, Stability, and Nuclear Weapons. Institute on Global Conflict and Cooperation. Policy Papers #15. University of California, Multi-Campus Research Unit. *Available at*: http://repositories.cdlib.org/igcc/PP/PP15

Waltz, Kenneth N. 2000. Structural Realism After the Cold War. *International Security*. 25(1): 5–41.

Waltz, Kenneth N. 2012. Why Iran Should Get the Bomb. *Foreign Affairs*, 91: 4.

Wan, W. 2013. *Institutional Change and the Nuclear Non-Proliferation Regime*. Irvine, CA: University of California.

Wan, W. and E. Solingen. 2015. Why do States Pursue Nuclear Weapons (or Not). In *Emerging Trends in the Social and Behavioral Sciences*. John Wiley & Sons, Inc.

Wan, W. and Etel Solingen. 2017. International Security: Nuclear (Non-) Proliferation. In William R. Thompson (ed.), *Oxford Research Encyclopedia of Politics*. (*Oxford Research Encyclopedia* (ORE) program). Oxford: Oxford University Press.

Way, C. and J. L. P. Weeks. 2014. Making It Personal: Regime Type and Nuclear Proliferation. *American Journal of Political Science*, 58(3): 705–19.

Wohlforth, William C. 1993. *The Elusive Balance: Power and Perceptions During the Cold War*. Ithaca, NY: Cornell University Press.

CHAPTER 26

THE GLOBAL SOUTH AND INTERNATIONAL SECURITY

RITA ABRAHAMSEN AND ADAM SANDOR

The countries of the global South have historically been relatively absent from both academic and policy debates about international security, figuring mostly at the margins as either Cold War pawns or the sites of bloody, but regionally contained conflicts. Already in 1988 Joseph Nye and Sean Lynn-Jones noted in a survey of International Security Studies that the field paid inadequate attention to "regional security issues" and attributed this to "ethnocentric biases," resulting from its development primarily in the United States (Nye and Lynn-Jones 1988: 27). International security studies today, in common with International Relations (IR) more broadly, remain preoccupied with great power politics and devoted to understanding the states "that make the most difference" (Waltz 1979: 73; Tickner and Wæver 2009), but the South is occupying an increasingly central, yet ambivalent and contradictory, position within contemporary security debates and policies. One the one hand, in the post-9/11 security landscape so-called weak states have emerged as the front line in the war against terrorism and violent extremism, their conflicts no longer perceived as regional or peripheral, but potentially destabilizing for the world at large. On the other hand, countries in the South are becoming increasingly powerful as their economies expand and their populations outnumber those of the North. There are also signs that countries in the South are seeking to speak with a more unified voice in international forums and through regional organizations, acquiring a new, more confident and assertive role in global affairs. Southern countries are now, for example, the main troop contributors to international peacekeeping missions, and the reluctance of rich Northern states to commit soldiers to the world's trouble spots has significantly increased the political agency and bargaining power of the South. The global South thus appears in contemporary international security in two main guises; that of the weak state and the intervener state.

This chapter seeks to capture this contradictory position of being part problem, part solution. In keeping with the focus of the Handbook, it does so by highlighting the themes of continuity and change, as well as the interplay of ideas and material factors in determining the South's position within security discourses and policies. As no short chapter can do justice to this vast topic, we begin by contextualizing the notion of a global South within historical efforts to make the former colonized countries speak with a more unified, powerful voice in international affairs. We argue that as much as the notion of a uniform "South" is a fiction, the belief in the virtues of a united South continues to inform efforts toward policy integration and coherence, despite frequently competing ideological and material interests. We then trace the emergence of the weak state as a security threat to post-Cold War ideas about human security and the subsequent merger of development and security, which lay the foundations for thinking about security in less state-centric and militaristic ways. We show how, following the attacks of 9/11, the weak state has emerged as a key international security problem, and argue that there are clear signs that the emphasis on human security and development is increasingly losing out to more hard-core material, geopolitical security interests. Finally, we show how, despite lofty ideas such as the "Responsibility to Protect," the reluctance of rich states to risk their soldiers' lives in faraway conflicts has made the South key actors in international security, both as individual intervener states and as regional organizations such as the African Union.

We conclude that taken together these developments mean not only that the global South is likely to continue to occupy a central place within international security, but also that the contradictions are likely to multiply. The current trends of armed conflict and violent extremism look set to continue, and many of the theaters of intervention will undoubtedly remain in spaces of the South. Regional southern interventions will therefore be required, but will remain dependent on northern actors for funding and equipment. As more actors from the global South come to act as interveners, the creation of competing interests and practices is inevitable. Southern actors will not only increasingly come to compete over how to solve security concerns that cross borders, but also over access to economic and material resources from Northern actors. The potential for southern cooperation and cohesion might thus become ever more elusive, an unintended political casualty of the present security landscape.

26.1 The Elusive "South"

To speak of the "the Third World" or "the global South" conjures up a set of questions and contradictions over the existence of such a political body. Instead of a fixed geographical point, the global South in the academic literature more commonly refers to a "symbolic designation" associated with places in the world that shared the political project of advancing decolonization in the mid-twentieth century (Grovogui 2011: 176). In the immediate post-Second World War period, there was certainly a sense that peoples from regions that had recently achieved decolonization (such as India, Burma, Iraq, Egypt, and others), or from those areas struggling to end colonization (Vietnam, Ghana, Algeria, South Africa, Cameroun, etc.), displayed a common set of insecurities connected to imperial domination. With varying degrees of success, many of these groups attempted to speak with a common voice to espouse similar political principles in favor of the norms of complete decolonization, non-intervention, non-interference, and non-alignment to bipolar imperialism in international forums (Lee 2009). The famed "Asian-African Conference" in Bandung in April 1955, and the subsequent efforts to consolidate a body of states into a formal institution—the Non-Aligned Movement (NAM)—against Cold War superpower manipulation, indicate that representatives from recently decolonized governments did indeed seek to exercise a larger degree of agency in the face of striking asymmetries of material and coercive power in the international system, perhaps even developing a collective identity in favor of emancipation, equal participation, and recognition on the international stage (Acharya 2014).

At the same time, the vision and consolidation of a collective identity of peoples of the global South were consistently challenged at multiple political scales across and within decolonized spaces. The NAM itself was riddled with competition and tense rivalries between its members (Vitalis 2013). Bandung and Belgrade Conference participants had significant disputes over the substance of their governments' foreign policies toward their former colonial powers and the new bipolar world order. Many participating members supported policies sponsored by either the United States or the Soviet Union based on the pursuit of their own sovereign and personal agendas. Bandung, Belgrade, and subsequent meetings, while helping to craft a general set of norms expressing resistance to superpower interference and manipulation, therefore, were comprised of a coalition of some like-minded heads of state that could not agree what their collective vision and political responses should be vis-à-vis NATO or Warsaw Pact countries.

The core principles of NAM, including the principle of non-interference and support of non-intervention, were themselves contested and often required adaptation to historical contingencies and developing insecurities, or were simply ignored (see Vieira 2016). For instance, even though they were strident members of the NAM, the People's Republic of China actively pursued policies supporting Communist armed movements across Southeast Asia; Keita's Mali received significant military equipment and support from the USSR with which it violently subjugated its nomadic populations; and Nasser's Egypt actively influenced the politics of Middle Eastern countries to support the establishment of Baathist political regimes. As a Bandung attendee, Nasser himself had received his briefing on the conference from the CIA (Vitalis 2013: 267). Thus, even during a period of postcolonial hope and shared commitment to de-colonial norms among governments and anti-colonial nationalist movements, political actors across "the global South" still defended and represented distinct agendas, interests, and practices that challenge, if not belie, notions of a common agency or identity based on a de-colonial ethos.

In today's security environment, just as in the past, speaking of a unified and coherent global South, whether politically or analytically, is equally problematic. The much-touted "rise of emerging powers" or the BRICS (Brazil, Russia, India, China, and South Africa) is but one example of difference and divergence (see Hurrell 2008; Flemes 2016), as are recent trends toward political fragmentation, decentralization, and transformation of state institutions (both in "the West" and "the global South") in favor of governing through transnational policy networks spanning public and private, national and international domains (see Sassen 2006; Abrahamsen and Williams 2011; Hameiri and Jones 2016). Many states that nominally fit under the label of the global South are currently growing in terms of economic, military, political, diplomatic, and symbolic might, and they are also contesting many of the principles that have come to define the liberal international world order (Stephen 2014). The growth of these economies and polities amplifies inter-global South competition for regional dominance within a potentially post-liberal international order. The purported "rise of the South" would thus more accurately be termed "the rise of the *souths*," and the transformation of global "*orders*," underlining the continuation of differences, divergences, and forms of competition.

Yet amidst the geopolitical, regional, personal, economic, and identity-based rivalries that inform the competitive heterogeneity of the global South, we nevertheless frequently see common "southern" positions against forms of economic, structural, military, and political domination by Western powers. In global forums ranging from the UN General Assembly to UNESCO and the WTO, southern political leaders often speak with a single voice on numerous political and security issues, such as international public resources and environmental preservation, the spread of nuclear weapons, and the Israeli Occupation of Palestine (Grovogui 2011: 187–8). Similarly, South African, Brazilian, and a host of other African and Asian governments (though not all) opposed the NATO intervention of Libya in 2011, not because they rejected the principle of protection against crimes against humanity or the Responsibility to Protect, but because of hard fought, shared beliefs in non-intervention and a preference for diplomatic over military solutions (see Jaganathan and Kurtz 2014; Stuenkel and Tourinho 2014; Beresford 2015). These examples, as well as the growing role of regional organizations like the African Union, point to the continuation of southern resistance and contestation of dominant forms of power and violence in the global system, and the fact that the aspirations of greater influence and voice through cooperation remain and can at times be effectively mobilized.

The purpose of this brief historical account is to highlight the difficulties and dangers of approaching the global South as an actually existing entity. On the one hand, the concept of a global South is nothing but an academic fiction; a heuristic device that conceals as much as it reveals about actors and actions in international affairs. It is also a term infused with romanticized myths of an alternative world order, and of a past ripe with the promise of future resistance and solidarity. On the other hand, the global South remains alive as a political ambition, and at crucial times the belief in the virtues of a united South continues to inform efforts toward policy integration and coherence, despite frequently competing ideological and material interests. Arguably, the divisions within the global South have increased in recent years, with some states gaining in economic and political power, while others have remained poor, or succumbed to violence and civil war. In the practice (and the study) of contemporary international security, this fractured global South is most evident in the two figures of the "weak state" and the "intervener state." Both, however, have traditionally been relatively absent from the study of international security. Before turning to the contemporary situation, it is therefore important to consider the ideas and intellectual shifts that facilitated the incorporation of the global South into international security studies.

26.2 The Rise of the Global South in International Security Studies

"The events of September 11, 2001 taught us that weak states, like Afghanistan, can pose as great a danger to our national interests as strong states" (White House 2002). This oft-quoted phrase from the United States' 2002 National Security Strategy epitomizes the central position of the global South in contemporary international security. To be sure, more traditional concerns such as the strategic balance, nuclear proliferation, and access to resources continue to figure prominently on the international security agenda, but they now vie for attention with the perceived dangers represented by weak states, frequently framed as "black holes" or "ungoverned spaces" whence terrorists and violent extremists are suspected of planning their attacks on a Western civilization whose values and lifestyles they allegedly despise.

The novelty of this situation should not be overlooked. Only a few decades ago, international security studies largely ignored the global South, or the Third World as it was generally referred to in the 1980s and 1990s. As Amitav Acharya (1995) observed, the exclusion of the Third World from the Cold War security studies agenda was evident in both policy and academic arenas; in the former "superpower diplomacy" carefully distinguished the "'central strategic balance' (involving superpower nuclear deterrence and their European allies) from regional conflict and regional security (conflict and conflict-management issues arising primarily in the Third World," while the latter was preoccupied by the East–West divide (Acharya 1995: 3). Despite the fact that most conflicts took place in the Third World, they were generally regarded as irrelevant to international security as they were primarily civil wars within rather than between states, or they were considered proxies for great power conflict, and hence did not fit the state-centric and war-centric focus of the discipline (see Barkawi and Laffey 2006). Put differently, ideas about what and who counted as international security mattered, and by the same token, the contemporary centrality of the global South in both academic and policy debates has to be understood with reference to ideas, knowledge, and politics.

The Western-centric and state-centric agenda of traditional security studies came under increasing criticism at the end of the Cold War. Within the academy, critics argued for a broadening and widening of the concept of security, encouraging a shift away from state-centrism and military issues toward a focus on individuals and non-military threats arising from social, economic, and environmental pressures (see e.g.

Buzan 1991; Krause and Williams 1997). The traditional security approach was found to be particularly unsuited to capturing the security concerns of the Third World where most wars were internal and where the state was often a source of insecurity for the citizens it was assumed to protect (see Ayoob 1995). National security, or the security of the state and its territorial integrity, critics therefore maintained, was not to be conflated with the security of the people, and a significant rethinking of the referent object of security, away from the state and toward the individual, thus took place within international security studies. This shift facilitated the incorporation of southern countries and peoples into international security studies, and has gone a long way toward improving our understanding of security in diverse areas of the globe.

In the policy arena, parallel developments gave rise to the concept of "human security." A milestone event was the publication of the United Nations Development Programme's first Human Development Report in 1994, which expanded the notion of security to take account of "freedom from want" (UNDP 1994). Human security, according to the report, is about people and not about territories; it is about development and not about arms. Framing security with reference to freedom from social and economic threats such as poverty, ill-health, and environmental degradation, the report conceptualized international security from the individual level up: "The world," it declared, "can never be at peace unless people have security in their daily lives" (UNDP 1994: 1). Not only might many future conflicts occur "within nations rather than between them—with their origins buried deep in growing socio-economic deprivations and disparities," but threats to human security are increasingly becoming global (UNDP 1994: 1–2). Poverty, AIDS, environmetal degradation, and terrorism respect no national borders, the report noted, and the search for security thus lies "in development, not in arms" (UNDP 1994: 1–2).

The report stands as a key maker of the merger of development and security and the association of underdevelopment with conflict. Over time, the idea that there can be "no security without development, and no development without security" has become so firmly entrenched in the international discourses of governments, development organizations, and NGOs as to require no further explanation. It is quite simply the new common sense, and as Mark Duffield perceptively argues, development has in this way re-invented itself as "a structural form of conflict prevention" and as a valuable and indispensable tool in the armory of liberal peace (Duffield 2001: 121). By the same token, security has also been repackaged and re-invented, and in the post-Cold War era militaries and security establishments eagerly began embracing the broadening of the security agenda to include non-military aspects as a means of maintaining their own relevance in a rapidly changing geopolitical environment that emphasized humanitarian intervention and peacekeeping rather than defence and warfare (Wæver 1995). Put differently, in terms of practical policy, both development and security organizations and professionals had much to gain from the merger of development and security. The result has been an increasing fusion of development and security policies and knowledges, so much so that the two are at times almost indistinguishable.

26.3 The Weak State: The Global South as an International Security Problem

The attacks of September 11, 2001 firmly cemented the merger of security and development in theory and in practice, and also pushed the international engagement with actors from the global South further away from development, humanitarianism, and human security toward increasingly militarized security policies and counter-terrorism strategies (Abrahamsen 2005; Albrecht and Stepputat 2015; Tschirgi this volume). Almost overnight the attacks of 9/11 came to be interpreted as demonstrating beyond dispute that conflict in distant parts of the world could spill over and destroy the lives of thousands on the other side of the globe, elevating so-called weak, fragile, or failed states to the top of the list of international security problems.

Barely a month after the attacks, the United States, supported by the UK, launched its military intervention in Afghanistan. Dubbed Operation Enduring Freedom, the declared purpose was to defeat al-Qaeda, eliminate its leader Osama Bin Laden and depose the Taliban government from power. When responsibility for the war passed to NATO in 2003, troops from over 40 countries were involved in this "weak" state perceived as the cradle of global terrorism. The same year saw the second major offensive against a "failed" state associated with terrorism; the invasion of Iraq by the United States, supported by the UK, Australia, and Poland among others. This time the stated aim of the invasion was to destroy Iraq's alleged weapons of mass destruction and to end Saddam Hussein's support for terrorism, but lacking an official UN Security Council Mandate the invasion and subsequent military occupation were—and remain—hugely controversial and legally contested. Both the war in Afghanistan and the military occupation of Iraq turned into long-term engagements, with foreign troops officially withdrawing from Afghanistan in 2014 and the Iraqi occupation ending in December 2011 (see Baily and Immerman 2015). But conflicts and political turmoil are by no means over in the two countries, and neither has the extensive involvement of foreign militaries, private security companies, and development agencies come to an end. The fighting has spread and the number of insurgent groups multiplied, with the rise of ISIS and the war in Syria perhaps the most serious fall-out from the Iraqi occupation. In this sense, Afghanistan and Iraq epitomize the strategic and political complexities of interventions informed by the logic of the security/development nexus, giving rise to seemingly never-ending wars that bleed into permanent reconstruction, development, and state-building.

While Afghanistan and Iraq are by far the most extensive post-9/11 security operations, military and security engagements of various kinds have proliferated since weak and fragile states were elevated to the top of the international security agenda. Some are large-scale, spectacular, and widely reported in the news, such as the multi-state NATO-led military intervention in Libya in 2011, allegedly to stop what the UN Security Council termed crimes against humanity by forces loyal to Colonel Muammar

Qaddafi, or the subsequent French Operation Serval in Mali in 2012, triggered in part by the influx of weapons and militants from Libya into northern Mali. Most international security activities in southern states, however, never earn a mention on the 24-hour news cycle, both by design and by default. Few details are disclosed about the numerous foreign Special Forces troops that now regularly operate in weak states like Somalia, Yemen, Sudan, Niger, and Pakistan, training local soldiers and actively fighting insurgents, rebels, and militias. The use of drones in so-called targeted killings of terrorists has also been a largely covert form of warfare, only rarely making the headlines, despite the Investigative Bureau of Journalists estimating that US drones killed between 384 and 807 civilians in Pakistan, Somalia, and Yemen during the Obama presidency (The Bureau 2017). Information about the continually expanding activities of the US Africa Command (AFRICOM), authorized by President Bush in 2005, has been equally hard to obtain (see Turse 2015). By now, the AFRICOM website lists 15 different regular military exercises and Theater Security Cooperation programmes, giving the United States an historically unprecedented military footprint on the continent. While no other country can match the United States' security spending, many, including the UK and France, are deeply committed to various forms of military training and security assistance in southern states. Because much of this security work—be it in terms of finances, equipment, or personnel—is routine and everyday, and sometimes dressed up as development and humanitarian assistance, it lacks the eye-catching cachet of a full-scale military invasion or war and by default passes largely unnoticed. Its significance, however, should not be overlooked, as it marks key shifts in strategic thinking and has important political implications.

Strategically, international security operations in weak states are increasingly informed by the view that bringing an end to war and violent extremism requires not only bombs and bullets, but also food and jobs. While winning "hearts and minds" has always been a part of warfare and strategic thinking, contemporary interventions entail novel institutional collaborations and practices. In policy discourse, this is frequently termed the three Ds-approach, where the three "Ds" of development, diplomacy, and defense are considered mutually reinforcing tools of foreign policy that are in turn integrated into an overall security strategy. Security policy, in other words, is simultaneously development policy, and vice versa. This was clearly articulated in President Obama's Presidential Directive on Global Development, which sought to forge a new bipartisan consensus on development policy "within the broader context of our National Security Strategy" (White House 2010). As the President put it, "My national security strategy recognizes development not only as a moral imperative, but as a strategic and economic imperative" (White House 2010). Other countries have followed strikingly similar routes of synchronizing defense and development; for example, the Department for International Development (DFID) is a permanent member of the new British National Security Council established in May 2010, mirroring the new patterns of institutional collaboration and coordination between USAID and the National Security Council (NSC). In the field, too, militaries and development organizations work side-by-side, with soldiers helping to build schools in Afghanistan and NGOs delivering security sector reform through human rights training for local police and military officers.

Politically (and ethically) there is of course much to be said in defense of such an integrated approach, and there is no doubt that combining hard security interventions with humanitarian relief and development projects can reduce human suffering, help win "hearts and minds," and thus lessen the chances of "blow-back" and further radicalization. But there are clear political dangers: The insistence that contemporary development assistance must not only reduce poverty, but also simultaneously serve the national security interest of donors is based on the straightforward assumption that "development and security goals can be pursued in a mutually reinforcing way" (DFID 2005: 13). Thus formulated, any possible contradiction between benevolence and self-interest is made to vanish in a seamless fusion of moral obligation and national interest. The possibility remains, however, that the security of donors might conflict with the welfare of the recipient—and that the former might triumph.

While development assistance has always been influenced by geopolitics and self-interest, the contemporary insistence that security and development are one and the same facilitates and justifies the redirection of funds from welfare and poverty reduction to security and militaries. The elevation of the weak states from development problem to security problem has meant that increasing proportions of the international aid budget are allocated to states that are also considered pivotal to international security and stability. For example, the British government in 2015, in a new aid strategy tellingly named *Tackling Global Challenges in the National Interest*, pledged to allocate a full 50 percent of DFID's budget to fragile states and regions (HM Treasury 2015: 14). The main benefactors have been countries such as Pakistan, Afghanistan, Ethiopia, and Somalia, each experiencing a sharp rise in their share of international assistance. While difficult to measure (due to the complexities of budgets and reporting criteria), more and more assistance is also directed toward security sector reform (SSR) programs, where the technical dimensions of "train and equip" have come to dominate over the more developmental and political aspects focused on democratic oversight, transparency, and accountability of security forces (Scheye 2010). Thus, at least 65 percent of EU expenditure on SSR is now directed toward police development and border management (Scheye 2010), leading some to speak of a militarization of SSR (Albrecht and Stepputat 2015). There are also fears that a preoccupation with security might result in aid being directed toward population groups that are considered at risk of radicalization (such as young Muslim men) rather than the poorest and most excluded (such as women and children) (see Lind and Howell 2010). Put differently, development assistance may come to be increasingly determined by donors' security interests rather than recipients' needs, and the merger of development and security risks reframing and repacking security interventions and warfare in weak and fragile states as non-destructive, humanitarian activities, giving them a developmental, morally acceptable face and thereby making critique and political questioning more difficult.

26.4 The Intervener State: The Global South as an International Security Solution

Due to the power of the discourse of the security/development nexus, interventions of various kinds figure prominently on the foreign policy agenda of the international community. UN peacebuilding interventions, increasingly referred to as "Stabilization Missions," are nearly universally located in the global South, and have taken on a renewed importance in the context of international security concerns over state fragility. In addition, the global South is witnessing the proliferation of ambitious and experimental transnational security governance arrangements in response to insecurities emanating from its so-called ungoverned spaces (Hameiri and Jones 2015; Sandor 2016a). Governments in Africa, Asia, and Latin America, however, must not be viewed as passive recipients of donor interventions, as they often capitalize on international discourses regarding the global South as a source of threats in order to refashion their identities, gain international credibility, and reap economic and diplomatic rewards from interventions. States and societies in the global South, therefore, are not simply recipients of international intervention; they actively transform themselves into "intervener states," a move that is consolidating into the principal solution for responding to insecurities globally. This raises important political and ethical questions regarding who should bear the brunt of the risks of physical violence, especially when these interventions are framed and often advanced as a mechanism to safeguard the West (see Duffield 2005).

Following troop casualties experienced in Somalia, Rwanda, and former Yugoslavia in the 1990s, western governments have developed a serial allergy to participating in UN interventions. As a result, economically powerful states contribute relatively little in terms of personnel for Stabilization Missions. They do, however, pay the weight of financial resources required for the UN to function and peace missions to occur, and thereby enjoy an overabundance of decision-making power over the mandates and conduct of interventions. The institutional features of the United Nations, notably the payment of member dues, make it possible for Security Council members and other wealthy governments to manage their risk aversion by displacing the potential for troop losses onto poorer states. It is firmly the case that security actors from the global South far outstrip European and North American actors in theaters of intervention, forming the primary operational backbone forces for UN and regional interventions. The burden of violence and death that these missions entail, therefore, falls on military and policing actors from the global South, which are financially and symbolically incentivized to participate in them (Cunliffe 2009). Observers of UN interventions even speak of an "Africanization" of peacekeeping, as actors from the continent now form at least half of all civilian and military mission personnel, surpassing contributions from Asian states that make up over a third of UN mission staff (Brosig 2017). In practice, therefore, while international actors in the North consider insecurities to emanate from states in the global South, these very spaces and their associated actors simultaneously become the solution to security concerns by direct involvement and their transformation into intervener states.

Many governments and regional organizations in Africa, Latin America, and Asia willingly respond to the opportunities tied to interventions as this yields multiple benefits, including a recognition of their new weight in global affairs and an ability to express their political agency via foreign policies (see Amar 2013a). Governments that share borders with politically unstable neighbors also have a clear interest in stemming armed conflict and other related security concerns connected to state fragility, as do regional organizations like the African Union (see Menkhaus 2010). Apart from political or security expediency, however, participation in interventions can also increase a government's international credibility as a force of regional leadership. Since 2003, Brazilian governments have advertised their international image as "a model of human security" for the global South (Amar 2013b: 193), and in an effort to position itself as the leading Latin American emerging power have selected Haiti as a space for increased humanitarian interventionism, surpassing all other troop-contributing countries to the UN MINUSTAH Operation. Governments that fashion their interventions as the most efficient and ethical response to threats in the global South, such as when African heads of state argue for "African solutions to African problems," more often than not increase their political support from national audiences who resent past colonial domination, foreign interference, and political meddling by Western powers (Beswick 2010). Finally, contributing troops and expert personnel to peace interventions also provides poor states with significant financial resources. For governments that fear the possibility of coup d'états, sending sizable segments of their national military and police personnel on interventions abroad may not only reduce the feasibility of military takeovers, but also placate participants in interventions as they receive significant pay increases in addition to their annual salaries. In short, becoming an intervener state can unlock multiple opportunities to acquire material and symbolic resources, as well as the chance to meet several practical interests tied to governing a state.

Of course, when state forces in the global South seek out intervention opportunities and frame participation in them as the only way forward, this suits the international community. Northern states and international organizations get to argue that their foreign policy activities are pursued in the guise of "partnerships" with actors from the global South in support of the latter's political goals of development and security, essentially depoliticizing their involvement in spaces of intervention (Abrahamsen 2004). It also allows the donor community to shape their approach to interventions through seemingly innocuous, banal measures like "capacity-building" and "community resilience," with the objective of developing "security exporters" in the global South, for the global South. Thus, since the mid-2000s, not only is the presence of southern security actors in complex peace operations increasingly the norm, but South–South security cooperation agreements and experimental transnational security governance initiatives that connect southern spaces are also becoming more common-place (Sandor 2016b). These measures are mostly initiated by the international donor community, and sold to governments and regional organizations in the global South as efforts to increase their security expertise. While framed in the trappings of comprehensive or integrated multi-stakeholder security solutions, many such capacity-building interventions—ranging from anti-drug trafficking projects to the creation of counter-terrorism units and the equipping of rapid response tactical teams—serve primarily to strengthen and fetishize the coercive apparatuses of states in the global South.

It is not readily evident, however, that enhancing the capacities for violence of government agencies in Africa, Asia, and Latin America will automatically translate into an increase in protection for ordinary people. As we argued in Section 26.3, states are frequently a source of insecurity for citizens and many governments in these regions premise their governance activities on regime security, maintaining political order, and quelling any forms of contentious dissent. The logic of security, on the lips of so many political and security elites from both the North and the South, may therefore provide the impetus for an increase in militarism, coercive state violence, and transformations of state institutions that benefit some social forces more than others (Fisher and Anderson 2015; Hameiri and Jones 2015).

26.5 Conclusion

As this chapter has shown, speaking about the global South as a singular unit or identifiable group of states is fraught with difficulties, both analytically and politically. While many countries in areas of the global South have, in the past and in the present, sought to speak with a unified voice on international security issues, their ideological and material interests and positions are too diverse to be contained within a singular label. At the same time, as a political strategy against domination, the aspiration of a global South remains alive, as expressed for example in the confident re-statement of pan-Africanism in the African Union.

Our analysis of the harsh realities of contemporary global security politics points to the possibility of a more fractured global South, where the differences between the rich and the poor and between what we have termed the "weak state" and the "intervener state" may intensify. The future security landscape may also increase competiton between intervener states, both for resources and for power to influence and determine security strategies and policies.

For international security studies this brings both challenges and opportunities. The discipline has a checkered history in relation to the global South, but as we have shown, these areas of the globe have moved from being largely ignored in both policy and academic debates to assuming a central position in contemporary security affairs and research. Ideas about what and who counts as international security issues have been important to these changes, and moving forward, international security studies should remain engaged with the manifold security issues in the South, while seeking approaches that can appreciate the divergent paths, diverse political histories of colonialism, the agency of southern actors, and their long-standing and deepening transnational connections.

References

Abrahamsen, Rita. 2004. The Power of Partnerships in Global Governance. *Third World Quarterly*, 25(8): 1453–67.

Abrahamsen, Rita. 2005. Blair's Africa: The Politics of Securitization and Fear. *Alternatives: Global, Local, Political*, 30(1): 55–80.

Abrahamsen, Rita and Michael C. Williams. 2011. *Security Beyond the State: Private Security in International Politics*. Cambridge: Cambridge University Press.

Acharya, Amitav. 1995. The Periphery as the Core: The Third World and Security Studies. YCISS Occasional Paper Number 28, York University, Toronto.

Acharya, Amitav. 2014. Who Are the Norm Makers? The Asian-African Conference in Bandung and the Evolution of Norms. *Global Governance: A Review of Multilateralism and International Organizations*, 20(3): 405–17.

Albrecht, Peter and Finn Stepputat. 2015 The Rise and Fall of Security Sector Reform in Development. In P. Jackson (ed.), *Handbook of International Security and Development*, pp. 150–64. Cheltenham: Edward Elgar Publishing.

Amar, Paul. 2013a. *Global South to the Rescue: Emerging Humanitarian Superpowers and Globalizing Rescue Industries*. London: Routledge.

Amar, Paul. 2013b. *The Security Archipelago: Human-Security States, Sexuality Politics, and the End of Neoliberalism*. Durham, NC: Duke University Press.

Ayoob, Mohammed. 1995. *The Third World Security Predicament: State-Making, Regional Conflict, and the International System*. Boulder, CO: Lynne Rienner Publishers.

Baily, Beth and Richard H. Immerman (eds.). 2015. *Understanding the U.S. Wars in Iraq and Afghanistan*. New York: New York University Press.

Barkawi, T. and M. Laffey 2006. The Postcolonial Moment in Security Studies. *Review of International Studies*, 32(2): 329–52.

Beresford, Alexander. 2015. A Responsibility to Protect Africa from the West? South Africa and the NATO Intervention in Libya. *International Politics*, 52(3): 288–304.

Beswick, Danielle. 2010. Peacekeeping, Regime Security and "African Solutions to African Problems": Exploring Motivations for Rwanda's Involvement in Darfur. *Third World Quarterly*, 31(5): 739–54.

Brosig, Malte. 2017. Rentier Peacekeeping in Neo-Patrimonial Systems: The Examples of Burundi and Kenya. *Contemporary Security Policy*, 38(1): 109–28.

The Bureau of Investigative Journalism. 2017. Obama's Drone War in Numbers: Ten Times More Strikes than Bush. *Available at:* https://www.thebureauinvestigates.com/stories/2017-01-17/obamas-covert-drone-war-in-numbers-ten-times-more-strikes-than-bush

Buzan, Barry. 1991. *People, States and Fear: An Agenda for International Security Studies in the Post-Cold War Era*, 2nd edn. Boulder, CO: Lynne Rienner Publishers.

Cunliffe, Philip. 2009. The Politics of Global Governance in UN Peacekeeping. *International Peacekeeping*, 16(3): 323–36.

Department for International Development (DFID). 2005. *Fighting Poverty to Build a Safer World: A Strategy for Security and Development*. London: Department for International Development.

Duffield, Mark. 2001. *Global Governance and the New Wars*. London: Zed Books.

Duffield, Mark. 2005. Getting Savages to Fight Barbarians: Development, Security and the Colonial Present. *Conflict, Security & Development*, 5(2): 141–59.

Fisher, Jonathan and David M. Anderson. 2015. Authoritarianism and the Securitization of Development in Africa. *International Affairs*, 91(1): 131–51.

Flemes, Daniel (ed.). 2016. *Regional Leadership in the Global System: Ideas, Interests and Strategies of Regional Powers*. Abingdon: Routledge.

Grovogui, Siba. 2011. A Revolution Nonetheless: The Global South in International Relations. *The Global South*, 5(1): 175–90.

Hameiri, Shahar and Lee Jones. 2015. *Governing Borderless Threats: Non-Traditional Security and the Politics of State Transformation*. Cambridge: Cambridge University Press.

Hameiri, Shahar and Lee Jones. 2016. Rising Powers and State Transformation: The Case of China. *European Journal of International Relations*, 22(1): 72–98.

HM Treasury. 2015. *UK Aid: Tackling Global Challenges in the National Interest*. London: HM Treasury.

Hurrell, Andrew. 2008. *On Global Order: Power, Values, and the Constitution of International Society*. Oxford: Oxford University Press.

Jaganathan, Madhan M. and Gerrit Kurtz. 2014. Singing the Tune of Sovereignty? India and the Responsibility to Protect. *Conflict, Security & Development*, 14(4): 461–87.

Krause, Keith and Michael C. Williams (eds.). 1997. *Critical Security Studies: Concepts and Cases*. Minneapolis: University of Minnesota Press.

Lee, Christopher J. 2009. Recovered Histories at the Rendezvous of Decolonization: The Final Communiqué of the Asian-African Conference, Bandung, Indonesia, 18–24 April 1955. *Interventions: International Journal of Postcolonial Studies*, 11(1): 81–93.

Lind, Jeremy and Jude Howell. 2010. Counter-terrorism and the Politics of Aid: Civil Society Responses in Kenya. *Development and Change*, 41(2): 335–53.

Menkhaus, Ken. 2010. Stabilisation and Humanitarian access in a Collapsed State: The Somali Case. *Disasters*, 34(3): 320–41.

Nye, Joseph S. Jr. and Sean M. Lynn-Jones. 1988. International Security Studies: Report on a Conference on the State of the Field. *International Security*, 12(4): 5–27.

Sandor, Adam. 2016a. Border Security and Drug Trafficking in Senegal: AIRCOP and Global Security Assemblages. *Journal of Intervention and Statebuilding*, 10(4): 490–512.

Sandor, Adam. 2016b. Tightly Packed: Disciplinary Power, the UNODC, and the Container Control Programme in Dakar. *African Studies Review*, 59(2): 133–60.

Sassen, Saskia. 2006. *Territory, Authority, Rights*. Princeton, NJ: Princeton University Press.

Scheye, Eric. 2010. *Realism and Pragmatism in Security Sector Development*. Washington, DC: United States Institute of Peace, Special Report.

Stephen, Matthew D. 2014. Rising Powers, Global Capitalism and Liberal Global Governance: A Historical Materialist Account of the BRICs Challenge. *European Journal of International Relations*, 20(4): 912–28.

Stuenkel, Oliver and Marcos Tourinho. 2014. Regulating Intervention: Brazil and the Responsibility to Protect. *Conflict, Security & Development*, 14(4): 379–402.

Tickner, Arlene B. and Ole Wæver (eds.). 2009. *International Relations Scholarship around the World*. London: Routledge.

Turse, Nick. 2015. *Tomorrow's Battlefield. US Proxy Wars and Secret Ops in Africa*. Chicago: Haymarket Books.

United Nations Development Programme (UNDP). 1994. *Human Development Report 1994*. Oxford/New York: Oxford University Press.

Vieira, Marco A. 2016. Understanding Resilience in International Relations: The Non-Aligned Movement and Ontological Security. *International Studies Review*. 18(2): 290–311.

Vitalis, Robert. 2013. The Midnight Ride of Kwame Nkrumah and Other Fables of Bandung (Ban-doong). *Humanity: An International Journal of Human Rights, Humanitarianism, and Development*, 4(2): 261–88.

Wæver, Ole. 1995. Securitization and Desecuritization. In Ronnie Lipschutz (ed.), *On Security*, pp. 46–86. New York: Columbia University Press.

Waltz, Kenneth. 1979. *Theory of International Politics*. Reading, MA: Addison-Wesley.

White House. 2002. *The National Security Strategy of the United States of America 2002*. Washington, DC: The White House.

White House. 2010. Remarks by the President at the Millennium Development Goals Summit in New York, New York. September 22, 2010. *Available at:* http://www.whitehouse.gov/the-press-office/2010/09/22/remarks-president-millennium-development-goals-summit-new-york-new-york

PART IV

CHALLENGES AND OPPORTUNITIES FOR TWENTY-FIRST-CENTURY SECURITY

CHAPTER 27

ARMS CONTROL

JENNIFER L. ERICKSON

ARMS control and disarmament are cornerstones of international security. By seeking to manage weapons acquisition and use, arms control attempts to tame the security dilemma, prevent the outbreak of war, and limit war's brutality. Yet in pursuing limits on states' core material power resources, arms control negotiations are typically long and fraught. Arms control has therefore been held up as a source of cooperation between adversaries and condemned as doomed to failure. Nevertheless, as concerns about weapons proliferation persist and the domains of conflict expand, arms control remains a central issue on the international agenda.

The future of arms control will be marked by growing complexity, as new technologies emerge, more actors (state and non-state) demand a seat at the table, and existing regimes require regular maintenance. Moreover, as security goals have broadened to include human security, the targets of arms control have also broadened, introducing once-acceptable weapons to new restrictions. Even as arms control evolves, however, understanding it will continue to depend on understanding the interplay between the material and normative pressures actors face in domestic and international politics. As I show, the power dynamics and normative considerations of arms control are consistent, even as new weapons challenge its foundations.

27.1 WHAT IS ARMS CONTROL?

There is no single accepted definition of arms control, but most scholars highlight cooperative action between potential adversaries to restrain levels of armaments or their use.[1] Quantitative arms control limits the numbers of specific weapons states can hold in their arsenals. Qualitative arms control regulates or prohibits specific weapons or types of weapons. Policy-makers, the public, and the media, however, tend view arms control more narrowly as formal treaties limiting or prohibiting particular weapons systems.

Before the 1950s, disarmament was the term of art. The shift to arms control terminology in the Cold War was meant to avoid the idealism that had become associated with disarmament. Today, disarmament is distinguished as a type of arms control by its explicit goal to reduce the number of weapons in states' arsenals. Thus, nuclear disarmament would reduce a state's nuclear weapons, while nuclear arms control in general could simply cap them. In practice, the two terms are often used in tandem, and the more common distinction is between conventional and unconventional (nuclear, biological, and chemical) arms control.

Scholars widely accept Schelling and Halperin's (1961: 2) arms control objectives as "reducing the likelihood of war, its scope and violence if it occurs, and the political and economic costs of being prepared for it." However, they disagree about whether these goals can be achieved (e.g. Krepon 1989; Betts 1992; Gray 1992). General theoretical debates over the prospects for interstate cooperation aside, arms control faces the persistent challenge of playing catch-up with technology. While states are obliged to follow the laws of war with all weapons, their obligation to review the compatibility of new weapons with the laws of war has not been well realized.[2] Arms control has therefore been the primary means to restrict weapons on a case-by-case basis. Unsurprisingly, this has been a regular source of debate in international politics.

27.2 Nineteenth-Century Foundations

The principles of contemporary arms control are rooted in nineteenth-century great power agreements. Scholars point to a mix of normative and material concerns motivating efforts to regulate weapons after 1860. Rapid industrialization and technological innovation introduced new weapons with more destructive potential as the century progressed. Russia, which convened the pivotal conferences, sought both to address humanitarian ideals and to spare the cost of keeping up with more technologically advanced states. Many other governments also wanted to avoid costly arms races and respond to growing public concerns about conflict brutality.[3] Yet although the resulting agreements articulated enduring principles of arms control, states were reluctant to place specific restrictions on both new and established weapons.

The first conference in 1868 produced the St Petersburg Declaration: the first instrument of modern international weapons law and the first to invoke "the exigencies of humanity" as a reason to limit war (Holquist 2004: 11). The Declaration establishes that "the only legitimate object" of war is to "weaken the military forces of the enemy" and that to "[uselessly] aggregate the sufferings of disabled men, or render their death inevitable" is "contrary to the laws of humanity." The 1899 and 1907 Hague Peace Conferences reinforced these principles, which have become binding on all states as part of customary international law and served as legal and normative foundations for contemporary weapons bans.

States could agree on few specific qualitative or quantitative limitations, however. The St Petersburg Declaration agreed only to ban the use of small-caliber high-explosive bullets weighing under 400 grams. The Hague Conferences made four prohibitions, covering mainly untested weapons. The most influential for subsequent agreements has been the prohibition on the diffusion of asphyxiating or deleterious gases, which later helped establish the chemical weapons ban.[4] All other proposals failed. Established weapons were largely off the table, and the ability to restrict weapons before they had proven their destructiveness (or merit) was also limited.

27.3 The League of Nations system

The First World War demonstrated the destructive potential of new weapons. In response, the interwar years saw a flurry of disarmament meetings backed by considerable public support. Arms reductions were seen as necessary to avoid arms races leading to war, and the League of Nations declared that disarmament was required for "the maintenance of peace." States also debated qualitative limitations based on prewar humanitarian principles. Nevertheless, they disagreed about new weapons regulations and sought to work around agreed-upon limitations.

27.3.1 Quantitative Limitations

The threat of a costly naval arms race prompted the first multilateral post-war disarmament conference, the Washington Naval Conference (1921–22). The resulting treaties largely detailed numerical parity and ratios, rather than humanitarian principles. In particular, delegates agreed to limit the tonnage and construction of capital ships. However, attempts to limit auxiliary ships failed, due to disagreements between strong and weak naval powers about whether submarines should be subject to quantitative limitations or be banned as offensive and inhumane.

In accordance with the standard of the time, the Washington treaties relied on "good faith" and diplomatic integrity for compliance. As a result, treaty violations and evasions—both actual and accused—were common (Buckley 1993: 652–3). In practice, Kaufman (1992) contends, domestic structure shaped governments' ability to commit violations. An open society and legislative oversight made violations more difficult to make and easier to detect, while more closed societies could better engage in clandestine construction.

Quantitative efforts broadened in the 1930s to include all types of weapons and national defense budgets. The Disarmament Conference ran from 1932 to 1936, but finding cuts in military forces that states considered comparable and acceptable proved too difficult (Jacobson 1984: 1590). States also disagreed about which weapons were offensive, and which were indispensable for national security rather than a threat to it.

Attempts to restrict arms acquisition by controlling the global arms trade also floundered under political rivalries and pushback by non-producing states to protect their access to arms (Goldblat 2002).

27.3.2 Qualitative Limitations

Poison gas, submarines, and airplanes—weapons largely untested in battle before the war—were the primary candidates for qualitative limitations after the war. Perceptions of military and commercial utility influenced success in doing so, but debates turned on disagreements about the application of humanitarian principles, including the potential harm to soldiers and civilians.

The most enduring agreement from this period is the 1925 Geneva Protocol banning the use of poison gas and bacteriological weapons.[5] Despite the Hague prohibitions, chemical weapons were deployed extensively in the war. Military analysts disagreed about their effectiveness, necessity, and humanity in practice, but post-war public opinion and concerns about potential future use on civilians were more decisive. Although there have been violations, states have mostly adhered to their non-use obligations. Normative-cultural explanations attribute non-use to a chemical weapons taboo, connected to broader taboos against the use of poison (Price 1997) and states' bureaucratic cultures (Legro 1996). Military-strategic explanations point to a decline in those weapons' strategic value (Mathews and McCormack 1999) or to effective deterrence (van Courtland Moon 1984).

Other restrictions found less support. As the target of Germany's submarine campaign in the war, Great Britain's push to ban submarines as inherently indiscriminate and inhumane was popular at home, but weaker naval powers argued (as before the war) that submarines were essential defensive weapons. States settled on regulating submarines by surface ship rules in the 1936 London Protocol. Most, however, viewed the rules as impossible to implement, thus creating—depending on who was asked—either a de facto ban or rules that were made to be broken. Whatever their intentions had been, most states quickly discarded the rules in the Second World War, raising questions about the constraining force of international law on wartime practices.

An aircraft ban was most controversial. States were aware of the offensive potential of aircraft but ruled out a ban based on their rapidly growing military and commercial value. Rules drafted in 1923 (never adopted) forbade direct attacks on civilian populations and bombardment on military targets that could not be hit without indiscriminately bombing civilians. Subsequent discussions to restrict aerial bombing also came and went without success as tensions escalated in the 1930s. By the Second World War, aerial bombing had become an accepted means of warfare that often targeted civilian populations.

Chemical weapons aside, the interwar years have therefore been seen as a resounding failure for arms control, leaving states in search of less "idealistic" measures after the Second World War. Critics faulted the interwar system with altering the balance of power in favor of the aggressors. Others concluded that it had mattered little for the pace of the arms race or deterrence.[6] Yet although states would seek a break with the past after the Second World War, binding treaties and quantitative limitations would also come to characterize Cold War arms control.

27.4 Arms Control in the Cold War

The United States' bombing of Japan in 1945 permanently changed the security landscape and placed nuclear weapons at the top of the international agenda. As the Cold War heated up, nuclear arms control also became the primary means of stabilizing US–Soviet relations. However, it left multilateral, conventional, and qualitative limitations (and the interests of smaller powers) largely on the sidelines.[7] Early comprehensive UN disarmament plans were popular but scuttled by superpower disagreements. The Vietnam War re-introduced humanitarian concerns about some conventional arms, but without superpower backing, efforts fell short of their goals.[8]

US–Soviet disagreements stymied UN nuclear disarmament attempts from the start. Both states proposed nuclear disarmament plans but could not agree on the sequencing of disarmament or the Security Council's role in dealing with violations. It was not until the 1962 Cuban Missile Crisis that the two sides recognized the need for bilateral cooperation. The first US–Soviet "risk reduction" treaty, the 1963 Hot Line Agreement establishing rapid communication links in times of emergency, proved valuable for avoiding misperceptions of military maneuvers and building understandings between the governments over time. Since then, a plethora of agreements have covered various aspects of nuclear weapons stockpiles, delivery, locations, testing, and anti-ballistic missile systems.[9] Verification was often a sticking point and led to complex combinations of national technical monitoring, data exchanges, and on-site visits.

Systemic conditions are often cited as the source of superpower insecurity and nuclear arms control during the Cold War (e.g. Betts 1992; Glaser 1994/95). Some scholars argue, however, that domestic and transnational pressures also helped generate bilateral nuclear cooperation. In the United States, popular protests, argues Knopf (1998), altered decisions to seek arms control cooperation and the substance of those policies. In addition, Adler (1992) observes, strategists and scientists influenced policy-makers to adopt their ideas and expectations about nuclear arms control. Similarly, Evangelista (1999) shows that Soviet scientists—members of the same transnational networks Adler identifies—gained access to high levels of government and shaped policy using their knowledge and ideas. In these ways, non-systemic factors substantively affected governments' perceptions of their security environment and responses to it.

In the multilateral realm, the 1968 Nuclear Nonproliferation Treaty (NPT) is the cornerstone of the nonproliferation regime. Its "central bargain" commits all signatories but the Permanent Five (P5) members of the UN Security Council to forego nuclear weapons in exchange for access to civilian nuclear technology.[10] It also commits the P5 to "pursue negotiations in good faith" on measures relating to nuclear disarmament. It is the only legally-binding agreement in which the recognized nuclear weapons states accept disarmament as a goal, although their compliance is disputed.

For many, the NPT is a success, with a broad membership that has helped curb nuclear proliferation (Potter 2010; Fuhrmann and Lupu 2016). Scholars point to a range of possible mechanisms behind its success, including NPT safeguards and transparency that reduce uncertainty about other states' activities, the empowerment of domestic actors, and the norms it helped create.[11] Others contend that the NPT has mattered little for managing nuclear proliferation,[12] arguing that its signatories had already decided to forego nuclear weapons (Betts 1999) and that its provisions are too weak to prevent others from developing them (Hymans 2006). Some scholars, for example, instead credit strong sanctions or other domestic economic interests with deterring proliferation (Solingen 1994, 2007; Miller 2014). Conversely, political-strategic considerations may favor proliferation, in spite of the NPT (Kroenig 2010; Monteiro and Debs 2014). Individual leaders' beliefs may also affect proliferation and counter-proliferation decision making (Hymans 2006; Whitlark 2017).

Yet despite extensive nuclear arms control efforts, there are no formal rules banning their use by those who possess them. Rationalists attribute the non-use of nuclear weapons after 1945 to states' interest in avoiding the high costs of mutually assured destruction (Jervis 1989; Sagan and Waltz 2003: 3–45). For others, it stems from strong taboos or traditions that have developed over time (Tannenwald 2007; Paul 2008). In recent years, however, the public foundations of a nuclear taboo have been questioned, with experimental evidence suggesting that Americans may not (or no longer) see the use of nuclear weapons as "unthinkable" (Press et al. 2013). Together, these findings raise questions about effective means of arms control, the role of the public, and the ability of formal institutions and informal norms to shape state behavior more broadly.

27.5 Arms Control after the Cold War

Post-Cold War arms control has shown the possibility for more fundamental change. Weapons of mass destruction (WMD) remain a top concern.[13] However, negotiations have paid renewed attention to conventional arms thought to harm human security or domestic stability and have sought to incorporate states adversely affected by their proliferation. This turn to "humanitarian" arms control has seen smaller states and non-state actors, often against great power preferences, take the lead to extend rules and norms to new *and* well-established weapons.

27.5.1 Blinding Laser Weapons (BLW)

At the first Review Conference on the 1980 Convention on CCW (Certain Conventional Weapons) in 1995, states agreed to ban the use of laser weapons designed to cause blindness. The few states familiar with blinding laser weapons (BLW) in the 1980s, like the United States, had originally opposed a ban.[14] Even so, by 1989, word of their production prompted the ICRC to convene expert meetings to examine BLW use, effects, and legality. Most importantly, the meetings collected evidence to address claims that BLW may not cause permanent blindness and that blindness was no worse than other battlefield injuries. Subsequent laser developments and a better understanding of their injuries helped national viewpoints to converge further (Carnahan and Robertson 1996: 487). Human Rights Watch also got involved, issuing a report in the lead-up to the 1995 conference that prompted the United States to revise its position to support a partial ban, clearing the way for the Review Conference to take up the issue.

In some ways, the new BLW protocol kept with the past. It reflected established humanitarian principles and accommodated US preferences: a ban only on weapons *intentionally* designed to blind soldiers in the field. Lasers are not inherently indiscriminate, and a ban on all lasers was not seen as politically feasible or militarily desirable. The need for more accurate precision-guided munitions also made an important humanitarian case for allowing some laser use to reduce collateral damage (Carnahan and Robertson 1996: 487).

What was new was, first, the ICRC's key role in gathering and disseminating information to make the case for weapons regulations. It showed "forcefully and graphically" that "blinding was in fact more severe and debilitating than most other war injuries" (Morton 1998: 700). Second, advocates' emphasis on the long-term costs of supporting "increasing numbers of blinded veterans for years after a war has ended" set a new precedent in which the "postwar social effects of weapons systems" became legitimate grounds on which to restrict a weapon (Carnahan and Robertson 1996: 489, 490).

27.5.2 Anti-personnel Landmines (APL)

The 1997 Ottawa Treaty banning the use, stockpiling, production, and transfer of anti-personnel landmines (APL) took non-state actor advocacy and the consideration of long-term social costs further. Scholars point to the pivotal role of the ICRC and other NGOs, in partnership with "like-minded" middle powers, in making the treaty a reality (Price 1998; Rutherford 2000). Humanitarian NGOs in the field identified the APL problem and collected evidence of their indiscriminate effects and long-term impact on post-conflict communities. Their reports helped show that APL violated international law despite existing CCW regulations. Under the aegis of the International Campaign to Ban Landmines, NGOs also coordinated a global campaign to mobilize publics to pressure their governments to support a ban.

The Ottawa Treaty broke with the past in breaking with great power preferences. The United States opposed a full APL ban and sought to keep negotiations within UN fora, where consensus rules would allow it to block such measures. Ban supporters responded by moving negotiations outside the UN to ensure a comprehensive ban. Although the United States participated in the final drafting conference, it declined to sign after organizers rejected its requested exceptions in favor of a strong treaty. As a result, Bower (2017) argues, the APL ban shows that treaties can succeed and gain widespread adherence without the support of materially powerful states.

The Ottawa Treaty does have its limits. It lacks signatures from several major powers and has no verification measures. Scholars note that it has nevertheless generated widespread behavioral change, including by the United States (Rutherford 2000; Bower 2017). In doing so, it established a normative shift and social pressures on states to participate in subsequent humanitarian arms control initiatives (Erickson 2015). Yet its success also stems from unique characteristics of APL: retired military personnel testified to their lack of strategic value, and industry found more profit to be made in landmine removal than in selling cheap APL on a saturated global market. Low material interests in APL thus eased the way for norm development but have been difficult to replicate elsewhere.

27.5.3 Small and Major Conventional Arms Transfers

Initiatives to regulate the global trade in small arms and light weapons (SALW) built on the landmine campaign. However, the process was much more state-dominated, NGOs more divided, and economic and strategic interests less conducive to concluding a strong agreement. The politically-binding 2001 Programme of Action on Small Arms asks states to implement national measures combatting illicit SALW transfers. Because the United States repeatedly blocked more binding measures to regulate legal SALW transfers, lead states and NGOs launched a separate Arms Trade Treaty (ATT) process in 2006. Even so, the United States makes up such a significant portion of the global arms market that supporters kept negotiations within the UN hoping the United States would eventually participate in the treaty. United States support came in late 2009, paving the way for negotiations that resulted in the 2013 ATT. The treaty sets legally-binding export standards to restrict state-sanctioned transfers of small and major conventional arms to human rights violators and conflict zones but contains no enforcement mechanisms.

After several failed attempts to regulate conventional arms transfers over the course of the twentieth century, scholars have sought to account for the ATT's success.[15] Bromley et al. (2012: 1030) argue that support has come partly because the ATT bridged North–South interests by incorporating "human security concepts into the field of arms export controls." Others focus on the role of international norms. Garcia (2011) views the ATT as a product of international norms and moral leadership that will restrict states' arms export sovereignty. Erickson (2015), in contrast, argues that states have used ATT support to bolster their international reputations in the post-Ottawa normative environment but still may not reliably constrain their export behavior. Stavrianakis (2016: 855) is the most skeptical about normative motivations, arguing that the ATT legitimizes "liberal war making and war preparation." Whether the ATT will change state practices remains to be seen. What is clear is that material interests complicated ATT negotiations and will likely complicate its implementation.

27.5.4 Cluster Munitions (CM)

The cluster munition (CM) ban more closely followed the landmine trajectory, with an NGO-middle power coalition leading a transnational campaign to ban a weapon based on its indiscriminate effects and social costs. Advocates even framed CM as "de facto landmines." As late as 1997, however, ban supporters were concerned that proposing a CM ban would be too controversial. As a result, campaigning started only in 1999–2000, propelled by the success of the Ottawa Treaty and reports of CM use in Chechnya and Kosovo. The final push came after the Israel–Lebanon conflict returned the CM problem to the spotlight in 2006. Like landmines, larger powers' opposition prompted supporters to remove negotiations from the CCW in 2007 to ensure a comprehensive ban. Yet the 2008 Cluster Munition Convention left room to maneuver by defining CM in such a way as to allow states to develop and use "smart" CM and engage in military cooperation with non-signatories, like the United States.

The CM case highlights again the pivotal role of NGOs and middle powers in setting the humanitarian arms control agenda, reframing a weapon as indiscriminate, and negotiating a ban. Petrova (2007) points to the particular importance of national campaigns in fostering "leadership competition" between states to adopt increasingly progressive domestic positions on CM and support multilateral agreements. Although several large military powers remain outside the convention, some previous CM users, including France and the UK, came to support it. Explanations that look only to military utility to understand support therefore fall short and may, for example, also require attention to how states define their roles in international politics, as Petrova (2007) suggests explains leadership variation among supporter states.

Collectively, these post-Cold War agreements further reinforce and expand arms control rooted in humanitarian principles. Yet their scope and membership have depended both on the strength of states' material interests and on supporters' ability to mobilize publics and governments by linking weapons to established norms. Even as defense technologies become more complex, these political dynamics promise to shape arms control regimes to come.

27.6 The Future of Arms Control

Contemporary research raises a wealth of complex questions for the future of arms control. When does technological change prompt new international rules and norms? Are formal, negotiated agreements necessary, or can less codified forms of cooperation restrain weapons use? When do normative pressures outweigh material interests in making and implementing agreements? What are the roles of domestic politics and non-state actors? These questions remain relevant for maintaining current regimes and for responding to new weapons developments. As in the past, regime creation will have to contend with power politics, and technological changes will complicate the normative foundations of the system.

27.6.1 Current Regimes

Among current arms control regimes, consensus is strongest—but not absolute—on WMD. Rules and norms against chemical and biological weapons reinforce one another, but the diffusion of technological know-how will complicate their enforcement. Active international support will be needed to deter interested actors from seeking "the poor man's nuclear bomb" but may be hard to come by, especially if Russian and US interests are at odds. How Syria's disputed gassing of civilians in 2013, for example, will affect chemical weapons norms remains to be seen. However, it points to a need to understand the conditions under which governments disregard established conventions to suit their strategic interests, and by what means the international community can or will enforce them, if at all.

Nuclear proliferation raises similar concerns. Bilateral cooperation between Russia and the United States remains uncertain at best. Regional nuclear powers with smaller arsenals and potentially more unstable governments, like North Korea and Pakistan, continue to provoke worries about willingness to proliferate and use.[16] Would-be nuclear powers also demand attention. Provided it endures, the 2015 Joint Comprehensive Action Plan with Iran will provide important lessons about the utility of sanctions and formal nonproliferation agreements. Perceptions of its successes and failures will in turn affect states' proliferation and counter-proliferation decision making.

Conventional weapons rules and norms are newer and, with the exception of the landmine ban, less established. The Cluster Munition Convention and ATT require actors to set implementation standards, build technical capacity, and generate political will. Without formal enforcement mechanisms, civil society will play a central role in government accountability (Erickson 2015). Consequently, these cases will provide important tests for the influence of domestic enforcement and non-state actors in generating state compliance. Moreover, as several major players remain unlikely to join these agreements, these cases will test whether treaty norms will shape non-member behavior, as with landmines, or undermine the institutionalization and effectiveness of new regimes. The passing of the UN Nuclear Ban Treaty in 2017, despite opposition form the nuclear weapons states and their allies will also test the limits of weapons norm creation.

The question of armed non-state actors looms largest for adapting current agreements to the realities of modern conflict. Arms control agreements are the domain of states, and their obligations do not technically apply to non-state actors. The growing capabilities of some terrorist groups have—rightly or wrongly—sounded the alarm about risks of nuclear terrorism (Bunn et al. 2016). Of course, armed groups already use a wide range of conventional arms and explosives. NGOs are therefore attempting to commit them to following international law, with varied success (Gleditsch et al. 2016). The results may further scholars' understanding of when and why actors follow or discard international rules and norms, and the consequences of their choices for conflict dynamics.

27.6.2 New Weapons

States are reluctant to accept restrictions on weapons before their military utility and humanitarian costs are demonstrated. Even then, material interests and normative pressures shape states' positions on new agreements. Contemporary technological developments further complicate arms control: New weapons may simultaneously make targeting more precise but injuries more severe. Increasingly, new technologies also blur the line between conventional and unconventional arms, challenge notions of responsibility, and push the domains of conflict further beyond the traditional battlefield.

Most immediately, arms control faces questions about the compatibility of international law with cyber weapons, drones, and autonomous weapons systems.[17] The answers are not clear-cut. Experts disagree on what constitutes cyber warfare, whether new agreements are needed to govern it, whether cyber weapons directly cause death and injury or avoid them, and what are appropriate and proportional responses to cyber attacks (Buchan and Tsagourias 2012). As cyber weapons push warfare into the virtual realm, armed unmanned aerial vehicles, or drones, push it further into civilian areas. Drones' ability to engage in targeted strikes and disrupt terrorist organizations' command and control make them appealing. However, their accuracy, use for extrajudicial killings, and impact on the ground raise important legal questions (Bergen and Rothenberg 2014). Most recently, activists have campaigned to ban "killer robots" that select and kill targets without human intervention after their initial programming. Such weapons have not yet been deployed, making them especially divisive. Ban supporters argue that killer robots violate international law by precluding the ability to determine legal responsibility and "attributability" (Garcia 2014). Others contend, however, that automation could "make the use of force more precise and less harmful for civilians caught near it" (Anderson and Waxman 2013). Regardless, such weapons push arms control into unchartered territory, in which established legal and normative principles may no longer provide a sufficient guide for international cooperation.

27.7 Conclusion

All of these weapons, and more, will challenge the politics and principles of arms control. New weapons may be framed as making war more humane or as violating long-established humanitarian principles. Yet, the more states use them, the more contentious negotiations may become. As usual, regulations must appeal to these states' wide-ranging security interests, legal commitments, and normative obligations. Where legal and normative standards less clearly transfer to new weapons, consensus may be more difficult to reach. Domestic pressures to encourage cooperation, moreover, will struggle where normative consensus is unclear and domestic actors are weak.

A more fundamental question is whether a formal treaty approach can keep up with the growing list of actors, technological developments, and challenges to international institutions. Future research can inform both scholarly understandings of and practical thinking about how to generate cooperation and compliance through a variety of formal and informal arrangements, especially as a means to advance arms control amidst political deadlock. Yet even at its best, arms control has limits in curbing the brutality of war. States and armed groups go back to basics when they lack access to weapons, building makeshift weapons and explosives from everyday parts. Arms control can seek to control the means violence, but it cannot cure it.

Notes

1. See Schelling and Halperin (1961); Bull (1965).
2. Most states have not implemented formal measures to comply with Article 36 of Additional Protocol I (1977) to the Geneva Conventions (Daoust et al. 2002).
3. In the realm of war, these changing sentiments originated with ICRC founder Henry Dunant's advocacy after witnessing the aftermath of the 1859 Battle of Solferino.
4. The other three address discharging explosives and projectiles from hot air balloons "or by other new methods of a similar nature," expanding bullets, and submarine contact mines.
5. Production and stockpiling prohibitions came with the Biological Weapons Convention (1972) and the Chemical Weapons Convention (1993).
6. Jacobson (1984), Buckley (1993), and Vagts (2000) outline the debate.
7. In a rare non-nuclear initiative, the United States opened the Conventional Arms Transfer Talks with the Soviet Union over arms export limitations in 1977. They fell apart in 1978. The Treaty on Conventional Armed Forces in Europe (1990) places quantitative limitations on five categories of conventional weapons.
8. Switzerland and Sweden led discussions in ICRC meetings on five categories of conventional weapons but were opposed by larger powers. The 1977 Additional Protocol has no weapons prohibitions, and the original protocols to the 1980 Convention on Certain Conventional Weapons (CCW) restrict but do not ban the use of anti-personnel landmines and napalm and other incendiary weapons. See Baxter (1977).
9. For a catalogue of nuclear arms control agreements, see Woolf et al. (2016).
10. On why non-nuclear states sign the NPT, see Way and Sasikumar (2004); Erickson and Way (2011).
11. For example, Sagan (1996/1997); Dai (2007); Rublee (2009).
12. For reviews of literature on the causes of nuclear proliferation, see Sagan (2011) and Bell (2016).
13. Members voted to extend the NPT indefinitely in 1995. Belarus, Kazakhstan, South Africa, and Ukraine voluntarily gave up their nuclear weapons in the early 1990s. Other post-1991 proliferation cases have met with mixed international attention and mixed success (i.e. India, Iran, Iraq, Libya, North Korea, and Pakistan).
14. The Judge Advocate General of the US Army ruled in 1988 that anti-personnel lasers would not create superfluous injury or unnecessary suffering. The United States and the

Soviet Union agreed to bilateral regulations on BLW use in peacetime in 1989, but several subsequent incidents were reported (Morton 1998: 697).

15. For historical overviews, see Garcia (2011); Bromley et al. (2012); Erickson (2015).
16. Narang (2014) discusses regional nuclear postures.
17. Space-based, hypersonic, and non-lethal weapons, as well as nanotechnologies, modular weapons, and new kinds of missiles, guns, and bullets may also soon belong on the list.

References

Adler, Emanuel. 1992. The Emergence of Cooperation: National Epistemic Communities and the International Evolution of the Idea of Nuclear Arms Control. *International Organization*, 46(1): 101–45.

Anderson, Kenneth and Matthew C. Waxman. 2013. *Law and Ethics for Autonomous Weapon Systems: Why a Ban Won't Work and How the Laws of War Can*. Stanford, CA: Hoover Institution.

Baxter, R. R. 1977. Conventional Weapons under Legal Prohibitions. *International Security*, 1(3): 42–61.

Bell, Mark S. 2016. Examining Explanations for Nuclear Proliferation. *International Studies Quarterly*, 60(3): 520–9.

Bergen, Peter L. and Daniel Rothenberg (eds.). 2014. *Drone Wars: Transforming Conflict, Law, and Policy*. New York: Cambridge University Press.

Betts, Richard K. 1992. Systems for Peace or Causes of War? Collective Security, Arms Control, and the New Europe. *International Security*, 17(1): 5–43.

Betts, Richard K. 1999. Universal Deterrence or Conceptual Collapse? Liberal Pessimism and Utopian Realism. In Victor A. Utgoff (ed.), *The Coming Crisis: Nuclear Proliferation, US Interests, and World Order*, pp. 51–85. Cambridge, MA: MIT Press.

Bower, Adam. 2017. *Norms without the Great Powers: International Law and Changing Social Standards in World Politics*. Oxford: Oxford University Press.

Bromley, Mark, Neil Cooper, and Paul Holtom. 2012. The UN Arms Trade Treaty: Arms Export Controls, the Human Security Agenda, and the Lessons of History. *International Affairs*, 88(5): 1029–48.

Buchan, Russell and Nicholas Tsagourias (eds.). 2012. Cyber War and International Law [Special Issue]. *Journal of Conflict and Security Law*, 17(2): 183–297.

Buckely, Thomas H. 1993. *The Washington Naval Limitation System 1921–1939*. In Richard Dean Burns (ed.), *Encyclopedia of Arms Control and Disarmament*, pp. 639–56. New York: Charles Scribner's Sons.

Bull, Hedley. 1965. *The Control of the Arms Race*, 2nd edn. New York: Frederick A. Praeger.

Bunn, Matthew, Martin B. Malin, Nickolas Roth, and William H. Tobey. 2016. *Preventing Nuclear Terrorism: Continuous Improvement or Dangerous Decline*. Cambridge, MA: Harvard Kennedy School.

Carnahan, Burrus M. and Marjorie Robertson. 1996. The Protocol on "Blinding Laser Weapons": A New Direction for International Humanitarian Law. *American Journal of International Law*, 90(3): 484–90.

Dai, Xinyuan. 2007. *International Institutions and National Policies*. New York: Cambridge University Press.

Daoust, Isabelle, Robin Coupland, and Rikke Ishoey. 2002. New Wars, New Weapons? The Obligation of State to Assess the Legality of Means and Methods of Warfare. *International Review of the Red Cross*, 84(846): 345–63.

Erickson, Jennifer L. 2015. *Dangerous Trade: Arms Exports, Human Rights, and International Reputation*. New York: Columbia University Press.

Erickson, Jennifer L. and Christopher R. Way. 2011. Membership Has Its Privileges: Conventional Arms and Influence within the Nuclear Non-Proliferation Treaty. In Robert Rauchhaus, Matthew Kroenig, and Erik Gartzke (eds.), *Causes and Consequences of Nuclear Proliferation*. New York: Routledge.

Evangelista, Matthew. 1999. *Unarmed Forces: The Transnational Movement to End the Cold War*. Ithaca, NY: Cornell University Press.

Fuhrmann, Matthew and Yonatan Lupu. 2016. Do Arms Control Treaties Work? Assessing the Effectiveness of the Nuclear Nonproliferation Treaty. *International Studies Quarterly*, 60(3): 530–9.

Garcia, Denise. 2011. *Disarmament Diplomacy and Human Security: Regimes, Norms and Moral Progress in International Relations*. New York: Routledge.

Garcia, Denise. 2014. Killer Robots: Why the US Should Lead the Ban. *Global Policy Journal. Available at:* http://www.globalpolicyjournal.com/blog/15/08/2014/killer-robots-why-us-should-lead-ban accessed June 29, 2016.

Glaser, Charles L. 1994/95. Realists as Optimists: Cooperation as Self-Help. *International Security*, 19(3): 50–90.

Gleditsch, Kristian Skrede, Simon Hug, Livia Isabella Schubiger, and Julian Wucherpfennig. 2016. International Conventions and Nonstate Actors: Selection, Signaling, and Reputation Effects. *Journal of Conflict Resolution*: 1–35. Doi: https://doi.org/10.1177/0022002716650924

Goldblat, Jozef. 2002. *Arms Control: The New Guide to Negotiations and Agreements*. London: Sage.

Gray, Colin S. 1992. *House of Cards: Why Arms Control Must Fail*. Ithaca, NY: Cornell University Press.

Holquist, Peter. 2004. *The Russian Empire as a "Civilized State": International Law as Principle and Practice in Imperial Russia, 1874–1878*. Washington, DC: National Council for Eurasian and East European Research.

Hymans, Jacques E.C. 2006. *The Psychology of Nuclear Proliferation: Identity, Emotions, and Foreign Policy*. New York: Cambridge University Press.

Jacobson, Harold K. 1984. The Crisis in Arms Control. *Michigan Law Review*, 82(5/6): 1588–1603.

Jervis, Robert. 1989. *The Meaning of the Nuclear Revolution*. Ithaca, NY: Cornell University Press.

Kaufman, Robert G. 1992. The United States and Naval Arms Control between the Two World Wars: Implications for Contemporary and Future Arms Control. *Millennium* 21(1): 29–52.

Knopf, Jeffrey W. 1998. *Domestic Society and International Cooperation: The Impact of Protest on US Arms Control Policy*. New York: Cambridge University Press.

Krepon, Michael. 1989. Has Arms Control Worked? *Bulletin of the Atomic Scientists*, (May): 27–8.

Kroenig, Matthew. 2010. *Exporting the Bomb: Technology Transfer and the Spread of Nuclear Weapons*. Ithaca, NY: Cornell University Press.

Legro, Jeffrey W. 1996. Culture and Preferences in the International Cooperation Two-Step. *American Political Science Review*, 90(1): 118–37.

Mathews, Robert J. and Timothy L. S. McCormack. 1999. The Influence of Humanitarian Principles in the Negotiation of Arms Control Treaties. *International Review of the Red Cross*, No. 834. *Available at:* https://www.icrc.org/eng/resources/documents/misc/57jpty.htm accessed May 31, 2016.

Miller, Nicholas L. 2014. The Secret Success of Nonproliferation Sanctions. *International Organization*, 68(4): 913–44.

Monteiro, Nuno P. and Alexandre Debs. 2014. The Strategic Logic of Nuclear Proliferation. *International Security*, 39(2): 7–51.

Morton, Jeffrey S. 1998. The Legal Status of Laser Weapons that Blind. *Journal of Peace Research*, 35(6): 697–705.

Narang, Vipin. 2014. *Nuclear Strategy in the Modern Era: Regional Powers and International Conflict*. Princeton, NJ: Princeton University Press.

Paul, T. V. 2008. *The Tradition of Non-Use of Nuclear Weapons*. Stanford, CA: Stanford University Press.

Petrova, Margarita Hristoforova. 2007. Leadership Competition and the Creation of Norms: A Cross-National Study of Weapons Restrictions. PhD dissertation, Cornell University.

Potter, William C. 2010. The NPT and the Source of Nuclear Restraint. *Daedalus*, 139(1): 68–81.

Press, Daryl G., Scott D. Sagan, and Benjamin A. Valentino. 2013. Atomic Aversion: Experimental Evidence on Taboos, Traditions, and the Non-Use of Nuclear Weapons. *American Political Science Review*, 107(1): 188–206.

Price, Richard M. 1997. *The Chemical Weapons Taboo*. Ithaca, NY: Cornell University Press.

Price, Richard M. 1998. Reversing the Gun Sights: Transnational Civil Society Targets Land Mines. *International Organization*, 52(3): 613–44.

Rublee, Maria Rost. 2009. *Nonproliferation Norms: Why States Choose Nuclear Restraint*. Athens, GA: University of Georgia Press.

Rutherford, Ken. 2000. The Evolving Arms Control Agenda: Implications of the Role of NGOs in Banning Antipersonnel Landmines. *World Politics*, 53(1): 74–114.

Sagan, Scott D. 1996/97. Why Do States Build Nuclear Weapons?: Three Models in Search of a Bomb. *International Security*, 21(3): 54–86.

Sagan, Scott D. 2011. The Causes of Nuclear Weapons Proliferation. *Annual Review of Political Science*, 14: 225–44.

Sagan, Scott D. and Kenneth N. Waltz. 2003. *The Spread of Nuclear Weapons: A Debate Renewed*. New York: W.W. Norton & Company.

Schelling, Thomas C. and Morton H. Halperin. 1961. *Strategy and Arms Control*. New York: The Twentieth Century Fund.

Solingen, Etel. 1994. The Political Economy of Nuclear Restraint. *International Security*, 19(2): 126–69.

Solingen, Etel. 2007. *Nuclear Logics: Contrasting Paths in East Asia and the Middle East*. Princeton, NJ: Princeton University Press.

Stavrianakis, Anna. 2016. Legitimising Liberal Militarism: Politics, Law and War in the Arms Trade Treaty. *Third World Quarterly*, 37(5): 840–65.

Tannenwald, Nina. 2007. *The Nuclear Taboo: The United States and the Non-Use of Nuclear Weapons since 1945*. New York: Cambridge University Press.

Vagts, Detlev F. 2000. The Hague Conventions and Arms Control. *American Journal of International Law*, 94(1): 31–41.

Van Courtland Moon, John Ellis. 1984. Chemical Weapons and Deterrence: The World War II Experience. *International Security*, 8(4): 3–35.

Way, Christopher and Karthika Sasikumar. 2004. Leaders and Laggards: When and Why Do Countries Sign the NPT. REGIS Working Paper No. 16. Montreal: University of Montreal/ McGill University.

Whitlark, Rachel Elizabeth. 2017. Nuclear Beliefs: A Leader-focused Theory of Counter-Proliferation. *Security Studies*, 26(4): 545–74.

Woolf, Amy F., Paul K. Kerr, and Mary Beth D. Nikitin. 2016. *Arms Controls and Nonproliferation: A Catalog of Treaties and Agreements*. CRS Report. Washington, DC: Congressional Research Service.

CHAPTER 28

NATIONALISM AND INTERNATIONAL SECURITY

BRENDAN O'LEARY AND NICHOLAS SAMBANIS

28.1 Introduction

Nationalism, the most potent principle of political legitimacy in most of the modern world, is the doctrine that nations have the right of self-determination; that is, the right freely to choose their political institutions, and to govern themselves. In a nation state, the governors must be co-national with the governed; in a multinational state, political and territorial institutions must reflect the equality of the constituent peoples or partners (Gellner 1983; O'Leary 1998; Hechter 2001). Nationalists therefore generally oppose empires, in which one nation typically dominates and exploits other nations—making exceptions when the dominating nation is their own. They are also generally skeptical of cosmopolitan doctrines that offer rival theocratic or secular accounts of political legitimacy, though nationalists may be internationalists and agree with particular "international" conventions, for example on universal human rights, or accept and practice certain universal political dispositions, for example conservatism, liberalism, or socialism. Nationalists are, in principle, democratic—the governors should derive their legitimacy from the consent of the governed—but generally argue that the nation is the basis of the demos in a democracy. Most nationalists would prefer their own independent state. While nationalists may regard multinational states as feasible, they also regard them as brittle, as do realists (see e.g. Mearsheimer 2001: 297).

Nationalism does not generate conflict in a deterministic way. The potential for conflict is inherent in the use of nationalism to cultivate the willingness to die for co-nationals; and nationalism often underlies exclusivist policies toward non-co-nationals, including in economic protectionism, or discrimination. While nationalism is a political doctrine of collective self-government, it may veer toward chauvinism and xenophobia—respectively, an excessive partiality and bias toward one's own nation, and hostility toward and fear of foreigners. Yet, in principle, nationalists can be internationalists who recognize the rights of other nations, and respect their collective symbols, and homelands. The context of international competition is what determines whether nationalism fuels interstate conflict. In domestic politics, shared nationalism, or a shared complementary national identity, might reduce the risk of internal violence between ethnic, religious, or other communities by inducing stronger identification with the nation and generating an aversion to actions, including violence, that destroy the nation's resources. However, where competition between the nation and its rivals is perceived as zero-sum, nationalism can fuel conflict.

28.2 Concepts and Definitions

Defining the nation presupposed by nationalism raises some difficulties. The nation is frequently conflated with related but not identical concepts, notably the state and the ethnic group. According to some, nations exist only in our imaginations or as "constructions." Precedence and causality are unclear, namely, do nations cause or precede nationalism, or is it the other way around?

Nations certainly vary in their implicit or explicit rules of membership, notably in the ease with which they accept new members; and co-nationals frequently disagree internally over whom should be counted as a co-national. When nations control states of their own, they decide who is to count as a co-national through their ability to define citizenship laws; when they do not they may define their co-nationals through one of three standard means: shared descent, that is, a narrow definition of ethnicity; shared culture, a broad definition of ethnicity, usually tapping a shared language or religion or both; or shared history, for example oppression at the hands of a foreign empire. Civic nationalism is more voluntarist, liberal, inclusionary, and open than ethnic nationalism, but both varieties have rules for adopting or co-opting members into their nation.

The late Anthony Smith defined the nation "as a named human community occupying a homeland, and having common myths and a shared history, a common public culture, a single economy and common rights and duties for all members" (2001: 13). This conception overlaps with common components in definitions of a state—a demarcated territory, citizens with common rights, and a common public culture. It also contains elements of national consciousness—the desire among members of an historically differentiated ethnic group to govern themselves. In that sense, nationalism precedes the nation because it is the desire for self-government that explains why some communities, many of them poly-ethnic (e.g. India), will perceive themselves as nations. Common culture, belief in shared ancestral origins, a shared economy, and geographic contiguity are certainly not sufficient to define a nation. If they were, then every territorially defined ethnic group, such as the Appalachian Hill People or the Amish in Western Pennsylvania, would be considered nations. Sufficient members of putative nations have to believe that the nation should be self-governing; and, the self-governing group can be a fusion of ethnic groups. Ernest Renan (1882) famously claimed that the nation was "a daily plebiscite," by which he meant a constantly remade political community that required active will and consent for its common public culture to endure.

Karl Deutsch (1966) and Ernest Gellner (1983) both saw a common high culture (in a modernized language) as the major defining attribute of modern nations—nationalists created this high culture according to Gellner, whereas for Deutsch nations emerged from networks of increasingly dense social communications, replacing smaller units of social life. Both agreed that nationalism flowed from modernization. Nationalism is what legitimizes state authority in a territory governed by the nation; it is also what delegitimizes authority where the nation does not control the state. That lack of legitimacy is at the core of the relationship between nationalism and violence, both domestically and internationally.

28.3 The Causes of Nationalism and of Nationalist Conflict

There are three foundational approaches to explaining the genealogy of nationalism: the idealist and diffusionist account developed in the writings of Elie Kedourie (2000); the materialist, modernist, and functionalist account exemplified in the works of Gellner (1983); and the ethno-symbolic approach developed by Anthony Smith and his collaborators (1986). These approaches differ in important respects, but share a view of nationalism and nations as social constructions. Whether the cultural antecedents of nations are invented or are pre-existing and rediscovered by nationalists, the common theme in all three approaches is that nationalism is seen as the product of agency and the political salience of the nation as a social identity varies with history. The stronger the salience of nationalism, the more likely it will be a source of war. Kedourie reminds us that "The First World War broke out over a national question, the South Slav question," and that another national question, that of the German minorities in the new nation states, "occasioned the outbreak of the Second World War." Kedourie challenges us to consider whether nation states have improved upon the empires they replaced as vehicles of political freedom, peace, and prosperity (2000: 129, 138–9). Gellner's account is more hopeful. It suggests that decolonization has been beneficial for the decolonized, and that once the world is through the transition from *agraria* to *industria* then the worst of nationalist-induced conflicts may be left behind. He also saw some meritorious role for international institutions, such as the United Nations, in managing nationalist conflicts. The ethno-symbolic approach, with its emphases upon the non-rational, the emotional, and the passions, offers less clear guidance to the future pattern of International Relations.

A crucial question in exploring the relationship between nationalism and conflict is whether the salience of nationalism is variable across elites and masses. If elites are able to use and abuse the identities and interests of the masses, that suggests that nationalism may be exploited both for domestic and international purposes (e.g. Snyder 2000). General "diversionary theory" suggests that nationalism can divert the attention of the masses away from domestic inequality, or from other true sources of their discontents, and thereby implies that nationalism may intensify in times of higher inequality (Posen 1993a: 88–9; Solt 2011). What underlies the "diversionary theory of war" is the assumption that policy elites can manipulate the shared tendency toward in-group bias and out-group prejudice among the population. An analogous literature on ethnic entrepreneurs in comparative politics seeks to explain identity formation and change as a process often exploited by elites who can mobilize groups or even construct new ethnic identities by manipulating affinities among members of an in-group and latent fears toward members of an out-group (Brass 1997; Laitin 1998; De Figueiredo and Weingast 1999).

The diversionary war perspective privileges domestic political-economy explanations for the external behavior of leaders and dismisses realists' concern with power distribution in the world system. While it is acknowledged in mainstream IR that nationalism has provided motives for major wars in history, cases such as Bismarck's wars against Denmark (1864), Austria (1866), and France (1871–71), are seen as anomalous exceptions that do not fit the dominant structural theories (Mearsheimer 2001: 288–97). Bridging this dominant IR perspective with domestic politics theories of nationalist conflict as emanating from inter-ethnic competition over resources is a view that flips diversionary war theory on its head: since nationalism can unify the nation and make it more powerful, *Realpolitik* competition among states may push some leaders to invest in strengthening national identification in their countries so that they can compete more effectively in the international arena (Sambanis et al. 2015). Nationalism is still used instrumentally by elites to fuel interstate conflict, but the aim is to increase the state's status and power in world politics, not to deflect attention from domestic problems of elites, a view that may be traced back at least to Max Weber.

Empirical evidence for diversionary war theories and strategic uses of nationalism is mixed and available observational data have insurmountable limitations (only the cases that can be reasonably expected to produce the desired outcome are observed). The mechanism underlying the "rally-around-the-flag" effect could be studied further using experimental methods; for example, in a recent study, Feinstein (2016) finds that the "rally-around-the-flag" effect in the United States becomes possible because of a successful nationalist framing of conflict, which increases perceived distance between the American nation and its enemies. That distance is thought to legitimize the leader's decision to go to war.

What, however, if elites themselves are as much constrained by their national identities as the masses? Both Gellnerian-materialist and ethno-symbolic accounts of identities and interests give us little reason to believe that elites will be more cosmopolitan, post-national, or simply less nationalist than the masses: after all they come from the same culture and have been through similar educational experiences. If so, those in charge of foreign or security policies will feel the same distance toward other nations and their preferences will be closer to their fellow citizens. Indirect evidence may be furnished from studies of the European Union, alleged by some to be the exemplary "post-national" polity. Eurobarometer survey and other data, even before the crisis of the Eurozone, suggested little shift from primary national loyalty and identifications among citizens of member states to the institutions of the European Union. It is true that the upper-class beneficiaries of European integration have been more consistently pro-European, and more likely to express some dual identifications than those in the lower classes, but few among the elites have replaced their national with a European identity (Fligstein 2008; Checkel and Katzenstein 2009). Not surprisingly therefore both inter-governmental and confederal explanations of the European Union appear to account well for its policy making, better than theories that would credit them with the ability to transcend their historic national identities *and* to manipulate those of their respective masses in a novel direction (Moravscik 1998; Majone 2005). If European elites, in historically favorable circumstances, have been unable, to date, to consolidate post-national integration by stealth that suggests significant limits to elites' abilities to transcend their national identities and to take their mass publics with them. The bleak may conclude that the EU requires a war to fuse its peoples into a significantly shared identity.

Macro-level theories of nationalist conflict or its opposite—the formation of supra-national institutions such as the EU—would benefit by integrating insights from micro-level research on altruism. Social psychologists have highlighted the innate human tendencies toward the formation of in-group bias and out-group prejudice, even on the basis of very "thin" and artificially induced differences in groups (Tajfel 1981). Such apparently universal dispositions provide some basis for primordialist accounts of the formation of strong collective identities that individuals experience as normal; and, ironically, such primordialist premises may be necessary to account for the exploitability of group-sentiments by manipulative political elites. Less persuasive are the efforts of rational choice theorists to provide exclusively utilitarian and methodologically individualist accounts of nationalist attitudes and behavior. Hechter (1987, 2001), for example, sees nationalism as a form of mobilization for collective action to supply excludable public goods, in which free-riding is discouraged through in-group policing and sanctioning, whereas Laitin (2007) argues that convergence on a national language may be best explained through an *n*-person coordination game, in which a tipping point will lead to a cascade of "choices" among ambitious families to select a particular language of schooling for their children. These examples, of ingenious efforts to supply rational choice micro-foundations for nationalist phenomena, perhaps simply serve the function of demonstrating limits to rationalist explanations in this field. After all, rational choice and instrumentalist perspectives have to depend on the existence of identities and affinities that can explain how leaders can mobilize a population. They thereby re-create the Gellner–Smith debate at a micro-level. If nationalism is necessary for the nation to form then the role of elites will be paramount in persuading a group (usually ethnic, narrowly or widely defined) to imagine or construct itself as a nation. But for that persuasion to be successful the group's members must already define themselves through attributes that distinguish them from other groups, which suggests some prior solidarity. Instrumental elites have to tap into pre-existing sources of solidarity to mobilize support.

An unresolved and likely unproductive debate about the causes and consequences of nationalism centers on whether national (and ethnic) identities are permanent or fluid, durable or malleable, and so on (see e.g. Eller and Coughlan 1993; Chandra 2012). Only an imaginary strawperson holds that some group somewhere has retained the same collective identity since the Stone Age. Equally only the hyper-constructivist believes that national identities can melt overnight. So the real question is to what extent, once formed, national identities are malleable, and with what repercussions for potential conflict, and conflict management. The entrenchment of the modern French national identity—through schooling, military service, and coercive linguistic assimilation—took at least six decades (Weber 1976), and it is not obvious how it could be dissolved now without the prolonged destruction of the French state through war. What is at stake in these discussions, arguably, is the malleability of the identifications of potentially secessionist national minorities. Rather than suggesting that all national identities are equally rapidly bio-degradable, or amenable to economic or multicultural therapy, it seems wiser to note that complementary regional and encompassing national identities *may* sometimes be developed within a polity (Stepan et al. 2011). For example, Bengalis may have come to regard themselves as a nation within the "state-nation" of India because they have not been obliged to prefer one identity to the other, even though Bengali nationalism arguably preceded Indian nationalism. Sometimes, however, identities are antagonistic rather than complementary, and engineering shifts toward complementary identities may be exceedingly difficult. While there may be no consensus on the nature of national identities, their degree of malleability, or their propensities to induce domestic or international conflict, there is agreement that the salience of nationalist sentiments may change over time (there are, after all, satisfied and unsatisfied nationalisms, which respectively have or do not have congruent polities). Equally there is some consensus that nationalism can only generate conflict and insecurity under some conditions, to which we return in Section 28.5.

28.4 Measuring Nationalism

The preceding discussion suggests that nationalism is hard to measure in a way that facilitates cross-country comparisons over time. In empirical research, the usual approach to testing hypotheses about the impact of nationalism on conflict is to use static demographic measures of ethno-linguistic fractionalization (ELF) to measure the propensity of countries toward conflict. Everything we have said thus far should advise against the soundness of that approach and inferences drawn from null findings on the relationship between ELF and armed conflict have no well-founded bearing on theories of nationalist violence.

Survey-based measures (e.g. Afro-barometer; World Values Survey) of the intensity of national identification are better than static country-level indicator measures, but they, too, have limitations as surveys are usually cross-sections rather than panel-structured, so they do not provide a perspective on the fluctuating salience of national identification. Moreover, in some countries, such as those with active ethnic civil wars where objective conditions would indicate low degrees of nationalism, survey measures of national identification still produce high readings, which suggests that the questions themselves do not capture what we understand by the term "identification." For example, in Iraq during the height of the sectarian war in 2006–08, 97 percent of respondents in the World Values Survey stated that they were "very proud" (83 percent) or "quite proud" (14 percent) of their country and nationality. Is that a reliable measure of national identification if by "identification" we understand caring about the nation and acting in ways that preserve its resources and international status? Even if only a small fraction of the Iraqi population was responsible for the violence, these survey results are likely due to sampling problems, which under-report views from the most violent areas and the survey question itself is inferior to true behavioral measures of social identification.

Recognizing the deficiencies of static measures of ethnic difference as proxies for nationalism, scholars have moved to combine demographic data on ethnic difference with information about the political context that characterizes inter-ethnic relations. Recent advances include data on the exclusion of ethnic groups from power (Wimmer et al. 2009) as well as Duclos et al.'s (2004) index of ethnic polarization that combines data on group size with information about ideological distance between the groups. The benefits of these approaches are clear, as they treat identities as politically-sensitive variables. Their limitation is that the measure itself can be endogenous to the conflict process that it seeks to explain.

28.5 The Consequences of Nationalism for Security

The necessary conditions for nationalism to be a potential source of domestic and international conflict are straightforward: a plurality of actual or potential nations which reject imperialist or cosmopolitan principles of legitimacy; nations that want a state with a defined territory of their own, or a political unit within a federal or confederal polity, and find these demands rejected; and nations with incompatible claims to statehood, sovereignty, and the allocation of territory, and which, by implication, reject power-sharing compromises.

28.5.1 Nationalism as a Driver of Domestic Conflict

Nationalist mobilization that leads to internal armed conflict is rare. Gellner calculated that judging by potential cultural (linguistic, religious, or ethnic) worldwide differentiations, there are several thousand potential nations, but the number of even partially mobilized nations has always been much smaller. The salience of nationalism has sometimes been latent rather than manifest because certain regimes successfully control subordinated nations. Empires in agro-literate polities, and European empires in Asia and Africa until the 1940s, were generally adept at incorporating potential nationalist elites (through allowing them to be indirect rulers (Hechter 2013)) and/or in disorganizing actual or potential nationalists through repression. And even when nationalism can generate demand for violent mobilization, supply-side constraints can impede the organization of nationalist conflict.

Nevertheless, the pattern of global regime change over two centuries has been striking. Whereas a dozen empires dominated much of the world's surface in 1900, by 2000 there were nearly 200 member states of the United Nations (O'Leary et al. 2001: Figs 1.1 and 1.2). Empires gave way to the world of professed nation states. The British, Spanish, and Portuguese empires were largely pushed out of the Americas between the 1770s and 1820s. The Habsburgs collapsed in central Europe in the First World War, when Germany also lost its African colonies. The Ottomans, previously weakened by the secession of Christian states in the Balkans, and by British control of Egypt and Sudan, were replaced by a Turkish nation state in Anatolia. In the Middle East and North Africa, French, British, and Italian empires did not last much beyond the Second World War. The termination of European empires was sometimes occasioned by nationalist insurrections, sometimes by peaceful decolonization movements, sometimes by both; and there were also prudent down-sizing decolonizations (not all nationalists had to fight or struggle vigorously for their freedom). More recently, the Soviet Empire, reconstructed by Lenin, Trotsky, and Stalin on the ruins of that of the Czars, dissolved into its constituent 15 republics, led by the Russian Federation. In the long-run, neither old-style imperialism nor Marxist-Leninist multinational pseudo-federations withstood their respective counter-nationalist movements. Indeed, the European and Russian empires arguably incubated many novel nation states that lack cultural homogeneity.

Yet despite the demise of these empires, many of today's states, new or old, nevertheless are seen as imperial or neo-colonial systems by some of their minority nationalities and ethnic groups, who often had no effective participation in the construction of their states. In many states, whether democratic, authoritarian or hybrid, the *Staats Volk* (the people who control the state) systematically dominates, excludes, and marginalizes ethnic groups or national minorities not perceived to be part of the official nation, or who are deemed to be potential threats to the regime's territorial integrity (traitors, collaborators, or fifth-columnists). Myanmar, a state dominated by Burman Buddhists, is an exemplary instance. Its regime has some 17 cease-fires with rebel groups and resolutely excludes the Muslim Rohingya from citizenship, and it has been indifferent toward or complicit in regular pogroms against the Rohingya on the grounds that they are illegal Bangladeshi immigrants (Smith 2007). Similarly, in many African states, for example Côte d'Ivoire, there are serious disputes over who rightfully has citizenship, sometimes stemming from previously more porous borders that led to uncertified migrations.

International Relations (IR) scholars have systematically shown in recent global datasets that states which systematically exclude one or more ethnic groups from political power are at greater risk of ethno-nationalist violence (Wimmer et al. 2009; Cederman et al. 2013). Three major patterns likely to trigger armed rebellions have been identified: the systematic exclusion of a group, for example the Kurds in Turkey; the experience of recent status reversals, for example formerly dominant minorities, such as Sunni Arabs in contemporary Iraq, who resent the transformation of their place within the state; and contests among former governmental partners, that is, the exclusion of a former ally in a coalition. The micro-foundations of these findings are sensible: exclusion from power matters politically to a group's members, especially when power has been previously possessed or shared. These patterns and explanations are consistent with powerful comparative studies of ethnic violence in Eastern Europe that employ political psychology to address configurations of inter-group violence driven by fear, hatred, resentment, or rage (Petersen 2002). Each of the three patterns driving violence—exclusion, reactions to status reversal, and combat among ex-allies—often has international security dimensions. The excluded may be regarded as potential irredentist targets of a neighboring state (e.g. Somalis in Ethiopia); status reversals may be caused by foreign invasions and occupations (e.g. the loss of dominance by Sunni Arabs in Iraq); and the break-up of domestic coalitions may be encouraged by outside powers (as has frequently occurred in the history of Lebanon).

Self-determination movements and secessionist conflicts are strongly driven by the perception that the group is not sufficiently represented in political decision making (Halperin et al. 1992). This perception results in greater polarization as exclusion increases the psychological distance between minority and majority populations (Sambanis et al. 2016). The greater that distance, the greater the "heterogeneity cost" that minorities would suffer by remaining part of a state that is controlled by a hostile majority. Autonomy or secession would reduce those costs, though it would generate others as the separatist group would now have to provide public goods while foregoing the economies of scale that benefited it when it was part of a larger state.

Given a demand for self-determination, conflict may result depending on the government's reaction. Governments may react in one of two ways to national or ethnic heterogeneity. They may seek to eliminate cultural differences or to manage them—and they may adopt different strategies toward different groups (O'Leary and McGarry 2012; Mylonas 2013). The most extreme forms of difference elimination include genocide and ethnic expulsions, which have typically occurred under the cover of war. Debates over their etiologies cannot be evaluated here, but it is common to implicate the nation state, nationalism, and its alleged cultural essentialism in the purification drives that typify these exterminationist policies (Semelin 2007). Others, however, seek to apply the rationalist logic of "security dilemmas" to account for expulsions (Posen 1993b). Genocide and ethnic expulsions have obvious troubling implications for international peace and security, and are widely recognized as justifications for humanitarian interventions.

The second form of difference elimination practiced within contemporary nation states is less extreme, but it may also generate conflict. This includes policies of *assimilation*, which promote either acculturation into the dominant group or inter-group fusion, or of *integration*, which promote equal citizenship within a common public culture while allowing for the preservation of private cultural differences. But when minorities reject such policies, or when they are applied unilaterally and coercively, conflict, including armed conflict, is likely, and such conflict has the potential to spill over across borders, especially if there is a kin-state or a kin-group to the targeted group in an adjacent country. Migratory and demographic stocks and flows may also affect the dispositions of both majorities and minorities toward assimilation and integration. Perceptions that new waves of migrants are rapidly changing the demographic composition of a state may lead to calls for increased controls and securitization at borders, the mass deportation of illegal migrants, and for the coercive assimilation of recent arrivals. Even the internal migration of citizens within the same state may generate tensions if demographic balances in particular perceived homelands change rapidly; such changes often give rise to "sons of the soil" movements (Weiner 1978).

Difference elimination can also be imposed through partition, that is, deliberately territorially separating groups through creating a fresh border to bring conflict to an end. This policy, however defined, has a much worse track-record than its partisans suggest (O'Leary 2007, 2011; Sambanis 2000). In particular, a recurrence of war (both civil and interstate) frequently follows partitions, and implementing partitions may lead to more death and mass flight than occurred before (as governments and militias create "facts on the ground"). Partitions, in short, may create more security dilemmas than they resolve.

Governments, by contrast, may seek to manage rather than eliminate national, cultural, ethnic, linguistic, or religious differences among their citizens and groups. When they adopt hierarchical control systems they typically seek to disorganize, co-opt, and repress the targeted minorities, and to sustain the unity of the dominant *Staats Volk* (Lustick 1979). These policies that overtly "securitize" minorities are highly likely to generate intermittent armed rebellion unless the controllers prove continuously adept at organizing quiescence. There are, however, benign ways in which governments may seek to manage national and ethnic differences, notably through forms of power sharing and arbitration, to which we shall turn in the concluding section.

28.5.2 Nationalism as a Driver of Interstate Conflict

If we define wars as events with more than 1,000 battle deaths in a given year, one estimate suggests that one-fifth of the wars between the Congress of Vienna and the Treaty of Versailles were conducted in the name of national liberation or ethnic autonomy; almost half of the wars conducted between the Versailles Treaty and the opening of the twenty-first century were nationalist or ethno-national; and no less than three-quarters of the wars since the collapse of the Soviet Union have been ethno-national (Wimmer and Min 2006). These estimates combine civil and interstate wars.

Plainly, national and ethnic groups and conflicts often transcend borders. What is the association between ethnic polarization and conflict in a widened strategic environment? Two obvious hypotheses have been explored (Forsberg 2008). First, when a state experiences ethnic conflict, neighboring states that are ethnically polarized may be more likely to experience ethnic armed conflict. In a global dataset (1989–2005) Forsberg found that polarized states are associated with an increased likelihood of contagion. Second, when a group involved in ethnic conflict has a kinship tie to a group in a neighboring state, the latter group is likely to be inspired to challenge the government and end up in ethnic conflict. These findings demonstrate that kinship links make contagion more likely; but the level of ethnic polarization in the neighboring state does not condition this effect.

Indeed, an understudied but likely important explanation for ethno-nationalist civil war onset is external intervention. Data on interventions are only available for ongoing conflicts, but scholars have established that interventions prolong civil wars (Regan 2000). However, intervention—actual or expected—could also create the conditions for conflicts to escalate from non-violent to violent (Sambanis et al. 2016). Given a positive level of ethnic polarization (which incorporates ideological distance between the majority-controlled state and a minority seeking self-determination), intervention can make rebellion and war more feasible for the minority. Further, if secession is successful, resulting in the down-sizing of the territory and resources of an established state, more conflicts could develop through a number of pathways. Specifically, the now diminished international power and status of the state would reduce national identification among other ethnic or other social groups in the country, generating more challenges to central authority (Sambanis et al. 2016). Under such conditions, the state becomes more vulnerable to external attack, so the risk of interstate war increases; or, returning to the logic of diversionary war, leaders in the declining state might pursue a "gambling for resurrection" strategy by escalating interstate conflict to unify the rest of the nation via a rally-around-the-flag effect. That logic, however, depends upon the masses failing to attribute the causation of increased violence to their own leaders (see Kaufman 2001, 2015 for caustic critiques of these rationalist accounts). Incorporating nationalism in modified rational choice models allows war to occur without incomplete information, commitment problems or other inefficiencies; the symbolic and affective dimensions of nationalism make some wars worth fighting.

These perspectives on intervention and social identification suggest that nationalism as a cause of war is compatible with some theories of international relations. To date, the study of war in International Relations has been dominated by structural theories. War was seen as the outcome of power transition cycles (Organski and Kugler 1980), economic decline and hegemonic ascent (Gilpin 1981), the type of system polarity (Waltz 1979; Wohlforth 1999; Mearsheimer 2001), or military technology (Van Evera 1999). Structural perspectives were refined by theories emphasizing decision making under conditions of anarchy (Jervis 1974; Glaser 2010), but even theories that emphasize the role of social identities took those identities as the products of systemic-level variables (Wendt 1999). Refinements and challenges to these structural approaches came from so-called "second-image" theories that emphasize the role of domestic political institutions (e.g. democratic peace theory) in shaping governments' foreign policies. But the usual approach was to "black-box" domestic actors without considering where their preferences came from.

The new literature on nationalism shifts focus from the structural level to the determinants of actors' preferences and to the interaction between unit-level (individuals, leaders) and structure (power-competition under anarchy). Incorporating nationalism in theories of International Relations implies that state power becomes a concept grounded in the social psychology of individual affinities. Thus, certain predictions of structural theories are to be revised accordingly. For example, if higher national status is important in forging nationalist sentiment and mitigating domestic sources of conflict, then leaders will benefit from stronger national identification, which should inform their strategies in world politics. It follows that hegemonic conflict becomes more likely as it would be implausible for rising powers to acquiesce indefinitely to a subordinate position in the global hierarchy. So questions such as whether China will challenge American hegemony become more complex and pose the need to consider affective components of state strategy in addition to the material incentives and constraints that are usually modeled in rationalist theories.

Nationalism can be part of what explains an actor's "type" in a bargaining model where the outcome can affect countries' relative status or power. While modeling conventions want types to be exogenous factors in the model, realizing the power of social identification—including nationalism—in explaining preferences over outcomes forces us to shift our attention to new models that explore the interaction of the systemic and unit level in international relations (Sambanis et al. 2015). Many of the old debates on hegemonic stability, power transition, and interstate cooperation will have to be revisited as we allow for the power of social identities, especially nationalism, to shape the preferences of domestic actors in world politics.

28.6 Managing Nationalist Conflicts

Writing in 1992 Elie Kedourie believed that national self-determination was a principle of disorder in international life, that the UN system could not prevent Russia from dominating ex-Soviet space, that both the EU and the UN would prove impotent in the Balkans, and that the "perils of Balkanization" would not be "confined to the Balkans" (2000: xvi, xvii, xviii). His pessimism about the capacity of the UN system and other international and transnational efforts to calm and manage nationalist conflicts remains a continuing challenge, both intellectually and institutionally. It is evident that "democratic peace theory," if broadly correct, offers hope for sustained interstate war reduction, especially over national questions, provided that democratization spreads, and deepens.

But it is much less evidently true that democracy *per se* should be regarded as the solvent of all domestic nationalist conflicts. Democracies, in principle, widen access and inclusion, and thereby may address the key sources of armed rebellion. Constitutional reconstruction to achieve integration, through "nation-building" may be successful in particular localities, but is likely to be resisted by those who have already been mobilized into a different national identity or who have already experienced broken promises of integration, repression, or worse. Moreover, democracies, infamously, can be tyrannies of the majority (or of a coalition of groups against the excluded), and if externally imposed on troubled regimes they may be flatly rejected by key components of a population. Lastly, democratization itself may trigger nationalist conflict—partly because it raises the question of the definition of the demos, and who will have power under conditions of electoral competition; and partly because newly established democracies are more likely "to elect to fight" (Mansfield and Snyder 1995, 2005).

That said, however, democratic government that enables power sharing among the representatives of national and ethnic groups, whether transitional or permanent, may facilitate the regulation of nationalist and ethnic conflicts. A minimum goal of international organizations would be to encourage inclusive government, both through the establishment of individual and collective rights, and through the use of proportional representation electoral systems that enable minorities to elect their own parties, if that is what they wish, and which, *ceteris paribus*, make coalition governments more likely. Evidence-based policy advice also suggests that the early and generous grant of territorial autonomy to compact groups that seek it may forestall violent secessionism (Rezvani 2014; Cederman et al. 2015). Enabling territorial autonomy may allow secession to occur peacefully later if it is still demanded; or, depending on other factors, such as the degree of economic integration of the regions, it might forge bridges that ultimately strengthen national identity and make secession less desirable. Multinational states, especially multinational federations, have had a bad press, partly in response to the experience of Communist regimes, but they need not fail, especially if they can combine territorial self-government for the major nations in their own states with power-sharing arrangements within key federal institutions, notably in the executive, the legislature, the judiciary, and in security institutions (McGarry and O'Leary 2009). Canada, Belgium, India, Switzerland, and, more recently, South Africa and Indonesia suggest that federal power sharing has its merits. Not all multinational federations can be expected to succeed, however. Ethnic power sharing in the aftermath of Iraq's civil war failed because it was not properly implemented and resulted in unilateral efforts at re-centralization. Consociational modes of power sharing, within federal or other forms of territorial government, may also help calm ethnic conflicts. They perm four principles: cross-community executive power sharing, proportionality, autonomy, and veto rights, and they *may* work in deeply divided places, where there is significant demographic mixing, and where divisions are based on language, religion, ethnicity, or race (Lijphart 1977).

Power-sharing principles, consociational or con/federal, may keep multi-ethnic states together. They will do so, however, only if the constituent peoples are all net beneficiaries, and only if over time a collective overarching complementary identity is built, one which may become a genuinely shared national identity. Leaders will also need to invest in power-sharing institutions and their maintenance to deepen citizens and groups attachments to the polity. In world politics going forward, whether nationalism will lead to more conflict largely depends on whether liberal institutionalists are right that democratization and conflict prevention can temper dispositions toward global anarchy. While many were quick to (over-)predict the decline of ethnic conflict in the mid-1990s, and again in the early twenty-first century, ongoing regional wars, particularly in the Middle East and North Africa, suggest a return to the world described by realists—in which aspirant regional hegemons vie for dominance in multipolar conflicts. The same may be true in sub-Saharan Africa and East Asia. Ethno-nationalism may be quickened in some places by widespread rejection of some of the consequences of economic globalization. If such trends weaken international institutions, reducing their ability to intervene to settle conflicts before they escalate, or to calm them when they begin, then nationalism will be part of the resurgence of violent conflict across the world.

References

Anderson, Liam. 2013. *Federal Solutions to Ethnic Problems: Accommodating Diversity*. Abingdon: Routledge.

Brass, Paul R. 1997. *Theft of an Idol: Text and Context in the Representation of Collective Violence*. Princeton, NJ: Princeton University Press.

Cederman, Lars-Erik, Kristian Skrede Gleditsch, and Halvard Buhaug. 2013. *Inequality, Grievances and Civil War*. Cambridge: Cambridge University Press.

Cederman, Lars-Erik, Simon Hug, Andreas Schádel, and Julian Wucherpfenniig. 2015. Territorial Autonomy in the Shadow of Conflict: Too Little, Too Late? *American Political Science Review*, 109: 354–70.

Chandra, Kanchan. 2012. *Constructivist Theories of Ethnic Politics*. Oxford: Oxford University Press.

Checkel, Jeffrey T. and Peter J. Katzenstein (eds.). 2009. *European Identity*. Cambridge: Cambridge University Press.

De Figueiredo, Rui and Barry Weingast. 1999. The Rationality of Fear: Political Opportunism and Ethnic Conflict. In B. Walter and J. Snyder (eds.), *Civil Wars, Insecurity, and Intervention*, pp. 261–302. New York: Columbia University Press.

Deutsch, Karl. 1966. *Nationalism and Social Communication: An Inquiry into the Foundations of Nationality*. Cambridge, MA: MIT Press

Duclos, J. Y., Joan Esteban, and Debraj Ray. 2004. Polarization: Concepts, Measurement, Estimation. *Econometrica*, 72(6): 1737–72.

Eller, Jack David, and Reed Coughlan, M. 1993. The Poverty of Primordialism: The Demystification of Ethnic Attachments. *Ethnic and Racial Studies*, 16(2): 183–202.

Feinstein, Yuval. 2016. Rallying Around the President: When and Why do Americans Close Ranks Behind their Presidents During International Crisis and War? *Social Science History*, 40(2): 305–38.

Fligstein, Neil. 2008. *Euroclash: The EU, European Identity, and the Future of Europe*. Oxford: Oxford University Press.
Forsberg, E. 2008. Polarization and Ethnic Conflict in a Widened Strategic Setting. *Journal of Peace Research*, 45(2): 283–300.
Gellner, Ernest. 1983. *Nations and Nationalism*. Oxford: Basil Blackwell.
Gilpin, Robert. 1981. *War and Change in World Politics*. Cambridge: Cambridge University Press.
Glaser, Charles L. 2010. *Rational Theory of International Politics*. Princeton, NJ: Princeton University Press.
Halperin, Morton, David Scheffer, and Patricia Small. 1992. *Self-Determination in the New World Order*. Washington, DC: Carnegie Endowment for International Peace.
Hechter, Michael. 1987. Nationalism as Group Solidarity. *Ethnic and Racial Studies*, 10(4): 415–26.
Hechter, Michael. 2001. *Containing Nationalism*. Oxford: Oxford University Press.
Hechter, Michael. 2013. *Alien Rule*. Cambridge: Cambridge University Press.
Jervis, Robert. 1974. *Perception and Misperception in International Politics*. Princeton, NJ: Princeton University Press.
Kaufman, Stuart J. 2001. *Modern Hatreds: The Symbolic Politics of Ethnic War*. Ithaca, NY: Cornell University Press.
Kaufman, Stuart J. 2015. *Nationalist Passions*. Ithaca, NY: Cornell University Press.
Kedourie, Elie. 2000. *Nationalism*. 4th edition. Blackwell.
Laitin, David. 1998. *Identity in Formation: The Russian-Speaking Populations in the Near Abroad*. Ithaca, NY: Cornell University Press.
Laitin, David. 2007. *Nations, States and Violence*. Oxford: Oxford University Press.
Lijphart, Arendt. 1977. *Democracy in Plural Societies*. New Haven, CT: Yale University Press.
Lustick, Ian S. 1979. Stability in Deeply Divided Societies: Consociationalism Versus Control. *World Politics*, 31(3): 325–44.
McGarry, John and Brendan O'Leary. 2009. Must Pluri-National Federations Fail? *Ethnopolitics (Special Issue: Federalism, Regional Autonomy and Conflict)*, 8(1): 5–26.
Majone, Giandomenico. 2005. *Dilemmas of European Integration*. Oxford: Oxford University Press.
Mansfield, Edward D. and Jack Snyder. 1995. Democratization and the Danger of War. *International Security*, 20(): 5–38.
Mansfield, Edward D. and Jack Snyder. 2005. *Electing to Fight: Why Emerging Democracies Go To War*. Cambridge, MA: MIT Press.
Mearsheimer, John J. 2001. *The Tragedy of Great Power Politics*. New York: Norton.
Moravcsik, Andrew. 1998. *The Choice for Europe: Social Purpose and State Power from Messina to Maastricht*. Ithaca, NY: Cornell University Press.
Mylonas, Harris. 2013. *The Politics of Nation-Building: Making Co-Nationals, Refugees, and Minorities*. Cambridge: Cambridge University Press.
O'Leary, Brendan. 1998. Gellner's Diagnoses of Nationalism: A Critical Overview *or* What is Living and What is Dead in Gellner's Philosophy of Nationalism? In John A Hall (ed.), *The State of the Nation: Ernest Gellner and the Theory of Nationalism*, pp. 40–90. Cambridge: Cambridge University Press.
O'Leary, Brendan. 2007. Analyzing Partition: Definition, Classification and Explanation. *Political Geography*, 26(8): 886–908.

O'Leary, Brendan. 2011. Debating Partition: Evaluating the Standard Justifications. In Kurt Cordell and Stefan Wolff (eds.), *The Routledge Handbook of Ethnic Conflict*, pp. 140–57. Abingdon: Routledge.

O'Leary, Brendan and John McGarry. 2012. The Politics of Accommodation and Integration in Democratic States. In Adrian Guelke and Jean Tournon (eds.). *The Study of Politics and Ethnicity: Recent Analytical Developments*, pp. 79–116. Leverkusen: Barbara Budrich.

O'Leary, Brendan, Ian S. Lustick, and Thomas M Callaghy (eds.). 2001. *Right-Sizing the State: The Politics of Moving Borders*. Oxford; Oxford University Press.

Organski, A. F. K. and Jacek Kugler. 1980. *The War Ledger*. Chicago: University of Chicago Press.

Petersen, Roger D. 2002. *Understanding Ethnic Violence: Fear, Hatred, and Resentment in Twentieth-Century Eastern Europe*. Cambridge: Cambridge University Press.

Posen, Barry. 1993a. Nationalism, the Mass Army, and Military Power. *International Security*, 18(2): 80–124.

Posen, Barry. 1993b. The Security Dilemma and Ethnic Conflict. *Survival*, 35(1): 27–47.

Regan, Patrick. 2000. *Civil Wars and Foreign Powers: Interventions and Intrastate Conflict*. Ann Arbor: University of Michigan Press.

Renan, Ernest. 1882 1996. What is a Nation? In Stuart Woolf (ed.), *Nationalism in Europe, 1815 to the Present*, pp. 48–60. Abingdon: Routledge.

Rezvani, David A. 2014. *Surpassing the Sovereign State. The Wealth, Self-Rule, and Security Advantages of Partially Independent Territories*. Oxford: Oxford University Press.

Sambanis, Nicholas. 2000. Partition as a Solution to Ethnic War: An Empirical Critique of the Theoretical Literature. *World Politics*, 52: 437–83.

Sambanis, Nicholas, Stergios Skaperdas, and William C. Wohlforth. 2015. Nation-Building Through War. *American Political Science Review*, 109: 279–96.

Sambanis, Nicholas, Stergios Skaperdas, and William C. Wohlforth. 2016. External Intervention and Civil War. Unpublished manuscript.

Semelin, Jacques. 2007. *Purify and Destroy: The Political Uses of Massacre and Genocide*. Trans. Cynthia Schoch. New York: Columbia University Press.

Smith, Anthony D. 1986. *The Ethnic Origins of Nations*. Oxford: Basil Blackwell.

Smith, Anthony. 2001. *Nationalism: Theory, Ideology, History*. Cambridge: Polity.

Smith, Martin. 2007. *State of Strife: The Dynamics of Ethnic Conflict in Burma*. Policy Studies (Southeast Asia) 36, East-West Center.

Snyder, Jack. 2000. *From Voting to Violence*. New York: Norton.

Solt, Frederick. 2011. Diversionary Nationalism: Economic Inequality and the Formation of National Pride. *Journal of Politics*, 73(3): 821–30.

Stepan, Alfred, Juan J. Linz, and Yogendra Yadav. 2011. *Crafting State-Nations: India and Other Multinational Democracies*. Baltimore, MD: The Johns Hopkins University Press.

Tajfel, Henri. 1981. *Human Groups and Social Categories*. Cambridge: Cambridge University Press.

Van Evera, Stephen. 1999. *Causes of War: Power and the Roots of Conflict*. Ithaca, NY: Cornell University Press.

Waltz, Kenneth N. 1979. *Theory of International Politics*. New York: McGraw-Hill.

Weber, Eugen. 1976. *Peasants into Frenchmen: The Modernization of Rural France, 1870–1914*. Stanford, CA: Stanford University Press.

Weiner, Myron. 1978. *Sons of the Soil. Migration and Ethnic Conflict in India*. Princeton, NJ: Princeton University Press.

Wendt, Alexander. 1999. *Social Theory of International Politics*. Cambridge: Cambridge University Press.

Wimmer, Andreas and Brian Min. 2006. From Empire to Nation-state: Explaining Wars in the Modern World, 1816–2001. *American Sociological Review*, 71(6): 867–97.

Wimmer, Andreas, Lars-Erik Cederman, and Brian Min. 2009. Ethnic Politics and Armed Conflict: A Configurational Analysis of a New Global Data Set. *American Sociological Review*, 74(2): 316–37.

Wohlforth, William. 1999. The Stability of a Unipolar World. *International Security*, 24(1): 3–41.

CHAPTER 29

ENERGY SECURITY

A Twentieth-Century Major Concern Becoming Irrelevant in the Twenty-First Century?

THIERRY BROS

29.1 From Churchill Definition to IEA Foundation: An insecure Twentieth Century

In the last 100 years, Winston Churchill's definition of energy security "safety and certainty in oil lie in variety and variety alone"[1] has proven right. For Churchill, oil was the most important fuel as this was powering British ships. This definition was also behind the foundation of the International Energy Agency[2] (IEA) during the oil crisis of 1973–74. The initial role of the IEA was to help member countries coordinate a collective response to major disruptions in the supply of oil (by potentially releasing strategic oil stocks). The IEA was also viewed as the energy watchdog of developed countries to counter-balance the producing countries cartel, the Organization of the Petroleum Exporting Countries (OPEC).[3] More energy has always been needed to sustain economic growth and for developed countries oil was, in the twentieth century, in the hands of a few unfriendly and unpredictable states. Security of supply in the twentieth century was not only about the supply itself but also about protecting big infrastructures (production areas (oil and gas fields or nuclear plants), pipelines, export terminals, electric lines, etc.).

29.1 Five Revolutions are Changing the Energy Security Concept at the Beginning of the Twenty-First Century

29.1.1 Three Revolutions on the Supply Side: US Shale Gas, US Shale Oil, and Worldwide Renewables

The US shale gas revolution[4] is only the first (and most documented) of three revolutions that have occurred on the supply side since the beginning of this century. The world has changed thanks to the US shale revolutions (gas first and then oil)[5] and a global quest for renewables. These revolutions have taken over a decade but will shape the twenty-first century. Australia followed in producing unconventional gas and is also now exporting it. It should take some time for unconventional oil and gas production to materialize in other places where the resource is available[6] (Argentina, Canada, China, Mexico, Russia, South Africa, etc.) but the US shale revolutions should be exploited in a few other countries.

Renewable policies were first designed in Europe (mostly based on subsidies as renewable energy at the time was much more expensive than any other form of energy) from 2001[7] to reduce CO_2 emissions. However, China is now also investing heavily as it needs clean energy in order to reduce air pollution in its big cities. The three biggest renewable producers in 2015 were the EU, the United States, and China. In 2015, China was the second largest producer of solar energy behind the EU but it has since become the biggest single solar producer (before Germany, the largest contributor to EU solar energy) (BP Statistical Review 2016). Thanks to technological improvements, the cost of renewables has gone down massively and can now compete with traditional electricity production (fossil or nuclear fuels). It can spread all over the world as it is no longer a fancy idea only for rich countries with an ecological mindset.[8] In the 2005–15 period, on a worldwide basis, renewable production grew by an astonishing 16 percent per annum when total primary consumption grew only by 2 percent per annum. In 2015, for the first recorded year, additions of renewable power generation capacity were higher than those for thermal capacity. If we assume this trend will continue, renewables should be the major contributor to the world primary energy mix by 2035. With more local supply (renewable), foreign dependency for energy is reduced and hence energy security will become less of an issue for any state (Figure 29.1).

But before renewables get the lion's share, in a few years' time, gas (as the cleanest fossil fuel) will become the major fuel in the worldwide energy mix. Although security of the gas supply has been high on the EU's agenda after the disruptions to supply in 2006 and 2009,[9] it is unlikely that, worldwide, gas security will be a major concern in the twenty-first century as this fuel should never represent more than

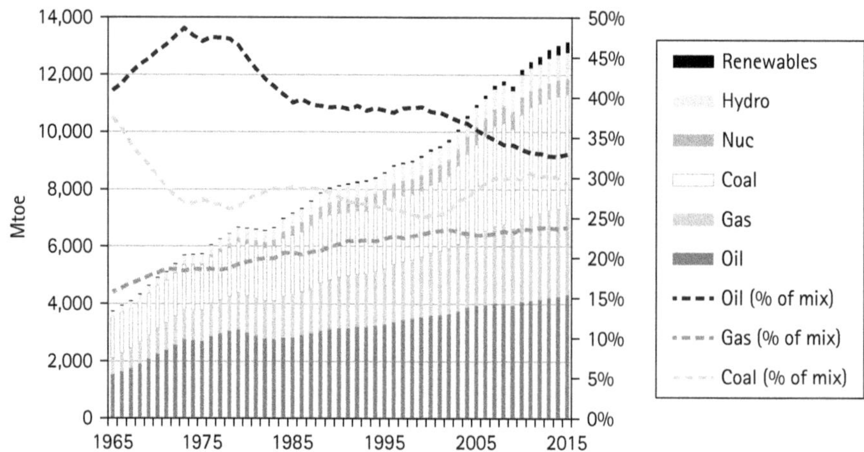

FIGURE 29.1 Worldwide primary energy mix

Source: thierrybros.com, BP Statistical Review – June 2016.

one-third of total energy needs. Even if gas reserves (where 50 percent of the reserve is shared by only three states: Iran, Russia, and Qatar) are more concentrated than oil reserves (where 50 percent of the reserve is shared by four states: Venezuela, Saudi Arabia, Canada, and Iran) on a worldwide basis, Liquefied Natural Gas (LNG) allows, as Churchill pointed out, diversity of supply. Thanks to LNG, which represents 10 percent of the global gas supply, any consuming state can increase diversity of supply and hence its energy security. Australia and the United States are exporting their unconventional gas (under LNG) and oil in the global market, increasing de facto diversification of supply for all consumers. For example, Russia provides 100 percent of Lithuania's and Poland's gas supply. However, both of these countries have invested in an LNG regas terminal (in 2014 and 2015, respectively) which will allow them to access waterborne LNG. These plants will mitigate the risk of having to reply on Russian supplies, a factor that was high on the political agenda of these two European states.

29.1.2 On the Demand Side, Efficiency Gains: An Ongoing Revolution

More energy has always been needed to sustain economic growth. Energy was first provided by slaves in Ancient Egypt, Greece, or the Roman Empire then by coal for steam machines during the Industrial Revolution in Europe and finally by oil during the twentieth century on a worldwide level. But for the first time, since 2006 (before the financial crisis), the European economy has been able to demonstrate growth utilizing less energy. This decoupling of economic growth and energy demand is now a European reality (Figure 29.2).

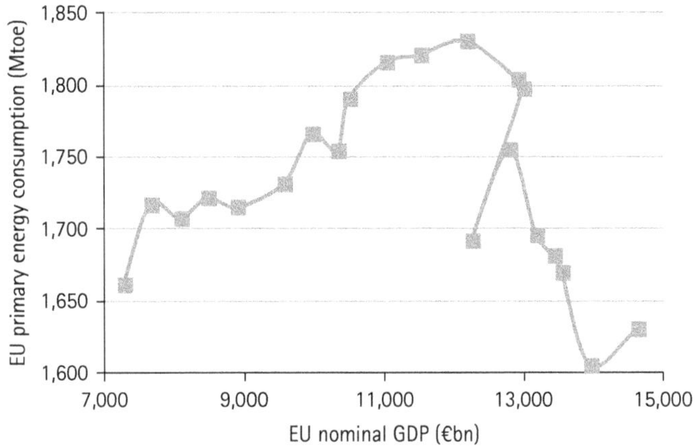

FIGURE 29.2 EU primary energy consumption vs GDP from 1995 to 2015: peaked in 2006

Source: thierrybros.com, SG Cross Asset Research, BP Statistical Review, Eurostat.

During the last decade, as in the 1970s, not only have we seen a reduction in demand as a result of higher prices (especially in Europe) but most policies are aimed at improving energy efficiency in the long run to avoid burning fossil fuels that have a negative impact on climate change. Europe is now definitively past its peak energy demand and could be followed by other developed states in the coming decade. This new trend is going to continue in Europe with the 2030 EU climate and energy roadmap.[10] In addition, the outcome of the Paris COP21 in December 2015 is putting further pressure at the world level on all fossil fuels (and in particular coal) that emit CO_2. The secular correlation between economic growth and energy was disrupted in Europe in 2006 and this is going to spread across the world (from developed to developing countries) in the coming decades. Even China has become more energy efficient (it uses less energy per unit of GDP) in the recent years. So the past growth of worldwide primary energy consumption (2 percent per annum in 2005–15) should slow down in the future (the 2014/2015 growth rate was only 1 percent), making renewables the biggest contributor to the world primary energy mix before 2035.

The power of the OPEC cartel over the oil market has disappeared in 2014/2015 thanks to the four revolutions of US shale gas and oil, renewables, and energy efficiencies and it is unlikely to resume any time soon. With a powerless OPEC, what is the exact aim of the IEA?

29.1.3 Energy Storage: The Next Revolution

We are witnessing an energy system where not only is supply widely available and demand is bound to peak, but some major technological breakthroughs in energy storage should soon materialize. This could completely alter the energy landscape where major companies were dealing with massive inflexible infrastructures (coal extraction, hydrocarbon production, nuclear plants, etc.). The future could look like a decentralized smart system where end-users select the kind of local energy they have (wind, hydro, solar), are able to store it, and then use it when needed. The intermittency of renewables that was a major obstacle in a centralized electricity transmission system should be solved with new batteries and new storage solutions (power-to-gas, molten salts, etc.). This should allow the share of renewables to continue to grow and to overtake fossil fuels around 2050. Energy storage is also needed for transportation which relies heavily on oil-based products. The number of electric cars on the road passed one million in 2015.

It is interesting to note that two of those revolutions started in the United States (shale gas and shale oil), two in Europe (the quests for renewables and energy efficiency). The ongoing fight to achieve the cheapest and most efficient energy storage is global; the highest prize is at stake as this could be the silver bullet to achieving a completely green energy supply. Companies and states are investing heavily to solve this problem and new products such as home batteries[11] are already appearing on the market. Like renewables in the early 2000s, batteries will be very expensive to start with, but costs should go down as R&D progresses. Finally, the manufacturing process should reduce the cost of batteries which would then be disseminated to all houses. With financial markets turning their back on coal, which faces strong policy reversals (because of the climate change risks), and limiting their exposure to oil,[12] vast sums of money are available for new technologies. The penetration of this dual technology (renewables and storage) could be as fast as mobile phones that, in developing countries in particular, leapfrogged landlines. This next revolution is just round the corner and will completely disrupt the energy landscape. Don't wait for 2035 for a new energy system, it is on its way and should appear around 2025.

29.2 How Vulnerable are the Key Trends to Contingent Events?

The two supply revolutions are contingent on the ability to effectively produce those unconventional hydrocarbons. So far, for example, Poland and China have not been able to produce their shale gas. In Poland's case, it is much deeper than the US resources; in China, it is in a place where water is too scarce to allow fracking. All three supply revolutions are dependent on the social acceptance of local population. France and a number of other countries decided to ban fracking for environmental issues. The effect of the "not in my backyard" (NIMBY) syndrome and lobbying from major oil and gas exporters, fighting to maintain their market position, could postpone any kind of local production whether it be hydrocarbon, wind turbines, etc. Prolonged low oil prices could make unconventional oil and gas as well as renewables less profitable (or even loss making), slowing their penetration in the energy market.

Energy efficiency has been very difficult to initiate in Europe but it seems likely that once the technology is available and affordable (for example LED lighting vs old bulb), people will stop using the old inefficient technology, even if an upfront investment is needed. But a prolonged period with low oil prices could limit the penetration of new technology into old buildings or its being retrofitted to old vehicles.

In terms of storing energy, the jury is still out. In the last 50 years, no real breakthroughs have been achieved in the storage of energy. However the recent level of investment in R&D should allow some progress. This chapter argues that if present trends continue, renewable energy should be the main contributor to the world primary energy mix by 2035. But if it proves impossible to achieve storage affordably, this would postpone the whole process of moving to a greener economy.

29.3 Energy Security still Relevant for States but for How Long?

In the twenty-first century, if there is more locally produced and stored green energy (renewables), the disruptions witnessed during the twentieth century—disasters, embargoes, wars, sanctions, etc.—will not disappear but should not pose as great a threat as they used to. The twenty-first century could be as (or even more) insecure than the twentieth century, but the energy insecurity witnessed in the last 100 years should recede. In addition, with renewables making the largest contribution to the energy market, the volatility of oil prices should have a lower impact on consumers' bills and be less dominant in the media.

At the end of the twentieth century, the world worried about energy security as it was assumed that hydrocarbon supply would be constrained as soon as the point of peak oil production was reached. In fact, the exact opposite has happened; we are now faced with unlimited supply before reaching peak demand risk. With more renewables and more proven oil and gas reserves, the security of supply on a worldwide level should not be such the major issue as it was in the twentieth century. In fact, in Europe, the major theme today is "security of demand."[13] This insecure demand market is leading to major changes. Oil and gas producers with expensive resources that are difficult to produce are no longer in a favorable position. Expensive highly polluting tar sands? Consumers can now say "No thanks." Expensive deep offshore oil production? No thanks. Expensive Alaska/Artic hydrocarbon exploration? No thanks.

In this new world, owners of cheap hydrocarbon resources have to decide quickly if they want to produce their oil and gas or leave it in the ground. Not all fossil reserves will be monetized. Iran was faced with a choice: if it wanted to monetize its huge hydrocarbon resources; it needed to produce them sooner rather than later or never. The fact that Iran agreed on July 14, 2015 to a 10-year hiatus in its nuclear development, in return for a lifting of sanctions, could be viewed as a consequence of this new energy world. If the window for oil and gas is going to close around 2050, Iran needs to start investing massively to capitalize on its hydrocarbon resources; failure to do this could leave Iran as the country with the highest stranded fossil reserve.

Since Churchill's time, markets have been created and are now a major instrument balancing supply and demand on a worldwide level. In the aftermath of the Fukushima disaster there was a major re-routing of LNG toward Japan to mitigate for the closure of all the nuclear power plants in the country. It is interesting to note that this has been achieved by market mechanisms alone without any state intervention.

Gas is a less fungible market than oil. There are major pipes linking Russia and Europe, and Russia is sometimes accused of using its gas exports as a weapon against neighboring states. To mitigate this risk (and this high import dependency (30 percent)), in the last 10 years Europe has improved its gas infrastructure to allow reverse flows (from West to East), allowing Eastern states like Lithuania and Poland to directly access LNG. Even Ukraine, which used to be 100 percent dependent on Russian imports, is now in a position to access "European" gas from its Western border. By building a resilient infrastructure and relying more on markets, the perceived threat of Russia using gas supplies as a weapon is declining. And the transit issues for gas (via Belorussia, Ukraine, or Turkey) can now be mitigated by long-distance offshore pipes and/or LNG. At the time of writing, Russia is wanting to finance and build more pipes to export more gas to Europe[14] and China,[15] as it needs to monetize its huge gas reserves before the world moves away from fossil fuels.

The indications are that the energy market is going to move from a rigid centralized system to a flexible decentralized one where storage is done by end-users. The need for strategic oil stocks should therefore recede. This is why, today, the IEA is working to ensure reliable, affordable, and clean energy for its 29 member countries. The IEA has four main areas of focus: energy security, economic development, environmental awareness, and engagement worldwide. Even the IEA—designed to mitigate oil disruption at a time of the world's worst oil crisis–is having to adapt as energy security is slowly becoming irrelevant. Once local renewables (with energy storage) represent the major part of the energy mix, energy security should become an irrelevant concept. In the same way as landline phones were the standard until the end of the twentieth century but have since been replaced by mobile phones, once the dual energy technology of renewables and storage becomes available all over the world, the IEA and energy security will become little more than a matter for historians.

For Winston Churchill, oil was the most important fuel as it powered British ships. Today, oil represents only 33 percent of the world energy mix and this should continue to decline in the years to come. Oil is still important for states as the world's militaries are using oil-based products to power their tanks, ships, and aircraft. So the concept of energy security will continue, but mainly for the military. Oil remains an easy to handle fuel and it has a high energy concentration. Militaries have not started to think about "energy efficient weapons." So in the first half of this new century, energy security will perhaps remain on the state agenda as armies will have no alternative to oil if they wish to embark on a war.

25.4 Implications for International Security Research

The mainstream IR literature seems to assume that what we have witnessed in the past in terms of oil can explain the future. But this disregards the fact that we now face a new world where supply is plentiful and demand should decrease in the future. This chapter strongly disagrees with this "cut and paste" approach to research, as the core implication of the findings discussed here is that analogies from the past are no longer valid.

The special section on energy recently published in the journal *Security Studies* provides interesting illustrations of the problems that arise when IR scholars rely on analogies from the past:

- In a paper entitled "The Petroleum Paradox" (Kelanic 2016: 181–213), the author—after looking at four historical cases ("specifically Great Britain's efforts to reduce coercive vulnerability at the close of the First World War, [and] Adolf Hitler's attempts across three periods to safeguard German oil access before and during World War II") concludes: "Despite the popular focus on oil's economic value, this alone cannot account for states' behavior. Military vulnerability plays a major, perhaps more important, role in spurring great power anticipation." She then adds a word of caution "A natural question raised by this paper concerns the applicability of coercive vulnerability theory to great power politics today and in the future.... First technological changes that significantly decrease oil's importance for military power could limit the theory's historical scope. If oil is no longer essential to war, this would diminish the impetus for strategic anticipation" but she then disregards her own words of warning. By looking back, Kelanic does not take into account the changes witnessed in the energy markets in the last 10 years, as described in this chapter. In fact, the great powers are doing now exactly the opposite of what was done before. The United States and the EU are putting sanctions on major oil producers (Iran, Russia) to force changes.
- If in "Oil Scarcity Ideology in US Foreign Policy, 1908–97" (Stern 2016: 214–57) Roger J. Stern's conclusion is that "aggressive polices to secure supply were never reassessed after scarcity failed to materialize," he stops short of predicting what could happen in the future with US oil demand declining and domestic supply growing.
- In "Dismantling the Oil Wars Myth", Emily Meierding (2016: 258–88) argues "that contrary to the assumptions of international relations scholars, policymakers, and the general public, states do not engage in oil wars". Again she only looks at the past but we could agree with her for an analysis of the future. The 1991 Gulf War could mark the end of a century of oil-related wars. It took place in an old world where oil reserves were believed to be limited and in the hands of a few states. The twenty-first-century sanctions against Iran and Russia were not just about oil but were

designed to put a ban on oil exports or oil technology imports to deprive those two oil-exporting countries of hard currency in a world where there is plenty of oil now available and demand is muted due to climate change policies. To be sure, future conflicts may occur in oil-exporting countries; however, those would probably not be wars for oil.

The IR literature on energy advances arguments that rely too much on the past, and fails to take into account recent key developments which are likely to have a significant impact on the future. Disregarding oil, in Chapter 23 of this Handbook, Daniel Deudney's argument is that "confidence in the stabilizing role of deterrence that marked the second round of the [nuclear] debate has been significantly weakened." According to him "sooner or later, and probably sooner, nuclear weapons will again be used in war." For Deudney, security of oil supply should be less relevant to nuclear warmaking in the twenty-first century compared to previous centuries. This chapter tends to agree with this conclusion just by observing that as more energy is available (due to the shale and renewable revolutions) and as demand is peaking (due to efficiency gains), the military should have plenty of oil available in the coming years.

With the technological breakthroughs mentioned in this chapter, energy is more widely available and the world needs to move away from fossil fuels (coal first, then oil, and finally gas) to avoid catastrophic climate changes. Energy security, after becoming irrelevant for citizens, should become less of an issue for states and their armies post-2050. In a buyers' market, energy security should slowly become irrelevant, but this will take time as any energy crisis will lead to an increase in market prices that could mistakenly be viewed as an issue of the security of supply. Thanks to mature markets and breakthroughs in technology, the *raison d'être* of the IEA should soon be questioned by member states needing to cut their overall expenses.

Notes

1. July 17, 1913, Winston Churchill (First Lord of the Admiralty) at the British House of Commons.
2. www.iea.org
3. www.opec.org. OPEC had the ability to curtail production (by a quota system) to manage prices.
4. By combining two technologies (fracking and horizontal drilling), US producers have been able, since 2005, to unlock shale gas reserves that previously could not be accessed on a commercial basis
5. The shale oil revolution tilted the pricing power away from OPEC as the United States was becoming the biggest worldwide oil (and gas) producer.
6. https://www.eia.gov/analysis/studies/worldshalegas/
7. Directive 2001/77/EC of the European Parliament and of the Council of September 27, 2001 on the promotion of electricity from renewable energy sources in the internal electricity market.

8. In 2015, in Denmark, renewable accounted for 25 percent of the total primary energy consumption vs 2 percent in China (BP Statistical Review, June 2016).
9. The risks were concerned more with transit via Ukraine than on Russian gas production.
10. http://ec.europa.eu/energy/en/topics/energy-strategy/2030-energy-strategy
11. For example https://www.teslamotors.com/powerwall or http://www.bollore.com/en-us/activities/electricity-storage-and-solutions
12. Some international oil companies, like Shell or Total, are claiming that they are now orientated more toward gas than oil.
13. The forecasting of future demand is so difficult that producers might not be willing to take the risk of investing to provide additional energy supply.
14. Nord Stream 2 would like to utilize an offshore Russia to Germany route via the Baltic. Howeer, this project faces resistance from Eastern European Member States and Ukraine as these latter areas risk losing transit fees.
15. The Power of Siberia that will link Russia to China (Eastern Route) is being built and should, from the next decade, provide a sizable share of Russian gas to China.

References

BP Statistical Review, June 2016.

Bros, Thierry. 2012. *After the US Shale Gas Revolution*. Paris: Editions Technip.

Kelanic, Rosemary A. 2016. The Petroleum Paradox: Oil, Coercive Vulnerability, and Great Power Behavior, *Security Studies*, 25(2): 181–213.

Meierding, Emily 2016. Dismantling the Oil Wars Myth, *Security Studies*, 25(2): 258–88.

Stern, Roger J. 2016. Oil Scarcity Ideology in US Foreign Policy, 1908–97, *Security Studies*, 25(2): 214–57.

CHAPTER 30

MIGRATION

AUDIE KLOTZ

30.1 Introduction

Migration inherently invokes change—people moving from one place to another—but the causes and consequences elude prediction. Outbreaks of violence sporadically spur flight, while economic fluctuations affect employment prospects. Networks reinvent pathways to desired destinations, while policy-makers continually seek ways to disrupt reliable routes. Micro-level personal relationships often defy the logic of markets or the demands of resettlement agencies, simultaneously playing a crucial role in recreating the underlying macro-level structures of global politics. How can we reconcile these apparent contradictions?

Too often, policy-makers and analysts separate myriad forms of migration into simplistic categories. Presumably, voluntary migrants—immigrants—seek jobs and citizenship, whereas forced migrants—refugees—lack agency as victims of violence beyond their control. Political economy thus becomes divorced from security, reinforcing the omission of cross-border migration, and demographics generally, from explanations of historical or contemporary security dynamics. As a consequence, security scholars prioritize a stylized notion of migration as a threat that sidelines a wide range of other considerations.

Instead, I argue that migration as a potential security concern should be analyzed through the politics of threat construction. In this chapter, I delineate the salience of migration along three dimensions of security: interstate, societal, and human. For each dimension, I draw upon iconic contributions to the literature and recent scholarly interventions. Along the way, I weave examples from around the world to underscore that the inclusion of migration within security studies also requires reassessment of the field's Eurocentric roots. In particular, I push for rethinking the nation state as a building block of our theories.

30.2 Interstate Security

Population movements feature prominently in interdisciplinary literatures on European nation building, imperial expansion, decolonization, and globalization. Unfortunately, few textbooks or survey courses in International Relations (IR) pay much attention to such debates about migration, even though demographics play key roles in both macro-historical structural shifts and foreign policy calculations. When migration does get acknowledged, refugees receive disproportionate attention, albeit typically as voiceless victims. To better comprehend the complex consequences of migration, IR scholars need to reconsider their core assumptions about states-as-actors.

Incrementally, narrow conventional wisdom is being challenged by linking transnational demographic shifts to interstate security. In his trail-blazing work, Weiner (1992/93) called for sustained attention to strategic manipulation of migration and mapped out multiple avenues through which population movements might be treated as threats. Others have gradually taken up his categories and claims. For example, Greenhill (2010) elaborated upon Weiner's suggestion that states might purposefully use mass expulsion, while Lischer (2005) explored how refugees might continue to play a role in the conflicts that led to their displacement. Adamson (2006: 175–85) also probed further his notion of state capacity.

Certainly deliberate expulsion or mobilization by diaspora can be linked to nation-building or strategic motives, and thus these studies add a welcome dose of agency. Contrary to claims that migration is a new security issue, however, such demographic effects are perpetually systemic phenomena, requiring the application of macro-historical perspectives, as other social scientists have long recognized.[1] Less dramatic migration flows also merit more sustained attention, not least for highlighting the structural underpinnings of key concepts such "expulsion" and "refugee." Both terms imply border-crossings, in turn suggesting the need for greater attention to relationships between territoriality and population.

One of the most prominent historical examples of the purposeful generation of refugees were Protestant Huguenots, who sought respite from religious persecution, especially by Catholics following revocation of the French Edict of Nantes in 1685 (Orchard 2014: 58–63). Within Europe, their destinations included the Netherlands, England, and areas now part of Germany and Switzerland. Their relocation was not geographically limited to Europe. Huguenots also arrived in Cape Town, then a southern African outpost of the Dutch Empire, where they merged with a small settler community (Thompson 1990: 35). At a time when few people had the right to move or the means to purchase mobility, empire served as a safety valve, providing a viable exit option that often dampened potential violence in countries of origin.

Nor was the Catholic–Protestant divide the only religious conflict. Various Protestant sects participated in settling North America, often due to limited opportunities if not outright persecution in Europe, which ironically often translated into intolerance of religious pluralism in many British colonies (Martin 2011: 27–34, 37–8). Yet relocation often generated new conflicts in the destinations. For instance, Pennsylvania proved more accommodating to diverse migrants, including those fleeing recurring conflicts in eighteenth-century Europe. Still, it was not immune to concerns over the security implications of too many Anabaptists, Irish Catholics, or German-speakers (Martin 2011: 52, 56–9).

Religion remained a crucial divide among Christians in the eighteenth century. Homes, marriages, education, livelihoods, and a whole host of other socio-economic conditions depended largely on religious affiliation. So too did political rights, with Catholics routinely barred from holding office or government jobs in Protestant-dominant colonies and vice versa. Thus conflicts in colonial North America, with lasting legacies for Canada and the United States, largely revolved around the legal status of Francophone Catholics under British rule after the 1763 Treaty of Paris acknowledged French defeat (Kelley and Trebilcock 2010: 31). For instance, due to fear of disloyalty, the British had forcibly expelled French settlers in the Acadia region (which spans the contemporary maritime provinces). Although some of those refugees did return after 1763, when British fears faded, many scattered throughout North America and to other outposts of the French Empire, including Louisiana (Kelley and Trebilcock 2010: 33–5).

Such migration-related tensions continued to impact both grand strategy and foreign policies even after the resolution of imperial competition in Britain's favor. In particular, the disputed rights of Francophone Catholics within Anglo-Protestant colonies mattered for the strategic balance of power in North America. Following British victory, its Proclamation Act of 1763 sought to assimilate Francophone settlers, but failure to recruit enough Anglophone settlers, combined with burgeoning discontent in its colonies further south, led to a dramatic shift in approach within a decade. The Quebec Act of 1774 reinstated many rights of Catholics—going beyond their rights within Britain itself—and reallocated to this newly consolidated colony substantial swaths of territory in the Ohio River Valley and Great Lakes region that had previously been granted to Indigenous allies (Kelley and Trebilcock 2010: 32; Ford 2010: 9–11; Jung 2015: 62).[2]

So outraged were the Americans that the Quebec Act features as one of the key complaints listed in their 1776 Declaration of Independence.[3] With the Quebec Act, however, Britain did succeed in keeping more colonies from joining the rebellion. And its ripple effects did not end with the outbreak of that war. After peace in 1783, many so-called Empire Loyalists fled to areas in the contemporary maritimes and Quebec, thereby dramatically increasing the proportion of Anglophone to Francophone populations, as well as bolstering politically conservative views (Kelley and Trebilcock 2010: 38–9). Unintentionally, Britain had finally found a way to address its North American demographic problem: the bulk of immigration to its Canadian colonies continued to come from the United States until the mid-1800s.

Attention to migration-related factors spurring US independence also highlights strategic interactions between colonists and Indigenous People, whose critical role is typically neglected (with a few exceptions such as Crawford 1994: 370–1). The military strength of Indigenous Peoples was in decline by 1774, hence the British ability to renege on land claims. After US independence, the British sought to accommodate the demands of Empire Loyalists by relocating Indigenous People in Canada (Kelley and Trebilcock 2010: 39–40). Meanwhile, the decentralized US federation enabled member states to lay claim to vast stretches of territory westward. Massive dispossession took hold starting in 1815, escalating throughout the 1820s and 1830s, in part due to voracious post-war demand for land conducive to growing cotton (Ford 2010: 129–35). The seeds of civil war had been planted long before 1860.

Despite its epic consequences, this North American (migration) history is overlooked in a field that routinely demarcates 1815 as the beginning of our modern international system, thereby omitting from analysis key strategic dynamics, including those with non-state actors such as Indigenous People. Such blinders are also unfortunate because the colonies, in North America and elsewhere, help us to understand the European core (Wolfe 1982; Ford 2010: 20–1; Vigneswaran 2013: ch.4). For example, Britain democratized partially in response to pressures from its settler dominions. London may have exported the formal institutions of its parliamentary model, but often as an ad hoc reaction to near-rebellion, first in Canada, then its other settler states—albeit not India, for reasons that Vigneswaran (2013: 72) links directly to an anomalous pattern of elite migration. And later, settler-subjects led the metropole to expand representation, not vice versa. For instance, Australia granted women the right to vote two decades before Britain (Towns 2010: 2).

One wider international consequence of this intra-imperial process of democratization, Vucetic (2011: 23–4) argues, was solidification during the nineteenth century of a racialized collective "Anglosphere" identity that ameliorated animosity toward Americans, culminating in (among other effects) pacification of the US–Canada border by the turn of the twentieth century.[4] As a result, we can trace one of the most stable alliances, and least militarized borders, to macro-historical demographic trends and the politics of migration management. On the flip side, British regulation of its South Asian subjects spurred imperial development of a passport system in the early 1900s, a boundary-building technology then internationalized through the League of Nations (Mongia 2003; Salter 2003: 77–80).

Furthermore, by the mid-twentieth century, reverse trends in migration impacted Britain significantly as colonial subjects and displaced Europeans provided much-needed labor, following devastating human losses during the First and Second World Wars (Paul 1997; Lucassen 2005: ch. 5). Anti-immigrant sentiment soon percolated, along with incrementally circumscribed intra-imperial mobility (Bevan 1986: 75–89; Gilroy 1987; Paul 1997: ch.7). Only in 1981 did Britain adopt something resembling a definition of nationality, once again trailing its settler colonies, this time by four decades. These policies—including a long history of playing off white Eastern European migrants against brown and black former colonial subjects—puts the Brexit referendum debate into context. An abiding disconnect between nationality and empire, manifest in xenophobic outbursts, underscores a fundamental uncertainty over the meaning of being English, British, or European.

Overall, this migration-infused analysis of Britain's multi-faceted imperial history illustrates why the field of IR needs to conceptualize *empire*-states instead of fetishizing the nation state (Cooper 2005: ch. 6; Ford 2010: 13; Vigneswaran 2013: 54–5). To do so requires, at minimum, scrutinizing assumptions about sovereignty and security. Combined with less Eurocentric historical knowledge, the insight that threats are socially constructed offers analytical tools for such a shift, starting with the concept of societal security.

30.3 Societal Security

Once a radical theoretical suggestion, the notion of threat as social construction has now attained the status of a conventional wisdom in IR. Nonetheless, divergent perspectives on the relationship between migration and threat reflect a deepening academic divide between US and European scholars. For example, both Weiner (1992/93) and Wæver (1993) sought to shift the security studies agenda after the Cold War by arguing that migration could be viewed as a threat to national identity. Based in the US, Weiner focused on ethnic communities and the potential impacts of social instability on national security. In contrast, Wæver, based in Europe, concentrated on the discursive ability of leaders to frame or "securitize" migration or other concerns as existential threats through a state-produced rhetoric of fear.

In part, this bifurcation reflects perceived political realities of migration: people-importing states in North America (and elsewhere) have viewed the intersection of migration and security through different lenses than people-exporting states in Europe (and elsewhere).[5] Theoretically, the oversimplified dichotomy between civic citizenship and ethno-nationalism replicates this historical divergence, with the partial exception of France.[6] Similarly, differences between national security and societal security frameworks have subsequently played out in competing analyses of European integration.

Initially work on societal security, with ethno-nationalist underpinnings, sought to understand the treatment of "new" migrants as a cultural threat, ostensibly a response to an increase in people, many of them Muslims, arriving from North Africa and the Middle East (Wæver 1993: 22–3). For example, starting with the Balkans crisis in the early 1990s, Germany has wrestled with escalating tensions between its constitutional commitments to refugees and xenophobia. The political salience of these tensions has heightened in light of burgeoning migration following the upheavals of the so-called Arab Spring, especially the Syrian war. Also, violent attacks in Paris perpetrated by second-generation European citizens got framed politically in religious terms, despite French secular civic nationalism.

As a distinctive securitization literature developed during the 1990s, its concern with societal security, conceived in terms of threats to collective identities, displaced attention to foreign policies as traditionally understood.[7] In response, Rudolph (2003, 2006) suggested linking these perspectives by positing an inverse relationship between national security and societal security. Specifically, he predicted that a stable strategic environment would enable domestic cultural schisms to thrive, whereas an intense strategic threat would foster domestic solidarity.[8] For example, assimilationist France, with a long history of low population growth and hence a ready reliance on imported labor, presents an unlikely setting for identity-based securitization of migration (Rudolph 2006: 127–8; also Lucassen 2005: ch. 3). Yet, consistent with trends elsewhere in Europe, xenophobia percolated from the 1960s, as sources of labor recruitment expanded beyond southern Europe to North Africa, especially with the expansion of family migration in the 1970s. Still, only after the collapse of Cold War strategic stability, Rudolph claims, did anti-immigrant extremism flare (Rudolph 2006: 141–2, 149–50, 154–5).

Other analysts place more emphasis on one or another of myriad variables, in part because conflating voluntary labor contracts, family unification, and asylum seekers (as Rudolph and many others often do) inevitably creates an inconsistent mix. For example, the courts have played a crucial role in protecting migrants' rights to family in France and elsewhere (Hollifield 1992: 186–96, 2000: 76, 94). And governments as well as academics tend to homogenize religions and nationalities, thereby under-appreciating sectarian divisions among Muslims or distinctive views of Kurds among Turks (Kastoryano 2002: 117–18). In addition, women's attire specifically has been the focal point of much anti-immigrant politics, suggesting the need for a gender component to any analysis (Raussiguier 1999: 436–7).

Furthermore, problems of methodological nationalism remain endemic in so many of these studies.[9] For instance, regional integration played a surprisingly minor role in Rudolph's analysis, mainly as an indicator of declining external threat rather than as a causal variable (Rudolph 2006: 154, 157–8). In contrast, Chebel d'Appollonia (2008: 205–6) eschewed methodological nationalism by analyzing the regionalization of societal security across Europe. Although distinctions between citizens and foreigners do vary by country, she argued that European governments participate in an overarching regional process that strengthens a collective sense of otherness and, with it, a tendency to scapegoat foreigners. For instance, policing procedures, including the development of biometric databases, linked migration to smuggling and terrorism (Chebel d'Appollonia 2008: 210, 213–14, 224). Consequently, in her framework, migration intersects simultaneously (rather than inversely, for Rudolph) with national security and societal security to produce both inclusionary and exclusionary policies.

To untangle the complexity of markets and mobility, Chebel d'Appollonia emphasized the multi-faceted institutional infrastructure of European integration. Securitization processes failed to resolve immigration issues, she concluded, and indeed exacerbated related factors, such as discrimination, which in turn foster terrorism (Chebel d'Appollonia 2008: 227–8). While no one seems to trumpet any European successes, others do see a more mixed record of intended and unintended consequences. For example, Zaiotti (2011), who looked at EU-level policy making, saw inconsistency due to overlapping approaches, the product of competing perspectives and balances of political power. He identified three "cultures" of security, promoted by clusters of countries as well as individual norm entrepreneurs, who produce competing policy solutions.

Perhaps satisfying empirically, because policies typically do have contradictory effects, Zaiotti's approach nonetheless, like so many others, smuggles in a naturalized European-based meta-narrative about the emergence of nation states and their purported sovereignty. After invoking Westphalia, he quickly segues to nation states and national security as the benchmark against which any shifts should be assessed (Zaiotti 2011: 25–7). Particularly problematic for security studies, the global history of migration directly challenges such a widely-proclaimed yet rarely examined assumption that control of migration is inherent to state sovereignty. Actually, macro-historical studies of migration demonstrate that mobility rights were often incorporated into international treaties, and migration was only enshrined as domestic jurisdiction in 1919, a result of the Versailles negotiations to end the First World War and establish the League of Nations (Lake and Reynolds 2008: ch. 12).

Unfortunately, few scholars will toss aside such theoretical blinders any time soon, because insufficient attention to territoriality is endemic in IR as a field (Vigneswaran 2013; Branch 2014). More optimistically, one way to confront these problems is to draw extensively on historical studies of empires (Vigneswaran 2013: 78–9). For example, migration to settler states demonstrates empirically that putatively non-ethnic civic nationalisms belie deep-rooted prejudices (Lake and Reynolds 2008; Klotz 2013). Furthermore, in this broader macro-historical context, the category of migration necessarily encompasses slavery (Quirk 2011), as well as European settlers' interactions with Indigenous Peoples (Ford 2010: 4, 210; Jung 2015: 59–63).

Directly addressing the concerns of security, such studies indicate that the strategic implications of migration across the Atlantic mattered less by the late 1800s than they had in the early colonial period. And control of mobility had little to do with sovereignty as currently defined: transportation regulations aimed merely to influence the number of European arrivals and their destinations, based mainly on class differentiation. Only as the cost of travel plummeted, due to steamship technology, did dramatic increases in immigration prompt a stronger desire among dominant elites to filter out certain social groups viewed as undesirable (Tichenor 2002: ch. 3; Martin 2011: ch. 7; Schneider 2011: ch. 1). Consequently, as both supply and demand altered, domestic debates over collective identity burgeoned, demonstrating securitization processes at work.

As the foremost migrant-receiving state, any US response directly and indirectly impacted migration around the globe. At the turn of the twentieth century, policy-makers sought to exclude radical ideologies, notably anarchism, then Communism, and less desirable religions, particularly Catholicism and Judaism. After a literacy test proved ineffectual in targeting these putative threats, a national-origins quota system directly linked these social concerns to source countries, mainly in Eastern and southern Europe (Tichenor 2002: ch. 5; Zolberg 2006: ch. 7). Meanwhile, starker explicitly exclusionary racist practices intensified in response to Asian migration, encompassing not only procedures that precluded entry but also laws carefully crafted to deny the rights of those few who had garnered citizenship (Tichenor 2002: ch. 4; Jung 2015: 76–9, 93–4).

These barriers did not forestall migration—people went elsewhere. Yet prejudices travelled across borders too. By the 1920s and 1930s, many other destinations had adopted various restrictions, from implicitly prejudiced literacy tests to explicitly discriminatory nationality quotas (Peberdy 2009; Fitzgerald and Cook-Martín 2014). These exclusionary dynamics, especially evident in the Pacific hemisphere, had gradually gained momentum following the abolition of the slave trade in 1807 and then abolition of slavery itself within the British realm, because global labor markets shifted to increase demand.

New forms of servitude filled some of the gap, primarily through an intra-imperial British system that carefully regulated flows of Indian indentured laborers throughout its colonies (Tinker 1974; Metcalf 2007; Quirk 2011: 198–9). In addition, British trade treaties with China allowed for unhindered migration, albeit with unintended consequences. Persistent efforts by the Australian colonies in particular to restrict Asian immigration ended up creating headaches for London, which sought to dampen both intra-imperial tensions over discriminatory treatment of Indians and geostrategic tensions with China and, later, Japan (Lake and Reynolds 2008: chs. 6–8; Klotz 2013: ch. 2). These are the racial dynamics that led hegemonic Britain and its allies to concede, in 1919, that migration would henceforth be treated as a matter of domestic jurisdiction, thereby rejecting Japan's efforts to make racial equality a foundational principle of world order. We can only speculate whether the opposite choice, recognizing Japan as a great power, might have prevented a Pacific theater in the Second World War.

Overall, this range of strategic reactions to migration, across centuries and across regions, reorients attention from individual countries to relationships between them, the hallmark of IR. Migration management in one location inevitably affects other places—cities, countries, even hemispheres. The ideas underpinning so-called best practices circulate just as readily. Incorporating such histories of migration more thoroughly also reveals how deeply racism has fueled efforts to block human mobility. The persistence of these issues underscores that people are remarkably creative in circumventing border controls. Thus any attempt to "secure" borders (for better or worse) needs to take human agency seriously.

30.4 Human Security

Few analysts claim that border controls can ever truly block population movements, even if xenophobic politicians continually try. Given that some people will overcome barriers, one way or another, migration will inevitably be a security concern for a subset of policy-makers. Efforts at border control exhibit performative motivations as well (Andreas 2009: ch. 5). Governments, therefore, will periodically tighten enforcement or devise new restrictions. For instance, the use of biometric data—currently invoked as an innovative technological solution—has a long lineage, back to the colonial era (Breckenridge 2014). Similarly, from trans-Atlantic shipping in the nineteenth century to trans-continental air travel in the twentieth century, modes of transportation have intersected with the regulation of population flows.

Notions of human security connect these macro-historical trends to migrants as people making choices rather than voiceless victims. In particular, international human rights norms play a critical role in contemporary definitions of human security, not least enshrining political persecution in the 1951 UN Convention as a key factor in granting refugee status.[10] Yet, as Bhabha (2014: 13) underscores, insufficient attention has been paid to "ambivalence" and "ambiguity" about rights for migrants, which results from an unchallenged presumption of the state as protector. Thus sanguine views of the refugee regime privilege treaty norms and portray the United Nations High Commissioner for Refugees (UNHCR) as a relatively effective node in a network of humanitarian actors (e.g. Hollifield 2000: 98–9, 105; Loescher 2001; Martin 2014), whereas attention to its limitations suggests a much more mixed record (e.g. Bhabha 2014: ch. 6).

One key tension revolves around the UN's narrow focus on individual persecution, which is rooted in twentieth-century European conflicts, as readily acknowledged when its members extended the geographical scope of the 1951 Convention in 1967.[11] In contrast, newly independent African states immediately recognized that the UN refugee regime did not adequately address threats to human security: the 1969 Organization of African Unity Convention encompassed upheaval linked to civil war or widespread unrest as well as environmental devastation.[12] Similarly, among the first academics to highlight the complexities of environmental impacts on migration, Richmond (1994: 80) offered multiple distinctions that spanned secondary effects of war on livelihoods, politically induced ecological disasters, as well as both short-term and long-term displacements due to weather or climate change. More recently, Betts (2013) has promoted recognition of so-called survival migration.

Because people who make choices about their movements acquire agency, any loosening of refugee status to cover, say, flight from famine, would require deeper rethinking, beyond receiving-state responses (Innes 2015: 5, 90). Thus Richmond (1994: 80–2) tried to differentiate systematically between proactive and reactive flight. Those fleeing likely combine an array of concerns when making decisions about timing and destination; individual stories of displacement poignantly illustrate such difficult decision making (e.g. Beah 2007; Steinberg 2015). In contrast, states following codified international law will seek to prioritize one "true" motive over another in order to determine procedurally whom to receive or reject. For example, since 2000, many Zimbabweans have fled a confluence of political, economic, and ecological disruptions, whereas South Africa has granted only a small fraction of them legal refugee status (Klotz 2013: ch. 4; Morreira 2016: ch. 4).

These complex realities are also increasingly manifest in Europe. For example, Greece currently plays a critical role in EU responses to the plight of Syrian refugees, not least because its geographical location on the Mediterranean with an extensive coastline, including many islands, provides innumerable opportunities for circumventing interdiction. Once on the ground, procedures create barriers to mobility, despite the porousness of intra-EU physical borders. Thus migrants in Athens (and elsewhere) learned to tailor their life stories to fit legalities; those who did not often failed to comprehend why their plights fell on deaf ears (Innes 2015: 99–103). These dynamics are hardly limited to contemporary asylum seekers or to Greece. For instance, British immigration policy and procedures have for decades sought to stymie family migration, in part due to the presumption of fraud (Bhabha et al. 1985).

Ironically, asylum registration processes or other immigration procedures can encourage dishonesty (e.g. packaging of legally acceptable life stories) and push desperate people into illegal activities (e.g. bribes for officials or human smugglers). This conundrum complicates any ethical considerations, because putative refugees no longer appear as hapless victims. Once tarred with criminality, their claims become humanitarian exceptions instead of principled obligations (Aradau 2004). Feminist insights into human security have gained the most traction in these interstitial areas of transnational mobility (Innes 2015: 33–6). Notably, the International Criminal Court now recognizes rape as a war crime, which also reduces the long-standing insulation of the refugee regime from the gender agenda within human rights arenas (Copeland 2003: 105–7, 110–11).

Still, the absence of explicit recognition of gender-based persecution in the UN refugee convention creates the misleading impression that recent adaptations mark a dramatic expansion of protection (Copeland 2003: 101–5). The main reform has been greater flexibility in applying the "social group" designation to gender issues, with few countries including gender-based violence in their domestic legislation or protocols (Copeland 2003: 104–6). In addition, specialists routinely fail to acknowledge that individual asylum seekers are predominantly men, while displaced groups are comprised disproportionately of women and children relegated to camps (Bhabha 2014: 208–9). And while UNHCR advocates for examiners to receive gender sensitivity training, many countries process married women's asylum claims as derivative of their husbands' applications (Copeland 2003: 102–3). The status of children remains even more tenuous (Bhabha 2014: ch. 6).

Indeed, gender is not an exception; few rights related to migration have gained acceptance within international treaties. Notoriously, a clear North–South divide marks the ratification pattern for the Convention on the Rights of Migrant Workers and Their Families.[13] In an exploration of this rights gap, Innes (2015: 69, 74, 77) underscored that asylum and nationality, although included in the 1948 UN Declaration of Human Rights, did not get included in the subsequent UN covenants (adopted two decades later) on civil and political rights or economic, social, and cultural rights. Even the widely supported and readily ratified Convention on the Rights of Children has proved to be highly contested when applied to migration matters (Bhabha 2014). Consequently, many migrants may face the prospect of statelessness.

Meanwhile, even accepted refugee rights are under assault. Before the Mediterranean refugee "crisis" of 2016 drew heightened media attention, receiving countries were already using innumerable strategies to reduce the types of claims that fall under the UN Convention definition (Orchard 2014: 237–8). One of these maneuvers has been the development of "safe country" provisions, particularly popular in Europe. These policies weaken the non-refoulement norm, by labeling countries of origin as safe (even when specific groups may be subject to discrimination) and categorizing transit countries as safe (often under dubious circumstances). In addition, when perilous ocean journeys did not sufficiently deter asylum seekers from Afghanistan or Iraq, Australian policy-makers opted for controversial offshore detention centers on allied small island states. Such designations then justify deportations without clearly abrogating international commitments.

Overall, most migration-related rights have garnered limited hortatory support in international conventions. Although the principle of domestic jurisdiction over transnational migration was only recognized in 1919, claims of sovereign control over population movement as an inherent right of states have proven remarkably successful (Dauvergne 2008). Ultimately, since states are the signatories and implementers of international law, domestic politics surrounding migration will limit any commitment to rights for migrants. In the foreseeable future, securitization of migration will likely increase, alongside rising populism across Europe and the United States, maybe even Canada.

30.5 Implications

Blurring the boundaries between voluntary and forced migration creates deep political and analytical challenges. Certainly no single theoretical perspective can capture the full scope of human mobility and its myriad international impacts. What migration does underscore for IR as a field is the limitations of relying primarily on European histories. The myth of Westphalia leads, among other problems, to the inaccurate assumption that control of population is inherent to state sovereignty. Instead, I have suggested that the concept of empire-state better captures global dynamics over the past three centuries and directs our attention to the politics surrounding recognition of domestic jurisdiction over migration in 1919. While securitization theory may avoid some of these presumptions, it too tends to overlook gender and race.

These theoretical concerns matter for people on the move, too. Compelling factors beyond individual political persecution lead to displacement and legitimate claims to protection. Writing at a time when the security implications of migration are grabbing headlines around the world, I hope that this reassessment will contribute to much-needed rethinking about rights-respecting responses at the local, national, and international levels.

Notes

1. Notably, in sociological studies of migration, world systems theory remains influential (Hollifield 2000: 86; Castles and Miller 2003: 25–6). In contrast, Marxist frameworks have declined in IR.

2. http://avalon.law.yale.edu/18th_century/quebec_act_1774.asp
3. http://www.archives.gov/exhibits/charters/declaration_transcript.html
4. These claims about the border merit deeper analysis. For instance, Ramirez (2001) points to increased border control in the 1920s. And much of the administrative infrastructure for border control started with concerns about Canada, not Mexico. See also Andreas (2009).
5. Many constructivists too readily accept such Eurocentric narratives of nation states. Lucassen (2005) among others effectively challenges this mythology that Europe has not been a region of immigration, by analyzing long-standing intra-European migration patterns.
6. Regularly invoked on this dichotomy, Brubaker (1992) contrasts secular France with ethno-nationalist Germany; cf. Kastoryano (2002) on the same pairing.
7. Methodologically, securitization analyses typically privilege micro-level processes linking threat construction to border regulation.
8. He explored this claim across a comparison of four advanced industrial democracies: the United States, Britain, France, and Germany. For a rationale defending this same European case selection, but excluding the US, see Lucassen (2005).
9. On perils of methodological nationalism for analyzing migration, see Money (1999: 47–53) and Jung (2015: 80–1, 107).
10. http://www.refworld.org/docid/3be01b964.html
11. http://www.refworld.org/docid/3ae6b3ae4.html
12. http://www.refworld.org/docid/3ae6b36018.html
13. https://treaties.un.org/Pages/ViewDetails.aspx?src=IND&mtdsg_no=IV-13&chapter=4&clang=_en

References

Adamson, Fiona. 2006. Crossing Borders: International Migration and National Security. *International Security*, 31(1): 165–99.

Andreas, Peter. 2009. *Border Games: Policing the U.S.—Mexico Divide*, 2nd edn. Ithaca, NY: Cornell University Press.

Aradau, Claudia. 2004. The Perverse Politics of Four-Letter Words: Risk and Pity in the Securitisation of Human Trafficking. *Millennium*, 33(2): 251–77.

Beah, Ishmael. 2007. *A Long Way Gone: Memoirs of a Boy Soldier*. New York: Farrar, Straus and Giroux.

Betts, Alexander. 2013. *Survival Migration: Failed Governance and the Crisis of Displacement*. Ithaca, NY: Cornell University Press.

Bevan, Vaughan. 1986. *The Development of British Immigration Law*. London: Croom Helm.

Bhabha, Jacqueline. 2014. *Child Migration & Human Rights in a Global Age*. Princeton, NJ: Princeton University Press.

Bhabha, Jacqueline, Francesca King, and Sue Shutter (eds.). 1985. *Worlds Apart: Women under Immigration and Nationality Law*. London: Pluto.

Branch, Jordan. 2014. *The Cartographic State: Maps, Territory, and the Origins of Sovereignty*. Cambridge: Cambridge University Press.

Breckenridge, Keith. 2014. *Biometric State: The Global Politics of Identification and Surveillance in South Africa, 1850 to the Present*. Cambridge: Cambridge University Press.

Brubaker, Rogers. 1992. *Citizenship and Nationhood in France and Germany*. Cambridge, MA: Harvard University Press.

Castles, Stephen and Mark Miller. 2003. *The Age of Migration: International Population Movements in the Modern World*, 3rd edn. New York: Guilford.

Chebel d'Appollonia, Ariane. 2008. Immigration, Security, and Integration in the European Union. In Ariane Chebel d'Appollonia and Simon Reich (eds.), *Immigration, Integration, and Security: America and Europe in Comparative Perspective*, ch. 11. Pittsburgh, PA: University of Pittsburgh Press.

Cooper, Frederick. 2005. *Colonialism in Question: Theory, Knowledge, History*. Berkeley: University of California Press.

Copeland, Emily. 2003. A Rare Opening in the Wall: The Growing Recognition of Gender-Based Persecution. In Niklaus Steiner, Mark Gibney, and Gil Loescher (eds.), *Problems of Protection: The UNHCR, Refugees, and Human Rights*. New York: Routledge.

Crawford, Neta. 1994. A Security Regime among Democracies: Cooperation among Iroquois Nations. *International Organization*, 48(3): 345–85.

Dauvergne, Catherine. 2008. *Making People Illegal: What Globalization Means for Migration and Law*. New York: Cambridge University Press.

Fitzgerald, David and David Cook-Martín. 2014. *Culling the Masses: The Democratic Origins of Racist Immigration Policy in the Americas*. Cambridge, MA: Harvard University Press.

Ford, Lisa. 2010. *Settler Sovereignty: Jurisdiction and Indigenous People in America and Australia*. Cambridge, MA: Harvard University Press.

Gilroy, Paul. 1987. *"There Ain't No Black in the Union Jack": The Cultural Politics of Race and Nation*. Chicago: University of Chicago.

Greenhill, Kelly. 2010. *Weapons of Mass Migration: Forced Displacement, Coercion, and Foreign Policy*. Ithaca, NY: Cornell University Press.

Hollifield, James. 1992. *Immigrants, Markets and States: The Political Economy of Postwar Europe*. Cambridge, MA: Harvard University Press.

Hollifield, James. 2000. Migration and the "New" International Order: The Missing Regime. In Bimal Ghosh (ed.), *Managing Migration: Time for a New International Regime?* pp. 75–109. Oxford: Oxford University Press.

Innes, Alexandria. 2015. *Migration, Citizenship and the Challenge for Security: An Ethnographic Approach*. Basingstoke: Palgrave Macmillan.

Jung, Moon-Kie. 2015. *Beneath the Surface of White Supremacy: Denaturalizing U.S. Racisms Past and Present*. Stanford, CA: Stanford University Press.

Kastoryano, Riva. 2002. *Negotiating Identities: States and Immigrants in France and Germany*, trans. Barbara Harshav. Princeton, NJ: Princeton University Press.

Kelley, Ninette and Michael Trebilcock. 2010. *The Making of the Mosaic: A History of Canadian Immigration Policy*, 2nd edn. Toronto: University of Toronto Press.

Klotz, Audie. 2013. *Migration and National Identity in South Africa, 1860–2010*. New York: Cambridge University Press.

Lake, Marilyn and Henry Reynolds. 2008. *Drawing the Global Colour Line: White Men's Countries and the International Challenge of Racial Equality*. Cambridge: Cambridge University Press.

Lischer, Sarah Kenyon. 2005. *Dangerous Sanctuaries: Refugee Camps, Civil War, and the Dilemmas of Humanitarian Aid*. Ithaca, NY: Cornell University Press.

Loescher, Gil. 2001. *The UNHCR and World Politics: A Perilous Path*. Oxford: Oxford University Press.
Lucassen, Leo. 2005. *The Immigrant Threat: The Integration of Old and New Migrants in Western Europe since 1850*. Urbana: University of Illinois Press.
Martin, Susan. 2011. *A Nation of Immigrants*. New York: Cambridge University Press.
Martin, Susan. 2014. *International Migration: Evolving Trends from the Early Twentieth Century to the Present*. New York: Cambridge University Press.
Metcalf, Thomas. 2007. *Imperial Connections: India in the Indian Ocean Arena, 1860–1920*. Berkeley: University of California Press.
Money, Jeannette. 1999. *Fences and Neighbors: The Political Geography of Immigration Control*. Ithaca, NY: Cornell University Press.
Mongia, Radhika. 2003. Race, Nationality, Mobility: A History of the Passport. In Antoinette Burton (ed.), *After the Imperial Turn: Thinking with and through the Nation*, pp.196–214. Durham: Duke University Press.
Morreira, Shannon. 2016. *Rights after Wrongs: Local Knowledge and Human Rights in Zimbabwe*. Stanford: Stanford University Press.
Orchard, Phil. 2014. *A Right to Flee: Refugees, States, and the Construction of International Cooperation*. Cambridge: Cambridge University Press.
Paul, Kathleen. 1997. *Whitewashing Britain: Race and Citizenship in the Postwar Era*. Ithaca, NY: Cornell University Press.
Peberdy, Sally. 2009. *Selecting Immigrants: National Identity and South Africa's Immigration Policies 1910–2008*. Johannesburg: Wits University Press.
Quirk, Joel. 2011. *The Anti-Slavery Project: From the Slave Trade to Human Trafficking*. Philadelphia, PA: University of Pennsylvania Press.
Ramirez, Bruno. 2001. *Crossing the 49th Parallel: Migration from Canada to the United States, 1900–1930*. Ithaca, NY: Cornell University Press.
Raussiguier, Catherine. 1999. Gender, Race and Exclusion: A New Look at the French Republican Tradition, *International Feminist Journal of Politics*, 1(3): 435–57.
Richmond, Anthony. 1994. *Global Apartheid: Refugees, Racism, and the New World Order*. Oxford: Oxford University Press.
Rudolph, Christopher. 2003. Security and the Political Economy of International Migration. *American Political Science Review*, 97(4): 603–20.
Rudolph, Christopher. 2006. *National Security and Immigration Policy Development in the United States and Western Europe*. Stanford, CA: Stanford University Press.
Salter, Mark. 2003. *Rights of Passage: The Passport in International Relations*. Boulder, CO: Lynne Rienner.
Schneider, Dorothee. 2011. *Crossing Borders: Migration and Citizenship in the Twentieth Century United States*. Cambridge, MA: Harvard University Press.
Steinberg, Jonny. 2015. *A Man of Good Hope*. New York: Vintage.
Thompson, Leonard. 1990. *A History of South Africa*. New Haven, CT: Yale University Press.
Tichenor, Daniel. 2002. *Dividing Lines: The Politics of Immigration Control in America*. Princeton, NJ: Princeton University Press.
Tinker, Hugh. 1974. *A New System of Slavery: The Export of Indian Labour Overseas, 1830–1920*. London: Oxford University Press.
Towns, Ann. 2010. *Women and States: Norms and Hierarchies in International Society*. Cambridge: Cambridge University Press.

Vigneswaran, Darshan. 2013. *Territory, Migration and the Evolution of the International System*. Basingstoke: Palgrave Macmillan.

Vucetic, Srdjan. 2011. *The Anglosphere: A Genealogy of a Racialized Identity in International Relations*. Stanford, CA: Stanford University Press.

Wæver, Ole. 1993. Societal Security: The Concept. In Ole Wæver, Barry Buzan, Morten Kelstrup and Pierre Lemaitre (eds.), *Identity, Migration and the New Security Agenda in Europe*, pp. 17–40. New York: St. Martin's Press.

Weiner, Myron. 1992/93. Security, Stability, and International Migration. *International Security*, 17(3): 91–126.

Wolfe, Eric. 1982. *Europe and the People without History*. Berkeley: University of California Press.

Zaiotti, Ruben. 2011. *Cultures of Border Control: Schengen & the Evolution of European Frontiers*. Chicago: University of Chicago Press.

Zolberg, Aristide. 2006. *A Nation by Design: Immigration Policy and the Fashioning of America*. Cambridge, MA: Harvard University Press.

CHAPTER 31

HUMANITARIAN INTERVENTION

JENNIFER M. WELSH

THERE are few issues related to peace and security that have engendered more controversy than the practice of humanitarian intervention. Indeed, ethical and political debates about the legitimacy of military action by outside actors to address humanitarian suffering within the sovereign jurisdiction of a state have been an integral part of the evolution of modern international society. It is therefore reasonable to assume, in taking up the future-oriented challenge of the editors of this volume, that such debates will continue to feature on the international security landscape of the twenty-first century. Nonetheless, as I will illustrate below, there are both material and psychological factors—operating at all three of Kenneth Waltz's three levels of analysis (Waltz 1959)—that will arguably constrain the practice of intervention for humanitarian purposes (though not necessarily interventions with other goals in mind). Despite the continuing power of individual-centric rather than state-centric notions of security, and the breadth of the consensus on the need to treat certain acts—commonly described as "atrocity crimes"[1]—as matters of *international* (as opposed to domestic) concern, the presence of a case for humanitarian intervention is much less likely to translate into an actual choice to intervene than it did during the last three decades.

This chapter starts from the premise that the trajectory of the practice of humanitarian intervention is best understood in reference to its historical development. As I will suggest, humanitarian intervention has always been facilitated, despite its potentially corrosive effect on sovereignty, by certain material and ideational conditions or "hierarchies" (Macmillan 2013: 1039). This was as true of the 1990s as it was of the mid-nineteenth century. But the past also matters in another sense: the willingness of states to intervene in the contemporary era has been profoundly shaped by previous instances of intervention (or non-intervention) and the perceived success or failures of such strategies. The importance of these "pivotal events" in the ongoing story of humanitarian intervention partly derives from the fact that such actions are rarely (if ever) responses to perceived existential security threats, but rather constitute political and moral *choices* involving assessments of cost and benefit—often on the basis of comparisons with interventions in the past. Of course, the perception of costs and benefits and the representation of past events are susceptible to change and could be consciously altered. I broadly concur with constructivist and critical scholars that decisions related to peace and security never proceed on the basis of objective or brute facts alone. It would therefore be premature to proclaim that the context has been forever altered in favor of non-intervention over intervention.

31.1 Early Interventions in the "Interests of Humanity"

The term "intervention"—though in usage in earlier centuries—only came to refer to coercive interference in the domestic affairs of a state in the middle of nineteenth century, at roughly the same time that John Stuart Mill penned his famous works on non-intervention (Mill 1875). It was in this period that diplomatic statements and broader public discourse began to refer to a form of coercion that was distinct both from interstate war and from formal empire: intervention constituted a discrete act of interference that did not seek to change the formal legal status of an "intervened party" (Macmillan 2013: 1041). The emergence of an identifiable class of great powers in the nineteenth century was critical to the spread and legitimation of this kind of coercive interference, as these custodians of order became leading political actors in maintaining stability and hierarchy in European international society—and beyond (Keene 2013). Intervention was deemed rightful if it was collective and based on great power consensus. The development of stark power differentials among actors was, however, only one factor in enabling the more particular phenomenon of humanitarian intervention; the latter was also made possible by the intensifying links between polities and peoples that made the suffering of others, in far-flung places, more accessible (Festa 2010).

But despite intervention's relatively modern standing as a term of art, its *practice*, and particularly the practice of humanitarian intervention, has a much longer history. From the sixteenth century onward, princes and state leaders deployed armed force in other jurisdictions, without the consent of those in that jurisdiction, and justified their actions on the basis of the appalling acts of foreign sovereigns. Oliver Cromwell's intervention on behalf of the Vaudois in the Savoy in 1656—though partially motivated by religious affinity to fellow Protestants—was primarily driven by outrage over their inhumane treatment by a tyrannical Duke of Savoy. The emotive language used by Cromwell, notes historian David Trim, suggests that he "conceived of the Vaudois as fellow suffering *human beings*, rather than simply types of Protestant martyr-heroes." (Trim 2013: 38; emphasis added). As this example shows, humanitarian intervention is not something peculiar to the past two centuries, as some have argued (Lawson and Tardelli 2013), but is also evident in the previous efforts of sovereigns to address "bad behavior" that transgressed commonly accepted standards of conduct toward populations.

There were a variety of humanitarian bases for intervention advanced in earlier centuries, ranging from the need to rescue fellow humans from egregious harm or vicious oppression by a tyrannical ruler, to the imperative to respond to massacres committed against members of particular religious groups. Nonetheless, given the gathering strength of the counteracting norm of non-intervention in intra-European relations (in relations between Europe and the non-European world, by contrast, intervention was widely practiced as a tool to reorder and "civilize"), and the value that was placed on its protection of diversity and autonomy, intervening princes and states were more likely to seek a change in the target's policy or behavior, rather than to change the regime itself (Trim 2013). The power of non-intervention as a brake on transgressions of sovereignty was also buttressed by the more general rise of positivism in international law. Whereas Hugo Grotius had established a right of sovereigns (though, crucially, not a duty) to wage war on behalf of the oppressed inside another state, the legitimate grounds for intervention gradually narrowed over the course of the eighteenth and nineteenth centuries. This reflected a shift away from the moral imperatives of the Middle Ages, toward the task of consolidating a modern international society, based on the emerging idea of *de jure* (if not *de facto*) sovereign equality.

Humanitarian intervention did develop into a coherent *political* notion in the nineteenth century, and was practiced widely by the ancestors of modern-day liberals in crises such as the Greek War of Independence, or the persecution of Christian minorities in the Ottoman Empire (Finnemore 2004; Bass 2008). However, these responses to massacre and atrocities were not based on a broad philosophy of "secular universalism," but rather, as David Rodogno argues, on threats to particular religious and ethnic groups. In short, "suffering Christianity" was the primary concern of policy-makers, and not suffering writ-large (Rodogno 2011: 11). Moreover, these modern instances of humanitarian intervention were not generally considered by international lawyers as constituting a legal exception to the hardening rule of non-intervention; instead, they helped to create the space for a more explicit normative discussion about where and when such coercive means, as infringements of sovereignty, were justified (Lawson and Tardelli 2013: 1236). Thus, while intervention in the late nineteenth century was not prohibited outright—given its frequent practice on Europe's periphery—it was carefully circumscribed (Winfield 1922–23). By the early twentieth century, intervention was legally sanctioned only in situations of civil war where clear lines could be drawn between a ruler and his people; it could not be justified as a defense of the rights of the oppressed in other jurisdictions against their sovereign. Most international lawyers, in fact, placed the question of humanitarian intervention outside the realm of law altogether, describing it as a matter of politics, policy, or morality (Chesterman 2001: 35–44).

The controversial place of humanitarian intervention in the nineteenth century also stemmed from a set of ethical and political concerns that have continued to shape debates about its practice in our contemporary era. These can be roughly summarized as problems related to *motives, consistency, scope*, and *participation*—all of which have continued to affect the legitimacy of using force for humanitarian purposes.

The first issue arises from the frequent (and some would argue inescapable) phenomenon of mixed motives: how can we condone the practice of humanitarian intervention if interveners have additional motives—beyond humanitarian ones—for employing military force? This question was as pressing for legal scholars in the late nineteenth century as it was in the beginning of the twenty-first. The second and related problem is that of inconsistency: why intervention on behalf of the Ottoman Greeks, but not to save Ottoman Armenians? Or, to take a contemporary example, why military action to protect Kosovar Albanians but not the victims of the Janjaweed militia in Darfur? The selectivity with which powerful states have acted to "save strangers" has always informed opposition to legitimizing the practice of humanitarian intervention.

The third source of concern is one of scope. If a case can be made that armed intervention is required to address a humanitarian emergency, what kind of military action and what level of force are appropriate? Are humanitarian objectives best served by a sharp and short show of force or do they require a more comprehensive and sustained commitment by outside powers—which in turn could embroil interveners in a long-term campaign? In the contemporary era, this dichotomy between "surgical strike" and "quagmire" (Macmillan 2013) often plays out in debates over whether air power alone can protect populations. But worries about how to define and contain the scope of humanitarian intervention have a longer history. The fear of stationing a large army in Asia Minor constrained European powers from responding decisively to the 1909 massacre of Armenians in Adana (Rodogno 2011), just as the reluctance to deploy significant numbers of American forces acted as a break on US intervention, just over a century later, in the Syrian civil conflict.

The final issue that frequently features in debates about humanitarian intervention relates to participation: Who has the right to act in the "interests of humanity"? Writing just prior to the First World War, French international lawyer Antonine Rougier insisted that not just any old power, no matter how capable, could respond to a violation of the laws of humanity. In order to minimize the risk of self-serving interventions by powerful states, unilateralism had to be outlawed (Rougier 1910). But what about those instances in which collective agreement is either unavailable, or too time-consuming to achieve? Despite the frustrations associated with multilateralism, most members of international society have insisted upon it as both a guarantor of greater impartiality and a means of placing checks and balances on military intervention—precisely at the moment when the use of coercive means is most controversial (Recchia and Welsh 2013: 4). As a result, the vast majority of interventions for humanitarian interventions since the Second World War have been undertaken multilaterally, through regional organizations or the United Nations. There is also some evidence to indicate that impartial multilateral interventions—which are directed at minimizing suffering rather than strengthening one or more parties in a conflict—are related to a decline in fatality rates (Dembinski and Gromes 2016).

31.2 The Multilateralization of Humanitarian Intervention in the Twentieth Century

While the United Nations Charter established clear limitations on the use of force, effectively outlawing aggression, it did not directly address the question of whether states can use military force to address a humanitarian crisis occurring within the sovereign jurisdiction of another member state of the UN. The language of Article 2(4) reflects the strong post-1945 commitment to delegitimizing acts of war outside the context of self-defence and to transferring any authorization for the use of force to the Security Council (Chesterman 2001: 48–9; Roberts 2004). At the same time, given the experience of brutality against civilian populations during the Second World War, state representatives maintained that the promotion and protection of human rights had to be one of the core purposes and principles of the new post-war organization. This concern is reflected in the strong human rights commitments in Articles 1(2), 1(3), and 55 of the Charter (which were expanded in subsequent declarations and conventions) and in the creation of legal instruments such as the Convention on the Prevention and Punishment of Genocide.

The result is what some have described as an irreconcilable conflict between two core principles of the United Nations system: sovereignty and human rights (Weiss 2012: 24). The former suggests that states should enjoy sovereign equality—defined internally as exclusive jurisdiction within a territory and externally as freedom from outside interference—while the latter indicates that individual rights are inalienable and transcend sovereign frontiers. But another way of interpreting the Charter is to recognize the ways in which it left open the possibility of interventions for humanitarian purposes through the directives of the Security Council. Those provisions containing collective obligations for the maintenance of international peace and security suggest that sovereignty is not a general and absolute barrier to action. While Article 2(7) is normally taken as *the* definitive statement of non-intervention, the final phrase of that same article allows for enforcement actions under Chapter VII. This opening, combined with the provisions of Articles 39 and 42, gives the Council the right to define what constitutes a threat to international peace and security and to decide on the appropriate type of military action—should it be deemed necessary to counter that threat.

As the empirical record shows, the Council proved reluctant to engage in an expansive definition of threats to peace and security for most of the Cold War period. There were only two instances throughout the first four decades of the UN's life in which the Security Council tilted toward human rights over the claims of sovereignty and imposed coercive measures: white-minority rule in Rhodesia (in 1966) and apartheid in South Africa (in 1977). Of the three main instances which most closely resemble humanitarian interventions in this period—India's military action in East Pakistan in 1971, Vietnam's intervention in Cambodia in 1979, and Tanzania's show of force in Uganda in 1979—only the former two were discussed within the Council, and in both cases the humanitarian rationale for military action were hotly contested (Wheeler 2000). Nonetheless, the UN Secretary General at the time of the Indian intervention, U Thant, pointed the way toward a new approach, by arguing that Pakistan's internal repression constituted a threat to international peace and security that the Council had a responsibility to address (U Thant 1978: 422–4).

Following the end of the Cold War, and the structural change which enabled more collaboration among the great powers, the Security Council began to take a more expansive approach in defining threats to peace and security—a power it theoretically always had—in dealing with a series of situations involving humanitarian crises. The shift was a product of not only the easing of East–West tensions, but also, inter alia, the proliferation of complex humanitarian emergencies that called for a different form of international engagement, normative developments related to human rights and human security (Wheeler 2000; Weiss 2012), and the role of media in mobilizing concern among Western domestic publics (Shaw 1996; Minear et al. 1996). This combination of "push" factors was particularly visible with respect to the Council's response to the plight of Kurds and Shiites in northern Iraq in 1991, the famine in Somalia in 1992, the destructive civil war in the Balkans during the 1990s, and the post-referendum violence in East Timor in 1999—all of which gave rise to Security Council authorized actions to address various forms of humanitarian crisis. This accumulated practice indicated that the Council had come to see "flagrant and widespread violations of international humanitarian and human rights law in situations of armed conflict" as a threat to the peace (United Nations Security Council, 2000). It also revealed at least toleration, if not active support in all cases, for UN-authorized military actions with an expressly humanitarian purpose.

It is crucial to note, however, that the practice from the 1990s legitimized *multilateral* action to save individuals in peril; the weight of state opinion and the majority opinion of international lawyers did not favour unilateral humanitarian intervention—by one state or a coalition of states acting without multilateral backing (Byers and Chesterman 2003; Wheeler 2004). In practice this meant that the legitimacy of intervention for humanitarian purposes clearly rested upon the condition of Security Council authorization—the body with "primary responsibility" for the maintenance of international peace and security.[2]

There were two core problems with this state of play at the end of the 1990s. First, despite the Security Council's evolving practice toward authorization of military measures in situations of humanitarian emergency, this trend was highly contingent on intergovernmental agreement. The 1994 genocide in Rwanda, and the inadequate international response, illustrated all too vividly how that contingency could cost lives (United Nations 1999). On the other hand, NATO's 1999 bombing campaign in Kosovo, which did not have explicit authorization, demonstrated how the Security Council's imprimatur remained essential to legitimizing intervention for humanitarian purposes (Independent International Commission on Kosovo 2000). If the international community's failure to act to the unfolding massacre in Rwanda provoked condemnation, so too did the West's military campaign to address the spectre of ethnic cleansing of Kosovar Albanians in 1999.

It was this stalemate that in part helped to propel the development of the principle of the Responsibility to Protect (R2P), first through the work of the International Commission on Intervention and State Sovereignty (2001) and later through former UN Secretary General Kofi Annan's proposals for UN reform that were tabled at the 60th anniversary World Summit (Annan 2005). In searching for a new consensus to respond more effectively to extreme humanitarian tragedies, the proponents of R2P advanced two principal claims: first, that the best path to protecting populations was to *prevent* situations involving atrocity crimes—and thereby avoid the need to resort to more costly, and controversial, military intervention later on; and second, that the best strategy was a partnership for protection between national authorities (who bore the primary responsibility to protect populations) and the international community (which could play a supportive and remedial role). The latter claim was based on the assumption that the rights of sovereignty were not absolute and unconditional, but rather depended upon a state's ability to ensure basic protection for its population. As the ICISS report put it: "Where a population is suffering serious harm, as a result of internal war, insurgency, repression or state failure, and the state in question is unwilling or unable to halt or avert it, the principle of non-intervention yields to the international responsibility to protect." (ICISS 2001: xi) Understood in this way, international efforts to assist in protection—including, if necessary, through military means—could be sovereignty *enhancing* if they were aimed at restoring the protective function of states. Unlike the more "confrontational" notion of humanitarian intervention, R2P was thus seen by its proponents as "a linking concept that bridges the divide between the international community and the sovereign state" (Thakur 2005: 123).

When the principle of R2P was ultimately endorsed by heads of state and government at the 2005 World Summit Outcome Document (United Nations 2005), it enunciated a broader framework for protection that included not only prevention, but also the use of non-military means of response. In other words, the Responsibility to Protect, while containing a provision for military action when peaceful means prove inadequate, is much broader and deeper than the older practice of humanitarian intervention. As a *political* principle, R2P was designed both to shift expectations about how the international community should view situations involving atrocity crimes, and to mobilize greater will and capacity to act at the national, regional, and international levels. Although its unanimous endorsement can be viewed as an authoritative interpretation of existing international law relating to international human rights, humanitarian law, and the use of force, it did not itself create any new legal obligations (Strauss 2009; Welsh and Banda 2010).

In particular, the intergovernmental consensus on R2P's coercive dimension—which is included under so-called Pillar Three[3]—reflects the continuing concern about unilateralism and thus rests firmly upon multilateral authorization. Legitimate military action in support of the principle is situated firmly within the existing collective security provision of the UN Charter, despite the frequently expressed concerns about the potential for Security Council paralysis (Welsh 2013). As Michael Doyle concludes, R2P can be seen as "both a *license for* and a *leash against* forcible intervention" (Doyle 2015: 110): it legitimizes greater international concern for atrocity-crime situations that occur (or are imminent) inside a state's sovereign jurisdiction, but insists that any coercive response to such situations must be undertaken through "case by case" decisions of the Security Council.

The permissive potential of R2P was illustrated by the Council's authorization, through Resolution 1973, of "all necessary measures" to protect civilians in Libya in the spring of 2011.[4] Although the relative weight and mix of motives for intervening have been hotly debated, there is strong evidence that the lessons of non-intervention in the past (especially the cases of Rwanda and Srebrenica) weighed heavily in the balance and were particularly dominant in the minds of the US President and Secretary of State (Adler-Nissen and Pouliot 2014: 13; Paris 2014: 587). Yet, when compared with previous humanitarian crises that had generated calls for a resolute international response, the civilian casualties in Libya prior to the passing of Resolution 1973 were relatively low (Doyle 2015: 109). The military action was therefore primarily *preventive* in nature, designed to respond to calls for the international community to forestall atrocity crimes, rather than to respond when mass killing has already taken place.

The Security Council's swift response to the mounting crisis in Libya was highly significant in that it represented the first time that the United Nations had authorized the use of force for civilian protection purposes, without the consent of the state in question. Moreover, the Resolution passed on March 17, 2011 referred not only to the "protection of civilians" but also to the "protection of civilian populated areas," suggesting to some that the international community had effectively inserted itself in the ongoing struggle, by putting particular cities out of bounds for Colonel Qaddafi and his forces. The potential for controversy was revealed all too quickly, when two days after the passing of Resolution 1973 former US President Barack Obama issued an ultimatum to Qaddafi to pull back from rebel strongholds, such as Ajdabiya and Misrata. Once the initial bombing campaign achieved the objective of preventing the further advance of Qaddafi's forces on Benghazi, NATO widened its list of targets to include more controversial sites (such as buildings hosting senior political officials in the Libyan chain of command) and some countries in the coalition began providing key support to fighters from the Libyan opposition—in apparent contravention of Security Council resolutions (Kuperman 2013; Paris 2014;).

It was these tactical moves by the NATO-led mission that sparked intense criticism of the intervention and claims that the legally mandated objective of civilian protection had been overtaken by the broader goal of regime change (Rieff 2011; Kuperman 2013; Singh Puri 2016). Post-facto assessments of the military campaign in Libya have thus been dichotomous. For some, March 2011 represented a "coming of age" for R2P and a sign that states could come together to defend humanitarian principles. As one proponent of the intervention put it: "Libya suggests that we can say no more Holocausts, Cambodias, and Rwandas—and occasionally mean it" (Weiss 2012: 172). Others—especially those Security Council members who had reluctantly allowed Resolution

1973 to pass—insisted they had been "hoodwinked" by Western powers and concluded that interventions for humanitarian purposes would always be manipulated by the powerful for their own purposes (Doyle 2015: 14; Brockmeier et al. 2016: 123). The conduct of the military campaign also gave rise to a Brazilian proposal to enhance the procedures for multilateral authorization, by establishing criteria on when and how force should be used to protect civilians and accountability mechanisms for those implementing a Security Council mandate (Stuenkel and Tourinho 2014).

31.3 The Power of the Past: Biases in Strategic Decision Making about Humanitarian Intervention

The controversy surrounding use of force for humanitarian purposes in Libya had a significant impact on subsequent policy making with respect to the ongoing crisis in Syria—most notably the failure of the Security Council to act decisively to address mounting evidence of atrocity crimes (Bellamy 2014; Singh Puri 2016). The question of whether the 2011 intervention had a negative effect on broader norms related to protection is less clear-cut (Brockmeier et al. 2016), and cannot be examined in detail here. What is certain is that several states—particularly Russia—referenced the experience in Libya as a rationale for opposing collective action against the Syrian government. Once again, the shadow of past interventions has loomed large in debates about whether or how to intervene in the present.

In employing the Libyan precedent, scholars and policy-makers have not only referenced the age-old concern about the potential for humanitarian rationale to mask deeper and "darker" objectives. They have also pointed to the aftermath of the 2011 intervention to emphasize the costs of using military means: outsiders sow chaos and destruction, they contend, leaving societies less stable, and more violent, than they would have been without external intervention (Singh Puri 2016). Military action to prevent or respond to atrocity crimes is therefore being judged not in terms of whether it meets its immediate goal, but rather in terms of whether the state in which intervention occurs becomes *generally* more stable. And when this test is applied, the verdict analysts often reach is that the costs outweigh the benefits. The combined experience of Western states in Afghanistan and Iraq—military actions that were not humanitarian interventions—have amplified the power of this "lesson learned."

By adopting the individual level of analysis, we can see how deliberation about humanitarian intervention has come to feature a set of systematic biases that currently appear to favor inaction. The philosopher Bashshar Haydar unpacks this phenomenon into a set of three "asymmetries" in the way that individuals assess the costs of intervention and non-intervention (Haydar 2017). The first asymmetry is between how decision-makers evaluate failed interventions and (relatively) successful interventions. The costs of the former are given much greater emphasis than the benefits of the latter, given the greater psychological impact of "bad" outcomes. Thus, even though *Operation Provide Comfort* (the intervention on behalf of Kurds in northern Iraq in 1991) was quite successful in meeting its stated objective, it has largely faded from memory.

A second asymmetry is between how policy-makers assess a failed intervention and a failure to intervene. The latter must incur a significant level of negative consequences before it becomes prominent in the minds of those making decisions about a subsequent intervention. Hence, Rwanda registers as a failure to act, but the inadequate intervention in southern Iraq to protect Shiites in 1991 does not. On the other hand, an intervention can be deemed to have failed if it generates any loss of life—even if its purpose was to avert a much greater catastrophe. This judgment reflects both the cognitive tendency to react more strongly to the actual damage inflicted (no matter what the level) rather than the hypothetical harm averted, as well as the contentious nature of counter-factual reasoning (Paris 2014: 575-6).

And finally, there is a clear asymmetry in the criteria used to evaluate the success of a strategy of intervention and a strategy of non-intervention. When assessing interventions, Haydar argues, the bar for success is set almost impossibly high—a stable and rights-respecting country in the aftermath of military action—while the bar for failure is set very low; a very modest level of civilian casualties, even if proven to be unintended "collateral damage," can render an intervention unsuccessful. As a result, even though the Human Rights Council Report into violations of international humanitarian law in Libya found that NATO had conducted a "highly precise campaign with a demonstrable determination to avoid civilian casualties" (United Nations Human Rights Council 2014), the judgment of the opponents of the 2011 intervention has had a longer-term impact. When it comes to the strategy of non-intervention, on the other hand, the bar for failure is very high. As suggested above, there has to be a humanitarian catastrophe on an epic scale before non-intervention is deemed a bad strategy. To put it another way, the "cost of doing" nothing is systematically underplayed—a trend that some, including the late British Member of Parliament Jo Cox, argue has been persistent in the West's response to the civil war in Syria (McGovern and Tugendhat 2017).

As of the start of 2017, it was difficult to see how one could apply the label "non-intervention" to the Syrian crisis. In fact, there was a great deal of involvement by external powers—both regional and international—in a variety of forms, from the supply of weaponry to participation in active combat. This is a civil war that has seen a great deal of external meddling, particularly when the campaign against Daesh is added into the mix. Still, the West's response to the commission of atrocity crimes in Syria has been consistently characterized as one of non-intervention. The costs of that strategy can be measured not only in the thousands of civilian deaths, but also in the mass movement of the Syrian population both within and beyond the country's borders. The counter-factual is challenging to determine: what would have happened if the West had intervened decisively?

31.4 Conclusion

There is, of course, a powerful justification for some of these asymmetries in moral philosophy: actively *doing* harm is viewed as a greater evil than not preventing harm. There is also strong support in psychological literature for the cognitive biases that drive the overestimation of costs or negative outcomes. Both suggest that the balance toward inaction will be difficult to change. The current strategic context for humanitarian intervention is thus one in which decision-makers view "damned if you do" as worse than "damned if you don't."

When we turn from the individual to the system level of analysis, the prospects for humanitarian intervention also look dimmer than they did at the beginning of the twenty-first century. As other contributors to this volume have noted, traditional security threats have resumed a prominent place in the calculus of Western policy-makers, and the possibility of conflict among major powers is greater than at any time since the end of the Cold War. This arguably leaves less space for so-called wars of choice, such as humanitarian interventions.

However, "less" does not necessarily mean "none." There are at least two reasons to believe that the case for using force, as a last resort, to address large-scale humanitarian crises will continue to find some support. First, despite frostier relations among the permanent members of the Security Council, the UN has continued to authorize robust peace operations, under the auspices of Chapter VII, with a clear mandate to protect civilians. Recent examples include South Sudan, Mali, and the Central African Republic. While these are not strictly humanitarian interventions, they do suggest that some of the trends that favor expanded conceptions of peace and security will continue for the foreseeable future. Second, the reluctance of states to engage in large-scale interventions—with the associated risks of escalation or quagmire—does not rule out the possibility of more contained shows of force to create so-called safe areas. The latter option was strongly advocated by Turkish President Erdogan during the Syrian crisis, and also found adherents in the form of French President Hollande and German Chancellor Merkel. Although the proponents of safe zones did not win the argument in Syria, the case for this limited form of intervention may be compelling in other instances, particularly if the problem of internal displacement of populations continues to grow in scale and severity.

This brings us to the state level of analysis, and the future shape of foreign policy in those countries that have always shown the greatest inclination to intervene in the "interests of humanity": Western liberal states. In addition to the systemic pressures pressing down upon these countries are internal voices calling for the prioritization of *national* interests, narrowly conceived. While globalization and liberal internationalism were (and are) different phenomena, they share some of the same sources and sensibilities—both of which are now under critical scrutiny from pockets of Western public opinion. Deploying force abroad to "save strangers" has always required heroic arguments that appeal to a community that transcends sovereign states. The political environment that state leaders now occupy—and have done much to create—is likely to make such arguments hard to make, and more difficult to accept, in the decade ahead.[5]

Notes

1. In this chapter, I use the term "atrocity crimes" to refer to the four acts commonly associated with the principle of the Responsibility to Protect, which are specified in paragraph 138 of the 2005 World Summit Outcome Document: genocide, war crimes, crimes against humanity, and ethnic cleansing (United Nations 2005).
2. It is important to note that I am employing a relatively broad conception of humanitarian intervention. Some scholars define humanitarian intervention as encompassing only those actions that are not authorized by a multilateral body, referring to the latter as collective security actions (Holzgrefe and Keohane 2003: 1). Yet, most of the instances of intervention for humanitarian purposes in the post-Cold War period involved Security Council resolutions that invoked Chapter VII—i.e. a threat to international peace and security. As I have argued elsewhere (Welsh 2004), one can conclude from this that states are still uncomfortable asserting that gross human rights violations by a government against its own people is, *in itself*, a sufficient justification for the use of force, and must be supplemented by concerns about so-called spillover effects that threaten regional or international security.
3. Building on paragraphs 138 and 139 of the World Summit Outcome, R2P is now commonly described as consisting of three pillars. Pillar One, drawing on pre-existing legal obligations, is the responsibility of individual states to protect their own populations (whether nationals or not) from genocide, war crimes, ethnic cleansing, and crimes against humanity. Pillar Two calls upon the international community (acting through the UN system and partner organizations) to help states fulfil these responsibilities (for example, by helping to build capacity for the prevention of these crimes). Finally, Pillar Three specifies that if the state in question is "manifestly failing" to protect its population, UN member states have a residual role and can respond collectively, in a "timely and decisive manner," using the full range of political, humanitarian, diplomatic, and—if necessary—military tools (Ban Ki-moon 2009: paras. 10–12).
4. The Resolution was passed with 10 votes in favor and 5 abstentions (China, Russia, Brazil, India, and Germany).
5. The research leading to this chapter has received funding from the European Research Council under the European Union's Seventh Framework Agreement (FP/2007-2013)/ERC Grant Agreement n. 340956.

References

Adler-Nissen, R. and Pouliot, V. 2014. Power in Practice: Negotiating the International Intervention in Libya, *European Journal of International Relations*, 20(4): 1–23.

Annan, K. 2005. *In Larger Freedom: Toward Development, Security and Human Rights for All*, UN doc. A/59/2005 (March 21, 2005).

Ban Ki-Moon. 2009. *Report of the Secretary-General on Implementing the Responsibility to Protect*, UN doc. A/63/677 (July 23, 2009).

Bass, G. 2008. *Freedom's Battle: The Origins of Humanitarian Intervention.* New York: Alfred Knopf.

Bellamy, A. J. 2014. From Tripoli to Damascus? Lesson Learning and the Implementation of the Responsibility to Protect, *International Politics*, 51: 23–44.

Brockmeier, S., O. Stuenkel, and M. Tourinho. 2016. The Impact of the Libya Intervention Debates on Norms of Protection, *Global Society*, 30(1): 113–33.

Byers, M. and S. Chesterman. 2003. Changing the Rules about Rules? Unilateral Humanitarian intervention and the Future of International Law. In J. L. Holzgrefe and R. O. Keohane (eds.), *Humanitarian Intervention: Ethical, Legal, and Political Dilemmas.* Cambridge: Cambridge University Press.

Chesterman, S. 2001. *Just War or Just Peace? Humanitarian Intervention and International Law.* Oxford: Oxford University Press.

Dembinski, M. and T. Gromes. 2016. *The PRIF Dataset on Humanitarian Military Interventions.* Frankfurt: Peace Research Institute of Frankfurt.

Doyle, M. 2015. *The Question of Intervention*, New Haven, CT: Yale University Press.

Evans, G. 2008. *The Responsibility to Protect: Ending Mass Atrocity Crimes once and for all.* Washington, DC: Brookings Institution.

Festa, L. 2010. Humanity without Feathers. *Humanity: An International Journal of Human Rights, Humanitarianism, and Development*, 1(1): 3–27.

Finnemore, M. 2004. *The Purpose of Intervention.* Ithaca, NY: Cornell University Press.

Haydar, B. 2017. The Bias against Intervention. Paper presented to the Symposium on Humanitarian Intervention and the Responsibility to Protect. American University of Beirut, January 26, 2017.

Holzgrefe, J. L. and R. Keohane. 2003. *Humanitarian Intervention: Ethical, Legal and Political Dilemmas.* Cambridge: Cambridge University Press.

Independent International Commission on Kosovo. 2000. *The Kosovo Report: Conflict, International Response, Lessons Learned.* Oxford: Oxford University Press.

International Commission on Intervention and State Sovereignty. 2001. *The Responsibility to Protect: Report of the International Commission on Intervention and State Sovereignty*, Ottawa: International Development Research Corporation.

Jones, B. 2005. Implementing "In Larger Freedom." In P. Heinbecker, P. and P. Goff (eds.), *Irrelevant or Indispensible? The United Nations in the 21st Century.* Waterloo: Wilfred Laurier University Press.

Keene, E. 2013. International Hierarchy and the Origins of the Modern Practice of Intervention, *Review of International Studies*, 39(5): 1077–90.

Kuperman, A. 2013. NATO's Intervention in Libya: A Humanitarian Success? In A. Hehir and R. Murray (eds.), *Libya, the Responsibility to Protect and the Future of Humanitarian Intervention.* New York: Palgrave Macmillan.

Lawson, G. and L. Tardelli. 2013. The Past, Present and Future of Intervention, *Review of International Studies*, 39(5): 1233–53.

McGovern, A. and T. Tugendhat. 2017. *The Cost of Doing Nothing: The Price of Inaction in the Face of Mass Atrocities.* London, Policy Exchange. *Available at:* www.policyexchange.org.uk.

Macmillan, J. 2013. Intervention in the Modern World, *Review of International Studies*, 39(5): 1039–56.

Mill, J. S. 1875. A Few Words on Non-Intervention. In: *Dissertation and Discussions: Political, Philosophical, and Historical.* Vol. III, pp. 153–78 2nd edn. London: Longmans,.

Minear, L., C. Scott, and T. G. Weiss. 1996. *The News Media, Civil War, and Humanitarian Action.* Boulder, CO: Lynne Reinner.

Paris, R. 2014. The "Responsibility to Protect" and the Structural Problems of Preventive Humanitarian Intervention, *International Peacekeeping*, 21(5): 569–603.

Recchia, S. and J. Welsh (eds.). 2013. *Just and Unjust Military Intervention: European Thinkers from Vitoria to Mill.* Cambridge: Cambridge University Press.

Rieff, D. 2011. R2P, R.I.P. *The New York Times*, November 7, 2011.

Roberts, A. 2004. The United Nations and Humanitarian Intervention. In J. M. Welsh (ed.), *Humanitarian Intervention and International Relations*. Oxford: Oxford University Press,.

Rodogno, D. 2011. *Against Massacre: Humanitarian Interventions in the Ottoman Empire, 1815–1914*. Princeton, NJ: Princeton University Press.

Rougier, A. 1910. Theorie de l'intervention d'humanite, *Revue Generale du Droit International Public*, 17(1): 468–526.

Shaw, M. 1996. *Civil Society and the Media in Global Crises*. London: Pinter Press.

Singh Puri. H. 2016. *Perilous Interventions: The Security Council and the Politics of Chaos.* Harper Collins India.

Strauss, E. 2009. A Bird in the Hand is Worth Two in the Bush—On the Assumed Legal Nature of the Responsibility to Protect. *Global Responsibility to Protect*, 1: 291–323.

Stuenkel, O. and M. Tourinho. 2014. Regulating Intervention: Brazil and the Responsibility to Protect, *Conflict, Security and Development*, 14(4): 379–402.

Thakur, R. 2005. Freedom from Fear. In P. Heinbecker and P. Goff (eds.), *Irrelevant or Indispensable? The United Nations in the 21st Century*. Waterloo: Wilfred Laurier Press.

Trim, D. 2013. Intervention in European History, *c.* 1520–1850. In S. Recchia and J. Welsh (eds.), *Just and Unjust Military Intervention: European Thinkers from Vitoria to Mill.* Cambridge: Cambridge University Press.

United Nations. 1999. *Report of the Independent Inquiry into the Actions of the United Nations during the 1994 Genocide in Rwanda*, UN doc. S/1999/1257 (December 16, 1999).

United Nations. 2005. *World Summit Outcome*, UN doc. A/Res/60/1 (September 16, 2005).

United Nations Human Rights Council. 2014. *Report of the International Commission of Inquiry on Libya*, UN doc. A/HRC/19/68.

United Nations Security Council. 2000. *Protection of Civilians in Armed Conflict*, UN doc. S/Res/1296 (April 19, 2000).

U. Thant. 1978. *View from the UN.* London: David and Charles.

Waltz, K. 1959. *Man, the State, and War: A Theoretical Analysis.* New York: Columbia University Press.

Weiss, T. G. 2012. *Humanitarian Intervention.* Cambridge: Polity Press.

Welsh, J. M. (ed.). 2004. *Humanitarian Intervention and International Relations.* Oxford: Oxford University Press.

Welsh, J. M. 2013. Norm Contestation and the Responsibility to Protect. *Global Responsibility to Protect*, 5: 365–96.

Welsh, J. M. and M. Banda. 2010. International Law and the Responsibility to Protect: Clarifying or Expanding States' Responsibilities? *Global Responsibility to Protect*, 2: 213–31.

Wheeler, N. 2000. *Saving Strangers: Humanitarian Intervention and International Society.* Oxford: Oxford Uniersity Press.

Winfield, P. H. 1922–3. The History of Intervention in International Law. *British Yearbook of International Law*, 131–34.

CHAPTER 32

ENVIRONMENTAL SECURITY

JOSHUA BUSBY

WHAT is the link between the environment and security? The answer depends on the meaning of "security" and the research methods used. Focused mainly on case studies, the first major wave of scholarship on environmental change and violence emerged just as advocates and scholars sought to redefine security in the late 1980s. A second wave starting in the mid-2000s zeroed in on whether climate change was associated with conflict and was joined by quantitative social scientists employing big data and innovative research designs. As this chapter shows, along the way aspirations for a transformation in how we conceive of security narrowed to more tractable research questions about violence.

The trajectory is understandable but unfortunate. With climate change and unprecedented pressures on the natural world, environmental degradation may pose an existential challenge for some places and key ecosystem services and systems like carbon dioxide storage, coral reefs, and more. A security agenda that solely looks at violence is impoverished, transforming global problems into largely local affairs. Since many environmental problems, including but not limited to climate change, emanate from external forces and intersect with trade, aid, and alliances, the challenge is how to study problems of unknowable gravity where past patterns offer limited guidance. To imagine how the future could be different, however, we need to understand the intellectual history.[1]

32.1 The First Debate: The Opening

The traditional meaning of national security has "meant protection from organized violence caused by armed foreigners" (Del Rosso 1995: 183). Though it historically referred to protecting the state's territorial integrity, it has a broader meaning than state survival. Countries have interests beyond their borders for which they may be willing to fight. These "vital interests" may be tied to the country's "way of life," its access to critical natural resources, and be considered so important that a challenge would threaten national security (Art 2003: 3).

Moves to link environmental issues to security date back to the mid-1980s when scholars and advocates sought to widen the concept to encompass environmental concerns, health, human rights, and development. In 1983, Richard Ullman wrote that defining security in military terms "causes states to concentrate on military threats and to ignore other and perhaps even more harmful dangers" (Ullman 1983: 129). He called for a different approach based on harms that could (1) quickly and drastically cause a degradation in the quality of life of a people; and (2) threaten to narrow the options governments and other actors had to respond. With this definition in hand, "natural" disasters such as droughts and floods or epidemics could rise to the level of concern long occupied by interstate war to internal violence (Ullman 1983: 133).

With the Cold War winding down, this demand gained more traction. There was considerable optimism that the environment could finally get the attention it deserved. Jessica Mathews (1989: 177) captured this perspective: "Man is still utterly dependent on the natural world but now has for the first time the ability to alter it, rapidly and on a global scale." The dystopian underpinning of environmental threats loomed large in this assessment. Journalist Robert Kaplan captured the zeitgeist in his 1994 essay "The Coming Anarchy" in which he suggested the environment would be the defining national security issue of the early twenty-first century (Kaplan 1994).

That essay helped bring Canadian scholar Thomas Homer-Dixon to the forefront. He and his collaborators delivered an ambitious and complex portrait of the links between the environment and conflict, drawing on case studies of Rwanda, South Africa, and other places (Homer-Dixon 1991, 1994, 1999; Homer-Dixon and Blitt 1998; Percival and Homer-Dixon 1998). Alongside Kaplan's cruder version, Homer-Dixon's scholarship helped catapult environmental security onto the agenda of the Clinton administration (Peluso and Watts 2001: 4).

Homer-Dixon foresaw a future of environmentally-driven scarcity potentially leading to violence, particularly within developing countries (Homer-Dixon 1991: 78). While inspired by the eighteenth-century cleric Thomas Malthus, Homer-Dixon sought to avoid criticism of being seen as an "environmental determinist."[2] He wrote that environmental factors were neither necessary nor sufficient for conflict (Homer-Dixon 1999: 7). Moreover, understanding the environmental contribution to conflict was complicated given a tangled chain of causation, interactions between environmental and social causes, effects that only occur above certain thresholds, and feedback loops (Homer-Dixon 1991: 86, 107, 1999: 105–6, 174). While he despaired of assessing the relative causal importance of environmental factors, Homer-Dixon argued that some conflicts cannot be understood without including environmental scarcity (Homer-Dixon 1999: 7–9).

He distinguished three different kinds of environmental scarcity that could, when coupled with social and political factors, lead to conflict. The first was *supply-induced scarcity* due to environmental degradation, the second *demand-induced scarcity* due to population growth, and the third *unequal resource-based distribution or structural scarcity* (Homer-Dixon 1994, 1999: 15). Whether situations lead to violence depends on the capacity for societies to innovate and overcome scarcity (Homer-Dixon 1994, 1999). Significantly, Homer-Dixon focused on renewable resources, such as fisheries and timber or processes like the hydrological cycle and the climate. Non-renewable resources like oil and minerals, which scholars think of as important drivers of conflict, are not part of his framework.

Homer-Dixon generated three hypotheses of conflict types: (1) simple scarcity between states; (2) group identity-based conflicts within states affected by internal migration; and (3) relative deprivation conflicts where economic decline disrupts social institutions and leads to domestic strife. He found little support for the first hypothesis but stronger support for the other two (Homer-Dixon 1994: 18–25). Needless to say, Homer-Dixon's was not the only research effort; other major initiatives, also largely case-study based, generated broadly similar results (e.g. Baechler 1998, 1999,).

While Homer-Dixon narrowed the focus to violent conflict, others sought to broaden the agenda under the umbrella concept of "human security" (UNDP 1994; Barnett et al. 2010). Efforts to promote this agenda culminated in a chapter on human security in the 2014 report of the Intergovernmental Panel on Climate Change (IPCC) (Adger et al. 2014; see also Dalby 2009). There, human security was defined "as a condition that exists when the vital core of human lives is protected." The "vital core" of human security extends beyond material well-being to include "culturally specific" non-material factors that people require to fulfill their interests (Adger et al. 2014: 759). This broad definition of security has its detractors. As Roland Paris argued, "human security seems to encompass everything from substance abuse to genocide" (Paris 2004: 371). Moreover, the definition makes causal analysis challenging since factors that could cause human security are part of the definition (Paris 2004: 371). While I largely agree that human security may conceptually stretch the concept of security too far, the attention to individual well-being has some salutary properties, emphasizing the safety and well-being of individuals and not just the territorial integrity of states.

Despite these efforts, the narrower research agenda on the environment and violence has dominated and been the primary focus of criticism. Dan Deudney's critique has continued resonance. He saw efforts to securitize the environment—that is to label the environment as a security issue—as a strategic ploy by advocates to generate more attention. While national security issues typically command higher priority and resources, securitizing the issue has risks, including the tendency for countries to interpret responses to security problems in terms of national self-interest rather than the collective good (Deudney 1990: 467).

Homer-Dixon's methodology also came in for criticism. Instead of selecting only cases of violence, Marc Levy (1995: 57) counseled that it would be better "to compare societies facing similar environmental problems but exhibiting different levels of violent conflict. That would permit some precision in identifying the conditions under which environmental degradation generates violent conflict and when it does not." Objections such as these (e.g. Gleditsch 1998) underlay efforts to leverage quantitative methods (for a defense, see Homer-Dixon and Levy 1995; Schwartz et al. 2001). But those studies faced a new set of challenges and generated mixed results. With rough estimates of environmental scarcity, Hauge and Ellingsen found that forest loss and freshwater availability were more highly correlated with lower-level armed conflicts than civil wars, though land degradation was significant for both. They conclude regime type and economic development are more important drivers of conflict (Hauge and Ellingsen 2001).[3] For his part, de Soysa brought in debates about whether greed or grievance is a more significant motivation for violence. He found that natural capital, including both renewable and non-renewable resources, is unrelated to the incidence of internal conflict but that mineral wealth on its own was so related (de Soysa 2000). While providing some support for greed-based theories, de Soysa's aggregate measure of natural capital is even cruder than Hauge and Ellingsen's indicators.[4] The US-government supported State Failure Task Force provided a third quantitative assessment but did not find any statistically significant direct relationship between environmental variables and state failure. They did, however, find environmental factors affected infant mortality, a strong predictor of state failure (Esty et al. 1999).

Beyond the critiques and efforts by quantitative scholars, criticism also emerged from political ecologists Nancy Peluso, Michael Watts, and their collaborators. Informed by Marxist approaches to political economy, they argued that Homer-Dixon perpetuated "automatic, simplistic linkages" between scarcity and conflict and gave insufficient attention to regime type (Peluso and Watts 2001: 5, 18). As Colin Kahl notes Peluso and Watts "focus mainly on questions of distribution without fairly considering the ways in which rapid population growth and environmental degradation exacerbate conditions of inequality" (Kahl, 2002a: 138).[5] Kahl's own work is something of a bridge to these arguments. He sought to understand under what conditions demographic and environmental stress (DES) could lead to conflict. Kahl focuses on *state exploitation*, where elites "capitalize on scarcities of natural resources and related social grievances to advance their parochial interests" (Kahl 1998: 82). Kahl argued states with exclusive institutions and stark cleavages (what he calls "groupness") are more vulnerable to environmental scarcity-related conflicts (Kahl 1998, 2002b, 2006).

32.2 The Second Debate: Climate Change and Security

A new literature on climate and security emerged in the mid-2000s and is awash with data, in terms of the variety of environmental indicators, their temporal coverage, and the degree of geographic disaggregation made possible by improved satellite and georeferenced coverage.[6] This revolution facilitated statistical tests of connections between proxies for climate change impacts (i.e. droughts, temperature change, and rainfall volatility) and security outcomes, namely the onset and incidence of violent conflict within states.

After nearly a decade, however, this research has produced mixed findings. As the 2014 IPCC chapter on human security concluded: "The evidence on the effect of climate change and variability on violence is contested. Although there is little agreement about direct causality, low per capita incomes, economic contraction, and inconsistent state institutions are associated with the incidence of violence" (Adger et al. 2014: 758; for summaries of the state of the literature, see also Nordås and Gleditsch 2007; Gleditsch 2012; Scheffran et al. 2012; Salehyan 2014). Where there are reasonably robust correlations between climate hazards and conflict, such as for temperature, there needs to be more development of causal mechanisms and the selection of paired cases (some with and some without conflict) to demonstrate the scope conditions for when climate factors lead to violence. To understand this assessment, it helps to walk through a number of studies.

The climate–conflict debate has largely, though not exclusively, been between quantitative scholars aligned with Norway's Peace Research Institute Oslo (PRIO) and California-based scholars Edward Miguel, Marshall Burke, and Solomon Hsiang (e.g. Hsiang et al. 2013). While Miguel and co-authors have found strong correlations between climate-related variables and conflict, PRIO scholars for the most part have not. At the risk of over-simplification, their disputes have largely become ones of model specification and differences over methodology. Other prominent scholars among many include Marc Levy (Levy et al. 2005, 2008; Levy 2014) and John O'Loughlin (O'Loughlin et al. 2014a, 2014b, 2012). Three special issues—a 2007 issue of *Political Geography*,[7] a 2012 issue of the *Journal of Peace Research*,[8] and a 2014 *Political Geography*[9]—included many other leading figures.

The connections between climate and security contemporaneously emerged in the mid-2000s in the policy community. Nigel Purvis and I wrote a study for the United Nations, where we emphasized climate-driven humanitarian emergencies as the most proximate concern (Purvis and Busby 2004). Debates accelerated after the release of several US think-tank reports around 2007, including one by the CNA Corporation, a joint CNAS-CSIS effort, and my paper for the Council on Foreign Relations (CNA Corporation 2007; Campbell et al. 2007).[10] These reports emphasized the potential role of climate change as a threat multiplier in the exacerbation of security problems, with a particular focus on US national security. Other countries like Germany and the UK also carried out similar efforts (WBGU 2007; Mabey 2008). Discussions culminated in high-level attention to climate and security by the US government and the United Nations Security Council (Busby 2016).

The policy literature often chooses high-profile conflicts and tries to surface a climate signal as a key driver. For example, UN Secretary General Ban Ki-Moon identified climate change as an important cause of the conflict in Darfur, Sudan, though scholars debated the relative importance of environmental versus political factors.[11] Similarly, think-tank scholars have suggested drought helped give rise to the Arab Spring through the impact on food prices and riots (Werrell and Femia 2013). The role played by drought in the lead up to the Syrian civil war has also received particular attention.[12] One troubling issue is that individual case studies that only examine instances of conflict suffer from the selection problem that faced Homer-Dixon. This is particularly true if advocates shoehorn prominent examples into the environmental conflict box. In some accounts, the causal pathways between environmental change and conflict are dealt with by assertion rather than detailed process tracing.

A parallel academic discussion emerged contemporaneously to the policy debates (Barnett 2003; Barnett and Adger 2007). This research focused largely on whether proxies for climate change were correlated with conflict, with Africa receiving particular attention. Early studies found promising results. In 2004, Edward Miguel and collaborators tested the relationship between economic growth and civil conflict in Africa (Miguel et al. 2004). Given reverse causality between violence and economic growth, they used rainfall variation as an instrumental variable: rainfall could affect conflict through economic growth but could not itself be affected by conflict. They found that negative growth shocks of 5 percent increase the likelihood of civil conflict by more than 12 percent in the following year. They argued that lower economic growth would both increase individual incentives to engage in conflict and undermine state capacity to repress violence (Miguel et al. 2004).[13]

In 2005, Marc Levy and collaborators took advantage of disaggregated subnational data to assess the connections between rainfall anomalies and conflict outbreak for the world. They found rainfall anomalies were correlated with high-intensity civil conflicts but not low-intensity ones. They argue that rainfall variability affects the economy and state capacity to manage conflicts (Levy et al. 2005).

Cullen Hendrix and Sarah Glaser in their paper on Africa also focused on civil conflict (Hendrix and Glaser 2007). They examined the contribution of long-term trends (including a location's climate suitability for agriculture and freshwater availability) to conflict onset. They also assessed the contribution of inter-annual deviations from normal rainfall to trigger the onset of conflicts. They found that higher than normal rains and land suitable for agriculture were negatively correlated with conflict, but only when controlling for other social, political, and economic factors. Good rains in a single year reduce the incentives for engaging in conflict because farming is more attractive. At the same time, areas that are amenable to agriculture over the long term have higher economic returns, also diminishing the likelihood of conflict (Hendrix and Glaser 2007).

Some scholars used temperature rather than rainfall measures as their climate variable. A 2009 paper by Burke and colleagues found for every 1 degree increase in Celsius, there was a 4.5 percent increase in the incidence of violent conflict (Burke et al. 2009). Buhaug found the results did not hold up when one included additional data, used alternative model specifications, or included other variables such as political exclusion (Buhaug 2010). Other studies also found limited effects for different kinds of climate-related phenomena, with stronger evidence that political institutions and population density were more important drivers of conflict (Raleigh and Urdal 2007). PRIO affiliated researchers found no association between drought and civil wars in Africa; marginalized ethnic groups were correlated with conflict onset, providing further support for the political exclusion argument (Theisen et al. 2012).

In Theisen's study of Kenya, water scarcity was actually correlated with reduced conflict (Theisen 2012). In other articles, it appeared that abundance might be a more potent mechanism triggering conflict as groups have more reason to clash in times of plenty. Better rains might give raiding parties engaged in communal conflict more cover to conceal attacks.[14] Raleigh and Kniveton (2012) found this pattern of rainfall abundance accentuating communal conflict (such as between herders and farmers) while anomalously dry conditions enhanced rebel conflict.[15]

Other studies emphasized political variables over environmental ones. Gates and Butler in their assessment of range wars between pastoralists and farmers in East Africa argued that asymmetric property rights rather than resources per se fuel banditry by poorer parties (Butler and Gates 2012). Similarly, Benjaminsen and colleagues in their examination of similar conflicts in the Sahel attributed the violence to agricultural encroachment that impeded mobility by pastoralists, opportunism in rural areas with the decline of the state, and rent-seeking behavior by elites (Benjaminsen et al. 2012).

A 2013 meta-analysis by Solomon Hsiang and co-authors fueled the debate further. They estimated the average effects of a variety of climate indicators (temperature increases, positive deviations in rainfall, negative deviations in rainfall) on violence across 60 different studies, examining both "personal violence" (which included studies of baseball pitchers beaning more batters on hot days) as well as "inter-group" violence (which included studies of state collapse, civil wars, and other measures). Their provocative claim was that every standard deviation of climate indicators increased the frequency of interpersonal violence by 4 percent and inter-group conflict by 14 percent (Hsiang et al. 2013). Buhaug and co-authors raised various objections—about model specification, choice of control variables, and other arcana—that resulted in a back and forth with Hsiang and his collaborators (Buhaug 2014; Buhaug et al. 2014; Hsiang and Meng 2014). The 2013 Hsiang et al. piece included studies of ancient Egypt and fifteenth-century China whose relevance to the contemporary period is questionable. In addition, as opposed to average effects, the field has been moving toward identifying discrete causal pathways between specific climate phenomena (such as too much rain) and particular kinds of conflict (such as communal violence).

Thus far, most studies have tested direct relationships between physical hazards and conflict rather than indirect pathways through economic growth or food prices. Recent contributions from Koubi et al. (2013) and Smith (2014) addresss these lacunae. Where Koubi et al. did not find a connection between rainfall and conflict through economic growth, Smith found rainfall shocks increased protests and other forms of social conflict through effects on local food prices in Africa.[16]

Other recent studies have taken advantage of refined data sources. For example, von Uexkull and colleagues found that negative rainfall anomalies during the growing season in Asia and Africa influenced conflict likelihood under certain conditions, namely when groups are highly dependent on agriculture and politically excluded from power (von Uexkull 2014). Another paper in this vein by Maystadt and Ecker connected drought to civil conflict in Somalia through the effects on livestock prices (Maystadt and Ecker 2014).

Some papers have tried to nail down pathways to violence through the effects on migration and disasters. Again, here the evidence is mixed. There is strong evidence migrants can increase the potential for conflict as groups struggle for access to resources (Salehyan and Gleditsch 2006). Reuveny argued climate-related migration could lead to inter-ethnic conflict over resources, distrust, and rivalry between socio-economic groups (Reuveny 2007; see also Reuveny and Moore 2009). However, other studies suggested movements related to climate might be temporary and less likely to trigger conflict (Gleditsch et al. 2007; Raleigh et al. 2008).

A different literature has examined the effects of natural disasters on conflict. Some studies have posited that disasters make conflict less likely by inducing cooperation between the state and rebels; others suggest really severe disasters can deprive rebels of the resources to continue the fight (Kelman 2006; see also Schaffer 2011; Walch 2014). Nel and Righarts showed the effects of disasters on conflict to be the most severe in low- and medium-income countries with high inequality, low economic growth, and mixed political regimes (either partially democratic or partially authoritarian). While the effects were stronger for earthquakes and volcanoes, the results held up for climate-related disasters (Nel and Righarts 2008). However, Slettebak found climate-related disasters actually made conflict less likely (Slettebak 2012; for similar results, see Bergholt and Lujala 2012). Other studies have examined connections between disasters and regime survival (Flores and Smith 2010; Quiroz Flores 2015).

An understudied area is the role played by institutions in dampening the potential for conflict in the face of climate shocks and competition over resources. One reason interstate disputes over water have thus far rarely resulted in armed conflict is because of transboundary institutions to manage river basins. Studies by Stefano et al. and Tir and Stinnett found the robustness of these institutions was correlated with lower incidence and risk of conflict (Stefano et al. 2012; Tir and Stinnett 2012).

Nearly all these studies use datasets and cases from the past to say something about the future. However, the geographic distribution and intensity of weather events in the future (of rainfall, temperature) may not resemble past patterns (Busby et al. 2012a). The policy community is less constrained by data and can posit possible future scenarios. Thus, we see more efforts by the policy community to explore the security significance of unfolding events such as Arctic sea ice melt and interstate rivalry over access to resources (Borgerson 2008). However, as Gleditsch argued, the future is not evidence for political scientists. He is generally dismissive of forecasting as akin to fortune telling (Gleditsch 1998). That said, some studies, including Hendrix and Glaser and Burke et al. have exploited climate projections to inform estimates of future conflict (Burke et al. 2009; Hendrix and Glaser 2007). Another study estimated potential conflict risk under different scenarios of future economic growth and various climate mitigation efforts (Hegre et al. 2016). I have used both historic data on physical exposure and projections of future climate change to identify likely climate security hot spots in Africa (Busby et al. 2012a, 2012b, 2013, 2014a, 2014b).

32.3 Concluding Thoughts

We have some directions for where the field is and ought to be headed. There is rightfully more emphasis on indirect causal pathways between climate hazards and conflict through economic growth, migration, and disasters, with particular attention to food prices and agricultural production. Scholars have exploited better geo-referenced datasets to examine subnational conflict patterns and a variety of kinds of conflict. We are also seeing scholarship on regions other than Africa, including Asia and the Middle East. The best work seeks to specify the conditions under which climate-related hazards lead to particular kinds of conflict, distinguishing between kinds of states (such as between exclusive and inclusive institutions, states with stark group cleavages), kinds of contexts (such as between urban and rural areas), and kinds of hazards (such as swift onset versus slow onset).[17]

As Hendrix (2016) suggests, it also time to revisit the earlier debate on the circumstances under which demographic and environmental stress lead to mass atrocities and other security outcomes. Since other forms of resource pressures such as poaching of wildlife and deforestation continue on a large scale, scholars of environment and security should also broaden their research beyond climate change.

Going forward, as responses to climate change take shape, there is the potential that measures to mitigate emissions and adapt to the consequences of climate change themselves may become a source of friction between and within states. These include whether countries meet their mitigation commitments, efforts to keep hydrocarbons in the ground, geo-engineering, support for clean energy, attempts to divert water or acquire foreign agricultural lands, as well as border fences.[18] All of these developments portend a rich research and challenging policy agenda going forward.

Notes

1. In what follows, issues such as conflicts related to water, fisheries, and timber are given short shrift. The environmental consequences of war itself are not discussed (cf. Chalecki 2010; Dalby 2010; Hendrix et al. 2016).
2. Malthus thought the rate of population growth would inexorably exceed the capacity of food production to expand, leading to boom–bust cycles of population growth and famine (Malthus 1798).
3. Theisen largely could not replicate these findings with the original data or with better time series data (Theisen, 2008).
4. An updated literature review found more support for abundance arguments than scarcity ones (Koubi et al. 2013).
5. The venue for Kahl and Homer-Dixon's rejoinders to Peluso and Watts was the report series from the Woodrow Wilson Center's Environmental Change and Security Program (ECSP).

Since 1994, ECSP has served as an important outlet for scholars interested in environment and security.

6. There is a different literature on water and conflict that finds interstate water wars have almost never occurred (Wolf 1998).
7. See http://www.sciencedirect.com/science/journal/09626298/26/6
8. See http://jpr.sagepub.com/cgi/collection/special_issue_on_climate_change_and_conflict?page=2
9. See http://www.sciencedirect.com/science/journal/09626298/43
10. See also my 2008 paper in *Security Studies* for a more theoretical account of the ways climate change could pose a threat to US national security (Busby 2008).
11. Ban Ki-Moon (2007). Homer-Dixon argued climate factors were key to understanding the origins of the conflict while De Waal discounted their significance (de Waal 2007; Homer-Dixon 2007).
12. The claim is that the drought was mismanaged by the Syrian state which led to rural–urban migration and those new migrants were among those who joined the early protests against Assad. His repression, in turn, escalated to violence and the formation of a violent rebellion (Friedman 2013; Polk 2013; Gleick 2014).
13. Ciccone provided a critique of this methodology and suggested these findings disappear if one uses rainfall levels rather than growth rates in rainfall (Ciccone 2011).
14. Meier et al. (2007). See also Hendrix and Salehyan (2012); Salehyan and Hendrix (2014).
15. Raleigh and Kniveton (2012). For their part, Fjelde and von Uexkull found the opposite—that large negative deviations in rainfall in Africa were associated with more conflict (Fjelde and von Uexkull 2012).
16. (Smith 2014). Buhaug has two pieces on food prices that conflict with Smith and with each other (Wischnath and Buhaug 2014; Buhaug et al. 2015. See also Hendrix and Brinkman 2013).
17. For a similar take, see Hendrix et al. (2016).
18. Dabelko et al. (2013).

References

Adger, W. N., J. M. Pulhin, J., Barnett, G. D. Dabelko, U. Oswald Spring, C. H. Vogel. 2014. Human Security. In C. B. Field, V. R. Barros, D. J. Dokken, K. J. Mach, M. D. Mastrandrea, T. E. Bilir, M. Chatterjee, K. L. Ebi, Y. O. Estrada, R. C. Genova, B. Girma, E. S. Kissel, A. N. Levy, S. MacCracken, P. R. Mastrandrea, and L. L. White (eds.), *Climate Change 2014: Impacts, Adaptation, and Vulnerability. Part A: Global and Sectoral Aspects*, pp. 755–91. Contribution of Working Group II to the Fifth Assessment Report of the Intergovernmental Panel on Climate Change. Cambridge and New York: IPCC.

Art, R. J. 2003. *A Grand Strategy for America, Cornell Studies in Security Affairs*. Ithaca, NY: Cornell University Press.

Baechler, G. 1998. *Why Environmental Transformation Causes Violence: A Synthesis*. Washington, DC: Woodrow Wilson Center.

Baechler, G. 1999. Environmental Degradation in the South as a Cause of Armed Conflict. In A. Carius and K. M. Lietzmann (eds.), *Environmental Change and Security: A European Perspective*, pp. 107–30. Berlin: Springer,.

Ban Ki-Moon. 2007. A Climate Culprit in Darfur [WWW Document]. *Washington Post. Available at:* http://www.washingtonpost.com/wp-dyn/content/article/2007/06/15/AR2007061501857_pf.html

Barnett, J. 2003. Security and Climate Change. *Global Environmental Change*, 13: 7–17.

Barnett, J. and W. N. Adger. 2007. Climate Change, Human Security and Violent Conflict. *Political Geography*, 26: 639–55.

Barnett, J., R. A. Matthew, and K. L. O'Brien. 2010. Global Environmental Change and Human Security: An Introduction. In R. A. Matthew, J. Barnett, B. McDonald, and K. L. O'Brien (eds.), *Global Environmental Change and Human Security*, pp. 3–32. Cambridge, MA: MIT Press, .

Benjaminsen, T. A., K. Alinon, H. Buhaug, and J. T. Buseth. 2012. Does Climate Change Drive Land-use Conflicts in the Sahel? *Journal of Peace Research*, 49: 97–111.

Bergholt, D. and P. Lujala. 2012. Climate-Related Natural Disasters, Economic Growth, and Armed Civil Conflict. *Journal of Peace Research*, 49: 147–62.

Borgerson, S. 2008. Arctic Meltdown: The Economic and Security Implications of Global Warming. *Foreign Affairs*, 87(2): 63–77.

Buhaug, H. 2010. Climate not to Blame for Africa's Civil Wars. *Proceedings of the National Academy of Science*, 107: 16477–82.

Buhaug, H. 2014. Concealing Agreements over Climate–Conflict Results. *Proceedings of the National Academy of Science*, 111: E636–E636.

Buhaug, H., J. Nordkvelle, T. Bernauer, T. Böhmelt, M. Brzoska, J. W. Busby, A. Ciccone, H. Fjelde, E. Gartzke, N. P. Gleditsch, J. A. Goldstone, H. Hegre, H. Holtermann, V. Koubi, J. S. A. Link, P. M. Link, P. Lujala, J. O'Loughlin, C. Raleigh, J. Scheffran, J. Schilling, T. G. Smith, O. M. Theisen, R. S. J. Tol, H. Urdal, and N. von Uexkull. 2014. One Effect to Rule Them All? A Comment on Climate and Conflict. *Climate Change*, 127: 391–7.

Buhaug, H., T. A. Benjaminsen, E. Sjaastad, and O. M. Theisen. 2015. Climate Variability, Food Production Shocks, and Violent Conflict in Sub-Saharan Africa. *Environmental Research Letters*, 10, 125015.

Burke, M. B., E. Miguel, S. Satyanath, J. A. Dykema, and D. B. Lobell. 2009. *Warming Increases the Risk of Civil War in Africa. Proceedings of the National Academy of Science*, 106: 20670–4.

Busby, J. 2007. *Climate Change and National Security: An Agenda for Action*. New York and Washington, DC: Council on Foreign Relations.

Busby, J. W. 2008. Who Cares About the Weather? Climate Change and U.S. National Security. *Security Studies*, 17: 468–504.

Busby, J. 2016. Climate Change and U.S. National Security: Sustaining Security Amidst Unsustainability. In J. Suri, and B. Valentino (eds.), *Sustainable Security: Rethinking American National Security Strategy*. Oxford: Oxford University Press.

Busby, J. W., J. Gulledge, T. G. Smith, and K. White. 2012a. Of Climate Change and Crystal Balls: The Future Consequences of Climate Change in Africa. *Air and Space Power Journal Africa and Francophonie*, 3(3): 4–44.

Busby, J. W., T. G. Smith, K. White, and S. M. Strange. 2012b. Locating Climate Insecurity: Where are the Most Vulnerable Places in Africa? In Michael Brzoska and Peter Michael Link (eds.), *Climate Change, Human Security and Violent Conflict, Hexagon Series on Human and Environmental Security and Peace*, pp. 463–512. Berlin: Springer.

Busby, J. W., T. G. Smith, K. White, and S. M. Strange. 2013. Climate Change and Insecurity: Mapping Vulnerability in Africa. *International Security*, 37: 132–72.

Busby, J. W., K. Cook, E. Vizy, T. Smith, and M. Bekalo. 2014a. Identifying Hot Spots of Security Vulnerability Associated with Climate Change in Africa. *Climate Change*, 124: 717–31.

Busby, J. W., T. G. Smith, and N. Krishnan. 2014b. Climate Security Vulnerability in Africa Mapping 3.0. *Political Geography*, Special Issue: Climate Change and Conflict 43: 51–67.

Butler, C. K. and S. Gates. 2012. African Range Wars: Climate, Conflict, and Property Rights. *Journal of Peace Research*, 49: 23–34.

Campbell, K. M., J. Gulledge, J. R. McNeill, J. Podesta, P. Ogden, L. Fuerth, R. J. Woolsey, A. T. J. Lennon, J. Smith, R. Weitz, and D. Mix. 2007. The Age of Consequences. [WWW Document]. Washington, DC: Center for a New American Security and the Center for Strategic and International Studies, *available at:* https://www.csis.org/analysis/age-consequences

Chalecki, E. L. 2010. Environment and Security. In R. A. Denemark (ed.), *The International Studies Encyclopedia*. International Studies Compendium Project. Oxford: Blackwell Publishing Online.

Ciccone, A. 2011. Economic Shocks and Civil Conflict: A Comment. *American Economic Journal Applied Economics*, 3: 215–27.

CNA Corporation. 2007. National Security and the Threat of Climate Change [WWW Document], *available at:* https://www.cna.org/cna_files/pdf/national%20security%20and%20the%20threat%20of%20climate%20change.pdf

Dabelko, G. D., L. H. Risi, S. Null, M. Parker, R. Sticklor. 2013. *Backdraft: The Conflict Potential of Climate Change Adaptation and Mitigation*. Washington, DC: Woodrow Wilson Center.

Dalby, S. 2009. *Security and Environmental Change*. Cambridge; Malden, MA: Polity.

Dalby, S. 2010. Environmental Security and Climate Change. In R. A. Denemark (ed.), *The International Studies Encyclopedia*. International Studies Compendium Project. Oxford: Blackwell Publishing Online.

de Soysa, I. 2000. The Resource Curse: Are Civil Wars Driven by Rapacity or Paucity. In M. Berdal and D. M. Malone (eds.), *Greed and Grievance: Economic Agendas in Civil Wars*, pp. 113–36. Ottawa: Lynne Rienner Publishers.

de Waal, A. 2007. Is Climate Change the Culprit for Darfur? [WWW Document]. Social Science Research Council, *available at:* http://africanarguments.org/2007/06/25/is-climate-change-the-culprit-for-darfur//

Del Rosso, S. J. J. 1995. The Insecure State: Reflections on "the State" and "Security" in a Changing World. *Daedalus*, 124: 175–207.

Deudney, D. 1990. The Case Against Linking Environmental Degradation and National Security. *Millennium* 19: 461–76.

Esty, D. C., J. A. Goldstone, T. R. Gurr, B. Harff, M. Levy, G. Dabelko, P. T. Surko, and A. N. Unger. 1999. *State Failure Task Force Report: Phase II Findings, Environmental Change and Security Project Report*. Washington, DC: Woodrow Wilson Center.

Fjelde, H. and N. von Uexkull. 2012. Climate Triggers: Rainfall Anomalies, Vulnerability and Communal Conflict in Sub-Saharan Africa. *Political Geography*, 31: 444–53.

Flores, A. Q. and A. Smith. 2010. Surviving Disasters [WWW Document]. New York University, *available at:* https://ncgg.princeton.edu/IPES/2010/papers/S345_paper3.pdf

Friedman, T. L. 2013. Without Water, Revolution. *New York Times*, May 18.

Gleditsch, N. P. 1998. Armed Conflict and the Environment: A Critique of the Literature. *Journal of Peace Research*, 35: 381–400.

Gleditsch, N. P. 2012. Whither the Weather? Climate Change and Conflict. *Journal of Peace Research*, 49: 3–9.

Gleditsch, N. P., R. Nordås, and I. Salehyan. 2007. Climate Change and Conflict: The Migration Link [WWW Document]. Coping Crisis Working Paper Series, *available at:* https://

web.archive.org/web/20081209131302/http://www.ipacademy.org/asset/file/169/CWC_Working_Paper_Climate_Change.pdf

Gleick, P. H. 2014. Water, Drought, Climate Change, and Conflict in Syria. *Weather, Climate, and Society*, 6: 331–40.

Hauge, W. and T. Ellingsen. 2001. Causal Pathways to Conflict. In P. F. Diehl and N. P. Gleditsch (eds.), *Environmental Conflict*, pp. 36–57. Boulder, CO: Westview Press.

Hegre, H., H. Buhaug, K. V. Calvin, J. Nordkvelle, S. T. Waldhoff, and Elisabeth Gilmore. 2016. Forecasting Civil Conflict along the Shared Socioeconomic Pathways. *Environmental Research Letters*, 11: 54002.

Hendrix, C. 2016. *Putting Environmental Stress (Back) on the Mass Atrocities Agenda*. Muscatine, IO: Stanley Foundation.

Hendrix, C. and H.-J. Brinkman. 2013. Food Insecurity and Conflict Dynamics: Causal Linkages and Complex Feedbacks. *Stability. International Journal of Security and Development*, 2(2): 1–18

Hendrix, C. S. and S. M. Glaser. 2007. Trends and Triggers: Climate Change and Civil Conflict in Sub-Saharan Africa. *Political Geography*, 26: 695–715.

Hendrix, C. S. and I. Salehyan. 2012. Climate Change, Rainfall, and Social Conflict in Africa. *Journal of Peace Research*, 49: 35–50.

Hendrix, C., S. Gates, and H. Buhaug. 2016. Environment and Conflict. In T. D. Mason, and S. M. Mitchell (eds.), *What Do We Know about Civil Wars?*, pp. 231–46. Lanham, MD: Rowman & Littlefield Publishers.

Homer-Dixon, T. F. 1991. On the Threshold: Environmental Changes as Causes of Acute Conflict. *International Security*, 16: 76–116.

Homer-Dixon, T. F. 1994. Environmental Scarcities and Violent Conflict: Evidence from Cases. *International Security*, 19: 5–40.

Homer-Dixon, T. F. 1999. Environment, Scarcity, and Violence. Princeton, NJ: Princeton University Press.

Homer-Dixon, T. 2007. Cause and Effect [WWW Document]. Social Science Research Council, *available at:* http://africanarguments.org/2007/08/02/cause-and-effect//

Homer-Dixon, T. F. and J. Blitt (eds.). 1998. *Ecoviolence: Links Among Enviroment, Population, and Security*. Lanham, MD: Rowman & Littlefield Publishers.

Homer-Dixon, T. F. and M. A. Levy. 1995. Environment and Security. *International Security*, 20: 189–98.

Hsiang, S. M. and K. C. Meng. 2014. Reconciling Disagreement over Climate-Conflict Results in Africa. *Proceedings of the National Academy of Science*, 111: 2100–3.

Hsiang, S., M. Burke, and E. Miguel. 2013. Quantifying the Influence of Climate on Human Conflict. *Science*, 341.

Kahl, C. H. 1998. Population Growth, Environmental Degradation, and State-Sponsored Violence: The Case of Kenya, 1991–93. *International Security* 23: 80–119.

Kahl, C. H. 2002a. *Review of Violent Environments (No. 8), Environmental Change and Security Project Report*. Washington, DC: Woodrow Wilson Center.

Kahl, C. H. 2002b. Demographic Change, Natural Resources and Violence, the Current Debate. *Journal of International Affairs*, 56: 257–82.

Kahl, C. H. 2006. *States, Scarcity, and Civil Strife in the Developing World*. Princeton, NJ: Princeton University Press.

Kaplan, R. 1994. The Coming Anarchy. *Atlantic Monthly*, 273: 44–76.

Kelman, I. 2006. Island Security and Disaster Diplomacy in the Context of Climate Change. *Cahiers de Sécurité*, 63: 61–94.

Koubi, V., G. Spilker, T. Böhmelt, and T. Bernauer. 2013. Do Natural Resources Matter for Interstate and Intrastate Armed Conflict? *Journal of Peace Research*, 51: 227–43.

Levy, M. A. 1995. Is the Environment a National Security Issue? *International Security*, 20: 35–62.

Levy, M. A. 2014. Trends in Climate Stress: Implications for Instability over the Coming Decade. Presented at the Over the Horizon Conference Convened by the Political Instability Task Force.

Levy, M. A., C. Thorkelson, C. Vörösmarty, E. Douglas, and M. Humphreys. 2005. Freshwater Availability Anomalies and Outbreak of Internal War: Results from a Global Spatial Time Series Analysis [WWW Document]. Columbia University, *available at:* http://www.cicero.uio.no/humsec/papers/Levy_et_al.pdf

Levy, M. A., B. Anderson, M. Brickman, C. Cromer, B., Falk, B. Fekete, P. Green, M. Jaiteh, R. Lammers, V. Mara, K. MacManus, S. Metzler, M. Muñiz, T. Parris, R. Pullen, C. Thorkelson, C. Vorosmarty, W. Wollheim, X. Xing, and G. Yetman. 2008. Assessment of Select Climate Change Impacts on U.S. National Security [WWW Document]. Columbia University, *available at:* http://www.ciesin.columbia.edu/documents/Climate_Security_CIESIN_July_2008_v1_0.ed.pdf

Mabey, N. 2008. *Delivering Climate Security. International Security Responses to a Climate Changed World*. London: Routledge.

Malthus, T. R. 1798. *An essay on the principle of population, as it affects the future improvement of society. With remarks on the speculations of Mr. Godwin, M. Condorcet and other writers.* London: J. Johnson.

Mathews, J. T. 1989. Redefining Security. *Foreign Affairs*, 68: 162–77.

Maystadt, J.-F. and O. Ecker. 2014. Extreme Weather and Civil War: Does Drought Fuel Conflict in Somalia through Livestock Price Shocks? *American Journal of Agricultural Economics*, 96: 1157–82

Meier, P., D. Bond, and J. Bond. 2007. Environmental Influences on Pastoral Conflict in the Horn of Africa. *Political Geography*, 26: 716–35.

Miguel, E., S. Satyanath, and E. Sergenti. 2004. Economic Shocks and Civil Conflict: An Instrumental Variables Approach. *Journal of Political Economy*, 112: 725–53.

Nel, P. and M. Righarts. 2008. Natural Disasters and the Risk of Violent Civil Conflict. *International Studies. Quarterly*, 52: 159–85.

Nordås, R. and N. P. Gleditsch. 2007. Climate Change and Conflict. *Political Geography*, 26: 627–38.

O'Loughlin, J., F. D. W. Witmer, A. M. Linke, A. Laing, A. Gettelman, and J. Dudhia. 2012. Climate Variability and Conflict Risk in East Africa, 1990–2009. *Proceedings of the National Academy of Science*, 109(45): 18344–9.

O'Loughlin, J., A. M. Linke, and F. D. W. Witmer. 2014a. Modeling and Data Choices Sway Conclusions about Climate-Conflict Links. *Proceedings of the National Academy of Science*, 111: 2054–5.

O'Loughlin, J., A. M. Linke, and F. D. W. Witmer. 2014b. Effects of Temperature and Precipitation Variability on the Risk of Violence in sub-Saharan Africa, 1980–2012. *Proceedings of the National Academy of Science*, 111: 16712–17.

Paris, R. 2004. Still an Inscrutable Concept. *Secur. Dialogue*, 35: 370–2.

Peluso, N. L. and M. Watts. (eds.), 2001. *Violent Environments*. Ithaca, NY: Cornell University Press.

Percival, V. and T. Homer-Dixon. 1998. Environmental Scarcity and Violent Conflict: The Case of South Africa. *Journal of Peace Research*, 35: 279–98.

Polk, W. R. 2013. Your Labor Day Syria Reader, Part 2: William Polk [WWW Document]. The Atlantic, *available at:* http://www.theatlantic.com/international/archive/2013/09/your-labor-day-syria-reader-part-2-william-polk/279255/

Purvis, N. and J. Busby. 2004. The Security Implications of Climate Change for the UN System [WWW Document]. Washington, DC: Woodrow Wilson Center, *available at:* http://www.wilsoncenter.org/topics/pubs/ecspr10_unf-purbus.pdf

Quiroz Flores, A. 2015. Protecting People from Natural Disasters: Political Institutions and Ocean-Originated Hazards. *Political Science Research and Methods*, FirstView, 1–24. doi:10.1017/psrm.2015.72

Raleigh, C. and D. Kniveton. 2012. Come Rain or Shine: An analysis of Conflict and Climate Variability in East Africa. *Journal of Peace Research*, 49: 51–64.

Raleigh, C. and H. Urdal. 2007. Climate Change, Environmental Degradation and Armed Conflict. *Political Geography*, 26: 674–94.

Raleigh, C., L. Jordan, and I. Salehyan. 2008. Assessing the Impact of Climate Change on Migration and Conflict [WWW Document]. Social Dimensions of Climate Change, *available at:* http://siteresources.worldbank.org/EXTSOCIALDEVELOPMENT/Resources/SDCCWorkingPaper_MigrationandConflict.pdf

Reuveny, R. 2007. Climate Change-induced Migration and Violent Conflict. *Political Geography*, 26: 656–73.

Reuveny, R. and W. H. Moore. 2009. Does Environmental Degradation Influence Migration? Emigration to Developed Countries in the Late 1980s and 1990s. *Social Science Quarterly*, 90: 461–79.

Salehyan, I. 2014. Climate Change and Conflict: Making Sense of Disparate Findings. *Political Geography*, Special Issue: Climate Change and Conflict 43: 1–5.

Salehyan, I. and K. S. Gleditsch. 2006. Refugees and the Spread of Civil War. *International Organization*, 60: 335–66.

Salehyan, I. and C. S. Hendrix. 2014. Climate Shocks and Political Violence. *Global Environmental Change*, 28: 239–50.

Schaffer, H. B. 2011. *Making Peace When Disaster Strikes: Sri Lanka, Aceh and the 2004 Tsunami*. Washington, DC: Institute for the Study of Diplomacy, Georgetown University.

Scheffran, J., M. Brzoska, J. Kominek, P. M. Link, and J. Schilling. 2012. Climate Change and Violent Conflict. *Science*, 336: 869–71.

Schwartz, D., T. Deligiannis, and T. Homer-Dixon. 2001. The Environment and Violent Conflict. In P. F. Diehl, and N. P. Gleditsch (eds.), *Environmental Conflict*, pp. 273–94. Boulder, CO: Westview Press .

Slettebak, R. T. 2012. Don't Blame the Weather! Climate-Related Natural Disasters and Civil Conflict. *Journal of Peace Research*, 49: 163–76.

Smith, T. G. 2014. Feeding Unrest. Disentangling the Causal Relationship between Food Price Shocks and Sociopolitical Conflict in Urban Africa. *Journal of Peace Research*, 51: 679–95.

Stefano, L. D., J. Duncan, S. Dinar, K. Stahl, K. M. Strzepek, and A. T. Wolf. 2012. Climate Change and the Institutional Resilience of International River Basins. *Journal of Peace Research*, 49: 193–209.

Theisen, O. M. 2008. Blood and Soil? Resource Scarcity and Internal Armed Conflict Revisited. *Journal of Peace Research*, 45: 801–18.

Theisen, O. M. 2012. Climate Clashes? Weather Variability, Land Pressure, and Organized Violence in Kenya, 1989–2004. *Journal of Peace Research*, 49: 81–96.

Theisen, O. M., H. Holtermann, and H. Buhaug. 2012. Climate Wars? Assessing the Claim That Drought Breeds Conflict. *International Security*, 36: 79–106.

Tir, J. and D. M. Stinnett. 2012. Weathering Climate Change: Can Institutions Mitigate International Water Conflict? *Journal of Peace Research*, 49: 211–25.

Ullman, R. 1983. Redefining Security. *International Security*, 8: 129–53.

United Nations Development Program. 1994. *New Dimensions in Human Security*. New York: Oxford University Press.

von Uexkull, N. 2014. Sustained Drought, Vulnerability and Civil Conflict in Sub-Saharan Africa. *Political Geography*, Special Issue: Climate Change and Conflict, 43: 16–26.

Walch, C. 2014. Collaboration or Obstruction? Rebel Group Behavior during Natural Disaster Relief in the Philippines. *Political Geography*, Special Issue: Climate Change and Conflict, 43: 40–50.

WBGU, 2007. Climate Change as a Security Risk: Summary for Policymakers [WWW Document], *available at:* http://www.wbgu.de/wbgu_jg2007_kurz_engl.html

Werrell, C. E. and F. Femia (eds.). 2013. *The Arab Spring and Climate Change*. Washington, DC: Center for American Progress, Stimson Center, and the Center for Climate and Security.

Wischnath, G. and H. Buhaug. 2014. Rice or Riots: On Food Production and Conflict Severity across India. *Political Geography*, Special Issue: Climate Change and Conflict, 43: 6–15.

Wolf, A. T. 1998. Conflict and Cooperation along International Waterways. *Water Policy*, 1: 251–65.

CHAPTER 33

THE CRIME SCENE

What Lessons for International Security?

ANJA P. JAKOBI

33.1 Introduction

Transnational crime is an integral part of studying international security today—yet, crimes differ in how relevant they are from a security perspective. This chapter critically assesses the importance of transnational crime for international security, showing that a differentiated and more fine-grained picture of criminal activities is needed. "Transnational crime" is a label for different activities, and not all of them are equally relevant for national and global security.

Three lines of arguments can usually be distinguished in the literature on crime and security: the broadest argument conceives transnational crime as a new, *sui generis* security threat, additional to security threats known before. Crime would threaten individual or public security in a new way, undermining morality, societal, and legal norms. The second line of arguments conceives transnational crime as one among other non-traditional security threats, with a higher significance than before, and embodying a growing relevance of non-state actors in security. From that perspective, crime is not a new threat, but its growing relevance is part of a larger change in the security environment. A third line of argument conceptualizes transnational crime primarily as a threat with links to other security threats—like its nexus to terrorism. From that perspective, crime facilitates traditional and non-traditional security threats by supporting organizations that pursue hostile political aims.

While each of these arguments is valid for some crimes, none of them applies to all types of crimes. This chapter starts with an introduction to transnational crime by showing that the definition of crime is a political process in which crime signals a security threat, even without referring to a substantive activity. Section 33.3 presents the governance of crime by distinguishing between internal and external governance. It elaborates on the most important current developments in global crime governance, and shows that any assessment of security risks needs to compare the opportunities of crime with the abilities of states. Section 33.4 outlines scenarios on three major aspects of governing transnational crime in the future: the use of data, the role of formal norms, and the dimensions of security.

33.2 What is Transnational Crime?

Transnational crime is a flexible threat, partly because its definition varies. The UN Convention against Transnational Organized Crime refers to a crime that is "serious" in its nature (usually punishable by a deprivation of liberty of four years or more), organized by a group of at least three persons, and transnational in its planning, pursuit, or impact. Additional crimes covered in the convention and its protocols include money laundering, corruption, obstruction of justice, being member of a crime group, human smuggling, human trafficking, and the trafficking of firearms (United Nations 2016a). Several other global conventions exist that cover corruption, drug trafficking, or terrorism. Furthermore, a multitude of regional conventions have been adopted as well; for instance, by the Council of Europe and the Organization of American States. Each of these instruments defines a specific crime, which might or might not overlap with other conventions: cybercrime is targeted in a convention of the Council of Europe; corruption is prohibited in UN and regional conventions; and counter-terrorism financing was initially covered in a UN convention, but was later more prominently disseminated by the Financial Action Taskforce, which is an international network.

Defining transnational crime is, therefore, difficult. In a strictly legal sense, crime is created by the states, themselves, by criminalizing an activity: without a law, there is no crime. Gray areas exist with regards to which activities are not deemed criminal, but rather, illegal or illicit (e.g. by exploiting loopholes or by wrongdoings in a moral sense). While these definitions may sound like an academic exercise, they have a huge impact on how security agencies and law enforcement can tackle crime. For instance, "legal highs" refers to substances that are legally available in shops, but whose distribution circumvents existing anti-drug laws. This open sale has been difficult to regulate even though they are seen as one of the biggest health risks among young consumers in Europe. The complexity of defining transnational crime increases even more due to cross-national variance in what is criminalized, illegal, or illicit—what looks like a legitimate business in one country can be criminal in another. Hence, the declaration of something as a "transnational crime" depends on national backgrounds.

In a functional sense, the security impact of transnational crime varies depending on the specific crime. However, political debates have often "securitized" crime in general, identifying it as a threat to national and international security. A typical argument found would be:

> In recent years, international organized crime has expanded considerably in presence, sophistication and significance—and it now threatens many aspects on how Americans live, work and do business. International organized crime promotes corruption, violence and other illegal activities, jeopardizes our border security, and causes human misery. It undermines the integrity of our banking and financial systems, commodities and securities markets, and our cyberspace. In short, international organized crime is a national security problem that demands a strategic, targeted and concerted U.S. government response. (US Department of Justice, quoted in Mandel 2011: 31)

Like in many other political analyses, transnational crime is presented as a ubiquitous, abstract, and foreign threat to all sectors of society. This idea of a uniform threat is sometimes brought together with the idea of "converging" threats, thus signifying that different criminal and terrorist organizations grow closer to each other, or that licit and illicit markets increasingly overlap (Miklaucic and Brewer 2013; Neuman 2013). The alarming tone that often comes with analyses has always been a constant in reporting about crime (Deflem 2005; Woodiwiss and Hobbs 2009). What is missing from a generalizing talk about crime are details on the multitude of crimes, the diversity of criminal groups, and the varying impact of different crimes on security.

The openness of the term "crime" is also beneficial for political agendas. Public awareness of crime is high and polls steadily list crime among the most important topics for the public (e.g. Eurobarometer 2016: 7). Counter-crime arguments are, therefore, likely to catch the public attention, and contested policies are easier to legitimize once they are framed as counter-crime activities. For example, European policy-makers who aimed to cut migration over the Mediterranean often claimed that their policies would destroy the criminal business of people smugglers and traffickers, while usually omitting that this market for criminals exists because of restrictive migration policies and problems in the countries of origin. By framing problems as criminal problems, policy-makers and others benefit from the negative bias toward crime and the positive bias toward counter-crime policies. The securitization of crime is, thus, an ongoing process that involves public debate about crime and counter-strategies against a background of national, societal, and individual vulnerability.

A generalizing concept of crime also eschews the reasons for criminal behavior, and the ways in which these relate to different aspects of security. An established dichotomy distinguishes the political motivations for crime from the economic motivations. Politically motivated crimes include crimes against humanity and terrorism (see Cronin, Chapter 34, this volume), including their transnational organization or transnational impact. Political crimes usually target the state, its legal system, or the social fabric. In contrast, crimes based on an economic motivation follow a rational choice idea of cost–benefit calculations, as criminals aim to maximize profit and do not primarily pursue political aims. As a consequence, they may even benefit from stability in a state, as this also enables smooth facilitation of their criminal business (Williams 2002). While political crimes are usually targeted from a security perspective, the responses to transnational crimes based on economic motivations vary. Some of them—for instance drug trafficking—attract a high level of publicity in the media and politics. Others—like car theft, smuggling of cigarettes, or product counterfeiting—lead to economic losses, but are dealt with mostly on the national level or in expert circles, and are not usually perceived as a security threat. Still, the dichotomy of political and economic motivations for crime is not always clear-cut: he FARC in Colombia brought together a political fight with the economic benefits from the drug trade, thus showing a mixed political and economic background of their activities (Rubio and Ortiz 2005). Crimes committed for economic reasons can also impact politics, when negative externalities, such as violence, become a larger societal problem. Furthermore, the benefits of crime committed with an economic motivation can be channeled to fund political crime, which is the case in the crime–terror nexus. Finally, different participants within the same criminal activity can be motivated by disparate factors: human smugglers in Turkey usually aim to make a financial profit when bringing Syrians to Europe, while their Syrian client base is motivated by wishing to escape from a war zone. Identifying the motivation for a specific criminal activity is a difficult, but necessary element in order to establish effective countermeasures.

Given the different understandings of what constitutes transnational crime, Table 33.1 lists a first selection of well-known transnational crimes, showing their different threat potentials. For instance, large-scale arms trafficking implies a threat to the population to which these arms are trafficked and where they intensify armed conflict. The trade can affect these war-torn countries, as well as international security as a whole, depending on the global dimension of the conflict. The same applies to the trade in conflict minerals, which helps to fund civil wars and local conflict parties. In the past, rebel groups in

Table 33.1 Transnational criminal activities and threat potential

Activity	Main threat to
Arms trafficking	Population in zones of conflict, international security
Trade in conflict minerals	Population in zones of conflict, international security
Corruption	Society, politics, rule of law, support crime
Money laundering	Society, integrity of banking system, support crime
Terrorism financing	Politics and society (local to global), support crime
Human smuggling	National border control, life of smuggled person
Human trafficking	Human rights of trafficked person
Drug trafficking and consumption	Individual and public health, behavioral norms
Maritime piracy	Shipping routes, world trade
Cybercrime	Individual user, critical infrastructure

Sierra Leone and Angola profited from the diamond trade to fund their war activities; today, Congolese rebel groups generate funds from mining minerals used in the electronics industry.

Another group of crimes listed can be classified as "support crimes" which facilitate other "predicate" crimes and whose threat potential differs. For instance, drug trafficking benefits by corrupting law enforcement or other governmental actors; corruption is, thus, supporting the predicate crime "drug trafficking." The same applies to money laundering, which is used to make assets appear as legitimate income: he laundering process enables effective use of criminal assets for the crime groups, while non-laundered money can be traced back more easily to the crime. While money laundering usually "cleans" dirty money, the support crime of terrorism financing can be linked to all types of sources: wealthy sponsors can use funds from their licit sources, or criminal activities can finance attacks—the source of the funds is irrelevant, supporting the predicate crime of terrorism is the main focus.

Human smuggling—the paid operation to move people across borders—is first and foremost a violation of countries' laws. Sometimes the individuals smuggled can be criminals, or even terrorists, but most often they are migrants seeking a better life. Human trafficking means that individuals are "acquired and sold" like a product, and often involves illegal border-crossing. The human rights of trafficked persons are, thus, violated, and the immigration laws of states undermined. The security threat emerging from trafficking is often the consequence of assumed effects such as the wealth of traffickers and corruption, or the undermining of market regulations by supplying cheap labor (Avdan 2012: 173).

The presence of these crimes in political debates also differs. Drug trafficking has been targeted for decades by intense efforts, while being framed as a threat to society and its norms. The health problems caused by drug consumption have often received less attention than moral arguments, or from a security perspective, the wealth and political influence accumulated by drug cartels. A very different problem was the re-emergence of maritime piracy, in particular, off the coast of Somalia: facilitated by conditions of a failed state, piracy targeted the shipping industry, ultimately generating millions for Somali criminal gangs. Despite the fact that its threat potential had been limited to the shipping industry, piracy was countered by global military cooperation, supplemented by legal and economic development aid to countries in the Aden region. Similarly, cybercrime and its "securitized" companion cyberwarfare have received substantial attention in recent years in the security community, as their threat potential is diverse and ranges from individually hacked computers to attacks on critical infrastructure.

Taken together, some transnational crimes genuinely represent new security challenges, the most prominent of which is cybercrime. Many transnational crimes have only limited or indirect effects on national security, but they enable other potentially more harmful crimes. Finally, not all potential criminal threats are transnational—state security can also be weakened from "home-grown" terrorists and criminals (George 2016: 21). Thus, international security is not only threatened by crime in general, but also in different ways, and by some crimes more than by others.

33.3 How is Transnational Crime Governed?

Governing transnational crime has two dimensions: the internal dimension and the external dimension. The internal dimension refers to how criminal actors carry out their operations, control market shares and territory, while the external dimension refers to how states and other actors prevent criminal activity, intervene in criminal operations, or prosecute criminals. The internal governance is typically relevant when it comes to how criminals relate to other security threats, and how they undermine law enforcement efforts—thus, a state's capacity to defend itself. The external dimension of governance is often highlighted as a new security threat in debates about crime. Analyses then focus on whether external governance can actually be carried out effectively.

The internal governance of crime depends on the structure of criminal groups, the crime committed, and the relation to the environment. Transnational crime can be committed through hierarchical organizations that resemble the classic Mafia model with a clear chain of command, even if some parts of the organization enjoy some degree of autonomy over decision-making. In contrast, a network model of organized crime groups links together individuals or small groups that carry out specific tasks for a criminal enterprise, from faking documents to finding an available passage across a border or knowing the local markets for illicit goods. Multiple forms of hierarchical and networked organizations exist, sometimes in combinations that span across countries and regions (Williams 2001; von Lampe 2012: 183–5).

Internal governance is also influenced by the specific requirements of a crime. Terrorist groups prepare their acts secretively, while human smugglers or drug traffickers need a semi-public client base for selling their services and goods. Local market structures require more openness of a criminal business, while illicit transnational financial transactions require knowledge about the best territories and banks to launder money. Cybercriminals can cooperate without ever meeting each other, while human traffickers have direct interaction with their victims. The internal governance of crime also depends on the environment and how risky the exposure of criminal activity is: contexts in which criminal activity is regular, for example due to a large black market, corrupt police officials, or a weak rule of law, will require less precautions from criminals than a context in which crime is prosecuted. The internal governance of crime differs widely in terms of risk-management, market strategies, and the use of violence; thus, the impact of crime on national or individual security varies.

The external dimension of governing crime is mostly based on law enforcement carried out by state agencies and other actors aiming to interfere in the conduct of criminals. Elements range from the prevention of crime to policing and prosecution; they include measures aimed to distort criminal markets, for instance, by changing regulations or certification. The external dimension of governance also crosses different levels, from international legal instruments to the involvement of private actors or citizens at the local level. International bodies like Europol, Interpol, the Financial Action Taskforce, or the United Nations Office against Drugs and Crime help spread information about criminal activities or support the enforcement of international standards (Andreas and Nadelmann 2006). Non-state actors problematize criminal activities, monitor agreements against crime, or even implement regulations (Jakobi and Wolf 2013; Liss and Sharman 2014; Avant and Haufler, Chapter 24, this volume).

Transnational crime is particularly challenging because law enforcement agencies operate against a specific national background of different laws, policing practices, and capabilities. These differences in external governance can be exploited by transnational criminal networks, adapting smuggling routes, or establishing production sites where the risk of discovery is low. International cooperation has, therefore, increased, representing the central means to enable a more effective external governance of crime across borders.

Assessing the success of external crime governance is difficult for a variety of reasons: any assessment suffers from the secret nature of crime and its abstractness. Terrorist attacks are clearly visible, but successful anti-terrorist policies would prevent these from happening at all; in this case, a non-event signals success. The debate on human trafficking produces very different figures on how many victims exist (Frimann 2010); successful anti-trafficking policies are, thus, influenced by the statistics on which they rely. Some crimes are "victimless," for example money laundering: he threat linked to it is not the financial transaction, but rather, the crimes surrounding it, and the benefits derived from it. Other crimes produce multiple victims: human smuggling is a crime, but the main victim can be either the state whose immigration laws are circumvented or the smuggled person who might be killed in a non-safe passage across borders. The security of states and individuals is impacted by human smuggling, and while it sounds cynical that there is a trade-off between both, policy reactions vary greatly depending on what the priority is.

If not focusing on victims, the assessment of effective policies against transnational crime could also rely on figures regarding how many criminals were caught or whether the criminal activity was disrupted. Due to the secret nature of transnational crime, statistics are difficult to rely on (Andreas and Greenhill 2010), but the history of anti-crime policies and analyses of major trends can provide information on whether global crime governance actually serves global, national, or individual security.

From a historical perspective, transnational crime has been a long-standing item on international agendas of major powers, and early efforts against crime have been successful. In the eighteenth century, the British Royal Navy took a lead in prosecuting and extinguishing maritime piracy; in the nineteenth century British politicians pushed for an international anti-slavery agreement (Nadelmann 1990; Löwenheim 2006). While a resurrection of maritime piracy has been noted in some places, and human trafficking today has some remembrance to early slavery, these early counter-crime policies have, nonetheless, been effective in terms of crime reduction. Other policies were less so: the United States became a leading force for fighting narcotic drugs in the twentieth century (Andreas and Nadelmann 2006); still, decades later, narcotic drug consumption is prevalent in many societies, and the tools to counter it are increasingly contested. In 2016, a special session of the UN General Assembly did not result in major changes, but many countries are increasingly promoting another strategy in fighting drug consumption and trafficking (United Nations 2016b).

Besides introducing substantive norms, cooperation in global crime governance has expanded continuously, which has meant introducing structures and processes in the loosely regulated sphere of world politics. European powers paved the way to international police cooperation and crime governance in the early twentieth century (Deflem 2002). Other early efforts against crime included bilateral treaties, in particular on extradition and mutual legal assistance. These instruments were based on diplomatic exchange, and did not guarantee regular and cooperative exchange of law enforcement.

The growth of global governance processes against crime took place by expanding institutions—what institutionalists would call "layering" (Pierson and Skocpol 2002). International police cooperation was initiated in the early twentieth century to counter anarchism and other political crimes, but the practice of police exchange soon turned to other crimes (Deflem 2002). The global anti-money laundering regime has helped in establishing global monitoring processes on financial transactions; the regime was later enlarged to track terrorism and proliferation financing, as well as other aspects of illicit finance (Nance 2015). European cooperation against crime started in the 1970s, with cooperation against terrorism; this later became institutionalized with the European Anti-Drug Unit, which ultimately became Europol (Deflem 2006).

The enlargement of global crime governance has not only led to new institutions, but also to new combinations of actors. In line with neoliberal policy making, states increasingly outsource state functions, and rely on non-state actors. On the national and local level, crime governance, today, includes private security providers or private prisons (Krahmann 2010). On the transnational level, non-state actors are involved in data collection, monitoring, and implementation (Jakobi and Wolf 2013). The external governance of crime, thus, increasingly involves more sectors of society (Schuilenburg 2015). Governments have not only decreased the distance to non-state actors in governing crime, but there is also a tendency to merge policing efforts with intelligence and military capabilities. The rise of security concerns from within societies, due to criminal and terrorist actors, has led democracies to converge military, law enforcement, and intelligence roles, even though these used to be separate (Andreas and Price 2001; Lutterbeck 2005).

The analysis of crime as a security threat often only recognizes changed conditions for the internal governance of transnational crime: a closer connectedness of economies and markets, facilitated transport and travel across borders, better communication, and networking. At the same time, however, the external governance of crime has increased as well, and state agencies have responded by establishing new international norms, coordination bodies, and processes to counter crime across borders. Balancing internal and external governance against one another, while taking into account the specificities of different crimes, would be needed to assess the potential security threat of crime. All in all, the current governance of global crime has expanded considerably compared to efforts only a few decades ago, and this trend seems to be continuing.

33.4 The Future of Crime Governance

Despite the expansion of global crime governance in recent decades, presenting the future of crime, security, and its governance faces many unknowns. The most certain aspect is that crime is unlikely to disappear. From an economic perspective, it is likely that incentives will continue to exist that lead people to violate existing rules and become criminal. Political ideas will also differ in the future, and some people might opt to use violence to realize these ideas. Moral guidelines for behavior differ as well, and are not necessarily accepted, resulting in yet another reason for criminal behavior.

What type of crime will be most prominent in the future is dependent on technological progress, regulatory frameworks, and on political agendas: technological progress enables criminals to develop new ways of committing crime—like online fraud or hacking computer systems. Regulatory frameworks can incentivize new crimes, for instance when prohibitions create lucrative black markets. Political agendas determine whether and how a specific crime is framed as a security problem, and for whom. The same reasons also determine how crime will be governed in the future. Technological progress had already changed crime governance before the invention of the fingerprint system and future methods of crime governance can change rapidly in ways still unknown. Regulatory frameworks will make some forms of crime governance more likely than others, for instance austerity policies are likely to place even more emphasis on non-state actors than other models. Finally, political agendas will be determined by what policy-makers perceive as feasible options to govern crime.

In addition to all these unknown background conditions, crimes differ in how they are governed today, and they are likely to differ in the future. Yet, three main points seem to be particularly important for future crime governance and security: the availability and use of data, the role of formal norms, and the different aspects of security—individual, national, and global. Different scenarios are plausible for each of these points, depending on whether to expect a linear development or major disruptions.

Data have increasingly been used to monitor transactions and track down criminals, but there have been changes with regard to who is collecting data, and who is accessing them. States continue gathering data through intelligence agencies, yet they can also access data collected by non-state actors involved in monitoring activities. The financial data of banks is used to trace illicit finance, such as money laundering or terrorism financing. Communications data from internet providers are used to find cybercriminals and fraudsters, or to uncover relations in criminal networks. Individuals can be identified when they buy suspicious chemicals with dual use. The availability of data not only facilitates the monitoring of transactions and networks, but also sparks controversy about surveillance and privacy.

Different scenarios can evolve from this status quo. The first scenario is a linear development that ends in the ever-increasing accessibility of data by state agencies, and increased monitoring obligations of non-state actors. The accessibility of data can be ensured by developing technical measures for data exchange and defined procedures for reporting by non-state actors. As more and more information is available electronically and collected by transnational corporations, the exchange of information across borders could become easier. Data collection is also facilitated by the fact that privacy becomes a more outdated societal concept, and "digital natives"—a generation that has grown up with social media and online access—are less likely to object to data collection. In this scenario, the amount of data availability increases, while privacy concerns move to the background. Government agencies could draw on more information for security purposes and for prosecuting transnational crime.

Another scenario would be a non-linear development caused by an increasing awareness of privacy, as well as skepticism toward data collection. The reasons for such a development could be an aging generation of digital natives who are keen to eradicate past data, or to protect the rights of their children in cyberspace. Regulations like "the right to be forgotten" (European Commission 2014) support this development. Simultaneously, the legitimacy of data collection might become more contested: The United States and some other Western states show a high acceptance of data collection, while other states, such as Germany, are more skeptical. While authoritarian regimes are usually collecting data as well, this is not necessarily seen as legitimate, and political activists usually try to find ways around them. A shift to democracy in authoritarian regimes could make data collection regarding citizens more unpopular, and, thus, could also work as a restricting force.

In between these two scenarios is a middle way: the continuation and extension of data collection combined with a growing awareness among citizens and users. In this scenario, the amount of data could increase, but the overall quality could decrease, when users—including those carrying out completely legitimate activities—try to circumvent monitoring and data collection. The consequence could be a large number of "false positives" in detecting suspicious patterns, undermining public trust and legitimacy in the data collection and making it increasingly unmanageable for law enforcement. At the same time, a growing awareness of privacy can make future law-making on surveillance more difficult, and this could result in more data being collected by intelligence agencies only—with the potential to undermine trust in the transparency of state agencies even further.

This links to the second important aspect of future global crime governance: the role of formal norms on the state level, as well as on the global level. In weak and failing states, crime and terrorism can flourish due to the absence of effective formal norms and law enforcement. Yet, even in stronger states, the retrenchment of state agencies and declining influence of the state on its population can strengthen criminal groups. Ultimately, these groups could succeed in creating "alternative governance" (Williams 2013), and their own informal rule-system. However, formal norms are not only pressured on the national level: formal prohibitions have been the basis of global crime governance, already codified in international conventions against slavery and piracy. After the Second World War, and, in particular, since the end of the Cold War, international agreements against crimes like drug trafficking, terrorism, and corruption proliferated and corresponding criminalization was implemented in national laws (Jakobi 2013). At the same time, global crime governance has also witnessed more informal procedures and soft law regulations, most prominently in the field of anti-money laundering (Tsingou 2010). Cybercrime is only regulated by the Council of Europe, while conflict diamonds have been regulated in the global network of the Kimberley Process.

Again, different scenarios can follow from this development. In the first scenario, states could agree on an ever-increasing number of international agreements against crime, including norms about which activities need to be criminalized and which procedural regulations apply for cross-border prosecution. This would mark a growing consensus on criminalization, could homogenize national laws, and enhance cross-national cooperation in law enforcement, as well as end safe havens for globally operating criminals. Quite the opposite is a scenario in which global crime governance becomes increasingly contested, and states cannot agree on common approaches. While the threat of crime might be shared, the solutions are not: established prohibition regimes, such as the one on narcotic drugs, are contested today and tend to become weaker. In other cases, states may not agree on a global regulation—for instance regarding cyberspace or global tax law. This disagreement on crime could give rise to fragmented approaches, as well as more informal instruments based on ad hoc coalitions. Effective international law enforcement would be limited, however, and safe havens would continue to exist.

It is likely that global crime governance will develop somewhere in between these scenarios: consensus on some crimes will continue to grow into international conventions—perhaps only restricted to those committed by non-state actors with a strong impact on national security—while others will be regulated differently or not at all. This would not imply that counter-crime activities cease to exist: states could increase the use of transnational businesses and use data collected by those, and they could regulate extraterritorially. Moreover, non-state activists have increasingly started to delegitimize social activities outside legal frameworks, for instance by drawing attention to labor rights, environmental protection, or corporate responsibility in global consumption. A large number of labels and certification measures have been adopted that are not legally required, but positively mark products and procedures. Global norms about right and wrong would, thus, be growing, but not necessarily on the basis of formal norms. In a security context, this informalization and extension of moral standards could imply a sharper division of crimes that are seen as being relevant for security and those that are not.

So far, the rise of crime as a security threat has been accompanied by an enlarged understanding of security, from all aspects of human security to global security. Security concerns today can arise from environmental crime and environmental degradation, threatening the livelihood of individuals, as well as collective security due to large population movements. Security can be threatened by hackers trying to damage critical infrastructure and by intruding into the "web of things," including airplanes—to name just a few possibilities. This ubiquity of security concerns is a societal and political development, and not a "given" (Balzacq 2011; Schuilenburg 2015). The future of security and crime can unfold in different scenarios.

In a linear development, security and crime policies continue to converge, making crime one of the most central transnational security threats. The costs to this could be an ever more generalizing talk about crime and security, and the continuous emphasis on the nexus of criminal groups to different security threats. What is less pronounced in such a scenario is differentiation regarding the crimes, their causes, and consequences. In the long run, however, permanent references to the threat of crime or an exaggeration of the "numbers game" (Andreas and Greenhill 2010) are likely to lose appeal and undermine trust in analyses. In a second scenario, a clear division would be established between security as being state or international security, and crime as a societal security problem. Apart from cyber-attacks, terrorism, and large-scale weapons trafficking, few crimes would qualify as being a national security threat. This would mean a narrower idea of security, and a clearer distinction between security threats and criminal threats; thus, establishing a sort of "high security" linked to global and national security and "low security" being individual and human security.

However, depending on the context, even "petty crime" can supply funds or other resources for major security incidents. Self-financing of low-cost terrorist attacks can be easier than moving funds across borders as in the case of French terrorist attacks in 2015 (Bloomberg 2015). Additionally, criminal organizations can change over time to become more political and, therefore, become a security threat to others outside the criminal context. Furthermore, the distinction of state security and criminal activity is not necessarily clear; for example when criminal groups infiltrate or corrupt state organizations.

The more likely scenario is, therefore, an enduring presence of security debates linked to crime. Crime will remain an integral part of security agendas—if only because it can flourish under conditions when security or other core institutions are weakened. Each crime can potentially impact a range of security issues: corruption can enable nuclear proliferation, threaten democratic stability, or the rule of law (Rotberg 2009), but not all at the same time. Illicit networks cause cyber-attacks, carry out weapons smuggling, or prevent state-building (Miklaucic and Brewer 2013), but one network will not necessarily carry out all these forms of crime. What is crucial from a research and policy perspective is a differentiated analysis on the conditions, the effects, and the threats of transnational crime. This includes more systematic analyses on the conditions where different crimes flourish, as well as the mechanisms by which they threaten security. In some cases, criminal activities are embedded in societal niches, while in others they are even supported by corrupt government agencies. Transnational crime is often a symptom of weak law enforcement, a low legitimacy of governmental authority, and other social-economic problems.

References

Andreas, Peter and Kelly M. Greenhill (eds.). 2010. *Sex, Drugs and Body Counts. The Politics of Numbers in Global Crime and Conflict*. Ithaca, NY: Cornell University Press.

Andreas, Peter and Ethan Nadelmann. 2006. *Policing the Globe. Criminalization and Crime Control in International Relations*. Oxford: Oxford University Press.

Andreas, Peter and Richard Price. 2001. From War Fighting to Crime Fighting: Transforming the American National Security State. *International Studies Review*, 3(3): 31–52.

Avdan, N. 2012. Human Trafficking and Migration Control Policy: Vicious or Virtuous Cycle? *Journal of Public Policy*, 32(3): 171–205.

Balzacq, Thierry (ed.). 2011. *Securitization Theory. How Security Problems Emerge and Dissolve* London: Routledge.

Bloomberg. 2015. *Why France's Terror Attacks Were Probably Self-Financed. Available at:* http://www.bloomberg.com/news/articles/2015-01-12/why-frances-terror-attacks-were-probably-selffinanced, last accessed in September 2016.

Deflem, Matthieu. 2002. *Policing World Society: Historical Foundations of International Police Cooperation*. Oxford: Clarendon.

Deflem, Mathieu. 2005. "Wild Beasts without Nationality": The Uncertain Origins of Interpol, 1889–1910. In Philip Reichel (ed.), *Handbook of Transnational Crime and Justice*, pp. 275–85. Thousand Oaks, London, and New Delhi: Sage.

Deflem, Matthieu. 2006. Europol and the Policing of International Terrorism: Counter-Terrorism in a Global Perspective. *Justice Quarterly*, 23(3): 336–59.

Eurobarometer. 2016. *First Results of Eurobarometer 2016. Available at.* ec.europa.eu/COMMFrontOffice/PublicOpinion/index.cfm/ResultDoc/download/DocumentKy/74264, last accessed in September 2016.

European Commission. 2014. *Factsheet on "The Right to Be Forgotten" ruling. Available at:* http://ec.europa.eu/justice/data-protection/files/factsheets/factsheet_data_protection_en.pdf, last accessed in September 2016.

Frimann, H. Richard. 2010. Numbers and Certification: Assessing Foreign Compliance in Narcotics and Human Trafficking. In Peter Andreas and Kelly M. Greenhill (eds.), *Sex, Drugs, and Body Counts. The Politics of Numbers in Crime and Conflict*, pp. 75–109. Ithaca, NY: Cornell University Press.

George, Justin. 2016. State Failure and Transnational Terrorism: An Empirical Analysis. *Journal of Conflict Resolution*. doi: 10.1177/0022002716660587

Jakobi, Anja P. 2013. *Common Goods and Evils? The Formation of Global Crime Governance*. Oxford: Oxford University Press.

Jakobi, Anja P. and Klaus Dieter Wolf (eds.). 2013. *The Transnational Governance of Violence and Crime: Non-State Actors in Security* Houndmills: Palgrave.

Krahmann, Elke. 2010. *States, Citizens and the Privatization of Security*. Cambridge: Cambridge University Press.

Liss, Carolin and Jason C. Sharman. 2014. Global Corporate Crime-fighters: Private Transnational Responses to Piracy and Money Laundering. *Review of International Political Economy*: 693–718. doi: 10.1080/09692290.2014.936482

Löwenheim, Oded. 2006. *Predators and Parasites: Persistent Agents of Transnational Harm and Great Power Authority*. Ann Arbor: University of Michigan Press.

Lutterbeck, Derek. 2005. Blurring the Dividing Line: The Convergence of Internal and External Security in Western Europe. *European Security*, 14: 231–53.

Mandel, Robert. 2011. *Dark Logic. Transnational Criminal Tactics and Global Security*. Stanford, CA: Stanford University Press.

Miklaucic, Michael and Jaqueline Brewer (eds.). 2013. *Convergence. Illicit Networks and National Security in the Age of Globalization* Washington, DC: National Defense University Press.

Nadelmann, Ethan A. 1990. Global Prohibition Regimes: The Evolution of Norms in International Society. *International Organization*, 44(4): 479–526.

Nance, Mark T. 2015. Naming and Shaming in Financial Regulation. Explaining Variation in the Financial Actions Task Force on Money Laundering. In H. Richard Frimann (ed.), *The Politics of Leverage in International Relations. Name, Shame and Sanction*, pp. 123–41. London: Palgrave.

Neumann, V. 2013. Grievance to Greed: The Global Convergence of the Crime–Terror Threat. *Orbis*, 57(2): 251–67.

Pierson, Paul and Theda Skocpol. 2002. Historical Institutionalism in Contemporary Political Science. In Ira Katznelson and Helen V. Milner (eds.), *Political Science. State of the Discipline*, pp. 693—721. New York and London: W.W. Norton.

Rotberg, Robert I. (ed.). *Corruption, Global Security and World Order.* Washington, DC: Brookings Institution.

Rubio, Mauricio and Román Ortiz. 2005. Organized Crime in Latin America. In Philip Reichel (ed.), *Handbook of Transnational Crime and Justice*, pp. 425–38. Thousand Oaks, London, and New Delhi: Sage.

Schuilenburg, Marc. 2015. *The Securitization of Society. Crime, Risk and Social Order*. New York: New York University Press.

Tsingou, Eleni. 2010. Global Financial Governance and the Developing Anti-Money Laundering Regime: What Lessons for International Political Economy? *International Politics*, 47(6): 617–37.

United Nations. 2016a. Treaty Collection: United Nations Convention against Transnational Organized Crime. *Available at:* https://treaties.un.org/Pages/ViewDetails.aspx?src=TREATY&mtdsg_no=XVIII-12&chapter=18&lang=en, last accessed on February 6, 2016."

United Nations. 2016b. *UNGASS 2016. Special Session of the United Nations General Assembly on the World Drug Problem Documentation. Available at:* http://www.unodc.org/ungass2016/en/documentation.html, last accessed in September 2016.

Von Lampe, Klaus. 2012. Transnational Organized Crime Challenges for Future Research. *Crime, Law and Social Change*, 58(2): 179–94.

Williams, Phil. 2001. Transnational Criminal Networks. In John Arquilla and David Ronfeldt (eds.), *Networks and Netwars: The Future of Terror, Crime, and Militancy*, pp. 61–97. Santa Monica: RAND.

Williams, Phil. 2002. Transnational Organized Crime and the State. In Rodney Bruce Hall and Thomas J. Bierstecker (eds.), *The Emergence of Private Authority in Global Governance*, pp. 161–82. Cambridge: Cambridge University Press.

Williams, Phil. 2013. Lawlessness and Disorder. An Emerging Paradigm for the 21st Century. In Michael Miklaucic and Jaqueline Brewer (eds.), *Convergence. Illicit Networks and National*

Security in the Age of Globalization, pp. 15–36. Washington, DC: National Defense University Press.

Woodiwiss, Michael and Dick Hobbs. 2009. Organized Evil and the Atlantic Alliance Moral Panics and the Rhetoric of Organized Crime Policing in America and Britain. *British Journal of Criminology*, 49(1): 106–28.

CHAPTER 34

TERRORISM

AUDREY KURTH CRONIN

THE study of terrorism changed dramatically in the first two decades of the twenty-first century, reflecting the vast number of academics and policy analysts who entered the field after the September 2001 attacks on the United States. This yielded mixed results. Improved academic rigor was a positive development. Many of the best academics turned their attention to this subject, analyzing the causes of terrorism, strategies of terrorism, the use of suicide attacks, and evolving ideologies, for example, often supported by large government grants. New and better terrorism incident databases enabled stronger quantitative analyses and reduced the politicization of the field. Thousands of books and articles emerged, some of them excellent contributions that enhanced our understanding of terrorism, how to respond to it, and how to prevent it.

But troubling cleavages also opened up in the study of terrorism, notably a sharp geographical divergence between the analysis of terrorism and those who experienced it. Analysts focused on the relatively small number of terrorist attacks in the United States and Western Europe (as horrible and tragic as they were), even as terrorism in the Middle East, South Asia, and North Africa skyrocketed. Keeping terrorism "over there" was a deliberate policy. During the 2000s, the top four countries in terms of terrorist attacks were Iraq, Pakistan, India, and Afghanistan, in that order (LaFree et al. 2015: 58). These were, not coincidentally, the countries (or their neighbors) where US and European militaries had intervened. The number of terrorist attacks in Iraq was more than 29,000, 98 percent after the invasion of 2003 (to 2012). By contrast, from 1970 to 2012, the United States homeland suffered a total of 3,496 attacks, only 32 of them between 2003 and 2012 (LaFree et al. 2015: 135 and Global Terrorism Database). Brutal attacks in Paris, Brussels, Orlando, and Nice horrified audiences in Europe and the United States, yet the contrasting levels of bloodshed still held. From 2015 to mid-2016, the death toll from attacks in Europe and the Americas was 658 in 46 attacks, even as the Middle East, Africa, and Asia suffered 28,031 deaths in 2,063 attacks (IHS Janes).

Another negative trend was uneven expectations about major acts of terrorism. Americans, especially, demanded zero risk of terrorism at home, while those in fractured regions bore the brunt of escalating terrorist violence. It was a kind of outsourcing of political violence, logical perhaps for a government whose top priority is to protect its own citizens, but solipsistic, short-sighted, and unsustainable over time. The vast majority of victims of terrorist attacks during the first two decades of the twenty-first century were Muslims from the Middle East, North Africa, and South Asia. Yet the vast majority of terrorism research focused on the small number of attacks perpetrated or inspired by Islamists in Europe and North America. US terrorism analyses that did look elsewhere focused first on terrorist attacks in Iraq and Afghanistan during the occupation (but very little afterwards), and then on the flow of foreign fighters to and from Syria (but very little on the people who lived there). Thousands of civilians were slaughtered by the Syrian regime or forced to flee; yet most of the academics still saw the situation there through the narrow lens of US and European counter-terrorism, especially the struggle between al Qaeda and ISIS. There are reasons for this, including the difficulty of traveling to unstable places, the greater availability of funding for US- and European-focused projects, and the lack of accessible data from active conflict zones or countries lacking a free press. But academics should at least acknowledge that the field of "terrorism studies" has been globally skewed.

The gap between the focus of terrorism studies and terrorist casualties will narrow in the future. Going forward, the post-9/11 seal between terrorism in those regions and in the United States and Europe has become porous and will break down further. Recent tragic attacks have already demonstrated this. The millions of desperate refugees fleeing the wars in the Middle East, and the xenophobic populist backlash in some places, will further polarize European and American societies. Distinctions between those who are logistically connected to terrorist groups and those who are "inspired" will be harder to draw. Even after the so-called Islamic State Caliphate disappears, the violence related to ISIS, al Qaeda, and their successors or affiliates will persist and become less coherent and less trackable. The future of terrorism studies must reflect a more mature geographical scope, a better understanding of the social and political context, and a more agile, interdisciplinary framework if it is to adapt.

This chapter will provide an overview of terrorism's current and future challenges, in five sections. Beginning with a short discussion of the definition, the chapter expands upon terrorism's neglected yet important symbolic nature. The third section analyzes time-tested strategies of terrorism, explaining how they have evolved over the centuries. Next is an overview of radicalization studies, an area of driving significance for the future, where more academic rigor, fresh framing, and new methods are needed. The conclusion offers five driving factors that will shape both the future of terrorism and the study of terrorism.

34.1 What is Terrorism?

A common understanding of the problem is a prerequisite to studying it. There is no universally agreed definition of terrorism, a fact that is also true of "war," "legitimacy," and "sovereignty." Still, terrorism is a uniquely value-laden term, often sloppily used, and always associated with creating public fear. It is murder with widespread symbolic meaning, a type of violence whose effects play out partly in audiences' minds afterwards. Non-state attackers killing or maiming innocent victims cause the principal wave of fear, as others watch in horror or deal with the aftermath. But irresponsible pundits, media members, politicians, and sometimes academics can drive the secondary wave, feeding the anxieties of domestic constituencies in an action/reaction cycle that heightens the incentive to strike again and surrenders the initiative to the terrorists. Understanding how terrorism works can avert that fundamental error, as we will discuss below.

Fortunately there are more commonalities than differences in what people consider terrorism. The core elements boil down to five factors. First, terrorism is an *act* that involves the threat or use of violence. The act may be in the name of good or bad causes: means and motivation are separate. Second, terrorism has a political aim. The violence can be in the service of a political ideology or a spiritual belief (religion is, after all, the most ancient type of "politics") but it must be more than self-serving. Terrorism is about seeking justice, or at least someone's conception of justice. There must be a sense of altruism on behalf of a broader community (misguided as it may be) or else the violence is strictly a criminal act. Third, the targets must be illegitimate, meaning innocent victims, non-combatants, or civilians. Those who are strong enough to attack active military forces and to hold territory (even temporarily) are insurgents (see Checkel, Chapter 11, this volume). Terrorists can transition to becoming insurgents but only if they gain strength and numbers, typically going from hundreds of operatives to thousands. Fourth, the perpetrators must be non-state actors. This is the hardest aspect to wrestle with, because state violence has led to far more misery and death than terrorism has, and ruling it out of the definition inevitably draws us closer to status quo state governments (Roberts 2015). When state force is used internationally, it is considered an act of war; when it is used domestically, it may be called law enforcement. But perfidious state actions are called crimes against humanity, a violation of the laws of war, genocide, and so on—there is a vocabulary to describe state uses of force (see Hendershot and Mutimer, Chapter 5, this volume). Not so for non-state uses of force. Analysts speak of "terror from above" and "terrorism from below." Only the latter is included here. Lastly, there must always be an audience, either to intimidate or inspire. Unless there is an audience, terrorism is indistinguishable from other types of violence against civilians. Killing innocents in the absence of symbolism or publicity is murder, not terrorism (Cronin 2002/3; Stohl 2014).

As we admitted at the outset, there are gray areas in every definition of terrorism, not least because the term has evolved in different historical contexts. For example, some people insist that states can be terrorists (as in the strategic bombing of cities during the Second World War) or that military forces can be illegitimate targets (as in the 1983 US Marine Barracks bombing in Beirut, Lebanon, killing 241 soldiers who were peacekeepers). These ambiguous cases spark bitter arguments when the definition is too narrow. Others call virtually every abhorrent act of violence "terrorism," because the word is so evocative and powerful. They make the definition too broad and ultimately meaningless. Because of the heavily political nature of the term, especially its pejorative usage, a perfect definition is impossible. But the perfect being the enemy of the good, the definition of terrorism for the purposes of this chapter is: the use or threat of use of symbolic violence against innocents by a non-state actor to achieve political ends.

34.2 The Role of Publicity

Symbolism relies upon publicity, which is at the heart of terrorist violence and always has been. The effect on an audience offers political leverage to otherwise weak political actors. This may seem odd, because terrorism is an ancient phenomenon that pre-dates modern media. David Rapoport claims that it dates at least to the Zealots and Sicarii of the first century BCE, Jewish groups that killed with a dagger (the Sicarii) or used violence to spark an uprising in Judea against the Romans (the Zealots) (Rapoport 1984). But even these two groups attacked their victims using public, demonstrative methods to force a popular reaction.

In the world of social media, the tie to symbolism and publicity is more direct than ever; but it is not new. Modern terrorism traces its lineage to the concept of propaganda of the deed (or propaganda *by* the deed, from the French *propaganda par le fait*), an old activist principle drawn from writings by French politician Pierre-Joseph Proudhon (1846), Italian revolutionary Carlo Pisacane (1857) and Russian anarchist Mikhail Bakunin (1870). During the late nineteenth century, the concept came to refer to publicized acts of killing, especially bombings. The goal was to engage in "creative destruction," shake the foundations of society, and shock the masses into revolution throughout the world (Woodcock 1962).

Between the invention of dynamite in 1867 and about 1934 (interrupted by the First World War), there was a global wave of political violence associated with propaganda of the deed. It included social revolutionaries (e.g. *Narodnaya Volya* in Russia, the group that in 1881 assassinated the tsar), anarchist groups and individuals (e.g. Mario Buda, an anarchist who blew up Wall Street in 1920, killing 38 and injuring 143), and nationalists (e.g. Irish nationalists, who carried out a campaign of violence in Britain between 1881 and 1885 and pioneered the use of timers and detonators) (Clutterbuck 2004). It was not a single coherent movement but more a worldwide wave of violence encompassing both networked organizations and lone individuals "inspired" to act, with the ideal means (dynamite) to do so (Rapoport 2004; Jensen 2014).

Modern terrorism would not have been born without the laying of cross-oceanic telegraph cables (1858+) and the boom in mass media newspapers (so-called "yellow journalism") that followed. During this period there were hundreds of bombings throughout the world, on every continent except Antarctica. Egypt, China, Japan, and Australia all had significant anarchist groups. Ordinary people died in the hundreds, and prominent leaders were assassinated. Between 1892 and 1901, more monarchs, presidents, and prime ministers of major powers were killed than at any other time in history, including

President Marie Francois Sadi Carnot of France in 1894, King Umberto of Spain in 1897, and American President William McKinley in 1901 (Jensen 2014: 31). All of the bombings and killings were meant move the populace, by demonstrating dissatisfaction with the current political system and inspiring a global uprising against it. Willingly or not, this agenda suited the worldwide press, competing for a mass readership by pricing newspapers very low and printing boldface banner headlines to attract buyers. This business model helped build both the Pulitzer and Hearst newspaper empires in the United States, for example. Each "anarchist" bombing was reported in sensational terms, reaching both the appalled and the inspired, perpetuating the cycle of violence.

The next watershed event was the Munich Olympics massacre, an unprecedented opportunity to reach almost a billion viewers from a global stage via television. On September 5, 1972 members of Palestinian group Black September kidnapped 11 Israeli athletes, killing two immediately and holding the remaining nine hostage over two days. Operationally the episode was a disaster for everyone involved, with both a lack of planning by the operatives and abysmal handling of the rescue attempt by the West German police. Threatening to kill a hostage every two hours, Black September demanded the release of 236 prisoners in Israeli jails and five in West Germany in exchange for the Israeli hostages, but its violence failed to compel either of those governments to comply. After 15 hours of negotiations, the bloody outcome was the deaths of all of the Israeli athletes, a West German policeman, and five of the eight Palestinian terrorists (Reeve 2000).

The immediate reaction to the Olympics massacre was global condemnation and revulsion; but the longer-term implications were entirely different. By striking at the Olympics, the Palestinians grabbed a huge publicity opportunity, with hundreds of print, radio, and television journalists broadcasting live to sports fans throughout the world. Horrified observers who condemned the violence also found it impossible not to watch. The image of a masked man pacing on the balcony of the athletes' quarters in the Olympic village, broadcast in real time over television networks, was seared into people's minds. Many for the first time saw the Palestinian people and their plight as a force to be reckoned with. Eighteen months later, Yassir Arafat was invited to address the United Nations, and the Palestinians gained UN special observer status shortly thereafter. Palestinian nationalism also drew increased revenue and thousands of new recruits in the immediate aftermath of the attack (Hoffman 2006: 67–71).

The Munich Olympics tragedy changed both terrorism and counter-terrorism in subsequent decades. It demonstrated how ill-prepared the Germans had been and led to the establishment of special counter-terrorist units there and in most major countries. It also spawned a wave of copycat terrorist attacks aimed at international publicity throughout the 1970s and well beyond. While direct cause and effect cannot be proven, the Global Terrorism Database shows that the total number of attacks worldwide began to increase in the 1970s, with a sharp uptick in 1978–79 (from 1,526 to 2,661 a 74 percent increase), peaking in 1992 (with more than 5,000 attacks). In other words, overall the number of terrorist attacks globally more than tripled and fatal attacks more than doubled between 1978 and 1992 (LaFree et al. 2015: 28–33, and Global Terrorism Database).

Terrorism had failed in Munich, and yet the promotional effect of the operation was seen as an enormous success.

34.3 The Strategies of Terrorist Campaigns

Any objective assessment of the terrorist attacks of 1972 would conclude that both "sides"—the Germans and the Israelis, on the one hand, and the Palestinians on the other—had lost in a big way. Yet the operation was celebrated and copied. This is because terrorism is much more than a dyadic relationship between terrorists and counter-terrorists. Strategies are always broader than tactics because they incorporate longer-term effects and take into account other actors.

The strategies of modern terrorism have evolved over the centuries to suit the vulnerabilities of the states or societies against which they are arrayed. Since the nineteenth century, there have been four major strategies engaged in by terrorist groups to achieve their broad political aims. These strategies, which are sometimes used in combination, provide an overarching logic for a terrorist campaign.

The first and best known is compellence—the use of threats to manipulate or influence another actor to stop doing an unwanted behavior or to start doing something that a group wants it to do. This concept comes directly from the writings of Thomas Schelling, whose notions of coercion and compellence are drawn from economics and are foundational to political science, especially the study of international security (Schelling 1966). Compellence may try to force a state to withdraw from territorial commitments through a strategy of punishment and attrition, to engage in terrorist attacks that make holding the territory so painful that the state abandons it. Most academic researchers agree that terrorists make rational strategic decisions in their campaigns (Crenshaw 1998). The bargaining framework is therefore a natural way for them to look at terrorism. It employs the same structure and methods, rationally matching terrorist means to ends, that academics employ for analyzing state behavior (Enders and Sandler 2006).

American policy-makers have also preferred this approach. Al Qaeda's strategy seemed perfectly suited to a compellence framework, for example, not least because the 9/11 attacks looked exactly like a surprise attack from the air. All of the basic axioms of air power, initially put forth by Italian Guiliot Douhet in *Command of the Air* 1921 and expanded in US nuclear strategy during the Cold War, seemed to be playing out, including the hopeless vulnerability of civilians to attack, the difficulty of effective defense, the benefits of sudden attack, and the need for immediate retaliation (Freedman 1981). Given their deep twentieth-century experience with air power and nuclear strategy, US defense policy-makers found the logic comfortably familiar and transferred it to counter-terrorism. Immediate retaliation even played a role in the Bush administration's mistaken 2003 invasion of Iraq, as when National Security Advisor Condoleeza Rice warned of the potential for a "smoking gun" to turn into a "mushroom cloud" (Blitzer 2003).

Compellence as a strategy of terrorism at times seems to work. There have been numerous examples, including the US and French withdrawals from Lebanon in 1983, the US withdrawal from Somalia in 1993, and the Israeli withdrawal from Lebanon in 2000. Bin Laden even mentioned Somalia in his public statements and interviews. The heavy focus of most terrorism studies on the anti-colonial struggles of ethno-nationalist groups, along with highly developed quantitative methods drawn from game theory, naturally led to reliance upon bargaining frameworks in analyzing the strategies of terrorism, resulting in many important insights (Enders and Sandler 2006; Kydd and Walter 2006).

But the approach also had its limitations. Terrorist campaigns have employed three other historically proven approaches, all strategies of leverage that maximize a weak hand yet operate very differently from compellence. Its symbolic nature means there are three sides to terrorism: the group, the target state (or states), and the various audiences who are watching. In terrorism, strategy is not just the application of means to ends, because the reactions of the various audiences involved can be a group's means, or its ends, or both.

The first strategy of leverage is provocation, which tries to force a state to react, to *do something*—not a specific policy, but a vigorous action that works against its interests. Provocation was firmly established as a purpose for terrorism during the nineteenth century and was at the heart of the strategy of the Russian populist group *Narodnaya Volya* (People's Will), for example. *Narodnaya Volya*'s goal was to attack representatives of the tsarist regime so as to provoke a brutal state response and inspire a peasant uprising. Other cases of provocation include the Basque group ETA's early strategy in Spain, the Sandinista National Liberation Front's strategy in Nicaragua, and the FLN's strategy in Algeria (Cronin 2009).

Provocation is a difficult strategy to apply effectively, however, since terrorist attacks often cause a state to behave in ways that no one expects. For this reason, beginning in 1950, terrorist groups targeting strong West European states chose a strategy of provocation less often than their predecessors of the nineteenth century had (Carter 2016/17). Afraid to look weak, policy-makers respond forcefully in the aftermath of an attack in ways that may alienate their supporters, invigorate the supporters of a terrorist group, draw in third parties (state or non-state), or even catalyze a broader systemic conflict—which is exactly what happened with the killing of Archduke Franz Ferdinand in 1914 at the outbreak of the First World War.

The next strategy, polarization, uses terrorist attacks to affect the domestic politics of a state, trying to divide people and delegitimize governments so it becomes impossible to govern. It often drives regimes sharply to the right, forcing populations to choose between the terrorist cause and brutal state repression, for example. The goal is to set people against each other, fragmenting societies to the extent that it is impossible to maintain a moderate middle within a functioning state. Polarization acts by intimidating neutral civilian populations, preventing them from being uninvolved in a campaign or cause. Sometimes the outcome is a failed state and escalation to a civil war.

Polarization is an attractive strategy against democracies and it appeared often during the twentieth century. But like the strategy of provocation, it results in unintended consequences. Examples include the Tamil Tigers in Sri Lanka and the Provisional Irish Republican Army in Northern Ireland. Terrorist activities in Germany, Austria, and Hungary after the First World War polarized and played a role in the arrival of the Second World War. In the United States, Timothy McVeigh's 1995 Oklahoma City terrorist attack on the Murrah Federal Building (168 killed and more than 600 injured) sought to ignite a white separatist war against the federal government. But the classic example of polarization is the Tupamaros' strategy in democratic Uruguay in the 1960s. They targeted the business community, inciting panic, prompting the Army to take over in 1973 and govern Uruguay for the next 12 years. The terrorist campaign had executed one hostage and assassinated eight counter insurgency personnel; the military regime that came to power "disappeared," tortured, or killed thousands (Cronin 2009: 130–1). In Uruguay a polarization strategy drove the government to destroy itself.

The last strategy of leverage, mobilization, tries to recruit and rally supporters to the cause. Terrorist attacks use the reaction of the state as a means, not an end. The violence may invigorate and energize potential recruits and raise the profile of the group internationally, drawing resources, sympathizers, and allies (Abrahms 2008). The symbolic nature of attacks draws additional attention, even when the terrorist group may be losing a direct confrontation against a stronger state or group of states (Bueno de Mesquita and Dickson 2007). This is why, going forward, the most important element of a sustainable terrorist campaign is an effective media operation, including traditional media, social media, and all relevant instantaneous platforms.

The central theme of all of these strategies of terrorism is that they are designed to exploit the vulnerabilities of the types of states against which they are directed. As the state and the international system have evolved, so the strategies of terrorism have followed a historical pattern. Provocation especially suited the nineteenth century, when aging autocratic regimes were struggling to hold on as popular suffrage gained ground. Their brittleness and vulnerability increased the incentives to provoke them as they coped with growing populist movements, especially in Europe and the United States. Compellence best fit the mid-twentieth century, as it aligned well with nationalist movements whose aims could be expressed in terms of territory. Many newly established postcolonial states (Israel, Algeria, Vietnam) began their fights for independence with terrorist attacks directed against colonial powers such as Britain and France, whose governments had touted self-determination during the Second World War. Polarization was at the heart of Marxist movements in the early twentieth century and it has reappeared now, with terrorist attacks designed to polarize along racial, religious, ethnic, tribal, linguistic, or sectarian lines. And mobilization plays directly into globalization, with its sweeping changes in communication, porous borders, alienation of those left behind, and direct access to violent non-state groups (Cronin, 2002/3).

Terrorist groups do use other approaches in specific situations. These include "spoiling," meaning carrying out terrorist attacks to undermine peace processes, and "outbidding," meaning using attacks to convince potential followers to follow one group instead of another (Bloom 2004). Specific operations can achieve these short-term purposes but they are tactics, not strategies. They aim at process goals (e.g. jockeying with other groups, showing strength, drawing attention, undermining talks, etc.) rather than outcome goals (e.g. changing the governance of a state, redistributing resources, attacking or protecting a racial or ethnic identity, promoting religious identity or values, etc.) (Cronin 2009: 77–82). Likewise, suicide attacks may be employed in the *service* of a strategy; but consciously committing suicide while engaging in violence is a tactic that has been used for millennia by individuals, terrorist groups, insurgencies, and even states (Gambetta 2006; Pape 2006). It is not a strategy of terrorism.

Going forward, the most effective strategies for terrorist groups will be polarization and mobilization, the two that best exploit the intense external and internal pressures on states. On the internal dimension, polarization is already yielding benefits for neo-Nazi and right-wing groups like Pegida (Patriotic Europeans Against the Islamization of the West) in Germany, for example, as more than a half million migrants seek asylum there. Even as it lost territory, the so-called Islamic State used the November 2015 attacks at the Bataclan theatre and several cafes in Paris to drive European societies apart and cause a violent backlash. On the external dimension, mobilization via social media provides violent groups with direct access to individuals, be they potential recruits, weak-minded seekers, supporters, thugs, antagonists, or potential victims. Porous borders, criminal networks, human trafficking, and other transnational ties all offer physical routes for violent actors; but mobilization via social media is more instantaneous. If a group is successful at "inspiring" individuals to carry out attacks, then even airtight borders will fail to prevent them. How to counter that kind of threat while preserving the rights and freedoms of all people in a democracy is what we will discuss next.

34.4 Radicalization and Extremism

Polarization is very dangerous to democratic countries. Terrorism often pits values such as freedom of speech, freedom of the press, and non-discrimination against protecting the lives of potential terrorist victims. It heightens fear even as other types of violence kill far more people. For example, the US Center for Disease Control and Prevention reports that annual firearm mortality (including mass shootings) in the United States is around 30,000, while deaths from terrorist attacks after 9/11 through 2016 (15 years) number fewer than 100. This is the result of robust defenses put into place and tips from local communities—the very communities that are alienated by polarizing political rhetoric in the wake of a terrorist attack. Every death from whatever source is a tragedy. But like good policing, good counter-terrorism always depends upon the cooperation of local communities.

In the absence of tips from friends or neighbors, it is almost impossible for intelligence services to track individuals who have no prior experience or logistical ties yet become "inspired" to engage in one-time attacks at home or abroad. For example, the attacks in Nice, France (July 14, 2016, 84 killed, 303 wounded), Orlando, Florida (June 12, 2016, 49 killed, 53 wounded) and San Bernardino, California (December 2, 2015, 14 killed, 22 wounded) were all committed in the name of the Islamic State yet without any direct logistical ties. In most earlier incidents, there were email connections, phone conversations, or some other kind of evidence of a plot underway. Not so now.

This autonomous pattern of terrorism is not yet well understood, but it will be important in the future. As one approach to protecting the broader community, many academics and policy-makers focus on "radicalization," or the process whereby a person begins to hold extreme views. In theory, looking at processes of "radicalization" could help prevent terrorist attacks at an earlier stage. But in practice, this framing of human behavior is problematic. Engaging in violence involves not only adopting radical viewpoints but also deciding to act upon them. Whether or not a person orchestrates a terrorist attack depends on social, political, and personal factors that can be idiosyncratic.

Some scholars compare the radicalization process to the complex factors that lead young people to build circles of friends or join gangs (Sageman 2008; Bjorgo 2009). Of course, context matters. At the societal level, belonging to a community that is marginalized, economically disadvantaged, victimized, or discriminated against may increase the likelihood of violence. Anger at political developments or government policies at home or abroad can play a role. Psychological vulnerabilities may also be relevant, including a sense of personal failure, a yearning for individual agency or adventure, deep empathy for victims, or an overwhelming need to belong to something. But beyond generalities, trying to identify who is or is not likely to be radicalized is impossible: well-funded scholars have been trying for years, without success, to build a single coherent "model" of radicalization.

A key focal point is the movement from ideas to action. A vast amount of research, under the burgeoning categories of "counter-radicalization" or "countering violent extremism," focuses on understanding how individuals go from adopting extremist ideas to engaging in violence. Scholars and policy-makers tend to divide along the thinking/action line. In the first category are abstract models of cognitive radicalization with a series of stages in the move from curiosity to adoption of an extreme ideology, especially violent radical Islamism (Neumann 2013: 874; Schmid 2013: 23–5). Those who focus on cognitive processes tend to be psychologists or criminologists, emphasizing the broad political and social contexts that contribute to violence. Analysts in the second category stress the point at which extremists cross over into action, via "action pathways" or "behavioral radicalization" for example (Neumann 2013: 875). They tend to be lawyers, political scientists, or security experts, typically focusing upon violent episodes and working backwards.

As with most research on human subjects, cognitive and behavioral explanations are complementary but inadequate. The relationship between human thinking and action is complex. Looking comparatively at recent cases can be misleading and has a selection bias. Studies rarely use randomized controls when they generalize about sources of radicalization, for example, examining why individuals with dangerous ideas decide *not* to act—that is, thinking without acting. Nor do they examine why individuals who lack any coherent internalized political ideology nonetheless cite political extremist groups as the reason they kill—that is, acting without thinking. And the overall number of terrorists who will talk frankly to researchers about their process of radicalization is tiny. There is reason to fear that the radicalization framework is alienating communities who feel as if "countering violent extremism" initiatives are too close to counter-terrorism and just another way to stigmatize them. If today's scholars were to transfer this intellectual approach to familiar cases less fraught with contemporary political bias—such as nineteenth-century Russian social revolutionaries or mid-twentieth-century Western anti-war movements, perhaps—they might see the problem more objectively and abandon the effort to create a single predictive "model" altogether.

Well short of a predictive model, however, there are common vectors in the spread of political violence. The vector can be impersonal access to information, such as Islamic State propaganda on the Internet, or a relationship or tie to someone who is already radicalized, either in person or via social media. There is ample evidence of traditional recruitment through clubs, prisons, or gangs. All of these are potential channels, and none has been sufficiently studied—as Chapter 22 on new geographies of global security explains.

But even they are insufficient in themselves. A final, rarely mentioned yet crucial ingredient for terrorism is knowledge of, or access to, the *means* to act. Going from radical ideas to taking action involves not just a mental or recruitment process but also practical tools and training—another essential dimension of terrorism that is woefully understudied.

34.5 Future Challenges and Opportunities for Terrorism Studies

A key challenge going forward is determining who the audience (or audiences) for a terrorist attack actually is. This is no longer as simple as reading public opinion polls in the place where the attack occurs (e.g. Jordan after the 2005 attacks by al Qaeda in Iraq on three popular hotels), or even in the countries where purported recruits may live (e.g. Muslim-majority countries with respect to al Qaeda). The ubiquity of social media means that individuals can be following a group's activities from anywhere, as is the situation with the so-called Islamic State. Individuals who become "radicalized" appear without the usual trail of plotting and planning that enables intelligence agencies to identify them, much less academics. Indeed, in the age of social media, the group may not even know for sure exactly who its audience is. In this respect, ISIS and al Qaeda echo the anarchists of the nineteenth century, who inspired hundreds of attacks by alienated workers, Irish nationalists, or ill-treated immigrants, individually or in small groups. Many of the "dynamitards" who carried out bombings were angry, inspired, weak-minded, or just desperate for attention and knew next to nothing about anarchist ideas. Yet their killing became associated with the anarchist movement, a global pattern of terrorist attacks that persisted for decades.

Another serious challenge for the analysis of terrorism is the limited historical scope and political depth of most academic studies. All of the major databases are collected and maintained in the United States, a fact that helps explain the geographical bias mentioned at the outset of this chapter. The periods they cover are short and very recent. For example, the ITERATE database begins in 1968, the RAND database begins in 1968, and the Global Terrorism Database begins in 1970 (Sheehan 2011). The Terrorism in Western Europe: Events Data (or TWEED), database does go a few decades earlier to 1950, but it only covers Western Europe. If we consider the age of modern terrorism to have begun in about 1881, with the killing of the Russian tsar kicking off what David Rapoport calls the first wave of terrorism, then more than half of the total period that has elapsed since then (~135 years at this writing) is not included (Rapoport 2004). There is a serious possibility that the period covered by our databases is anomalous—or at least not accurately representative of the phenomenon of terrorism either in the past or the future.

Related to this problem, the focus of the field has shrunk to myopic questions that can be addressed by looking at the data that are available. Academics divide topics for analysis into smaller and smaller fragments so as to permit clear, unchallengeable conclusions. This is understandable for young scholars still trying to prove themselves but it is also true of seasoned writers, who increasingly divide big strategic questions into data-driven fragments. The field is driven by segmentation, looking for example at certain tactics (e.g. suicide attacks, drone strikes), certain types of operatives (e.g. women, children), or certain geographic territories (Afghanistan, Iraq). At the same time, US policy is driven by tactics such as the use of unmanned aerial vehicles ("drones"), the use of special operations raids, or the training of rebel groups (e.g. in Syria). The parallels are striking. Both academics and practitioners are getting more and more into the weeds, even as terrorist attacks in Europe and the United States are going up, hundreds of thousands of refugees are fleeing the violence, and reality is less and less reflective of our elegant theories. To take one obvious example, neither academics nor practitioners have seriously examined the strategic effectiveness of kinetically attacking terrorism at its source, the idea that led to the military interventions in Afghanistan, Iraq, and now Syria and Iraq (again) to begin with (Roberts 2015).

A fourth problem is the lack of knowledge of the histories, languages, and cultures of societies that are most affected by terrorism, either producing the violence or absorbing it. The growth in quantitative analyses and databases, as well as a shift to the functional approach to terrorism and counter-terrorism of the past two decades, has given the research much more rigor. But it has also crowded out the seasoned regional experts who lent perspective and expertise regarding local situations. Qualitative comparative analyses across cases are very useful but they must be done in depth. If we are to draw strong conclusions about terrorism as a phenomenon, we must ensure that the research is not based on superficial knowledge of the societies under examination.

Finally, the relationship between terrorism and other types of violence must be examined more carefully in the future. Terrorism is neither a hermetically sealed phenomenon nor the worst type of violence that can occur. Most terrorist groups aspire to engage in types of political violence that are stronger and more effective in achieving their aims, such as insurgency or even conventional war. For example, in 2014 the so-called Islamic State of Iraq and Syria rapidly morphed beyond a terrorist group yet analysts still saw it strictly in that framework (Cronin 2015). Academics who study criminology, insurgency, civil war, and conventional war will have to be more intellectually agile and collaborate more if they are to reflect the future reality of terrorism.

References

Abrahms, Max. 2008. What Terrorists Really Want: Terrorist Motives and Counterterrorism Strategy. *International Security*, 32(4): 78–105.

Bjorgo, Tore. 2009. Processes of Disengagement from Violent Groups of the Extreme Right. In Tore Bjorgo and John Horgan (eds.), *Leaving Terrorism Behind: Individual and Collective Disengagement*. London: Routledge.

Blitzer, Wolf. 2003. Search for the "Smoking Gun." January 10. CNN.com/U.S. *Available at:* http://www.cnn.com/2003/US/01/10/wbr.smoking.gun/

Bloom, Mia M. 2004. Palestinian Suicide Bombing: Public Support, Market Share, and Outbidding. *Political Science Quarterly*, 119(1): 61–88.

Bueno de Mesquita, Ethan and Eric S. Dickson. 2007. The Propaganda of the Deed: Terrorism, Counterterrorism, and Mobilization. *American Journal of Political Science*, 51(2): 364–81.

Carter, David B. (2016/17) Provocation and the Strategy of Terrorist and Guerrilla Attacks. *International Organization*, 70(1): 133–73.

Clutterbuck, Lindsay. 2004. The Progenitors of Terrorism: Russian Revolutionaries or Extreme Irish Republicans? *Terrorism and Political Violence*, 16(1): 154–81.

Crenshaw, Martha. 1998. The Logic of Terrorism: Terrorist Behavior as a Product of Strategic Choice. In Walter Reich (ed.), *Origins of Terrorism: Psychologies, Ideologies, Theologies, States of Mind*, p. 24. Baltimore, MD: The Johns Hopkins University Press.

Cronin, Audrey Kurth. 2002/03. Behind the Curve: Globalization and International Terrorism. *International Security*, 27(3): 30–58.

Cronin, Audrey Kurth. 2009. *How Terrorism Ends: Understanding the Decline and Demise of Terrorist Campaigns*. Princeton, NJ: Princeton University Press.

Cronin, Audrey Kurth. 2015. ISIS is Not a Terrorist Group: Why Counterterrorism Won't Stop the Jihadist Threat. *Foreign Affairs* (March/April): 87–98.

Douhet, Giulio. 1942. *The Command of the Air*, trans. Dino Ferrari. New York: Coward-McCann. (Reprinted edition Washington, DC: Office of Air Force History, 1983.)

Enders, Walter and Todd Sandler. 2006. *The Political Economy of Terrorism*. New York: Cambridge University Press.

Freedman, Lawrence. 1981. *The Evolution of Nuclear Strategy*. New York: Macmillan.

Gambetta, Diego (ed.). 2006. *Making Sense of Suicide Missions*. Oxford: Oxford University Press.

Global Terrorism Database (www.start.umd.edu).
Hoffman, Bruce. 2006. *Inside Terrorism*. New York: Columbia University Press.
IHS Jane's Terrorism and Insurgency Centre Research Database. *Available at:* https://www.ihs.com/products/janes-terrorism-insurgency-intelligence-centre.html
International Terrorism: Attributes of Terrorism Events (ITERATE) Database. *Available at:* http://vinyardsoftware.com/researchprojectsusingvinyardproducts.html
Jensen, Richard Bach. 2014. *The Battle Against Anarchist Terrorism: An International History, 1878–1934*. Cambridge: Cambridge University Press.
Kydd, Andrew H. and Barbara F. Walter. 2006. The Strategies of Terrorism. *International Security*, 31(1): 49–80.
LaFree, Gary, Laura Dugan, and Erin Miller. 2015. *Putting Terrorism in Context: Lessons from the Global Terrorism Database*. London: Routledge.
Neumann, Peter. 2013. The Trouble with Radicalization. *International Affairs*, 89(4): 873–93.
Pape, Robert. 2006. *Dying to Win: The Strategic Logic of Suicide Terrorism*. New York: Random House.
Rapoport, David C. 1984. "Fear and Trembling": Terrorism in Three Religious Traditions. *The American Political Science Review*, 78(3): 658–77.
Rapoport, David C. 2004. The Four Waves of Modern Terrorism. In Audrey Kurth Cronin and James M. Ludes (eds.), *Attacking Terrorism: Elements of a Grand Strategy*, pp. 46–73. Washington, DC: Georgetown University Press.
Reeve, Simon. 2000. *One Day in September: The Story of the 1972 Munich Olympics Massacre*. London: Faber and Faber.
Roberts, Adam. 2015. Terrorism Research: Past, Present, and Future. *Studies in Conflict & Terrorism*, 38: 62–74.
Sageman, Marc. 2008. *Leaderless Jihad: Terror Networks in the Twenty-First Century*. Philadelphia, PA: University of Pennsylvania Press.
Schelling, Thomas. 1966. *Arms and Influence*. New Haven, CT: Yale University Press.
Schmid, Alex P. 2013. *Radicalisation, De-Radicalisation, Counter-Radicalisation: A Conceptual Discussion and Literature Review*. ICCT Research Paper, The Hague, Netherlands.
Sheehan, Ivan Sascha. 2011. Assessing and Comparing Data Sources for Terrorism Research. In C. Lum and L.W. Kennedy (eds.), *Evidence-Based Counterterrorism Policy*. New York: Springer.
Stohl, Michael. 2014. Don't Confuse Me with the Facts: Knowledge Claims and Terrorism. In David Miller, Jessie Blackbourn, Helen Dexter, and Rani Dhanda, (eds.), *Critical Terrorism Studies Since 11 September 2001: What Has Been Learned?*, pp. 31–50. London: Routledge.
US Centers for Disease Control and Prevention. 2014. National Center for Health Statistics. *Available at:* https://www.cdc.gov/nchs/fastats/injury.htm
Woodcock, George. 1962. *Anarchism: A History of Libertarian Ideas and Movements*. Cleveland: The World Publishing Co.

CHAPTER 35

INTELLIGENCE AND INTERNATIONAL POLITICS

ROBERT JERVIS

DESPITE being as old as recorded history, intelligence remains under-appreciated when it is not being used as the explanation for all our ills. "Send men to spy out the land," Moses said on his approach to Canaan. To make the story even more modern, the information the spies returned with was false. The history of the Second World War has had to be re-written on the basis of revelations about intelligence, and the history of the Cold War will similarly have to be revised as we learn more about participants' intelligence activities and penetrations.[1] It is not likely to be possible to understand any international interaction, especially a hostile one, without learning what information each state had about the other and what it made of it.

Note that the term "spy" is not only both a noun and a verb, but has two meanings. The most obvious is to surreptitiously gather information, but it can also mean to look and see. In parallel, the term "intelligence" has two main meanings. The narrower one, which will be my focus here, centers on individuals and organizations whose task it is to gather, analyze, and convey information that is usually secret. But in a broader sense intelligence refers to an individual's or entity's ability to make sense of its environment and to understand the capabilities and intentions of others and the vulnerabilities and opportunities that result. In this broad sense then, intelligence starts with the first humans, or rather with the first life on earth, since even microbes and plants need to be able to sense their environment. In fact, this distinction is more than academic because it reminds us that intelligence professionals are not the only ones who gather and analyze information and hints at possible conflicts between intelligence services and their masters.

Actors—to use a term that encompasses individual, organized groupings, and states—need to estimate who their friends and enemies are, what others might be able to do to help or harm them, and how others are likely to respond to alternative courses of action they might take. Every official paper that discusses the state's fundamental foreign policy makes assumptions about or analyses how the other is likely to behave in the future,[2] and many foreign policy debates and choices, at least in the modern (i.e.

post-1815 era) turn on this question. To take the most salient examples, this debate was central to British foreign policy before both World Wars, animated the debates within the United States and its allies during the Cold War, and is the focus of current disagreements about policy toward China. When the other side does something that harms the state, the state has to diagnose the situation and try to understand why the other acted as it did and to infer the characteristics and motives of the other that are likely to guide how it will behave in the future.[3]

Not only is intelligence central to foreign policy, but it intersects with a number of political science topics and approaches, most obviously with the notion that information is a potent form of power and the "informational turn" in the study of bargaining (Schelling 1960; Jervis 1970; Fearon 1995). More generally, although it uses secret sources, the general task of intelligence parallels that of social science: it seeks to understand the world.

Intelligence in the broadest sense depends in part on the observer's theories, often implicit, about state behavior. Some observers place great weight on the personalities of the other state's leaders, in contrast to those who believe that individuals matter much less than the domestic interests that support them or the nature of the other's regime. Some see a large role for ideology, while others tend to dismiss it as window-dressing. Still others believe in the importance of ineradicable national characteristics, a view that was widely held in the nineteenth century but that has reappeared in the slightly different guise in some analyses of "Islamic fundamentalism." In other words, although national leaders and intelligence analysts usually pride themselves in being pragmatic and fact-driven, intelligence is necessarily a theory-laden enterprise. People and organizations not being completely consistent, there may be contradictions here. For example, although British intelligence in the early Cold War stressed that power was concentrated in Stalin's hands (which they believed made Soviet policy more difficult to predict), when he died they predicted that whoever replaced him would follow a policy that was fundamentally the same (Goodman 2014: 263–5).

If intelligence in the broad sense is close to being coterminous with knowledge and so is an enormous subject, even intelligence in the narrower sense of the activities of individuals and organizations dedicated to the gathering and analysis of information about foreign entities is also dauntingly large and my coverage cannot be complete. Among other things, mirroring the English-language literature I will concentrate on the West in general and the United States in particular. From the start, the whole enterprise has seemed questionable both because of inherent difficulties involved and because of the underground and dishonorable behavior required. Clausewitz famously said of military intelligence that "most intelligence is false, and the effect of fear is to multiply lies and inaccuracies" (Clausewitz 1976: 117) and his skepticism is widely shared. Since intelligence depended at least to a considerable degree on spying, it mattered that throughout much of history "the spy was [seen] as someone lacking both personal honor and loyalty to anything besides his purse strings" (Bauer 2016: 661). Of course this does not mean that spies were not used or were not listened to, but it does help explain the combination of fascination and distaste that surrounds the subject. In some cases, the spy betrays his (most spies are men) country; in other cases the spy's job is to recruit others who will betray their country. Not only is this morally repugnant, but it raises questions about the validity of the information. If someone is willing to betray his country, perhaps he is also willing to deceive and lie to his masters. Those who receive the information need to at least wonder whether it is fictitious or even, in the more extreme cases touched on later, manufactured in order to deceive (double-agents) (Goldman 2006; Olson 2006; Le Carré 2012).

Nasty or not, the field is large enough to have two dedicated journals, *Intelligence and National Security* and the *International Journal of Intelligence and CounterIntelligence*, in addition to being able to draw on the unclassified version of the Central Intelligence Agency's in-house journal *Studies in Intelligence*. Excellent surveys of the field and of the literature also have appeared in recent years (Kent 1951; Hilsman 1956; Knorr 1964; Herman 1996; Dujmovic 2005; Betts 2007; Gill et al. 2009; Pillar 2011; Marrin 2013; Varouhakis 2013; Immerman 2014; Lowenthal 2014; May 2014; Warner 2014; Maddrell 2015; Lowenthal and Clark 2016; Marrin 2016; Wilford 2016).

35.1 Secrecy

"We steal secrets" is how Michael Hayden, former director of the National Security Administration and CIA, described his organizations. Secrecy indeed is at the heart of intelligence: gaining access to information the other side wants to keep hidden and hiding a great deal about what the state is thinking and what it knows about the other side. Secrecy is joined at the hip with deception as intelligence has the two-fold job of penetrating others' deception schemes and deceiving them when this is appropriate to supporting policy (Jervis 1970; Bowyer 1982; Holt 2010). Secrecy is often multi-layered in that it is often important for the state to keep secret the fact that it had stolen secrets. This is not always true, however. The United States was glad to publicize Nikita Khrushchev's "Secret Speech" denouncing Stalin in 1956, once it obtained a copy from Israel's secret service. To take a hypothetical case, a state that developed the means of detecting whether an adversary was about to attack might make this known as long as doing so did not allow the adversary and others to thwart this asset. But more often a stolen secret loses much of its value if it becomes known, and therefore the secret needs to be wrapped in elaborate protective measures. An obvious case in point is that the ability of the British to read the German codes produced by the seemingly fool-proof Enigma machine would have lost its value if the Germans had learned of this feat. States then often have to go to great lengths to disguise the source of their information. To take another Second World War example, decoded intercepts (known as Ultra) allowed the Allies to track convoys re-supplying German and Italian forces in North Africa. Bombing them was then easy, but to do so risked giving away the Ultra secret. So the British sent out reconnaissance planes which the convoy would spot. Since it was plausible that planes were blanketing the

Mediterranean, the Germans would have no reason to suspect the truth. An extreme case is represented by the incorrect but plausible story that when the British learned that a German bombing raid was on its way to Coventry in 1940, Churchill ordered that no protective measures be taken lest the Germans be alerted to the vulnerability of their codes.

If deception may be used to enhance security, the latter is usually necessary for the former. Deception works best when the misleading information is conveyed though channels that the other side believes are reliable. So if one state learns that another has broken some of its codes, instead of changing them, it may use them to send misleading information (or accurate information that it wants other side to believe). History is full of examples, but the Second World War provides probably the best known and most successful one. Acting on earlier intelligence, at the start of the war the British rounded up all the German spies on the island. But instead of merely cutting Germany off from what could have been sources of very valuable information, the British "turned" several of the German agents, gaining their collaboration in what became a giant sting operation. Known by the XX committee that managed (the "Double Cross") system, the British were able to systematically deceive Germany. Of course this had to be done with great care and in order to establish and maintain the agents' credibility, some valuable information had to be conveyed (damage was limited by a number of tricks such as sending valid information about a planned military operation only at the last minute so that the Germans could not take advantage of it). All this was put into service by misleading Hitler into believing that the Allied invasion of the continent would come at Calais, not Normandy. I do not believe it is an exaggeration to say that this deception saved the world (or at least spared Germany being attacked by atomic bombs) because the Allies would have been pushed off the beaches had the Germans guessed correctly. (A qualification must be noted: although the deception indeed was an exceptionally skillful one, it probably would not have succeeded if Hitler had not been pre-disposed to expect the Allies to land at Calais.)

The game does not end here, however. The awareness of the possibility of deception maybe as important as deception itself. States cannot believe their senses, or rather have to question whether they can. Most simply, they are aware that others may be lying to them—in the negotiations over a possible second Security Council Resolution that would justify a war against Iraq in 2003, the British Ambassador to Paris advised the Foreign Office that "Nothing the French say at this stage, even privately, should be taken at face value" (Chilcot 2016: executive summary, p. 28). Of course the whole point of spying, code-breaking, and the like is to get sources that are more reliable than this. The difficulty is that states know that spies can be turned and that adversaries may know you have broken their codes. Nothing, then, is completely trustworthy, and both Type I and Type II errors are possible. In many cases, states have been deceived by accepting information from what they incorrectly believe are reliable sources, but they have also rejected a great deal of valid information. Stalin provides a good example. He disregarded the innumerable reports that Hitler would attack him in the spring of 1941, including ordering the execution of a defecting German soldier who reported that the attack was only a few hours away, believing that the British were trying to trick him into provoking Hitler. During the war he also rejected the initial reports about the Manhattan Project in the belief that the American security apparatus was good enough to prevent penetrations. It was only after separate spy rings reported the same thing that he credited the information. In parallel, more than once American intelligence spurned the approaches of Soviet officials who volunteered to be spies only to eventually accept them and gain valuable information (in other cases, of course, they took in people who were in fact taking them in). The most famous recent case concerns not one agent or channel but an entire program: one reason why American and British intelligence believed that Iraq had active WMD programs before 2003, despite the fact that there were few visible traces, was the conviction that Iraq was skilled at concealment and deception.

Despite the elaborate protocols for vetting sources and judging whether communication channels are secure, certainty is beyond reach. How people react to this varies. Some are quicker to detect deception than others, which means that they are less likely to be fooled but more likely to reject valid information. When information about the adversary is sparse and sources are hard to come by, however, subjecting every bit of evidence to intense suspicion can make it impossible to produce any intelligence at all, with the result that the possibility of deception is not analyzed as thoroughly as it might be (Jervis 2010: 9–11).

Technology can change the possibilities for secrecy. The balance between code-making and code-breaking has changed over the years not only due to human ingenuity and organizational skill, but to the sorts of machines and mathematics that were developed. The most dramatic change, however, is with overhead photography. Balloons saw some usage in the nineteenth century and aerial photography came into its own during the First World War and greatly expanded in the next war. An even greater change came with space satellites, and current imagery is no longer restricted to the visible spectrum, involving radar, infra-red, and perhaps other forms. The result has been an enormous increase in transparency in quite a literal sense. In 1960 the first satellite photographs, along with the reporting of Colonel Rudolf Penkovsky, one of the most important spies who aided the West, revealed that the Soviets were behind the United States in the production of missiles, rather than ahead as many people had believed.

Overhead photography of course is not perfect, even if we ignore the limits imposed by clouds and night. The United States was not able to keep an accurate count of the number of Soviet intermediate-range missiles deployed in Europe in the 1980s and in the wake of the Kosovo war it became clear that NATO had expended a great deal of ordnance on destroying cardboard replicas of Serbian military equipment. The change is still massive, however. Furthermore, a great deal of satellite data is now available for purchase by third parties, which has not only produced important economic and social benefits, but also gives significant information to the public and to countries that lack satellites of their own.

35.2 Democracy and Secrecy

At first glance, democracy and secrecy seem antithetical, and even after closer analysis there are painful tensions here. This is most obvious with undercover activities by intelligence agencies: if what the government has done remains secret, the public cannot pass judgment on it. The very notion of plausible deniability, central to covert action, clashes with the idea of democratic accountability. Questions concerning International Relations (IR) theories arise as well, most sharply with whether covert actions by democracies against other democracies (e.g. American actions against the arguably-democratic regimes in Guatemala, Iran, and Chile) violate the theory of democratic peace (Treventon 1987; Prados 2006; Daugherty 2008; Poznansky 2015; Barkawi 2015). More broadly, secrecy can inhibit the public (and legislators) from curbing belligerent foreign policies that the executive branch may pursue (ISSF Forum 2013; Schuessler 2015).

Related, the secrecy surrounding intelligence makes it hard for the public to apportion the blame for foreign policy failures between intelligence and policy-makers. Are President George W. Bush and Prime Minister Tony Blair to be absolved of guilt for the Iraq war (assuming that the war was a mistake) because the blame falls on faulty intelligence for a vastly exaggerated picture of the threat they were facing? Did Bush fail to take adequate measures against terrorism before September 11, 2001, or did he do as well as we could expect given the information provided by the CIA and FBI? Turning the question around, how are intelligence agencies to be held accountable when so much of what they do cannot be divulged? (Zegart 2011; Lester 2015). And if to muster domestic support leaders distort intelligence judgments, should the intelligence service issue corrections?

Of course the veil of secrecy is often pierced in democracies, and conventional wisdom has it that they have a much harder time keeping information confidential than do dictatorships. There is something to this but we should not exaggerate. Tens of thousands of people know of Ultra, but none talked for 25 years. (One might ask why it was necessary to keep the secret after the war, and one of the reasons is that the United States and the UK sold variants of the Enigma machine to other countries.) It was also generally believed that democracies have a harder time managing their intelligence establishments than do dictatorships, in part because secrecy is antithetical to democracy. But in fact there are very few cases of American or British intelligence acting against or even in the absence of instructions from their political masters.[4] Senator Frank Church made his famous remark about the CIA being a "rogue elephant" before he led the hearings on its activities, he then changed his mind as the result of the investigation. The domestic abuses of the CIA and the FBI uncovered in the wake of the Watergate scandal, while clearly hampering democracy, were undertaken at the behest of presidents, not behind their backs. The other side of this coin is that dictators have to worry that their intelligence services will play a role in their overthrow, and in parallel to the need to "coup-proof" the army, they must often hinder the effectiveness of intelligence in order safeguard their own security.

Furthermore, democracies probably are superior in their ability to use intelligence information. Democratic leaders tend to have a better understanding of the world and other countries than do dictators, partly because of the different career paths in the two kinds of systems, although impressions may be biased because we get to read the records of dictators who are overthrown, partly because they badly misread their environments, as Saddam did. Empathy is essential for good intelligence, and extremely difficult to come by. It is at least plausible that officials at all levels of democratic governments are better able to empathize with others, especially adversaries, than are their opposite number in dictatorships. Pure power, especially violent power, cannot be used in democratic systems, and attempts to see world from the others' point of view are rarely encouraged in dictatorships. In some cases intelligence services in democracies have sought to mimic the assessments they thought other countries would make, something dictators appear never to have done. The enterprise is difficult and the incentives against it are significant: who is the intelligence official who wants to tell a policy-maker that the other side holds an image of her and her state that is very discrepant from what she believes?[5] But if this is distasteful in a democratic system, it is much more than that in a dictatorship, and this brings up the second advantage democratic intelligence systems have. Bringing bad news or challenging the prevailing policy may not be career-enhancing, but at least it is not life-threatening, as it is in many authoritarian regimes. It may be presumptuous of intelligence services in democracies to believe that they are telling truth to power, but this is their self-conception and is not entirely removed from reality.

The third and perhaps most obvious reason why democracies are most likely to hold a more accurate picture of the world is that their societies are much more open, with multiple and generally conflicting sources of information and biases (White 1991). Granted that democratic leaders and their intelligence services sometimes live in a bubble; those in authoritarian regime almost always do.

35.3 Effects of Intelligence

The "so what?" question is as hard to avoid as it is to answer. What difference has intelligence made to individual states' foreign policies and to the shape of international politics? The question is difficult not only because it is hard to trace the influence of any factor like intelligence, but because it is hard to know what the counterfactual comparison is: a world without intelligence is unimaginable. Nevertheless some observations are possible. First, during the Cold War intelligence was probably a stabilizing factor in that on the Western side and, as far as we can tell, on the Soviet side as well, intelligence services were able to reassure decision-makers that the adversary was not about to attack. Since nuclear weapons heightened both the sense of vulnerability and the temptation to disarm the other side by striking first, dangers growing out of what Schelling called "the reciprocal fear of surprise attack" were great (Schelling 1960: ch. 9). Although intelligence often had to admit that it could not promise much advanced notice of any surprise attack and each side made heavy investments in developing weapons that could survive one, the services were able to provide sufficient knowledge so that another Pearl Harbor (or, for the Soviets, another June 22, 1941) seemed unlikely. With the glaring exception of the Western failure to detect the large Soviet (and, after 1991, Russian) biological weapons program, intelligence apparently ensured that each side had ample warning of the other's deployment of major weapons systems as well. Spy satellites also enabled arms control agreements, and the provision in the SALT I treaty prohibiting interference with "national technical means of inspection" meant that each side agreed to refrain from damaging the other's satellites or putting obstructions over missile sites that would shield them from view.

The means of acquiring information, however, may have heightened tensions (Herman 2011). The Americans were deeply disturbed to learn of the extensive Soviet spy networks in the 1940s, and this may have lead President Truman to harden his stance in the negotiations with the Soviets about controlling nuclear weapons (Craig and Radchenko 2008). Throughout the Cold War, tensions were increased when each side discovered the other's spies and while space satellites were accepted as legitimate means of intelligence-gathering, the U-2 flights enraged Khrushchev and the shooting down of one in May 1960 scuttled the Paris Summit and created a brief but intense crisis.[6] Currently, the American intelligence-gathering flights and sailings near China's coast are a source of continuing friction.

Did intelligence also heighten conflict by overestimating the other side's capabilities and misreading its intentions? During the Cold War there were bitter and highly politicized debates about this, and while retrospective judgments are possible in some areas (e.g. there was neither a bomber gap in the mid-1950s nor a missile gap in the late 1950s and early 1960s), a full scorecard is still not available (Freedman 1977; Prados 1982). A related question is how accurate we (or decision-makers) can expect intelligence to be. It is easy to recite a long list of surprises and errors, many of which have been followed by soul-searching by intelligence services, national commissions, and recommendations for doing things differently. Since some of these have been adopted, this might imply that intelligence services have gotten better over time. It would be difficult to test this proposition, however, and no one has tried. Even if intelligence has improved, so may have the abilities to conceal and deceive, and I think the basic point remains the one made by Richard Betts that in an uncertain world surprises are inevitable (Betts 1978; Tetlock 2006; Tetlock and Gardner 2015). In some cases of specific but highly important actions, the other side may be indecisive and change its mind at the last minute, as was true for the decisions of the Chinese to join the Korean War and the Soviets to intervene in Hungary in 1956. In other cases, the state's behavior is foolish and indeed suicidal (e.g. Japan in 1941, Saddam Hussein in 2002–03), and empathy is hard to come by in these cases. Those who think we can come close to eliminating surprises should remember that despite the enormous amount of information at their disposal, people are frequently horrified to learn that their business or romantic partners have been cheating on them.

Looking at what intelligence has said is only part of the story and leaves unanswered the question of whether these judgments influence policies. Definitive answers are beyond reach, and undoubtedly there is great variance over time, circumstances, and countries. Two distinguished scholars have rendered quite negative judgments about the impact of intelligence on American policy during the Cold War, (Gaddis 1993; Immerman 2008; Treverton and Miles 2015) and I would make six points. First, impact may mean not only providing the right answer, but asking the right questions, increasing knowledge within the government, and raising the level of sophistication of the discussion. Important as this is, it is hard to document, however. Second, intelligence in the general sense of expertise certainly can matter, and a crucial case occurred at the climax of the Cuban Missile Crisis when Kennedy's skepticism that he could get the Soviet missiles out without an open trade for the American ones in Turkey was reduced when the leading government Kremlinologist, Llewellyn Thompson, said that he believed that Khrushchev would settle for something less. Third, while intelligence can spark specific actions (Priess 2016: 32), its impact is often indirect in triggering inquiries and deliberations that affect subsequent policy. Fourth, intelligence will have most impact (and is most likely to be correct) when it is derived from a solid body of information. Strong analytical methods ("tradecraft," as practitioners call it) are vital but in terms of convincing skeptics nothing beats photographs, reports from reliable agents, or intercepted communications (although these can be misleading, of course—there is much wisdom in the British saying that "reading a gentleman's mail is not the same as reading his mind"). Fifth, intelligence has most impact when it can resolve decision-makers' doubts or modify (but not reverse) their views. When leaders are torn over what to do or uncertain in their beliefs about others, they are more likely to be open to influence. Sixth, the impact is greatest in areas where decision-makers have least knowledge of their own. Intelligence on technical matters is likely to find receptive audiences, but on the broadest issues of the day dealing with the essential nature of others states and whether they are adversaries or not, leaders are likely to have their own strong opinions, as well as perhaps having staked their political fates on a line of policy. These questions are also necessarily difficult and not amenable to answers in terms of information to which intelligence has privileged access. Sometimes, as in the early years of the Cold War, decision-makers do change their minds on these questions, and here they might seem to be following the lead of their intelligence services. But it is more likely that both have reacted to important events in the same way (Wark 1985; Yarhi-Milo 2015).

The influence of intelligence is limited by the fact that it is often inconvenient. When it is doing its job well, it raises doubts and notes alternative possibilities, and it may point out that current policies are not going well. Lyndon Johnson put the point in his usual colorful style, but most of his peers would agree:

> Let me tell you about these intelligence guys. When I was growing up in Texas, we had a cow named Bessie. I'd go out early and milk her. I'd get her in the stanchion, seat myself and squeeze out a pail of fresh milk. One day I'd worked hard and gotten a full pail of milk, but I wasn't paying attention, and old Bessie swung her shit-smeared tail through the bucket of milk. Now, you know that's what these intelligence guys do. You work hard and get a good program or policy going, and they swing a shit-smeared tail through it. (Gates 1989: 42)

35.4 New Intelligence for a New World

Much has changed with advanced technologies after the end of the Cold War, but the basic tasks and problems of intelligence remain. The decline of interstate violence is of extraordinary importance, but states still have adversaries if not enemies, employ and are the victims of deception, and need to estimate future trends and what others are likely to do. If anything, the demands on intelligence are likely to increase with greater uncertainty in world politics and the expansion of the agenda beyond traditional security issues to include economic developments, human rights, and ecological threats.[7]

Both politics and technology will change how intelligence is conducted, however. Traditional sources and methods will not disappear, but will be supplemented and refracted by new ones.

For one thing, while some countries will be able to concentrate their intelligence on the US and one or two regional powers, setting priorities will be increasingly difficult for the US. In this respect the Cold War made life easy. Ten or even five years ago few would have expected that the US would need the sort of fine-grained analysis of the Russian military that was built up during the Cold War. Knowledge-bases like this cannot be produced on a crash basis; investment deficits will take years to overcome. In today's Washington, you probably could not give away intelligence on Central Africa or much of Latin America, but next year such expertise might be invaluable. A generation ago, knowledge of how pandemics spread and what new developments in biology were emerging would not have seemed central to national security; now, thanks in part to the relative decline of more traditional threats, they are. Needless to say, terrorism, never absent as an intelligence concern, will be central for the indefinite future.

The importance of terrorism, the growth of other transnational concerns, and the need for intelligence to have a very wide aperture increases the imperative for information sharing. What are called "liaison relations" with other services have always been important and because of their political sensitivity are generally shrouded in layers of secrecy. But it is clear that even a country with as large and diverse an intelligence apparatus as the US cannot succeed without close and multiple relationships. The fact that secrets are particularly hard to keep in the US poses problems for partners, but on the other hand, while cooperation with them is important for the US, it is absolutely vital for them. Cooperative arrangements among many but obviously not all countries are likely to extend and deepen, but they will always be both subject to political disturbances and potential sources of political friction.

Intelligence lives on technologies; it strives to understand the newer ones that others are developing and depends on the most advanced means in order to gather information and communicate with sources. Some secret means are remarkably durable, and it was only in 2011 that the CIA revealed 75-year-old methods of secret writing. Many are new, however, and even changes in the ways that information can be secretly conveyed that are publicly available are coming thick and fast. What is happening in the intelligence world obviously is not known to us, but this environment is likely to be highly dynamic, with the race between the ability to keep the communications secret and the technologies to uncover them requiring huge expenditures and producing uncertain outcomes.

There is likely to be an interaction with the emerging area of cyber conflict. It seems highly likely that increasing amounts of intelligence will be derived not from intercepting others' communications as they are sent through the air or by tapping communication lines, or even by related but esoteric means (Easter 2016), but by penetrating computer networks. Among other things, this will render even more problematic the already extraordinarily difficult effort to bring cyber within the ambit of arms control agreements or norms.

35.5 The End of Secrecy?

Although we are accustomed to a prevalence of overhead photography, it is nevertheless easy to forget what changes it has produced. Although, as I noted, it is not a panacea, it routinely reveals what in past eras would have been some of the state's deepest secrets. Furthermore, advanced techniques are surely being developed and will produce even more information, especially if they themselves are successfully kept secret. In some instances, furthermore, space satellites can be supplemented by silent drones. It would be an exaggeration to say that nothing can be hidden from all these eyes, but surely less can be hidden than was true in the past, and it is likely that finders will continue to gain ground over hiders in the future (Larkin 2016).

The increased prevalence of leaks, at least in the US, has decreased secrecy. As the 2016 presidential election illustrates, new tools have been added to the kit of countries that want to meddle in others' elections, not that these were entirely lacking in the past. Probably more important are domestic leakers, with Edward Snowden being the obvious but undoubtedly not the last example. An increasingly aggressive media links up with individuals who, for motives ranging from principal to ego, want to divulge information. As Hillary Clinton put it in a talk to Goldman Sachs in 2013 (itself leaked), "We used to be much better at [covert action] than we are now [because officials now will] tell their friendly reporters ... 'Look what we're doing, and I want credit for it'" (Sanger 2016). Indeed, the fear of leaks can inhibit the government from even studying possible contingencies.

A more general trend is at work. Intelligence scholars have distinguished between questions involving secrets and mysteries (Nye 1994; Treverton 2003). The former can be answered by information that the adversary is trying to keep hidden, for example military plans, weapons specifications, and bargaining strategies. The latter are not clear-cut and are less amenable to classified information. Examples would be the stability of a country, the likelihood that religious extremism will spread, and the prospects for economic prosperity. The obvious point is that the balance between the importance of secrets and mysteries has shifted toward the latter, and this has important implications for intelligence services that specialize in secrets. (Indeed, intelligence services have a professional bias that gives heaviest weight to the most highly classified information even when it is not highly diagnostic.)

Although countries still have adversaries whose intentions and capabilities need to be judged, other questions also loom large. This poses real challenges for organizations whose job it is to steal and analyze secrets. This still needs to be done, but is not enough. Secret information would have been very useful in predicting the attempted coup in Turkey in July 2016, but would not have been very much help in assessing its chances of success. Is the CIA better positioned than others without access to secrets to analyze the likely future course of the Sisi regime in Egypt, the ability of the world to cope with climate change, or even the ways in which China's neighbors are likely to react to its rise? In recent years, the American intelligence community has placed increased stress on "open sources"—that is, unclassified information. The rise of "big data" poses both challenges and opportunities here (Degaut 2016). But without a major change of incentives and culture, analysts who work with these materials will not be rewarded and the analyses will not gain prominence. Traditional intelligence will not go away, but the heightened salience of mysteries poses an intellectual and organizational challenge of some magnitude.

Notes

1. For an excellent example of how an understanding of the information yielded by intelligence changes the picture on central questions see Green and Long (2015).
2. The classic case is Eyre Crowe's (Crowe 1907: 397–431) memo about Germany (reprinted in Gooch and Temperly 1928: 397–431). This paper is not only careful, but is good social science methodology and, furthermore, is followed by a rebuttal by another high-ranking member of the Foreign Office and Crowe's re-rebuttal.
3. Notice that this assumes both some consistency in the other's behavior over time and a variability among actors or kind of actors.
4. There is at least one case of the CIA misleading and trying to trap a president: contrary to what CIA director Allen Dulles and his top subordinates told President Kennedy, they believed that to succeed, the Bay of Pigs invasion in 1961 probably would require American airpower. They disregarded the president's statements that he did not want the American hand to be shown in the (incorrect) expectation that if the president was faced by a choice of having the invasion fail and changing his mind, he would do the latter.
5. For a brief discussion of the CIA's resistance to doing this see Preiss (2016: 180).
6. Kennedy's White House delayed aerial reconnaissance of Cuba in the fall of 1962 because of fears that a plane might be shot down, roiling the waters before the Congressional elections: Barrett and Holland (2012).
7. The tension between surveillance and civil liberties is very important but too large a topic to cover here.

References

Barkawi, T. 2015. Scientific Decay. *International Studies Quarterly*, 59: 827–9.

Barrett, D. and M. Holland. 2012. *Blind over Cuba: The Photo Gap and the Missile Crisis*. College Park, TX: Texas A&M Press.

Bauer, D. 2016. Planting the Espionage Tree: The French Military and the Professionalization of Intelligence at the End of the Nineteenth Century. *Intelligence and National Security*, 31: 659–73.

Betts, R. 1978. Analysis, War, and Decision: Why Intelligence Failures Are Inevitable, *World Politics*, 31: 61–89.

Betts, R. 2007. *Enemies of Intelligence: Knowledge and Power in American National Security*. New York: Columbia University Press.

Bowyer, J. (a pseudonym for J. Bowyer Bell and Barton Whaley) 1982. *Cheating*. New York: St. Martin's Press.

Chilcot Report. 2016. *Available at:* http://www.iraqinquiry.org.uk/the-report/. Executive Summary.

Clausewitz, Carl von. 1976. *On War*. Ed. and trans. H. Howard and P. Paret. Princeton, NJ: Princeton University Press.

Craig, C. and S. Radchenko. 2008. *The Atomic Bomb and the Origins of the Cold War*. New Heaven, CT: Cornell University Press.

Daugherty, W. 2008. *Executive Secrets, Covered Action and the Presidency*. Lexington, KY: University of Kentucky Press.

Degaut, M. 2016. Spies and Policymakers: Intelligence in the Information Age. *Intelligence and National Security*, 31: 509–31.

Dujmovic, N. 2005. Fifty Years of Studies in Intelligence: Building an Intelligence Literature. *Studies in Intelligence*, 49: 6–13.

Easter, D. 2016. Soviet Bloc and Western Bugging of Opponents' Diplomatic Premises During the Early Cold War. *Intelligence and National Security*, 31: 28–48.

Fearon, J. 1995. Rationalist Explanations for War. *International Organization*, 49: 379–414.

Freedman, L. 1977. *US Intelligence and the Soviet Strategy Threat*. Princeton, NJ: Princeton University Press.

Gaddis, J. 1993. The Tragedy of Cold War History. *Diplomatic History*, 17: 1–16.

Gates, R. 1989. An Opportunity Unfulfilled: The Use and Perceptions of Intelligence in the White House. *Washington Quarterly*, 12: 35–44.

Gill, P., S. Marrin, and M. Phythian (eds.). 2009. *Intelligence Theory: Key Questions and Debates*. New York: Routledge.

Goldman, J. 2006. *Ethics of Spying: A Reader for the Intelligence Professional*. Lanham, MD: Scarecrow Press.

Gooch, G. P. and H. Temperly (eds.). 1928. *British Documents on the Origins of the War, 1898–1914, Vol. 3, The Testing of the Entente, 1904–6*. London: His Majesty's Stationery Office.

Goodman, M. 2014. *The Official History of the Joint Intelligence Committee*, Volume I: *From the Approach of the Second World War to the Suez Crisis*. London: Routledge.

Green, B. and A. Long. 2015. Stalking the Secure Second Strike: Intelligence, Counterforce, and Nuclear Strategy. *Journal of Strategic Studies*, 38: 38–73.

Herman, M. 1996. *Intelligence Power in Peace and War*. New York: Cambridge University Press.

Herman, M. 2011. Intelligence as Threats and Reassurance. *Intelligence and National Security*: 791–817.

Hilsman, R. 1956. *Strategic Intelligence and National Decisions*. Glencoe, IL: The Free Press.

Holt, T. 2010. *The Deceivers: Allied Military Deception in the Second World War*. New York: Skyhorse Publishing.

Immerman, R. 2008. Intelligence and Strategy: Historicizing Psychology, Policy, and Politics. *Diplomatic History*, 32: 1–23.

Immerman, R. 2014. *The Hidden Hand: A Brief History of the CIA*. Malden, MA: Wiley Blackwell.

International Security Studies Forum. 2013. Democracy, Deception, and Entry into War, Vol. V, No. 4, May 17, 2013. *Available at:* http://www.h.net.org/~diplo/ISSF/PDF/ISSF~Roundtable-5-4.pdf

Jervis, R. 1970. *The Logic of Images in International Relations*. Princeton, NJ: Princeton University Press (1989 2nd edn. New York: Columbia University Press).

Jervis, R. 2010. *Why Intelligence Fails: Lessons from the Iranian Revolution and the Iraq War*. Ithaca, NY: Cornell University Press.

Kent, S. 1951. *Strategic Intelligence for American World of Policy*. Princeton, NJ: Princeton University Press.

Knorr, K. 1964. Foreign Intelligence and the Social Sciences. *Research Monograph No. 17*. princeton, NJ: Center of International Studies, Woodrow Wilson School of Public and International Affairs, Princeton University.

Larkin, S. 2016. The Age of Transparency: International Relations without Secrets. *Foreign Affairs*, 95: 136–46.

Le Carré, J. 2012. *The Spy Who Came in from the Cold*. New York: Penguin Books.

Lester, G. 2015. *When Should State Secrets Stay Secret? Accountability, Democratic Governance, and Intelligence*. New York: Cambridge University Press.

Lowenthal, M. 2014. *Intelligence: From Secrets to Policy*, 6th edn. Washington, DC: CQ Press.

Lowenthal, M. and R. Clark. 2016. *The Five Disciplines of Intelligence Collection*. Washington, DC: CQ Press.

Maddrell, P. (ed.). 2015. *The Image of the Enemy: Intelligence Analysis of Adversaries since 1945*. Washington, DC: Georgetown University Press.

Marrin, S. 2016. Improving Intelligence Studies as an Academic Discipline. *Intelligence and National Security*, 31: 266–79.

May, E. (ed.). 2014. *Knowing One's Enemies*. Princeton, NJ: Princeton University Press.

Nye, J. 1994. Peering into the Future. *Foreign Affairs*, 73: 82–93.

Olson, J. 2006. *Fair Play: The Moral Dilemmas of Spy*. Washington, DC: Potomac Books.

Pillar, P. 2011. *Intelligence and U.S. Foreign Policy: Iraq, 9/11, and Misguided Reform*. New York: Columbia University Press.

Poznansky, M. 2015. Stasis or Decay? Reconciling Covert War and the Democratic Peace. *International Studies Quarterly*, 59: 815–26.

Prados, J. 1982. *The Soviet Estimate: U.S. Intelligence Analysis and Russian Military Strength*. New York: Dial.

Prados, J. 2006. *Safe for Democracy: The Secret Wars of the CIA*. Chicago: Ivan Dee.

Priess, D. 2016. *The President's Book of Secrets: The Untold Story of Intelligence Briefings to America's Presidents from Kennedy to Obama*. New York: Public Affairs.

Sanger, D. 2016. Clinton Liked Covert Action if It Stayed Covert, Hacked Transcript Shows. *New York Times*. October 16.

Schelling, T. 1960. *The Strategy of Conflict*. Cambridge, MA: Harvard University Press.

Schuessler, J. 2015. *Deceit on the Road to War*. Ithaca, NY: Cornell University Press.

Tetlock, P. 2006. *Expert Political Judgment: How Good Is It? How Can We Know?* Princeton, NJ: Princeton University Press.

Tetlock, P. and Dan Gardner. 2015. *Superforecasting: The Art and Science of Prediction*. New York: Crown.

Treverton, G. 1987. *Covert Action: Central Intelligence Agency and the Limits of American Intervention in the Post-War World.* New York: Basic Books;

Treverton, G. 2003. *Reshaping National Intelligence for an Age of Information.* Cambridge: Cambridge University Press.

Treverton, G. and R. Miles. 2015. *Unheeded Warning of War: Why Policymakers Ignored the 1990 Yugoslavia Estimate.* Washington, DC: CIA Center for the Study of Intelligence.

Varouhakis, M. 2013. What is Being Published in Intelligence? A Study of Two Scholarly Journals. *International Journal of Intelligence and CounterIntelligence*, 26: 176–89.

Wark, W. 1985. *The Ultimate Enemy: British Intelligence in Nazi Germany 1933–1939*. Ithaca, NY: Cornell University Press.

Warner, M. 2014. *The Rise and Fall of Intelligence: An International Security History*. Washington, DC: Georgetown University Press.

White, R. 1991. Empathizing with Saddam Hussein. *Political Psychology*, 12: 291–308.

Wilford, H. 2016. Still Missing: The Historiography of U.S. Intelligence. *Passport: The Society of Historians of American Foreign Relations Review*, 47: 20–7.

Yarhi-Milo, Keren. 2015. *Knowing the Adversary: Leaders, Intelligence, and Assessment of Intentions in International Relations*. Princeton, NJ: Princeton University.

Zegart, A. 2011. The Domestic Politics of Irrational Intelligence Oversight. *Political Science Quarterly*, 126: 1–25.

CHAPTER 36

TRAJECTORIES FOR FUTURE CYBERSECURITY RESEARCH

RONALD DEIBERT

36.1 Introduction

Whether it is a major corporate data breach, evidence of secret mass surveillance, or extremism on social media, nearly a day does not go by without a cybersecurity related news headline. The reasons are not surprising: human societies are going through a sea-change in communications as far-reaching as anything that has come before in modern history, but now compressed within a span of a little more than a decade. Variously referred to as "big data," the "Internet of Things," or just "cyberspace," the communications environment in which we live has been vastly transformed. Cybersecurity is, therefore, a topic of obvious policy importance, but highly contested. How it is secured and by whom and for what purpose will touch upon the most basic of political questions, as infamously defined by Harold Laswell (1936): "who gets what, when, and how."

The challenges of securing cyberspace are unique because doing so inevitably involves multiple stakeholders, including businesses, government agencies, and civil society. Since the bulk of what we call cyberspace is in the hands of the private sector, governments are compelled to enlist or otherwise compel companies in their efforts. Added to the competitive dynamic is that civil society groups and other non-state actors have been empowered by digital media, and seek to shape cyberspace to their own diverse ends, often putting them in direct competition, and in the case of militant non-state actors—*violent* confrontation, with states and the private sector.

Cybersecurity is also characterized by a unique convergence of national security and business interests around *surveillance*. For states, the threat environment has shifted over the last few decades. Whereas for most of modern history the primary security concern of most states was the threat posed by other states, today the primary threat is dispersed across all of society, inside and outside of states. On the part of businesses, the economic engine at the heart of cyberspace is the commodification of personal information—likes, habits, movements, relationships—acquired through acquisition of users' communications by companies such as Google and Facebook. In between the two engines of mass surveillance is a multi-billion dollar data analysis economy that services both governments and companies. This convergence of interests is where "Big Brother" meets "Big Data," creating a powerful, and very difficult-to-reverse set of forces around mass surveillance. (Lesk 2013: 86)

Because the issue is so new and dynamic, social science research on cybersecurity is still in its infancy. In this chapter, I review some of the major topics around cybersecurity and highlight some of the outstanding questions or areas for further research. This survey is not meant to be exhaustive, but rather illustrative of some of the core international political questions that require further attention from scholars.

36.2 What is Cyberspace? What is Cybersecurity?

What is "cyberspace"? The term is used widely, often undefined, or defined in many different ways, and is connected to a long history of metaphors that have their origins in science fiction (Rid 2016a: Preface). One of the widely used definitions of cyberspace, and a good starting point for historical reasons, is the one devised by the United States government. According to the "U.S. Strategic Command, The Cyber Warfare Lexicon," published in 2009, cyberspace is a "global domain within the information environment consisting of the interdependent network of information technology infrastructures, including the Internet, telecommunications networks, computer systems, and embedded processors and controllers" (US Strategic Command 2009, 8; Richelson 2016).[1]

What is notable about this definition is that it describes cyberspace as a "domain" equivalent to the domains of sea, air, land, and outer space (Kuehl 2009: 24–42). The recognition that cyberspace is a warfighting domain naturally led to the creation of the US Cyber Command, which centralizes command of cyberspace operations across the US military. That the world's largest military defines cyberspace as a domain within which to project power, and to fight and win wars, inevitably has system-wide repercussions, both materially and ideationally. In basic terms, the reorganization of the US military prompts reorganization among allied armed forces who need to be synched up operationally in order to cooperate. Their discursive framing of cyberspace as a warfighting domain also leads to strategic and tactical explorations among theorists and practitioners, and to the development of new tools, techniques, and procedures from the defense industrial base, companies within which profit from the reorganization and new acquisition cycles. At the same time, adversaries notice the shift, the reorganization, and the build-up of forces and capabilities, and respond in ways they see fit, opening up yet more market opportunities.

Settling on a definition of cyberspace for operational purposes also leads to theoretical explorations of how the material properties of the "domain" differ in character from other "domains," like land, sea, air, and space. An exemplary in this respect is that put forward by Joseph Nye, who distinguishes cyberspace from other domains because it is a "man-made" environment:

> The cyber domain is a complex man-made environment. Unlike atoms, human adversaries are purposeful and intelligent. Mountains and oceans are hard to move, but portions of cyberspace can be turned on and off by throwing a switch. It is cheaper and quicker to move electrons across the globe than to move large ships long distances through the friction of salt water. (Nye 2011: 20)

Dorothy Denning, however, challenges this perspective, arguing that cyberspace is actually a mixture of natural and man-made variables, and that geography matters in cyberspace as much as in the other domains. She also takes issue with the alleged malleability of the environment, arguing that path dependencies constrain cyberspace. "While some things are easy to change in cyberspace," explains Denning, "the overall malleability of the domain is severely limited by standards, interoperability requirements, legacy software, regulations, and the resources and inertia needed to make changes" (2015: 10). Cyberspace has deep institutional and material roots that, while maybe not as fixed as a mountain, are still very formidable.

Seeing cyberspace as a single "domain" is also limited in that it masks important distinguishing features. A different way of breaking down cyberspace is the four part definition developed by David Clark. Clark (2010) defines cyberspace as the people who participate in it, the information that is stored, transmitted, and transformed within it, the logical building blocks that make it up (i.e. the software and applications), and finally the physical foundations that support the logical elements. Breaking down cyberspace in this manner allows for more specification of characteristics across the different layers of the domain. Cyberspace is better thought of as an ecosystem with multiple components that vary depending on the country and the region. In other words, there is a continuously evolving and interacting *mixture* of characteristics to cyberspace which are *contingent* on local politics, culture, geography, and technology.

There are many areas for further research related to this characterization of cyberspace, much of which requires skills that are typically not part of the toolkit of a typical social science researcher. First, mapping the infrastructure of cyberspace is an essential part of any analysis of the geopolitics of the domain in light of the fact that the infrastructure of cyberspace varies from country to country and is highly dynamic. There are numerous tools and existing data sources that can be marshalled to undertake different slices of this type of mapping. Several university-based and community-based projects exist that aim to map Internet infrastructure. The OpenNet Initiative (a project the author helped lead) undertook network measurement tests in more than 70 countries on an annual basis for several years until its cessation in 2013. A complementary project is the Open Observatory of Network Interference (OONI), "a free software, global observation network for detecting censorship, surveillance and traffic manipulation on the Internet." The researchers involved in this area are maturing to the point of becoming a self-identified community, including extensive discussions concerning the ethics of network measurement tests. Their research outputs have provided evidence of national Internet censorship and surveillance, and disruptions to Internet and cellphone networks around significant events, like elections or major anniversaries.

Beyond technical measurements, and recalling Clark's other layers of cyberspace, mapping should include the cultural, social, and political variables that affect cyberspace contingently. While there are similarities among countries, and significant transmission of ideas and practices from one country to another, no one country is identical to another in terms of the historical path dependencies, agencies and institutions, and unique security issues. Laws, regulations, and practices vary extensively from country to country and are important to map as part of an accurate understanding of the dynamics of cybersecurity, a challenge that requires extensive field research and understanding of local languages and cultures (Deibert et al. 2008, 2010, 2011).

36.3 Security for Whom and What?

That cyberspace does not have fixed properties across time and space, means that it is also an essentially contested space, and thus inherently political. Technologists may bristle at this suggestion, and feel that the best way to secure cyberspace would be to "leave politics out of it." But as always in life, politics—meaning the decision as to who gets what, how, and when—is inescapable. The same is no less true when it comes to cybersecurity. Regardless of whether "fixes" to cybersecurity problems are couched in techno-functional terms, cybersecurity is a contest among different worldviews, ideologies, and strategic interests even if they are obscured as unquestioned assumptions.

Myriam Dunn Cavelty has published on the social construction of cybersecurity. Drawing from securitization theory, Dunn Cavelty shows how (2013: 108) "[t]he way cyberspace is imagined and defined has consequences for the way any type of action or strategy is conceptualized." Different communities of stakeholders have differing "threat perceptions" which in turn contain different conceptual assumptions about cyberspace as a space and place. These threat perceptions compete with each other, sometimes overlapping but other times projecting different "realms of the possible." Differing threat perceptions also delimit the range of possible policies, leaving some options out of the equation. As Dunn Cavelty (2012) explains, different ways of framing cyber threats "come with political and social effects."

Extending Dunn Cavelty's social construction of cybersecurity to the international realm, we can see how competing threat perceptions of cybersecurity manifest themselves. For liberal democratic countries, cybersecurity is primarily about protecting information networks and databases from compromise, while simultaneously freeing up information flows for the functioning of the global economy. However, as shown earlier, for a variety of historical and institutional reasons, military and intelligence agencies dominate cybersecurity. State-directed mass surveillance has been largely normalized and extensive resources have now been devoted to offensive cyber-espionage and warfare. The dominant position of these agencies sometimes leads to conflicts over the "referent object" of security—and whether the protection of national security should trump "network" or "user" security. A good example is the stockpiling by government agencies of computer software vulnerabilities as potential "weapons" of warfare or espionage, and the targeting of computer networks in "foreign" jurisdictions. Here, the referent object of "free, open, and secure networks" bumps up against the much more deeply entrenched paradigm of the national-security state and the defense of networks within state boundaries. Protecting "our country's" networks takes precedence over the networks of foreign countries, networks that may in fact be targeted for disruption, degradation, or even destruction.

Civil society perspectives on cybersecurity do overlap with this paradigm, but also conflict in important areas—such as around limits to mass surveillance against both government and corporations. Rather than a "domain," civil society organizations would prefer to think of cyberspace as a global *commons*—a public good—that should be shared by all, without boundaries or borders, and in which basic human rights are entrenched (Broeders 2015). Some would like to go further, drawing on theories of "liberation technology" and Internet freedom that imply cyberspace would be better off without governments altogether. But this notion seems increasingly naïve in light of seemingly unstoppable government and corporate efforts. That said, it is noteworthy that the multi-dimensional contests between liberal democratic states, companies, and civil society means that cyberspace as it is presently constituted is subject to an informal system of mutual restraints, and a kind of "republican"-style system of checks and balances—what I have elsewhere called "distributed security" (Deibert 2012). Keeping this tug-of-war alive may be the best means to ensure Internet freedom.

Moving from liberal democratic to other countries, we see a diversification of threat models, paradigms, and stakeholder interests. China's cybersecurity paradigm, for example, while sharing some important referents with other countries around data protection, places more weight on the protection of the ruling Communist party from domestic challenges. (Lindsay 2014/15: 15–16) This attention to threats from regime challengers is operationalized into extensive controls on content, downloading of policing networks to private sector service providers, and targeted digital attacks on civil society.

China also places a premium on state sovereignty in cyberspace over the multi-stakeholder model, a priority that is expressed internationally in Internet governance forums in which China increasingly participates as a major player and where it has been pushing a coalition of countries toward a common Internet governance model (Lindsay 2014/15: 37–8; Cornish 2015: 161). Whether China and other like-minded countries can succeed in promoting this agenda globally remains to be seen, but their prospects get brighter as more Internet users come from the developing world and from countries that have hybrid, mixed, or authoritarian regimes (Deibert 2015a).

Further research in this area could examine how threat perceptions come to be shared by different countries. Ideas, norms, and practices can be transmitted from one country to another, but the mechanisms by which they do so are unclear. Drawing from research done in other issue areas, for example environmental or trade governance, cybersecurity researchers could examine the role of norm entrepreneurs as "transmission belts," or the ways in which companies transmit practices through products and services (Deibert and Crete-Nishihata 2012). Comparative country studies on the implementation of cybersecurity policies are needed, including those that analyze new laws passed, institutions created, and practices transformed because of cybersecurity concerns (ADC and Cyber Stewards 2016).

36.4 Lifting the Lid on the Digital Environment

In spite of differing perceptions of cybersecurity, there are some inescapable trends tied to the material properties of cyberspace. One of them is the growing volume of data shared by users with third parties, and a greater number of devices connected to each other and the Internet which in turn collect, share, and transmit huge volumes of personally identifiable information. Today, we leave a digital trail wherever we go, whatever we do. How that data is protected, with whom it is shared, how it is accessed, are all important public policy and security questions.

At the most basic level, the growing number of Internet-connected devices, while convenient, presents a growing attack surface with possible cascading security consequences. Think of your Internet-enabled fridge: it allows you to remotely track the contents and see if products that are on sale at the grocery are available for purchase. But that same Internet-enabled fridge offers a potential entry point to your entire home network. If the fridge's network security is flawed, it could be the "soft underbelly" to other parts of your network. And that's just the fridge. Today there are approximately 15 billion Internet-enabled devices connected to the Internet. When we view this issue through the lens of a household, fraud, privacy violations, and theft of personal data are principal concerns. But consider the issue at a higher level: so-called "critical infrastructure," like hydroelectric dams, nuclear power plants, hospitals, or electrical grids. Cascading problems found in the software of these systems can wreak havoc on society, and even bring about significant loss of life (Schneier 2016). Software developers do not always foresee how their systems will integrate with other systems in ways that might bring out negative externalities. Even worse is the prospect of unpatched systems "living" undetected on an ecosystem for years because the developers have stopped maintaining them. We have dramatically increased the number of digital connected devices, but the alarming number of breaches show that we have not yet figured out the security problem. As one author put it, "societies today network first, and ask questions later" (Eichensehr 2016: 320).

Yet another factor contributing to the security issues around our interconnected world, ironically perhaps, are actions undertaken by governments themselves in the name of national security. For example, in 2016, an unattributed group called "ShadowBrokers" released an archived repository of software exploits that they claimed were taken from the US National Security Agency's "TAO" unit. Experts who analyzed the files verified the likelihood of their source. Among the files were tools that took advantage of previously unknown vulnerabilities in a variety of widely used network routers (Biddle 2016). The revelations underscored the severity of the risks involved in network security when governments hold on to software bugs in order to use them as weapons of espionage and warfare, or to aid in law enforcement. As Schwartz and Knacke (2016: 3) say "[w]hen federal agencies discover vulnerabilities as part of carrying out law enforcement and intelligence missions, the government must determine whether knowledge of these vulnerabilities should be restricted and used for these purposes or disclosed in the national interest of improving cybersecurity." The issue underlines well the competing paradigms of cybersecurity: should the interests of national security trump user security? If so, when?

One line of evidence-based research that the Citizen Lab (a research lab at the University of Toronto, directed by the current author) has developed has been to combine technical with legal, political, and social analysis of popular instant messaging, live-streaming, and other mobile applications in order to discover hidden privacy and security risks. Several of these studies have shown that popular applications used by millions of users, most of them in China, contain hidden keyword-based censorship and surveillance functionalities presumably implemented to comply with government policies on the policing of their users. As the universe of big data progresses, this type of research will become more critical to better understanding the exercise of power "beneath the surface" of the information systems upon which we depend. Future research should explore whether applications developed in other country contexts outside of China contain similar "policing" functions.

36.5 Cybersecurity and Threats to Civil Society

As cybersecurity practices spread, governments are allocating considerable resources to new institutions (e.g. cyber commands) or to older institutions that were previously in the shadows (e.g. national security agencies). Of course the precise character of these developments vary, but one general trend is the impact of cybersecurity practices on the prospects for civil society and the flourishing of democracy.

Today, the fastest Internet growth rates are occurring within the world's weak, authoritarian, or mixed regimes, within countries that face governance challenges in the form of domestic insurgencies or various forms of popular discontent and digitally-empowered mass mobilization. The Arab Spring demonstrated to power elites in these countries the need to take counter-measures against groups using digital technologies. Meanwhile, state security agencies in these countries now have available to them a wide array of sophisticated products and services that allow them to undertake deep packet inspection, cellphone tracking, social media monitoring, automated trolling, and computer network attack and exploitation.

One area of concern is so-called "dual-use" technologies that provide capabilities to surveil users or to censor online information at the country network level. These technologies are referred to as "dual-use" because, depending on how they are deployed, they may serve a legitimate purpose, or, equally well, a purpose that undermines human rights. For example, certain deep packet inspection and Internet filtering technologies that private companies can use for traffic management can also be used by government-controlled Internet service providers to prevent entire populations from accessing politically sensitive information. (Dalek et al. 2016; Marquis-Boire et al. 2016) The term "dual-use" also covers malware billed as a tool for "lawful intercept," for example software exploits and remote access trojans that enable surveillance through a user's device.

It is private industry, often based in the West, that supplies much of the dual-use technology of concern (Privacy International 2016). This supply-side is now only at the very early stages of regulation and operating with little to no transparency, oversight, or accountability. Most companies in the surveillance industry have poor corporate social responsibility procedures while some have flagrantly defied such norms (Dalek et al. 2016; Dalek et al. 2015). The combination of rapid advancements in technical capabilities, lack of transparency, and the close ties of surveillance technology manufacturers with the apparatus of state security, has resulted in legal and regulatory gray areas in which companies have thus far operated with relative impunity.

Civil society organizations are bearing the brunt of this combination of forces, and are particularly vulnerable to targeted digital attacks (Deibert 2016a). Civil society organizations now depend on and have benefited from social media to conduct their campaigns and communicate with each other. Yet that same dependence on social media has become a principal point of exposure and risk, exploited by criminals, intelligence agencies, and other adversaries determined to silence dissent. Civil society is connecting at a rate that is far outpacing their capacity to secure. Many civil society organizations lack technological support, and have no means to contract with large cybersecurity firms to remediate their problems.

In the course of the last few years, research groups like the Citizen Lab have documented numerous cases of human rights defenders and other civil society actors being targeted with advanced commercial spyware (e.g. Hacking Team, Finfisher, and NSO Group) (Marczak et al. 2014; Scott-Railton et al. 2016), commercial off-the-shelf malware (in the cases of Latin America, Syria, and Iran) (Scott-Railton et al. 2014; Scott-Railton and Kleemola 2015; Scott-Railton et al. 2015), and by so-called Advanced

Persistent Threats (APT) campaigns (in the cases of Tibetan and Hong Kong activists) (Citizen Lab 2014). Using network scanning techniques, Citizen Lab has also been able to map the proliferation of dual-use technology to a large and growing global client base, many of which are countries that have notoriously bad human rights records (Marczak et al. 2015; Deibert 2016b). Nonetheless, these findings are only touching on a small area of what is a disturbingly larger picture. The market for dual-use technologies, particularly spyware, is escalating. Government demand for these technologies may actually be increasing following the Snowden disclosures, which raised the bar on what is deemed *de rigueur* in digital surveillance (Deibert 2015a). Far from accelerating positive democratic change and liberalization, the Internet and social media may correlate with a resurgence of authoritarianism and the gradual strangling of civil society (Deibert 2015b). Unless efforts are undertaken to address in a wholesale manner the silent epidemic of targeted digital attacks on civil society, we could be facing a crisis of democracy. Further comparative research is required on how "cybersecurity" is employed to justify the implementation of policies and practices that end up furthering hybrid democracies, autocracies, and authoritarian forms of rule, and how civil society can better secure themselves from such trends.

36.6 Cybersecurity and Warfare/ Armed Conflict

One important cybersecurity debate concerns the prospects of armed conflict as a result of the perceived "advantage" offense has over defense in cyberspace (Applegate 2013; Calvo 2014). It is much easier to penetrate computer networks than it is to defend them, as evidenced by the number of breaches of corporate and government networks. With the growing number of targets multiplying through the Internet of Things, and governments racing to develop capabilities to exploit those vulnerabilities (serviced by a growing market for offensive services), it seems reasonable to conclude that it is only a matter of time before a serious armed conflict erupts, either out of design or by accident (Greenberg 2015).

On the other side of the equation, however, there are those who point out the self-serving hyperbole about cyber-war (Walt 2010). Individuals associated with the defense and intelligence sectors stand to benefit by trumpeting concerns about cyber-warfare. Others express skepticism that we will ever witness a pure cyber-attack crossing the threshold to meet the Clausewitzian definition of war. The most elaborated version of this argument comes from Thomas Rid, who has pointed out there has not been a single cyber-attack resulting in loss of life. (Rid 2012) The so-called Stuxnet cyber-attack on Iranian nuclear enrichment facilities (thought to be engineered at great cost by the United States and Israel), though causing considerable setbacks to the nuclear program, did not directly cause a single loss of life. Likewise, the digital attack on the Ukrainian power grid in 2015, largely thought to be the responsibility of a Russian state-organized cybercrime nexus, did not result in a loss of life, and power was restored with a few hours (E-ISAC 2016). As Erik Gartzke explains "[s]hutting down power grids, closing airports, or derailing communication could be tremendously costly, but most damage of this type will be fixed quickly and at comparatively modest investment of tangible resources" (2013: 57).

One of the reasons we have not yet seen, and may never see, a full-blown cyber-attack resulting in massive loss of life is that governments, even those that are adversaries, are mutually entangled in cyberspace. Insofar as we can attribute rationality to their decisions, leaders of all countries realize that attempts to disrupt cyberspace may come back to bite them, and so deterrence applies in cyberspace for the same reasons as it does with respect to deterrence in relation to kinetic attacks (Lindsay and Gartzke 2016).

While we may never see a pure cyber-war, it is important to bracket this discussion with two important caveats. First, all of armed conflict today has a some kind of digital component to it. Consider the ongoing Syrian armed conflict, where one study showed that fake female avatars on social media were used to entice opposition fighters to click on malicious links in order to get inside their computers. Using information gleaned from these computers allowed the Syrian regime to arrest and kill opposition fighters (Regalado et al. 2015). A recent Citizen Lab report showed that ISIS had used targeted digital attacks to get inside the mobile devices of opposition groups in Raqqa for the purposes of physical tracking, ostensibly for targeted murders or kidnapping (Scott-Railton et al. 2014). The same type of dynamic interplay between intelligence derived from digital technologies and their use of kinetic attacks happens on a daily basis in the War on Terror, as illustrated in targeted drone attacks (Currier and Maass 2015). So while warfare may not result solely from the use of digital "weapons," digital technologies are integral to all armed conflict today.

Second, just because it is rational for leaders to choose not to undertake cyber-attacks, the reality is that people often in engage in suboptimal or irrational behavior; accidents can happen, and misunderstandings can bring about outcomes that no one desires. Consider, in this respect, the tense situation involving China, the United States, and countries engaged in territorial disputes in the South China Seas. Should tensions emerging out of territorial disputes rise to the precipice of an armed conflict, a major cyber-related incident—like a distributed denial of service attack on critical infrastructure—could be interpreted by one of the protagonists as an "opening shot," leading to the eruption of hostilities (Libicki 2012).

In response to these contingencies, analysts and policy-makers have started to explore ways to limit warfare in cyberspace through the articulation of "rules of the road," and by elaborating on principles concerning the laws of armed conflict as they apply to cyberspace, the so-called Tallinn Manual being the most well-known of them (Meyer 2015). These efforts are complicated by the unique properties of state competition in cyberspace, including difficulties attributing the sources of cyber-attacks, deliberate efforts to disguise the origins of operations to provide plausible deniability, the use of third-parties, or "proxies" in cyber operations, and by the blurring of cyber-espionage and -warfare. In spite of these challenges, it will be important for research to explore ways to limit state behavior in cyberspace to avoid armed conflict, but also to better refine ways to "verify" state and non-state behavior in cyberspace—a challenge that will require technical as well as social science methods.

One type of warfare that may become more prevalent in cyberspace is known as "hybrid warfare," which consists of the combination of subversion and propaganda with traditional strategies of kinetic warfare. One recent example of hybrid warfare is the digital infiltration of the Democratic National Committee (DNC) and other Democratic Party individuals and organizations leading up to the 2016 US Presidential election. Email accounts associated with these groups were breached and the data released to and published on Wikileaks, which led to embarrassing revelations. Forensic work undertaken by companies and security researchers, later reinforced by the US government itself, attributed the attacks to groups associated with the Russian government (Rid 2016b). The DNC episode was one example of a long-standing Russian approach to disinformation, which "consists of a deliberate disinformation campaign supported by actions of the intelligence organs designed to confuse the enemy and achieve strategic advantage at minimal cost" (Snegovaya 2015).

Hybrid warfare involving the use of social-media enabled propaganda, combined with targeted digital attacks, may be especially attractive to authoritarian regimes that are accustomed to exploiting the criminal underworld to accomplish their goals, and have few meaningful checks on clandestine activities. According to Katy Pearce, "Social media affords inexpensive and undemanding opportunities for an authoritarian regime to subtly harass opposition in front of a large domestic audience, while eschewing direct responsibility for the harassment, and measuring the spread of the harassing content" (2015: 1158). It may also be an area in which liberal democratic countries have a distinct *disadvantage*, given the role of a relatively independent and adversarial press in checking their operations.

There are many promising areas of further research around better understanding hybrid warfare. For example, Philip Howard's "Political Bots" project uses techniques from different disciplines to understand the "impact of automated scripts, commonly called bots, on social media" (Political Bots 2016). The project aims to discover how bots are used to manipulate public opinion and sow disinformation. Research that documents information disruptions around major events, such as the severing of Internet cellphone connections—what I have elsewhere called "just-in-time" blocking—offers a good complement to Howard's work (Deibert and Rohozinski 2008; Crete-Nishihata and York 2011). As in most areas of cybersecurity research, progress in this area will require the integration of technical and social science methods that are still unorthodox in the International Relations field.

36.7 Conclusion

The burgeoning universe of digital technologies and "big data" shows no signs of abating. As it continues to expand so too will the security issues that come alongside it.

Securing cyberspace will inevitably involve highly detailed engineering and computer science techniques. But those disciplines alone can only ever provide partial answers to what are inherently political questions. The security of cyberspace is essentially contested, and is as much a struggle of power and influence as is securing other areas of life.

This chapter has provided a survey of some cybersecurity topics where evidence-based and theoretically informed social science research will be sorely needed. In order to be successful, however, researchers will need to explore methods that are not typically within the social science toolkit: techniques drawn from computer science, engineering, data analysis, and software development. Doing so will require bridging disciplinary divides that are not easily overcome—a challenge that may, in reality, take generations to overcome. Given the swift pace of change in our digital mediated world, and the enormous stakes involved for human security, one can only hope that the process of overcoming disciplinary divides can be accelerated.

Note

1. The US military has spent enormous resources and published extensive documents on cyberspace lexicon, the volume itself an indication of the importance which the US military attaches to the domain.

References

ADC and Cyber Stewards. 2016. Surveillance and Intelligence in the Latin American Cybersecurity Agenda. *ADC Digital*, October. *Available at:* https://adcdigital.org.ar/wp-content/uploads/2016/10/Cybersecurity-comparative-cl-ar.pdf

Applegate, Scott D. 2013. The Dawn of Kinetic Cyber. In *2013 5th International Conference on Cyber Conflict*, edited by K. Podins, J. Stinnisen, and M. Maybaum. Tallinn, NATO CCD COE Publications, 2013. *Available at:* https://ccdcoe.org/sites/default/files/multimedia/pdf/d2r1s4_applegate.pdf

Biddle, Sam. 2016. The NSA Leak is Real, Snowden Documents Confirm. *The Intercept*, August 19. *Available at:* https://theintercept.com/2016/08/19/the-nsa-was-hacked-snowden-documents-confirm/

Broeders, Dennis. 2015. The Public Core of the Internet: An International Agenda for Internet Governance. *WRR-Policy Brief no.* 2, The Hague: WRR. *Available at:* https://www.gccs2015.com/sites/default/files/documents/WRR%20Policy%20Brief%20(2015)%20The%20Public%20Core%20of%20the%20Internet.pdf

Calvo, Alex. 2014. Cyberwar is War: A Critique of "Hacking Can Reduce Real-World Violence." *Small Wars Journal*, April 6. *Available at:* http://smallwarsjournal.com/jrnl/art/cyberwar-is-war

Citizen Lab. 2014. Communities @ Risk: Targeted Digital Threats Against Civil Society. *Communities @ Risk*. *Available at:* https://targetedthreats.net/.

Clark, David. 2010. Characterizing Cyberspace: Past, Present and Future. *MIT Computer Science and Artificial Intelligence Laboratory*, March 12. *Available at:* https://projects.csail.mit.edu/ecir/wiki/images/7/77/Clark_Characterizing_cyberspace_1-2r.pdf

Cornish, Paul. 2015. Governing Cyberspace through Constructive Ambiguity. *Survival: Global Politics and Strategy*, 57(3): 153–76. *Available at:* https://www.researchgate.net/publication/277134499_Governing_Cyberspace_through_Constructive_Ambiguity

Crete-Nishihata, Masashi and Jillian C. York. 2011. Egypt's Internet Blackout: Extreme Example of Just-in-time Blocking. *OpenNet Initiative*, January 28. *Available at:* https://opennet.net/blog/2011/01/egypt%E2%80%99s-internet-blackout-extreme-example-just-time-blocking

Currier, Cora and Peter Maass. 2015. The Drone Papers: Firing Blind. *The Intercept*, October 15. *Available at:* https://theintercept.com/drone-papers/firing-blind/

Dalek, Jakub, Ronald Deibert, Sarah McKune, Phillipa Gill, and Adam Seft. 2015. Information Controls During Military Operations: The Case of Yemen during the 2015 Political and Armed Conflict. Citizen Lab, October 21. *Available at:* https://citizenlab.org/2015/10/information-controls-military-operations-yemen/

Dalek, Jakub, Ronald Deibert, Bill Marczak, Sarah McKune, Helmi Noman, Irene Poetranto, and Adam Senft. 2016. Tender Confirmed, Rights at Risk: Verifying Netsweeper in Bahrain. Citizen Lab, September 21. *Available at:* https://citizenlab.org/2016/09/tender-confirmed-rights-risk-verifying-netsweeper-bahrain/

Deibert, Ronald. 2012. Distributed Security as Cyber Strategy: Outlining a Comprehensive Approach for Canada in Cyberspace. *Canadian Defence and Foreign Affairs Institute*, August. *Available at:* https://citizenlab.org/wp-content/uploads/2012/08/CDFAI-Distributed-Security-as-Cyber-Strategy_-outlining-a-comprehensive-approach-for-Canada-in-Cyber.pdf

Deibert, Ron. 2015a. The Geopolitics of Cyberspace After Snowden. *Current History*, 114(768): 9–15. *Available at:* http://www.currenthistory.com/Deibert_CurrentHistory.pdf

Deibert, Ron. 2015b. Authoritarianism Goes Global: Cyberspace Under Siege, *Journal of Democracy*, 26(3): 64–78.

Deibert, Ron. 2016a. How Foreign Governments Spy using PowerPoint and Twitter. *The Washington Post*, August 2. *Available at:* https://www.washingtonpost.com/posteverything/wp/2016/08/02/how-foreign-governments-spy-using-email-and-powerpoint/?utm_term=.995b323c9ced

Deibert, Ron. 2016b. What an "MRI of the Internet" Can Reveal: Netsweeper in Bahrain. Citizen Lab, September 21. *Available at:* https://deibert.citizenlab.org/2016/09/what-an-mri-of-the-internet-can-reveal-netsweeper-in-bahrain/

Deibert, Ron and Masashi Crete-Nishihata. 2012. Global Governance and the Spread of Cyberspace Controls. *Global Governance*, 18(3): 339–61.

Deibert, Ronald and Rafal Rohozinski. 2008. Good for Liberty, Bad for Security? Global Civil Society and the Securitization of the Internet. In Ronald Deibert, John Palfrey, Rafal Rohozinski, and Jonathan Zittrain (eds.), *Access Denied: The Practice and Policy of Global Internet Filtering*, pp. 123–149. Cambridge, MA: MIT Press. *Available at:* http://access.opennet.net/wp-content/uploads/2011/12/accessdenied-chapter-6.pdf

Deibert, Ronald, John Palfrey, Rafal Rohozinski, and Jonathan Zittrain (eds.). 2008. *Access Denied: The Practice and Policy of Global Internet Filtering*. Cambridge, MA: MIT Press.

Deibert, Ronald, John Palfrey, Rafal Rohozinski, and Jonathan Zittrain (eds.). 2010. *Access Controlled: Shaping of Power, Rights, and Rule in Cyberspace*. Cambridge, MA: MIT Press.

Deibert, Ronald, John Palfrey, Rafal Rohozinski, and Jonathan Zittrain (eds.). 2011. *Access Contested: Security, Identity, and Resistance in Asian Cyberspace.* Cambridge, MA: MIT Press.

Denning, Dorothy E. 2015. Rethinking the Cyber Domain and Deterrence. *Joint Force* (2): 8–15. *Available at:* http://faculty.nps.edu/dedennin/publications/Rethinking%20the%20Cyber%20Domain%20and%20Deterrence%20-%20jfq-77_8-15.pdf

Dunn Cavelty, Myriam. 2012. The Militarisation of Cyberspace: Why Less May Be Better. In C. Czosseck, R. Ottis and K. Ziolkowski (eds.), *2012 4th International Conference on Cyber Conflict.* Tallinn: NATO CCD COE. *Available at:* https://ccdcoe.org/publications/2012proceedings/2_6_Dunn%20Cavelty_TheMilitarisationOfCyberspace.pdf

Dunn Cavelty, Myriam. 2013. From Cyber-Bombs to Political Fallout: Threat Representations with an Impact in the Cyber-Security Discourse. *International Studies Review*, 15(108): 105–22. *Available at:* https://www.researchgate.net/publication/264669823_From_Cyber Bombs_to_Political_Fallout_Threat_Representations_with_an_Impact_in_the_Cyber-Security_Discourse

Eichensehr, Kristen E. 2016. Giving Up On Cybersecurity. *UCLA Law Review Discourse*, 64(320): 320–39. *Available at:* http://www.uclalawreview.org/giving-up-on-cybersecurity/

E-ISAC. 2016. Analysis of the Cyber Attack on the Ukrainian Power Grid: Defense Use Case. *SANS ICS*, March 18. *Available at:* http://www.nerc.com/pa/CI/ESISAC/Documents/E-ISAC_SANS_Ukraine_DUC_18Mar2016.pdf

Gartzke, Erik. 2013. The Myth of Cyberwar: Bringing War in Cyberspace Back Down to Earth. *International Security*, 38(2): 41–73.

Gartzke, Erik and Jon R. Lindsay. 2015. Weaving Tangled Webs: Offense, Defense, and Deception in Cyberspace. *Security Studies*, 24(2): 316–48. *Available at:* http://deterrence.ucsd.edu/_files/Weaving%20Tangled%20Webs_%20Offense%20Defense%20and%20Deception%20in%20Cyberspace.pdf

Greenberg, Andy. 2015. New Dark-Web Market is Selling Zero-Day Exploits to Hackers. *Wired*, April 17. *Available at:* https://www.wired.com/2015/04/therealdeal-zero-day-exploits/

Kopstein, Joshua. 2014. Inside Citizen Lab, the "Hacker Hothouse" Protecting you from Big Brother. *ARS Technica*, July 30. *Available at:* http://arstechnica.com/security/2014/07/inside-citizen-lab-the-hacker-hothouse-protecting-you-from-big-brother/2/

Kuehl, Daniel T. 2009. From Cyberspace to Cyberpower: Defining the Problem. In Franklin D. Kramer, Stuart H. Starr, and Larry K. Wentz (eds.), *Cyberpower and National Security*, pp. 24–42. Dulles: Potomac Books.

Laswell, Harold D. 1936. *Politics: Who Gets What, When, How.* New York: Whittlesey House.

Lesk, Michael. 2013. Big Data, Big Brother, Big Money. *IEEE Security & Privacy*, 11(4): 85–9. *Available at:* http://resolver.scholarsportal.info.myaccess.library.utoronto.ca/resolve/15407993/v11i0004/ 85_bdbbbm.xml

Libicki, Martin C. 2012. Crisis and Escalation in Cyberspace. *RAND: Project Air Force. Available at:* https://www.rand.org/content/dam/rand/pubs/monographs/2012/RAND_MG1215.pdf

Lindsay, Jon R. 2014/15. The Impact of China on Cybersecurity: Fiction and Friction. *International Security*, 39(3): 7–47. *Available at:* http://www.mitpressjournals.org.myaccess.library.utoronto.ca/doi/pdf/10.1162/ISEC_a_00189

Lindsay, Jon R. and Eric Gartzke. 2016. Cross-Domain Deterrence as a Practical Problem and a Theoretical Concept. *Cross-Domain Deterrence, UC San Diego*, July 2. *Available at:* http://deterrence.ucsd.edu/_files/CDD_Intro_v2.pdf

MacKinnon, Rebecca. 2012. *Consent of the Networked: The Worldwide Struggle for Internet Freedom.* New York: Basic Books. iBooks Edition.

Marczak, Bill and John Scott-Railton. 2016. The Million Dollar Dissident: NSO Group's iPhone Zero-Days used against a UAE Human Rights Defender. Citizen Lab and Lookout Security, August 24. *Available at:* https://citizenlab.org/2016/08/million-dollar-dissident-iphone-zero-day-nso-group-uae/

Marczak, Bill, Claudio Guarnieri, Morgan Marquis-Boire, and John Scott-Railton. 2014. Hacking Team and the Targeting of Ethiopian Journalists. Citizen Lab, February 12. *Available at:* https://citizenlab.org/2014/02/hacking-team-targeting-ethiopian-journalists/

Marczak, Bill, John Scott-Railton, Adam Senft, Irene Poetranto, and Sarah McKune. 2015. Pay No Attention to the Server Behind the Proxy: Mapping FinFisher's Continuing Proliferation. Citizen Lab, October 15. *Available at:* https://citizenlab.org/2015/10/mapping-finfishers-continuing-proliferation/

Marquis-Boire, Morgan, Collin Anderson, Jakub Dalek, Sarah McKune, and John Scott-Railton. 2016. Some Devices Wander by Mistake: Planet Blue Coat Redu., Citizen Lab, July 9. *Available at:* https://citizenlab.org/storage/bluecoat/CitLab-PlanetBlueCoatRedux-FINAL.pdf

Meyer, Paul. 2015. Is Cyber Peace Possible? *Open Canada*, October 28. *Available at:* https://www.opencanada.org/features/cyber-peace-possible/

Nye Jr., Joseph S. 2011. Nuclear Lessons for Cyber Security? *Strategic Studies Quarterly*, 5(4): 18–38. *Available at:* http://myaccess.library.utoronto.ca/login?url=http://search.proquest.com.myaccess.library.utoronto.ca/docview/1242014564?accountid=14771

Pearce, Katy E. 2015. Democratizing kompromat: The Affordances of Social Media for State-sponsored Harassment. *Information, Communication & Society*, 18(10): 1158–74.

Political Bots. 2016. Project Description. *Available at:* http://politicalbots.org/?page_id=129

Privacy International. 2016. The Global Surveillance Industry. July. *Available at:* https://privacyinternational.org/sites/default/files/global_surveillance_f.pdf

Regalado, Daniel, Nart Villeneuve, and John Scott-Railton. 2015. Behind the Syrian Conflict's Digital Front Lines. *FireEye Threat Intelligence*, February. *Available at:* https://www.fireeye.com/content/dam/fireeye-www/global/en/current-threats/pdfs/rpt-behind-the-syria-conflict.pdf

Richelson, Jeffrey. 2016. The United States and Cyberspace: Military, Organization, Policies, and Activities. *National Security Archive Electronic Briefing Book No. 539*, January 20. *Available at:* http://nsarchive.gwu.edu/NSAEBB/NSAEBB539-Declassified-Documents-on-US-Military-Activities-in-Cyberspace/

Rid, Thomas. 2012. Cyber War Will Not Take Place. *Journal of Strategic Studies*, 35(1): 5–32.

Rid, Thomas. 2016a. *Rise of the Machines: A Cybernetic History*. New York: W.W. Norton & Company, Inc.

Rid, Thomas. 2016b. All Signs Point to Russia Being Behind the DNC Hack. *Motherboard*, July 25. *Available at:* http://motherboard.vice.com/read/all-signs-point-to-russia-being-behind-the-dnc-hack

Schneier, Bruce. 2016. Real-World Security and the Internet of Things. *Schneier on Security*, July 28. *Available at:* https://www.schneier.com/blog/archives/2016/07/real-world_secu.html

Schwartz, Ari and Rob Knacke. 2016. Government's Role in Vulnerability Disclosure: Creating a Permanent and Accountable Vulnerabilities Equity Process. *Belfer Center for Science and International Affairs*, June. *Available at:* http://belfercenter.ksg.harvard.edu/files/vulnerability-disclosure-web-final3.pdf

Scott-Railton, John and Katie Kleemola. 2015. London Calling: Two-Factor Authentication Phishing from Iran. Citizen Lab, August 27. *Available at:* https://citizenlab.org/2015/08/iran_two_factor_phishing/

Scott-Railton, John, Seth Hardy and Cyber Arabs. 2014. Malware Attacks Targeting Syrian ISIS Critics. Citizen Lab, December 18. *Available at:* https://citizenlab.org/2014/12/malware-attack-targeting-syrian-isis-critics/

Scott-Railton, John, Morgan Marquis-Boire, Claudio Guarnieri, and Marion Marschalek. 2015. Packrat: Seven Years of a South American Threat Actor. Citizen Lab, December 8. *Available at:* https://citizenlab.org/2015/12/packrat-report/

Scott-Railton, John, Bahr Abdul Razzak, Adam Hulcoop, Matt Brooks, and Katie Kleemola. 2016. Group5: Syria and the Iranian Connection. Citizen Lab, August 2. *Available at:* https://citizenlab.org/2016/08/group5-syria/

Snegovaya, Maria. 2015. Russia Report 1: Putin's Information Warfare in Ukraine. *Institute for the Study of War*, September. *Available at:* http://understandingwar.org/sites/default/files/Russian%20Report%201%20Putin's%20Information%20Warfare%20in%20Ukraine-%20Soviet%20Origins%20of%20Russias%20Hybrid%20Warfare.pdf

US Strategic Command. 2009. The Cyber Warfare Lexicon: A Language to Support the Development, Testing, Planning and Employment of Cyber Weapons and Other Modern Warfare Capabilities. January 5. *Available at:* http://nsarchive.gwu.edu/dc.html?doc=2692102-Document-1

Walt, Stephen M. 2010. Is the Cyber Threat Overblown? *Foreign Policy*, March 30. *Available at:* http:// walt.foreignpolicy.com/posts/2010/03/30/is_the_cyber_threat_overblown

CHAPTER 37

COUNTER INSURGENCY

AUSTIN LONG

In 1955, Bernard Brodie wrote an article for *Harper's Magazine* entitled "Strategy Hits a Dead End." The article described how the newly developed hydrogen bomb had created an environment where military means had become impossible to connect to political ends. The destructive power of the new weapons was simply too great to imagine what objective could be worth their use (Brodie 1955).

Brodie may have been wrong about nuclear weapons and strategy but an analogous situation may be true of Western counter insurgency and strategy in the twenty-first century. The theoretical underpinnings and operational techniques of Western counter insurgency have scarcely progressed in over five decades. While this could indicate convergence on a proper paradigm, the lack of success in Western counter insurgency campaigns from Algeria to Vietnam to Iraq and Afghanistan suggests the opposite.

This chapter reviews the history and current state of counter insurgency, proceeding in four parts. First it defines both insurgency and counter insurgency in historical context. Second, it reviews the intellectual origin and evolution of counter insurgency as a theoretical and operational construct beginning in the Cold War. Third, it describes the post-September 11, 2001 renaissance in counter insurgency. Fourth, it concludes with discussion of the future of counter insurgency.

37.1 Insurgency and Counter Insurgency: Definitions and Origins

Insurgency is the use of political and military means by irregular forces to change an existing political order. These forces typically mingle with civilians in order to hide from the forces defending the political order. This form of warfare began to emerge in the nineteenth century, though war among the people was not novel at that point. Counter insurgency, defined as a systematic political military campaign to negate insurgency, likewise was not novel in the nineteenth century but became more organized and professional in response to these new challenges.

Yet just as nationalism and industrial technology enabled conventional warfare to transform in both degree and kind, it likewise changed war among the people. Nationalism generated a potent motivating force for dispersed forces mixing with the population. Industry provided a cornucopia of lethal weapons to these forces. Crucially important was the breech-loading rifle, which provided the ability to attack at long range with surprise, while dynamite provided the ability to destroy structures. Industrial organization was the last ingredient making "people's war" in the late nineteenth century vastly more capable than in previous centuries. The new effectiveness of insurgency was apparent in the US Civil War. Southern guerillas harassed the Union, especially as Union logistics grew more challenging with the advance to the south later in the war.[1]

While the Civil War was viewed by many in Europe as an aberration, the power of people's war quickly became apparent on the continent as well. In 1870, the Prussian Army triumphed over the French Army in a short campaign ending in September with the Battle of Sedan. When Emperor Napoleon III was captured, a new Government of National Defense was formed to mount a people's war (Howard 1961).

In contrast to this new model of a people's war, imperial wars often fought premodern irregulars lacking arms, nationalism, and organization. Most imperial wars were characterized by set-piece battles (won by European forces) followed by negotiations. Colonial administration did lay the theoretical and operational groundwork for what would become counter insurgency. Both the British and French developed colonial information and intelligence regimes, as the intermingling of insurgent and native colonial populations put a premium on local information. Both also became accustomed to raising both regular and irregular forces from the native population. The French also developed a system of military administration designed to spread the writ of the state in a gradual fashion, likened to the spreading of an "oil spot" (Singer and Langdon 2008; Rid 2010; Bayly 2011). Each of these elements of colonial administration would find an analog in twentieth-century counter insurgency.

In the early twentieth century, new communications along with the education of native populations began to generate challenges to imperial powers. The groundwork of insurgency was laid across the world, from French North Africa to British India. The British and French redoubled their investments in intelligence in the colonial possessions to maintain control (Porch 2003; Thomas 2007; Andrew 2009).

37.2 The Cold War: A New Paradigm for Insurgency

The next great leap forward in insurgency began after the Second World War, as the Cold War dawned. The war weakened the imperial powers such as the French and

British, while it also expanded the capability and opportunity of many potential insurgents. Many nationalists had been armed and trained by combatants in the war, such as the Viet Minh in Indochina, supported by the Allies against the Japanese (Karnow 1983: 135–40).

The Soviets, having successfully consolidated most of the old Russian Empire into the new Soviet Union, saw insurgency as a tool against the capitalist West. The Communist strategy of supporting insurgency in current and former colonies of Western powers prompted an interest in countermeasures. The new discipline of counter insurgency was born in this environment. It had roots in the earlier colonial experience but with a modern twist.

Much of the initial effort emphasized the perils of modernization along with political and economic development. Analysts believed the central problem of insurgency was the speed with which former (and sometimes current) colonies were modernizing.[2] While the West had centuries to adjust to the transition from premodern to modern society, the developing former colonies were experiencing it in years or decades. As the economic foundations of society changed, political pressure grew. This in turn put pressure on colonial regimes or newly independent former colonies. Institutions could not keep pace with newly mobilized forces in society, leading to disorder, instability, and vulnerability to Communist influence.[3]

The answer, these early counter insurgency theorists argued, entailed providing security to a population by shielding them from insurgent forces while ameliorating the negative consequences of economic development and enhancing the positive. Increasing political representation, reducing corruption and abuse by the government, and ensuring that economic development was widely shared were the central elements of this strand of counter insurgency thinking. This school of counter insurgency thought came to be known as "winning the hearts and minds of the people," a phrased used by Sir Gerald Templer, who led the British counter insurgency campaign in Malaya. "Hearts and minds" became the dominant theory of counter insurgency in the West during the early 1960s. The vast majority of both analysts and practitioners of counter insurgency believed in this period that the support of the population was the *sine qua non* of counter insurgency.

However, by the mid-1960s some analysts began to question this orthodoxy. Charles Wolf, an analyst at the RAND Corporation, argued in 1965 that popular support was not actually required for insurgency. He argued, using the language of the new discipline of systems analysis: "[f]rom an operational point of view, what an insurgent movement requires for successful and expanding operations is not popular support, in the sense of attitudes of identification and allegiance, but rather a supply of certain inputs ... at a reasonable cost, interpreting cost to include expenditure of coercion as well as money" (Wolf 1965: 5).

Wolf also noted that increasing the livelihoods of a population would not necessarily reduce insurgency. Economic development would provide resources to a population but insurgents could then extract those resources through some combination of coercion and suasion. Paradoxically, efforts to reduce popular support for insurgents could actually make it easier for insurgents to obtain things like food.

At its core, Wolf's alternative counter insurgency theory, known as the cost–benefit or coercion theory, sought to apply systems analysis and econometrics to confront insurgency. Insurgency and counter insurgency were simply competing systems seeking more effective ways to extract resources and employ them to consolidate control of the state. Populations were rational actors responding to incentives and disincentives from the competing systems. The population's attitudes were not what mattered but rather its actions. Wolf, along with fellow RAND analyst Nathan Leites, further refined this theory in the seminal work *Rebellion and Authority* (Leites and Wolf 1970).

The cost–benefit theory of counter insurgency received additional support from other scholars. Samuel Popkin conducted fieldwork among Vietnamese peasants, concluding that they did behave as more or less rational actors when deciding whether and how to engage with insurgent and counter insurgent. While Popkin did not endorse the Leites and Wolf theory explicitly, his work nonetheless underscored that rational calculations about costs and benefits rather than emotions or attitudes were what mattered (Popkin 1970, 1979).[4]

Popkin's work was an explicit challenge to James Scott's work, also in Vietnam, arguing that peasant calculations were based heavily on norms of reciprocity and subsistence. Scott's work hinged on perceptions of the *legitimacy* of the extraction of resources rather than extraction itself (Scott 1976). This was consonant with the "hearts and minds" view of counter insurgency and communal norms would remain a major component of subsequent study of insurgency and rebellion.

The debate about the importance of legitimacy was continued by several of Leites and Wolf's colleagues at RAND. Daniel Ellsberg argued that the cost–benefit theory of counter insurgency erred in taking preferences as a given. The implicit assumption of cost–benefit theory was the population's indifference to insurgent and counter insurgent, so the better package of incentives and incentives was what was important. This meant the cost of extraction was, at the margin, the same for both sides. Ellsberg argued preferences mattered in terms of marginal costs. Government extraction could, if viewed as illegitimate, decrease the marginal costs paid by insurgents to extract other resources. As Ellsberg put it, using Leites and Wolf's language (P for population, R for rebellion, A for authority): "With new attitudes in P—then, with P providing more help for R, and less for A, for given inducement and effort by each—R could grow from its small beginnings, press A increasingly, perhaps win" (1970: 2).

RAND analyst Albert Wohlstetter came to similar conclusions, further noting that for counter insurgents operating as third parties abroad the impact of tactics on the view of their home population were equally troublesome (Wohlstetter 1968). This proved empirically true with the French war in Algeria and to a lesser extent the US war in Vietnam, as tactics used abroad undermined support for the war (Merom 2003).[5] Wohlstetter also noted the distribution of preferences in a given population would likely shape the "tipping points" where general dissatisfaction with the political order boiled over into insurgency (Wohlstetter 1968).[6] The issue of third-party counter insurgency and the role of preferences in mobilizing insurgency would remain perennial topics.

In practice, most counter insurgency campaigns seemed to rely on elements of both of these theories. Even in the British campaign in Malaya, where the term "hearts and minds" originated, there was extensive reliance on a variety of inducements (such as rewards for providing intelligence on insurgents) as well as control mechanisms such as population relocation and controlling the population's access to food. The British relied on similar tactics in Kenya in the 1950s but at the same time British military leaders worried a great deal about the legitimacy not only of the colonial government generally but the specific leadership in place.[7] The US-supported counter insurgency campaign in the Philippines led by Ramon Magsaysay in the same period also mixed concern for legitimacy with a variety of costs and benefits for the population.

The end of the US war in Vietnam in 1975 led to a rapid decline in interest in counter insurgency in both the policy research and academic communities.[8] Indeed, the Vietnam War had destroyed much of the Cold War consensus linking the academy to the US military and intelligence community. Symbolically, this was perhaps best demonstrated by the decision of RAND analyst Daniel Ellsberg to leak the so-called "Pentagon Papers," a compilation of documents detailing the evolution of US decision making on Vietnam. University campuses became hostile to research seen to be supporting an "imperialist" agenda.

However, one of the more important works on counter insurgency appeared in 1975, perhaps as a punctuation mark on the conflict. Andrew Mack's "Why Big Nations Lose Small Wars," emphasized the importance of asymmetry of interest in so-called small wars, which often trumped the asymmetry of power between large powers (like the United States) and weaker regional actors (like North Vietnam) (Mack 1975). The regional actor was vastly more committed to achieving its political objectives than the large power, which meant—absent a quick victory (unlikely but not impossible)—the large power would grow weary of the conflict and withdraw.

Even as US interest in counter insurgency waned, it became a major focus of the United Kingdom, which in the 1970s became embroiled in two counter insurgency campaigns. The first was in the Gulf state of Oman while the second was in the UK's constituent country of Northern Ireland. In Oman, a very small contingent of UK troops was able to work with the country's British educated Sultan Qaboos (who had overthrown his reactionary father in a bloodless coup) to defeat an insurgency in the province of Dhofar in a few years. In contrast, the Northern Ireland conflict proved long running, politically divisive, and relatively costly, at one point tying down tens of thousands of British troops.[9]

A major part of the difference in these experiences was the nature of the political order the British were seeking to defend. In Oman, Sultan Qaboos was as close to the ideal type of a canny benevolent despot as one is likely to find. He was willing to reorganize Oman's military and security and also able to make political and economic changes that addressed many of the causes animating the insurgency. This ensured both perception of the Sultan as a legitimate authority (hearts and minds) as well as offering specific costs and benefits (most notably amnesty for those agreeing to leave the insurgency willingly).

In Northern Ireland, the British government had to manage its own domestic politics as well as the politics of Irish unionists (who made up much of the police and political class in Northern Ireland) and republicans. This was vastly more difficult than the relatively straightforward politics of Oman and the Sultan. However, the British would persist in Northern Ireland, gradually squeezing the insurgency down to a relative handful of urban terrorists.

Britain's 1970s experience with counter insurgency highlighted the importance of the relationship between counter insurgent forces, local elites or governments, and the broader population. In the case of Oman, a close alignment between the interests and views of the British government and the sultan allowed for a very effective counter insurgency campaign. In Northern Ireland, there was little alignment between counter insurgents, local elites, and the population. Thus, paradoxically, the United Kingdom was much more effective in fighting insurgency thousands of miles away than it was inside its own borders.

After a lull in the late 1970s, in the 1980s there was a modest resurgence in US academic and policy interest in counter insurgency, driven again by Cold War concerns. The first cause of this renewed focus was insurgency in Central America, particularly in El Salvador. The second was the Soviet intervention in Afghanistan, which prompted the Soviets to develop counter insurgency techniques which the US military and intelligence community in turn examined.

Wary of "another Vietnam" the US commitment to El Salvador in the 1980s mirrored the UK effort in Oman in terms of personnel, as only a relative handful of US advisors were committed. Unlike the UK approach in Oman, the United States was willing to provide substantial military and economic aid to support the Salvadoran government. However, as with the UK in Oman, the United States also sought to convince the Salvadoran government to undertake significant economic and political reforms.[10] Here the two conflicts diverged radically, as the United States had modest, even minimal, success in convincing the government of El Salvador to make reforms despite providing vastly more aid to the government than the British did in Oman. Only late in the war, as the Cold War was ending and US threats to cut aid became more plausible, did the United States start to gain in influence (Schwarz 1991; Ladwig 2016).

This paradox—more aid leading to less rather than more influence or leverage over a client state in counter insurgency—was not entirely new (there were echoes in the US' experience in Vietnam). Yet the El Salvador experience, where the disparity between the US and El Salvador was so enormous (El Salvador is less than 0.25 percent the size of the US), underscored that Mack's insight on asymmetry of interest did not apply only to insurgent and counter insurgent. It applied at least as much to counter insurgents and notional allies when the ally's survival was viewed as crucial to the counter insurgent. As long as the ally believed aid was not conditional, as withdrawal of aid would lead to the collapse of the ally, then leverage was minimal.

Even as the war in El Salvador raged, the Soviet Union was embroiled in a counter insurgency campaign in Afghanistan, where Communist policies and attempts to centralize power had provoked a major insurgency.[11] The Soviets experienced many of the same challenges France, the US, and the UK faced despite having very limited domestic opposition.[12] In particular, the Soviets came to rely heavily on a variety of quasi-state militias to support their beleaguered ally, the People's Democratic Republic of Afghanistan.[13] The West made extensive study of the Soviet campaign, in part because it was supporting the insurgency (as the Soviets were supporting the insurgency in El Salvador) (Grau 1996; Grau and Gress 2002).

The insurgencies in El Salvador and Afghanistan, despite both receiving significant external support, were organized very differently with significant consequences. The conditionality of that external support was crucial to shaping these different insurgencies. There were five major factions opposing the state in El Salvador in the 1970s with differing ideologies and agendas. Following the victory of the leftist Sandinistas in 1979, Cuba and the Soviet Union were able to use the newly friendly Nicaragua as a base to supply. In Afghanistan there were at least half a dozen major insurgent groups by the early 1980s and many smaller groups, which the US was able to support through Pakistan.

In the case of El Salvador, the Cubans were adamant the factions unite as a condition of receiving support. As Andrea Onate notes "the Cuban administration made its position clear: it would provide large-scale aid through armaments, financial backing, and military training if, and only if, the groups agreed to unite and coordinate their efforts" (Onate 2011: 10). While the resulting unity under the auspices of the new Frente Faribundo Marti para la Liberacion Nacional (FMLN), formed in Havana in 1980, was not always perfect, the conditionality of Cuban aid forced the groups to eventually form a strong united organization. In contrast, the US and Pakistan did not impose significant conditions for unity on aid, in part because the Pakistanis did not want to provide aid equally to all groups, favoring some ethnic groups over others. Afghan insurgents thus remained divided and even fratricidal (Coll 2002).

While there were a variety of consequences to this differential aid and unity, including limited efficacy in large military operations for the Afghan insurgents, the most obvious effect was on war termination. The war in El Salvador ended in 1992 with a negotiated peace between the government and the FMLN, the latter being able to prevent significant defection or spoiling of the peace process from within its own ranks.[14] The war in Afghanistan did not end when, following Soviet withdrawal in 1989, the People's Democratic Republic of Afghanistan collapsed in 1992 . Instead, the various insurgent groups, after a brief attempt at a unity government, turned to fighting one another in shifting collections of loose alliances of convenience.[15] Conditionality of aid therefore can have major consequences not just for allied counter insurgents but also for insurgents.

37.3 Civil Wars: Parallel Evolution of Theory

The end of the Cold War brought this renaissance in counter insurgency studies to an end, particularly in terms of policy analysis. However, the perceived increase in civil wars in the 1990s, with war fueled—if not always caused—by the end of the Cold War, led to continued interest in certain aspects of rebellion and political violence that were intellectually akin to insurgency. This produced a growing body of work serving as an intellectual heir to the Cold War-focused study of counter insurgency but with different agendas (and intellectual baggage).

Most notable in this respect was renewed interest in the theoretical roots of political violence inside states, whether termed an insurgency or a civil war. Rather than the terms hearts and minds vs costs and benefits, the civil wars literature framed the debate more pithily: grievance vs greed. Yet the intellectual concepts were acutely similar. "Greed" corresponded to the costs and benefits model, with the principal causes of civil war being economic incentives. "Grievance" corresponded to hearts and minds, with a focus on legitimacy and identity.

In contrast to the early Cold War focus on legitimacy, much of this literature emphasized material factors. One of the most widely cited studies of civil war onset argued that, while grievance was not irrelevant, greed was a more powerful explanation (Collier and Hoeffler 2004). Another equally widely cited study made a parallel argument for thinking of civil war as primarily driven by material conditions favoring insurgency and guerilla warfare—for example weak state capabilities and rough terrain where weak states would have difficulty projecting power (Fearon and Laitin 2003). Grievance was thus perhaps a necessary condition for civil war and insurgency but not a sufficient one.

Other studies of civil war and rebellion found a much stronger role for norms, preferences, and thresholds, echoing the critiques of the costs and benefit model. One study of El Salvador concluded that popular support for the insurgency did not hinge on cost–benefit calculations but rather around considerations of legitimacy and citizenship (Wood 2003). Another found that norms of reciprocity along with low thresholds for action among some of the population were crucial for generating and sustaining rebellion against the Soviet Union in Lithuania after the Second World War (Petersen 2001). In addition to extending debate about the theoretical foundations of insurgency, the civil wars literature also examined the organization of insurgents. This combination began to make sense of previously "senseless" violence by rebel groups (Kalyvas 1999; Weinstein 2006).

37.4 The Return of Counter Insurgency in Iraq and Afghanistan

The attacks of September 11, 2001 indirectly returned counter insurgency to the center of policy and academic analysis. Following those attacks, the US invaded and overthrew the governments of Afghanistan and Iraq, seeking to replace both with democratic regimes. These efforts soon provoked insurgencies in both countries, forcing the US military to confront a challenge it had not seen in decades.

Classic texts of counter insurgency returned to vogue during this period and the US military generated a much discussed new counter insurgency doctrine.[16] This US doctrine was echoed in NATO's "comprehensive approach" (Williams 2011). However, what is most striking about the "new counter insurgency era" is the extent to which it did not engage to any significant degree with either the costs and benefits theory of counter insurgency developed during the late Vietnam period or virtually any of the subsequent civil wars literature.[17]

Instead, the new counter insurgency orthodoxy, in terms of the theory of insurgency, was essentially the original counter insurgency orthodoxy—a return to "hearts and minds." From an intellectual perspective this was a perplexing development, particularly given the significant involvement of academics in the drafting of the new counter insurgency doctrine. What could explain this rather curious development?

The answer appears to be that the new counter insurgents had taken to heart the importance of domestic politics for those conducting counter insurgency abroad. The war in Iraq proved incredibly divisive inside the US and between the US and its allies from the beginning. These divisions were heightened by subsequent events such as the massive operation to seize the Iraqi city of Fallujah and the revelation of abuse at Abu Ghraib prison, both in 2004.

Moreover, unlike the Cold War, there was no clear and compelling strategic rationale to support long-running counter insurgency campaigns in Iraq or Afghanistan. However questionable support to the government of South Vietnam or El Salvador was, at least it was clear they were part of a global contest. The major strategic argument for involvement in Iraq or Afghanistan after the initial invasions was to prevent these states from becoming bases for terrorist attacks on the US. Yet the US had, by the mid-2000s, demonstrated the ability to conduct counter-terrorism campaigns in Yemen, Somalia, Pakistan, and elsewhere without conducting major counter insurgency campaigns. Counter-terrorism might not prove enough to maintain support in the US or with its allies (Long 2010).

If the US and allied publics and political elites were to ensure the support they needed for counter insurgency, it would have to appear normatively positive—bringing democracy and development to these countries. Leaving aside questions of whether this constituted a sort of benevolent imperialism, at least this old/new "hearts and minds" orthodoxy seemed to be kinder and gentler than what had been seen in Fallujah and Abu Ghraib. The involvement of academics, including a prominent role for those focused on human rights, helped give the orthodoxy a further imprimatur.

Ignoring the development of the costs and benefits theory of counter insurgency, along with the civil wars literature emphasizing "greed" and opportunity in driving insurgency, was thus not a simple oversight. It was in all likelihood a fairly deliberate decision for political purposes.[18] While understandable in some ways, this decision created subsequent problems.

First, ignoring developments in counter insurgency theory and the civil wars literature created a gap between the theoretical foundations of "new" counter insurgency and the requirements of operations. The most telling example of this gap was the view espoused in the 2006 US counter insurgency doctrine on the role of extragovernmental militias in counter insurgency. The official doctrine, derived from a theory that modernization and the creation of an effective central state apparatus were the keys to solving grievances, described militias in negative terms—essentially rivals to the state.

However, the Anbar Awakening (and later broader Sunni Awakening) presented US forces with the opportunity to work with such militias against more lethal insurgents. These militias would prove extraordinarily useful in counter insurgency (see overview in Long et al. 2012). Yet making use of these militias, which were often composed of former insurgents or tribal smugglers, required US forces to pragmatically ignore the promulgated doctrine.

This leads to a second problem, which was that the adherence to promulgated doctrine was highly variable and often at odds with reality at the local level in Iraq and Afghanistan. In some cases, adherence to doctrine led to unfortunate concepts such as "government in a box"—the idea that after US and allied military units cleared an area of insurgents then a technocratic local government apparatus, staffed by the host nation, could be immediately brought in. The unreflective modernization view of doctrine in a major military effort in Helmand ran aground on the shoals of shallow theory (Jackson 2014).

In contrast, other military efforts paid little attention to the promulgated doctrine, as in the Anbar Awakening. In other instances, the disconnect between doctrine and reality was as pragmatic as it was problematic. In Uruzgan and Kandahar provinces in Afghanistan the US and its allies relied heavily on strongmen who showed little interest in modernization and technocracy but nonetheless fought hard against the Taliban. Yet these strongmen by their very existence challenged the notion of building a technocratic modern state and their often casual disregard for due process and human rights made efforts to cast counter insurgency in a positive normative light challenging (Aikins 2009, 2011; Reuth 2009; McGeogh 2015).

This "new" counter insurgency doctrine, with its emphasis on modernization and building a strong central state, dominated US policy in Iraq and Afghanistan despite years of failure to achieve decisive results. It would only be in August 2015 that President Barack Obama allegedly stated in a National Security Council meeting "The fever in this room has finally broken. . . . We're no longer in nation-building mode" (Landler 2017). Yet it is far from clear what will replace the "new" counter insurgency.

In parallel, the US remained frustrated by its inability to convince either the Iraqi or Afghan governments to undertake the reforms it believed was necessary to end the insurgencies in those countries. This echoed its experience in El Salvador, as, despite vast aid and commitment of troops, it had insufficient leverage to convince local elites to act against their own perceived interests. Yet, again, having a doctrine built on reform and modernization as a solution, despite historical and contemporary evidence such reform is rare, was a serious flaw. Unfortunately, the only means to gain leverage was to make US support contingent, which meant demonstrating the US was not endlessly committed to Iraq and Afghanistan, as with El Salvador at the end of the Cold War.

But the possibility of terror attacks combined with the need to convince the US public that counter insurgency was really necessary meant the US commitment could not be framed as highly contingent.

37.5 Counter insurgency: The Future

The drawdown of US forces in Afghanistan and Iraq as with the end of the Vietnam War has taken some of the wind from the sails of the study of counter insurgency. However, the problem of counter insurgency is unlikely to recede entirely, at least in an era of global terrorism, leaving dilemmas for Western democracies. The theoretical underpinning of Western counter insurgency doctrine is driven by political necessity but that doctrine is, at its core, trapped in the 1960s, unwilling to embrace much of the insight produced since and with a track record of failure (with the exception of Oman—but benevolent despots are rare indeed). The requirement to mobilize domestic political support in Western democracies makes it all but inevitable that leverage over host nations will be low.

Has counter insurgency strategy thus hit a dead end? It seems likely it has from a Western policy perspective but analysts and academics may have fruitful times ahead of them. In addition to increasing data from Afghanistan and Iraq as declassification proceeds, there are non-Western campaigns that may provide a useful comparative perspective. Most notable is the Russian effort in Chechnya, which has combined the "costs and benefits" and "hearts and minds" approaches to produce a much more stable outcome than Afghanistan or Iraq—but at a high cost.[19]

Notes

1. See Robert Mackey (2004) and Janda (1995).
2. See Gilman (2003); Long (2006); Shafer (1988); and Marquis (2000).
3. Examples of this generation of research include Rostow (1959), Pye (1957), and Huntington (1968).
4. See parallel discussion of incentives in Donnell (1966).
5. On France and the impact of tactics see also Horne (1987); Melnik (1964); Bigeard (1997).
6. See also Gurr (1970).
7. See summary in Long (2016).
8. For a review of the decline in US military interest in counter insurgency see Fitzgerald (2013).
9. On these campaigns see Bell (1993), Petersen (2008); Hughes (2009); and Mockaitis (1995).
10. For an overview of the conflict see Greentree (2008) and Byrne (1996).
11. For an overview see Giustozzi (2000) and Edwards (2002).
12. For Russian senior military veteran perspectives see Gromov (1994) and Lyakhovskiy (1995). For a retrospective look see Braithwaite (2011).

13. See Long et al. (2012: ch. 8) for an overview.
14. On in the importance of spoiling see, inter alia, Greenhill and Major (2007).
15. On this period see, inter alia, Christia (2012).
16. On this period see, inter alia, Ucko (2009); and Long (2016). For a more critical perspective see Gventer et al. (2014) and Gentile (2013).
17. Many of these observations echo those of Kalyvas (2008).
18. See related discussion in Smith and Jones (2015).
19. See for example Šmíd and Mareš (2015).

References

Aikins, Matthieu. 2009. The Master of Spin Boldak. *Harper's Magazine*, December.

Aikins, Matthieu. 2011. Our Man in Kandahar. *The Atlantic*, November.

Andrew, Christopher. 2009. *Defend the Realm: The Authorized History of MI5*. New York: Alfred A. Knopf).

Bayly, C. A. 2011. *Empire and Information: Intelligence Gathering and Social Communication in India, 1780–1870*. Cambridge: Cambridge University Press.

Bell, J. Bowyer. 1993. *The Irish Troubles: A Generation of Violence, 1967–1992*. New York: St. Martin's Press.

Bigeard, Marcel-Maurice. 1997. *Pour Une Parcelle de Gloire*. Paris: Edition 01.

Braithwaite, Roderic. 2011. *Afgantsy: The Russians in Afghanistan, 1979–89*. London: Profile Books.

Brodie, Bernard. 1955. Strategy Hits a Dead End. *Harper's Magazine*: October.

Byrne, Hugh. 1996. *El Salvador's Civil War: A Study of Revolution*. Boulder, CO: Lynne Rienner Publishers.

Christia, Fotini. 2012. *Alliance Formation in Civil Wars*. Cambridge: Cambridge University Press.

Coll, Steve. 2002. *Ghost Wars*. New York: Penguin.

Collier, Paul and Anke Hoeffler. 2004. Greed and Grievance in Civil War. *Oxford Economic Papers*, 56(4): 563–95.

Donnell, John. 1966. *Viet Cong Recruitment: How and Why Men Join*. Santa Monica, CA: RAND.

Edwards, David. 2002. *Before Taliban: Genealogies of the Afghan Jihad*. Berkeley, CA: University of California Press.

Ellsberg, Daniel. 1970. *Revolutionary Judo: Working Notes on Vietnam*. Santa Monica, CA: RAND.

Fearon, James and David Laitin. 2003. Ethnicity, Insurgency, and Civil War. *American Political Science Review*, 97(1): 75–90.

Fitzgerald, David. 2013. *Learning to Forget: US Army Counterinsurgency Doctrine and Practice from Vietnam to Iraq*. Stanford, CA: Stanford University Press.

Gentile, Gian. 2013. *Wrong Turn: America's Deadly Embrace of Counterinsurgency*. New York: New Press.

Gilman, Nils. 2003. *Mandarins of the Future: Modernization Theory in Cold War America*. Baltimore, MD: Johns Hopkins University Press.

Giustozzi, Antonio. 2000. *War, Politics, and Society in Afghanistan 1978–1992*. Washington, DC: Georgetown University Press.

Grau, Lester. 1996. *The Bear Went Over the Mountain: Soviet Combat Tactics In Afghanistan.* Washington, DC: National Defense University Press.

Grau, Lester and Michael Gress. 2002. *The Soviet War: How A Superpower Fought and Lost.* Lawrence, KS: University of Kansas Press.

Greenhill, Kelly and Solomon Major. 2007. The Perils of Profiling: Civil War Spoilers and the Collapse of Intrastate Peace Accords. *International Security*, 31(3).

Greentree, Todd. 2008. *Crossroads of Intervention: Insurgency and Counterinsurgency Lessons from Central America.* Boulder, CO: Praeger.

Gromov, Boris. 1994. *Ogranichennyi Kontingent [Limited Contingent]*. Moscow: Progress.

Gurr, Ted. 1970. *Why Men Rebel.* Princeton, NJ: Princeton University Press.

Gventer, Celeste Ward, M. L. R Smith, and D. Jones (eds.). 2014. *The New Counter-insurgency Era in Critical Perspective.* London: Palgrave Macmillan.

Horne, Alistair. 1987. *A Savage War of Peace: Algeria, 1954–1962.* New York: Penguin Books.

Howard, Michael. 1961. *The Franco-Prussian War: The German Invasion of France, 1870–1871.* London: Rupert Hart-Davis.

Hughes, Geraint. 2009. A "Model Campaign" Reappraised: The Counter-Insurgency War in Dhofar, Oman, 1965–1975. *Journal of Strategic Studies*, 32(2).

Huntington, Samuel. 1968. *Political Order in Changing Societies.* New Haven, CT: Yale University Press.

Jackson, Colin. 2014. Government in a Box? Counter-Insurgency, State Building, and the Technocratic Conceit. In Celeste Ward Gventer, M. L. R Smith, and D. Jones (eds.), *The New Counter-insurgency Era in Critical Perspective.* London: Palgrave Macmillan.

Janda, Lance. 1995. Shutting the Gates of Mercy: The American Origins of Total War, 1860–1880. *Journal of Military History*, 59(1).

Kalyvas, Stathis. 1999. Wanton and Senseless? The Logic of Massacres in Algeria. *Rationality and Society*, 11(3): 243–85.

Kalyvas, Stathis. 2008. Review Symposium: The New U.S. Army/Marine Corps Counterinsurgency Field Manual as Political Science and Political Praxis. *Perspectives on Politics*, 6(2).

Karnow, Stanley. 1983. *Vietnam: A History.* New York: Viking Press.

Ladwig, Walter. 2016. Influencing Clients in Counterinsurgency: U.S. Involvement in El Salvador's Civil War, 1979–92. *International Security*, 41(1): 99–146.

Landler, Mark. 2017. The Afghan War and the Evolution of Obama. *New York Times*, January 1.

Leites, Nathan and Charles Wolf. 1970. *Rebellion and Authority: An Analytic Essay on Insurgent Conflicts.* Santa Monica, CA: RAND.

Long, Austin. 2006. *On "Other War": Lessons from Five Decades of RAND Counterinsurgency Research.* Santa Monica, CA: RAND.

Long, Austin. 2010. Small is Beautiful: The Counterterrorism Option in Afghanistan. *Orbis*, 54(2): 199–214.

Long, Austin. 2016. *The Soul of Armies: Counterinsurgency Doctrine and Military Culture in the U.S. and U.K.* Ithaca, NY: Cornell University Press.

Long, Austin, et al. 2012. *Locals Rule: Historical Lessons for Creating Local Defense Forces for Afghanistan and Beyond.* Santa Monica, CA: RAND.

Lyakhovskiy, Aleksandr. 1995. *Tragediya I Doblest' Afgana [Afghan Tragedy and Valor].* Moscow: Iskona.

McGeogh, Paul. 2015. Death of New Age Warlord Matiullah Khan Leaves Oruzgan at Edge of Abyss. *Sydney Morning Herald*, March 20.

Mack, Andrew. 1975. Why Big Nations Lose Small Wars: The Politics of Asymmetric Conflict. *World Politics*, 27(2): 175–200.

Mackey, Robert. 2004. *The Uncivil War: Irregular Warfare in the Upper South, 1861–1865*. Norman: University of Oklahoma Press.

Marquis, Jefferson. 2000. The Other Warriors: American Social Science and Nation Building in Vietnam. *Diplomatic History*, 24(1).

Melnik, Constantin. 1964. *Insurgency and Counterinsurgency in Algeria*. Santa Monica, CA: RAND.

Merom, Gil. 2003. *How Democracies Lose Small Wars: State, Society, and the Failures of France in Algeria, Israel in Lebanon, and the United States in Vietnam*. Cambridge: Cambridge University Press.

Mockaitis, Thomas. 1995. *British Counterinsurgency in the Post-Imperial Era*. New York: Manchester University Press.

Onate, Andrea. 2011. The Red Affair: FMLN–Cuban Relations During the Salvadoran Civil War, 1981–92. *Cold War History*, 11(2): 10.

Petersen, J. E. 2008. *Oman's Insurgencies: The Sultanate's Struggle for Supremacy*. London: Saqi Books.

Petersen, Roger. 2001. *Resistance and Rebellion: Lessons from Eastern Europe*. Cambridge: Cambridge University Press.

Pye, Lucian. 1957. *Lessons from the Malayan Struggle against Communism*. Cambridge, MA: Center for International Studies.

Popkin, Samuel. 1970, Pacification: Politics and the Village. *Asian Survey*, 10(8): 662–71.

Popkin, Samuel. 1979. *The Rational Peasant: The Political Economy of Rural Society in Vietnam*. Berkeley, CA: University of California Press.

Porch, Douglas. 2003. *The French Secret Services: From the Dreyfus Affair to the Gulf War*. New York: Farrar, Strauss, and Giroux.

Reuth, Christoph. 2009. The Warlord of the Highway. *Vice*, November.

Rid, Thomas. 2010. The Nineteenth Century Origins of Counterinsurgency Doctrine. *Journal of Strategic Studies*, 33(5): 727–58.

Rostow, Walt. 1959. *Economic Growth: A Non-Communist Manifesto*. Cambridge, MA: Center for International Studies.

Schwarz, Benjamin. 1991. *American Counterinsurgency Doctrine and El Salvador: Frustrations of Reform and the Illusions of Nation Building*. Santa Monica, CA: RAND.

Scott, James. 1976. *The Moral Economy of the Peasant: Rebellion and Subsistence in Southeast Asia*. New Haven, CT: Yale University Press.

Shafer, D. Michael. 1988. *Deadly Paradigms: The Failure of U.S. Counterinsurgency Policy*. Princeton, NJ: Princeton University Press.

Singer, Barnett and John Langdon. 2008. *Cultured Force: Makers and Defenders of the French Colonial Empire*. Madison, WI: University of Wisconsin Press.

Šmíd, Tomáš and Miroslav Mareš. 2015. Kadyrovtsy': Russia's Counterinsurgency Strategy and the Wars of Paramilitary Clans. *Journal of Strategic Studies*, 38(5).

Smith, M. L. R. and David Martin Jones. 2015. *The Political Impossibility of Modern Counterinsurgency: Strategic Problems, Puzzles, and Paradoxes*. New York: Columbia University Press.

Thomas, Martin. 2007. *Empires of Intelligence: Security Services and Colonial Disorder After 1914*. Berkeley, CA: University of California Press.

Ucko, David. 2009. *The New Counterinsurgency Era: Transforming the U.S. Military for Modern Wars*. Washington DC: Georgetown University Press.

Weinstein, Jeremy. 2006. *Inside Rebellion: The Politics of Insurgent Violence*. Cambridge: Cambridge University Press.

Williams, M. J. 2011. Empire Lite Revisited: NATO, the Comprehensive Approach and State-building in Afghanistan. *International Peacekeeping*, 18(1): 64–78.

Wohlstetter, Albert. 1968. *Comments on the Wolf-Leites Manuscript: 'Rebellion and Authority*. Santa Monica, CA: RAND.

Wolf, Charles. 1965. *Insurgency and Counterinsurgency: New Myths and Old Realities*. Santa Monica, CA: RAND.

Wood, Elisabeth Jean. 2003. *Insurgent Collective Action and Civil War in El Salvador*. Cambridge: Cambridge University Press.

CHAPTER 38

INTERNATIONAL SECURITY AND DEVELOPMENT

NECLA TSCHIRGI

38.1 Introduction

Drawing upon the rich body of theory, policy, and practice since the end of the Cold War, this chapter examines two interrelated questions: How do challenges in the development arena contribute to global insecurity today? What types of research, policies, and strategies can best contribute to alleviating, mitigating, and preventing these threats? The chapter argues that after a lengthy period during the Cold War when development and security theories, institutions, and policies were artificially separated, these twin agendas gradually started to come closer in the 1990s under a new era of liberal internationalism. However, the re-emergence of hard security concerns threatening the Westphalian international order after 9/11 seriously affected efforts toward greater alignment between the development and security agendas. With the Global War on Terror (GWOT) and the military interventions in Afghanistan and Iraq, governments reverted to traditional political and military instruments while development actors were increasingly called upon to address the pressing humanitarian consequences of new security threats as part of their development programming. With the ongoing civil wars in the Middle East after the Arab Spring and the rise of ISIS, the recent Countering Violent Extremism (CVE) agenda is heavily driven by hard security concerns—leading to further divergence between security and development. This is unfortunate since many of the challenges that currently confront the international system have their roots in the development arena and require concerted efforts by development and security analysts and actors.

The chapter is organized as follows: Section 38.2 provides a quick overview of the growing recognition of the interplay between security and development in the aftermath of the Cold War by researchers and policy-makers and draws out key insights that were gained on the so-called security–development nexus. Section 38.3 reviews the responses to the re-emergence of hard security threats following 9/11 and the unraveling of the regional order in the Middle East after the occupation of Iraq. Section 38.4 analyzes key developmental drivers of contemporary threats to international security. Finally, Section 38.5 offers some concluding thoughts as to why current fragmented approaches to international security and development are inadequate to address some of the key challenges that lie ahead and what might be done about them.

38.2 The Security–Development Nexus after the End of the Cold War

Recognition of the interplay between security and development is not particularly novel. Socio-economic factors have always been considered an important dimension of national power and international security. Conversely, the impact of war and conflict on socio-economic progress has been recognized long before the recent aphorism of conflict as "development in reverse" (Collier 2003). Indeed, starting with the Truman Doctrine and the Marshall Plan, the entire infrastructure of international development as we know it today has its origins during the Cold War when the two superpowers exported their economic models and sought to win friends among the newly-emerging states through foreign aid. Yet, what distinguished the Cold War era was its singular focus on avoiding war between the two nuclear superpowers and their allies. Security was thus pursued primarily through increased military power and a web of alliances. Other lower-level security threats (including underdevelopment, anti-colonial wars, intra-state conflicts, and insurgencies) were important to the extent they affected the precarious balance of power between the two rival blocs.

Thus, throughout the Cold War there was a marked divide between security studies, institutions, and policies, on the one hand, and development studies, institutions, and policies, on the other. The former focused on interstate wars and threats to the bipolar international order while the latter focused on the macro-economic development of the so-called Third World countries. The lion's share of foreign aid went to prop up friendly governments and client states and to strengthen their military and security institutions rather than to address deep-rooted developmental problems. With the end of the Cold War, protracted local conflicts, intra-state wars, and complex political emergencies in developing countries were catapulted to the international stage, although the major powers did not consider these as direct threats to their vital interests. Thus, there was an unusual opportunity to re-think the concept of security and examine ways of addressing new types of threats with deep developmental roots.

The security studies literature of the 1990s reflects both a deepening and widening of the concept of security, and growing contestation of the state-centric, post-Westphalian security paradigm (Buzan and Hansen 2007). Given the changing international context, traditional security institutions assumed new roles as reflected in the rapid expansion of UN peacekeeping and NATO's engagement in the Balkans. Development actors, who until the end of the Cold War worked "*in*" or "*around*" conflict, finally started working "*on*" conflict—an area that was considered the domain of political and security actors (Goodhand 2006). This allowed many non-state actors (including the growing number of international nongovernmental organizations (NGOs)) to work on the complex socio-economic-political drivers of conflict as well as on issues of conflict resolution, peacemaking, and peacebuilding—tasks that had hitherto been considered outside their mandate (Tschirgi 2004; Goodhand 2006).

It is in this context that the concepts of peacebuilding and the security–development nexus emerged and led to a growing industry of academic literature as well as myriad innovations aiming to bridge the chasm between the security and development institutions, policies, and practices that had taken shape during the Cold War. Largely informed by a "human security" lens and focusing primarily on addressing the twin challenges of security and development in conflict-affected countries, the new interest in the security–development nexus generated increased understanding of the range of developmental factors that contribute to the onset, duration, and ending of violent conflicts. There was exciting new research on the links between conflict and poverty, horizontal inequality, displacement, poor governance, environmental and demographic pressures, the resource curse, and other socio-economic factors. Recognizing the developmental dimensions of these new security challenges, policy-makers and practitioners responded with new peacebuilding programs such as rule of law, security sector reform, and disarmament, demobilization, reintegration which would have been unthinkable only a few decades earlier. The UN Security Council was called upon to play an active role in peacemaking, peacekeeping, and peacebuilding after having been in paralysis for much of the Cold War. There was growing convergence at the intersection of an expanded development and peace and security agenda as reflected in successive UN reports, *An Agenda for Peace, An Agenda for Development*, and *An Agenda for Democratization* (United Nations 1992, 1994, 1997).

Throughout the 1990s the main question that motivated research, policy, and practice was how to avert the outbreak or recurrence of low-level security threats in developing countries through structural prevention by addressing long-standing problems in the development domain (Carnegie Commission 1997). The new conflict and peacebuilding agendas at the United Nations, the OECD Development Assistance Committee (DAC) and the bilateral and multilateral donor agencies involved a serious examination of development policies and strategies through a conflict lens—leading to new insights and tools such as Do No Harm, conflict sensitivity, peacebuilding, and Peace and Conflict Impact Assessment (Anderson 1999; OECD DAC 2001).

The conceptual, policy, and practical innovations of the 1990s were part of liberal internationalism of the post-Cold War era and seemed to herald paradigmatic changes on the part of key international actors. Security was no longer conceived primarily in military and state-centric terms while the developmental challenges of developing countries became an international concern. Yet, many of these efforts were in fact mostly at the level of policy pronouncements and aspirational commitments. There were hardly any fundamental reforms in either the development or security domains. A closer look at international priorities, resource allocations, and institutional reforms of the 1990s confirm that the security–development nexus was more rhetorical than real (Tschirgi et al. 2010; Amer et al. 2012). In retrospect, it is evident that there were serious obstacles to greater synergy between development and security after decades of disconnect. The two fields had differing guiding paradigms, institutional cultures, policy priorities, and instruments as well as vastly different time frames for anticipated results. It would have required an extension of the favorable international environment to bring about fundamental shifts in both fields to better align them conceptually and operationally. This was not to be.

38.3 The Paradox of 9/11: Securing or Securitizing Development

The terrorist attacks of 9/11 had a direct and profound impact on the burgeoning concept and practice of the security–development nexus (Dannreuther 2007; Baranyi 2008; Hintjens and Zarkov 2015). 9/11 elevated problems originating in zones of conflict, especially through terrorism and state failure, to the level of direct threats to international security (Tschirgi 2013). The United States and its key allies declared terrorism an existential threat requiring military action—opening the door to the US-led Global War on Terror, the US interventions in Afghanistan and Iraq, as well as the doctrines of counter insurgency and counter-terrorism. The forceful military responses to 9/11 transformed the international security context—ushering in a new era of foreign wars by the United States and its key allies. They also reshaped the discourse on the security-development nexus.

Initially, there were high hopes for a "great bargain" after 9/11 whereby the international community would prioritize both development and security as twin goals requiring strategic attention, collective action, pooled resources and sustained collaboration by all relevant actors. As was the case after the the Second World War and the Cold War, at the United Nations and various international fora the links between deep-rooted development problems and international peace and security were affirmed and calls for integrated strategies reiterated (United Nations 2004; Annan 2005). Even as they fought open wars in Afghanistan and Iraq, many Western governments committed to greater collaboration between their departments of diplomacy, development, and defense (the "3Ds") to synchronize their efforts for "whole-of-government" approaches (OECD 2007; Patrick and Brown 2007). However, the real consequence of 9/11 was not to deepen the links between security and development but to "securitize" development by subordinating it to a militarized security agenda (Baranyi 2008; Newman 2010; Tschirgi 2013). The conflict prevention and peacebuilding agendas of the 1990s had been motivated by the need to address deep-rooted development problems to bring greater stability and security in conflict-affected countries and to avoid their regional and international spill-overs. After 9/11 the security–development nexus was co-opted and re-conceptualized as the cornerstone of a new stabilization and state-building strategy as a new hard security agenda took shape (Baranyi 2008; Tschirgi 2013).

State failure was already on the international agenda in the 1990s with the break-down of political order in various Balkan and African countries. However, it gained prominence after 9/11 with al-Qaeda's success in flourishing in "ungoverned" spaces in Somalia, Sudan, and Afghanistan. The 2002 US National Security Strategy set the tone when it declared that "America is now threatened less by conquering states than we are by failing ones" (United States 2002). In the following years, other countries and institutions followed suit in identifying state failure, and its antidote state-building, as key challenges due to increased security threats—especially terrorism—resulting from state fragility (United Kingdom, 2008; United States 2008).

Thus, state-building emerged as a central priority at the nexus of security and development. Yet, there was no consensus on what state-building required. Instead, security and development actors approached the new state-building agenda from different perspectives and with different agendas. Recognizing that effective statehood required legitimacy as well as the capacity to govern, development actors took a longer-term approach rooted in the concept of sustainable peace (OECD 2005; OECD DAC 1997, 2001; World Bank 2009, 2011; UNDP 2012). Meanwhile, defense departments and national security agencies tended to view conflict and state fragility primarily as a security issue—approaching state-building instrumentally from a stabilization perspective. They focused largely on a state's capacity to maintain security, ignoring the fact that many instances of state failure witnessed in the 1990s were in fact the result of the security-oriented strategies promoted by external actors during the Cold War. The new stabilization and security agenda was less concerned with the domestic foundations of good governance than with governments' ability to crack down on terrorism and transnational security threats. In many instances development and security actors found themselves working at cross-purposes. As the OECD (2007) noted regarding the *Principles of Good International Engagement in Fragile States & Situations* that had been adopted by donor governments:

> The challenge for governments involved in fragile states is to establish clarity on and coherence in objectives. These objectives are likely to differ among the departments involved. ... Therefore, ministries may promote national interests rather than the interests of a partner country, which, from the perspective of development cooperation, is problematic. When dealing with the problems of precarious statehood— and in particular the wide range of potential threats emanating from them—the issue therefore is how governments determine their priorities for engagement in fragile states. From the perspective of the OECD-DAC, the question more specifically is where development outcomes should rank *vis-à-vis* trade, counter-terrorism, national defence and other political objectives of donor countries. (OECD 2007: 17)

Despite competing agendas, interest in the security–development nexus flourished in the decade after 9/11—leading to a small industry of books, policy statements, reports, and documents. There was, however, little agreement on how to bring them together (Duffield 2001; Stern and Öjendal 2010; Tschirgi et al. 2010; Mavrotas 2011). As Spear and Williams (2012: 21) masterfully summarize—reproduced here in Table 38.1—there are at least eight different ways in which the security–development relationship has been conceptualized.

Different analysts and actors have taken entirely different approaches to explaining, as well as responding to, the interplay between security and development, depending upon their analytical perspectives, political agendas, institutional mandates, and the level at which they work (Stern and Öjendal 2010; Spear and Williams 2012). Irrespective of their differences, there is broad agreement that, unlike the dangerous clarity of the Cold War or the heady optimism of the post-Cold War years, the second decade of the twenty-first century is witnessing a shrinking world in constant turmoil; what happens in any part of the world has almost instant repercussions globally. In such a context, the interplay

Table 38.1 Conceptualizing the security–development relationship

Zero-sum	Security and development are framed in either–or terms where allocating resources to one detracts from the potential to achieve the other; e.g. the guns-versus-butter debate.
Positive-sum	Security and development are understood as mutually reinforcing; the provision of one increases the likelihood of achieving the other.
Distinct	Security and development are both viewed as important goals but are understood as distinct enterprises best pursued using different methods.
Synonymous	Security and development are basically about the same thing: ensuring that the referent object can pursue its cherished values effectively.
Sequential	Security and development are conceived as preconditions for the other; e.g. development can only progress in a secure environment, or genuine national security requires a certain level of economic development.
Hierarchical	Security priorities are said to structure the choice of development projects undertaken. For some, this has produced a situation where the development industry has become a project to support the peace and stability of the North.
Selectively co-constitutive	Security and development are interconnected but in complex and not necessarily similar ways; e.g., only in certain contexts or with respect to particular issues.
Sui generis	Security and development issues are always entirely context dependent; hence, it is impossible to draw meaningful conceptual generalizations across different times and places.

Note: Table reproduced with permission from Joanna Spear and Paul D. Williams (eds.), *Security and Development in Global Politics: A Critical Comparison*. Washington, DC: Georgetown University Press 2012, p. 21.

between security and development becomes even more complex. The two agendas do not necessarily operate in synch—requiring continuous investigation of their interplay at the domestic as well as the international level and crafting contextualized responses.

38.4 The Security–Development Nexus in a Turbulent World

There is increasing recognition that the contemporary scourge of terrorism and violent extremism flourish in conditions of socio-economic deprivation and political exclusion (United Nations 2006, 2015c). Similarly, analysts recognize that the Arab Spring and the ongoing civil wars in Syria, Libya, and Yemen have been fueled by long-standing failures of development in these countries (Al-Sumait et al. 2015; Sadiki, 2015). Meanwhile, the UN's Sustainable Development Goals (SDGs) have explicitly made the case for the interplay between developmental factors and security (United Nations 2015b). In other words, there is strong evidence that neither approaching security and development as separate areas of concern nor securitizing development has yielded positive results. The challenge is in viewing developmental risks through a long-term, security and conflict-prevention lens. That requires taking development seriously and committing the necessary tools and resources to addressing structural development problems before they become imminent security threats.

Based on a review of the extensive body of literature generated since the end of the Cold War, Section 38.4.1 aims to illustrate what we have learned about how developmental factors affect international security. Development is an all-encompassing concept, evolving from its early equation with macro-economic growth to its expanded definition embracing economic, social, political, and environmental dimensions of well-being. As a result, the discussion in Section 38.4.1 is highly selective—focusing on several long-term development trends that are steadily converging to threaten international security.

38.4.1 A Perfect Storm: Convergence of Demography, Poverty, Inequality, and Environmental Degradation

In the words of former UN Secretary General Kofi Annan, poverty, inequality, demographic, and environmental pressures are "problems without passports" (Annan 2009). They are not only transnational in nature; they take place in a context of heightened globalization whereby their scope and impacts are greatly magnified. The security implications of each of these development problems have been investigated extensively by experts. While these problems do not necessarily cause direct or immediate security threats, they do pose particular risk factors which, combined with other factors, can help to create a perfect storm. For example, several demographic trends that have been developing over time (namely, the divergent age structure of populations in developing and industrialized countries; the youth bulge in developing countries; the mass movement of populations through urbanization, migration, and refugee flows) seem to have reached a dangerous point today. The statistics are telling.

It is projected that the global population of 7.3 billion in 2015 will continue to grow—reaching 9.7 billion people by 2050 (United Nations 2015a). The growth will be concentrated in only a few regions and countries—many of which are not only among the world's lowest income countries, but are also in regions of conflict in Africa and the Islamic world (Goldstone 2012). Meanwhile, population growth will be slow, or negative, in many industrialized countries. It is projected that by 2050, the population of the developed countries will stagnate while the population of the rest of the world will grow by 50 percent—from 5.3 billion people in 2005 to 8 billion in 2050 (Goldstone 2012). Perhaps the most pressing issue is the so-called youth bulge. In countries where the proportion of the population aged 15 or younger ranges from 30 to 40 percent, the pressure for education, health, basic services, and jobs will increase in the coming decades—creating heavy burdens on governments. Concurrent with the population increase and the youth bulge, massive migration from the countryside to cities is expected to continue. For less-developed regions, the urban population is projected to increase from 42.7 percent in 2005 to 67 percent by 2050 (Goldstone 2012; United Nations 2015a), leading to competition for scarce resources in urban settings. Equally importantly, migration and refugee flows from developing to developed countries are expected to accelerate due to civil wars, domestic conflicts, natural disasters, and economic pressures.

These demographic trends and the growing population discrepancies across the North–South axis are sufficiently alarming. Yet, they are also accompanied by an equally dramatic change in global incomes. It is expected that the share of income going to developed countries with the richest billion people in the world is likely to fall from roughly 60 percent in 2005 to less than 30 percent by 2050 (Goldstone 2012). This, however, does not mean that the great divide in wealth between the global North and the South—the haves and the have-nots—will disappear. On the contrary, as the 2017 Oxfam briefing paper, *An Economy for the 99%*, argues, "the global inequality crisis continues unabated." According to Oxfam (2017), eight men now own the same amount of wealth as the poorest half of the world. In 2010, that number was 388 individuals. "Since 2015, the richest 1% has owned more wealth than the rest of the planet," the report finds and "the incomes of the poorest 10% of people increased by less than $3 a year between 1988 and 2011, while the incomes of the richest 1% increased 182 times as much." Strikingly, "Since 2015, the richest 1% has owned more wealth than the rest of the planet."

The consequences of global inequality are manifold—undermining growth, perpetuating poverty, fragility, and conflict. Researchers have shown that a country's rate of growth is inversely correlated with the risk of conflict (Collier 2001, 2008; Fukuda-Parr 2010). It is estimated that the risk of war is three times greater for a country with a per capita income of $1,000 than for a country with a per capita income of $4,000 (Humphreys 2003; Fukuda-Parr 2010). The countries at the bottom of the Human Development Index are also the countries that face state fragility or conflict (World

Bank 2011). Nonetheless, researchers do not posit a direct causal link between poverty and international insecurity. Instead, the links are intermediated through such factors as horizontal inequalities, poor governance, urban pressures, heightened competition for scarce resources, high unemployment, globalization, technological connectivity, greater access by young men to criminal and terrorist networks, conflict, and state failure. During most of the Cold War "mainstream security studies relegated poverty to the category of low politics" (Williams 2012: 193). This is no longer the case as the complex interplay between poverty, inequality, population growth, urbanization, and globalization have become increasingly more evident. In a rapidly globalizing and interdependent world, the persistence of an unequal world order that fails to address interlocking global problems is a contributing factor to insecurity and conflict. These problems have been exacerbated by environmental degradation which has emerged as a multi-faceted threat (Dannreuther 2007; Matthew 2010).

Until the end of the Cold War, "the notion of the environment as a significant source of insecurity was not on the radar screen" (Dannreuther 2007). This has changed radically even though researchers and analysts continue to differ on the nature and dynamics of the interplay between the environment and security. Some scholars refer to an "environmental crisis" whereby unrestrained human activity, intensified by a growing population, is destroying the carrying capacity of the earth. They foresee heightened competition over natural resources with grave consequences for security. There is a rich body of literature on the links between natural resources and civil conflict—variably explained in terms of resource scarcity or the resource curse. Others point to climate change as a growing threat in light of mounting evidence of its adverse impacts on the world economy, affecting economic growth in both the industrial and developing countries. Climate change is also expected to lead to extreme weather conditions and a significant loss of productive agricultural lands—fueling poverty as well as mass migration (United Nations 2016). As with other developmental factors, environmental problems have a direct impact on the poor and the vulnerable; they also have a North–South equity dimension which adds to their complexity. It is generally accepted that the relationship between security and the environment is indirect and multi-directional. Researchers have identified various feedback loops through which environmental factors generate conflicts and security threats and vice versa (Homer-Dixon 1999; Dannreuter 2007; Matthew 2010). It is, however, quite evident that mounting environmental problems can no longer be ignored as a security issue—especially when coupled with changing demographic and economic factors.

38.4.2 The Challenges of Governance in an Insecure World

The interlocking dynamics between the long-term trends identified in Section 8.4.1 demonstrate the gravity of the potential threats they pose to human security, political stability, state failure and, indirectly, to international security. None of these problems lend themselves to quick and easy solutions. Moreover, although anchored in concrete contexts, they traverse the globe. From a prevention perspective, the challenge is how best to manage their progression and mitigate their negative impacts through more effective governance in a world where nation states and fragmented approaches still dominate. Indeed, this is where security studies and developmental studies have a common agenda: greater understanding of the challenges of governance both at the domestic and international levels.

Development studies has—albeit belatedly—recognized the importance of good governance as an essential element of socio-economic development. Security studies, on the other hand, has traditionally taken a narrow view of the institutional underpinnings of security—focusing primarily on the security institutions of the state. With development trends posing long-term security challenges, there is need for a conceptualization of governance beyond the security oriented state-building model discussed in this chapter.

At the domestic level, governance is not about stronger states but about how power is exercised to manage public affairs; it is increasingly understood in terms of state–society relations based on legitimate and accountable institutions, norms, and processes within an inclusive political framework. State-centric security approaches that are not based on a social contract between the government and its citizenry are unlikely to provide either development or security—as repeatedly demonstrated in weak, fragile, and failing states. Good governance (variably defined as democratic participation, inclusive politics, or state legitimacy) has to do with more than building state institutions and capacities. It is correlated with citizens' perceptions of their ability to shape the decisions that affect their lives (World Bank 2011; UNDP 2012). In that light, governance deficits are not exclusively confined to fragile or conflict-affected states. There is a serious crisis of governance in many countries around the world. Economic and financial crises, terrorism, unrestrained migration, and the negative impacts of globalization are creating deep distrust in politics and established governance systems with serious implications for their ability to ensure security. Perhaps one of the most telling examples of the crisis of governance was the discordant responses of European governments to the 2015 Syrian refugee crisis and the rise of populist, right-wing political movements contesting official policies.

At the international level, the governance challenges are of a different order. There is growing recognition that there have been fundamental changes in the world system without corresponding changes in global governance. From the bipolar world of the Cold War, to the unipolar world of the 1990s, we are living in an era of tectonic shifts in economic and political power. As has been noted: "We have not any time since 1800 seen a world in which the majority of economic growth occurs outside of the United States and Europe, in which any countries had sixty-year-olds constitute 30–40% of their populations, and in which large countries at relatively modest levels of income per capita reached urbanization levels of 60%. Yet that is the world of the next half century" (Goldstone 2012: 288–9). The impacts of these trends are compounded by traditional as well as non-traditional security threats including violent extremism, terrorism, cybersecurity, and organized crime. Largely created in the aftermath of the Second World War, current global institutions are unable to deal with the number and complexity of these challenges. Equally importantly, they do not represent the important shifts of power in the international system ranging from the rise of China and India to the growing role of non-state actors. Clearly, there is a pressing need for more representative and effective institutions of governance at the international level that can deal with global problems. Yet, paradoxically, even as the need for global governance grows, there is public suspicion and lack of faith in multilateralism and the post-Second World War international architecture as prominently reflected in the election of Donald Trump as US President in November 2016. From both a security and development perspective, addressing the deficits of governance emerges as a high priority.

38.5 Implications and Possible Directions

What are the implications of the preceding analysis for future research and policy? It is clear that security studies and development studies cannot continue on separate tracks as they have done for much of the last 60 years. This chapter has shied away from claiming any automatic causal connection between development and international security. Indeed, both fields need to continue deepening their understanding of development and security as distinct issue areas. Nonetheless, there is also need for multi-disciplinary research focusing on issues at the intersection of international security and development. There is already a rich body of literature on specific aspects of the nexus—poverty and civil conflict, urbanization and criminal violence, terrorism and marginalization, climate change and environmental migration. What is missing is a concerted and long-term research agenda that brings researchers from both fields to apply the qualitative and quantitative tools of their disciplines to map out and investigate the complex interplay of development and security challenges that face us in the twenty-first century. Such a research program requires a prevention mindset which goes beyond the "clear and present danger" perspective of many security analysts without securitizing development. The development challenges described above are long-term threats; nonetheless, in combination they can cause a "perfect storm." We need to understand the conditions that can create such a perfect storm using both development and security frameworks and tools while exploring new governance mechanisms to manage local, national, and global challenges.

Yet, focusing only on structural factors or material conditions will not suffice. Guided by insights from traditional security studies, threat perceptions by both policy-makers and publics in a world in turmoil should be part of any research at the nexus of security and development. Public perceptions of loss of national sovereignty, community, or identity should be taken into account alongside deteriorating socio-economic conditions or hard security threats. Rise of right-wing leaders and populist resistance to immigration and refugee flows as security threats in the US and Europe demonstrates the challenges policy-makers face in reconciling domestic pressures with the need for multilateral action in a dangerous world. Thus, multi-disciplinary research needs to include disciplines that can bring an understanding of both the objective conditions and subjective perceptions of insecurity in a shrinking world.

Turning to policy implications, as the preceding analysis demonstrates, threats emanating from the development arena are not sectoral in nature and do not lend themselves to fragmented solutions. They are products of long-term historical and socio-economic trends, exacerbated by far-reaching changes in the international system due to globalization, technological advances, the end of the Cold War, and the rise of transnational threats like global terrorism. Thus, policy responses should be informed by historically grounded and contextually specific analysis. While useful, simply adding band-aid solutions like security sector reform to the development toolbox is not enough. Similarly, strategies of containment or stabilization promoted by security actors are not viable over the long-haul. Meanwhile, including Goal 16 to "promote peaceful and inclusive societies for sustainable development, provide access to justice for all and build effective, accountable and inclusive institutions at all levels" as part of the Sustainable Development Goals is far from adequate (United Nations 2015c). Going beyond Goal 16, there is need for a fundamental re-thinking of all the sustainable development goals from a peace and security perspective.

However, a more coherent or comprehensive policy framework is not sufficient without corresponding resources. According to the US Department of State (United States 2015) which tracks military expenditures and arms transfers globally: "From 2002 through 2012, in constant 2012 U.S. dollar terms, the annual value of world military expenditures appears—despite declining slightly after 2009—to have risen about 40–52%, from about $1.28–.59 trillion in 2002 to about $1.79–2.42 trillion in 2012, and to have averaged between $1.59 and $2.04 trillion for the 11-year period." During this same 11-year period, "the share of GDP to which military expenditure was equivalent—an indicator sometimes called 'the military burden'—appears to have averaged between 2.1% and 2.5%, peaking at between 2.2% and 2.8% in 2009" (United States 2015). According to SIPRI, in 2015 global military expenditure was $1.67 trillion, equivalent to 2.3 per cent of global gross domestic product (SIPRI, 2016). Meanwhile, in 2015 official development assistance (ODA) by the 28 countries in the OECD Development Assistance Committee (2015) stood at $131.6 billion, averaging 0.30% of gross national income.

The allocation of resources outlined in the previous paragraph is indicative of the continuing gap between security and development priorities. It also reflects the challenges of mobilizing resources for preventive purposes in a global system based on sovereign states. Despite various waves of internal reforms, the United Nations is straining to address the growing range of issues on its agenda. Moreover, it is highly compartmentalized with different parts of the system dealing with climate change, population, poverty, and security. The relations between the UN Security Council and ECOSOC—the

UN's Economic and Social Council responsible for development—remain shaky. The UN's relations with the Bretton Woods Institutions have traditionally been constrained due to member state policies and preferences even though there is growing collaboration at least on the development front. The World Bank's publication of the 2011 World Development Report, *Conflict, Development and Security*, was a breakthrough. However, the global system remains as siloed as ever. Beyond the UN, there are no global institutions with the mandate to address security and development challenges in a coherent manner.

The imperative for conflict prevention and peacebuilding, as a joint agenda for security and development analysts and actors, rests on the viability of the idea of global interdependence and global governance. There are numerous institutional, political, and procedural obstacles to the realization of this agenda. However, perhaps the most serious is the increasing push-back against globalization and the idea of a liberal one-world system that seemed on the ascendancy in the immediate aftermath of the Cold War. This push-back manifests itself in different ways in different parts of the world (Barber 1995; Ikenberry 2011; Haidt 2016). It is found in the ideology of political Islam which, in its extreme form, has led to the scourge of global terrorism.

However, there are other forces at work which were further accelerated with globalization that also challenge the post-Second World War liberal international world order. The economic rise of China, the resurgence of a nationalist Russia, the British vote to exit the European Union, President Trump's America First policies in the United States, and populist, isolationist movements in Europe seem to signify a return to a more fragmented, inward-looking worldview across the globe. Thus, it is particularly ironic that while the range of threats and challenges discussed in this chapter require greater global collaboration for effective preventive action, we might in fact witness the strengthening of the Westphalian state system based on traditional concepts of nationalism and national security in an increasingly globalized world.

References

Al-Sumait, F. N. Lenze, and M. C. Hudson, M.C. (eds.). 2015. *The Arab Uprisings: Catalysts, Dynamics, and Trajectories*. London: Rowman & Littlefield.

Amer, R. A. Swain, and J. Öjendal. 2012. *The Security–Development Nexus: Peace, Conflict and Development*. London: Anthem Press.

Annan, K. 2005. *In Larger Freedom: Towards Security, Development and Human Rights for All*. New York; United Nations.

Annan, K. 2009. Problems without Passports. *Foreign Policy*, Special Report.

Anderson, M. 1999. *Do No Harm*. Boulder, CO: Lynne Rienner Publishers.

Baranyi, S. 2008. *The Paradoxes of Peacebuilding Post-9/11*. Vancouver: UBC Press.

Barber, B. 1995. *Jihad vs. McWorld: How Globalism and Tribalism Are Reshaping the World*. London: Ties Books, Random House.

Buzan, B. and L. Hansen. 2007. *Debating Security and Strategy and the Impact of 9-11*. Reader on International Security. Thousand Oaks, CA: Sage Publications especially Vol 4.

Buzan, B., O. Wæver, and J. de Wilde, J. 1998. *Security: A New Framework for Analysis*. Boulder, CO: Lynne Rienner Publishers.

Carnegie Commission. 1997. *Preventing Deadly Conflict*. New York: Carnegie Commission.

Collier, P. 2001. Economic Causes of Civil Conflict and Their Implications for Policy. In C. Crocker, F. Hampson, and P. Aall (eds.), *Turbulent Peace: The Challenges of Managing International Conflict*, pp. 143–61. Washington, DC: United States Institute of Peace.

Collier, P. 2003. *Breaking the Conflict Trap: Civil War and Development Policy*. Washington, DC: World Bank.

Collier, P. 2007. *The Bottom Billion: Why the Poorest Countries Are Failing and What Can Be Done About It*. Oxford: Oxford University Press.

Dannreuther, R. 2007. *International Security: The Contemporary Agenda*. Cambridge: Polity Press.

Duffield, M. 2001. *Global Governance and the New Wars: The Merging of Development and Security*. London: Zed Books.

Fukuda-Parr, S. 2010. Poverty and Violent Conflict: Rethinking Development. In N. Tschirgi, M. Lund, and F. Mancini (eds.), *Security and Development: Searching for Critical Connections*. Boulder, CO: Lynne Rienner.

Goldstone, A. 2012. Demography: A Security Perspective. In J. Spear, and P. Williams (eds.), *Security and Development in Global Politics: A Critical Comparison*. Washington, DC: Georgetown University Press.

Goodhand, J. 2006. *Aiding Peace? The Role of NGOs in Armed Conflict*. Boulder, CO: Lynne Rienner.

Haidt, J. 2016. When and Why Nationalism Beats Globalism. *The National Interest*. 12(1).

Hintjens, H. and D. Zarkov. 2015. *Conflict, Peace, Security and Development: Theories and Methodologies*. Abingdon: Routledge.

Homer-Dixon, T. 1999. *Environment, Scarcity and Violence*. Princeton, NJ: Princeton University Press.

Humphreys, M. 2003. *Economics and Violent Conflict*. Cambridge, MA: Harvard University Press.

Ikenberry, John G. 2011. *Liberal Leviathan: The Origins, Crisis, and Transformation of the American World Order*. Princeton, NJ: Princeton University Press.

Matthew, A. 2010. Environment, Conflict, and Sustainable Development. In N. Tschirgi, M. Lund, and F. Mancini (eds.), *Security and Development: Searching for Critical Connections*. Boulder, CO: Lynne Rienner.

Mavrotas, G. (ed.). 2011. *Security and Development*. Cheltenham: Edward Elgar Publishers.

Newman, E. 2010. Peacebuilding as Security in "Failing" and Conflict-Prone States. *Journal of Intervention and Statebuilding*, 4: 305–22.

OECD. 2005. *Principles for Good International Engagement in Fragile States*. OECD document DCD, 11/REV.2.

OECD. 2007. *Whole of Government Approaches in Fragile States. Available at:* www.oecd.dac/dataoecd/15/24/37826256pdf, accessed December 8, 2016.

OECD. 2008. *3rd High Level Forum on Aid Effectiveness, 2–4 September, Accra, Ghana, Roundtable Summary*. Paris: OECD.

OECD DAC. 1997. *DAC Guidelines on Conflict, Peace and Development Co-operation*. Paris: OECD.

OECD DAC. 2001. *DAC Guidelines: Helping Prevent Violent Conflict. Available at:* http://www.gtz.de/security-sector/download/DAC_Guidelines.pdf, accessed December 8, 2016.

OECD DAC. 2015. *Development aid rises again in 2015, spending on refugees doubles. Available at:* http://www.oecd.org/dac/development-aid-rises-again-in-2015-spending-onrefugees-doubles.htm, accessed December 8, 2016.

Oxfam. 2017. *An Economy for the 99%. Available at:* https://www.oxfam.org/en/research/economy-99, accessed on May 15, 2017.

Patrick, S. and K. Brown. 2007. *Greater than the Sum of Its Parts? Assessing "Whole of Government Approaches" to Fragile States.* Washington, DC: Center for Global Development.

Sadiki, L. 2015. *Routledge Handbook of the Arab Spring: Rethinking Democratization,* London: Routledge.

SIPRI. 2016. *Yearbook 2016, Armaments, Disarmament and International Security. Available at:* https://www.sipri.org/sites/default/files/YB16-Summary-ENG.pdf, accessed December 8, 2016.

Spear, J. and P. Williams (eds.). (2012). *Security and Development in Global Politics: A Critical Comparison.* Washington, DC: Georgetown University Press.

Stern, M. and J. Öjendal. 2010. Mapping the Security–Development Nexus: Conflict, Complexity, Cacophony, Convergence? *Security Dialogue*, 41(1); 5–31.

Stern, M. and J. Öjendal. 2012. Exploring the Security-Development Nexus. In A. Swain, and J. Öjendal, *The Security–Development Nexus: Peace, Conflict and Development.* London: Anthem Press.

Tschirgi, N. 2004. Post-Conflict Peacebuilding Revisited: Achievements, Limitations, Challenges. *International Peace Academy*, IPA Policy Paper.

Tschirgi, N. 2013. Securitization and Peacebuilding. In Roger Mac Ginty (ed.), *Routledge Handbook of Peacebuilding.* London: Routledge.

Tschirgi, N., M. Lund, and F. Mancini (eds.). 2010 *Security and Development: Searching for Critical Connections*, Boulder, CO: Lynne Rienner.

United Kingdom. 2008. *National Security Strategy.* Norwich: Her Majesty's Stationery Office.

United Nations. 1992. *An Agenda for Peace: Preventive Diplomacy, Peacemaking and Peacekeeping.* Report of the Secretary-General pursuant to the statement adopted at the Summit Meeting of the security Council on January 31, 1992. UN Doc A/47/277-S/2411

United Nations. 1994. *An Agenda for Development: Report of the Secretary-General.* UN Doc A/48/935.

United Nations. 1997. *An Agenda for Democratization, Report of the Secretary-General.* UN Doc S/1997/712.

United Nations. 2004. *A More Secure World: Our Shared Responsibility. Report of the High Level Panel on Threats, Challenges and Change.* New York: United Nations.

United Nations. 2006. *The United Nations Global Counter-Terrorism Strategy.* UN Doc A/Res?60/288.

United Nations. 2015a. *World Population Prospects*, 2015 Revisions. *Available at:* https://esa.un.org/unpd/wpp/publications/files/key_findings_wpp_2015.pdf, accessed on December 8, 2016.

United Nations. 2015b. *Transforming Our World: The 2030 Agenda for Sustainable Development.* UN Doc A/69/L.85.

United Nations. 2015c. *Plan of Action to Prevent Violent Extremism.* UN Doc A/70/674.

United Nations. 2016. *Framework Convention on Climate Change. Available at:* http://unfccc.int/paris_agreement/items/9485.php, accessed December 8, 2016.

United Nations Development Programme (UNDP) 2012. *Governance for Peace: Securing the Social Contract. Available at:* http://www.undp.org/content/undp/en/home/librarypage/

crisis-prevention-and-recovery/governance_for_peacesecuringthesocialcontract.html, accessed September 12, 2017.

United States. 2002. *The National Security Strategy of the United States of America. Available at:* http://www.state.gov/documents/organization/63562.pdf, accessed December 9, 2016.

United States. 2008. *National Defense Strategy*. Washington, DC: Department of Defense.

United States. 2015. *World Military Expenditures and Arms Transfers. Available at:* http://www.state.gov/documents/organization/251075.pdf, accessed on December 8, 2016.

Williams, Paul D. 2012. Poverty: A Security Perspective. In J. Spear and P. Williams (eds.), *Security and Development in Global Politics: A Critical Comparison*. Washington, DC: Georgetown University Press.

World Bank. 2004. *The Role of the World Bank in Conflict and Development: An Evolving Agenda*. Washington, DC: World Bank: Conflict Prevention and Reconstruction Unit.

World Bank. 2009. Securing Development by World Bank President Robert B. Zoellick, a presentation at USIP. *Available at:* http://siteresources.worldbank.org/NEWS/Resources/RBZUSIPSpeech010809.pdf, accessed September 12, 2017.

World Bank. 2011. *World Development Report 2011: Conflict, Security and Development*. Washington, DC: World Bank.

CHAPTER 39

DRONE PROLIFERATION IN THE TWENTY-FIRST CENTURY

SARAH E. KREPS, MATTHEW FUHRMANN, AND MICHAEL C. HOROWITZ

ONE of the most significant, if contentious, developments on the twenty-first century battlefield has been the use of unmanned aerial vehicles (UAVs), or drones, to carry out counter-terrorism strikes.[1] Although unmanned platforms had been used for surveillance and reconnaissance for decades, they were first used for strike missions in Afghanistan in the fall of 2001. The United States, in particular, has used drones to target suspected terrorists and insurgents around the globe, beginning with a strike in Yemen in 2002 against the suspected perpetrator of the USS *Cole* bombing in 2000. Between then and 2015, the United States carried out more than 500 counter-terrorism strikes in countries ranging from Pakistan to Yemen to Somalia.

The use of drones, particularly beyond declared war zones, has raised questions about their legality. A report by the United Nations Special Rapporteur on Extrajudicial, Summary or Arbitrary Executions, Philip Alston, argued that "there has been a highly problematic blurring and expansion of the boundaries of the applicable legal frameworks . . . [and] a tendency to expand who may permissibly be targeted and under what conditions" (United Nations 2010). Scholars have also debated whether using drones for targeted strikes effectively reduces terrorist violence, or leads to more terrorist attacks in the future (Johnston 2012; Byman 2013; Cronin 2013; Jordan 2014).

Against this backdrop, the proliferation of drones beyond the United States, an on-going reality, means that the relevance of current-generation drones in the international security environment is likely to grow, rather than shrink. This chapter therefore evaluates the use and proliferation of drones, along with the consequences for the international security environment. It first traces the United States' use of drones in combat since the September 11, 2001 attacks. We then discuss proliferation trends and outline several explanations for why states desire armed drones. In the next section, we present arguments for why drone proliferation could theoretically affect regional and international security, evaluating the arguments in light of the capabilities of current-generation drones and the likely context of their use. The penultimate section examines the turn to stealth, speed, swarms, and smaller drones by way of considering how the development of future-generation drones may change the landscape considerably. We then conclude by discussing implications for the future.

39.1 The Use of Armed Drones Since 9/11

The use of drones on the battlefield long precedes highly publicized uses by the United States since the September 11, 2001 attacks. During the Vietnam War, the United States used the Firebee drone to conduct reconnaissance, with a C-130 Hercules launching the drone, which then parachuted down and ultimately was retrieved by helicopters. While the United States used MQ-1 Predator drones for surveillance and reconnaissance in the Balkans wars (Becker 1999), it opted against arming drones until after the 9/11 attacks, when it armed Predators with Hellfire missiles and began using them in Afghanistan.

More controversial is the use of drones by the United States outside active combat zones, in countries such as Pakistan, Yemen, and Somalia. The United States has conducted about 500 such strikes in the last decade (Bureau of Investigative Journalism 2017). These counter-terrorism strikes have drawn criticism. By eliminating the risk of death to soldiers on the attacking side, some critics worry drones may create a moral hazard that makes states more reckless with drones than they would be if their soldiers faced the risk of death (Kaag and Kreps 2012). President Obama said, "[I]t wasn't until about a year, year and a half in where I began to realize that the Pentagon and our national-security apparatus and the CIA were getting all too comfortable with the technology as a tool to fight terrorism" (Coates 2016).

Along similar lines, the use of drones for counter-terrorism also raises legal criticisms, including compatibility with *jus ad bellum* (the recourse to force), particularly for uses outside active combat zones. Scholars such as Mary Ellen O'Connell (2010/2011) argue that international law hinges on territory rather than specific individuals. Insofar as the United States is not at war with either Pakistan or Yemen, then strikes against individuals in these countries are not consistent with international law in terms of the recourse to force. Another is that if drones were used at some points that did not properly distinguish between civilians and combatants, it would raise *jus in bello* issues (Kaag and Kreps 2012; Walzer 2016).

If concerns raised about US drone strikes are correct, the prospect of proliferation to other countries might appear significant for the international security environment. What is the reality of drone proliferation today? And what can we expect the consequences to be as more countries around the world acquire armed and advanced drones? Subsequent sections answer these questions by examining why countries might proliferate, how they are proliferating, and what the consequences might be. The conclusions temper concerns about proliferation by suggesting that the strategic context for the use of drones—which would likely be different for many countries other than the United States—are likely to mitigate the security risks of proliferation in most contexts. Before turning to that analysis, the next section outlines the state of proliferation by way of situating the analysis about proliferation consequences.

39.2 Why Proliferate? Explaining Trends in UAV Diffusion

For several years, many thought that the United States had a virtual monopoly on the use of armed drones. However, other countries are catching up. Israel has been one of the leading producers and exporters of UAVs for decades. China has also emerged as a leader in the development of drone technology. Moreover, states such as Iraq, Nigeria, and Pakistan, have now used armed drones in combat. According to data compiled by Fuhrmann and Horowitz (2017), 29 countries had an active program to acquire armed drones by the end of 2014. The list of armed drone aspirants includes countries such as India, North Korea, Saudi Arabia, South Korea, Taiwan, and Turkey. Moreover, more than a dozen countries possess advanced drones, or drones that can spend more than 20 hours in the air and conduct significant intelligence, surveillance, and reconnaissance (ISR) missions, whether armed or not (Fuhrmann and Horowitz 2017). Why are so many countries interested in armed and advanced drones? We briefly review four explanations for drone proliferation in contemporary world politics.

39.2.1 Augmenting Strategic Capacity for Counter-terrorism

From an operational standpoint, current-generation drones have appeal for many states. Manned strike aircraft tend to have "short legs"; they cannot fly long distances before requiring refueling, and refueling requires both tankers and additional crews that have mandatory limits on their operational duration. Unmanned aircraft can operate between 14–36 hours, giving them considerable range (Kreps 2013). Not only do these aircraft have an extraordinary duration, they are able to carry out surveillance and reconnaissance as well as strike missions by virtue of being able to loiter and persist over targets while also being armed. The ability to persist and loiter means that the crew can watch for hours at a time and ensure that they correctly identify the target. The ability to strike from the same aircraft simply means deploying fewer types of aircraft, which has important implications for logistics.

One might argue that all states should value the loitering-related advantages of drones to some degree. Yet clearly countries are pursuing armed drones with varying degrees of intensity. The reason is simple: some states have much more to gain than others by augmenting their loitering capacity. For countries that face terrorist threats, in particular, drones provide a potentially useful tool, as the US use of drones in counter-terrorism operations since 9/11 underscores. According to analysis carried out by Fuhrmann and Horowitz (2017), experiencing just one additional terrorist attack annually triples the probability of a state having an armed drone program. Turkey, for instance, seems to value armed drones in part because of the terrorist threat it faces from groups such as ISIS and the Kurdistan Workers' Party (PKK) (Matthews 2011).

39.2.2 Technological Availability

Supply-side factors can also shape the weapons proliferation process. Current-generation drones are significantly less capable—and sophisticated—than modern combat aircraft, and the underlying technology is dual-use in nature. This makes the acquisition of advanced and armed drones an arguably natural step for countries seeking to obtain updated military capabilities (Horowitz 2010). For shorter-range systems in particular, that cannot operate beyond the line of sight, systems are widely available on the commercial market. Even for slightly more advanced systems, there are willing exporters such as Israel willing to supply unarmed systems, and China has become increasingly willing to export armed drones such as the CH-3 or CH-4 for unarmed systems. This makes the technology-push factors driving current-generation drone proliferation strong, as most theories of proliferation predict.

The most advanced current-generation drones, those that require significant ISR processing and satellite connectivity, whether armed or unarmed, remain harder to operate and outside the grasp of many countries (see Gilli and Gilli 2016). To be sure, very few countries operate Reaper-like drones today. Yet, the barriers to entry for current-generation drones seem to be declining yearly, as more countries, including Canada and India by late 2016, seek to acquire advanced and armed drones. Moreover, due to the dual-use nature of the technology, it may be more plausible for countries to build their own systems, over time, than to simply rely on imports, as they often do in areas such as combat aircraft.

39.2.3 Domestic Political Institutions

A state's regime type can make certain military technologies more (or less) attractive (Lyall and Wilson 2009; Sechser and Saunders 2010; Way and Weeks 2014). Domestic political institutions affect defense acquisition strategies by shaping how leaders may wield military power, and by potentially constraining them from pursuing their desired policy.[2]

Drones likely appeal to both democracies and autocracies, albeit for different reasons. The fact that drones reduce the risk of casualties makes them potentially attractive for leaders in democracies who fear the public opinion consequences of wartime casualties. At the same time, drones allow countries to maintain more centralized control over the use of force. Leaders who are distrustful of the military, as is the case in many authoritarian regimes, may therefore seek drones to lessen their reliance on commanders in the field. From a centralized location, a dictator may be able to oversee an entire operation with greater confidence that its order will be carried out. As US Undersecretary of Defense Robert Work (2015) put it, "authoritarian regimes who believe people are weaknesses in the machine, that they are the weak link in the cog, that they cannot be trusted, that they will naturally gravitate toward totally automated solutions."

Fuhrmann and Horowitz (2017) find evidence that domestic political incentives influence drone proliferation. They show that 90 percent of the states with armed drone programs, for example, are autocracies or democracies, despite the fact that mixed regimes (countries that are in between being an autocracy and a democracy) constitute 30 percent of all countries. A total of 32 percent of autocracies and 24 percent of democracies are seeking armed drones—compared to just 5 percent for mixed regimes.

39.2.4 Emulation and Precedent Setting

The American experience, in part, could also motivate the drone ambitions of other countries by serving as a role model, as Micah Zenko argues (quoted in Shane 2011). The implication is that the United States' use of armed drones created a precedent that other countries would follow. As then US Counter-terrorism Advisor John Brennan (2012) stated in a 2012 speech, "if we want other nations to use these technologies responsibly, we must use them responsibly … we cannot expect of others what we will not do ourselves."

US political leaders appear well aware that, by reducing the risk to US forces, drones generate more flexibility for US decision-makers. Minimizing casualties is an advantage in its own right, but it also has instrumental value for leaders. As former US President Obama (2013) admitted, drone strikes "end up shielding our government from the public scrutiny that a troop deployment invites." Obama suggested that the Libya intervention in 2011 did not require Congressional authorization because there were no "boots on the ground" but rather stand-off airpower, including drone strikes, and a somewhat similar argument has been made for Syria. Policy elites outside the United States are likely to find this type of decision-making latitude quite attractive, as it allows them a free hand in their conduct of foreign policy. Thus, observing the freedom of latitude that using drones has given US policy-makers may make drones more attractive to elites elsewhere.

39.3 Arguments about the Strategic Consequences of Proliferation

The discussion in Section 39.2 helps explain why drones are spreading internationally. Having examined the causes of UAV proliferation, we now turn to the consequences for the international security environment, especially for advanced, armed current-generation drones that can carry out surveillance, reconnaissance, *and* strikes. One view suggests that drone proliferation will generate challenges for international stability. This argument hinges on the notion that drones, by eliminating risk, create a moral hazard and lead to more frequent and questionably legal uses of force than would otherwise occur.

Indeed, President Obama's own comments about being shielded from scrutiny in ways that made drones feel like the "cure-all for terrorism," (2013) lend credence to the argument. A number of other observers have made similar claims, from United Nations Special Rapporteur on Extrajudicial, Summary or Arbitrary Executions Christof Heyns to some scholars (Boyle 2015; Cole 2016). The empirical record suggests some basis for the argument. For example, drone strikes constitute 98 percent of all targeted killings by the United States of suspected terrorists. Moreover, despite the stated preference for capturing versus killing suspected militants—given the intelligence advantages of capturing—the United States has captured few suspected terrorists, instead simply killing them and most often through drone strikes. If drones did not alter the way states use force, then we might have expected that the United States should have captured more suspected terrorists than it does.

Those who are pessimistic about the prospects of proliferation advance several potential contexts in which the introduction of current-generation drones could be destabilizing. Perhaps most salient are cross-border scenarios in regions that are already quite tense such as the Middle East and East Asia. One concern is that if drones lower the cost of using force, states will deploy drones more cavalierly across borders, whether to test boundaries or simply carry out surveillance, risking provocations in areas that are already fraught with problems. Given the lack of clear rules of engagement for how to respond to incursions by unmanned aircraft, an already-tense atmosphere could escalate quickly as either or both side misperceives the intentions of the other (Zenko and Kreps 2014: 10). The East and South China Seas could be especially ripe for this type of exchange, given the existing tensions, nationalism, and contested borders. South Asia, with a history of cross-border incursions and low intensity conflict, might also be primed for such escalation especially since both Pakistan and India have or are acquiring armed drones.

The proliferation of drones could also make the domestic use of force, for the purposes of repression, more likely. A number of states appear to face domestic-based opposition groups that they believe threaten their rule. In some of these cases, from Russia with the Chechens to Pakistan with the Taliban, the government has designated these groups terrorists, giving them license to attack. Drones could present leaders with an alternative that might seem easier to use and at lower cost. Moreover, the centralization of force possible with drones could make it easier to use force repressively for regimes concerned about the loyalty of far-flung forces who might not follow orders.

A third major context that could present security challenges is use by violent non-state actors or militant groups. Acting either on behalf of a terrorist group or as lone wolves, drones could have the advantage of being directed into high density areas, or areas with high-value targets, then deploying a gun or explosive. Even if the attack does not kill dozens or thousands, such attacks could certainly lead to mass terror, largely because of the unexpected and unpredictable uses possible—and the perceived difficulty of defending against weaponized low-flying, commercial drones that will increasingly saturate the skies of many countries in general. In that sense, Senator Diane Feinstein argued that drones are "a perfect assassination weapon," since they could be deployed strategically at a moment when an important individual was present (Zenko and Kreps 2014: 12).

39.4 Putting Proliferation in Context

The scenarios outlined in Section 39.3 offer a helpful first step in analyzing the possible range of proliferation consequences, but require additional context. This section assesses each scenario, given the capabilities of current generation drones, and discusses the implications for interstate and intra-state conflicts.

39.4.1 Interstate Conflict Mediators

In the period since the Second World War, the incidence of interstate conflict has become exceedingly rare (Lacina and Gleditsch 2005). While interstate war is uncommon, however, there remain dozens of territorial disputes between two or more countries around the world. Many of these are already armed to the hilt with anti-air defenses, providing a clear restraint on the utility of current generation drones. With rare exceptions such as the United States' RQ-170, even the most advanced current generation drones are slow-flying and lack low-observability characteristics such as stealth, making them extremely vulnerable to standard air defense systems. The sophistication of air defense systems is also increasing. For example, Russia recently sold S-400 battalions to China, giving China the ability to track 100 airborne targets, including both low observable aircraft and precision-guided munitions (Heath 2016). It would be impossible for a current-generation drone to penetrate that type of air defense without saturating the airspace with so many drones that, based on current procurement models, it would not be affordable for any country. Thus, given their lack of utility in what experts call denied airspace, current-generation drones are unlikely to be a tool for lowering the threshold for using force in an interstate context.

Evidence for the limited capabilities of drones in the interstate context is that even the United States has restricted its use of drones in countries such as Syria that have particularly rudimentary air defenses compared to those of more advanced countries such as China. In March 2015, the US Air Force lost a Predator over Syria when it was allegedly shot down by air defenses. American officials had earlier defended the use of drones in the region because of the "permissive" environment (Everstine 2015). At best, then, drones are likely to be just a complement to other platforms. As a former Air Force General put it, drones are "useless in a contested environment" (Whitlock 2013).

39.4.2 The Potential Appeal in Intra-state Conflict

Unlike interstate environments where air defenses are likely to be potent, intra-state settings that pit governments against insurgent or opposition groups are likely to be more asymmetric, involving a government equipped with a drone versus an opposition group lacking sophisticated air defenses. In this context, authoritarian leaders might find drones an attractive tool for controlling the domestic population, as discussed in Section 39.2.3. One typical barrier to an authoritarian leader using force against his or her own people is that he or she must enlist the military to fight against their own citizens. In addition, the same efficient forces that would be useful in defeating opposition groups are also those that could be a challenge to the authoritarian leader himself (Talmadge 2015).

Drones could thereby provide a helpful tool for autocratic leaders seeking to overcome these obstacles. They have the added advantage of being operable from a centralized location close to the regime itself, meaning that the technology could be available even to regimes such as North Korea that have not acquired longer-range drones but might find an interest in controlling its populations with the use of force. Already, countries such as China (in Xinjiang) have used drones for the surveillance of domestic dissidents.

Drones will also have utility as a complement to other means of using force for conventional intra-state conflicts. For example, Pakistan used its recently acquired armed Burraq drone in 2015 against the Taliban. In its initial strikes, the drone killed "several" Taliban militants compared to 22 in a previous airstrike that month, suggesting a capability difference (*Express Tribune* 2015). Much of the fight against the Taliban is also carried out by the Pakistani Army, suggesting an additional limited use of airpower in this context, with air strikes "softening" targets before army components mount ground offensives in thickly forested regions.

Similarly, Nigeria has generally fought Boko Haram with ground forces rather than its air force, and the CH-3 drone Nigeria imported from China in 2015 became another weapon in the overall fight. It did not, however, change the nature of the conflict. Arguably of more value to the Nigerian military were the armored vehicles imported from the United States (*Newsweek* 2016).

39.4.3 Non-State Actors

Another context in which drones might be considered attractive and have not yet been used at all is the case of non-state actors such as terrorist groups. Drones could generate a low-tech form of precision strike, allowing militant groups to vector bombs precisely to particular locations to maximize the impact. This is a non-trivial contribution for groups or individuals looking for the next counter-measure for states such as the United States that are often fighting the last terrorist attack; witness the Shoe Bomber and subsequent requirements that passengers take off their shoes.

Drones would certainly have advantages for militant groups. Hezbollah appears to have acquired some armed drones from Iran, and Israel has reportedly shot down several less-advanced Hezbollah drones. For militant groups seeking to demonstrate their capacity, however, the ability to use a drone to conduct a strike in Israel could be important, as Hamas demonstrated when it publicly unveiled its acquisition of basic drone capabilities. For militant groups, the limited range would not necessarily limit the operation, since most of its objectives would be local anyway.

On the other hand, both militant groups and non-state actors can already carry out attacks without drones. Hamas and Hezbollah have sophisticated rockets that are far more capable than drones, and lone wolf terrorists have rudimentary devices that can also wreak havoc, as the Boston marathon bombers showed when they left homemade devices near the finish line and killed several people. Drones would simply be a new frontier in older terrorism tactics.

The emerging battlefield threat has reached the highest levels of the US Defense Department and Central Intelligence Agency, which have requested increased funds for counter-drone measures (Schmidt and Schmitt 2016). The United States has already been developing counter-drone systems. In 2013, the US military successfully tested a truck-mounted laser, also designed to lock on to and shoot down small UAVs (Panda 2014). China has developed a laser weapon system, designed to shoot down small drones flying at low altitudes. Chinese officials were particularly worried about the security risks associated with small drones, as they are cheap and easy to use (making them ideal for terrorists; *The Guardian* 2014).

39.5 Future Technologies

Our conclusions are based on the technology of today and the specific capabilities of current-generation drones, up to and including the MQ-9 Reaper, arguably the most advanced current armed drone in the world. Drones are just a subset of the broader area of robotics, however, which is experiencing a period of rapid technological innovation in the commercial sector, as well as significant investments on the part of national militaries. Thus, the effects of drones, as well as the broader category of military robotics, could change dramatically in the coming generation as they are further integrated into the arsenals of militaries and militant groups. In general, the key limitation on current-generation drones is their vulnerability to air defenses, which arises from limited speed and a lack of stealth capabilities.

Countries are pursuing the integration of stealth technology into next-generation drones, a capability that entered the public sphere with the revelation of the US-built RQ-170 stealthy surveillance drone. A stealth drone would provide an additional set of defenses against both air defenses and jamming, which would make them more useful, but also prohibitively expensive for many countries. Equipped with this technology, however, stealth drones would thereby become more valuable in interstate contexts insofar as they would overcome the vulnerabilities that would limit their current usefulness. In combination with larger bomb bays, especially, stealth capabilities would make drones significantly more capable in denied airspace. China's Sharp Sword test platform, along with the experimental X-47B in the United States, have demonstrated the sweeping physical form factors necessary for low observability aircraft.

Second, advancements in the speed of drones could improve the utility of drones, especially in an interstate context. Again, what limits the utility of drones in an interstate setting is that they are vulnerable to enemy fire, mostly because they fly far more slowly than manned fighters such as an F-16. Improvements in speed (and maneuverability) could address some of these limitations. In principle, the early vision for the Unmanned Combat Aerial Vehicle would have offered this feature (as well as being low observable), with speeds approaching high subsonic (Mach 0.9) (Northrop Grumman 2012) but the US military shifted the program instead to the development of an uninhabited air-to-air refueling aircraft. Current-generation drones cannot operate at the speeds necessary for operations in denied airspace.

A larger area for change involves the development of new types of drones, combined with new tactics for their usage. Current-generation drones are generally considered as one-to-one replacements for inhabited aircraft. An alternative development pathway would involve focusing on the production of large numbers of cheap, replaceable drones.

Small, even unarmed, drones could be used as a swarm to override enemy air defenses (Scharre 2014). While the size could imply a lack of sophistication, the ability to swarm—flying in formation over reasonably long distances—is no trivial matter. As University of Pennsylvania Engineering Dean Vijay Kumar argues "These devices take hundreds of measurements each second, calculating their position in relation to each other, working cooperatively toward particular missions, and just as important, avoiding each other despite moving quickly and in tight formations" (O'Connor 2014). A limitation, though, will be advances in battery power as well as the cost of production.

Another, more dangerous application of drones, particularly by less-powerful states or non-state actors, could involve the creation of "dirty drones" that could be armed with agents such as Sarin. The US military appears to be concerned about this, and is soliciting ideas for technologies that can defend against these drones. Indeed, the offensive value of drones such as this is that they are almost imperious to traditional sensor systems such as Joint Surveillance Target Attack Radar Systems (JSTARS) that are typically oriented toward larger assets. The technology challenge arises from the fact that any sensor must be sensitive enough to detect these smaller drones but not so sensitive that they detect everything that moves (Tucker 2014).

A final area of current research and development involves the creation of drones designed for very different missions—small-scale tactical activities enabled by miniaturization. As one technology reporter observed, "in keeping with its vision for a 'smaller and leaner' military that's agile, flexible, fast, and cutting-edge, the DoD will work on 'miniaturizing' drones and drone weapons to make them smaller, lighter and less energy-consuming." That comment draws on the Defense Department's 25-year Unmanned Roadmap, which observes that by going in the direction of miniaturization, it will also make the systems more affordable (Neal 2013). Many of the technologies mimic nature in order to "hide in plain sight," such that they can move into an open window, land on a wall, and collect surveillance video (Kreps 2016: 122). In his review of micro-drone technology, Adam Piore (2014) writes that "until recently, inventors lacked the aerodynamics expertise to turn diagrams into mechanical versions of something as quotidian as a fly or a bee." Because of the small size, they would not have the direct lethal impact, but would be quite effective in terms of surveillance. They are also virtually unstoppable, as it would be nearly impossible to regulate their use (Ball 2013).

39.6 Discussion and Conclusion

Scholars typically analyze drones in two contexts: the success or failure of targeting killing and the application of international law. These contexts arise almost entirely, though not completely, from the use of drones by one country, the United States, in one scenario, targeted strikes against suspected militants.

Now that current generation drones are proliferating more broadly due to a combination of indigenous production and exports from China, Israel, and the US, widening the aperture is necessary. Our analysis suggests that the US experience with counter-terrorism may not be generalizable to other countries, particularly given the varying contexts in which other countries may use drones. Thus, even though other countries may be acquiring armed drones, some that are nearly as capable as those that the United States uses, we should exercise caution in extrapolating from the US experience.

First, even American leaders suggest that advanced current-generation drones are only useful in permissive airspace, such as counter-terrorism operations where the opponent is an insurgent or militant who lacks sophisticated air defenses. Few other countries will be faced with exactly this setting to begin with, and those that are, such as Israel, use drones for targeted killings on a very sporadic basis.

Second, interstate war has become less frequent since the end of the Cold War, and states—especially those that are nuclear-armed—have a number of incentives to avoid escalation. Introducing drones into the international security environment will not suddenly cause conflicts where they did not exist. Rather, the prospect for uncertainty and tension is far more likely. States still have not defined the rules of engagement for how to respond to an unmanned incursion across borders. The costs of responding militarily could be lower, but responding militarily to an unmanned aircraft being shot down might also seem far less legitimate or legal. The point is that some uncertainty exists, and that uncertainty in regions with territorial disputes could create grounds for confusion; but confusion is unlikely to become synonymous with conflict. Moreover, given that current-generation drones mostly fly slowly, they are unlikely to be useful in the types of interstate settings where either or both side has sophisticated air defenses.

Third, the intra-state setting produces a more permissive environment and therefore could create incentives for the repressive use of drones. This is especially the case for authoritarian leaders who could find it attractive to be able to control the technology from central locations, meaning they can engage in violent repression without having to rely on ground forces firing at the country's own citizens in person. This could also reduce authoritarian concerns about equipping a military with sophisticated, efficient tools that could later be used against it. Drones could therefore provide a useful platform for controlling domestic populations.

Lastly, violent non-state actors and militant groups are already utilizing drones to advance their interests. In addition to surveillance benefits, drones could offer militant groups new opportunities for a precision strike, in much the same way suicide bombing did in the previous generation. Moreover, given that militant groups such as ISIS have already demonstrated the ability to modify commercial drone platforms to carry small arms, controlling that technology will prove nearly impossible. However, current-generation drones are unlikely to represent game changing technologies for militant groups, since, outside of the novelty value from the first few times they are used, the actual destructive capabilities they offer are similar to other means of attack that militant groups already possess.

It is important to underscore, however, that our conclusions are necessarily preliminary. As drones move from the current generation to stealthier, speedier, smaller, and swarming drones in the future, the strategic and political consequences of drone proliferation will warrant continued examination.

Notes

1. This chapter draws partially on arguments we have made elsewhere (Horowitz et al. 2016; Kreps 2016; Fuhrmann and Horowitz 2017). Drones are also called *uninhabited* aerial vehicles, remotely piloted vehicles (RPAs), or unmanned aerial systems (UAS).
2. For example, one reason why no democracy has pursued nuclear weapons since 1970 might be a combination of institutional veto players and public aversion (Fuhrmann and Berejikian 2012).

References

Aviation Week Network. 2014. U-2 Has the Edge Over Global Hawk. *Aviation Week and Space Technology*. *Available at:* http://aviationweek.com/awin/u-2-has-edge-over-global-hawk, accessed November 29, 2016.

Ball, J. 2013. Drones Should be Banned From Private Use, Says Google's Eric Schmidt. *The Guardian*.

Becker, E. 1999. Crisis in the Balkans: The Drones; They're Unmanned, They Fly Low, and They Get the Picture. *The New York Times*.

Boyle, M. 2015. The Race for Drones. *Orbis*, 59(1): 76–94.

Brennan, J. 2012. The Ethics and Efficacy of the President's Counterterrorism Strategy. Wilson Center. *Available at:* https://www.wilsoncenter.org/event/the-efficacy-and-ethics-us-counterterrorism-strategy, accessed November 29, 2016.

Bureau of Investigative Journalism. *Available at:* use this website instead: https://www.thebureauinvestigates.com/stories/2017-01-01/drone-wars-the-full-data, accessed November 19, 2017.

Byman, Daniel. 2013. Why Drones Work: The Case for Washington's Weapon of Choice. *Foreign Affairs*, 92(4): 32–43.

Coates, T. 2016. "Better is Good": Obama on Reparations, Civil Rights, and the Art of the Possible. *The Atlantic*, December 21.

Cole, C. 2016. Drones Do "Lower Threshold for Use of Lethal Force" Academic Study Finds. Drone Wars UK. *Available at:* https://dronewars.net/2016/02/12/drones-do-lower-threshold-for-use-of-lethal-force-academic-study-finds/, accessed November 29, 2016.

Cronin, A. 2013. Why Drones Fail: When Tactics Drive Strategy. *Foreign Affairs*. 92(4): 44–54.

Drone Wars UK. 2016. *UK Drone Strike Stats*. *Available at:* https://dronewars.net/uk-drone-strike-list-2/, accessed November 29, 2016.

Everstine, B. 2015. Air Force: Lost Predator was Shot Down. *Air Force Times*.

Express Tribune. 2015. Pakistan's Indigenous Armed Drone Conducts First Night-Time Strike. *Express Tribune*, October 22, 2015. *Available at:* http://tribune.com.pk/story/977517/21-militants-killed-in-airstrikes-near-pak-afghan-border/, accessed November 29, 2016.

Fuhrmann, M. and J. Berejikian. 2012. Disaggregating Noncompliance: Predation versus Abstention in the Nuclear Nonproliferation Treaty. *Journal of Conflict Resolution*, 56(3): 355–81.

Fuhrmann, M. and M. Horowitz. 2017. Droning On: Explaining the Proliferation of Unmanned Aerial Vehicles. *International Organization*, 71(2): 397–418.

Gilli, A. and M. Gilli. 2013. Attack of the Drones: Should We Fear the Proliferation of Unmanned Aerial Vehicles? In American Political Science Association Annual Conference, Chicago.

Gilli, A. and M. Gilli. 2016. The Diffusion of Drone Warfare? Industrial, Organizational, and Infrastructural Constraints. *Security Studies*, 25(1): 50–84.

Guardian, The. 2015. China unveils laser drone defence system. *Guardian*, November 3.

Heath, T. 2016. How China's New Russian Air Defense System Could Change Asia. War on the Rocks. *Available at:* http://warontherocks.com/2016/01/how-chinas-new-russian-air-defense-system-could-change-asia/ , accessed November 29, 2016.

Horowitz, M. 2010. *The Diffusion of Military Power: Causes and Consequences for International Politics*. Princeton, NJ: Princeton University Press.

Horowitz, M., S. Kreps, and M. Fuhrmann. 2016. The Consequences of Drone Proliferation: Separating Fact from Fiction. *International Security*, 41(2): 7–42.

International Security Data Site. 2016. *World of Drones: Military, Available at:* http://security-data.newamerica.net/world-drones.html , accessed November 29, 2016.

Johnston, Patrick. 2012. Does Decapitation Work? Assessing the Effectiveness of Leadership Targeting in Counterinsurgency Campaigns. *International Security*, 36(4): 47–79.

Jordan, J. 2014. Attacking the Leader, Missing the Mark: Why Terrorist Groups Survive Decapitation Strikes. *International Security*, 38(4): 7–38.

Kaag, J. and S. Kreps. 2012. The Moral Hazard of Drones. *The New York Times*.

Kilcullen, D. and A. Exum. 2009. Death from Above, Outrage Down Below. *The New York Times*.

Kreps, S. 2013. Ground the Drones? The Real Problem with Unmanned Aircraft. *Foreign Affairs*.

Kreps, S. 2016. *Drones: What Everyone Needs to Know*. Oxford: Oxford University Press.

Lacina, Bethany and Nils Petter Gleditsch. 2005. Monitoring Trends in Global Combat: A New Dataset of Battle Deaths. *European Journal of Population*, 21(2–3): 145–66.

Lyall, J. and I. Wilson. 2009. Rage Against the Machines: Explaining Outcomes in Counterinsurgency Wars. *International Organization*, 63(1): 67–106.

Matthews, O. 2011. Turkey's Tricky Drone Diplomacy. The Daily Beast. *Available at:* http://www.thedailybeast.com/articles/2011/09/13/turkey–s–tricky–drone–diplomacy–with–israel–and–u–s–over–pkk.html, ccessed November 29, 2016.

Neal, M. 2013. The Pentagon's Vision for the Future of Military Drones. *Vice. Available at:* http://motherboard.vice.com/blog/the pentagons-vision-for-the future of military dro nes , accessed November 29, 2016.

Newsweek. "US Gives Nigeria 24 Armored Vehicles to Fight Boko Haram," *Newsweek*, January 8, 2016.

Northrop Grumman. 2012. Unmanned Combat Air System Carrier Demonstration. *Available at:* http://www.northropgrumman.com/Capabilities/X47BUCAS/Documents/X-47B_Navy_UCAS_FactSheet.pdf, accessed November 29, 2016.

Obama, B. 2013. Remarks by the President at the National Defense University. The White House: Office of the Press Secretary. *Available at:* https://www.whitehouse.gov/the-press-office/2013/05/23/remarks-president-national-defense-university, accessed November 29, 2016.

O'Connell, M. 2010/2011. Remarks: The Resort to Drones Under International Law. *Denver Journal of International Law*, 585(39): 585–600.

O'Connor, M. 2014. Here Come the Swarming Drones. *The Atlantic*.

Panda, Ankit. 2014. China Develops Anti-Drone Lasers. *The Diplomat*, November 5.

Pinker, S. 2011. *The Better Angels of our Nature: Why Violence Has Declined*. New York: Penguin.

Piore, A. 2014. Rise of the Insect Drones. *Popular Science. Available at:* http://www.popsci.com/article/technology/rise-insect-drones, accessed November 29, 2016.

Robson, S. 2014. Air Force Plans Drone Upgrade to Replace U-2 Planes. Stars and Stripes. *Available at:* https://www.stripes.com/news/air-force-plans-drone-upgrade-to-replace-u-2-planes-1.272289, accessed November 29, 2016.

Scharre, P. 2014. Robotics on the Battlefield Part Ii: The Coming Swarm. *Center for a New American Security*, October. *Available online at:* http://www.cnas.org/sites/default/files/publications-pdf/CNAS_TheComingSwarm_Scharre.pdf

Schmidt M. and E. Schmitt. 2016. Pentagon Confronts a New Threat from ISIS: Exploding Drones. *New York Times*, October 11.

Sechser, T. and E. Saunders. 2010. The Army You Have: The Determinants of Military Mechanization, 1979–2001. *International Studies Quarterly*, 54(2): 481–511.

Shane, S. 2011. Coming Soon: The Drone Arms Race. *The New York Times.*

Singh, R. 2013. *A Meta-Study of Drone Strike Casualties.* [Blog] Lawfare. *Available at:* https://www.lawfareblog.com/meta-study-drone-strike-casualties, accessed November 29, 2016.

Strawser, B. 2013. *Killing by Remote Control: Ethics of an Unmanned Military.* Oxford: Oxford University Press.

Talmadge, C. 2015. *The Dictator's Army: Battlefield Effectiveness in Authoritarian Regimes.* Ithaca, NY: Cornell University Press.

Tayler, L. 2014. The Truth about the United States Drone Program. *Human Rights Watch. Available at:* https://www.hrw.org/news/2014/03/24/truth-about-united-states-drone-program, accessed November 29,. 2016.

Tucker, P. 2014. The Military Wants New Technologies to Fight Drones. Defense One. *Available at:* http://www.defenseone.com/technology/2014/11/military-wants-new-technologies-fight-drones/98387/, accessed November 29, 2016.

United Nations General Assembly. 2013. Extrajudicial, Summary or Arbitrary Executions: Note by the Secretary-General. *Available at:* https://www.justsecurity.org/wp-content/uploads/2013/10/UN-Special-Rapporteur-Extrajudicial-Christof-Heyns-Report-Drones.pdf, accessed November 29, 2016.

United Nations General Assembly Human Rights Council. 2010. Report of the Special Rapporteur on Extrajudicial, Summary or Arbitrary Executions, Philip Alston. *Available at:* http://www2.ohchr.org/english/bodies/hrcouncil/docs/14session/A.HRC.14.24.Add6.pdf, accessed November 19, 2016.

Walzer, M. 2016. Just & Unjust Targeted Killing & Drone Warfare. *Daedalus*, 145(4): 12–24.

Way, C. and J. Weeks. 2014. Making it Personal: Regime Type and Nuclear Proliferation. *American Journal of Political Science*, 58(3): 705–19.

Whitlock, C. 2013. Drone Combat Missions May Be Scaled Back Eventually, Air Force Chief Says. *The Washington Post.*

Work, R. 2015. Deputy Secretary of Defense Speech: CNAS Defense Forum. U.S. Department of Defense. *Available at:* http://www.defense.gov/News/Speeches/Speech-View/Article/634214/cnas-defense-forum, accessed November 29, 2016.

Zenko, M. and S. Kreps. 2014. *Limiting Armed Drone Proliferation.* New York: Council on Foreign Relations Press.

CHAPTER 40

IMAGES AND INTERNATIONAL SECURITY

LENE HANSEN

IMAGINE if there had been no images of the planes hitting the World Trade Center on September 11, or if the US government had suppressed photos from the Abu Ghraib prison, or if the Danish cartoons of Muhammed had never been drawn. If you think any of these changes in the dissemination of images would have altered international security behavior and outcomes, then you agree that images matter—and yet the field of security studies only began to address these issues recently. Starting in the early 1990s, post-structuralist security studies was the approach from which the first explicit studies of images appeared. Michael J. Shapiro (1990) traced how images played central roles in how security policies were represented, for example in popular culture. James Der Derian (1992) analyzed how the first Gulf War in 1991 was mediated through television and how videogames blurred the line between war and play. It took more than a decade, however, before these early studies led to the formulation of an explicit visual security studies agenda. This agenda connects with critical security studies more broadly, in particular with securitization theory and the debate over whether the referent object of security should be deepened beyond the traditional referent object of the state and widened beyond the concern with military-political issues. Taking stock of visual security studies in 2017, there is now a substantial body of works theorizing the distinctive ways that images communicate threats and insecurity. Most studies have examined one or a small number of images, including iconic photographs such as Napalm Girl and Flag Raising at Iwo Jima (Kirkpatrick 2015: 209; Gartner and Gelpi 2016: 173–4); most have been located within critical security studies; and most have employed a post-positivist epistemology and qualitative methodologies.

Yet, "most" does not mean "all." Recently, the effect of images on popular support for military intervention has been measured in large-n, quantitative experimental studies (Gartner 2011; Gartner and Gelpi 2016). Visual content analysis that codes a large number of images has also started to appear (Bleiker et al. 2013; Methman 2014). Looking to the future, it seems likely that not only the number of studies of images and international security will grow, but that epistemological and methodological diversity will increase. As Roland Bleiker (2015) argues, analysis of images requires multiple methods and collaborations across the epistemological divides that have historically characterized the field of security studies.

This chapter has two goals: to provide an understanding of how and why a research agenda has formed on images within security studies, particularly in the past decade, and to demonstrate that images matter for contemporary international security. The two goals are connected in that security problems that arise "out there" in the world always interact with the theories and conceptualizations within security studies. Images produce different research agendas depending on the concept of security that is adopted, the theorization of the image, and the choice of epistemology and methodology. In order to show the current breath and future potential of a visual security studies agenda, this chapter adopts a broad conception of security akin to the one found—and contested—within security studies itself (Buzan and Hansen 2009). In terms of a definition of the image, this chapter examines images in the form of visual representations, usually in the form of photographs, video, film, drawings, paintings, etc., as these are produced, circulated, and consumed.

The chapter falls into three parts. The first provides an examination of the way that images as an object of study have entered security studies. The second part points to a longer history within security studies for drawing attention to the dangers of aesthetic politics. This literature is of relevance, not only for historical reasons, but because it draws our attention to debates over the politics of images today. The third part of the chapter asks which epistemological and methodological positions may best support current and future work on images in IR.

40.1 How Images Entered Security Studies

From a disciplinary sociological perspective, the relatively recent interest in images draws attention to a broader question, namely what leads security studies scholars to add new issues to their research agenda? Why did it take more than a decade from the first post-structuralist studies to the formation of a more explicit visual security research agenda? Why has critical security studies been the dominant approach from which images have been engaged? And why is the study of images likely to grow and expand in the years ahead? Three driving factors—and the interplay between them—help answer these questions: the internal dynamics of academic debates, that is how disciplines draw upon other disciplines and how debates evolve over substance, theory, and methods; technology; and events (Buzan and Hansen 2009; Hansen 2011: 52).

40.1.1 The Internal Dynamics of Academic Debates

International Relations (IR) and its sub-fields, including security studies, have a tradition of looking to other disciplines for intellectual inspiration and support (Buzan and Little 2001; Lebow 2007). Critical security studies, and post-structuralism in particular, has been influenced by literatures and trends in the humanities. The linguistic turn of the 1960s and 1970s was drawn upon by security scholars who argued that security is a discourse and thus that security problems need to be constituted through language before they can be meaningfully understood by politicians and publics (Wæver 1995). As the visual turn was launched within the humanities in the 1990s, it seemed logical for critical security scholars to follow suit arguing that there are crucial differences between "language discourse" and "visual discourse" (Williams 2003; Möller 2007). The lag between the first post-structuralist studies and an explicit visual security studies agenda is also related to the academic debates within security studies. Post-structuralism became the subject of much criticism in the early 1990s (Walt 1991) and post-structuralist security scholars of the 1990s made less explicit calls for research agendas to be built than did most other security studies approaches. As a consequence, "post-structuralism"—the first mover on visual security analysis—became a vanishing label (Hansen 2010: 5876–8). Another explanation of the lag between the first studies and a full-blown visual security studies research agenda is a "non-finding," a body of literature that could have happened, but did not. In the early 1990s, there was much talk about the so-called CNN-effect, that is, the assumption that news coverage can cause humanitarian interventions, not least because of touching images. Yet, as the CNN-effect was subjected to more rigorous academic scrutiny, scholars found very little support for there being a simple "images cause policy" maxim (Livingston and Eachus 1995; Robinson 2002). Work on the relationship between media and foreign policy continued within communication studies, but the interface between security studies and political communication did not grow as fast as it might have had the CNN-effect been empirically verified by large-n studies.

40.1.2 Technology

Technology is a crucial factor in understanding the trajectory of security studies in general as well as the particular route through which images became an object of study. Yet, it is important to warn against technological determinism, that is a view of technology as acting independently of human agency. Technology has a social and political side in that decisions are made about which technologies are going to be produced and, once invented, how they are going to be used. In the case of images, two aspects of technology, namely production and circulation, are important for understanding the way images impact international security "in the world" and in turn have become objects of study within security studies. Since images first entered security studies in the early 1990s, we have seen a dramatic expansion in the reach, interactivity, and integration across different communication devices. Old models of the media as producers and populations as consumers of news have been undermined by the embedding of cameras in cellphones and digital technologies. The expansion in the number and kinds of image producers, the increased capacity of images to circulate across linguistic and state boundaries, and the speed with which image flows take place is crucial for how international security issues and events become known to the wider public. Perhaps the best example of how images play central roles in establishing and communicating global events is the live coverage on September 11, 2001, where audiences worldwide watched the two planes fly into the World Trade Center in New York, and then the towers collapsing. An important consequence of the narrowing down of the time between production and circulation is that politicians are expected to make decisions more quickly than when it took days before footage from the battlefield reached audiences (Der Derian 1992: 174). The pressure on decision making is further added by the ability of images to move much more easily than words across linguistic and cultural boundaries (Hansen 2011). This is not to say that everybody, across the globe, will interpret an image in exactly the same way, but there is an expectation that one is able to "read" an image across context. The ability of images to reach large audiences is further aided by how they can generate emotional responses that textual accounts of the same events do not (Bleiker 2015). Images become, as a consequence, potentially powerful tools for activists and human security advocates who draw attention to insecurities worthy of international concern. Yet, in response, governments and digital technology corporations have developed a range of "counter technologies" that block visual content from being uploaded, accessed, and circulated, and which trace those who do (Deibert 2013).

40.1.3 Events

Events, like technology, have a material as well as a social side. Major wars like the Second World War and attacks like the ones on September 11, 2001, obviously involve a long list of material factors, yet there is also a social discourse about that materiality that grants it a particular "event status." The status of the Second World War as a historical event is reproduced through commemorative discourses and practices; September 11 would have been a different kind of event had the George W. Bush administration adopted a discourse of the attacks being the work of an isolated group of madmen rather than the beginning of a War on Terrorism. Visual events come in three forms. The first form of events are those like September 11 where images play an integral part in providing an event with a particular shape and status. The second form of event is when images have an independent impact on the making of an event. An example is "Abu Ghraib," that is the shorthand for the scandal produced in 2004 by the release of a large number of photos where American military personnel abused Iraqi inmates in the Abu Ghraib prison. Textual accounts of what happened at the prison that appeared before the photos had generated little discussion (Hansen 2015). Thus it was the appearance of images that caused the shift from relative indifference to global attention. The third form of visual events are those that involve non-documentary images, for example artworks, popular culture, and cartoons. The Danish Muhammad Cartoons and cartoons by the French magazine *Charlie Hebdo* provide the strongest illustration thereof. Here it is the decision to produce such images, what those images "say," and their circulation which is securitized (Buzan et al. 1998; Hansen 2011). In that sense, there is nothing happening unless images are created.

40.1.4 Interplays and Futures

The internal dynamics of academic debate, technology, and events are factors that have impacted the genesis and formation of a visual security studies agenda. We get the best understanding of their impact if we trace the interplay between them, rather than measure each of them seperately. Agency is also crucial: scholars make choices about which academic theories to bring into security studies, companies make decisions about which technologies to develop and users adopt and adapt them, and politicians and mass media provide "things that happens" with event status. The interplay between the factors that drive visual security studies and the important status that agency has make it rather difficult to predict the future of visual security studies. New technologies keep appearing and "accidental images" such as "Abu Ghraib," where images produced for an insider circle reached a global audience, are hard to foresee. What does seem certain though is that more visual events will be produced; that technologies will continue to offer new possibilities for production, circulation and interactivity between users/producers; and that developments in other academic fields, for example the use of experiments to trace emotional responses to images in political psychology, will make their way into visual security studies.

40.2 Aesthetic Politics and the Conflict Potential of Images

The story in the previous section was one of images as absent—except for a few poststructuralist studies—from the agenda of security studies until the early 2000s. In that story, images enter partly because of the interplay between technology and important security events, partly because of the visual turn reaching security studies from the humanities. That story is true insofar as it dates the establishment of an explicit visual security studies agenda. Yet, it is not the full or the only story to be told about the relationship between images and security studies. There is another, less explicit story, about the concern that classical realist security studies scholars including Kennan and Niebuhr had about the dangers of aesthetic politics, that is the way in which evocative images and words rally populations behind totalitarian regimes (Williams 2016). Uncovering this story is important, not just because it makes the overall account of the relationship between images and security studies more accurate, but because it enables us to make important observations about visual politics in the twenty-first century.

40.2.1 Classical IR and the Mobilizing Power of Images

The less told story about images and security studies evolves around the ability of visual communication to mobilize individuals, in particular to make them feel like they are part of a larger community: a nation, a state, an ethnic group, or a religious community. Simply put, politics depends on individuals coming together whether to fight wars, combat climate change or devote resources to ameliorate famine and epidemics. A key question in international political theory is therefore how such "coming togethers" are produced. Is politics a rational process where people calculate and maximize their individual utility? Or is politics a process driven as much, if not more, by emotions and affective bonds as by one's own rational interest (Hutchison 2016)? Most political theorists adopt a view of politics as both rational and emotional, yet there are still differences in how much emphasis is bestowed upon each, and whether emotions are seen as desirable or dangerous for politics. As a classical realist, Hans Morgenthau (1946) was, for example, highly critical of what he saw as liberalism's exaggeration of the extent to which politics could be conducted as a rational, almost technocratic measuring of interests. Writing in the wake of the Second World War, Morgenthau and his generation had witnessed how German and Italian populations had been mobilized—some would say manipulated—by Hitler's and Mussolini's regimes in the 1930s (Bleiker 2009: 10–11). German Nazism and Italian Fascism were highly skilled in their use of film and photography to project the strength and unity of their own populations. Leni Riefenstahl's *Triumph des Willens* brought, for example, Hitler's powerful speech and the exuberant response at the Nuremberg rally in 1934 to those who had not been present at the scene, and the opportunity to relive the experience for those who were.

The dangers of such spectacles was summed up by German social theorist Walter Benjamin's (1936: 234) famous phrase: "All efforts to render politics aesthetic culminate in one thing: war." The concept of the aesthetic has multiple usages. In one usage it refers to works of art, and aesthetic forms of expression are contrasted to factual, non-artistic ones. In another usage, as in Benjamin's case, the aesthetic refers to how politicians—and others—use images and texts to create and enforce myths about national and individual superiority and power. Aesthetic politics, not least as forged through images, is affective and endangers rational deliberation, thus it is a powerful way of rallying an "us" against "them." This connects with works in security studies and peace research on the importance of misperceptions for the escalation of the security dilemma (Jervis 1978) and on the news media's role in fortifying enemy images (Galtung and Ruge 1965). Aesthetic politics creates a dilemma: it comes with clear dangers to democratic principles, including deliberation and tolerance, yet, if as Morgenthau held, it is impossible to understand politics simply as the calculation of individual interests, it is likely impossible to get rid of aesthetic politics entirely (Williams 2016). The question is thus not *if* an aesthetic politics exists, but how it is applied.

40.2.2 Aesthetic Politics and the Twenty-first-century Security Agenda

The concern with visual, aesthetic politics is of relevance for twenty-first-century visual security politics in several ways. First, images are capable of speaking to the emotions of individuals and societies in ways that exceed those of words. At the same time, photography, film, and video are privileged as more factually correct than an oral or textual account of the same event. As a consequence, there are events and problems that come onto the security agenda, because they tap into aesthetic politics. Stephen Walt argued for example that the bombing at the Boston marathon in 2013, though a tragic event was not the national security issue that much of the US media took it to be (Walt 2013). From the perspective of assessing the number of deaths and the connections of the two bombers to wider terrorist networks, Walt made a valid point, yet his argument ran up against the wide, visual, and emotional coverage that brought the event to an American public. The importance of aesthetic politics also implies that security studies should analyze the way in which non-state actors such as, most prominently, ISIS, draw upon carefully crafted techniques and an astute understanding of how to capture multiple audiences, including Western ones (Friis 2015).

Second, the emotional status of images is intimately linked with their ability to create communities (Hutchison 2016). Images are mobilized by patriotic discourses about the need for defending "us" and the sacrifice of those who do, as exemplified by the iconic photography of the American troops in the Second World War, Flag Raising at Iwo Jima. This image use fits well with the traditional concept of security as the political-military defense of national security and community. Looking beyond national security, images mobilize support for wider conceptions of security as well. Images may speak to concerned citizens within particular states, but also to a wider—sometime more diffuse—international community and global citizenry. The acknowledgment of HIV/AIDS as a human security issue has for example, been linked with photographs of those suffering from the disease (Bleiker and Kay 2007; Richey and Ponte 2011). It is important to underscore that the emotional is a capacity of images, not an inevitability. As debates over "compassion fatigue" have brought out, images of atrocities and famine can generate a willingness to help, but they might also accumulate to create an emotional numbing (Campbell 2004). Particular motifs can become visual clichés and lose their capacity to make those who watch care and act.

Third, aesthetic politics is at the heart of visual conflicts that arise over what it is appropriate to show in images. Art history includes numerous examples of paintings, sculptures, and other works of art that have been censored and vandalized. Political theory has a tradition of being engaged with the question of where boundaries to visual representation should be set. The field of journalism studies is concerned with news criteria and production, including which images should be shown and which should not. For security studies the particular question is how images generate international conflicts and impact debates over national, religious, or other collective concepts of security. One form of visual conflict is when an image is securitized because it is claimed to transgress a taboo on depiction (Hansen 2011). For example, the so-called Muhammad Cartoons were published by the Danish newspaper *Jyllands-Posten* in September 2005. As those images—and narratives about them—circulated from a local Danish context to the Middle East and beyond in early 2006, embassies were attacked and an estimated 250 people were killed (Klausen 2009). Conflicts also arise over documentary images, for example photographs from diplomatic encounters where one party is represented in a disgraceful manner. This was the case in a photograph from 2010 which documented how the Turkish Ambassador to Israel, Ahmet Oguz Celikkol, was put in a lower chair in a meeting with the Deputy Foreign Minister Danny Ayalon. As the photograph was circulated by global news media, it was widely understood as a humiliation of Celikkol, and through him, Turkey itself. Another form of visual conflict arises not over taboos or insulting images, but because images are seen as too beautiful and aesthetically pleasing. This concern comes through in critiques of, for example, war photography for glorifying the suffering and destruction that war entails (Reinhardt et al. 2007). The charge is that such representations influence the ability of audiences to ask critically whether war is worthy of support or not. A particular form of visual aesthetic conflict involves depiction of "the other" in too flattering a light. The August 2013 cover of *Rolling Stone* magazine featured Dzhokhar Tsarnaev, charged with the bombing at the 2013 Boston Marathon. This generated widespread and passionate condemnation as *Rolling Stone* was accused of glorifying Tsarnaev and making terrorism "cool."

40.3 Capturing Twenty-first-century Security Images—Methods and Epistemology

Looking to the diversity of security studies, including the debate between traditional approaches and those in favor of widening and deepening the agenda, a complete consensus on how images should be studied is unlikely to appear. Given the multiple ways that images matter to contemporary security politics, this is most likely a good thing: a pluralist research agenda is what serves visual security studies best (Bleiker 2015). The goal of this section is not therefore to lay out one approach that all others should follow, but rather to provide four suggestions for which methodological and epistemological principles best support a pluralist agenda.

First, we should theorize images as polysemic, that is as open to interpretation (Barthes 1979: 38–9). Yet, as Roland Barthes pointed out, individuals do not choose interpretations randomly, within any given society there are "anchoring practices," including textual discourse, that guide interpretation. Photos of flag-draped coffins may, for example, come to tell a standardized story of painful personal loss rather than of a glorious patriotic defense of one's nation (Gartner 2011). Or, images of one or a small number of victims may be more likely to evoke sympathy and willingness to donate money that those featuring larger groups (Slovic 2007). The process through which polysemic images come to "speak security" is inherently political and dependent on agency. Some images are very contested, others have come to "speak security" in highly accepted ways. Each lend themselves to particular research strategies. In the case of contested images, it is important that the security discourses that "read" images differently are closely analyzed. For example, the most famous of the Muhammad cartoons published by *Jyllands-Posten* in 2005 showed Muhammad with a bomb in his turban. This cartoon has been read as arguing that all Muslims are terrorists; a competing reading is that the cartoon is a critique of those who use religion, including Islam, to legitimize terrorism. These readings lead to very different positions on who is attacked and what the necessary policy response is. As security studies scholars we might be best advised not to seek to determine which of the two readings are correct, but rather analyze how multiple interpretations of the same image are made. Research projects working with highly institutionalized images have a much clearer view of what an image says and what policy response it invokes. Roland Bleiker et al. (2013) analyzes, for example, the extent to which boat refugees are depicted as identifiable human beings or as masses and thus whether a politics of humanitarianism or of fear is in place.

Second, we should adopt a pluralist epistemology when studying the impact of images on security politics. Everyday flows of images can be understood as signs adding up to a visual environment that forms the backdrop to policy making even if we cannot establish simple causal connections between images and specific policy decisions (Andersen and Hansen 2016). The role that the visual environment plays for establishing security agendas is in need of further theoretical and empirical research (Livingston 2011). To take an example, the European refugee crisis in 2015 was visualized through photography and video that captured crossings of the Mediterranean Sea as well as hundreds of thousands of people walking through the Balkans toward northern Europe. These were two very different visual environments: the dangerous crossings at sea were harder to depict than people arriving on shores and moving on land. Land photos provided the possibility of showing the refugee as an individual in ways that sea photos did not. One way to assess the importance of this shift in visual environment would be to conduct interviews with political decision-makers and diplomats involved in European policy making. Another way is to use experiments to ask whether the difference in images (land or sea) impacts policy preferences (Gartner 2011; Bleiker 2015).

Looking to the impact of specific images, relative to the number of images produced and circulated, there are thankfully few that directly cause violence. Yet, as the attacks on the office of *Charlie Hebdo* in January 2015 showed, the effects of such attacks can be substantial, especially when the logic of terrorism, which is less about the number of casualties than about installing a general sense of insecurity among the broader public, is invoked. Iconic images—that is "those [photographic] images appearing in print, electronic, or digital media that are widely recognized and remembered, are understood to be representations of historically significant events, activate strong emotional identification or response, and are reproduced across a range of media, genres, or topics" (Hariman and Lucaites 2007: 27)—have a capacity to capture the political agenda. A recent example is the photograph of the dead 3-year-old boy, Alan Kurdi, who drowned as his family was trying to cross from Turkey to Greece in September 2015. This image was instantly circulated and led numerous European heads of states to speak of the need for solving the European refugee crises. Though not the only factor, the prevention of another "Kurdi" probably played a role in the agreement between the EU and Turkey in March 2016 that virtually stopped boat migration from the former to the latter. For most iconic images, however, the impact on policy is indirect and requires a longer time frame to be fully understood. In some cases, the impact of the icon is to engender a story about the policy impact an icon is said to have had (Perlmutter 1998). This enables icons to become "visual nodal points," that is symbols that enter into the representation not only of the event or situation an image originally referred to, but of a larger phenomenon (Hansen 2015). For example, the Hooded Man has become a symbol of American atrocities beyond the site of the Abu Ghraib prison. Measuring the impact of icons is further complicated by the tricky question of when to make that measure. An iconic photo by Ron Haviv of Serbian paramilitaries kicking an old woman they had just shot from the early days of the Bosnian War in 1992 was not followed by a robust international intervention. Yet, this and other photos may gradually over the next three and a half years have accumulated as a slowly building call for action that eventually, propelled by the massacre in Srebrenica in 1995, led NATO to enter the war.

Third, at least in this early stage of visual security research, it is important to ask theoretical questions that concern the specificity of visual security discourse. One crucial question concerns the visualization of the referent object of security. At the meta-level security studies has featured heated discussions over the expansion of the referent object beyond the state for close to 30 years. Within the part of security studies that adopts an expanded concept of the referent object, there is a wealth of work on specific sectors of security, including the societal, environmental, economic, religious, and cybersecurity sectors (Buzan et al. 1998; Laustsen and Wæver 2000; Hansen and Nissenbaum 2009). Theoretical and empirical work on the referent object also includes, for example, the gendered referent object (Shepherd 2008; MacKenzie 2012) and the migrant (Huysmans 2006; Aradau 2008). How are referent objects formed in visual discourse? Is the environmental referent object(s), for example, constituted differently in textual (spoken and written) discourse than in images that are featured alongside such discourse? Methodologically, one way to begin such research is to identify texts that securitize—here the environment—then the images that are selected to document or illustrate this discourse. If certain motifs are recurring we might draw on these in generating a theory of visual referent objects (Andersen and Hansen 2016; Rose 2012: 188–226).

Fourth, the epistemological potential of aesthetic representations is worthy of further study. Drawing on a romantic notion of aesthetics, Roland Bleiker has argued that there is a more positive role for aesthetics to play than the one envisioned by Benjamin. Aesthetic-artistic representations, including images, enable creativity and imagination and "more sensuous and perhaps more tangible, yet equally important forms of insights" (Bleiker 2009: 2). In this view, aesthetic politics may move people—including researchers—in ways that open up space for reflection and critical engagement with reigning understandings of security. This reading of aesthetic politics has been explored in analyses in critical security studies, for example of the representation of the Bosnian War through post-atrocity art photography and comics (Lisle 2011; Lowe 2014; Hansen 2017).

40.4 Conclusion

This chapter has examined the way that images have entered the research agenda of security studies over the past decade; it has drawn attention to the concern with aesthetic politics that has been a part of security studies since the 1940s and the implications thereof for the contemporary security agenda; and it has discussed the epistemological and methodological challenges that the study of images brings forth. It seems apt to point out, in conclusion, that though security studies has come late to the question of images, it has an important contribution to make to those other disciplines and fields of study that are concerned with the visual. Security studies foregrounds the political constitution of images and analyzes their significance for world politics. As the policy implications of images are constituted through discourse, there are limitations to how firmly we can predict the conflict potential of the years ahead. There is very little to suggest that we will see a shrinking in the number of images produced and circulated across national borders. Yet, it is not the number of images in itself which causes conflicts, but the constitution of images as threats to identities and security. Images hold the potential for conflict, but image crises also offer an opportunity for publishers, journalists, diplomats, politicians, and corporations to reflect on the securitizing potential of images. Decisions such as that of the Obama administration not to release photos of the dead body of Osama bin Laden and his burial on the grounds that these might entice further violence are an indication that visual strategic decisions are being made. Whether international "image norms," for example on how visual representations of war and death are made public or how satirical cartoons are responded to, develop in the years ahead is an important question. It is also one which is very hard to answer: it requires not only that governments and media institutions make strategic decisions, but that a dialogue on visual conflict resolution is established. Finally, it is important to stress that as the number of images produced and circulated increases, those who want to draw attention to security problems stand a much better chance if these problems are visualized. This pressure to visualize is not neutral: not all security problems are equally easy to render through images or some may struggle more to find their iconic representation.

References

Andersen, K. E. and L. Hansen. 2016. Visual International Relations: Ontologies, Methodologies and Migration Across the Mediterranean. Paper prepared for the *International Studies Association's Annual Conference*, Atlanta, Georgia, March 16–19.

Aradau, C. 2008. *Rethinking Trafficking in Women: Politics out of Security*. Houndmills, Basingstoke: Palgrave Macmillan.

Barthes, R. 1979. *Image, Music, Text*. Glasgow: William Collins Sons & Co. Ltd.

Benjamin, W. 1936. The Work of Art in the Age of Mechanical Reproduction. Reprinted in W. Benjamin, *Illuminations*, pp. 217–35. London: Pimlico, 1999.

Bleiker, R. 2009. *Aesthetics and World Politics*. Houndmills, Basingstoke: Palgrave Macmillan.

Bleiker, R. 2015. Pluralist Methods for Visual Global Politics. *Millennium*, 43(3): 872–90.

Bleiker, R. and A. Kay. 2007. Representing HIV/AIDS in Africa: Pluralist Photography and Local Empowerment. *International Studies Quarterly*, 51(1): 139–63.

Bleiker, R., D. Campbell, E. Hutchison, and X. Nicholson. 2013. The Visual Dehumanisation of Refugees. *Australian Journal of Political Science*, 48(4): 398–416.

Buzan, B. and L. Hansen. 2009. *The Evolution of International Security Studies*. Cambridge: Cambridge University Press.

Buzan, B. and R. Little. 2001. Why International Relations has Failed as an Intellectual Project and What to do About it. *Millennium*, 30(1): 19–39.

Buzan, B., O. Wæver, and J. de Wilde. 1998. *Security: A New Framework for Analysis*. Boulder, CO: Lynne Rienner.

Campbell, D. 2004. Horrific Blindness: Images of Death in Contemporary Media. *Journal for Cultural Research*, 8(1): 55–74.

Deibert, R. J. 2013. *Black Code: Surveillance, Privacy, and the Dark Side of the Internet*. Toronto: McClelland & Stewart.

Der Derian, J. 1992. *Antidiplomacy: Spies, Terror, Speed, and War*. Oxford: Basil Blackwell.

Friis, S. M. 2015. "Beyond anything we have ever seen": Beheading Videos and the Visibility of Violence in the War against ISIS. *International Affairs*, 91(4): 725–46.

Galtung, J. and M. H. Ruge. 1965. The Structure of Foreign News. *Journal of Peace Research*, 2(1): 64–91.

Gartner, S. S. 2011. On Behalf of a Grateful Nation: Conventionalized Images of Loss and Individual Opinion Change in War. *International Studies Quarterly*, 55(2): 545–61.

Gartner, S. S. and C. F. Gelpi. 2016. The Affect and Effect of Images of War on Individual Opinion and Emotions. *International Interactions*, 42(1): 172–88.

Hansen, L. 2010. Poststructuralism and Security. In R. A. Denemark (ed.), *The International Studies Encyclopedia Volume IX*,pp. 5876–92. Chichester, West Sussex: Wiley-Blackwell.

Hansen, L. 2011. Theorizing the Image for Security Studies: Visual Securitization and the Muhammad Cartoon Crisis. *European Journal of International Relations*, 17(1): 51–74.

Hansen, L. 2015. How Images Make World Politics: International Icons and the Case of Abu Ghraib. *Review of International Studies*, 41(2): 263–88.

Hansen, L. 2017. Reading Comics for the Field of International Relations: Theory, Method and the Bosnian War. *European Journal of International Relations*, 23(3): 581–608.

Hansen, L. and H. Nissenbaum. 2009 Digital Disaster, Cyber Security, and the Copenhagen School, *International Studies Quarterly*, 53(4): 1155–75.

Hariman, R, and J. L. Lucaites. 2007. *No Caption Needed—Iconic Photographs, Public Culture, and Liberal Democracy*. Chicago: University of Chicago Press.

Hutchison, E. 2016. *Affective Communities in World Politics: Collective Emotions after Trauma*. Cambridge: Cambridge University Press.

Huysmans, J. 2006. *The Politics of Insecurity: Fear, Migration and Asylum in the EU*. London: Routledge.

Jervis, R. 1978. Cooperation Under the Security Dilemma. *World Politics*, 30(2): 167–214.

Kirkpatrick, E. 2015. Visuality, Photography, and Media in International Relations Theory: A Review. *Media, War & Conflict*, 8(2): 199–212.

Klausen, J. 2009. *The Cartoons that Shook the World*. New Haven, CT: Yale University Press.

Laustsen, C. B. and O. Wæver. 2000. In Defence of Religion: Sacred Objects for Securitization. *Millennium*, 29(3): 705–39.

Lebow, R. N. 2007. Texts, Paradigms and Political Change. In M. C. Williams (ed.), *Realism Reconsidered: The Legacy of Hans Morgenthau in International Relations*, pp. 241–68. Oxford: Oxford University Press.

Lisle, D. 2011. The Surprising Detritus of Leisure: Encountering the Late Photography of War. *Environment and Planning D: Society and Space*, 29(5): 873–90.

Livingston, S. 2011. The CNN Effect Reconsidered (Again): Problematizing ICT and Global Governance in the CNN Effect Research Agenda. *Media, War & Conflict*, 4(1): 20–36.

Livingston, S. and T. Eachus. 1995. Humanitarian Crises and U.S. Foreign Policy: Somalia and the CNN Effect Reconsidered. *Political Communication*, 12(4): 413–29.

Lowe, P. 2014. The Forensic Turn: Bearing Witness and the "Thingness" of the Photograph. In L. Kennedy and C. Patrick (eds.), *The Violence of the Image: Photography and International Conflict*, pp. 211–34. London: I.B. Tauris.

MacKenzie, M. 2012. *Female Soldiers in Sierra Leone: Sex, Security, and Post-Conflict Development*. New York: New York University Press.

Methman, C. 2014. Visualising Climate-Refugees: Race, Vulnerability, and Resilience in Global Liberal Politics. *International Political Sociology*, 8(4): 416–35.

Möller, F. 2007. Photographic Interventions in Post-9/11 Security Policy. *Security Dialogue*, 38(2): 179–96.

Morgenthau, H. J. 1946. *Scientific Man versus Power Politics*. Chicago: University of Chicago Press.

Perlmutter, D. D. 1998. *Photojournalism and Foreign Policy: Icons of Outrage in International Crisis*. Westport, CT: Praeger.

Reinhardt, M., H. Edwards, and E. Duganne, E. 2007. *Beautiful Suffering: Photography and the Traffic in Pain*. Chicago: University of Chicago Press.

Richey, L. A. and S. Ponte. 2011. *Brand Aid—Shopping Well to Save the World*. Minneapolis: University of Minnesota Press.

Robinson, P. 2002. *The CNN Effect: The Myth of News, Foreign Policy and Intervention*. London: Routledge.

Rose, G. 2012. *Visual Methodologies. An Introduction to Researching with Visual Materials*, 3rd edn. London: Sage.

Shapiro, M. J. 1990. Strategic Discourse/Discursive Strategy: The Representation of "Security Policy" in the Video Age. *International Studies Quarterly*, 34(3): 327–40.

Shepherd, L. J. 2008. *Gender, Violence and Security: Discourse as Practice*. London: Zed Books.

Slovic, P. 2007. "If I Look at the Mass I Will Never Act": Psychic Numbing and Genocide. *Judgment and Decision Making*, 2(2): 79–95.

Wæver, O. 1995. Securitization and Desecuritization. In R. D. Lipschutz (ed.), *On Security*, pp. 46–86. New York: Columbia University Press. Reprinted in B. Buzan and . Hansen, L. (eds.) 2007 *International Security. Volume II: Widening Security*, pp. 66–98. London: Sage.

Walt, S. M. 1991. The Renaissance of Security Studies. *International Studies Quarterly*, 35(2): 211–39.

Walt, S. M. 2013. On the Boston Marathon Attacks. *Foreign Policy*, April 16, 2013. *Available at:* Http://www.foreignpolicy.com/posts/2013/04/16/on_the_boston_marathon_attacks, accessed December 16, 2016.

Williams, M. C. 2003. Words, Images, Enemies: Securitization and International Politics. *International Studies Quarterly*, 47(4): 511–29.

Williams, M. C. 2016. Images of Violence: Elements of an Alternative Genealogy of International Political Theory. Paper presented at the *57th Annual Conference of the International Studies Association*, Atlanta, Georgia, March 16–19.

CHAPTER 41

MARITIME SECURITY

SARAH PERCY

MARITIME security issues are central to broader questions of international security. They rest at the heart of many core strategic disputes, from China's claims in the South China Sea, to Canada's concerns over melting sea ice in the Northwest Passage and how best to secure its Arctic region, (Kraska 2011: 295–99) to disputes between China and Japan over the Senkaku Islands (Koo 2009: 207).[1] The oceans are highways of crime as well as highways of prosperity, and in many cases these crimes constitute security threats. The ability to move people, weapons, narcotics, and other smuggled goods in effective and clandestine ways challenges security both directly (in that weapons or people can pose a specific threat to states) and indirectly (in that the proceeds of crime can be channelled into insurgency or terrorism).

This chapter will examine two main types of maritime security challenges, both with a long history. Conventional maritime security issues center around issues of geostrategic importance, such as access to natural resources, or freedom of transit across the oceans. Unconventional maritime security challenges stem from criminal threats at sea that can have an impact upon national security.

The potential of maritime issues to cause serious security problems is not surprising, and indeed maritime security challenges have been responsible for a wide range of strategic disputes between states. Growing naval competition was a leading factor that led to the crisis and origins of the First World War (Maurer 1997). The failure of naval arms agreements in the interwar period has been cited as a contributing factor in Japanese–British–American rivalries and consequently the development of the Second World War (Pelz 1974). States have long sought (and have largely been prevented by geography) to develop overland routes between the interior of Eurasia to the Indian Ocean, as a component of a strategy to either access or dominate the Indian Ocean. China has recently been spending vast sums to produce a long-sought overland route to the Pakistani port city of Gwadar (Brewster 2016).

Criminal predation at sea has a long history, and has challenged state security by impeding trade. The need to control piracy was so significant in the Roman Empire that controlling piracy was "a cause and legitimation of Roman imperialism and territorial expansion" (Braund 1993: 203). Likewise, nineteenth-century efforts to eradicate piracy off the coast of North Africa (the so-called Barbary pirates) facilitated significant international cooperation, including the first major overseas operations of the US Marine Corps (Leiner 2007). States have long worked to control smuggling, and to counter threats to their successful trade at sea (Karras 2009).

This chapter will proceed in four sections. First, it will examine how the relationship between rules, order, and ungoverned spaces is essential for understanding maritime security. In particular I will argue that maritime security challenges often stem from the conflict between two competing strategic imperatives, both of which are reflected in law: the desire of states to control the oceans nearest to them, and the simultaneous necessity of recognizing the importance of free movement of shipping. I will consider how maritime crime becomes a security threat through the application and enforcement of other legal rules. Second, I will outline the main security threats currently visible in the maritime sphere, and explain their relationship with rules and order. In the third and fourth sections, I will argue that while geostrategic maritime issues are always likely to be present and that major changes in this space will likely be driven by challenges to rules, the most rapid current change comes in the form of unconventional security threats at sea in the form of maritime crime. The former is predictable, and the latter is much less predictable. The third section considers the future of conventional maritime security in the geostrategic realm, and the fourth examines the future of unconventional security threats. I conclude by considering the relationship between continuity, change, and contingency in the future of maritime security.

41.1 Rules, Order, and Maritime Security

Maritime security provides a fascinating test case of the relationship between rules, order, power, and security. As the Emperor Antoninus wrote in his *Digest* of the *de lege Rhodia*, "I am the master of the earth but the law is the mistress of the sea" (quoted in O'Connell 1975). It may come as some surprise to scholars of international security unfamiliar with the maritime sphere that the are subject to "a remarkably complex and distinctive legal order consisting of ancient custom and state practice alongside modern treaties, codes and guidelines that govern virtually all activities at sea" (Kraska 2016b: 88). The legal control of the seas has a long history, and has always sought to preserve a balance between the requirements of states to protect their own maritime access and resources, and the recognition that the common good of all states requires the freedom of the oceans, or *mare liberum* (Booth 1985). Both of these factors are highly strategic. Protecting a state's territorial waters or maritime access contributes strongly to national security. However, states also must be able to navigate freely to preserve their security, particularly around maritime "chokepoints," and they must be able to ensure that trade proceeds smoothly in order to preserve economic security. States have relied on the law to protect both of these ideas, but their inherent contradiction can lead states into conflict.

Balancing disputes between national rights to the ocean and *mare liberum* can be traced back to at least the seventeenth century. Grotius first wrote about the concept of *mare liberum* in 1608 (Klein 2011: 12). A series of seventeenth-century naval disputes over the freedom of the seas ranging from the Adriatic to the Baltic were eventually solved by diplomacy, but, as O'Connell writes, law "gave formal structure and normative character to the diplomatic achievement." By the eighteenth century, "the adroit shaping of the law became a significant adjunct of the effective use of sea power," including the creation of rules "that protected the weak and circumscribed the powerful" (O'Connell 1975: 17).

Contemporary international law still seeks to balance the concept of the freedom of the seas with individual state claims to those seas. The United Nations Convention on the Law of the Sea (UNCLOS), ratified in 1982, both codified existing maritime law as well as developing new areas. Fundamentally, UNCLOS balances the right of freedom of navigation with the desire of states to preserve their sovereign coastal rights. UNCLOS divides the world's oceans into different areas, all of which are subject to different rules. The high seas are the areas in which no one state is sovereign, and all states have the right to freedom of navigation and fishing. States have sovereignty over two different parts of the ocean: their own territorial waters, which extend 12 nautical miles from the shore; and the exclusive economic zone (EEZ), which extends out 200 nautical miles. Territorial waters are under the full sovereign control of the state. Within the EEZ, the state has access to natural resources such as seabed minerals, fish, or the ability to generate electricity from waves or wind. Kraska argues that EEZs are the most important part of the oceans in geostrategic and political-military terms, because they include most of the world's maritime resources (Kraska 2011: 6). In each of these areas, different rules apply. Many of today's most significant maritime disputes involve the latter two categories, either because of the potential for states to lawfully prevent transit of other states or over the presence of strategically significant resources in these zones.

The notion of an EEZ was formally established by UNCLOS, and as early as the 1980s, observers noticed the potential for overlapping EEZs to create conflict over natural resources or the right to military navigation (Boczek 1988). EEZs constitute 35.81 percent of the world's oceans, and many areas are "zone-locked" by EEZs (areas where it is impossible to reach the high seas without crossing an EEZ). These zone-locked areas include, among others, the South China Sea, the Bay of Bengal, the Sea of Japan, the Arabian Gulf, the Black Sea, and the North Sea (Kraska 2011: 6).[2] Clearly, many of these areas are of current or past strategic importance, and the increasingly improved access to seabed natural resources renders them even more strategically important.

It is important to recognize here that not every strategic dispute or maritime dispute that has security implications emanates from international law; this is particularly true in wartime or in crisis, where issues like maritime chokepoints can create strategic challenges simply by virtue of their geography. In peacetime, however, the overarching, well-developed, and historic nature of the laws of the sea mean that many disputes relate to the law. On a related note, it must be acknowledged that the United States is not a signatory to UNCLOS. However, the United States was closely involved in the UNCLOS negotiation process, and abides by the rules it sets out (Kraska 2016a: 6).

41.2 Current Challenges to Maritime Security

Maritime security challenges today have a clear relationship with the rules that govern the world's oceans. In some cases, the security dispute stems from the collision caused by the imperative to "enclose" national waters and the competing pressure to keep the freedom of the seas. In other cases, the age of the rules means that they no longer have clear application to state behavior. And increasingly, maritime security challenges are simple incidences of breaking the law: they are crimes that have become security issues. I will now explore these three ideas.

41.2.1 Security Problems Caused by Enclosure versus Freedom

Maritime security problems tend to arise when the desire to enclose or preserve maritime space clashes with the desire to keep navigation free. Both of these are strategic imperatives. States wish to extend their sovereignty over the resources in their immediate maritime neighborhood, and doing so gives them the potential to control the passage of other states through their waters. But at the same time, all states must be able to navigate the world's oceans freely in order to pursue trade. Booth calls this the problem of " 'territorialization' " (1985: 40) of the oceans. He notes that "the basic problem in the interplay between naval strategy and the present and future evolution of the law of the sea arises from the fact that the 'blue water' of the naval power is invariably somebody else's maritime backyard. And it is likely to be a backyard over which the coastal state has a stronger sense of ownership and a greater desire to exploit its resources unilaterally" (Booth 1985: 97). The laws of the sea reflect these competing imperatives: on the one hand, they preserve the right to freedom of navigation, especially on the high seas, while on the other, the creation of EEZs moves to territorialize the oceans. As states seek to assert claims over the oceans, they will inevitably conflict with states seeking to preserve freedom of navigation.

The South China Sea provides a clear example of the security problems created by these competing imperatives. In the South China Sea, EEZs and territorial water claims are particularly useful for two reasons: securing seabed and marine natural resources, and allowing or preventing navigation through an important but very narrow maritime shipping route. China has made two moves in the South China Sea challenging the current demarcation of territorial waters and EEZs: it has argued that it has historical sovereignty over much of these waters, inside the so-called "nine-dash line." To solidify these claims, China has used dredging and construction to develop maritime features[3] into "islands." Maritime features create entitlements for states to claim varying amounts of territorial seas. Rocks unfit for human habitation only create territorial waters extending out 12 nautical miles while "low tide elevations," only above water at low tide, create no territorial claims at all. Islands can allow a state to claim an EEZ that extends out 200 nautical miles. If China's building works constitute islands, it would then have access to seabed natural resources, as well as potentially limit the freedom of navigation of other states through this crucial maritime chokepoint.

Accordingly, other states have been concerned about Chinese actions and their impact on freedom of navigation. The Philippines took the issue of China's activities in the South China Sea, particularly its island development and attempts to restrict the activities of Filipino fishing vessels, to an UNCLOS Arbitral Tribunal (in this case the Permanent Court of Arbitration). The Philippines asked for a ruling on a number of questions, related to the validity of China's claims regarding the nine-dash line, the nature of the maritime features China claimed and whether their development was lawful (Stephens 2016: 73).

The Tribunal ruled overwhelmingly in favour of the Philippines, in what has been described as an "extraordinary, sweeping win" (Guilfoyle 2016: 2). Most saliently for maritime security, the Tribunal comprehensively rejected the nine-dash-line claim regarding China's historical rights in the region; asserted that Chinese fishing within Philippine territorial waters was unlawful; clarified that the construction of artificial islands was unlawful and violated Philippine sovereignty; and clarified that Spratly Islands and other features under dispute are maritime features and generate no territorial waters, even though they have now been developed into artificial islands. The net effect of the judgment is to reject completely Chinese claims for different interpretations of the demarcation between territorial waters and EEZs.

China's actions in the South China Sea have undoubtedly raised the temperature of maritime security in the region higher than it has been for a long time. The United States has launched three freedom of navigation operations to challenge China's maritime activities since October 2015.[4] The Tribunal decision, having technically settled the legal question, now must be interpreted by states, which may lead to further deterioration of the security situation in the South China Sea. The United States, Japan, and Australia jointly declared that China must abide by the tribunal decision. China responded angrily to the Tribunal decision, criticizing Australia as a "paper cat" with "an inglorious history"[5] and suggesting that the judges were unlawfully influenced by Japan.[6] China also sent fighter jets near Okinawa into the Western Pacific for the first time in September 2016; Japan responded by scrambling its fighters, prompting China to warn that the Japanese were "playing with fire."[7] The dispute over the rules in this case has now exacerbated the security situation, with the world and the region closely observing to see if China changes course in response to the decision, and how the local parties respond to a decision so resoundingly in their favor.

China's activities in the South China Sea are clearly high-order strategic maneuvering closely tied to the national interest. So too are the responses of the United States and other neighboring countries; for them it is a strategic imperative to keep navigation in the South China Sea free, and thus to prevent China from gaining a foothold that gives it the potential power to control maritime traffic and develop resources that would enhance its power. China is not contesting the validity of the law. Rather, its island-building efforts seek to work within a particular interpretation of the law. The current tension in the South China Sea would simply be unintelligible without a clear understanding of the legal structure that undergirds the world's oceans.

The South China Sea represents the most contemporary maritime security episode that occurs at the nexus of different strategic positions on the oceans, or the debate between *mare liberum* and enclosure. However, they are not the first such disputes. Kraska points out that the first four wars fought by the United States after independence were largely over freedom of navigation, as was American entry into the Vietnam War, precipitated by the Gulf of Tonkin incident (Kraska 2016a: 2).

41.2.2 Security Problems Caused by Breaking the Rules: Crime

Unconventional maritime security threats also result from the violation of domestic and international rules: in other words, they are crimes. Maritime crime's security impact is now widely accepted (Bueger 2015; Klein 2011; UNGA 2008). The UN Secretary General outlined in a 2008 report on oceans and the law of the sea that eight maritime criminal threats constituted significant security challenges: piracy; terrorism; the smuggling of weapons of mass destruction, narcotics, and people; illegal, unauthorized and unreported (IUU) fishing; and wilful damage to the marine environment (UNGA 2008). Many of these maritime crimes are closely intertwined, as illegal fishing vessels can be used for piracy and smuggling, and maritime smuggling routes easily repurposed to carry different illegal goods (Percy 2016).

Some of these crimes may pose a direct security threat, such as the smuggling of weapons or insurgents. Others pose a security threat because they have been securitized. Securitization is the process through which an issue comes to be treated as a security problem. Securitizing an issue allows states to deploy a wider range of control methods, because "the special nature of security threats justifies the use of extraordinary measures to handle them" (Buzan et al. 1998: 21). In order to securitize an issue, states or other actors with authority must successfully persuade an audience that the issue at hand poses an existential or serious threat (via a "speech act," or a public declaration), thus allowing extraordinary measures (Buzan et al. 1998).

Maritime crimes have been securitized in varying degrees and with differing levels of intensity in different states. Securitization of migration is a commonly noted phenomenon (Bourbeau 2011; Huysmans 2000; McDonald 2011). Somali piracy has been presented as a severe threat to all states because of its impact on shipping (Percy and Shortland 2013: 35; World Bank 2013: 15). IUU fishing is also securitized, as evidenced by the "commitment both in rhetoric and resources allocated" (Österblom et al. 2011: 261). Narcotics smuggling is treated as a significant threat in most states, but in the United States is most obviously securitized as a result of the long-standing "war on drugs." There is a long-standing linked relationship between terrorism, crime, and migration, emphasized in increased domestic controls on migration after the terrorist attacks of 9/11, and despite the fact that the terrorists involved in these attacks had arrived in the United States legally (Hammerstad 2011: 269).

Securitizing an issue has the benefit of allowing policy-makers to extend emergency measures, which include distorting aspects of regular practice (such as altering the status of Australian territory to prevent migrants from claiming asylum) and using the military to deal with these threats (McDonald 2011). In the case of piracy, securitization has facilitated an extremely expensive multinational naval mission, which may not be in proportion to the actual threat posed by Somali pirates (Bowden 2010).[8]

Maritime crime lends itself easily to securitization. Securitization is easy for any criminal threat, because of the simplicity with which we equate criminal behaviour with danger. There has been a long-standing tendency to securitize transnational crime, by politicians and academics alike; not only has crime been declared to be a security issue, many commentators have argued that it may be one of the most, if not the most, critical security issue for states (Emmers 2003: 421).

Threats in the maritime space are also easily securitized because navies are the only actor that can operate and control crime on the high seas, and for many states, also in territorial waters. In other words, the only tool most states have to deal with some of these threats is military, or, in the case of movement onto shore, border protection (which in many states is notably militarized). Once a major security actor like the state's military is involved, it is not only easier to consider the problem a security threat but probably essential to do so. Why would we need to use the navy to counter, say, migration, if it were not a security threat?

41.2.3 Security Problems Caused by Inappropriate Rules or Unclear Rules

The long history of the law of the sea also means that many of its rules were created to control a very different world. The security problems posed by maritime crimes such as IUU fishing, the trafficking and smuggling of people and other goods at sea, and other types of maritime crime are undoubtedly facilitated by the legal edifice that surrounds the boarding of ships suspected of crimes and the system of flags of convenience.

The law holds that on the high seas, states can only board vessels without the permission of the owner when these vessels are suspected of slavery, piracy, or illegal broadcasting. This motley collection of crimes reflects some historical challenges simply no longer pressing for states, such as illegally transmitting radio broadcasts; others, like slavery, that now take a very different form; and others, like piracy, which occur in particular regions but are not widespread. The right to board is thus highly restricted.

The system of "flags of convenience" is a historical artifact making the rules harder to enforce. A "flag of convenience" is a term describing a situation when a ship originating from one state is nonetheless registered in and flies the flag of a different state. This system first appeared in the 1920s as a method for US vessels to avoid the restrictions of prohibition laws on cruise ships: by flying a Panamian flag, these vessels could serve alcohol (Wing 2003: 175) Other businesses began to avoid local tax, labor, and other regulations by seeking foreign registries (Wing 2003: 175).

Flags of convenience are lucrative both for states and for ship owners. Liberia's registry earns one-sixth of the state's total revenue (DeSombre, p. 182). Agents for the Cambodian registry marketed its financial benefits, claiming that ships flying the Cambodian flag could save $15,000 for each port call (DeSombre 2008: 182).

The flag of convenience system is also beneficial, and therefore lucrative, for criminals. The restrictions on boarding vessels on the high seas except in certain circumstances mean that permission must be sought from ship owners in order to board vessels suspected of a wide range of crimes, including illegal fishing, and all types of smuggling. Authorities must determine who the ship owner is. Sometimes registries are located in states that lack effective administration. In other cases, the registry is in fact located in another state entirely. For example, the Marshall Islands registry is located in Reston, Virginia, and the Liberian registry in Vienna, Virginia (Sharife 2010: 112). Contacting the registry may only be the first step in locating the ship owner, because vessels are often owned in extremely complicated shell company arrangements (Sharife 2010: 112).[9] The delays and difficulties created by the flag of convenience system mean that suspected criminal vessels often escape before an owner can be found.

41.3 The Future of Conventional Maritime Security

The pattern of states competing over resources, trade routes, or geostrategically significant areas is nothing new. In fact, the long history of rules in the maritime sphere has created a situation where potential conflicts are relatively predictable. Geostrategic conflict in the maritime sphere is usually over natural resource access and management (as is this case in, among others, the East Timor Sea;[10] the Senkaku Islands;[11] and in the South China Sea) or access to strategically significant chokepoints such as the South China Sea, the Gulf of Aden, or the Straits of Malacca.

Of course, the future of maritime security in situations of outright hostility differs. As the noted international lawyer D. P. O'Connell wrote in 1975, "the only prediction that can be made with assurance is that the lower the level of conflict, the more localised the situation and the more restricted the objectives, the more predominant will be the element of law in the governing of naval conflict; and that the law will assume a diminished role ... when the conflict becomes global, when the neutrals have been mostly drawn into it ... and when an element of desperation has entered into operational planning" (O'Connell 1975: 3). Guilfoyle notes that O'Connell's logic plays out precisely in the South China Sea, where the conflict is currently of a low scale and between fishing boats and coast guard vessels from China and neighboring states (Guilfoyle 2016). In an actual conflict, it is likely that the maritime legal system governing the waters would have less influence.

Crisis can also arise when states contest the rules, so that their interpretation is more aligned with the national interest. This is precisely the course of action taken by China in the South China Sea. China is not trying to suggest that there are no rules operating in the region, or that the rules do not apply to them, but rather trying to manipulate the rules through the creation of artificial islands in order to facilitate control over the South China Sea. Guilfoyle remarks that "as a trading nation and rising naval power, it is not in China's ultimate interests to challenge fundamental doctrines of the law of the sea.... China's difficulty is that ... it wants the benefit of those universal rules and also a special set of rules applicable in its own backyard" (Guilfoyle 2016).

The combination of obvious maritime chokepoints and clear rules that states nonetheless contest mean that geostrategic maritime security issues are reasonably predictable. Observers have been concerned about the South China Sea's potential for conflict since long before China began to demonstrate its power in the region. In 1974, South Vietnam and China fought a battle over the Paracels archipelago, a land feature in the South China Sea that also featured in the 2016 case.[12] Likewise, observers have noted that the Senkaku Islands, Canada's Arctic, and a number of other strategically significant areas pose possible security threats. In 1978, Buzan identified the likely sources of potential maritime dispute given the pending codification of the laws of the sea (what would become UNCLOS). He was particularly interested in the impact of ownership and rights pertaining to islands, and maritime features. Islands, Buzan argued, can "increase the area coming under a state's control in two ways: by acting as an anchor-point from which to draw baselines ... and by serving as a territorial basis from which to make claims to the continental shelf or economic zone". The "evolution of the new ocean regime has greatly increased the incentive for states to establish their title to any islands within reach—a marked contrast to the situation which existed until quite recently, when many islands were unclaimed"(Buzan 1978: 6). Buzan goes on to argue that the impact of islands, and low tide elevations will be to create a number of disputes (Buzan 1978: 6). Very little about the South China Sea dispute nearly 30 years later would be surprising from this perspective. There is relative predictability in geostrategic maritime issues: states will have disputes in situations where the desire to enclose the oceans conflicts with the imperative to keep them open.

The areas where such conflict will occur are also reasonably predictable: in the parts of the world where states have directly overlapping EEZs, or competing claims to the same waters, there is the potential for argument over resources and transit. The world's maritime chokepoints map on to these areas, because overlapping EEZs are created by areas where states are very close together along their coastlines, as is the case in the South China Sea or the Straits of Malacca. It is likely that states with very diverse strategic interests, such as China, the US, Russia, Canada, and Australia, nonetheless have the same list of potential maritime security hotspots. They would disagree only on which state has the right side in the dispute, not that the potential for dispute is there.

While the location of disputes and even the players are reasonably predictable, states can be extremely creative in how they contest the rules. The South China Sea demonstrates the high level of creativity states can bring to contesting the rules in order to further their own security. While it has been no surprise that China would wish to exert claims to control a maritime route it finds essential for security and containing potentially lucrative resources, it is very surprising that it has chosen to do so by artificially extending coral reefs and low tide elevations in order to have them considered to be "islands." Predicting that there will be a problem is easy; predicting the myriad creative ways that states will respond to security imperatives is not.

41.4 The Future of Unconventional Maritime Security

The future of unconventional maritime security challenges is more contingent and accordingly less predictable. Unlike conventional maritime security threats, which stem from the conflict between self-interest and rules, unconventional threats stem from new applications of rules or new threats. It is not always clear when and why states will securitize a particular threat. For example, the securitization of migration, now common, would have been surprising in the context of the 1970s, when migration by sea was also a political issue. The idea of *non-refoulement*, or that refugees should not be turned away at sea or on land, is a commonly accepted fact of customary international law, treaty law, and doctrine (Goodwin-Gill 2011: 444). The only way that it has been possible to act outside these clearly articulated laws is to claim an exceptional situation—an "emergency." If an issue like migration by sea can be successfully securitized, in particular the treatment of unarmed people as threats, then it is equally possible that other maritime issues as yet unexplored may become security "threats" in the future.

Moreover, once these issues become securitized by some states, there is a contagion effect whereby other states also treat maritime crime as a security problem. Both the case of countering maritime smuggling of narcotics, which began as a US initiative in the Caribbean but is now seen around the world, and the Australian program of maritime interdiction of refugees have been adopted elsewhere. Thus, one national decision can quickly be adopted around the world and alter the wider maritime security landscape. While navies counter all types of maritime crime, when an issue becomes securitized it leads to more elaborate and institutionalized responses, which in turn alter the maritime security landscape.

Once maritime crimes have reached the status of a security issue, they are controlled at the highest levels of the state and by military means as well as conventional policing. However, their essential criminal nature does not go away. A further reason for the unpredictability of maritime security threats is that crime evolves unpredictably in response to control measures. For example, the narcotics trade in the Caribbean has become dramatically more sophisticated, and smugglers are able to use technologically complex submarines to evade detection (Papastavridis 2013: 27). In turn, naval and coastguard operations have evolved to counter these more sophisticated threats. Both criminal threat and control effort can evolve in unpredictable ways, that will be contingent on factors such as the desire of criminals to stay in business, and the will of authorities to continue their control.

A major contingent factor in controlling some maritime security threats is the challenge and expense posed by indefinite commitments. Crime control is not normally designed to eliminate crime, but to reduce it to acceptable minimum levels; if control efforts cease, crime is likely to be resurgent. Thus, complex crime control operations are usually indefinite, and often result in a situation where criminals and authorities operate in symbiosis (Hill 2006). While states have, in some cases, shown an appetite to persist with extremely expensive indefinite operations—as has been the case with the control of narcotics—they may not do so in all areas. For example, the multinational efforts to control piracy off the Somali coast are very costly, and the apparent successful eradication of pirates may prompt states to withdraw. Somali pirates appear to have turned to other forms of smuggling and appear likely to return to piracy if control efforts cease (Percy 2016).

Indeed, the complexity of responding to maritime crime has placed new issues in the security landscape and presented new security challenges. The legal division of the world's oceans into categories where different rules apply has meant that responding to maritime threats boasts its own particular ecosystem of challenges. For example, the maritime threat of people smuggling (whether or not the people in question are trafficked) originates as a crime within one domestic state. As a boat smuggling people crosses territorial waters into an EEZ and then on to the high seas, and then back into the territorial waters of the destination state, a different series of rules apply as to how and when that boat might be investigated, boarded, or stopped. Once a vessel is in the territorial waters of a state, it is up to that state and that state only to police its activity (Klein 2011: 68). Exceptions that allow the pursuit of a criminal vessel of any type into the territorial waters of another state are very rare. For example, naval interdiction of Somali piracy within Somali territorial waters had to be facilitated by a Security Council resolution.[13]

41.5 Conclusion

If maritime security has a past characterized by two issues, criminal threat and geostrategic challenge, and their interactions with law, what will characterize the future? The pattern of rules and challenge in the geostrategic realm means that it will be much less subject to contingency than in other domains. There will always be disputes over strategically significant maritime areas, or over access to strategically important natural resources in the seabed. These may sharpen as resources continue to become more scarce. Unpredictability in this realm will come from the relationship between rules and power. When will states abide by the rules and when will they choose to ignore them? However, the study of International Relations itself demonstrates that there is nothing new in this debate.

Studying maritime security is not only of inherent importance, but it also demonstrates the complex relationship between rules and security. Many maritime security disputes, even those that cut to the heart of the national interest, exist *only* because of the rules that govern the maritime space. States contest and challenge these rules, but the rules set the parameters for their action. Even when states fully intend to bend the rules and ignore the consequences, the laws of the sea are governing which rules they wish to bend and which consequences they will seek to ignore.

An international maritime order shaped profoundly by the rules will, as a consequence, have areas of comparative predictability. States will have conflicts over the reach, interpretation, and applicability of the rules. However, the multiplicity of ways that states can challenge the rules, and the way other states respond, is far less predictable.

While we tend to see criminals as the archetypal rule-breakers, in fact rules shape unconventional maritime security problems in very similar ways. The decision to make some activities illegal makes them lucrative, and therefore open to criminal exploitation. Decisions about which rules to create and which rules to enforce can also lead to an element of predictability for future maritime security. If an activity becomes illegal, and states enforce that law, it is possible to predict a new area of unconventional security problems.

The close relationship between law and both conventional and unconventional maritime security may also serve as a useful reminder for students of International Relations. When we seek to examine how security plays out in situations where states contest territory in a literal anarchy, we should look to the maritime as an immediate example. The fact that the high seas are not subject to hierarchical government but nonetheless heavily disciplined by rules is another piece of evidence demonstrating that state interaction ungoverned by rules is perhaps rarer than is often thought.

Notes

1. Koo also points out that the nature of the relationship between territorial waters, EEZs, and islands in East Asia creates a very significant number of maritime territorial disputes.

2. In total there are 16 areas partially or totally blocked.
3. A maritime feature is a noticeable land element that stops short of being an island, such as rocks, coral reefs, or sandbanks.
4. http://www.lowyinstitute.org/issues/south-china-sea
5. http://www.globaltimes.cn/content/997320.shtml
6. http://www.abc.net.au/news/2016-07-13/china-reasserts-claims-over-south-china-sea-after-hague-ruling/7625114
7. http://www.japantimes.co.jp/news/2016/09/30/national/china-warns-japan-playing-fire-south-china-sea/#.WA79YS195tQ
8. Oceans Beyond Piracy "found that maritime piracy cost the global economy between $5.7 and $6.1 billion in 2012. This figure reflects a drop in the cost of piracy to the global community of around $850 million, or 12.6% from 2011." <http://oceansbeyondpiracy.org/publications/economic-cost-somali-piracy-2012>. Even at the height of Somali pirate attacks, less than 1 percent of all shipping in the region was attacked (Percy and Shortland 2013: 69).
9. See also http://www.defenddemocracy.org/media-hit/an-inconvenient-flag/ and http://www.globalsecurity.org/military/world/liberia/registry.htm for more on ship registries.
10. http://www.abc.net.au/news/2016-08-28/east-timor-australia-maritime-border-to-be-negotiated-the-hague/7791778
11. http://www.bbc.com/news/world-asia-pacific-11341139
12. On the Battle of the Paracels, see O'Connell (1975: 11).
13. S/RES/1814 (2008).

References

Boczek, B. A. 1988. Peacetime Military Activities in the Exclusive Economic Zone of Third Countries. *Ocean Development & International Law*, 19(6): 445–68.

Booth, K. 1985. *Law, Force and Diplomacy at Sea*. London: George Allen & Unwin.

Bourbeau, P. 2011. *The Securitization of Migration: A Study of Movement and Order*. London: Taylor & Francis.

Bowden, A. 2010. *The Economic Cost of Maritime Piracy*, Working Paper, December 2010, One Earth Future Foundation.

Braund, D. 1993. Piracy under the Principate and the Ideology of Imperial Eradication. In J. Rich and G. Shipley (eds.), *War and Society in the Roman World*, pp. 195–212. London: Routledge.

Brewster, D. 2016. Silk Roads and Strings of Pearls: The Strategic Geography of China's New Pathways in the Indian Ocean. *Geopolitics*, 1–23.

Bueger, C. 2015. What is Maritime Security? *Marine Policy*, 53: 159–64.

Buzan, B. 1978. A Sea of Troubles? Sources of Dispute in the New Ocean Regime. *The Adelphi Papers*, 18: 143.

Buzan, B., O. Wæver, and J. De Wilde. 1998. *Security: A New Framework for Analysis*. Boulder, CO: Lynne Rienner Publishers.

DeSombre, E. R. 2008. Globalization, Competition, and Convergence: Shipping and the Race to the Middle. *Global Governance*, 14(2): 179–98.

Emmers, R. 2003. ASEAN and the Securitization of Transnational Crime in Southeast Asia. *The Pacific Review*, 16(3): 419–38.

Goodwin-Gill, G. S. 2011. The Right to Seek Asylum: Interception at Sea and the Principle of Non-Refoulement. *International Journal of Refugee Law*, 23(3): 443–57.

Guilfoyle, D. 2016. The South China Sea Abritration: The Influence of Law on Sea Power, *Richard Cooper Memorial Lecture, Available at:* SSRN: https://ssrn.com/abstracoup837586

Hammerstad, A. 2011. UNHCR and the Securitization of Forced Migration, in A. Betts and G. Loescher (eds.), *Refugees in International Relations*, pp. 237–61. Oxford: Oxford University Press.

Hill, P. B. E. 2006. *The Japanese Mafia: Yakuza, Law and the State*. New York: Oxford University Press.

Huysmans, J. 2000. The European Union and the Securitization of Migration. *JCMS: Journal of Common Market Studies*, 38(5): 751–77.

Karras, A. L. 2009. *Smuggling: Contraband and Corruption in World History*. Lanham, MD: Rowman and Littlefield.

Klein, N. 2011. *Maritime Security and the Law of the Sea*. Oxford: Oxford University Press.

Koo, M. G. 2009. The Senkaku/Diaoyu Dispute and Sino-Japanese Political-Economic Relations: Cold Politics and Hot Economics? *The Pacific Review*, 22(2): 205–32.

Kraska, J. 2011. *Maritime Power and the Law of the Sea*. New York: Oxford University Press.

Kraska, J. 2016a. *The Struggle for Law in the South China Sea*, September 21, 2016. *Available at:* http://docs.house.gov/meetings/AS/AS28/20160921/105309/HHRG-114-AS28-Wstate-KraskaSJDJ-20160921.pdf

Kraska, J. 2016b. Tyrants, Terrorists, and Traffickers int he Ungoverned Oceans. *SAIS Review of International Affairs*, 36(1): 87–96.

Leiner, F. 2007. *The End of Barbary Terror: America's 1815 War against the Pirates of North Africa*. New York: Oxford University Press.

McDonald, M. 2011. Deliberation and Resecuritization: Australia, Aslyum-Seekers and the Normative Limits of the Copenhagen School. *Australian Journal of Political Science*, 46(2).

Maurer, J. H. 1997. Arms Control and the Anglo-German Naval Race before World War I: Lessons for Today? *Political Science Quarterly*, 112(2): 285–306.

O'Connell, D. P. 1975. *The Influence of Law on Sea Power*. Manchester: Manchester University Press.

Österblom, H., A. Constable, and S. Fukumi. 2011. Illegal Fishing and the Organized Crime Analogy. *Trends in Ecology and Evolution*, 26(6): 261–2.

Papastavridis, E. 2013. *Combating Transnational Organized Crime at Sea*, United Nations Office on Drugs and Crime, Geneva. *Available at:* www.unodc.org/documents/organized-crime/GPTOC/Issue_Paper_-_TOC_at_Sea.pd

Pelz, S. E. 1974. *Race to Pearl Harbor: The Failure of the Second London Naval Conference and the Onset of World War II*. Cambridge, MA: Harvard University Press.

Percy, S. 2016. Maritime Crime and Naval Response. *Survival*, 58(3): 155–86.

Percy, S. and A. Shortland. 2013. Contemporary Maritime Piracy: Five Obstacles to Ending Somali Piracy. *Global Policy*, 4(1): 65–72.

Sharife, K. 2010. Flying a Questionable Flag: Liberia's Lucrative Shipping Industry. *World Policy Journal*, 27(4): 111–18.

Stephens, T. 2016. International Law of the Sea: China's Claims Dashed in South China Sea Arbitration. *LSJ: Law Society of NSW Journal*, 25: 73–5.

UNGA. 2008. *Oceans and the Law of the Sea: Report of the Secretary General*. New York: United Nations General Assembly.

Wing, M. J. 2003. Rethinking the Easy Way Out: Flags of Convenience in the Post-September 11th era. *Tulane Maritime Law Journal*, 28(1): 173–90.

World Bank. 2013. The pirates of Somalia: ending the threat, rebuilding a nation. *Available at:* http://www.worldbank.org/africa/piratesofsomalia

CHAPTER 42

GLOBAL HEALTH AND SECURITY

Reassessing the Links

SUSAN PETERSON

In September 2014 US President Barack Obama cited the "profound political and economic and security implications for all of us" of the surging Ebola epidemic in West Africa. "This is an epidemic that is not just a threat to regional security. . . . It's a potential threat to global security" (Mason and Giyahue 2014). By October the President announced the deployment of up to 4,000 US engineers and military personnel to stem an Ebola outbreak that ultimately killed 11,310 people (Kamradt-Scott 2015: 175; CDC 2014). In the midst of the crisis, the United Nations Security Council (UNSC) declared the Ebola epidemic "a threat to international peace and security" and established the United Nations Mission for Ebola Emergency Response, the first UN health mission ever undertaken (UNSC 2014; UNGA 2014).

It seems an appropriate time to ask whether health issues, particularly infectious diseases (IDs), pose security threats. Should scholars and practitioners highlight the connections between the two arenas? The answer is not obvious. By definition, IDs threaten human security—that is, safety from threats to people, individually and collectively, caused by a range of dangers, including but not limited to military force (Paris 2001). But health issues have not permeated the national security field, which traditionally has focused on the preservation of the state from physical threats.

Paradoxically, awareness of health issues is pervasive in many policy-making circles. In 1998 President Bill Clinton added a Special Advisor for International Health Affairs to the National Security Council (NSC). Today, the Office of the President includes both the Senior Director for Global Health Security and Biothreats and the Director for Global Health and International Development. The US Intelligence Community has released at least four major reports on the effects of global health, especially IDs, on

US national security (NIC 2000, 2002, 2003, 2008), and the previous three US presidents included global health issues in their National Security Strategies (Bush 2006; Clinton 1998; Obama 2015). After 1996 the Department of Defense's mission "expanded to include support of global surveillance, training, research, and response to emerging infectious disease threats" (White House 1996), and in the 1990s the World Health Organization (WHO) launched a "global health security" initiative (Weir 2015).

While extensive, these and related efforts are rooted in a narrow, contested notion of the relationship between health and security that privileges defense against biological weapons and pathogens that might threaten the developed world. To attract resources to global health, scholars and practitioners have brought national security thinking to a topic for which it is ill-suited. For theoretical, normative, and instrumental reasons, security provides a poor rationale for addressing health concerns and, ultimately, efforts to link health and security will not achieve the result their advocates seek—global cooperation on pressing health issues. That these advocates mean well does not change the fact that casting health as a national security issue has led and will continue to lead to the "garrisoning of states behind national boundaries and national security rhetoric" (Peterson 2002/03: 81).

The foreseeable future will be marked by major disease outbreaks. Growing resistance to modern drugs, refugee flows, and high-speed travel permit increasing numbers of microbes to jump the boundary between animal and human hosts and spread around the globe. Slow, inadequate, and uncoordinated responses to such outbreaks, such as we saw in 2013–14 in West Africa, may seem to confirm the need for a securitized approach to disease. In reality, however, outbreaks will be worsened by policies based on such claims, which have a self-fulfilling quality: treating global health primarily as a security issue encourages national, self-interested responses and exacerbates health disparities that may, in turn, facilitate the outbreak and spread of disease.

The news is not all bad, however; early efforts to trace the national security implications of IDs have attracted attention to global health and embedded disease experts within many security and foreign policy bureaucracies. Within the academy, these efforts have helped produce a wave of interest in global health and helped create a vibrant, interdisciplinary, and policy-oriented field that views health as a global governance issue. This field—which benefits from the study of medicine, politics, human rights, economics, development, and security—may finally convince International Relations (IR) scholars to bring global health in from the cold.

The rest of the chapter proceeds in four parts. Section 42.1 briefly outlines attempts over the past two decades by scholars and practitioners to link health and security. The second section highlights the resistance in some academic and policy circles to securitizing health, and Section 42.3 explores the reasons efforts to connect health and security will not succeed in producing greater resources for global health challenges. The chapter concludes by looking to the future of the global health governance field.

42.1 Linking Health and Security

Throughout human history disease has threatened people and states. By the nineteenth century diseases like cholera were widely perceived as external threats to Western states. At the end of the Second World War, the charter of the World Health Organization (WHO) enshrined health as a basic human right, and by mid-century—when developed states had acquired potent medical, pharmaceutical, and public health tools to counter disease within their own borders—health became a development issue largely affecting countries in the global South. It was not until the 1990s, following the end of the Cold War and the emergence of Acquired Immune Deficiency Syndrome (AIDS) and the human immunodeficiency virus (HIV) that causes it, that health re-emerged as a security issue—that is, a largely external threat to states (Kamradt-Scott 2015: 193). Calls from academics and practitioners to expand our traditional notion of security to include health followed developed states' increasing awareness of their vulnerability to IDs and often were driven by attempts to garner resources for disease prevention and control.

The end of the Cold War brought a reduction in the superpower rivalry that had dominated security thinking for half a century. Alone, this might have generated new thinking about the relationship between security and health, but it was accompanied by a major new viral outbreak, HIV, and the recognition that global changes heralded new and re-emerging microbial threats. Increasing economic and cultural integration—globalization—carried the potential for unintended effects, including the emergence and spread of disease. By the late twentieth century, air travel allowed individuals to circumnavigate the globe in a single day; trade, finance, and food production required the movement of large numbers of people and goods everyday; the flow of economic and political refugees soared; and advanced telecommunications brought news from across the world within minutes. Together, these forces created a world that is far more interconnected in far more ways, including pathogenically, than ever before (see Lee 2003).

Some IR scholars responded with a call to action; they sought to expand traditional definitions of national and international security to encompass a broader range of potential dangers, including health threats. As early as 1983 Richard Ullman (1983: 133) had redefined a national security threat as "an action or sequence of events that (1) threatens drastically and over a relatively brief span of time to degrade the quality of life for the inhabitants of a state, or (2) threatens significantly to narrow the range of policy choices available to the government of a state or to private, nongovernmental entities (persons, groups, corporations) within the state." This reconceptualization invited others (e.g. Homer-Dixon 1999) to examine the relationship between environmental factors and security.

Beginning in the 1990s academics also explored the links between health and security. One approach, human security, views security from the individual level of analysis (see Buzan 1983). The human security concept dates from the influence of Mahbub ul Haq's work on the United Nations Development Programme's (UNDP) 1994 annual Human Development Report (Caballero-Anthony and Amul 2015: 33). The report called for a "profound transition in thinking" and criticized the concept of security for "relat[ing] more to nation-states than to people. . . . Forgotten were the legitimate concerns of ordinary people who sought security in their daily lives. For many of them, security symbolized protection from the threat of disease, hunger, unemployment, crime, social conflict, political repression and environmental hazards" (UNDP 1994: 22).

A second approach to the study of health and security emerged from traditional security studies, more narrowly defined as the "study of the threat, use, and control of military force" (Walt 1991: 212). These works also call for "a fundamental reconceptualization of standard definitions of national and international security" (Price-Smith 1999: 432), but they explore ways in which IDs can threaten international and domestic conflict and stability through: the weakening of military and peacekeeping forces; significant loss of life within the general population; increased refugee flows; increasing numbers of orphans; higher crime levels; the gutting of governance and civil service institutions; and economic devastation (Price-Smith 1999, 2002; Fidler 2001; Peterson 2002/03; Singer 2002). Scholars began exploring the security implications of HIV/AIDS, in particular (Rosen 1987; de Waal 2003; Elbe 2003), although more recently the logic has been extended to other emerging and re-emerging diseases, including SARS (Caballero-Anthony 2005) and influenza (Enemark 2009).

The third approach, securitization theory, emerged from the Copenhagen School. Barry Buzan's (1983: 6) claim that security is a contested concept paved the way for the insight that framing an issue as a security threat raises it to the level of "high politics," necessitating "exceptional measures" (Buzan et al. 1998: 24). Infectious disease becomes a security threat when securitizing actors, including academics and practitioners, engage in speech acts that persuade an audience with the ability to authorize extraordinary measures that pathogens pose an existential threat (Wæver 1995; Buzan et al. 1998). By 2007, David Fidler (2007: 41) argued, "securitization ha[d] happened" and global health governance had entered a "post-securitization phase" in which it was widely accepted that health issues threaten security.

Finally, a growing literature on health threats to security embodies a global health security approach, which focuses on global efforts to detect and respond to disease outbreaks (Weir 2015). Scholars in this tradition (e.g. Davies et al. 2015; Kamradt-Scott 2015) explore global health governance, often studying the WHO's attempts to "minimize vulnerability to acute public health events that endanger the collective health of populations living across geographical regions and international boundaries" (WHO 2007: ix). They explore the 2005 revision of the WHO's International Health Regulations (IHR), as well as other surveillance and rapid response efforts by the WHO, nongovernmental entities, national governments, and public–private partnerships.

Various efforts to link health and security have resonated with policy officials.[1] In 1991 the US Institute of Medicine convened an interdisciplinary committee on emerging microbial threats that concluded that "some infectious diseases that now affect people in other parts of the world represent potential threats to the United States because of global interdependence, modern transportation, trade, and changing social and cultural patterns" (Lederberg et al. 1992). President Clinton addressed "new diseases, such as AIDS, and other epidemics" in his 1996 National Security Strategy and issued a Presidential Decision Directive ordering the Department of Defense to integrate emerging disease threats into its work (White House 1996). USAID (2001: 17-18) outlined HIV/AIDS' effects on elements of national security, and a US National Intelligence Estimate (NIC 2000) concluded that global infectious diseases will endanger US citizens, armed forces, and interests. In 2003, then Director of Central Intelligence George Tenet (2003) testified to Congress that "[t]he national security dimension of [HIV/AIDS] is plain: it can undermine economic growth, exacerbate social tensions, diminish military preparedness, create huge social welfare costs, and further weaken already beleaguered states. And the virus respects no border."

Today, US national security documents routinely reference the risk of pandemic disease. The 2006 National Security Strategy explicitly acknowledged the threat posed by a wide range of "public health challenges like pandemics (HIV/AIDS, avian influenza)" (Bush 2006: 47), while the 2007 Joint Forces Command report on future security challenges warned that a plague-like "pandemic in North America would be protracted and pervasive, causing substantial societal impact and persistent economic losses in almost every state" (USJFCOM 2007: 53). The most recent National Security Strategy (Obama 2015) discusses health security, including fighting pandemics, as an "enduring national interest."

The events of September 11, 2001, and the subsequent anthrax attacks, accelerated US leaders' concerns over disease threats and highlighted their potential to contribute to state failure and terrorism. In 2002 the US Congress created the Department of Homeland Security (DHS), including an Office of Health Affairs that now works on detection of biological attacks and emergency preparedness, and passed the Public Health Security and Bioterrorism Preparedness and Response Act of 2002 to restrict access to biological agents and toxins. The Centers for Disease Control established the Office of Public Health Preparedness and Response in 2002 to strengthen "the nation's health security" (CDC 2016). President Bush proposed and in 2004 Congress created BioShield to purchase and stockpile vaccines against biological agents and facilitate research, development, and use of medical countermeasures to biological, chemical, radiological, and nuclear agents (Bush 2004; Elbe 2010: 88–97). After 2001 the United States also launched the Global Health Security Initiative—an informal, international partnership to improve efforts to detect and respond to biological, chemical, radiological, and nuclear terrorism (GHSI n.d.).

US and Western security concerns also infused the WHO's efforts. From 1995 to 2005, member states and WHO staff created a "sociotechnical apparatus for early outbreak detection and rapid response." WHO documents "recontextualized the [emerging infectious disease] concept from U.S. domestic public health onto international public health at WHO . . . . [T]he United States, Canada, and the European Union . . . formed an alliance around EID as a need of the global north" (Weir 2015: 20). In the mid-1990s the World Health Assembly (WHA), the WHO's legislative body, approved resolutions authorizing revision of the IHR and development of improved strategies for combatting emerging infectious diseases. The organization began using an NGO network to search nongovernmental sources for evidence of outbreaks, including many diseases not covered by the existing IHR. In 1997 WHO started operating its own Global Outbreak Alert and Response Network (GOARN), which it formally established in 2000 (Fidler 2004: 63, 66–67, 2005: 347). The IHR were approved in 2005 and came into force in 2007 as part of the WHO's global health security initiative, an agenda to prevent the international spread of IDs that took its name from the WHA's 2001 resolution, *Global Health Security: Epidemic Alert and Response* (Aldis 2008: 370; Weir 2015: 21).

The language of threat, risk, and security permeated WHO documents for a decade. In 2002 the organization's Communicable Disease Report was entitled *Global Defense Against the Infectious Disease Threat*. The next year, the WHO Commission on Macroeconomics and Health found "the massive amount of disease burden in the world's poorest nations poses a huge threat to global wealth and security" (quoted in Davies 2010: 143). In 2006 the WHO identified "individual and global health security" as one of the international organization's two top goals (quoted in Kamradt-Scott 2015: 160). And the 2007 WHO report (2007: ix), "A Safer Future: Global Public Health Security in the 21st Century," defined "global public health security" to include "the activities required, both proactive and reactive, to minimize vulnerability to acute public health events that endanger the collective health of populations living across geographical regions and international boundaries."

42.2 Health and Security: An Idea That Didn't Quite Catch On

Despite all the ink that has been spilled on the subject, the securitization of global health remains, as Jeremy Youde (2016: 161) tells us, "partial and incomplete at best." The traditional security field has not embraced health studies, despite efforts to incorporate non-military threats. Health is central to the concept of human security, and academic work in that field has grown exponentially, but not within the Western academy. Less than 2 percent of IR scholars in the United States and 1.1 percent in the United Kingdom reported in 2014 that human security was their primary research area; another 5.3 percent and 3.4 percent, respectively, described it as a secondary sub-field (TRIP 2015).

Traditional security studies still focus on the use of force. Only 27.6 percent of US scholars and 33.1 percent of British scholars who teach security include any health-related material in their classes; in all, 34.8 percent of scholars in the 33 countries surveyed in 2014 included such content (TRIP 2015). Only 3.5 percent of IR scholars identify health or epidemic disease among the three most important foreign policy issues facing their countries today. On the 2014 TRIP survey, when scholars were asked to name the three most important issues *over the next ten years*, concern for global health issues increased modestly, with 5.1 percent selecting disease/health. Not surprisingly, relatively few IR scholars study global health issues. In 2014 less than 1 percent listed health as their primary sub-field, and another 1.3 percent called it a secondary research area (TRIP 2015).

The dearth of interest among IR scholars in global health is partially reflected in the dominant security texts. Fewer than half of an admittedly unscientific sample of 21 major security textbooks include significant material on health and/or IDs, including biological weapons. Many of the textbooks that do devote space to health address "new threats and new actors" (Krahmann 2005) or "contemporary" security studies (Collins 2007).

By definition, health issues suffuse the study of human security, although this field remains analytically distinct from international security. In some academic communities, particularly in Asia, the study of human security is more common than it is in the United States (Caballero-Anthony and Amul 2015; Howe 2013). Western security textbooks (e.g. Reveron and Mahoney-Harris 2011) sometimes discuss human security, but the idea generally is broached only when defining the contours of the security discipline or considering emerging security issues (e.g. Kay 2015; Caldwell and Williams 2016). Students of international security often critique the human security idea as overly expansive and vague. The term may be useful as a political rallying cry, according to Roland Paris (2001), but it is not analytically useful (also Macfarlane and Khong 2006). Stefan Elbe (2009: 34) similarly concludes that calling a disease like AIDS a human security threat amounts to a "definitional fiat."

Securitization theory's insight that threats are socially constructed has strongly influenced the IR discipline. But securitization explores how issues come to be framed as security problems, not whether and to what extent a threat such as disease materially threatens a state or its inhabitants. Despite the growth of securitization theory, moreover, McInnes and Rushton (2011) argue that even HIV/AIDS was incompletely securitized and, in the last decade, has been at least partly de-securitized and moved back toward the realm of normal politics (also Youde 2016).

A major reason security scholars have not fully embraced global health issues is that the empirical links between the two remain weak. As new medications became available, the fears that drove much of the AIDS and security rhetoric faded. A wave of revisionist research further suggested that earlier claims, particularly about the security implications of HIV/AIDS, were overdrawn (DeWaal 2006; Elbe 2009). HIV/AIDS continues to pose a humanitarian crisis, but the security concerns of the 1990s and early 2000s, including high rates of HIV prevalence in national military forces, have faded. It was thought that hard-hit forces, with infection rates of 60 percent or more, would face threats to: military readiness, morale, and recruitment; ability to contribute to regional peacekeeping efforts; medical systems; and government control of armed forces (Heinecken 2001; Elbe 2003: chs. 2–3). Within a few years, however, many students of the pandemic realized that the feared decimation of national military forces by AIDS was not materializing; military prevalence levels, in fact, are considerably lower than initially forecast and, in some cases, lower than those in the general population (de Waal 2006; Elbe 2009: 35–9). Even general prevalence rates have been overstated;

the tendency to focus on prevalence levels within only a portion of the adult population, rather than on overall mortality rates, may have exaggerated the epidemic (Elbe 2009: 43–4).

Dire predictions that AIDS would lead to state failure, civil war, civil–military conflict, and/or interstate war through its effects on economic, political, and social structures (e.g. Elbe 2003: ch. 4; Price-Smith 1999, 2002) also have not materialized. As Pieter Fourie (2015: 105) notes "there is no empirical proof to support the hypothesis that AIDS, even in the context of mature, high-prevalence epidemics, poses any significant threat to state survival." The states that have or are in danger of failing do not match those hardest hit by HIV/AIDS. A 2005 meeting of US experts on sub-Saharan Africa (NIC 2005: 2) concluded that, although increasing numbers of people would continue to die from AIDS, "it is not clear if AIDS can be directly tied to state collapse in the way that was feared and anticipated a few years ago." The rhetoric may linger, but the idea that IDs threaten national and international security, driven mainly by the effects of AIDS, has been largely exposed as what Elbe (2009) calls a "noble lie."

The global health security agenda also faces challenges from developing countries. From the beginning, some WHO members mistrusted the security logic behind global health efforts and specifically questioned US efforts to include chemical, biological, radiological, and nuclear (CBRN) threats in the IHR (Weir 2015: 24–6). Developing states worried that the global disease surveillance and response system had been initiated by the United States and its allies to prevent the deliberate or inadvertent spread of IDs from the South to the North (Weir 2015). In 2006 Indonesia refused to continue sharing H5N1 samples with the WHO. When that country, which had the highest number of people succumbing to H5N1, subsequently sought to purchase vaccines created using samples it had provided, it was sent to the back of the line (Aldis 2008: 372; Kamradt-Scott 2015: 158–9). Brazil, Thailand, and India also opposed the security concept, more generally, with Brazil complaining that the WHO's 2007 World Health Report contained "confrontational language that was more appropriate to the UN Security Council than to the International Health Regulations" (cited in Kamradt-Scott 2015: 159).

Opposition from developing countries chipped away at the WHO's global health security initiative. References to CBRN were deleted from the final IHR, and the language of "threat" and "security" in that document was replaced with "public health risk" (Aldis 2008: 370). The "WHO has an international security mandate under the IHR (2005), but one narrower than the United States had desired" (Weir 2015: 26). By 2012, indeed, the WHO had almost completely abandoned the phrase "global health security" (Kamradt-Scott 2015: 160–2).

42.3 Why Not Securitize Health?

Advocates of securitizing health seek resources to address dangers to human well-being, but depicting health concerns as national security threats is counter-productive.

Certainly, some health issues may threaten national security and/or international stability. Over the last two decades, however, efforts to securitize health have been based on a narrow, contested idea of the link between health and security that privileges defense against infectious pathogens that might threaten developed states. Such national thinking is not well suited to problems that so easily cross borders and require medical, development, and public health—not national military—solutions.

Attempts to securitize IDs are not new. There was no medical treatment for the repeated cholera epidemics that spread from India to Russia and Europe in the nineteenth century, so states responded with a dizzying array of national quarantine policies designed to protect their own citizens (Goodman 1971). Of limited value in preventing the spread of disease, these policies inhibited trade and travel, propelling national governments to coordinate their policies. This collaboration only became possible through a series of 14 international conferences at which states shared medical and scientific knowledge (Howard-Jones 1975). Those meetings eventually led to the creation of the WHO. But when the developed world acquired powerful new drugs to battle disease, they took their new weapons and went home to fight pathogens in their own countries. In the 1990s, as the effects of globalization and growing resistance to the West's pharmaceutical weapons again raised the ID specter, the United States and other countries jumped back onto the international stage. There is every reason to believe that if the West succeeds in establishing a strong outbreak detection and response system and developing vaccines and treatments to protect its civilian and military populations, it will again retreat behind national borders, rather than help the developing world control disease.

Observers raise a number of additional arguments, beyond these historical reasons, and the theoretical reasons discussed above, for keeping health and security analytically distinct. I extrapolate from Elbe's (2006) ethical objections to securitizing HIV/AIDS two major arguments against focusing on the security effects of IDs more generally. First, using security language to draw attention to health problems locates solutions within the military and other security institutions of the state. This can lead to the erosion of basic human rights, lack of support for public health programs, loss of medical and public health authority, and inappropriate and ineffective health policies (Elbe 2006; Kamradt-Scott 2015).

Second, the logic of defense against security threats may undermine efforts to prevent and control the spread of IDs. Encouraging international efforts by highlighting narrowly self-interested reasons for developed states to share the health burden in the developing world implies that health is less important than security and relieves the West of a moral obligation to help developing nations (Zelikow 2000; Peterson 2002/03; Elbe 2006). Focusing on a security rationale also inevitably prioritizes some diseases over others based on the degree of threat they pose to the developed world. HIV/AIDS, SARS, and influenza receive more attention and resources, for example, than other IDs and chronic conditions that may kill significant numbers of people, albeit in limited geographic regions outside the West (Garrett 2007; Davies 2010; McInnes and Lee 2012; Kamradt-Scott 2015). Linking health to security may reduce funding for national health systems in developing countries (Stevenson and Moran 2015) and divert funding within those systems away from poverty-related challenges and core infrastructural needs toward diseases such as HIV/AIDS (Aldis 2008; DaLaet 2015: 339). Finally, framing disease control as a national security issue may undermine global health efforts by prioritizing funding for political and military elites, and it may weaken public health and anti-discrimination efforts to normalize public perceptions of the disease (Elbe 2006).

These normative concerns also suggest a set of instrumental reasons developed states should downplay the security rationale for their global health policies. The developed world pursued an effective alert and response system through the 2005 IHR. In the process WHO members recognized that preventing and responding to outbreaks requires strong national health systems, so the IHR mandates that all states develop minimum surveillance, detection, and response capabilities. Developed states provided no new resources to developing countries to build this infrastructure, however, and as of the 2012 deadline for implementing the 2005 IHR only 22 percent of WHO states had fully developed core capacities (Gostin and Phelan 2014: 27). Helping lower- and middle-income states develop stronger national health systems may not be an obvious security strategy for wealthier states concerned with stopping disease at their borders, but it will have significant positive effects on surveillance, detection, and response.

Second, US and Western advocacy of global health security has politicized the WHO in ways that could further undermine the organization's ability to provide continued leadership in health governance. In years past, the United States objected when the WHA passed resolutions perceived to be more political than health-related, such as those warning of the dangers of nuclear weapons or the epidemiological effects of the Vietnam War and those supporting Palestinians' right to self determination (Jacobson 1973: 187; Williams 1987: 63–4; Karns and Mingst 1992: 223). Attempts to include CBRN incidents in the 2005 IHR—indeed, the whole global health security initiative—represent for some a similarly political attempt to incorporate "an international security matter outside WHO's remit" (Weir 2015: 22).

42.4 The Future of Global Health and International Relations

In recent decades a growing awareness of bioterrorist threats and the emergence and re-emergence of disease-causing pathogens—such as those linked to HIV/AIDS, SARS, Ebola, avian and swine influenza, extensive drug-resistant tuberculosis, and Zika—have mobilized many in the Western academy and policy-making circles to shine a brighter light on health issues. Linking health and security raised the profile of disease within the study of IR (Taylor 2004: 501; Davies 2010: 151) and changed the discourse, staffing, and mission of some national and international agencies. IDs were securitized, but not fully. Only diseases with a potential to threaten the West were framed as security threats;

forecasts of the calamitous security consequences of HIV/AIDS were downgraded over time; and the field of security studies, at least in the West, did not embrace the concepts of human security or health security.

More significantly, the security logic used to investigate and respond to incipient IDs reinforced prevailing trends and biases. In previous historical eras developed states cooperated to contain pathogens originating in the developing world. Once those states secured their own populations and trade routes, however, interest waned. The current interest in global health, linked as it is to Western notions of security and defense against pathogenic threats, will again likely produce a garrison mentality, not global cooperation. Calls for global health action, in short, may create a self-fulfilling prophecy. The failure of the WHO, weakened by years of budgetary cuts and declining support from developed states, to quickly respond to the 2013 Ebola outbreak in West Africa until Western nations framed the disease as a security threat may seem to confirm the claim that securitizing health is an effective strategy for attracting greater resources and awareness. In reality, however, it suggests that health policy may imitate academic and advocacy rhetoric: if developed states only provide significant bilateral health assistance or extra-budgetary funding through the WHO when national leaders believe a disease threatens their own states' security, health crises in developing countries will be allowed to emerge and fester unless or until they threaten developed nations.

There is cause for optimism, however; security is just one of many ways to cast our thinking about global health. Colin McInnes and Kelly Lee (2012) outline at least five competing, but overlapping frames for global health—medical, human rights, economic, security, and development—that each highlight different norms, actors, and interests. Together, these approaches suggest the growth of an interdisciplinary, policy-oriented sub-field of global health governance within International Relations (not the narrower sub-field of international security) that explores the institutions and processes by which states, IOs, and non-state actors collectively meet health challenges that cross national borders (Fidler 2010: 3). It is not difficult to envision global health as a field akin to global environmental politics, although one still relatively early in its development. A focus on global health governance, as Davies (2010: 4) notes, creates the "possibility of studying health issues without the need to justify such studies through the language of security, which inevitably narrows the scope of health issues that can be explored and frames the way in which they are studied." Outside a strict security frame, scholars examine a range of topics, such as: diseases of the developing world; human rights implications of health policies; and the role of civil society, markets, and NGOs in health governance.

National and international leaders will not and should not decide that health and security are unrelated. They clearly are linked, particularly when pathogens threaten to kill significant numbers of people, gut military forces, or significantly damage the economy. Many disease threats can be controlled through national policies inspired by the logic of defense against security threats. But the increased mobility of people and goods wrought by globalization, the emergence and re-emergence of a host of IDs, unprecedented refugee flows, and the contemporary bioterrorist threat make disease control more difficult than in earlier eras. The speed and distance of the recent Zika outbreak suggest that the world will continue to confront epidemic and pandemic diseases. Purely national policies based on a security logic of the defense of the state against external threats, as the authors of nineteenth-century quarantine policies discovered, cannot address global health challenges in ways that facilitate trade and travel; nor can they reduce health disparities between the developed and developing worlds. Certainly, we should not cast aside the security lens when studying and responding to global health issues, but national security is not the only or even the most appropriate vehicle for confronting the major health challenges of the twenty-first century.[2]

Notes

1. I discuss only US examples, but US agencies and leaders were not alone in their attempts to link pathogenic safety and national security (e.g. Elbe 2010: 32).
2. I thank Amy Oakes, Heather Scully, and Michael Tierney for helpful comments, and Hali Czosnek, Brendan Helm, and Elizabeth Martin for research assistance.

References

Aldis, W. 2008. Health Security as a Public Health Concept: A critical analysis. *Health Policy and Planning*, 23: 369–75.

Bush. G. W. 2004. President Bush Signs Project Bioshield Act of 2004. *Available at:* http://georgewbush-whitehouse.archives.gov/news/releases/2004/07/20040721-2.html, accessed June 25, 2016.

Bush, G. W. 2006. *National Security Strategy of the United States of America*. White House. *Available at:* http://www.state.gov/documents/organization/64884.pdf, accessed July 10, 2016.

Buzan, B. 1983. *People, States and Fear: The National Security Problem in International Relations*. Chapel Hill: University of North Carolina Press.

Buzan, B., O. Wæver, and J. de Wilde, J. 1998. *Security: A New Framework for Analysis*. Boulder, CO: Lynne Rienner Publishers.

Caballero-Anthony, M. 2005. SARS in Asia: Crisis, Vulnerabilities and Regional Responses. *Asian Survey*, 45: 475–95.

Caballero-Anthony, M. and G. G. Amul. 2015. Health and Human Security: Pathways to Advancing a Human-centered Approach to Health Security in East Asia. In S. Rushton and J. Youde (eds.), *Routledge Handbook of Health Security*, pp. 32–47. London and New York: Routledge.

Caldwell, D. and R. E. Williams Jr. 2016. *Seeking Security in an Insecure World*, 3rd edn. Lanham, MD: Rowman & Littlefield Publishers.

Centers for Disease Control (CDC). 2014. *2014 Ebola Outbreak in West Africa—Case Counts*. *Available at:* http://www.cdc.gov/vhf/ebola/outbreaks/2014-west-africa/case-counts.html, accessed June 15, 2016.

Centers for Disease Control (CDC). *Office of Public Health Preparedness and Response*. *Available at:* http://www.cdc.gov/phpr/about.htm, accessed June 25, 2016.

Clinton, W. 1996. *A National Security Strategy of Engagement and Enlargement*. White House. *Available at:* http://nssarchive.us/NSSR/1996.pdf, accessed July 10, 2016.

Clinton, W. 1998. *A National Security Strategy for a New Century*. White House. *Available at:* http://history.defense.gov/Portals/70/Documents/nss/nss1998.pdf?ver=2014-06-25-121250-857, accessed July 10, 2016.

Collins, A. (ed.). 2007. *Contemporary Security Studies*. Oxford: Oxford University Press.

DaLaet, D. L. 2015. Whose Interest is the Securitization of Health Serving? In S. Rushton and J. Youde (eds.), *Routledge Handbook of Health Security*, pp. 339–348. London and New York: Routledge.

Davies, S. E. 2010. *Global Politics of Health*. Cambridge: Polity Press.

Davies, S., A. Kamradt-Scott, and S. Rushton. 2015. *Disease Diplomacy: International Norms and Global Health Security*. Baltimore, MD: Johns Hopkins University Press.

de Waal, A. 2003. How Will HIV/AIDS Transform African Governance? *African Affairs*, 102(406): 1–23.

de Waal, A. 2006. *AIDS and Power: Why There Is No Political Crisis—Yet*. London: Zed Books.

Elbe, S. 2003. *Strategic Implications of HIV/AIDS (Adelphi Papers)*. Oxford: Oxford University Press.

Elbe, S. 2006. Should HIV/AIDS Be Securitized? The Ethical Dilemmas of Linking HIV/AIDS and Security. *International Studies Quarterly*, 50(1): 119–44.

Elbe, S. 2009. *Virus Alert: Security, Governmentality, and the AIDS Pandemic*. New York: Columbia University Press.

Elbe, S. 2010. *Security and Global Health*. Cambridge: Polity.

Enemark, C. 2009. Is Pandemic Flu A Security Threat? *Survival*, 51(1): 43–81.

Fidler, D. 2001. The Return of "Microbialpolitik." *Foreign Affairs* (January/ February): 80–1.

Fidler, D. 2004. *SARS, Governance, and the Globalization of Disease*. Basingstoke: Palgrave Macmillan.

Fidler, D. 2005. From International Sanitary Conventions to Global Health Security: The New International Health Regulations. *Chinese Journal of International Law*, 4(2): 325–92.

Fidler, D. 2007. A Pathology of Public Health Securitism: Approaching Pandemics as Security Threats. In A. F. Cooper, J. J. Cooper, and T. Schrecker (eds.), *Governing Global Health: Challenge, Response, Innovation*, pp. 41–64. Abingdon: Routledge.

Fidler, D. 2010. *The Challenges of Global Health*. New York: Council on Foreign Relations Press.

Fourie, P. 2015. AIDS as a Security Threat: The Emergence and the Decline of an Idea. In S. Rushton and J. Youde (eds.), London and New York, *Routledge Handbook of Health Security*, pp. 105–17. London and New York: Routledge.

Garrett, L. 2007. The Challenge of Global Health. *Foreign Affairs* (January/February). *Available at:* https://www.foreignaffairs.com/articles/2007-01-01/challenge-global-health, accessed July 10, 2016.

Global Health Security Initiative (GHSI). n.d. *GHSI Background*. *Available at:* http://www.ghsi.ca/english/background.asp, accessed June 25, 2016.

Goodman, N. 1971. *International Health Organizations and Their Work*. 2nd edn. Edinburgh: Churchill Livingstone.

Gostin, L. and A. Phelan. 2014. The Global Health Security Agenda in an Age of Biosecurity. *JAMA*, 312(1): 27–8.

Heinecken, L. 2001. Strategic Implications of HIV/AIDS in South Africa, *Conflict, Security & Development*, 1(1): 109–15

Homer-Dixon, T. 1999. *Environment, Scarcity and Violence*. Princeton, NJ: Princeton University Press.

Howard-Jones, N. 1975. The Scientific Background of the International Sanitary Conferences 1851–1938, *History of International Public Health*. Geneva: WHO.

Howe, B. 2013. *The Protection and Promotion of Human Security in East Asia*. Basingstoke: Palgrave Macmillan.

Jacobson, H. K. 1973. WHO: Medicine, Regionalism, and Managed Politics. In R. W. Cox and H. K. Jacobson (eds.), *The Anatomy of Influence: Decision Making in International Organization*. New Haven, CT: Yale University Press

Kamradt-Scott, A. 2015. Health, Security, and Diplomacy in Historical Perspective. In S. Rushton and J. Youde (eds.), *Routledge Handbook of Health Security*. London and New York: Routledge.

Karns, M. and K. Mingst. 1992. The United States and the World Health Organization. In M. Karns and K. Mingst (eds.), *The United States and Multilateral Institutions: Patterns of Changing Instrumentality and Influence*. London: Routledge.

Kay, S. 2015. *Global Security in the Twenty-First century: The Quest for Power and the Search for Peace*. Lanham, MD: Rowman and Littlefield.

Krahmann, E. (ed.). 2005. *New Threats And New Actors In International Security*. Basingstoke: Palgrave Macmillan.

Lederberg, J., R. E. Shope, and S. C. Oaks, Jr. (eds.). 1992. *Emerging Infections: Microbial Threats to Health in the United States*. Washington, DC: National Academy Press.

Lee, K. 2003. *Globalization and Health: An Introduction*. Basingstoke: Palgrave Macmillan.

MacFarlane, S. and Y. F. Khong. 2006. *Human Security and the UN: A Critical History*. Bloomington: Indiana University Press.

McInnes, C. and K. Lee. 2012. Health, Security, and Foreign Policy, *Review of International Studies*, 32(1): 5–23.

McInnes, C. and S. Rushton. 2011. HIV/AIDS and Securitization Theory. *European Journal of International Relations*, 19(1): 115–38.

Mason, J. and J. Giahyue. 2014. Citing Security Threat, Obama expands U.S. role fighting Ebola. *Reuters. Available at:* http://www.reuters.com/article/us-health-ebola-obama-idUSKBN-0HB08S201409167, accessed October 19, 2016.

National Intelligence Council (NIC). 2000. The Global Infectious Disease Threat and Its Implications for the United States, NIE 99-17D. (17 November). *Available at:* http://fas.org/irp/threat/nie99-17d.htm, accessed July 10, 2016.

National Intelligence Council (NIC). 2002. The Next Wave of HIV/AIDS: Nigeria, Ethiopia, Russia, India, and China, *Intelligence Community Assessment* 2002-04D. *Available at:* http://fas.org/irp/nic/hiv-aids.html, accessed July 11, 2016.

National Intelligence Council (NIC). 2003. SARS: Down But Still A Threat (August). *Available at:* https://www.dni.gov/files/documents/Special%20Report_SARS%20Down%20But%20Still%20a%20Threat.pdf, accessed July 11, 2016.

National Intelligence Council (NIC). 2005. Mapping Sub-Saharan Africa's Future. *Available at:* http://www.au.af.mil/au/awc/awcgate/nic/africa_future.pdf, accessed June 4, 2016.

National Intelligence Council (NIC). 2008. Strategic Implications of Global Health, *Intelligence Community Assessment* 2008-10D (December). *Available at:* https://www.dni.gov/files/documents/Special%20Report_ICA%20Global%20Health%202008.pdf, accessed July 11, 2016.

Obama, B. 2015. *National Security Strategy*. White House. *Available at:* https://www.whitehouse.gov/sites/default/files/docs/2015_national_security_strategy.pdf, accessed July 10, 2016.

Paris, R. 2001. Human Security: Paradigm Shift or Hot Air? *International Security*, 26(2): 87–102.

Peterson, S. 2002/03. Epidemic Disease and National Security. *Security Studies*, 12(2): 43–81.

Price-Smith, A. 1999. Ghosts of Kigali: Infectious Disease and Global Stability at the Turn of the Century, *International Journal*, 54(3): 432.

Price-Smith, A. 2002. *The Health of Nations: Infectious Disease, Environmental Change, and Their Effects on National Security and Development.* Cambridge, MA: MIT Press.

Reveron, D. S. and K. A. Mahoney-Norris. 2011. *Human Security in a Borderless World.* Boulder, CO: Westview Press.

Rosen, S. 1987. Strategic Implications of AIDS. *The National Interest*, 9: 64–73.

Singer, P. W. 2002. AIDS and International Security, *Survival*, 44(1): 145–58.

Stevenson, M. A. and M. Moran. 2015. Health Security and the Distortion of the Global Health Agenda. In S. Rushton and J. Youde (eds.), *Routledge Handbook of Health Security*, pp. 328–38. London and New York: Routledge.

Taylor, A. L. 2004. Governing the Globalization of Public Health. *Journal of Law, Medicine, and Ethics*, 32: 1073–105.

Tenet, G. 2003. DCI's Worldwide Threat Briefing The Worldwide Threat in 2003: Evolving Dangers in a Complex World (as prepared for delivery). *Available at:* https://www.cia.gov/news-information/speeches-testimony/2003/dci_speech_02112003.html, accessed June 12, 2016.

TRIP. 2015. TRIP Faculty Survey Data, Version 1.0.0 (September 30). *Available at:* https://trip.wm.edu/charts/, accessed July 10, 2016.

Ullman, R. H. 1983. Redefining Security. *International Security*, 8(1): 129–53.

United Nations Development Programme (UNDP). 1994. *Human Development Report 1994.* Oxford: Oxford University Press.

United Nations General Assembly (UNGA). 2014. Resolution Adopted by the General Assembly on 19 September 2014, 69/1. Measures to contain and combat the recent Ebola outbreak in West Africa. (23 September). *Available at:* http://www.un.org/en/ga/search/view_doc.asp?symbol=A/RES/69/1, accessed July 11, 2016.

United Nations Security Council (UNSC). 2014. Resolution 2177 (2014) (18 September). *Available at:* http://www.securitycouncilreport.org/atf/cf/%7B65BFCF9B-6D27-4E9C-8CD3-CF6E4FF96FF9%7D/S_RES_2177.pdf, accessed July 11, 2014.

United States Agency for International Development (USAID). 2001. *Leading the Way: USAID Responds to HIV/AIDS, 1997–2000.* Washington, DC: USAID.

United States Joint Forces Command (USJFCOM). 2007. *Joint Operating Environment: Trends & Challenges for the Future Joint Force Through 2030. Available at:* http://www.au.af.mil/au/awc/awcgate/jfcom/joe_dec2007.pdf, accessed July 10, 2016.

Wæver, O. 1995 Securitisation and Desecuritisation In R. Lipshutz (ed.), *On Security*, New York: Columbia University Press.

Walt, S. M. 1991. The Renaissance of Security Studies. *International Studies Quarterly*, 35(2): 211–39.

Weir, L. 2015. Inventing Global Health Security, 1994–2005. In S. Rushton and J. Youde (eds.), *Routledge Handbook of Health Security*, pp. 18–31. London and New York: Routledge.

White House. 1996. Presidential Decision Directive NSTC-7 http://fas.org/irp/offdocs/pdd/pdd-nstc-7.pdf, accessed July 10, 2016.

Williams, D. 1987. *The Specialized Agencies and the United Nations: The System in Crisis.* New York: St. Martin's Press.

World Health Organization (WHO). 2007. A Safer Future: Global Public Health Security in the 21st Century. *The World Health Report 2007.* Geneva: World Health Organization.

Youde, J. 2016. High Politics, Low Politics, and Global Health. *Journal of Global Security Studies*, 1(2): 157–70.

Zelikow, P. 2000. Review of The Global Infectious Disease Threat and Its Implications for the United States. *Foreign Affairs*, 74(4): 154.

PART V

TWENTY-FIRST-CENTURY INTERNATIONAL SECURITY ACTORS

CHAPTER 43

GREAT POWERS

BARRY BUZAN

43.1 Introduction

This chapter starts by arguing the need to differentiate between great powers and superpowers at the global level. From there, it looks at the structural implications, both material and ideational, of analyzing the major powers in this way. The third section sets out the shifting balance between, on the one hand, the traditional security agenda of great powers managing relations among themselves, and on the other, the rising new security agenda of how to manage a variety of shared fate problems. The last section features the pathology of *autism* in great powers, and how that affects the prospects for great power management in the decades ahead. The theoretical perspective combines a critique of the excessively broad category of "great power" common to much realist and liberal theory, with an English School concern not just about conflict among great powers, but also with great power management as an institution of international society. In contrast to most realist thinking (e.g. Mearsheimer 2001), this perspective rejects the ingrained pessimism that conflict among great powers is inevitable, though it certainly accepts that such conflict is possible. In contrast to most liberal thinking, it takes a wider view of the possibilities for cooperation among the great powers than mere rational choice, focusing more on international society as an expression of the desire for a degree of order among the great powers (Bull 1977).

43.2 Classification and Definition

This chapter builds on a book I wrote on great powers and polarity theory more than a decade ago (Buzan 2004: see also Buzan 2013). In that work, I understood great powers as both material and ideational constructs, and reviewed in detail the long-standing difficulties and uncertainties about how to identify and define them (Buzan 2004: 13–80).

Central to the argument was that what Hansen (2000: 18) called neorealism's commitment to a single stratification of states into great powers and other states, is deeply flawed. This flaw goes beyond the long-standing difficulty of finding plausible metrics to distinguish great powers from lesser ones (Brooks and Wohlforth 2015–16: 7–15). It is about a category error that is revealed in the approach to contemporary world politics more common among practitioners, of distinguishing between great powers and superpowers. This approach is both more descriptively accurate and more theoretically rewarding than "simple polarity theory" based on a single differentiation between great powers and all others. The key analytical move was therefore to distinguish between *superpowers* and *great powers* at the global level. These distinctions not only set up the actors to be discussed, but also define structural arrangements of "great powers" that are radically different from what comes out of "simple polarity theory" because they focus on superpowers and great powers and the interplay between them.

The criteria for superpower status are demanding in that they require broad spectrum capabilities exercised across the whole of the international system. Superpowers must possess first class military-political capabilities (as measured by the standards of the day), and the economies to support such capabilities. They must be capable of, and also exercise, global military and political reach. They need to see themselves, and be accepted by others in rhetoric and behavior, as having this rank. Superpowers must be active players in processes of securitization and desecuritization in all, or nearly all, of the regions in the system, whether as threats, guarantors, allies, or interveners. Except in extremely conflictual international systems, superpowers will also be fountainheads of "universal" values of the type necessary to underpin international society. Their legitimacy as superpowers will depend substantially on their success in establishing the legitimacy of such values. Taking all of these factors into account, during the nineteenth century only Britain unquestionably had this rank (Ferguson 2004: 222). After the First World War, it was held by Britain, the United States, and the Soviet Union. After the Second World War it was held by the United States and the Soviet Union. And after the Cold War it was held only by the United States.

Achieving great power status is less demanding in terms of both capability and behavior. Great powers need not necessarily have big capabilities in all sectors, and they need not be actively present in the securitization or economic processes of all areas of the international system. Great power status rests mainly on a single key: what distinguishes great powers from merely regional ones is that they are responded to by others on the basis of system-level calculations, as well as regional ones, about the present and near future distribution of power. A state may be awarded great power status by successfully trading on its potential as well as its actual capability. This single key is observable in the foreign policy processes and discourses of other powers. It means that actual possession of material and legal attributes is less crucial for great powers than for superpowers. They will generally think of themselves as more than regional powers, and possibly as prospective superpowers, and they will usually be capable of operating in more than one region. Mostly, great powers will be rising in the hierarchy of international power, but a second route into the category is countries declining from acknowledged superpower status. During the later nineteenth century, Germany, France, Russia, the United States, and Japan had great power rank. After the First World War, it was still held by Germany, Japan, and France. During the Cold War it was held by China, Germany, and Japan, with Britain and France coming increasingly into doubt. Here there was the difficult question of how to treat the EU, which as time wore on acquired more and more actor quality in the international system, and was by the 1970s being treated as an emergent great power, albeit of an unusual kind, and with some serious limitations. After the Cold War it was held by Britain/France/Germany–EU, Japan, China, and Russia. By the second decade of the twenty-first century, India was moving into the great power club in terms of capability, recognition, and place in the calculations of others.[1]

In identifying superpowers and great powers, the qualification noted just a few paragraphs above of "as measured by the standards of the day" is important. As Buzan and Lawson (2015: 240–70) argue, the multiple revolutions of modernity during the nineteenth century comprehensively redefined the qualifications for being a great power. The agrarian criteria of population size and wealth rapidly gave way to modern criteria built around industrialism, the rational state, and a new set of ideologies of progress. Countries that were too slow to acquire the revolutions of modernity, such as China and the Ottoman Empire, quickly fell out of the ranks of great powers, whereas countries that were quick to adopt them, such as Japan, Germany, and the United States, rose rapidly into great power ranks. Modernity not only redefined who counted as a great power, it also permanently destabilized great power relations by introducing rapid and continuous advances in military technology into their relations with each other. Failure to keep up with this hugely expensive technological treadmill spelt either or both of defeat or loss of standing as a great power. Because the onset and embedding of modernity was a highly uneven process, for more than a century this meant that the ranks of great and superpowers were almost exclusively filled by European/Western states. Only Japan broke this mold, doing so a century before what Fareed Zakaria (2009) nicely labels "the rise of the rest." As illustrated by the history of Britain, and indeed Japan, this power gap undercut population size as a key to power, and underpinned the colonial international society that lasted up until 1945. During the nineteenth century, a small, but highly modernized country such as Britain could simultaneously occupy India and defeat China, the two most populous societies on earth. What the rise of the rest means is that the modern foundations of power are diffusing more widely through the international system. As the revolutions of modernity spread rapidly beyond the West, this enables other non-Western states to enter the great power ranks. And as China and India modernize, they are restoring the significance of demography to the material foundations of great power standing.

43.3 Structures

Differentiating between superpowers and great powers requires a much more complex polarity theory in which there are many possible combinations and permutations of the two types. In material perspective, since the end of the Cold War there has been one superpower (United States) and several great powers (China, EU, Russia, with Japan and India on the edges). Note that this post-Cold War model is not truly "unipolar." It is one superpower and several great powers "1 + X," whereas true unipolarity would be one superpower and zero great powers "1 + 0," an unlikely distribution. Here I will focus only on the two models that are the most likely successors to the current "1 + X" structure: "2 + X" and "0 + X." The "2 + X" model captures the much discussed rivalry between the United States as the established superpower and China as the rising one, though most discussion concentrates on the "2" and ignores the great power part of the equation. The "0 + X" model is such a radical departure from simple polarity theory that it has not yet been much discussed (Buzan and Lawson 2015: 271–304). Simple polarity theory assumes that the "poles" interact and compete on a global scale and therefore must be superpowers. But the relative decline of the United States, when combined with the diffusion of power flagged by the rise of the rest, opens a real possibility of a world without any superpowers (the United States becomes the biggest of the great powers), but having several great powers (China never gets to be a superpower because too many others are rising as well). A "0 + X" world would not be multipolar in the traditional sense of that term because the great powers might well have neither the capacity nor the will to contest with each other for global dominance or to lead international society. They might well have a more regional and inter-regional focus. The "2 + X" scenario is about contestation for global hegemony, but the "0 + X" one raises questions about under-provision of global management by the leading powers. These two models can be reconciled to some extent by seeing the United States–China rivalry as a great power inter-regional contest in Asia rather than as a superpower one on a global scale.

Structure is ideational as well as material, and in thinking about great power structures one therefore needs to consider both the distribution and the character of the ideologies in play.[2] In terms of the distribution of ideology, one can also begin by using a polarity approach. In abstract, it is easy to imagine worlds in which there is one dominant ideology (e.g. *Tianxia* in the classical Chinese order); or two (e.g. democratic liberalism vs communism during the Cold War); or multipolar (e.g. democracy, fascism, and Communism during the interwar years). The suggestion in this approach is that cooperation among the great/super powers would become easier if all shared the same ideology, and more difficult the more ideologies there were in play. Cui and Buzan (2016) argue that in practice this has not been the case, and that great power cooperation has functioned under all three forms of ideational polarity. The keys to such cooperation are, first, willingness among the powers to take a pluralist attitude of tolerance toward difference, and to give priority to a logic of co-existence, and second, the presence of shared interests strong enough to overcome ideological difference. Thus during the Cold War, when each camp found the other both morally intolerable and existentially threatening, the United States and the Soviet Union were still able to conduct arms control negotiations driven by a mutual interest in survival. So even where differences are substantial, the existence of a strong shared interest or value can suffice to override them. In this perspective, for both of the materialist models set out above (2 + X and 0 + X), the prospect looks to be one of ideological bipolarity in terms of the post-Cold War divide between democratic and authoritarian states. In either model, this puts China and Russia in the authoritarian camp, and the Western powers, Japan, India, and Brazil in the democratic one. This divide is a very old one in the history of human government, and although it is deep, it is perhaps not as deep as the ideological polarizations of the Cold War or the nineteenth century, which involved wholly different systems of political economy.

On top of the basic framing of ideological polarity, the English School concepts of *pluralism* and *solidarism* provide another handle on the normative structure of international society. Pluralism means acceptance among the great powers of a logic of coexistence, which requires tolerance of difference, and an acknowledgment of shared interests that necessitate a degree of cooperation if they are to be realized. Solidarism means that the great powers are, or want to be, more alike, and therefore share a range of important values around which to organize cooperation. Solidarism points to ideological unipolarity, or if there are two or more ideologies in play that the differences between them should be neither so deep nor so wide as to eliminate any common ground.

In order to interpret the prospect for pluralism and solidarism in relation to material and ideational polarity, one needs to look at the ideological character of the great and superpowers in play. Ideological character ranges across a spectrum from universalist, open, and inclusive at one end, to parochial, closed, and exclusive at the other. Universal, open, inclusive ideologies rest on the principle (and practice) that all people can join them if they agree to take on the necessary beliefs and practices. Examples are proselytizing religions such as Buddhism, Christianity, and Islam, and political ideologies such as liberalism, social democracy, and Communism. Parochial, closed, and exclusive ideologies are those that apply only to particular people and are either impossible or very difficult for outsiders to join. Examples are race ideologies positing the superiority of one race or people over others; "chosen people" religions; or nationalisms defined in terms of strong and exclusionary cultural exceptionalism.

This fairly simple classification offers some general insights into the scope for pluralism and solidarism. Where ideological bipolarity takes the form of two offensive universalist ideologies, the scope for solidarism will be zero, and for pluralism low, as during the Cold War. Such a pairing is by definition zero-sum unless there is some exceptionally strong intervening shared interest (e.g. survival during the Cold War) to mediate it. But where a universalist ideology is widely shared, or more defensive, it can provide firm foundations for pluralism or even solidarism, as suggested by the idea of democratic peace. At the other end of the spectrum parochial ideologies also come in offensive and defensive forms. Defensive parochialism is where a cultural group simply wants the right to survive and coexist (e.g. American isolationism during the nineteenth century). Offensive parochialism is where a culture group claims the right to absorb, or dominate, or exterminate and replace, others (e.g. imperialist white supremacy; the Nazi *lebensraum* and eugenics projects; the Japanese empire). Defensive, parochial ideologies might well provide quite fertile ground for pluralism. Offensive parochialisms will not.

Both kinds of parochial ideology will have trouble coexisting with a universal one. An offensive parochial one will create a zero-sum situation comparable to that of two competing universalisms. An example here might be the conflict that shaped the Second World War between two offensive parochialisms (Germany and Japan) and two universalist ones (liberalism and Communism). A defensive parochial ideology will necessarily resist the pressure from the universal one to homogenize the system. Contemporary examples of countries that might be thought of as mainly defensive parochial—such as Russia, Iran, and China—clearly feel under siege by what they see as the intrusive tyranny of liberal universalism.

A quick ideological overview of the likely powers in play in the 2 + X and 0 + X scenarios suggests a mixed picture. The United States and the EU still represent liberal universalist ideology, but their material position is weaker, and the legitimacy of their ideology somewhat battered. After Trump and Brexit, liberal ideology is under serious question even in its Anglosphere core. A case could be made that these two universalists are now in a more defensive mode. They have substantially abandoned the offensive liberalism of their imperial and Cold War days, and adopted a position more like that of the United States before it took on global engagement. Isolationism would be much too strong a term, but these two are now more inclined to play the "city on the hill," preaching by example, rather than actively proselytizing for converts. Given its internal troubles and weakness, the EU seems likely to remain that way. The United States, however, might just be in a phase, and revert to more offensive form.

All of the other main candidates for the 2 + X and 0 + X scenarios are on the parochial side. Brazil, India, and Japan are pretty clearly defensive parochial. Russia has abandoned the offensive universalism of its Soviet days, and now seems to be basically parochial, mainly defensive, but with some limited offensive intent around its edges. China is the most difficult call. The ideological universalism of the Maoist period has been decisively abandoned, and the government's main aim is the parochial one of domestic social stability and continuing economic growth under Communist Party rule. China's long-standing mantra of "Chinese characteristics" suggests a defensive desire to preserve a distinctive culture and politics from the intrusions of offensive liberal universalism. Whether China is a defensive or offensive parochialism is, however, difficult to say. Up until 2008, its rhetoric of "peaceful rise/development," and much of its behavior, suggested a defensive parochialism. Since then, China's apparent assertive turn has generated increasing international concerns that it might be an offensive parochial power (see Ross 2011; Wang 2011; Kai and Feng 2012; Zhang 2012; Johnston 2013). Its increasing propensity for military swaggering, and the subtext in its rhetoric of a big power having the right to regional primacy in East Asia, point to a more offensive parochialism. One solution to this puzzle is to say that the shift simply represents China's response to its rising power. Another is to say that China was always an offensive parochial power, but it adopted a rhetoric of peaceful rise/development to hide this, and bide its time until it was strong enough to show its real face: a classic, *Art of War* strategy of deception. Yet another is to say that Chinese foreign policy making is incoherent, often sending contradictory signals, and hence causing confusions and misperceptions to outsiders (Wang 2011: 77–9; Shambaugh 2013: 46–53, 61–71, 99; Hameiri and Jones 2015).

This structural combination of several great powers, ideological bipolarity moderated by shared capitalism, and a mix of parochial and universalist powers, contains several potentialities. As shown by the hot contestation over human rights and democracy, it rules out any kind of generalized solidarism. Yet as Buzan and Lawson (2014) argue, all of the major powers now share a substantial commitment to global capitalism, in other words the market as an institution of international society, as the basis of their power and prosperity. Capitalism won the Cold War even though liberal democracy did not. Maintaining a global market is a solidarist institution, and marks a substantial ideological development in the character of international society. Global economic governance requires much broader cooperation than the Cold War interest in nuclear survival. Agreement on the principle of the market not only reduces the degree of ideological difference among the major powers, but also generates a compelling shared fate, and thus a powerful collective interest in managing the global economy. It might even be argued that global economic governance has superseded the management of war as the first priority for the great powers. In addition, the contemporary group of great powers faces a variety of other shared fate problems including the environment, terrorism, and the proliferation of nuclear weapons, that pressure them to cooperate. This structure therefore supports important elements of solidarism.

In terms of pluralism, there is already a substantial substrate of agreement on an impressive range of pluralist primary institutions underpinning international society—that is, those institutions that mainly reflect a logic of coexistence. Regardless of their differences the great powers (and most other states) are in broad agreement about sovereignty, territoriality, international law, diplomacy, the irrationality of great power war (but see Copeland, Chapter 15, this volume), and human equality. The potential between pluralism and disorder hangs on the uncertainties about China and the United States, and to a much lesser extent Russia. On the worst scenario for international society (the United States reverts to offensive liberal universalism, and China and Russia become offensive parochial) there will be little scope for tolerance and a logic of coexistence. On the best scenario (the United States stays a defensive universalist, China and Russia become clearly defensive parochial), then the scope for pluralism increases. It is too early to tell whether coexistence logic and shared interests will play out in a pluralist "Concert of Capitalist Powers," or in a disorderly "two-camps" world where the powers focus mainly on their political differences. These evaluations would be true regardless of whether the material structure is interpreted as 2 + X or 0 + X.

43.4 Challenges and Capabilities

Within this framing of material and ideational structures, what kind of challenges face the contemporary set of great and superpowers, and how do their capabilities measure up to these challenges? In the classical English School discussions of great power management (GPM), the main responsibility of the great powers was to manage relations among themselves. But as suggested above, the issue of great power war has declined in importance, and there is now an increasing number of shared fate issues from the global economy to the global environment that are becoming ever more pressing.

Bull (1977: 207) argued that the basic role of great powers was to manage their relations with each other and to "impart a degree of central direction to the affairs of international society as a whole." More specifically he identified six functions for great powers:

1. to preserve the general balance of power;
2. to avoid or control central crises;
3. to limit or contain central wars;
4. to exploit their local preponderance to maintain regional order;
5. to respect each other's spheres of influence; and
6. to take joint actions.

The obvious model for this view was the Concert of Europe, which operated for several decades during the nineteenth century. Bull (1977: 228–9, 1980) also argued that excessively disorderly relations among the great powers would undermine the legitimacy of GPM, and that they needed to cultivate that legitimacy by paying at least some attention to the justice demands of the lesser powers.

While this traditional security agenda has certainly not disappeared, both the ending of the Cold War and increasing restraints on racism, imperialism, and great power war and violence mean that it has declined in importance. It is conceivable that the issue of great powers managing their relations with each other could regain its centrality: scenarios of Russian expansionism, and Chinese seeking of primacy in East Asia, could unfold into a new kind of spheres of influence game, and even cold war. This would pitch the parochial, authoritarian great powers against the universalist, democratic ones. The ongoing attempts to restrict the spread of nuclear weapons and their delivery systems fall into this set, and Bull's fourth and fifth functions could become important in a more regionalized "0 + X" world. As Lasmar (2015) argues, transnational terrorism is in one sense an extension of the traditional GPM agenda. Transnational terrorism threatens the sovereignty and territoriality of all states, not just great powers, and can never be eliminated, only managed. It is hardly surprising that on this issue Russia and China quickly got on side with the United States regardless of their ongoing hostility to it. The threat from transnational terrorism links to that from nuclear proliferation, making these the dominant post-Cold War issues on the traditional military-political security GPM agenda.

The threat from terrorism took the great powers out of their traditional comfort zone of dealing with the balance of power among themselves, and into the problem of how collectively to confront shared transnational threats. In that sense, terrorism, although still about violence issues, looks more like the new agenda of shared fate challenges such as pollution, financial crises, migration, disease, cybersecurity, and transnational crime, that can and do spill over territorial borders and create a wide range of security threats and sources of instability. Since no single country can address these threats on its own, the challenge facing the great powers is how to achieve the necessary cooperation (Cui 2013). Issues such as climate change and disease are clearly shared threats/fates faced by all. But some issues cut both ways: terrorism and cybersecurity could be as much about rivalry between powers as about shared fates.

In part because of both the rise of the global economy as a factor of international order, and the decline of great power war as a daily concern, other issues have moved strongly onto the contemporary GPM agenda. The violence problem is now much less about state-to-state conflict than about violence either within states (weak and failed states—where the state, or those who compete to control it, are the main threat to the citizens), or between non-state transnational actors and states (terrorism and crime). These problems at least fit into the traditional agenda in being threats that are for the most part intentionally made by organized groups of human beings against each other. Especially in relation to weak and failed states, this type of violence also raises issues of human rights and human security. Human rights and human security make individuals and people the main referent object, which creates significant tensions with the sovereign state framing of international society.

Alongside these non-traditional forms of violence has arisen another agenda of threats to international order that are for the most part unintentional, and usually not made by humans against each other. These range from epidemic diseases, through the risk from space rocks hitting earth, to climate change, but also social ones such as when migration is constructed as a threat to identity. As Hurrell and Woods (1999: 259) note, many non-military security threats, such as transnational crime, drug/human trafficking, refugees, pandemics, and environmental degradation, have emerged "not from state strength, military power, and geopolitical ambition, but rather from state weakness." These threats have mainly natural causes, but some of them, particularly migration, transnational crime, and cybersecurity are driven by the same dramatic economic and technological developments that have shrunk time and space, and elevated the global economy to the first rank of great power concerns. The outcome of the Paris 2015 climate summit made it conceivable that climate change could challenge the global economy as the first priority issue for GPM. Such issues draw the focus of international order away from the relations among the great powers themselves. One indicator of this is the rising role of Peacekeeping Operations, and their attraction to states such as China and Japan seeking to strengthen their legitimacy as great powers (Suzuki 2008; Gill and Huang 2009).

This new agenda makes the military capabilities of great powers much less central to their function than was the case for the traditional agenda. Military capability will of course remain relevant for some issues, but dealing with shared fate problems will require much more in the way of political skills, economic and technological capabilities, and social adaptability, with military power playing a background role. In the twenty-first century, international order will depend much less on the capabilities of the great powers to win wars against each other or lesser states, and much more on their ability to create and maintain consensual international societies at both the regional and global levels. That raises the question about the relationship between GPM, on the one hand, and the whole range of intergovernmental organizations (IGOs), global civil society, and non-governmental organizations, on the other. How do global governance and GPM relate to each other? As Hurrell (2007: 20, 35, 295) notes, the hierarchical order established by the great powers during the nineteenth century remained "extraordinarily powerful and influential throughout the twentieth century." The great powers will continue to play a crucial role in world order even as the wider range of players involved in global governance extends beyond mere GPM: "unsurprisingly, in debates on world order, it is the voices of the most powerful that dominate the discussion." Even the work of a dedicated liberal institutionalist such as Ikenberry (2009, 2011) makes strong links between great powers and the creation and function of IGOs. So while global governance involves both a wider range of actors and a more consensual, horizontal, and negotiated character, it might still be seen more as an extension of GPM than as a displacement of it. The great powers still have the resources and interests to dominate IGOs.

43.5 Pathologies and Prospects

How one defines a pathology depends on what one sees as normal. Given the pressing need to deal with a variety of shared fate problems, some people might well see as pathological continued great power rivalry of a traditional sort, as exemplified by the tensions between Russia and the EU, and between China and both the United States and Japan. Those of a more realist disposition might just see such rivalry as normal behavior. Rather than engage in this unresolvable normative debate, about which readers can decide for themselves, I want to focus here on a problem that is generic to all great powers, and up to a point all states: *autism*. The problem is that for a variety of reasons, all of the likely great powers for the coming decades are likely to be more than usually autistic.

In humans, autism is a condition that produces impaired social interaction because those who suffer from it are much more internally referenced than shaped by interactions with others, and are easily overwhelmed by inputs from outside. In states, autism can be understood as reaction to external inputs much more based on the internal processes of the state than on rational, fact-based, assessment of and engagement with the other states and societies that constitute international society. To some extent autism in this sense is a normal feature of states. It is built into their political structure that domestic factors generally take priority over foreign policy. That might be because prioritizing domestic concerns is seen as necessary for regime survival. Or it might be because the government is designed in such a way as to represent its citizens, and far more people are concerned about their local issues than care much about foreign policy. At the level of states, therefore, autism is where behavior toward other states is primarily driven by domestic political bargains (e.g. party rivalries; pandering to public opinion, whether it be nationalist or isolationist; trying to put the government in a good light, and such like) and also by the mistaken assumption that others think, and see the world, in the same way as they do (Senghaas 1974; Buzan 2007 [1991]: 277–81; Luttwak 2012: 13–22).

Autistic states tend to be self-centered, insensitive to the perspectives of others, or to social conventions, and to have prickly or even violent responses to anything perceived as criticism, obstruction, or insult.

Such internally driven behavior is visible in the foreign policies of most states, and is often observed in analyses of US foreign policy (e.g. Bacevich 2002: 90; Prestowitz 2003: 1–17) and indeed of many other countries from Israel and Iran to Russia and Serbia. Luttwak (2012) makes the general case that autism is particularly strong in big states. He then focuses on China as being exceptionally prone to it not only because of its size and internal complexity, but also because of some of its cultural characteristics (see also Wang 2012). To the extent that states have autistic foreign policies they lose touch with their social environment, and fail to see how their policies and behaviors affect the way that others see and react to them. In such conditions a cycle of action–overreaction is likely to prevail, and building trust becomes difficult or even impossible. Everyone sees only their own interests, concerns, and "rightness," and is blind to the interests, concerns, and "rightness" of others, a process already visible in United States–China and Russia–EU relations. This dynamic is also very visible in the current disputes about islands, rocks, and reefs in the East and South China Seas, where all the parties are behaving autistically.

Autism is important because it affects, perhaps crucially, whether the emerging set of great and superpowers will be responsible enough to coordinate their behavior in relation to shared fate threats, or whether they will become, in Bull's (1980) phrase, "great irresponsibles." Autistic great powers focus more on *raison d'etat*, and the pursuit of their own interests, obsessions, and advantages, than on *raison de système*, the belief that it pays to make the system work (Watson 1992: 14). This returns to the question put in the previous section: can a diverse set of great powers that remain ideologically divided, yet economically quite interdependent, and also face a whole set of shared fate problems, pull together sufficiently to create a pluralist international order?

In addition to the propensity to autism of states generally, and great powers particularly, in the current and near future great powers autism will be strong for two additional reasons. First, the old, advanced industrial great powers (the United States, the EU, Japan) are exhausted, weakened both materially and in terms of legitimacy, and are increasingly unable or unwilling to take the lead. The EU and Japan have deep economic problems and lack effective foreign policy-making structures able to override their domestic political constraints. The United States has strong foreign policy-making structures, but has been burned by many costly foreign policy failures, is paralyzed by its deeply polarized domestic politics, and no longer enjoys the legitimacy in much of the world that underpinned its leadership during the second half of the twentieth century. Russia is unable to see itself in anything other than imperial terms, and therefore seeks dominance over its neighbors as part of its self-definition as a great power. Its material foundations as a great power are thin, and given that of all the great powers it is the one that remains the most resistant to capitalism, its prospects for development look poor. The rising great powers (China and India, possibly Brazil) are very keen to claim great power status, but equally keen not to let go of their status as developing countries. That combination leads them to give priority to their own development, to argue that that is a big and difficult job for them, and on that basis to resist being given wider global managerial responsibilities. They seek to shift responsibility onto the older great powers for having caused current problems. Both India and China have relatively weak foreign policy-making establishments, and are favoring inward-looking exceptionalism, respectively in the form of "Hindutva" and "Chinese characteristics."

The simultaneous autism of all the great powers is not just a coincidence. It results from a historical conjuncture much larger than a mere power transition crisis among a handful of leading states. What underpins it is the ending of a structure defined by two centuries of Western/Anglosphere hegemony in which a small, modernized core dominated a large unmodernized periphery. The rise of the rest means that the huge power gap that existed between those who acquired modernity early and those who did not, is fast fading away. As more states and peoples find their way into modernity, and acquire the wealth and power it enables, so the core becomes bigger and the distribution of power more even. This process still has a long way to go, but it has come far enough to bring us to the point at which the old Western/Anglosphere core has lost both its edge and its will to lead, while the rising powers are developed enough to claim great power status, but still developing, and so neither able nor willing to take on leadership (Buzan and Lawson 2015).

If this diagnosis of autism turns out to be correct, then we are unlikely to see responsible great powers or any kind of great power concert to manage the growing set of shared fate issues. Autistic great powers lack much global vision other than their own self-interest, and will quickly lose the legitimacy necessary for GPM. In the scenario of a world of autistic great powers, great power war will still remain unlikely (though not impossible), and the global level will be undermanaged. The United States will try to maintain its privileges as sole superpower, and alienate the rising powers in the process. This is already visible in US resistance to reform of the IMF and its campaign against China's Asian Infrastructure Investment Bank. China and Russia will both seek old style primacy in their neighborhoods, China as part of its "return to normality" after the century of humiliation. This will mean edgy and tense relations between China and not only the United States, but also Japan and India. Russia will have similar edgy and tense relations with the EU and the United States. For a time China and Russia will be content to stand back to back against the West, but as China gets stronger, Russia will confront difficult choices about whether to become its junior partner, or whether to realign itself to balance China.

The pathology of great power autism applies to both the 2 + X and 0 + X models. It stands against the counter-pressure from both the narrower ideological bandwidth of an international society with the global market as one of its core institutions, and the strong collective interest in addressing shared fate issues. It will be this tension that shapes great power relations in the coming decades, and in the process determines the shape and character of international society.

Notes

1. These definitions are drawn from Buzan (2004: 63–73) where further elaboration and reasoning can be found.
2. This discussion draws on Cui and Buzan (2016).

References

Bacevich, Andrew J. 2002. *American Empire: the Realities and Consequences of U.S. Diplomacy*. Cambridge, MA: Harvard University Press.

Brooks, Stephen G. and William C. Wohlforth. 2015–16. The Rise and Fall of the Great Powers in the Twenty-first Century: China's Rise and the Fate of America's Global Position. *International Security*, 40(3): 7–53.

Bull, Hedley. 1977. *The Anarchical Society: A Study in World Politics* London: Macmillan Press.

Bull, Hedley. 1980. The Great Irresponsibles? The United States, The Soviet Union and World Order. *International Journal*, 35(3): 437–47.

Buzan, Barry. 2004. *The United States and the Great Powers: World Politics in the Twenty-First Century*. Oxford, Polity.

Buzan, Barry. 2007 [1991]. *People, States and Fear: An Agenda for International Security Studies in the Post-Cold War Era*, Colchester: ECPR Press.

Buzan, Barry. 2013. Polarity. In Paul Williams (ed.), *Security Studies: An Introduction*, pp. 155–69. Abingdon: Routledge.

Buzan, Barry and George Lawson. 2014. Capitalism and the Emergent World Order. *International Affairs*, 90(1): 71–91. In Chinese in *Journal of International Security Studies*, 32(1): 78–100.

Buzan, Barry and George Lawson. 2015. *The Global Transformation: History, Modernity and the Making of International Relations*, Cambridge: Cambridge University Press.

Cui, Shunji. 2013. Beyond History: Non-Traditional Security Cooperation and The Construction of Northeast Asian International Society. *Journal of Contemporary China*, 22(83): 868–86.

Cui, Shunji and Barry Buzan. 2016. Great Power Management in International Society. *Chinese Journal of International Politics*, 9(2): 181–210.

Ferguson, Niall. 2004. *Empire: How Britain Made the Modern World*. London: Penguin.

Gill, Bates and Chin-Hao Huang. 2009. China's Expanding Peacekeeping Role: Its Significance and the Policy Implications, *SIPRI Policy Brief. Available at:* http://books.sipri.org/files/misc/SIPRIPB0902.pdf, accessed March 13, 2009.

Hameiri, Shahar and Lee Jones. 2015. Rising Powers and State Transformation: The Case of China. *European Journal of International Relations*, 22(1): 72–98.

Hansen, Birte. 2000. *Unipolarity and the Middle East*. Richmond: Curzon Press.

He Kai and Huiyin Feng. 2012, Debating China's Assertiveness: Taking China's Power and Interests Seriously. *International Politics*, 49(5): 639.

Hurrell, Andrew. 2007. *On Global Order: Power, Values and the Constitution of International Society*. Oxford: Oxford University Press.

Hurrell, Andrew and Ngaire Woods. (eds.). 1999. *Inequality, Globalization and World Politics*. Oxford: Oxford University Press.

Ikenberry, John. 2009. Liberal Internationalism 3.0: America and the Dilemmas of Liberal World Order. *Perspectives on Politics*, 7(1): 71–86.
Ikenberry, John. 2011. *Liberal Leviathan*. Princeton, NJ: Princeton University Press.
Johnston, Alastair Iain. 2013. How New and How Assertive is Chinas New Assertiveness? *International Security*, 37(4): 7–48.
Lasmar, Jorge. 2015. Managing Great Powers in the Post-Cold War World: Old Rules New Game? The Case of the Global War on Terror. *Cambridge Review of International Affairs*, 28(3): 396–423.
Luttwak, Edward N. 2012. *The Rise of China Vs. the Logic of Strategy*. Cambridge MA: The Belknap Press of Harvard University Press. Kindle edn.
Mearsheimer, John. 2001. *The Tragedy of Great Power Politics*. New York: W.W. Norton.
Prestowitz, Clyde P. 2003. *Rogue Nation: American Unilateralism and the Failure of Good Intentions*. New York: Basic Books.
Ross, Robert. 2011. Chinese Nationalism and its Discontents, *The National Interest*, No. 116.
Senghaas, Dieter. 1974. Towards an Analysis of Threat Policy in International Relations. In Klaus von Beyme (ed.), *German Political Studies*, pp. 59–103. London: Sage.
Shambaugh, David. 2013. *China Goes Global: The Partial Power*. Oxford: Oxford University Press. Kindle edn.
Suzuki, Shogo. 2008. Seeking "Legitimate" Great Power Status in Post-Cold War International Society: China's and Japan's Participation in UNPKO. *International Relations*, 22(1): 45–63.
Wang Jisi. 2011. China's Search for a Grand Strategy. *Foreign Affairs*, 90(2): 68–79.
Wang, Zheng. 2012. *Never Forget National Humiliation: Historical Memory in Chinese Politics and Foreign Relations*. New York: Columbia University Press, Kindle edn.
Watson, Adam. 1992. *The Evolution of International Society: A Comparative Historical Analysis*. London: Routledge.
Zakaria, Fareed. 2009. *The Post-American World and the Rise of the Rest*. London: Penguin.
Zhang, Feng. 2012., Rethinking China's Grand Strategy: Beijing's evolving National Interests and Strategic Ideas in the Reform Era. *International Politics*, 49(3): 318–45.

CHAPTER 44

ALLIANCES

STEN RYNNING AND OLIVIER SCHMITT

44.1 INTRODUCTION

ALLIANCES have an intuitive conceptual feel to them that all too easily breaks down upon closer scrutiny. The first difficulty concerns the nature of security arrangements among states where alliances are only one form of cooperation next to coalitions, concerts, and ententes, while the next difficulty concerns the variety of alliance formats where sub-categories—such as military alliances, tacit alliances, de facto alliances, wartime alliances, etc.—have been created to capture distinct realities.

In his seminal book on the origins of alliances, Stephen Walt (1987: 1) defines an alliance as "a formal or informal relationship of security cooperation between two or more sovereign states." This definition is concise but problematic in two distinct respects (Duffield 2009). First, it is so large that it can encompass virtually all security arrangements between states. Analytically speaking, the definition blurs the fundamental distinction between an alliance, on the one hand, and a collective security arrangement, on the other. An alliance is primarily, if not exclusively, outwardly oriented, intended to enhance the security of its members vis-à-vis external parties. In contrast, a collective security arrangement is designed to enhance the security of its participants vis-à-vis each other. The definition thus confuses policies designed to control and manage external threats and policies designed to enable and coordinate security governance.

The other problem with the definition is the conflation of various forms of security cooperation. The definition embraces all manners of security cooperation, including instances of security cooperation limited to supportive diplomacy or economic aid. Traditionally, alliances have distinguished themselves from other security arrangements by the emphasis they place on military assistance, especially the use of force.

Our purpose in this article is not to generate consensus on a certain definition of alliances but rather to provide an overview of main trends, historical and current. Still, in light of the slippery nature of the concept itself, it might be useful to sketch the definition of alliances that we have employed here as a tool for sorting out the literature. We understand alliances as entailing *a formal or informal association of states for the (threat of) use of military force, in specified circumstances, against actors external to the alliance.* This definition emphasizes the military aspect of alliances, highlights the distinction between alliances and collective security agreements, and encompasses both permanent and institutionalized alliances (such as NATO) and non-institutionalized collective military activities (such as various US-led coalitions in the Middle East).

With this in mind we turn to the alliance literature. Our ambition is to create an overview of the classical alliance literature but also and more importantly to assess trending debates on the relationship between alliances and, on the one hand, the maintenance of international order and, on the other, the nature of multinational military interventions.

44.2 Classical Research on Alliances

Because of their strong impact on the organization and structure of the international system, alliances have generated an important literature in security studies. The two main areas of focus concern the formation of alliances and the impact of alliances on war (do alliances make war more or less likely?). This literature has already been expertly summarized elsewhere (Sprecher and Krause 2006; Weitsman 2010), so the presentation below must be considered as a general roadmap and needs to be completed with more granular overviews. However, this is a deliberate choice that follows from our preference for concentrating on the evolution of contemporary alliances and coalitions in Sections 44.3 and 44.4 of this chapter.

44.2.1 Alliance Formation and Management

Several explanations exist regarding alliance formation, which grant more or less weight to the importance of an external threat. Essentially, states face a dilemma when there is a change in the distribution of power in the international system: should they balance the emerging threat, or bandwagon in order to accommodate it?

The first motivation concerns a state's willingness to reduce the gap between its military capabilities and those of a potential adversary, thus its desire for allies to augment its military power against an external threat. This mechanism is called *balancing*. The literature has discussed whether states were balancing power or perceived threats (Walt 1987), but the mechanism is the same: an alliance is an institutional mechanism facilitating the aggregation of military capabilities to deter potential adversaries and/or maximize the chances of victory in cases of conflicts. In multipolar systems in which states face a common threat and defensive military strategies are perceived as superior, states will tend to adopt buck-passing behaviors and let other states deal with the threat—simply because passing the buck is less costly than balancing. In contrast, in bipolar systems in which offensive military strategies are perceived as superior, the weaker states will tend to strongly tie themselves to alliances they hope will guarantee their survival. In such situations, and depending on the alliance's internal management, moderate states can be rendered more bellicose, or aggressive states can be constrained by their allies (Tierney 2011). Allies' reputation is also important in the process of alliance formation (Crescenzi et al. 2012).

The second motivation to join an alliance is *bandwagoning*. In this situation, instead of countering a threat, states join the threatening state in order to ensure their survival, or, less frequently argued, to secure a profit from the spoils of victory. Bandwagoning for survival is typically observed among small states geographically close to the threatening states and willing to secure strategic gains despite their material disadvantage. Bandwagoning seems to occur less frequently than balancing (Schweller 1998), but bandwagoning is nonetheless implicit in many foreign policy speeches and decision making processes. For example, the metaphor of the "domino theory," most famously pushed forward to justify the US intervention in Vietnam, but which regularly comes back in the American public debate, is in fact based on an implicit bandwagoning argument.

Finally, the third motivation is called *tethering*. As counterintuitive as it sounds, an alliance can be formed in order to manage the adversarial relationships between states. From this perspective, an alliance functions like other international institutions, improving the exchange of information between states and raising the costs of defection, thus making cooperation more attractive, and more likely. Despite their adversarial relationship, Turkey and Greece are both NATO members. As such, their membership to the NATO alliance does not formally augment their theoretical potential power, since their adversary is also a member of the same alliance. Nevertheless, being an "adversary-ally" within NATO grants them institutional advantages, in particular in terms of mutual transparency on their defense budgets and as a framework for conflict management.

In terms of alliance management, the main issue that states have to solve is the alliance security dilemma. In essence it is the dilemma between small states fearing abandonment, and large states fearing entrapment (Snyder 1998): small states fear that the large states would not honor their defense commitments if they enter a conflict, and large states do not want to join a conflict initiated by small states that they would be forced to join. Mitigating this dilemma is a common problem for alliance relationships.

44.2.2 Alliances and War

The academic literature on alliances has long tackled the issue of whether alliances make war more or less likely in the international system.

Several important works argue that alliances are rather useful to maintain peace (Levy 1981). The traditional realist literature argues that alliance creation is a balancing act, which forms the theoretical foundation for arguing that alliances are means of deterrence and systemic stability (Waltz 1979). Divergences do emerge regarding the mechanism through which alliances maintain peace. To both classical realists and neorealists, alliances maintain peace by balancing power and deterring aggression, which is an external effect, but recent works have emphasized an internal effect, namely alliances as a constraint on adventurous allies (Gelpi 1999; Pressman 2008; Tierney 2011). For this strand of research, internal constraint is a side effect of the alliance, and not the reason why it was created in the first place.

Other works argue that military alliances create a more dangerous world. The main argument is that alliances reinforce the security dilemma and culminate in the formation of counter-alliances, increased polarization, widespread misperception, hostility, and war. An alliance paradox follows: the more effective an alliance is at maintaining peace and cohesion within, the more it raises the level of systemic insecurity by way of its apparent impressive capabilities (Weitsman 2004). As the security dilemma intensifies, moreover, cohesion maintenance supersedes the urge to peacefully resolve conflicts with adversarial alliances. Such "rigidity" of alliances enables allies to drag their fellow allies into wars they would have otherwise wished to avoid. This makes alliances dangerous: allied nations intervene far more in wars than non-allied nations, and wars become bloodier since they involve more states (Levy 1981; Oren 1990).

Most of this strand of research is based on large-n quantitative analyses lumping together all forms of alliances regardless of the historical context of their formation, and types of management. As such, these results appear somehow disconnected from the evolving relationship between coalitions, alliances, and security institutions that emerged after the Cold War, on which we will now focusing.

44.3 Alliances and International Order

Alliances have increasingly become tied into the management of International Relations and partnerships. Naturally, alliances and global organization coexisted through much of the twentieth century, but with the end of the Cold War, the increased pace of globalization, and the emerging pluralization of power, the need to manage alliances in concert with global networks has qualitatively increased. Where the United States could once focus on running its bi- and multilateral alliances and then the structuring of debates in the United Nations Security Council, it must now comprehensively integrate the two. The United States military strategy of 2015 defines three National Military Objectives in support of national interests, one of which is the ability to "strengthen our global network of allies and partners" (Department of Defense 2015: 5). This emphasis on "networks" of both allies and partners likewise figures prominently in the US Navy's Cooperative Strategy for 21st Century Seapower where "allies and partners" brought together in "formal and informal networks" form a "global network of navies" with a "robust capacity" to face new and emerging challenges (US Navy 2015: 1–2). This connectivity is driven not only by broad processes of globalization but also changes in warfare. We begin with the latter and move toward the former, ending with an assessment of future implications.

44.3.1 Changing Character of War

War is at the heart of alliances because they form, essentially, to prevent or win wars. As war changes in character, therefore, so will the role and shape of alliances.

A big trend in recent decades has been the growth in small wars whose center of gravity is not the armed forces of the adversary but the loyalty of the population. In these small wars—or wars among the people—the ultimate objective is to capture the will of the people, something which industrial-sized and organized military organizations, including alliances, are poorly equipped to grasp (Smith 2006). The extended argument is that wars have changed in a qualitative way, feeding successive "generations" of warfare that bring with them an enhanced emphasis on psychology, communication, social organization extending into globalized crime and illicit networks, and various hybrid versions hereof (Hammes 2004; Hoffman 2007).

The importance of this shift is up for debate, though. Other scholars continue to emphasize the structuring impact of prospective great power war—rare and perhaps even unlikely, but sobering in its potential effect. States and their alliances are therefore pushed to engage with transformative technologies and organization and to integrate these into their grand strategies (Dombrowski 2015).

In either case the effect on alliances is considerable. One considerable effect is to open up alliances. To cope with either small wars or transformative preparations for big war, alliances must move beyond their cloak and dagger past and embrace societal actors around them to secure support, import ideas, and create partnerships by generating new ways of managing emerging challenges. In terms of small wars, the challenge comes under the heading of "comprehensive approach" (CA), lately also stabilization, which signifies the coordination of security, governance, and development efforts. The lineages of such comprehensive approaches can be traced back into the history of counter insurgency, the "defense and diplomacy" turn of the 1970s, as well as humanitarian interventions in the 1990s, but its modern version was crafted inside NATO in response to the challenge of stabilizing Afghanistan. With the CA, NATO insisted that it could not solve Afghanistan by its own efforts and invited the whole international community to join in. In terms of major war, opening implies an engagement with the most innovative sectors of the economy, especially the IT sector with its fast pace of innovation both in terms of products and networked organizations. When new IT and new organization come together in the manufacturing of new arms—from missiles to cyber—new ways of war become possible.

For alliances, the pace and scope of innovation, both in terms of CA outreach and transformative warfare, harden the challenge of sharing burdens and distributing benefits. Transformative warfare aggravates the asymmetry linked to budgets and adaptive organizations, while CA engagement aggravates the politics of linking or limiting the political presence and impact of an alliance.

44.3.2 Global Organization

The drive to open alliances and institutionalize partnerships in support of comprehensive approaches has rekindled questions of global governance and regional alliances. The United Nations Charter foresees the integration of such alliances under the authority of the UNSC, something that the Cold War prevented but which has become both more likely and more contentious in the new era of small wars and crisis management.

Some scholars argue that global governance must be strengthened. The key argument is that if a war effort is just a small piece in a more comprehensive puzzle, then it is the wider political process that must gain precedence. This political process ultimately takes us to the UNSC and its authority to mandate the use of armed force. The strengthening of the UN was on the agenda in the early 1990s when UN Secretary General Boutros Boutros-Ghali suggested in his *Agenda for Peace* report ways to more firmly embed nations in a strengthened collective security system, including by "special arrangements" whereby member states make armed forces available to the UNSC. More broadly, the theory of security governance suggested that a more fluid system of specialized and "structurally neutral" coalitions of states and non-state actors take the place of fixed and antagonistic alliances (Krahmann 2005).

Alliances are a collective defense in nature, however, and the underlying schism between security and defense was not resolved. Rather, it caused the end of Boutros-Ghali's tenure at the UN helm, just as it caused the sidelining of the UN in Bosnia and the concomitant rise of NATO in the business of peacemaking and -keeping. In a globalizing context NATO had both more adaptable general institutional assets (Wallander 2000) and greater political purpose (Rynning 2005). Revealingly, when NATO intervened in Kosovo in 1999 to establish peace, it did so without a legal UN mandate but, it argued, with the legitimate purpose of providing for "human security and development"—an agenda that once had been UN anchored (Commission on Global Governance 1995) but now had become appropriated by an alliance that wished to labor in favor of certain global norms while retaining its collective defense character.

44.3.3 Concert of Power

If the relationship between alliances and global organization can be difficult, the dynamic solution is to exploit various intermediary formats for concerting power. Concerts are not new, of course, and have been likened to "central coalitions" (Rosecrance 1992) that supersede the balance of power. Typically they do so in the aftermath of systemic wars when the desire for stability is overwhelming (Jervis 1985), and they last only as long as the shock of war is felt. In time, alliances and the balance of power revive.

However, a new mechanism has emerged whereby concerts form to reinforce alliances. Concerts have thus become instrumental to alliance management and a tool rather than a replacement of the balance of power. Such concerts come in the shape of "contact groups" that an alliance can form on top of or in parallel to its operational mission and in order to garner support for it. In Bosnia, NATO allies established a contact group with five principal allies and then Russia. This instance of concerted power had limited success, and practice evolved into a two-phase approach by the time of the Libya campaign in 2011 when NATO allies first formed a contact group of like-minded partners to garner legitimacy and support and then, once the mission was firmly on track, broadened the contact group into a wider "friends of Libya" group that included China and Russia (Rynning 2013).

Interestingly, by instrumentalizing concerts in this way, alliances borrow a diplomatic mechanism from the UN system that had grown dramatically in use since the end of the Cold War, namely the use of groups of Friends to support UN peacekeeping and crisis management (Whitfield 2007). Though alliances can claim to build bridges between the world of collective defense where allies and like-minded partners operate and then the world of collective security and diverse groups of Friends, in reality alliances are tipping the scales in favor of collective defense.

A similar phenomenon is taking place in the heart of Asia where China, Russia, and a host of other mostly Central Asian countries take part in the Shanghai Cooperation Organization (SCO), which from 2001 has existed as a hybrid between an alliance (to keep the United States out of the region), a collective security arrangement (to engender peaceful coexistence within its membership), and a concert of power (led notably by China and Russia). The concert is the most prevalent facet of the SCO whereby the two big powers draw in diverse groups of Friends to manage this geopolitical domain, most recently with the inclusion of rivals India and Pakistan, traditionally aligned with Russia and China, respectively. Russia has since 1992 sought to build up a Collective Security Treaty Organization (CSTO) for the post-Soviet space, and while the CSTO is in effect, it is a clear-cut case of Russian-led alliance-building with junior and former vassal states which is nowhere near the SCO in terms of the complexity of its underlying concert of power.

44.3.4 The Future of Alliances and International Order

In this rivalry between collective defense and collective security orders, the defining element will likely be the role of political belief systems that historically have tended to be local or regional (as in nationalism or Atlanticism) but which may—or may not—be fusing into a global consciousness (as in cosmopolitanism). If belief systems are stubborn and remain national or regional, the world will be pluralist, and collective defense systems will follow. If, on the other hand, global governance generates a considerable global layer of beliefs, then the world could become one, at least sufficiently to allow for a type of rational or legalistic collective security system. In short, collective consciousness enables strategic obligations among multiple actors, and the key question is whether consciousness will predominantly form regionally or globally (Kissinger 2014). The trend in the post-Cold War decades, which appears likely to continue, is for continued pluralism though with a significant element of cosmopolitan thinking. Alliances—collective defense arrangements—have thus remained bedrocks of international relations. NATO has with some difficulty, but ultimately successfully, adapted to the cosmopolitan condition by appropriating tools in the collective security toolbox. Key questions for the future include whether China's (and also Russia's) engagement in the SCO and other regional organizations will similarly adapt to the cosmopolitan agenda or inversely reject it as a Western phenomenon, and whether the alliances of these great powers will enable a degree of concerted power or rather, by way of their competition, engender new ways of covert or overt warfare.

44.4 Alliances, Coalitions, and the Challenges of Multinational Military Interventions

Alliances can be large and unwieldy, even if politically useful, and a high operational tempo or prolonged or particularly difficult campaign thus tends to shift the balance in favour of more informal "strike" coalitions of dedicated countries. These coalitions are still multinational or multilateral, and they can form intimate links with established alliances, but they are by nature more pragmatic and improvised, and also less durable. Western states have since the end of the Cold War sought to combine these two multinational formats—coalitions and alliances—which have posed a number of specific challenges.

44.4.1 The Military Challenges of Coalition Warfare

After the Kosovo intervention in 1999, US policy-makers and analysts debated and often criticized NATO's cumbersome warmaking procedures in contrast to the alleged flexibility of "coalitions of the willing," effectively paving the way for coalition-based intervention in Afghanistan (2001) and Iraq (2003). Patricia Weitsman (2013) theorizes this insight by making a conceptual distinction between coalition and alliances, a coalition being formed in order to counter a specific threat only (being an ad hoc institution), whereas an alliance has political weight it can translate from peace to wartime conditions. Weitsman then argues that the institutional design of the former makes them more militarily effective than the latter: basically, states in coalition focus principally on operational effectiveness, while states in alliances are primarily concerned with political effectiveness.

Yet, while the idea of a difference in nature between wartime alliances and coalitions is interesting, it is also highly disputable. Weitsman creates ideal-types of coalitions and alliances, while in reality the distinction is not that clear-cut. During the Gulf War the effectiveness of the ad hoc coalition probably benefited from the fact that some of its core members were part of NATO and shared a history of military cooperation. And regarding operations in Afghanistan, it seems difficult to oppose the Operation Enduring Freedom (OEF) as a case of coalition warfare while the International Security Assistance Force (ISAF) would be a case of wartime alliance. Both faced the same type of problems, and the difference between the two is one of degree, not kind. As such, it is probably more appropriate to talk about a multinational military intervention (MMI), which may or may not use the planning and execution facilities offered by a standing alliance such as NATO.

An enduring question to which Weitsman alerts us concerns the military effectiveness of multinational military interventions. This question must be appreciated via an underlying dilemma between rival military and political logics inherent in MMIs. On the one hand, the logic of military effectiveness and less friction push for the integration of all armed forces under a single chain of command. On the other, the logic of sovereignty makes states reluctant to relinquish control over their troops, as they ultimately are politically accountable for their actions and may have interests diverging from those of coalition partners. This tension between (military) integration and (political) autonomy is at the heart of the contemporary challenges of coalition warfare and explain multiple phenomena such as the existence of parallel chains of command, uneven burden sharing, or caveats (Auerswald and Saideman 2014).

Those few studies that do examine this topic identify a trade-off between the political benefits for the United States of operating with allies and the military constraints these allies impose on the conduct of operations. The most powerful state leading a coalition (in this case the United States) has to accept a degree of operational ineffectiveness in order to gain political benefits from the participation of junior partners in a multinational military intervention (Bensahel 2007).

The trade-off between military effectiveness and political value and legitimacy ties in with what "any officer knows intuitively," according to a military analysis, namely that "interoperability of equipment and compatibility of doctrine and operational procedures pose significant challenges in any coalition" (Scales 1998: 4). Accepting a loss of a degree of military effectiveness would thus seem to be premised on a plan for acquiring a political gain that can offset the military setback. Yet we know little about how this trade-off actually works—about the level of political benefits that might compensate for potential or actual military ineffectiveness, or whether the "trade-off" in some cases might be annulled by, say, the combined political and military contributions junior partners can make.

Schmitt (2018) has questioned the practical reach of the trade-off. He argues that the utility of a junior partner's contribution depends on whether this junior partner has a high degree of standing in the international system, or on its military contribution which can be both integrated (a large number of troops deployed and the willingness to use them) and of a superior technological quality. Contrary to what the trade-off perspective suggests, cases of countries with high standing but no real military integration and quality are rare and limited to very peculiar geostrategic contexts, such as Syria's participation in the 1991 Gulf War. Instead, junior partners tend to be both militarily and politically effective, or they tend to be militarily effective but with little political weight. In both instances the trade-off does not apply.

44.4.2 The Quest for Legitimacy

In the post-Cold War era, multilateralism has become a key factor legitimizing military interventions. We refer here to multilateralism not as an ambitious set of procedures shared by all the great powers, which it could be, but less dramatically as a shared understanding among multiple states cooperating militarily, and this regardless of the specific decision mechanisms and arrangements between them. Thus, as Martha Finnemore (2003: 82) notes, "multilateralism legitimizes action by signaling broad support for the actor's goals. Interveners use it to demonstrate that their purpose is not merely self-serving and particularistic but is joined in some way to community interests that other states share." In other words, the current international normative context regarding the use of force encourages multilateralism and incentivizes states to build international coalitions in order to signal support for their cause.

States employing military force sometimes struggle to meet this expectation. In 2003, when unable to secure a formal UN Security Council resolution for the Iraq intervention, the United States attempted to replace multilateralism by multinationalism, making the sheer number of participants in the intervention a value in itself. In effect, mass became a substitute for principled legitimacy. However, judging by the record, it is a poor substitute. In the Iraq intervention, which lacked a UN mandate, the United States struggled to mobilize support even from close allies, such as Turkey; in Afghanistan, where the campaign was consistently anchored in UNSC resolutions, operations and logistics were comparatively easy to organize in widespread networks of allies and partners (Mattox and Grenier 2015).

The attempt to establish "legitimacy by mass" in order to compensate for the absence of principled multilateral legitimacy is thus problematic. Coalition-building strategies based on an alleged "legitimacy-aggregation model" should therefore be subjected to scrutiny, as they likely promise more operational effectiveness and impact than they can deliver. Schmitt (2018) shows that no relationship (positive or negative) between the international public support (consistently under 30 percent) and the number of states participating in Afghanistan or Iraq interventions can be identified: in other words, the "legitimacy-aggregation" strategy that drove the make-up of large coalitions had no observable effect on the perceptions of the interventions by international audiences. Revealingly, Stefano Recchia (2015) demonstrates that US military officers are usually more inclined than their civilian counterparts to operate within a multilateral framework in spite of the operational challenges involved, given their awareness of the operational impact of legitimacy. Military officers may thus be inclined to consider the diplomatic-strategic dimension of the deployment one of several preconditions for operational success, a point which suggests that coalitions' comparative advantage in terms of military effectiveness—discussed in the previous section—should be appreciated in a wider context. In fact, durable alliances and other multilateral frameworks based on principles in addition to the pragmatics that inform coalitions, have competitive advantages that pull coalitions back into their fold. The outcome is not the dominance of one institutional form over the other but rather a difficult and contested relationship between coalitions and alliances, each of which have distinct but incomplete advantages.

44.4.3 The Future

Ultimately, and as previously noted, military cooperation is shaped by the expectation of war and the desire to prevent it or prevail in it. As the character of war changes, the format and shape of military cooperation will change alongside it. Several trends in contemporary warfare are likely to have an impact on future multinational military interventions.

First, it seems that the rise of what has been called "compound warfare" will continue as a major battlefield phenomenon. This type of fighting implies technologically superior forces enabling and supporting local combatants through airpower, limited ground forces, naval power, or other capabilities (cyber, intelligence, etc.). This model refers to the NATO-led intervention in Libya in 2011, the French-led intervention in the Sahel since 2013, the US-led coalition in Iraq and Syria since 2014 in support of the Iraqi armed forces and rebel groups, the Russian intervention in support of rebels in Ukraine's Donbass region, and the Russian intervention in Syria since 2015 in support of the Assad regime.

Compound warfare is less costly than the large ground deployments of Afghanistan and Iraq and on the face of it offers the distinct advantage of political gain at less cost. However, this type of warfare also intensifies the traditional challenges of coalition warfare. For instance, in the relationship between local forces and the technologically superior power, the latter will become politically responsible for the former's behavior. In a sense, this is a new version of the "alliance security dilemma" of entrapment and abandonment: the outside great power will want to orient the intervention's strategy in a certain direction but risks entrapment by local maneuvers and strategizing; conversely, the local troops can only go so far in pulling the great power's string because they risk its severing and thus their own abandonment on the battlefield. All these considerations are compounded by the technical challenges of coordinating and integrating distinctively different levels of organizational and technical skill into a cohesive military force. There is a risk that great powers will be overtly focused on form, which local forces will mimic, at the expense of operational impact along local lines and traditions. Thus, it is thought provoking that Russia has had more success coordinating with the Syrian regime than

NATO had coordinating with rebels in Libya, and there seem to be two main reasons for this. First, the imbalance of military skill between Russia and the Syrian regime is less pronounced than between NATO and the Libyan rebels, which makes operational coordination easier and more effective. Second, political alignment between two actors is smoother than between an alliance of 28 member states and a plurality of rebel movements. Indeed, the record suggests that compound warfare will inherently put alliances' cohesion under stress.

Another important aspect for alliances and coalitions to consider in the future is their capability to create cohesive strategic narratives aimed at external parties and also their own publics. Strategic narratives are an important way for political entities to shape their environment by justifying and implementing their preferred policies (Miskimmon et al. 2013). Yet, the coordination of strategic narratives is challenging for an alliance that has to balance cohesiveness toward external audiences with member states' attention to their own public opinion. In the Afghan campaign, NATO allies upheld multiple and sometimes competing strategic narratives, which inevitably impacted negatively on public opinion (De Graaf et al. 2015). Considering the new media ecology (De Franco 2012) and the growth of connectivity (Betz 2015), the necessity to establish cohesive narratives in order to maximize strategic effect is here to stay, which is to say that potential political disagreements among alliance members will develop under a magnifying glass.

Third, multinational military exercises (MMEs) are becoming increasingly important in the establishment and maintenance of strategic partnerships, and have become a diplomatic tool in their own right. Data compiled by the *Military Balance* since the end of the Cold War show a constant rise in the number, and variety, of multinational military exercises, in particular in Europe and in Asia. Such exercises fulfill a number of important functions. They may first of all, and in quite traditional fashion function as a deterrent tool as they signal resolve and readiness. Moreover, they may serve as track-two diplomacy between military powers that are strategic rivals. For instance, China and the United States train together once a year (alongside many other countries) during the RIMPAC exercise. MMEs also benefit the individual domains of great powers, as they facilitate the establishment of security networks with partner countries not ready for formal alliance commitments. Such partnerships typically evolve around the adoption and maintenance of common procedures and ways of war. MMEs also facilitate defense exports as the great power can demonstrate defense know-how and partner countries can demonstrate allegiance by buying into the patron's defense equipment.

Future research on alliances should therefore pay careful attention to MMEs as vehicles for both alliance formation—even if informal—as well as international security governance. If MMEs fulfill their potential, they can help stabilize both patron–patron and patron–client relations. However, MMEs are as vulnerable to the dynamics of the security dilemma as other forms of security cooperation and should be studied within this broad context.

Finally, trends in warfare will change the dynamics of intra-alliance diplomacy. Traditionally, such diplomacy has evolved around questions of burden sharing, which has been measured in terms of shares of GDP or manpower and fighting power amassed for defensive postures or military operations. New technologies—or, emerging security challenges in NATO-speak—offer new opportunities for alliance diplomats, in particular in regards to cyber and information warfare, though opportunities also emerge from broader issues of societal resilience and hybrid warfare. Resilience can refer to energy security, border security, or even the inclusion of social minorities in the constitutional order. This range of emerging security challenges offers allies a broader menu for choice in terms of their alliance contribution but also makes the political task of striking a "fair" burden sharing deal more complex. Such complexity in turn tempts populist leadership, which promises to rigorously sort out affairs, but which in effect should be considered another facet of the intricacy of intra-alliance management.

This broader context of alliance diplomacy should thus be part of the research agenda. The central question concerns the ability of "reluctant" allies to argue for broad measures of collective defense and the inverse ability of "spearhead" allies to narrow the strategic agenda to suit their key interests, and how this relationship is upended by new technologies and security challenges.

44.5 Conclusion

The study of alliances has traditionally focused on states and war, with alliances being a tool with which the former could manage the latter. In recent years, the field has widened, taking into account alliances' evolving and contested relationship to both broader collective security institutions and narrower and supposedly more effective coalitions. In this chapter we have emphasized this evolution of the study of alliances, beginning with traditions and moving on to collective security and coalitions.

Alliances have advantages in both directions. Compared to collective security institutions, they offer a sharper combination of capacity and purpose, something that led NATO to appropriate some of the collective security thinking of the 1990s without giving up its collective defense character. Compared to coalitions, alliances have staying power and thus political weight, just as they confer a greater degree of legitimacy to military operations. With these advantages, it is unlikely that we will see any weakening of alliances as a phenomenon in international relations.

The politics of alliances, their character and impact should be carefully scrutinized, though. Their changing boundaries vis-à-vis collective security institutions could well weaken the UNSC concert of power and thus intensify great power rivalry. Likewise, informal alliances will as a type of networked coalition pretend to offer security governance but will simultaneously be tied to spheres of great power influence that are contested and must be diplomatically managed. And finally, widened scope for internal alliance diplomacy suggests new opportunities for building cohesion but inversely also enhanced space for recriminations of free riding and unfair burden sharing. As they thus change in character, alliances will continuously define the frontier between cooperation and conflict and be of central concern to security studies scholars.

References

Auerswald, D. and S. Saideman. 2014. *NATO in Afghanistan*, Princeton, NJ: Princeton University Press.

Bensahel N. 2007. International Alliances and Military Effectiveness: Fighting Alongside Allies and Partners. In Risa. A. Brooks and Elizabeth. A. Stanley (eds.), *Creating Military Power*. Stanford, CA: Stanford University Press.

Betz, D. 2015. *Carnage and Connectivity. Landmarks in the Decline of Conventional Military Power*. London: Hurst Publishers,.

Commission on Global Governance. 1995. *Our Global Neighbourhood*. Oxford: Oxford University Press.

Crescenzi M. J. C., J. D. Kathman, K. B. Kleinberg, and R. M. Wood. 2012. Reliability, Reputation and Alliance Formation. *International Studies Quarterly*, 56(2): 259–74.

De Franco, C. 2012. *Media Power and the Transformation of War*. Basingstoke: Palgrave Macmillan.

De Graaf, B., G. Dimitriu, and J. Ringsmose. (eds.). 2015. *Strategic Narratives, Public Opinion and War. Winning Domestic Support for the Afghan War*. Abingdon: Routledge.

Department of Defense. 2015. *The National Military Strategy of the United States of America, 2015*. Washington, DC: Department of Defense.

Dombrowski, Peter. 2015. America's Third Offset Strategy: New Military Technologies and Implications for the Asia Pacific, RSIS Policy Report, June.

Duffield, John S. 2009. Alliances. In Paul D. Williams (ed.), *Security Studies*, pp. 291–306. London: Routledge.

Finnemore M. 2003. The Purpose of Intervention: Changing Rules About the Use of Force. Ithaca, NY: Cornell University Press.

Gelpi, C. 1999. Alliances as Instruments of Intra-Allied Control. In H. Haftendorn, R. O. Keohane, and C. Wallander (eds.), *Imperfect Unions. Security Institutions over Time and Space*, pp. 107–39. Oxford: Oxford University Press.

Hammes, Thomas X. 2004. *The Sling and the Stone: On War in the 21st Century*. St. Paul, MN: Zenith Press.

Hoffman, Frank G. 2007. *Conflict in the 21st Century: The Rise of Hybrid Wars*. Arlington: Potomac Institute.

Jervis, Robert. 1985. From Balance to Concert: A Study of International Security Cooperation. *World Politics*, 38(1): 58–79.

Kissinger, H. 2014. *World Order*. New York: Penguin.

Krahmann, Elke. 2005. American Hegemony or Global Governance? Competing Visions of International Security. *International Studies Review*, 7(4): 531–45.

Levy, J. S. 1981. Alliance Formation and War Behavior: An Analysis of the Great Powers, 1495–1975. *Journal of Conflict Resolution*, 25(4): 581–613.

Mattox, G. A. and Grenier, S. M. (eds.). 2015. *Coalition Challenges in Afghanistan. The Politics of Alliance*. Stanford, CA: Stanford University Press.

Miskimmon, A., B. O'Loughlin, and L. Roselle, 2013. *Strategic Narratives. Communication Power and the New World Order*. Abingdon: Routledge.

Oren, I. 1990. The War Proneness of Alliances. *Journal of Conflict Resolution*, 34(2): 208–33.

Pressman, J. 2008. *Warring Friends: Alliance Restraint in International Politics*. Ithaca, NY: Cornell University Press.

Recchia, S. 2015. *Reassuring the Reluctant Warrior. U.S Civil-Military Relations and Multilateral Intervention*. Ithaca, NY: Cornell University Press.
Rosecrance, Richard. 1992. A New Concert of Powers. *Foreign Affairs*, Spring: 64–82.
Rynning, Sten. 2005. *NATO Renewed: The Power and Purpose of Transatlantic Cooperation*. New York: Palgrave.
Rynning, Sten. 2013. Coalitions, Institutions and Big Tents: The New Strategic Reality of Armed Intervention. *International Affairs*, 89(1): 53–68.
Scales, R. H. Jr. 1998. Trust, Not Technology, Sustains Coalitions. *Parameters*, XXVIII: 4–10.
Schmitt, O. 2018. *Allies That Count. Junior Partners in Coalition Warfare*. Washington, DC: Georgetown University Press.
Schweller, R. L. 1998. *Deadly Imbalances*. New York: Columbia University Press.
Smith, Rupert. 2006. *The Utility of Force: The Art of War in the Modern World*. London: Penguin.
Snyder, G. 1998. *Alliance Politics*. Ithaca, NY: Cornell University Press.
Sprecher C. and V. Krause. 2006. Alliances, Armed Conflicts and Cooperation: Theoretical Approches and Empirical Evidences. *Journal of Peace Research*, 43(4): 363–9.
Tierney, D. 2011. Does Chain-Ganging Cause the Outbreak of War? *International Studies Quarterly*, 55(2): 285–304.
US Navy. 2015. Forward, Engaged, Ready: A Cooperative Strategy for 21st Century Seapower. March.
Wallander, Celeste A. 2000. Institutional Assets and Adaptability: NATO after the Cold War. *International Organization*, 54(4): 705–35.
Walt, S. 1987. *The Origins of Alliances*. Ithaca, NY: Cornell University Press.
Waltz, K. N. 1979. *Theory of International Politics*. Reading: Addison Wesley.
Weitsman, P. A. 2004. *Dangerous Alliances: Proponents of Peace, Weapons of War*. Palo Alto, CA: Stanford University Press.
Weitsman, P. A. 2010. Alliances and War. In R. Denemark and R. Marlin-Bennett (eds.), *The International Studies Encyclopedia. Available at:* http://www.oxfordreference.com/view/10.1093/acref/9780191842665.001.0001/acref-9780191842665.
Weitsman, P. A. 2013. *Waging War. Alliances, Coalitions and Institutions of Interstate Violence*. Stanford, CA: Stanford University Press.
Whitfield, Teresa. 2007. *Friends Indeed? The United Nations, Groups of Friends, and the Resolution of Conflict*. Washington, DC: USIP.

CHAPTER 45

THE UN SECURITY COUNCIL

IAN HURD

THE UN Security Council was created in 1945 as the central body on international security issues in the new United Nations. It combines international legal and political authority in a way that had never been seen before in the Westphalian state system. I explore here how the expansive mandate to resolve "threats to international peace and security" on behalf of all members of the United Nations creates a legalized international hierarchy with the Council at the peak and governments in subordinate positions. This system of legal and political authority comes to life when the Permanent Members of the Council decide to use it. It lies dormant when they do not. The combination of absolute legal authority and a commitment to the substantive goals of the great powers gives the Security Council an imperial character; it is a world state (from Wendt), empire (from Hardt and Negri), and global sovereign (from Schmitt).

The Charter of the UN set out an ambitious agenda for a post-Second World War global order which included lofty aspirations for "friendly relations among nations" and "respect for human rights and for fundamental freedoms" as well as concrete legal obligations on governments to "settle their international disputes by peaceful means" and "refrain ... from the threat or use of force".[1] The political organs of the UN link the high-minded language of the aspirations to the formal realities of legal obligation. To the designers of the UN system, these would help bring about a more peaceful and well-governed international system.

The Security Council is the crucial piece of this institutional architecture. It is the body in the UN system that deals exclusively with international peace and security and the only body with the legal authority to compel governments to abide by its decisions. It was also intended to function as a kind of central committee for the great powers, a place of the highest diplomacy on the political and military management of world affairs and perhaps also of compromise and accommodation among the leading states.

Textbooks of international politics commonly refer to the Security Council as a kind of problem-solving device to fill in gaps in good governance for global order. It is said, for instance, that "the Security Council dispatches peacekeeping forces to trouble spots" and has "the primary responsibility to decide, coordinate and supervise acts of collective security" (Goldstein and Pevehouse 2011: 238).[2] It "was kept small to facilitate swift decision making in response to threats to international peace and security" (Mingst and Arreguín-Toft 2014: 209). These writers see the Council in terms borrowed from liberal international theory: as a solution to security externalities of the sovereign state system, acting for the shared goal of international order.[3]

In practice, the Council reveals something different. Its legal authority is decidely un-liberal, in that it possesses unlimited, unchecked authority to impose itself on governments and demand their obedience. It has endless legal authority but its practical power is entirely dependent on the Permanent Members—that is, on "great powers." Its agenda therefore reflects their desires. This dependence opens the Council to the common complaint that it acts inconsistently in addressing international crises: for instance, it acted with force against Gaddafi in Libya in 2011 but meekly or not at all in Rwanda in 1994, Syria from 2011, and elsewhere. These complaints are right on the substance of the issue—that is the Council does indeed act inconsistently—but they are wrong on their normative interpretation—this isn't a failure of the system, but rather the system working as it was designed to do.

In what follows I explore the Council's legal authority as defined in the UN Charter and then look at how it has been put to use in practice. The two main parts of the chapter come together in the conclusion as the combination of absolute legal authority and specific political interests suggest an "imperial" model of the Security Council.

45.1 The Competence of the Security Council

The authority of the Security Council is constituted by Chapters V and VII of the UN Charter. These set out its structure, membership, and capacities. They list its five permanent members (the UK, the United States, France, China, and Russia) and the rules for selecting the ten non-permanent members (chosen for two-year terms by regionally defined voting groups).[4]

The Security Council is granted the authority to "determine the existence of any threat to the peace, breach of the peace, or act of aggression" in the world and to "decide what measures shall be taken ... to maintain or restore international peace and security" (UN Charter, Article 39). These measures can be anything that the Council decides, from diplomatic solutions to economic sanctions to military enforcement—or nothing. Every UN member has the right to bring issues to the attention of the Council but the Council alone decides what if anything to do about them.

The Charter makes clear that the Council has sole authority to determine what constitutes a threat to international peace and the appropriate response. Its choices on these cannot be second-guessed by any other institution; there is no form of judicial review by the International Court of Justice or any other court or institution.[5] This authority is both limiting and empowering for the Council: it is constraining in that it limits the Council's authority to issues that involve international peace and security and so it ensures that the Council will not take action on any other topics. But it is empowering because it leaves it up to the Council itself to decide what counts as "international peace and security" and also because it gives the Council unlimited authority within that area of competence. This displaces the general prohibition against any UN action on "matters which are essentially within the domestic jurisdiction of any state" (Art. 2(7) of the Charter) since anything the Council finds to be an "international" matter is by definition not a domestic matter. The practical consequences are evident as, for instance, the Council increasingly identifies dire humanitarian conditions within states as a potential "threat to international peace and security," with the effect that the Council is then authorized to intervene in them if it wants.[6]

When taking a decision, the Council follows the voting rule set out in Article 27 of the Charter. This says that "every member of the Security Council shall have one vote" and decisions on substantive matters "shall be made by an affirmative vote of nine members including the concurring votes of the permanent members" (UN Charter, Article 27(1) and 27(3)). Council decisions therefore require at least nine of the 15 members of the Council in favor, and no permanent members voting against. The phrase "concurring votes" was originally understood to mean that all five permanent members must vote in favor for a decision to pass, but that was very quickly (i.e. by 1946) superseded by the practice that accepted abstentions by permanent members as "concurring" (Bailey and Daws 1998: 251). The new interpretation was pushed by the United States and UK against Soviet resistance, though the Soviet Union quickly came to appreciate the greater flexibility this gave to veto-holders and thus the controversy went quiet.[7] The ease with which this clause was reinterpreted hints at the influence of great power interests in shaping the actions and power of the Council, to which I return in Section 45.2.

All states that join the UN agree in advance to accept and carry out the decisions of the Security Council. This is an explicit obligation (Art. 25) that brings with it wide-ranging legal, political, and even conceptual implications. It creates a formal legal hierarchy in world politics with the Security Council at the peak. It gives a foundation to the more general commitment in Article 24(1) which states that UN "members confer on the Security Council primary responsibility for the maintenance of international peace and security, and agree that . . . the Security Council acts on their behalf."[8]

As a consequence, UN members are legally subordinate to the Security Council on matters of international peace and security. When the Council demands that they do something—for instance, that Iraq withdraw from Kuwait in 1990 (S/RES/660), that the International Criminal Court investigate crimes against humanity in Sudan in 2005 (S/RES/1593), that Libya end its violence against civilians in 2011 (S/RES/1970), or that all countries must enact domestic laws that criminalize the "collection . . . of funds . . . to carry out terrorist acts" (S/RES/1373)—all governments are legally obligated to comply. These powers are greater than anything ever given to any international organization in the history of the Westphalian system.

The five Permanent Members of the Council are in control of this power. The veto ensures that nothing can come out of the Council that is opposed by any of them. The idea of a directorship of the great powers emerged in 1943 and 1944 in discussions between the United States, the UK, and the Soviet Union. The "Big Three" thought of themselves as the natural leaders of the globe with the material capacity to project power around the world. They brought on China, for regional representativeness, and France, to renew its historical global position, to make up the eventual Permanent Five (P-5). They considered themselves the great powers of the age and wrote themselves into the Charter to institutionalize that status. It has largely worked, in the sense that as political power has shifted the permanent seats remain as inked in 1945. These five countries get extra influence in world politics as a result of the Charter, and since their assent is necessary for any change to the Charter there is little prospect of that changing.[9]

The Council is a legal-political supreme authority over states (at least with respect to international security questions). This directly contradicts Kenneth Waltz's famous axiom on international "anarchy," that in the anarchic international system "none is entitled to command; none is required to obey" (Waltz 1979: 88). On this premise he differentiated domestic from international politics and constructed the edifice of international "self-help," power balancing, and perpetual state insecurity that came to be known as neorealism.[10] But with the UN in mind, we can see that he was wrong from the start. All states are obligated to obey the Security Council[11] and the international political system does contain the "relations of super- and subordination" among its parts that Waltz said it could not have. Moreover, Charter rules on war are binding on everyone and so it is no longer true that "each state decid[es] for itself whether or not to use force" (Waltz 1979: 102; see also Weller 2016). The authority to decide when to use force has, since 1945, been in the Security Council, not individual governments. Even the "inherent right" to individual self-defense in Article 51 is constrained by the legal primacy of the Security Council.[12] The central premise of the "anarchy problematique," shared by realists, liberals, and many constructivists, has been empirically wrong since 1945.[13] The Security Council *governs* world politics. It exercises legalized hegemony.

And yet, as Leonard Cohen said, "There is a crack in everything—that's how the light gets in" (Cohen 1992). The crack in the Council's hegemony appears at the intersection between international and domestic constitutional orders. This has recently become evident as people who have been targeted by the Council for punishment have used domestic courts against the authority of the Council. The most famous case is of Yassin Abdullah Kadi who in 1999 was identified by the Security Council as a member of al Qaida. It ordered domestic authorities to seize his assets around the world (UN S.S. Res. 1267 1999 and S.C. Res. 1333 2000). The European Union complied in 2001 and in response Kadi filed a challenge at the European Court of First Instance claiming that his rights were violated. Prior to the seizure, he had not been charged with any crime or been given an opportunity to respond to the accusations made against him. He was essentially disposed of his property by the Security Council without so much as a note telling him that it had been done.

The legal processes became highly complex as it moved through the layers of the EU legal system[14]—but at heart, the question was simple: Can domestic courts stand up to the Security Council? The questions is highly charged, since to answer "yes" would apparently contradict the paramount authority over domestic institutions promised to the Council by the UN Charter, but to answer "no" would delete the due-process legal protections that many people feel are a key accomplishment of the rule of law in domestic legal systems. The European Court of Justice eventually ruled in Kadi's favor. In 2008, it ordered that EU governments to return his property and stop enforcing UN sanctions that lacked due process protections for their targets. Kadi got his bank accounts back and the Security Council amended its sanctioning procedures. It now gives individuals or their governments more information about accusations and in some instances provides a channel to oppose them (Kokott and Sabotta 2012).[15] The Kadi case and others like it appear to have put a hole in the Council's legal authority, empowering domestic courts to review Council decisions.[16]

The Council's authority—Kadi notwithstanding—is a major concession of sovereignty by states to a centralized authority. It replaces the basic model of statehood on which much of International Relations (IR) is based, which Siba Grovogui has called "the Westphalian commonsense,"[17] with a hierarchical political-legal system. It trades away state autonomy in favor of collectivization, with the P-5 driving the collective body. To those who value national sovereignty, this may make the Council an instance of what Ben Schonthal (2016: 12) calls "pyrrhic constitutionalism," that is, a step toward legalization whose long-term or systemic repercussions turn out to undermine the goals of the designers. To the P-5, however, it is a very favorable arrangement: it empowers a central agent which they themselves control, backed by all the discursive power of international legalization.

45.2 The Security Council in Practice

Having set out the legal bases of Council power, it should be immediately obvious that real-world international politics matches these rules only partially or with significant caveats. Despite their obligations, governments routinely evade, ignore, or reinterpret the demands of the Security Council, and disagreements over who owes what under Council resolutions is a notable site for international political contestation. These disagreements have high stakes precisely because they invoke the legal and political power of the Council in the service of particular goals.[18] But they also show that it is worth considering the Council's legal authority and its power in practice as somewhat separate: the legal centralization of authority over security affairs in the Council is hardly the last word in international politics—it may not even be the operative organizing principle.

Despite the comprehensive and absolute legal authority of the Security Council, its practical impact in world politics is something less. The Council only rarely puts into practice the powers given to it by the Charter. Its periods of activism and latency are a function of the changing interests of the permanent members: the Council becomes active when its permanent members agree that it should and it stays dormant when they do not. This result is precisely what was intended by the designers of the Council. They wanted a governing body that would be entirely unbounded when there was great power consensus and entirely inert when there was not. In Barry Buzan's terms, it accepts the "autism" of the great powers and also that they nonetheless may sometimes find that their desires coincide (Buzan, Chapter 43, this volume).

This design served the Council well in the Cold War since it ensured that it would remain on the sidelines through all of the great power confrontations of that time. The main security conflicts in these years were largely engineered by the superpowers and they had no shared interest in using the enforcement powers of the Council to resolve them. The veto gave all parties confidence that the Council would not be used by one great power against another. The Council therefore had virtually no role in any of the headline conflicts of the Cold War—it made no resolutions on the Vietnam War, the Cuban Missile Crisis, or the Berlin Wall and blockade, and it had little to say on any of the many proxy wars and overthrows engineered by the United States and the Soviet Union. Before 1990, it imposed economic sanctions only twice (in the 1960 against Southern Rhodesia and in 1977 against South Africa) and the only application of its authority for military intervention (in 1950 regarding Korea) occurred when the Soviet Union was boycotting the Council and missed its chance to veto the resolutions.

The Council was useful to the superpowers in the Cold War in its role as a third-party observer to conflicts. This is how UN "peacekeeping" was invented in the 1950s. These missions are authorized by the Security Council but rely on negotiations between the UN and the parties rather than outright coercion.[19] Peacekeepers are typically lightly armed soldiers or police officers and they are authorized to use force only if directly attacked.[20] Their mandates range from monitoring a peace agreement (Cyprus, India–Pakistan, Israel and several neighbors, El Salvador), to arranging elections (Namibia, Haiti, Cambodia, Nicaragua), to providing basic policing or security (Cambodia, Haiti, Somalia), among other functions. The fact that they are negotiated with the local government means that peacekeeping operations rest on consent rather than the legal enforcement authority of the Security Council. It also means they naturally respect Article 2(7) on non-interference in domestic affairs. But it also means that they must remain in the good graces of the government. This can seriously compromise the goals or integrity of a peace operation—the prime example coming from the unwillingness of the UN in Rwanda to protect innocent people from government-sponsored mass killing in 1994 (United Nations 1996; Dallaire 2003).

The change in United States–Soviet relations in the 1980s allowed an expansion of the possibilities for action by the Security Council. The era began in the mid-1980s with negotiations to end the Cambodian wars—after backing opposite sides in Cambodia over many years, the United States and the Soviet Union agreed on the terms of a negotiated settlement and used the Council to implement it (de Cuéllar 1997). This led to the most interventionist peacekeeping mission to date (UNTAC, from 1991 to 1995), which was deeply and actively involved in governing Cambodia for several years (United Nations 1995). It also provided the model for the 1990s version of the Security Council: with the Permanent Members agreeing among themselves more often about how some regional disputes should be resolved, the great powers found the Council to be a tool with which to jointly administer the rest of the world. The United States and the Soviet Union had sustained many of these conflicts during the Cold War and now found reason to work together using the Security Council to wind them down (Matheson 2006).

The 1990s saw a series of high-profile interventions by the Council. Most important may be the 1990 resolutions that authorized collective military action to reverse Saddam Hussein's takeover of Kuwait. This case also illustrates the fact that the Council itself controls no military—when it decides to use force, it relies on the contributions of member states, which are voluntary. This is true both of the militarized "peace enforcement" missions such as Iraq–Kuwait and also peacekeeping operations. Beyond Kuwait, the Council in the 1990s also broke new ground by authorizing a new kind of international criminal court in Yugoslavia and Rwanda. These stretched the Council's authority under Article 29 of the Charter which empowers it to create "such subsidiary bodies as it deems necessary for the performance of its functions."

The dependence on great power unanimity should make it clear why it is wrong to describe the Security Council as a collective security system.[21] This is a common but mistaken way to conceive of the Council.[22] Kupchan and Kupchan say that "collective security rests on the notion of all against one. While states retain considerable autonomy over the conduct of their foreign policy, participation in a collective security organization entails a commitment by each member to join a coalition to confront an aggressor with opposing preponderant strength" (Kupchan and Kupchan 1991: 118).[23] Many commentators advance the view that this principle is institutionalized, albeit imperfectly, in the Security Council.[24] In fact, the Council does the opposite: it empowers the great powers to intervene in global affair as they wish, but does not require that they come to the aid of anyone if they do not want to.

The obligations of the permanent members were explicitly discussed during the negotiations over the Charter in 1944–45. A group of smaller states presented the great powers with a proposal to actively require that the Council defend individual member states who were under attack—that is, they proposed a collective security mechanism. The idea was quickly killed. The big four (who became the P-5 once France was added) made it clear they would sooner abandon the UN project entirely than accept an automatic obligation to intervene militarily on behalf of another state (Russell 1958; Hurd 2007). What the great powers wanted—and what they eventually got—was a security system which left it up to them to decide whether a security crisis merited their intervention. Charles Webster, a British diplomat involved in drafting the Charter, called this system "an alliance of the great powers embedded in a universal organization" (Mazower 2013b: 63). It is a great power compact, not a collective security system.

The recent history of Responsibility to Protect (R2P) helps to illustrate how the Council's activism is opportunistic rather than automatic. As the concept of R2P was popularized through the 2000s, a central question was whether it could be used to legitimize military interventions for humanitarian rescue without the approval of the Security Council. This was part of the aspiration of pro-R2P activists who sought a path for intervention that could by-pass a deadlocked Council. It was, after all, precisely the Council's failure to help the people of Rwanda in 1994 that provided the energy for R2P in the first place. They were convinced that the Council could not be relied upon to put human welfare ahead of great power politics. But absent an amendment to the Charter, there was no way for R2P to overcome the obvious fact that it was advocating a use of force that was illegal. China and Russia (among others) have been clear that they do not accept that R2P authorizes the use of force without Council approval and the issue has been obfuscated in international reports to avoid having to resolve the underlying tension between the law of the Charter and the idea that the Council will always supply less intervention than activists desire.[25]

Into this gap, the Council has inserted itself. It has asserted its own capacity to use R2P to justify intervention and so has embraced the concept insofar as it enhances its own powers. It made explicit reference to R2P in Resolution 1973, authorizing the use of force against the government of Libya in 2011 (Weiss 2011). It suggested that "the responsibility of the Libyan authorities to protect the Libyan population" was not being met and thus that the international community should act forcefully in its place. By appropriating the language of R2P, the Council expanded its own capacity to intervene militarily in world affairs, secure in its legal authority under Chapter VII of the Charter.[26] If the result of R2P is that the Council's interventionist powers expand while others are forbidden to use it, then the pro-R2P norm entrepreneurs are likely to be very disappointed.

Some observers misunderstand the relationship between the Council and the great powers. Seeing the dependence of the former on the latter, they conclude that the Council itself is relatively powerless and its rules and symbols relatively unimportant.[27] This is a mistake that is made by IR realists and IR liberals alike—both imagine that the power of international organizations comes from their capacity to *constrain* powerful states.[28] They overlook the fact that international organizations may instead be designed to *enhance* the power of governments—Charlotte Peevers calls this the "facilitative aspect of international law" (Peevers 2013: 127). The Security Council is an excellent example: it was envisioned as a device which would facilitate the governance of the international system by the strongest states on behalf of "everyone."[29] With the Council, the Charter gives to the great powers powers which they would not have in its absence: they can legally oblige other states to go along with their desires and take military action against them if they refuse. This power is legitimated by the institutional and discursive forms of law, diplomacy, and negotiation but behind these markers of consensual "global governance" lie the desires of the strong (Hurd 2015). The Council facilitates global domination—though of course only so far as the great powers are in agreement among themselves.

45.3 Leviathan/Empire/Nomos

Authority, said Hannah Arendt, is a relation "between the one who commands and the one who obeys" (Arendt 1997: 93). The Security Council is in a position of authority over the governments of the world. The UN Charter centralizes decisions on the use of force in the Security Council and invests that new institution with the substantive goals and interests of the great powers. The combination of unchecked legal authority and great-power interests makes the Council an institution of global empire. It institutionalizes the dominance of the P-5 and legitimates it through international legalization. With the legal powers of Leviathan and the political interests of the great powers, the Security Council is an imperial super-sovereign, an agent of global governance that transcends the conventional distinctions of liberal political theory between public and private power and between domestic and international affairs.

In the place of "international anarchy," the Security Council brings into being a global Empire, a world state. For Hardt and Negri, "empire" describes a constellation of political and military power that gives "the right of duty of the dominant subjects of the world order to intervene in the territories of other subjects in the interest of preventing or resolving humanitarian problems, guaranteeing accords, and imposing peace" (Hardt and Negri 2000: 18). Alexander Wendt aimed at a similar idea with the "world state," which he defined as a "universal supranational authority—a procedure for making binding and legitimate decisions about the exercise of ... common power."[30] The Security Council is the institutional home of that authority. It embodies the world-governing imperial council that Carl Schmitt called for in his mid-century analysis of world governance—it is the *Nomos* of the earth (Schmitt 2006).

Both liberals and realists in IR theory are likely to overlook this imperial power since they are both committed to the view that international law constitutes a *constraint* on state power.[31] My analysis here offers evidence that international law should also be recognized for its *enabling* capacity, by which governments might become empowered by international law to do things which they previously could not.[32] The Council is important in international politics because it helps the great powers do things which they could not do without it. Its role in legitimizing enforcement action through legal forms amplifies the power of its strongest members and enables them to more effectively pursue the interests in global governance that they share with each other.

45.4 Conclusion

In popular mythology, the Security Council is a place of "decision-making mechanisms that give voice to countries of diverse cultures and regions [that] help to counterbalance self-regarding judgments and discourage unwarranted action," and where the misbehaving states are brought back to the common good through the multilateral diplomacy and collective enforcement of the "international community" (Wedgwood 2003: 576). A clear-headed analysis of the law and politics of the Council suggests something different.

The Security Council is the leading body in the United Nations system for questions of international peace and security. It has the primary responsibility among UN organs to determine the existence of threats to and breaches of international peace and to design responses to deal with them. In doing so, it is empowered to act on behalf of all UN members and may demand of them anything that it deems necessary to restore international peace. These powers are contingent on the agreement of all five of the Permanent Members of the Council. This significantly weakens the Council's activism and has ensured that its full legal and political power has been on display relatively infrequently since 1945. When it is unleashed, as in Iraq in 1990, Libya in 2011, and in creating ad hoc criminal courts for specific countries, its effective power is tremendous.

The legal authority and the power of the Council in practice combine in such moments to create a global hegemonic order above states. This is a remarkable transformation of the anarchic, decentralized, Westphalian system into a hierarchical legal, political, and military order. The Security Council has unlimited legal authority to impose itself on the world and it is guided by the interests of the P-5. The rest of the community of states is legally obligated to go along with it. It results in a paradox: the global dominance of the great powers set within a legal infrastructure that legitimizes their collective rule, but always at the brink of irrelevance when these five governments find themselves moving in different directions.

Notes

1. UN Charter, Arts. 1(2), 1(3), 2(3), and 2(4).
2. See *A Plea Against the Abusive Invocation of Self-Defense as a Response to Terrorism*, open letter by a group of international lawyers on the interpretation of the UN Charter, June 29, 2016, http://cdi.ulb.ac.be/wp-content/uploads/2016/06/A-plea-against-the-abusive-invocation-of-self-defence.pdf
3. See for instance John Owen, Chapter 8 this volume.
4. The line between formal Charter rules and informal UN practices is blurry, and often the latter are allowed to change the former. For instance, the regional groups are hinted at but not defined in the Charter. And Russia and China sit in seats that are specified in the Charter for the USSR and the Republic of China.
5. See the discussion in Alvarez (2005).
6. This theme has been explored extensively by Jennifer M. Welsh in theory in a 2004 chapter in practice, as reported in a 2011 paper.
7. South Africa tried to resuscitate the controversy at the International Court of Justice in the 1960s, arguing that the Council's decisions against it were illegal because some of them passed with P-5 abstentions. It lost. The Court said "the proceedings of the Security Council extending over a long period ... have consistently and uniformly interpreted

the practice of voluntary abstention by a permanent member as not constituting a bar to the adoption of resolutions." See Advisory Opinion on the *Legal Consequences of the Continued Presence of South Africa in Namibia* 1970, cited in Schweigman (2001: 43, fn 203).

8. The phrase 'primary responsibility' in Art. 24(1) is provocative because the Charter never specifies where "secondary" or other responsibilities lie for international peace and security. One possibility is that states themselves retain "secondary" responsibility in the form of the right to use force in self-defense in Art. 51 (though this is complicated by the reference in Art. 51 to the "inherent" (i.e. not secondary) right to self-defense). Another possibility is that the General Assembly has a responsibility for peace and security which is "secondary" to the council. This was invoked by the United States and some allies in 1950 to permit the General Assembly to authorize military operations in Korea in the face of Soviet veto in the Security Council. See A/RES/377.
9. On SC membership reform debates, see Nadin (2016).
10. Adam Quinn calls this the 'second realism' in Quinn, Chapter 6, this volume.
11. The status of non-members of the UN is murky—to a legal positivist, a government that chose not to join the UN would not be obligated to comply with the Council or any other part of the treaty; to others the Charter has constitutional status in world affairs and some parts of it may therefore be binding *erga omnes* even without consent. Since there are today no widely recognized nation states that are not UN members, there is no urgent need to resolve the ambiguity.
12. Article 51 on self-defense affirms a broad self-interested "inherent right of individual or collective self-defense" by states but it places that right inside a legal box defined by the Charter: the right to self-defense exists only once "an armed attack occurs against a Member of the United Nations" and only "until the Security Council has taken measures necessary to maintain international peace and security." The controversies over what that allows, forbids, and implies for state agency are extensive. See, among others, O'Connell (2008), Corten (2012), Hathaway (2014), Hurd (2016).
13. The term "anarchy problematique" is taken from Ashley (1988).
14. See the account in Tzanakopoloulos (2013).
15. See also "The Targeted Sanctions Initiative" at the Graduate Institute of International and Development Studies, Geneva, http://graduateinstitute.ch/un-sanctions. Accessed July 28, 2016. Farrall (2016).
16. James Crawford wrote a poem about the Kadi case, at http://www.ejiltalk.org/mr-kadi-and-article-103-by-james-crawford-a-poem/. Accessed July 29, 2016. Thanks to Ian Johnstone for bringing it to my attention.
17. Grovogui (2002).
18. For instance, some interpret the overthrow of Gaddafi in Libya in 2011 as authorized by Council resolutions and others as a violation of them. Similarly, the United States argued in 2003 that its invasion of Iraq was permitted, perhaps even required, under Council decisions from the early 1990s. This interpretation had virtually no support outside the US government. On Libya, see "Russia Accuses NATO of Going Beyond UN Resolution on Libya," rt.com, April 17, 2011, https://www.rt.com/news/russia-nato-un-resolution-libya/. On Iraq, see Taft and Buchwald (2003); Grey, (2008).
19. It is conceivable that a peacekeeping operation might be authorized by the General Assembly or another unit of the UN but this is very much a marginal possibility compared with the Council's role.

20. Many good histories exist including Dobbins (2014) and Howard (2008).
21. This section draws on Hurd (2006).
22. Mohamed S. Helal (2015: 389) notes that "depicting the Security Council as a collective security system misrepresents its nature and structure."
23. See also, Mingst and Arreguín-Toft (2017: 305–7).
24. See among others, Kupchan and Kupchan (1991); Ruggie (1993); Lipson (1994); Murphy (1997); Pease (2000: 64); Curtis et al. (2014: 154); Russett and Oneal (2001); Dunne et al. (2014: 84). Among those who resist describing the Council a form of collective security are Mingst and Arreguín-Toft (2017).
25. For instance, in the 2005 World Summit Outcome document, A/RES/60/1.
26. A list of all SC uses of R2P is here: http://www.globalr2p.org/resources/335. Accessed August 9, 2016.
27. For instance, Mearsheimer (2002) and Glennon (2003).
28. On law as constraint, see for instance Ikenberry (2012) and Guzman (2010).
29. Recent work in global and intellectual history has provided new insight into how this "everyone" was understood at the time, particularly with regards to race. See for instance Mazower (2013a), Pedersen (2015), and Vitalis (2015).
30. Wendt (2003: 505. See also Chimni (2004).
31. The idea that international law is a constraint on states is conventional wisdom for scholars of international law and international politics. For instance, Rosa Brooks (2014) says "the core notion of the rule of law is that all power must be constrained by law." Beth Simmons (2009: 5) says "it is precisely because of their potential power to constrain that treaty commitments are contentious in domestic and international politics."
32. On the "permissive power" of international law, see Hurd (2016).

References

Arendt, Hannah. 1997. *Between Past and Future.* Harmondsworth: Penguin.

Alvarez, José E. 2005. *International Organizations as Law-Makers.* Cambridge: Cambridge University Press.

Ashley, Richard K. 1988. Untying the Sovereign State: A Double Reading of the Anarchy Problematique. *Millennium*, 17(2): 227–62.

Bailey, Sydney D. and Sam Daws. 1998. *The Procedure of the UN Security Council.* 3rd edn. Oxford: Oxford University Press .

Brooks, Rosa. 2014. Cross-Border Targeted Killings: "Lawful but Awful?" *Harvard Journal of Law and Public Policy*, 38: 233–50.

Chimni, B. S. 2004. International Institutions Today: An Imperial Global State in the Making. *European Journal of International Law* 15(1): 1–37.

Cohen, Leonard. 1992. "Anthem" *The Future.*

Corten, Olivier. 2012. *The Law Against War: The Prohibition on the Use of Force in Contemporary International Law.* Oxford: Hart.

Curtis, Devon et al. 2014. International Law and Nonstate Actors. In Steven L. Lamy, John S. Masker, John Baylis, Steve Smith, and Patricia Owens (eds.), *Introduction to Global Politics.* New York: Oxford University Press.

Dallaire, Roméo. 2003. *Shake Hands with the Devil: The Failure of Humanity in Rwanda.* Toronto: Random House Canada.

de Cuéllar, Javier Pérez. 1997. *Pilgrimage for Peace: A Secretary-General's Memoir.* New York: St. Martin's Press.

Dobbins, James. 2014. A History of UN Peacekeeping. In Ian Shapiro and Joseph Lampert (eds.), *Charter of the United Nations: Together with Scholarly Commentaries and Essential Historical Documents.* New Haven, CT: Yale University Press.

Dunne, Tim et al. 2014. Theories of Global Politics. In Steven L. Lamy, John S. Masker, John Baylis, Steve Smith, and Patricia Owens (eds.), *Introduction to Global Politics.* New York: Oxford University Press.

Farrall, Jeremy. 2016. Sanctions. In Jacob Jatz Cogan, Ian Hurd, and Ian Johnstone (eds.), *Oxford Handbook of International Organizations.* Oxford: Oxford University Press.

Glennon, Michael. 2003. Why the Security Council Failed. *Foreign Affairs.*

Goldstein, Joshua S. and Jon C. Pevehouse. 2011. *International Relations* 10th edn. Pearson.

Grey, Christine. 2008. *International Law and the Use of Force*, 3rd edn, pp. 354–66. Oxford: Oxford University Press.

Grovogui, Siba. 2002. Regimes of Sovereignty: International Morality and the African Condition. *European Journal of International Relations*, 8(3): 315–38.

Guzman, Andrew. 2010. *How International Law Works: A Rational Choice Analysis.* Oxford: Oxford University Press.

Hardt, Michael and Antonio Negri. 2000. *Empire.* Cambridge, MA: Harvard University Press.

Hathaway, Oona. 2014. Fighting the Last War: The United Nations Charter in the Age of the War on Terror. In Ian Shapiro and Joseph Lampert (eds.), *Charter of the United Nations: Together with Scholarly Commentaries and Essential Historical Documents.* New Haven, CT: Yale University Press.

Helal, Mohamed S. 2015. Am I my Brother's Keeper? The Reality, Tragedy, and Future of Collective Security. *Harvard National Security Journal*, 6: 389.

Howard, Lise Morjé. 2008. *UN Peacekeeping in Civil Wars.* Cambridge: Cambridge University Press.

Hurd, Ian. 2006. Unrealizable Expectations: Collective Security, The UN Charter, and Iraq. In Harvey Starr (ed.), *Approaches, Levels, and Methods of Analysis in International Politics: Crossing Boundaries.* Basingstoke: Palgrave.

Hurd, Ian. 2007. *After Anarchy: Legitimacy and Power in the UN Security Council.* Princeton, NJ: Princeton University Press.

Hurd, Ian. 2015. The International Rule of Law and the Domestic Analogy. *Global Constitutionalism*, 4(3): 365–95.

Hurd, Ian. 2016. The Permissive Power of the Ban on War. *European Journal of International Security*, 2(1): 1–18.

Ikenberry, G. John. 2012. *Liberal Leviathan.* Princeton, NJ: Princeton University Press.

Kokott, Julianne and Christoph Sobotta. 2012. The Kadi Case—Constitutional Core Values and International Law—Finding the Balance. *The European Journal of International Law*, 23(4): 1015–24.

Kupchan, Charles A. and Clifford A. Kupchan. 1991. Concerts, Collective Security, and the Future of Europe. *International Security*, 16(1): 114–61 .

Lipson, Charles. 1994. Is the Future of Collective Security Like the Past? In George W. Downs (ed.), *Collective Security Beyond the Cold War.* Ann Arbor, MI: University of Michigan Press.

Matheson, Michael J. 2006. *Council UN-Bound: The Growth of UN Decision Making on Conflict and Postconflict Issues after the Cold War.* Washington, DC: United States Institute for Peace, ch. 4.

Mazower, Mark. 2013a. *Governing the World: The History of an Idea, 1815 to the Present*. Harmondsworth: Penguin.

Mazower, Mark. 2013b. *No Enchanted Palace: The End of Empire and the Ideological Origins of the United Nations*. Princeton, NJ: Princeton University Press.

Mearsheimer, John. 2003. *The Tragedy of Great Power Politics*. London: Norton.

Mingst, Karen A. and Ivan M. Arreguín-Toft. 2014. *Essentials of International Relations*. 6th edn. London: Norton.

Murphy, John F. 1997. Force and Arms. In Christopher C. Joyner (ed.), *The United Nations and International Law*. Cambridge: Cambridge University Press.

Nadin, Peter. 2016. *UN Security Council Reform*. Abingdon: Routledge.

O'Connell, Mary Ellen. 2008. *The Power and Purpose of International Law: Insights from the Theory and Practice of Enforcement*. Oxford: Oxford University Press.

Pease, Kelly-Kate. 2000. *International Organizations: Perspectives on Governance in the Twenty-First Century*. London: Prentice-Hall.

Pedersen, Susan. 2015. *The Guardians: The League of Nations and the Crisis of Empire*. Oxford: Oxford University Press.

Peevers, Charlotte. 2013. *The Politics of Justifying Force: The Suez Crisis, the Iraq War, and International Law*. Oxford: Oxford University Press.

Ruggie, John Gerard.1993. Multilateralism: Anatomy of an Institution. In John Gerard Ruggie (ed.), *Multilateralism Matters: The Theory and Praxis of an Intitutional Form*. New York: Columbia University Press.

Russell, Ruth B. 1958. *A History of the United Nations Charter: The Role of the United States, 1940–1945*. Washington: Brookings Institution.

Russett, Bruce M. and John R. Oneal. 2001. *Triangulating Peace: Democracy, Interdependence, and International Organizations*. London: Norton.

Schmitt, Carl. 2006. *The* Nomos *of the Earth in the International Law of* Jus Publicum Europaeum. Candor, NY: Telos Press.

Schonthal, Benjamin. 2016. *Buddhism, Politics and the Limits of Law*. Cambridge: Cambridge University Press.

Schweigman, David. 2001. *The Authority of the Security Council Under Chapter VII of the UN Charter*. Kluwer Law.

Simmons, Beth A. 2009. *Mobilizing for Human Rights: International Law in Domestic Politics*. Cambridge: Cambridge University Press.

Taft, William H. IV and Todd F. Buchwald. 2003. Preemption, Iraq, and International Law. *American Journal of International Law* 97(3): 557–63.

Tzanakopoloulos, Antonios. 2013. *Kadi* Showdown: Substantive Review of (UN) Sanctions by the ECJ, *EJIL Talk*, July 19, 2013. *Available at:* http://www.ejiltalk.org/kadi-showdown/#more-8613. Accessed July 29, 2016.

United Nations. 1995. *The United Nations and Cambodia 1991–1995*. New York: UN Department of Public Information,.

United Nations. 1996. *The United Nations and Rwanda 1993–1996*. New York: UN Department of Public Information.

Vitalis, Robert. 2015. *White World Order, Black Power Politics: The Birth of American International Relations*. Ithaca, NY: Cornell University Press.

Waltz, Kenneth. 1979. *Theory of International Politics*. New York: McGraw Hill.

Wedgwood, Ruth. 2003. "The Fall of Saddam Hussein: Security Council Mandates and Preemptive Self-Defense," *American Journal of International Law* 97(3): 576–85.

Weiss, Thomas. 2011. RtoP Alive and Well after Libya. *Ethics and International Affairs*, 25(3): 287–92.

Weller, Marc. 2016. The Use of Force. In Jacob Katz Cogan, Ian Hurd, and Ian Johnstone (eds.), *Oxford Handbook of International Organizations*. Oxford: Oxford University Press.

Welsh, Jennifer M. 2004. Authorizing Humanitarian Intervention. In Richard M. Price and Mark W. Zacher (eds.), *The United Nations and Global Security*, pp. 177–92. Abingdon: Routledge.

Welsh, Jennifer M. 2011. Civilian Protection in Libya: Putting Coercion and Controversy Back into RtoP, *Ethics and International Affairs*, 25(3): 255–62.

Wendt, Alexander. 2003. Why a World State is Inevitable. *European Journal of International Relations*, 9(4): 491–542.

CHAPTER 46

REGIONAL SECURITY COMPLEXES AND ORGANIZATIONS

MATTEO LEGRENZI AND FRED H. LAWSON

SCHOLARLY attention to regional aspects of international security has increased markedly since the end of the Cold War. The focus on regions is evident in structural realist writing (Grieco 1997), in rationalist accounts of international institutions (Wallander and Keohane 1999), among scholars who chart the evolution of underlying conventions and practices (Hurrell 2007), and among those who analyze how states construct their security interests (Acharya 2001). The most promising research programme that explores security matters at the regional level is the extensive body of scholarship that focuses on regional security complexes (RSCs). This concept makes it possible to explicate the emergence and impact of a wide range of threats confronting policy-makers, most notably the tendency for conflicts that break out in one country to spread across the border into neighboring countries and the growing incidence of disputes over scarce water resources. The increasing interconnectedness of internal and external threats in the contemporary world gives adjacent states a strong incentive to coordinate their security policies, thereby creating renewed impetus to long-dormant regional organizations (Tavares 2010).

46.1 Regional Security Complexes

Regional dynamics lie at the core of the analytical framework advanced by Karl Deutsch and his colleagues to explain why states sometimes coalesce into "security communities," that is, discernible groupings among whose constituents the use of military force is inconceivable. Security communities take shape whenever economic and cultural transactions among member states reach the level at which there develops "a matter of mutual sympathy and loyalties; of 'we feeling,' trust, and mutual consideration; of partial identification in terms of self-images and interests; [and] of mutual successful predictions of behavior," which convinces leaders and general publics alike to expect that interstate disputes will be settled only by non-violent means (Deutsch et al. 1957: 36; Deutsch 1961). Some security communities, so-called "amalgamated" ones, entail the political unification of member states; others, designated "pluralistic security communities," consist of independent states that engage in coordinated action to deal with major security problems. The failure of pluralistic security communities to take shape anywhere outside Western Europe led scholars to abandon this line of inquiry, and although recent developments have sparked renewed interest in the notion of security communities, newer studies explain their emergence and consolidation in terms different from those proposed in the original theory (Acharya 1996; Adler and Barnett 1998; Schoeman 2002; Ngoma 2003; Nathan 2009).

Robert Jervis (1982) offers a compelling alternative explanation for the rise of regional security orders. Sustained cooperation among governments in the face of severe external threats results from a combination of four factors: a shared preference for the existing state of affairs; a consensus that no country intends to overturn the status quo; general agreement that security cannot be achieved through expansionism; and a recognition that warfare and arms races are inordinately costly (Jervis 1982: 361–2). In addition, regional security orders take shape whenever circumstances make defensive weapons and strategies more effective than offensive ones, and it is possible to distinguish between attack weaponry and protective armaments. These conditions explain the emergence of the Concert of Europe in the years following the Napoleonic Wars (Jervis 1985), and may well lay the foundation for robust security arrangements in the contemporary world.

Jervis's theory of security regimes has been overshadowed by Barry Buzan's (1983: 106) concept of "regional security complexes," or "group[s] of states whose primary security concerns link together sufficiently closely that their national securities cannot realistically be considered apart from one another." The distinctive features of regional security complexes are produced by specific combinations of local state interaction and great power intervention in regional affairs, although such structures increasingly reflect "the importance of actors at the bottom of the [global] power hierarchy" (Buzan 1983: 113). Buzan and Ole Wæver (2003: 45) also describe regional security complexes as "durable patterns of amity and enmity taking the form of subglobal, geographically coherent patterns of security interdependence."

What exactly constitutes security interdependence remains unclear in Buzan and Wæver's analytical framework. The concept is quickly replaced by the looser notion of "security interaction," which is said to increase in line with "simple physical adjacency" (Buzan and Wæver 2003: 45). The defining characteristic of regional security complexes is subsequently reduced to the observed activity of states in a particular part of the world: "The standard form for an RSC is a pattern of rivalry, balance-of-power, and alliance patterns among the main powers *within* the region: to this pattern can then be added the effects of penetrating external powers" (Buzan and Wæver 2003: 47). Regional security complexes get further redefined in terms of the "securitisation practices of practitioners," so that the constituents and boundaries of such complexes come to be "dependent on what and whom [the actors at hand choose to] securitise" (Buzan and Wæver 2003: 48). It is therefore not surprising to learn that regional security complex theory "is mostly a descriptive language, a method for producing order out of complicated data, and for writing structured history" (Buzan and Wæver 2003: 52; see also Khong 1997: 319).

David Lake (1997) offers a more satisfactory analytical perspective, which demarcates regional security complexes on the basis of the unintended consequences of the security-related actions undertaken by governments in some parts of the world. For Lake (1997: 48–9), "a regional system [consists of] a set of states affected by at least one transborder but local externality that emanates from a particular geographical area" and that "poses an actual or potential threat to the physical safety of individuals or governments in other states." Such externalities can be either harmful or beneficial, and tend to be inherently "nonexcludable," so states suffer or profit from the security-related activities that take place around them, whether or not they had a hand in producing those activities (Lake 1997: 49 note 4).

Security externalities associated with the outbreak and subsequent evolution of armed conflicts play a crucial role in configuring regional security complexes. Conflicts can be interstate or intra-state, small or large, sporadic or intense; they can affect some adjacent countries more than others, or all neighbors equally; they can generate one substantial externality at a time, or a cluster of significant externalities all at once (Lake 1997: 52–3). Lake (1997: 53) claims that conflicts that spin-off lots of security externalities will on the whole be easier to manage, due to the "greater scope for strategies of tactical linkage and conditional cooperation" that multiple conflicts accord the states involved; similarly, states that confront several externalities at once will be "more likely to form institutions or regimes to manage their relations, spreading the fixed costs of institutional construction across a greater number of spillovers." By contrast, conflicts that generate fewer or less intense externalities will be harder to manage and give states an incentive to "negotiate more ad hoc agreements" instead of stable institutions. In addition, regional security complexes that contain unipolar or bipolar distributions of interstate power can be expected to have an easier time managing armed conflicts, whereas multipolarity makes it difficult for states to cope with the effects of conflict (Lake 1997: 60–1).

Regional power distributions play an equally central role in the analytical framework proposed by Robert Stewart-Ingersoll and Derrick Frazier (2012). As in Lake's theory, much hinges on how many actors exist in a given part of the world, with "regional powers" defined as "states who [*sic*] possess sufficient capabilities to project power throughout and who disproportionately influence the security dynamics within their regional security complex" (Stewart-Ingersoll and Frazier 2012: 7). Having fewer regional powers facilitates a higher degree of orderliness. Order is even more likely to prevail if regional powers are satisfied with the existing situation, and therefore more inclined to collaborate with one another (Stewart-Ingersoll and Frazier 2012: 12–13). Taken together, these factors determine "the [region's] governing arrangements, including [the] rules, principles and institutions that define the regional security order" (Stewart-Ingersoll and Frazier 2012: 21).

Recent scholarship highlights the concept of regional security governance. Studies initially focused on the European Union (Webber et al. 2004; Kirchner 2006), then set out to incorporate other parts of the world (Kirchner and Dominguez 2011). Emanuel Adler and Patricia Greve (2009) assert that regions in which power balancing constitutes the predominant mode of security governance will operate differently from ones that approximate Deutschian security communities. Emil Kirchner (2014) posits a four-fold typology of regulatory modes: conflict prevention, policies that assure (or reassure) regional partners, strategies that protect the existing order, and efforts to compel recalcitrant states to comply with regional norms. A more comprehensive set of "general forms of security governance" is sketched by James Sperling (2014: 109): "impermanent alliances, cooperative security, concerts, collective defense, collective security and two types of security community—contractual and fused."

Current work on security governance assays to show what types of regulation are most effective in dampening or precluding conflict (Aris 2009; Caballero-Anthony 2010; Barbarinde 2011; Jackson 2014). The research program thus displays an inherent normative thrust, with "governance" used to mean "good governance," or "successful governance." One set of case studies finds that regional security governance is more likely to exist whenever states are well-articulated, there is widespread "commitment to the region as a site of governance" and two mutually antagonistic adversaries are not present (Breslin and Croft 2012: 16). Another survey of 14 regional institutions finds that security governance is associated with high scores for human development and economic freedom, as well as with a high degree of commonality among member states (Kirchner and Dominguez 2014).

Out of this diverse assortment of writings, a synthetic theory of regional security complexes can be derived that illuminates crucial features of the contemporary international arena. The theory rests on the premise that a regional security complex consists of countries whose security interests are deeply affected by the externalities of policies that their respective governments adopt in response to severe internal and external challenges. It asserts that each state's defense policies emerge from the securitization of particular matters, rather than from abstract and unchanging threats-in-principle. It hypothesizes that security externalities are more dangerous and harder to manage whenever the region includes more than two powers, and whenever attack weapons and strategies enjoy a clear advantage over protective ones. It expects states to take more vigorous steps to coordinate their security policies, and construct or strengthen regional organizations, as externalities grow more numerous and pressing. And it posits that the robustness of regional cooperation increases as member states become more fully articulated and firmly established.

46.2 Cross-Border Diffusion of Civil Wars

One danger that confronts states in the contemporary world is the cross-border spread of internal warfare. Quantitative studies show that civil wars in one country are highly correlated with armed conflicts in adjacent countries (Sambanis 2002; Gleditsch and Salehyan 2008; Salehyan 2009). Maarten Bosker and Joppe de Ree (2014: 207) present strong evidence that it is "only ethnic [civil] wars [that] tend to spill over [interstate boundaries], and they are more likely to spread along ethnic lines." Nevertheless, the precise mechanisms and processes that cause the cross-border spread of so-called "ethnic civil wars" remain obscure (Forsberg 2016).

Whether or not ethno-sectarian conflicts spill across international borders depends on the extent to which the combatant community in the adjacent state(s) finds itself in circumstances that are similar to those in the country where a civil war is transpiring (Hill et al. 1998; Bosker and de Ree 2014: 214–15; Forsberg 2014: 148–9). Warfare is more likely to spread whenever a combatant community straddles the border (Brown 1996). Armed conflict is also more likely to spread whenever the combatant community in the adjacent country is clustered in space (Toft 2002–03). The chances that a civil war will jump across the border are particularly high if a spatially concentrated community in the neighboring country constitutes the majority in a particular district close to the frontier (Fearon 1998; Cederman et al. 2009).

Ethno-sectarian conflict will be more likely to spill over national boundaries if the combatant community in the adjacent country occupies rough terrain (Fearon and Laitin 2003; Hendrix 2011) and inhabits territory that lies at a distance from national or provincial capitals (Buhaug et al. 2008). Civil wars are more likely to cross the border if the adjacent state possesses a minimal degree of institutional capacity (Braithwaite 2010: 314) and the neighboring country's political system is neither a liberal democracy nor a repressive autocracy—in other words, if it is "anocratic" (Hegre et al. 2001). Finally, civil wars exhiibit a greater potential to spread whenever the neighboring country is an autocracy that has introduced a limited number of political reforms (Maves and Braithwaite 2013).

46.2.1 Strategic Interaction

Whenever armed conflict breaks out in one state, the authorities in the adjacent state(s) can be expected to take steps to head off outbreaks of violence inside their own domain(s) (Danneman and Ritter 2014). Such measures occasionally block the diffusion of the conflict, but they more often provoke belligerent responses from one or more of the combatant communities whose members reside in neighboring countries (Forsberg 2014: 149). Furthermore, policies that surrounding governments adopt to prevent the spread of ethno-sectarian fighting tend to increase the salience of distinctions among latent ascriptive communities, thereby creating antagonistic collectivities that had previously lain dormant (Fearon and Laitin 2000: 856).

More broadly, ethno-sectarian warfare spreads whenever the dominant community in a neighboring country becomes unable credibly to commit itself not to exploit the minority (Fearon and Laitin 2000). Commitment problems are likely to be more profound for regimes whose institutional structure is comparatively weak (Walter 2009). The collapse of the majority's credible commitment to refrain from exploiting the minority is particularly important if it coincides with a drop in the latter's capacity to protect itself, or if a decline in certainty regarding the outcome of a prospective conflict accompanies a higher degree of general polarization (Forsberg 2008: 286).

46.2.2 Impact of Refugees

Civil wars usually generate waves of displaced persons, which entail a host of "negative externalities" for the countries in which the refugees end up (Salehyan and Gleditsch 2006: 338). Refugees upset the inter-communal equilibrium in the receiving country (Salehyan and Gleditsch 2006: 342). An increase in the size of one community can be expected to increase the overall salience of ascriptive ties, which in turn "improve[s] an ethnic group's ability to act collectively in high-risk situations" (Krcmaric 2014: 190). If refugees align with a minority community in the receiving country, they pose a threat to the majority, which will take steps to protect the established order. If, on the other hand, refugees align with the majority, then "minority groups may feel that the influx of foreigners further dilutes their strength," giving them an incentive to attack the new arrivals before their position deteriorates any further (Salehyan and Gleditsch 2006: 343).

Displaced persons generate a broad range of economic difficulties in receiving countries (Salehyan and Gleditsch 2006: 341). The new arrivals depress wages and inflate housing costs (Salehyan and Gleditsch 2006: 344), especially in the districts where they take up residence (Buhaug and Gates 2002). Refugees often push out long-time inhabitants, who can be expected to mobilize into "sons of the soil" movements to take back their lost rights and prerogatives concerning the land (Fearon and Laitin 2011). Moreover, refugees challenge the dominance of the existing leadership of the combatant community in the receiving country, which has an incentive to resort to violence to preserve or restore the status quo ante (Fearon and Laitin 2000: 856).

46.2.3 Civil Wars and Regional Security Complexes

Civil wars affect the security of adjacent countries in a variety of ways. They disrupt routine transactions, scare away foreign investment and tempt extra-regional powers to intervene in local affairs. Yet it is when ethno-sectarian fighting spills across interstate boundaries that the externalities associated with internal warfare pose particularly severe threats to neighboring governments. Future research would do well to investigate instances of the cross-border diffusion of ethno-sectarian conflict in detail, in order to determine the mechanism(s) and process(es) whereby different types and admixtures of externalities become actively securitized (Lawson 2016b). It would be useful as well to find out whether civil wars are more likely to spread in multipolar regions, and under circumstances that accord attack weapons and strategies an advantage over protective forces.

46.3 Regional Water Conflicts

Disagreements over water constitute a security problem in several parts of the contemporary world. The incidence of militarized interstate disputes jumps if the adversaries are part of the same river basin (Toset et al. 2000), and there is a much greater likelihood of armed conflict if a river cuts across the border that divides two states than if it constitutes the boundary between them (Gleditsch et al. 2006). Numerous case studies illustrate the intimate connection between disputes over water and the outbreak and perpetuation of armed conflict (Schultz 1995; Freeman 2001; Horsman 2001; Zakhirova 2013).

Why disagreements over water sometimes get managed or resolved peacefully has provoked considerable controversy. The prevailing explanation channels hegemonic stability theory, and argues that cooperative arrangements take shape whenever one state is so much more powerful than the others that it can both enforce compliance and provide public goods to compensate the loser(s) (Furlong 2006; Tir and Ackerman 2009). Mark Zeitoun and Jeroen Warner (2006) assert that regional institutions appear in the context of "hydro-hegemony," in which "the benefits [that states derive from not exploiting one another] ([such as] international public goods in the form of order, stable expectations and the option of free-riding) outweigh the negatives." By contrast, whenever a regional hydro-hegemon turns in the direction of "the negative, dominative form of hydro-hegemony[,] a certain degree of conflict may [become] inevitable, whether or not the conflict will manifest itself overtly" (Zeitoun and Warner 2006: 439).

Whether or not water disputes erupt into actual warfare depends on the degree to which states find themselves under stress with regard to water supply, as well as on the symbolic importance of this particular natural resource to the actors involved (Selby 2003; Link et al. 2016). More important, the potential for armed conflict increases sharply whenever water becomes securitized (Stetter et al. 2011). And disputes over water tend to be much harder to manage or resolve if one or more of the riparian countries exhibits a high level of domestic instability (Keskinen et al. 2008).

46.3.1 Water Conflicts and Regional Security Complexes

Current scholarship on the regional implications of interstate disputes over water remains rudimentary and largely descriptive. Future work could spell out analytically distinct types of security externalities that accompany states' attempts to exercise control over shared aquifers, and investigate the circumstances and dynamics whereby the distribution of water resources becomes securitized (Lawson 2016a). The peculiar conditions that induce regional hydro-hegemons to adopt collaborative—rather than an exploitative—postures vis-à-vis the other riparian countries merit careful investigation as well (Prys 2010).

46.4 Resurgence of Regional Organizations

Regional organizations that were created to deal with economic affairs or had long lain dormant have become increasingly involved with security matters (Wolff and Dursun-Oezkanca 2012). The Economic Community of West African States (ECOWAS) "has not intervened in every military conflict [that has occurred in western Africa between 1992 and 2012], but has had a diplomatic role in almost all of them," and even dispatched troops to Liberia, Sierra Leone, Guinea-Bissau, Côte d'Ivoire, and Mali (Iwilada and Agbo 2012; Gandois 2014: 50–1). The Association of Southeast Asian Nations set up the ASEAN Regional Forum to address questions regarding mutual security (Haacke 2009). The Shanghai Co-operation Organization now concerns itself with a wide range of threats, and its member states "have begun to note that their security is being impacted on [*sic*] by actors beyond [the former Soviet] space, in particular by Afghanistan and external interference in its members['] information space" (Aris 2014: 150). And in South America, "converging conceptions of security and similar threat perceptions have developed within Mercosur, and the regional organisation has served as a forum, however limited, for coordinating political action in the realm of security" (Oelsner 2014: 206).

Nowhere is this trend more prounounced than in the Middle East and North Africa. Two regional organizations, the League of Arab States (or Arab League) and the Co-operation Council of the Arab States of the Gulf (or Gulf Co-operation Council [GCC]), were founded decades ago to pursue ambitious diplomatic and economic objectives (MacDonald 1965; Legrenzi 2011), almost none of which has been accomplished. Until recently, scholars highlighted the evident shortcomings of both organizations as instruments to promote the security of their respective members and the region as a whole (Barnett and Solingen 2007; Ehteshami 2012; Dakhlallah 2012).

These two organizations nevertheless undertook notable initiatives in the wake of the popular uprisings of 2010–11. The Arab League authorized the establishment of a no-fly zone over Libya, in an unprecedented break with the principle of non-interference in domestic affairs (Beck 2015: 196). The Arab League Council subsequently adopted a resolution insisting that Syria's President Bashshar al-Asad relinquish power. Meanwhile, the GCC's Peninsula Shield Force intervened in Bahrain to crush anti-regime protests (Nuruzzaman 2013), and Saudi Arabia mustered a coalition of GCC forces to carry out air and ground operations in Yemen (Beck 2015: 201). The latter offensive prompted the Arab League to announce plans to set up a rapid reaction force to combat future threats to internal and regional security (Mustafa 2015).

Why long-slumbering regional organizations sometimes revive and undertake innovative initiatives regarding security has yet to be explained. Existing studies point to the end of the Cold War and the "obvious limitations" of the United Nations as factors that set the stage for a resurgence of regionalism (Fawcett 2013: 6; Stein and Lobell 1997; Diehl and Cho 2006). One research program concludes that regionalist activism results from a combination of "the interests and objective conditions that make communal [*sic*] peacemaking a beneficial venture in the assessment of member states" and "the normative congruence among these states that enables them to engage in close political co-operation in order to prevent and end conflict" (Nathan 2010: 3). In these terms, the ECOWAS states shifted their attention to security as sustained growth and economic integration became "unattainable in the context of large-scale violence" (Nathan 2010: 11), and Nigeria found itself predisposed to exercise military force to pacify the region (Nathan 2010: 19).

More compelling explanations for the resuscitation of regional organizations can be derived from the dynamics of regional security complexes (Haacke and Williams 2008, 2009). It might well be argued that regional organizations coalesce and gather strength whenever a cluster of states confronts severe internal challenges to the authorities at the same time that the actions of a nearby state become securitized into a salient external threat. Escalating political challenges at home prevent governments from mobilizing the resources required to parry the foreign threat acting individually, so the leaderships of the countries affected by the securitized externality have a compelling incentive to set up a collaborative security arrangement (Lawson 1999). Such initiatives have a greater chance of succeeding if one, or at most two, of the prospective member states is substantially stronger than the others.

As the conjunction of internal and external threats recedes, states can be expected to scale back their commitment to regional organizations. Multilateral institutions created by governments in crisis are unlikely to evaporate, however, particularly if the circumstances under which those institutions emerged have not been eradicated. The mistrust and uncertainty inherent in international anarchy ensure that once a regional organization gets formed, member states will hold it in reserve for the next time that domestic and foreign dangers converge. It seems likely as well that a ratcheting effect characterizes regional organizations, so that their revivification and expansion into new realms occur in response to externalities that are more numerous or intense than the ones that sparked their initial founding.

46.5 Conclusion

Regional aspects of security play a crucial role in shaping the contemporary international arena, and have attracted burgeoning scholarly interest. Recent work revives the notion of security communities, albeit in a loose and largely untestable fashion. Other studies focus on security governance, but ignore the Foucauldian insight that governance can be either conducive or detrimental to general welfare. More promising is the concept of regional security complexes, particularly ones delineated by the externalities that accompany the policies implemented by adjacent states to deal with convergent internal challenges and securitized external developments. Such complexes vary according to the number of regional powers they contain and the comparative advantage of attack and protective armaments. Conflicts that generate several intense externalities prompt states to create or resuscitate regional organizations, whereas ones that produce fewer or more diffuse externalities result in transient collaborative arrangements. The developmental trajectory of regional security organizations reflects the changing dynamics of regional security complexes.

References

Acharya, A. 1996. A Regional Security Community in Southeast Asia? In D. Ball (ed.), *The Transformation of Security in the Asia/Pacific Region*, pp. 175–200. London: Frank Cass.

Acharya, A. 2001. *Constructing a Security Community in Southeast Asia: ASEAN and the Problem of Regional Order*. London: Routledge.

Adler, E. and M. Barnett 1998. A Framework for the Study of Security Communities. In E. Adler and M. Barnett (eds.), *Security Communities*, pp. 29–65. Cambridge: Cambridge University Press.

Adler, E. and P. Greve 2009. When Security Community Meets Balance of Power: Overlapping Regional Mechanisms of Security Governance. *Review of International Studies*, 35(supplement): 59–84.

Aris, S. 2009. The Shanghai Cooperation Organisation: "Tackling the Three Evils." A Regional Response to Non-Traditional Security Challenges or an Anti-Western Bloc? *Europe-Asia Studies*, 61(3): 457–82.

Aris, S. 2014. The Shanghai Cooperation Organisation: A Eurasian Security Actor? In S. Aris and A. Wenger (eds.), *Regional Organisations and Security*, pp. 141–60. London: Routledge.

Barbarinde, O. 2011. The African Union and the Quest for Security Governance in Africa. In E. Kirchner and R. Dominguez (eds.), *The Security Governance of Regional Organizations*, pp. 273–99. London: Routledge.

Barnett, M. and E. Solingen 2007. Designed to Fail or Failure of Design: The Origin and Legacy of the Arab League. In A. Acharya and A. Johnston (eds.), *Crafting Cooperation*. Cambridge: Cambridge University Press.

Beck, M. 2015. The End of Regional Middle Eastern Exceptionalism? The Arab League and the Gulf Cooperation Council after the Arab Uprisings. *Democracy and Security*, 11(2): 190–207.

Bosker, M. and J. de Ree 2014. Ethnicity and the Spread of Civil War. *Journal of Development Economics*, 108: 206–21.

Braithwaite, A. 2010. Reisisting Infection: How State Capacity Conditions Conflict Contagion. *Journal of Peace Research*, 47(3): 311–19.

Breslin, S. and S. Croft 2012. Researching Regional Security Governance: Dimensions, Debates and Discourses. In S. Breslin and S. Croft (eds.), *Comparative Regional Security Governance*, pp. 1–22. London: Routledge.

Brown, M. 1996. The Causes and Regional Dimensions of Internal Conflict. In M. Brown (ed.), The International Dimensions of Internal Conflict, pp. 571–602. Cambridge, MA: MIT Press.

Buhaug, H. and S. Gates 2002. The Geography of Civil War. *Journal of Peace Research*, 39(4): 417–33.

Buhaug, H., L. Cederman, and J. Rod 2008. Disaggregating Ethno-Nationalist Civil Wars. *International Organization*, 62(3): 531–51.

Buzan, B. 1983. *People, States and Fear*. Chapel Hill: University of North Carolina Press.

Buzan, B. and O. Wæver 2003. *Regions and Powers*. Cambridge: Cambridge University Press.

Caballero-Anthony, M. 2010. Non-Traditional Security Challenges, Regional Governance and the ASEAN Political-Security Community (APSC). Working Paper No. 7. Asia Security Initiative Policy Series. S. Rajaratnam School of International Studies. Singapore.

Cederman, L., L. Girardin, and K. Gleditsch 2009. Ethnonationalist Triads. *World Politics*, 61(3): 403–37.

Dakhlallah, F. 2012. The League of Arab States and Regional Security: Towards an Arab Security Community? *British Journal of Middle Eastern Studies*, 39(3): 393–412.

Danneman, N. and E. Ritter 2014. Contagious Rebellion and Preemptive Repression. *Journal of Conflict Resolution*, 58(2): 254–79.

Deutsch, K. 1961. Security Communities. In J. Rosenau (ed.), *International Politics and Foreign Policy*. New York: Free Press.

Deutsch, K., S. Burrell, R. Kann, J. Lee, M. Lichterman, R. Lindgren, F. Loewenheim, and R. Wagenen 1957. *Political Community and the North Atlantic Area*. Princeton, NJ: Princeton University Press.

Diehl, P. and Y. Cho 2006. Passing the Buck in Conflict Management: The Role of Regional Organizations in the Post-Cold War Era. *Brown Journal of World Affairs*, 12(2): 191–202.

Ehteshami, A. 2012. MENA Region: Security and Regional Governance. In S. Breslin and S. Croft (eds.), *Comparative Regional Security Governance*, pp. 131–53. London: Routledge.

Fawcett, L. 2013. Security Regionalisms: Lessons from Around the World. EUI Working Paper RSCAS 2013/62. European University Institute, Florence.

Fearon, J. 1998. Commitment Problems and the Spread of Ethnic Conflict. In D. Lake and D. Rothchild (eds.), *The International Spread of Ethnic Conflict*, pp. 107–26. Princeton, NJ: Princeton University Press.

Fearon, J. and D. Laitin 2000. Violence and the Social Construction of Ethnic Identity. *International Organization*, 54(4): 845–77.

Fearon, J. and D. Laitin 2003. Ethnicity, Insurgency and Civil War. *American Political Science Review*, 97(1): 75–90.

Fearon, J. and D. Laitin 2011. Sons of the Soil, Migrants and Civil War. *World Development*, 39(2): 199–211.

Forsberg, E. 2008. Polarization and Ethnic Conflict in a Widened Strategic Setting. *Journal of Peace Research*, 45(2): 283–300.

Forsberg, E. 2014. Transnational Transmitters: Ethnic Kinship Ties and Conflict Contagion 1946–2009. *International Interactions*, 40(2): 143–65.

Forsberg, E. 2016. Transnational Dimensions of Civil Wars. In T. Mason and S. Mitchell (eds.), *What Do We Know about Civil Wars?*, pp. 75–90. Lanham, MD: Rowman and Littlefield.

Freeman, K. 2001. Water Wars? Inequalities in the Tigris-Euphrates River Basin. *Geopolitics*, 6(2): 127–40.

Furlong, K. 2006. Hidden Theories, Troubled Waters: International Relations, the "Territorial Trap" and the Southern African Development Community's Transboundary Waters. *Political Geography*, 25(4): 438–58.

Gandois, H. 2014. Security Regionalism in West Africa: Conceptions and Practices. In S. Aris (ed.), *Regional Organisations and Security*, pp. 41–58. London: Routledge.

Gleditsch, K. and I. Salehyan 2008. Civil Wars and Interstate Disputes. In M. Oberg and K. Strom (eds.), *Resources, Governance and Civil Conflict*, pp. 58–76. London: Routledge.

Gleditsch, N., K. Furlong, H. Hegre, B. Lacina, and T. Owen 2006. Conflicts over Shared Rivers: Resource Scarcity or Fuzzy Boundaries? *Political Geography*, 25(4): 361–82.

Greico, J. 1997. Systemic Sources of Variation in Regional Institutionalization in Western Europe, East Asia and the Americas. In E. Mansfield and H. Milner (eds.), *The Political Economy of Regionalism*, pp. 164–87. New York: Columbia University Press.

Haacke, J. 2009. The ASEAN Regional Forum: From Dialogue to Practical Security Cooperation? *Cambridge Review of International Affairs*, 22(3): 427–49.

Haacke, J. and P. Williams 2008. Regional Arrangements, Securitization and Transnational Security Challenges: The African Union and the Association of Southeast Asian Nations Compared. *Security Studies*, 17(4): 775–809.

Haacke, J. and P. Williams 2009. Regional Arrangements and Security Challenges: A Comparative Analysis. Working Paper No. 52. Crisis States Working Papers Series No. 2. Development Studies Institute. London School of Economics and Political Science. July.

Hegre, H., T. Ellingsen, S. Gates, and N. Gleditsch 2001. Toward a Democratic Civil Peace? *American Political Science Review*, 95(1): 33–48.

Hendrix, C. 2011. Head for the Hills? Rough Terrain, State Capacity and Civil War Onset. *Civil Wars*, 13(4): 345–70.

Hill, S., D. Rothchild, and C. Cameron 1998. Tactical Information and the Diffusion of Peaceful Protests. In D. Lake and D. Rothchild (eds.), *The International Spread of Ethnic Conflict*, pp. 61–88. Princeton, NJ: Princeton University Press.

Horsman, S. 2001. Water in Central Asia: Regional Cooperation and Conflict? In R. Allison and L. Jonson (eds.), *Central Asian Security*, pp. 69–94. Washington, DC: Brookings.

Hurrell, A. 2007. One World? Many Worlds? The Place of Regions in the Study of International Society. *International Affairs*, 83(1): 127–46.

Iwilade, A. and J. Agbo 2012. ECOWAS and the Regulation of Regional Peace and Security in West Africa. *Democracy and Security*, 8(4): 358–73.

Jackson, N. 2014. Trans-Regional Security Organisations and Statist Multilateralism in Eurasia. *Europe-Asia Studies*, 66(2): 181–203.

Jervis, R. 1982. Security Regimes. *International Organization*, 36(2): 357–78.

Jervis, R. 1985. From Balance to Concert: A Study of International Security Cooperation. *World Politics*, 38(1): 58–79.

Keskinen, M., K. Mehtonen, and O. Varis 2008. Transboundary Cooperation vs. Internal Ambitions: The Role of China and Cambodia in the Mekong Region. In N. Pachova, M. Nakayama, and L. Jansky (eds.), *International Water Security*, pp. 79–109. Tokyo: United Nations University Press.

Khong, Y. 1997. ASEAN and the Southeast Asian Security Complex. In D. Lake and P. Morgan (eds.), *Regional Orders*, pp. 318–39. University Park: Pennsylvania State University Press.

Kirchner, E. 2006. The Challenge of EU Security Governance. *Journal of Common Market Studies*, 44(5): 947–68.

Kirchner, E. 2014. Theoretical Debates on Regional Security Governance. EUI Working Papers RSCAS 2014/40. European University Institute. Florence.
Kirchner, E. and R. Dominguez 2011. *The Security Governance of Regional Organizations*. London: Routledge.
Kirchner, E. and R. Dominguez 2014. Security Governance in a Comparative Regional Perspective. *European Security*, 23(2): 163–78.
Krcmaric, D. 2014. Refugee Flows, Ethnic Power Relations and the Spread of Conflict. *Security Studies*, 23(1): 182–216.
Lake, D. 1997. Regional Security Complexes: A Systems Approach. In D. Lake and P. Morgan (eds.), *Regional Orders*, pp. 45–67. University Park: Pennsylvania State University Press.
Lawson, F. 1999. Theories of Regional Integration in a New Context: The Gulf Cooperation Council. In K. Thomas and M. Tetreault (eds.), *Racing to Regionalize*, pp. 7–31. Boulder, CO: Lynne Rienner.
Lawson, F. 2016a. Desecuritization, Domestic Struggles and Egypt's Conflict with Ethiopia over the Nile River. *Democracy and Security*, 12(1): 1–22.
Lawson, F. 2016b. Explaining the Spread of Ethnosectarian Conflict: Syria's Civil War and the Resurgence of Kurdish Militancy in Turkey. *Nationalism and Ethnic Politics*, 22(4): 478–96.
Legrenzi, M. 2011. *The GCC and the International Relations of the Gulf*. London: I. B. Tauris.
Link, P., J. Scheffran, and T. Ide 2016. Conflict and Cooperation in the Water-Security Nexus. *WIREs Water*, 3: 495–515.
MacDonald, R. 1965. *The League of Arab States*. Princeton, NJ: Princeton University Press.
Maves, J. and A. Braithwaite 2013. Autocratic Institutions and Civil Conflict Contagion. *Journal of Politics*, 75(2): 478–90.
Mustafa, A. 2015. Arab League Sets New Defense Force at 40,000. *Defense News*, 1 April.
Nathan, L. 2009. Domestic Instability and Security Communities. *European Journal of International Relations*, 12(2): 275–99.
Nathan, L. 2010. The Peacemaking Effectiveness of Regional Organizations. Working Paper No. 81. Crisis States Working Papers Series No. 2. Development Studies Institution. London School of Economics and Political Science. October.
Ngoma, N. 2003. SADC: Towards a Security Community? *African Security Review*, 93(375): 17–28.
Nuruzzaman, M. 2013. Politics, Economics and Saudi Military Intervention in Bahrain. *Journal of Contemporary Asia*, 43(2): 363–78.
Oelsner, A. 2014. Aritculating Mercosur's Security Conceptions and Practices. In S. Aris and A. Wenger (eds.), *Regional Organisations and Security*, pp. 203–21. London: Routledge.
Prys, M. 2010. Hegemony, Domination, Detachment: Differences in Regional Powerhood. *International Studies Review*, 12(4): 479–504.
Salehyan, I. 2009. *Rebels Without Borders*. Ithaca, NY: Cornell University Press.
Salehyan, I. and K. Gleditsch 2006. Refugees and the Spread of Civil War. *International Organization*, 60(2): 335–66.
Sambanis, N. 2002. A Review of Recent Advances and Future Directions in the Quantitative Literature on Civil War. *Defence and Peace Economics*, 13(3): 215–43.
Schoeman, M. 2002. Imagining a Community: The African Union as an Emerging Security Community. *Strategic Review for Southern Africa*, 24(1): 1–26.
Schulz, M. 1995. Turkey, Syria and Iraq: A Hydropolitical Security Complex. In L. Ohlsson (ed.), *Hydropolitics*, pp. 91–122. London: Zed Press.

Selby, J. 2003. Dressing Up Domination as "Cooperation": The Case of Israeli-Palestinian Water Relations. *Review of International Studies*, 29(1): 121–38.

Sperling, J. 2014. Regional Security Governance. In J. Sperling (ed.), *Handbook of Governance and Security*, pp. 98–119. Cheltenham: Edward Elgar.

Stein, A. and S. Lobell 1997. Geostructuralism and International Politics: The End of the Cold War and the Regionalization of International Security. In D. Lake and P. Morgan (eds.), *Regional Orders*, pp. 101–22. University Park: Pennsylvania State University Press.

Stetter, S., E. Herschinger, T. Teichler, and M. Albert 2011. Conflicts about Water: Securitizations in a Global Context. *Cooperation and Conflict*, 46(4): 441–59.

Stewart-Ingersoll, R. and D. Frazier 2012. *Regional Powers and Security Orders*. London: Routledge.

Tavares, R. 2010. *Regional Security*. London: Routledge.

Tir, J. and J. Ackerman 2009. Politics of Formalized River Cooperation. *Journal of Peace Research*, 46(5): 623–40.

Toft, M. 2002–03. Indivisible Territory, Geographic Concentration and Ethnic War. *Security Studies*, 12(2): 82–119.

Toset, H., N. Gleditsch, and H. Hegre 2000. Shared Rivers and Interstate Conflict. *Political Geography*, 19(8): 971–96.

Wallander, C. and R. Keohane 1999. Risk, Threat and Security Institutions. In H. Haftendorn, R. Keohane, and C. Wallander (eds.), *Imperfect Unions*, pp. 21–47. Oxford: Oxford University Press.

Walter, B. 2009. Bargaining Failures and Civil War. *Annual Review of Political Science*, 12: 243–61.

Webber, M., S. Croft, J. Howorth, T. Terriff, and E. Krahmann 2004. The Governance of European Security. *Review of International Studies*, 30(1): 3–26.

Wolff, S. and O. Dursun-Oezkanca 2012. Regional and International Conflict Regulation. *Civil Wars*, 14(3): 297–323.

Zakhirova, L. 2013. The International Politics of Water Security in Central Asia. *Europe-Asia Studies*, 65(10): 1994–2013.

Zeitoun, M. and J. Warner 2006. Hydro-Hegemony: A Framework for Analysis of Trans-Boundary Water Conflicts. *Water Policy*, 8(2): 435–60.

CHAPTER 47

INTERNATIONAL CRIMINAL ACCOUNTABILITY AND TRANSNATIONAL ADVOCACY NETWORKS (TANS)

HANS PETER SCHMITZ

47.1 Introduction

On May 30, 2016, Hissène Habré, president of Chad from 1982 to 1990, was sentenced by a Senegalese court[1] to life in prison for crimes against humanity, torture, and sex crimes. For the first time, the judiciary of one country prosecuted the former leader of another for gross human rights violations. The sentencing was the end result of more than 20 years of activism by his victims and the mobilization of local and international civil society forming a transnational advocacy network (TAN) that campaigned against impunity.[2] Habré's conviction is another high-profile case added to the list of more than 70 prosecutions of state leaders for human rights violations and serious financial crimes since the end of the Cold War (Lutz and Reiger 2009: 295–304).

This rising tide of prosecutions has not gone unchallenged, especially on the African continent where resistance against international criminal justice is increasing. The African Union has demanded immunity for sitting heads of states (African Union 2016), while Burundi and South Africa have declared their intentions to withdraw from the International Criminal Court (ICC). The ICC has a weak record of only four convictions since its creation in 2002 (all cases in the Democratic Republic of Congo), and a much higher acquittal rate than similar criminal tribunals created since the Second World War (Smeulers et al. 2013). And while Habré is being held accountable for torture, government officials in the United States responsible for torture committed between 2001 and 2008 are unlikely to ever face prosecution (Schabas 2013: 551).

Increasingly diverging views on international criminal justice not only pervade the policy world, but also characterize scholarly debates. Proponents argue that there can be no peace and security without justice, and that prosecutions are key to deterring future atrocities. Skeptics disagree and argue that peace after major episodes of violence requires political solutions that are often undermined by prosecutions (Snyder and Vinjamuri 2003). A third position based on ideas of transformative justice critiques prosecutions as unable to address root causes of mass atrocities. This perspective views criminal justice as crowding out more comprehensive post-violence. It faults trials as externally imposed and ill-equipped to foster collective agency against future atrocities (Gready and Robins 2014).

The divergent views on international criminal justice raise questions about why and how this practice has emerged as well as the effectiveness of using individual prosecutions to address gross human rights violations and enhance peace and security domestically and internationally. The first question will be addressed in the next section by focusing on the relative importance of TANs and their activism in support of international criminal justice. The subsequent section then takes a closer look at arguments about the effectiveness of prosecutions. The chapter closes with a discussion on the future role of TANs, in particular in what ways our current, and still limited, knowledge about the impact of such trials can foster institutional learning.

47.2 What Explains the Rise of International Criminal Justice?

The idea of individual criminal responsibility gained attention for short periods after the First and Second World Wars (Schabas 2013: 546), and was more permanently established after the end of the Cold War based on a combination of international law criminalizing heinous crimes as well as domestic, foreign, and international prosecutions (Sikkink and Kim 2013: 275, figure 3). The Nuremberg and Tokyo military tribunals of 1945–46[3] set a precedent, but the idea of prosecuting state leaders only took hold with the democratic transitions in Greece and Portugal during the 1970s and in Argentina during the 1980s (Sikkink 2011: chs. 2 and 3). In 1993–94, the United Nations Security Council established ad hoc tribunals to address mass atrocities in Rwanda and the former Yugoslavia. In 1997, the ICC was established as a more permanent judicial response to gross human rights violations.

In explaining this rise of international criminal justice norms, the scholarly literature offers both agency-driven explanations focused on the role of norm entrepreneurs (Finnemore and Sikkink 1998) and structuralist accounts either highlighting the role of states and material power or identifying diffusion and acculturation processes that have unfolded based on a culture of modernity (Goodman and Jinks 2013; Kim and Sharman 2014).

Scholars focused on the role of power and politics argue that the global rise of individual criminal accountability is the result of Western hegemony and the geopolitical trends of the post-Cold War era (Vinjamuri and Snyder 2015: 309). Evidence includes the growth in prosecutions since the end of the Cold War, the preference for Western legal approaches, and the uneven application of the norms across the globe. For example, the complementarity principle enshrined in the ICC statute protects powerful states from prosecution while exposing weak states to external intervention (Vinjamuri and Snyder 2015: 313).[4]

A focus on power and politics can also be applied domestically when explaining the likelihood of prosecutions in transition processes. While trials in Argentina were enabled by the collapse of the military regime, military elites in Chile and Brazil remained influential after transitions and either delayed or prevented prosecutions. When considering the results of trials and tribunals, skeptics highlight their institutional weaknesses and the need for coercive action by Western states to secure the arrest of accused war criminals (Peskin 2008). They also insist that prosecutions can backfire and politically strengthen those indicted. The Sudanese President Omar al-Bashir or Kenya's leaders Uhuru Kenyatta and William Ruto experienced steady or increased domestic support after being indicted by the ICC prosecutor. This scholarship recommends amnesties during peaceful transitions to democracy in order to remove potential spoilers.

Although a power perspective can offer some insights into the politics of global justice norms, it does not offer a more systematic account of how criminal accountability norms emerged or why states and individuals either promote or deny the validity of these norms. Sociological institutionalism offers some answers here by highlighting a long-term process of expanding individual rights and accountability (Meyer et al. 1997; Kim and Sharman 2014: 436). This rights discourse is expressed in the Universal Declaration of Human Rights (UDHR, 1948), the subsequent constitution of major human rights groups (Amnesty International, founded in 1961; Human Rights Watch, founded in 1978), and the ongoing diffusion of these norms across various international nongovernmental organization (INGO) sectors (Uvin 2007).

Institutionalist accounts rely on a range of mechanisms to explain the diffusion of norms, including material pressures (Keck and Sikkink 1998: 208), persuasion or acculturation (Goodman and Jinks 2013; Johnston 2007). Social change takes place as "progressive structural evolutions, often catalyzed and facilitated by contingencies and exogenous shocks" (Kim and Sharman 2014: 426), and debates in this literature focus attention on the relative importance of different diffusion mechanisms. For example, Goodman and Jinks view compliance resulting from material pressures as much less effective than processes of acculturation based on deep ties of the target state to the larger international community (Goodman and Jinks 2013).

Agency-driven accounts add norm entrepreneurs (Finnemore and Sikkink 1998) not only as key players producing the ties across borders, but also as independent shapers of norms and their implementation. Individual and collective norm entrepreneurs (Flohr et al. 2010), TANs (Keck and Sikkink 1998), epistemic communities (Cross 2013), and small states at the periphery of the dominant global North (Sikkink 2014; Ingebritsen 2006) can all play important roles ignored in structural- or power-based explanations of normative change.

Raphael Lemkin, a Polish lawyer and norm entrepreneur, represented such norm entrepreneurship during and after the Second Word War when he established the term "genocide" and rejected the non-binding UDHR as too weak to defend against gross human rights violations (Frieze 2013). Instead, in his writings he promoted the idea of a legally binding treaty focused on protecting ethnic, religious, and other groups from extermination. Lemkin rejected the idea of individual rights and emerged as a successful norm entrepreneur outside of the culture of modernity and its claim to advance impersonal rules and secularization. While the UDHR became the basis for a significant part of transnational human rights activism emerging in the 1960s and 1970s, the Genocide Convention struggled to gain traction mainly because states feared that ratification would open scrutiny of their own domestic conduct (LeBlanc 1991). The Cold War pushed both approaches to the sidelines, but they endured in becoming constitutive documents for new human rights-focused INGOs (Korey 1998).

In addition to the power of individual norm entrepreneurs, domestic legal struggles at the periphery turned out to be more crucial to advancing international criminal justice than powerful states or the spread of a culture of modernity. The idea of holding state leaders accountable re-emerged during the 1970s in Portugal and Greece after the end of authoritarian rule. The Greek prosecutions had a more limited regional impact in shaping the work of Amnesty International and the emerging European human rights system (Sikkink 2011: 88). A the global level, international criminal justice norms emerged when the Inter-American Commission on Human Rights in the early 1980s recommended prosecuting the former members of the Argentinian military junta. Based on a relatively independent judicial system and lawyers using domestic law in novel ways (Sikkink 2011: 82), Argentina became "ground zero" for the rise of a wide range of transitional justice mechanisms, including truth commissions and reparations (Roht-Arriaza 2009: 51).

What set Latin America in the 1980s apart was a more mature human rights movement promoting Argentinian experiences abroad as well as greater regional interest as neighboring countries experienced their own transitions from authoritarian rule (Brysk 1994). As the idea of prosecuting state officials diffused through networks of lawyers and activists, the response in other countries varied. Chile explicitly rejected individual criminal responsibility until 1998 when former President Augusto Pinochet was arrested in London. South Africa also took a close look at the Argentinian experience, but ultimately opted for amnesty combined with truth-telling in the effort to deal with decades of apartheid as a system of governance (Gade 2013).

TANs in the human rights field became major proponents of criminal justice because it mirrored their existing emphasis on high-profile advocacy and legal strategies targeting individual "villains" to address injustice. TANs were able to exert agenda-setting power especially during the 1990s when failures to prevent mass atrocities in the former Yugoslavia and Rwanda left Western states vulnerable to moral pressures that featured both an explanation for the problem (individuals' decisions to unleash mass violence) and a feasible solution (trials promising justice and future deterrence). The key advantage for TANs supporting criminal justice was not simply that they promoted universalism and human rights and exposed atrocities, but that they promised a policy solution that was broadly compatible with existing norms of Western legal systems. Rather than relying only on "naming and shaming" efforts, advocates offered policy solutions for states to adopt.

47.3 What Difference do International Criminal Justice Norms Make?

TANs make choices about how to organize, deploy their resources, respond to counter-mobilization, and adapt their strategic approaches. These choices are not simply a reflection of an ever-expanding culture of modernity, but they shape the nature and reach of rights. As the idea of prosecuting individuals for heinous crimes takes hold, important new questions emerge about who should be indicted and how trials should be conducted. What matters is not simply that there are more prosecutions over time, but what outcomes can be attributed to them and other measures implemented in a specific national context (Fischer 2016).

Two challenges emerge when assessing the effects of these prosecutions and trials. The first entails the definition of relevant outcomes as well as an account of possible intended or unintended consequences. The second focuses on how to measure outcomes and link them causally to specific criminal justice policies. In addition, these policies and institutions are new and evolving and prosecutions take place in a wide variety of political and social contexts. Current research does not support definitive claims about the impact of prosecutions on subsequent levels of peace and security, although it may be possible to identify short-term effects and reasonably assert likely mid- and long-term consequences.

Arguments for and against criminal prosecutions rely on assumptions about how trials affect the decision making of those considering mass atrocities. Scholars of democratic transitions in southern Europe and Latin America highlighted the need for elite pacts and argued that prosecutions may precipitate coup attempts (O'Donnell and Schmitter 1986: 32). Similar arguments emerged after the end of the Cold War as scholars questioned the wisdom of prosecuting former government officials for major crimes. As former leaders maintain power resources and democratic institutions are still weak, prosecutions create incentives to disrupt transitions to democracy (Snyder and Vinjamuri 2003). Securing peace required giving up on justice, at least in the short- or medium-term.

Critics of international justice claim that prosecutions drive government officials to use the threat of violence as a bargaining chip, while proponents see no link between a threat of prosecutions and increased violence and human rights abuses (Sikkink and Kim 2013: 280). Proponents have also promoted alternative views on leaders' decision making in facing prosecutions. This literature links improved human rights records in Latin America directly to prosecutions and highlights mechanisms of short-term deterrence and long-term socialization (Sikkink 2011: 231). Deterrence has also been a core claim of TANs agitating for prosecutions, in addition to assertions of cost-effectiveness, enhanced rule of law and security, and justice for victims. Logics of appropriateness play a much more limited role here (Vinjamuri 2010) as both sides agree on assessing prosecutions primarily based on their consequences, while disagreements largely focus on the actual effects of justice mechanisms.

What remains unclear in the accounts of both proponents and critics is how large-scale social outcomes, such as more or less violations, are linked to the individual decision making that drives these arguments. A first issue arises when seeking to establish that individual leaders are actually responsive to incentives emanating from a prosecution threat. Sikkink relies on criminology research to argue that an increased likelihood (not severity) of punishment alters leaders' calculations by increasing the costs of repression (Sikkink 2011: 171). Critics have challenged this claim as unreliable and not based on evidence directly collected from such state leaders. Mendeloff emphasizes that the key to deterrence is timing, not likelihood, and as "people heavily discount the future, punishment has little impact on behavior when delayed" (Mendeloff 2011: 291). In addition, everyday criminal behavior may not be a very good predictor of decision making during episodes of mass atrocities (Rodman 2008). Such rational choice assumptions (shared by both critics and proponents) may not hold if relevant information is not available or calculations of risks differ substantially across individuals and cultures.

A second issue emerges when drawing causal linkages between individuals' decision making and large-scale violence. Even if leaders are rational in their calculations of risks, it remains unclear how important their decisions are for violent or peaceful outcomes. Only a few studies acknowledge these complexities of analyzing the effects of prosecutions. Focused on four ICC indictments in the African context, Geis and Mundt identified two key conditions for a positive impact of prosecutions, including the "degree of international cohesion and the subsequent will to impose real costs" and the ICC's ability to generate the "respect and legitimacy of the national populations" (Geis and Mundt 2009: 19). Similarly, research considering both the effects of trials and amnesty laws has argued that a combination of trials and amnesties is most effective in deterring future abuses (Olsen et al. 2010). This position strikes a balance between competing arguments and makes a case for considering how to most effectively sequence different transitional justice mechanisms.

Apart from deterrence, court proceedings are said to contribute to norm socialization by creating a collective memory removing mass atrocities from the repertoire considered by future leaders (Sikkink 2011: 174). A norm of impunity is replaced by a norm of accountability supported by shared understandings of historical events. Establishing a case for such a long-term process is certainly even harder to accomplish than measuring short-term effects, in particular since multiple social, economic, and cultural factors will likely intervene over time and shape changes in levels of repression and human rights violations. Some have argued that pronounced normative shifts are more likely when trial proceedings are embedded in broader social movements where groups outside of the "transitional system" are more important than the narrow criminal proceedings that represent professionalized, top-down efforts unlikely to address the root causes of past atrocities (Fischer 2016: 13).

Arguments for transformative, rather than limited transitional justice are based on the claim that Sikkink's focus on Latin American cases reflects a biased case selection focused on individual leaders using tools of state violence. Many other cases of mass atrocities, including the former Yugoslavia, Rwanda, or Darfur/Sudan, suggest a need for responding in a more comprehensive manner to "chronic structural violence and unequal social relations" (Gready and Robins 2014: 342). Although prosecutions could serve as complementary to other measures, the diffusion of international criminal justice norms establishes a "transitional justice industry" (Nassar 2014: 69) and may crowd out other approaches. Court proceedings risk hiding the context of violence behind assumptions of individual responsibility (Gready and Robins 2014: 347) and privilege the spread of professionalism at the expense of local empowerment (Bush 2015). Such risks have also been identified in research on the securitization of mass sexual violence, arguing that advocacy efforts fetishize and dislocate causes of violence (Meger 2016) by creating abstract legal categories such as "gender-based violence" or "genocide" (Henry 2014). This may unintentionally incentivize local actors to engage in more violence, either to gain access to external resources or to improve their bargaining power in political negotiations (Autesserre 2012: 217).

The focus on individual criminal responsibility also risks reducing victims of past violence to witnesses without agency (Madlingozi 2010: 213). Advocates for transformational justice reject superficial efforts of expanding victims' assistance and argue that deep-seated causes of communal violence require sustained local engagement, rather than a performance of justice. "Both a trial and a truth commission are events, not processes, and they fail to engage substantively and over time with those most affected by the violations they seek to address on their own terms" (Gready and Robins 2014: 357). In contrast, scholars have emphasized that the creation of substantive equality among all citizens is a precondition for successful participation in criminal justice efforts (Bundschuh 2015).

The failed prosecution of Kenya's political leaders Uhuru Kenyatta and William Ruto serves as a key lesson in this regard. Unable to access local evidence with regard to the 2007/08 election violence, witness statements became the key source of prosecutorial evidence marshaled at the ICC. As witnesses mysteriously died or recanted their statements (Mueller 2014), the case fell apart and exposed the weaknesses of a narrow, prosecutorial approach to addressing long-standing ethnic and social inequalities. It is probably not unreasonable to claim that the indictments contributed to eliminating violence during the 2013 elections, but it is also fair to claim that prosecutions are insufficient. While many supporters of the ICC have lobbied to give the ICC more enforcement powers as well as improve witness protection, this approach would offer very limited answers to the challenge posed by the idea of transformational justice. In Kenya, it would have not been able to undercut the domestic backlash against an external intervention viewed as foreign and neo-colonial (Lynch 2015).

In sum, international criminal justice norms today play a significant role in efforts to secure peace and security after mass atrocities. Many of the strong claims by supporters and critics of these tools are not supported by the limited empirical evidence. There is a particular need for more research into how prosecutions are perceived by those they are supposed to deter as well as the scope conditions under which prosecutions combined with other measures contribute to a path toward a rule of law and governance (Skaar et al. 2015; Vinjamuri and Snyder 2015: 306). Most promising are approaches that combine a range of tools and consider how each case requires unique sequencing of judicial and non-judicial measures aimed at supporting local agency. Elite-driven approaches favored by both proponents and critics of prosecutions converge on the idea that "certain options are no longer even considered" (Sikkink 2011: 173), while a bottom-up approach focuses on how social movements and their long-term activism keeps repression off the table while also expanding protections and rights enjoyment.

47.4 Lessons for TANs and International Criminal Justice

The prosecution of Hissène Habré supports arguments made by both supporters and critics of international criminal justice. Supporters can point to a new step in the justice cascade, while critics may highlight that the defendant had little power to prevent prosecution and the case lacked geopolitical importance. Those calling for transformative justice will likely question the focus on the past and Habré as an individual perpetrator. Although International Relations (IR) scholarship has spent much time arguing for and against criminal justice norms, the more prescient and compelling lessons for TANs emerge from the ideas of transformative and social justice. They move beyond the contentious views on prosecutions by addressing weaknesses of prosecutorial approaches and framing them within more explicitly emancipatory peace and justice efforts (Sharp 2015). Three main lessons highlight the need to take account of the broader context of mass violence as well as the role of monitoring and evaluation in improving criminal justice practices over time.

The first lesson applies insights from the transformative justice literature as well as from research on transnational activism more broadly. The cascade metaphor describes well the rise in prosecutions since the 1990s, but the justice pursued remains narrowly focused on retributive outcomes (Moyn 2012) and TANs spent limited time and resources on validating the wide-ranging claims about the positive effects of trials. The rise in prosecutions has been accomplished by what Kenneth Roth, the Executive Director of Human Rights Watch, has defended as the core three steps of (1) exposing human rights violation, (2) naming a perpetrator, and (3) proposing a remedy (Roth 2004: 68). This "naming and shaming" approach is prevalent in many international criminal justice cases, but typically oversimplifies the underlying root causes of atrocities. For example, research on the 2004 Rwandan genocide identified a complex set of contributing factors, including environmental changes, threat perceptions during a civil war, and the nature of state institutions (Straus 2006). A narrow focus on "who did it" in human rights fact-finding produces a simplified form of reporting that foregrounds victims and perpetrators at the expense of hidden structural forces. The bias introduced not only reduces justice to a relationship between the individual and the state, but also expresses clear preferences for retributive and legal solutions (Nagy 2008; Sharp 2016: 75).

There are several challenges in moving away from the current, professionalized model of human rights fact-finding. First, efforts to engage in broader framing and analysis will likely create more uncertainty with regard to individual responsibility and causes. Second, the generation of expertise about structural forces has to rely on local sources, which often lack the capacities of powerful INGOs. Increasing the bottom-up input from communities requires investment in local capacity to articulate narratives as well as expanded capacities among INGOs to listen to and process diverging opinions. One way of enhancing local agency from the outside is to document resistance and not just violations (Leebaw 2011) and prioritize a focus on processes of ongoing political mobilization, rather than narrow judicial procedures (Gready and Robins 2014: 356).

If research on gross violations is transformed to reflect more local input, then powerful external activists will take a less prominent role in defining the meaning of justice and choosing the appropriate responses (Mutua 2015: 7). Sikkink's description of the paradigmatic case of Argentina elucidates the limited role of external actors, as domestic social movements and lawyers led the efforts to prosecute former leaders. Similar lessons are emerging in the African context where truly legitimate efforts to prevent or end major crimes highlight the need for leadership by regional organizations, including the African Union (Mamdani 2017). Such devolution of control over campaigns may lead to increased tensions within TANs as local groups could be more reluctant to engage in "naming and shaming" than their international counterparts (Sharp 2016: 79). As the governance of TANs evolves to reflect more balanced local and international control, these types of global actors will be able to strengthen their collaborative properties.

If TANs produce more locally-driven research on the root causes of human rights problems, how would this then translate into more comprehensive approaches either to prosecuting or to preventing atrocities? This is a particularly challenging question if different local communities disagree about the causes of violations and the meaning of justice. The fundamental idea behind talking not only about retributive, but also restorative and distributive justice is to enable external actors to better understand why local actors may have complex and diverging perspectives on root causes of human rights violations. While such a broadened approach may not provide immediate answers to how external actors should intervene in a given situation, it provides an improved knowledge base that is no longer limited by the exclusive framing of the "naming and shaming" approach. For example, taking into consideration how communities can move forward by explicitly addressing contemporary social and economic rights represents one way of complementing the more backward-looking emphasis on individual responsibilities for past abuses.

The second main lesson complements the need for more local involvement with a push to invest more resources into monitoring and evaluation focused on the short- and mid-term effects of trials. TANs have not only claimed that prosecutions deter future atrocities, but are cost-effective and have a positive impact on democracy and the rule of law. These broad claims are aimed at attracting support from outside the human rights community where many decision-makers care less about the norms and more about the costs of humanitarian interventions or the persistence of instability during and after political transitions. The argument for rigorous monitoring and evaluation is widespread across INGO fields, and it faces two important challenges in the area of international criminal justice. First, mid- and long-causality are difficult to establish because of the complexity of post-conflict and democratization processes. Second, good evaluations are costly and take away resources from fact-finding and other activities. In order to address these challenges, TANs must collaborate more closely with academic researchers and foundations in advancing monitoring and evaluation practices.

Leading researchers have established and shared data on prosecutions and other transitional measures,[5] while more evidence about the positive effects of trials is emerging in journals typically read by a small number of academic peers (Appel 2016). While there are links between activists and researchers, they remain limited (Shucksmith 2016) and are often biased toward bringing together those already in agreement on the criminal justice agenda. More sophisticated monitoring and evaluation requires not only more resources, but also has to grapple with the inclination of INGOs to "seek to measure, or take credit for, impacts that extend well beyond the scale and scope of what they actually do" (Ebrahim and Rangan 2014: 134). A more legitimate approach would concentrate on identifying positive or negative short-term effects, while relying on academic scholarship to develop theoretical frameworks that are capable of establishing testable hypotheses about the likely mid- and long-term contributions of criminal justice efforts to peace and democratization. This may not always produce evidence supporting the actions of TANs, but it would provide more incentives for learning and strategic adaptation.

Finally, TANs may have recently relied too heavily on consequentialist arguments in defending criminal justice norms. Even if more evidence supports the case for prosecutions in the future, the current legitimacy crisis of the ICC indicates that expanding popular support for criminal justice requires not only the mobilization of rational arguments or the insistence on abstract universal norms. The case of Chile is instructive in this regard. Even if Augusto Pinochet had been put on trial and convicted, the effects of his prosecution on domestic public discourse reveal how tenuous the recognition of past atrocities remains and why trials do not settle deep societal divides (Collins et al. 2013). The focus on fact-finding creates a false sense of trust in the past truth, which ignores the fact that the long-term success of criminal justice ideas requires popular support based on constant positive reaffirmation in daily experiences. International actors may disappear quickly after the end of trials, while domestic social movements are left with creating and maintaining emotional ties between past events and current politics.[6]

Notes

1. The Extraordinary African Chambers were established in early 2013 based on an agreement between the African Union (AU) and the government of Senegal (www.chambresafricaines.org).
2. Transnational advocacy networks (TANs) are coalitions of individuals and organizations dedicated to a particular advocacy issue (Keck and Sikkink 1998: 9). TANs often exhibit typical collective action problems and their differences in power and strategies may be important factors shaping their internal workings (Jordan and Van Tuijl 2000). In the case of international criminal justice, the Coalition for the ICC (http://www.coalitionfortheicc.org/) was founded in 1995 and is made up of regional networks of activists as well as prominent global groups such as Amnesty International or Human Rights Watch.
3. Individual criminal responsibility, crimes against peace, and crimes against humanity represented major innovations of the Nuremberg and Tokyo Tribunals (Greppi 1999).
4. For defenders of the ICC, complementarity serves as a back-up to domestic prosecution and reduces "the control that perpetrators . . . have in preventing prosecution" (Sikkink and Kim 2013: 272).
5. The Transitional Justice Research Collaborative founded by Kathryn Sikkink and Leigh Payne offers the most comprehensive data (https://transitionaljusticedata.com/).
6. I am grateful to Dustin N. Sharp and the two editors of this volume for their helpful feedback and comments.

References

African Union. 2016. *Summary Report of the African Union Open-Ended Ministerial Commitee of Ministers of Foreign Affairs on ICC*. Addis Ababa: African Union.

Appel, Benjamin J. 2016. In the Shadow of the International Criminal Court. *Journal of Conflict Resolution*, doi:10.1177/0022002716639101.

Autesserre, Séverine. 2012. Dangerous Tales: Dominant Narratives on the Congo and their Unintended Consequences. *African Affairs*, 111(443): 202–22.

Brysk, Alison. 1994. *The Politics of Human Rights in Argentina: Protest, Change, and Democratization*. Stanford, CA: Stanford University Press.

Bundschuh, Thomas. 2015. Enabling Transitional Justice, Restoring Capabilities: The Imperative of Participation and Normative Integrity. *International Journal of Transitional Justice*, 9(1): 10–32.

Bush, Sarah Sunn. 2015. *The Taming of Democracy Assistance: Why Democracy Promotion Does Not Confront Dictators*. Cambridge: Cambridge University Press.

Collins, Cath., Katherine Hite, and Alfredo Joignant (eds.). 2013. *The Politics of Memory in Chile: From Pinochet to Bachelet*. Boulder: Lynne Rienner.

Cross, Mai'a K. Davis. 2013. Rethinking Epistemic Communities Twenty Years Later. *Review of International Studies*, 39(1): 137–60.

Ebrahim, Alnoor and V. Kasturi Rangan. 2014. What Impact?: A Framework for Measuring the Scale and Scope of Social Performance. *California Management Review*, 56(3): 118–41.

Finnemore, Martha and Kathryn Sikkink. 1998. International Norm Dynamics and Political Change. *International Organization*, 52(4): 887–917.

Fischer, Martina. 2016. Struggling with the Legacy of War—Croatia, Serbia, and Bosnia-Hercegovina 1995–2015. In M. Fischer and O. Simic (eds.), *Transitional Justice and Reconciliation: Lessons from the Balkans*. Abingdon: Routledge.

Flohr, Annegret, Lothar Rieth, Sandra Schwindenhammer, and Klaus Dieter Wolf. 2010. *The Role of Business in Global Governance: Corporations as Norm-Entrepreneurs*. Houndmills: Palgrave Macmillan.

Frieze, Donna-Lee. 2013. *Totally Unofficial: The Autobiography of Raphael Lemkin*. New Haven, CT: Yale University Press.

Gade, Christian B. N. 2013. Restorative Justice and the South African Truth and Reconciliation Process. *South African Journal of Philosophy*, 32(1): 10–35.

Geis, Jacqueline and Alex Mundt. 2009. *When to Indict? The Impact of Timing of International Criminal Indictments on Peace Processes and Humanitarian Action*. Washington, DC: Brookings-Bern Project on Internal Displacement.

Goodman, Ryan and Derek Jinks. 2013. *Socializing States: Promoting Human Rights through International Law*. Oxford: Oxford University Press.

Gready, Paul and Simon Robins. 2014. From Transitional to Transformative Justice: A New Agenda for Practice. *International Journal of Transitional Justice*, 8(3): 339–61.

Greppi, Edoardo. 1999. The Evolution of Individual Criminal Responsibility under International Law. *Revue Internationale de la Croix-Rouge/International Review of the Red Cross*, 81(835): 531–53.

Henry, Nicola. 2014. The Fixation on Wartime Rape: Feminist Critique and International Criminal Law. *Social & Legal Studies*, 23(1): 93–111.

Ingebritsen, Christine. 2006. *Small States in International Relations*. Reykjavik: University of Iceland Press.

Johnston, Alastair Iain. 2007. *Social States: China in International Institutions, 1980–2000*. Princeton, NJ: Princeton University Press.

Jordan, Lisa and Peter Van Tuijl. 2000. Political Responsibility in Transnational NGO Advocacy. *World Development*, 28(12): 2051–65.

Keck, Margaret E. and Kathryn Sikkink. 1998. *Activists Beyond Borders. Advocacy Networks in International Politics*. Ithaca, NY: Cornell University Press.

Kim, Hun Joon and Jason Campbell Sharman. 2014. Accounts and Accountability: Corruption, Human Rights, and Individual Accountability Norms. *International Organization*, 68(2): 417–48.

Korey, William. 1998. *NGOs and the Universal Declaration of Human Rights. A Curious Grapevine*. Houndmills/Basingstoke: Macmillan.

LeBlanc, Lawrence J. 1991. *The United States and the Genocide Convention*. Durham, NC: Duke University Press.

Leebaw, Bronwyn Anne. 2011. Review of Kathryn Sikkink's The Justice Cascade: How Human Rights Prosecutions Are Changing World Politics. *Journal of Human Rights*, 11(2): 301–7.

Lutz, Ellen L. and Caitlin Reiger. 2009. *Prosecuting Heads of State*. Cambridge: Cambridge University Press.

Lynch, Gabrielle. 2015. The International Criminal Court and the Making of a Kenyan President. *Current History*, May: 183–8.

Madlingozi, Tshepo. 2010. On Transitional Justice Entrepreneurs and the Production of Victims. *Journal of Human Rights Practice*, 2(2): 208–28.

Mamdani, Mahmood. 2017. Can the African Union Save South Sudan from Genocide? *New York Times*, January 9, A1.

Meger, Sara. 2016. The Fetishization of Sexual Violence in International Security. *International Studies Quarterly*, 60(1): 149–59.

Mendeloff, David. 2011. Deterrence, Norm Socialization, and the Empirical Reach of Kathryn Sikkink's The Justice Cascade: How Human Rights Prosecutions Are Changing World Politics. *Journal of Human Rights*, 11(2): 289–95.

Meyer, John W., John Boli, George M. Thomas, and Francisco O. Ramirez. 1997. World Society and the Nation-State. *American Journal of Sociology*, 103(1): 144–81.

Moyn, Samuel. 2012. Of Deserts and Promised Lands: The Dream of Global Justice. *The Nation*, 294(12): 32–5.

Mueller, Susanne D. 2014. Kenya and the International Criminal Court (ICC): Politics, the Election and the Law. *Journal of Eastern African Studies*, 8(1): 25–42.

Mutua, Makau. 2015. What Is the Future of Transitional Justice? *International Journal of Transitional Justice*, 9(1): 1–9.

Nagy, Rosemary. 2008. Transitional Justice as Global Project: Critical Reflections. *Third World Quarterly*, 29(2): 275–89.

Nassar, Habib. 2014. Transitional Justice in the Wake of Arab Uprisings. In K. J. Fisher and R. Stewart (eds.), *Transitional Justice and the Arab Spring*. Abingdon: Routledge.

O'Donnell, Guillermo and Philippe C. Schmitter. 1986. *Transitions from Authoritarian Rule. Tentative Conclusions about Uncertain Democracies*. Baltimor, MD: Johns Hopkins University Press.

Olsen, Tricia D., Leigh A. Payne, and Andrew G. Reiter. 2010. The Justice Balance: When Transitional Justice Improves Human Rights and Democracy. *Human Rights Quarterly*, 32(4): 980–1007.

Peskin, Victor. 2008. *International Justice in Rwanda and the Balkans: Virtual Trials and the Struggle for State Cooperation*. Cambridge: Cambridge University Press.

Rodman, Kenneth A. 2008. Darfur and the Limits of Legal Deterrence. *Human Rights Quarterly*, 30: 529–60.

Roht-Arriaza, Naomi. 2009. Prosecutions of Heads of States in Latin America. In E. L. Lutz and C. Reiger (eds.), *Prosecuting Heads of States*. Cambridge: Cambridge University Press.

Roth, Kenneth. 2004. Defending Economic, Social and Cultural Rights: Practical Issues Faced by an International Human Rights Organization. *Human Rights Quarterly*, 26(1): 63–73.

Schabas, William A. 2013. The Banality of International Justice. *Journal of International Criminal Justice*, 11(3): 545–51.

Sharp, Dustin N. 2015. Emancipating Transitional Justice from the Bonds of the Paradigmatic Transition. *International Journal of Transitional Justice*, 9(1): 150–69.

Sharp, Dustin N. 2016. Human Rights Fact-Finding and the Reproduction of Hierarchies. In P. Alston and S. Knuckey (eds.), *The Transformation of Human Rights Fact-Finding*. Oxford: Oxford University Press.

Shucksmith, Mark. 2016. *InterAction. How can Academics and the Third Sector Work Together to Influence Policy and Practice?* Dunfermline: Carnegie UK Trust.

Sikkink, Kathryn. 2011. *The Justice Cascade. How Human Rights Prosecutions are Changing World Politics*. New York: W.W. Norton.

Sikkink, Kathryn. 2014. Latin American Countries as Norm Protagonists of the Idea of International Human Rights. *Global Governance*, 20(3): 389–404.

Sikkink, Kathryn and Hun Joon Kim. 2013. The Justice Cascade: The Origins and Effectiveness of Prosecutions of Human Rights Violations. *Annual Review of Social Science and Law*, 9: 269–85.

Skaar, Elin, Camila Gianella Malca, and Trine Eide (eds.). 2015. *After Violence. Transitional Justice, Peace, and Democracy*. Abingdon: Routledge.

Smeulers, Alette, Barbora Hola, and Tom van den Berg. 2013. Sixty-Five Years of International Criminal Justice: The Facts and Figures. *International Criminal Law Review*, 13(1): 7–41.

Snyder, Jack and Leslie Vinjamuri. 2003. Trials and Errors: Principle and Pragmatism in Strategies of International Justice. *International Security*, 28(3): 5–44.

Straus, Scott. 2006. *The Order of Genocide. Race, Power, and War in Rwanda*. Ithaca, NY: Cornell University Press.

Uvin, Peter. 2007. From the Right to Development to the Rights-based Approach: How Human Rights entered Development. *Development in Practice*, 17(4–5): 597–606.

Vinjamuri, Leslie. 2010. Deterrence, Democracy, and the Pursuit of International Justice. *Ethics & International Affairs*, 24(2): 191–211.

Vinjamuri, Leslie and Jack Snyder. 2015. Law and Politics in Transitional Justice. *Annual Review of Political Science*, 18: 303–27.

CHAPTER 48

CIVIL–MILITARY RELATIONS

LINDSAY COHN, DAMON COLETTA, AND PETER FEAVER

How has our understanding of the military as a political and social actor evolved, and how might that understanding change in the future? It is hard to talk about academic progress in a sub-field when the questions that most engage researchers are the same ones that were raised by philosophers thousands of years ago. The stubborn persistence of old questions and old answers is vividly evident when the most-quoted aphorism was penned by first-century Roman poet, Juvenal—"who will guard the guardians?" (Satire VI, lines 347–8)—and the most cited theory was published 60 years ago (Huntington 1957).

In the classic clash of paradigms—realism vs liberalism vs constructivism—civil–military relations falls primarily within the liberal paradigm as a study of domestic factors that shape state capabilities and international behavior. Within the sub-field, however, elements of realism—in the form of concern for external material threats—and elements of constructivism—in the form of competing conceptions of military professionalism—have also been prominent. In terms of positivism vs critical security studies, the US-focused literature tends to the positivist, while the non-US literature features a full spectrum of approaches.

Patterns of civil–military relations are typically studied according to three distinct sets of interactions: the relationship between the government and the military—focused on civilian control, best military advice, defense budgets, etc.; the relationship between the military and the larger society—focused on recruiting, mutual perceptions of servicemembers and civilians, race, gender, and class issues, etc.; and the relationship between society and government—focused on public opinion and oversight with respect to military, defense, and foreign policy issues.

The sub-field has four noteworthy and idiosyncratic features that have limited the development of general theory. First, the most thoroughly researched case, the United States, is arguably *sui generis* and thus a poor basis for generalization. Second, the core problem in one area (coups in fragile democracies) is all but non-existent in other areas (advanced industrial democracies). Third, a dominant theoretical model (Samuel Huntington's) is widely challenged by scholars but generally embraced, at least as a normative ideal, by many key practitioners (senior military officers). Fourth, questions about "what is" and "what ought to be" are closely intertwined in the thinking and action of the military as a political actor, and thus hard to separate.

Despite these challenges, the sub-field of civil–military relations has been both central and fertile for the field of international security studies. The scholarly interest is fueled by still greater policy interest. Even in countries where the extreme pathology of a military coup is a non-concern, the broader question of civilian control of the military—how can civilian political leaders ensure that military tools align with, and do not undermine, political objectives—remains a central preoccupation of policy-makers and the engaged public. Political science must remain interested in civil–military relations in part because practicing politicians—at least successful politicians—remain so.

This chapter proceeds with a brief discussion of general theory, a focus on the widely covered American case, and then a summary of military politics in other cases. We conclude with observations on likely emerging trends.

48.1 The Civil–Military Problematique and Huntington–Janowitz Baseline Theory

The central problem in the sub-field of civil–military relations is as old as Plato's *Republic*. How could warrior auxiliaries of the state be trusted to obey the polity's unarmed philosopher kings, and protect a vulnerable citizenry, but not use the very same strength to enslave them for corrupt or self-centered purposes? (Bloom [Plato] Book II, 375d–376c). Huntington noted in his classic *Soldier and the State* (1957) that some solutions to this problem only introduced other problems: keep the military weak so it is not a political threat and your society is at risk from foreign enemies.

Huntington's preferred solution involved a particular understanding of *professionalism*: if military personnel were allowed to exercise their professional competence free of interference, they would return the courtesy to the civilian policy-makers, whose competence was the crafting of national strategy and policy. The warriors guarding a liberal society would be trustworthy as well as militarily effective because their professional competence and identity required them to police themselves. Huntington called this objective control, and distinguished it from subjective control, where each civilian faction equates maximizing civilian control with maximizing its own political control over the military, thus politicizing the military by dragging it into fights between powerful civilians.

Huntington's approach attracted a strong sociological critique from Morris Janowitz (1960), who argued that professionalism was endogenous to deeper societal and technological forces. Contra Huntington, there was not a single pure form of military professionalism and therefore not a single optimal pattern of civil–military relations (Janowitz

1960; Moskos et al. 2000; Schiff 2009). And yet, Janowitz's approach relied as much as Huntington's did on the military embracing an ethic of subordination (Feaver 1996).

One promising approach to general theory that moves beyond Huntington and Janowitz is agency theory (Feaver 2003). Agency theory framed relations as a game of strategic interaction between a military agent and a civilian principal, each holding distinct rational preference orderings. If military preferences differed strongly from those of civilian authority, and if there was a low probability of being caught or punished, military officers might "shirk" unpalatable tasks handed down by civilian authority (cf. Avant 1994; Weiner 1996; Brooks 2008).

The principal–agent approach continues to be a productive line of inquiry (Sowers 2005; Coletta and Feaver 2006; Ruffa 2013), though a controversial one (Burk 1998; Owens 2011). It has also led to a revival of the Huntingtonian approach in an effort to redefine military professionalism after the Cold War (Snider et al. 2002; Nielsen and Snider 2009).

48.2 The American Case and the Evolution of the Military as a Political and Social Actor

Huntington wrote during the first decade of the Cold War, and as America's geostrategic environment shifted in the ensuing decades, so too did the kinds of problems raised by the military as a political and social actor. These problems included retaining political control as both superpowers married hydrogen bombs with thousands of aircraft and intercontinental missile launchers (Feaver 1992); rebalancing civil–military relations after the political disillusionment and societal upheavals of Vietnam (Moskos 1979); and redefining characteristics of civilian control for irregular threats and high operations tempo after the Cold War (Avant 1996–97; Desch 1999; Strachan 2006). Throughout, the United States military maintained a high degree of professionalism, Huntington's essential ingredient for healthy civil–military relations; yet the American military also engaged in bureaucratic subterfuge that raised concerns about civilian control.

This pattern reached what some considered a crisis point with the end of the Cold War and the arrival of an inexperienced, socially liberal administration that campaigned on domestic economic concerns and vowed to harness the military for progressive social change and humanitarian goals (Powell 1992–93; Kohn 1994). The concerns focused particularly on the military as a social actor, one operating across a wide gap from the rest of civilian society, or at least civilian elite society (Holsti 1998–99; Feaver and Kohn 2001; Dempsey 2010). Some warned about (and others welcomed) the possibility that the military would act to bring civilian values more in alignment with theirs (Dunlap 1992–93; Milburn 2010).

The terrorist attacks of 9/11 opened a new chapter in civil–military relations. Secretary of Defense Donald Rumsfeld had been fighting bureaucratic wars inside the Pentagon to advance a transformation agenda before 9/11, and continued to fight them even as the military establishment ramped up to launch a series of shooting conflicts (Brooks 2008; Herspring 2008). The ambivalent progress of the Iraq War sent shockwaves through American civil–military relations. Was the problem that civilian authority, first under President Bush and then under President Obama, cavalierly dismissed professional military advice (Ricks 2006; Desch 2007)? Or was the military, by reason of intimidation, inadequate education, or failure of Congress to exercise its prerogatives under the Constitution, too cowed to insist when civilians were wrong (McMaster 1997; Moten 2014)? Alternatively, were top officers availing themselves of levers in American democracy—among them sworn testimony before Congress; the threat of resignation; commentary before the media; and punditry of retired officers—to resist civilian preferences and otherwise constrain civilian leadership (Kohn 2009)? How should civil–military operations function when civilian leaders and military leaders fundamentally disagreed on the way forward in Iraq (Feaver 2011)?

The historic election of the first African-American President, and President Obama's decision to keep Republican Robert Gates on as Defense Secretary, brought only the briefest of respites in actual civil–military relations. By the end of his first year, Obama was stuck in a bitter civil–military dispute over strategy and resources in Afghanistan, and civil–military tensions continued throughout the rest of his tenure (Owens 2011; Davidson 2013; Herspring 2013; Moten, 2014).

Continued prominence of civil–military conflict in American policy making has been matched by continued fertility in American civil–military relations scholarship. Research has tracked the effects *of* and effects *on* civil–military relations with respect to decisions on the use of force (Feaver and Gelpi 2004; Saunders 2015; Recchia 2015); public support for war (Gelpi et al. 2009; Golby et al. 2013; Baum and Potter 2015); inter-branch politics (Campbell and Auerswald 2015); combat effectiveness (Farrell et al. 2013); the role of civilian partners and quasi-military surrogates in operations (Avant 2005; Dunigan 2011; Ruffa 2013); the political behavior of the military (Brooks 2013a; Golby et al. 2013; Golby 2015; Inbody 2016); and the age-old question of the sociological gap between those who serve and those who are served (Golby et al. 2012; Bacevich 2013).

48.3 Comparative Civil–Military Relations in Theory and Practice

48.3.1 Theory

The study of comparative civil–military relations has followed a roughly similar evolution, in part because comparativists found it necessary to respond to theoretical and empirical developments that were pioneered in the data-rich American case. Of course, there is far more variance on the dependent variables of interest when the aperture is widened to consider the rest of the world. As a consequence, while the comparative sub-field sometimes runs into data limitations, the breadth of concepts, theories, and issues covered more than compensates.

The problem of political control arises for any society in which leadership of the armed forces is distinct from political leadership, whether that society is democratic or not. Mulvenon (2001) and Broemmelhoerster and Paes (2003), however, note that "civilian control," in the sense of the government having full and direct control over the armed forces, is a fairly recent historical development, associated primarily with Western democracy. This explains the dichotomy in the literature between developed and developing states, and indicates caution for efforts to generalize from the United States or other cases of mature democracies to the rest of the world.

The literature on political control of the military agent is largely in agreement on three points (cf. Cohn 2011: 385ff.): civilians must have the institutions and authority to issue orders; they must not be subject to undue influence in the formulation of the orders; and the orders must be obeyed. While some scholars discuss the significance of good policy making (e.g. Huntington 1957; Avant 1994; Cohen 2002), most simply assume the government is issuing competent and legitimate orders. This neglects what Cottey et al. (2002) called "governance": if the government fails to issue clear orders, or abdicates its policy-making responsibilities, the relationship is no longer one of "control" (Cottey et al. 2002, 2005; Born et al. 2003; Cohn 2011; Mannitz 2013).

Three main mechanisms drive civilian/political control: belief in the legitimacy or authority of the principal; shared ideals, beliefs, and preferences; and self-interest. Belief in authority shows up as appeals to "professionalism," "duty," "service ethic," etc.—anything that relies on the military agent's self-control. In Nordlinger's classic (1977) treatment, this is described as the liberal model of civilian control, and is the one most heavily relied upon by democracies and those states hoping to become democratic. Shared ideals, beliefs, and preferences are prominent in Nordlinger's traditional and penetration models, as well as several of Quinlivan's (1999) "coup-proofing" techniques. Finally, the rationalist models (Avant 1994; Feaver 2003) highlight the role that pure self-interest can play.

Synthesizing these theories, Cohn (2011) proposes six variables for evaluating the strength of control: (1) institutions that place civilians in positions of authority over the military; (2) civilian leader competence for good governance, understood as issuing reasonable and legitimate policies; (3) an agent culture of duty/obedience; (4) effective systems of agent monitoring and punishment; (5) preference compatibility between the principal and the agent; and (6) coherence within the agent organization.

48.3.2 Practice: Developing/Democratizing States

The literature on the developing world focuses on three main concerns: the military as a player in the struggle for ultimate power in the state; the lack of military effectiveness due to measures taken to keep them subordinate; and the military as a distorter of the economy through their economic activities.

48.3.2.1 *Power Struggles*

The military often becomes an important faction in the struggle for power in weak states, either on its own or as a key supporter courted by other groups (see, e.g., Fossum 1967; Barany 2011; Brooks 1998, 2013b). The developing and non-democratic worlds are thus dominated by Traditional and Penetration models of civilian control, which tend to involve one or more "coup-proofing" techniques (Quinlivan 1999). These include exploiting family/ethnic/religious loyalties; creating multiple competing military-like organizations; creating multiple security institutions with overlapping jurisdictions as a form of intrusive monitoring; fostering professionalism/apolitical culture among the officers; and manipulating how the institutions are financed (to create mutual self-interest between officers and regime).

These methods have had mixed success. Research indicates that creating multiple security organizations, fostering professionalism (without also creating legitimate governance), and giving military officers independent economic interests can all lead to *more* coups (Quinlivan 1999; Broemmelhoerster and Paes 2003). There is some evidence that relying on family, ethnic, or religious loyalties is a more effective form of coup-proofing than any of the others (Barany 2011; Bellin 2012; Makara 2013), but it may also lead to militaries that cannot perform well on the battlefield.

48.3.2.2 *Military Weakness*

The weakness and/or limited resources of developing states frequently mean that the military is tasked with a number of missions that fall to other agencies in more developed states. These include civil defense, response to natural disasters, law enforcement/maintenance of public order, and, sometimes, defender of the constitution against corruption (Bruneau and Matei 2013; Pion-Berlin 2016). These roles tend to politicize the military, undermining the possibility of control passing smoothly and democratically from one administration to another.

Another result of this is that the military's attention and resources are diverted away from strictly military effectiveness, leaving the state potentially vulnerable to enemies (Talmadge 2015). Thus, contrary to popular perception, most non-democracies are forced to come down on the side of military weakness, if they wish to keep their militaries under control (Quinlivan 1999; Pilster and Bohmelt 2011; Powell 2012; Talmadge 2015).

48.3.2.3 *Militaries in Business*

Finally, a weak state that has trouble collecting taxes and/or allocating sufficient funding to defense will frequently encourage the armed forces to find their own funding (Broemmelhoerster and Paes 2003, 9f.; Mani 2007). This can range from individual moonlighting to the military organization owning large enterprises and using military assets for business purposes (Mulvenon 2001; Broemmelhoerster and Paes 2003; Cheung 2003; Mani 2007). This means, however, that the militaries are in full control of those revenue streams, which reduces the amount of oversight and control civilians can exercise over them (Broemmelhoerster and Paes 2003: 1; Barany 2011).

There is enormous variation in the ways that militaries can be involved in economic activity, and the type of involvement can lead to very different historical trajectories. Some militaries in Latin America, for example, tended to engage in heavy industry (Argentina) and more consumer-oriented sectors (e.g. commodities, banking, and finance in Honduras, Guatemala, El Salvador, and Nicaragua). Now, however, they have either exited those entirely or are on their way out, as the enterprises became inefficient or the public mood shifted against such involvement (Castro and Zamora 2003; Scheetz 2003; Mani 2007; Pion-Berlin and Trinkunas 2010). In many states in sub-Saharan Africa, individual members of the military engage in enterprise to augment their sometimes unreliable incomes, and use their status as uniformed (and armed) personnel to economic advantage (Paes and Shaw 2003). This is unlikely to change while state weakness persists. Siddiqa-Agha (2003) argues that the Pakistani military's involvement in the business world has been detrimental to its military readiness and effectiveness, as funds that ought to have gone toward military ends have been diverted to improving market competitiveness. Because of the domestic political power wielded by the military, however, it is unlikely that this situation will change any time soon.

48.3.3 Practice: Post-Communist and Other Single-Party Rule Transitioning States

Most of the literature on control in the post-Communist transitioning states of Central and Eastern Europe has focused on two issues: "professionalizing" military establishments that had been highly political, and working to develop civilian defense expertise so that the governments would not be wholly dependent upon their armed forces for policy advice and decisions (Cottey et al. 2002; Malesic et al. 2003).

The first of these enterprises appears to have gone well, and most militaries in Central and Eastern Europe are not inappropriate players in governmental politics, although they may still be subject to corruption and nepotism. Their biggest challenge was moving away from being party instruments to being democratic instruments (Cottey et al. 2002, 2005; Barany 2012). Building civilian expertise has been slower and more difficult. However, these militaries have benefited significantly from their association with NATO (Cottey et al. 2005; Gheciu 2005), and the main concern now is a lack of funding for modernization and training. Despite their concerns about Russian intentions, this is not likely to change significantly, due to the economic and social stress these countries have been experiencing. As populations decline, budgets stay stagnant, and Russia becomes more of a threat, we may see several of these countries revert to some form of conscription.

In the now-mature democracies of Asia, such as Japan, South Korea, and Taiwan, literature on civilian control of the military focused similarly on how to construct institutions of control. The difference with these states is that the military had been a strong independent player in governance before democratization, as opposed to a party instrument (Cottey et al. 2002: 36; Fravel 2002). As Chinese, North Korean, and Russian assertiveness increase, we may see the militaries of these and other Asian democracies return to traditional roles and become bolder in their policy participation.

48.3.3.1 *Russia*

The USSR was a prime example of a successful Penetration model (Nordlinger 1977), but what about the post-Cold War period? Evidence indicates that the Russian military under both Yeltsin and early Putin tended to engage in public criticism of the regime and make their own policy decisions (Belkin 2003; Brannon 2009). Under Medvedev, a series of reforms were undertaken, aimed at the modernization of both equipment and personnel practices. These reforms and investments did produce some modernization and increased capability—though not as much as the investment warranted, and their effects have been complicated and delayed by corruption (Kofman 2016). One initiative aimed to reduce the number of conscripts and increase the number of contract personnel, which would likely make the military a more effective and reliable tool of national strategy (Golts 2016: 12f.; Kofman 2016: 7). To be successful, however, this sort of reform required a move toward a more meritocratic and less politicized personnel system (Golts 2016: 15), and it hit a significant snag in 2012 when Putin fired its architect for corruption (Golts 2016: 15ff.). Since the beginning of Putin's third term as president in 2012, the interests of the military appear to have converged with his (Cottey et al. 2005; Golts 2016).

It is unclear, however, how long Putin's Russia can continue active military operations before the economic and domestic political underpinnings become untenable (Kofman 2016). Golts (2016: 18) argues that professionalism and morale problems continue. Even so, the military at this writing appears to have little incentive to resist Putin's policies, be they domestic or in Eastern Europe or Syria.

48.3.3.2 *China*

Civil–military relations in China are increasingly murky, largely because of the shifting role played by the Chinese Communist Party (CCP) and the People's Liberation Army's (PLA) and Navy's (PLAN) bids for greater autonomy (Shambaugh 2002). China is another salient example of Nordlinger's penetration model, in which the military is under total Party control, both at the level of top officers and through political commissars placed throughout as monitoring agents.

Although the PLA's business activities did produce valuable resources, training, and employment for many members and dependents, party leadership worried about its effects on professionalism, cohesiveness, and military preparedness (Mulvenon 2001: esp. 138ff.; Cheung 2001, 2003: 65ff.). It led to an enormous amount of corruption and economic criminality, and in 1998 the party issued a directive requiring all military enterprises to be shut down or transferred out of the military. This led to only partial divestiture, but did result in cleaning up some corruption and modernizing political control over the military (Mulvenon 2001; Cheung 2003). Cheung (2001, 2003) believes that the PLA(N)'s current focus on professionalism, effectiveness, and operational readiness indicates a low likelihood that the military will try to regain its old market share any time soon.

48.3.4 Practice: Consolidated Democracies

In advanced democracies aside from the United States, the scholarly conversation has focused much less on the professionalism or monitoring of the military institution and more on the roles of legislative branches and civil society. This discussion of "governance" calls for more parliamentary oversight and significantly more informed participation by citizens, academia, and the press (Cottey et al. 2002; Fravel 2002: 76ff.; Born et al. 2003; Malesic et al. 2003; Barany 2012; Bruneau and Matei 2013; Mannitz 2013).

48.4 Conclusion

The civil–military relations sub-field has remained lively, with waves of scholarship reflecting new methodological or theoretical trends seen in other areas of political science, despite being preoccupied with the same basic sets of questions identified in the earliest scholarly work. These underlying questions are all aspects of the same fundamental dilemma the institution that protects can also threaten. Steps taken to protect the polity *from* the military complicate the effectiveness of protection *by* the military, and vice versa.

In other words, the future of civil–military relations theory and practice is likely to look a lot like the past. Even so, we see trends in the scholarship worth flagging. First, the concerns (and literature) of civil–military relations and the concerns (and literature) of democratization and development are converging. The factors identified as problematic for civil–military relations also tend to be those that weaken democratic governance and/or result from weak or corrupt state structures. In the developing world, the concerns stem primarily from the dynamics of power consolidation, but power consolidation is inevitably linked with popular legitimacy. In the transitioning world, the biggest problems are the development of tenacious and legitimate democratic institutions and civil society. In consolidated democracies, attention focuses on problems of political apathy and bureaucratic politics, which raise questions about the legitimacy of foreign policy decisions.

Second, if democratization continues, the canonical threat of a coup may begin to give way to concerns about nuanced forms of domestic or transnational power and influence that militaries could wield in the future. In consolidated democracies, militaries can accomplish more through political influence than they could through coup. Whether this takes the form of being the only source of security and defense expertise, as in many former Communist states, or of being the most trusted institution in society, as in the United States, Pakistan, and several other places in the Middle East and Latin

America, or of being so important to the economy that their voices must be considered, these are the challenges to true "control."

Third, the sub-field may increasingly attend to the functional side of the civil–military dilemma, rebalancing away from preoccupation with the complexities of democratic control as states in all three of our regime categories are forced to respond to rapidly evolving security challenges. We expect to see more debate over how configurations of civil–military relations affect variables such as war-initiation, conflict and crisis escalation/de-escalation, strategic innovation, operational and tactical proficiency, risk portfolios, and so on.

Fourth, the sub-field will increasingly focus on mid-range theorizing, at the expense of proposing grand civil–military paradigms. We also expect research to take advantage of growing large-n databases relevant to civil–military relations and to use a wider range of analytical tools to study the military as a political actor. Of course, this simply follows trends in the larger discipline, but the civil–military sub-field may be especially ripe for this because here more traditional forms of analysis have remained prominent much longer than in other political science scholarship.

In the practical realm, we expect that the configuration of the civil–military relationship will continue to be a key factor in states' behavior and capabilities, and will continue to pose important concerns to those in power or attempting to consolidate power within states. In the United States, this issue will be closely connected to the polarization of partisan politics, increasing pressure on the national budget, and strong disagreement about the nature of the threats facing the country. As recent survey research has shown, there is the potential for serious breakdown in norms of civil–military relations in the US (Golby et al. 2016), and this is a trend that must be actively managed.

In other consolidated democracies, where publics and the press may not be very engaged with defense and security issues and militaries constitute small, largely content, and socially marginal organizations, the result may be a further de-militarization of foreign and security policy. This prediction may hold true particularly for many European states, and may contribute to disagreements within both the EU and NATO. For those states facing significant threats to their territorial integrity, however, both consolidated and transitioning democracies may turn to conscription and/or alliance structures to keep their budgets manageable. In those states where the military used to be a key political actor before democracy, we may see a return to more military influence.

In developing and democratizing countries, the patterns of power struggle, coup-proofing, and independent economic activities are likely to continue; these will be brought under control only by consolidation of democratic institutions and civil society. It is particularly important to understand the domestic dynamics of such states, as militaries are likely to play very different roles in, for example, popular uprisings, depending on factors such as co-ethnicity, external support for the regime, and the overall structure of the state security apparatus.

One promising hypothesis worth exploring is the possibility that the spread of information technologies has created a new and different balance of power between society and the coercive institutions of the state. On the one hand, it may be that new technologies have made it possible for citizens to respond quickly in the face of an unfolding coup, making it harder for coup plotters to create a *fait accompli* without confronting the painful choice of inflicting mass violence on the citizenry. On the other hand, the same technologies may have so improved the surveillance capacity of the state that citizens enjoy less privacy and autonomy than they previously expected even in unstable polities. On the third hand, it is possible that the new technologies will result in a distribution of lethality across a wider spectrum of actors, narrowing the gap that separated the armed forces from all other rivals; if so, the field of civil–*military* relations could morph into something else, with multiple (potentially) coercive institutions in play.

A prediction that the future of civil–military concerns will resemble the past is based on the assumption that political change in consolidated democracies will proceed in gradual, evolutionary fashion. Of course, it is at least imaginable that a period of revolutionary change might disrupt even consolidated democracies. If that happens, the implications for civil–military relations are very hard to predict with confidence, save this: that the armed forces will be a hinge institution on which the political trajectory will turn, for good or ill. Either way, with or without revolutionary change, it will remain important for students of international security to heed the military as a political actor, for it can shape policy as well as constitute power.

References

Avant, Deborah. 1994. *Political Institutions and Military Change: Lessons from Peripheral Wars*. Ithaca, NY: Cornell University Press.

Avant, Deborah. 1996–97. Are the Reluctant Warriors Out of Control? Why the U.S. Military Is Averse to Responding to Post-Cold War Low-Level Threats. *Security Studies*, 6(2): 51–90.

Avant, Deborah. 2005. *The Market for Force: The Consequences of Privatizing Security*. Cambridge: Cambridge University Press.

Bacevich, Andrew. 2013. *Breach of Trust: How Americans Failed Their Soldiers and Their Country*. New York: Metropolitan Books.

Barany, Zoltan. 2011. Comparing the Arab Revolts: The Role of the Military. *Journal of Democracy*, 22(4): 24–35.

Barany, Zoltan. 2012. *The Soldier and the Changing State: Building Democratic Armies in Africa, Asia, Europe, and the Americas*. Princeton, NJ: Princeton University Press.

Baum, Matthew and Philip Potter. 2015. *War and Democratic Constraint: How the Public Influences Foreign Policy*. Princeton, NJ: Princeton University Press.

Belkin, Alexander. 2003. Civil–Military Relations in Russia After 9-11. *European Security*, 12 (3–4): 1–19.

Bellin, Eva. 2012. Reconsidering the Robustness of Authoritarianism in the Middle East: Lessons from the Arab Spring, *Comparative Politics*, 44(2): 127–49.

Bloom, Allan (trans. intro.). 1968. *The Republic of Plato*, 2nd edn. New York: Basic Books.

Born, Hans, Karl Haltiner, and Marjan Malesic. 2003. Democratic Control of Armed Forces: Renaissance of an Old Issue. In H. Born, K. Haltiner, and M. Malesic (eds.), *Renaissance of Democratic Control of Armed Forces in Contemporary Societies*, pp. 1–9. Baden-Baden: Nomos.

Brannon, Robert. 2009. *Russian Civil–Military Relations*. Burlington, VT: Ashgate.

Broemmelhoerster, Joern and Wolf-Christian Paes (eds.). 2003. *The Military as an Economic Actor: Soldiers in Business*. Basingstoke: Palgrave Macmillan.

Brooks, Risa. 1998. *Political–Military Relations and the Stability of Arab Regimes*. International Institute for Strategic Studies Adelphi Paper 324. New York: Oxford University Press.

Brooks, Risa. 2008. *Shaping Strategy: The Civil–Military Politics of Strategic Assessment*. Princeton, NJ: Princeton University Press.

Brooks, Risa. 2013a. The Perils of Politics: Why Staying Apolitical Is Good for Both the U.S. Military and the Country. *Orbis*, 57(3): 369–79.

Brooks, Risa. 2013b. Abandoned at the Palace: Why the Tunisian Military Defected from the Ben Ali Regime in January 2011. *Journal of Strategic Studies*, 36(2): 205–20.

Bruneau, Thomas and Florina Cristiana Matei (eds.). 2013. *The Routledge Handbook of Civil–Military Relations*. London: Routledge.

Burk, James. 1998. The Logic of Crisis and Civil–Military Relations Theory: A Comment on Desch, Feaver, and Dauber. *Armed Forces & Society*, 24(3): 455–62.

Campbell, Colton and David Auerswald (eds.). 2015. *Congress and Civil-Military Relations*. Washington, DC: Georgetown University Press.

Castro, Arnoldo Brenes and Kevin Casas Zamora. 2003. Soldiers as Businessmen: The Economic Activities of Central America's Militaries. In J. Broemmelhoerster and W.-C. Paes (eds.), *The Military as an Economic Actor: Soldiers in Business*. Basingstoke: Palgrave Macmillan.

Cheung, Tai Ming. 2001. *China's Entrepreneurial Army*. Oxford: Oxford University Press.

Cheung, Tai Ming. 2003. The Rise and Fall of the Chinese Military Business Complex. In J. Broemmelhoerster and W.-C. Paes (eds.), *The Military as an Economic Actor: Soldiers in Business*. Basingstoke: Palgrave Macmillan.

Cohen, Eliot. 2002. *Supreme Command: Soldiers, Statesmen, and Leadership in Wartime*. New York: Free Press.

Cohn, Lindsay. 2011. It Wasn't in My Contract: Security Privatization and Civilian Control. *Armed Forces & Society*, 37(3): 381–98.

Coletta, Damon and Peter Feaver. 2006. Civilian Monitoring of U.S. Military Operations in the Information Age. *Armed Forces & Society*, 33(1): 106–26.

Cottey, Andrew, Timothy Edmunds, and Anthony Forster. 2002. The Second Generation Problematic: Rethinking Democracy and Civil-Military Relations. *Armed Forces & Society*, 29(1): 31–56.

Cottey, Andrew, Timothy Edmunds, and Anthony Forster. 2005. Civil–Military Relations in Postcommunist Europe: Assessing the Transition. *European Security*, 14(1): 1–16.

Davidson, Janine. 2013. Civil–Military Friction and Presidential Decision Making: Mending the Broken Dialogue. *Presidential Studies Quarterly*, 43(1): 129–45.

Dempsey, Jason. 2010. *Our Army: Soldiers, Politics, and American Civil-Military Relations*. Princeton, NJ: Princeton University Press.

Desch, Michael. 1999. *Civilian Control of the Military: The Changing Security Environment*. Baltimore, MD: Johns Hopkins University Press.

Desch, Michael. 2007. Bush and the Generals. *Foreign Affairs*, 86(3): 97–108.

Dunigan, Molly. 2011. *Victory for Hire: Private Security Companies' Impact on Military Effectiveness*. Stanford, CA: Stanford University Press.

Dunlap, Charles. 1992–93. The Origins of the American Military Coup of 2012. *Parameters*, Winter: 2–20.

Farrell, Theo, Sten Rynning, and Terry Terriff. 2013. *Transforming Military Power since the Cold War: Britain, France, and the United States, 1991–2012*. Cambridge: Cambridge University Press.

Feaver, Peter. 1992. *Guarding the Guardians: Civilian Control of Nuclear Weapons in the United States*. Ithaca, NY: Cornell University Press.

Feaver, Peter. 1996. The Civil–Military Problematique: Huntington, Janowitz, and the Question of Civilian Control. *Armed Forces & Society*, 23(2): 149–78.

Feaver, Peter. 2003. *Armed Servants: Agency, Oversight, and Civil–Military Relations*. Cambridge, MA: Harvard University Press.

Feaver, Peter. 2011. The Right to be Right: Civil–Military Relations and the Iraq Surge Decision. *International Security*, 35(4): 87–125.

Feaver, Peter and Christopher Gelpi. 2004. *Choosing Your Battles: American Civil-Military Relations and the Use of Force*. Princeton, NJ: Princeton University Press.

Feaver, Peter and Richard Kohn (eds.). 2001. *Soldiers and Civilians: The Civil–Military Gap and American National Security*. Cambridge, MA: MIT Press.

Fossum, Egil. 1967. Factors Influencing the Occurrence of Military Coups d'etat in Latin America, *Journal of Peace Research*, 4(3): 228–51.

Fravel, M. Taylor. 2002. Towards Civilian Supremacy: Civil–Military Relations in Taiwan's Democratization. *Armed Forces & Society*, 29(1): 57–84.

Gelpi, Christopher, Peter Feaver, and Jason Reifler. 2009. *Paying the Human Costs of War*. Princeton, NJ: Princeton University Press.

Gheciu, Alexandra. 2005. *NATO in the New Europe: The Politics of International Socialization after the Cold War*. Stanford, CA: Stanford University Press.

Golby, James. 2015. Beyond the Resignation Debate: A New Framework for Civil–Military Dialogue. *Strategic Studies Quarterly*, 9(3): 18–46.

Golby, James, Kyle Dropp, and Peter Feaver. 2012. *Military Campaigns: Veterans' Endorsements and Presidential Elections*. Washington, DC: Center for a New American Security.

Golby, James, Kyle Dropp, and Peter Feaver. 2013. *Listening to the Generals: How Military Advice Affects Public Support for the Use of Force*. Washington, DC: Center for a New American Security.

Golby, James, Lindsay Cohn, and Peter Feaver. 2016. Thanks for Your Service: Civilian and Veteran Attitudes after Fifteen Years of War. In Kori Schake and Jim Mattis (eds.), *Warriors & Citizens: American Views of Our Military*, pp. 97–142. Stanford, CA: Hoover Institution Press.

Golts, Alexander. 2016. The Inherent Limits of Russian Military Reform: Another Lost Opportunity. In Alexander Golts and Michael Kofman (eds.), *Russia's Military: Assessment, Strategy, and Threat*, pp. 13–19. Washington, DC: Center on Global Interests.

Herspring, Dale. 2005. Vladimir Putin and Military Reform in Russia. *European Security*, 14(1): 137–55.

Herspring, Dale. 2008. *Rumsfeld's Wars: The Arrogance of Power*. Lawrence, KS: University Press of Kansas.

Herspring, Dale. 2013. *Civil–Military Relations and Shared Responsibility: A Four-Nation Study*. Baltimore, MD: Johns Hopkins University Press.

Holsti, Ole. 1998–99. A Widening Gap between the U.S. Military and Civilian Society? Some Evidence, 1976–1996. *International Security*, 23(2): 5–42.

Huntington, Samuel. 1957. *The Soldier and the State: The Theory and Politics of Civil-Military Relations*. Cambridge, MA: Harvard University Press.

Inbody, Donald. 2016. *The Soldier Vote: War, Politcs, and the Ballot in America*. Basingstoke: Palgrave Macmillan.

Janowitz, Morris. 1960. *The Professional Soldier: A Social and Political Portrait*. Glencoe, IL: The Free Press.

Kofman, Michael. 2016. The Russian Military: A Force in Transition. in *Russia's Military: Assessment, Strategy, and Threat*, pp. 3–12. Washington, DC: Center on Global Interests.

Kohn, Richard. 1994. Out of Control. *National Interest*, 35(Spring): 3–31.

Kohn, Richard. 2009. Always Salute, Never Resign: How Resignation Threatens Military Professionalism. *Foreign Affairs*, November 10.

McMaster, H. R. 1997. *Dereliction of Duty: Johnson, McNamara, the Joint Chiefs of Staff, and the Lies that Led to Vietnam*. New York: HarperCollins.

Makara, Michael. 2013. Coup-Proofing, Military Defection, and the Arab Spring, *Democracy and Security*, 9(4): 334–59.

Malesic, Marjan, Hans Born, and Karl Haltiner. 2003. What Have We Learned and Where Do We Go From Here? In H. Born, K. Haltiner, and M. Malesic (eds.), *Renaissance of Democratic Control of Armed Forces in Contemporary Societies*. Baden-Baden: Nomos.

Mani, Kristina. 2007. Militaries in Business—State-making and Entrepreneurship in the Developing World. *Armed Forces & Society*, 33(4): 591–611.

Mannitz, Sabine. 2013. The "Democratic Soldier": Comparing Concepts and Practices in Europe. Geneva: the Centre for the Democratic Control of Armed Forces.

Milburn, Andrew. 2010. Breaking Ranks: Dissent and the Military Professional. *Joint Force Quarterly*, 59(4th Quarter): 101–7.

Moskos, Charles. 1979. The All-Volunteer Force. *Wilson Quarterly*, 3(2): 131–42.

Moskos, Charles, John Allen Williams, and David Segal (eds.). 2000. *The Postmodern Military: Armed Forces after the Cold War*. Oxford: Oxford University Press.

Moten, Matthew. 2014. *Presidents and Their Generals: An American History of Command in War*. Cambridge, MA: Harvard University Press.

Mulvenon, James. 2001. *Soldiers of Fortune: The Rise and Fall of the Chinese Military-Business Complex, 1978–1998*. London: M.E. Sharpe.

Nielsen, Suzanne and Don Snider (eds.). 2009. *American Civil–Military Relations: The Soldier and the State in a New Era*. Baltimore, MD: Johns Hopkins University Press.

Nordlinger, Eric. 1977. *Soldiers and Politics: Military Coups and Government*. Upper Saddle River, NJ: Prentice-Hall.

Owens, Mackubin Thomas. 2011. *U.S. Civil–Military Relations after 9/11: Renegotiating the Civil-Military Bargain*. New York: Continuum International.

Paes, Wolf-Christian and Tim Shaw. 2003. Praetorians or Profiteers? The Role of Entrepreneurial Armed Forces in Congo-Kinshasa. In J. Broemmelhoerster and W.-C. Paes (eds.), *The Military as an Economic Actor: Soldiers in Business*. Basingstoke: Palgrave Macmillan.

Pilster, Ulrich and Tobias Bohmelt. 2011. Coup-Proofing and Military Effectiveness in Interstate Wars, 1967–99. *Conflict Management and Peace Science*, 28(4): 331–50.

Pion-Berlin, David. 2016. *Military Missions in Democratic Latin America*. New York: Springer.

Pion-Berlin, David and Harold Trinkunas. 2010. Civilian Praetorianism and Military Shirking During Constitutional Crises in Latin America. *Comparative Politics*, 42(4): 395–411.

Powell, Colin. 1992–93. U.S. Forces: Challenges Ahead. *Foreign Affairs*, 71(5): 36–41.

Powell, Jonathan. 2012. *Coups and Conflict: The Paradox of Coup-Proofing*, PhD dissertation, University of Kentucky.

Quinlivan, James T. 1999. Coup-proofing. *International Security*, 24(2): 131–65.

Recchia, Stefano. 2015. *Reassuring the Reluctant Warriors: U.S. Civil-Military Relations and Multilateral Intervention*. Ithaca, NY: Cornell University Press.

Ricks, Thomas. 2006. *Fiasco: The American Military Adventure in Iraq*. New York: Penguin Press.

Ruffa, Chiara (ed.). 2013. Special Issue: Explaining Coordination and Breakdown in Complex Operations. *Small Wars & Insurgencies*, 24(2).

Saunders, Elizabeth. 2015. War and the Inner Circle: Democratic Elites and the Politics of Using Force. *Security Studies*, 24(3): 466–501.

Scheetz, Thomas. 2003. Military Business in Argentina. In J. Broemmelhoerster and W.-C. Paes (eds.), *The Military as an Economic Actor: Soldiers in Business*. Basingstoke: Palgrave Macmillan.

Schiff, Rebecca. 2009. *The Military and Domestic Politics: A Concordance Theory of Civil–Military Relations*. London: Routledge.

Shambaugh, David. 2002. *Modernizing China's Military: Progress, Problems, and Prospects*. Berkeley, CA: University of California Press.

Siddiqa-Agha, Ayesha. 2003. Power, Perks, Prestige, and Privileges: The Military's Economic Activities in Pakistan. In J. Broemmelhoerster and W.-C. Paes (eds.), *The Military as an Economic Actor: Soldiers in Business*. Basingstoke: Palgrave Macmillan.

Snider, Don, Gayle Watkins, and Lloyd Matthews (eds.). 2002. *The Future of the Army Profession*. New York: McGraw-Hill.

Sowers, Tommy. 2005. Beyond the Soldier and the State: Contemporary Operations and Variance in Principal–Agent Relationships. *Armed Forces and Society*, 31(3): 385–409.

Strachan, Hew. 2006. Making Strategy: Civil–Military Relations after Iraq. *Survival: Global Politics and Strategy*, 48(3): 59–82.

Talmadge, Caitlyn. 2015. *The Dictator's Army: Battlefield Effectiveness in Authoritarian Regimes*. Ithaca, NY: Cornell University Press.

Weiner, Sharon. 1996. Resource Allocation in the Post-Cold War Pentagon. *Security Studies*, 5(4): 125–42.

INDEX

Tables, figures, and endnotes are indicated by an italic *t*, *f*, and *n* following the page number.

Ingram Content Group UK Ltd.
Milton Keynes UK
UKHW030203210423
420546UK00001B/1

9 780198 854623